D1257801

Contributors

Monica Biernat Department of Psychology, University of Kansas, Lawrence, Kansas 66045

Henry E. Brady Department of Political Science, University of California, Berkeley, California 94720

Jack Citrin Department of Political Science, University of California, Berkeley, California 94720

Christian S. Crandall Department of Psychology, University of Kansas, Lawrence, Kansas 66045

Stanley Feldman Department of Political Science, State University of New York at Stony Brook, Stony Brook, New York 11794

Steven E. Finkel Woodrow Wilson Department of Government and Foreign Affairs, University of Virginia, Charlottesville, Virginia 22901

Stan Humphries Department of Political Science, George Washington University, Washington, DC 20063

Jon Hurwitz Department of Political Science, University of Pittsburgh, Pittsburgh, Pennsylvania 15260

Kathleen Knight Department of Political Science, University of Houston, Houston, Texas 77204

David Knoke Department of Sociology, University of Minnesota, Minneapolis, Minnesota 55455

Jon A. Krosnick Department of Psychology, University of Ohio, Columbus, Ohio 43210

Christopher Muste Department of Political Science, University of California, Berkeley, California 94720

Mark Peffley Department of Political Science, University of Kentucky, Lexington, Kentucky 40506

Vincent Price Annenberg School for Communication, University of Pennsylvania, Philadelphia, Pennsylvania 19104

Mary Jo Reef Department of Sociology, Clarion University, Clarion, Pennsylvania 16214

John P. Robinson Department of Sociology, University of Maryland, College Park, Maryland 20742

J. Merrill Shanks Department of Political Science, University of California, Berkeley, California 94720

Phillip R. Shaver Department of Psychology, University of California, Davis, California 95616

Lee Sigelman Department of Political Science, George Washington University, Washington, DC 20063

Herbert F. Weisberg Department of Political Science, Ohio State University, Columbus, Ohio 43210

Lawrence S. Wrightsman Department of Psychology, University of Kansas, Lawrence, Kansas 66045

Measures of
Political Attitudes

Volume 2 of Measures of Social Psychological Attitudes

Edited by

John P. Robinson

Department of Sociology
University of Maryland
College Park, Maryland

Phillip R. Shaver

Department of Psychology
University of California
Davis, California

Lawrence S. Wrightsman

Department of Psychology
University of Kansas
Lawrence, Kansas

ACADEMIC PRESS
An Imprint of Elsevier

San Diego   London   Boston   New York   Sydney   Tokyo   Toronto

Academic Press
An Imprint of Elsevier
525 B Street, Suite 1900, San Diego, California 92101-4495, USA
http://www.apnet.com

Academic Press Limited
24-28 Oval Road, London NW1 7DX, UK
http://www.hbuk.co.uk/ap/

Library of Congress Catalog Card Number: 98-84427

International Standard Book Number: 0-12-590242-5 (case)
International Standard Book Number: 0-12-590245-X (pb)

PRINTED IN THE UNITED STATES OF AMERICA
04   05   06   LN   10   9   8   7   6   5   4   3

Contents

CHAPTER 3

Liberalism and Conservatism   59
Kathleen Knight

CHAPTER 6

Racial Attitudes   297

Monica Biernat and Christian S. Crandall

CHAPTER 7

Political Alienation and Efficacy   413

Mary Jo Reef and David Knoke

CHAPTER 8

CHAPTER 9

CHAPTER 10

Political Information   591

Vincent Price

CHAPTER 11

Political Agendas   641

J. Merrill Shanks

CHAPTER 12
_____

Political Partisanship   681
Herbert F. Weisberg

CHAPTER 13
_____

Political Participation   737
Henry E. Brady

Preface

Our attitude measurement series, originally published by the Institute for Social Research of the University of Michigan almost 30 years ago, has reached a wide international audience. Colleagues tell us that these volumes are among the most frequently borrowed and stolen publications in their libraries.

The original series needed revising for some time, but we were daunted by the prospect of again doing it alone. The number of measures has increased enormously since 1970. We kept looking toward a time when we could enlist the help of experts and specialists to produce an authoritative and timely collection of reviews. We are extremely pleased with the reviews and insights of the chapter authors who contributed to this volume, and to Volume 1 (published in 1991).

Our series is intended as a basic reference work in the social sciences and is directed to three different audiences:

- Professionals actively involved in social science, especially those conducting survey research in the fields of political science, psychology, sociology, and communications.
- Students taking courses in social research methods who are interested in becoming familiar with the measuring instruments of the social sciences or students who wish to conduct their own research projects.
- Nonacademic professionals in fields related to the social sciences, such as social commentators, journalists, political analysts, and market researchers.

Our aim has been to provide a comprehensive guide to the most promising and useful measures of important social science concepts. We aspired to make the measures maximally accessible, so that readers can decide which one to use in a particular situation. Whenever possible—given copyright restrictions and authors' justifiable reservations—we have included actual scale items and scoring instructions. Nevertheless, these materials and our brief comments on them are no substitute for reading the original sources and subjecting the instruments to further item analyses and validation studies. This book is meant to be a starting point, an idea generator, a guide—not the last stop on the way to a perfect measure.

We are grateful to the Society for the Psychological Study of Social Issues (SPSSI), which helped make this new series possible. The warm encouragement and skillful diplomacy of Louise Kidder, former SPSSI Publications Chair, are especially appreciated.

Susan Bilek expertly prepared numerous chapter rewrites. Richard Brody offered crucial substantive advice.

Most important of all, we acknowledge the creative and dedicated scale authors whose work lies at the heart of this volume. Without their curiosity, imagination, and high technical standards, we would have nothing to pass along to you. Many scale authors not only granted permission to reproduce their work but also supplied supplementary references and information about recent research. It's a pleasure to showcase their work.

One final word: If all necessary information concerning a particular scale is included here, you are welcome to use the scale in your research. If more information is needed, please contact the scale's author or publisher. In many cases, we provide an address where permission or copies of commercial test forms can be obtained.

John P. Robinson
Phillip R. Shaver
Lawrence S. Wrightsman

CHAPTER 1

Scale Selection and Evaluation

John P. Robinson, Phillip R. Shaver, and Lawrence S. Wrightsman

The original idea for a series of handbooks of attitude and personality measures came from Robert Lane, a political scientist at Yale University. Like most social scientists, Lane found it difficult to keep up with the proliferation of social and political attitude measures. In the summer of 1958, he first compiled a broad range of scales that would be of interest to researchers in the field of political behavior. Subsequently this work was continued and expanded at the Survey Research Center of the University of Michigan under the general direction of Philip Converse, with support from a grant by the National Institute of Mental Health. The result was a three-volume series, the focal one being *Measures of Political Attitudes*. That is the focus of our second update of the original volumes.

Readers will note several differences between this work and its predecessors. Most important, we have given responsibility for each topic to experienced and well-known researchers in each field rather than choosing and evaluating items by ourselves. These experts were also limited to identifying the 10 or 20 most interesting or promising measures in their area rather than covering all available instruments. This new structure has resulted in more knowledgeable review essays, but also in less standardized evaluations of individual instruments and less than universal coverage.

There are many reasons for creating a volume such as this. Political attitude and behavior measures are likely to appear under thousands of book titles, in dozens of social science journals, in seldom circulated dissertations, and in the catalogues of commercial publishers as well as in undisturbed piles of manuscripts in the offices of social scientists. This is a rather inefficient grapevine for the interested researcher. Too few scholars stay in the same area of study on a continuing basis for several years, so it is difficult to keep up with all of the empirical literature and instruments available. Often the interdisciplinary investigator is interested in the relation of some new variable, which has come to his or her attention casually, to a favorite area of interest. The job of combing the literature to pick a proper instrument consumes needless hours and often ends in a frustrating decision to forego measuring that characteristic, or worse, it results in a rapid and incomplete attempt to devise a new measure. Our search of the literature has revealed unfortunate replications of previous discoveries as well as lack of attention to better research done in a particular area.

Measures of Political Attitudes
Copyright © 1999 by Academic Press.
All rights of reproduction in any form reserved.

The search procedure used by our authors included thorough reviews of *Social Science Abstracts* and *Psychological Abstracts,* as well as the most likely periodical sources of standardized political measurements (i.e., *American Political Science Review, Journal of Politics,* and *Public Opinion Quarterly*) and sociological and psychological measures (e.g., *American Sociological Review, Journal of Personality and Social Psychology, Journal of Social Psychology, Social Psychology Quarterly, Journal of Social Issues,* and *Journal of Applied Psychology*). Doctoral dissertations were searched by examining back issues of *Dissertation Abstracts.* Personal contact with the large variety of empirical research done by colleagues widened the search, as did conversations with researchers at annual meetings of the American Political Science Association and the American Sociological Association, among others. Papers presented at these meetings also served to bring a number of new instruments to our attention.

Our focus in this volume is on political attitude and behavior *scales* (i.e., series of items with homogeneous content), scales that are useful in survey research settings as well as in laboratory situations. We have not attempted the larger and perhaps hopeless task of compiling single attitude items, except for ones that have been used in large-scale studies such as the General Social Survey (GSS) and the American National Election Studies (ANES). While these often tap important variables, a complete compilation of them is beyond our scope.

Although we have attempted to be as thorough as possible in our search, we make no claim that this volume contains every important scale pertaining to our chapter headings. We do feel, however, that the chapter authors have identified most of the high-quality instruments.

Contents of This Volume

This volume can be viewed as being divided into three sections, the first methodological, the second attitudinal, and the third more behavioral, including not only political activity, but also political information, political salience, and party affiliation. In the rest of Chapter 1 we review the main methodological factors used to evaluate the quality of survey measures, namely, thoroughness, reliability, and validity; we then propose the rough guidelines that we asked reviewers to use in evaluating the nearly 150 measures covered in this volume. These evaluative criteria fall into three groups:

1. Item construction criteria (sampling of relevant content, wording of items, and item analysis);
2. Response set criteria (controlling the spurious effects of acquiescence and social desirability response sets); and
3. Psychometric criteria (representative sampling, presentation of normative data, reliability [both internal consistency and test–retest reliability], and validity [both convergent and discriminant]).

Of course, meeting or not meeting these criteria does not fully determine the value of a scale. For example, one can construct a scale with high internal consistency merely by including items that express the same idea in much the same way, and one can ensure significant discrimination between known groups merely by sampling two groups that are so divergent that they would be unlikely to respond the same way to any item. For this reason we recommend that the choice of a scale from this volume be based as much as possible on decision theoretic criteria, such as those originally outlined by Cronbach and

Gleser (1965). The present chapter concludes with reviews of a number of political measures that could not be included under any of the subsequent chapter headings, such as cosmopolitanism, social responsibility, and political power.

In Chapter 2 Jon Krosnick reviews the major methodological concern in constructing measures of political attitudes and behavior, question framing. This involves issues of wording and form, number of response alternatives, labeling of alternatives, open versus closed questions, and the like. Agreement or acquiescence response set is particularly troublesome because most of the measures in this book have been applied to cross-sectional samples of the public, and less-educated respondents in such surveys are particularly likely to agree with survey questions regardless of their content. An analyst, therefore, cannot tell when respondents are agreeing with a policy or attitude position and when they are simply agreeing (or not disagreeing) with a statement. Much the same problem arises with the response set of social desirability. Krosnick reviews the extensive literature on these topics and cites their relevance for measuring political attitudes. He concludes with some general suggestions for improving questionnaire quality in attitude and behavior scales.

Chapter 3 begins the reviews of measures of particular political attitudes by focusing on the central concept in the study of politics, political ideology. Kathleen Knight reviews 15 separate scales measuring this construct, 3 of which attempt to cover the spectrum most broadly, 6 of which appear more tied to research on authoritarianism, 3 of which are more directed to radicalism and the "left" extreme of the ideological spectrum, and 3 of which examine the "right" end of the spectrum. She provides an extensive review of the vast number of single liberal-conservative items used by most survey organizations. Although they may not yield agreement on what proportion of the country is liberal or conservative, these different organizational measures all seem to show that there has been no simple, consistent shift to the right or to the left over the last quarter century. Knight concludes her chapter with a useful summary guide concerning which aspects of ideology each of the 15 scales does (or does not) address.

One of the major attitudes that separates liberals and conservatives intellectually concerns the role of government intervention, particularly in the economy and especially in providing "welfare" and more equitable treatment to those in economic need. In Chapter 4 Stanley Feldman reviews seven scales related to this set of issues, most of which come from national studies and focus on the values of egalitarianism and individualism, which are thought to underlie debate on these issues (but in fact may not, as he notes in the conclusion to the chapter). The chapter also contains responses to more than 60 questions on inequality and related government policy that have appeared on the General Social Survey (GSS) since 1972. As with the case of internationalism in Chapter 9, this is an area in which measurement seems badly out of date with regard to political developments, particularly given the major ongoing political debates about the proper role and size of government and the unlikelihood that such questions will be resolved in the foreseeable future.

One of the central elements of the democratic form of government is tolerance of those with opposing and minority viewpoints. In Chapter 5 Steven Finkel, Lee Sigelman, and Stan Humphries provide a comprehensive review of the dynamic debates that have taken place among political scientists since Samuel Stouffer's and others' classical treatises on this topic in the 1950s. Of the 14 scales reviewed in the chapter, about half deal with the topic of general democratic values and the others with the specific topic of political tolerance. The authors conclude by noting the promising new methodological and international developments in this area, but they also note the need for more research on the larger political consequences of holding more or less tolerant views.

The topic of tolerance touches on one of the major aspects of what has been perhaps the most explosive area of public opinion in this country, race. In Chapter 6 Monica Biernat and Christian Crandall review 18 measures of race-related attitudes, although all but 4 of them have yet to be applied in larger community settings outside the college classroom. Nonetheless, that means that the scales tend to be richer and more multifaceted than typical survey measures, and several tap more subtle and "modern" aspects of racism (sometimes called "symbolic racism"). These measures may be important, as older and straightforward attitude items (like those in the GSS) show that fewer and fewer white Americans agree explicitly with these more blatant racial views. Biernat and Crandall conclude by noting some promising new methodological developments in this increasingly complex area of attitude research.

Chapter 7 addresses the classic topic of political alienation, the aspect of political life that was at the heart of the theorizing by Karl Marx and his disciples. Mary Jo Reef and David Knoke first note the philosophical disagreements that still plague this concept and then provide reviews of 14 measures that (mainly) tap feelings of powerlessness in affecting political outcomes. The 2 main measures in this area, however, reflect the opposite end of this alienation dimension, *political efficacy*—even though the measures of this construct are very short and do not cohere well. More recent measures have been designed to overcome both problems, but not entirely successfully. Reef and Knoke also note the lack of data on causes and consequences of alienation.

Political trust can be seen as one counterpoint to political alienation. In Chapter 8 Jack Citrin and Christopher Muste review 25 separate political trust measures, defining trust as citizen "confidence that authorities will observe the rules of the game and serve the general interest." The reviewed scales include 4 focused on the short-term incumbent level, 5 examining trust of Congress or other specific institutions, and 4 covering cynicism about politicians in general. The final 11 measures deal with longer-term confidence in the general methods of governance and political institutions, several from other countries. Citrin and Muste see the need for future measures that would focus on the different levels and branches of government, examine what citizens expect from their government, and relate political trust to trust at more basic and personal levels of social interaction. A matter of some concern is that confidence in U.S. institutions has steadily decreased over time.

Chapter 9 turns attention to the international arena. Jon Hurwitz and Mark Peffley review 10 measures, the first 4 of which cover feelings of patriotism and nationalism; the next 2, national "distinctiveness"; and the last 4, internationalism or policy support. A major problem of measurement in this area is the perceived lack of interest and information about foreign affairs, both among the public and among political scholars. This problem is exacerbated by the rapidly changing nature and landscape of international politics, which limit the ability of researchers to invest effort in developing long-term scales (most notably in the case of the collapse of the Soviet Union, the focal point of U.S. foreign policy between 1945 and 1990). There seem to be few efforts to tap even such recurring and basic issues as American intervention to correct perceived human rights abuses in other countries, assistance to third world countries, the global economy, and worldwide environmental issues.

One of the fastest growing areas of empirical research in the last decade has been focused on political information. Vincent Price discusses the unique issues involved in constructing knowledge scales and reviews 10 such scales in Chapter 10. Most of these are national knowledge measures that come from American National Election Studies (ANES) involving representative samples of Americans

Chapter 11 on political agendas marks the transition in this volume from more attitudinal measures to more behavioral ones. Here the measurement is not of pro versus con divisions of opinion on an issue, but of how politically *important* an issue itself is seen to

Table 1-1
Outline of Chapters 3–13

Attitudes	Orientations/Dispositions	Behavior
3. Liberal-conservative	10. Political information	13. Political participation
4. Government intervention	11. Political agendas	
5. Tolerance	12. Party identification	
6. Race		
7. Political alienation		
8. Trust		
9. International attitudes		

be. Merrill Shanks (with the assistance of Douglas A. Strand) describes 10 different sets of measures that have been developed, 5 in his own Surveys of Governmental Objectives. In addition, Shanks considers responses to open-ended questions from Gallup, ANES, and other national surveys on "the most important problem facing the country." Shanks contrasts these direct measures of issue importance with "indirect" statistical approaches, in which differences in actual opinion are correlated with vote outcome. He presents original analyses in which close-ended questions seem to predict vote better than open-ended measures. He concludes with a brief review of how these results contrast with a third and even more sophisticated statistical procedure aimed at isolating the crucial issues in an election.

A behavioral predisposition, political partisanship, is covered by Herbert Weisberg in Chapter 12. Party identification continues to be the major predictor of vote, despite academic arguments about shifts toward more issue-oriented voting in the 1970s. Weisberg notes the many issues that surround the use of this multicategory scale as well as some new variants to capture independent voters and the multiple party affiliations found in other societies. He sees a need for more concentrated cognitive psychological research to improve measurement of the strength of party affiliation as well as the dynamics of how partisanship changes across different electoral contests.

In Chapter 13 Henry Brady examines the various measures of political participation. He first reviews the historical contributions of the six major studies of participation that have been conducted, including the ANES, GSS, and Roper longitudinal studies; he presents the correlations of participation measures with each other and with background factors, suggesting that there is no simple unidimensional scale of participation. He then reviews two alternatives to the closed-ended-question approach, one based on societal institutions and the other on political problems. He concludes with a list of participation items that can usefully be included in future studies as well as with a call for further validation of specific measures. He notes how measures of political behavior suffer from the same problems as measures of political attitudes.

Stepping back from the specific contents of the 11 scale-review chapters, one could arrange them as in Table 1–1. The more purely attitudinal variables are listed in the left-hand column; those variables involving more cognitive or behavioral dispositions in the middle column; and the activity or behavioral variables in the right-hand column. As can be seen, most of the conceptual differentiation has occurred in the domain of political *attitudes*.

Evaluative Criteria

We have tried to go beyond a simple listing of potential instruments and their psychometric properties. While most scale authors do provide useful statistical data in their scale presentations, it is one thing to present statistical data and another to interpret them. The casual reader or part-time researcher may find it difficult to assess such assets and liabilities when different authors use different statistical procedures. For example, few researchers seem to know that a Guttman reproducibility coefficient of .91 can be obtained from a series of items with interitem correlation coefficients around .30 or that a test–retest reliability correlation of .50 may indicate a higher reliability than a split-half reliability of .80.

Nor may scale authors be disposed to point out the limitations of their instruments when they are writing articles for publication. Thus many authors fail to alert readers to their restricted samples, failure to deal with response sets, items that are too complicated for respondents to understand, lack of item analyses, or failure to include certain behaviors and attitudes relevant to the construct at hand. We have tried, where possible, to make such liabilities visible to the reader, although it was simply not feasible with the space and resources available to note all such shortcomings. Originally we had hoped to order the instruments in each chapter according to their probable research value, or to their ability to meet certain desirable standards; that also was not possible. Within each topic area the instruments we have space to consider often differ so much in purpose or focus that they cannot be arranged along a single quality dimension.

At present, when experienced researchers disagree with our reviewers' assessments, they need to supplement them with their own. We hope that our reviewers have alerted readers to a number of psychometric considerations, not only when deciding which instrument to use, but also in evaluating their own new scales. We have tried to be fair, honest, consistent, and not overly demanding in our evaluations, and we have tried to highlight the merits as well as the limitations of each instrument.

The following brief description of our evaluative criteria proceeds in the general chronological sequence in which attitude instruments are constructed.

Writing the Items

The first step for scale builders, and the first dimension on which their work can be evaluated, is writing or locating items to include in a scale. It is usually assumed that the scale builder knows enough about the field to construct an instrument that will cover an important theoretical construct well enough to be useful to other researchers. If it covers a construct for which instruments are already available, sound improvements over previous measures should be demonstrated.

Three minimal considerations in constructing a scale are the following:

1. *Proper Sampling of Content:* Proper sampling is not easy to achieve, nor can exact rules be specified for ensuring its achievement (as critics of Louis Guttman's concept of "universe of content" have noted). Nonetheless, one must be aware of the critical role of item sampling procedures in scale construction. Future research may better reveal the population of behaviors, objects, and feelings that ought to be covered in any area, but some examples may suggest ways in which the interested researcher can provide better coverage of a construct domain. Thus investigators of the authoritarian personality lifted key sentiments expressed in small-group conversations, personal interviews, and written remarks and transformed them into scale items; some of the items consisted of direct verbatim quotations from such materials. In the job satisfaction area, Robinson, Athanasiou, and Head (1967) presented open-ended responses to such questions as "What things do you like best (or don't you like) about your job?" Responses to such questions offer invaluable guidelines to researchers concerning both the universe of factors to be covered

and the weight that should be given to each factor. Other instruments in the job satisfaction area (as elsewhere) were built on the basis of either previous factor analytic work or responses to questions concerning critically satisfying or dissatisfying situations. Decisions remain to be made about the number of questions needed to cover each factor, but the important first step is to make sure that the main factors have been identified and covered.

2. *Simplicity of Item Wording:* One of the great advantages of obtaining verbatim comments from group discussions or open-ended questions, as people in advertising have discovered, is that such sentiments are usually couched in language easily comprehended and recognized by respondents. Comparing earlier and contemporary instruments, we see that more recently constructed scales contain question wording that is far less stuffy, complex, and esoteric. Even today, however, items developed from college student samples must be edited and adapted for use with more heterogeneous populations. Some helpful advice on these matters is contained in Sudman and Bradburn (1982), Robinson and Meadow (1982), and Converse and Presser (1986).

Many other undesirable item-wording practices seem to be going out of style as well: double-barreled items, which contain so many ideas that it is hard to tell why a person agrees or disagrees with them (e.g., "The government should provide low-cost medical care because too many people are in poor health and doctors charge so much money."), items that are so vague they mean all things to all people ("Everybody should receive adequate medical care."), and items that depend on familiarity with little-known facts ("The government should provide for no more medical care than that implied in the Constitution."). Advice about writing items in the negative versus the positive is offered in our discussion of response set.

3. *Item Analysis:* While item wording is something an investigator can manipulate to ensure coverage of intended content, there is no guarantee that respondents will reply to the items in the manner intended by the investigator. Item analysis is one of the most efficient methods for checking whether people are responding to the items in the manner intended. We have encountered several scales whose authors assumed that some a priori division of scale items corresponded to the way their respondents perceived them.

Many methods of item analysis are available; in general, multidimensional analyses (described under homogeneity in our subsequent discussion of statistical procedures) can be considered the ultimate item analytic procedure. Researchers need not go so far as to factor-analyze their data to select items to be included or discarded, but an item intercorrelation matrix (on perhaps a small subsample, or pretest sample) can be a simple and convenient surrogate for determining which items to include, particularly when using most of the statistical packages available for personal computers. If it is hypothesized that five items in a large battery of items (say, those numbered 1, 2, 6, 12, and 17) constitute a scale of conservatism, then the majority of the 10 interitem correlations between these five items should be substantial. At the minimum they should be significant at the .05 level. While this minimum may seem liberal, it is in keeping with the degree to which items in the most reputable scales intercorrelate for heterogeneous populations. If items 1, 2, and 17 intercorrelate substantially with each other, but item 6 does not correlate well with any of them, then item 6 should be discarded or rewritten. Measuring the degree to which each of the five items correlates with external criteria or outside variables is a more direct device for the selection of items; this may even be preferable to high interitem correlations. Such item validity approaches provide a built-in validational component for the scale. Wendt (1979), for example, used canonical correlation methods to find that a general alienation scale factored into two distinct scales with different demographic correlates. Exercises using LISREL programs may be similarly useful.

Robinson (1969) reported learning a valuable lesson about the myriad pitfalls in writing items from a simple item analysis of value questions in a national survey. Twelve items had been selected from a previous study that had uncovered four dimensions of value (authoritarianism, expression, individualism, and equalitarianism). One of the individualism items ("It is the man who starts off bravely on his own who excites our admiration.") seemed in particular need of reframing for a cross-sectional survey. Accordingly the item was reworded: "We should all admire a man who starts out bravely on his own." Item analysis revealed that this reformulated item was more closely associated with the three authoritarianism items than with the other two individualism items. Thus this seemingly innocuous wording change completely altered the value concept tapped by the item.

For researchers who do not have the luxury of pretesting as a way to eliminate or revise unsatisfactory items, the item analysis phase of scale construction can be incorporated into the determination of the dimensionality or homogeneity of the test items. This will ensure that there is an empirical as well as a theoretical rationale for combining the information contained in various items into a scale.

Avoiding Response Set

A second large area of concern to scale builders is the avoidance of response set. Response set refers to a tendency on the part of individuals to respond to attitude statements for reasons other than the content of the statements. Thus a person who might want to appear generally agreeable with any attitude statement is said to show an agreement response set. One defense against response set is to make the scale as interesting and pleasant for respondents as possible. The more that respondents find the instrument dull or unpleasant, the greater the chance that they will not answer carefully or will attempt to finish it as quickly as possible, agreeing indiscriminately or simply checking off the same answer column for each item.

As Krosnick details in Chapter 2, two major sources of response set need to be controlled:

1. *Acquiescence:* Most of us have observed people whose attitudes change in accord with the situation. Such people are said to acquiesce in anticipation of opposition from others. In the same way some people are "yeasayers," willing to go along with anything that sounds good, while others (perhaps optimists) are unwilling to look at the negative side of any issue. These dispositions are reflected in people's responses to attitude questions. Fortunately it is often possible to separate their "real" attitudes from their tendency to agree or disagree.

There are various levels of attack, all of which involve abandoning a simple agree–disagree or yes–no format. One can first control simple order effects by at least an occasional switching of response alternatives between positive and negative. For simple yes–no alternatives a few no–yes options should be inserted. Similarly for the strongly agree–agree–uncertain–disagree–strongly disagree or Likert format, the five alternatives should occasionally be listed in the opposite order. This practice will offer some possibility of locating respondents who choose alternatives solely on the basis of the order in which they appear. It may also encourage overly casual respondents to think more about their answers, although at the cost of some confusion to respondents.

It is more difficult to shift the entire item wording from positive to negative, as those who have tried to reverse authoritarianism items (e.g., Christie, Havel, & Seidinberg, 1958) have found. A logician may argue that the obverse of "Obedience is an important thing for children to learn" is not "Disobedience is an important thing for children to learn," and the investigator is on shaky ground in assuming that a respondent who agrees with both the first and the second statements is completely confused or vulnerable to agreement response set. Along the same line the practice of inserting a single word in order to reverse an item can produce rather awkward sentences, while changing one word in an unusual context can produce items in which most respondents may not notice the change. In sum, writing item reversals requires considerable sensitivity and care. The interested researcher should check previous work on the subject (as referenced in Chapter 10 of our 1991 volume).

A third and more difficult, yet probably more effective, approach involves the construction of forced-choice items. Here two (or more) replies to a question are listed, and respondents are told to choose only one: "The most important thing for children to learn is (obedience) (independence)." Equating the popularity or social desirability of each of these alternatives provides even greater methodological purity, but also entails more intensive effort on the part of both scale constructors and respondents. At the same time, the factor of social desirability is an important response set variable in its own right and needs to be considered independently of acquiescence, as Krosnick notes in Chapter 2.

2. *Social Desirability:* In contrast to the theory that acquiescent persons reveal a certain desire for subservience in their willingness to go along with any statement, Edwards (1957) proposed more positively that such people are just trying to make a good impression. Decreasing social desirability responding usually involves the use of forced-choice items in which the alternatives have been equated on the basis of social desirability ratings. In more refined instruments the items are pretested on social desirability, and alternative pairings (or item pairings) that do not prove to be equated are dropped or revised. DeMaio (1984) discusses approaches to the social desirability factor in the context of cross-sectional surveys.

We have mentioned the major sources of response set contamination, but there are others of which investigators should be aware. One of the more prevalent sources of contamination is the faking of responses according to some preconceived image that the respondent wants to convey. On a job satisfaction scale, for example, the respondent may try to avoid saying anything that might put his or her supervisor in a bad light or involve a change in work procedures. College students may be aware of a professor's hypothesized relationship between two variables and try to answer in ways that confirm (or disconfirm) this prediction. Other undesirable variations of spurious response patterns that an investigator may wish to minimize can result from the respondents' wanting (a) to appear too consistent, (b) to use few or many categories in their replies, or (c) to choose extreme alternatives.

Incorporating Statistical Procedures

The third area of instrument evaluation concerns the various statistical and psychometric procedures incorporated into its construction. These include respondent sampling, presentation of norms (usually means and standard deviations), reliability, and validity. While each of these statistical considerations is important, inadequate performance on any one of them does not render the scale worthless. Nevertheless, inadequate performance or lack of concern with many of them does indicate that the scale should be used with reservation. Recent scale authors have paid more heed to these considerations than their predecessors did, but few scales can be said to be ideal on all these factors.

The following eight statistical standards cover the basic requirements in the construction of a well-designed scale.

1. *Representative Sampling:* Too many researchers remain unaware of the fallacy of generalizing results from samples of college students to an older and much less well-educated general population (for an excellent review, see Sears, 1986). Indeed, some statisticians argue that a sample of a single classroom should be treated as a sample size of one, not the number of students in the classroom. Moreover, college students as a whole represent less than 5% of the population of the United States and diverge from the population on two characteristics that survey researchers usually find most distinctive in predicting attitude differences: age and education. Among college students significant differences are also likely to be found between freshmen and seniors, engineering and psychology students, and students at different colleges, so that one must be careful in expecting results from one classroom sample to hold for all college students. In the political attitude area, distinctions made by political elites may not be recognized by typical citizens, or even by politically sophisticated college students.

This is meant not to discourage researchers from improving the representativeness of whatever populations they do have available for study, but rather to caution against generalizing from their findings to people not represented by their samples. Nor is it meant to imply that samples of college students are useless groups on which to construct scales. In areas like foreign affairs, one might well argue that college exposure is the best single criterion of whether a person can truly appreciate the intricacies of the issues involved.

However, an instrument constructed from replies of a random cross section of all students in a university has much more to offer than the same instrument developed on students in a single class in psychology (even if there are more students in the classroom than in the university sample). The prime consideration is the applicability of the scale and scale norms to respondents who are likely to use them in the future.

Problems arise with many samples of noncampus respondents as well. Poor sampling frames and low response rates are not uncommon, even for scales that are otherwise carefully designed and administered to community samples.

2. *Normative Information:* The adequacy of norms (mean scale scores, percentage agreements, etc.) is obviously dependent on the adequacy of the sample. The most basic piece of normative information is the difference between the researcher's sample and the sample on which the scale was developed in terms of mean scale score and standard deviation.

Additional useful statistical topics include item means (or percentage agreements), standard deviations, and median scores (if the scale scores are skewed). Most helpful are means and standard deviations for certain well-defined groups (e.g., men and women, Catholics and Baptists) who have high or low scale scores. When such differences have been predicted, the results bear on the validity of the scale, which is discussed subsequently. Validity and reliability are also important areas of basic normative information, of course, and they are covered in more detail below.

3. *Reliability (Test–Retest): Reliability* is one of the most ambiguous terms in psychometrics. There are at least three major referents: (1) the correlation between the same sets of items at two separate points in time (for a particular sample), (2) the correlation between two different sets of items at the same time (called parallel forms if the items are presented in separate formats and split-half if the items are all presented together), and (3) the correlation among the scale items for all who answer the items. The latter two indices refer to the internal structure or homogeneity of the scale items (the next criterion), while the former indicates stability of a respondent's item responses over time. It is unfortunate that test–retest measures, which require more effort and sophistication on the part of scale authors and may generate lower reliability figures for their efforts, are available for so few instruments. While the test–retest reliability level may be approximately estimated from

indices of homogeneity, there is no substitute for the actual test–retest data. Some attempts to assess reliability and stability are discussed in Wheaton et al. (1977) and Bohrnstedt, Mohler, and Muller (1987).

4. *Internal Consistency:* In addition to split-half, parallel forms, and interitem indices of the internal homogeneity of scale items, there exist other measures of reliability. Some of these item-test and internal consistency measures have known statistical relationships with one another, as Scott (1960) and others have shown. Even between such "radically" different procedures as the traditional psychometric approach and the Guttman cumulative approach, however, there likely exist reasonably stable relationships between indices based on interitem, item-total, and total test homogeneity; as yet, however, these have not been charted. This includes the major reliability coefficient, Cronbach's α (1951).

Currently the major difference among the indices seems to lie in a researcher's preference for large or small numbers. Interitem correlations and homogeneity indices based on Loevinger's concepts seldom exceed .40. If one prefers larger numbers, a reproducibility coefficient or split-half reliability coefficient computed on the same data could easily exceed .90. While there is currently no way of relating the various indices, one minimal, but still imperfect, criterion is that of statistically significant correlations. Many researchers complain that this criterion depends too heavily on the sample sizes involved. To make the job even more difficult, statistical distributions of these various indices are not always available so that significance can be ascertained.

Of all the proposed indices, none combines simplicity with amount of information conveyed as well as does the interitem correlation matrix. Computing Pearson r correlation coefficients for more than five items is no longer a time-consuming operation for any researcher with access to a personal computer. Even the interitem correlation matrix for a 20-item scale can now be generated in a matter of seconds. In the case of dichotomous (two-choice) items, the coefficient Yule's Y or Kendall's τ_β can easily be calculated to determine interitem significance. Cronbach's α is now calculated on personal-computer scaling programs. These, however, constitute only rule-of-thumb procedures for deciding whether a group of items should be added together to form a scale or an index. Similarly the criterion of statistical significance is proposed only because it is a standard that remains fairly constant across the myriad measures that are now, or have been, in vogue. Perhaps more satisfactory norms will be proposed in the future.

When the number of items goes beyond 10, however, the interitem matrix becomes quite cumbersome to analyze by inspection. One is well advised to have the data analyzed by a multidimensional computer program. Program packages such as SPSS and SAS have the ability to factor-analyze 10–50 item intercorrelations in a few seconds or minutes, given a reasonably sized sample. These sorts of analyses will help one locate groups of items that go together much faster than could be done by inspecting the correlation matrix.[1] There are many kinds of factor analysis programs and options; under most circumstances, however, the differences among them usually do not result in radically different factor structures.

To say that factor analytic programs do not usually vary greatly in their output is not to imply that structures uncovered by factor analysis are without serious ambiguities. In particular, one common structure of attitudinal data seems to produce an indeterminant factor structure. This occurs when almost all the items are correlated in the range from about .15 to .45. Sometimes only a single factor will emerge from such a matrix, and sometimes a solution will be generated that more clearly reflects item differentiation on a

[1]Researchers should not be deceived by what appear to be high factor loadings. Factor loadings need to be squared to reach levels that are equivalent to correlation coefficients.

series of factors. We have encountered one instance in which an instrument that was carefully constructed to reflect a single dimension of inner- versus other-directedness (according to a forced-choice response format) was found to contain eight factors when presented in Likert format. Thus one can offer no guarantee that building scales based on interitem significance will invariably generate unidimensional scales. Nonetheless, only by these procedures can scale authors properly separate the apples, oranges, and coconuts in the fruit salad of items they have assembled.

One final word of caution: It is possible to devise a scale with very high internal consistency merely by writing the same item in a number of different ways. Obviously such scales tap an extremely narrow construct. Sampling of item content, therefore, is crucial in assessing internal consistency. Internal consistency is a very desirable property, but it needs to be balanced by concept coverage, proper norms, and careful validity work.

5. *Convergent Validity* (*Known Groups*): Validity is the more crucial indicator of the value of the scale. Nevertheless, group discrimination is not necessarily the most challenging hurdle to demonstrated validity. It is rather difficult to construct a liberalism–conservatism scale that will *not* show significant differences between members of The Heritage Foundation and members of the American Civil Liberties Union, or a religious attitude scale that will not separate Mormons from Jews or ministerial students from engineers. The more demanding criterion is whether the scale scores reliably distinguish happy people from miserable people, liberals from conservatives, or agnostics from believers within heterogeneous samples—or predict which of them will demonstrate behavior congruent with their attitudes.

6. *Convergent Validity (Predictions from Theory):* A second and more usual test of convergent validity involves obtaining results from the scale consistent with one's theory. For example, one might find that older people or better educated people or students with higher grades score higher on the scale, which would be consistent or convergent with some theoretical expectation or prediction. One might also expect that the scale scores would be higher among people who engaged in some type of behavior (such as joining a social group or contributing money) or expressed a particular attitude. The persuasiveness of this convergent or construct validation depends, of course, on the comprehensiveness and plausibility of the theory and the strength of the outside correlations. More formal attempts to establish construct validity have been attempted through causal modeling (e.g., Andrews, 1984).

7. *Cross-validation:* Cross-validation requires two different samples and measures of some criterion variable on each sample. The question to be answered by the test is whether the combination of items for sample *A* that best correlates with the criterion variable will also work for sample *B*, and conversely whether the best set of sample *B* items works for sample *A*. Note that the crux of the procedure involves first identifying the items from sample *A* and then testing them independently on sample *B*.

8. *Discriminant Validation:* A more refined and powerful standard is the multitrait–multimethod matrix proposed by Campbell and Fiske (1959). The method requires more than one index of each of the several constructs (say, *x*, *y*, and *z*) one wants to measure with the instrument. It is best to include as many measures or indices of each construct as possible as well as to measure for control purposes such variables as intelligence and response set that could also explain apparent relationships. In the resulting correlation matrix, the various items measuring each single construct (say, *x*) should first correlate highly among themselves; second, the correlations among these items should be higher than their correlations with the items intended to measure construct *y* or *z*, or any of the control variables. The latter is evidence of the scale's ability to discriminate from these other measures.

Needless to say, this is a gross oversimplification of the Campbell–Fiske criteria, and interested readers should examine the authors' article thoroughly before attempting com-

Table 1-2

Some Criteria for Evaluating Attitude Measures

Criterion rating	4. Exemplary	3. Extensive	2. Moderate	1. Minimal	0. None
Theoretical development/ structure	Reflects several important works in the field plus extensive face validity check	Either reviews several works or has extensive face validity	Reviews more than one source	Reviews one (no sources)	Ad hoc
Pilot testing/item development	More than 250 items in the initial pool; several pilot studies	100–250 items in the initial pool; more than two pilot studies	50–100 items in the initial pool; two pilot studies	Some items eliminated; one small pilot study	All initial items included; no pilot study
Available norms	Means and SDs for several subsamples and total sample; extensive information for each item	Means and SDs for total and some groups; some item information	Means for some subgroups; information for some items	Means for total group only; information for 1–2 items	No means or SDs; no item information
Samples of respondents	Random sample of nation/community with response rate over 60%, of college students	Cross-sectional sample of nation/community; random national sample	Some representation of noncollege groups; random sample of college students in same departments or colleges	Two or more college classes (some heterogeneity)	One classroom group only (no heterogeneity)
Interitem correlations	Interitem correlation average of .30 or better	Interitem correlation average of .20–.29	Interitem correlation average of .10–.19	Interitem correlations below .10	No interitem analysis reported

Continued

Table 1-2
Some Criteria for Evaluating Attitude Measures—cont'd

Criterion rating	4. Exemplary	3. Extensive	2. Moderate	1. Minimal	0. None
Coefficient α	.80 or better	.70–.79	.60–.69	<.60	Not reported
Factor analysis	Single factor from factor analysis	Single factor from factor analysis	Single factor from factor analysis	Some items on same factors	No factor structure
Test-retest	Scale scores correlate more than .50 across at least a 1-year period	Scale scores correlate more than .40 across a 3- to 12-month period	Scale scores correlate more than .30 across a 1- to 3-month period	Scale scores correlate more than .20 across a 1-month period	No data reported
Known groups validity	Discriminates between known groups highly significantly; groups also diverse	Discriminates between known groups highly significantly	Discriminates between known groups significantly	Discriminates between known groups	No known groups data
Convergent validity	Highly significant correlations with more than two related measures	Significant correlations with more than two related measures	Significant correlations with two related measures	Significant correlation with one related measure	No significant correlations reported
Discriminant validity	Significantly different from four or more unrelated measures	Significantly different from two or three unrelated measures	Significantly different from one unrelated measure	Different from one correlated measure	No difference or no data
Freedom from response set	Three or more studies show independence	Two studies show independence	One study shows independence	Some show independence; others do not	No tests of independence

parable analyses. At the time they were writing, Campbell and Fiske found only a few personality scales that met their conditions. One more recent example of an attitude scale that meets them is Andrews and Crandall's (1976) life-quality scale.

In certain chapters in our earlier volumes, in which a sufficient number of instruments to warrant comparison were present, we attempted to rate each scale on all such considerations.

Readers might consider using the rating scheme shown in Table 1–2 to evaluate the adequacy of measures they propose to use. Readers are also referred to the psychometric standards of the American Psychological Association (1985) and those in Heise and Bohrnstedt (1970), Bohrnstedt and Borgatta (1981), and Werts and Linn (1970) for "quick methods" of ascertaining reliability and validity.

Even this extensive list of proposed criteria is far from exhaustive. The actual choice of an instrument should be dictated by decision theoretic considerations. Thus the increasing of homogeneity by adding questionnaire items needs to be balanced against corresponding increases in administrative analysis and cost (as well as respondent fatigue and noncooperation) before one decides on how many attitude items to use. For assessing general levels of some attitude (e.g., separating believers from atheists), well-worded single items may do the job just as well as longer scales no matter how competently the scales are devised.

Future Volumes

As noted earlier, this is the second or our updated measurement volumes. The next volume in this series will deal with measures of role- and relationship-related attitudes (e.g., work, love, marriage, parenthood). Areas for further volumes are being considered, and further revisions of the present volume will appear as demand and changes in the field warrant.

Appendix: Specialized Political Attitude Scales

(John P. Robinson & Martha Kropf)

In this appendix we include several attitude scales and items that did not fit easily into the following chapters. The first three scales, for example, measure various aspects of political "cosmopolitanism"—looking to outside, universal norms rather than to what may be more prevalent or popular in one's own community or neighborhood:

1. Cultural Cosmopolitanism Scale (Robinson & Zill, 1997)
2. Local Cosmopolitanism Scale (Dye, 1963)
3. Cosmopolitanism Scale (Jennings, 1965)

Dictionaries typically define cosmopolitanism as "being free of local/national interests or prejudices." The most recent scale tapping this construct was developed from five items dealing with culture that were asked in the 1993 GSS. Robinson and Zill (1997) found that responses to these five items told a great deal about a respondent's attitudes on a variety of political issues, such as race relations, welfare, abortion, and internationalism; responses also correlated strongly with whether GSS respondents considered themselves to be politically liberal rather than conservative. Similar relations were found with the earlier measures of political cosmopolitanism included in this appendix, the first by Dye (1963) in a community study and the second by Jennings (1965) in a national study of high school seniors. The Jennings scale has the advantage of being simpler and freer of agreement response set than the Dye scale.

The second set of scales included in this appendix deals with the concept of general political responsibility—in particular, whether one takes the concerns of the wider society into account rather than simple self-interest:

4. Social Responsibility Scale (SRS) (Berkowitz & Lutterman, 1968)
5. Citizen Duty Scale (Campbell, Gurin, & Miller, 1954)
6. Sociotropic Evaluations (MacKuen, Erikson, & Stimson, 1992)

The SRS has the advantages of being developed on a statewide sample and of showing relations with a wide variety of political behaviors, in both field and college settings. The Campbell *et al.* Citizen Duty Scale was developed as a predictor of various forms of political participation. It did rather well in the early 1950s, but newer versions have been created to predict other aspects of political behavior, such as paying taxes and participating in the census. The Sociotropic Evaluations measures are derived from traditional economic measures of consumer sentiment but have been adapted to predict presidential evaluation and voting, as demonstrated in the MacKuen *et al.* article.

The final three scales cover diverse topics:

7. Diffuse Support for the Supreme Court (Caldeira & Gibson, 1992; Tanenhaus & Murphy, 1981)
8. Beliefs about the Distribution of Power (Form & Rytina, 1969)
9. New Ecological Consciousness (Ellis & Thompson, 1997)

The Caldeira and Gibson scale represents an attempt to distinguish between "diffuse" and "specific" support, the latter being support for the Court's specific decisions. Tanenhaus and Murphy's items are included for comparison purposes. The Form and Rytina scale is based on an unusual approach to the study of political beliefs. It focuses on ways in which respondents view the distribution of political power in society, whether determined mainly by business interests (as claimed by Marx), a power "elite" (Mills), or pluralistic interests that may cut across class lines (Riesman). The final scale (by Ellis and Thompson) refers to the specific issue of the environment, which should become increasingly salient in the future. Although this scale needs to be applied to broader samples, it appears to correlate with a number of political and social attitudes and could be a model for other issues likely to emerge in the future, such as the role and size of government.

Cultural Cosmopolitanism Scale

(J. P. Robinson & N. Zill, 1997)

Variable

This scale measures a variety of attitudes about broad cultural issues that have surprising correlations with a number of political attitudes.

Description

These 1993 GSS questions tapped a number of unexplored aspects of the public's views concerning cultural differences in society, such as the educational emphasis on "Great

Books" and the skill and artistry evident in abstract modern art. Common to each of the items is the sense that artistic and cultural distinctions are mainly made arbitrarily or by a few elites whose views are hard to understand or justify (and who may even be undemocratic in the sense of advocating cultural views not prevalent among most Americans). Opposing them involves a conviction that cultural distinction and excellence take many forms. Such a mindset goes along with a general openness to mix with people who have different cultural views.

The Cultural Cosmopolitanism Scale consists of five items rejecting a sense that art and culture are the province of a privileged few and endorsing a general openness to new ideas and people. It fits the standard dictionary definition of a cosmopolite as someone free of local/national interests or prejudices. Scores on the scale are roughly normally distributed, meaning that there is a balance of agree and disagree responses to each item.

Sample

The 1993 GSS was based on a nationally representative sample of 1650 respondents. The response rate was over 75%.

Reliability

Internal Consistency

The items intercorrelate in the .20–.30 range and emerge as a single factor in a factor analysis. The value of alpha is .74.

Test–Retest

No data are available.

Validity

Convergent

Respondents with Democratic Party identification have higher Cosmopolitanism scores. But the major political correlate is ideological identification. Self-defined liberals tend to be more cosmopolitan than either moderates or conservatives, and the extent of ideological differences on the Cosmopolitanism questions is among the greatest of the differences on more than 100 politically relevant questions included in the GSS—higher than the differences between self-defined liberals and conservatives on international isolationism, support for government intervention on welfare issues, abortion, support for capital punishment, and policies on interracial busing. The difference in cosmopolitanism is almost on a par with differences on the major GSS issues dividing liberals and conservatives, namely sexual issues, such as involvement in premarital or extramarital affairs and views on homosexuality.

Higher Cosmopolitanism scores go along with higher scores on other GSS measures related to culture and values. Thus, those higher in cosmopolitanism are also higher in cultural salience and lower in Darwinian worldview. The cultural salience items asked respondents about various characteristics of friends that are important to them; to the extent that they rated "intelligent," "cultured," and "creative" as more important characteristics, cultural salience scores were higher.

As expected, cosmopolitanism is substantially related to education, especially after adjusting for gender, age, and the like. Just as important as years of education are qualitative distinctions among kinds of education. Those who say they enjoyed their literature and humanities courses most in high school scored above average, as did those who remembered science and psychology courses most positively.

Larger differences are found in courses taken at the college level. Those who majored in literature and fine arts in college were above average in cosmopolitanism compared with others who attended college, but the highest scores were obtained by people who majored in psychology and political studies. Those who majored in business and vocational studies scored below average, but the lowest scores were obtained by engineers, whose scores were slightly lower than those of high school graduates. Thus simply having a college education is not a guarantee of cultural openness. Differences by college major remained after controlling for gender, age, and other background factors.

As might be expected, higher Cosmopolitanism scores are found in geographic areas with more exposure to other cultures, such as the East and West Coasts and large cities; lower scores are found in southern and less urban areas. After controlling for education, age, and so on, however, the regional differences are not large.

Discriminant

People with higher incomes are above average in their Cosmopolitanism scores; but when education is controlled, the difference reverses direction, and wealthier people obtain below-average scores.

Location

Robinson, J. P., & Zill, N. (1997). Matters of culture. *American Demographics, 19,* 48–52.

Results and Comments

The following demographic differences in cultural cosmopolitanism were found:

1. Women scored significantly higher than men, and the differences became larger after the lower education and higher age of women were taken into account.
2. Higher scores were found among black respondents, who may have responded favorably to the value placed on diversity.
3. Older people obtained lower average scores, even when education and age were controlled. For respondents under age 55 higher scores were obtained by those aged 35–54 than by younger people.

Higher Cosmopolitanism scores go along with an optimistic view of life. Respondents who are happier also have higher scores, as do those who are satisfied with their financial status. Among both affluent and poorer respondents, the more satisfaction, the higher the Cosmopolitanism score—again after controlling for other variables.

There is a second cultural attitude factor inherent in the nine GSS cultural issue items, and it is unrelated to cosmopolitanism. The more a person agrees that there is too much emphasis on politically correct art, that folk/popular art can share equal excellence with high art, and that the human element is what defines great literature, the more ecumenical or universal is the person's cultural orientation. It might be thought that these ecumenicism items simply reflect the other end of cosmopolitanism, but that is not how people in the GSS sample responded to them. Instead, they reflect a different kind of openness, one that treats literature and art on their own merits, not on how they are labeled or categorized in terms of audience appeal. The scale implies relativism in what qualifies as worthwhile cultural content. One feature of ecumenicism that it shares with cosmopolitanism is a correlation with education. It differs from cosmopolitanism, however, in that there are no age or gender differences, and differences due to income, location, and other background factors are also very small. Moreover, the relation between ecumenicism and race is different, with blacks being significantly less likely to be ecumenical in the sense measured by these items:

1. The greatest books are universal in their appeal: there is no "white literature," "black literature," or "Asian literature"; there is only human literature.
2. It is a shame when traditional American literature is ignored while other works are promoted because they are by women or by members of minority groups.
3. Artistic excellence can be found in popular and folk culture just as much as in the fine arts.

Higher scores are associated with agreement on each item.

Cultural Cosmopolitanism Scale
(Robinson & Zill, 1997)

1. Only a few people have the knowledge and ability to judge excellence in the arts. (47%)*

1	2	3	4	5
STRONGLY AGREE	AGREE	NEITHER AGREE NOR DISAGREE	DISAGREE	STRONGLY DISAGREE

2. High schools and colleges spend too much time making students read classics that have little relevance in today's world. (56%)
3. Modern painting is just slapped on: a child could do it. (55%)
4. It is better for everyone if English is the only language used in public schools. (50%)
5. I would feel uncomfortable entertaining people I don't know in my home. (45%)

*Percentage who disagree (which indicates cosmopolitanism)

Local Cosmopolitan Scale
(T. R. Dye, 1963)

Variable

This instrument was designed to characterize an individual as more "local" or more "cosmopolitan" according to the level of social environment in which he or she feels most comfortable.

Description

Items were intended to identify persons whose scale of social experience is limited, whose primary interest and involvement are in local rather than national or international affairs, who perceive themselves primarily as members of a local community rather than of larger social organizations, and who identify with and allocate respect toward individuals with local rather than national reputations. The five 6-point Likert-type items were distributed at random throughout a mailed questionnaire. Agreement with each item was in the local direction, and scores on the scale ranged from 5 (least local) to 30 (most local).

Sample

The sample of 340 residents and 105 elected public officials was drawn from 16 suburban municipalities in the Philadelphia metropolitan area. The municipalities were selected to represent social types (six upper, five middle, five lower), using occupational and educational characteristics as criteria. Respondents returning the mailed interviews were probably biased toward those most interested in politics.

Reliability

Internal Consistency

The reliability of each item was established by showing that it distinguished significantly between respondents in the highest and lowest quartiles on the scale.

Test–Retest

No data were reported.

Validity

Convergent

The relevance of the attitude tapped by the scale to local-cosmopolitan policy choices was tested by relating scale scores to answers on a short opinion poll concerning three recurring metropolitan issues. With community social rank held constant, significantly more cosmopolitans than locals favored improving mass transit and areawide government and opposed discriminatory zoning.

Discriminant

No data were reported.

Location

Dye, T. R. (1963). The local-cosmopolitan dimension and the study of urban politics. *Social Forces, 41,* 239–246.

Results and Comments

It was found that localism was inversely related to status: the mean of residents from upper-ranked municipalities was 16.3 as compared to means of 17.2 and 19.3 for residents of middle and lower-ranked municipalities, respectively. In each type of community, leaders possessed significantly higher "local" mean scores than their constituents, even though the leaders' means varied consistently with the social rank of their communities.

This scale is vulnerable to agreement response set, especially in lower-socioeconomic-status communities, which might partially account for this group's higher localism scores. Still the construct measured by the scale taps a useful distinction in one's political outlook and is amenable to less biased measurement in future studies.

Local Cosmopolitan Scale
(Dye, 1963)

1. The most rewarding organizations a person can belong to are local clubs and associations rather than large nationwide organizations.

1	2	3	4	5	6
STRONGLY DISAGREE	DISAGREE	SLIGHTLY DISAGREE	SLIGHTLY AGREE	AGREE	STRONGLY AGREE

2. Despite all the newspaper and TV coverage, national and international happenings rarely seem as interesting as events that occur right in the local community in which one lives.

3. No doubt many newcomers to the community are capable people; but when it comes to choosing a person for a responsible position in the community, I prefer a man whose family is well established in the community.

4. Big cities may have their place but the local community is the backbone of America.

5. I have greater respect for a man who is well established in his local community than a man who is widely known in his field but who has no local roots.

Cosmopolitanism Scale
(M. K. Jennings, 1965)

Variable

This instrument taps an individual's orientations toward multiple levels of government.

Description

The scale consists of a simple rank-ordering of the degree to which an individual follows local, state, national, or international affairs.

These four items can be rank-ordered in any of 24 ways. Only 7 of these orderings fit Coombs's (1964) criteria for a unidimensional scale. These orderings, from most cosmopolitan (1) to least cosmopolitan (7), are as follows:

Ordering	% of population
1. International-National-State-Local	21
2. National-International-State-Local	33
3. National-State-International-Local	18
4. State-National-International-Local	17
5. State-National-Local-International	5
6. State-Local-National-International	3
7. Local-State-National-International	3
	100%

Only 53% of the sample gave one of the above 7 orderings, the remaining 17 orderings being assigned to the most similar acceptable ordering. (Thus, International-National-Local-State and National-International-Local-State were given the same code as ordering 2).

Sample

The sample consisted of 1669 seniors selected to represent a national cross-section of high school seniors in the United States. The interviews were conducted in the spring of 1965, with a response rate of 97%.

Reliability

Internal Consistency

No data bearing directly on the internal structure of the scale are reported, although as noted above 53% of the sample gave one of the seven acceptable response patterns. An alternative scale-ordering running from Local-International-National-State to State-National-International Local resulted in 66% of the students fitting the scale.

Test–Retest

No data were reported.

Validity

Convergent

Cosmopolitanism was found to be moderately related to political knowledge (*gamma* = .35) and notably related to interest in the United Nations. These relations held when controls were applied for three variables related to cosmopolitanism: general concern with public affairs, student grade average, and mother's educational level.

Discriminant

No data were reported.

Location

Jennings, M. K. (1966, April). *Pre-adult orientations to multiple systems of government.* Paper prepared for the Midwest Conference of Political Scientists, Survey Research Center, University of Michigan, Ann Arbor.

Results and Comments

The items can be administered in less than three minutes. The following total distribution of rankings was obtained:

Rank of how closely followed	Level of affairs				
	International	National	State	Local	
First	39%	44%	6%	11%	100%
Second	26%	38%	18%	18%	100%
Third	16%	14%	45%	25%	100%
Fourth	19%	3%	32%	46%	100%

The relatively high proportion of response patterns that did not fit the model and the fact that an alternative scale ordering fits the data better suggest that more than one dimension is needed to account for the data.

   Students in the south proved less cosmopolitan than students in other geographical regions, as did students who had experienced more permanent residency. No differences were found between urban and rural dwellers or between boys and girls. When compared with their parents, students were found to voice much greater interest in international affairs. Thus, while over half the students scored 1 or 2 on the cosmopolitan end of the scale, less than a third of their parents did.

Cosmopolitanism Scale
(Jennings, 1965)

1. Which one do you follow most closely—international affairs, national affairs, state affairs, or local affairs?
2. Which one do you follow least (interviewer reads the three remaining levels)?
3. Of the other two (interviewer reads the two remaining levels), which one do you follow most closely?
(The residual level occupies the third rank.)

Social Responsibility Scale
(L. Berkowitz & K. Lutterman, 1968)

Variable

This scale assesses a person's traditional social responsibility, an orientation toward helping others even when there is nothing to be gained from them.

Description

Six of the eight items in the Social Responsibility Scale (SRS) are drawn from a similar scale for children designed by Harris (1957). These, in turn, are similar to items constructed earlier by Gough *et al.* (1952). The items in the present scale are linked with traditional values and are, therefore, likely to have a conservative cast. The scale was conceptualized as measuring a construct that is the opposite of alienation. Items are administered in Likert format, with five response options ranging from Strongly Agree to Strongly Disagree. Four items are worded in the responsible direction and four in the opposite direction. The SRS closely follows earlier measures of this concept, but it benefits from having been applied to a statewide probability sample in which correlations with a wide variety of associated behaviors and attitudes were obtained. The items in the scale have been constructed to control for agreement response set.

Sample

The SRS was administered to a statewide probability sample of 766 Wisconsin adults in early fall 1963. The response rate was 88%.

Reliability

While the scale was constructed on the basis of item analyses with samples of college students, no statistical data are reported. No test–retest data were reported.

Validity

Convergent

Among both working-class and middle-class respondents those scoring high on the SRS were more likely to

1. Make financial contributions to an educational or a religious institution.
2. Be active in organizations or church work.
3. Show greater interest in national and local politics and be more active politically.
4. Vote in elections and know the names of candidates for office.
5. Oppose greater government involvement with the problem of unemployment and oppose extending Social Security.

Discriminant

No data were reported.

Location

Berkowitz, L., & Lutterman, K. G. (1968). The traditionally socially responsible personality. *Public Opinion Quarterly, 32,* 169–185.

Results and Comments

High SRS scorers among both middle- and working-class respondents tended to affiliate more with the Republican Party. It was concluded that "all in all, high scorers on SRS generally were least inclined to deviate from the political traditions of their class and community." High SRS scorers were not "other-directed conformists," however. They were less likely (than those with low SRS scores) to place a high value on children being well liked or popular and more likely to place a high value on thinking for oneself. High SRS scorers in the working class were less likely than low SRS scorers to disagree with the view that big business was too powerful.

The SRS was strongly associated with education, but the laboratory behavior of college students (all with roughly equal education) was congruent with their SRS scores. Finally, the results run counter to McClosky's (1958) well-known description of conservatives as alienated and hostile.

Social Responsibility Scale
(Berkowitz & Lutterman, 1968)

*1. It is no use worrying about current events or public affairs; I can't do anything about them anyway.

1	2	3	4	5
STRONGLY AGREE	AGREE	UNDECIDED	DISAGREE	STRONGLY DISAGREE

2. Every person should give some of his time for the good of his town or country.

*3. Our country would be a lot better off if we didn't have so many elections and people didn't have to vote so often.

*4. Letting your friends down is not so bad because you can't do good all the time for everybody.

5. It is the duty of each person to do his job the very best he can.

*6. People would be a lot better off if they could live far away from other people and never have to do anything for them.

7. At school I usually volunteered for special projects.

8. I feel very bad when I have failed to finish a job I promised I would do.

* Reverse scored.

Citizen Duty Scale
(A. Campbell, G. Gurin, & W. E. Miller, 1954)

Variable

Sense of citizen duty is defined as the feeling that people ought to participate in the political process, regardless of whether such political activity is deemed as efficacious.

Description

The Citizen Duty Scale was expected to correlate positively with, and therefore to help explain, the authors' Index of Political Participation. The scale is composed of four agree–disagree items forming a five-point Guttman scale. Scores were 0 (6%), 1 (3%), 2 (7%),

3 (40%), and 4 (44%). Negative responses to all items are coded as indicating a sense of civic duty.

Reliability

Internal Consistency

The coefficient of reproducibility was .96, with a maximum error of 5%, giving a plus percentage ratio of .77.

Test–Retest

No test–retest data were reported.

Validity

Convergent

The Citizen Duty Scale was positively correlated with the Index of Political Participation. The Participation Index scores ranged from +17 for those with the highest Citizen Duty score to −69 for those with the lowest, and there were no reversals among intervening scale types.

Discriminant

No data were reported.

Location

Campbell, A., Gurin, G., & Miller, W. E. (1954). *The voter decides.* Evanston, IL: Row Peterson & Co.

Results and Comments

The relationship between citizen duty and political participation persisted even when eight demographic variables were held constant. The items are susceptible to agreement response set, since they are all phrased in the same direction. More recently Citizen Duty items have been developed for actions other than voting, such as filling out census forms (Couper, Singer, & Kulka, 1998) and paying taxes (Schloz & Lubell, 1998; Schloz & Pinney, 1995).

Citizen Duty Scale
(Campbell, Gurin, & Miller, 1954)

1. It isn't so important to vote when you know your party doesn't have a chance to win.
   0. AGREE   1. DISAGREE
2. A good many local elections aren't important enough to bother with.

3. So many other people vote in the national elections that it doesn't matter much to me whether I vote or not.

4. If a person doesn't care how an election comes out, he shouldn't vote in it.

Sociotropic Evaluations

(M. B. MacKuen, R. S. Erikson, & J. A. Stimson, 1992)

Variable

This scale is composed of evaluations of the state of the national economy, which presumably reflect concern about the overall state of the country (in relation to one's personal economic state).

Description

The scale is composed of three items from the University of Michigan's Index of Consumer Sentiment, which asks respondents to rate whether current business conditions have improved and will improve over the next year and the next five years. These are often contrasted with three similar items asking about the respondent's personal economic situation, or "pocketbook" concerns. The scale is scored and weighted differently by different authors.

Sample

These items have been routinely administered since the 1950s in consumer behavior studies done at the University of Michigan's Survey Research Center and were often included in its ANES surveys of cross-sectional probability samples of the American public. The usual sample size was about 1500.

Reliability

Internal Consistency

The items generally cluster together with the exception of item 5, on current buying conditions.

Test–Retest

No data could be located.

Validity

Convergent

The items were found by these authors and others to predict presidential approval.

Discriminant

MacKuen *et al.* found that the items dealing with the future (particularly the longer five-year period) predicted approval better than items dealing with the present.

Location

MacKuen, M. B., Erikson, R. S., & Stimson, J. A. (1992). Peasants or bankers: The American electorate and the U.S. economy. *American Political Science Review, 86,* 597–611.

Results and Comments

Several investigators have used various of these items to predict not only presidential approval, but also presidential vote (e.g., Marcus, 1988), and to indicate that concern about the overall economy supersedes concern about personal pocketbook issues (e.g., Funk & Garcia-Monet, 1997). An expanded set of personal and collective economic expectation items from the EuroBarometer surveys is reported in Lewis-Beck (1988, p. 44).

Sociotropic and Pocketbook Items
(MacKuen, Erikson, & Stimson, 1992)

These items were all derived from consumer sentiment surveys.

Sociotropic Items

1. Would you say that at the present time business conditions are better or worse than they were a year ago?
   1. BETTER   2. WORSE

2. Now turning to business conditions in the country as a whole—do you think that during the next 12 months we'll have good times financially, or bad times, or what?
   1. GOOD TIMES   2. BAD TIMES

3. Looking ahead, which would you say is more likely—that in the country as a whole we'll have continuous good times during the next 5 years or so, or that we will have periods of widespread unemployment or depression, or what?
   1. CONTINUOUS GOOD   2. PERIODS OF UNEMPLOYMENT

Pocketbook Items

4. Would you say that you (and your family living with you) are better off or worse off financially than you were a year ago?
   1. BETTER OFF   2. WORSE OFF

5. Generally speaking, do you think now is a good or a bad time for people to buy major household items?
   1. GOOD TIME   2. BAD TIME

---

6. Now looking ahead—do you think that a year from now you (and your family living there) will be better off financially, or worse off, or just about the same as now?
1. BETTER OFF   2. ABOUT SAME   3. WORSE OFF

Diffuse Support for the Supreme Court
(G. A. Caldeira & J. L. Gibson, 1992; J. Tanenhaus
& W. F. Murphy, 1981)

Variable

These two sets of scale items tap diffuse support, defined as "a reservoir of favorable attitudes or good will that helps members to accept or tolerate outputs to which they are opposed or the effects of which they see as damaging to their wants" (Easton, 1965, p. 273).

Description

Caldiera and Gibson's (1992) scale differs from previous measures of this concept in using "items that concern willingness to support elemental changes in the powers, process, and structures of the high bench" (p. 639). The emphasis in the five items is on fundamental changes, not procedural or minor details. It is not clear how the scale was scored, but scores presumably run from 5 (least supportive) to 25 (most supportive). Item 5 is presumably reverse scored.

Sample

The items were included in a reinterview of 1106 respondents in the 1987 GSS, a national probability survey of adults aged 18 and older with an original response rate of about 75%.

Reliability

Internal Consistency

The items loaded on a single factor, with loadings ranging from .74 for item 1 to .46 for item 5. Item correlations with the total scale score ranged from .84 for item 1 to .51 for item 5.

Test-Retest

No data were reported.

Validity

Convergent

As predicted, the scale showed no relation to "specific support" for the Court, that is, support for the Court's decisions on specific cases or issues. The authors criticize previous scales for their inability to separate diffuse from specific support.

Discriminant

The above evidence also suggests discriminant validity, although one would ideally like to have the authors' scale and alternative scales administered to the same sample.

Location

Caldeira, G. A., & Gibson, J. L. (1992). The etiology of public support for the Supreme Court. *American Journal of Political Science, 36,* 635–664.

Tanenhaus, J., & Murphy, W. F. (1981). Patterns of public support for the Supreme Court: A panel study. *Journal of Politics, 43,* 24–39.

Results and Comments

The authors find much less support for the Court among blacks than whites. In general, respondents with more "liberal" attitudes were found to be more supportive of the Court, but none of the relationships with issue positions was particularly strong.

Tanenhaus and Murphy's (1981) alternative set of items measuring diffuse Court support, based on ANES samples in 1966 and 1975, is provided here for contrast and as a potential resource for future scaling efforts.

Diffuse Support for the Supreme Court (Caldeira & Gibson, 1992)

1. The power of the Supreme Court to declare acts of Congress unconstitutional should be eliminated.

1	2	3	4	5
STRONGLY AGREE	AGREE	NEITHER AGREE NOR DISAGREE	DISAGREE	STRONGLY DISAGREE

2. If the Supreme Court continually makes decisions that the people disagree with, it might be better to do away with the Court altogether.
3. It would not make much difference to me if the U.S. Constitution were rewritten so as to reduce the powers of the Supreme Court.
4. The right of the Supreme Court to decide certain types of controversial issues should be limited by the Congress.
5. People should be willing to do everything they can to make sure that any proposal to abolish the Supreme Court is defeated.

*Revised item.

Diffuse Support for the Court Scale
(Tanenhaus & Murphy, 1981)

1. How well do you think the Supreme Court does the job: very well or not very well? (Supreme Court's main job in the government as R understands it)
   1. VERY WELL   3. PRO-CON   5. NOT VERY WELL   7. IT DEPENDS

2. Some people think that the Supreme Court gets too mixed up in politics. Others don't feel that way. How about you? Do you think the Supreme Court gets too mixed up in politics or not?
   1. YES   5. NO   7. IT DEPENDS

3. Sometimes people tell us they trust the Supreme Court more than Congress. Others disagree with that. Which do you trust more, the Supreme Court or Congress?
   1. SUPREME   2. CONGRESS   3. BOTH   5. NEITHER   7. IT DEPENDS
      COURT

4. Do you think that in its decisions the Supreme Court favors any particular group or groups in this country?
   1. YES   5. NO   7. IT DEPENDS

Beliefs about the Distribution of Power

(W. H. Form & J. Rytina, 1969)

Variable

This scale assesses whether individuals believe that power in the United States is distributed according to the positions advocated by David Riesman (political pluralism), C. Wright Mills (power elite), or Karl Marx (control by big business).

Description

The task for the respondent is to pick one of the three formulations of how power is distributed in the United States. The following distribution was obtained:

Pluralistic	63%
Elitist	19%
Economic dominance	18%
	100%

Statements concerning an "employee and managerial society" were originally included but later dropped because so few respondents considered them meaningful.

The measure consists of a single question asking the respondent to choose which of three descriptions best fits the way power is distributed in America. The three descriptions follow the basic philosophies of Reisman, Mills, and Marx.

Sample

The sample consisted of a cross-section of 186 respondents in Muskegon, Michigan, plus supplementary samples of poor and rich respondents, bringing the total up to 354. They were interviewed in the mid-1960s.

Reliability

No reliability data were reported, although only test–retest indicators would be possible, given the single-item format.

Validity

No data bearing directly on validity were reported. However, the authors say that because the pluralistic belief is reported more often by those with higher incomes, there is support for their hypothesis that this view would appeal to people who get more rewards from the system. On the other hand, the authors note that although higher-income respondents reported belief in the pluralist ideology, very few rejected the task of selecting which groups were most powerful when asked to give such ratings. (Such ratings would constitute a violation of the pluralistic conception of politics.)

Location

Form, W. H., & Rytina, J. (1969). Ideological beliefs on the distribution power in the United States. *American Sociological Review, 34,* 19–31.

Results and Comments

Larger differences were found in ideological beliefs by education than by the factors of income or race. The pluralistic view was endorsed by 73% of college graduates but only 33% of those who had completed just grade school. This view was held by 55% of the poor and 65% of the rich. Those choosing the economic dominance model varied from 40% of the less-than-grade-school educated to 8% of college graduates. Blacks (37%) were much more likely to take this view than whites (18%) and poor whites (23%) more than rich whites (12%).

Distribution of Power Scale
(Form & Rytina, 1969)

I am going to read you three ways in which people think that power in this country is distributed. Which of these, in your opinion, is the most accurate description?

a. No one group really runs the government in this country. Instead, important decisions about national policy are made by a lot of different groups such as labor, business, religious, and educational groups, and so on. These groups influence both political parties, but no single group can dictate to the others, and each group is strong enough to protect its own interests. (Riesman)*

b. A small group of men at the top really run the government in this country. These are the heads of the biggest business corporations, the highest officers

in the Army, Navy, and Air Force, and a few important senators, congressmen and federal officials in Washington. These men dominate both the Republican and Democratic parties. (Mills)

c. Big businessmen really run the government in this country. The heads of the
large corporations dominate both the Republican and Democratic parties.
This means that things in Washington go pretty much the way big businessmen want them to. (Marx)

*The theorists' names are not included when the measure is administered.

New Ecological Consciousness

(R. J. Ellis & F. Thompson, 1997)

Variable

This scale taps general feelings about the degradation of the environment, including catastrophic concerns about overpopulation and limits to economic growth.

Description

The items cover 10 aspects of ecological consciousness using a 7-point Likert format, so
that scores can presumably vary from −30 (lowest consciousness) to +30 (highest consciousness). Since all items are worded and scored in the same direction, they are open to
agreement response set.

Sample

The items were asked of a sample of about 700 environmental activists from the Salem,
Oregon Audubon Society, the Oregon chapter of the Sierra Club, and Earth Island International organizations in Oregon and Washington. Response rates to mail surveys of these
organizations varied from 51 to 60%. A less intense set of items was administered to a
cross-sectional sample of nonactivists.

Reliability

Internal Consistency

An alpha of .83 was reported, with item to total scale correlations ranging from .42 to .65.

Test–Retest

No data were reported.

Validity

Convergent

Among the activists, environmental concern was positively correlated with being a Democrat ($r = .24$) and ideologically liberal ($r = .29$), as expected. It also correlated .39 (.31 after adjustment for other predictors) with egalitarianism and −.34 with individualism, con-

sistent with some characterizations of environmental activists. Even higher correlations were found with the less intense version of the scale administered to the general public.

Discriminant

No data were reported.

Location

Ellis, R. J., & Thompson, F. (1997). Culture and the environment in the Pacific Northwest. *American Political Science Review, 91*, 885–897.

Results and Comments

The authors also developed a scale of environmental concern that was applied to a public sample of about 375 residents of Salem and Yamhill County, Oregon. That scale had an alpha of .87 and consisted of items 1 and 10 below, plus "We are fast using up the world's natural resources," "The problems of the environment are not as bad as most people think" [reverse-scored item], and "People worry too much about human progress harming the environment" [reverse-scored item].

New Ecological Consciousness (Ellis & Thompson, 1997)

1. If things continue on their present course, we will soon experience a major ecological catastrophe.

−3	−2	−1	0	+1	+2	+3
STRONGLY DISAGREE	DISAGREE	SOMEWHAT DISAGREE	NEITHER AGREE NOR DISAGREE	SOMEWHAT AGREE	AGREE	STRONGLY AGREE

2. What human beings are currently doing to nature can be fairly characterized as an "ecoholocaust."
3. Humans are no more important than any other species.
4. We would be better off if we dramatically reduced the number of people on this earth.
5. No wild place will be safe from us until we reconsider our devout belief that economic growth is always good.
6. We can only save the planet by radically transforming our social lives with each other.
7. Unrelenting exploitation of nature has driven us to the brink of ecological collapse.
8. We have reduced natural beauty to postcard prettiness, just another commodity for our consumption.
9. Human happiness and human reproduction are less important than a healthy planet.
10. The oceans are gradually dying of oil pollution and dumping of waste.

References

American Psychological Association. (1985). *Standards for educational and psychological tests.* Washington, DC: Author.

Andrews, F. (1984). Construct validity and error components of survey measures: A structural modeling approach. *Public Opinion Quarterly, 48,* 409–422.

Andrews, F., & Crandall, R. (1976). The validity of measures of self-reported well-being. *Social Indicators Research, 3,* 1–19.

Berkowitz, L., & Lutterman, K. G. (1968). The traditionally socially responsible personality. *Public Opinion Quarterly, 32,* 169–185.

Bohrnstedt, G., & Borgatta, E. (Eds.). (1981). *Social measurement: Issues.* Newbury Park, CA: Sage.

Bohrnstedt, G., Mohler, P., & Muller, W. (Eds.). (1987). *Empirical study of the reliability and stability of survey research items.* Newbury Park, CA: Sage.

Caldeira, G. A., & Gibson, J. L. (1992). The etiology of public support for the Supreme Court. *American Journal of Political Science, 36,* 635–664.

Campbell, A., Gurin, G., & Miller, W. E. (1954). *The voter decides.* Evanston, IL: Row Peterson & Co.

Campbell, D., & Fiske, D. (1959). Convergent and discriminant validation by the multitrait multimethod matrix. *Psychological Bulletin, 56,* 81–105.

Christie, R., Havel, J., & Seidenberg, B. (1958). Is the F scale irreversible? *Journal of Abnormal and Social Psychology, 56,* 143–159.

Converse, J., & Presser, S. (1986). *Survey questions: Handcrafting the standardized questionnaire.* Newbury Park, CA: Sage.

Coombs, C. H. (1964). *A theory of data.* New York: Wiley.

Couper, M., Singer, E., & Kulka, R. A. (1998). Participation in the 1990 decennial census: Politics, privacy, pressures. *American Politics Quarterly, 26,* 59–80.

Cronbach, L. (1951). Coefficient alpha and the internal structure of tests. *Psychometrika, 31,* 93–96.

Cronbach, L., & Gleser, G. (1965). *Psychological tests and personnel decisions* (2nd ed.). Urbana: University of Illinois Press.

DeMaio, T. (1984). The social desirability variable in survey research. In C. Turner & E. Martin (Eds.), *Surveying subjective phenomena* (Vol. 2). New York: Russell Sage Foundation.

Dye, T. R. (1963). The local-cosmopolitan dimension and the study of urban politics. *Social Forces, 41,* 239–246.

Easton, D. A. (1965). *A systems analysis of political life.* New York: Wiley.

Edwards, A. (1957). *The social desirability variable in personality assessment and research.* New York: Dryden Press.

Ellis, R. J., & Thompson, F. (1997). Culture and the environment in the Pacific Northwest. *American Political Science Review, 91,* 885–897.

Form, W. H., & Rytina, J. (1969). Ideological beliefs on the distribution power in the United States. *American Sociological Review, 34,* 19–31.

Funk, C. L., & Garcia-Monet, P. A. (1997). The relationship between personal and national concerns in public perceptions about the economy. *Political Research Quarterly, 50,* 317–342.

Gough, H. G., McClosky, H., & Meehl, P. E. (1952). A personality scale for social responsibility. *Journal of Abnormal and Social Psychology, 47,* 73–80.

Harris, D. B. (1957). A scale for measuring attitudes of social responsibility in children. *Journal of Abnormal and Social Psychology, 55,* 322–326.

Heise, D. R., & Bohrnstedt, G. W. (1970). Validity, invalidity, and, reliability. In E. F. Borgatta & G. W. Borhnstedt (Eds.), *Sociological methodology.* San Francisco: Jossey-Bass.

Jennings, M. K. (1966, April). *Pre-adult orientations to multiple systems of government.* Paper prepared for the Midwest Conference of Political Scientists, Survey Research Center, University of Michigan, Ann Arbor.

Lewis-Beck, M. S. (1988). *Economics and elections: The major Western democracies.* Ann Arbor: University of Michigan Press.

MacKuen, M. B., Erikson, R. S., & Stimson, J. A. (1992). Peasants or bankers: The American electorate and the U.S. economy. *American Political Science Review, 86,* 597–611.

Marcus, G. B. (1988). The impact of personal and national economic conditions on the presidential vote. *American Journal of Political Science, 32,* 829–834.

McClosky, H. (1958). Conservatism and personality. *American Political Science Review, 52,* 27–45.

Robinson, J. P. (1969). Values. In J. P. Robinson & P. Shaver (Eds.), *Measures of social psychological attitudes.* Ann Arbor, MI: Institute for Social Research (also see review of 1965 Withey scale, p. 533).

Robinson, J. P., Athanasiou, R., & Head, K. (1967). *Measures of occupational attitudes and characteristics.* Ann Arbor, MI: Institute for Social Research.

Robinson, J. P., & Meadow, R. (1982). *Polls apart.* Cabin John, MD: Seven Locks Press.

Robinson, J.P., Shaver, P. R., & Wrightsman, L. S. (Eds.). (1991). *Measures of personality and social psychological attitudes.* San Diego, CA: Academic Press.

Robinson, J. P., & Zill, N. (1997). Matters of culture. *American Demographics, 19,* 48–52.

Schloz, J. T., & Lubell, M. (1998). Trust and taxpaying: Testing the heuristic approach to collective action. *American Journal of Political Science, 42,* 398–417.

Schloz, J. T., & Pinney, N. (1995). Duty, fear, and tax compliance: The heuristic basis of citizenship behavior. *American Journal of Political Science, 39,* 490–512.

Scott, W. A. (1960). Measures of test homogeneity. *Educational and Psychological Measurement, 20,* 751–757.

Sears, D. (1986). College sophomores in the laboratory: Influences of a narrow data base on social psychology's view of human nature. *Journal of Personality and Social Psychology, 51,* 515–530.

Sudman, S., & Bradburn, N. (1982). *Asking questions.* San Francisco: Jossey-Bass.

Tanenhaus, J., & Murphy, W. F. (1981). Patterns of public support for the Supreme Court: A panel study. *Journal of Politics, 43,* 24–39.

Wendt, J. (1979). Canonical correlation as an explanatory technique for attitude scale construction. *Public Opinion Quarterly, 43,* 518–531.

Werts, C. E., & Linn, R. L. (1970). Cautions in applying various procedures for determining the reliability and validity of multiple item scales. *American Sociological Review, 34,* 757–759.

Wheaton, B., et al. (1977). Assessing reliability and stability in panel models. In D. R. Heise (Ed.), *Sociological methodology.* San Francisco: Jossey-Bass.

CHAPTER 2

Maximizing Questionnaire Quality

Jon A. Krosnick

Measurement tools are tremendously important in science because they are the lenses through which we see the world. To the biologist, reality is observed through a microscope. To the astronomer, learning takes place through a telescope. Geographers analyze photographs taken by satellites far from the earth's surface. Regardless of whether the measuring instrument is on a desk in front of the investigator or thousands of miles away, if there is a scratch or a spec of dust on the lens or if it is miscalibrated, a scientific analysis can end up far from the truth.

To many, and perhaps most, social scientists, measurement occurs via questionnaires. And most often our goal is to place people on measurement continua, whether they range from strong liberal to strong conservative, or from strong internationalist to strong isolationist, or from strongly pro–legalized abortion to strongly anti–legalized abortion. Just as for biologists, astronomers, and geographers, if our measuring instruments are flawed or miscalibrated, we can be seriously misled as well, placing people in the wrong places on a continuum relative to one another and/or relative to the continuum's endpoints.

In the literature on good measurement in the social sciences, a number of truisms about effective questionnaire design have been widely accepted. For example, the words used in questions should be understandable to all respondents, and the meanings imputed to those words should be as universal as possible among respondents (e.g., Oppenheim, 1992; Warwick & Lininger, 1975). Second, question wordings should avoid bias that would push answers one way or another (e.g., Parten, 1950; Young, 1939). Third, in order to minimize the impact of the idiosyncrasies of item wordings, it is best to aggregate answers to a battery of items into a single index (e.g., Likert, 1932; Thurstone, 1928). And the items used should be the few most efficient and effective ones tapping the construct of interest, to maximize validity, minimize respondent burden, and minimize the financial costs of data collection.

During the past five decades, social scientists have been following this advice and building batteries of questions to measure many important constructs, and this book documents just how much has been accomplished by these individuals: a lot. Thanks to large-scale collective enterprises, such as the National Election Study, small-scale research projects by lone investigators, and everything in between, we now have batteries to measure ideology, political partisanship, trust in government, political alienation and efficacy, racial attitudes, international attitudes, political information, values, participation, and much more. Most of these batteries are tried and true, having been employed in many

Measures of Political Attitudes
Copyright © 1999 by Academic Press.

empirical investigations that reassure us about their validity and reliability. And they have been built largely following the general pieces of advice about good questionnaire design mentioned above.

Beyond that very general advice, however, there has been relatively little empirically validated and widely accepted wisdom in the questionnaire design literature about exactly how to word and structure the individual items that compose a battery. Consequently designers of most of the batteries in this book were left to their own devices when making a series of necessary decisions. For example, when constructing closed-ended questions, should one use rating scales or ranking tasks? If one uses rating scales, how many points should be on the scales, and how should they be labeled with words? Should respondents be explicitly offered "no opinion" response options, or should these be omitted? In what order should response alternatives be offered?

Every researcher's goal is to maximize the reliability and validity of the data he or she collects, so each of these design decisions should presumably be made so as to maximize these two indicators of data quality. Fortunately thousands of empirical studies provide clear and surprisingly unanimous advice on the issues listed above, but most of these studies have been unacknowledged in contemporary reviews of this literature (see, e.g., Bradburn, Sudman, & Associates, 1981; Converse & Presser, 1986; Schuman & Presser, 1981; Sudman, Bradburn, & Schwarz, 1996). Consequently it should come as no surprise that many batteries described in this book do not conform to the guidelines for good measurement suggested by this literature.

This chapter previews portions of a forthcoming book that will review this literature in detail, bringing to bear a rich set of evidence dating from the beginning of the 20th Century to the present (Krosnick & Fabrigar, in press). Most of this evidence comes from experimental studies comparing one method of question construction to another. And when brought together, these studies are remarkably consistent with one another in suggesting clear guidelines about how to maximize reliability and validity. This chapter offers a brief review of some of the implications of this literature, particularly in light of the sorts of items employed in the chapters that follow. The chapter's primary goal is to help readers see the design strengths of some batteries presented in later chapters and to suggest possibilities for experimentation with other batteries in order to increase their reliability and validity through subtle redesign.

The chapter begins with an issue of relevance to most chapters in the book: acquiescence. Subsequent sections consider issues of relevance to only some chapters: (1) the design of rating scales, including how many points should be offered, verbal labeling of them, and the branching approach to asking multiple, interrelated questions; (2) the impact of the order of response choices on answers; (3) the potential value of offering "no opinion" options to respondents and of directly measuring dimensions of attitude strength; (4) the impact of social desirability response bias on data quality; (5) the relative merits of rating scales versus ranking tasks; (6) the relative merits of open-ended versus closed-ended questions; and (7) the validity of questions asking people to describe their own mental processes.

Acquiescence

Defining Acquiescence

Many items in this book offer response choices such as "agree or disagree," "true or false," or "yes or no" (see especially Chapters 3–9). This sort of item format is very appealing from a practical standpoint because such items are easy to write. If one wants to identify people who have positive attitudes toward bananas, for example, one simply needs to write a statement expressing an attitude (e.g., "I like bananas") and ask people whether they agree or disagree with it or whether it is true or false. Also, these formats can be used to measure a wide range of different constructs efficiently. Instead of having to change the response options from one question to the next as one moves from measuring liking to frequency to probability, one can use the same set of response options without having to re-read them to respondents. In line with this logic, a series of studies suggests that it takes people about 75% longer to answer a multiple choice test question than to answer a comparable true-false question (e.g., Wesman, 1947). The popularity of agree–disagree and true–false item formats is, therefore, no surprise.

Despite this popularity, there has been a great deal of concern expressed over the years that these question formats may be seriously problematic. The danger is that some respondents may sometimes say "agree," "true," or "yes," regardless of the question being asked of them. So, for example, a person might agree with a statement that the United States should forbid speeches against democracy and might also agree with a statement that the United States should allow such speeches. This behavior, labeled *acquiescence,* can be defined as endorsement of an assertion made in a question, regardless of the content of the assertion.

In theory, acquiescence could result from a desire to be polite rather than confrontational in interpersonal interactions (Leech, 1983), from a desire of individuals of lower social status to defer to individuals of higher social status (Lenski & Leggett, 1960), or from an inclination to satisfice rather than optimize when answering questionnaires (Krosnick, 1991). According to this latter explanation, people sometimes shortcut the cognitive processes they execute when answering questions, and when they do so, they fall prey to a confirmatory bias. This bias inclines people toward accepting assertions, rather than thinking more extensively and seeing the flaws in those assertions.

Documenting Acquiescence

The evidence documenting acquiescence is now voluminous and consistently compelling, based on a range of different demonstration methods. For example, consider first just agree–disagree questions. When people are given such answer choices, are not told any questions, and are asked to guess what answers an experimenter is imagining, people guess "agree" much more often than "disagree" (e.g., Berg & Rapaport, 1954). In other studies pairs of statements were constructed stating mutually exclusive views (e.g., "I enjoy socializing" versus "I don't enjoy socializing"), and people were asked to agree or disagree with both. Although answers to such pairs should be strongly negatively correlated, 41 studies yielded an average correlation of only $-.22$. This correlation may be far from -1.0 partly because of random measurement error, but studies that corrected for such error suggest that the departure from -1.0 is also because of acquiescence.

Consistent with this claim, combining across 10 studies, an average of 52% of people agreed with an assertion, whereas an average of only 42% of people disagreed with the opposite assertion. Thus, people are apparently inclined toward agreeing rather than disagreeing, manifesting what might be considered an acquiescence effect of 10%. Another set of 8 studies compared answers to agree–disagree questions with answers to forced choice questions where the order of the views expressed by the response alternatives was the same as in the agree–disagree questions. An average of 14% more people agreed with an assertion than expressed the same view in the corresponding forced-choice question. Averaging across 7 studies, 22% of people, on average, agreed with both a statement and its reversal, whereas only 10% of people disagreed with both. Thus, all of these methods suggest an average acquiescence effect of about 10%.

Other evidence indicates that acquiescence reflects a general tendency of some individuals across questions. For example, the average cross-sectional reliability of the tendency to agree with assertions is .65 across 29 studies. Furthermore, the over-time consistency of the tendency to acquiesce is about .75 over one month, .67 over four months, and .35 over four years (e.g., Couch & Keniston, 1960; Hoffman, 1960; Newcomb, 1943).

These same sorts of results (regarding correlations between opposite assertions, endorsement rates of items, their reversals, forced-choice versions, and so on) have been produced in studies of true–false questions and of yes–no questions, suggesting that acquiescence is present in these items as well. And there is other evidence regarding these response alternatives as well. For example, people are much more likely to answer yes–no factual questions correctly when the correct answer is "yes" than when it is "no" (e.g., Larkins & Shaver, 1967; Rothenberg, 1969), presumably because people are biased toward saying "yes." Similarly, a person's answer to a factual yes–no question (e.g., "Did you go shopping for food last week?") is more likely to disagree with an informant's account of that fact when the yes–no question is answered "yes" than when it is answered "no," again presumably because of a bias toward "yes" answers (Sigelman & Budd, 1986). When people say they are guessing the answer to a true–false question, 71% of answers were "true" in one study, and only 29% were "false." Acquiescence appeared just as clearly in studies using dichotomous items (e.g., "agree or disagree") and in studies offering more elaborate scales (e.g., "agree a lot, agree somewhat, neither agree nor disagree, disagree somewhat, disagree a lot").

The only body of evidence inconsistent with the acquiescence hypothesis involves forbid–allow questions. Rugg (1941) was the first to demonstrate that more people say "no" when asked whether something should be "allowed" than say "yes" when asked whether the same thing should be "forbidden" (see also Budd, Sigelman, & Sigelman, 1981; Schuman & Presser, 1981; Shaw & Budd, 1982). This pattern is in the opposite direction to what acquiescence would produce. Hippler and Schwarz (1986) argued that this tendency occurs because large numbers of people do not wish to take sides on these issues and "no" is the only response option offered that allows them to avoid taking a side. Such a bias toward saying "no" may have been quite a bit more common than acquiescence in responses to these items, masking it completely. Regardless, though, this is the only exception in the results of over 100 studies documenting the presence of acquiescence.

When Acquiescence Occurs

Acquiescence is most common among respondents of lower social status (e.g., Gove & Geerken, 1977; Lenski & Leggett, 1960), with less formal education (e.g., Ayidiya & McClendon, 1990; Narayan & Krosnick, 1996), of lower intelligence (e.g., Forehand, 1962; Hanley, 1959; Krosnick, Narayan, & Smith, 1996), of lower cognitive energy (Jackson, 1959), who do not like to think (Messick & Frederiksen, 1958), and of lower bias toward conveying a socially desirable image of themselves (e.g., Goldsmith, 1987; Shaffer, 1963). Also, acquiescence is most common when a question is difficult to answer (Gage, Leavitt, & Stone, 1957; Hanley, 1962; Trott & Jackson, 1967), after respondents have become fatigued answering a lot of prior questions (e.g., Clancy & Wachsler, 1971), and during telephone interviews rather than during face-to-face interviews (e.g., Calsyn, Roades, & Calsyn, 1992). Although some of these results are consistent with the notion that acquiescence results from politeness or deferral to people of higher social status, all of the results are consistent with the satisficing explanation. Thus it appears that acquiescence occurs when people lack the skills and motivation to answer thoughtfully and when a question demands difficult cognitive tasks be executed in order for a person to answer precisely (Krosnick, 1991).

Correcting for Acquiescence

A number of studies now demonstrate how acquiescence can distort the substantive conclusions a researcher reaches from a study involving agree–disagree, true–false, or yes–no questions (e.g., Jackman, 1973; Winkles, Kanouse, & Ware, 1982). One of the best-known illustrations of the problem involved the F-scale used by Adorno and colleagues in *The Authoritarian Personality* to measure working-class authoritarianism (Adorno, Frenkel-Brunswik, Levinson, & Sanford, 1950). In fact, this scale turned out mostly to measure acquiescence (Christie 1991), and the substantive value of Adorno *et al.*'s. (1950) findings was completely undercut.

Although a number of methods for eliminating the distorting impact of acquiescence have been considered and employed over the years, only one seems to work effectively: avoiding agree–disagree, true–false, and yes–no question formats altogether. In order to understand why this is the optimal approach, it is useful to review the logic of other approaches and empirical evidence on their effectiveness.

One alternative method is based upon the presumption that certain people have acquiescent personalities and are likely to do all of the acquiescing. Therefore one simply needs to identify those people and statistically adjust their answers to correct for this tendency (e.g., Couch & Keniston, 1960). To this end many batteries of items have been developed to measure a person's tendency to acquiesce, and people who offer lots of "agree," "true," or "yes" answers across a large set of items can then be spotlighted as likely acquiescers. However, the evidence reviewed earlier suggests that acquiescence is not simply the result of having an acquiescent personality; rather, it is influenced by circumstantial factors as well. Because this "correction" approach does not take that into account, the corrections performed are not likely to fully and precisely account for acquiescence. Furthermore, if a set of agree–disagree items is asked of people and the acquiescers are then identified, there is no way to know how these people would have answered the questions had they not acquiesced. So post hoc statistical controlling for acquiescence seems unlikely to be fully effective.

Another popular technique thought to control acquiescence is measuring a construct with a large set of agree–disagree or true–false items, half of them making assertions opposite to the other half (called *item reversals;* see Altemeyer, 1996; Paulhus, 1991). This approach is designed to place acquiescers in the middle of the latent measurement dimension. However, it will do so only if the assertions made in the reversals are equally as extreme as the statements in the original items. Making sure this is true requires extensive pretesting and is, therefore, cumbersome to implement. Furthermore, it is difficult to write large sets of item reversals without using the word *not* or other such negations, and evaluating assertions that include negations is cognitively burdensome and error-laden for respondents, thus adding measurement error and increasing respondent fatigue (e.g., Eifermann, 1961; Wason, 1961).

Even after all this effort, the balancing approach only partially solves the problem. Acquiescers who agree with every statement end up at a point on the measurement dimension where most of them probably do not belong. Instead, these people are arbitrarily placed there. And people who acquiesce on only some items end up with final scores that are closer to the dimension's midpoint than would validly represent their opinions. If enough people acquiesce, arbitrarily placing the acquiescers (who have various distinctive characteristics, e.g., low education) at or near the dimension's midpoint can significantly distort correlations. If acquiescers were instead induced to answer items thoughtfully, their final index scores would be more valid than placing them at or near the midpoint. Nothing valid is learned from these people simply by balancing a battery; instead, valuable information about them is foregone.

The fatal flaw inherent in agree–disagree, true–false, and yes–no questions becomes obvious when one recognizes that answering such a question always requires a respondent to answer a comparable rating question in his or her mind first. For example, if a man is asked to agree or disagree with the assertion, "I am not a friendly person," he must first decide how friendly a person he is (perhaps concluding "extremely friendly"). Then he must translate that conclusion into the appropriate selection in order to answer the question he was asked ("disagree" to the original item). Researchers who use questions like this presume that the arraying of respondents along the agree–disagree dimension corresponds monotonically to the arraying of those individuals along the underlying substantive dimension of interest. That is, the more a person agrees with the assertion "I am not a friendly person," the lower he or she truly is in actual friendliness.

But consider the following scenario. Our hypothetical extremely friendly respondent answers a series of agree–disagree questions with stems such as "I am an extremely generous person," "I am never helpful to others," and "I always do well at everything I do." And the next stem in the question sequence is: "I am a friendly person." Given how extremely the previous stems were phrased, this one seems quite moderate (i.e., simply "friendly" instead of "extremely friendly"). Therefore our hypothetical respondent may feel that the word *friendly* does not adequately express the full extent of his gregariousness, so he may respond "disagree." Thus some people who disagree may feel they genuinely are not friendly, and other people who disagree may feel they are substantially more affable than the word *friendly* suggests. This clearly violates the monotonic equivalence of the response dimension and the underlying construct of interest.

This example points us to the solution to the acquiescence problem: Simply ask respondents directly how friendly they are. In fact, every agree–disagree, true–false, or yes–no question implicitly requires the respondent to rate an object along a continuous dimension in his or her mind, so asking about that dimension directly is bound to be less burdensome. In this light, it should be no surprise that the reliability and validity of rating-scale and forced-choice questions that present multiple competing points of view are higher than the reliability and validity of comparable agree–disagree, true–false, and yes–no questions, which focus on only a single point of view (e.g., Ebel, 1982; Mirowsky & Ross, 1991; Ruch & DeGraff, 1926; Wesman, 1946). Consequently it seems best to avoid agree–disagree, true–false, and yes–no formats altogether and instead ask just a few questions using other rating-scale or forced-choice formats.

Rating-Scale Formats

When designing a rating scale, one must begin by specifying the number of points on the scale, and the scales described in this book are of varying lengths, ranging from dichotomous items up to scales of 101 points (see, e.g., Chapters 11 and 12). A great number of studies have compared the reliability and validity of scales of varying lengths (for a review, see Krosnick & Fabrigar, in press). For bipolar scales, which have a neutral or status-quo point in the middle (e.g., running from positive to negative), reliability and validity are highest for about 7 points (e.g., Matell & Jacoby, 1971). In contrast, the reliability and validity of unipolar scales, with a zero point at one end (e.g., running from no importance to very high importance), seem to be optimized for a bit shorter scales, approximately 5 points long (e.g., Wikman & Warneryd, 1990). Techniques such as magnitude scaling (e.g., Lodge, 1981), which offer scales with an infinite number of points, yield data of lower quality than do more conventional rating scales and should, therefore, be avoided (e.g., Cooper & Clare, 1981; Miethe, 1985; Patrick, Bush, & Chen, 1973).

A good number of studies suggest that data quality is better when all scale points are labeled with words than when only some are (e.g., Krosnick & Berent, 1993). Furthermore respondents are more satisfied when more scale points are verbally labeled (e.g., Dickinson & Zellinger, 1980). When selecting labels, researchers should strive to select ones that have meanings that divide up the continuum into approximately equal units (e.g., Klockars & Yamagishi, 1988). For example, "very good, good, and poor" is a combination that should be avoided because the terms do not divide the continuum equally: The meaning of "good" is much closer to the meaning of "very good" than it is to the meaning of "poor" (Myers & Warner, 1968). Guidelines provided by Krosnick and Fabrigar (in press) can help researchers select labels.

The Order of Response Alternatives

The answers people give to closed-ended questions are sometimes influenced by the order in which the alternatives are offered. When response choices are presented visually, as in self-administered questionnaires, people are inclined toward selecting answer choices offered early in a list, yielding primacy effects (e.g., Krosnick & Alwin, 1987; Sudman, Bradburn, & Schwarz, 1996). But when the answer choices are read aloud to people, recency effects tend to appear, whereby people are inclined to select the options offered last (e.g., McClendon, 1991). These effects are most pronounced among respondents who have limited cognitive skills and when questions are more cognitively demanding (Krosnick & Alwin, 1987; Payne, 1949–1950). All this is consistent with the theory of satisficing (Krosnick, 1991), which posits that response order effects are generated by the confluence of a confirmatory bias in evaluation, cognitive fatigue, and a bias in memory favoring response choices read aloud most recently. Therefore it seems best to minimize the difficulty of questions and to rotate the order of response choices across respondents. Almost none of the scales described in this book are accompanied by advice to rotate response order, but the evidence of such effects is so consistent as to suggest that doing so is well worthwhile.

No-Opinion Filters and Attitude Strength

Concerned about the possibility that respondents may feel pressure to offer opinions on issues when they truly have no attitudes (e.g., Converse, 1964), questionnaire designers have often explicitly offered respondents the option to say they have no opinion. And indeed, many more people say they "don't know" what their opinion is when this is done than when it is not (e.g., Schuman & Presser, 1981). People tend to offer this response under conditions that seem sensible (e.g., when they lack knowledge on the issue, Donovan & Leivers, 1993), and people prefer to be given this option in questionnaires (Ehrlich, 1964). Furthermore offering a "don't know" option significantly reduces the number of people who offer substantive evaluations of obscure or fictitious attitude objects, such as the Agricultural Trade Act (Schuman & Presser, 1981).

However, most "don't know" responses are due to conflicting feelings or beliefs (rather than lack of feelings or beliefs) or to uncertainty about exactly what a question's response alternatives mean or what the question is asking (e.g., Coombs & Coombs, 1976–1977). When people are pushed to offer an opinion instead of saying "don't know," the reliability and validity of data collected is no lower than when a "no opinion" option is offered and people are encouraged to select it (e.g., McClendon & Alwin, 1993). That is, people who would have selected this option if offered nonetheless report meaningful opinions when it is not offered. In fact, this is true even of opinions about obscure or fictitious attitude objects; people base their attitude reports on their best guesses about the objects' likely characteristics (Schuman & Presser, 1981). Therefore it is wise that most of the items described in this book do not offer explicit "don't know" response alternatives.

A better way to accomplish the goal of differentiating "real" opinions from "nonattitudes" is to measure the strength of an attitude using one or more follow-up questions. Krosnick and Petty (1995) recently proposed that strong attitudes can be defined as those that are resistant to change, are stable over time, and have powerful impact on cognition and action. Many empirical investigations have confirmed that attitudes vary in strength, and the respondent's presumed task when confronting a "don't know" response option is to decide whether his or her attitude is sufficiently weak as to be best described by selecting that option. But because the appropriate cut point along the strength dimension seems exceedingly hard to specify, it seems preferable to ask people to describe where their attitude falls along the strength continuum.

Unfortunately there are many different aspects of attitude strength, and they are largely independent of each other (see, e.g., Krosnick, Boninger, Chuang, Berent, & Carnot, 1993). For example, people can be asked how important the issue is to them personally or how much they have thought about it or how certain they are of their opinion or how knowledgeable they feel about it (for details on measuring these and many other dimensions, see Wegener, Downing, Krosnick, & Petty, 1995). And one can measure the length of time it takes a person to answer a question, which reflects construct accessibility (Bassili & Fletcher, 1991). Each of these dimensions can help to differentiate attitudes that are crystallized and consequential from those that are not.

Social Desirability

The Notion of Social Desirability Response Bias

An issue potentially applicable to many chapters in this volume is that of social desirability response bias (for an earlier review, see Paulhus, 1991). One instance illustrating this potential problem in the context of politics involved the 1989 Virginia gubernatorial race, in which Douglas Wilder, an African-American Democrat, ran against Marshall Coleman, a Caucasian Republican. Preelection polls consistently gave Wilder a lead of between 4% and 11%, but on election day Wilder won by a mere .6%. Finkel, Guterbock, and Borg (1991) claimed the poll error was due to respondent dishonesty based on race. They argued that especially when interviewed by African Americans, Caucasian respondents are reluctant to express an intention to vote for a Caucasian candidate in a race against an African-American candidate. Finkel et al. (1991) demonstrated that a race-of-interviewer effect along these lines was especially powerful among respondents who did not identify with a major political party (i.e., "independents") and respondents who initially said they were undecided and were then pushed by the interviewer to express a candidate preference.

Finkel *et al.* (1991) concluded that this is evidence of a bias in reports toward presenting a socially desirable self-image to one's interviewer.

For this bias to have fully explained the error in all preelection polls in Virginia, a very large proportion of the interviewers involved would have had to be African-American and would have had to be identifiable as such by voice. This seems a bit implausible. Furthermore, there is another compelling possible explanation for the polls' error that does not involve race at all. In an extensive analysis of numerous candidate elections and referenda, Visser, Krosnick, Marquette, and Curtin (in press) showed that preelection polls have routinely overestimated the margin of victory of the winner. One possible explanation for this is the sort of bandwagon effect described by Noelle-Neumann's (1984) notion of the "spiral of silence." From publicity of preelection poll results, people often learn that a particular candidate is leading over his or her challengers. And when later interviewed for another poll, some supporters of a challenger may be reluctant to seem out of step with the majority and may, therefore, express support for the leading candidate or may say "don't know." This, too, would constitute measurement error due to intentional misrepresentation by a respondent to present a favorable self-image to an interviewer.

The Plausibility of the Threat

A number of different lines of research endorse the plausibility of the notion that people might lie to interviewers and researchers. For example, DePaulo, Kashy, Kirkendol, Wyer, and Epstein (1996) had people complete daily diaries in which they recorded any lies that they told during a seven-day period. On average, people reported telling one lie per day, with some people telling many more, and 91% of the lies involved misrepresenting oneself in some way. This evidence is in line with theoretical accounts from sociology (Goffman, 1959) and psychology (Schlenker & Weigold, 1989) asserting that an inherent element of social interaction is constructing an image of oneself in the eyes of others in pursuit of relevant goals. The fact that being viewed favorably by others is more likely to bring rewards and minimize punishments than being viewed unfavorably may motivate people to construct favorable images, sometimes via deceit. If this sort of behavior is common in daily life, why wouldn't people lie when answering questionnaires as well?

In fact, there are a number of reasons to believe that the motivation to lie in surveys might be minimal. First, when filling out an anonymous questionnaire, no rewards or punishments can possibly be at stake. And second, in most surveys and laboratory experiments, the respondent's relationships with an interviewer and/or a researcher are likely to be so short-lived and superficial that very little of consequence is at stake as well. Certainly even a small frown of disapproval from a total stranger can cause a bit of discomfort, but this is not likely to be especially noxious. And the cognitive task of figuring out which response to each question will garner the most respect from an interviewer and/or a researcher is likely to be demanding enough to be worth doing only when the stakes are significant. So perhaps there is not so much danger here after all. And perhaps the tendency of preelection polls to overpredict the margin of victory of the winner is due to a process having nothing to do with intentional lying to present a respectable image of oneself to others.

It would be nice if that were true, but unfortunately there is another potential source of systematic distortion in responses to even self-administered anonymous questionnaires: self-deception. Not only do people want to maintain favorable images of themselves in the eyes of others, but they want to have such images in their own eyes as well. According to many psychological analyses, the pursuit of self-esteem is a basic human motive (see, e.g.,

Sedikides & Strube, 1997), and it is driven partly by such inevitable realities as the prospect of death (e.g., Greenberg, Solomon, & Pyszczynski, 1997). So people may be motivated to convince themselves that they are respectable, good people, and doing so may at times entail misconstrual of facts (see Paulhus, 1984, 1986, 1991). If people fool themselves in this way, such misconstrual will find its way into questionnaire responses, even when respondents want to accurately report their perceptions to an interviewer and/or a researcher. Obviously it is tricky business to fool oneself because part of the mind might need to know that it is fooling another part. But such self-deception can be so automatic and may even unfold outside of consciousness that people would not be aware of it at all.

What a mess! Questionnaire research is based on the assumption that people can and will accurately report information. If this is not true, either because of other-deception or because of self-deception, this threatens the value of questionnaire-based data. Many of the scales described in this book are potentially vulnerable to this problem because it seems socially desirable to express interest and involvement in politics, not to express racial prejudice, to endorse classically American values instead of repudiating them, to appear nationalistic instead of cynical about one's own country, and so on. Given this threat, researchers have been very interested over the years in exploring whether social desirability response bias is truly a source of data distortion, assessing its magnitude, and developing techniques to overcome it.

Evidence of Social Desirability Bias

The evidence documenting systematic and intentional misrepresentation is now quite voluminous and very convincing, partly because the same conclusion has been supported by studies using many different methods. One such method is the *bogus pipeline technique*, which involves telling respondents that the researcher can otherwise determine the correct answer to a question they will be asked, so they might as well answer it accurately (see, e.g., Roese & Jamieson, 1993). Under these conditions, people are more willing to report substance use (Evans, Hansen, & Mittlemark, 1977; Murray & Perry, 1987). Likewise, white respondents are more willing to ascribe undesirable personality characteristics to African-Americans (Pavlos, 1972, 1973; Sigall & Page, 1971) and are more willing to report disliking African Americans (e.g., Allen, 1975) under bogus pipeline conditions. Women are less likely to report supporting the women's movement under bogus pipeline conditions than under normal reporting conditions (Hough & Allen, 1975). And people are more likely to admit having been given secret information under bogus pipeline conditions (Quigley-Fernandez & Tedeschi, 1978).

Another approach to documenting such distortion is to compare responses given when people believe their answers will have significant consequences for them to responses given when no such consequences exist. For example, in one study respondents who believed that they had already been admitted to an apprenticeship program admitted to having less respectable personality characteristics than did comparable respondents who believed they were being evaluated for possible admission to the program (Michaelis & Eysenck, 1971).

Yet another approach to this problem involves the *randomized response technique* (Warner, 1965). Here respondents answer one of various different questions, depending on what a randomizing device instructs. Thus the interviewer and the researcher do not know exactly which question each person is answering, so the respondents can presumably feel freer to be honest. In one such study Himmelfarb and Lickteig (1982) had respondents secretly toss three coins before answering a yes–no question. Respondents were instructed to say "yes" if all three coins came up heads, to say "no" if all three coins came up tails, and to answer the yes–no question truthfully if any combination of heads and tails came up. People answering in this fashion admitted to falsifying their income tax reports and enjoying soft-core pornography more than did respondents who were asked these questions directly.

Still another approach to assessing the impact of social desirability is by studying interviewer effects. The presumption here is that the observable characteristics of an interviewer may suggest to a respondent which answers he or she would consider most respectable. So if answers vary in a way that corresponds with interviewer characteristics, it suggests that respondents tailored their answers accordingly. For example, various studies have found that African Americans report more favorable attitudes toward whites when their interviewer is white than when the interviewer is African-American (Anderson, Silver, & Abramson, 1988a, 1988b; Campbell, 1981; Schuman & Converse, 1971). Likewise, white respondents express more favorable attitudes toward African Americans and the principle of racial integration to African-American interviewers than to white interviewers (Campbell, 1981; Cotter, Cohen, & Coulter, 1982; Finkel *et al.*, 1991). In another study, people expressed more positive attitudes toward firefighters when they thought their interviewer was a firefighter than when they did not hold this belief (Atkin & Chaffee, 1972–1973).

Another approach to this issue involves comparisons of different modes of data collection. In general, pressure to appear socially desirable is presumably greatest when a respondent is being interviewed by another person, either face-to-face or over the telephone. But when respondents complete written questionnaires alone, this pressure is presumably lessened. Consistent with this reasoning, Catholics in one study were more likely to report favoring legalized abortion and birth control when completing self-administered questionnaires than when being interviewed by telephone or face-to-face (Wiseman, 1972). And people report being happier with their lives in interviews than on self-administered questionnaires (Cheng, 1988).

The anonymity of some self-administered questionnaires further reduces social pressure, so it, too, offers an empirical handle for addressing this issue. In one study, Gordon (1987) asked respondents about dental hygiene on questionnaires; half the respondents (selected randomly) were asked to write their names on the questionnaires, whereas the other half were not. Dental checkups, brushing, and flossing were all reported to have been done more often when people wrote their names on the questionnaires than when they did not. Thus socially desirable responses were apparently more common under conditions of high identifiability. Likewise people reported having more desirable personality characteristics when they wrote their names, addresses, and telephone numbers on questionnaires than when they did not (Paulhus, 1984).

Taken together, these studies all suggest that some people sometimes distort their answers in surveys in order to present themselves as having more socially desirable or respectable characteristics or behavioral histories. But the social desirability driven distortions documented above represent only those involving other deception. There may be significant amounts of self-deception going on as well, and when combined with other deception, social desirability driven error may be even more substantial. Needless to say, there is no easy way of documenting self-deception in studies that involve only self-reports. When records can be checked, researchers can validate self-reports against, for example, official records of whether a person voted in a particular election. So if respondents are asked (using a randomized response technique, for example) whether they voted or not in an election and more people say they voted than can be confirmed in the official records, that would provide a suggestive estimation of the magnitude of self-deception. Unfortunately, few, if any, such studies have been done, so it is difficult to draw any conclusions at the moment about the prevalence of such error in data.

Controlling for Social Desirability Response Bias

One approach to correcting for social desirability bias involves making a big assumption. According to this perspective, some people are especially likely to distort their responses to all questions in socially desirable directions, whereas other people are especially unlikely to do so. Therefore all respondents can be asked a battery of questions with strong social desirability connotations, and the people who offer especially large numbers of socially desirable responses would be considered suspect. A researcher could then retest hypotheses after removing these respondents from a data set to see what effect doing so has. Also a researcher can statistically control for the tendency to answer such a battery in a socially desirable fashion when analyzing correlational associations among other variables in a data set (see Paulhus, 1991).

The big assumption involved in this approach is that the tendency to answer one set of questions with a social desirability bias can effectively predict the extent of such bias in a single other question. But it seems likely that whether a particular person answers this single other question with such bias depends on a number of other factors (e.g., the match of the race of the respondent and the interviewer if the question involves a racial issue, but not if the topic is unrelated to race). Therefore this approach probably at best can detect only a portion of the social desirability bias present and may in fact claim to detect such bias in answers that are not in fact thusly contaminated.

Perhaps the most important reason to hesitate when considering this correction method is that it involves after-the-fact adjustment. Methods like the bogus pipeline and the randomized response technique lead each respondent to answer honestly, so valid data are available for all respondents. But when suspect respondents are identified by their answers to a social desirability battery, there is no way to know how they would have answered target questions if they had done so accurately. Statistical correction using answers to a battery is also suspect, as there is no way to know whether a bias toward socially desirable answers among suspect respondents had no real impact because the "correct" answers to target questions for these people also happened to be the socially desirable ones. Thus there is good reason to hesitate before presuming that statistical detection or correction using social desirability response bias batteries is an effective solution to the problem.

The better approach to solving the intentional misrepresentation problem is employing one or more of the techniques outlined above that either reduce pressure to appear socially desirable (e.g., via anonymity) or create new pressures to be honest (e.g., via the bogus pipeline). If a researcher is concerned that social desirability pressures might be distorting answers to a particular question, that hypothesis can be evaluated in a pretest by randomly assigning some respondents to answer using an ordinary self-report approach, and other respondents to provide reports in a way that reduces the likelihood of social desirability based distortion. If the distribution of answers is different in these two groups, then one knows that a measurement method must be employed in the final study that solves this problem (e.g., by allowing completely anonymous responses).

Promising New Techniques

Very new techniques are being developed to solve not only the intentional misrepresentation problem but also the self-deception problem. One such technique involves bypassing respondents' reports altogether and measuring cognitive processes more directly. For example, people's attitudes toward an object are revealed by tiny movements of facial muscles upon observation of the object (Cacioppo, Petty, Losch, & Kim, 1986), and electrical activity in the brain indicates attitudes as well (Crites, Cacioppo, Gardner, & Berntson, 1995). Measurement of such phenomena is quite cumbersome and not suitable for most surveys and laboratory experiments, but another measure—reaction time—may be more practical.

According to an accumulating body of studies, the length of time it takes a person to make a judgment can be used to gauge evaluations. For example, a person may be asked to place his or her right index finger on one key of a computer keyboard and his or her left index finger on another key. Then he or she may be asked to read a word that appears in the middle of the computer screen and decide as quickly as possible whether it refers to a good–pleasant concept or a bad–unpleasant concept. The person can be instructed to press the right-hand button in the former case and the left-hand button in the latter case. The computer can then measure the amount of time between the appearance of a word, such as "good" or "bad," and a button press.

Recent research has shown that the length of time it takes to press the button, usually a fraction of a second, can be influenced by a very fast, subliminal flash of another word on the computer screen, just before the appearance of the word to be evaluated (e.g., Hermans, De Houwer, & Eelen, 1994). If the subliminal flash is of a positive word (e.g., "nice"), people are a little bit quicker at recognizing that "good" is a positive word. If the subliminal word is negative (e.g., "rotten"), then people are a little bit slower at recognizing that "good" is a positive word. This technique can be used to measure people's attitudes toward objects when they think they are simply being asked to identify words as good and bad.

If on a given trial the subliminal word is "pizza" and the supraliminal word is "good," then a researcher can assess whether pizza speeds up or slows down identification of "good" as a positive word and by how much. The more speeding up a person manifests, the more positive his or her attitude toward pizza presumably is. And the more slowing down a person manifests, the more negative his or her attitude toward pizza probably is. Fazio, Jackson, Dunton, and Williams (1995) have used this technique to measure racial prejudice and have found evidence that such measurements are quite valid. In theory, these attitude measurements may be more valid than self-reports because the former are uncontaminated by any other-deception or self-deception biases. However, some new evidence suggests that self-reports may be more accurate predictors of some behaviors, whereas the reaction-time measurements may be better predictors of other behaviors (e.g., Dovidio, Kawakami, Johnson, Johnson, & Howard, 1997).

This procedure is obviously easy to execute in a laboratory, and it is also easy to execute in in-home surveys when field interviewers carry laptop computers. Although some recent work suggests that reaction-time measurement can be done validly over the telephone (e.g., Bassili & Fletcher, 1991), no evidence yet documents whether the very quick reaction-time differences of interest here can be captured with that methodology. Perhaps more importantly, ethical considerations are raised by the fact that respondents are asked to participate in a procedure but are not told what is being measured. Nonetheless, there may be some potential use for this technique in survey research generally, and it may provide a way to overcome social desirability-based response distortion.

Rating versus Ranking

Although most questions in this book involve rating scales, some involve ranking tasks (see, e.g., Chapter 11). In fact, many have argued that ranking is the superior method for measuring political values (e.g., Ingelhart, 1977; Rokeach, 1973). And the choice between these two approaches can be quite consequential. Imagine that one wishes to determine whether people prefer to eat carrots or peas. Respondents could be asked this question directly (a ranking question), or they could be asked to rate their attitudes toward carrots and peas separately, and the researcher could infer which is preferred. With this research goal, asking the single ranking question seems preferable and more direct than asking the two rating questions. But rank ordering a large set of objects takes much longer and is less enjoyed by respondents than a rating task (Elig & Frieze, 1979; Taylor & Kinnear, 1971). Furthermore, ranking might force respondents to make choices between objects toward which they feel identically, and ratings can reveal not only which object a respondent prefers but also how different his or her evaluations of the objects are.

Surprisingly, however, rankings are more effective than ratings because ratings suffer from a significant problem: non-differentiation. According to Krosnick's (1991) theory of survey satisficing, some respondents are not especially motivated to think carefully about the questions they are asked, or doing the cognitive work required is especially demanding for them. Under such circumstances, people may choose to shortcut the response process via a series of specific response strategies. When a person is asked to rate a large set of objects on a single scale, one satisficing strategy is to select what appears to be a reasonable point to rate most objects on the scale and rate all objects at or near that point (i.e., non-differentiation), rather than thinking carefully about each object and rating different objects differently (see Krosnick, 1991; Krosnick & Alwin, 1988; Krosnick, Narayan, & Smith, 1996). So, for example, if a respondent is asked to rate the importance of a series of objects (e.g., child qualities such as honesty, intelligence, and responsibility), satisficers may rate each one "very important" (Krosnick & Alwin, 1988). At least partly as a result, the reliability and validity of ranking data are superior to those of rating data (e.g., Miethe, 1985; Munson & McIntyre, 1979; Nathan & Alexander, 1985; Rankin & Grube, 1980; Reynolds & Jolly, 1980).

Batteries of items using the same response scale (as many of the batteries in this book do) are at risk for this sort of satisficing. Such non-differentiation is most likely to occur when respondent motivation and/or ability to answer optimally are low (e.g., Krosnick, Narayan, & Smith, 1996). Therefore, the problem might be reduced by taking steps to minimize the cognitive difficulty of the items and to maximize respondent motivation to answer carefully and precisely (see Krosnick, 1991). However, it is not yet clear whether such strategies can be completely effective. Therefore, although rankings do not yield interval-level measures of the perceived distances between objects in respondents' minds and are more statistically cumbersome to analyze (see Alwin & Jackson, 1982), these measures are apparently more useful when a researcher's goal is to ascertain rank orders of objects. At the very least, researchers interested in implementing a series of ratings might consider ordering questions so that no two adjacent questions offer the same response alternatives.

Open versus Closed Questions

Although the vast majority of items listed in this book are closed-ended (meaning that they ask respondents to choose among offered sets of response choices), a few are open-ended, allowing respondents to answer in their own words (see, e.g., Chapters 10, 11, and 12). For example, one of the most frequently asked and widely publicized survey items inquires about what people consider to be the most important problem facing the country, usually presented in an open-ended format (see Chapter 11). But a closed-ended version of this question might be used instead, asking, "What is the most important problem facing the country today: inflation, unemployment, crime, the federal budget deficit, or some other problem?"

The biggest challenge in using open-ended questions is the task of coding responses. In a survey of 1000 respondents, nearly 1000 different answers will be given to the "most important problem" question if considered word for word. But in order to analyze these answers, they must be clumped into a relatively small number of categories. This requires that researchers must develop a coding scheme for each question; multiple people must read and code the answers into the categories; the level of agreement between the coders must be ascertained; and the procedure must be refined and repeated if agreement is too low. The time and financial costs of such a procedure, coupled with the added challenge of requiring interviewers to carefully transcribe answers, have led many researchers to favor closed-ended questions, which in essence ask respondents to directly code themselves into categories that the researcher specifies.

When closed-ended questions are used to ascertain categorical judgments of this sort (where the options represent different objects rather than different points along a single continuum), researchers often do not want to confine respondents to the list, so they offer an "other" response alternative. However, respondents tend to confine their answers to the choices offered, even when the "other" opportunity is offered (Jenkins, 1935; Lindzey & Guest, 1951). If the list of choices presented by a question is incomplete, even the rank ordering of the choices that are explicitly offered can be different from what would be obtained if a longer or shorter list were offered instead. Therefore a closed-ended categorical question can be used effectively only if its answer choices are comprehensive, and this can usually be assured only if an open-ended version of the question is administered in a pretest using a reasonably large sample. Given that, it may be more practical simply to ask the open-ended question in the final survey.

Introspection

Because researchers are often interested in identifying the causes of people's thoughts and actions, it is tempting to ask people directly why they thought a certain thing or behaved in a certain way. For example, political scientists have routinely asked people to explain why they voted as they did in a particular election (see Chapter 11). Whether employing an open-ended question or a closed-ended one, this approach requires people to introspect and describe their own cognitive processes, which was one of modern psychology's first core research methods (Hothersall, 1984).

Early in this century, though, it became clear that this method can often yield misleading results (Hothersall, 1984). And Nisbett and Wilson (1977) articulated an argument about why this is so, reviewing a great deal of evidence in support of their theoretical account. Studies done since their landmark paper have further reinforced the conclusion that many cognitive processes occur very quickly and automatically "behind a black curtain" in people's minds, so they are unaware of them and cannot describe them. Consequently questions asking for such descriptions seem best viewed skeptically.

Conclusion

This review illustrates only a tiny fraction of the wealth of knowledge about questionnaire design buried in the journals of many social science disciplines. Many, if not most, of the

batteries described in this book were developed long before the accumulated wisdom of
this literature was apparent. Consequently many of these batteries do not fully conform to
the advice offered in this chapter. It clearly seems worthwhile, then, to consider experi-
menting in future studies with slight alterations in format to see whether reliability and validity can be improved.

Some readers, after plowing through the above review, might say instead: How much
can we hope to gain from such efforts? Aren't the reliabilities and validities sufficiently
high to suggest that the batteries are just fine as they are? Furthermore why should we
view these items as potentially "broken" when they have been used successfully in numerous investigations? This is certainly an understandable perspective, so it seems quite reasonable that some readers might feel this way.

However, the literature backing the above advice is both so voluminous and so consistent in its findings that it is hard to disregard the possibility that the accuracy of just
about any measuring instrument can be improved by following it. Likewise what may appear to be high reliability in some scales may actually be highly reliable systematic measurement error rather than reliable substantive assessment. And correlations between items
that appear to suggest high validity may instead be associations due to systematic measurement error rather than substance (see, e.g., Krosnick & Alwin, 1988). So batteries that
appear not to be "broken" may indeed be improvable through systematic, theory-guided
experimentation. And the literature reviewed in this chapter points to some possible av-
enues for such exploration.

Acknowledgments

This chapter was written partly while the author was a Fellow at the Center for Advanced Study in
the Behavioral Sciences, supported by National Science Foundation Grant SBR-9022192. The author wishes to express his thanks to Michael Tichy for his help with manuscript preparation. Correspondence should be addressed to Jon A. Krosnick, Department of Psychology, Ohio State University, 1885 Neil Avenue, Columbus, Ohio 43210 (e-mail: Krosnick@osu.edu).

References

Adorno, T. W., Frenkel-Brunswick, E., Levinson, D. J., & Sanford, R. N. (1950). *The authoritarian
     personality.* New York: Harper.
Allen, B. P. (1975). Social distance and admiration reactions of "unprejudiced" whites. *Journal of
     Personality, 43,* 709–726.
Altemeyer, B. (1996). *The authoritarian specter.* Cambridge, MA: Harvard University Press.
Alwin, D. F., & Jackson, D. J. (1982). Adult values for children: An application of factor analysis
     to ranked preference data. In K. F. Schuessler (Ed.), *Sociological methodology 1980* (pp. 311–
     329). San Francisco: Jossey-Bass.
Anderson, B. A., Silver, B. D., & Abramson, P. R. (1988a). The effects of race of the interviewer
     on measures of electoral participation by Blacks in SRC national election studies. *Public Opin-
     ion Quarterly, 52,* 53–83.
Anderson, B. A., Silver, B. D., & Abramson, P. R. (1988b). The effects of the race of the interviewer
     on race-related attitudes of black respondents in SRC/CPS national election studies. *Public
     Opinion Quarterly, 52,* 289–324.
Atkin, C. K., & Chaffee, S. H. (1972–1973). Instrumental response strategies in opinion interviews.
     Public Opinion Quarterly, 36, 69–79.

Ayidiya, S. A., & McClendon, M. J. (1990). Response effects in mail surveys. *Public Opinion Quarterly, 54*, 229–247.

Bassili, J. N., & Fletcher, J. F. (1991). Response-time measurement in survey research. *Public Opinion Quarterly, 55*, 331–346.

Berg, I. A., & Rapaport, G. M. (1954). Response bias in an unstructured questionnaire. *Journal of Psychology, 38*, 475–481.

Bradburn, N. M., Sudman, S., & Associates (1981). *Improving interview method and questionnaire design.* San Francisco: Jossey-Bass.

Budd, E. C., Sigelman, C. K., & Sigelman, L. (1981). Exploring the outer limits of response bias. *Sociological Focus, 14*, 297–307.

Cacioppo, J. T., Petty, R. E., Losch, M. E., & Kim, H. S. (1986). Electromyographic activity over facial muscle regions can differentiate the valence and intensity of affective reactions. *Journal of Personality and Social Psychology, 50*, 260–268.

Calsyn, R. J., Roades, L. A., & Calsyn, D. S. (1992). Acquiescence in needs assessment studies of the elderly. *Gerontologist, 32*, 246–252.

Campbell, B. A. (1981). Race-of-interviewer effects among southern adolescents. *Public Opinion Quarterly, 45*, 231–244.

Christie, R. (1991). Authoritarianism and related constructs. In J. P. Robinson, P. R. Shaver, & L. S. Wrightsman (Eds.), *Measures of Personality and Social Psychological Attitudes* (pp. 501–571). San Diego, CA: Academic Press.

Cheng, S. (1988). Subjective quality of life in the planning and evaluation of programs. *Evaluation and Program Planning, 11*, 123–134.

Clancy, K. J., & Wachsler, R. A. (1971). Positional effects in shared-cost surveys. *Public Opinion Quarterly, 35*, 258–265.

Converse, J. M., & Presser, S. (1986). *Survey questions: Handcrafting the standardized questionnaire.* Beverly Hills, CA: Sage.

Converse, P. E. (1964). The nature of belief systems in the mass public. In D. E. Apter (Ed.), *Ideology and discontent* (pp. 206–261). New York: Free Press.

Coombs, C. H., & Coombs, L. C. (1976–1977). "Don't know": Item ambiguity or respondent uncertainty? *Public Opinion Quarterly, 40*, 497–514.

Cooper, D. R., & Clare, D. A. (1981). A magnitude estimation scale for human values. *Psychological Reports, 49*, 431–438.

Cotter, P., Cohen, J., & Coulter, P. B. (1982). Race of interviewer effects in telephone interviews. *Public Opinion Quarterly, 46*, 278–294.

Couch, A., & Keniston, K. (1960). Yeasayers and naysayers: Agreeing response set as a personality variable. *Journal of Abnormal and Social Psychology, 60*, 151–174.

Crites, S. L., Jr., Cacioppo, J. T., Gardner, W. L., & Berntson, G. G. (1995). Bioelectrical echoes from evaluative categorization: II. A late positive brain potential that varies as a function of attitude rather than attitude report. *Journal of Personality and Social Psychology, 68*, 997–1013.

DePaulo, B. M., Kashy, D. A., Kirkendol, S. E., Wyer, M. M., & Epstein, J. A. (1996). Lying in everyday life. *Journal of Personality and Social Psychology, 70*, 979–995.

Dickinson, T. L., & Zellinger, P. M. (1980). A comparison of the behaviorally anchored rating and mixed standard scale formats. *Journal of Applied Psychology, 65*, 147–154.

Donovan, R. J., & Leivers, S. (1993). Using paid advertising to modify racial stereotype beliefs. *Public Opinion Quarterly, 57*, 205–218.

Dovidio, J. F., Kawakami, K., Johnson, C., Johnson, B., & Howard, A. (1997). On the nature of prejudice: Automatic and controlled processes. *Journal of Experimental Social Psychology, 33*, 510–540.

Ebel, R. L. (1982). Proposed solutions to two problems of test construction. *Journal of Educational Measurement, 19*, 267–278.

Ehrlich, H. J. (1964). Instrument error and the study of prejudice. *Social Forces, 43*, 197–206.

Eifermann, R. R. (1961). Negation: A linguistic variable. *Acta Psychologica, 18*, 258–273.

Elig, T. W., & Frieze, I. H. (1979). Measuring causal attributions for success and failure. *Journal of Personality and Social Psychology, 37*, 221–231.

Evans, R. I., Hansen, W. B., & Mittlemark, M. B. (1977). Increasing the validity of self-reports of smoking behavior in children. *Journal of Applied Psychology, 62,* 521–523.

Fazio, R. H., Jackson, J. R., Dunton, B. C., & Williams, C. J. (1995). Variability in automatic activation as an unobtrusive measure of racial attitudes: A bona fide pipeline? *Journal of Personality and Social Psychology, 69,* 1013–1027.

Finkel, S. E., Guterbock, T. M., & Borg, M. J. (1991). Race-of-interviewer effects in a preelection poll: Virginia 1989. *Public Opinion Quarterly, 55,* 313–330.

Forehand, G. A. (1962). Relationships among response sets and cognitive behaviors. *Educational and Psychological Measurement, 22,* 287–302.

Gage, N. L., Leavitt, G. S., & Stone, G. C. (1957). The psychological meaning of acquiescence set for authoritarianism. *Journal of Abnormal and Social Psychology, 55,* 98–103.

Goffman, E. (1959). *The presentation of self in everyday life.* Garden City, NY: Doubleday/Anchor Books.

Goldsmith, R. E. (1987). Two studies of yeasaying. *Psychological Reports, 60,* 239–244.

Gordon, R. A. (1987). Social desirability bias: A demonstration and technique for its reduction. *Teaching of Psychology, 14,* 40–42.

Gove, W. R., & Geerken, M. R. (1977). Response bias in surveys of mental health: An empirical investigation. *American Journal of Sociology, 82,* 1289–1317.

Greenberg, J., Solomon, S., & Pyszczynski, T. (1997). Terror management theory of self-esteem and cultural worldviews: Empirical assessments and conceptual refinements. *Advances in Experimental Social Psychology, 29,* 61–139.

Hanley, C. (1959). Responses to the wording of personality test items. *Journal of Consulting Psychology, 23,* 261–265.

Hanley, C. (1962). The "difficulty" of a personality inventory item. *Educational and Psychological Measurement, 22,* 577–584.

Hermans, D., De Houwer, J., & Eelen, P. (1994). The affective priming effect: Automatic activation of evaluative information in memory. *Cognition and Emotion, 8,* 515–533.

Himmelfarb, S., & Lickteig, C. (1982). Social desirability and the randomized response technique. *Journal of Personality and Social Psychology, 43,* 710–717.

Hippler, H.-J., & Schwarz, N. (1986). Not forbidding isn't allowing: The cognitive basis of the forbid-allow asymmetry. *Public Opinion Quarterly, 50,* 87–96.

Hoffman, P. J. (1960). Social acquiescence and "education." *Educational and Psychological Measurement, 20,* 769–776.

Hothersall, D. (1984). *History of psychology.* New York: Random House.

Hough, K. S., & Allen, B. P. (1975). Is the "women's movement" erasing the mark of oppression from the female psyche? *Journal of Psychology, 89,* 249–258.

Ingelhart, R. (1977). *The silent revolution.* Princeton, NJ: Princeton University Press.

Jackman, M. R. (1973). Education and prejudice or education and response-set? *American Sociological Review, 38,* 327–339.

Jackson, D. N. (1959). Cognitive energy level, acquiescence, and authoritarianism. *Journal of Social Psychology, 49,* 65–69.

Jackson, D. N. (1967). Acquiescence response styles: Problems of identification and control. In I. A. Berg (Ed.), *Response set in personality assessment* (pp. 71–114). Chicago: Aldine.

Jenkins, J. G. (1935). *Psychology in business and industry.* New York: Wiley.

Klockars, A. J., & Yamagishi, M. (1988). The influence of labels and positions in rating scales. *Journal of Educational Measurement, 25,* 85–96.

Krosnick, J. A. (1991). Response strategies for coping with the cognitive demands of attitude measures in surveys. *Applied Cognitive Psychology, 5,* 213–236.

Krosnick, J. A., & Alwin, D. F. (1987). An evaluation of a cognitive theory of response order effects in survey measurement. *Public Opinion Quarterly, 51,* 201–219.

Krosnick, J. A., & Alwin, D. F. (1988). A test of the form-resistant correlation hypothesis: Ratings, rankings, and the measurement of values. *Public Opinion Quarterly, 52,* 526–538.

Krosnick, J. A., & Berent, M. K. (1993). Comparisons of party identification and policy preferences: The impact of survey question format. *American Journal of Political Science, 37,* 941–964.

Krosnick, J. A., Boninger, D. S., Chuang, Y. C., Berent, M. K., & Carnot, C. G. (1993). Attitude strength: One construct or many related constructs? *Journal of Personality and Social Psychology, 65,* 1132–1151.

Krosnick, J. A., & Fabrigar, L. R. (In press). *Designing good questionnaires: Insights from psychology.* New York: Oxford University Press.

Krosnick, J. A., Narayan, S., & Smith, W. R. (1996). Satisficing in surveys: Initial evidence. *New Directions for Evaluation, 70,* 29–44.

Krosnick, J. A., & Petty, R. E. (1995). Attitude strength: An overview. In R. E. Petty & J. A. Krosnick (Eds.), *Attitude strength: Antecedents and consequences* (pp. 1–24). Hillsdale, NJ: Erlbaum.

Larkins, A. G., & Shaver, J. P. (1967). Matched-pair scoring technique used on a first-grade yes-no type economics achievement test. *Utah Academy of Science, Art, and Letters: Proceedings, 44-1,* 229–242.

Leech, G. N. (1983). *Principles of pragmatics.* London: Longman.

Lenski, G. E., & Leggett, J. C. (1960). Caste, class, and deference in the research interview. *American Journal of Sociology, 65,* 463–467.

Likert, R. (1932). A technique for the measurement of attitudes. *Archives of Psychology, 104,* 44–53.

Lindzey, G. E., & Guest, L. (1951). To repeat—checklists can be dangerous. *Public Opinion Quarterly, 15,* 355–358.

Lodge, M. (1981). *Magnitude scaling: Quantitative measurement of opinions.* Beverly Hills, CA: Sage.

Matell, M. S., & Jacoby, J. (1971). Is there an optimal number of alternatives for Likert scale items? Study I: Reliability and validity. *Educational and Psychological Measurement, 31,* 657–674.

McClendon, M. J. (1991). Acquiescence and recency response-order effects in interview surveys. *Sociological Methods and Research, 20,* 60–103.

McClendon, M. J., & Alwin, D. F. (1993). No-opinion filters and attitude measurement reliability. *Sociological Methods and Research, 21,* 438–464.

Messick, S., & Frederiksen, N. (1958). Ability, acquiescence, and "authoritarianism." *Psychological Reports, 4,* 687–697.

Michaelis, W., & Eysenck, H. J. (1971). The determination of personality inventory factor patterns and intercorrelations by changes in real-life motivation. *Journal of Genetic Psychology, 118,* 223–234.

Miethe, T. D. (1985). The validity and reliability of value measurements. *Journal of Personality, 119,* 441–453.

Mirowsky, J., & Ross, C. E. (1991). Eliminating defense and agreement bias from measures of the sense of control: A 2 × 2 index. *Social Psychology Quarterly, 54,* 127–145.

Munson, J. M., & McIntyre, S. H. (1979). Developing practical procedures for the measurement of personal values in cross-cultural marketing. *Journal of Marketing Research, 16,* 48–52.

Murray, D. M., & Perry, C. L. (1987). The measurement of substance use among adolescents: When is the bogus pipeline method needed? *Addictive Behaviors, 12,* 225–233.

Myers, J. H., & Warner, W. G. (1968). Semantic properties of selected evaluation adjectives. *Journal of Marketing Research, 5,* 409–412.

Narayan, S., & Krosnick, J. A. (1996). Education moderates some response effects in attitude measurement. *Public Opinion Quarterly, 60,* 58–88.

Nathan, B. R., & Alexander, R. A. (1985). The role of inferential accuracy in performance rating. *Academy of Management Review, 10,* 109–115.

Newcomb, T. E. (1943). *Personality and social change.* New York: Dryden Press.

Nisbett, R. E., & Wilson, T. D. (1977). Telling more than we can know: Verbal reports on mental processes. *Psychology Review, 84,* 231–259.

Noelle-Neumann, E. (1984). *The spiral of silence.* Chicago: University of Chicago Press.

Oppenheim, A. N. (1992). *Questionnaire design, interviewing, and attitude measurement.* London: Pinter Publishers.

Parten, M. (1950). *Surveys, polls, and samples: Practical procedures.* New York: Harper and Brothers.

Patrick, D. L., Bush, J. W., & Chen, M. M. (1973). Methods for measuring levels of well-being for a health status index. *Health Services Research, 8,* 228–245.

Paulhus, D. L. (1984). Two-component models of socially desirable responding. *Journal of Personality and Social Psychology, 46,* 598–609.

Paulhus, D. L. (1986). Self-deception and impression management in test responses. In A. Angleitner & J. Wiggins (Eds.), *Personality assessment via questionnaires: Current issues in theory and measurement* (pp. 143–165). New York: Springer-Verlag.

Paulhus, D. L. (1991). Measurement and control of response bias. In J. P. Robinson, P. R. Shaver, & L. S. Wrightman (Eds.), *Measures of personality and social psychological attitudes,* Vol. 1 (pp. 17–59). San Diego: Academic Press.

Pavlos, A. J. (1972). Racial attitude and stereotype change with bogus pipeline paradigm. *Proceedings of the 80th Annual Convention of the American Psychological Association, 7,* 292.

Pavlos, A. J. (1973). Acute self-esteem effects on racial attitudes measured by rating scale and bogus pipeline. *Proceedings of the 81st Annual Convention of the American Psychological Association, 8,* 165–166.

Payne, S. L. (1949–1950). Case study in question complexity. *Public Opinion Quarterly, 13,* 653–658.

Quigley-Fernandez, B., & Tedeschi, J. T. (1978). The bogus pipeline as lie detector: Two validity studies. *Journal of Personality and Social Psychology, 36,* 247–256.

Rankin, W. L., & Grube, J. W. (1980). A comparison of ranking and rating procedures for value system measurement. *European Journal of Social Psychology, 10,* 233–246.

Reynolds, T. J., & Jolly, J. P. (1980). Measuring personal values: An evaluation of alternative methods. *Journal of Marketing Research, 17,* 531–536.

Roese, N. J., & Jamieson, D. W. (1993). Twenty years of bogus pipeline research: A critical review and meta-analysis. *Psychological Bulletin, 114,* 363–375.

Rokeach, M. (1973). *The nature of human values.* New York: Free Press.

Rothenberg, B. B. (1969). Conservation of number among four- and five-year-old children: Some methodological considerations. *Child Development, 40,* 383–406.

Ruch, G. M., & DeGraff, M. H. (1926). Corrections for chance and "guess" vs. "do not guess" instructions in multiple-response tests. *Journal of Educational Psychology, 17,* 368–375.

Rugg, D. (1941). Experiments in wording questions: II. *Public Opinion Quarterly, 5,* 91–92.

Schlenker, B. R., & Weigold, M. F. (1989). Goals and the self-identification process: Constructing desires identities. In L. A. Pervin (Ed.), *Goal concepts in personality and social psychology* (pp. 243–290). Hillsdale, NJ: Erlbaum.

Schuman, H., & Converse, J. M. (1971). The effect of black and white interviewers on black responses. *Public Opinion Quarterly, 35,* 44–68.

Schuman, H., & Presser, S. (1981). *Questions and answers in attitude surveys.* San Diego: Academic Press.

Sedikides, C., & Strube, M. J. (1997). Self-evaluation: To thine own self be good, to thine own self be sure, to thine own self be true, and to thine own self be better. *Advances in Experimental Social Psychology, 29,* 209–269.

Shaffer, J. W. (1963). A new acquiescence scale for the MMPI. *Journal of Clinical Psychology, 19,* 412–415.

Shaw, J. A., & Budd, E. C. (1982). Determinants of acquiescence and naysaying of mentally retarded persons. *American Journal of Mental Deficiency, 87,* 108–110.

Sigall, H., & Page, R. (1971). Current stereotypes: A little fading, a little faking. *Journal of Personality and Social Psychology, 18,* 247–255.

Sigelman, C. K., & Budd, E. C. (1986). Pictures as an aid in questioning mentally retarded persons. *Rehabilitation Counseling Bulletin, 29,* 173–181.

Smith, T. W. (1987). That which we call welfare by any other name would smell sweeter: An analysis of the impact of question wording on response patterns. *Public Opinion Quarterly, 51,* 75–83.

Sudman, S., Bradburn, N. M., & Schwarz, N. (1996). *Thinking about answers: The application of cognitive processes to survey methodology.* San Francisco: Jossey-Bass.

Sussman, B. (1985, November 28). Hidden racial attitudes distorted Virginia polls. *The Washington Post.*

Taylor, J. R., & Kinnear, T. C. (1971). Numerical comparison of alternative methods for collecting proximity judgements. In *Proceedings of the Fall Conference* (pp. 547–550). Chicago: American Marketing Association.

Thurstone, L. L. (1928). Attitudes can be measured. *American Journal of Sociology, 33,* 529–554.

Tourangeau, R., & Rasinski, K. A. (1988). Cognitive processes underlying context effects in attitude measurement. *Psychological Bulletin, 103,* 299–314.

Trott, D. M., & Jackson, D. N. (1967). An experimental analysis of acquiescence. *Journal of Experimental Research in Personality, 2,* 278–288.

Visser, P. S., Krosnick, J. A., Marquette, J., & Curtin, M. (In press). Improving election forecasting: Allocation of undecided respondents, identification of likely voters, and response order effects. In P. Lavrakas & M. Traugott (Eds.), *Election polls, the news media, and democracy.*

Warner, S. L. (1965). Randomized response: A survey technique for eliminating evasive answer bias. *Journal of the American Statistical Association, 60,* 63–69.

Warwick, D. P., & Lininger, C. A. (1975). *The sample survey: Theory and practice.* New York: McGraw-Hill.

Wason, P. C. (1961). Response to affirmative and negative binary statements. *British Journal of Psychology, 52,* 133–142.

Wegener, D. T., Downing, J., Krosnick, J. A., & Petty, R. E. (1995). Measures and manipulations of strength-related properties of attitudes: Current practice and future directions. In R. E. Petty & J. A. Krosnick (Eds.), *Attitude strength: Antecedents and consequences* (pp. 455–487). Hillsdale, NJ: Erlbaum.

Wesman, A. G. (1946). The usefulness of correctly spelled words in a spelling test. *Journal of Educational Psychology, 37,* 242–246.

Wesman, A. G. (1947). Active versus blank responses to multiple-choice items. *Journal of Educational Psychology, 38,* 89–95.

Wikman, A., & Warneryd, B. (1990). Measurement errors in survey questions: Explaining response variability. *Social Indicators Research, 22,* 199–212.

Winkler, J. D., Kanouse, D. E., & Ware, J. E. (1982). Controlling for acquiescence response set in scale development. *Journal of Applied Psychology, 67,* 555–561.

Wiseman, F. (1972). Methodological bias in public opinion surveys. *Public Opinion Quarterly, 36,* 105–108.

Young, P. V. (1939). *Scientific social surveys and research.* New York: Prentice-Hall.

CHAPTER 3

Liberalism and Conservatism

Kathleen Knight

The meanings of the terms *liberal* and *conservative* may be familiar to readers of this chapter, but the same can be said for only about half of the American public—according to repeated studies employing representative samples (Converse, 1964; Knight, 1990; Knight & Erikson, 1997; Luttbeg & Gant, 1985). Philosophical and scholarly differences about the meanings of these ideological labels are evident in the variety of scales that have been proposed to measure liberalism–conservatism and in the critiques of them. William Stone's (1994) essay in the *Encyclopedia of Human Behavior* provides a cogent discussion of the origins and meanings of the terms and describes the multiple usages to which they are put:

> The terms conservative and liberal are much misunderstood. . . . A *conservative* person is one who is devoted to the status quo and who accepts authority and the norms of society. A *liberal* is change-oriented and places great emphasis on individual freedom, being opposed to the external imposition of authority. In reality, neither people nor philosophies are that simple and unalloyed. They are all mixtures, to some degree, of opposing tendencies. (p. 701)

Not all of the scales presented here have been titled measures of *liberalism* and/or *conservatism* by their developers, although the selection is biased in favor of measures that explicitly use the words *liberal, conservative, radical, progressive, left,* and/or *right* in their titles.[1] Other scales have been selected because their authors refer to them in discussion as measures of liberalism and/or conservatism, because these authors call the groups identified by the scales "liberal" or "conservative," or because subsequent researchers have employed the scales as indicators of ideological leanings.

[1]No information on scales resulted from searches of the word *progressive.* The selection of scales presented here has been limited to those that have been reported in literature published since the early 1970s. To identify these scales, a search of the following computerized data bases was conducted: "PsychLit," "Sociofile," and the Social Science Index. These searches were keyed on the names of authors of known scales as well as on the titles of the scales and the keywords identified in the text. A few scales identified in this search process were excluded from the review because they were used only once, were presented without any validation data, or addressed only issues of a topical nature that were clearly outdated.

Dimensionality and the Bipolar Assumption

In political discourse liberalism is generally conceived as the opposite of conservatism. The liberal–conservative distinction is portrayed as a *unidimensional* construct—the more liberal individuals are, the less conservative they are generally considered to be. Therefore individuals who score "low" on scales identified as measuring conservatism are frequently called "liberals," and vice versa. However, even here agreement is far from complete.

Kerlinger (1984), a prominent educational psychologist, proposed a *dualistic* model of ideology wherein liberalism and conservatism may be viewed as orthogonal dimensions. In Kerlinger's theory the bipolar, or unidimensional, structure of ideology is a special case. It occurs only when the same issue is favored by one side, while being just as strongly opposed by the other. Such an issue is defined as "polarized." Very few issues become polarized in this fashion because liberals and conservatives generally pay attention to different issues. Even when both liberals and conservatives attend to the same issue, they may define it differently or bring different values to bear (see also Rotunda, 1986; Schattschneider, 1960).

Kerlinger's criticism of unidimensional conceptualizations can be stated as follows: If we are interested in what liberals think, or how they behave, but we have identified them only by default (as "not conservative"), then our scales may not capture the concepts that are important, or central, to liberals' attitudes and behavior. One possible consequence of this is that the scales may be less effective in predicting some ideologically based attitudes than others. Following this logic, if one is interested in both liberals and conservatives, one should include scales measuring each. Theoretically these scales will be only slightly correlated.[2] And considering what we know about the general degree of ideological awareness in the public at large, the sum of the two sets of individuals who can be legitimately identified by the scales may be less than the whole public.

The question of whether one conceives of liberalism and conservatism as a single bipolar dimension is partly theoretical, perhaps even philosophical. Some scales are flexible enough to allow empirical tests of the underlying dimensionality of the construct; others assume a general unidimensional structure. In addition, because of the theoretical breadth of the construct, many scales that assume an overarching unidimensionality in theory still allow for a multidimensional measurement model that identifies different components of liberalism and conservatism. Thus the adequacy of the unidimensional assumption for the population addressed by the research should be considered carefully when scales and subscales are chosen.

Scope of the Definition

It is also necessary to consider the breadth of the conception of ideology appropriate to the research objective. For some scholars liberalism–conservatism is a fundamental and comprehensive general personality factor that underlies reactions and preferences across a wide variety of human endeavors (e.g., Comrey & Newmeyer, 1965; Tomkins, 1965; Wilson, 1973a). For other scholars ideology is a general orientation that mediates between the personality and values (e.g., Eysenck, 1954). For still others it *is* a value system (e.g.,

---

[2]There will be high negative correlations between liberal and conservative subscales only under special circumstances (polarization) that have been most completely addressed in Kerlinger (1984). The dualistic conceptualization is also an important part of Tomkins's (1964) *polarity theory,* which is best described in Stone and Schaffner (1988).

Rokeach, 1973; Kerlinger, 1984). Further complicating the picture, some scholars are interested in predicting a wide variety of political, social, and economic attitudes, while others are interested in attitudes that apply only within a specific domain.

For scholars interested in broad trends in the public, ideology is sometimes defined as some product of policy preferences or issue opinions, occasionally including additional ideological categories, such as "libertarian" and "populist" (Maddox & Lillie, 1984). When taken on a case-by-case basis, there is a substantial agreement in the scholarly community about which "end" of a given issue is liberal and which is conservative, but not necessarily about trends or their timing. Smith (1982, 1985) and Robinson (1984) have provided very useful survey evidence about liberal and conservative trends in issues covered by the General Social Survey (GSS) that suggests a "liberal plateau" in the 1970s. Using a complex algorithm to adjust for instrument effects, Stimson (1991) found shorter term shifts in issue "policy mood."

Efforts to use issue opinions as indirect measures of ideological sentiments also resulted in the broad literature on issue constraint and issue dimensionality (e.g., Barton & Parsons, 1977; Campbell, Converse, Miller, & Stokes, 1960; Converse, 1964; Stimson, 1975; Weisberg & Rusk, 1970). The best known of the general findings on issue dimensionality is that of separate, not necessarily correlated, social and economic dimensions. This allows some citizens to define themselves as, for example, social liberals and economic conservatives without experiencing any of the discomfort hypothesized to arise with the holding of "dissonant" political attitudes (Heider, 1958).

Indeed, the American public at large may deserve to be described in this fashion. Robinson notes in his appendix to this chapter that the percentage of the public in the GSS saying that birth control information should be available to teenagers increased from 80% in 1972 to nearly 90% by the 1990s, and the percentage of the public in the GSS saying that premarital sex is always wrong declined from 37% to 27% over the same period. In the same surveys support for euthanasia increased from 39% in 1977 to 65% in 1994. However, 65% of GSS respondents felt their taxes were still too high in 1994, compared to 60% in 1976. At the same time support for the death penalty rose from 64% in 1975 to 78% in 1994, and the percentage of GSS respondents who said that the courts were not harsh enough with criminals rose from 74% in the 1970s to nearly 90% by the 1990s. Clearly, then, care must be taken with the selection of issue items used to produce a liberal–conservative scale based on issue opinions (Erikson & Tedin, 1995).

This chapter proceeds from a discussion of the general domain of liberalism–conservatism to consider more specific dimensions of values and attitudes that may be of use in particular research objectives. In some cases these can be drawn from subscales of the more general measures. Emphasis is also placed on scales that are current and widely employed, although some older scales are included either because they are the best available for a particular conceptualization of ideology or because they provide the cornerstones for subsequent development. We turn first to simple general questions that have been asked repeatedly of representative cross-section samples of the American public.

Direct Measures of Liberalism–Conservatism

Scholarly disagreement over the philosophical meaning of the terms *liberal* and *conservative* in political science has led to increased reliance on simple self-definition, or identification as a liberal or conservative, as an alternative to the use of indirect multi-item scales. This method is extremely economical and reasonably effective, but succeeds by finessing the question of "what it is." While a generation ago direct self-labeling tended to be dismissed (e.g., Free & Cantril, 1968), direct measures of liberalism–conservatism are now the dominant means of assessing individual ideology in political science. In fact, ideological self-identification is so well accepted today that it is used to validate indirect scales.

The fundamental question that arises when employing direct measures of liberal–conservative identification is whether, or to what extent, the response represents a "non-attitude" (Converse, 1975). Earlier scholars who assumed the terms would *not* be generally understood by the public-at-large placed a premium on indirect multi-item scales. Luskin's (1987) excellent review of the literature examined the adequacy of public understanding of common distinctions between liberals and conservatives as an indicator of political sophistication. The consensus that simple methods of direct measurement will be contaminated to some extent by "thoughtless" responses is reflected in the general tendency to refer to them as expressions of "symbolic" ideology (Conover & Feldman, 1981; Levitin & Miller, 1979). Nonetheless, even very simple undifferentiated items measuring liberal–conservative identification yield significant correlations with a large number of relevant criterion variables, such as voting. This has resulted in the common practice of including at least one direct measure in most questionnaires measuring political attitudes, if only to have it available as a control variable or for secondary analyses.

The reliability and predictive power of direct measures of liberalism–conservatism are presumably enhanced by a *multi-item scale*. For example, Levitin and Miller (1979) employed a three-item scale constructed from American National Election Study (ANES) data in their influential article on the "non-ideological use of ideological labels." This scale combined (a) responses to a seven-point scale labeled *extremely liberal* at one end and *extremely conservative* at the other, with a filter for *no opinion* (Table 3–1.A), (b) "thermometer" ratings of liberals and conservatives (Table 3–1.D); and (c) self-reports of feeling "close to" each of the two ideological groups. The items were obtained at different points in the 1972 postelection interview and were distributed across preelection and postelection interviews in 1976, thus building in some control for the temporal stability of ideological self-labeling.

When considerations of time and space rule out the construction of a multi-item scale, the wording and format of the single item chosen become more important. A vast array of different item wordings have been employed in national surveys. These are detailed in Robinson and Fleishman (1984) along with response frequencies across time. Fortunately a substantial amount of experimental research on differences in question wording and format has been undertaken, which can provide guidance on the choice of the item. Most of these items assume the bipolarity (unidimensionality) of liberalism–conservatism and make this assumption explicit to the respondent in the wording of the question.

Numerical Rating Scales

The best known of the direct indicators of liberalism–conservatism is the seven-point scale, employing a "show-card" (see Table 3–1.A) in in-person interviews and in paper-and-pencil questionnaires. The major advantage of this format is that respondents can be asked to use the scale to locate other political objects (candidates and parties) as well as themselves. This facilitates the creation of *proximity* and *difference* measures to contrast

Table 3-1

Question Wording for Different Versions of Liberal–Conservative Identification Items

---

A. The Traditional Seven-Point Visual Scale

We hear a lot of talk these days about liberals and conservatives. Here is a 7-point scale on which the political views that people might hold are arranged from extremely liberal to extremely conservative.

1	2	3	4	5	6	7
Extremely Liberal	Liberal	Slightly Liberal	Moderate: Middle of the Road	Slightly Conservative	Conservative	Extremely Conservative

Where would you place yourself on this scale [or haven't you thought much about this]?

____   0. Haven't thought   8. Don't know

Rating

Probe: If you had to choose, would you consider yourself a liberal or a conservative?

[The probe can be asked of all respondents who do not initially place themselves on the scale and of those who initially locate themselves at the moderate point, Point 4.]

B. The Seven-Point Imaginary Ruler

Think of a ruler for measuring political views that people might hold from liberal to conservative. Point 1 means [very/extremely/strongly] liberal political views, and Point 7 means [very/extremely/strongly] conservative political views. Just like a regular ruler, it has points in between at 2, 3, 4, 5, or 6. Where would you place yourself on this ruler, remembering that Point 1 is [very/strongly] liberal and Point 7 is [very/strongly] conservative [or haven't you thought much about this]?

____   0. Haven't thought   8. Don't know

Rating

Probe: Do you think of yourself as closer to liberals or closer to conservatives?

C. The Branching Question (used to construct a seven-point scale)

Generally speaking, would you consider yourself to be a liberal, a conservative, a moderate, or what, or haven't you thought much about this?

If liberal or conservative: Do you consider yourself to be [very/strongly] liberal/conservative or just [liberal/conservative]?

If other than liberal or conservative: Do you think of yourself as closer to liberals or conservatives?

D. The Feeling Thermometer, In-Person Administration

Please turn to page *x* of this booklet. I'd like to get your feeling toward some of our political leaders and people/groups who are in the news these days. I'll read the name of a person/group, and I'd like you to rate that person/group using something we call a feeling thermometer.

   Ratings between 50 degrees and 100 degrees mean that you feel favorable and warm toward that person/group. Ratings between 0 degrees and 50 degrees mean that you don't feel favorable toward that person/group and that you don't care too much for that person. [You would rate a person/group at 50 degrees if you don't feel particularly warm or cold toward that person. If we come to a person whose name you don't recognize, you don't need to rate that person/group. Just tell me, and we'll move on to the next one.]

   The first person/group is ____.

Record actual number: ____   997. Doesn't recognize.   998. Can't judge.

After the candidate list: And still using the feeling thermometer, how would you rate ____?

[The "show card" depicts a lengthwise equal-interval scale with 100 at the top and 0 at the bottom, but only Points 15, 30, 40, 50, 60, 70, and 85 are numbered.]

Continued

Table 3-1

Question Wording for Different Versions of Liberal–Conservative Identification Items—cont'd

---

E. The Feeling Thermometer, Telephone Administration

I'd like to get your feeling toward some of our political leaders and other people who are in the news these days. I'll read the name of a person/group, and I'd like you to rate that person/group using something we call a feeling thermometer.

   You can choose any number between 0 and 100. The higher the number, the warmer or more favorable you feel toward that person/group; the lower the number, the colder or less favorable. [You would rate a person/group at the 50 degree mark if you feel neither warm nor cold toward them. If we come to a person/group whose name you don't recognize, you don't need to rate that person/group. Just tell me, and we'll move on to the next one.]

   Our first person/group is ____. How would you rate him/her/them using the feeling thermometer?

Record actual number: ____   997. Doesn't recognize.   998. Can't judge.

After the candidate list: And still using the feeling thermometer, how would you rate ____?

F. The Zero- to Ten-Point Rating Scale

I'd like to get your feeling toward some of our political leaders and other people who are in the news these days. I'll read the name of a person/group, and I'd like you to rate that person/group. You can choose any number between 0 and 10.

   The higher the number, the more favorable you feel toward that person/group; the lower the number, the less favorable. [You would rate the person/group at 5 if you feel neither favorable nor unfavorable toward them. If we come to a person/group whose name you don't recognize, just tell me, and we'll move on to the next one.]

   Our first person/group is ____. How would you rate him/her/them on a scale of 0 to 10?

Record actual number: ____   997. Doesn't recognize.   998. Can't judge.

Names of groups are continued after candidates with no additional instruction.

---

the respondent's position with his or her perception of candidates or political groups. The versions of the *seven-point scale* employed in the major national academic data collections are identical except that the GSS does not include a filter for *no opinion,* while the ANES does (see Table 3–1.A). The correlation between the same items asked at roughly a two- to four-month interval in the preelection and postelection interviews of the 1980 ANES was .69. The filter "or haven't you thought much about this?" generally is chosen by 25% to 30% of national samples.

   A version of the seven-point scale suitable for telephone administration asks the respondent to imagine a "ruler" with Point 1 labeled *extremely (or very) liberal* and Point 7 labeled *extremely (or very) conservative* (Table 3–1.B). Even without explicit labeling of the midpoint, this item yields the same distribution as the visual representation obtained in in-person interviews. Nonresponse due to acceptance of the filter increases by about 5% in the telephone administration mode, but otherwise the items appear to be fully substitutable. Contrary to conventional wisdom labeling the midpoint does not seem to increase respondents' propensity to choose it. The test–retest reliability for the telephone administration of the "imaginary ruler" over a two-month interval in the 1989 ANES Pilot Study was .77.

   The *Eurobarometer* and the General Social Surveys between 1983 and 1987 used a 1-to-10 scale without a natural midpoint labeled *left* and *right.* A 1-to-6 *left–right* scale was used by Stone, Ommundsen, and Williams (1985) to validate scales by Eysenck (1954) and Tompkins (1965). The fact that no natural midpoint is available obviously forces respondents to "take sides," but little methodological information is available on the effect of this omission.

Very few respondents place themselves at the endpoints of the seven-point scale in either the telephone or the in-person administration. Changing the labeling of the endpoints from *extremely* to *very* has no effect on the distribution of responses. While the resulting distributions are quite appropriate for regression formulations, it may be necessary to combine the endpoints with their adjacent categories for some kinds of analyses (Miller & Shanks, 1996; Miller & Traugott, 1989).

Direct Self-Labeling

There are a large number of straightforward identification, or self-labeling, questions available with only slight variations in wording. A full listing of the wordings used in major surveys in the United States was provided by Robinson and Fleishman (1984). When direct questions are employed, the major issues involve (1) the number of response options provided, (2) the provision of a middle category (Miller, 1984; Presser & Schuman, 1980), (3) whether follow-up probes are employed, and (4) the use of a filter for *no opinion*. It is currently common to include an explicit "moderate" alternative; even when one is not provided, a fairly high percentage of national samples (10–20%) may volunteer "moderate" or "neither." Failure to provide a middle alternative in a direct self-labeling question may also increase the number of responses that are likely to be treated as missing.

When a moderate category is provided, it is usually selected by 30 to 40% of the public depending on the other response categories presented. For some analyses, however, this large undifferentiated middle may be a source of concern. One solution to this problem is to include a follow-up question phrased in forced-choice terms. The follow-up question "Are you more like a liberal or more like a conservative?" works better than "If you had to choose, would you call yourself a liberal or a conservative?" The latter phrasing seems to evoke a degree of resistance to self-labeling among respondents. However, both succeed in depopulating the pure moderate category. This malleability, coupled with lower temporal stability and consistency with other identification items among those who identify only after a probe (Knight & Lewis, 1986), suggests that care should be taken in assuming any great degree of ideological motivation on the part of such respondents.

When a probe of this sort is employed for moderates, it is worthwhile also asking the same follow-up question of respondents who initially choose a *filter*, such as "or haven't you thought much about that?" It has been repeatedly found that a majority of initially filtered respondents accept a label after probing. The same caveats about the meaningfulness of such responses that apply to probed moderates should be kept in mind here. In general, however, the rule of thumb is to obtain as much information as there is time for, if only to avoid regrets during subsequent analysis. It is also worth noting that the same question can be employed as a follow-up probe of "don't know" and "moderate" responses to the seven-point scale. This follow-up has been included in ANES surveys since 1980. Data from such responses are most appropriately incorporated into the analysis by recoding them to points 3 and 5 on the standard seven-point scale.

A follow-up question asking initial identifiers to assess the intensity of their identification using the modifier "strong"/"not so strong" has been found to yield a seven-point scale whose categories are all well populated and well behaved (Feldman, 1984). The evidence overwhelmingly favors the term *strong* over the terms *very* and *extremely*. Such a follow-up should be included if time allows. The full sequence of branching questions is presented in Table 3–1.C. When the full sequence is employed, the responses can be converted into an approximation of a seven-point scale with "strong" identifiers at Points 1 and 7, "not strong" immediate identifiers at Points 2 and 6, and initial moderates who identify in response to the probe at Points 3 and 5. Because scales created from the branching questions will be much more strongly bimodal than the numerical scale, they should be identified as such to avoid confusion about differences in results.

The test–retest correlation for the branching question for the two-month interval in the 1987 ANES Pilot Study was .77 when the filter was employed. This dropped to .70 when respondents originally excluded by the filter who identified in the forced-choice follow-up question were included in the calculation. The test–retest figure for the nationwide ANES sample in the 1984 pre- and post-election interviews was .64 when no filter was employed (Haltom, 1990; Knight, 1990).

Feeling Thermometers

Feeling thermometers ranging from 0 to 100, with 50 identified as the neutral point (Table 3–1.D), have become a quite popular means of collecting evaluations of a wide range of political objects. In part this is because once the "stem," or introduction, has been administered, additional objects can be evaluated in the same metric very quickly. While imposing a similar metric by standardizing the format is convenient for many analytic purposes, care must be taken to avoid method artifacts. With respect to the feeling thermometers, the most common artifact seems to take the form of a "positivity" bias (Green, 1988; Knight, 1984; Wilcox, Sigelman, & Cook, 1989). As a consequence one generally finds in national samples that the mean feeling thermometer rating for both liberals and conservatives will be above the 50-degree neutral point. Wilcox *et al.* (1989) reported the results of tests of several different "correction" techniques that can be employed if the individual ratings are used as unidimensional measures of affect, as, for example, in correlational analyses.

Other scholars (most prominently Conover and Feldman, 1981, and Weisberg, 1980) argue that the low negative correlations between the raw ratings of groups generally considered to be "opposites" are evidence for a lack of bipolarity reminiscent of Kerlinger's (1984) dualistic structure. If the analyst is willing to assume that liberalism–conservatism is unidimensional, then one thermometer rating can simply be subtracted from the other to create a relative indicator of affect toward the two ideological groups, with a theoretical range of -100 to $+100$. Test–retest correlations for a liberal–conservative feeling thermometer *difference* using a panel of respondents from the 1986 ANES and its 1987 Pilot Study averaged about .59 over a six-month interval and .69 for a one-month interval in 1987. The Heise 3-wave reliability figure for this panel was .78 (Knight, 1990).

Recently more scholars have been adopting a simpler variation on the feeling thermometer ratings employing an 11-point scale (Table 3–1.F). The argument here is that "zero" and "ten" are naturally occurring concepts, which are easier for the average individual to understand. Scales based on the 0-to-10 metric can be introduced and administered somewhat faster, particularly on the telephone. Experimental evidence suggests that 11-point scales produce the same distribution as feeling thermometers divided by 10 and rounded to the nearest integer. The correlation between a thermometer difference recoded to a 21-point scale and a 21-point scale difference created by subtracting one 11-point scale from the other was .69 when administered to the same national sample after an interval of roughly 10 months.

Macroideology: The Problem of Trends

The question of whether there are discernible ideological trends in the general public has been a matter of some contention, at least since *The American Voter* (Campbell, Converse,

Miller, & Stokes, 1960). One element in that contention has focused on issue-based ideology and will always remain to some degree a matter of which issues are included. The fact that ideological identification, or preference for a liberal or conservative party, was collected only occasionally from the 1930s through the 1960s seems to reflect a politician–press consensus that the public could not, or should not, be swayed by ideological appeals (see, for example, Shils, 1958). Indeed, the "lesson" of the Goldwater debacle given precedence at the time was that ideological appeals did not penetrate to the public at large. In essence the Goldwater forces mistook enthusiasm among the politically involved for numbers of votes (Converse, Clausen, & Miller, 1965).

From the perspective of the 1990s, it is not necessary to recall the whole of "the elitist/populist debate" in order to assert that *something* changed in the 1960s. Pierce (1970) suggested that the electorate began to tune in to ideological appeals in 1964, and even more in 1968. Nie, Verba, and Petrocik (1979) suggested that the public had become more ideological, but all were buried in the methodological morass that overwhelmed the debate (Barton & Parsons, 1977; Bennett, 1980). News organizations began to collect estimates of ideological identification more regularly in the late 1960s, but the questions did not become standard until the 1970s.

Figure 3–1 traces the pattern of ideological identification for three different survey houses [GSS, ANES, and CBS/New York Times (CBS/NYT)] that have maintained consistent question wording from the 1970s to the 1990s. The percentage conservative estimated by each house is based on the total number of ideological identifiers (excluding "moderate" and "don't know" respondents). Based on the beginning points at hand, the trend, if any, is toward greater conservative identification for all three houses. The ANES

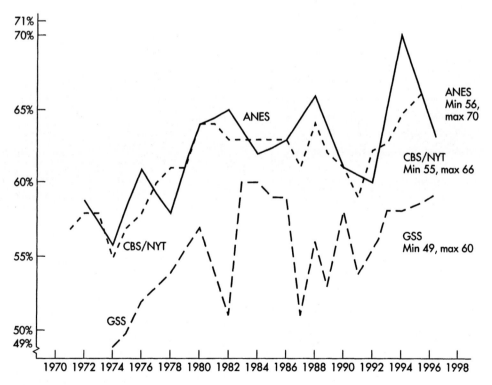

Fig. 3–1 Trends in Ideological Identification: Percent Conservative among Identifiers. (Percent Conservative = C/C+L, Moderates excluded.)

estimates are the most conservative and depict a strong conservative tide in 1994. ANES and CBS/NYT estimates track each other fairly closely. GSS shows less movement overall, particularly in the later years, and provides estimates that suggest that the public is somewhat less conservative (or more liberal) on balance.

The largest differences in the estimated percentages conservative for GSS and ANES are 14, 10, and 12 points in 1982, 1988, and 1994, respectively. For most years, however, differences are small enough to be attributed to sampling error. As mentioned previously, GSS does not screen out people who say they "have not thought much about" the ideological terms, which leaves a larger number of people in the denominator; but neither does CBS/NYT. The GSS and ANES both feature in-person interviews with proper multistage random probability samples of the American public and response rates of better than 70%. The CBS/NYT series includes both telephone interviews and exit polls weighted by their own algorithm.

The larger substantive point, however, is that there is little discernible movement in macroideology (Box-Steffensmeier, Knight, & Sigelman, 1998) over the period for which estimates are plentiful (see also Cohen & Krassa, 1990; Erikson & Tedin, 1995; Robinson & Fleishman, 1989). At the same time there has been a significant increase in the correlation between party identification and ideological identification in the public at large (Knight & Erikson, 1997). It also appears that when the sample is restricted to look only at the ideologically sophisticated segment of the electorate, some of the causal dynamics of macropartisanship and macroideology can be discerned (Box-Steffensmeier & DeBoef, 1997).

Correlates of Ideological Identification

In general, the demographic correlates of the ideological identification questions follow a not unexpected pattern. In the GSS, male voters are slightly more conservative in their self-identification than females ($r = -.02$); older people rate themselves more conservative than younger people ($r = -.13$); the more educated are slightly more conservative ($r = -.04$), and blacks are more liberal than whites ($r = .08$). The strongest correlation, not surprisingly, occurs with party identification ($r = -.32$), although "weak" Democrats rate themselves as more liberal than strong Democrats.

Summary and Recommendations

There is sufficient evidence of the validity of direct *liberal–conservative self-identification* to warrant its inclusion in almost any survey of political attitudes. However, the attitude will be more likely to be meaningful, and a more important predictor of other attitudes, among politically sophisticated citizens (Knight, 1985).

The provision of a middle/neutral category and the use of a screening question or filter for no sense of identification are consistent with empirical evidence that suggests that the liberal and conservative labels are meaningful to only about half of the American public (Knight & Erikson, 1997; Levitin & Miller, 1979; Luttbeg & Gant, 1985). The use of a filter for no opinion and a follow-up probe seeking any vague sense of identification from those who initially accept the filter and from those who describe themselves as moderate provides the greatest flexibility for later analysis. One can then define identification both strictly and loosely and see if it makes any difference in a particular specification.

Use of a seven-point scale will provide the greatest comparability with other current academic surveys, but with the prevalence of telephone interviewing, the branching question will become more common. In cybersurveys graphic depiction of a seven-point scale may be worthwhile, but care should be taken to ascertain and report background and labeling.

Multi-Item Measures
of Liberalism–Conservatism

When choosing among the various indirect multi-item indicators of liberalism–conservatism, the question of what the concept means to the analyst must be addressed. Most scholars would probably find much to agree with in the following comprehensive definitions offered by Kerlinger (1984):

> *Liberalism* is a set of political, economic, religious, educational, and other social beliefs that emphasize freedom of the individual, constitutional participatory government and democracy, the rule of law, free negotiation, discussion and tolerance of different views, constructive social progress and change, egalitarianism and the rights of minorities, secular rationality and rational approaches to social problems, and positive government action to remedy social deficiencies and to improve human welfare. (p. 15)

> *Conservatism* is a set of political, economic, religious, educational, and other social beliefs characterized by emphasis on the status quo and social stability, religion and morality, liberty and freedom, the natural inequality of men, the uncertainty of progress, and the weakness of human reason. It is further characterized by distrust of popular democracy and majority rule and by support for individualism and individual initiative, the sanctity of private property, and the central importance of business and industry in society. (pp. 16–17)

However, different facets of these definitions have been emphasized by different scholars.

The notion that concepts and values salient to one ideological side might not be equally salient to the other, or attract the same intensity of affect, is reflected in concerns over "balance" in several critiques of unidimensional scales. Interest in the dualistic approach is reflected in Conover and Feldman's (1981, 1986) work on issues and reference groups. Duality is also a hallmark of Tomkins's *polarity theory.* As in the Rokeach "two-value model," *humanistic* and *normative* orientations are both ideals, and they are not mutually exclusive (Stone & Schaffner, 1997). Ultimately, as Sidanius and Duffy (1988) pointed out, the question of whether a bipolar structure exists in any particular population is amenable to testing if scale items are constructed in a way that allows it. A large number of studies (Converse, 1964; Knight, 1985; Knight & Erikson, 1997; Stimson, 1975), including Sidanius's cross-national work on university students (Sidanius, Brewer, Banks, & Ekehammar 1987), suggest that the most important variable affecting this dimensionality will be political—or even more explicitly, ideological—sophistication.

Disagreement is also evident concerning whether liberals can automatically be said to value the exact opposite of what conservatives value with respect to various aspects of the definitions. Thus Tomkins (1965) proposed that "left–right" ideology pervades every aspect of human endeavor, but that its essence can be encompassed in a single humanistic–normative continuum: "Is man the measure, an end in himself, an active creative, thinking, desiring, loving force in nature? Or must man realize himself, attain his full stature only through struggle toward, participation in, conformity to a norm, a measure, an ideal essence basically prior to and independent of man" (1965, p. 79). Loye (1977) distilled this conceptualization into "norm violating" and "norm maintaining" and, following

Knutson (1972), linked these poles with Maslow's (1968) distinction between defensive and growth needs.

Thomas (1976, 1978) adapted 60 Tomkins items for Q-sort analysis and found nearly orthogonal liberal and conservative factors. De St. Aubin (1996) also investigated Tomkins's polarity theory, but split the polar opposites offered in the traditional item format into equal sets of randomly ordered humanistic and normative items to which subjects responded in Likert-type format. Again, the humanistic and normative scores were not found to be significantly correlated. Stone and Schaffner (1988, 1997) and Milburn (1991) recommended the Tomkins formulation, but suggested that the liberal (humanistic) and conservative (normative) items be scored separately, in essence supporting a dualistic interpretation.

Rokeach (1973) provided a cogent description of difficulties encountered in attempting to define the liberal–conservative continuum with respect to a single underlying dimension. He offered an alternative *two-value model* based on people's relative ranking of the terminal values of *equality* and *freedom*. Based on a content analysis of political documents, Rokeach (1973) proposed that the two dimensions resolved into four quadrants identified with different political philosophies: communist—high equality/low freedom; socialist—high equality/high freedom; capitalist—low equality/high freedom; fascist—low equality/low freedom. While theoretically satisfying, this formulation has received only partial empirical validation (Cochrane, Billig, & Hogg, 1979; Mueller, 1974; Rokeach, 1973).

In commenting on Kerlinger's (1967, 1972) earlier work, Rokeach (1973) also suggested that the liberal referents emphasized *equality* and the conservative referents emphasized *freedom*. Feather (1979) found that conservatives identified by the Wilson–Patterson (1968; Wilson, 1973a) C-Scale downgraded both freedom and equality. While a theoretical relationship between liberalism–conservatism and the Rokeach Value Survey has been suggested by a number of researchers, the empirical relationship is far from clear. The Rokeach Value Scale is conceptually broader than liberalism–conservatism. It is thoroughly reviewed by Braithwaite and Scott in the first volume in this series (Robinson, Shaver, & Wrightsman, 1991).

Politics and Personality

Eysenck (1954) proposed a substantially different two-factor model of ideology, which remains useful in disentangling other definitional issues. Both Eysenck and Kerlinger based their arguments about the structure of ideology on the extraction of consistent second-order factors using instruments designed to provide broad coverage of all relevant domains and to work with a variety of different subjects. While Kerlinger's two general factors are liberalism and conservatism, Eysenck's first general factor—the so-called R factor—is bipolar *radicalism–conservatism*. His second general factor is defined as *tough-mindedness–tendermindedness*—the T factor. The term *radical* avoids confusion in the British context, where the Labour Party is to the left of the Liberal Party. In this sense radicalism is simply the antonym for conservatism and, as such, can be considered a synonym for liberalism in the American context. Commenting on the British case, Eysenck (1954) described liberals as "tender-minded radicals."

In a later study Eysenck (1975) described the R factor as "a kind of philosophical conservatism characterized by anti-progressive attitudes" (reprinted in Eysenck & Wilson, 1978, p. 260) and identified a third general factor—*economic conservatism*. He attributed the discovery of this third general factor to the greater variance in the random sample of the British public used in the 1975 study. Drawing on similarities in cross-national findings, Kerlinger (1984) identified three first-order factors associated with liberalism (equality, civil rights, and social welfare) and four associated with conservatism [religiosity, economic conservatism, traditional conservatism (order), and morality].

There is considerable debate about whether the factor Eysenck identified as T is independent of the direction of ideological orientation (Birenbaum & Zak, 1982; Stone & Russ, 1976). Some attention to the foundations of this debate is useful in addressing another conceptual strand in the measurement of ideology. As numerous scholars have noted, the theory underlying the *authoritarian personality* (Adorno, Frenkel-Brunswick, Levinson, & Sanford, 1950) assumes that the personality syndrome captured in the F scale is inextricably tied to right-wing political values. The "good-liberal, bad-conservative stereotypes" (Stone, 1983, p. 217) arising from this pivotal work generated a firestorm of criticism and a whole separate avenue of research. The fundamental basis of the argument is well represented by Shils's (1954) essay "Authoritarianism: Right and Left." Shils argued that if the political system could generate the totalitarian socialistic regimes characteristic of the Soviet Union and Eastern Europe during that period, then the impulse to support or acquiesce in such systems must be independent of the left–right content of political values.

For Eysenck this is the toughmindedness–tendermindedness factor—"the projection on to the social attitudes field of a *set of personality variables* [italics added]" (Eysenck, 1954, p. 170). In a later review Eysenck and Wilson (1978) argued that the T factor is also represented by constructs such as *dogmatism* (Rokeach, 1960), *Machiavellianism* (Christie & Geis, 1970), and *"non-directional" authoritarianism*. What these scales, along with Ray and Lovejoy's (1986) "directiveness" measures, have in common is the attempt to measure a psychological orientation toward social values and relations that is free of left–right content. As such, they are outside the scope of this presentation. Authoritarianism has been covered in detail in Richard Christie's chapter in the first volume in this series (Robinson *et al.*, 1991). Brief attention is devoted to the concept here because of its theoretical relationship with the politics of the right.

Scales Reviewed in This Chapter

The first three scales in this chapter can be considered the most comprehensive because they give equal theoretical weight to conservatism and liberalism, although dimensionality assumptions differ. The dates listed are those of the versions included in this presentation. In several instances the scale authors are engaged in ongoing research to refine and update the scales, and it would be wise to contact them about current versions.

1. Social Attitudes Statements and Referents Scales (Kerlinger, 1984)
2. Polarity Scale (Tomkins, 1964) PS43 (Stone & Schaffner, 1997)
3. Public Opinion Inventory (Eysenck, 1951)

The central element of Kerlinger's scale is its conception of liberalism–conservatism as *dualistic*. The liberal scale is expected to be nearly orthogonal to (independent of) the conservative one. This is because the concepts that distinguish the groups of individuals who can be called liberal are not "criterial" or central to conservatives, and vice versa. One can predict how conservatives will respond to conservative referents (positively), but one cannot predict how they will respond to liberal ones, and again vice versa. In essence both "sides" respond favorably to criteria they consider relevant, but not necessarily negatively to referents from the *other* side. When the public, or segments of it, becomes polarized, it is because elements of the ideological debate normally irrelevant to the other side become negatively criterial. Only in the special case of "negative criteriality" will the attitude structure of the population examined be bipolar (Kerlinger, 1984, pp. 50–53).

The Kerlinger (1984) scale operationalized a dualistic theory of liberalism and conservatism. The theory underlying Tomkins's (1964) polarity scale proposes a single humanistic–normative dimension underlying left–right attitudes, although it has been argued that the two orientations are orthogonal (Stone, 1983, 1986; Stone & Schaffner, 1988, 1997; Thomas, 1976, 1978). Eysenck (1954) conceives of a general bipolar factor of radicalism–conservatism.

Conservatism and Authoritarianism

The next six instruments are explicitly identified as scales of conservatism. All assume a single underlying left–right continuum.

4. Right-Wing Authoritarianism Scale (Altemeyer, 1990)
5. Conservatism Scale, or C-Scale (Wilson & Patterson, 1989)
6. S Conservatism Scale (Nilsson & Ekehammar, 1989; Sidanius, 1991)
7. Conservatism of American Public Opinion (Ray, 1982)
8. Classical Conservatism Scale (McClosky, 1958); Conservatism–Liberalism Scale (McClosky & Bann, 1979)
9. Ideological Agreement with Goldwater Scale (Selznick & Steinberg, 1966)

Of these, the Right-Wing Authoritarianism (RWA) Scale developed by Altemeyer (1981, 1988, 1996) is most explicitly modeled after the theoretical construct developed in *The Authoritarian Personality* (Adorno *et al.*, 1950). However, the selection of defining characteristics for the Wilson–Patterson (1968) C-Scale was also influenced by the authoritarianism tradition. Sidanius's (1976a) scale of social attitudes began as a revision of the Wilson–Patterson (1968) C-Scale, while Ray's (1983) measure of conservative attitudes was generated from Ray's (1982) more comprehensive effort to test the dimensional models of ideology proposed by Eysenck (1954). McClosky's (1958) Classical Conservatism Scale was intended to capture a broad philosophical orientation toward conservatism; the Conservatism–Liberalism Scale of McClosky and Bann (1979) focuses more explicitly on the variety of social and economic attitudes thought to underlie ideological orientation in the mass public.

Authoritarianism spans two major areas of political science research—political tolerance and liberalism–conservatism. Objections to the F scale (Adorno *et al.*, 1950) have been methodologically driven as well as philosophical. Methodological difficulties (most prominently response set bias and attempts at balanced presentation) led Altemeyer (1981, 1988) to propose a revised measure of explicitly right-wing authoritarianism—the RWA Scale—which has been extensively tested in Canada and the United States.

For Altemeyer, Right-Wing Authoritarianism is politically significant because it creates a climate of opinion that supports repressive action by government; it is "a state of mind, a willingness to see democratic institutions destroyed" (1988, p. 3). In this sense it could be regarded as a measure of political (in)tolerance, but it is included here because of its theoretical relationship to conservatism. The Altemeyer scale seeks to measure a complex of the three major traits identified by Adorno *et al.* (1950) as predictive of pre-Fascist tendencies: *submissiveness, conventionality,* and *authoritarian aggression.* These are explicitly linked to the political right by the theoretical definition of "authoritarian aggression." Here Altemeyer (1988) has refined the notion of "hostility toward outgroups," focusing on agreement with aggressive–punitive actions toward *authority-sanctioned* targets.

> Aggression is authoritarian when it is accompanied by the belief that established authority at least tacitly approves it or that it will help preserve established authority. . . . The perception of authoritative approval . . . extends beyond individual authorities . . . to vaguer and larger powers . . . "God wants sinners punished." (p. 106)

> Authoritarians are "rightist" because they support traditional authority. Current usage of the term "conservative" to describe "hardline Communists" in the Soviet Union illustrates the generality of this connotation. (p. 264)

Altemeyer's explanation of authoritarian aggression is particularly enlightening in this respect because it makes clear that the aggressive impulse can be stirred up in opposition to an established government when that government is portrayed as violating the norms of an even "higher" authority. In this sense the Altemeyer conceptualization provides some insight into the historical attractiveness of reactionary movements (e.g., Lipset & Raab, 1978) and organizations operating outside established law like vigilantes or militias. These connections are explored in more depth in Altemeyer's (1996) *The Authoritarian Specter.*

It should also be noted that it is Altemeyer's critics (most particularly Ray, 1985c) who equate right-wing authoritarianism with conservatism. Altemeyer (1988) argued that RWA is not synonymous with conservatism. He defined conservatism as a disposition to "preserve the status quo, and maintain social stability . . . close to conventionalism, *one* of the attitude clusters I use to define authoritarianism" (1988, p. 8). Nonetheless, the political significance of the RWA Scale derives from the implications of the co-occurrence of the three attitude clusters. Some of Altemeyer's most striking findings were obtained from responses to questionnaires that included the RWA Scale sent to members of several legislative bodies in Canada and the United States. While carefully noting variability in RWA scores within parties, Altemeyer reported differences among party members significant enough to suggest that the RWA Scale "appears to be a more precise . . . definition of what the basic 'left/right' dimension really is" (1988, p. 256).

Two other versions of the F scale that may be of particular interest to those engaged in political research are: the Authoritarian-Rebellion Scale developed by Kohn (1972) and the short version of the F scale (Lane, 1955), which is carried in some years of the ANES or GSS surveys. The Kohn scale is intended to be a balanced F scale explicitly containing items that might be answered affirmatively by members of the radical left. It yielded significant differences across the political spectrum in Canada. Both appear in Christie's (1991) review of measures of authoritarianism.

The Wilson and Patterson (1968) *C-Scale* appears to be the most popular measure of conservatism in recent research, judging by the number of citations obtained by computerized search. At least part of its popularity stems from its ease of administration and scoring. Wilson popularized a "catchphrase" approach to attitude measurement in which respondents are asked to provide an affective reaction to short words or phrases rather than considering detailed statements with causal or action implications (Wilson, 1985). Subsequently a number of scholars have chosen this less cognitively demanding format (see Kerlinger, 1984; Ray, 1971; Sidanius, 1976a, 1976b; Suziedelis & Lorr, 1973).

The original version of the Wilson–Patterson C-Scale (Wilson & Patterson, 1968) consisted of a list of 50 phrases that alternated between referents that would be positively evaluated by a conservative and referents that would be negatively evaluated by a conservative. This is the crucial theoretical and operational difference between the Wilson–Patterson C-Scale and Kerlinger's (1984) referent scale, in which half of the items would be *positively* evaluated by a *liberal*. To define low scorers on the C-Scale as "liberals" requires the assumptions that liberals value the exact opposite of what conservatives value and that no other considerations enter into their evaluative systems. It also requires the somewhat less obvious assumption of equal weight or impact of positive and negative affect.

Wilson (1973a, p. 3) proposed that conservatism is "a general factor underlying an entire field of social attitudes" or a " 'dimension' of personality that is inferred on the basis of the organization of such attitudes." He chose the term *conservative* to describe this factor because "it is relatively free of derogatory value-tone" (1973a, p. 4), but makes clear that its conceptualization is nearly synonymous with "a variety of labels such as 'fascism,' 'authoritarianism,' 'rigidity,' and 'dogmatism' " (1973a, p. 4). The seven characteristics of the "ideal conservative" listed in the theory and scale construction sections of several articles are clearly reminiscent of, but not identical to, the "traits" explored by Adorno *et al.* (1950). They include religious dogmatism, punativeness, ethnocentrism, conventionality, antihedonism, and superstition/resistance to scientific progress (Wilson, 1973a, p. 51).

A truly vast literature generally testifies to the validity and reliability of the C-Scale as a measure of general conservatism, although, as might be anticipated, support for a single-factor interpretation is not unanimous (e.g., Robertson & Cochrane, 1973) and the issue of acquiescent response set has been raised (Ray, 1980; Ray & Pratt, 1979). In 1975 Wilson presented an updated and revised version of the C-Scale, which he subsequently referred to as the WPAI. Wilson (1975) also provided information allowing the 50 items to be scored in three alternative dimensional configurations: traditional conservative versus liberal, orthogonal realism versus idealism dimension, and four content subscales (militarism–punativeness, antihedonism, ethnocentrism, and religious puritanism).

The C-Scale has been validated on an American sample (Lapsley & Enright, 1979), and it has been translated into a number of different languages. Shea and Jones (1982) developed a pictorial format of 25 items validated in Papua New Guinea, which appears to have some promise for nonliterate populations (although the authors caution against expecting that a truly universal attitude scale can be developed).

General conservatism has been found to be strongly related to political conservatism. Wilson (1973a, p. 68) reported the results of a small "known groups" study conducted on New Zealand political activists, which revealed little overlap in the C-Scale scores of left- and right-wing college students. He also reported results obtained from a German version of the scale, which found a correlation of .51 between total scale score and self-placement on a scale running from *extreme left* to *extreme right*. While such a correlation is respectably high for social science research, it caused Wilson to properly caution "that the conservatism dimension as measured by the C-Scale is not supposed to be synonymous with the political 'left-right' continuum" (1973a, p. 68). Only one of the defining characteristics of the "ideal conservative" is explicitly political, and Wilson noted that even this one excludes consideration of the laissez-faire economic attitudes that have come to be associated with conservatism since World War II.

High C-Scale scores have also been found to be associated with relatively lower rankings of equality and freedom on the Rokeach Value Survey (Feather, 1977b, 1979), and with masculine attitudes (Miller & Martin, 1995). In a large mail survey of the United States (30,000 returned questionaries), Truett (1993) found that C-Scale scores increased with age.

Both the Altemeyer RWA Scale and the Wilson–Patterson C-Scale are clearly grounded in the Adorno *et al.* (1950) tradition. Subsequent revisions of the Wilson–Patterson (1968) items (e.g., Ekehammar, Nelson, & Sidanius, 1989; Ray, 1972) have not recognized this theoretical focus as explicitly. McClosky (1958) developed a scale of classical conservatism explicitly rooted in the writings of conservative political philosophers.

McClosky's (1958) scale was not explicitly intended to measure authoritarianism, but many of the undesirable social psychological and personality traits identified as part of the authoritarianism syndrome were found to be related to his scale of classical conservatism. The report on his findings did much to fuel the "good liberal, bad conservative" debate (Stone, 1983).

Whether it is possible to successfully identify an authoritarianism of the left depends to a great extent on both one's definition of conservatism and one's definition of authoritarianism. As explained in the earlier discussion of Eysenck (1954) and Shils (1954), there is a certain basic logic in the assumption of opposites—particularly when liberalism and conservatism are characterized in spatial terms. At one level, if the left is the logical opposite of the right, one should expect mirror-image characteristics. At a deeper level it is frequently the case that analysts disagree about the precise definitions of the opposing poles. These disagreements have led to lengthy debates in research journals (Eckhardt, 1988; Ray, 1985a, 1988b, 1989; Sidanius & Duffy, 1988; Stone, 1983; Ward, 1988).

Part of the difficulty comes from the fact that Adorno et al. (1950) offered a very broad definition of authoritarianism. Because the Horkheimer (1936) and Adorno et al. (1950) research groups were interested in the rise of fascism at the societal level, the central definition of authoritarianism subsumed conservatism. But, as Altemeyer (1988) pointed out, to say that *all authoritarians are conservative* is not the same as saying *all conservatives are authoritarian.* And neither of these statements is the same as saying that conservatives and authoritarians share *some* of the same defining characteristics.

Two recent sets of research findings shed some light on these distinctions. Feldman (1989) identified separate factors of moral traditionalism and authoritarianism. He proposed that conservative issue positions reflect both of these factors, but that a crucial distinction must be made between "evaluations of the appropriateness of specific activities, and judgments of proper societal actions to limit transgression" (p. 27). He argued that it is considerations of the second kind—implying government intervention to enforce desired standards—that are central to the conceptualization of authoritarianism. Research in the Soviet Union using the Altemeyer scale has found that the "right-wing" authoritarians are more supportive of the old-line Communist regime. McFarland, Ageyev, and Abalakina (1990) reported that the translated version of the RWA Scale correlated at .71 with hostility toward capitalists and dissidents in the USSR. Altemeyer (1990) reported that high RWA scores predicted own-country nationalistic biases in student samples in the USSR and the United States.

From the standpoint of choosing the appropriate scale, the first task of the researcher is to explicate his/her understanding of the theoretical linkage between the personality and politics. In the work of the Horkheimer group (Adorno et al., 1950; Horkheimer, 1936), Eysenck (1954), and Tomkins (1963) individual differences are theorized to be the result of differences in socialization and child-rearing style (Milburn 1991). The implications of the personality variables for political attitudes is explored at length in *The Politics of Denial* (Milburn & Conrad, 1996). Then, one needs to consider the theoretical linkage between authoritarianism and conservatism. This linkage is quite explicit in Altemeyer's (1981, 1988) conceptualization and clearly evident in Wilson's original formulation of the problem (Wilson & Patterson, 1968). Authoritarianism has not been as explicit in a number of other scales, but it may be useful to explore their intellectual parentage to determine if one buys all of the underlying assumptions.

Other Conservatism Scales

Sidanius (1976a) has developed a 36-item referent scale based on his efforts to revise the Wilson–Patterson (1968) scale for use in Sweden, and he has subsequently validated it in the United States and elsewhere. He has defined the scale simply as a measure of socio-political attitudes, but has presented some evidence that it is related to intolerance of ambiguity in the manner suggested by the Adorno group. Sidanius and his colleagues (Sidanius, Ekehammar, & Ross, 1979; Sidanius et al., 1987) have also identified various subdimensions of conservatism—political–economic conservatism, social inequality, racism, religion, and punitiveness. These traits appear to be stable cross-nationally, and they are related to ideological self-designation and party preference.

The Sidanius measure is designed as a balanced scale, but is identified only as a measure of conservatism. This is in keeping with Sidanius's conceptualization of liberalism–conservatism as bipolar. He did not entirely reject Kerlinger's notion of attitude duality, but argued that liberalism and conservatism are seldom strictly orthogonal. He also argued that even relatively modest levels of political sophistication produce bipolar attitude structures. Thus bipolarity is much more common than a strict reading of Kerlinger's theory might suggest (e.g., Sidanius & Duffy, 1988).

Sidanius's colleagues Nilsson and Ekehammar (1989, 1990) have presented a revised version of the Sidanius scale composed of 24 items. The scale was revised to update some referents, to provide an equal number of balanced items for each of the five most frequently occurring dimensions, and to add an environmentalism dimension. Analysis suggested that the factor structure identified by Sidanius remains in the revised scale. The environmental subscale was found to be the least reliable of the six, but still satisfactory. A second scale was developed for administration to children (Nilsson & Ekehammar, 1989).

Ray (1971, 1980, 1984) has criticized the Wilson–Patterson (1968) scale for acquiescent response set problems and has provided both a revised catchphrase-type scale and a statement version covering the same dimensions. These have been validated on samples of Australian army recruits and university students (Ray, 1971). He has also provided a more extensive set of subscales measuring various aspects of conservatism (Ray, 1984) and a *neoconservatism* scale that focuses heavily on attitudes about government intervention in economic arrangements (Ray, 1987). While all of these scales demonstrated high reliability in the various Australian samples that were used in their construction, none of them seem to have been employed again in the same form in which they were created—even in subsequent research by Ray.

Ray has also provided a short (22-item) statement scale to measure the conservatism of American public opinion (Ray, 1983). This scale produced an alpha reliability of .85 in a small random sample of Californians. It covers a wide range of issues that are part of the conservative belief system. The wording and selection of items remain quite contemporary despite the passage of time.

Since the publication of the Classical Conservatism Scale (McClosky, 1958), McClosky has expanded his interest in liberalism–conservatism and has engaged in an extensive enterprise aimed at developing more comprehensive and reliable scales. While a full explication of his approach awaits the publication of a book on liberalism–conservatism, McClosky and Bann (1979) have provided an interim measure that shows some promise based on a sample of the mass public. The original Classical Conservatism Scale (McClosky, 1958) was explicitly rooted in the writings of political philosophers. While it successfully discriminated between liberals and conservatives in samples of political elites, it does not seem to yield reliable results in samples of ordinary citizens (Owens, 1979). This appears to be due both to the abstract nature of the final nine items of the scale and to an agreement bias resulting from the fact that all conservative responses are worded positively.

To address the response set problem, McClosky and Bann (1979) presented a 19-item forced-choice sentence completion scale, which was validated on criterion groups of liberal and conservative elites and on a national sample of adults. Whereas the original Classical Conservatism Scale was not related to ideological self-designation among samples of the public at large (Owens, 1979), it was positively related among elites (McClosky, 1958; McClosky & Bann, 1979). The revised version of the scale was related to self-identification and presidential vote intent among both mass and elites, although the relationships were stronger in the elite samples. McClosky recommended the addition of seven social welfare items, also presented in the 1979 article, to produce a general revised Conservatism–Liberalism Scale (McClosky, 1991).

Another early effort to come to terms with the resurrection of the conservative ideology in American politics that is frequently overlooked is the Ideological Agreement with Goldwater Scale (Selznick & Steinberg, 1966). The sociological foundation of the theory underlying it is evident from the way in which the respondent is asked to make *relative judgments across time*. It could be argued that the relational nature of the evaluative dimensions (e.g., "how great a danger") insures that the items cannot become outdated, but, currently, it is difficult to justify survey time to ask about American communists, or socialism. For the few people who answer in the extreme, the items are likely to be a very good predictor that the respondent is an ideologue of some kind. The specific referents in the other three items (government/basic freedoms; state of morals; US power in the world) are abstract enough to remain relevant over time. While the moralistic dimension of liberalism-conservatism is a focus in a large number of scales, perceptions of US power in the world and government control over citizens' lives may be overlooked. However, if one is willing to make some compromises on question wording and format, it is fairly easy to construct a reasonable facsimile of the scale from items generally available in academic surveys.

Liberalism, Radicalism, and the New Left

The next three scales pay particular attention to the attitudes and values of the left.

10. New Left Ideology Scale (Gold, Christie, & Friedman, 1976)
11. Radicalism-Conservatism Scale (Nettler & Huffman, 1957; Raden, 1979)
12. Radicalism–Conservatism Scale (Comrey & Newmeyer, 1965)

Gold, Christie, and Friedman's (1976) New Left Ideology Scale can be disaggregated into components of philosophy and tactics. Raden's (1979) update of Nettler and Huffman's (1957) Radicalism–Conservatism Scale focuses on economic redistribution and the status of workers. Comrey and Newmeyer's (1965) Radicalism–Conservatism Scale is more comprehensive in terms of the number of dimensions covered, and has served as a source for a number of other, shorter scales. Given historical oscillation in attention to concerns of the left and the right, it seems prudent to include scales designed to measure both "traditional" and "radical" aspects of leftist ideology.

When one reviews the research literature devoted to the measurement of ideology, one is struck by the fact that the overwhelming preponderance of attention is devoted to the conceptualization and measurement of conservatism. To some extent this focus can be traced back to the original theoretical concern with authoritarianism and its association with ideologies of the right. Another part of the explanation for the concentration on conservatism may lie in the fact that conservatism is more fashionable than liberalism. Rotunda (1986), for example, argued that liberalism as a symbol was appropriated by the politicians of the New Deal and had essentially become saturated with multiple meanings and exhausted by the 1960s. In this respect it is interesting to note that the older the scale is, the more likely it is to be identified as a measure of liberalism or radicalism. Still another reason for the preoccupation with conservatism may be traced to Mannheim's (1936) observation that conservatism is relatively easily definable as a political philosophy, while liberalism involves the progressive approximation of an ideal that changes as its goals are achieved.

If, as most authors assume, liberalism is simply the opposite of conservatism, then little harm is done to the measurement of the concept simply by labeling the scales as measures of conservatism. If, on the other hand, liberalism is something different from, but not necessarily the exact opposite of, conservatism, then the exclusive focus on conservatism may leave social scientists stranded when it comes time to assess the attitudes and values of movements of the left.

Gold, Christie, and Friedman (1976) found themselves in this kind of dilemma when faced with student protests at Columbia in 1968. They devised a series of scales designed to measure student attitudes that were grounded in the work on authoritarianism and Machiavellianism (Christie & Geis, 1970) but sought to measure the new values that seemed to emerge during this period. The most relevant of these measures are the New Left Philosophy sub-scale and the Revolutionary Tactics sub-scale. These are part of a 90-item New Left Ideology Scale (Gold et al., 1976) which has been employed in various forms in subsequent research.

The sentiments and philosophy captured in many of these items are not reflected in any other of the left–right scales available. While many of these sentiments are not very salient at the present time, they remain part of the discourse of the "Radical Left." Thus the scale would appear to provide a psychometrically well-grounded foundation for additional analyses of left–liberalism. Gold et al. (1976), however, pointed out that since the scale was validated on college students, care should be taken to make sure that agreement response set bias does not produce a falsely liberal picture among less politically cognizant members of the public.

Raden (1979) has provided a 10-item update of Nettler and Huffman's (1957) Radicalism–Conservatism Scale, which focuses exclusively on questions of economic redistribution and the status of workers. The original scale incorporated items from Centers (1949) and the Adorno et al. (1950) Political Economic Conservatism (PEC) Scale. Radin (1979) found that the Adorno PEC Scale items were the least reliable and that change in their association with the scale suggested changes in the public's perception of labor unions. The Comrey and Newmeyer (1965) Radicalism–Conservatism Scale provides a much broader range of coverage, including more specific items related to unions. While the full scale has not been incorporated into much subsequent research, subsets of items have formed the foundation for other investigations.

Moral Conservatism and the New Right

While moral and religious considerations have traditionally been included in the more comprehensive measures of conservatism, the Reagan Revolution of the 1980s and the increasing salience of the politics of the Religious Right (e.g., Wald, 1992; Wilcox, 1996) suggest some attention to scales designed to capture this dimension exclusively.

13. Moral Traditionalism Scale (Conover & Feldman, 1986)
14. Moral Conservatism Scale (Wald, Owen, & Hill, 1988)
15. Moral Conservatism Index (Woodrum, 1988)

Two scales are identified as explicit measures of *moral conservatism*. The Wald et al. (1988) scale has been validated on samples of religious congregations. The Woodrum

(1988) index focuses on political issues of specific concern to the New Right. This index was found to be strongly associated with denominational membership and with political self-identification and presidential preference. Conover and Feldman (1986) developed a scale of *moral traditionalism* theorized to be related to, but distinct from, religious fundamentalism. Four of the items from this scale were retained in the American National Election Study; Feldman's (1989) subsequent work suggests that moral traditionalism can be distinguished from authoritarianism, but that both influence social conservatism.

Moral conservatism has frequently been a component in general scales of conservatism, but the rise of the New Right and religion-based political activism has resulted in additional interest in the moral foundation of conservatism. In the GSS, for example, it is lifestyle issues that more clearly distinguish self-identified liberals from conservatives. Robinson (1984) estimated differences of 20–25% between liberals and conservatives in support for the Equal Rights Amendment, legalization of marijuana, and premarital–extramarital–homosexual sex, the largest of more than 100 sociopolitical issues covered in the GSS.

Both Conover and Feldman (1986) and Wald *et al.* (1988) have attempted to disentangle the effects of religious beliefs and moral values on political conservatism. The Wald *et al.* (1988) Moral Conservatism Scale is a 10-item balanced index focusing on specific aspects of traditional sex roles and practices like birth control and abortion, attitudes toward marijuana and pornography, and interracial marriage. It has been validated on samples of religious congregations in the South. The Conover and Feldman (1986) scale contains abstract statements focusing on the evaluations of changes in moral values and practices of society.

The Woodrum (1988) Moral Conservatism Index is a five-item scale aimed at assessing the policy attitudes that form the core of the New Right agenda. Four of these items propose an explicit role for government—outlawing abortion, homosexuality, and pornography and institutionalizing prayer in school. The last item concerns the morality of premarital sex. The scale has been found to correlate with membership in conservative denominations and ideological identification. The fact that all items are worded so that agreement represents the conservative position might be a cause of concern. Moreover, following Feldman (1989), it is possible that some of the Wald *et al.* (1988) items and all but one of the Woodrum (1988) items confound the impact of personal values and the impulse to *enforce* those values on society. The latter is captured in work on social dominance by Sidanius and his colleagues (Sidanius *et al.,* 1992, 1996).

New Concerns: Postmaterialism, Environmentalism, and Feminism

From time to time since the sixties, scholars have focused on the potential changes in ideological structure that might result from an "age of affluence." For some, affluence was thought to presage the end of ideology (Bell, 1960) or an era of consensus (Lane, 1965). Subsequently, the central focus has been on the redefinition of cleavages along generational lines. Miller and Levitin (1976) provided some evidence of a generational shift toward "New Politics." Inglehart (1977) proposed a simple, but comprehensive, "postmaterialist" thesis.

In essence Inglehart's (1977) theory argues that the experience of relative affluence (satisfaction of material wants) produces new sensitivity to higher-order goals of political actualization and democratic decision making. Since this new world view is socialized young, it is relatively impervious to short-term setbacks in the economic climate. This shift in emphasis produces a fundamental difference in the meaning assigned to the left–right continuum between the generations. For older citizens the continuum is defined in terms of economic and security issues. Among younger citizens, in the "first world," issues of lifestyle freedom, environmental protection, and an expanded concept of social equality define the cleavage (Inglehart, 1984).

Since *post-materialism* is not theoretically posed as an alternative definition of the left–right continuum per se, it is not reviewed here in detail. However, a standard version of the Post-Materialism Scale (Inglehart, 1977; see Table 3–2) has been adopted in several of the large survey-based data collection enterprises. The relative rankings of the four statements are generally used to produce a threefold classification. Individuals who rank "maintaining order" and "fighting rising prices" as more important are classified as "materialists," regardless of which of the two goals takes precedence. Those who rank democratization of government decision making and freedom of speech as more important are defined as "post-materialists"; all other response patterns are classified as "mixed."

Environmentalism has been proposed not only as an additional dimension of general liberalism–conservatism (e.g., Nilsson & Ekehammar, 1989, 1990), but also as a more comprehensive world view. Milbraith (1984, 1986) has articulated the components of the new environmental paradigm in great detail and has contrasted it with what he describes as the dominant social paradigm. In essence values of the new environmental paradigm subsume liberal social and political values, and post-materialism, but organize these according to a revised set of assumptions and priorities. The dominant social paradigm encompasses dimensions of values usually measured by the traditional scales of conservatism. Ray (1988a) operationalized a small part of this theory and reported minimal support for the hypothesis that the more "compassionate" were less supportive of an explicitly capitalistic political candidate.

Like post-materialism the implications of environmental values and attitudes have been more extensively studied in Western Europe, where their political significance can be seen in the rise of various "Green" parties. Given reports of widespread environmental devastation under the command economies, the advent of political and economic reform in the former Eastern bloc provides the opportunity for some interesting investigations of dimensionality. The variety of scales developed to measure aspects of environmentalism are, however, beyond the scope of this chapter. Milbraith (1984) presented an example of what he terms a "useful" environmentalism scale, but did not report its statistical properties.

Table 3–2
Inglehart Post-Materialism Scale

There is a lot of talk these days about what the aims of the country should be for the next ten years. On this card are listed some of the goals which different people would give as top priority. Would you please say which of these you consider the most important? And which would be the next most important?

a ☐ Maintaining order in the nation
b ☐ Giving people more say in important government decisions
c ☐ Fighting rising prices
d ☐ Protecting freedom of speech

Scoring: a & c ranked at 1 & 2 = materialist
         b & d ranked first & second = post-materialist
         other combinations = mixed

Finally, there have been various efforts to confront the liberal–conservative continuum with the values of *feminism* and sexual equality. Many of the general conservatism scales explicitly incorporate support for traditional sex roles (see Lenney in Volume 1) and family arrangements as part of the definition of conservatism. However, scales that focus on liberal and radical definitions of the left–right continuum are not as explicit about incorporating a gender equality dimension. While this omission might be attributed to the era in which they were created, Eisler and Loye (1983) suggested that the "failure" of liberalism results from liberal ambivalence about the role of women. In essence they argue that the latent ideology of gender inequality is supported in the manifest ideology of the right. On the liberal side, while the manifest ideology may avow sexual equality, the latent ideology tends to undermine it by assigning "women's issues" a low priority or ignoring them altogether.

Again the wide variety of scales designed to measure feminism, feminist consciousness, and sex role orientations is beyond the scope of this chapter, but the implications of the measurement of such attitudes for the liberal–conservative debate might be briefly considered. At its broadest scope the feminist perspective argues for a reexamination of deeply held societal beliefs about the organization of society and even the gender of God. On this point Greeley (1988) has offered some interesting observations based on GSS data indicating that liberal attitudes correlate with a maternal conception of God.

Mosher and Tomkins (1988), working with script theory, have suggested that the U.S. culture and media provide a "hypermasculine" socialization, producing a "macho personality constellation consisting of callous sexual attitudes, violence as manly, and danger as exciting" (p. 60) that provides affective reinforcement of conservative values. Sidanius and his colleagues have undertaken a series of studies examining the relationship among social dominance, gender, and sex role orientation (e.g., Sidanius, Cling, & Pratto, 1991; Sidanius *et al.*, 1994; Pratto *et al.*, 1994). Lakoff (1996) has proposed that the essence of conservatism can be found in socialization to a "strict father" morality. Whether gender and sex role attitudes become fully incorporated into left–right distinctions, or come to supersede them, remains to be seen.

Summary and Recommendations

Wide-ranging philosophical and theoretical differences in the definitions of liberalism and conservatism complicate any decision about the choice of scales to measure ideological predispositions. Such choices must ultimately be driven by one's research objective, but some explicit attention to the definitional issues at the outset will help to clarify future research on liberalism and conservatism. As this review has suggested, arguments about *how* to measure liberalism–conservatism frequently disguise disagreements about *what* aspects are being measured. And both the choice of instrument and the interpretation of results may occasionally be influenced by the researcher's own ideological predispositions (Ray, 1989; Stone, 1983). Because of differences in conceptualization, there is no simple statistical criterion that can be used to determine the "best" measure in all circumstances.

Table 3–3 is an attempt to delineate the different aspects of the definition encompassed by the scales reviewed here. Clearly there is some degree of consensus about the components of liberalism–conservatism in the more comprehensive scales, but it is by no means complete. The footnotes to Table 3–3 identify a variety of terms that have been used by different authors as synonyms or subdimensions for the major factors and illustrate the degree of conceptual overlap among them. While the table should prove helpful in sorting out some of the differences in content it cannot at the same time capture differences in the

Table 3-3

Components of Liberalism/Conservatism: Dimensions Identified in Factor Analytic Studies, or Assumed to be Measured in the Scales Reviewed

Scales[a]	Nationalism[b]/ racism	Liberalism/ equality	Economic	Traditional morality	Religion	Punitive/ aggressive	Authority submission	Realism	Government power
Kerlinger	X	X	X	X	X			X	
Tomkins[1]		X				X		X	
Eysenck[2]	X	X	X	X	X				
Altemeyer				X			X		
Wilson	X			X	X	X		X	
Sidanius	X	X	X		X	X			
Ray			X			X			
McClosky		X	X	X					
Selznick[3]				X					X
Gold[4]				X					
Nettler			X						
Comrey[5]	X		X		X	X			
Wald				X	X				X
Woodrum				X					
Conover				X					
Inglehart		X	X						

[a]Scales are identified by first author only.

[b]Synonyms/antonyms for factor/dimension labels used by different authors include: Nationalism/racism—civil rights, ethnocentrism, nationalism, racial tolerance, xenophobia; Liberalism/equality—progressivism, social inequality, social liberalism; Economic—economic conservatism, capitalism, laissez-faire, government aid, welfare state, labor; Traditional Morality—anti-hedonism, conventionality, permissiveness; Religion—religiosity, puritanism; Punitive/Aggressive—punitiveness, authoritarian aggression; Realism—anti-superstition, pragmatism, science.

[1]Tomkins: Humanism/Normativeness, factor structure has not been explored.

[2]Eysenck: additional first-order factors identified include: pacifism, reactionary individualism, human nature, and libertarianism.

[3]Selznick & Steinberg: factor structure not examined; additional items measure individualism, perception of communists/socialists.

[4]Gold et al.: additional factors (subscales) include: New Left Philosophy, Revolutionary Tactics, Machiavellian Cynicism, and Machiavellian Tactics.

[5]Comrey & Newmeyer: additional first-order factors include: pacifism, weak federal government, world government, service to government, service to individual.

theoretical locus of the predispositions. In deciding what scales to employ in a particular study, it needs to be kept in mind that for some authors left–right orientation is considered to be a fundamental part of the personality, while for others this ideology operates at the level of values and beliefs (Stone, 1983). These considerations will have an impact on the appropriateness of different validation strategies and particularly on the choice of criterion variables.

Finally, choices among different measuring instruments must also be informed by the nature of the population being addressed. If the sample is taken from a fairly sophisticated population (e.g., college students or political activists), there need be little concern about understanding of the concepts presented in the items or agreement response set biases. In addition, the degree of sophistication of the sample may influence findings concerning dimensionality. Only a few of the scales currently in existence have been validated with representative samples of the general public. However, even where scales have been subjected to relatively extensive validation, it is possible to argue that the passage of time may have weakened or changed the implications of some items. Greater attention to the reporting of sampling and validation procedures in the future may ultimately lend more coherence to the conceptual debates.

Social Attitudes Statement and Referent Scales

(F. N. Kerlinger, 1984)

Variable

These scales are designed to measure general factors of liberalism and conservatism thought to underlie a wide variety of social and political attitudes.

Description

The Social Attitudes Statement and Referent Scales considered here represent the cumulative effort of a lengthy research agenda reflected in the book *Liberalism and Conservatism* (Kerlinger, 1984). As explained in more detail in the text, Kerlinger developed an extensive theoretical rationale for *separate* "dualistic" dimensions of liberalism and conservatism. The Referent Scale's most recent revision (REF–X) consists of 28 referents (or catchphrases) similar in format to those of Wilson and Patterson (1968).

Kerlinger (1984) strongly recommends that the scales be scored separately. Theoretically the liberal scale is expected to be nearly orthogonal to (independent of) the conservative one, mainly because the concepts that distinguish liberals are not "criterial" or central to conservatives, and vice versa. While both "sides" respond favorably to criteria they consider relevant, they do not necessarily respond negatively to referents from the other "side." "Negative criteriality" is a special case generally characteristic of extreme or radical positions (on either side).

The scales contain an equal number of items, half of which can be responded to positively by liberals and half of which can be responded to positively by conservatives based on the assumption that positive and negative affect are not equally weighted in most people's minds. If one wishes to *assume* unidimensionality, a single score on a continuum running from liberal to conservative can be constructed by subtracting the liberal scale score from the conservative one.

Kerlinger's (1967) first Social Attitudes Statement Scale (SA–I) consisted of 20 liberal and 20 conservative items that were selected from an initial pool of more than 100 items based on the following criteria: (1) represent the social attitude domains of religion, economics, politics, education, and general social areas; (2) are nonredundant; and (3) appear relevant and appropriate. Respondents indicated their degree of agreement or disagreement on a seven-point Likert scale (where +3 is *strongly agree* and −3 is *strongly disagree*). This format has been maintained for all subsequent scales. The SA–II, presented here, contains the 13 best responses from each scale.

Kerlinger was influenced by the Wilson–Patterson (1968) scale to adopt an item format that was more directly linked to his criterial referents theory. He formally defined a *referent* as "any object or construct of psychological regard . . . toward which an attitude can be directed" (1984, p. 31). The first Referent Scale, REF–I (Kerlinger, 1972), consisted of 24 liberal and 24 conservative items from an initial pool of 400 attitude referents. Fifty items were then selected on the basis of their meeting the same criteria used for the SA–I. The REF–IV has 58 item referents based on their loading on the same factor arrays as the REF–I, augmented with referents selected from previous research literature. The 29 liberal and 29 conservative items were designed to measure both attitudes and values. The REF–VI is the 78-item American version of the scale employed in cross-cultural studies. English, German, Dutch, and Spanish versions containing 40 to 78 items have been selected on the basis of their fulfilling known psychometric properties.

The REF–IX, presented here, was developed by taking the best 25 liberal and 25 conservative items with the highest factor loadings and item-total correlations; the REF–X is a shorter version of the REF–IX, consisting of only the best 28 items (as indicated by an X following each item).

Sample

The subject pool for the SA–I consisted of 210 graduate students in education, 251 undergraduates, and 205 noncollege respondents. Respondents for the SA–II were 530 teachers and graduate students along with some noncollege individuals.

REF–I norms are based on five different samples, three samples of teachers and graduate students ($N = 746$) and two samples of business and noncollege persons ($N = 270$). The REF–IV was administered to 237 graduate education students. The REF–VI was given to 135 education students and 365 graduate education students in the United States, 427 graduate students in education in Spain, and one random sample of households and one sample of university students in the Netherlands ($N = 955$).

Reliability

Internal Consistency

For the SA–I, split-half reliabilities of .78 for the Liberalism subscale and .79 for the Conservatism subscale were found for 168 unidentified individuals (Robinson, Rusk, & Head, 1969). For the SA–II, alpha coefficients ranged from .77 to .86 for the Liberalism subscale and from .74 to .83 for the Conservatism subscale.

For the REF–I, alpha reliability coefficients ranged from .83 to .85 for the Liberalism subscale and from .84 to .89 for the Conservatism subscale. For the REF–IV, alpha coefficients of .85 and .92 were reported for the subscales of Liberalism and Conservatism, respectively. For the REF–VI, reliability for the Liberalism subscale was found to be .85 in the U.S. samples, .74 for the Spanish sample, and .83 for the Dutch sample. For the Conservatism subscale, reliabilities were .90, .92, and .92 for the U.S., Spanish, and Dutch student samples, respectively.

Test–Retest

No test–retest data are reported for the SA–I. For the SA–II, repeat reliability coefficients were found to be .85 for the Liberalism subscale and .84 for the Conservatism subscale over a three-month period. No test–retest data are reported for any of the Referent Scales.

Validity

Convergent

The correlations between the Referent Scale (REF–I) and the Social Attitudes Statement Scale (SA–II) ranged between .46 and .53 for the Liberal subscale and between .54 and .66 for the Conservative subscale. Using the REF–VI, correlations between the Liberal subscale and self-identification as a "Progressive" are reported as .38 for a Dutch random sample and .47 for a sample of Dutch students, with correlations for the Conservative subscale in the same range.

Further cross-national investigations employing the REF–VI revealed that the conservative factors of religiosity, economic conservatism, and traditional conservatism appeared in a similar form in the United States, Spain, and the Netherlands. The same analysis revealed liberal factors of sexual freedom, feeling and affection, and social welfare; however, the evidence was not as obvious.

Known groups in Holland who perceived themselves as being associated with the Left, Socialism, or Progressivism tended to score high on Liberalism and conversely for subjects who identified as Conservative, Traditional, or Right.

Discriminant

In general, few studies have demonstrated that these scales discriminate from other scales or constructs. However, the low correlations between the Liberalism and Conservatism subscales support the dualism hypotheses. For the REF–I, correlations between the Liberalism and Conservatism subscales for the samples studied ranged from $-.01$ to $-.21$ in the United States. For the SA–II, they ranged from .02 to $-.23$. However, one U.S. sample, identified as progressive graduate students of education, yielded a correlation of $-.64$. This last sample is one Kerlinger would characterize as sophisticated about education policy and, therefore, polarized.

Employing various translations of the REF–VI, cross-national correlations between liberalism and conservatism tended to vary with the nature of the samples. In one U.S. undergraduate sample, the scales were positively correlated at .37. In other U.S., Spanish, and German student samples, correlations between the Liberalism and Conservatism subscales ranged from $-.02$ to $-.26$. In the Netherlands a random sample of Dutch citizens yielded a correlation of .05, although in a sample of social science students the correlation was $-.35$.

Location

Kerlinger, F. N. (1984). *Liberalism and conservatism: The nature and structure of social attitudes.* Hillsdale, NJ: Lawrence Erlbaum Associates.

Results and Comments

Most of Kerlinger's efforts were directed toward testing the duality theory using second-order factor analysis and, later, LISREL techniques. Other researchers who confirmed the existence of duality include Ziegler and Atkinson (1973), who found a "general" conservatism factor and a separate "general" liberalism factor for both high and low information groups; Marjoribanks and Josefowitz (1975) conducted factor analyses in which two orthogonal factors emerged. Birenbaum and Zak (1982) examined the validity of the criterial referent theory compared to Eysenck's (1954, 1976) theory of social attitudes, which posits liberalism–conservatism as bipolar. Their analyses generally supported the duality hypothesis. They concluded, however, that the two theories were complementary and that "Kerlinger explains the structure, whereas Eysenck provides the motivational background of the underlying process" (p. 512).

Baggaley (1976) also found that the Conservatism and Liberalism subscales loaded on different factors, and Zak (1973, 1976) validated the existence of the duality hypothesis of two orthogonal factors among Israelis living in Israel and in the United States.

Not all studies have supported Kerlinger's duality hypothesis. Sontag and Pedhavuz (1972) intercorrelated five subscales [two from Kerlinger's scale of educational attitudes and three from Oliver and Butcher's (1962) Survey of Opinions about Education] with a mix of positive and negative loadings on both factors along with high negative correlations between the two instruments. Rambo (1972) administered a liberalism–conservatism scale that he constructed to groups known to be different according to their degrees of liberalism and conservatism. Out of the three samples, two showed no bipolarity, but one yielded three of four factors that were each bipolar.

Ray (1980) found that liberalism and conservatism were not orthogonal using balanced scales for radicalism and conservatism (although assumptions about the weight of negative affect in the Ray instrument were contrary to those made by Kerlinger). Sidanius and his colleagues (e.g., Sidanius, 1985; Sidanius & Duffy, 1988; Sidanius & Lau, 1989) have also undertaken various investigations of the duality hypothesis. They concluded that bipolarity is a result of "sophistication" and that its occurrence is not as rare as a strict reading of Kerlinger's theory might suggest.

Social Attitudes Statement Scale (SA–II) (Kerlinger, 1984)

Instructions: Given below are statements on various social problems about which we all have beliefs, opinions, and attitudes. We all think differently about such matters, and this scale is an attempt to let you express your beliefs and opinions. There are no right and wrong answers. Please respond to each of the items as follows:

Agree very strongly:	+3	Disagree very strongly:	−3
Agree strongly:	+2	Disagree strongly:	−2
Agree:	+1	Disagree:	−1

For example, if you agree very strongly with a statement, you would write +3 on the short line preceding the statement, but if you should happen to disagree with it, you would put −1 in front of it. Respond to each statement as best you can. Go rapidly but carefully. Do not spend too much time on any one statement; try to respond and then go on. Don't go back once you have marked a statement.

_____ 1. Individuals who are against churches and religions should not be allowed to teach in colleges.

_____ *2. Large fortunes should be taxed fairly heavily over and above income taxes.

_____ *3. Both public and private universities and colleges should get generous aid from both state and federal governments.

_____ 4. Science and society would both be better off if scientists took no part in politics.

_____ *5. Society should be quicker to throw out old ideas and traditions and to adopt new thinking and customs.

_____ *6. To ensure adequate care of the sick, we need to change radically the present system of privately controlled medical care.

_____ 7. If civilization is to survive, there must be a turning back to religion.

_____ 8. A first consideration in any society is the protection of property rights.

_____ 9. Government ownership and management of utilities lead to bureaucracy and inefficiency.

_____ 10. If the United States takes part in any sort of world organization, we should be sure that we lose none of our power and influence.

_____*11. Funds for school construction should come from state and federal government loans at no interest or very low interest.

_____ 12. Inherited racial characteristics play more of a part in the achievements of individuals and groups than is generally known.

_____*13. Federal Government aid for the construction of schools is long overdue, and should be instituted as a permanent policy.

_____*14. Our present economic system should be reformed so that profits are replaced by reimbursements for useful work.

_____*15. Public enterprises like railroads should not make profits; they are entitled to fares sufficient to enable them to pay only a fair interest on the actual cash capital they have invested.

_____ 16. Government laws and regulations should be such as first to ensure the prosperity of business since the prosperity of all depends on the prosperity of business.

_____*17. All individuals who are intellectually capable of benefiting from it should get a college education, at public expense if necessary.

_____ 18. The well-being of a nation depends mainly on its industry and business.

_____*19. True democracy is limited in the United States because of the special privileges enjoyed by business and industry.

_____*20. The gradual social ownership of industry needs to be encouraged if we are ever to cure some of the ills of our society.

_____ 21. There are too many professors in our colleges and universities who are radical in their social and political beliefs.

_____ 22. There should be no government interference with business and trade.

_____ 23. Some sort of religious education should be given in public schools.

____*24. Unemployment insurance is an inalienable right of the working man.

____ 25. Individuals with the ability and foresight to earn and accumulate wealth should have the right to enjoy that wealth without government interference and regulations.

____*26. The United Nations should be whole-heartedly supported by all of us.

*Indicates Liberal subscale items.

Referent Scale (REF–IX)
(Kerlinger, 1984)

Instructions: Given below are statements on various social problems about which we all have beliefs, opinions, and attitudes. We all think differently about such matters, and this scale is an attempt to let you express your beliefs and opinions. There are no right and wrong answers. Please respond to each of the items as follows:

Agree very strongly:	+3	Disagree very strongly:	−3
Agree strongly:	+2	Disagree strongly:	−2
Agree:	+1	Disagree:	−1

For example, if you agree very strongly with a statement, you would write +3 on the short line preceding the statement, but if you should happen to disagree with it, you would put −1 in front of it. Respond to each statement as best you can. Go rapidly but carefully. Do not spend too much time on any one statement; try to respond and then go on. Don't go back once you have marked a statement.

____ *1. economic reform

____ 2. social stability (X)

____ *3. feeling (X)

____ *4. women's liberation

____ 5. real estate

____ 6. discipline (X)

____ *7. government price controls (X)

____ *8. freedom (X)

____ 9. business (X)

____ 10. authority (X)

____ 11. faith in God (X)

____*12. racial integration

____*13. free abortion (X)

____*14. sexual freedom

____ 15. corporate industry

____ 16. obedience of children (X)

____ 17. morality

____ 18. respect for elders

____*19. liberalized abortion laws

____*20. social equality

____*21. collective bargaining (X)

____*22. socialized medicine (X)

____ 23. church

____ 24. law and order (X)

____*25. racial equality (X)

____ 26. private property (X)

____*27. birth control

____ 28. capitalism (X)

____ 29. money

____ 30. social status (X)

____ 31. religious education

____*32. social change (X)

____ 33. moral standards (X)

____ 34. patriotism (X)

____ 35. profits

____*36. equality (X)

____ 37. education as intellectual training

____*38. federal aid to education

____*39. social planning (X)

____ 40. competition

____*41. human warmth

____ 42. family

____ 43. free enterprise (X)

____*44. civil rights (X)

____*45. world government

____ 46. religion (X)

____*47. children's interests (X)

____*48. labor unions (X)

____*49. equality of women (X)

____*50. United Nations

*Identifies Liberal subscale items.
X Indicates recommended short-form items.

Polarity Scale

(S. S. Tomkins, 1964; W. F. Stone & P. E. Schaffner, 1997)

Variable

Tomkins's Polarity Scale is based on his theory of affect, which proposes a humanistic–normative continuum as the essential definition of left–right ideology.

Description

The original Polarity Scale consisted of 59 pairs of opposing choices designed to measure tendencies of humanism and normativeness in a variety of domains. These tendencies are theoretically related to basic personality orientations (Tomkins, 1962, 1963, 1991). While little statistical information has been presented by the author on scale development, the scale has been adopted and further refined by several researchers. Stone's PS43 version adapts the format so that responses can be processed on a standard OCR ("scantron").

The scale items are presented in pairs to reflect Tomkins's theory about the fundamental polarity of human nature. In addition to choosing one of the polar opposites, subjects may choose a *both* or a *neither* option. Stone recommends scoring responses separately on each dimension by tallying the number of endorsements. He and his colleagues have provided substantial information validating this "dualistic" conception. Carlson and Brincka (1987) ignored *both* and *neither* responses and subtracted humanistic responses from normative ones to create a continuum. Stone and Schaffner (1988) have also proposed the percentage of humanistic responses as an indicator of relative learning. (In this instance the number of humanistic responses is divided by the total number of humanistic plus normative responses.)

Sample

The initial subject pool consisted of approximately 500 males and females. Subjects included high school students, university students, older normals aged 45–60, psychotic depressives, and schizophrenics. Information was not provided pertaining to sample size for each group or to more specific demographic characteristics.

Reliability

Internal Consistency

Stone and Schaffner (1988) reported reliability coefficients of .80 for humanism and .81 for normativeness for the 59-item scale for a sample of 305 students from U.S. and Canadian colleges. Similar reliability coefficients (.78 humanist, .79 normative) were obtained for a revised 40-item scale. Stone (1991) reported alphas of .76 for the Humanistic subscale and .86 for the Normative subscale. Using the PS43, Stone (1997) reported alpha reliabilities of .82 for the Humanistic subscale and .78 for the Normative subscale.

Test–Retest

Carlson and Brincka (1987) found a test–retest reliability on a shorter 20-item version of the Polarity Scale of .74 for a unidimensional humanistic–normative scale.

Validity

Convergent

Several studies have related the humanistic and normative tendencies to other constructs. Tomkins (1965) found that scores on the Polarity Scale predicted performance on the Tomkins–Horn Picture Arrangement Test (a standardized projective personality test). Humanists were found to be sociophilic (i.e., attracted to others), whereas normative subjects were more sociophobic and, as such, anticipated more aggression from others. Tomkins noted that humanistic subjects were significantly more likely than the normative subjects to see a smiling face when shown photographs depicting fused feelings. This finding was validated and extended by Vasquez (1976), who found left-oriented subjects (i.e., those with humanistic tendencies) to smile more and to reflect more enjoyment. Rightist subjects (i.e., those with normative tendencies), on the other hand, showed more disgust.

Williams (1984) noted that normative subjects were more likely to blame the victim than were humanistic subjects in both welfare and theft situations. In a similar vein Suedfeld, Hakstian, Rank, and Ballard (1985) found a positive correlation between normative scores on the Polarity Scale and traditional focused responsibility (a belief in traditional authority figures).

Thomas (1976, 1978) conducted a *Q*-methodology study that found two orthogonal factors. Higher loadings on the first factor were produced by left-wing (i.e., humanistic) subjects, and higher loadings on the second factor were obtained for the right-wing (i.e., normative) subjects. In a second study ideoaffective dispositions explained a significant proportion of the variance in right–left ideology. Alker and Poppen (1973) found that humanism was highly associated with principled morality on Kohlberg's (1963) moral maturity instrument and that normativism and dogmatism (as measured by Rokeach's (1960) D scale) were highly associated. Humanists have also been found to place more value on qualities such as commitment, love, and care, whereas normatives have been found to place a greater emphasis on values such as purpose and competence (Carlson & Levy, 1970). When gender differences obtain, it is usually found that men are more normative and women more humanistic (Stone, 1986; Stone & Schaffner, 1988).

In a more political vein, Carlson and Brincka (1987) found that the 1984 Republican candidates (Reagan and Bush) were more frequently associated with the normative dimension, while the Democratic candidates (Mondale and Ferraro) were associated with the humanistic dimension. Loye (1977) found that a modified six-item Polarity Scale correlated at .46 with ideological self-identification in a sample of Princeton students.

Stone (1997) also reported that the Normative subscale correlated positively with the Altemeyer (1981) RWA Scale and with the McClosky (1958) Classical Conservatism Scale ($r = .55$ and $.46$, respectively) and that the Humanism subscale was negatively correlated with the RWA Scale ($-.26$) and mildly positively correlated with the McClosky scale ($.17$). The Normative subscale was also correlated at .37 with the Sidanius Social Dominance Scale. Yelland and Stone (1996) found that Humanistic subscale scores were associated with the belief that the Holocaust was a true event and with resistance to denial propaganda. Schultz, Stone, and Christie (1997) found that mental rigidity was related to authoritarianism (using the RWA Scale) and to low scores on the Humanist subscale, but not directly to higher scores on the Normative subscale.

Discriminant

No research has been reported.

Location

Tomkins, S. S. (1964). *Polarity scale.* New York: Springer.
  Stone, W. F., & Schaffner, P. E. (1997). *Tomkins' Polarity Scale: Recent developments.* Paper prepared for presentation at the annual convention of the International Society of Political Psychology, Montreal.

Results and Comments

Tomkins's approach is unique because he was trying to relate personality to ideology across many domains, including not only politics, but also such diverse domains as belief in the scientific method, child-rearing practices, and mathematics (Stone, 1986). Tomkins (1979) later expanded his theory using the term *scripts,* referring to an underlying ideo-affective posture, which is a set of feelings, and ideas about feelings, that define left–right personality differences. This posture is assumed to result from differences in the socialization of affects (Tomkins, 1965).

Polarity Scale[1]
by Silvan S. Tomkins

Instructions: Consider each of the following pairs of ideas, A and B, and decide which of them you agree with. If you agree with both ideas, you can answer "C" on your answer sheet. If you agree with neither, answer "D."

Blacken A if you agree with the idea on the left.

Blacken B if you agree with the idea on the right.

If you agree with the idea on the left, and also the idea on the right, blacken C.

If you disagree with both ideas, blacken circle D for that item.

Remember:

  A = you choose the *left* idea
  B = you choose the *right* idea
  C = you like *both* ideas
  D = you care for *neither* idea

1. (A) Children should be taught to obey what is right even though they may not always feel like it.

1. (B) Children should be encouraged to express themselves even though parents may not always like it.

2. (A) If I break the law, it is not always to my advantage or to the advantage of society that I be punished.

2. (B) If I break the law, I should be punished for the good of society.

3. (A) The most important aspect of science is that it enables you to realize yourself by gaining understanding and control of the world around you.

3. (B) The most important aspect of science is that it enables you to separate the true from the false, the right from the wrong, reality from fantasy.

4. (A) Play is childish. Although it is proper for children to play, adults should concern themselves with more serious matters.

4. (B) Play is important for all human beings. No one is too old to enjoy the excitement of play.

5. (A) The maintenance of law and order is the most important duty of any government.

5. (B) Promotion of the welfare of the people is the most important function of a government.

6. (A) To assume that most people are well-meaning brings out the best in others.

6. (B) To assume that most people are well-meaning is asking for trouble.

7. (A) Parents should first of all be gentle with children.

7. (B) Parents should first of all be firm with children.

8. (A) Children must be loved so that they can grow up to be fine adults.

8. (B) Children must be taught how to act so that they can grow up to be fine adults.

9. (A) A government should allow freedom of expression even though there is some risk in permitting it.

9. (B) A government should allow only such freedom of expression as is consistent with law and order.

10. (A) What children demand should be of little consequence to their parents.

10. (B) What children demand, parents should take seriously and try to satisfy.

11. (A) When people are in trouble, they should help themselves and not depend on others.

11. (B) When people are in trouble, they need help and should be helped.

12. (A) Competition brings out the best in human beings.

12. (B) Cooperation brings out the best in human beings.

13. (A) The most important thing in the world is to know yourself and be yourself.

13. (B) The most important thing in the world is to try to live up to the highest standards.

14. (A) The main purpose of education should be to enable the young to discover and create novelty.

14. (B) The main purpose of education should be to teach the young the wisdom of the remote and recent past.

15. (A) Juvenile delinquency is simply a reflection of the basic evil in human beings. It has always existed in the past and it always will.

15. (B) Juvenile delinquency is due to factors we do not understand. When we do understand these we will be able to prevent it in the future.

16. (A) When you face death you learn how basically insignificant you are.

16. (B) When you face death, you learn who you really are and how much you loved life.

17. (A) Great achievements require first of all great imagination.

17. (B) Great achievements require first of all severe self-discipline.

18. (A) If human beings were really honest with each other, there would be a lot more antipathy and enmity in the world.

18. (B) If human beings were really honest with each other, there would be a lot more sympathy and friendship in the world.

19. (A) The beauty of theorizing is that it has made it possible to invent things that otherwise never would have existed.

19. (B) The trouble with theorizing is that it leads people away from the facts and substitutes opinion for truth.

20. (A) Imagination leads people into self-deception and delusions.

20. (B) Imagination frees people from the dull routines of life.

21. (A) Thinking is responsible for all discovery and invention.

21. (B) Thinking keeps people on the straight and narrow.

22. (A) It is disgusting to see an adult cry.

22. (B) It is distressing to see an adult cry.

23. (A) Fear can make the bravest person tremble. We should not condemn a failure of nerve.

23. (B) Cowardice is despicable and in a soldier should be punished.

24. (A) When a person feels sorry for himself, he really needs more sympathy from others.

24. (B) When a person feels sorry for himself, he really should feel ashamed of himself.

25. (A) Some people can only be changed by humiliating them.

25. (B) No one has the right to humiliate another person.

26. (A) Human beings are basically evil.

26. (B) Human beings are basically good.

27. (A) Those who err should be forgiven.

27. (B) Those who err should be corrected.

28. (A) Anger should be directed against the oppressors of mankind.

28. (B) Anger should be directed against those revolutionaries who undermine law and order.

29. (A) Familiarity like absence makes the heart grow fonder.

29. (B) Familiarity breeds contempt.

30. (A) Numbers were invented.

30. (B) Numbers were discovered.

31. (A) Reason is the chief means by which human beings make great discoveries.

31. (B) Reason has to be continually disciplined and corrected by reality and hard facts.

32. (A) The changeableness of human feelings is a weakness in human beings.

32. (B) The changeableness of human feelings makes life more interesting.

33. (A) Human beings should be loved at all times, because they want and need to be loved.

33. (B) Human beings should be loved only if they have acted so that they deserve to be loved.

34. (A) There are a great many things in the world which are good for human beings and which satisfy them in different ways. This makes the world an exciting place and enriches the lives of human beings.

34. (B) There are a great many things which attract human beings. Some of them are proper, but many are bad for human beings, and some are very degrading.

35. (A) Children should be seen and not heard.

35. (B) Children are entirely delightful.

36. (A) In order to live a good life you must act like a good person, i.e. observe the rules of morality.

36. (B) In order to live a good life you must satisfy both yourself and others.

37. (A) Mystical experiences may be sources of insight into the nature of reality.

37. (B) So-called mystical experiences have most often been a source of delusion.

38. (A) You must always leave yourself open to your own feelings— alien as they may sometimes seem.

38. (B) If sanity is to be preserved, you must guard yourself against the intrusion of feelings which are alien to your nature.

39. (A) To act on impulse is to act childishly.

39. (B) To act on impulse occasionally makes life more interesting.

40. (A) Human beings should be treated with respect at all times.

40. (B) Human beings should be treated with respect only when they deserve respect.

41. (A) There is no surer road to insanity than surrender to the feelings, particularly those which are alien to the self.

41. (B) There is a unique avenue to reality through the feelings, even when they seem alien.

42. (A) Life sometimes smells bad.

42. (B) Life sometimes leaves a bad taste in the mouth.

43. (A) The mind is like a lamp which illuminates whatever it shines on.

43. (B) The mind is like a mirror which reflects whatever strikes it.

Scores, Key, Interpretation (Form PS43)[1]

Major Scores

The major scores in the Polarity Scale are:
1. *The number of L* (Left Wing or Humanistic)*responses.*
This is the sum of all responses keyed as Left Wing (either A or B).

2. The number of Both responses.

This is the sum of all "C" responses. Each such double response is given a score of one on the *Both* score. Thus if a subject answered "C" to every item-pair in the entire test her *Both* response score would be 43.

3. The number of R (Right Wing or Normative) responses.

This is the sum of all responses keyed as Right Wing (A *or* B). (It is possible for a subject to have a zero Left Wing score *and* a zero Right Wing score if he has a *Both* score of 43 obtained by answering "C" on every item-pair).

4. The number of Neither responses.

This is the sum of all the subject's "D" responses. (In the original Polarity Scale, "Neither" was scored when the subject made no response to either item of the pair, thus it was uncertain whether she meant "neither" or simply had skipped that item-pair).

How to Score

The Scoring Key appears on the following page. Humanistic, Normative, Both, and Neither scores sum to 43.

PS43 Scoring Key

Starting with the item-pair #1, the following gives the key for an "A" response. Thus, for item-pair 1, an "A" is a Right Wing (Normative) response (R). For item-pair 2, an "A" is a Left Wing (Humanistic) response (L), etc.

1. R	12. R	23. L	34. L
2. L	13. L	24. L	35. R
3. L	14. L	25. R	36. R
4. R	15. R	26. R	37. L
5. R	16. R	27. L	38. L
6. L	17. L	28. L	39. R
7. L	18. R	29. L	40. L
8. L	19. L	30. L	41. R
9. L	20. R	31. L	42. R
10. R	21. L	32. R	43. L
11. R	22. R	33. L	

Interpretation of Major Scores

The rationale of the Polarity Scale has been described in Tomkins, S. S., and Izard, C. (Eds.) (1965), *Affect, Cognition, and Personality* (Springer) in the chapter "The Psychology of Knowledge," and in White, R. W. (Ed.) (1963), *The Study of Lives* (Atherton) in the chapter "Left and Right: A Basic Dimension of Ideology and Personality." Pages 399 to 411 of the latter book contain an analysis not found in "The Psychology of Knowledge" chapter. Additional material on the differences in types of socialization (rewarding and punitive) which are postulated to determine left and right wing ideas—affective postures [now *scripts*]—will be found in Volume II, Tomkins, S. S. (1963), *Affect, Imagery and Consciousness* (Springer). [Further discussion, with additional research, will be found in Tomkins's (1991) Volume III].

The score *Number of L responses* and the score *Number of R responses* indicate in general how humanistic and how normative in orientation the individual is. In general, there is a negative relationship between the scores. But in individual cases scores may be equally high: in some areas, e.g., child rearing, attitudes toward play, attitudes toward friendship, they may be humanistic in orientation, whereas in such areas as government, science, and aesthetics they may be normative in orientation. In such a case there might have been a golden age in childhood which was sharply reversed in late adolescence so that the severity of later experience influenced attitudes toward adult concerns. Another possibility would be an identification with the mother which determined attitudes about childhood and an identification with the father who held articulate normative views on government, science, and aesthetics.

Although the scale was designed to represent several specific ideological domains, or dimensions, it is not always the case that the individual person, or even groups of subjects, will always categorize their experience in these categories. Items 22 and 23 deal with tolerance for distress and fear respectively. They were designed to test for tolerance toward negative affect in general. Indeed, many subjects will respond to these two items in the same way, but for specific individuals or groups (such as adolescents) there may be tolerance for one negative affect (either fear or distress) but not for the other. Furthermore, some items are responded to in the same way by almost all subjects of one age or class; e.g., almost all college graduates have *one* answer to Item 4—Play is important for all human beings—whereas older subjects are divided equally. In general then, the factor structure of the test varies for different groups of subjects, and one must examine carefully the groups of items on which the individual (or group) are normative and humanistic. These variations will reveal important differences in the structure of ideology and personality.

The number of *Both* responses may be interpreted in a number of different ways. In contrast to an even distribution of *L* and *R* responses, it indicates more conscious conflict between *L* and *R* positions, and an unwillingness to commit oneself to one or the other position. As such it is a more temperate, graded posture. It may also indicate heightened empathy with all human beings. It may arise from identification with both mother and father, but in a different way from where *L* and *R* are equal in frequency. In the case of the high *Both* score, it is more probable that the mother and father did not hold opposing ideological positions about non-overlapping issues (such as child rearing and politics) but rather had different views on *all* issues and were in open conflict with each other. In this case the child *may* identify with both positions and his high *Both* score arises from his wish to reduce the conflict between his conflicted parents and between his divided selves, and to increase communication and agreement between the parents—which becomes equivalent to integration within his own personality. Such individuals are commonly drawn to the mediating professions—the law, government, etc.—and to domains of knowledge that are concerned with conflict, e.g., communication theory, the drama. A high *Both* score may also arise from a failure of commitment or excessive indecision, or an obsessive neurosis. Or, again, it may arise from a very high intelligence which is sensitive to the complexities of the issues involved and therefore reluctant to affirm either extreme position. In most studies thus far (but not all) the high *Both* score has occurred when the rest of the score was predominantly Left Wing, indicating in all probability heightened empathy as a concomitant of conflicted identification.

In the high *Neither* score we may be dealing either with high negativity or with an ideological position orthogonal to the theory on which the Polarity scale is based. The significance of the rationale of the Polarity Scale is suggested by the small number of records in which very high *Neither* scores appear. This, however, may also indicate the strength of yea-saying over nay-saying trends within the American culture. . . .

[1]These instructions for the 43-item version (PS43) are adapted from Silvan S. Tomkins's 1966 instructions. His comments are reproduced here with little modification, as they reflect his original thinking (W. F. Stone, July, 1997).

Inventory of Social Attitudes
(H. J. Eysenck, 1951)

Variable

This scale is based on two primary dimensions that presumably underlie people's social attitudes and beliefs: radicalism–conservatism (the R factor) and tendermindedness–toughmindedness (the T factor).

Description

Eysenck's (1954) *The Psychology of Politics* provides the most comprehensive discussion of his influential theory. Difficulties in employing the scale arise from the multiple versions introduced by the author. In addition, subsequent researchers have haphazardly selected subsets of items from various versions. The 14 items comprising the Radicalism–Conservatism Scale developed and validated by Eysenck (1947) were presented in the first edition of *Measures of Political Attitudes* (Robinson, Rusk, & Head, 1969). The version of the scale reproduced here is taken from a 1951 article, which provided further validation and expanded the pool of R items. Items included in Robinson *et al.* (1969) are indicated by the letter *R*.

In addition to the scale version presented here, three others worth considering for some research purposes include the Public Opinion Inventory (POI) (40 items that are scored for both the R and the T factors), a 1971 revision of 28 items administered to a BBC Viewing Panel (Eysenck, 1971), and a subsequent revision (Eysenck, 1975) that lengthened the POI to 88 statements. In 1976 Eysenck developed a Wilson–Patterson-type scale consisting of 68 catchphrases (Eysenck, 1976). Since question selection can influence the structure of the scale, it is important to consult the original sources.

The 40 statements of the original scale were selected from a pool of 500 items. Fourteen of the 40 attitude statements were scored for radicalism–conservatism based on their loading on the R factor. Response choices range from *strongly agree* to *neutral* to *strongly disagree* on a five-point Likert scale. Responses are summed after appropriate reverse scoring.

Sample

The initial scale was developed on 750 British middle-class, urban residents in 1947. Respondents were equally drawn from the Conservative, Liberal, and Labour Parties and matched on education, gender, and age. The 1951 sample was augmented to include Communists and samples of working-class respondents.

Subjects for the first revision (Eysenck, 1971) were 2000 male and female members of a BBC Viewing Panel. For the second revision (Eysenck, 1975), 368 males and females stratified by social classes were interviewed. The updated C-Scale (Eysenck, 1976) was used in interviews with 1442 persons selected by quota sampling procedures.

Reliability

Internal Consistency

A split-half correlation of .81 was found for the entire group for the initial scale. Correlations ranged from .63 for the Conservatives to .73 for Labourites.

Test–Retest

No test–retest data are reported for any of the versions.

Validity

Convergent

Discrepancies in the percentages of Conservatives and Labourites agreeing with each statement correlated .98 with item saturations for the R factor (Eysenck, 1954). For the original scale there is some evidence for the R factor if one compares the percentages.

Analysis of the responses of known groups demonstrates the validity of the R factor for the initial scale. For instance, the small number of Fascists were found to rank lowest in radicalism (and highest in toughmindedness); this group was followed by the Conservative Party and then the Liberal and Labour Parties. Communists ranked highest in radicalism and exceeded both working- and middle-class members of the other three organized parties in toughmindedness (Eysenck, 1951). Dator (1969) studied Japanese judges using a modified version of the scale and found them to be conservative as a whole, with self-identification corresponding highly to subjects' scores on the R factor.

Stone, Ommundsen, and Williams (1985) reported a correlation of .55 between a scale composed of six Eysenck R items and self-location on a left–right scale in Norway. In a sample of U.S. college students, this correlation was only .26. Analysis of responses to Eysenck's 1971 revision revealed differences between respondents according to class, age, and gender. Women were found to be more conservative than men. The working class was found to be more conservative than the middle class, and more conservatism was found for older subjects. These findings were replicated by Eysenck (1975).

Discriminant

Eysenck (1976) reported radicalism to be negatively associated with measures of dominance and aggression.

Location

Eysenck, H. J. (1947). Primary social attitudes: I. The organization and measurement of social attitudes. *International Journal of Opinion and Attitude Research, 1*, 49–84.

Eysenck, H. J. (1951). Primary social attitudes as related to social class and political party. *British Journal of Sociology, 11*, 198–209.

Eysenck, H. J. (1954). *The psychology of politics.* London: Routledge & Kegan Paul Ltd.

Eysenck, H. J. (1975). The structure of social attitudes. *British Journal of Clinical and Social Psychology, 14*(4), 323–331.

Eysenck, H. J. (1976). Structure of social attitudes. *Psychological Reports, 39*, 463–466.

Eysenck, H. J., & Wilson, G. D. (1978). *The psychological basis of ideology.* Lancaster, England: MTP Press, Ltd.

Results and Comments

In general, research has focused on validating or refuting the existence of Eysenck's two orthogonal dimensions. The existence of the radical–conservative and toughminded–tenderminded dimensions has tended to be replicated by other researchers regardless of the version of the scale employed (Eysenck, 1971, 1975, 1976; Hewitt, Eysenck, & Eaves, 1977; Smithers & Lobley, 1978; Stone & Russ, 1976) and in cross-cultural settings (Bruni & Eysenck, 1976; Singh, 1977). However, support for an orthogonal T factor is not unanimous (Birenbaum & Zak, 1982; Stone & Russ, 1976).

The number and content of first-order factors have not always been identical, but radicalism–conservatism has always emerged as the primary second-order factor. In the 1975 study Eysenck greatly expanded the sample of questions included and identified a third second-order factor, in addition to R and T, that he defined as "politico-economic conservatism."

Public Opinion Inventory, R Factor
(Eysenck, 1951)
Attitude Statements

Instructions: After each statement, you are requested to record your personal opinion. You should use the following system of marking:

++   If you strongly agree with the statement
+   If you agree on the whole
0   If you can't decide for or against, or if you think the question is
     worded in such a way that you can't give an answer
−   If you disagree on the whole
−−   If you strongly disagree

Please answer frankly. Remember this is not a test; there are no "right" or "wrong" answers. The answer required is your own personal opinion. Be sure not to omit any questions. Do not consult any other person while you are giving your answers.

　1. Colored people are innately inferior to white people

＊2. Present laws favour the rich as against the poor

3. War is inherent in human nature (R)

*4. The marriage bar on female teachers should be removed

*6. Our treatment of criminals is too harsh; we should try to cure, not to punish them (R)

*8. In the interests of peace, we must give up part of our national sovereignty (R)

*9. Sunday observance is old fashioned, and should cease to govern our behavior (R)

*12. Ultimately, private property should be abolished, and complete socialism introduced (R)

13. Conscientious objectors are traitors to their country, and should be treated accordingly

*15. The laws against abortion should be abolished

16. Only by going back to religion can civilization hope to survive

17. Marriages between white and colored people should be strongly discouraged (R)

*18. Jews are as valuable, honest, and public-spirited citizens as any other group (R)

*20. There should be far more controversial and political discussion over the radio

*23. Divorce laws should be altered to make divorce easier

*24. Patriotism in the modern world is a force which works against peace

25. Modern life is too much concentrated in cities; the government should take steps to encourage a "return to the country"

26. Crimes of violence should be punished by flogging (R)

27. The nationalization of the great industries is likely to lead to inefficiency, bureaucracy, and stagnation (R)

28. It is right and proper that religious education in schools should be compulsory (R)

*29. Men and women have the right to find out whether they are sexually suited before marriage (e.g., by companionate marriage) (R)

30. The principle "Spare the rod and spoil the child" has much truth in it, and should govern our methods of bringing up children

33. The Jews have too much power and influence in this country (R)

*34. Differences in pay between men and women doing the same work should be abolished

35. Birth control, except when medically indicated, should be made illegal

*36. The death penalty is barbaric, and should be abolished (R)

38. Scientists should take no part in politics

39. The Japanese are by nature a cruel people (R)

*Indicates liberal "radical" items.
Items appearing in Robinson, Rusk, & Head (1969) are identified by an R.

Right-Wing Authoritarianism Scale (RWA)
(B. Altemeyer, 1988, 1990, 1996)

Variable

Following Adorno *et al.* (1950), Altemeyer conceptualizes right-wing authoritarianism in terms of three major attitudinal constructs: authoritarian aggression, authoritarian submission, and conventionality (Altemeyer, 1981, 1988, 1996).

Altemeyer emphasizes that it is the *combination* of these attitudinal clusters that defines right-wing authoritarianism and distinguishes it from more general conservatism. The scale has been updated and refined on a number of occasions. Researchers desiring to employ it are encouraged to contact the author for more recent revisions.

Description

Altemeyer's theory of right-wing authoritarianism and extensive validations of the scale are provided in three books: *Right-Wing Authoritarianism* (1981), *Enemies of Freedom* (1988), and *The Authoritarian Specter* (1996). The complex of attitudes measured by the scale can be briefly defined as follows:

> authoritarian submission—a high degree of submission to the authorities who are perceived to be established and legitimate in the society in which one lives.
>
> authoritarian aggression—a general aggressiveness, directed against various persons, that is perceived to be sanctioned by established authorities.
>
> conventionalism—a high degree of adherence to the social conventions that are perceived to be endorsed by society and its established authorities. (Altemeyer, 1981, p. 148)

Christie (1991), in his review of measures of authoritarianism, comments favorably on the strict psychometric criteria followed in the development of the scale. After considerable experimentation with item response formats, Altemeyer has settled on a nine-point scale ranging from *very strongly agree* (+4) to *very strongly disagree* (−4) with *neutral–no opinion* defined as 0.

Sample

Construction of the scale has been conducted using thousands of students recruited from the subject pool at the University of Manitoba. Validation studies have included students from a large number of universities in the United States and Europe as well as U.S. legislators and Canadian M.P.s.

Reliability

Internal Consistency

An alpha of .88 was obtained for a sample of 956 Manitoba students in 1973 (Altemeyer, 1981). Zwillenberg (1983) reported reliabilities ranging from .77 to .95 for numerous American college samples, with an alpha of .90 for the combined samples. Ray (1985c) found an alpha of .89 for a random cluster sample of 84 persons surveyed in Australia. Heaven (1984) found alpha coefficients of .81 and .90 for samples of 52 psychology undergraduates and 130 adult contacts of the first sample. Alphas for small mail samples of provincial legislators ranged from .88 to .97 (Altemeyer, 1988). Two studies conducted in the Soviet Union yielded alphas of .92 (McFarland, Agayev, & Abalakina, 1990) and .81 (Altemeyer, 1990).

Test–Retest

Reliabilities of .95 for a period of 1 week and .85 for a 28-week interval were reported for samples of Canadian students (Altemeyer, 1988).

Validity

Convergent

When the RWA Scale was given to student samples in conjunction with other prominent measures of authoritarianism, it consistently outperformed them. Scales aimed at measuring (1) orientation toward endorsement of established authority and law, (2) approval of law as the cornerstone of morality, and (3) punitiveness toward "sanctioned targets" (such as minority groups, social deviants, and "common criminals") showed the highest correlations with RWA. The RWA Scale was also found to have a high correlation ($-.52$) with acceptance of government injustice, such as illegal wiretapping and police harassment (Altemeyer, 1981). The scale was also found to have a high correlation ($+.44$) with persistence of "shocking" the learner in a modified version of Milgram's (1974) obedience paradigm (Altemeyer, 1981). Heaven (1984) found the RWA to be highly correlated with Ray's Balanced F scale, a measure of authoritarianism (Meleon, VanderLinden, & De Witte, 1996).

Altemeyer (1981) reported significant differences in RWA scores by party affiliation among Canadian students and American students, but he also notes a great deal of overlap in RWA scores between the parties. Eta values have ranged in the neighborhood of .20 to .26 among both Canadian and U.S. student samples. Party explains RWA scores much better among Canadian legislators, with eta values averaging .85 (Altemeyer, 1988).

Heaven (1984) reported a correlation of .51 between the RWA and observer ratings of conservative behavior. Ray (1985) reported a correlation of .81 between the RWA and his scale of conservatism. Stone (1997) reported a correlation of .55 between the RWA and the Normative scale of the Tomkins Polarity Scale. Duckitt and Farre (1994) reported that high RWA scores among white South Africans were associated with intolerance of opposition to the new government—a finding that they suggested emphasizes authoritarian aggression as a component of the syndrome.

Discriminant

Ray (1985c) argued that the right-wing authoritarianism scale "measures nothing more than conservatism," both because it is not related to his measure of directiveness and because it is correlated with his conservatism scale. Altemeyer (1988) argued that the directiveness measure might be useful among the politically involved, but fails to capture the element of authoritarian submission that is crucial to the classical definition of authoritarianism. Validity here is very much dependent on the theoretical requirements of the model.

Location

Altemeyer, B. (1981). *Right-wing authoritarianism.* Winnipeg: University of Manitoba Press.

Altemeyer, B. (1988). *Enemies of freedom.* San Francisco: Jossey-Bass. (1990 version of the scale provided by the author.)

Altemeyer, B. (1996). *The authoritarian specter.* Cambridge MA: Harvard University Press.

Results and Comments

Altemeyer's theoretical interest is in right-wing authoritarianism, not general conservatism. He views the attitude clusters that define the syndrome as having important political consequences, many of which are examined in his second and third books (1988, 1996). The scale has been designed to be unidimensional, and factor analysis revealed only one factor that accounted for 23.3% of the variance. Because each of the three attitude clusters contributes to the factor, Altemeyer cautions against disaggregating the items or using shortened versions of the scale.

Right-Wing Authoritarianism (Altemeyer, 1990)

1. Our country will be great if we honor the ways of our forefathers, do what the authorities tell us to do, and get rid of the "rotten apples" who are ruining everything.

$$-4 \quad -3 \quad -2 \quad -1 \quad 0 \quad +1 \quad +2 \quad +3 \quad +4$$
VERY STRONGLY DISAGREE   NEUTRAL   VERY STRONGLY AGREE

*2. It is wonderful that young people can protest against anything they don't like, and act however they wish nowadays.

3. It is always better to trust the judgment of the proper authorities in government and religion, than to listen to the noisy rabble-rousers in our society who are trying to create doubt in people's minds.

*4. People should pay *less* attention to the Bible and the other old traditional forms of religious guidance, and instead develop their own personal standards of what is moral and immoral.

5. What our country *really* needs, instead of more "civil rights," is a good stiff dose of law and order.

6. Our country will be destroyed someday if we do not smash the perversions eating away at our moral fiber and traditional beliefs.

*7. The sooner we get rid of the traditional family structure, where the father is the head of the family and the children are taught to obey authority automatically, the better. The old-fashioned way has a lot wrong with it.

*8. There is nothing wrong with premarital sexual intercourse.

9. The facts on crime, sexual immorality, and the recent public disorders all show we have to crack down harder on deviant groups and troublemakers if we are going to save our moral standards and preserve law and order.

*10. There is nothing immoral or sick in somebody's being a homosexual.

*11. It is important to protect fully the rights of radicals and deviants.

12. Obedience is the most important virtue children should learn.

*13. There is no "one right way" to live your life; everybody has to create his *own* way.

14. Once our government leaders condemn the dangerous elements in our society, it will be the duty of every patriotic citizen to help stomp out the rot that is poisoning our country from within.

*15. Government, judges and the police should never be allowed to censor books.

16. Some of the worst people in our country nowadays are those who do not respect our flag, our leaders, and the normal way things are supposed to be done.

17. In these troubled times laws have to be enforced without mercy, especially when dealing with the agitators and revolutionaries who are stirring things up.

18. Atheists and others who have rebelled against the established religions are no doubt every bit as good and virtuous as those who attend church regularly.

19. Some young people get rebellious ideas, but as they get older they ought to become more mature and forget such things.

*20. There is nothing really wrong with a lot of the things some people call "sins."

*21. Everyone should have his own lifestyle, religious beliefs, and sexual preferences, even if it makes him different from everyone else.

22. The situation in our country is getting so serious, the strongest methods would be justified if they eliminated the troublemakers and got us back on our true path.

23. Authorities such as parents and our national leaders generally turn out to be right about things, and the radicals and protestors are almost always wrong.

*24. A lot of our rules regarding modesty and sexual behavior are just customs which are not necessarily any better or holier than those which other people follow.

*25. There is absolutely nothing wrong with nudist camps.

26. The *real* keys to the "good life" are obedience, discipline, and sticking to the straight and narrow.

*27. We should treat protestors and radicals with open arms and open minds, since new ideas are the lifeblood of progressive change.

28. What our country really needs is a strong, determined leader who will crush evil, and take us back to our true path.

*29. Students must be taught to challenge their parents' views, confront the authorities, and criticize the traditions of our society.

30. One reason we have so many troublemakers in our society nowadays is that parents and other authorities have forgotten that good old-fashioned physical punishment is still one of the best ways to make people behave properly.

*Indicates reverse scored items.

Wilson–Patterson Attitude Inventory (WPAI) Conservatism Scale

(G. D. Wilson & J. R. Patterson, 1989)

Variable

The Wilson–Patterson Conservatism Scale (or C-Scale) is defined as measuring a general factor of conservatism that is thought to underlie all social attitudes.

Description

The Wilson–Patterson Attitude Inventory, or WPAI (Wilson, 1975), is a revision of the C-Scale that includes the replacement of seven items. Items were replaced to update their meanings (e.g., *beatniks* has been replaced by *hippies*), to enhance understanding across cultures, to decrease overlap in item content, to better the balance of differing scales, to delete items that failed to discriminate statistically, and to introduce meaningful new issues that previously had not been included, such as pornography (Wilson, 1973a, 1975). The 1989 revision presented here was provided by the authors.

Construction of the scale started with a list of characteristics assumed to measure the "ideal conservative" in terms of the following domains: (1) religious fundamentalism; (2) right-wing political orientation; (3) insistence on strict rules and punishments; (4) intolerance of minority groups; (5) preference for conventional art, clothing, and institutions; (6) antihedonistic outlook; and (7) superstitious resistance to science. The authors selected a pool of 130 items that were intuitively considered to measure these characteristics. The final 50 items, chosen on the basis of item analyses, met the following criteria: (1) demonstrated a positive association with the whole-test scores, (2) had power to discriminate among dimensions for different groups, (3) were understandable, (4) were not redundant in meaning, (5) represented the attitude areas in roughly equal numbers, (6) were expected to maintain validity over time, and (7) were expected to be usable in other cultures.

Wilson and Patterson (1968) sought to overcome social desirability and agreement response biases in the existing measures by constructing a scale of 50 brief labels or "catchphrases" representing familiar and controversial issues. Wilson (1985) maintained that the use of catchphrases should elicit uncomplicated emotional responses that should be of greater use in samples of the mass public. Nonetheless, Ray (1971, 1980) argued that the Wilson–Patterson items were still prone to response biases and proposed his own "catchphrase" inventory (Ray, 1972).

In the original scale, liberal items were alternatively presented with conservative ones, but they are now randomly presented. Respondents simply answer *yes, no,* or *?* to indicate whether or not they favor the item. After appropriate reverse coding, a "yes" response is scored 2, "?" receives a 1, and "no" is scored 0. The scale has a theoretical range of 0 to 100, with a higher score indicating more conservatism. The same scoring system was retained with the WPAI.

The WPAI can also be scored to measure five other scales besides conservatism–liberalism (Wilson, 1973b, 1975): particularly realism–idealism, but also (1) militarism–punitiveness, (2) antihedonism, (3) ethnocentrism, and (4) religion–puritanism. The conservatism–liberalism factor is scored using all 50 items, 25 of which are positive and 25 of which are negative. The realism–idealism factor is keyed using 36 items, with 18 being positive and 18 being negative. Each of the four oblique factors is scored using 12 items. Each of the subscales is balanced except for the religion–puritanism factor. The various scoring keys are identified in the version of the scale presented here, but they were developed in conjunction with work on the 1975 revision. Complete instructions are given in Wilson's (1975) manual.

Sample

The original scale was administered to 496 males and females from the following occupational categories: (1) university students, (2) laboratory technicians, (3) professionals, (4) secondary school pupils, (5) unskilled workers, (6) college teachers, (7) typists, (8) businessmen, and (9) housewives. Subsequent studies have involved a variety of samples in many areas of the world.

Reliability

Internal Consistency

Split-half reliability, corrected for test length by using the Spearman–Brown Prophecy Formula, was .94 ($N = 244$) for the initial scale. Subsequent investigators have estimated the scale's reliability at .83 to .94. Wilson (1970) reported a split-half reliability of .93 and an alpha coefficient of .91 for a sample of heterogeneous males in the United Kingdom. Bagley, Wilson, and Boshier (1970) found the split-half reliability to be .89 for a sample of heterogeneous males in the United Kingdom, and Insel and Wilson (1971) reported a split-half reliability of .84 for U.K. schoolgirls. Ray (1971) reported an alpha coefficient of .83 for first-year psychology students in Australia. The split-half reliability for university students in Germany was reported to be .86 by Schneider and Minkmar (1972; as summarized by Wilson, 1975). Orpen and Rodenwoldt (1973) found a split-half reliability of .90 for first-year school students in South Africa. Lapsley and Enright (1979) reported an alpha reliability of .80 for a sample of male and female university students in the United States. The one exception to these findings of high reliability was reported by Ray (1971). He found an alpha coefficient of .63 for a sample of army conscripts in Australia.

Feather (1984) reported an alpha coefficient of .81 for introductory Australian psychology students. Katz and Ronen (1986) reported Cronbach's alpha reliability coefficients of .82 for Israeli citizens of Western origin and .74 for Israeli citizens of Eastern origin. Katz (1988b) found Spearman–Brown reliability coefficients of .86 for Jewish subjects and .78 for Arab students. Becona (1985) reported an alpha of .86 for 405 students attending university in Spain. A shortened version of the scale by Kirton (1978) yielded coefficients of .86 and .87 for two heterogenous samples of British men and women. In validating the Children's Scale of Social Attitudes, Katz (1988a) reported a Spearman–Brown reliability coefficient of .75 for Israeli school children.

Test–Retest

Nias, Wilson, and Woodbridge (1971) administered the scale twice to four groups of female students in a college setting during an interval of 12 weeks. Reliabilities ranged from
.82 to .94 depending on the testing environment. Schneider and Minkmar (1972; as summarized by Wilson, 1975) gave the scale to 28 psychology students and reported a test–
retest coefficient of .94. Kirton (1978) reported a coefficient of .92 using his shortened
version of the C-Scale.

Validity

Convergent

As hypothesized, C scores increased monotonically with age and were somewhat higher
for females than males (Feather, 1975, 1977a, 1977b, 1979; Shea & Jones, 1982; Wilson,
1973a). Much research has been conducted demonstrating that known groups respond differently to the C-Scale, as one would expect. For instance, Wilson and Patterson (1968)
found that the New Left Club, a liberal organization, endorsed fewer conservative items
than did the Junior National Party, a conservative organization. Wilson and Lillie (1972)
found that Salvation Army officer cadets scored high on the scale and Young Humanists
scored low. Orpen and Rodenwoldt (1973) found high C scorers to be advocates of the
prosegregationist, ruling National Party in South Africa.

In terms of other theoretically appropriate constructs, Crano (1969; as summarized by
Wilson, 1975) found a correlation of .68 between the C-Scale and the California F-Scale.
Orpen and Rodenwoldt (1973) found a positive correlation of .69 between self-ratings of
conservatism and scores on the C-Scale. Scores on principle morality were significantly
associated with scores on the WPAI in the expected direction (Fincham & Barling, 1979).

High scorers on the WPAI have been found to desire the restriction of environmental
complexity and uncertainty in order to prevent information overload (Gillies & Campbell,
1985; Glasgow, Cartier, & Wilson, 1985). Scores on the C-Scale were positively correlated with measures of the Protestant ethic (Feather, 1984). Appreciation of incongruity–
resolution humor was found to be associated with scores on the C-Scale in which these
same persons were found to desire control or reduced uncertainties in life (Hehl & Ruch,
1990). Feather (1979) found high scorers to value the following: family security; national
security; salvation; being clean; and being honest, obedient, and polite. High scorers demonstrated lower sexual responsivity (Joe, Kostyla, & Jones, 1985). Wilson and Caldwell
(1988) found parties on the right to be higher on the WPAI than parties on the left. Finally,
Walkey *et al.* (1990) suggested that the "general factor" relates to Judeo-Christian religious tradition.

Discriminant

Lapsley and Enright (1979) found that the C-Scale was negatively related to intelligence.
Feather (1979) found a negative relationship between scores on the C-Scale and the relative importance designated by respondents to values associated with more liberal thinking
using the Rokeach (1973) value survey.

Location

Wilson, G. D., & Patterson, J. R. (1968). A new measure of conservatism. *British Journal
of Social and Clinical Psychology, 7,* 264–269.

Wilson, G. D. (1975). *Manual for the Wilson–Patterson Attitude Inventory (WPAI)*. Windsor, England: NFER–Nelson Publishing Co. (1989 version obtained from the author.)

Results and Comments

The literature search suggests that the WPAI is the most frequently used conservatism scale in recent research. This is likely due to the ease of administration and scoring, the extensive information about its statistical properties, and the breadth of attitude objects covered. Wilson (1975) emphasizes that it is not meant strictly to be a measure of political conservatism and that it explicitly excludes the economic dimension. Wilson and Patterson's (1968) definition of conservatism includes a number of characteristics that other researchers have defined as part of authoritarianism. Wilson (1975) notes that the measure is "presumed to reflect a dimension of personality similar to that which has been previously described in terms of a variety of labels such as 'fascism,' 'authoritarianism,' 'rigidity,' and 'dogmatism' " (p. 10).

Many investigators have been concerned with trying to replicate the six factors reported by Wilson and the amount of variance accounted for by these factors. As pointed out by Green, Reynolds, Walkey, and McCormick (1988), only seldom do more than three items fall jointly on the factors studied. Furthermore the replication of more extensive structures has not been substantiated (Green *et al.*, 1988). In general, most studies have found the first unrotated factor to account for under 20% of the total variance (Bagley, 1970; Boshier, 1972; Feather, 1975; Joe, 1984; Wilson, 1970). The characteristics of the rotated factor structure of the scale are still open to debate (Green *et al.*, 1988). Reported differences frequently depend on the criteria used in determining how many factors should be extracted for a correlation matrix and subsequently rotated. The scale is based on the assumption that liberalism–conservatism is unidimensional. Though low scorers on the WPAI have tended to be associated with liberal groups, evidence for a single-dimension interpretation is not unanimous (e.g., Bahr & Chadwick, 1974; Boshier, 1974; Robertson & Cochrane, 1973).

Wilson–Patterson Attitude Inventory (WPAI) Conservatism Scale (Wilson, 1989)

Instructions: WHICH OF THE FOLLOWING DO YOU FAVOR OR BELIEVE IN? (Circle "yes" or "no". If absolutely uncertain, circle "?". There are no right or wrong answers; do not discuss; just give your first reaction. Answer all items.)

1. Death penalty	YES ? NO	R+, M+[1]
*[2]2. Evolution theory	YES ? NO	R−, P−
3. White superiority	YES ? NO	R+, E+
*4. Working mother	YES ? NO	E−
5. Divine law	YES ? NO	R−, P+
*6. Pornography	YES ? NO	R+, H−
*7. Disarmament	YES ? NO	R−, M−
8. Learning Latin	YES ? NO	R−, E−
*9. Smoking pot	YES ? NO	R+, H−

10. Royalty	YES ? NO		R−, M+
*11. Legal abortion	YES ? NO		P−
12. Church authority	YES ? NO		R−, P+
13. Conventional clothes	YES ? NO		R+
*14. Fluoridation	YES ? NO		R−, P−
*15. Modern art	YES ? NO		H−
16. Strict rules	YES ? NO		M+
17. Corporal punishment	YES ? NO		R+, M+
18. Miracles	YES ? NO		R−, P+
*19. Socialism	YES ? NO		R−, M−
*20. Hippies	YES ? NO		E−
21. Chaperones	YES ? NO		R+, H+
22. Straightjackets	YES ? NO		R+, M+
23. Racial segregation	YES ? NO		R+, E+
24. Moral training	YES ? NO		R−, H+
25. Censorship	YES ? NO		R−, H+
*26. Birth control	YES ? NO		P−
*27. Foreign immigration	YES ? NO		R−, E−
28. Self-denial	YES ? NO		R−, H+
*29. Cousin marriage	YES ? NO		R+, P−
*30. Bible truth	YES ? NO		R−, P+
*31. Jazz	YES ? NO		E−
32. Military drill	YES ? NO		M+
33. Inborn conscience	YES ? NO		R−, P+
*34. Co-education	YES ? NO		R−, M−
35. Sabbath observance	YES ? NO		R−, P+
*36. Computer music	YES ? NO		R−
*37. Casual living	YES ? NO		R+, H−
*38. Women judges	YES ? NO		R−, E−
39. Patriotism	YES ? NO		M+
*40. Easy divorce	YES ? NO		R+, P−
41. School uniforms	YES ? NO		M+
*42. Student pranks	YES ? NO		E−
43. Licensing laws	YES ? NO		H+
*44. Teenage drivers	YES ? NO		E−
45. Chastity	YES ? NO		R−, H+
*46. Striptease shows	YES ? NO		R−, H−
*47. White lies	YES ? NO		R+, M−
48. Empire building	YES ? NO		R+, E+

| *49. Mixed marriage | YES ? NO | E– |
| *50. Euthanasia | YES ? NO | R–, H– |

[1]The letters after each item indicate the subscale and direction of scoring. R = realism–idealism; M = militarism–punitiveness; H = antihedonism; E = ethnocentrism & out-group hostility; P = religion–puritanism.

[2]*Indicates reverse scored item—i. e., on the C-Scale a "yes" on these items is scored 0, a "no" is scored 2.

S Swedish Conservatism Scale
(J. Sidanius, 1976, 1991; I. Nilsson & B. Ekehammar, 1989)

Variable

The scale was designed to provide an equal number of balanced items for five prominent subdimensions of conservatism found in the work of Sidanius and his collegues, plus an environmentalism dimension.

Description

The S Swedish Conservatism Scale was originally constructed to be employed as a measure of sociopolitical attitudes in Sweden. The objective was to develop a Swedish version of the Wilson–Patterson C-scale. The S4 version retained only 13 items from the original C-Scale (Wilson & Patterson, 1968). As in the C-Scale, items were selected to measure the following content areas: (1) punitiveness, (2) religion, (3) racism, (4) political–economic conservatism, (5) sexual repression, (6) social conservatism, and (7) ethnocentrism. These content areas were chosen because of their similitude to the attitude scales of Eysenck (1975) and Kerlinger (1967). The item format is similar to that of the Wilson–Patterson C-Scale (1968) and thus consists of single words or short phrases.

In the earlier versions (i.e., S4 and S5), respondents were to reply *yes, no,* or *?* to each item in order to indicate a positive, negative, or neutral reaction. For the more recent versions, response choices range from 1 (very negative) to 7 (very positive). With appropriate reverse scoring, a higher score indicates a higher degree of conservatism. The current version of the Swedish Scale of Social Attitudes is referred to as S9. The name of the scale is slightly misleading, since it has been validated on samples of American and Australian students as well as Swedes. The scale is a 36-item, balanced, "catchphrase" type of attitude inventory, which has been frequently updated.

The most recent scale by Nilsson and Ekehammar (1989, 1990) consists of 24 items that were chosen according to a stratified sampling plan (Rajaratnam, Chronbach, & Glesser, 1965) instead of selecting items randomly from the universe as a whole. As in the earlier versions of the S Scale, respondents are asked to provide their immediate response to various statements. Specifically they are to indicate whether they have a positive reaction with a *yes,* a negative reaction with a *no,* or a neutral response with a *?.* "Yes" responses are scored a 2, "no" responses a 0, and "?" responses a 1. Half of the items are reversed; once recoded, a higher score indicates more conservatism.

Sample

The initial sample studied for the first S Scale (i.e., S4 Scale) consisted of 87 psychology students attending the University of Stockholm. Three independent samples were used to validate the S5 version. One consisted of 190 undergraduate psychology students attending the University of Stockholm, and the second was composed of 195 high school students in Stockholm. The third sample was composed of 157 students from a second-year high school class. Subjects studied using the S6 version were 783 gymnasium students attending five different schools in Stockholm. Two American samples composed of 267 psychology undergraduates and 225 undergraduates from a government class were investigated using S7. The sample used by Nilsson and Ekehammar (1989, 1990) consisted of 445 students, aged 14–17, from metropolitan Stockholm schools.

Reliability

Internal Consistency

A Spearman–Brown split-half reliability coefficient of .91 was reported for the S4. A KR 20 coefficient of .89 was obtained for the S4 (Sidanius, 1976a). Sidanius (1976b) found reliability coefficients of .90 for a sample of undergraduate psychology students and .88 for a diverse sample of high school students. For the S5 version Sidanius (1976b) reported reliabilities ranging from .90 to .92. An alpha coefficient of .85 was obtained for a sample of Australian psychology students by Sidanius, Ekehammar, and Ross (1979). For the S6 and S7 versions, alpha coefficients of .89 for a sample of gymnasium students in Sweden and .85 for a sample of undergraduates in the United States were found (Sidanius & Duffy, 1988).

Sidanius, Brewer, Banks, and Ekehammar (1987) calculated a goodness of fit and a total coefficient of determination (TCD) as measures of reliability for their three samples of gymnasium students from Stockholm, psychology undergraduate students in the United States, and undergraduates attending a government class in the United States. The goodness of fit index was .90, and the TCD was .99. In this study Sidanius and his colleagues also calculated Cronbach's alpha for the five subdimensions of the scale for both men and women in the Swedish and the American samples. For Swedish men the coefficients ranged from .75 to .92, whereas for the women the range was from .66 to .87. In general, lower coefficients were calculated for the American samples. The range was from .72 to .85 for men and .71 to .86 for the women. Nonetheless, these are still acceptable. Nilsson and Ekehammar (1989, 1990) reported an alpha coefficient of .76 for their sample of gymnasium students. Split-half coefficients were .78 for each age group and .79 for the total sample.

Test–Retest

No test–retest data are reported for any versions of the S Scale. The test–retest correlation for the Revised Swedish Scale of Social Attitudes was found to be .85 for the total sample (Nilsson & Ekehammar, 1989, 1990).

Validity

Convergent

Analyses of responses to the S4 Scale by respondents of known political groups revealed that the conservative groups responded as one would expect (Sidanius, 1976a, 1976b).

Furthermore self-labeling of political preferences (i.e., radical, liberal, conservative) was highly associated with one's scores on the S4 scale (Sidanius, 1976b). The S4 version was found to be highly correlated with political party preferences, educational status, and political self-identification (Sidanius, 1985). The five subdimensions—racism, political–economic conservatism, religion, sexual repression, and authoritarian aggression—were found to be significantly related to two indices of cognitive functioning. In general, Sidanius found that the greater one's general conservatism, the lesser one's cognitive flexibility. Furthermore it was demonstrated that the more racist, sexually repressive, and punitive the individual was, the more cognitively rigid he/she was.

For the S5 the Australian sample was found to be more conservative than a Swedish sample (Sidanius et al., 1979). Sidanius and Duffy (1988) found a monotonic increase in S6 scores among respondents with progressively more conservative political party preferences for their Swedish sample. This same relationship was also observed with the S7 scale among the U.S. sample. Furthermore high alpha coefficients were obtained for respondents who were found to be more sophisticated in their thinking, thus demonstrating more attitude constraint. This finding was characteristic of both the Swedish and the American samples. Also, for the S6 version, Ekehammar, Nilsson, and Sidanius (1989) noted that the higher a person's social status, the more sociopolitically conservative that person's attitudes. Additionally they found the political–economic conservatism (PEC) subdimension to be highly related to social class, social economic status (SES), income, occupation, and education in Sweden. In the U.S. sample PEC was associated only with social class and SES. From their study Sidanius et al. (1987) concluded that the more conservative one's political self-concept is, the more conservative one will be found to be as measured by the S6 Scale. Additionally they found the subdimensions of PEC, racism, religion, and punitiveness to be significantly related to political party preference and political self-concept.

Analyses performed on the revised scale constructed by Nilsson and Ekehammar (1989, 1990) suggested that the factor structure identified by Sidanius remained. The environmental subscale, which the authors added, was found to be the least reliable of the six, but still satisfactory.

Discriminant

Ekehammar, Nilsson, and Sidanius (1989) found a negative relationship between social class and the subdimensions of the S6 Scale measuring noneconomic conservatism (i.e., religion, punitiveness, social inequality, and racism) for the U.S. sample. However, this relationship was not maintained for their Australian sample as had been hypothesized.

Location

Sidanius, J. (1976a). *A Swedish scale of conservatism* (Rep. No. 465). Stockholm: Department of Psychology, University of Stockholm.

Sidanius, J., & Duffy, G. (1988). The duality of attitude structure: A test of Kerlinger's criterial referents theory within samples of Swedish and American youth. *Political Psychology, 9*, 649–670. (1991 version of the scale provided by the authors.)

Nilsson, I., & Ekehammar, B. (1989). *A revised Swedish social attitudes scale*. (Rep. No. 688). Stockholm: Department of Psychology, University of Stockholm.

Results and Comments

The scale is defined by Sidanius (1976a) as a measure of sociopolitical attitudes. Nonetheless, he has presented some evidence that it is related to intolerance of ambiguity in the manner suggested by the Adorno group (Adorno *et al.*, 1950). Furthermore Sidanius describes his scale as a measurement of conservatism, which is in keeping with his conceptualization of liberalism–conservatism as bipolar. He does not reject Kerlinger's (1984) notion of attitude duality, but argues that liberalism and conservatism are seldom strictly orthogonal. He also argues that even relatively modest levels of political sophistication produce bipolar attitude structures, and thus bipolarity is much more common than a strict reading of Kerlinger's theory might suggest (e.g., Sidanius & Duffy, 1988).

One criticism to be noted is the variability in terms of the number of factors found to be associated with the scale. The number of factors has ranged anywhere from four to six, and they may not always be the same ones. For the S4 version Sidanius (1976a) reported the following five subdimensions as a result of using an oblique factor analysis: (1) racism, (2) PEC, (3) religion, (4) sexual repression, and (5) authoritarian aggression. For the S5 version Sidanius *et al.* (1979) employed a principal-factors extraction and found six factors for their Australian and Swedish samples. In the Australian sample the factors were (1) authoritarian aggression–punitiveness, (2) social inequality, (3) religion, (4) pro-West, (5) PEC, and (6) racism. For the Swedish respondents the factors found were as follows: (1) PEC, (2) religion, (3) authoritarian aggression–punitiveness, (4) social inequality, (5) xenophobia, and (6) racism. In a later investigation Sidanius *et al.* (1987) found the subdimensions of PEC, racism, religion, and punitiveness for the S6 version. That the same factors for subdimensions are not always obtained has not been addressed by Sidanius and his associates. Sidanius now appears to have become convinced that social dominance orientation is a more theoretically satisfying construct for explaining attitudes generally thought to be predicted by conservatism (see, for example, Sidanius & Pratto, 1993; Sidanius, Pratto, & Bobo, 1996).

Conservatism Scale
(Sidanius, 1991)

Instructions: Which of the following objects or events do you have a positive or a negative feeling towards? Place one of the numbers below beside that object or event towards which you have a positive or negative feeling.

    1. Tougher measures against criminals.

1	2	3	4	5	6	7
VERY NEGATIVE						VERY POSITIVE

    2. Eliminate affirmative action.

    3. Belief in authority.

 *4. Increased taxation of the rich.

 *5. Improved relations with Vietnam.

    6. Increased support of the military.

    7. American military intervention in Latin America.

 *8. Socialism.

    9. White superiority.

*10. Increased aid to the poor.

11. Castration of rapists.

*12. Racial equality.

13. Religion.

*14. Greater equality in salaries.

15. Jesse Helms.

16. Privately owned prisons.

*17. Government supported, national health care.

*18. Interracial marriage.

19. The death penalty.

20. Lower minimum wage.

*21. Increased equality.

22. Increased religious instruction in the schools.

23. Capitalism.

*24. Racially integrated neighborhoods.

*25. Decreased weapons development.

*26. A Black President of the USA.

*27. Nationalization of private companies.

28. Longer prison sentences.

*29. Social equality.

*30. Employee ownership of corporations.

31. Law and order.

*32. Increased democracy on the job.

33. Lower taxes on corporations.

34. Religious faith.

*35. A woman President of the USA.

*36. Better medical care for the poor.

*Indicates reverse scored items.

Conservatism of American Public Opinion

(J. J. Ray, 1983)

Variable

Of the large number of different scales of conservatism and related constructs Ray has developed, this 22-item counterbalanced conservatism scale was designed for American subjects as a unidimensional measure of liberalism–conservatism.

Description

The 22 items were selected from an earlier 68-item scale (Ray, 1982) that had been designed to assess the existence of two orthogonal dimensions, libertarian–authoritarian and radicalism–conservatism. [The libertarian–authoritarian dimension failed to emerge as hypothesized (Ray, 1982).] Items were selected that demonstrated the highest correlation with the total score obtained on the 68-item scale. Response choices range from *strongly agree,* which is scored as 1, to *strongly disagree,* which is scored as 7. Half of the items are reversed scored.

Ray (1972) has also provided a revised version of the Wilson–Patterson (1968) C-Scale and the Neoconservatism Scale (Ray, 1987), which may be of interest to researchers, although some testing will be necessary to determine the effects of revisions for non-Australian subjects.

Sample

The initial subject pool consisted of 500 persons randomly selected from the voter registration lists of Los Angeles and Orange Counties in California. The final sample consisted of 70 individuals. In terms of demographic characteristics, the average age was 43.4 years, 59% were male, the averaged education level obtained was between senior in high school and college, and 33% were employed in manual occupations.

Reliability

Internal Consistency

Ray (1983) reports an alpha reliability of .85. A correlation of .43 was found between the positively and negatively scored halves of the scale, thus suggesting that the items are moderately free of an acquiescence contamination.

Test–Retest

No test–retest data are reported.

Validity

Convergent

No data are presented for this version. For the initial 68-item scale (Ray, 1982), the conservatism–radicalism dimension was found to dominate. For example, respondents who favored conservative positions of a libertarian nature were also more likely to favor conservative positions of an authoritarian nature.

Discriminant

No research has been reported.

Location

Ray, J. J. (1983). A scale to measure conservatism of American public opinion. *Journal of Social Psychology, 119*, 293–294. Reprinted with permission of the Helen Dwight Reid Educational Foundation. Published by Heldref Publications, 1319 Eighteenth St., N.W., Washington, D.C. 20036-1802. Copyright © 1983.

Results and Comments

Ray has devised a number of scales relevant to the measurement of liberalism–conservatism and has contributed heavily to debates over methodological and philosophical issues. Of potential additional interest are two revisions of the Wilson–Patterson C-Scale, the accompanying statement scale used for concurrent validation (Ray, 1972, 1984), and the Neoconservatism Scale (Ray 1987). In 1985 Ray presented a more comprehensive analysis identifying subscales measuring political, social, economic, aesthetic, religious, and moral conservatism. The major difficulty with the many scales devised by Ray results from their sheer number and from the fact that most have been developed for Australian subjects. Although additional validation is in order, the 22-item scale presented here seems to capture the range of concerns relevant to conservatism, and despite Ray's (1972) caveat, the substance of the items continues to be relevant.

Scale to Measure Conservatism of American Public Opinion
(Ray, 1982)

*1. A free dental service should be provided by the Federal government.

1	2	3	4	5	6	7
AGREE STRONGLY						DISAGREE STRONGLY

2. Schoolchildren should have plenty of discipline.

3. The government should not attempt to limit business profits.

4. Erotic and obscene literature should be prohibited from public sale.

*5. The Federal government should introduce a health insurance scheme which would cover every American no matter what he does.

*6. Labor unions should make more efforts to grab corporate profits for the workers.

*7. People should be allowed to hold demonstrations in the streets without police interference.

8. The police deserve more praise for the difficult job they do.

9. Law and order is more important than letting every kook have his say.

10. People who are always protesting to have something banned or stopped would probably howl the loudest if they themselves were banned.

*11. Government attempts to prevent people using marijuana are just about as stupid as prohibition of alcohol was.

*12. The rebellious ideas of young people are often a constructive source of change for the better.

*13. Laws against homosexuality are old-fashioned and wrong.

14. People should be free to get on with their own lives without being pestered by governments and do-gooders.

15. Busing of children to school outside their own neighborhoods is an unforgivable infringement of individual liberties.

16. People who show disrespect for their country's flag should be punished for it.

17. The government should make sure that our armed forces are stronger than those of Russia at all times.

*18. The right of strikers to picket a firm they are striking against should not be interfered with.

*19. The police are generally corrupt and brutal.

*20. The government should do everything it can to eradicate poverty in this country.

*21. Military training is unnatural and has a tendency to warp people.

22. People who want more money should work harder for it instead of trying to get it off the government in one way or another.

*Indicates reverse scored items.

Conservatism Scale

(H. McClosky, 1958, 1979)

Variable

The initial 12-item scale was designed to measure "classical conservatism" at the philosophical level, theorized to be broader and more abstract than other scales of personality or political attitudes.

Description

The original scale consisted of 12 agree-disagree statements that were chosen from an initial pool of 43 items based on the writings of a variety of conservative thinkers. The final 12 were selected because of their greater internal consistency, but correlated .83 with the original 43-item pool. The scale was refined and reduced to nine items in a succeeding investigation. Agreement responses are scored as indicating conservatism. Therefore, the higher the score, the greater the degree of conservatism being exhibited. Endorsement of 7–9 items was considered extremely conservative, 5–6 as moderately conservative, 3–4 as moderately liberal, and 2–0 as extremely liberal.

The 1979 revision (McClosky & Bann, 1979) contains 26 balanced items that closely resemble in substance the initial 43-item pool used for the original scale. The format is a forced-choice sentence completion test, and liberal and conservative alternatives are presented in random order. The seven-item social welfare subscale follows the same format. The items can be scored −1 for liberal responses, 0 for neutral, or no opinion, and +1 for conservative responses.

Sample

Subjects were 1200 persons from Minneapolis-St. Paul, Minnesota, for the first scale. Two samples were employed for analyses with the revised 1979 version. The first sample was a national cross-section of 938 adults. The other sample was composed of 2142 members randomly selected from 19 known ideological groups representing all ranges of

the political spectrum. From the 19 groups, responses from 6 liberal and 5 conservative groups were chosen for analysis.

Reliability

Internal Consistency

No data are reported.

Test-Retest

No data are reported.

Validity

Convergent

McClosky's (1958) original findings generated a good deal of controversy. McClosky reported that the 12-item scale correlated highly (r = .83) with the pool of 43 items.

Furthermore, he reported that 90% of a "validation group," which was comprised of 48 seniors or graduate students in a political theory class, marked subsets of the items from the scale as conservative. Those who scored high on the scale were also found to endorse other items representing conservative sentiment more often than those who scored low on the scale (i.e., liberals). McClosky (1958) also reported that conservatives were most often the uninformed, the poorly educated, and in general those with a variety of undesirable personality characteristics. Campbell, Converse, Miller, and Stokes (1960) substantiated these results on a more limited basis finding that the scale successfully differentiated voters who had switched party loyalty (i.e., Republicans who were previously Democrats scored high and Democrats who were previously Republicans scored low). Photiadis and Biggar (1962) found the scale to be associated with religious orthodoxy and extrinsic religious beliefs, in addition to confirming many of the earlier correlates reported by McClosky. Recently, Stone (personal communication) reported the McClosky scale to correlate .46 with the Normative scale of the Tomkins (1964) Polarity Scale among a sample of college students.

Other researchers have not supported McClosky's findings, and have been particularly critical of agreement response set problems (e.g., Campbell et al., 1960). As pointed out by Polsby, Dentler, and Smith (1963), McClosky's findings do not "incriminate any politically meaningful group in the population" (p. 167–168). Moreover, as noted by Flanigan (1972), McClosky's scale is not directly associated with political parties or public policy. Stone (1974) examined responses of members of the John Birch Society and found that almost 80% of these members were classified as liberals on the scale. Finally, Owens (1979) found that liberals on the McClosky scale tended to self-identify as conservatives. Similar reversals were reported in terms of respondents' endorsements of social welfare issues, and conservative scorers were not found to endorse conservative political candidates.

McClosky and Bann (1979), however, pointed out that while the scale failed to correlate with self-designation and candidate preference in the mass public, significant positive associations were found for a large national sample of party convention delegates. It is also possible that some of the scale's disjuncture with self-identification comes from public misunderstanding of the ideological terms. McClosky and Bann (1979) reported that responses to the new version are very much associated with ideological self-identification and to reported presidential voting for both the samples of the mass public and groups with known ideological predispositions.

Discriminant

No data are reported.

Location

McClosky, H. (1958). Conservatism and personality. *American Political Science Review,* *52,* 27–45.
  McClosky, H., & Bann, C. A. (1979). On the reappraisal of the classical conservatism scale. *Political Methodology, 6,* 149–172.

Results and Comments

The chief difficulty with the Classical Conservatism scale has been its relatively weak performance against relevant criterion variables when the scale is employed in samples of the mass public. McClosky has responded that this is because the ideas of philosophical conservatism are not commonly understood in the mass public. The fact that the concepts are relatively sophisticated, coupled with the agreement response bias in the original, argues against employing the items on a mass sample. In his response to Owens, McClosky also noted that the scale "was not designed to encompass the entire constellation of beliefs composing liberal and conservative ideologies" and that "liberalism and conservatism are multidimensional belief systems encompassing important ideas and principles that are related to, but not part of the (more philosophical) classical conservatism" (McClosky & Bann, 1979, p. 150).

  The revised scale was developed to represent liberalism–conservatism more comprehensively and to provide a statement style and response format that would be more appropriate to the general public. The preliminary analysis of this scale suggests that it has substantial utility as a broader measure of liberalism–conservatism. It should be kept in mind, however, that this scale is part of a larger index which is still undergoing analysis and refinement.

Classical Conservatism Scale
(McClosky, 1958)

Instructions: This scale concerns opinions on a variety of social issues. You will probably find that you *agree* with some of the statements and *disagree* with others, to varying degrees. Please indicate the extent of your agreement or disagreement with each statement.

1. All groups can live in harmony in this country without changing the system in any way.

1	2	3	4	5
STRONGLY AGREE				STRONGLY DISAGREE

2. If something grows up over a long time, there will always be much wisdom in it.

3. If you start trying to change things very much, you usually make them worse.

4. I prefer the practical man any time to the man of ideas.

5. No matter how we like to talk about it, political authority really comes not from us but from some higher power.

6. We must respect the work of our forefathers and not think that we know better than they did.

7. It's better to stick by what you have than to be trying new things you really don't know about.

8. A man doesn't really get to have much wisdom until he's well along in years.

9. I'd want to know that something would really work before I'd be willing to take a chance on it.

Conservatism–Liberalism Scale
(McClosky & Bann, 1979)

Instructions: Mark the alternative that is closest to your opinion.

1. People who are always trying to reform things are usually:
   ____ people who really care about other people
   ____ busybodies who do more harm than good
   ____ neither/undecided

2. Replacing traditional policies with new ones that seem attractive but have not been tested by experience is:
   ____ often necessary for progress
   ____ usually shortsighted and dangerous
   ____ neither/undecided

3. Trying to make sweeping reforms in a society as complicated as ours is usually:
   ____ worth trying, despite the risks
   ____ much too risky
   ____ neither/undecided

4. If you had to choose, whom would you trust to solve the country's problems:
   ____ "practical" people who know how to run things
   *____ "thinking" people who have lots of ideas
   ____ neither/undecided

5. Can you depend on a man more if he owns property than if he doesn't?
   ____ yes
   *____ no
   ____ neither/undecided

6. Efforts to make everyone as equal as possible should be:
   ____ increased
   ____ decreased
   ____ neither/undecided

7. All groups can live in harmony in this country:
____ only if big changes are made in the system
____ without changing the system very much
____ neither/undecided

8. Which of these opinions do you think is more correct?
____ all people would be about the same if they were treated equally
____ like some fine race horses, some classes of people are just naturally better than others
____ neither/undecided

9. In making changes in our society or government, it's usually better to be guided by:
____ a plan that tries out new ideas
____ the practical experience of the past
____ neither/undecided

10. The best way to improve our society is:
____ to follow an overall program or theory
____ to allow changes to develop naturally by themselves
____ neither/undecided

11. Most crime is caused by:
____ poverty and social injustice
____ the bad character of criminals
____ neither/undecided

12. Laws and institutions which have existed for a long time:
____ usually have much wisdom in them
*____ are often too old-fashioned to be useful
____ neither/undecided

13. Public ownership of large industry would be:
____ a good idea
____ a bad idea
____ neither/undecided

14. The way property is used should mainly be decided:
____ by the individuals who own it
*____ by the community, since the earth belongs to everyone
____ neither/undecided

15. When it comes to poverty:
____ we could easily wipe it out if we really tried
____ some people will remain poor no matter what we do for them
____ neither/undecided

16. The profit system:
____ brings out the worst in human nature
____ teaches people the value of hard work and success
____ neither/undecided

17. A person's wage should depend on:
____ the importance of his job
*____ how much he needs to live decently
____ neither/undecided

18. Private ownership of property:
    ____ is as important to a good society as freedom
    *____ has often done more harm than good
    ____ neither/undecided

19. Working people in this country:
    ____ do not get a fair share of what they produce
    ____ usually earn about what they deserve
    ____ neither/undecided

20. Providing medical care for everyone at public expense would:
    ____ greatly improve the health of the nation
    ____ reduce the general quality of medical care
    ____ neither/undecided

21. If some people can't afford good housing:
    ____ the government should provide it
    ____ they should work harder and save, until they can afford it
    ____ neither/undecided

22. Money spent by the government to relieve poverty is:
    ____ mostly a waste
    *____ a worthwhile investment
    ____ neither/undecided

23. Spending tax money to provide a college education for those who can't afford it is:
    ____ a bad idea
    *____ a good idea
    ____ neither/undecided

24. In the matter of jobs and standards of living, the government should:
    ____ see to it that everyone has a job and a decent standard of living
    ____ let each person get ahead on his own
    ____ neither/undecided

25. Who should bear the main responsibility for taking care of our senior citizens?
    ____ the elderly themselves and their families
    ____ the community
    ____ neither/undecided

26. Which of these comes closer to your own opinion?
    ____ no American family should be allowed to live in poverty, even if they don't work
    ____ any person who is able to work should not be allowed to receive welfare
    ____ neither/undecided

Liberal responses are presented first except where indicated by *.

Ideological Agreement
with Goldwater Scale
(G. Selznick & S. Steinberg, 1966)

Variable

This scale was intended to measure agreement with "ideological" tenets of conservative political beliefs expressed by Goldwater in his campaign for the presidency in 1964.

Description

The scale contains five items. Two of them are in Likert format, and the others are answered in a multiple-choice format. One point is added for each item judged to be in agreement with Goldwater. Scores range from 0 to 5.

Sample

A national cross-section of about 2000 respondents was interviewed in the weeks immediately prior to the election of 1964.

Reliability

Internal Consistency

No data are reported.

Test–Retest

No data are reported.

Validity

Convergent

As reported in Robinson, Rusk, and Head (1969), a substantial correlation was found between scale scores and reported vote for Goldwater.

Discriminant

No data are reported.

Location

Selznick, G., & Steinberg, S. (1966). *Class and ideology in the 1964 election: A national survey.* Paper presented at the annual meeting of the American Sociological Association.

Results and Comments

This is a short scale that has been frequently overlooked. The item content suggests that it may remain a useful scale of conservatism. Items have been included in serveral national studies, but not as a battery.

Ideological Agreement with Goldwater Scale (Selznick & Steinberg, 1966)

Instructions: Choose the answer that comes closest to your own opinion.

1. The Federal government is gradually taking away our basic freedoms.
   AGREE
   Disagree
   Don't Know

2. In the past twenty-five years this country has moved dangerously close to Socialism.
   AGREE
   Disagree
   Don't Know

3. Which of these statements comes closest to expressing how you feel about the state of morals in this country at the present time?
   THEY ARE PRETTY BAD AND GETTING WORSE.
   They are pretty bad, but getting better.
   They are pretty good, but getting worse.
   They are pretty good, and getting better.
   Don't Know, or Same as ever.

4. How great a danger do you feel that American communists are to this country at the present time?
   A VERY GREAT DANGER
   A GREAT DANGER
   Some danger
   No danger
   Don't Know

5. Do you feel the United States is losing power in the world, or is it becoming more powerful? [IF LOSING POWER]: How much does this disturb you—a great deal, somewhat, or very little?
   LOSING POWER, DISTURBED A GREAT DEAL
   LOSING POWER, DISTURBED SOMEWHAT
   Losing power and disturbed very little
   Becoming more powerful
   Staying the Same
   Don't Know

Scoring Key: Responses in capital letters are awarded one point each.

New Left Ideology Scale
(A. R. Gold, R. Christie, & L. N. Friedman, 1976)

Variable

This scale is made up of items created for a 1968 study of student activism at Columbia University and for continuing research on authoritarianism and Machiavellianism.

Description

Sixty-two items comprise the *New Left Ideology Scale* (Gold, Christie, & Friedman, 1976). These are marked R+ and R−. Much of the research was conducted with a 90-item inventory reproduced below. The 90-item inventory also provides for the recovery of five sub-scales containing twelve items each. These are New Left Philosophy, Revolutionary Tactics, Traditional Moralism, Machiavellian Cynicism, and Machiavellian Tactics (Christie & Geis, 1970). Scale construction and validation are detailed in the book *Fists and Flowers* (Gold, Christie, & Friedman, 1976).

Hypotheses concerning the process of radicalization were tested on a panel of freshmen who entered Columbia in 1968. According to the model, radicalization proceeds in three stages: Decreased belief in traditional morality is followed by increased cynicism and belief in the political philosophy of the New Left; this results in greater attention to radical tactics and support for broad structural change.

Although the language of some of the items is dated, most of the concepts have retained their meaning, and many are not reflected in other measures of liberalism or conservatism. The New Left Philosophy and Radical Tactics subscales focus on the structure of society and government, attitudes about human nature and participation in governing and decision making, and tactics for achieving change. The Traditional Moralism subscale focuses on attitudes toward order, property, and the status quo and is much broader than the focus on religion and sexual morality factors in traditional measures of conservatism. While the Machiavellian Cynicism and Machiavellian Tactics subscales employ some items from the Mach IV version of the Machiavellianism Scale (Christie & Geis, 1970), they also include new items developed for the study that focus more directly on the political structure.

Responses are obtained in a seven-point format running from *strongly agree* (1) to *strongly disagree* (7), with the midpoint (4) designated as *no opinion*. Responses can be scored for the full 62-item scale or for the five subscales. Items comprising the full New Left Scale are designated with an R in the version of the scale presented here (a − indicates reverse-scored items). Items composing each of the subscales are designated by initials following each item in the original scale. The entire 90-item inventory is presented here in order to provide flexibility in item selection and scoring. Items are ordered, as they were in Robinson and Shaver (1973), according to the descending magnitude of the item's correlation with the original 62-item scale.

A shorter 60-item scale with revised wording has been administered to a number of different samples, but it is not recommended by Gold, Christie, and Friedman (1976, p. 23). A 30-item scale was developed from the revised scale for high school students. They used simplified language that might be appropriate for less sophisticated subjects (see Gold *et al.*, 1976, Appendix B2a).

Sample

In addition to the main Columbia University sample ($N = 122$) and their parents ($N = 165$), the 90-item scale was administered to students at several different types of colleges and universities and to small samples of the Berkeley counterculture ($N = 31$), New York City police ($N = 23$), and construction workers ($N = 20$). A shortened 15-item scale (designated by the letter Y) was administered to a national sample of college students ($N = 747$) conducted by Daniel Yankelovich (see Yankelovich, 1972). Hicks (1974) employed a 50-item version of the scale with a sample of 167 liberal arts college students.

Reliability

Internal Consistency and Test–Retest

Information about statistical reliability was generally reported for the Columbia student sample for the five separate subscales and is presented in the table below. The subscales were constructed from the 12 items with the highest loading on each factor. The alpha reliabilities are from the fall 1968 freshman administration. The test–retest correlations represent an interval of about one year (freshman–sophomore, $N = 122$) (Gold *et al.*, 1976, pp. 15, 24, 114).

	Alpha	Test–Retest
New Left Philosophy	.82	.64
Revolutionary Tactics	.80	.66
Traditional Moralism	.85	.71
Machiavellian Cynicism	.78	.57
Machiavellian Tactics	.73	.54

A split-half reliability of .89 was calculated for a shortened version of the scale consisting of the first 20 items.

Validity

Convergent

Scores on the 62-item New Left Scale were found to be associated with activism and with presidential candidate preference in 1968. In the Columbia University sample, activists with radical candidate preferences generally scored lowest on the Traditional Morality subscale and highest on the New Left Philosophy subscale. They also scored higher than nonactivists and those with traditional and moderately liberal candidate preferences on Machiavellian Cynicism. Construction workers and police officers scored well below the student samples on Traditional Moralism. The Berkeley counterculture sample was the only one to score higher on Revolutionary Tactics than on New Left Philosophy.

Hicks (1974) found a correlation of .39 between the New Left Scale and a conservatism index derived from subjects' preferences for political candidates. Lichter and Rothman (1981–1982) found the New Left Scale discriminated well between selected samples of "New Left participants" and socially active traditional middle Americans. In a study of

Indian political activists, Pandey, Sinha, Prakash, and Tripathi (1982) found a strong relationship among an abridged (24-item) New Left Scale from Robinson and Shaver (1973), political affiliation, and perceived causes of poverty.

Discriminant

Gold, Christie, and Friedman (1976) focused on the relationship between the five subscales and found that the strongest negative relationship existed between Traditional Moralism and Revolutionary Tactics ($-.52$). New Left Philosophy was also negatively related to Traditional Moralism ($-.39$) and Machiavellian Tactics ($-.23$), but positively related to Machiavellian Cynicism (.39). Machiavellian Cynicism was unrelated to Machiavellian Tactics in the sample as a whole, but among activists an interesting distinction was found between the left and the right. While both groups would tend to score in the middle of a combined measure of Machiavellianism, leftists tended to score high on cynicism and low on tactics, while rightists tended to score low on cynicism and high on tactics.

Hicks (1974) found a moderate negative relationship ($r = -.26$) between the New Left Scale and the Lane's (1955) 4-item F scale. Hicks also found a mild positive relationship ($r = .12$) between the New Left Scale and the Comrey and Newmeyer (1965) Radicalism–Conservatism Scale. He further reported that the New Left Scale was unrelated to a 20-item Mach IV version of the Machiavellianism Scale developed in Christie and Geis (1970).

Location

Gold, A. R., Christie, R., & Friedman, L. N. (1976). *Fists and flowers: A social psychological interpretation of student dissent.* New York: Academic Press (pp. 167–173).

Results and Comments

A number of values and attitudes measured by the New Left Scale, particularly those in the New Left Philosophy and Revolutionary Tactics subscales, are not adequately addressed in the other scales reviewed in this volume. They remain relevant, albeit perhaps to a smaller share of the contemporary public.

The items comprising the original New Left Scale have been adopted in different ways by a number of different researchers, and the exact items employed are not always carefully reported. While the Gold *et al.* (1976) book provided a substantial amount of validating information, this is generally not the case with subsequent uses of the scale. For example, no information about the validity or reliability of the 15 items selected for the CBS–Yankelovich survey (Yankelovich, 1972) appears to be available to check whether it is the best shortened version of the scale.

Robinson and Shaver (1973) suggested that the first 10 or 20 items of the 62-item New Left Scale might be sufficient for most purposes. While it is true that these are the items with the highest part–whole correlation with the original 90-item scale, they underrepresent the New Left Philosophy and Revolutionary Tactics items, which are the main focus of the book. Moreover, the 12 items making up the New Left Philosophy subscale are all worded in a positive direction, making them prone to acquiescence response set in less sophisticated samples. Despite these difficulties the work of Gold, Christie, and Friedman (1976) represents a firm foundation for the investigation of leftist radicalism should it ever reemerge as an important element in American political life.

New Left Scale
(Gold, Christie, & Friedman, 1976)

Instructions: Circle only one alternative for each item on your answer sheet. Listed below are a number of statements. We have collected them from a variety of sources and there are no right or wrong answers. You will probably disagree with some items and agree with others. We are interested in the extent to which you agree or disagree with such matters of opinion.

Read each statement carefully. Then indicate the extent to which you agree or disagree by circling the corresponding alternative on your answer sheet.

The number of the alternatives and their meanings are:

If you disagree strongly	circle 1
If you disagree somewhat	circle 2
If you disagree slightly	circle 3
If you have no opinion	circle 4
If you agree slightly	circle 5
If you agree somewhat	circle 6
If you agree strongly	circle 7

First impressions are usually best in such matters. Read each statement, decide if you agree or disagree and the strength of your opinion, and then circle the appropriate alternative on the answer sheet. Read the items carefully, but work as rapidly as you can. Give your opinion on every statement. If you find that the numbers to be used in answering do not adequately indicate your own opinion, use the one that is closest to the way you feel.

1. The "Establishment" unfairly controls every aspect of our lives, we can never be free until we are rid of it. (R+, NL, Y)[1]

1	2	3	4	5	6	7

2. You can never achieve freedom within the framework of contemporary American Society. (R+, MC)

3. The United States needs a complete restructuring of its basic institutions. (R+, NL)

4. A mass revolutionary party should be created. (R+, RT, Y6)

5. Authorities must be put in an intolerable position so they will be forced to respond with repression and thus show their illegitimacy. (R+, RT, Y)

6. The solutions for contemporary problems lie in striking at their roots, no matter how much destruction might occur. (R+, TM−)

7. Disruption is preferable to dialogue for changing our society. (R+, RT, Y)

8. Even though institutions have worked well in the past, they must be destroyed if they are not effective now. (R+, TM−)

9. The structure of our society is such that self-alienation is inevitable. (R+, NL)

10. Sexual behavior should be bound by mutual feelings, not by formal and legal ties. (R+, Y)

[1]See scoring key at the end of this scale presentation.

11. A problem with most older people is that they have learned to accept society as it is, not as it should be. (R+, TM−)

12. The bureaucracy of American society makes it impossible to live and work spontaneously. (R+, MC)

13. Radicals of the left are as much a threat to the rights of the individual as are the radicals of the right. (R−, RT−, Y)

14. While man has great potential for good, society brings out primarily the worst in him. (R+, NL, Y)

15. The processes of rebuilding society are of less immediate importance than the processes of destroying it. (R+, Y)

16. The political structure of the Soviet Union is more like that of the United States than that of Red China. (R+)

17. The streets are a more appropriate medium for change in our society than printing presses. (R+)

18. Competition encourages excellence. (R−, MT, Y)

19. Marriage unfairly restricts one's personal freedom. (R+)

20. The right to private property is sacred. (R−, TM, Y)

21. Most people in government are not really interested in the problems of the average man. (AN+, MC)

22. No one should be punished for violating a law which he feels is immoral. (R+)

23. If it weren't for the rebellious ideas of youth there would be less progress in the world. (TM−)

24. The courts are a useful vehicle for responsible change. (R−, RT−)

25. There are legitimate channels for reform which must be exhausted before attempting disruption. (R−, RT−, Y)

26. You learn more from 10 minutes in a political protest than 10 hours of research in a library. (R+, NL)

27. Although our society has to be changed, violence is not a justified means. (R−, RT−)

28. Society needs some legally based authority in order to prevent chaos. (R−, Y)

29. Representative democracy can respond effectively to the needs of the people. (R−, MC−, Y)

30. Police should not hesitate to use force to maintain order. (R−, TM)

31. Real participatory democracy should be the basis for a new society. (R+, NL)

32. If people worked hard at their jobs, they would reap the full benefits of our society. (R−, TM)

33. Groups with a formal structure tend to stifle creativity among their members. (R+, NL)

34. A social scientist should not separate his political responsibilities from his professional role. (R+, NL)

35. People should not do research which can be used in ways which are contrary to the social good. (R+, NL)

36. Abrupt reforms in society usually lead to such a severe backlash that they will be self-defeating. (R−)

37. People ought to pay more attention to new ideas, even if they seem to go against the American way of life. (TM−)

38. Traditions serve a useful social function by providing stability and continuity. (R−)

39. The very existence of our long-standing social norms demonstrates their value. (R−, TM)

40. If the structure of our society becomes nonrepressive, people will be happy. (R+, NL)

41. The distinction between public and private life is unnecessary. (R+)

42. Most people don't realize how much our lives are controlled by plots hatched in secret places. (AN+, MC)

43. Compromise is essential for progress. (R−, RT−, Y)

44. Extensive reform in society only serves to perpetuate the evils; it will never solve problems. (R+, RT)

45. Voting must be a pragmatic rather than moral decision. (R−, MT)

46. Anyone who violates the law for reasons of conscience should be willing to accept the legal consequences. (R−, RT−)

47. It is possible to modify our institutions so that the blacks can be incorporated on an equal basis into our contemporary society. (R−, MC−)

48. If you try hard enough, you can usually get what you want. (DT−, MT)

49. Although men are intrinsically good, they have developed institutions which force them to act in opposition to their basic nature. (R+, NL)

50. Educational institutions should espouse political doctrines. (R+)

51. The biggest difference between most criminals and other people is that criminals are stupid enough to get caught. (AN+)

52. Every person should have complete faith in a supernatural power whose decisions he obeys without question. (TM+)

53. The findings of science may some day show that many of our most cherished beliefs are wrong. (TM−)

54. People suffering from incurable diseases should have the choice of being put painlessly to death. (TM−)

55. Change in our society should be based primarily on popular elections. (R−, RT−)

56. A minority must never be allowed to impose its will on a majority. (R−, Y10)

57. Spontaneity is often an excuse for irresponsibility. (R−)

58. An individual can find his true identity only by detaching himself from formal ideologies. (R+, MC)

59. When you ask someone to do something for you, it is best to give the real reasons for wanting it rather than giving reasons which carry more weight. (DP−, MT)

60. Books and movies ought to give a more realistic picture of life even if they show that evil sometimes triumphs over good. (TM−)

61. Being put in positions of leadership brings out the best in men. (R−, MC−)

62. Most people can still be depended on to come through in a pinch. (DT−, MC−)

63. Political factions cannot cooperate with each other without sacrificing their integrity. (R+)

64. It is more important that people be involved in the present rather than concerned with the past or the future. (R+, MT)

65. Most people who get ahead in the world lead clean, moral lives. (DT−, TM)

66. No sane, normal, decent person could even think of hurting a close friend or relative. (DT+)

67. A commitment to action is more socially relevant than a commitment to any specific philosophy. (R+)

68. Commitment to a meaningful career is a very important part of a man's life. (R−)

69. One's personal life can be kept separate from one's political life. (R−)

70. It is wise to flatter important people. (DP+, MT)

71. A group without a clear-cut pattern of leadership cannot function effectively. (R−)

72. All in all, it is better to be humble and honest than to be important and dishonest. (DP−, MT)

73. Next to health, money is the most important thing in life. (DP+, MT)

74. Freedom of expression should be denied to racist and neofascistic movements. (R+, MC)

75. Provocation of the police should only be a byproduct, not a goal, of mass action. (R−)

76. A liberal society is more conducive to revolutionary change than is a fascistic one. (R−)

77. We must strive for the democratization of decision-making bodies within the existing government. (R−, RT)

78. Most people will go out of their way to help someone else. (DT−, MC−)

79. Anyone who completely trusts anyone else is asking for trouble. (AN+, MT)

80. The only way to combat violence is to use violent means. (R+)

81. Honesty is the best policy in all cases. (DP−)

82. Most men are brave. (DT−)

83. Most people are basically good and kind. (DT−, MC)

84. You should always be candid with your friends even though you may hurt their feelings. (R+)

85. Most honest people admit to themselves that they have sometimes hated their parents. (TM−)

86. Most of our social problems could be solved if we could somehow get rid of the immoral, crooked, and feeble-minded people. (AN+, MT)

87. The best way to handle people is to tell them what they want to hear. (DP+, MT)

88. There is no excuse for lying to someone else. (DP−)

89. Generally speaking, men won't work hard unless they're forced to do so. (AN+)

90. It is safest to assume that all people have a vicious streak and it will come out when they are given a chance. (AN+, MT)

Scoring Key: The following code has been used to indicate the scale from which the item was originally taken:

R = New Left	DT = Distrust of People
AN = Affirmative–Negative	TM = Traditional Moralism
DP = Duplicity (Machiavellian Tactics)	

The last four scales were taken from the FacMac Scale (Christie & Lehmann, 1970).
     The signs following each letter indicate the direction of scoring:

R+ = an agree response scored high; R− = a disagree response scored high

Letters indicate the subscale in which the item was validated:

NL = New Left Philosophy	RT = Revolutionary Tactics
TM = Traditional Moralism	MC = Machiavellian Cynicism
MT = Machiavellian Tactics	

Y designates items used in the 1992 CBS–Yankelovich national survey.

Radicalism–Conservatism Scale

(A. L. Comrey & J. A. Newmeyer, 1965)

Variable

Through the application of the factored homogeneous-item-dimension approach, Comrey and Newmeyer developed two forms of a 30-item sociopolitical attitude statement scale.

Description

A pool of 120 items was initially examined. Subjects indicated their degree of agreement with each item on a nine-point Likert scale ranging from *agree very strongly* (1) to *disagree very strongly* (9). Factor analysis revealed nine first-order factors that resolved into five second-order factors: (1) welfare-state attitudes, (2) punitive attitudes, (3) nationalism, (4) religious attitudes, and (5) racial tolerance attitudes. Sixty-seven items from the original 120 items loaded on these primary second-order factors, which together were designated *radicalism–conservatism.*

     Two parallel forms (A and B) were then constructed from these 67 items; each form contains 30 items using the same nine-point Likert scale. After appropriate reversals, scores range from 30 to 270, with higher scores indicating more radical positions. The average scores obtained were 159.0 (s.d. = 41.3) for Form A and 158.4 (s.d. = 41.8) for Form B. The distribution of scores was reported as approximately normal around these means.

Sample

The sample consisted of 212 volunteers recruited from universities, organizations, and randomly selected blocks in Los Angeles. A third of the sample was composed of females. The median age was 29, and the median education was 15 years. Republicans and Democrats were approximately equally represented. Fewer than 10% were categorized by the original authors as possessing "extreme" political beliefs.

Reliability

Internal Consistency

A correlation of .96 between Forms A and B was reported.

Test–Retest

No data are reported.

Validity

Convergent

Hicks (1974) reported a correlation of .46 for Form A of the Radicalism–Conservatism Scale and a conservatism index developed from subjects' preferences for political candidates and parties.

Discriminant

No data are reported.

Location

Comrey, A. L., & Newmeyer, J. A. (1965). Measurement of radicalism–conservatism. *Journal of Social Psychology, 67,* 357–369. Reprinted with permission of the Helen Dwight Reid Educational Foundation. Published by Heldref Publications, 1319 Eighteenth St., N.W., Washington, D.C. 20036-1802. Copyright © 1965.

Results and Comments

Both the length and the datedness of some items limit the usefulness of the full versions of the scale as measures of liberalism–conservatism. Levenson and Miller (1974, 1976) adopted some of the items in their scale development, and Emihovich and Gaier (1983) employed Form A in a study of ideology among adolescents. Guy and Norvell (1977) examined the impact of not having a neutral point on the response format for this scale. They found that the frequency of nonresponse increased when the neutral position was omitted and that subjects who had previously taken the equivalent form of the instrument with a neutral response option used the extreme points of the response scale less frequently.

Radicalism–Conservatism Scale
(Comrey & Newmeyer, 1965)

Form A

(Religiosity)

1. Every child should have religious instruction.
2. God exists, in the form in which the Bible describes him.
3. This country would be better off if religion had a greater influence in daily life.
4. All people alive today are the descendants of Adam and Eve.

(Pacifism)

*5. This country should disarm regardless of whether or not other countries do.

*6. If my country had been destroyed, I still would not push the button to wipe out the attacking enemy nation.

7. Our country should be engaged constantly in research to develop superior weapons for our national defense.

(Welfarism)

*8. The average man today is getting less than his rightful share of our national wealth.

*9. The government should guarantee every citizen enough to eat.

(Anti-Unionism)

10. Many large unions have officers with criminal records.
11. Most unions do not elect officers by honest, secret ballot elections.

(Weak Federal Government)

12. Central Government should run only those things which cannot be run effectively at the local level.
13. The federal government has too much power over citizens and local government.
14. Greater decentralization of power would be better for this country.
15. A greater degree of government control over business would result in a weakening of this country's economy.

(Moral Censorship)

16. If a man is showing a sex movie to friends in his own home, the police should stop it.
17. Every city should prevent the sale of objectionable books.
18. Sexual relations between unmarried people should be illegal.
19. The police should hunt down homosexuals and put them in jail.

(Contraception)

*20. Abortion should be legalized.

(Racial Tolerance)

*21. Employers should be prevented by law from hiring only people of their own race.

(Severe Treatment of Criminals)

22. Criminals convicted of three separate felonies should never be released.

23. In our country, the sentences handed out to criminals are usually too light.

(Capital Punishment)

24. A mentally ill man who attacks and kills a little girl should be executed.

25. A gunman who kills someone in an armed robbery should receive the death sentence.

(Service to Country)

26. Every able male should willingly serve for a period of time in his country's military service.

27. A man who is ready to die for his country deserves the highest honor.

(World Government)

*28. The United States should work peacefully for a strong world government.

*29. The United States should be willing to surrender some of its rights to strengthen the United Nations.

(Service to the Individual)

*30. Laws which benefit the people are more important than laws which strengthen the nation.

Form B

(Religiosity)

1. School teachers should believe in God.

2. It should be against the law to do anything which the Bible says is wrong.

3. Moses got the ten commandments directly from God.

4. All the miracles described in the Bible really happened.

(Pacifism)

*5. Under no circumstances should our country use nuclear bombs against anybody.

*6. I would rather have a foreign power take over our country than start another world war to stop it.

7. Our country should prepare to employ every available weapon to destroy any major power that seriously attacks us.

(Welfarism)

*8. It is the responsibility of the government to take care of people who can't take care of themselves.

*9. If the government must go deeper in debt to help people, it should do so.

(Anti-Unionism)

10. Most unions try to prevent the efficient use of labor.

11. Many union leaders use threats and violence to keep themselves in power.

(Weak Federal Government)

12. The federal government should not interfere in the affairs of individual states unless absolutely necessary.

13. The strength of this country today is largely a product of the free enterprise system.

14. Regulation of business by government usually does more harm than good.

15. When something is run by the government, it is apt to be inefficient and wasteful.

(Moral Censorship)

16. Motion pictures which offend any sizeable religious group should be banned.

17. Public libraries should contain only books which are morally sound.

18. A woman who has sexual relations with a man for money should go to jail.

19. More restrictions should be imposed to prevent young people from having sexual relations before marriage.

(Contraception)

*20. Birth control devices should be made readily available to anyone who wants to use them.

(Racial Tolerance)

*21. Marriages between persons of different races should be socially acceptable.

(Severe Treatment of Criminals)

22. Teenage hoodlums should be punished severely.

23. Our laws give too much protection to criminals.

(Capital Punishment)

24. A dictator who orders the extermination of thousands of innocent people should be executed for his crimes.

25. Someone who plans and carries out the murder of his or her spouse should be executed.

(Service to Country)

26. If called upon to do so, a citizen should be willing to sacrifice his life for his country.

27. Patriotism is one of the great virtues.

(World Government)

*28. The United States eventually should give up its military power to a strong world government.

*29. Present nations should become states within an all powerful world Government.

(Service to the Individual)

*30. The welfare of the individual is more important than the welfare of the country.

*Indicates reverse scored items.

Moral Traditionalism Scale
(P. J. Conover & S. Feldman, 1985)

Variable

This eight-item balanced scale was designed to measure support for traditional moral and social values separately from other aspects of conservatism.

Description

The traditional moralism items focus on individuals' tolerance of modern moral standards and their evaluations of the impact of changing mores on society. The items focus on sexual freedom, cohabitation, divorce, and traditional family ties. They are phrased directly, but without explicit mention of hot issues, like abortion and homosexuality. Several evaluations are phrased in terms of the contribution of the "new morality" to social and national decline, but no explicit policy action (e.g., outlaw) is implied. The four best items were retained in the 1988 ANES. Responses are obtained in a five-point agree–disagree format, which can be summed after appropriate reverse scoring.

Sample

The original sample consisted of a random national sample of 306 respondents reinterviewed as part of the 1985 ANES Pilot Study.

Reliability

Internal Consistency

An alpha reliability of .74 was reported for the 1985 sample.

Test–Retest

No data are reported.

Validity

Convergent

Scores on traditional morality were found to contribute to evaluations of social groups identified with the new morality (e.g., homosexuals, feminists) and to evaluations of policy and candidates. These effects were generally larger than those for ideological self-identification.

Discriminant

Effects of religious beliefs and moral traditionalism varied across social groups and policy areas, suggesting that the two constructs reflect independent influences.

Location

Center for Political Studies. (1985). *Codebook for American National Elections Study: Pilot Study; Codebook for American National Election Study* 1988–1996.

Results and Comments

This scale was constructed as part of an examination of the Religious Right in American politics (Conover & Feldman, 1985). The underlying construct is defined as moral *traditionalism* rather than conservatism per se, but it is viewed as a central component of conservatism. Items were phrased in general language rather than incorporating specific references to political issues, allowing the scale to be used as an independent predictor of public policy preferences.

Moral Traditionalism Scale
(Conover & Feldman, 1985)

*1. We should be more tolerant of people who choose to live according to their own moral standards, even if they are different from our own. (A)

1	2	3	4	5
STRONGLY AGREE				STRONGLY DISAGREE

2. There is too much sexual freedom and loose living today.

3. Changes in lifestyles, such as divorce and men and women living together without being married, are signs of increasing moral decay.

4. The newer lifestyles are contributing to the breakdown of our society. (A)

*5. The world is always changing, and we should accommodate our view of moral behavior to those changes. (A)

*6. There will always be some people who think and act differently, and there is nothing wrong with that.

*7. Society should be more accepting of people whose appearance or values are very different from most.

8. This country would be better off if there were more emphasis on traditional family ties. (A)

*Indicates reverse scored items.
Items retained in the 1988 American National Election Study are indicated with an A.

Moral Conservatism Scale

(K. D. Wald, D. E. Owen, & S. S. Hill, 1988)

Variable

This is a balanced 10-item scale designed to measure the moral aspect of liberal and conservative sentiments.

Description

The Moral Conservatism Scale taps individuals' preferences on public issues containing an underlying moral tone: abortion, cohabitation, homosexuality, traditional sex roles, censorship, birth control, family, drug use, and racial intermarriage. For each item, respondents are to indicate their degree of agreement or disagreement on a five-point Likert scale. After appropriate reverse scoring, a higher score indicates a higher degree of moral conservatism.

Sample

Respondents included 657 males and females from 21 different Protestant churches in the Gainesville, Florida, metropolitan area. No other demographic information is provided.

Reliability

Internal Consistency

An alpha reliability coefficient of .80 was obtained.

Test–Retest

No data are reported.

Validity

Convergent

Scores on the Moral Conservatism Scale were found to contribute significantly to individual self-identification as a political conservative.

Discriminant

No data are reported.

Location

Wald, K. E., Owen, D. E., & Hill, S. S., Jr. (1988). Churches as political communities. *American Political Science Review, 82,* 531–548.

Results and Comments

The study for which the scale was developed was primarily concerned with testing hypotheses about the influence of denominational context on religious and political attitudes.

The moral conservatism items focus on a range of lifestyle issues of particular interest to the Religious Right, but none is explicitly religious in content. A small number of the items also imply government intervention. Further validation is needed, but the scale may be of use to those interested in a finer-grained measurement of moral conservatism.

Moral Conservatism Scale
(Wald, Owen, & Hill, 1988)

1. Local governments should be allowed to ban books and movies that they think are harmful to the public.

1	2	3	4	5
STRONGLY AGREE				STRONGLY DISAGREE

*2. Birth control devices should be available to any adult who wants them.

*3. Men and women should have the same legal rights.

4. There are too many shows on television that make fun of traditional family values.

5. Women are happiest if they stick to keeping a home and raising children.

6. There should be laws against marriage between blacks and whites.

*7. Abortion should be a private matter between a woman and her doctor.

8. The government should prohibit the private use of marijuana.

*9. Homosexuals should be able to do what they want to so long as they don't hurt other people.

*10. If a man and a woman want to live together without getting married, that's their business.

*Indicates reverse scored items.

Moral Conservatism Index
(E. Woodrum, 1988)

Variable

This five-item index was constructed to ascertain agreement with conservative stands on contemporary issues with moral implications.

Description

The scale consists of statements written to represent traditional, morally conservative stances on abortion, pornography, prayer in the schools, homosexuality, and sexual relationships outside of marriage. Respondents indicate their degree of agreement on a five-point Likert scale, with higher scores (maximum = 25) indicating greater endorsement of a morally conservative world view. Information pertaining to the selection and construction of these statements was not reported.

Sample

A probability sample of 378 male and female adults living in Raleigh, North Carolina, was selected on the basis of 1980 census tract data and stratified by education.

Reliability

Internal Consistency

A Cronbach's alpha coefficient of .81 was reported.

Test–Retest

No data are reported.

Validity

Convergent

As hypothesized, respondents who were less educated, were older, and belonged to conservative religious denominations scored the highest on this index. A correlation of .38 was reported between moral conservatism and ideological self-identification.

Discriminant

No data are reported.

Location

Woodrum, E. (1988). Moral conservatism and the 1984 presidential election. *Journal for the Scientific Study of Religion, 27*, 192–210.

Results and Comments

This scale focuses on the major political issues of interest to the Religious Right, with explicit focus on the role of government in the enforcement of traditional values. Because none of the items is written in the negative direction, the scale may be subject to agreement response set bias.

Moral Conservatism Index
(Woodrum, 1988)

1. Abortion should be outlawed except for rape, incest, or threat to the mother's life.

1	2	3	4	5
STRONGLY AGREE				STRONGLY DISAGREE

2. Pornography is harmful and should be outlawed.

3. Organized prayer should be a regular part of public school activities.

4. Homosexuality is immoral and should be prosecuted by law.

5. Sexual relationships outside marriage are immoral.

Acknowledgments

Research for this chapter was partially supported by the Division of Humanities and Social Sciences, California Institute of Technology, and by the Limited Grants in Aid Program of the University of Houston. Special thanks are due to Heather Kellert Cecil for her care with the bibliographic search and preliminary reviews, and to Christopher J. Carman for updates of data. Errors remain the responsibility of the author.

Appendix: Ideological Trends from General Social Survey Items

(John P. Robinson)

It is widely accepted that life in America has become more conservative over the last three decades. But how exactly have the beliefs and lifestyles of the American public become more conservative in the last third of the 20th century?

The answer is not as simple as the question. On one hand, we have seen more conservative political candidates elected to the White House and Congress, beginning on the coattails of Ronald Reagan's victories in 1980 and 1984. That mood seemed to gain renewed strength with many conservative causes elevated to prominence with the 1994 election of Republicans to Congress and their famous Contract with America. These congressmen continue to push their conservative views, with reducing benefits for welfare recipients, reducing government controls on business, and eliminating the National Endowment for the Arts high on their political agenda.

While future historians may consider this part of a continuous shift to the right in American politics since the 1960s, the evidence from opinion surveys has been far less conclusive. While social surveys rarely yield simple answers to simple questions, the empirical evidence becomes especially murky on matters of political ideology and beliefs.

Public opinion research offers a wealth of apparent contradictions and exceptions to the convenient lines of debate offered by political elites:

- After reviewing extensive public opinion data on political issues in the 1960s, pollster Louis Harris described what he referred to as "Karl Marx upside down." He found resistance to new ideas and social changes among the working classes, who might expect to benefit most from them; he also found more tolerance of minorities, greater support of foreign aid and other internationalist polices, and more support of social welfare policies among supposedly more conservative businessmen than among working-class Americans.
- In their book *The Political Beliefs of Americans*, Free and Cantril (1968) described the public as basically conservative on abstract issues (government regulation of business, private property) but liberal on specific government programs and policies (Medicare, Social Security, and urban renewal).

- As noted in this chapter, educational psychologists Fred Kerlinger and E. J. Ped-hazur have conducted several studies over the last three decades in which endorsement of a liberal stand on one item did not guarantee rejection of a conservative stand on another issue. Many people scored just as high (or low) on the liberal scale as they did on the conservative scale.
- Political scientist Everett Ladd has noted that on many issues there were greater differences among conservatives (particularly between grade-school- and college-educated conservatives) than between liberals and conservatives.

The varied findings suggest the myriad problems that await those who would look to survey data for simple answers and trends about the public's political beliefs. The General Social Survey (GSS) of the University of Chicago's National Opinion Research Center, for example, provides the following evidence of movement in a consistently *conservative* direction over the last quarter century:

1. While 64% of the public favored capital punishment for murderers in 1975, 72% favored it in 1980 and up to 78% in the 1990s.
2. In 1972, 74% of the public said that courts were not harsh enough with criminals; that figure rose to the 85–89% range in the mid-1980s survey, where it stands today.
3. In 1973, 56% agreed that pornography leads to a breakdown in morals; in 1984, 65% did, which is about where it is currently; those favoring laws outlawing the sale of pornography to teenagers increased from 47% in the 1970s to 60% in the 1990s.

On the other hand, the 1990s have also seen a rebound of opinion toward the *liberal* direction after *conservative gains* in the 1980s.

1. Some 65% of Americans in 1994 felt their federal income taxes were too high—down from 73% in 1982 but up from 60% in 1976 and 58% in 1991.
2. In 1974, 44% felt that divorce should be more difficult to obtain; by 1994, 49% felt that way—down from 56% in 1985.
3. In 1973, 44% believed that Communism was the worst form of government, and 61% did in 1984, but in the 1990s, after the Berlin wall torn down, the figure had fallen to around 50%.

Over the same period, however, GSS data show just as much evidence of movement in a *liberal* direction:

1. *Racial issues:* 25% of whites in 1972 rejected the assertion that "Blacks shouldn't push themselves where they're not wanted"; in 1982 that figure rose to 39% and in 1994 to 55%; only about one in five favored school busing for racial integration in the 1970s, compared to one in three currently.
2. *Sexual issues:* For example, in 1972, 37% said premarital sex relations were "always wrong"; in 1983, 27% said that, which is about where it is in the 1990s. Similarly, those saying that birth control information should be available to teenagers rose from 80% in 1974 to 87% in 1983; no change in these attitudes has been found over the last decade.
3. *Gender issues:* Those saying that they would vote for a woman for president rose from 74% in 1972 to 87% in 1983 to 92% in 1994. Proportions saying women should only run their homes and let men run the country drooped from 38% in 1977 to 14% in 1994.
4. *Life and death issues:* Approval of euthanasia when a person has an incurable disease went from 39% in 1977 to 46% in 1984 and 65% in 1994; proportions

approving abortion for any reason rose from 35% in 1977–1978 to 46% in 1994.

5. *Tolerance issues:* In 1972 some 45% of GSS respondents felt that a book written by an admitted Communist should be removed from a public library; by the 1990s that proportion had gradually shrunk to 31%; those favoring removing a book by someone advocating military rule of the United States similarly dropped from 40% in 1976 to around 30% in the 1990s.

Two other GSS questions on ideology, however, have shown relatively little liberal movement over the years. One is approval of marijuana use, which at 24% in 1994 is 6 points higher than the 18% in the mid-1980s, but below the 30% in the 1967–1978 surveys. The other is personal adherence to strict literal interpretation of the Bible, which has dropped, but only slightly, from 37% in the early 1970s to about 33% in the mid-1990s.

The Effect of Education

Demographic changes help explain much of the more liberal "climate" of opinion. The major predictor of liberal attitudes over the years, particularly on questions of tolerance, has been the respondent's level of education. In general, the more educated the respondent, the more tolerant his or her attitudes, and the average level of education over the years has been rising steadily. In 1960, 17% of the adult population had had a college education; in 1994, that figure was 52%.

The rising level of education among the public, then, helps explain part of this complicated picture—their greater tolerance of homosexuals, of changing roles for women, and of minority rights, for example. But it does not explain the political emergence of such conservative concerns as escalating taxes, the increasing role of government bureaucracy, diminished respect for marriage and the family, and a lack of adequate punishment for lawbreakers.

The lack of clear-cut ideological trends does not mean that public liberals and public conservatives are virtually indistinguishable on the issues. People who describe themselves as conservatives do differ from those who describe themselves as liberal on most of the political questions the GSS asks, with self-identified conservatives usually taking what is thought of as the more conservative stand. Thus conservatives are more opposed to abortion under a variety of circumstances, to racial integration, to the United Nations, to government spending on social programs, to atheist and homosexual rights, to pornography, to legalized marijuana, to Communist governments, and to abolition of the death penalty.

Nonetheless, on many of these issues the differences between liberals and conservatives are surprisingly small. On the abortion questions mentioned above, for example, self-identified conservatives are only 10 to 15 percentage points more opposed than are self-identified liberals. Moreover, on other subjects that are considered litmus tests for one ideological camp or the other—gun control and high taxes, for instance—there is virtually no difference between liberals and conservatives.

These differences are arrayed in Table 3–4, which gives the range of correlations that reflect how much self-identified conservatives differ from liberals on several matters. The table also reveals the issues that *most* distinguish conservatives from liberals, even though few of these differences are very dramatic. The most ideological concerns turn out to be "lifestyle" matters, such as the Equal Rights Amendment, legalized marijuana, sex outside marriage, and affinity toward modern art and high culture.

Indeed, the single issue in the GSS battery that most sharply separates liberals from conservatives, at the bottom of Table 3–4, is the propriety of extramarital sexual

Table 3-4
What Separates Conservatives from Liberals?

On these issues, the difference between conservatives and liberals is	Tolerance	Social controls	Traditions/Morals	Government/Spending	Foreign affairs
.05–.09		Approve police striking vulgar male Courts not harsh enough with criminals Oppose police permit before buying gun	Divorce should be more difficult to obtain Person has right to end own life Not vote for black president	Federal income tax too high	U.S. should stay out of world affairs
.10–.14	Oppose racial busing	Approve of wire-tapping	Oppose legal abortion Birth control information should not be available to teenagers Would not vote for female presidential candidate Disapprove of married woman working if husband is employed Attend religious services frequently Disapprove of Supreme Court ruling on prayer in public schools	Government should not reduce income differences between rich and poor	Dislike Russia and dislike China Pull out of United Nations

.15–.19	Approve laws against interracial marriage Whites have right to exclude blacks from their neighborhoods Don't allow atheist to speak in community Don't allow Communist to speak in community Don't allow homosexual to speak in community	Favor death penalty for murderers	Should be laws against pornography	Country spends too much on Improving environ-ment Improving health Improving education Solving urban prob-lems Improving conditions of blacks Welfare	Communism is worst form of government Country spends too little on defense
.20+	Cultural cosmopolitan-ism		Oppose Equal Rights Amendment Don't legalize marijuana Wrong to have sex before marriage Wrong to have extra-marital sex Wrong to have homo-sexual sex		

relations—an issue that is almost completely outside the political arena and least subject to political control. Differences between liberals and conservatives on this issue are about 25 percentage points. This suggests that for the public the scale is more of a *"libertine-conservative"* scale than one following the classical liberal versus conservative lines of debate.

Thus it is moral issues rather than political ones that most divide the ideological extremes in the mass public. This holds true even though moral issues are rarely mentioned in open-ended responses the public describes as distinguishing liberals from conservatives. In their open-ended definitions of what separates them, self-identified liberals emphasize broader concerns about social change and social justice, while conservatives most often worry about the threat of big government to free enterprise.

Party and Ideology

Adding to our confusion about movement in one philosophical direction or the other is the role of party identification and its effect on ideology. Some political observers have all but dismissed the importance of the issues and ideological differences described above. But they overlook one significant aspect: ideology does a far better job of distinguishing the public's political beliefs than party affiliation does. For example, in some cases people who label themselves Democrats take far more conservative stands than do those who label themselves Republicans. On other issues, mainly social welfare matters, Democrats take more liberal stands. But even these differences are not as clear or as consistent as those found in Table 3–4.

We can look again at education for a partial explanation. Republicans, on the whole, average a few more years of formal education than Democrats do; this leads them to more liberal, or tolerant, attitudes on many issues. It is for that reason that political observers face such a difficult task in attempting to describe electoral outcomes in simple ideological, partisan, or issue terms. Education, partisanship, and ideology are so intricately interconnected that they defy easy explanation.

At the same time, that is not to deny the significant correlation between party affiliation and ideological identification that exists. More Republicans than Democrats identify themselves as conservatives, and more Democrats identify themselves as liberals. In this one area, party affiliation does relate to political beliefs as expected.

Both ideology and party identification also relate to the most crucial political variable, how people vote in presidential elections. Party is the more important predictor, but ideology remains an important predictor in its own right. Moreover, there is one important area not included in Table 3–4 that might put more ideological meaning into mass politics. The GSS has repeated four questions that had been asked in 1975 about an expanded role for the federal government (versus more individual responsibility) in social programs; support has been down about 10 percentage points on each item since 1983. There has been no movement back to the liberal direction on these items over the last decade.

References

Adorno, T. W., Frenkel-Brunswick, E., Levinson, D. J., & Sanford, R. N. (1950). *The authoritarian personality.* New York: Harper and Row.

Alker, H. A., & Poppen, P. J. (1973). Personality and ideology in university students. *Journal of Personality, 41,* 653–671.

Altemeyer, B. (1981). *Right-wing authoritarianism.* Winnipeg: University of Manitoba Press.

Altemeyer, B. (1988). *Enemies of freedom.* San Francisco: Jossey-Bass.

Altemeyer, B. (1990, July). *The mirror image in U.S.–Soviet perceptions.* Paper presented at the annual convention of the International Society of Political Psychology.

Altemeyer, B. (1996). *The authoritarian specter.* Cambridge, MA: Harvard University Press.

Altemeyer, B., & Hunsberger, B. (1993). Religion and prejudice: Lessons not learned from the past: Reply to Gorsuch. *International Journal for the Psychology of Religion, 3,* 33–37.

Baggaley, A. (1976). Countercultural and opposing values at a two-year college. *Multivariate Experimental Clinical Research, 2,* 57–62.

Bagley, C. R. (1970). Racial prejudice and the conservative personality. *Political Studies, 18,* 134–141.

Bagley, C. R., Wilson, G. D., & Boshier, R. (1970). The Conservatism Scale: A factor-structure comparison of English, Dutch, and New Zealand samples. *Journal of Social Psychology, 81,* 267–268.

Bahr, H. M., & Chadwick, B. A. (1974). Conservatism, racial intolerance, and attitudes towards racial assimilation among whites and American Indians. *Journal of Social Psychology, 94,* 45–56.

Barton, A. H., & Parsons, R. W. (1977). Measuring belief system structure. *Public Opinion Quarterly, 41,* 159–180.

Becona, E. (1985). Relations among conservatism scales. *Journal of Social Psychology, 125,* 795–796.

Bell, D. (1960). *The end of ideology.* New York: Free Press.

Billings, S. W., Guastello, S. J., & Rieke, M. L. (1993). A comparative assessment of the construct validity of three authoritarianism measures. *Journal of Research in Personality, 27,* 328–348.

Birenbaum, M., & Zak, I. (1982). Contradictory or complementary? Reassessment of two competing theories of the structure of attitudes. *Multivariate Behavioral Research, 17,* 503–514.

Block, J. H. (1973). Conceptions of sex role: Some cross-cultural and longitudinal perspectives. *American Psychologist, 28,* 512–526.

Boshier, R. (1974). To rotate or not to rotate: The question of the Conservatism Scale. *British Journal of Social and Clinical Psychology, 11,* 313–323.

Box-Steffensmeier, J., Knight, K., & Sigelman, L. (1998). The interplay of macropartisanship and macroideology. *Journal of Politics,* (in press).

Box-Steffensmeier, J. M., & DeBoef, S. (1997). *Political sophistication and the relationship between ideological and partisan trends.* Presented at the Annual Meeting of the Midwest Political Science Association, Chicago, IL.

Braithwaite, V. A., & Scott, W. A. (1991). Values. In J. P. Robinson, P. R. Shaver, & L. S. Wrightsman. (Eds.), *Measures of personality and social psychological attitudes* (pp. 661–753). New York: Academic Press.

Bruni, P., & Eysenck, H. J. (1976). Structure of attitudes—An Italian sample. *Psychological Reports, 38,* 956–958.

Campbell, A., Converse, P. E., Miller, W. E., & Stokes, D. E. (1960). *The American voter.* New York: John Wiley & Sons, Inc.

Carlson, R., & Brincka, J. (1987). Studies in script theory: III. Ideology and political imagination. *Political Psychology, 8,* 563–574.

Carlson, R., & Levy, H. (1970). Self, values, and affects: Derivations from Tomkins' polarity theory. *Journal of Personality and Social Psychology, 16,* 338–345.

Centers, R. (1949). *The psychology of social class.* New York: Russell and Russell (reprinted 1961).

Christie, R. (1991). Authoritarianism and related constructs. In J. P. Robinson, P. R. Shaver, & L. S. Wrightsman (Eds.), *Measures of personality and social psychological attitudes* (pp. 501–571). New York: Academic Press.

Christie, R., & Geis, F. L. (1970). *Studies in Machiavellianism.* New York: Academic Press.

Cloud, J., & Vaughan, G. M. (1969). Using balanced scales to control acquiescence. *Sociometry, 33,* 193–202.

Cochrane, R., Billig, M., & Rokeach, M. (1979). Politics and values in Britain: A test of Rokeach's two value model. *British Journal of Clinical and Social Psychology, 18,* 159–167.

Cohen, J., & Krassa, M. (1991). *The rightward drift in American public opinion: Trends and themes in aggregate national conservatism, 1974–1989.* Prepared for presentation at the Annual Convention of the American Political Science Association, Washington, DC.

Comrey, A. L., & Newmeyer, J. A. (1965). Measurement of radicalism–conservatism. *Journal of Social Psychology, 67,* 357–369.

Conover, P. J., & Feldman, S. (1981). The origins and meaning of liberal/conservative self-identification. *American Journal of Political Science, 25,* 617–645.

Conover, P. J. & Feldman, S. (1986). *Religion, morality, and politics.* Paper prepared for presentation at the Annual Convention of the American Political Science Association, Washington, DC.

Converse, P. E. (1964). The nature of belief systems in mass publics. In D. Apter (Ed.), *Ideology and discontent* (pp. 206–261). New York: Free Press of Glencoe.

Converse, P. E. (1975). Public opinion and voting behavior. In F. I. Greenstein (Ed.), *The handbook of political science* (Vol. 4, pp. 75–169). Reading, MA: Addison-Wesley Press.

Converse, P. E., Clausen, A. R., & Miller, W. E. (1965). Electoral myth and reality: The 1964 election. *American Political Science Review, 59,* 321–336.

Dator, J. A. (1969). Measuring attitudes across cultures: A factor analysis of the replies of Japanese judges to Eysenck's inventory of conservative–progressive ideology. In G. Schubert & D. J. Danelski (Eds.), *Comparative judicial behavior* (pp. 71–102). London: Oxford University Press, Inc.

Davis, J. A. (1992). Changeable weather in a cooling climate atop the liberal plateau: Conversion and replacement in forty-two General Social Survey items 1972–1989. *Public Opinion Quarterly, 56,* 261–306.

Demorest, A. P., & Irving, I. E. (1992). *Journal of Personality, 60,* 645–663.

De St. Aubin, E. (1996). Personal ideological polarity. *Journal of Personality and Social Psychology, 71,* 152–165.

Duckitt, J., & Farre, B. (1994). Right-wing authoritarianism and political intolerance among whites in the future majority-rule South Africa. *Journal of Social Psychology, 134,* 735–741.

Eckhardt, W. (1971). Conservatism, east and west. *Journal of Cross Cultural Psychology, 2,* 109–128.

Eckhardt, W. (1988). Comment on Ray's "Why the F scale predicts racism: A critical review." *Political Psychology, 9,* 681–691.

Eisler, R., & Loye, D. (1983). The "failure" of liberalism: A reassessment of ideology from a new feminine–masculine perspective. *Political Psychology, 4,* 375–391.

Ekehammar, B., Nilsson, I., & Sidanius, J. (1989). Social attitudes and social status: A multivariate and multinational analysis. *Personality and Individual Differences, 10,* 203–208.

Emihovich, C. H., & Gaier, E. L. (1983). Ideology and idealism in early adolescence. *Adolescence, 18,* 787–798.

Emler, N., Renwick, S., & Malone, B. (1983). The relationship between moral reasoning and political orientation. *Journal of Personality and Social Psychology, 45,* 1073–1080.

Erikson, R. S., & Tedin, K. L. (1995). *American public opinion: Its origin, content and impact.* Boston: Allyn & Bacon.

Eysenck, H. J. (1947). Primary social attitudes: I. The organization and measurement of social attitudes. *International Journal of Opinion and Attitude Research, 1,* 49–84.

Eysenck, H. J. (1951). Primary social attitudes as related to social class and political party. *British Journal of Sociology, 11,* 198–209.

Eysenck, H. J. (1954). *The psychology of politics.* London: Routledge & Kegan Paul, Ltd.

Eysenck, H. J. (1971). Social attitudes and social class. *British Journal of Clinical and Social Psychology, 10,* 210–212.

Eysenck, H. J. (1975). The structure of social attitudes. *British Journal of Clinical and Social Psychology, 14,* 323–331.

Eysenck, H. J. (1976). Structure of social attitudes. *Psychological Reports, 39,* 463–466.

Eysenck, H. J., & Wilson, G. D. (1978). *The psychological basis of ideology.* Lancaster, England: MTP Press, Ltd.

Farre, B., & Duckitt, J. (1994). The validity of the Tomkins Polarity Scale among white South Africans. *Journal of Social Psychology, 134*, 287–296.

Feather, N. T. (1975). *Values in education and society.* New York: Free Press.

Feather, N. T. (1977a). Value importance, conservatism, and age. *European Journal of Social Psychology, 7*, 241–245.

Feather, N. T. (1977b). *Values in education and society* (2nd ed.). New York: Free Press.

Feather, N. T. (1979). Value correlates of conservatism. *Journal of Personality and Social Psychology, 37*, 1617–1630.

Feather, N. T. (1984). Protestant ethics, conservatism, and values. *Journal of Personality and Social Psychology, 46*, 1132–1141.

Feldman, S. (1984, May). *Memo to the Planning Committee and NES Board of Overseers on the measurement of liberal–conservative self-identification.* Center for Political Studies, University of Michigan.

Feldman, S. (1989, June). *Moral values and social order.* Paper presented at a meeting of the International Society of Political Psychology, Tel Aviv, Israel.

Ferguson, L. (1939). Primary social attitudes. *Journal of Psychology, 8*, 217–223.

Ferguson, L. (1973). Primary social attitudes of the 1960s and those of the 1930s. *Psychological Reports, 33*, 655–664.

Fincham, F., & Barling, J. (1979). Moral judgment and psychological conservatism. *Journal of Social Psychology, 107*, 139–140.

Fink, H. C., & Hjelle, L. A. (1973). Internal and external locus of control and ideology. *Psychological Reports, 33*, 967–974.

Flanigan, W. H. (1972). *Political behavior of the American electorate* (2nd ed.). Boston: Allyn & Bacon, Inc.

Fleishman, J. A. (1988). Attitude organization in the general public: Evidence for a bidimensional structure. *Social Forces, 67*, 159–184.

Free, C. A., & Cantril, H. (1968). *The political beliefs of Americans: A study of public opinion.* New York: Simon and Schuster.

Gillies, J., & Campbell, S. (1985). Conservatism and party preferences. *British Journal of Social and Clinical Psychology, 24*.

Glascow, M. R., Cartier, A. M., & Wilson, G. D. (1985). Conservatism, sensation-seeking, and music preferences. *Personality and Individual Differences, 6*, 395–396.

Gold, A. R., Christie, R., & Friedman, L. N. (1976). *Fists and flowers: A social psychological interpretation of student dissent.* New York: Academic Press.

Gorsuch, R. L. (1993). Religion and prejudice: Lessons not learned from the past. *International Journal for the Psychology of Religion, 3*, 29–31.

Grant, M. J., Hannah, T. E., Ross, A. S., & Button, C. M. (1995). Structure and processing of the perceived attitudes of others: Beyond "liberal" and "conservative." *Social Behavior and Personality, 23*, 1–22.

Greeley, A. M. (1988). Evidence that a maternal image of God correlates with liberal politics. *Sociology and Social Research, 72*, 150–154.

Green, D. E., Reynolds, N. S. M., Walkey, F. H., & McCormick, I. A. (1988). The Conservatism Scale: In search of a replicable factor. *Journal of Social Psychology, 128*, 507–516.

Green, D. P. (1988). On the dimensionality of public sentiment toward partisan and ideological groups. *American Journal of Political Science, 32*, 758–780.

Guy, R. F., & Norvell, M. (1977). The neutral point on a Likert scale. *Journal of Psychology, 95*, 199–204.

Haltom, W. (1990). Liberal–conservative continua: A comparison of measures. *Western Political Quarterly, 43*, 387–401.

Heaven, P. C. L. (1984). Predicting authoritarian behavior: Analysis of three measures. *Personality and Individual Differences, 5*, 251–253.

Heaven, P. C. L. (1986). Directiveness and dominance. *Journal of Social Psychology, 126*, 271–272.

Hehl, F. J., & Ruch, W. (1990). Conservatism as a predictor of responses to humour: III. The prediction of appreciation of incongruity–resolution based humour by content saturated attitude scales in five samples. *Personality and Individual Differences, 11*, 439–445.

Heider, F. (1958). *The psychology of interpersonal relations.* New York: Wiley.

Hewitt, J. K., Eysenck, H. J., & Eaves, L. J. (1977). Structure of social attitudes after twenty-five years: A replication. *Psychological Reports, 40*, 183–188.

Hicks, J. M. (1974). Conservative voting and personality. *Social Behavior and Personality, 2*, 43–49.

Hicks, J. M., & Wright, J. H. (1970). Convergent–discriminant validation and factor analysis of five scales of liberalism–conservatism. *Journal of Personality and Social Psychology, 14*, 114–120.

Horkheimer, M. (Ed.). (1936). *Studies in authority and family.* Paris: Felix Alcam.

Inglehart, R. (1977). *The silent revolution.* Princeton, NJ: Princeton University Press.

Inglehart, R. (1981). Post-materialism in an environment of insecurity. *American Political Science Review, 75*, 880–900.

Inglehart, R. (1984). Changing cleavage alignments in Western democracies. In R. Dalton, S. Flanagan, & P. Beck (Eds.), *Electoral change in advanced industrial democracies.* Princeton, NJ: Princeton University Press.

Insel, P. M., & Wilson, G. D. (1971). Measuring social attitudes in children. *British Journal of Clinical and Social Psychology, 10*, 84–86.

Joe, V. C. (1984). Factor analysis of the Conservatism Scale. *Journal of Social Psychology, 124*, 175–178.

Joe, V. C., Kostyla, S., & Jones, R. N. (1985). Conservatism as a factor of sexual responding to a word association test. *Journal of Social Psychology, 125*, 275–276.

Katz, Y. J. (1988a). Conservatism of Israeli children. *Journal of Social Psychology, 128*, 833–835.

Katz, Y. J. (1988b). Conservatism of Israeli Arabs and Jews. *Journal of Social Psychology, 128*, 695–696.

Katz, Y. J., & Ronen, M. (1986). A cross cultural validation of the conservatism scale in a multi-ethnic society: The case of Israel. *Journal of Social Psychology, 126*, 555–557.

Kerlinger, F. N. (1967). Social attitudes and their critical referents: A structural theory. *Psychological Review, 74*, 110–122.

Kerlinger, F. N. (1972). The structure and content of social attitude referents: A preliminary study. *Educational and Psychological Measurement, 32*, 613–630.

Kerlinger, F. N. (1976). The structure of social attitudes in three countries: Tests of a criterial referents theory. *International Journal of Psychology, 11*, 265–279.

Kerlinger, F. N. (1980). Analysis of covariance structure: Tests of a criterial referents theory of attitudes. *Multivariate Behavioral Research, 15*, 403–422.

Kerlinger, F. N. (1984). *Liberalism and conservatism: The nature and structure of social attitudes.* Hillsdale, NJ: Lawrence Erlbaum Associates.

Kerr, W. (1946). *Tulane factors of liberalism–conservatism: Manual of instruction.* Chicago: Psychometric Affiliates.

Kerr, W. (1952). Untangling the liberalism–conservatism continuum. *Journal of Social Psychology, 35*, 111–125.

Kerr, W. (1955). *Manual of instruction for Tulane factors of liberalism–conservatism.* Chicago: Psychometric Affiliates.

Kirton, M. J. (1978). Wilson and Patterson's Conservatism Scale: A shortened alternative form. *British Journal of Social and Clinical Psychology, 17*, 319–323.

Knight, K. (1984). The dimensionality of partisan and ideological affect. *American Politics Quarterly, 12*, 305–334.

Knight, K. (1985). Ideology in the 1980 election: Ideological sophistication does matter. *Journal of Politics, 47*, 828–853.

Knight, K. (1990, February). *Comparison of liberal–conservative items in the ANES 1989 Pilot Study.* Report to the Pilot Study Committee and Board of Overseers. Center for Political Studies, University of Michigan.

Knight, K. (1990). Ideology and public opinion. In N. Long (Ed.), *Research in micropolitics* (Vol. 3, pp. 59–82). New York: JAI Press.

Knight, K., & Erikson, R. S. (1997). Ideology in the 1990s. In B. Norrander & C. Wilcox (Eds.), *Understanding public opinion* (pp. 89–110). Washington, DC: CQ Press.

Knight, K., & Lewis, C. (1986). *The growth of conservatism in the American mass public: Measurement and meaning*. Paper presented at the annual convention of the Southwest Social Science Association, San Antonio, Texas.

Knutson, J. C. (1972). *The human basis of the polity*. New York: Aldine Publishers.

Kohlberg, L. (1963). The development of children's orientations toward a moral order. *Vita Humana, 6*, 11–331.

Kohn, P. M. (1972). The authoritarianism–rebellion scale: A balanced F scale with left-wing reversals. *Sociometry, 35*, 176–189.

Lakoff, G. (1996). *Moral politics: What conservatives know that liberals don't*. Chicago: University of Chicago Press.

Lane, R. E. (1955). Political personality and electoral choice. *American Political Science Review, 49*, 173–190.

Lane, R. E. (1965). The politics of consensus in an age of affluence. *American Political Science Review, 59*, 874–895.

Lapsley, D. K., & Enright, R. D. (1979). The effects of social desirability, intelligence, and milieu on an American validation of the Conservatism Scale. *Journal of Social Psychology, 107*, 9–14.

Lederer, G. (1988). Young Austrians and the election of Kurt Waldheim. *Political Psychology, 9*, 633–647.

Lenney, E. (1991). Sex roles: Measurement of masculinity, femininity, and androgyny. In J. P. Robinson, P. R. Shaver, & L. S. Wrightsman. (Eds.), *Measures of personality and social psychological attitudes*, (pp. 573–660). New York: Academic Press.

Levenson, H., & Miller, J. (1974). Development of a current scale to measure conservatism–liberalism. *Journal of Psychology, 88*, 241–244.

Levenson, H., & Miller, J. (1976). Multidimensional locus of control in sociopolitical activists of conservative and liberal ideologies. *Journal of Personality and Social Psychology, 33*, 199–208.

Levitin, T. E., & Miller, W. E. (1979). Ideological interpretations of presidential elections. *American Political Science Review, 73*, 751–771.

Lichter, S. R., & Rothman, S. (1981–1982). Jewish ethnicity and radical culture. *Political Psychology, 3*, 116–157.

Lipset, S. M., & Raab, E. (1978). *The politics of unreason*. Chicago: University of Chicago Press.

Loye, D. (1977). *The leadership passion: A psychology of ideology*. San Francisco: Jossey-Bass.

Luskin, R. C. (1987). Measuring political sophistication. *American Journal of Political Science, 31*, 856–899.

Luttbeg, N. R., & Gant, M. M. (1985). The failure of liberal/conservative ideology as a cognitive structure. *Public Opinion Quarterly, 49*, 80–93.

Maddox, W. D., & Lillie, S. A. (1984). *Beyond liberal and conservative: Reassessing the political spectrum*. Washington, DC: Cato Institute.

Mannheim, K. (1936). *Ideology and utopia*. New York: Harcourt, Brace and World.

Marjoribanks, K., & Josefowitz, N. (1975). Kerlinger's theory of social attitudes: An analysis. *Psychological Reports, 37*, 819–823.

Maslow, A. (1945). A clinically derived test for measuring psychological security–insecurity. *Journal of General Psychology, 33*, 21–41.

Maslow, A. (1968). *Toward a psychology of being*. New York: Van Nostrand Reinhold.

McClosky, H. (1958). Conservatism and personality. *American Political Science Review, 52*, 27–45.

McClosky, H. (1991, May). Personal communication.

McClosky, H., & Bann, C. A. (1979). On the reappraisal of the Classical Conservatism Scale. *Political Methodology, 6*, 149–172.

McFarland, S., Agayev, V., & Abalakina, M. (1990). Russian authoritarianism. In W. F. Stone & G. Lederer (Eds.), *Strengths and weaknesses: The authoritarian personality today.* New York: Springer-Verlag.

McHoskey, J. W. (1996). Authoritarianism and ethical ideology. *Journal of Social Psychology, 136,* 709–717.

Meloen, J. D., Van der Linden, G., & De Witte, H. (1996). A test of the approaches of Adorno et al., Lederer, and Altemeyer on authoritarianism in Belgian Flanders: A research note. *Political Psychology, 7,* 643–656.

Milbraith, L. W. (1984). *Environmentalists: Vanguard for a new society.* Albany, NY: State University of New York Press.

Milbraith, L. W. (1986). Environmental beliefs and values. In M. G. Hermann (Ed.), *Political psychology* (pp. 97–138). San Francisco: Jossey-Bass.

Milburn, M. A. (1991). *Persuasion and politics.* Pacific Grove, CA: Brooks/Cole Publishing.

Milburn, M. A., & Conrad, S. D. (1996). *The politics of denial.* Cambridge, MA: MIT Press.

Milgram, S. (1963). Behavioral study of obedience. *Journal of Abnormal and Behavioral Psychology, 67,* 371–378.

Miller, P. V. (1984). Alternative question forms for attitude scale questions in telephone interviews. *Public Opinion Quarterly, 48,* 766–778.

Miller, W. E., & Levitin, T. (1976). *Leadership and change.* Boston: Winthrop Publishing Co.

Miller, W. E., & Traugott, S. A. (1989). *American National Election Studies data sourcebook: 1952–1986.* Cambridge, MA: Harvard University Press.

Mosher, D. L., & Tomkins, S. S. (1988). Scripting the macho man. *Journal of Sex Research, 25,* 60–84.

Mueller, D. J. (1974). The relationship of political orientation to the values of freedom and equality. *Journal of Psychology, 86,* 105–109.

Nathanson, D. L. (1994). Shame transactions. *Transaction Analysis Journal, 24,* 121–129.

Nettler, G., & Huffman, J. (1957). Political opinion and personal security. *Sociometry, 20,* 51–66.

Nias, D. K. B., Wilson, G. D., & Woodbridge, J. M. (1971). Test–retest results in the Conservatism Scale completed under conditions of anonymity and identification. *British Journal of Clinical and Social Psychology, 10,* 282–283.

Nie, N. S., Verba, & Petrocik, J. R. (1979). *The changing American voter.* Chicago: University of Chicago Press.

Nilsson, I., & Ekehammar, B. (1989). *A revised Swedish Social Attitudes Scale* (Rpt. No. 688). Stockholm: Department of Psychology, University of Stockholm.

Nilsson, I., & Ekehammar, B. (1990). A new Swedish Social Attitude Scale: Reliability and construct validity. *Scandinavian Journal of Psychology, 31,* 55–64.

Olivier, R., & Butcher, H. (1962). Teachers' attitudes to education. *British Journal of Clinical and Social Psychology, 1,* 56–69.

Open, C., & Rodenwoldt, E. (1973). The Wilson–Patterson Conservatism Scale in a "conservative" culture. *British Journal of Clinical and Social Psychology, 11,* 313–323.

Owens, W. H., Jr. (1979). The McClosky "Conservatism Scale" reappraised. *Political Methodology, 6,* 129–148.

Pandey, J., Sinha, Y., Prakash, A., & Tripathi, R. C. (1982). Right–left political ideologies and attributes of the causes of poverty. *European Journal of Social Psychology, 12,* 327–331.

Photiadis, J., & Biggar, J. (1962). Religiosity, educational and ethnic distance. *American Journal of Sociology, 67,* 666–672.

Pierce, J. C. (1970). Party identification and the changing role of ideology in American politics. *Midwest Journal of Political Science, 14,* 25–42.

Polsby, N. W., Dentler, R. A., & Smith, P. A. (1963). *Politics and social life: An introduction to political behavior.* Boston: Houghton, Mifflin.

Pratto, F., Sidanius, J., Stallworth, L. M., & Malle, B. F. (1994). Social dominance orientation: A personality variable predicting social and political attitudes. *Journal of Personality and Social Psychology, 67,* 741–763.

Presser, S. A., & Schuman, H. (1980). The measurement of a middle position in attitude surveys. *Public Opinion Quarterly, 44,* 70–85.

Raden, D. (1979). An item analysis based update of the Nettler–Huffman Radicalism–Conservatism Scale. *Psychological Reports, 45,* 429–430.

Rajaratnam, N., Cronbach, L. J., & Glesser, G. C. (1965). Generalizability of stratified-parallel tests. *Psychometrika, 30,* 39–56.

Rambo, W. (1972). Measurement of broad spectrum social attitudes: Liberalism–conservatism. *Perceptual and Motor Skills, 35,* 463–477.

Ray, J. J. (1971). A new measure of conservatism: Its limitations. *British Journal of Clinical and Social Psychology, 10,* 79–80.

Ray, J. J. (1972). A new balanced F-scale and its relation to social class. *Australian Psychologist 7,* 155–166.

Ray, J. J. (1973a). Conservatism, authoritarianism, and related variables: A review and empirical study. In G. D. Wilson (Ed.), *The psychology of conservatism* (pp. 17–35). New York: Academic Press.

Ray, J. J. (1973b). Dogmatism in relation to sub-types of conservatism: Some Australian data. *European Journal of Social Psychology, 3,* 221–232.

Ray, J. J. (1976). Do authoritarians hold authoritarian attitudes? *Human Relations, 29,* 307–325.

Ray, J. J. (1980). Orthogonality between liberalism and conservatism. *Journal of Social Psychology, 112,* 215–218.

Ray, J. J. (1982). Authoritarianism/liberalism as the second dimension of social attitudes. *Journal of Social Psychology, 117,* 33–44.

Ray, J. J. (1983). A scale to measure conservatism of American public opinion. *Journal of Social Psychology, 119,* 293–294.

Ray, J. J. (1984). Alternatives to the F scale in the measurement of authoritarianism: A catalog. *Journal of Social Psychology, 122,* 105–119.

Ray, J. J. (1985a). Authoritarianism of the left revisited. *Personality and Individual Differences, 6,* 272.

Ray, J. J. (1985b). Using multiple class indicators to examine working-class ideology. *Personality and Individual Differences, 6,* 557–562.

Ray, J. J. (1985c). Defective validity in the Altemeyer authoritarianism scale. *Journal of Social Psychology, 125,* 271–272.

Ray, J. J. (1987). Radicalism and alienation. *Journal of Social Psychology, 127,* 219–220.

Ray, J. J. (1988a). Why the F scale predicts racism: A critical review. *Political Psychology, 9,* 671–679.

Ray, J. J. (1988b). Cognitive style as a predictor of authoritarianism, conservatism, and racism: A fantasy in many movements. *Political Psychology, 9,* 303–308.

Ray, J. J. (1989). The scientific study of ideology is too often more ideological than scientific. *Personality and Individual Differences, 10,* 331–336.

Ray, J. J., & Lovejoy, F. H. (1986). A comparison of three scales of directiveness. *Journal of Social Psychology, 126,* 249–250.

Ray, J. J., & Pratt, G. J. (1979). Is the influence of acquiesence of the "catchphrase" type scale not so mythical after all? *Australian Journal of Psychology, 31,* 73–78.

Robertson, A., & Cochrane, R. (1973). The Wilson–Patterson Conservatism Scale: A reappraisal. *British Journal of Social and Clinical Psychology, 12,* 428–430.

Robinson, J. (1984). The ups and downs and ins and outs of ideology. *Public Opinion,* 12–15.

Robinson, J. P. (1997). *Ideological trends, tunes, and lifestyles: The public moves right (or is it left?)* Ms. Dept. of Sociology, University of Maryland, College Park, MD.

Robinson, J. P., & Fleishman, J. A. (1984). Ideological identification: Trends and interpretations of the liberal–conservative balance. *Public Opinion Quarterly, 52,* 134–145.

Robinson, J. P., Rusk, J. G., & Head, K. B. (1969). *Measures of political attitudes* (2nd ed.). Ann Arbor: Institute for Social Research, University of Michigan.

Robinson, J. P., & Shaver, P. R. (Eds.). (1973). *Measures of social psychological attitudes.* Ann Arbor: Institute for Social Research, University of Michigan.

Rokeach, M. (1960). *The open and closed mind.* New York: Basic Books.

Rokeach, M. (1973). *The nature of human values.* New York: Free Press.

Rokeach, M. (1979). The two-value model of political ideology. *British Journal of Clinical and Social Psychology, 18,* 169–172.

Rotunda, R. D. (1986). *The politics of language.* Iowa City: University of Iowa Press.

Rubinstein, G. (1996). Two peoples in one land: A validation study of Altemeyer's Right-Wing Authoritarianism Scale in the Palestinian and Jewish societies in Israel. *Journal of Cross Cultural Psychology, 27,* 216–230.

Rusk, J. G., & Weisberg, H. F. (1972). Perceptions of presidential candidates: Implications for electoral change. *Midwest Journal of Political Science, 16,* 388–410.

Santos, M., & Pedhazur, E. (1972). Dimensions of educational attitudes: Factorial congruence of two scales. *Journal of Educational Measurement, 9,* 189–198.

Schaffner, P. E., & Stone, W. F. (1992). *Empirical distinctions among ideologies: Humanism, normativism, conservatism, authoritarianism.* Paper presented at a meeting of the International Society of Political Psychology, San Francisco.

Schattschneider, E. E. (1960). *The semi-sovereign people.* Hinsdale, IL: The Dryden Press.

Schultz, P. W., Stone, W. F., & Christie, R. (1997). Authoritarianism and mental rigidity: The Einstellung problem revisited. *Personality and Social Psychology Bulletin, 23,* 3–9.

Selznick, G. & Steinberg, S. (1966) *Class and ideology in the 1964 election: A national survey.* Paper presented at the Annual Meeting of the American Sociological Association.

Shea, J. D. C., & Jones, J. (1982). A model for the use of attitude scales across cultures. *International Journal of Psychology, 17,* 331–343.

Shils, E. A. (1954). Authoritarianism: Right and left. In R. Christie & M. Jahoda (Eds.), *Studies in the scope and method of the authoritarianism personality* (pp. 24–49). Glencoe, IL: Free Press.

Shils, E. A. (1958). Ideology and civility. *The Sewanee Review, 66,* 450–480.

Sidanius, J. (1976a). *A Swedish Scale of Conservatism* (Rep. No. 465). Stockholm: Department of Psychology, University of Stockholm.

Sidanius, J. (1976b). *Further tests of a Swedish Scale of Conservatism* (Rep. No. 467). Stockholm: Department of Psychology, University of Stockholm.

Sidanius, J. (1985). Cognitive functioning and sociopolitical ideology revisited. *Political Psychology, 6,* 637–661.

Sidanius, J., Brewer, R. M., Banks, E., & Ekehammar, B. (1987). Ideological constraint, political interest and gender: A Swedish–American comparison. *European Journal of Political Research, 15,* 471–492.

Sidanius, J., Cling, B. J., & Pratto, F. (1991). Ranking and linking as a function of sex and gender role attitudes. *Journal of Social Issues, 47*(3), 131–149.

Sidanius, J., Devereux, E., & Pratto, F. (1992). A comparison of symbolic racism theory and social dominance theory as explanations for racial policy attitudes. *Journal of Social Psychology, 132,* 377–395.

Sidanius, J., & Duffy, G. (1988). The duality of attitude structure: A test of Kerlinger's criteria referent theory within samples of Swedish and American youth. *Political Psychology, 9*(4), 649–670.

Sidanius, J., Ekehammar, B., & Ross, M. (1979). Comparisons of social–political attitudes between two democratic societies. *International Journal of Psychology, 14,* 225–240.

Sidanius, J., & Lau, R. R. (1989). Political sophistication and political deviance: A matter of context. *Political Psychology, 10,* 85–109.

Sidanius, J., & Pratto, F. (1993). Racism and support of free-market capitalism: A cross-cultural analysis. *Political Psychology, 14,* 381–401.

Sidanius, J., Pratto, F., & Bobo, L. (1996). Racism, conservatism, affirmative action, and intellectual sophistication: A matter of principled conservatism or group dominance? *Journal of Personality and Social Psychology, 70,* 476–490.

Sidanius, J., Pratto, F., & Mitchell, M. In-group identification, social dominance orientation and differential intergroup social allocation. *Journal of Social Psychology, 134,* 151–167.

Singh, A. (1977). Structure of social attitudes: A Canadian sample. *Psychological Reports, 40,* 165–166.

Smith, T. W. (1982). General liberalism and social changes in post World War II America: A summary of trends. *Social Indicators Research, 10,* 1–28.

Smith, T. W. (1985). Atop a liberal plateau? A summary of trends since World War II. *Research in Urban Policy, 1,* 245–257.

Smithers, A. G., & Lobley, D. M. (1978). Dogmatism, social attitudes, and personality. *British Journal of Clinical and Social Psychology, 17,* 135–142.

Sontag, M., & Pedharuz, E. (1972). Dimensions of educational attitudes. *Journal of Educational Measurement, 9,* 189–198.

Stimson, J. A. (1975). Belief systems: Constraint, complexity, and the 1972 election. *American Journal of Political Science, 19,* 393–417.

Stimson, J. A. (1991). *Public opinion in America: Moods, cycles, and swings.* Boulder, CO: Westview.

Stone, B. S. (1974). The John Birch Society: A profile. *Journal of Politics, 36,* 184–197.

Stone, W. F. (1980). The myth of left-wing authoritarianism. *Political Psychology, 2,* 3–19.

Stone, W. F. (1981). Left and right in personality and ideology. *Journal of Mind and Behavior, 4,* 211–220.

Stone, W. F. (1983). Left and right in personality and ideology: An attempt at clarification. *Journal of Mind and Behavior.*

Stone, W. F. (1986). Personality and ideology: Empirical support for Tomkins' polarity theory. *Political Psychology, 7,* 689–708.

Stone, W. F. (1991, July). *Right-wing authoritarianism and normative and humanistic personality orientation.* Ms. Dept. of Psychology, University of Maine, Orono, ME.

Stone, W. F., & Garzon, A. (1992). Personalidad e ideologia: La escala de polaridad (Personality and ideology: The Polarity Scale). *Psicologia Politica, 4,* 65–84.

Stone, W. F., Ommundsen, R., & Williams, S. (1985). The structure of ideology in Norway and the United States. *Journal of Social Psychology, 125,* 169–179.

Stone, W. F., & Russ, R. C. (1976). Machiavellianism as tough-mindedness. *Journal of Social Psychology, 98,* 213–220.

Stone, W. F., & Schaffner, P. E. (1988). *The psychology of politics* (2nd ed.). New York: Springer-Verlag.

Stone, W. F., & Schaffner, P. E. (1997). *Tomkins' Polarity Scale: Recent developments.* Paper prepared for presentation at the annual convention of the International Society of Political Psychology, Montreal, Ontario, Canada.

Suedfeld, P., Hakstian, A. R., Rank, D. S., & Ballard, E. J. (1985). Ascription of responsibility as a personality variable. *Journal of Applied Social Psychology, 15,* 285–311.

Suziedelis, A., & Lorr, M. (1973). Conservative attitudes and authoritarian values. *Journal of Psychology, 83,* 287–294.

Tarr, H., & Lorr, M. (1991). A comparison of right-wing authoritarianism, conformity and conservatism. *Personality and Individual Differences, 12,* 307–311.

Tetlock, P. E. (1983). Cognitive style and political ideology. *Journal of Personality and Social Psychology, 45,* 118–126.

Thomas, D. B. (1976). Exploring the personality–ideology interface: *Q*-sort of Tomkins' polarity theory. *Experimental Study of Politics, 5,* 47–87.

Thomas, D. B. (1978). Political belief systems and ideo-affective resonance: The structuring principle revisited. *Experimental Study of Politics, 6,* 34–89.

Thurstone, L. L., & Chave, E. J. (1929). *The measurement of attitude.* Chicago: University of Chicago Press.

Tomkins, S. S. (1962, 1963, 1991). *Affect, imagery and consciousness.* (Vols. 1–3). New York: Springer Publishing Co.

Tomkins, S. S. (1963). Left and right: A basic dimension of ideology and personality. In R. W. White (Ed.), *The study of lives: Essays on personality in honor of Henry A. Murray* (pp. 389–411).

Tomkins, S. S. (1964). *Polarity Scale.* New York: Springer Publishing Co.

Tomkins, S. S. (1965). Affect and the psychology of knowledge. In S. S. Tomkins & C. E. Izard (Eds.), *Affect, cognition, and personality: Empirical studies* (pp. 72–97). New York: Springer Publishing Co.

Tomkins, S. S. (1979). Script theory: Differential magnification of affects. In H. E. Howe & R. A. Dienstbier (Eds.), *Nebraska symposium on motivation* (Vol. 26). Lincoln: University of Nebraska Press.

Truett, K. R. (1993). Age differences in conservatism. *Personality and Individual Differences, 14*, 405–411.

Vasquez, J. F. (1976). The face and ideology. *Dissertation Abstracts International, 36*, 5365B. (University Microfilms No. 76-7341).

Wald, K. D. (1992). *Religion and politics in the United States* (2nd ed.). Washington, DC: Congressional Quarterly Press.

Wald, K., Owen, D. E., & Hill, S. S., Jr. (1988). Churches as political communities. *American Political Science Review, 82*, 531–548.

Walkey, F. H., Katz, Y. J., & Green, D. E. The general factor in the conservatism scale: A multinational multicultural examination. *Personality and Individual Differences, 7*, 985–988.

Ward, D. (1988). A critic's defense of the criticized. *Political Psychology, 9*, 317–320.

Weisberg, H. (1980). A multidimensional conceptualization of party identification. *Political Behavior, 2*, 33–60.

Weisberg, H. F., & Rusk, J. G. (1970). Dimensions of candidate evaluation. *American Political Science Review, 64*, 1167–1185.

Wilcox, C. (1996). *Onward Christian soldiers: The Religious Right in American politics.* Boulder, CO: Westview.

Wilcox, C., Sigelman, L., & Cook, E. (1989). Some like it hot: Individual differences in responses to group feeling thermometers. *Public Opinion Quarterly, 53*, 246–257.

Williams, S. (1984). Left–right ideological differences in blaming victims. *Political Psychology, 5*, 573–581.

Wilson, G. D. (1970). Is there a general factor in social attitudes? Evidence from a factor analysis of the Conservatism Scale. *British Journal of Clinical and Social Psychology, 9*, 101–107.

Wilson, G. D. (Ed.). (1973a). *The psychology of conservatism.* London: Academic Press.

Wilson, G. D. (1973b). The factor structure of the C-Scale. In G. D. Wilson (Ed.), *The psychology of conservatism* (pp. 71–92). London: Academic Press.

Wilson, G. D. (1975). *Manual for the Wilson–Patterson Attitude Inventory (WPAI).* Windsor, England: N.F.E.R. Publishing Co. Ltd.

Wilson, G. D. (1985). The "catchphrase" approach to attitude measurement. *Personality and Individual Differences, 6*, 31–37.

Wilson, G. D., & Caldwell, F. (1988). Social attitudes and voting intentions of members of the European Parliament. *Personality and Individual Differences, 9*, 147–153.

Wilson, G. D., & Lillie, F. J. (1972). Social attitudes of humanists and salvationists. *British Journal of Clinical and Social Psychology, 11*, 220–224.

Wilson, G. D., & Patterson, J. R. (1968). A new measure of conservatism. *British Journal of Social and Clinical Psychology, 8*, 264–269.

Woodrum, E. (1988). Moral conservatism and the 1984 presidential election. *Journal for the Scientific Study of Religion, 27*, 192–210.

Wright, J. H., & Hicks, J. M. (1966). Construction and validation of a Thurstone scale of liberalism–conservatism. *Journal of Applied Psychology, 50*, 9–12.

Yankelovich, D. (1972). *The changing values on campus: Political and personal attitudes of today's college students.* New York: Simon and Schuster.

Yelland, L. M., & Stone, W. F. (1996). Belief in the Holocaust: Effects of personality and propaganda. *Political Psychology, 17*, 551–562.

Zak, I. (1973). Dimensions of Jewish–American identity. *Psychological Reports, 33*, 891–900.

Zak, I. (1976). Structure of ethnic identity of Arab–Israeli students. *Psychological Reports, 38*, 239–246.

Ziegler, M., & Atkinson, T. H. (1973). Information level and dimensionality of liberalism–conservatism. *Multivariate Behavioral Research, 8*, 195–212.

Zwillenberg, D. F. (1983). *Predicting bias in the punishment of criminals as a function of authoritarianism.* Unpublished doctoral dissertation, Columbia University. UM microfilm 8311876.

CHAPTER 4

Economic Values and Inequality

Stanley Feldman

The welfare state has been a dominant feature of industrialized nations for much of the 20th century. Along with this has come conflict over the nature and scope of social welfare. Public support for the welfare state varies both cross-nationally and within nations (see Coughlin, 1980; Smith, 1987; Verba, 1987; Verba & Orren, 1985). The major issues of the welfare state have been central to politics in this century: inequality; wealth, poverty, and fairness; and government assistance to the poor and redistribution of income. Conflict over social welfare has helped to define ideological divisions in many societies, and attitudes toward social welfare strongly influence the shape of public opinion (Feldman, 1983; Ladd & Lipset, 1980).

Understanding attitudes and opinions toward the welfare state and social welfare policy has been, therefore, a major research area in the social sciences. A sizable literature has attempted to explain preferences on a range of public policy issues central to the welfare state. Although much can be learned from studying the determinants of specific attitudes and opinions, the salience of specific policies may vary significantly over time, and attitudes toward issues may have idiosyncratic components that obscure more basic orientations toward welfare state policies. It is, therefore, of particular interest to uncover the underlying principles that help to structure preferences. This has led Rokeach (1968, 1973) and other researchers to focus on certain core beliefs and values that they hypothesize structure more specific opinions about social welfare policy.

The literature that deals with these economic beliefs and values goes well beyond the analysis of preferences on public policy issues. Many discussions of the concept of political culture revolve around these same dimensions. This should not be surprising, since issues of work, production, and the distribution of resources are clearly central to the organization of society and the shape of a political culture. A long tradition of political and social analysis—going back to Tocqueville—has attributed much of the distinctive character of American society and politics to a distinctive political culture characterized by a set of values and beliefs such as equality, freedom, individualism, opportunity, religion, and voluntarism (see Lipset, 1979; Williams, 1970). The emphasis in this perspective is on predominant cultural patterns of beliefs and values rather than variations in specific opinions. It is frequently argued that these values and beliefs help to define a political culture based on the principles of 19th-century liberalism (Devine, 1972; Feldman & Zaller, 1992; Hartz, 1955). This literature on the American political culture provides an important basis for definitions of economic values and beliefs and a source of hypotheses concerning the effects of economic values and beliefs on opinion formation and public policy.

Social and economic values and beliefs are central not only to analyses of the American political culture, but also to a body of research that examines the nature and consequences of cultures in comparative perspective. Although there is a large literature on comparative political culture in political science, much of this has tended to deal with the participatory aspects of cultural variation (see, for example, Almond & Verba, 1963; Rosenbaum, 1975). Cross-cultural research in psychology, however, has been more concerned with differences in cultures that revolve around fundamental orientations toward work, interpersonal relations, and the self (Hofstede, 1980; Triandis, McCusker, & Hui, 1990). This literature helps to place the discussions of the American political culture and economic values and beliefs in a broader context. This should prove useful for interpreting measures developed and evaluated entirely with U.S. data.

Individualism and Egalitarianism

Although a wide range of specific terms appears in these discussions of social and economic beliefs, the concepts of individualism and egalitarianism are most frequently referred to in the literature. They play a prominent role in discussions of the American political culture and cross-national support for the welfare state. However, individualism and egalitarianism are not always clearly or consistently defined. Both are broad concepts that must be further broken down into their constitutive parts before they can be fully understood or defined for measurement.

Economic Individualism

The topic of this chapter deals with only part of the general concept of individualism. Economic individualism is the commitment to merit as the basis for the distribution of rewards in society and the belief that hard work ought to be rewarded and is a value in and of itself. This is clearly related to, but not necessarily equivalent to, the Protestant work ethic initially discussed by Weber (1958). Social and economic individualism also has historically been tied to the desire for limited government. As commonly argued, people must be free from external constraints to pursue their self-interest, the major potential constraint being the government. From a somewhat broader perspective, socioeconomic individualism is subsumed by the dimension of individualism–collectivism. The general concept of individualism also deals with personal freedom and moral values (Bellah, Madsen, Sullivan, Swindler, & Tipton, 1985); this review will not deal with those dimensions.

Socioeconomic individualism, the belief that people should get ahead on their own through hard work, is a core element in most accounts of American values and beliefs (Feldman, 1983; Lipset, 1979). Many consider it to be the most important component of American political culture. Some of the earliest European settlers in the New World brought with them a commitment to the work ethic already entrenched in industrializing Britain. Originally an outgrowth of ascetic Protestantism (Weber, 1958), the work ethic was refashioned in industrializing America into a powerful secular religion. Although the Great Depression and the New Deal response tempered the extremism of the Horatio Alger and Social Darwinism period (Beer, 1978), evidence of widespread belief in the work ethic is still apparent in mass opinion surveys and in-depth interviews (Devine, 1972; Lamb, 1974; Lane, 1962; McClosky & Zaller, 1984).

The literature on socioeconomic individualism in the United States focuses very heavily on one end of what is conceptually a value *dimension*. This gives a very good description of what a belief system based on the value of individualism looks like, but a much sketchier portrait of the other end of the continuum. Decreasing commitment to individualism in the United States is generally associated with an increasing likelihood of perceiving factors beyond individual effort to be significant influences on economic achievement. Luck, poor education, and discrimination are among the causes of poverty attributed to a lessened commitment to individualism (see Feagin, 1975; Kluegel & Smith, 1986). In the cross-national literature the opposite end of the continuum from individualism is often labeled *collectivism*. This more clearly suggests that the continuum varies from an exclusive concern with self and personal achievement to an awareness of the interdependence of members of society and concern for the collective well-being (Triandis, McCusker, & Hui, 1990).

Egalitarianism

Egalitarianism has several distinct dimensions that must be distinguished. There is first *equality of opportunity*, the view that each person should have the same initial chance of succeeding. Then there is formal or *legal equality*, the view that all people should be treated equally. Finally there is *equality of rewards*, a desire usually less for complete equality than for a limited range of wealth—a floor on income or an income limit (Hochschild, 1981; Verba & Orren, 1985). This chapter focuses on socioeconomic values and beliefs, not formal or legal equality; a good discussion of the complexities involved here is Rae, Hochschild, Morone, and Fessler (1981).

Given these distinctions, it may be misleading to treat egalitarianism as a single continuum of value or belief. A key problem is how to deal with both equality of opportunity and equality of results. It would be technically possible to posit a continuum defined by formal equality at one end and equality of results at the other, with equality of opportunity being somewhere in the middle. However, this specification does not appear to be correct either conceptually or empirically. A separate continuum of support for equality of results is easy to write down: At one end are people who want absolute equality within some defined population, and at the other end are those who would tolerate any degree of inequality that the social system produced. Even this may be an oversimplification. There are several routes to greater economic equality—placing upper and lower limits on income, for example—and the desire for more equality will not necessarily be strongly correlated with all methods for accomplishing it.

The dimension of equality of opportunity is even less straightforward. It may be possible simply to measure the strength of belief in the value of equal opportunity. However, those at the low end of the scale would be opposed to equal opportunity in principle. How should that be interpreted? Would that be due to their belief in an ascriptive (or hierarchical) system or to their desire to keep specific groups of people from achieving upward mobility?

A more useful conceptual definition probably focuses on the social commitment to equal opportunity. Should society do everything possible to foster equal opportunity, or is it sufficient to recognize the formal existence of opportunity? Some people may believe that society needs only to commit itself to the principle of equal opportunity. Others may argue that it is necessary to take action to make sure that opportunities are in fact equal.

Discussions of socioeconomic values in the United States have clearly focused on equality of opportunity rather than equality of results. Equality of opportunity is typically cited as the companion belief to economic individualism. Despite obvious discrimination against racial minorities and women, the United States was the first nation to break with the aristocratic tradition and acknowledge that formal equality is a right of all people, regardless of social status (Lipset, 1979). However, in their pure form individualism and equality do not easily coexist. To minimize the potential conflict, Americans have generally rejected equality of results in favor of formal or political equality and equality of opportunity. As Potter (1954, p. 92) has noted, "[E]quality came to mean, in a major sense, parity in competition. Its value was as a means to advancement rather than as an asset in itself." In fact, equality of opportunity is solidly based in the individualistic tradition.

The modern welfare state raises issues that go beyond equal opportunity to equality of results. Much of the activity of the welfare state goes toward providing a floor (safety net) through assistance for those who are unable to adequately support themselves. Those programs necessarily produce some redistribution of income. As noted by Verba and Orren (1985, p. 6), "Equality of result can be achieved only by containing the effects of equality of opportunity."

Much more attention may, therefore, be required to assess commitment to greater equality of results in the United States. In many other industrialized nations—particularly those with a history of political participation by socialist parties—equality of results has been more clearly on the national agenda, and this may dominate discussion of equality of opportunity. An increasingly important aspect of conflict over the welfare state may be the perceived trade-off between equality of opportunity and equality of results. This has so far received little attention in the empirical literature (but see Verba & Orren, 1985).

Humanitarianism

Although there is certainly evidence that belief in egalitarianism is associated with support for social welfare policies in representative national samples (Feldman, 1988; Kluegel & Smith, 1986), there is also reason to believe that egalitarianism is insufficient to account for expressed levels of support for welfare programs. Just by examining marginal distributions, there appears to be more support for many social welfare programs than support for the principle of egalitarianism (compare Free & Cantril, 1968). Except when the specific term *welfare* is used, studies have consistently shown high levels of public approval of many domestic welfare programs and support for greater spending on those programs (Sears & Citrin, 1985; Smith, 1987). On the other hand, Americans are not particularly supportive of (and are often vociferously opposed to) measures to achieve equality of income or equality of results more generally (Gans, 1988; Kluegel & Smith, 1986; McClosky & Zaller, 1984; Verba & Orren, 1985).

In addition, egalitarianism does not appear to be able to account for the *nature* of the welfare support that we find in the United States. If egalitarianism truly were the driving force behind welfare attitudes, we would expect Americans to express support for precisely those policies that they tend to reject, namely, redistributive policies. These policies are logically most closely related to egalitarianism, while the link between egalitarianism and policies like Social Security and assistance to the poor is much more tenuous. The latter policies do not necessarily contribute to the goal of equality, yet they receive the widest support in the American public (Weaver, Shapiro, & Jacobs, 1995).

Arguments like these have led to a consideration of other values that may lead to support for social welfare policies. Although it is not nearly as prominent in discussions of the American political culture as egalitarianism and individualism, there is evidence that humanitarian or social compassion has long been part of the culture as well. This can be seen in Tocqueville's (1955) observation that self-reliance and individualism do not appear to prevent Americans from providing assistance for others. Wuthnow (1991) made a remarkably similar observation from his analysis of people who are engaged in voluntary efforts to assist the needy. Researchers are starting to measure more systematically variations in humanitarian sentiments and their impact on social welfare attitudes and other policy positions.

Big Government

One of the components of individualism is typically opposition to big government. It would be easy to conclude that opposition to big government should be a prominent, or even the prominent, basis for opposition to social welfare policy. It is clearly the case that political rhetoric would lead one to believe that debates over the scope of the welfare state centrally involve the size of government. However, analyses of public opinion data that have compared the impact of belief in limited government with values like egalitarianism, individualism, and humanitarianism find that opposition to big government is a statistically significant, but relatively weak, predictor (Feldman & Steenbergen, 1993; Kinder & Sanders, 1996; Steenbergen, 1995). Feldman and Steenbergen (1993) found that egalitarianism and humanitarianism are substantially better predictors of a range of opinions on social welfare policy than is belief in limited government or economic individualism. On the other hand, there are few studies that have systematically examined either the nature of belief in limited government or its effects on public opinion.

     One way to understand the limitations of opposition to big government as a predictor of attitudes toward economic and social welfare policies is to consider the difference between procedure and outcome. Values like egalitarianism and humanitarianism may be good predictors of attitudes toward social welfare policy because they reflect the outcomes that people desire from social policies. While it may be true that increased social welfare spending is inconsistent with limited government, people may be more likely to base their opinions on their desires for public assistance or redistribution rather than on the principle of limited government itself. In addition, the concept of limited government does not easily map onto the liberal–conservative dimension in the United States. While conservatives generally prefer a more limited role for government in matters of social welfare and the economy, many conservatives argue for a more active government role in regulating moral and social behavior. The opposite is typical of many liberals. As a result, the very definition of "big government" may depend on people's ideologies (see Fee, 1981).

Measuring Socioeconomic Values and Beliefs

Despite the central role of concepts like egalitarianism and economic individualism in several large bodies of literature, specific scales that measure these values and beliefs are difficult to find. A major vehicle for studying the nature and effects of core beliefs and values like individualism and egalitarianism has been in-depth interviews with a small number of subjects (Hochschild, 1981; Lamb, 1974; Lane, 1962). Survey-based studies of political attitudes, policy preferences, and belief systems have devoted relatively little attention to this. In particular, there have been few studies that attempt to build and evaluate multi-item scales. Multiple uses of a scale—and direct replication—are rarer yet.

     The existing scales also tend to suffer from several common problems. First, in many cases the conceptualization of the dimension to be measured is too loose, ignoring many of the issue distinctions just discussed. Second, because equality of opportunity, the work ethic, and humanitarianism tend to be highly valued, at least in the United States, there is the further potential problem of social desirability. It may be difficult to get people to endorse statements counter to these values—even among people who are not strongly committed to them. Third, most existing scales are fairly short—often a constraint imposed by an otherwise long interview schedule and competition for space. Partly as a consequence of this, estimated reliabilities are generally mediocre at best.

The most difficult problem may be constructing and interpreting measures of values and beliefs based on research conducted entirely within a single nation—particularly the United States. Consider the case of individualism, for which cross-national studies have indicated that U.S. respondents are most supportive (Hofstedte, 1980; Hofstede & Bond, 1984). What are the implications of this for constructing and evaluating measures of individualism in the United States? Suppose an individual-level measure of the concept is constructed from combined samples of many nations that differ substantially in individualism (measure A). The existing cross-national studies suggest that the mean score for the United States on this measure will be quite high. There will, of course, be some variance around this mean because, even in a highly individualistic society, some people are more individualistic than others. The important question is, How much variance will be observed for Americans on a measure that has a range wide enough to capture all the cross-national variation? Suppose the variance in individualism for Americans on this measure is fairly low. Now consider a measure of individualism constructed wholly from U.S. data (measure B). If the analyst starts with a pool of items written to measure individualism, the common practice will be to retain those items that have substantial marginal variance, discarding items with little or no variance. The resulting scale will assign people scores that will vary over a substantial range.

Suppose we now try to interpret scores from measure B. Given its construction there will some people who get very low scores. It is natural to describe such people as low on individualism. But what if we also have scores for these same people on measure A? Will they still appear to be low on individualism, or will we now find that they are relatively high when judged in the broader context? If we find such a discrepancy, the meaning of variance in measure B is now suspect. Are items that find significant numbers of Americans to be "nonindividualistic" really tapping individualism? While it is usually possible to write survey questions that produce response variance, the problem is to identify the source of that variance.

Researchers who develop scales of values and beliefs with potentially large cross-national variation often seem not to appreciate the consequences of this problem for scale construction. In the extreme, if the American political culture is really characterized by commitment to individualism and equality of opportunity, there may be no cross-sectional variance to measure. Reality is almost certainly not this simple. Cross-sectional variance on these dimensions is probably nontrivial, but failure to think about the implications of the full range of observable cross-cultural variance for scale construction may undermine the final products.

Measures Reviewed in This Chapter

The measures included in this chapter are all attempts to construct multi-item scales of socioeconomic values or core beliefs. Single-item measures of concepts like egalitarianism, individualism, and limited government are common, but are not evaluated in this section. Scales composed of specific policy items rather than general orientations are also not included in this section. Due to the complexities of reactions to individual policy options, it is often difficult to know how to interpret the resulting scales. Their status as independent variables in analyses of public opinion is also suspect. As noted previously, there have been few efforts to develop multi-item measures of economic values and beliefs, with the scales typically being short and the estimated reliabilities (when calculated) often far from desired levels. Few of the scales are strongly recommended as finished products, and they should be seen as initial efforts needing higher reliabilities and validities.

1. American National Election Studies Egalitarianism Scale (Feldman, 1988)
2. Egalitarianism and Inegalitarianism Scales (Kluegel & Smith, 1986)

The American National Election Studies (ANES) Egalitarianism scale was first developed in the 1983 ANES Pilot Study and has been included in these election year studies since 1984. The six items in this scale focus on equality of opportunity, although equal rights are also explicitly dealt with. The Kluegel and Smith Egalitarianism and Inegalitarianism Scales were developed from a factor analysis of 11 items that broadly tap the sources and consequences of income inequality.

The next three scales deal with other value constructs:

3. Protestant Ethic Scale (Mirels & Garrett, 1971)
4. American National Election Studies Individualism Scales (Markus, 1990)
5. Capitalist Values Scale (Chong, McClosky, & Zaller, 1983; McClosky & Zaller, 1984)

Of the scales discussed in this chapter, the Protestant Ethic Scale is by far the instrument with the most substantial history and use. Almost all the research using it, however, has been in psychology and sociology. Developed directly from Weber's (1958) discussion of the role of the Protestant work ethic in the development of capitalism, the scale taps the hard-work aspect of economic individualism, placed in a somewhat broader context of moral obligation and the value of leisure time.

The ANES Individualism Scales are a result of recent work to bring survey data to bear on issues of individualism that have received a great deal of attention in social science analyses of American politics (see Markus, 1990). Four subdimensions of individualism were identified using data from the 1989 ANES Pilot Study. A subset of the original 11 items was subsequently included in the 1990 election year survey, and a smaller subset appeared in the 1992 and 1996 ANES studies.

The Capitalist Values Scale (Chong, McClosky, & Zaller, 1983; McClosky & Zaller, 1984) is another attempt to broadly measure those aspects of economic individualism relevant to support for limited government and capitalism. In this case a single instrument combines the various aspects of economic individualism and support for capitalism. This differs from the ANES Individualism Scales, in which the various aspects of the concept are separately operationalized.

Another approach to measuring beliefs in economic individualism focuses on explanations for poverty:

6. Explanations for Poverty Scales (Feagin, 1975; Kluegel & Smith, 1986)

Those who believe strongly in individualism should endorse explanations that assert that the poor are themselves responsible for their condition and reject assertions that societal factors are responsible. A version of these scales was used in Feagin (1975), and a related measure was included in the 1972 CPS (Center for Political Studies) election year study (see Feldman, 1983). Kluegel and Smith (1986) have updated these scales.

One of the first attempts to develop a multi-item measure of humanitarianism or social compassion distinct from egalitarianism is the following:

7. American National Election Studies Humanitarianism Scale (Steenbergen, 1995)

The scale was tested in the 1995 ANES Pilot Study, and four of the items appeared in the 1996 Election Study.

Conclusions

As should be clear from this review, there has been increasing attention given to measuring people's support for the basic elements of the free enterprise–capitalist system. Although it has long been common practice to solicit opinions on specific aspects of welfare state policy, the measurement of economic beliefs and values has lagged behind. There have been scattered attempts to measure constructs like individualism and egalitarianism for many years, but except for the Protestant Ethic Scale, these efforts have not resulted in reliable, well-validated scales. The scales reviewed in this chapter generally represent work done in the past 5 to 10 years. It is perhaps best to view them as early efforts toward scale construction rather than finished products. Often the estimated scale reliabilities are uncomfortably low, and evidence of validity is scarce.

Aside from problems with particular scales, there are more general problems evident in this review of existing instrumentation. Concepts like individualism, egalitarianism, and support for capitalist values are complex and probably multidimensional. It is hard to imagine that 6 or 10 survey questions could possibly do justice to such concepts. Further conceptualization is required to better identify what is being measured by these scales. There is no shortage of both theoretical discussions of these values and beliefs and qualitative studies of American politics to draw on. Reliability and validity will almost certainly improve if longer scales are constructed to measure more precisely defined concepts. This would clearly lead to the proliferation of scales and would require careful studies to establish convergent and discriminant validity. The hope is that such a strategy would begin to shed some light on the key beliefs and values that are driving public support for social welfare policy.

As valuable as theoretical discussions of economic values and beliefs may be to conceptualization, it is also important not to lose sight of the way in which members of the public actually understand these values and beliefs. It is easy to write questions that reflect theoretical discussions of values like individualism and egalitarianism. If these questions are not too difficult, most respondents will select a response alternative that most appeals to them. This does not necessarily show that they independently hold that value. For example, suppose one created a series of items to measure commitment to the free enterprise system. It would be reasonable to write questions that posed an alternative between an unregulated market system and some government oversight of business. It is possible that such a set of questions could scale nicely, even if the respondents do not possess a consistent belief in free enterprise. A cynical attitude toward government or a belief in governmental inefficiency could lead to a consistent rejection of government regulation, even if there is no strong support for free enterprise.

Feldman and Zaller (1992) found a situation similar to this. Responses to an egalitarianism scale—a variant of the ANES Egalitarianism scale reviewed in this chapter—were compared to responses to open-ended probes attached to standard social welfare issue questions. These probes asked respondents to report the thoughts they had while answering the issue questions. The responses to the standard egalitarianism questions suggested that people vary significantly in their commitment to this value. Scale scores were also strongly related to responses to the closed-ended issue questions. However, the open-ended probes gave almost no evidence that egalitarianism was a factor in answering the issue questions. Instead, expressions of sympathy and humanitarianism were prevalent among those most supportive of social welfare policy. Although a large body of literature suggests that egalitarianism should be a central value to Americans that structures their opinions on social welfare, the open-ended probes failed to confirm this. It is thus possible that concepts like egalitarianism and individualism may be too abstract to be employed by ordinary people. Feelings of sympathy and social benevolence may be simpler, more basic dimensions that could be driving responses to a variety of survey questions—including scales measuring egalitarianism and issue preferences.

There is thus much more work required to specify and construct measures of key economic values and beliefs. Further conceptual and empirical work is necessary to deal with these complex issues. Those interested in measuring these values and beliefs should find the scales reviewed in this chapter a good starting point. They also would be well advised to consider the numerous conceptual and measurement problems discussed here in some detail before beginning any new data collection.

American National Election Studies Egalitarianism Scale

(S. Feldman, 1988)

Variable

The ANES Egalitarianism scale was designed to measure commitment to the value of equal opportunity in American society.

Description

The ANES Egalitarianism scale is composed of six agree–disagree items. The direction of three of the items is reversed to deal with potential problems of agreement response set. Several of the items refer directly to equal opportunity, while others ask about equal rights. In the development of this scale, other items that dealt with the inherent equality of individuals (or talents) were also explored, but those items formed a dimension distinct from belief in equal opportunity.

Sample

The scale was developed in the 1983 ANES Pilot Study, a national sample of 314 respondents. It was subsequently modified—lengthened to six items—and has been included in the ANES election year studies since 1984.

Reliability

Internal Consistency

Kinder and Sanders (1996) report alpha coefficients for the six-item measure of .52 to .71 in subsamples of whites and African-Americans from two different national samples.

Test–Retest

There is no reported test–retest correlation. Feldman (1988) reports a corrected stability coefficient of .86 from a two-wave confirmatory factor analysis.

Validity

The egalitarianism measure is inversely correlated to income and education. African-Americans score higher on the scale than do whites (Feldman, 1988). The egalitarianism scale is a strong predictor of a range of domestic issue preferences: social welfare, support for women's rights, and racial policy (Feldman, 1988; Kinder & Sanders, 1996). In the original study there was a negative correlation of only .21 between egalitarianism and a measure of economic individualism, and comparable correlations with ideological self-identification and party identification (Feldman, 1988).

Location

Original scale: Feldman, S. (1988, May). Structure and consistency in public opinion: The role of core beliefs and values. *American Journal of Political Science, 32,* 416–440. Reprinted by permission of the University of Wisconsin Press.

Revised six-item scale: Codebooks for the 1984 through 1996 ANES election year surveys.

Results and Comments

The reliability of this measure appears quite poor, although the coefficient alpha provides only a lower bound to reliability and the reversal of half the items almost certainly causes even further underestimation. Given the complexities of equality as a concept, the variation in the item wording leaves some uncertainty as to what aspect of equality is really being measured. Still the measure shows high levels of temporal stability when corrected for unreliability and is a substantial predictor of a wide range of issue preferences. It is also available in several ANES data sets.

American National Election Studies
Egalitarianism Scale
(Feldman, 1988)

I am going to read several statements. After each one I would like you to tell me whether you AGREE STRONGLY with the statement, AGREE SOMEWHAT, NEITHER AGREE NOR DISAGREE, DISAGREE SOMEWHAT, or DISAGREE STRONGLY.

1. Our society should do whatever is necessary to make sure that everyone has an equal opportunity to succeed.

Agree strongly†	46%
Agree somewhat	35
Neither agree nor disagree	8
Disagree somewhat	7
Disagree strongly	4

*2. We have gone too far in pushing equal rights in this country.

Agree strongly	20%
Agree somewhat	34
Neither agree nor disagree	14
Disagree somewhat	17
Disagree strongly	14

*3. This country would be better off if we worried less about how equal people are.

Agree strongly	20%
Agree somewhat	33
Neither agree nor disagree	16
Disagree somewhat	20
Disagree strongly	12

*4. It is not really that big a problem if some people have more of a chance in life than others.

Agree strongly	8%
Agree somewhat	28
Neither agree nor disagree	19
Disagree somewhat	29
Disagree strongly	15

5. If people were treated more equally in this country we would have many fewer problems.

Agree strongly	24%
Agree somewhat	36
Neither agree nor disagree	16
Disagree somewhat	17
Disagree strongly	6

6. One of the big problems in this country is that we don't give everyone an equal chance.

Agree strongly	17%
Agree somewhat	31
Neither agree nor disagree	16
Disagree somewhat	24
Disagree strongly	11

†Frequencies are from the 1996 ANES Election Study
*Indicates reverse worded item

Egalitarianism and Inegalitarianism Scales
(J. R. Kluegel & E. R. Smith, 1986)

Variable

The Egalitarianism and Inegalitarianism Scales were developed to measure popular beliefs about inequality.

Description

These two scales were created from a factor analysis of a pool of 11 items. All the items deal explicitly with income inequality. More specifically the items concern the causes and consequences of income inequality. The statements were developed to represent three major theories of income inequality: the Marxist or conflict perspective, structural functionalism, and classical economic theory. Agree–disagree responses to the 11 items were factor-analyzed, and the resulting two-factor solution assigned the 4 positively worded items to the Egalitarianism Scale and the 7 negatively worded items to the Inegalitarianism Scale.

Sample

The data come from a national probability phone sample of English-speaking residents of the contiguous 48 states of the United States. The data were collected in 1980, and the sample size is 2212.

Reliability

Internal Consistency

Kluegel and Smith report an alpha coefficient of .68 for the Egalitarianism Scale and .76 for the Inegalitarianism Scale.

Test–Retest

No test–retest correlations are available.

Validity

Results published in Kluegel and Smith (1986) show that both scales are related in the expected direction to income and race. The two scales are also related to a variety of issue questions, including redistributive policy, affirmative action for African-Americans and women, and support for the equal rights amendment. The two scales often relate in different ways to these issue preferences, and there is no obvious pattern to the observed relationships.

Location

Kluegel, J. R., & Smith, E. R. (1986). *Beliefs about inequality: Americans' views of what is and what ought to be.* New York: Aldine de Gruyter. Copyright © 1986 James R. Kluegel and Eliot R. Smith.

Results and Comments

These two scales do appear to predict a range of domestic issue preferences, even in regression equations that control for many other variables. The reliability estimates are reasonable for scales of this length. There is a potential problem with agreement response set. All four of the egalitarianism items are worded positively (*agree* is a more egalitarian response), while all of the inegalitarianism items are worded negatively. This raises several potentially difficult issues. To the extent that agreement response set relates to other variables (for example, education), the relationships between these variables will be affected. In addition, because the division of the 11 items into two scales perfectly matches the direction of item wording, it is possible that there is only one dimension of egalitarianism underlying these questions. The factor analysis results may be an artifact of the direction of item wording. More analysis is required to demonstrate that these items measure two distinct dimensions of egalitarianism.

Egalitarianism and Inegalitarianism Scales
(Kluegel & Smith, 1986)

Egalitarianism Items

1. More equality of incomes would allow my family to live better.
   1. STRONGLY   2. AGREE   3. DISAGREE   4. STRONGLY
      AGREE   DISAGREE
2. More equality of incomes would avoid conflicts between people at different income levels.
3. Incomes should be more equal, because every family's needs for food, housing, and so on, are the same.
4. Incomes should be more equal, because everybody's contribution to society is equally important.

Inegalitarianism Items

5. If income were more equal, nothing would motivate people to work hard.
6. Incomes cannot be made more equal since people's abilities and talents are unequal.
7. Incomes should not be more equal since the rich invest in the economy, creating jobs and benefits for everyone.
8. If incomes were more equal, life would be boring because people would all live in the same way.
9. Incomes cannot be made more equal since it's human nature to always want more than others have.
10. Incomes should not be made more equal since that would keep people from dreaming of someday becoming a real success.
11. Making incomes more equal means socialism, and that deprives people of individual freedoms.

Protestant Ethic Scale
(H. Mirels & J. Garrett, 1971)

Variable

This scale was developed to operationalize Weber's (1958) Protestant ethic thesis as an individual differences variable.

Description

The scale is composed of 19 agree–disagree items. Three of the items are reverse worded. Most deal with the virtues of individual effort: Hard work—and often suffering—results in strong character development and is an indicator of character. Conversely other questions derogate leisure time and the "easy" acquisition of money. The 19 items in this scale were selected from a larger pool of items written to conform to Weber's description of the Protestant ethic.

Sample

The scale was originally developed on data from samples of college students ($N = 117$ and 222). It has subsequently been administered to many convenience samples, most relatively small.

Reliability

Internal Consistency

Mirels and Garrett (1971) report a Kuder–Richardson coefficient of .79. Furnham (1990) reports coefficient alphas from other studies ranging from .70 to .75 and a Spearman–Brown split-half reliability estimate of .67.

Test–Retest

No test–retest correlations have been reported.

Validity

Furnham (1990) summarizes the findings of many studies that have used the Mirels and Garrett scale. The scale correlates well with other scales designed to measure the same construct. Various studies have found the scale related to achievement motivation, internal locus of control, postponement of gratification, belief in a just world, conservatism, and authoritarianism. In addition, it predicts negative attitudes toward the poor, individualistic explanations for poverty, and opposition to social welfare.

Location

Mirels, H., & Garrett, J. (1971). The Protestant ethic as a personality variable. *Journal of Consulting and Clinical Psychology, 36*, 40–44. Copyright © 1971 by the American Psychological Association. Reprinted with permission.

Results and Comments

This scale taps a somewhat more basic aspect of economic individualism than the other scales reviewed in this chapter. It is centrally concerned with orientations toward work and leisure. The Mirels and Garrett scale has also been used in many more studies than any other scale in this chapter, although political scientists have largely ignored it. There is a sizable literature on the work ethic in psychology, much of it reviewed in Furnham (1990). The scale appears to be more reliable than most of the others reviewed here, although that may be largely due to its length.

Protestant Ethic Scale
(Mirels & Garrett, 1971)

The response format for each item was a scale ranging from −3 (I disagree strongly) to +3 (I agree strongly), with the 0 excluded.

1. Most people spend too much time in unprofitable amusements.

−3	−2	−1	+1	+2	+3
DISAGREE STRONGLY	DISAGREE	DISAGREE MORE THAN AGREE	AGREE MORE THAN DISAGREE	AGREE	AGREE STRONGLY

2. Our society would have fewer problems if people had less leisure time.
3. Money acquired easily (e.g., through gambling or speculation) is usually spent unwisely.
4. There are few satisfactions equal to the realization that one has done his best at a job.
5. The most difficult college courses usually turn out to be the most rewarding.
6. Most people who don't succeed in life are just plain lazy.
7. The self-made man is likely to be more ethical than the man born to wealth.
8. I often feel I would be more successful if I sacrificed certain pleasures.
*9. People should have more leisure time to spend in relaxation.
10. Any man who is able and willing to work hard has a good chance of succeeding.
11. People who fail at a job have usually not tried hard enough.
12. Life would have very little meaning if we never had to suffer.
*13. Hard work offers little guarantee of success.
14. The credit card is a ticket to careless spending.
*15. Life would be more meaningful if we had more leisure time.
16. The man who can approach an unpleasant task with enthusiasm is the man who gets ahead.
17. If one works hard enough he is likely to make a good life for himself.
18. I feel uneasy when there is little work for me to do.
19. A distaste for hard work usually reflects a weakness of character.

*Indicates reverse worded item

American National Election Studies
Individualism Scales

(G. Markus, 1990)

Variable

This set of items was designed to measure the concept of individualism as discussed in analyses of American politics and the American political culture.

Description

The items for this scale were constructed as paired-alternative or forced-choice items. The set of 11 items is intended to measure four aspects of individualism: personal autonomy (3 items), self-reliance (2 items), limited government (4 items), and laissez-faire capitalism (2 items). A factor analysis of responses to these items appeared to support the fourfold distinction. There are positive correlations among the four factors, but these are small, ranging from .10 to .29.

Sample

The scale was initially developed and examined using data from the 1989 ANES Pilot Study. This was a national probability phone sample with 609 respondents. Eight of the items were included in the 1990 ANES election year survey.

Reliability

Internal Consistency

The estimated reliabilities (alpha coefficients) of these four scales are low, in part because of the small number of items in each. The best of the four is Limited Government, with $\alpha = .66$. The alpha coefficients for the three-item Personal Autonomy scale and the two-item Laissez-Faire scale are .35. The estimated reliability of the two-item Self-Reliance scale is only .31. There is some reason to believe that the actual reliabilities may be higher than this, although no better estimates are available (see Markus, 1990).

Test–Retest

Cross-time correlations would be useful here, but none is yet available.

Validity

Evidence on validity comes from correlations between the four scales and a large battery of issue questions and from four regressions in which constructed issue dimensions were regressed on the four scales and several other variables (see Markus, 1990). Limited Government has a pronounced effect on social welfare opinions and weaker effects on racial policy opinions and support for free enterprise. Self-Reliance has its strongest effect on racial policy opinions and a weak, but statistically significant, effect on social welfare attitudes. Personal Autonomy is a good predictor of civil liberties attitudes, and the Laissez-Faire scale has only weak effects on social welfare conservatism and civil liberties attitudes.

Location

Markus, G. (1990). *Measuring popular individualism.* Report to the Board of Overseers for the American National Election Studies.

The entire set of 11 items is included in the 1989 ANES Pilot Study. Eight of those items are also in the 1990 ANES Election Study.

Results and Comments

Of the four individualism scales, Limited Government appears to be the strongest. It is the most reliable, it is strongly related to a number of social welfare issue positions, and it is correlated with racial policy attitudes. Conversely Laissez-Faire is the weakest scale. Its estimated reliability is low, and it is not correlated with issue preferences. Personal Autonomy and Self-Reliance do better than Laissez-Faire, but are not very strong scales. All these scales could benefit from the addition of new items. The marginal distributions of many of these items are curious: Despite descriptions of Americans that highlight their presumed individualism, majorities choose the nonindividualistic option in many of these items.

American National Election Studies Individualism Scales

I am going to read two statements. Please tell me which one is closer to your own view.

Limited Government

1. 1. The less government the better or, 2. There are more things that government should be doing?

The less government the better†	45%
There are more things government should do	54
DK/NA	1

2. 1. The government should try to ensure that all Americans have such things as jobs, health care, and housing or, 2. The government should not be involved in this?

3. 1. The main reason that government has gotten bigger over the years is because it has gotten involved in things that people should do for themselves or, 2. Government has gotten bigger because the problems we face have gotten bigger?

Gotten involved in things people should do	49%
Problems we face have gotten bigger	50
DK/NA	1

4. 1. We need a strong government to handle today's complex economic problems or, 2. The free market can handle these problems without government being involved?

Need a strong government	61%
Free market can handle these problems	38
DK/NA	1

Personal Autonomy

5. 1. It is more important to be a cooperative person who works well with others or, 2. It is more important to be a self-reliant person able to take care of oneself?

6. 1. When raising children it is more important to teach them to be independent-minded and think for themselves or, 2. It is more important to teach them obedience and respect for authorities?

Self-Reliance

7. 1. Is it better to fit in with the people around you or, 2. Is it better to conduct yourself according to your own standards, even if that makes you stand out?

8. 1. People should take care of themselves and their families and let others do the same or, 2. People should care less about their own success and more about the needs of society?

9. 1. Most poor people are poor because they don't work hard enough or, 2. They are poor because of circumstances beyond their control?

Laissez-Faire

10. 1. Government regulation of big businesses and corporations is necessary to protect the public or, 2. That government regulation does more harm than good?

11. 1. Society is better off when businesses are free to make as much profit as they can or, 2. Businesses should be prohibited from earning excessive profits?

†Frequencies are from the 1996 ANES Election Study.

Capitalist Values Scale

(H. McClosky & J. Zaller, 1984; D. Chong, H. McClosky, & J. Zaller, 1983)

Variable

This scale is intended to measure support for the values and practices of capitalism.

Description

The 26 items in this scale are constructed in a sentence completion form. Each question has a beginning stem and two (forced-choice) options that complete the stem. The options of *neither* and *undecided* are also offered. The items reflect two major aspects of capitalist values: private enterprise and the work ethic. Items on private enterprise deal with the profit system, private property, laissez faire, and the fair distribution of economic rewards. Work ethic questions deal with individual achievement, the value of hard work, and self-reliance.

Sample

These items were included in surveys conducted between 1975 and 1977. One was a national probability sample, while the other two were surveys of "opinion leaders and members of groups active in public affairs."

Reliability

Internal Consistency

The authors present no overall measure of reliability, although coefficient alphas calculated separately for those low, medium, and high in political awareness had values of .74, .83, and .91, respectively (Chong, McClosky, & Zaller, 1983).

Test–Retest

No data were reported.

Validity

The scale is correlated with other measures assumed to tap basic ideological sentiments: belief in social change, social benevolence, and faith in human nature. In addition, the scale is inversely related to support for measures that increase equality (McClosky & Zaller, 1984).

Location

McClosky, H., & Zaller, J. (1984). *The American ethos.* Cambridge, MA: Harvard University Press. Reprinted by permission of the publisher. Copyright © 1984 by the Twentieth Century Fund.

Results and Comments

This is by far the longest and most reliable scale reviewed in this chapter. Its length allows it to be a reliable measure of support for capitalism, even among those relatively low in political sophistication. The Capitalist Values Scale is also the broadest of the scales discussed here.

Capitalist Values Scale
(McClosky & Zaller, 1984; Chong, McClosky, & Zaller, 1983)

Which answer comes closest to the opinion you actually hold.

1. When it comes to making decisions in industry: 1. Workers should have more to say than they do now, 2. The important decisions should be left to management.*

2. The profit system: 1. Teaches people the value of hard work and success,* 2. Brings out the worst in human nature.

3. The private enterprise system: 1. Is generally a fair and efficient system.*
2. Mostly leads to depression and widespread poverty.

4. A lumber company that spends millions for a piece of forest land: 1. Has the right to cut down enough trees to protect its investment,* 2. Should, nevertheless, be limited by law in the number of trees it can cut.

5. If the system of private industry were abolished: 1. Most people would work hard anyway, 2. Very few people would do their best.*

6. The poor are poor because: 1. They don't try hard enough to get ahead,* 2. The wealthy and powerful keep them poor.

7. Unskilled workers (such as janitors, dishwashers, and so on) usually receive wages that are: 1. About right, considering the amount of skill required,* 2. Much too low for the dirty work they do.

8. Workers and management: 1. Have conflicting interests and are natural enemies,* 2. Share the same interests in the long run.

9. Getting ahead in the world is mostly a matter of: 1. Ability and hard work,* 2. Getting the breaks.

10. Trade unions: 1. Have too much power for the good of the country,* 2. Need the power they have to protect the interests of working people.

11. A person's wages should depend on: 1. How much he needs to live decently, 2. The importance of his job.*

12. When people fail at one thing after another it usually means: 1. They are lazy and lack self-discipline,* 2. They weren't given a good enough chance to begin with.

13. Under a fair economic system: 1. All people would earn about the same, 2. People with more ability would earn higher salaries.*

14. The way property is used should mainly be decided: 1. By the individuals who own it,* 2. By the community, since the earth belongs to everyone.

15. Public ownership of property: 1. Is as important to a good society as freedom,* 2. Has often done mankind more harm than good.

16. The use of strikes to improve wages and working conditions: 1. Is almost never justified,* 2. Is often necessary.

17. Men like Henry Ford, Andrew Carnegie, J. P. Morgan and John D. Rockefeller should be held up to the young people as: 1. Models to be admired and imitated,* 2. Selfish and ambitious men who would do anything to get ahead.

18. When businesses are allowed to make as much money as they can: 1. Everyone profits in the long run,* 2. Workers and the poor are bound to get less.

19. The land of this country should be: 1. Turned over to the people, 2. Left in the hands of private owners.*

20. Government regulation of business: 1. Usually does more harm than good,* 2. Is necessary to keep industry from becoming too powerful.

21. Working people in this country: 1. Do not get a fair share of what they produce, 2. Usually earn about what they deserve.*

22. Can you depend on a man more if he owns property than if he doesn't?
    1. Yes,* 2. No.

23. When people don't work hard on a job it's usually because: 1. They just
    don't care about doing an honest day's work,* 2. Their job is dull, un-
    pleasant, or unimportant.

24. When it comes to taxes, corporations and wealthy people: 1. Don't pay
    their fair share, 2. Pay their fair share and more.*

25. The free enterprise system: 1. Survives by keeping the poor down, 2. Gives
    everyone a fair chance.*

26. Competition, whether in school, work or business: 1. Leads to better perfor-
    mance and desire for excellence,* 2. Is often wasteful and destructive.

*Indicates support for capitalist values

Explanations for Poverty Scales
(J. R. Feagin, 1975; J. R. Kluegel & E. R. Smith, 1986)

Variable

This series of items was designed to measure popular beliefs about the causes of poverty
in the United States.

Description

These 12 items cover a range of explanations that people might use to account for poverty.
They are presented as possible reasons for poverty, and respondents are asked how important each reason is. A basic distinction is between explanations involving personal characteristics of the poor (lack of effort, talent, and ability) and structural characteristics of
society (inadequate schools, low wages, not enough jobs). Factor analyses of these items
have confirmed the existence of these two dimensions, with most of the items loading on
one dimension. The correlation between the two dimensions is quite low.

Sample

These items first appeared on a 1969 national survey. The updated items were included in
a 1980 national probability phone sample of English-speaking residents of the contiguous
48 states of the United States. The sample size is 2212.

Reliability

Internal Consistency

There is no reported evidence on the reliability of these scales. Similar scales were constructed from items included in the 1972 CPS election study. The wordings were somewhat different, and the response format was agree–disagree. The estimated reliability of
the Individualistic Explanations scale (four items) was .57 (theta coefficient). The corresponding estimate for the seven-item Structural Explanations scale was .75.

Test–Retest

No data were reported.

Validity

The two Explanation for Poverty Scales correlate moderately with similar dimensions of explanations for wealth. Structural explanations are more prevalent among whites and the more wealthy, while individualistic explanations are less related to social status and are more associated with religion (Feldman, 1983; Kluegel & Smith, 1986). The two scales are related to a variety of measures of opinion on social welfare and racial issues. The Structural Explanations scale is the more consistent predictor of these issue preferences, although the Individualistic Explanations scale does strongly predict preferences on welfare and certain racial policy preferences (Feldman, 1983; Kluegel & Smith, 1986).

Location

Feagin, J. R. (1975). *Subordinating the poor.* Englewood Cliffs, NJ: Prentice-Hall.
    Kluegel, J. R., & Smith, E. R. (1986). *Beliefs about inequality.* New York: Aldine De Gruyter.

Results and Comments

These two scales appear to do a good job of capturing variations in the application of economic individualism. A fundamental aspect of individualism is the explanation of success and failure. The two dimensions that emerge from these items seem to be robust: They appeared in data collected in 1969 and 1986 (Feagin, 1975; Kluegel & Smith, 1986) and when using somewhat different items with an alternate response format (Feldman, 1983). The way Americans account for poverty also is very stable over these years. There was little or no change in responses to the individual items from 1969 to 1986, with individualistic explanations being more widely endorsed than structural explanations.

Explanations for Poverty Scale
(Feagin, 1975; Kluegel & Smith, 1986)

Respondents were asked to judge the following reasons "why there are poor people in the U.S." Response categories are: 1. VERY IMPORTANT, 2. SOMEWHAT IMPORTANT, 3. NOT TOO IMPORTANT, and 4. NOT AT ALL IMPORTANT.

I   1. Lack of thrift and proper money-management skills.

I   2. Lack of effort by the poor themselves.

I   3. Lack of ability and talent.

I   4. Their background gives them attitudes that keep them from improving their condition.

S   5. Failure of society to provide good schools for many Americans.

I	6. Loose morals and drunkenness.
	7. Sickness and physical handicaps.
S	8. Low wages in some business and industries.
S	9. Failure of private industry to provide enough jobs.
S	10. Prejudice and discrimination against blacks.
S	11. Being taken advantage of by rich people.
	12. Just bad luck.

I = item in Individual Explanations scale
S = item in Structural Explanations scale

American National Election Studies Humanitarianism Scale

(M. Steenbergen, 1995)

Variable

The ANES Humanitarianism scale was designed to measure variations in beliefs that people should care about the well-being of others and be willing to help them.

Description

The scale is composed of six agree–disagree items. Three of the items are reversed to deal with potential problems of agreement response set. Four of the items tap feelings of concern for the well-being of others, while the other two ask about willingness to provide assistance. A confirmatory factor analysis provides strong evidence for the unidimensionality of the scale. Agreement response set effects are very evident in the factor analysis results, but the items still load highly on a single substantive dimension, and the six items are balanced to deal with response set.

Sample

The scale was validated in the 1995 ANES Pilot Study, a national sample of 486 respondents. The sample was randomly split so that the agree–disagree format for the humanitarianism items could be compared with a paired-alternative format. Thus the effective sample size for the analysis of the agree–disagree items was 247. Four of the items appeared in the 1996 ANES election study.

Reliability

Internal Consistency

Steenbergen reports a reliability of .805 for the six-item scale. This estimate is derived from the Spearman–Brown prophecy formula using polyserial correlations among the items.

Test–Retest

There is no reported test–retest correlation.

Validity

The Humanitarianism scale is only weakly correlated with egalitarianism (in the range of .2 to .3), measured either as commitment to equality of opportunity (Steenbergen, 1995) or as support for redistribution (Feldman & Steenbergen, 1993). Correlations with party identification, liberal–conservative ideology, individualism, and limited government are in this range or lower. The Humanitarianism scale is a strong predictor of attitudes toward social welfare policies, especially on "safety net" issues. It also predicts positions on non-economic issues like crime and foreign policy.

Location

Steenbergen, M. (1995). *Compassion and American public opinion: An analysis of the NES Humanitarianism scale.* Report to the Board of Overseers for the American National Election Studies.

Eight humanitarianism items are included in the 1995 ANES Pilot Study. Four of those items are also in the 1996 ANES Election Study.

Results and Comments

The Humanitarianism scale appears to be fairly reliable and is distinct from other predictors of social welfare attitudes, especially egalitarianism. This strongly suggests that it is an independent dimension that needs to be considered in the analysis of attitudes toward economic policy and the welfare state. The major potential concern with this scale is social desirability. The responses to the Likert-type items show very high levels of humanitarianism in the U.S. adult population. This could be an accurate assessment, or pressures to appear humanitarian may be very strong. An experiment in the 1995 ANES Pilot Study compared the Likert items to a paired forced-choice format. Although the forced-choice format should have reduced social desirability bias, there were still very high levels of reported humanitarianism.

American National Election Studies
Humanitarianism Scale

I am going to read several statements. After each one I would like you to tell me whether you AGREE STRONGLY with the statement, AGREE SOMEWHAT, NEITHER AGREE NOR DISAGREE, DISAGREE SOMEWHAT, or DISAGREE STRONGLY.

    1. One should always find ways to help others less fortunate than oneself.

Agree strongly†	44%
Agree somewhat	46
Neither agree nor disagree	7
Disagree somewhat	2
Disagree strongly	1

2. A person should always be concerned about the well-being of others.

Agree strongly	45%
Agree somewhat	45
Neither agree nor disagree	6
Disagree somewhat	3
Disagree strongly	1

3. It is best not to get too involved in taking care of other people's needs.*

Agree strongly	5%
Agree somewhat	29
Neither agree nor disagree	17
Disagree somewhat	34
Disagree strongly	15

4. People tend to pay more attention to the well-being of others than they should.*

Agree strongly	5%
Agree somewhat	17
Neither agree nor disagree	20
Disagree somewhat	43
Disagree strongly	14

5. The dignity and well-being of all should be the most important concerns in any society.

6. One of the problems of today's society is that people are often not kind enough to others.

†Frequencies are from the 1996 ANES Election Study
*Indicates reverse worded item

Additional Sources of Questions

Although there are not many scales developed to measure economic values and beliefs, there are many other sources of individual survey questions. The questions in Free and Cantril (1968) may be somewhat dated, but they do cover both support for specific government policies and, more relevant for this chapter, questions on the principles of individualism and limited government. Several questions on economic individualism—especially beliefs about success, failure, and mobility in the United States—can be found in Schlozman and Verba (1979). There are also questions here on perceptions of class and class consciousness. A very good review of the concept of the Protestant work ethic can be found in Furnham (1990). He reviews a number of alternative measures as well as the research that has used them. A wide range of questions on equality can be found in Verba and Orren (1985), including many on income inequality. In addition to the Capitalist Values Scale, there are questions on economic individualism, egalitarianism, and support for free enterprise in McClosky and Zaller (1984).

In addition to the multi-item scales in the American National Election Studies that have been reviewed here, these studies contain a large number of individual questions that tap beliefs about the economy and social welfare policy. Many of these are questions of policy preference, which people have sometimes combined to create more general measures of social welfare orientation. Many of these questions have been carried without change in ANES studies since 1968. These data thus provide a growing basis for examining patterns of support for social welfare policy over time.

Appendix: National Data from the General Social Survey

(John P. Robinson)

The General Social Survey (GSS) has included more than 60 individual items related to inequality and government intervention in the economy since 1973, as shown in Table 4–1. A major problem with all but 5 of these items is that they have been asked only once, making it impossible to track trends across time. Moreover, the responses point to few congruent conclusions, largely because the different items approach the inequality–intervention issues from different perspectives.

Table 4–1

GSS Items on Government Role and Inequality

72. On these cards are some opinions about the government and the economy. For each one I'd like you to tell me whether you strongly agree, somewhat agree, somewhat disagree, or strongly disagree.

A. In our society everyone must look out for himself. It is of little use to unite with others and fight for one's goals in politics or unions. (EQUAL1)

Responses
Strongly agree	8
Somewhat agree	24
Somewhat disagree	34
Strongly disagree	32
Don't know	2

B. The economy can run only if businessmen make good profits. That benefits everyone in the end. (EQUAL2)

Responses
Strongly agree	24
Somewhat agree	45
Somewhat disagree	20
Strongly disagree	8
Don't know	3

C. The government must see to it that everyone has a job and that prices are stable, even if the rights of businessmen have to be restricted. (EQUAL3)

Responses
Strongly agree	14
Somewhat agree	29
Somewhat disagree	34
Strongly disagree	21
Don't know	2

D. It is the responsibility of government to meet everyone's needs, even in case of sickness, poverty, unemployment, and old age. (EQUAL4)

Responses

Strongly agree	21
Somewhat agree	35
Somewhat disagree	29
Strongly disagree	14
Don't know	1

E. If social welfare benefits such as disability, unemployment compensation, and early retirement pensions are as high as they are now, it only makes people not want to work anymore. (EQUAL5)

Responses

Strongly agree	13
Somewhat agree	32
Somewhat disagree	33
Strongly disagree	20
Don't know	2

F. All in all, one can live well in America. (EQUAL6)

Responses

Strongly agree	45
Somewhat agree	42
Somewhat disagree	9
Strongly disagree	3
Don't know	1

G. Generally speaking, business profits are distributed fairly in the United States. (EQUAL7)

Responses

Strongly agree	5
Somewhat agree	29
Somewhat disagree	38
Strongly disagree	22
Don't know	6

H. If someone has a high social or economic position, that indicates the person has abilities or great accomplishments. (EQUAL8)

Responses

Strongly agree	12
Somewhat agree	37
Somewhat disagree	31
Strongly disagree	17
Don't know	3

73. Here are different opinions about social differences in this country. Please tell me for each one whether you strongly agree, somewhat agree, somewhat disagree, or strongly disagree.

A. In the United States traditional divisions between owners and workers still remain. A person's social standing depends upon whether he/she belongs to the upper or lower class. (USCLASS1)

Responses

Strongly agree	16
Somewhat agree	52
Somewhat disagree	22
Strongly disagree	6
Don't know	4

B. In the United States there are still great differences between social levels, and what one can achieve in life depends mainly upon one's family background. (USCLASS2)

Responses

Strongly agree	9
Somewhat agree	35
Somewhat disagree	32
Strongly disagree	22
Don't know	2

C. America has an open society. What one achieves in life no longer depends on one's family background, but on the abilities one has and the education one acquires. (USCLASS3)

Responses

Strongly agree	40
Somewhat agree	43
Somewhat disagree	13
Strongly disagree	2
Don't know	2

D. What one gets in life hardly depends at all on one's own efforts, but rather on the economic situation, job opportunities, union agreements, and the social services provided by the government. (USCLASS4)

Responses

Strongly agree	8
Somewhat agree	34
Somewhat disagree	35
Strongly disagree	21
Don't know	2

E. Personal income should not be determined solely by one's work. Rather, everybody should get what he/she needs to provide a decent life for his/her family. (USCLASS5)

Responses

Strongly agree	11
Somewhat agree	22
Somewhat disagree	34
Strongly disagree	31
Don't know	2

F. Only if differences in income and social standing are large enough is there an incentive for individual effort. (USCLASS6)

Responses
Strongly agree   11
Somewhat agree   45
Somewhat disagree   28
Strongly disagree   10
Don't know   6

G. Differences in social standing between people are acceptable because they basically reflect what people made out of the opportunities they had. (USCLASS7)

Responses
Strongly agree   17
Somewhat agree   54
Somewhat disagree   20
Strongly disagree   5
Don't know   4

H. All in all, I think social differences in this country are justified. (USCLASS8)

Responses
Strongly agree   8
Somewhat agree   44
Somewhat disagree   33
Strongly disagree   11
Don't know   4

74. Does everyone in this country have an opportunity to obtain an education corresponding to their abilities and talents? (EDUCOP)

Responses
Yes   70
No   28
Don't know   2

75. For some time there have been discussions about how concerned the government should be about the social welfare of people. We have listed here two different opinions [HAND CARD]. With which opinion do you agree the most. (GOVCARE)

Response

A. Our system of social services goes much too far. It takes too much care of people and deprives them of too much individual responsibility.   25

B. Our system of social services is on the right track. It provides security for the elderly, the sick, and other people in distress without depriving people of individual responsibility.   70

No opinion   5

76. Some people think that the government in Washington ought to reduce the income differences between the rich and the poor perhaps by raising the taxes of wealthy families or by giving income assistance to the poor. Others think that the government should not concern itself with reducing this income difference between the rich and the poor.

Here is a card with a scale from 1 to 7. Think of a score of 1 as meaning that the government ought to reduce the income differences between rich and poor, and a score of 7 as meaning that the government should not concern itself with reducing income differences. What score between 1 and 7 comes closest to the way you feel? (EQWLTH)

Response

Government should		
	1	21
	2	12
	3	15
	4	17
	5	13
	6	8
Government should not	7	12
Don't know		2

78. Do you consider the amount of federal income tax which you have to pay as too high, about right, or too low? (TAX)

Response

Too high	62
About right	33
Too low	1
R pays no income tax (vol.)	2
Don't know	2

280. Some people feel that the government in Washington should make every possible effort to improve the social and economic position of blacks and other minority groups, even if it means giving them preferential treatment. (Suppose these people are at one end of the scale at point number 1.) Others feel that the government should not make any special effort to help minorities because they should help themselves. (Suppose these people are at the other end, at point 7. And of course, some other people have opinions somewhere in between at points 2, 3, 4, 5, or 6.)

Where would you place yourself on this scale, or haven't you thought much about this? (HLPMINR)

Response

Government should help		
	1	5
	2	5
	3	9
	4	23
	5	17
	6	14
Minorities should help themselves	7	20
Haven't thought much		5
Don't know		2

281. Some people think the government should provide fewer services, even in areas such as health and education, in order to reduce spending. Other people feel it is important for government to continue the services it now provides even if it means no reduction in spending.

Where would you place yourself on this scale, or haven't you thought much about this? (CUTSPDR)

Response

Government should reduce	1	8
	2	9
	3	12
	4	19
	5	13
	6	11
Government should continue	7	18
Haven't thought much		8
Don't know		2

309. I'd like to talk with you about issues some people tell us are important. Please look at CARD RR. Some people think that the government in Washington should do everything possible to improve the standard of living of all poor Americans; they are at Point 1 on this card. Other people think it is not the government's responsibility, and that each person should take care of himself; they are at Point 5.

Where would you place yourself on this scale, or haven't you made up your mind on this? (HELPPOOR)

Response

Government	1	19
	2	13
Agree with both	3	42
	4	13
People	5	10
Don't know	8	3

310. Now look at CARD SS. Some people think that the government in Washington is trying to do too many things that should be left to individuals and private businesses. Others disagree and think that the government should do even more to solve our country's problems. Still others have opinions somewhere in between.

Where would you place yourself on this scale, or haven't you made up your mind on this? (HELPNOT)

Response

Government do more	1	15
	2	14
Agree with both	3	39
	4	16
Government doing too much	5	14
Don't know	8	2

311. Look at CARD TT. In general, some people think that it is the responsibility of the government in Washington to see to it that people have help in paying for doctors and hospital bills. Others think that these matters are not the responsibility of the federal government and that people should take care of those things themselves.

Where would you place yourself on this scale, or haven't you made up your mind on this? (HELPSICK)

Response		
Government help	1	29
	2	20
Agree with both	3	32
	4	10
People take care	5	8
Don't know	8	1

312. Now look at CARD UU. Some people think that (Blacks/Negroes) have been discriminated against for so long that the government has a special obligation to help improve their living standards. Others believe that the government should not be giving special treatment to (Blacks/Negroes).

Where would you place yourself on this scale, or haven't you made up your mind on this? (HELPBLK)

Response		
Government help	1	10
	2	10
Agree with both	3	29
	4	18
No special treatment	5	32
Don't know	8	1

409. Some people think those with high incomes should pay a larger proportion (percentage) of their earnings in taxes than those who earn low incomes. Other people think that those with high incomes and those with low incomes should pay the same proportion (percentage) of their earnings in taxes.

Do you think those with high incomes should pay a much larger proportion, pay a larger proportion, pay the same amount as those who earn low incomes, pay a smaller proportion, pay a much smaller proportion? (PROGTAX)

Response	
Much larger	18
Larger	40
Same	37
Smaller	1
Much smaller	*
Can't choose	4

410. What is your opinion of the following statement?

It is the responsibility of the government to reduce the differences in income between people with high incomes and those with low incomes. (EQINCOME)

Response	
Agree strongly	11
Agree	21
Neither agree nor disagree	24
Disagree	30
Disagree strongly	14
Don't know	*

422. Here are some things the government might do for the economy. Circle one number for each action to show whether you are in favor of it or against it.

A. Control of wages by legislation. (SETWAGE)

Response
Strongly in favor of   8
In favor of   16
Neither in favor nor against   23
Against   35
Strongly against   16
Don't know   2

B. Control of prices by legislation. (SETPRICE)

Response
Strongly in favor of   9
In favor of   27
Neither in favor nor against   23
Against   27
Strongly against   11
Don't know   3

C. Cuts in government spending. (CUTGOVT)

Response
Strongly in favor of   39
In favor of   40
Neither in favor nor against   13
Against   4
Strongly against   1
Don't know   3

D. Government financing of projects to create new jobs. (MAKEJOBS)

Response
Strongly in favor of   25
In favor of   43
Neither in favor nor against   19
Against   9
Strongly against   2
Don't know   2

E. Less government regulation of business. (LESSREG)

Response
Strongly in favor of   13
In favor of   31
Neither in favor nor against   36
Against   15
Strongly against   3
Don't know   2

F. Support for industry to develop new products and technology. (HLPHITEC)

Response

Strongly in favor of	24
In favor of	48
Neither in favor nor against	20
Against	6
Strongly against	1
Don't know	1

G. Support declining industries to protect jobs. (SAVEJOBS)

Response

Strongly in favor of	16
In favor of	35
Neither in favor nor against	26
Against	18
Strongly against	4
Don't know	1

H. Reducing the work week to create more jobs. (CUTHOURS)

Response

Strongly in favor of	7
In favor of	17
Neither in favor nor against	32
Against	31
Strongly against	11
Don't know	2

429. And what about the federal government, does it have too much power or too little power? (GOVTPOW)

Response

Far too much power	14
Too much power	38
About the right amount of power	43
Too little power	4
Far too little power	*
Can't choose	*

430. What do you think the government's role in each of these industries should be?

A. Electric power. (OWNPOWER)

Response

Own it	9
Control prices and profits but not own it	60
Neither own it nor control its prices and profits	31
Can't choose	(8)

B. Local mass transportation. (OWNMASS)

Response

Own it	10
Control prices and profits but not own it	48
Neither own it nor control its prices and profits	42
Can't choose	(8)

C. The steel industry. (OWNSTEEL)

Response
Own it   2
Control prices and profits but not own it   37
Neither own it nor control its prices and profits   61
Can't choose   (12)

D. Banking and insurance. (OWNBANKS)

Response
Own it   4
Control prices and profits but not own it   52
Neither own it nor control its prices and profits   44
Can't choose   (12)

E. The automobile industry. (OWNAUTOS)

Response
Own it   2
Control prices and profits but not own it   37
Neither own it nor control its prices and profits   61
Can't choose   (7)

431. On the whole, do you think it should or should not be the government's responsibility to . . .

A. Provide a job for everyone who wants one. (JOBSALL)

Response
Definitely should be   17
Probably should be   27
Probably should not be   30
Definitely should not be   26
Can't choose   (6)

B. Keep prices under control. (PRICECON)

Response
Definitely should be   26
Probably should be   49
Probably should not be   17
Definitely should not be   8
Can't choose   (3)

C. Provide health care for the sick. (HLTHCARE)

Response
Definitely should be   38
Probably should be   49
Probably should not be   10
Definitely should not be   3
Can't choose   (3)

D. Provide a decent standard of living for the old. (AIDOLD)

Response
Definitely should be   40
Probably should be   48
Probably should not be   10
Definitely should not be   2
Can't choose   (2)

E. Provide industry with the help it needs to grow. (AIDINDUS)

Response
Definitely should be   18
Probably should be   50
Probably should not be   25
Definitely should not be   7
Can't choose   (7)

F. Provide a decent standard of living for the unemployed. (AIDUNEMP)

Response
Definitely should be   16
Probably should be   38
Probably should not be   31
Definitely should not be   15
Can't choose   (7)

G. Reduce income difference between the rich and poor. (EQUALIZE)

Response
Definitely should be   17
Probably should be   25
Probably should not be   29
Definitely should not be   29
Can't choose   (6)

452. Some people earn a lot of money while others do not earn very much at
     all. In order to get people to work hard, do *you* think large differences in
     pay are . . . (INCENTIV)

Response
Absolutely necessary   20
Probably necessary   52
Probably not necessary   20
Definitely not necessary   8
Can't choose   (6)

453. Do you agree or disagree . . .

A. People would not want to take extra responsibility at work unless they were
   paid extra for it. (INEQUAL1)

Response
Strongly agree   19
Agree   51
Neither agree nor disagree   11
Disagree   15
Strongly disagree   2
Don't know   2

B. Workers would not bother to get skills and qualifications unless they were paid extra for having them. (INEQUAL2)

Response

Strongly agree	14
Agree	43
Neither agree nor disagree	14
Disagree	23
Strongly disagree	3
Don't know	3

C. Inequality continues to exist because it benefits the rich and powerful. (INEQUAL3)

Response

Strongly agree	15
Agree	35
Neither agree nor disagree	26
Disagree	18
Strongly disagree	4
Don't know	2

D. No one would study for years to become a lawyer or doctor unless they expected to earn a lot more than ordinary workers. (INEQUAL4)

Response

Strongly agree	27
Agree	42
Neither agree nor disagree	10
Disagree	17
Strongly disagree	2
Don't know	2

E. Large differences in income are necessary for America's prosperity. (INEQUAL5)

Response

Strongly agree	7
Agree	27
Neither agree nor disagree	28
Disagree	31
Strongly disagree	5
Don't know	2

F. Allowing business to make good profits is the best way to improve everyone's standard of living. (INEQUAL6)

Response

Strongly agree	10
Agree	37
Neither agree nor disagree	23
Disagree	24
Strongly disagree	4
Don't know	2

G. Inequality continues to exist because ordinary people don't join together to get rid of it. (INEQUAL7)

Response
Strongly agree	11
Agree	36
Neither agree nor disagree	26
Disagree	22
Strongly disagree	4
Don't know	1

723. Do you agree or disagree?

A. Differences in income in America are too large. (INCGAP)

Response
Strongly agree	16
Agree	42
Neither agree nor disagree	21
Disagree	15
Strongly disagree	3
Don't know	3

*Indicates less than 1%

In general, these trend and nontrend questions indicate considerable and continued ambivalence in the public on these issues. For example:

- In the 1974 GSS 69% agreed that business profits are good for the economy (Q72B), but only 34% agreed that such profits are distributed fairly in practice (Q72G). Similarly 56% agreed that it was the government's responsibility to meet everyone's basic needs (Q72D), but 45% agreed that current government welfare benefits reduce incentives to work (Q72E).
- In the 1984 GSS 51% said they were against government control of wages (Q422A) versus 24% in favor, but on control of prices the 38% against control were almost balanced by the 36% in favor (Q422B). Those in favor of government creating new jobs were 68% versus only 11% against (Q422D), and of government support of industry developing new technology, 72% were in favor versus 7% against (Q422F).
- In 1984 three times as many respondents agreed that income differences were too large as disagreed (Q723A), but only 29% then agreed (versus 57% that disagreed) that it was government's responsibility to reduce these differences (Q723B), and even fewer (21%) agreed it should guarantee a minimum income.

At the same time, the general edge in public opinion has seemed to favor business rather than government control. For example:

- In 1993 there was almost a 2-to-1 ratio of support (58% agree versus 30% disagree) for allowing people to accumulate as much wealth as possible, even if some people got very little (Q455B). In terms of a direct and clear pairing, 84% chose "equal opportunity" versus only 12% for "equal outcomes" in terms of distributing societal wealth (Q456, not shown).
- In 1984 only 32% agreed that government had a responsibility to reduce income differences versus 44% who disagreed (Q410); asked in a different format later

(Q431G) in the interview, 42% said it should be the government's responsibility versus 58% who said it should not be.

- Some 52% said the government in general had too much power versus 43% saying the right amount and 4% saying too little power (Q429). Only 2–10% felt the government should own and run power companies, banks, or transport (Q430).
- Some 47% agreed business profits were the best way to improve everyone's living standard versus 28% who disagreed (Q453F), and 34% agreed large income differences were necessary for America's prosperity (Q453E).
- In 1984–1987, 72% agreed that large pay differences were necessary to get people to work hard (Q452).
- In the 1984 GSS as well, 71% agreed (versus 25% disagreed) that differences in social standing reflected effort and were acceptable (Q73G), and 65% disagreed (versus 33% agreed) that one's income should depend on need rather than work effort (Q73E). In that same survey 70% agreed that educational opportunities were open to everyone (Q74), and 70% also agreed that government provision of social services was "on the right track" (Q75). Opposition to government help to African-Americans and other minorities is expressed at an even higher rate than is general opposition to government help (Q312).
- At the same time there was general agreement in the 1984 GSS (Q409) that the rich should pay higher income taxes (58% versus 37% for the same tax rate and 1% for lower taxes). When it comes to one's own taxes, of course, those saying they are "too high" outnumber those saying they are "about right" by almost a 2-to-1 margin (Q78).

GSS Trends

Table 4–2 shows the GSS trends in those government intervention items that have been repeated over the years. It can be seen that there was an initial drop in public support for intervention between 1975 and 1983, but that the 1996 figures end up being remarkably close to the 1983 figures. There were some fluctuations during the last 13 years in that support for intervention rose during the late 1980s, but it declined 4–8 points in the mid-1990s—being particularly low in 1994, the year of the Republican victory in the congressional elections, in which the public mood was reported to have turned sharply to the right, with its emphasis on minimal government.

Overall, then, it appears that public support for intervention in these economic matters did show a decline in the early Reagan years (in relation to 1975 figures), that it showed some comeback in the later years of his administration and during the Bush years, but that it has generally returned to early Reagan administration levels during the Clinton presidency. How much this is a function of their policies or statements on these issues is not clear. Moreover, responses over the years have varied by only about 10–15 points from high to low readings.

Relationship with Background Factors

Responses to the government help items have a notably consistent pattern of correlations with background factors. All of the correlations in Table 4–3 are statistically significant at the .05 level, but some of them are very small—such as the relationship between age and reducing the income gap and the relationship between education and aiding minorities.

Table 4-2

Trends in Government Help Items

Government should	1975	1978	1980	1983	1984	1986	1987	1988	1989	1990	1991	1993	1994	1996
1. Help poor	40			33	29	31	35	30	32	35	34	27	27	30
2. Do more	38			25	29	26	34	30	29	30	31	29	27	26
3. Help sick	50			46	44	50	51	49	54	57	57	52	48	49
4. Help minorities	25			18	20	18	27	18	19	23	23	18	16	17
5. Reduce gap		47	43	47	49	49	49	47	50	51	48	48	40	45

Table 4-3

Demographic Correlates of Government Help Items

Government should	Sex	Age	Race	Educ	Party	Lib–Con
1. Help poor	−.08	.10	−.24	.13	.25	.20
2. Do more	−.09	.11	−.24	.15	.25	.20
3. Help sick	−.03	.07	−.17	.07	.22	.22
4. Help minorities	−.04	.06	−.39	−.03	.20	.20
5. Reduce gap	−.09	.02	−.19	.20	.18	.24

The more general patterns are as follows:

- Gender: In general, women tend to be more prohelp, although the larger correlations generally result from men being more opposed than from women being in favor. Gender differences are minimal for help to the sick and to minorities.
- Age: Older people are more opposed to government help, which is perhaps surprising, given that they have enjoyed the benefits of Social Security and are more likely to remember what life was like not having it. Older and younger people are much less different in relation to support for the government reducing income differences.
- Race: African-Americans are much more supportive of government help than are whites, generally by about 2-to-1 margins. The differential, of course, becomes even larger when it comes to help for minorities.
- Education: Here is one area in which education differences are relatively small— and it is the college educated who are most "conservative" or anti-intervention on this issue (presumably because they have more to conserve). However, on the issue of helping minorities, the college educated are slightly more supportive.
- Party Identification: Consistent with voting behavior, Democrats are much more supportive of government intervention than Republicans, by 2-to-1 margins on some issues.
- Ideology: Consistent with the conservative principle of minimal government intervention, conservatives are much less supportive of government help. The percentage differences are generally larger than for party identification, but the correlations do not reflect this because the numbers of extreme liberals and conservatives are small and because extreme conservatives are not much different from moderate conservatives on these issues.

Dimensionality of the GSS Items

In general, factor analyses of the GSS items in Table 4–1 do not cluster into a simple set of two or three dimensions. Although we were unable to complete a dimensional analysis on all of the 1984 items together, analyses of subsets of them showed little clustering.

Thus the equality and class questions (Q72A–H, Q73A–H, Q74–76) break into five dimensions, the most common one combining Items 72C and D, 73D and E, 75 (reversed), and 76, which generally deal with support of government intervention and meeting everyone's minimal needs; a second factor combines Items 73 F, G, and H, which deal with support of inequalities, and a third factor combines Items 72 A and E, which deal with individualism.

Similarly, factor-analyzing Items 409 through 429 produces four fragmented factors, the main one being 422D, F, G, and H, which deals with government programs to increase jobs. A second factor isolates government control of wages and prices, and a third factor combines Items 409 and 410 on progressive taxes and reducing inequality. The items on inequality (453A–G) break into three factors, one on the need for incentives, another on why inequality exists, and a third on the need for large differences.

At the same time there is some clustering on certain sets of items. For example, the trend items on help in Table 4–3 do constitute a single factor. The same type of single dimension can be found for the five items dealing with government ownership of industries (430A–E) and the seven items on government responsibilities (431A–F); indeed, these last two dimensions also show notable correlation with each other. More detailed and refined analyses may reveal further areas of overlap in these question areas and may help in the development of a unidimensional or bidimensional instrument.

References

Almond, G. A., & Verba, S. (1963). *The civic culture.* Princeton, NJ: Princeton University Press.

Beer, S. H. (1978). In search of a new public philosophy. In A. King (Ed.), *The new American political system* (pp. 5–44). Washington, DC: American Enterprise Institute.

Bellah, R. N., Madsen, R., Sullivan, W. M., Swindler, A., & Tipton, S. M. (1985). *Habits of the heart.* Berkeley: University of California Press.

Chong, D., McClosky, H., & Zaller, J. (1983). Patterns of support for democratic and capitalist values in the United States. *British Journal of Political Science, 13,* 401–440.

Coughlin, R. M. (1980). *Ideology, public opinion, and welfare policy.* Berkeley, CA: Institute of International Studies.

Devine, D. J. (1972). *The political culture of the United States.* Boston: Little, Brown.

Feagin, J. R. (1975). *Subordinating the poor.* Englewood Cliffs, NJ: Prentice-Hall.

Fee, J. F. (1981). Symbols in survey questions: Solving the problem of multiple word meanings. *Political Methodology, 7,* 71–95.

Feldman, S. (1983). Economic individualism and American public opinion. *American Politics Quarterly, 11,* 3–29.

Feldman, S. (1988). Structure and consistency in public opinion: The role of core beliefs and values. *American Journal of Political Science, 32,* 416–440.

Feldman, S., & Steenbergen, M. (1993). *Explaining social welfare attitudes: The role of egalitarianism and humanitarianism.* Paper presented at the annual meeting of the Midwest Political Science Association, Chicago, IL.

Feldman, S., & Zaller, J. (1992). The political culture of ambivalence: Ideological responses to the welfare state. *American Journal of Political Science, 36,* 268–307.

Free, L. A., & Cantril, H. (1968). *The political beliefs of Americans.* New York: Simon and Schuster.

Furnham, A. (1990). *The Protestant work ethic.* London: Routledge.

Gans, H. J. (1988). *Middle American individualism.* New York: Free Press.

Hartz, L. (1955). *The liberal tradition in America.* New York: Harcourt Brace Jovanovich.

Hochschild, J. L. (1981). *What's fair: American beliefs about distributive justice.* Cambridge, MA: Harvard University Press.

Hofstede, G. (1980). *Culture's consequences.* Beverly Hills, CA: Sage.

Hofstede, G., & Bond, M. H. (1984). Hofstede's culture dimensions: An independent validation using Rokeach's value survey. *Journal of Cross-Cultural Psychology, 15,* 417–433.

Kinder, D. R., & Sanders, L. M. (1996). *Divided by color: Racial politics and democratic ideals.* Chicago: University of Chicago Press.

Kluegel, J. R., & Smith, E. R. (1986). *Beliefs about inequality.* New York: Aldine De Gruyter.

Ladd, E. C., & Lipset, S. M. (1980). Public opinion and public policy. In P. Duignan & A. Rabushka (Eds.), *The United States in the 1980s* (pp. 49–84). Stanford, CA: Hoover Institution.

Lamb, K. A. (1974). *As Orange goes.* New York: Norton.

Lane, R. E. (1962). *Political ideology.* New York: Free Press.

Lipset, S. M. (1979). *The first new nation.* New York: Norton.

Markus, G. (1990). *Measuring popular individualism.* Report to the Board of Overseers for the American National Election Studies.

McClosky, H., & Zaller, J. (1984). *The American ethos.* Cambridge, MA: Harvard University Press.

Mirels, H., & Garrett, J. (1971). The Protestant ethic as a personality variable. *Journal of Consulting and Clinical Psychology, 36,* 40–44.

Potter, D. M. (1954). *People of plenty.* Chicago: University of Chicago Press.

Rae, D., Hochschild, J., Morone, J. & Fessler, C. (1981). *Equalities.* Cambridge, MA: Harvard University Press.

Rokeach, M. (1968). *Beliefs, attitudes, and values.* San Francisco: Jossey-Bass.

Rokeach, M. (1973). *The nature of human values.* New York: Free Press.

Rosenbaum, W. (1975). *Political culture.* New York: Praeger.

Schlozman, K. L., & Verba, S. (1979). *Injury to insult.* Cambridge, MA: Harvard University Press.

Sears, D. O., & Citrin, J. (1982). *Tax revolt.* Cambridge, MA: Harvard University Press.

Smith, T. (1987). The welfare state in cross-national perspective. *Public Opinion Quarterly, 51,* 404–421.

Steenbergen, M. (1995). *Compassion and American public opinion: An analysis of the ANES Humanitarianism scale.* Report to the Board of Overseers for the American National Election Studies.

Tocqueville, A. de. (1955). *Democracy in America.* New York: Vintage.

Triandis, H. C., McCusker, C., & Hui, C. H. (1990). Multimethod probes of individualism and collectivism. *Journal of Personality and Social Psychology, 59,* 1006–1020.

Verba, S. (1987). *Elites and the idea of equality.* Cambridge, MA: Harvard University Press.

Verba, S., & Orren, G. R. (1985). *Equality in America.* Cambridge, MA: Harvard University Press.

Weaver, R. K., Shapiro, R. Y., & Jacobs, L. R. (1995). Trends: Welfare. *Public Opinion Quarterly, 59,* 606–627.

Weber, M. (1958). *The Protestant ethic and the spirit of capitalism.* New York: Scribner's.

Williams, R. H. (1970). *American society.* New York: Knopf.

Wuthnow, R. (1991). *Acts of compassion: Caring for others and helping ourselves.* Princeton, NJ: Princeton University Press.

CHAPTER 5

Democratic Values and Political Tolerance

Steven E. Finkel, Lee Sigelman, and Stan Humphries

How willing are citizens to endorse the values, norms, and procedures of the democracy in which they live? How willing are they to apply them in concrete situations, particularly situations involving people or groups they oppose? Theorists from Rousseau to Tocqueville to Rawls have viewed citizen consensus on democratic values as a prerequisite for a stable and effective democratic system. A government may have characteristics we associate with democracy—competitive elections with majority rule, political equality, inclusive political participation, and civil liberties, such as freedom of speech and the like—but as Pennock (in Griffith, 1956) noted, "Unless the *bulk of the society* is committed to a high valuation of these ideals [liberty and equality] it can hardly be expected that institutions predicated upon them will work successfully or long endure" (p. 131).

More recently cultural theorists of democratic development have re-echoed these themes, arguing that tolerance and interpersonal trust are essential elements of a democratic culture (Almond & Verba, 1963; Inglehart, 1988). Although the precise nature of the causal relationship between democratic structures and mass political orientations is not altogether clear, "[v]irtually every scholar who has thought about the process of democratization has ascribed an important role to political culture" (Gibson, Duch, & Tedin, 1992, p. 331).

The degree to which citizens endorse basic democratic norms also figures prominently in the debate between the "classical" and "elite" perspectives on the desirability of widespread mass political participation. If citizens subscribe to democratic principles and are willing to extend civil liberties even to those with whom they disagree, as the "classical" theory seems to mandate, then high levels of mass political participation should certainly be encouraged. If, however, individuals do not endorse basic democratic values and are intolerant of their opponents, then high levels of mass participation might endanger the political system itself. As Dahl (1956, p. 89) put it, "If an increase in political activity brings the authoritarian-minded into the political arena, the consensus on the basic norms among the politically active must certainly be declining. . . . In the light of all this we cannot assume that an increase in participation is always associated with an increase in [democracy]." Moreover, if endorsement of democratic norms is concentrated among those who are highly active in political life, as "elite" theorists contend, then political elites may be responsible for ensuring the viability of the political system *despite* the antidemocratic tendencies of the masses.

The First Studies

Given the centrality of political tolerance and democratic values in theories of democratization, participation, and system effectiveness, it is hardly surprising that the topic has spawned a massive empirical literature. In the 1950s and 1960s Stouffer (1956), Prothro and Grigg (1960), and McClosky (1964) constructed the first empirical measures of support for democratic principles and of political tolerance to analyze the beliefs of the mass public and political elites in the United States. After these initial studies uncovered widespread agreement among both masses and elites on abstract democratic principles—such as the belief in majority rule, political equality, and support for democracy as the best form of government—scholars for the next three decades focused primarily on the more problematic "applied" belief of political tolerance in the United States and elsewhere.

Among the key questions and controversies motivating this research have been the following:

- To what extent are citizens willing to extend procedural democratic liberties (such as freedom of speech and association) to unpopular political groups? How widespread is political intolerance?
- What are the cultural, demographic, social, psychological, economic, and political sources of political tolerance and intolerance? Are certain types of citizens (e.g., the less educated) more intolerant?
- Is the mass public becoming more tolerant than it once was? If so, why?
- Does intolerance tend to be concentrated on a few unpopular groups, or is it more widely dispersed? In other words, to what extent is intolerance "pluralistic"?
- Are elites more tolerant than the rank and file? If so, why? And is the elite–mass tolerance gap widening or narrowing?
- Are there significant cross-national differences in tolerance, whether in the general public or among elites? How can such differences be explained?
- What individual-level behaviors and system-level outcomes does political tolerance or intolerance foreshadow?

New Democracies

The wave of democratization in Latin America, Eastern Europe, and the former Soviet Union in the 1980s and early 1990s has generated renewed, and intense, scholarly interest in support for democratic values in all forms, abstract as well as concrete. Although consensus on the basic principles, structures, and procedures of democracy seemed fairly well established in the United States and in many nations of Western Europe, it was not at all clear that citizens in the new democracies of Latin America and the former Soviet bloc shared these beliefs—either at the onset of the transition to democracy or after some years of experience with democratically elected governments. Equally unclear was the extent to which citizens in countries that had only recently emerged from revolutionary convulsions or civil wars would be willing to tolerate political opponents or groups associated with previous regimes.

Consequently scholars over the past decade have investigated a wide range of democratic attitudes in these emerging democracies, using these "natural laboratories" to test theories of democratic development and to assess the extent to which the existence of democracy in previously infertile cultural ground could bring about changes in a country's political orientations. The following questions have figured prominently in this literature:

- How "democratic" are the attitudes of citizens in the newly emerging democracies? How do these attitudes compare to those found in the United States and other Western countries? Do the levels of support for democratic values in systems changing from communist and authoritarian regimes differ from the levels seen in the transitions from fascist regimes after World War II?
- What accounts for the levels of support for democratic values seen at the onset of democratization in these countries? What accounts for cross-national differences in democratic beliefs within the former Soviet bloc?
- What is the relationship between support for democracy and support for capitalism? Do citizens in newly emerging democracies endorse both sets of values, or is there greater consensus on one of these aspects of "Western-style" political and economic arrangements than on the other?
- How deeply entrenched are democratic values in the newly emerging democracies? Have these attitudes been successfully internalized, or are they dependent on favorable short-term economic and/or political conditions?

Each of these questions is a matter of genuine substance. But as is so often the case, questions of substance cannot be divorced from questions of measurement, which in turn cannot be divorced from theoretical and conceptual issues. Many of the controversies that swirl around the literature on political tolerance are ultimately reducible to disagreements about what political tolerance means and how to measure it. Similarly scholars have had enormous difficulty in specifying the precise orientations that correspond to "support for democratic principles"; indeed, these disagreements often reflect basic theoretical differences about what norms, procedures, and values constitute a democratic political system.

Despite these formidable conceptual and measurement difficulties, impressive progress has been made over the past four decades. Scholars are now acutely aware of the ways that different measurement strategies can produce different assessments of the nature of mass political tolerance, and much is now known about the relative advantages and disadvantages of alternative measurement techniques. In assessing support for more general democratic principles, progress has also been made by expanding the dimensions of democratic attitudes that are investigated and by developing scales that tap the concepts highlighted in particular versions of democratic theory.

We begin by summarizing three studies that set the agenda for research—Stouffer's *Communism, Conformity, and Civil Liberties* (1955), Prothro and Grigg's "Fundamental Principles of Democracy: Bases of Agreement and Disagreement" (1960), and McClosky's "Consensus and Ideology in American Politics" (1964). We then review the long and often controversial lines of research that these studies spawned. We conclude our historical review by considering the most recent work, mainly in new democracies.

The Early Classics

Stouffer on Political Tolerance

As enshrined forever in Voltaire's ringing avowal, "I disapprove of what you say, but I will defend to the death your right to say it," political tolerance has long been recognized as a central component of the democratic ethos. Modern political observers also view acceptance of Voltaire's formulation as vital to the maintenance of democracy: "The more tolerant citizens are of the rights of others, the more secure are the rights of all, their own included; hence the special place of political tolerance in contemporary conceptions of democratic values and democratic citizenship" (Sniderman, Tetlock, Glaser, Green, & Hout, 1989, p. 25). Yet, beginning with Stouffer's (1955) landmark work, empirical research has often made it painfully obvious that political tolerance in the United States and other nations is more an unfulfilled aspiration than an accomplished fact.

Although Stouffer was not the first social scientist who sought to gauge the political tolerance of the American public (see, e.g., the historical reviews by Erskine, 1970, and Hyman & Sheatsley, 1953), the importance of *Communism, Conformity, and Civil Liberties* cannot be overstated. It presented the results of the first comprehensive national survey of political tolerance in the United States, it painted an unsettling portrait of Americans' political values, and it constituted a point of departure for scores of new analyses of political tolerance that would be undertaken in the ensuing decades.

Conceived at the height of the McCarthy hysteria of the early 1950s, *Communism, Conformity, and Civil Liberties* was a product of its times (Ruggiero, 1979). Stouffer set out to determine the American public's "degree of willingness to tolerate nonconformists such as people whose loyalty has been criticized" and more specifically the "degree to which the internal Communist threat is regarded as a serious threat" (Stouffer, 1955, p. 21). His test of political tolerance was simple (too simple, it would turn out): People were considered politically intolerant to the extent that they would deny civil liberties to socialists, atheists, or accused or admitted communists.

In two 1954 national opinion surveys, Stouffer uncovered evidence of widespread intolerance in the American public. For example, two-thirds of those polled said an admitted communist should not be permitted to make a speech in their community. An equal proportion agreed that books written by a communist should be removed from a public library. Nine in 10 said an admitted communist should be fired from a college teaching position. Nor was such treatment reserved for admitted communists: More than 60% would not allow "somebody who is against all churches and religion" to make a public speech in their community.

From a measurement standpoint Stouffer's primary innovation was to examine the public's tolerance for various hypothetical actions taken by specific "target groups." Until then (and even thereafter), political tolerance had been measured via a hodgepodge of general questionnaire items, some of which referred to specific types of behavior without mentioning the circumstances or groups involved; still other items asked about certain groups without referring to the activities in which they might be engaged. In contrast, Stouffer devised a composite scale of "willingness to tolerate nonconformists." This scale was based on responses to 15 questions concerning the rights of members of four target groups: admitted communists, suspected communists, socialists, and antireligionists. The items focused on whether

- members of these groups should be permitted to make speeches in public,
- books they had written should be removed from public libraries,
- products with which they were associated should be boycotted,
- they should be fired from jobs of various sorts, and
- they should be jailed.

To the extent that a person favored repressing these target groups, he or she was considered politically intolerant.

Stouffer (1955, pp. 89–155) also examined the linkages between several personal background factors and scores on his scale of "willingness to tolerate nonconformists." Intolerance was most prevalent among the elderly, the less educated, Southerners, rural and small town dwellers, women, Protestants, and regular church attenders. Education stood out as having by far the greatest impact on tolerance; for example, among those in the 21–29 age group, 77% of college graduates scored high versus only 30% of those who had not completed high school. Despite the prevalence of intolerance in the American public, then, Stouffer found cause for optimism about the future. Because the United States was in the midst of "an almost revolutionary uplift in the schooling of its population" (Stouffer, 1955, p. 91), he considered it likely that the future would usher in a new era of tolerance.

Stouffer also presented results from a parallel elite survey of community leaders in more than 100 cities nationwide. He considered these results reassuring, for the leaders were significantly more respectful of the civil liberties of unpopular groups than were members of the mass public. These findings were taken as evidence that becoming a political leader opened one's mind to democratic norms of pluralism and minority rights (see Jackman, 1972, for a good summary) and lent support to emerging elite-oriented theories of democracy, which characterized political elites as the guardians of the democratic character of the political system.

Prothro and Grigg and McClosky on Consensus and "The American Creed"

Stouffer's depiction of a mass public indifferent to the protection of democratic rights for unpopular groups was reinforced in Prothro and Grigg's "Fundamental Principles of Democracy: Bases of Agreement and Disagreement" (1960) and McClosky's "Consensus and Ideology in American Politics" (1964), both of which undertook assessments of more general democratic norms and values—such as belief in majority rule, free speech, and political equality. As such, these studies represented important early efforts to develop survey measures of support for democratic principles and to gauge the degree of congruence between these general attitudes and the applied attitude of political tolerance. Further, McClosky explicitly compared the responses of samples of the mass public and political elites, thus extending Stouffer's mass–elite comparisons on tolerance to the more general orientations toward democracy.

In both studies the central question was whether democratic "consensus in a meaningful sense (at both the abstract and specific levels) exists among some segment(s) of the population (which can be called the 'carriers of the creed')" (Prothro & Grigg, 1960, p. 281). To assess consensus at the "abstract" level, Prothro and Grigg (1960, p. 282) designed items to tap "the principles regarded as most essential to democracy . . . —majority rule and minority rights (or freedom to dissent)." McClosky (1964, p. 362) based his items more broadly on

> uniformly recognized . . . elements of American democratic ideology such [as] consent, accountability, limited or constitutional government, representation, majority rule, minority rights, the principle of political opposition, freedom of thought, speech, press and assembly, equality of opportunity, religious toleration, equality before the law, the rights of juridical defense, and individual self-determination over a broad range of personal affairs.

Examples of these items ranged from "Public officials should be chosen by majority vote" and "People in the minority should have an equal chance to influence government policy"

(Prothro & Grigg) to "The majority has the right to abolish minorities if it wants to"; "No matter what a person's political beliefs are, he is entitled to the same legal rights and protections as anyone else"; and "I believe in free speech for all no matter what their views might be" (McClosky). To measure consensus at the specific level, Prothro and Grigg (1960) included variants of Stouffer's items referring to freedom of speech for communists and atheists and the rights to run for and hold public office for communists and "Negroes"; McClosky, in contrast, constructed new items applying the general principles in concrete situations, where other values or attitudes might come into play (e.g., "When the country is in great danger we may have to force people to testify against themselves even if it violates their rights"). The Prothro–Grigg surveys were administered to voters in Ann Arbor, Michigan, and Tallahassee, Florida, while McClosky surveyed a national mass sample as well as samples of Democratic and Republican activists.

The basic finding of both studies quickly became part of the conventional wisdom concerning American public opinion: Members of the mass public expressed overwhelming support for democratic principles in the abstract, but were unwilling or unable to apply these principles in practice. Agreement on the generalized principles of majority rule, minority rights, and whether democracy is the "best form of government" ran well over 90% in the Prothro–Grigg surveys, and McClosky also reported large majorities endorsing the principles of free speech and opinion and supporting the democratic "rules of the game" (e.g., not abolishing minorities or "taking the law into one's own hands"). However, consensus broke down completely when people were asked to apply these principles in particular situations: As in the Stouffer study, fewer than 50% of the Prothro–Grigg respondents said they would allow a communist to speak in public or hold political office; between one-third and three-quarters of McClosky's respondents were unwilling to extend the right of free speech to those who "teach foreign ideas" or hold "wrong political views" or to extend due process rights to anyone who "hides behind the laws when he is questioned about his activities" or has been convicted of crimes by "illegal evidence."

McClosky also documented significantly more prodemocratic responses to items referring to abstract principles and their specific applications among political activists than among the mass public. For example, whereas 28% of the general public agreed that "The majority has the right to abolish minorities if it wants to," only 7% of McClosky's elite sample gave this response. On the specific application items, differences were often more pronounced: Fifty percent of the mass sample, but only 18% of the elite sample, agreed that "A book that contains wrong political views cannot be a good book and does not deserve to be published." McClosky (1964, p. 366) concluded that although elite consensus on democratic norms was "far from perfect," members of the political elite "not only . . . exhibit stronger support for democratic values than does the electorate, but they are also more consistent in applying the general principle to the specific instance. The average citizen has greater difficulty appreciating the importance of certain procedural or juridical rights, especially when he believes the country's internal security is at stake."

The Stouffer, Prothro–Grigg, and McClosky studies had far-reaching theoretical implications and jointly set the agenda for future research. Theoretically they indicated that democratic societies could apparently survive and flourish despite a lack of consensus among members of the mass public on basic procedural norms and values. This was accomplished in part by the apathy of large numbers of the masses, as the systemic consequences of their antidemocratic impulses were mitigated by their generally low levels of political participation. In addition, democracy could be sustained by political elites, who "serve as the major repositories of the public conscience and as the carriers of the Creed" (McClosky, 1964, p. 374). By virtue of their relative social homogeneity and their exposure to democratic norms through involvement in the political process, members of the political elite were more likely to comprehend, accept, and act on those norms than were members of the mass public.

The influence of these three studies on later empirical research was enormous. Virtually every study conducted in the field in the ensuing 20 years returned to one or more of the issues first raised by Stouffer, Prothro and Grigg, or McClosky: the extent of mass intolerance toward unpopular political groups; the influence of age, education, and other factors on support for democratic principles; whether, and if so, why, differences in democratic orientations exist between masses and elites; and whether citizens can and do make connections between abstract democratic principles and their specific applications. Equally important, because of the overwhelming public agreement on the abstract principles relating to the "rules of the game," free speech, judicial rights, and the like, researchers in the United States moved away from developing and analyzing new measures of these concepts, instead focusing primarily on measuring and estimating the levels, sources, and consequences of political tolerance.

More recently, though, in response to developments around the world, a significant body of research has emerged that assesses the extent to which mass publics and elites in the newly emerging democracies of the former Soviet bloc and Latin America endorse democratic values both in the abstract and in specific applications. Some of this research builds directly on measures used by Prothro and Grigg, McClosky, and several Western European scholars; other researchers have developed new and more comprehensive scales to gauge support for democratic structures, procedures, norms, and values and to assess the relationship between these orientations and the more applied measures of political tolerance. We shall discuss each of these literatures and the controversies they have generated in turn.

Reconsidering Political Tolerance

For a long time, research on political tolerance did not stray far from Stouffer's footsteps; prior to the late 1970s, the literature was replete with updates, extensions, specifications, and refinements of his work—for example, attempts to follow up on Stouffer's ideas about the variability of tolerance across various segments of the mass public or toward different target groups—and these issues have continued to attract attention in the decades since then (e.g., Abrahamson & Carter, 1986; Beatty & Walter, 1984; Bobo & Licari, 1989; Cutler & Kaufman, 1975; Ellison & Musick, 1993; Gay & Ellison, 1993; Grabb, 1979; Hougland & Lacy, 1981; Irwin & Thompson, 1977; Jelen & Wilcox, 1990; McCutcheon, 1985; Smith & Petersen, 1980; Weston & Ruggiero, 1978; Wilson, 1985, 1991, 1994; Wilcox & Jelen, 1990).

However, in the last two decades attention turned from replication and extension of Stouffer's work to more fundamental reconsiderations. While acknowledging Stouffer's vital contributions to the study of political tolerance, later waves of researchers began thinking of tolerance in fresh ways, measuring it in innovative fashions and in different settings, and reaching new conclusions about his primary findings.

Mass versus Elites

One area of intense controversy that emerged from the early literature was the alleged difference in tolerance between political elites and the mass public. Reconsidering the notion that the elite–mass tolerance gap was wider than would be expected based on differences in education and socioeconomic status, Jackman (1972) concluded that the heightened tolerance Stouffer had observed among community elites was wholly a function of educational differences and had nothing to do with socialization experiences, role expectations, or elite culture. Jackman's conclusions proved controversial (see St. Peter, Williams, & Johnson, 1977; Jackman, 1977), and a subsequent study by McClosky and Brill (1983), analyzing fresh national surveys of the U.S. public and opinion leaders in the late 1970s, reported findings that bore out Stouffer's and McClosky's earlier conclusions (see also Sullivan, Walsh, Shamir, Barnum, & Gibson, 1993).

More recently, however, Sniderman, Fletcher, and their colleagues have argued that the elite–mass tolerance gap has been greatly overstated, based on Canadian surveys (Fletcher, 1989; Sniderman, Fletcher, Russell, Tetlock, & Boyd, 1990; Sniderman, Fletcher, Russell, Tetlock, & Gaines, 1991; Sniderman, Fletcher, Russell, & Tetlock, 1996). To be sure, on the question most similar to Stouffer's in the Canadian survey, whether "members of extreme political groups should be allowed to hold public rallies in our cities, or should not be allowed to do so," the traditional differences between masses and elites did emerge (Sniderman *et al.*, 1991, p. 355). But on several questions requiring respondents to choose between support for competing values, such as freedom of assembly or public safety ("Should a town or city be able to limit public demonstrations that city officials think might turn violent against persons and property?"), the political elite appeared to be little more pro–civil libertarian (and perhaps even less so) than the general public. Moreover, elite–mass differences in support for civil liberties were eclipsed by deep differences *within* the elite. In the view of Sniderman *et al.* (1991, p. 350), the "fallacy of democratic elitism" is that it failed to consider the degree to which political parties themselves "divide on issues of civil liberties [in part] out of political advantage, in part out of political conviction," rendering it vital from the standpoint of democratic stability *which* elites predominate in a given political conflict.

Over the years, then, the image of elites as guardians of civil liberties, prominent in the early literature, has been both reinforced by considerable research and subjected to sharp challenge. All that seems certain at this point is that this key issue in democratic theory remains unsettled.

Trends in Tolerance and the Sullivan *et al.* Reassessment

For a quarter of a century, Stouffer's optimistic prediction that the American mass public would grow more tolerant with the passage of time went unchallenged. A number of follow-up studies (see especially Corbett, 1982; Davis, 1975; Nunn, Crockett, & Williams, 1978; see also, e.g., Erskine & Siegel, 1975; Weston & Ruggiero, 1978) uniformly documented a substantial increase in tolerance after the 1950s, just as Stouffer had predicted. For example, Nunn *et al.* (1978) concluded that the proportion of the American public with scores in the "most tolerant" category of Stouffer's 15-item scale almost doubled between 1954 and 1973, growing from 31% to 55%. Moreover, education, the most powerful predictor of tolerance in the Stouffer study, proved to be even more closely tied to tolerance in 1973 than it had been during the 1950s (Nunn *et al.*, 1978, ch. 4). However, between 1954 and 1973 tolerance rose in every educational category. Accordingly the rising level of education could not be given all the credit for the increase in tolerance. On the basis of these studies, the sources of the trend toward greater tolerance remained unclear (see especially Davis, 1975, pp. 509–510), but the trend itself seemed indisputable.

In the late 1970s Sullivan and his colleagues undertook a truly fundamental reconsideration of Stouffer's conceptualization and measurement of, and conclusions about, political tolerance (see especially Sullivan, Piereson, & Marcus, 1979, 1982; Sullivan, Marcus, Feldman, & Piereson, 1981). Sullivan and his colleagues argued that the conclusions Stouffer and his successors reached were by no means indisputable and were, in many important respects, simply incorrect. The apparent trend toward more widespread tolerance was illusory, and the connection between education and tolerance had been overstated.

This critique was based on Stouffer's anchoring of his measure of tolerance on expressions of repressiveness toward members of *leftist* groups (socialists, atheists, and admitted or suspected communists). The point that the target groups in Stouffer's tolerance scale occupied a relatively narrow band on the left end of the political spectrum had been raised numerous times before Sullivan and his colleagues raised it anew (see, e.g., Ferrar, 1976; Lawrence, 1976; Zellman, 1975). Indeed, Stouffer (1955, p. 111) advised readers to "continually keep in mind the fact that we are not here measuring tolerance in general." However, his caveat was generally discounted or ignored by those who sought to build on his work, and Stouffer (1955) himself repeatedly referred generically to "tolerance for nonconformity."

Moreover, not all the target groups incorporated in post-Stouffer studies of political tolerance had been leftists. Holt and Tygart (1969), for example, counterbalanced two leftist groups (communists and socialists) and two rightist ones (members of the American Nazi Party and the John Birch Society), and Herson and Hofstetter (1975) focused on the rights of communists and members of the Ku Klux Klan. But these were exceptions to the prevailing practice. This leftist measurement bias was problematic because it left open the possibility that seemingly tolerant survey respondents might actually be quite intolerant, but of nonleftist groups. For example, Stouffer had found that Jews were unusually tolerant. But if tolerance were measured in terms of willingness to accord civil liberties to Nazis or Klansmen rather than to communists and socialists, would Jews still seem so tolerant?

The scope of the tolerance measure seemed to require a more diverse array of target groups. Yet for Sullivan and his colleagues, even such an expansion would not address the basic problem. "One is tolerant," Sullivan *et al.* (1979, pp. 784) argued, "to the extent one is prepared to extend freedoms to those whose ideas one rejects, whatever these might be." Different people oppose different groups and reject different ideas. For example,

> Smith may be particularly concerned about communists, while Jones is concerned about the Ku Klux Klan, and so on. . . . While one might be tolerant of communists or other radical groups, one might at the same time be quite intolerant of other groups on the right, such as racists, fascists, or nativists. (Sullivan *et al.,* 1979, pp. 784–785)

From this perspective the real test of tolerance is whether Smith would repress communists, toward whom he is ill-disposed, and whether Jones would repress Klan members, toward whom she is ill-disposed. Indeed, McCutcheon (1985) has shown that more than 20% of the American public is neither *generally* tolerant nor *generally* intolerant. Many respondents' willingness to permit others to exercise civil liberties depends on the political coloration of the group in question.

Sullivan *et al.*'s (1979) conceptualization requires that the target groups chosen to measure a particular individual's degree of tolerance be tailored to suit the individual's specific pattern of likes and dislikes. That is, if one wants to know how tolerant a particular person is, one must ask about a target group he or she is known to dislike. When Sullivan *et al.* (1979, p. 790) employed such a "content-controlled" measurement strategy, they found that fewer than half of their respondents selected communists, socialists, or atheists from a heterogeneous list as the group they liked least. This suggested that, at least in the United States in the late 1970s, it was inappropriate to measure tolerance solely in terms of repressiveness toward left-wing groups. Thus the lower repressiveness expressed toward members of leftist groups during the 1970s than the 1950s did not necessarily mean that the American public had become more tolerant. Americans may simply have diverted their repressiveness from extreme leftists toward other targets. Thus studies conducted by Stouffer's successors may have demonstrated a shift in the *targets* of intolerance rather than a diminution of intolerance.

Most of Sullivan *et al.*'s (1979) respondents also said they would deprive members of the particular target group they liked least of basic liberties—at the same time that the same respondents were giving the "tolerant" responses to the original Stouffer items about the rights of atheists and communists (Sullivan *et al.,* 1979, p. 787). This evidence made it

> difficult to escape the conclusion that the Stouffer items generate larger proportions of tolerant responses than do the content-controlled questions. Since the latter is the more valid approach, these results raise questions about the claims . . . that levels of tolerance in the American public are now very high relative to the 1950s. (Piereson, Sullivan, & Marcus, 1980a, p. 168)

Sullivan *et al.* (1982) then formulated and tested an alternative model of the sources of political tolerance. In contrast to earlier researchers who had uncovered moderate to strong relationships among tolerance and religion and urbanization, Sullivan *et al.* (1982) found these relationships "almost totally vitiated" by the content-controlled measurement strategy. Education's correlation with tolerance dropped to .29 when respondents selected a target group rather than .41 for four of Stouffer's original items concerning the rights of communists and atheists (Piereson *et al.,* 1980a, pp. 171, 177). It thus seemed reasonable to infer (Sullivan *et al.,* 1979, p. 792) that previously reported relationships between tolerance and various background characteristics were to some extent artifacts of the specific groups Stouffer and his successors had chosen as points of reference.

By far the best predictor of intolerance, Sullivan *et al.* (1982) reported, was the extent to which a respondent felt threatened by the target group he or she selected as the most disliked. In the absence of a sense of real threat, negative affect toward a group was significantly less likely to carry over into a willingness to prohibit group members from exercising liberties commonly granted to others.

The revisions Sullivan *et al.* (1979, 1982) made to earlier understandings of both the level and the sources of political tolerance had important theoretical implications as well. The observed low level of tolerance, combined with the relatively weak effects of age and education, cast doubt on whether the high standards desired for citizens in classical democratic theories could ever be met. Elite theories were also undermined, as even the most politically active respondents in the sample were generally intolerant, although somewhat less so than the mass public. Instead, Sullivan *et al.* (1982) argued that their results supported a kind of Madisonian theory, wherein democratic liberties are protected because the public and its politically active strata do not agree on *which* groups to target for intolerance. While most people are likely to deny civil liberties to groups they oppose, this "pluralistic intolerance," combined with constitutional safeguards of diffused and divided power, prevents the emergence of a consensus in favor of acts of repression against any particular political group.

The Countercriticisms

The Sullivan *et al.* (1979, 1982) critique of the Stouffer line of research initially won widespread, if often grudging, acceptance. But just as tolerance researchers now recognized fundamental problems in Stouffer's approach, so, too, did some of Sullivan *et al.*'s own ideas come under fire.

Much criticism focused on Sullivan *et al.*'s (1979) contention that the American public in the late 1970s was no more politically tolerant than it had been 25 years earlier—a contention that flatly contradicted one of Stouffer's most important predictions. Though acknowledging Sullivan *et al.*'s critique of Stouffer's measurement strategy, Abramson (1980) and Immerwahr (1980) could not accept the contention that apparent increases in tolerance since the 1950s were mere illusions. Without content-controlled data from the 1950s to contrast with Sullivan *et al.*'s 1978 findings, absolute levels of tolerance as measured by the two different strategies simply could not be compared. In response, Sullivan and his colleagues granted that the evidence on behalf of their "illusory" interpretation was inconclusive, but still characterized their evidence as highly consistent with their interpretation (Piereson, Sullivan, & Marcus, 1980b).

Almost a decade later Mueller (1988) reanalyzed trends in political tolerance, using measures that reflected Sullivan *et al.*'s (1979) content-controlled approach to the extent possible. He concluded that there had indeed been a marked increase in political tolerance over the years, but that it had occurred largely because the American public had grown less concerned about threats from leftist groups as the perceived threat of communism receded and was not replaced by a rightist counterpart. In responding to Mueller's analysis, Sullivan and Marcus (1988) retreated from their earlier position, now taking essentially the same agnostic position on the question of trends in tolerance as had Abramson and Immerwahr: "Given our conceptualization," they conceded, "it is probably most accurate to say that our percentage tolerant and intolerant cannot, in a strict sense, be compared with Stouffer's tolerant and intolerant percentages" (Sullivan & Marcus, 1988, p. 29). The question of whether the American public had become more tolerant since the 1950s simply did not admit of an answer, positive or negative.

A more fundamental critique goes to the conceptual heart of the Sullivan *et al.* (1979) content-controlled measurement strategy. The basis of that strategy is the assumption that negative affect toward a group is a precondition of tolerance toward the group—that is, that one cannot be considered "tolerant" (or "intolerant") of a group if one approves of it. After all, as Sniderman *et al.* (1989, p. 28) put it, "It would be odd to describe a person as a committed civil libertarian on the ground that he supports the right of fascists to hold a public rally—if he is himself a fascist."

However, according to McCutcheon (1985) this restraint should be rejected on two grounds. First, the willingness to curtail civil liberties to any group, no matter whether one is positively or negatively disposed toward it, is an intolerant attitude. The subtle, but important, change here is that whereas Sullivan *et al.* (1979) held that willingness to grant civil liberties to a group one *likes* does not constitute *tolerance*, McCutcheon contended that refusal to extend civil liberties to any group, *liked or disliked*, constitutes *intolerance* (McCutcheon, 1985, p. 476). Second, McCutcheon (1985, p. 476) noted that Sullivan *et al.*'s own data indicate that people are sometimes very tolerant of groups they like the least. McCutcheon's conclusion that affect toward a group is thus essentially irrelevant for measurement purposes represents a stark contrast to the Sullivan *et al.* position.

In a similar vein Sniderman and his colleagues (1989, 1991) and Gibson (1989b) criticized what may be termed the "emotivist," or affect-driven, view of tolerance. If the Sullivan *et al.* (1979) approach were correct, they argued, then there should be great variability in individual tolerance judgments, depending on which groups are targeted in a particular question. Moreover, following the "pluralistic intolerance" argument, one would expect ideological liberals to be more intolerant toward politically conservative targets, and vice versa, for the negative affect that individuals hold for groups at opposite ends of the political spectrum would produce intolerant responses. In the Sniderman *et al.* and Gibson (1989b) analyses, however, neither prediction appeared to hold. Sniderman *et al.* analyzed data from the 1977 General Social Survey (GSS), which contained Stouffer-like items on a wide range of minority political and social groups—atheists, racists, communists, militarists, and homosexuals. Confirmatory factor-analysis models with indicators representing the target groups and the acts toward which individuals made tolerance judgments showed that neither the group nor the act made much difference in individual responses. In addition, while conservatives in general were less tolerant than liberals, there was little difference between them in terms of which target groups were considered most objectionable: Both were more likely to say they would deny militarists and racists the right to speak in public than to say they would deny the same right to atheists, communists, or homosexuals. Gibson's (1989b) analysis of a 1987 U.S. national survey resulted in similar conclusions, as tolerance (and intolerance) judgments toward communists and members of the Ku Klux Klan were strongly correlated.

Sniderman, Brody, and Tetlock (1991) interpreted these and other findings to indicate that respondents' judgments about the rights that should be accorded members of certain groups are more reflective of a "principled," non-group-specific application of the abstract value of tolerance than of positive or negative feelings about these groups. As they argued (Sniderman, Brody, & Tetlock, 1991, p. 135), "The person who does not honor and protect the rights of those whose point of view clashes with his own is . . . a bad bet to protect the rights even of those whose point of view supports his own. . . . It is the racial bigot, not the person committed to racial tolerance, who is the more likely to oppose free speech for racists." This view was vividly supported in Duckitt and Farre's (1994) analysis of tolerance among South African college students, where it was shown that right-wing authoritarianism was related to support for a future black-majority government's repression of dissent—even though right-wing South Africans would likely be the targets of such repression.

Finally, Sullivan *et al.*'s (1979) focus on a single target group for each respondent, while avoiding some measurement problems, raises others. According to Sullivan and his colleagues, one is intolerant to the extent that one would deny civil liberties to members of that particular group, irrespective of one's willingness or unwillingness to extend civil liberties to any other groups—perhaps even to all other groups. However, refusal to tolerate a specific act or group does not necessarily define one as intolerant. Wagner (1986) argued that the content-controlled measurement strategy makes it difficult to distinguish contextually conditioned, transient responses from stable attitudes cued to a certain act or group or from a general tendency or behavioral disposition—and it is only those with a general tendency or latent disposition toward intolerance who should be considered intolerant. More generally Sullivan *et al.*'s (1979) measurement strategy may tap a respondent's least typical response tendency—a tendency triggered by being asked questions about the particular group toward which one's feelings are most extreme and negative. This measurement strategy cannot establish whether intolerance is focused (that is, restricted to a certain group or type of group) or diffuse (that is, directed against a wide array of groups).

These views suggest that the content-controlled method of gauging tolerance contains a fundamental analytic blindspot—the insistence that tolerance and intolerance come into play only in the presence of negative group affect. The ultimate measurement challenge is to determine how tolerant people are of the groups they *tolerate* the least, not necessarily the groups they *like* the least. The two are not necessarily synonymous and should be kept conceptually distinct. This is not a mere quibble because intolerance of one's second most disliked group on Sullivan *et al.*'s own measure outruns intolerance of one's most disliked group (Sullivan, Piereson, & Marcus, 1982, p. 65). Affect toward a group is undoubtedly a key factor influencing tolerance. But it need not be the defining consideration any more than, say, perceptions of the group as disruptive or threatening, which Sullivan and his colleagues treat as a predictor of tolerance rather than as part of the measurement of tolerance.

In sum, the advantages of the Sullivan *et al.* (1979) content-controlled measure in overcoming certain limitations of prior tolerance research have been widely acknowledged. At the same time this approach has itself been the target of considerable criticism. As a result, studies based on variants of the content-controlled measure (e.g., Barnum & Sullivan, 1989; Sullivan, Shamir, Walsh, & Roberts, 1985) as well as on Stouffer-like questions across an ideologically balanced set of targets (e.g., Nie, Junn, & Stehlik-Barry, 1996) can be found in the current literature—with the most comprehensive studies employing both types of questions (e.g., Gibson, 1989a; Gibson, Duch, & Tedin, 1992; Sniderman *et al.*, 1990, 1996). Unfortunately the levels of tolerance that are implied by the various measures differ considerably, thus rendering comparisons of the results across different studies problematic.

However, researchers can take comfort in Gibson's (1992a) demonstration that the etiology of tolerance judgments is remarkably the same, regardless of which of the currently popular measures is utilized in a given analysis. That is, the same set of independent variables, including education, psychological insecurity, and perceptions of group threat, tends to do equally well in predicting the level of tolerance as measured by both the Sullivan *et al.* (1979) approach and alternative measures. So although the different scales produce decidedly different distributions of tolerance and intolerance, and even though there appear to be limited amounts of shared variance among them, "on the key criterion—the implication for substantive conclusions—the alternative measures perform equally well" (Gibson, 1992a, pp. 573–574).

Subsequent Research on Support for Democratic Values

To this point we have focused largely on measuring and interpreting political tolerance in the United States. Yet tolerance is not the sole democratic value of interest, nor are concerns about tolerance and democratic values confined to the United States. Because democracy involves norms and processes other than the willingness to extend civil liberties to unpopular groups (norms such as majority rule, popular sovereignty, and the like), orientations toward political tolerance should not be equated with orientations toward "democracy." Building on Almond and Verba's *The Civic Culture* (1963) and Dahl's (1971) influential writings on the development of beliefs conducive to "polyarchy" (a type of regime characterized by extensive competition for political power and inclusive political participation), Gibson *et al.* (1992, p. 332) characterize a democratic citizen as one who believes in individual liberty and who is politically tolerant, who holds a certain amount of distrust of political authority but at the same time is trustful of fellow citizens, who is obedient but nonetheless willing to assert rights against the state, who views the state as constrained by legality, and who supports basic democratic institutions and processes.

Consistent with this multifaceted conceptualization, much scholarly attention has been devoted to these broader aspects of mass beliefs in democratic norms, structures, and processes in a variety of national settings.

Understanding the levels and sources of mass beliefs in democratic values is important for at least two reasons. First, since the early Prothro–Grigg (1960) and McClosky (1964) studies, it has been argued that tolerance is or ought to be rooted in the application of more general democratic principles to specific situations. Stouffer viewed a tolerant response as the result of a "sober second thought" to the perceived threat of communism— where an individual's belief in abstract democratic norms would override the visceral impulse to stifle a potentially dangerous group (compare Kuklinski, Riggle, Ottati, Schwarz, & Wyer, 1991). Accordingly analysis of general democratic principles, norms, and values may be critical for predicting the more applied attitude of political tolerance.

More generally, although research in the 1950s and 1960s appeared to demonstrate widespread acceptance of these general values in the United States, support may be weaker in the less established democracies of Western Europe and weaker still in the emerging democracies of the former Soviet bloc and Latin America. Widespread public acceptance of democratic values may be an important aspect of the democratization process—either by pressuring a former authoritarian or communist regime to instigate democratic reforms or by facilitating reforms that originate at the elite level (Dalton, 1994; Gibson *et al.*, 1992; Reisinger, Miller, Hesli, & Maher, 1994; Seligson & Booth, 1993). By tracking levels of these values over time, we may also gain a sense of the consolidation of a democratic regime and of the extent to which a country's political culture is changing as a result of the installation of democratic political structures (Toka, 1995; Weil, 1989, 1993; Whitefield & Evans, 1996). Consequently more and more research on mass support for both abstract and applied democratic values has been conducted outside the United States—especially since the wave of democratization occurred in Eastern Europe, the former Soviet Union, and Latin America in the late 1980s.

Increased interest in these issues in turn has sparked the development of new strategies for measuring public support for abstract democratic values. Some of the new measures are direct descendants of those developed by Prothro and Grigg (1960) and McClosky (1964), others are derived from work designed to assess the commitment of West Europeans to democracy in the post–World War II era, and still others are responses to the collapse of the Soviet bloc. As in the literature on political tolerance, we shall see that different measuring instruments can yield significantly different substantive conclusions regarding the levels and sources of support for abstract democratic principles.

Abstract and Applied Democratic Values

One method of measuring generalized beliefs in democracy arose through the efforts of Lawrence (1976), Sullivan *et al.* (1982), and others who questioned the notion that individuals were unable or unwilling to apply abstract democratic norms to specific situations. Recall that although the Prothro–Grigg (1960) and McClosky (1964) studies showed large majorities agreeing with general statements such as "Public officials should be chosen by majority vote" and "I believe in free speech for all, no matter what their views might be," much disagreement existed on the application of these norms to situations involving unpopular groups. Sullivan *et al.* (1982, pp. 202–207) correctly pointed out that neither of the two earlier studies explicitly linked the abstract principles with concrete applications. To probe these relationships, Sullivan *et al.* (1982) created a General Norms of Democracy Scale from the following six items, the first of which came from Prothro and Grigg (1960) and the remainder from McClosky (1964):

1. People in the minority should be free to try to win majority support for their opinions.
2. No matter what a person's political beliefs are, he is entitled to the same legal rights and protections as anyone else.
3. I believe in free speech for all no matter what their views might be.
4. If someone is suspected of treason or other serious crimes, he shouldn't be entitled to be let out on bail.
5. When the country is in great danger, we may have to force people to testify against themselves even if it violates their rights.
6. Any person who hides behind the laws when he is questioned about his activities doesn't deserve much consideration.

Based on their 1978 national survey, Sullivan *et al.* (1982) found, first, that support for these abstract democratic values was at nearly the same level as had been registered in the 1950s. In particular, the first three questions evoked "agree" responses from approximately 85–90% of those interviewed, much as Prothro and Grigg (1960) and McClosky (1964) had found. Second, these generalized attitudes were significantly related to Sullivan *et al.*'s (1979) content-controlled measure of political tolerance; in fact, after the perceived threat of the target group, an individual's belief in general democratic norms was the strongest predictor of tolerance in the Sullivan study. Subsequent analyses showed that support for democratic norms was positively related to tolerance in Israel and New Zealand (Sullivan *et al.*, 1985), though inconsistent effects have been found in Western Europe and the former Soviet Union (Duch & Gibson, 1992; Gibson & Duch, 1993a).

By demonstrating that abstract democratic principles can be measured and linked to more specific group-related tolerance items, these studies represent important additions to the field. At the same time the General Norms of Democracy Scale has several deficiencies that exemplify the problems researchers face in developing comprehensive measures of support for democratic beliefs.

- Little justification is given for why these six items, and not others, were taken from the Prothro–Grigg (1960) and McClosky (1964) surveys. No factor analysis or other data reduction technique appears to have been performed on the original items, and the empirical basis for the selection of questions is unclear.
- Although some scale items focus on central components of liberal democracy, such as minority rights, equality under the law, and abstract support for free speech, other, perhaps equally important, values are ignored, such as support for majority rule, competitive elections, and political opposition. Further the scale includes several items (4 through 6) that Sullivan *et al.* (1982, p. 204) conceded are "perhaps less fundamental to democratic procedure, such as the right to bail and protection against self-incrimination." As a practical matter, then, the scale represents only a portion of what is needed to gauge support for abstract democratic norms and procedures. And as in many studies in this domain, theoretical justification is lacking for why certain aspects of the "democratic creed" were chosen for analysis and not others.
- This scale highlights the practical difficulty of distinguishing between "abstract" and "specific" democratic beliefs. In the McClosky (1964) survey, only Items 2

and 3 above were considered Support for General Statements of Free Speech and Opinion, with Items 4–6 treated as Specific Applications of Free Speech and Procedural Rights. Item 5, for example, requires respondents to consider extending legal protection under a specific condition, "when the country is in great danger," in contrast to Item 1, which is pitched at a much higher, context-free level of abstraction. Sullivan *et al.* (1982) recognized that these items are more specific than the others in the scale, and in later analyses they combined Items 4 and 6 into a Legal Norms scale, separate from General Norms, measured by Items 1 through 3. It turned out, not surprisingly, that the Legal Norms scale outperformed the more abstract (and more consensual) General Norms scale in predicting applied tolerance in the United States, Israel, and New Zealand (Sullivan *et al.*, 1985).

At one level the issue is one of correctly labeling the orientation measured by a survey item, that is, describing it as either a measure of adherence to an abstract principle or a specific application of that principle. More fundamentally this work indicates that there are several different levels of abstraction at which survey items may be pitched, and researchers need to consider the kinds of information about democratic values that each type of question can provide.

First, highly abstract items like those in the General Norms scale can provide important information about generalized support for basic democratic principles, structures, and procedures. Sullivan *et al.* (1985), for example, showed that Israeli respondents were less likely to endorse the abstract principles related to minority political rights (Item 1 above) than were respondents in the United States and New Zealand, who were thought to be influenced more strongly by Anglo-Saxon libertarian traditions. In many settings, however, these types of context- and situation-free questions often yield highly consensual responses, and as such they will be of relatively little use in predicting other political attitudes.

At a lower level of abstraction are items that attempt to clarify the boundaries and limits of democratic support by posing situations in which abstract democratic values conflict with other considerations, such as public order, national security, or traditional morality. Sullivan *et al.*'s (1985) Legal Norms items fit squarely in this category. Similarly Lawrence's (1976) work showed that individuals may endorse free speech or free expression in general, yet may qualify that support when specific kinds of behaviors, such as protest demonstrations or blocking entrances to government buildings, are considered. The strategy of presenting respondents with situations where democratic values must be balanced against other values and considerations has been utilized in several other important studies of democracy in the United States and Canada (Chong, McClosky, & Zaller, 1983; McClosky & Zaller, 1984; Sniderman *et al.*, 1996).

Items that activate conflicting values typically yield lower levels of democratic support than do the "context-free" questions in the first category. To this extent they provide a more nuanced view of the mass public's belief in democratic norms, as they can clarify the conditions under which democratic values are trumped by other considerations. In addition, these types of items are more successful in classifying individuals according to their commitment to democratic values—the more individuals would apply democratic norms in situations where conflicting values come into play, the more they may be viewed as committed to the norm. Accordingly these items are likely to be more successful in predicting responses to questions relating to political tolerance, where individuals must balance their support for abstract democratic values against other values, such as public order or morality, as well as against the negative affect and perceived threat that individuals presumably feel toward specific target groups or issues.

Democratic Values in Other Political Systems

All the measures we have considered thus far were developed originally to assess support for democratic values in long-standing Anglo-American democracies, and the fact that democratic political structures were firmly established in these countries had important substantive and methodological implications. Substantively the prior consolidation of a democratic regime helps explain the mass public's overwhelming consensus in favor of certain abstract procedural norms and principles. However, when attention is confined to these countries, it is difficult to analyze the linkage between political structures and democratic beliefs because there has been so little variation in either factor over time. Over the past several decades, though, a significant body of research has emerged that examines the development of mass democratic attitudes during times of democratic transformation, first in Western Europe after World War II and more recently after the collapse of communism in the former Soviet bloc in the late 1980s. Some of this work has adapted measures of political tolerance and support for abstract democratic values discussed above, while in other studies entirely new measures have been constructed.

Democratization in Postwar Western Europe

In a pioneering study of democratic values in post–World War II Europe, Kaase (1971) analyzed surveys of West Germans conducted in 1968. The main purpose of Kaase's work was to determine the extent to which Germany's two decades of democracy had reshaped a political culture characterized by authoritarianism, intolerance, and vestiges of sympathy for the Nazi regime and fascist political ideals. From various perspectives on democratic theory, Kaase (1971, p. 142; see also Dalton, 1994, pp. 475–476) identified five basic principles of democratic government:

- Guaranteeing the right of individual participation, including the protection of minority rights
- Organizing political institutions on the basis of popular control through regular elections with a possibility of changes in leadership
- Recognizing the legitimacy of conflict over political means and ends
- Opposing violence as a means of settling political disputes
- Reaching consensus on the fundamental democratic attitudes, especially the presumption of legal settlement of conflicts

These five principles broadly encompass individual liberties and legal protections; basic structures of democratic government, such as a functioning opposition; and behavioral norms, such as nonviolent settlement of legitimate societal conflict. From items tapping each of these dimensions (e.g., "It is not conceivable to have a viable democracy without a political opposition"; "In principle, every democratic party should have a chance to govern"; and "Everyone should have the right to express his opinion even if he differs from the majority"), Kaase constructed a nine-item Democracy Scale.

The survey results suggested that by 1968 the West German public was highly supportive of abstract democratic values and that the structure of the German public's democratic beliefs was generally similar to that observed in the United States and elsewhere. Nearly universal support was registered in West Germany on questions relating to the rotation of power, the necessity of political opposition, and the abstract rights of free speech and assembly. As in other national settings, however, support eroded considerably when democratic values came into conflict with values such as public order ("A citizen forfeits the right to protest if order is threatened") and threats to the public good ("Conflicts between interests are adverse to the public interest"). Nevertheless, Kaase's (1971) analysis suggested that large-scale changes could occur in mass democratic values after a change in political regimes, and several subsequent studies identified similar processes in other countries, such as Spain, Italy, and Japan, that made transitions from authoritarian rule to democracy in the postwar years (e.g., Gunther, Sani, & Shabad, 1986; McDonough, Barnes, & Pina, 1986; Richardson & Flanagan, 1984; Sani, 1980).

Many factors, ranging from favorable economic performance to educational reforms and the public's negative attitudes toward previous regimes, have been cited to account for these value changes in postwar transitional systems. In an important analysis Weil (1989) developed a model of "democratic legitimation" based on the structure and long-term operation of a country's party system. Weil (1989, p. 684) argued that the longer people live in a democracy with a "responsive opposition structure"—one that "presents voters with clear alternatives, each capable of rotating into office, and none likely to destroy democracy"—the more likely they become to develop generalized support for democratic values. Using indicators of party system fractionalization, polarization, and the size of governing coalitions in six democracies, Weil demonstrated that these factors were more strongly related to "support for democracy" than were indicators of economic or political performance.

These results have important implications for understanding more recent transitions to democracy, and we shall return to Weil's work. For now, we note that his conclusions were based on measures of democratic support that differ slightly from what we have been considering thus far. In contrast to the scales developed by McClosky, Sullivan and his colleagues, and Kaase, which focus on the norms, processes, and principles of democratic government, Weil's (1989) items asked respondents to evaluate "democracy" as a form of government directly and in comparison to other kinds of political systems, either real or imagined ("Which form of government do you feel is best for us as Germans? Democracy; Monarchy; Dictatorships?"; "Do you believe the democracy which we have in the Federal Republic is the best form of state or is there another form of state which is better?"). These questions are more analogous to Prothro and Grigg's (1960) "Democracy is the best form of government"; interestingly, whereas more than 90% of Prothro and Grigg's American samples agreed with that statement, only three-quarters of West Germans in the late 1960s did so (Weil, 1993).

Clearly items of this type tap democratic values in a different sense than do items relating to the norms or values embodied in democratic governance. Prothro and Grigg (1960) called their scale item a measure of support for the "principle of democracy"; subsequent scholars have labeled similar items "evaluation of democracy" (Shin, 1995; Weil, 1993) or "normative commitment to democracy" (Evans & Whitefield, 1995; Whitefield & Evans, 1996). To some extent such questions tap into attitudes of regime support and legitimacy, and there is considerable overlap in scholarly discussions of legitimacy and support for democratic values (e.g., Dalton, 1994; Fuchs, Guidorossi, & Svensson, 1995; Weil, 1996). As Fuchs *et al.* (1995, p. 327) observed, "[L]egitimization is based on fundamental values, such as freedom and justice, but also on democracy in the sense of government by the people. A country's democratic system has been successfully legitimized to the extent that its citizens believe that the structural arrangements correspond with the fundamental values."

In this regard "normative commitment" items appear to measure support for democracy as a structural arrangement rather than support for fundamental democratic values per se. Such items also attempt to measure general evaluations of a country's political structure as distinct from more specific evaluations of system performance, or "democracy in practice" (Evans & Whitefield, 1995), although there is likely to be slippage on this point.

We regard disentangling the relationships among "normative commitments" to democracy, beliefs in democratic principles, and evaluations of system performance as an important task for future research. And obviously these conceptual distinctions need to be kept in mind in interpreting a given survey's results.

Democratization in the Post–Cold War Period

The transitions to democracy that began to occur across Eastern Europe, the former Soviet Union, and Latin America in the late 1980s have presented fresh opportunities for understanding the relationship between democratic values and the installation and consolidation of democratic regimes. Fortunately many surveys were conducted just before or shortly after the onset of these regime changes, and we are now beginning to see the results of longitudinal surveys tracking democratic orientations over this period. These studies have sparked considerable controversy about both the level and the sources of support for democratic values in the postcommunist world.

Perhaps the most striking finding is the extraordinary extent to which mass publics in many countries appeared to embrace democratic values and principles almost immediately after the collapse of communism. Dalton (1994), Klingemann and Hofferbert (1994), and Weil (1993), for example, all documented very high levels of support for democratic values in East Germany, based in part on surveys conducted in 1990, shortly after the fall of the Berlin Wall. Indeed, East and West Germans registered similar responses on Kaase's Index of Democratic Values in 1990 and 1991 (Dalton, 1994; Weil, 1993). Seligson and Booth (1993) showed similarly high levels of support for democratic values in Nicaragua and Costa Rica in the late 1980s, just prior to the elections that installed Nicaragua's first democratically elected regime. And although there is still no scholarly consensus, several studies have provided relatively strong evidence for the emergence of certain democratic values—notably those pertaining to competitive elections and the rights of individuals against the state—in the former Soviet Union and other East European countries (e.g., Finifter & Mickiewicz, 1992; Gibson et al., 1992; Hahn 1991; Reisinger et al., 1994; Rose & Mishler, 1994; Tedin, 1994).

The high levels of democratic support registered in many of these countries—all considerably higher than initial readings from earlier transitions in Germany and Spain—pose something of a puzzle for theories of democratization. According to traditional views of political culture, a country's political structures and democratic orientations should become more congruent over time—hence the expectation that East Germans, after four decades of communist rule, should be less supportive of democratic principles than their counterparts in the West. Similarly Seligson and Booth (1993) argued that Nicaraguans, in a country with virtually no experience in democracy and a legacy of "Iberian authoritarianism," were expected to show much lower levels of support for democracy than Costa Ricans, in a stable country with a long history of democratically elected governments and peaceful transfers of power. Moreover, Weil (1993, 1996) suggested that citizens need to experience some years with a responsive opposition structure before they begin to fill a "reservoir of legitimation" and adhere to democratic norms and principles. Modernization theories stress the role of economic growth in stimulating the growth of democratic norms, but this interpretation is inconsistent with (1) weak correlations between indicators of social-structural position and support for democratic values in East Germany and (2) conflicting findings regarding the influence of such variables in other countries of Eastern Europe and the former Soviet Union (Gibson et al., 1992; Gibson & Duch, 1993b; McIntosh & MacIver, 1992; Rose & Mishler, 1994; Reisinger et al., 1994).

Several explanations have been proposed to account for the high initial support for democratic values in these countries. One possibility is that there were relatively few clear philosophical differences in the first place between communism ("democratic socialism") and democracy as understood in the West (Dalton, 1994; Westle, 1994). According to this view citizens had already adopted democratic norms within the context of the previous socialist regime. This hypothesis, however, does not fare very well when subjected to empirical test, since both Dalton (1994) and Weil (1996) have shown that those who scored high on a "socialist values" index or who were supporters of the previous regime scored low on Kaase's Index of Democratic Values and on the question of whether "democracy is the best form of state." Similarly Rose and Mishler (1994) uncovered a negative correlation between support for the former communist system in Eastern Europe and support for democracy, suggesting that democratic orientations are adopted in part as a reaction to an earlier unpopular regime. This kind of process appears to have occurred in Nicaragua as well, for Seligson and Booth (1993) argued that opponents of the Sandinistas strategically embraced support for freedom of expression and the right to dissent as a means of furthering the overthrow of an unpopular regime.

No less important in explaining democratic values in recent transitional societies may be the "demonstration effect" of the successful West European democracies, which served as models that citizens in the East wished their countries to emulate. In this view Western-style democracies, through the mass media, personal contacts, and active propaganda efforts, had exported their political values to the communist world, and especially to newer generations coming of political age (Dalton, 1994; Gibson *et al.*, 1992; Klingemann & Hofferbert, 1994; Weil, 1996). Although empirical support for this interpretation is limited (Gibson *et al.*, 1992; Weil, 1996), the interpretation is widespread in the literature. As Dalton (1994, p. 490) argued, "[T]he socialization of political cultures is not a closed process; in the modern world political norms can also be learned by observing other national experiences. . . . [T]he political model of the Federal Republic and the transmission of this information to the Eastern public must have played a large role in the creation of support for democratic attitudes in the East."

Many scholars believe that these processes—"demonstration effects" from the West and the rejection of previous political regimes—produced a honeymoon period for democratic values at the onset of democratization in East Europe and the former Soviet Union. Most agree further that some early support was based on the novelty of democracy and on the euphoria associated with initial experiences with political and personal freedom (McIntosh & MacIver, 1992; Toka, 1995). To this extent the widespread initial enthusiasm for democratic principles may have rested on relatively shallow foundations.

Other evidence supports an even more cautious interpretation of the embrace of democratic values in former Soviet bloc countries. First, responses to questions measuring commitment to democracy or overall evaluation of democracy as a form of government are less supportive than responses to questions about norms or specific values associated with democratic government. Whitefield and Evans (1996), for example, showed that in the former Soviet Union fewer than 50% of those polled in 1993, and only 40% in 1995, were supporters of "the aim of building democracy." Moreover, such "normative commitment" to democracy was only in the 40–60% range in each of seven East European countries, while registering a much higher level only in Romania (Evans & Whitefield, 1995). Even in East Germany only one-third of respondents in 1991 believed that the "democracy that we have in Germany is the best form of state" (Weil, 1993). As noted above, "normative commitment" questions may well be tapping attitudes about system performance more than support for democratic values, but it bears emphasis that these items originally were developed to be distinguished from performance evaluations of the regime.

Second, even on questions relating to beliefs in democratic values, there is ambivalence in the former Soviet bloc. In their investigation of mass attitudes on seven measures of democratic orientations (tolerance, support for liberty, "rights conscious-ness," support for dissent, Sullivan and his colleagues' Norms of Democracy Scale, support for competitive elections, and support for independent media), Gibson *et al.* (1992) and Gibson and Duch (1993b) reported considerable variation in prodemocratic responses in Moscow and the European regions of the U.S.S.R. Substantial majorities supported the abstract norms of democracy as measured by the Norms of Democracy Scale: competitive elections, multipartyism, and the right of individuals to assert liberties against the state (see also Finifter & Mickiewicz, 1992; Miller, Hesli, & Reisinger, 1995; Tedin, 1994). But on some of the remaining measures, there was less enthusiasm for democratic principles. For example, only 38% of those polled in the former Soviet Union in 1990 disagreed that "Free speech is just not worth it if it means that we have to put up with the danger to society of extremist political views," and fewer than 25% disagreed that "It is better to live in an orderly society than to allow people so much freedom that they can become disruptive." Whitefield and Evans (1996) have reported similar responses to many of the questions asked in a 1995 survey in the former Soviet Union, and 42% of East Germans in 1993 agreed that "A citizen forfeits the right to protest if order is threatened" (Dalton, 1994).

These are clear signs that citizens in the former Soviet bloc do not embrace demo-cratic norms unconditionally. According to Gibson and Duch (1993b), the former Soviet mass public is committed much more strongly to "majoritarian" democratic principles, such as popular sovereignty and competitive elections, than to "minoritarian" principles, such as civil liberties and the right of dissent: "The people extended fairly broad support to competitive electoral structures, and . . . were quite willing to claim a variety of rights of democratic citizenship . . . but . . . not everyone was willing to embrace liberty if its cost is social disruption" (Gibson & Duch, 1993b, p. 87). Further, levels of applied toler-ance, as measured by either Sullivan- or Stouffer-type items, are extremely low in the former Soviet Union (Gibson & Duch, 1993a) and East Germany (Weil, 1993). It must be noted, however, that the trade-off between liberty and order has long vexed Western so-cieties as well, and there is a limited willingness to extend civil liberties to unpopular groups in contemporary Western democracies as well as in transitional systems (Duch & Gibson, 1992; Sniderman *et al.,* 1996; Thomasson, 1995).

Along with this dispute over the precise level of mass support for democratic values comes disagreement regarding the relative durability of democratic orientations in the former Soviet bloc and the extent to which these orientations are dependent on favorable economic and political performance. Some studies of the effects of short-term economic perceptions on democratic orientations indicate that economic evaluations are positively associated with democratic values (Dalton, 1994; McIntosh & MacIver, 1992; Rose & Mishler, 1994), but others show weak or nonexistent correlations (Evans & Whitefield, 1995; Gibson, 1996a, 1996b; Weil, 1996).

Those who argue that the relationship is relatively strong caution that consistently poor economic performance could undermine the former Soviet bloc's fledgling demo-cratic political cultures. Others argue that more than short-term economic performance, factors such as *political* performance, the successful rotation of political oppositions, and the behavior of political elites will determine the future of democracy in postcommunist systems. There is no scholarly consensus on this point. However, our reading of the litera-ture suggests that in more fully specified models, economic perceptions are weak predic-tors of democratic support once political performance factors are controlled. As Evans and Whitefield (1995, p. 503) argued: "People support democracies because they are seen to work, reflecting respondents' experience of the pay-offs from democracy itself, rather than on the basis of a simple cash nexus."

Perhaps the strongest evidence of the crystallization of opinions supportive of democracy in the former Soviet bloc comes from two later studies by Gibson (1996a, 1996b). In the only extant panel survey of attitudes toward democracy, Gibson (1996a) uncovered a correlation of .41 in Russia and Ukraine between a Support for Democratic Institutions and Processes factor and a similar factor in 1992, which represents "considerable stability" over time in democratic orientations. Changes in the main democracy factor were only weakly related to economic perceptions, indicating that the period's "severe economic malaise seems not to have weakened enthusiasm for democracy" (Gibson, 1996a, p. 413).

In the second study Gibson correlated the Support for Democracy factor with attitudes toward "market-based institutions and processes" in order to determine whether the political and economic attitudes associated with liberal Western democracies may be converging in Russia and Ukraine. Many scholars have characterized the two dimensions as only weakly related, with people often endorsing democratic principles while expressing much less support for, and deep skepticism about, economic reforms and capitalistic values (Finifter & Mickiewicz, 1992; Rose & Mishler, 1994; Westle, 1994; Whitefield & Evans, 1996). As Rose and Mishler (1994, p. 177) argued, in 1991 "[i]n most countries of Eastern Europe the median citizen [was] in favor of the new political regime and against the new economic regime." Others, though, have found stronger positive interrelationships between democratic and capitalist values (Duch, 1993; Miller, Hesli, & Reisinger, 1994, 1995; Miller, Reisinger, & Hesli, 1996)

According to Gibson (1996b), both camps may have been partially correct. As of 1992 the correlation between support for democratic values and support for market-based values was .50 in Russia and .48 in Ukraine, substantially higher than the .26 and .08 recorded in 1990. Moreover, the direction of causality between the two dimensions appeared to flow primarily from democratic attitudes to market orientations and not the reverse. The implication is that while democratic values may have been far stronger than market-based values at the onset of democratization, by 1992 support for capitalist values seemed to have increased and to have become more closely tied to support for democracy.

Gibson's analyses are problematic in some respects. Different indicators for the political and economic values were used in different years, different subdimensions loaded on different democracy factors in 1990 and 1992, and the panel effects were weakened somewhat in the context of fully specified models. Obviously this work will not be the last word on the subject, and much research remains to be conducted on these relationships in other settings and over time. Provisionally, though, it would seem that by the early to mid-1990s many citizens in East Europe had developed a relatively stable set of beliefs favoring "political and economic systems that reward individual initiative [and] that allow individual opportunity" (Gibson, 1996b, p. 980).

Future Research Directions

The past four decades have witnessed substantial progress in efforts to understand the levels and sources of political tolerance and support for democratic values in the mass public. Much of this progress can be traced to new conceptualizations of political tolerance and democratic values, which in turn have produced new measurement strategies and scales. Instead of measures of tolerance based on an ideologically restricted range of target groups, scholars now routinely use either a variant of Sullivan *et al.*'s (1979) "most disliked group" measure or a measure that gauges tolerance across a wide range of acts and target groups. And in addition to measuring democratic values that reflect only abstract principles of free speech and legal rights, scholars now tap support for a broad array of democratic norms, processes, and structures.

With the development of new scales has come increased concern for basic measurement issues, such as scale validity and reliability. The reporting of factor analyses or reliability coefficients for primary scales is now widespread in research on political tolerance (e.g., Duch & Gibson, 1992; Nie *et al.*, 1996; Sniderman, Brody, & Tetlock, 1991) and is increasingly common in work on support for more general democratic values (e.g., Gibson, 1996a, 1996b; Gibson *et al.*, 1992; Miller *et al.*, 1995; Weil, 1996). Studies have also begun to appear that compare the measurement properties of different tolerance scales and assess the substantive implications of alternative measurement strategies (Gibson, 1992a). This heightened attention to measurement concerns should facilitate a more orderly cumulation of research findings than that which characterized the field in its first few decades.

Still, many measurement issues remain unresolved. We know very little, for example, about the overall structure of democratic values, either in the former Soviet bloc or in more established Western democracies. Gibson and his colleagues have argued that political values in the former Soviet Union are configured in a "loose" democratic belief system with two subdimensions—one corresponding to majoritarian principles, such as support for competitive elections, and the other corresponding to "minoritarian" principles, such as political tolerance. Yet the factor structure Gibson (1996a) reported in one article showed Russians' and Ukrainians' support for competitive elections loading on the same minoritarian subdimension as political tolerance in one year of the panel study and on a different subdimension two years earlier. Moreover, the relationship between political tolerance and more general norms of democracy is inconsistent from study to study, with some reporting a moderately positive relationship (Gibson & Duch, 1993a; Sullivan, Piereson, & Marcus, 1982; Sullivan, Shamir, Walsh, & Roberts, 1985) and others a weak and in some cases a negative relationship (Duch & Gibson, 1992). Clearly we are still far from understanding the complex interrelationships among the dimensions of democratic values, let alone the relationships between these orientations and other attitudes—such as support for capitalism, prejudice, authoritarianism, and regime support (Altemeyer & Hunsberger, 1992; Duckitt & Farre, 1994; Fuchs *et al.*, 1995; Heath, Evans, & Martin, 1993; Sniderman *et al.*, 1996).

Nor is much known about the stability of democratic attitudes. There have been few panel analyses of either political tolerance or more general support for democratic values in Western democracies (Jennings, van Deth, *et al.*, 1990), and Gibson's (1996a, 1996b) work represents the sole panel analysis conducted in the former Soviet bloc. This is unfortunate. Given the historic and rapid nature of political change in many contemporary democracies, panel studies could clarify several critical issues: how changes in economic and political performance influence orientations toward democracy (Finkel, Muller, & Seligson, 1989; Remmer, 1991); how individuals develop tolerance and adherence to democratic norms through political participation, civic education, or other processes; and how democratic values may be undermined or channeled into support for extremist or antidemocratic parties.

Besides panel studies researchers will need other creative ways of addressing these important questions. Several innovations in research design are especially promising. One involves experimental or quasi-experimental methods, whether employed in a laboratory setting or by incorporating elements of experimental designs into attitude surveys. Such studies have yielded valuable insights concerning the impacts of cognitive and affective factors on tolerance judgments (Kuklinski *et al.,* 1991; Marcus, Sullivan, Theiss-Morse, & Wood, 1995; Theiss-Morse, Marcus, & Sullivan, 1993), of group stereotypes on intolerance toward individual group members (Golebiowska, 1996), and of perceptions of group threat on tolerance (Marcus *et al.,* 1995). Perhaps the most fruitful application has been the "counterargument technique," in which, after staking out a position in response to a given question or set of questions, survey respondents are presented with reasons why they might reconsider their view (Gibson, 1997; Marcus *et al.,* 1995; Sniderman *et al.,* 1996). These studies are calling into question much received wisdom in the field. For one thing tolerance judgments are often relatively pliable. For another it is sometimes as easy to convert individuals from tolerance to intolerance as vice versa. That is, in contrast to Stouffer's (1955) view of tolerance as a "sober second thought," reconsidering a tolerance scenario can make people *more* likely to favor repression and *less* likely to extend procedural liberties to target groups. More generally, studies using the counterargument technique are succeeding in simulating the rhetoric of conflicts over civil liberties in the "real world," where the clash between liberty and social order is often resolved through intense argumentation and persuasion (Gibson & Bingham, 1985; Sniderman *et al.,* 1996).

Two especially important innovations in the designs used in more traditional survey-based research are also noteworthy. One is the proliferation of cross-national research (Duch & Gibson, 1992; Evans & Whitefield, 1995; Gibson & Duch, 1993c; Hahn, 1991; McIntosh & McIver, 1992; Reisinger *et al.,* 1994; Seligson & Booth, 1993; Sullivan *et al.,* 1985; Toka, 1995; Weil, 1989). Besides the obvious advantage of providing information about cross-national variation in tolerance and support for democratic values, comparative survey research allows the researcher to test the generalizability of individual-level models as well as the extent to which models can explain cross-national differences (Evans & Whitefield, 1995; see also Anderson & Guillory, 1997). With enough countries in the analysis, variables such as a nation's years of experience with democracy, the polarization of its party system, and its level of economic development can be incorporated into models of tolerance and support for democratic values, along with micro-level factors like age, education, and gender (Duch & Gibson, 1992; Evans & Whitefield, 1995; Gibson & Duch, 1993c; Weil, 1989).

Finally, in perhaps the most welcome substantive development in the field, scholars are turning increasing attention to the *consequences* of political tolerance and support for democratic values. In a pioneering set of studies, Gibson (1988, 1989a) showed that repressive state policies during the McCarthy era and the Vietnam War era in the United States were unrelated to mass intolerance, and in some cases they were better predicted by levels of intolerance among political elites—exactly the opposite of what theories of democratic elitism would lead one to expect. Gibson (1992b) has also presented evidence that political tolerance in the United States has important cultural consequences, as levels of intolerance in one's family, peer group, and community tend to limit one's perceptions of political freedom and willingness to voice views that may be unpopular.

Far more exploration is needed into the effects of tolerance and other democratic values. What are the behavioral consequences of democratic orientations? Are intolerant attitudes good predictors of intolerant political behavior? Do beliefs in democratic principles correlate with voting or other forms of political participation? Do antidemocratic beliefs underlie support for antidemocratic political parties or candidates? We simply do not know the answers to these questions. Nor do we know much about the effects of mass attitudes on the process of democratization, the implementation of economic and political reforms, and the overall stability of democratic systems (Inglehart, 1988; Muller & Seligson, 1994). These critical theoretical issues demand attention as future research is conducted on a broad range of democratic attitudes in established as well as emerging democracies throughout the world.

Scales Reviewed Here

The scales reviewed in this chapter cover a broad array of attitudes related to democratic values, tolerance, and civil liberties. We will begin with scales designed primarily to measure broad support for democratic values, norms, and structures (although some of these scales include items that also tap specific applications of broader values and principles). We will next present scales that relate primarily to political tolerance.

Democratic Values
1. Fundamental Principles of Democracy (Prothro & Grigg, 1960)
2. Democratic Principles and Applications (McClosky, 1964)
3. Support for Democratic Principles (Kaase, 1971)
4. Democratic Values Scale (McClosky & Zaller, 1984)
5. Multi-Dimensional Scale of Democratic Values (Gibson, Duch, & Tedin, 1992)
6. Index of Pro-Democracy Orientation (Miller, Hesli, & Reisinger, 1995)
7. Attitudes towards Democracy (Whitefield & Evans, 1996)
8. Support for Democracy (Weil, 1989, 1993, 1996)

Political Tolerance
9. Willingness to Tolerate Nonconformists (Stouffer, 1955)
10. Repression Potential (Marsh & Kaase, 1979)
11. Content-Controlled Measure of Political Tolerance (Sullivan, Piereson, & Marcus, 1982)
12. Dimensions of Political Tolerance (Gibson & Bingham, 1982)
13. Omnibus Civil Liberties Scale (McClosky & Brill, 1983)
14. Political Tolerance Scale (Duckitt & Farre, 1994)

Democratic Values

Prothro and Grigg's (1960) Fundamental Principles of Democracy Scale represents one of the first attempts to evaluate support for general aspects of democracy. The scale, consisting of 15 items, identifies three important dimensions of support for democratic principles: (1) support for a majoritarian form of government, including support for universal suffrage and equality before the law; (2) "abstract" support for minoritarian values, such as the right to dissent; and (3) support for the specific application of minoritarian values, such as political tolerance in concrete situations (i.e., with reference to specific out-groups). In addition to tapping these particular dimensions of democracy, Prothro and Grigg also address overall support for democracy through a question about whether democracy is the best form of government.

McClosky's (1964) approach is similar to that of Prothro and Grigg. The three subscales reviewed here (consisting of 29 items) relate to abstract support for general procedural norms, such as universal suffrage, rule of law, and the illegitimacy of force; abstract support for freedom of expression; and support for specific applications of both procedural norms and freedom of expression. The specific applications address the willingness to extend rights and liberties in circumstances involving disliked groups (e.g., traitors, communists) or competing values, such as social order.

Kaase (1971) has identified several concepts central to democratic governance, including the right of individual participation, popular control of government, electoral competition, and the right of dissent and opposition. Thus, like others, he has identified both competitive majoritarian and minoritarian features of democracy. His Support for Democratic Principles Scale consists of nine items that tap support for these values. Some items elicit opinions using abstract, noncontroversial language, while others tap support for a value with reference to more concrete or problematic situations.

McClosky and Zaller (1984) include 44 items in their Democratic Values Scale, addressing a variety of attitudes toward rights and liberties of various groups, equality under the law, and due process and privacy rights. The principal focus of this scale is support for minoritarian values either in the abstract or in applied situations; there are also a few items related to institutional features of democratic systems, such as majority rule, electoral competition, and suffrage. Based on the distribution of elite opinion on the various items, McClosky and Zaller differentiate between "clear" and "contested" democratic values, with the former having consensual support among elites and the latter being characterized by ideological or other differences among elites.

Gibson, Duch, and Tedin (1992) have developed a multidimensional scale that addresses several aspects of democracy. They conceptualize democratic support as composed of seven major subdimensions: political tolerance, valuation of liberty, support for norms of democracy, consciousness of political rights, support for political dissent, support for independent media, and support for electoral competition. The subscales measuring support for norms of democracy and for political dissent gauge support for democratic values, such as political expression and due process rights, at a fairly abstract level. The Political Tolerance subscale (derived from Sullivan *et al.*, 1982) and the Valuation of Liberty subscale elicit support for similar concepts, but in situations involving specific groups or trade-offs with social order.

The Index of Pro-Democracy Orientation developed by Miller, Hesli, and Reisinger (1995) consists of five items relating to support for individual political participation, political dissent, electoral competition, and minority rights. This scale does not assess support for procedural norms or political tolerance when applied to specific unpopular groups or in circumstances involving competing values, such as social order.

While most of the previous scales focus on support for democratic values either in the abstract or in applied situations, Weil (1989, 1993, 1996) and Whitefield and Evans (1996) explore explicit support for democracy as a system of governance in addition to support for the values that are associated with democracy. Weil's (1996) scale of democratic ideals taps support for electoral competition, political opposition, and freedom of expression, and another of his scales taps support for democracy as opposed to other forms of government.

Whitefield and Evans (1996) identify commitment to democracy as support for the *aim* of building democracy. They differentiate this concept from support for the actual practice of democracy and from support for particular democratic values and institutions, such as freedom of expression, political opposition, and competitive elections.

Political Tolerance

Stouffer's (1955) pathbreaking work on political tolerance sought to assess willingness to extend civil liberties to certain out-groups, specifically communists, socialists, and atheists. The Stouffer items ask about a range of actions targeted against a given out-group, such as removing a book written by a group member from the public library, firing a group member from his or her job, and jailing a group member. A more ideologically balanced set of out-groups has been used in a revised version of the Stouffer items that is included in the GSS. The GSS version used until 1974 includes 18 items about three specific acts (allowing a public speech, teaching, and removing a book from the library) in reference to six outgroups (racists, communists, militarists, homosexuals, those who favor government ownership of industry, and those who oppose religion); in 1974 references to socialists were dropped.

Marsh and Kaase's (1979) Repression Potential Scale attempts to measure willingness to grant the government power to exert authority. The Marsh–Kaase scale includes items about support for harsh court sentences for protesters, use of force against demonstrators, and use of troops to break strikes. However, the items do not refer to particular groups. A similar measurement approach is reported by Simon and Mann (1977), Simon and Barnum (1978), and Simon and Landis (1990), asking about wire tapping, reading mail, and limiting the freedom of movement of religious groups and far-right and far-left political groups that oppose the Israeli state.

A fundamentally different approach to measuring political tolerance has been introduced by Sullivan, Piereson, and Marcus (1982). Sullivan *et al.* conceived of tolerance as the "willingness to permit the expression of ideas or interests one opposes." Unlike Stouffer's (1955) measurement strategy, this approach demands that tolerance be assessed with respect to groups identified unfavorably by the respondent. This "least-liked" approach is incorporated into Sullivan *et al.*'s Content-Controlled Measure of Political Tolerance, which has been used in numerous assessments of political tolerance in the United States and other nations.

Gibson and Bingham (1982, p. 604) define political tolerance much more broadly than Sullivan *et al.*, as "opposition to state actions that limit opportunities for citizens, individually or in groups, to compete for political power." This approach expands the scope of the scale to include questions related to general due process and privacy rights (e.g., the right to a jury trial and the use of government wiretaps), in addition to the more traditional tolerance questions related to freedom of expression and repression of unpopular groups. Their Dimensions of Political Tolerance Scale consists of four subscales, totaling 31 items.

McClosky and Brill's (1983) Omnibus Civil Liberties Scale contains 69 items arranged in nine subscales that address general and specific applications of freedom of expression and various other civil liberties. Like Gibson and Bingham's Dimensions of Political Tolerance Scale, this scale taps attitudes on general due process and privacy rights, some of which seem less related to political tolerance toward specific groups.

Duckitt and Farre (1994) developed a six-item scale that addresses fairly nonspecific applications of civil liberties in South Africa, such as expressive rights, right to a public trial, and tolerance toward political opposition. Specific target groups are not referred to, and most items refer to "enemies of the state" or "those who oppose the people."

Fundamental Principles of Democracy

(J. W. Prothro & C. M. Grigg, 1960)

Variable

These items are intended to measure (1) support among members of the mass public for abstract democratic principles, specifically the principles of majority rule and minority rights, and (2) the extent to which support for democratic principles in the abstract is translated into approval of both principles in concrete circumstances.

Description

There are 15 items. The first 5 are extremely abstract statements of support for democratic principles (1 concerning support for democracy as a form of government, 2 relating to support for majority rule, and 2 relating to support for minority rights, such as free expression and political opposition). The remaining 10 items are intended to be specific applications of these abstract statements (5 each relating to support for majority rule and minority rights in specific situations). Agreement or disagreement with the application items is assumed to follow logically from agreement or disagreement with the abstract statements.

Sample

Questionnaires were administered to random samples of registered voters in Ann Arbor, Michigan ($N = 144$), and Tallahassee, Florida ($N = 100$), in the late 1950s.

Reliability

Internal Consistency

We encountered no information regarding internal consistency.

Test–Retest

We encountered no information regarding test–retest reliability.

Validity

We encountered no information regarding validity.

Location

Prothro, J. W., & Grigg, C. M. (1960). Fundamental principles of democracy: Bases of agreement and disagreement. *Journal of Politics, 22,* 276–294. Reprinted by permission of the authors and the University of Texas Press. All rights retained by the University of Texas Press.

Results and Comments

Although virtually unanimous support was voiced for the 5 items related to abstract democratic principles (agreement ranged from 95 to 98%), consensus broke down on the 10 items related to the specific application of these principles. A majority of the Ann Arbor sample gave "undemocratic" responses to 4 items (7, 9, 10, and 15), while a majority of the Tallahassee sample gave "undemocratic" responses to 6 items (6, 7, 9, 10, 13, and 15). In addition, there was significantly less tolerance toward blacks in the Tallahassee sample, as compared to the Ann Arbor sample. More highly educated respondents were more likely to offer prodemocratic responses to the application items, but even among this group democratic support exceeded 75% on only 4 of the 10 specific application items (8, 11, 12, and 14).

There is some potential for a directionality problem with these items. Agreement with each of the abstract principles statements signifies support for civil liberties. On the other hand, agreement with 6 of the 10 application items signifies *lack* of support for civil liberties. To the extent that an acquiescence bias is at work, it could account for (1) the apparently greater support for abstract liberties than for the application of these abstract liberties and (2) the wider gap between support for abstract liberties and concrete expressions among less educated than among more highly educated respondents.

Fundamental Principles of Democracy
(Prothro & Grigg, 1960)

Scaling: The items are all presented in simple agree-disagree format. Prothro and Grigg assess each item individually and do not attempt to develop a composite scale of democratic support using all of the items.

Principle of Democracy Itself

1. Democracy is the best form of government.
   1. AGREE   0. DISAGREE

Principle of Majority Rule

2. Public officials should be chosen by majority rule.
3. Every citizen should have an equal chance to influence government policy.

Principle of Minority Rights

4. The minority should be free to criticize majority decisions.
5. People in the minority should be free to try to win majority support for their opinions.

Principle of Majority Rule in Specific Terms

6. In a city referendum, only people who are well informed about the problem being voted on should be allowed to vote.*
7. In a city referendum deciding on tax-supported undertakings, only tax-payers should be allowed to vote.*
8. If a Negro were legally elected mayor of this city, the white people should not allow him to take office.*
9. If a Communist were legally elected major of this city, the people should not allow him to take office.*
10. A professional organization like the AMA (the American Medical Association) has a right to try to increase the influence of doctors by getting them to vote as a bloc in elections.

Principle of Minority Rights in Specific Terms

11. If a person wanted to make a speech in this city against churches and religion, he should be allowed to speak.
12. If a person wanted to make a speech in this city favoring government ownership of all the railroads and big industries, he should be allowed to speak.

13. If an admitted Communist wanted to make a speech in this city favoring Communism, he should be allowed to speak.
14. A Negro should not be allowed to run for mayor of this city.*
15. A Communist should not be allowed to run for mayor of this city.*

*Disagreement represents the "democratic" response.

Democratic Principles and Applications
(H. McClosky, 1964)

Variable

As in the Prothro–Grigg (1960) study, this scale focuses on the measurement of abstract democratic principles and their application in concrete circumstances.

Description

McClosky has formulated six sets of agree–disagree items. Three of these (tapping political cynicism; sense of political futility; and belief in political, social, ethnic, and economic equality) do not directly pertain to political tolerance or support for democratic values and therefore are not reviewed here. The three remaining subscales are (1) Rules of the Game (12 items focusing on fairness and consideration for the rights of others), (2) Support for General Statements of Free Speech and Opinion (8 items), and (3) Support for Specific Applications of Free Speech and Procedure Rights (9 items).

Sample

Findings for the general population were based on a national survey of approximately 1500 Americans. An elite sample consisted of 1788 Democratic and 1232 Republican delegates to the 1956 national presidential nominating conventions.

Reliability

Internal Consistency

We encountered no information regarding internal consistency, although coefficients of reproducibility for Guttman scales were apparently calculated.

Test–Retest

We encountered no information regarding test–retest reliability.

Validity

We encountered no direct evidence of convergent validity, but McClosky reported that the items were subjected to "an empirical validation procedure employing appropriate criterion groups," and apparently experts were asked to assess the face validity of the items.

Location

McClosky, H. (1964). Consensus and ideology in American politics. *American Political Science Review, 58,* 361–382.

Results and Comments

A "high" level of support (a scale score equal to the top one-third of the population sample) was registered by 58 percent of elites on the Rules of the Game subscale, by 63 percent for the Support for General Statements of Free Speech and Opinion subscale, and by 61 percent for the Support for Specific Applications of Free Speech and Procedural Rights subscale.

   Members of the elite sample scored higher than did members of the mass public on all three scales, and they were also more consistent in applying general principles to specific situations. Despite the greater democratic support among elites, their level of agreement about democratic values was still far from consensual. McClosky draws the conclusion that, contrary to frequent claims otherwise, democracy can survive amidst widespread disagreement about basic democratic values. He asserts that consensus might not be essential during periods of social stability.

   Response acquiescence is a potential problem with parts of this scale, since each subscale is highly imbalanced in terms of the substantive meaning of a "democratic" response. (McClosky attempted to correct for response set by correcting respondents' scores on each subscale by a specially constructed acquiescence scale.)

Democratic Principles and Applications (McClosky, 1964)

Scaling: For each subscale, a score is derived by summing the number of "democratic" responses.

Rules of the Game

("Democratic" response = 1, undemocratic response = 0; agreement is the "democratic" response unless item is starred; scale scores range from 0 to 12)

  1. There are times when it almost seems better for the people to take the law into their own hands rather than wait for the machinery of government to act.*
     1. DISAGREE   0. AGREE
  2. The majority has the right to abolish minorities if it wants to.*
  3. We might as well make up our minds that in order to make the world free a lot of innocent people will have to suffer.*
  4. If congressional committees stuck strictly to the rules and gave every witness his rights they would never succeed in exposing the many dangerous subversions they have turned up.*
  5. I don't mind a politician's methods if he manages to get the right things done.*

6. Almost any unfairness or brutality may have to be justified when some good purpose is being carried out.*

7. Politicians have to cut a few corners if they are going to get anywhere.*

8. People ought to be allowed to vote even if they can't do so intelligently.

9. To bring about great changes for the benefit of mankind often requires cruelty and even ruthlessness.*

10. Very few politicians have clean records, so why get excited about the mud slinging that sometimes goes on?*

11. It's all right to get around the law if you don't actually break it.

12. The true American way of life is disappearing so fast that we may have to use force to save it.*

General Free Speech and Opinion

("Democratic" response = 1, "undemocratic" response = 0; agreement is the "democratic" response unless item is starred; scale scores range from 0 to 8)

1. People who hate our way of life should still have a chance to talk and be heard.

2. No matter what a person's political beliefs are, he is entitled to the same legal rights and protections as anyone else.

3. I believe in free speech for all no matter what their views might be.

4. Nobody has a right to tell another person what he should and should not read.

5. You can't really be sure whether an opinion is true or not unless people are free to argue against it.

6. Unless there is freedom for many points of view to be presented, there is little chance that the truth can ever be known.

7. I would not trust any person or group to decide what opinions can be freely expressed and what must be silenced.

8. Freedom of conscience should mean freedom to be an atheist as well as freedom to worship in the church of one's choice.

Specific Applications of Free Speech and Procedural Rights Scale

("Democratic" response = 1, "undemocratic" response = 0; agreement is the "democratic" response unless item is starred; scale scores range from 0 to 9)

1. Freedom does not give anyone the right to teach foreign ideas in our schools.*

2. A man ought not to be allowed to speak if he doesn't know what he's talking about.*

3. A book that contains wrong political views cannot be a good book and does not deserve to be published.*

4. When the country is in great danger we may have to force people to testify against themselves even if it violates their rights.*

5. No matter what crime a person is accused of, he should never be convicted unless he has been given the right to face and question his accusers.

6. If a person is convicted of a crime by illegal evidence, he should be set free and the evidence thrown out of court.

7. If someone is suspected of treason or other serious crimes, he shouldn't be allowed to be let out on bail.*

8. A person who hides behind the laws when he is questioned about his actions doesn't deserve much consideration.*

9. Dealing with dangerous enemies like the Communists, we can't afford to depend on the courts, the laws and their slow and unreliable methods.*

*Disagreement represents the "democratic" response.

Support for Democratic Principles
(M. Kaase, 1971)

Variable

This scale taps attitudes on a number of consensual and contested principles common to democratic systems, including basic democratic values and support for political rights versus social order.

Description

Kaase has identified five key principles common to democratic systems: (1) the right of individual political participation, (2) popular control of government through regular elections in which a change of leadership is possible, (3) understanding the legitimacy of political conflict, (4) opposition to violence as a legitimate means of resolving political conflict, and (5) consensus on fundamental democratic attitudes. Nine items measure support for these key principles. Items 1–4 and 9 relate to broadly held democratic values, while Items 5–8 involve competing values of political rights and social order. In order to minimize response set, agreement with five of the items represents a "democratic" answer, while disagreement with the other four items represents a "democratic" answer.

Sample

This scale was originally used in five surveys conducted by Kaase in West Germany in 1968. Two surveys were administered to a random sample of West German university students ($N = 3027$ and $N = 492$). Another survey was administered to a random sample of West Germans over the age of 14 ($N = 1964$). A fourth sample consisted of nonacademic West German youth between the ages of 18 and 25 ($N = 995$). The respondents for the nonacademic youth sample were selected on the basis of preselected characteristics rather than randomly. Finally a number of respondents from the first student sample were resurveyed, thus forming a panel of university students ($N = 1004$).

Dalton (1994) reports a number of subsequent uses in both West and East Germany as well as in reunified Germany, including the 1982 and 1988 ALLBUS (German General Social Survey) surveys, the 1990 German Identity Survey, the 1990 ISSP (International

Social Survey Program) survey in East Germany, the 1991 survey in both eastern and western Germany conducted by Weil (1993), and the 1993 survey in both eastern and western Germany conducted by Kaase and Westle. Dalton (1994) focuses on the 1990 German Identity Survey of East and West Germans. Rohrschneider (1994) has used a modified, shorter version of the Kaase scale in a 1991–1992 survey of 168 parliamentarians of the united Berlin Parliament (with three items related to general democratic principles and three items related to trade-offs between conflict and order).

Reliability

Internal Consistency

Kaase reports the results of a factor analysis of the nine items composing the scale. A four-factor solution was indicated. Items 2 and 4 loaded on the first factor, which Kaase calls Affirmation of Democratic Institutions. Depending on the sample, some combination of Items 5, 6, 8, and/or 9 loaded on the second factor, which Kaase calls Affirmation of Conflict. In all samples Item 7 loaded on the third factor, "Rejection of Violence." The composition of the fourth factor also varied among the samples. For the overall population Items 4 and 8 loaded on this factor (which was interpreted as Conflict-Related Understanding of Opposition). For the student and youth samples, Items 1 and 2 loaded on the fourth factor (Affirmation of the Right to Participate). Despite the four-factor solution, all nine items were combined into one overall scale.

Kaase also reports the average interitem correlation of each item for each sample as well as the average interitem correlation of all nine items for each sample (ranging from .05 to .11 for the various samples). Also reported is the correlation of each item with the overall scale index (ranging from −.01 to .36).

In his analysis of the 1990 German data, Dalton (1994) reports that a two-factor solution was indicated, with the first factor relating to support for consensual democratic values and the second to support for order over conflict. Items 1, 2, 3, and 4 loaded positively on the first factor (factor loadings ranging from .63 to .73). Items 5, 6, and 8 loaded positively on the second factor (and negatively on the first factor), as did Item 9 even though Kaase considered it a consensual democratic value (factor loadings ranging from .49 to .67). Item 7 loaded negatively on both factors. A composite measure of democratic attitudes was constructed using the factor scores of each item on the first factor only.

Test–Retest

Because one of the university student samples was sampled twice (thus creating a subset of panel responses), Kaase reports the across-time correlations and gamma coefficients of each item for this sample. The correlation of each item between the two surveys ranged from .12 to .43, and the gammas ranged from .32 to .54. The questions tapping consensual democratic values (Items 1–4) had relatively low across-time correlations (partially due to the lack of variance in the items), whereas those questions tapping contested values (Items 5–9) showed relatively higher across-time correlation.

Validity

Kaase compares the overall Support for Democratic Principles Scale with responses to a number of other items that he argues should be related to support for democratic values, such as support for student demonstrations (γ = .29 and .27 for the two student samples), negative evaluation of the Grand Coalition (gamma coefficients ranging from .10 to .28 for the various samples), attitudes toward state-of-emergency laws (gamma coefficients ranging from $-.20$ to $-.35$), support for a single dominant party or leader (gamma coefficients ranging from $-.18$ to $-.48$), and participation in a demonstration with political goals (gamma coefficients ranging from .37 to .61). Generally there was a stronger relationship between the Support for Democratic Principles Scale and these other democratic items for students than for the overall population.

Location

Original Use

Kaase, M. (1971). Demokratische Einstellung in der Bundesrepublik Deutschland. In R. Wildenman (Ed.), *Sozialwissenschaftliches Jahrbuch für Politik* (Vol. 2). Munich: Günter Olzog Verlag.

Subsequent Uses

Dalton, R. (1994). Communists and democrats: Democratic attitudes in the two Germanies. *British Journal of Political Science, 24,* 469–493.

Results and Comments

In Kaase (1971), agreement with Item 9 is coded as the "democratic" response, although Dalton (1994) acknowledges some ambiguity about the democratic response to this item.

In the overall population sample of his 1968 West German survey, Kaase finds that 6.2% of respondents had a scale score of less than 20 (most democratic), 41.7% scored between 21 and 28, and 43.2% scored between 29 and 52 (least democratic). There was broad popular support for consensual democratic principles, such as freedom of speech and electoral competition, with more than 85% supporting most items. The items related to trade-offs between conflict and order revealed less support for democratic principles when counterposed against other values. Fewer than one-third disagreed that citizens forfeit the right to protest if order is threatened.

In a 1990 survey Dalton (1994) finds extremely strong support for the consensual democratic principles (Items 1–4 and 9) in both the East and the West German samples (support near or exceeding 90%). As in Kaase's analysis, consensus broke down on the contested democratic principles (Items 5–8). Less than half of West Germans indicated a democratic response on Items 5, 6, and 8. Interestingly there was an increase of approximately 20 percentage points in the number of East Germans making the democratic response on these items. Approximately 80% of both samples rejected violence as a means of settling political conflicts.

Dalton (1994) finds socioeconomic explanations of support for democratic values in East Germany unconvincing because factors such as education and income were unrelated to democratic attitudes, unlike the situation in West Germany, where increasing education was correlated with support for democratic attitudes. Instead, support for democratic attitudes among East Germans seemed attributable to countercultural socialization and positive economic evaluations, which were associated with the impending reunification of the two Germanies. Dalton argues that a generational effect was at work in East Germany, making successive cohorts increasingly more democratic (and less supportive of the communist regime) over time. In contrast, age and democratic attitudes were unrelated in West Germany. Among East Germans democratic attitudes were also strongly related to personal economic evaluations, whereas there was no such relationship for West Germans. This may point to the fragility of democratic attitudes in East Germany.

Support for Democratic Principles
(Kaase, 1971)

Scaling: Respondents answer on a six-point scale ranging from "full agreement" = 1, "agreement for the most part" = 2, "low level of agreement" = 3, "low level of rejection" = 4, "rejection for the most part" = 5, and "complete rejection" = 6. The overall scale score is based on the sum of the responses to each of the nine questions. Items for which disagreement represents the "democratic" response are reverse-scored. The overall scale ranges from 9 (most democratic) to 54 (least democratic).

1. Every citizen has the right to take his convictions to the street if necessary.
2. Everyone should have the right to express his opinion even if he differs from the majority.
3. It is not conceivable to have a viable democracy without a political opposition.
4. In principle, every democratic party should have a chance to govern.
5. Conflicts between different interest groups and their demands on the government are adverse to the welfare of all.*
6. A citizen forfeits the right to strike and demonstrate if he threatens the public order.*
7. In every democratic society there are some conflicts which call for violence.*
8. It is not the job of the political opposition to criticize the government, rather it should support the government's work.*
9. The interests of the people at large should always have priority over the special interests of an individual.

*Disagreement represents the "democratic" response.

Democratic Values Scale
(H. McClosky & J. Zaller, 1984)

Variables

A large number of items are used to gauge support for "clear" and "contested" democratic norms related to rights and liberties accorded to various groups, political equality, due process, and privacy rights.

Description

McClosky and Zaller attempted to identify the structure of mass and elite attitudes toward democracy and capitalism. With this purpose in mind, they developed three primary scales, one each related to democratic and capitalist values and one related to individual political sophistication. The Democratic Values Scale is composed of 44 items that tap a variety of values related to support for rights and liberties of various groups, attitudes toward equality, and support for due process and privacy rights. All items are phrased in a sentence-completion format, in which the respondent must choose between two alternative responses to a given item. This format reduces the problem of acquiescence response set inherent in some agree–disagree response formats. Both alternative answers are phrased in moderate and neutral terms, but the choice between the two responses often requires a trade-off between a democratic value and some other value, perhaps related to morality, desire for order, or social prejudices. Both responses are equally plausible, although only one represents unequivocal or unconditional support for the given democratic value.

McClosky and Zaller differentiate a number of the items as either "clear" or "contested" democratic norms, depending on the distribution of elite opinion on the issue. By making this distinction McClosky and Zaller have sought to separate issues on which elites were united and which were not the subject of ideological conflict from issues on which elites held conflicting views. Items related to clear norms are those in which at least 75% of elite members expressing an opinion supported the norm. Items related to contested norms are those in which there was a substantial elite division on the norm and the difference in responses on the item by self-identified liberal and conservative elites was greater than 30 percentage points. Chong, McClosky, and Zaller (1983) report a slightly different method of defining clear and contested norms.

Sample

Three different sets of data were analyzed by McClosky and Zaller. The first was the 1975–1977 Opinions and Values of Americans Survey (OVS) of 938 randomly selected persons in the general public and 2142 members of the elite who were randomly selected from organizations and groups widely known for their ideological nature. The second data set included 845 elite respondents randomly selected from membership lists of five different nonpartisan elite subgroups—*Who's Who in America, Black Who's Who in America,* the Conference of Editorial Writers, the League of Women Voters, and Common Cause; both of the *Who's Who* lists were filtered to remove individuals engaged in activities clearly not related to public affairs. The third data set was the national Civil Liberties Survey of 1993 members of the general public and 1891 community leaders (leaders in local government, the media, business, labor, education, and civic associations) conducted in 1978 and 1979.

The Democratic Values Scale was constructed using 44 items from the OVS. Chong, McClosky, and Zaller (1983) selected the clear and contested norms from the OVS, whereas McClosky and Zaller (1984) selected them from the Civil Liberties Survey (CLS) (see the section on McClosky and Brill's (1983) Omnibus Civil Liberties Scale for a description of the items included in the CLS). The Democratic Values Scale reproduced here presents the OVS items, with notations on those items identified as either clear or contested by Chong, McClosky, and Zaller (1983).

Reliability

Internal Consistency

Chong, McClosky, and Zaller (1983) report scale reliabilities for the Democratic Values Scale ranging from .85 for the least politically aware members of the general public to .95 for ideological elites.

Test–Retest

We encountered no information regarding test–retest reliability.

Validity

We encountered no information regarding validity.

Location

McClosky, H. & Zaller, J. (1984). *The American ethos: Public attitudes toward capitalism and democracy.* Cambridge, MA: Harvard University Press.

Results and Comments

McClosky and Zaller find that while there was substantial disagreement about some democratic and capitalist values, there was generally broad support for the fundamental values of both democracy and capitalism (e.g., majority rule and private ownership of property), especially among members of the political elite. This pattern is consistent with the frequent assertion that ideological conflict in the United States occurs within a limited issue spectrum because of widespread commitment to basic democratic and capitalist values. Beyond this base of fundamental agreement, however, there was a somewhat inverse relationship between support for democratic and capitalist values (i.e., persons with highly prodemocratic attitudes were less supportive of capitalist values than persons with less democratic attitudes).

In contrast to the overwhelming support for democratic values among the elite, there was wide variation in support for capitalist values. This variation in support for capitalism produced two dominant ideologies among elites: welfare-state capitalism (high democratic support, low capitalist support) and nineteenth-century liberalism (high democratic support, high capitalist support). Although less prevalent among elites, two other ideologies could also be identified: strong conservatism (low democratic support, high capitalist support) and an antiregime pattern (low democratic support, low capitalist support).

McClosky and Zaller report that the mean acceptance score on the "clear" democratic norms scale was 12.95 (SD = 2.98), while the mean acceptance score on the "contested" democratic norms scale was 6.37 (SD = 3.71). Members of the public who were more knowledgeable about and involved in public affairs not only were more supportive of clear democratic norms, but also held positions on contested norms consistent with one of the three ideologies espoused by elites (welfare-state capitalism, nineteenth-century liberalism, or strong conservatism). McClosky and Zaller contend that responses consistent with the antiregime pattern were less an alternative ideological vision than a reflection of a lack of political acculturation into any political vision.

Democratic Values Scale (OVS Sample)
(McClosky & Zaller, 1984)

Scaling: "Neither" and "Undecided" response options were also provided for each item. It appears that the composite scale is constructed by summing the number of "democratic" responses on all the items, although this is not explicit; nor do McClosky and Zaller indicate the values given to the response options.

1. The employment of radicals by newspapers and TV: is their right as Americans* / should be forbidden. (Clear)

2. If a speaker at a public meeting begins to make racial slurs, the audience should: stop him from speaking / let him have his say and then answer him.* (Clear)

3. For children to be properly educated: they should be protected against ideas the community considers wrong or dangerous / they should be free to discuss all ideas and subjects, no matter what.*

4. Which of these opinions do you think is more correct? Like fine race horses, some classes of people are just naturally better than others / all people would be about the same if they were treated equally.*

5. When a criminal refuses to confess his crimes, the authorities: are entitled to pressure him until he does / have no right to push him around, no matter what.* (Clear)

6. Meetings urging America to make war against an enemy nation: are so inhuman that we should not allow them to be held / have as much right to be held as meetings that support peace.* (Clear)

7. The use of federal agents to spy on radical organizations: is necessary for national security / violates their right to political freedom.* (Contested)

8. Most of the people who are poor and needy: could contribute something valuable to society if given the chance* / don't have much to offer society anyway.

9. A radio or TV station that always speaks for the rich and powerful against the poor and oppressed: should be required by law to present a more balanced picture / should have the right to favour or oppose any group it chooses.*

10. "Crackpot" ideas: have as much right to be heard as sensible ideas* / sometimes have to be censored for the public good. (Clear)

11. Should a community allow the American Nazi Party to use its town hall to hold a public meeting? Yes* / No.

12. In enforcing the law, the authorities: sometimes have to break the rules in order to bring criminals to justice / should stick to the rules if they want other people to respect the law.*

13. Giving everyone accused of crime the best possible lawyer, even if the government has to pay the legal fees, is: necessary to protect individual rights* / wasteful and goes beyond the requirements of justice.

14. A newspaper has a right to publish its opinions: only if it doesn't twist the facts and tell lies / no matter how false and twisted its opinions are.*

15. Which of these comes closer to your own view? Nobody has the right to decide what should or should not be published* / To protect its moral values, a society sometimes has to forbid certain things from being published.

16. If minorities aren't receiving equal treatment in jobs or housing: they should try to act better so that they will be accepted / the government should step in to see that they are treated the same as everyone else.* (Clear)

17. Our laws should aim to: enforce the community's standards of right and wrong / protect a citizen's right to live by any moral standards he chooses.*

18. The freedom of atheists to make fun of God and religion: should not be allowed / is a legally protected right.* (Clear)

19. Tapping telephones of people suspected of planning crimes: is necessary to reduce crime / should be prohibited as an invasion of privacy.*

20. When it comes to free speech, extremists: should have the same rights as everyone else* / should not be allowed to spread their propaganda. (Clear)

21. Prayers in the public schools should be: permitted / forbidden.*

22. Laws protecting people accused of crime from testifying against themselves should be: strengthened* / weakened or abolished.

23. Is it a good idea / a bad idea* for the government to keep a list of people who take part in protest demonstrations?

24. A person who holds a position of great responsibility, such as a doctor, a judge, or an elected official: is entitled to be treated with special respect / should be treated the same as everyone else.*

25. On issues of religion, morals, and politics, high school teachers have the right to express their opinions in class: even if they go against the community's standards* / only if those opinions are acceptable to the community.

26. Teaching that some kinds of people are better than others: goes against the American idea of equality* / only recognizes the facts.

27. Censoring obscene books: is necessary to protect community standards / is an old-fashioned idea that no longer makes sense.*

28. Requiring policemen to tell a suspect that he has the right to remain silent: prevents the police from doing their job properly / is necessary to a fair system of law enforcement.* (Clear)

29. Complete equality for homosexuals in teaching and other public service jobs: should be protected by law* / may sound fair, but is not really a good idea. (Contested)

30. In dealing with crime, the most important consideration is to: protect the rights of the accused* / stop crime even if we have to violate the rights of the accused.

31. When the country is at war, people suspected of disloyalty: should be watched closely or kept in custody / should be fully protected in their constitutional rights.*

32. Freedom in sexual conduct between adults should be: left up to the individual* / regulated by law. (Clear)

33. Books that preach the overthrow of the government should be: banned from the library / made available by the library, just like any other book.*

34. Keeping people in prison without trial: is never justified, no matter what the crime is* / is sometimes necessary when dealing with people who are dangerous.

35. An American citizen: should not mind having his record checked by patriotic groups / is entitled to have his privacy respected, no matter what he believes.* (Clear)

36. Searching a person's home or car without a search warrant: should never be allowed* / is sometimes justified in order to solve a crime.

37. How do you feel about movies that use foul language or show nudity and sexual acts on the screen? They should be banned / They have as much right to be shown as other films.*

38. The right of a minority family to move into a particular neighborhood: should depend on whether the neighbors want them or not / should be the same as that of any other family.* (Clear)

39. If a person is found guilty of a crime by evidence gathered through illegal methods: he should be convicted no matter how the evidence was collected / he should be set free.*

40. If some minorities haven't succeeded in business or the professions the main reason is that: they don't have the natural ability / they haven't been given enough training and opportunity.*

41. Efforts to make everyone as equal as possible should be: increased* / decreased.

42. If an employer is forced to lay off some employees, he should: let the women go first, especially if they are married / treat men and women employees exactly the same.* (Clear)

43. The laws guaranteeing equal job opportunities for blacks and other minorities: should be made even stronger* / sometimes go too far.

44. Government efforts to bring about racial integration have been: too fast* / too slow. (Contested)

*Indicates the "democratic" response.
(Clear) Indicates the item is included in the Clear Norms subscale.
(Contested) Indicates the item is included in the Contested Norms subscale.

Multi-Dimensional Scale of Democratic Values

(J. L. Gibson, R. Duch, & K. Tedin, 1992)

Variables

The authors conceive of democratic support as composed of seven major subdimensions relating to basic democratic rights, liberties, and institutions: political tolerance, valuation of liberty, support for broad norms of democracy, consciousness of political rights, support for political dissent, support for independent media, and support for electoral competition.

Description

These subdimensions are measured via several distinct subscales: Support for the Value of Liberty, Support for the Norms of Democracy, Rights Consciousness, Support for the Value of Dissent, Support for Independent Media, and Support for Competitive Elections. Political tolerance is measured using the content-controlled (or "least-liked") methodology of Sullivan *et al.* (1982).

(1) The Support for the Value of Liberty subscale consists of four items relating to trade-offs between political participation and the desire for societal order.

(2) The four items in the Support for the Value of Dissent subscale, borrowed from the World Values Survey, are designed to tap attitudes about the ability of citizens to disagree with the government and support for the notion that the government should respect such disagreement.

(3) The Support for the Norms of Democracy subscale consists of four items relating to various civil liberties and rights, such as political expression, right against self-incrimination, and equal protection under the law. The Support for the Norms of Democracy subscale is a variant of the General Norms of Democracy Scale developed by Sullivan *et al.* (1982), which in turn is a combination of one question from Prothro and Grigg's (1960) Fundamental Principles of Democracy Scale and five questions from McClosky's (1964) Democratic Principles and Applications Scale. The Norms of Democracy subscale is not used in Gibson and Duch's (1993b) U.S.S.R. study.

(4) Gibson, Duch, and Tedin (1992) use three items in the Support for Independent Media subscale; Gibson and Duch (1993b) eliminate two of these questions, leaving only a single item on support for private as well as public sector media.

(5) Gibson, Duch, and Tedin (1992) use a six-item scale of Support for Competitive Elections, tapping attitudes about multiple-candidate elections, legalization of parties other than the communists, and assessments of the benefit or harm of competitive elections. Gibson and Duch (1993b) eliminate three of these questions in the non-Moscow sample (multicandidate elections, banning elections to allow Communist Party of the Soviet Union (CPSU) rule, and legalizing parties other than the CPSU) because of a lack of variance in their previous Moscow sample.

(6) The Rights Consciousness subscale asks respondents whether 11 different particular rights ought to be protected by the state.

Sample

The data reported in Gibson, Duch, and Tedin (1992) were collected between February and March 1990 from 504 citizens of the Moscow oblast. This scale was also used in a May 1990 survey of 1561 individuals in the entire European portion of the U.S.S.R., reported by Gibson and Duch (1993b). It was used again in a 1992 survey of 4309 persons in the former Soviet Union (representative of the former U.S.S.R., Russia, Moscow, Leningrad, Ukraine, Soviet Central Asia, and the remaining territory in the European portion of the former Soviet Union) and was reported in Gibson (1996a). Approximately 700 respondents in the 1992 survey had been interviewed in the 1990 survey of the entire European portion of the U.S.S.R., thus creating a subset of panel respondents.

Reliability

Internal Consistency

Factor analysis results are reported in support of the internal consistency of the composite scale and subscales by Gibson, Duch, and Tedin (1992); Gibson and Duch (1993b); and Gibson (1996a, 1996b). For the sample reported in Gibson, Duch, and Tedin (1992), factor analysis of the composite index revealed a single dominant factor accounting for 46% of the original variance. Five of the subscales have factor loadings on the composite scale of greater than .64. The Political Tolerance and Rights Consciousness subscales have relatively low loadings on the composite index (.25 and .41, respectively). The authors attribute the low loading of Political Tolerance to the specific, applied nature of the subscale and the low loading of Rights Consciousness to the lack of variance of the rights index. Cronbach's alpha for the six subscales (excluding Rights Consciousness) ranges from .31 (Independent Media) to .85 (Political Tolerance) and is reported in the article. Gibson and Duch (1993b) also report a single-factor solution to the factor analysis of the six subscales (accounting for 37.3% of the variance). Cronbach's alpha for the composite scale is .61. The factor analysis results and alphas for the composite scale and subscales are reported in the article. A two-factor solution with slightly different items is reported in Gibson (1996a, 1996b).

Test–Retest

We encountered no information regarding test–retest reliability.

Validity

We encountered no information regarding validity.

Location

Original Use

Gibson, J. L., Duch, R., & Tedin, K. (1992). Democratic values and the transformation of the Soviet Union. *Journal of Politics, 54,* 329–371. Reprinted by permission of the authors and the University of Texas Press. All rights retained by the University of Texas Press.

Subsequent Uses

Gibson, J. L., & Duch, R. (1993b). Emerging democratic values in Soviet political culture. In A. Miller, W. Reisinger, & V. Hesli (Eds.), *Public opinion and regime change: The new politics of post-Soviet societies* (pp. 69–94). Boulder, CO: Westview Press.

Gibson, J. L. (1996a). A mile wide but an inch deep (?): The structure of democratic commitments in the former USSR. *American Journal of Political Science, 40,* 396–420.

Gibson, J. L. (1996b). Political and economic markets: Changes in the connections between attitudes toward political democracy and a market economy within the mass culture of Russia and Ukraine. *Journal of Politics, 58,* 954–984.

Results and Comments

Gibson, Duch, and Tedin (1992) find fairly widespread support for some democratic values in the Moscow region, especially among the better educated, men, and the young. Education, gender, and age also predict support for democratic values in the Soviet Union at large (Gibson & Duch, 1993b), although gender has only a modest effect, and the effect of education is less powerful than in the Moscow sample. Gibson and Duch (1993b) suggest that the effect of education may depend on the availability of information. The better educated are likely to be more attuned to new information (some of it about democracy), but if less information is available (as in more isolated regions of the Soviet Union), then education will not affect attitudes toward democracy. Gibson and Duch (1993b) also report that opinion leaders are not more supportive of democratic principles than ordinary Soviet citizens, after controlling for other factors.

Although using a slightly different factor structure for democratic values for the 1990 and 1992 data, Gibson (1996a) finds no substantial decline in support for democratic values between 1990 and 1992. Moreover, panel data reveal considerable across-time stability of democratic attitudes. Finally, an important finding with respect to democratic legitimation, Gibson finds that evaluations of economic performance have relatively little impact on democratic support (at least in the short run).

Multi-Dimensional Scale of Democratic Values

Scaling: The scoring of the individual subscales is given below. After scoring each subscale as described, Gibson, Duch, and Tedin (1992) use the scores derived from a factor analysis of the seven subscales to construct a composite index of support for basic democratic rights, liberties, and institutions. Gibson and Duch (1993b) construct a composite index using a factor analysis of only six subscales since, as noted above, they do not use the Norms of Democracy subscale.

Political Tolerance Subscale

Following the procedure devised by Sullivan *et al.* (1982), the authors allow respondents to select target groups for themselves, either from a prepared list of groups or from groups they designate themselves. Each respondent is then asked four tolerance questions about each of the two groups the respondent has identified as his or her most disliked. For each group, respondents are asked whether the group should be allowed to make a speech, should be allowed to hold public rallies, should be outlawed, or should be banned from running for public office. The exact wording of the questions is provided in the

Sullivan *et al.* (1982) section of this chapter. The score on the Political Tolerance subscale is the sum of tolerant positions taken on the four statements for the two most disliked groups, thus creating a scale ranging from 0 (least tolerant) to 8 (most tolerant).

Support for the Value of Liberty Subscale

(Response options for each item are "agree strongly," "agree," "uncertain," "disagree," and "disagree strongly;" factor analysis of the component items is used to derive scores for the subscale)
1. Society shouldn't have to put up with political views that are fundamentally different from the views of the majority.*
2. Because demonstrations frequently become disorderly and disruptive, radical and extremist political groups shouldn't be allowed to demonstrate.*
3. Free speech is just not worth it if it means that we have to put up with the danger to society of extremist political views.*
4. It is better to live in an orderly society than to allow people so much freedom that they can become disruptive.*

Support for the Norms of Democracy Subscale

(Response options for each item are "agree strongly," "agree," "uncertain," "disagree," and "disagree strongly;" factor analysis of the component items is used to derive scores for the subscale)
1. No matter what a person's political beliefs are, he is entitled to the same legal rights and protections as anyone else.
2. It is necessary that everyone, regardless of their views, can express themselves freely.
3. When a country is in great danger we may have to force people to testify against themselves even if this violates their civil rights.*
4. If someone is suspected of treason or other serious crimes, he can be sent to prison without trial.*

Rights Consciousness Subscale

(Response options are "always respected" and "depends on circumstances;" the score of the subscale is the mean of the responses to the items with "always respected" = 1, "don't know" = 0.5, and "depends on circumstances" = 0, thus the overall subscale can have a value from 0 (least conscious of rights) to 1 (most conscious of rights)).
1. For each of the following rights and liberties, can you tell me if you think that they should always be observed or does it depend on the circumstances?
   Freedom of speech
   Right to personal safety and protection
   Freedom of association, groups, unions
   Right of people to their own language and culture
   Religious liberty and freedom of conscience
   Equality before the law

Right of asylum (not asked in all surveys)
Right to work
Right to own property
Right to education and training
Freedom of information (not asked in all surveys)
Right to privacy of personal correspondence, telephone conversations, and so on
Right to travel abroad

Support for the Value of Dissent Subscale

(Response options for each item are "agree strongly," "agree," "uncertain," "disagree," and "disagree strongly;" factor analysis of the component items is used to derive scores for the subscale)

1. Our government should become much more open to the public. (In some versions, "The people should know more about their government.")
2. Political reform in this country is moving too rapidly.*
3. People should be able to participate in any organization even if this activity opposes some current laws.
4. We are more likely to have a healthy economy if the government allows more freedom for individuals to do as they wish.

In some versions, the second question is deleted and the following question is added: "If an unjust law were passed, I could do nothing about it."*

Support for Independent Media Subscale

(Response options for each item are "agree strongly," "agree," "uncertain," "disagree," and "disagree strongly;" factor analysis of the component items is used to derive scores for the subscale)

1. The press should be protected by the law from persecution by the government.
2. Private radios, television, and newspapers should exist alongside state-owned media.
3. There is currently too much criticism in Soviet newspapers and magazines.*

In some versions, only the second question is used.

Support for Competitive Elections Subscale

(Response options for each item are "agree strongly," "agree," "uncertain," "disagree," and "disagree strongly;" factor analysis of the component items is used to derive scores for the subscale)

1. Elections to local Soviets should be conducted in such a way that there are several candidates for each post.
2. It is necessary to ban elections and allow the CPSU to rule the country without elections.*
3. Political parties other than the Communist party should be legalized.

4. Those supporting competitive elections are doing harm to the country.*

5. Competition between the Communist party and other parties will improve the way the authorities work in the Soviet Union.

6. A one-party system in the USSR promotes the development of democracy.*

In some versions, the first three questions are eliminated.

*Disagreement represents the "democratic" response.

Index of Pro-Democracy Orientation
(W. Reisinger, A. Miller, V. Hesli, & K. Maher, 1994; A. Miller, V. Hesli, & W. Reisinger, 1995)

Variable

The purpose is to identify those who support democratic values, which are viewed as a combination of values pertaining to civil liberties and to the form of government (e.g., competitive elections and majority rule).

Description

Reisinger, Miller, Hesli, and Maher (1994) assert that three specific values or beliefs are essential to democracy: (1) diffuse support for the institutions of democracy and belief in the superiority of democratic rule; (2) a high degree of interpersonal trust, which makes the concept of loyal opposition more credible; and (3) the assertion by citizens of individual rights. They operationalize these values and beliefs with five items measuring interpersonal trust, support for values such as free speech and popular political influence, support for party competition, support for the rights of political opposition, and rights consciousness. The Index of Democratic Values scale contains only the latter three items because the first two are not closely related to the others.

Miller, Hesli, and Reisinger (1995) report a new version of the Index of Democratic Values, which they refer to as the Index of Pro-Democracy Orientation. The items composing this new scale were identified from an exploratory factor analysis of 30 questions related to a range of political, economic, and cultural beliefs and values. The five items comprising the Index of Pro-Democracy Orientation all load on the same factor and relate to support for features of a democratic government (e.g., popular participation, competition, and compromise) as well as to support for First Amendment rights and protection of minority rights. Miller, Hesli, and Reisinger do not explain why rights consciousness is excluded.

Sample

The data reported by Reisinger, Miller, Hesli, and Maher (1994) were collected in surveys conducted in Lithuania, Ukraine, and European Russia during 1990, 1991, and 1992; the total sample size for the three surveys is 7500. Apparently, however, all of the items necessary for the construction of the Index of Democratic Values are available only in the 1992 survey ($N = 2700$).

Miller, Hesli, and Reisinger (1995) use the Index of Pro-Democracy Orientation in the analysis of a 1992 survey of 2200 Russian and Ukrainian citizens and a survey of 112 Russian elites and 65 Ukrainian elites. Miller, Reisinger, and Hesli (1996) report an additional use of the Index of Pro-Democracy Orientation in a 1995 survey of 2820 citizens of Lithuania, Ukraine, and European Russia.

Reliability

Internal Consistency

Reisinger, Miller, Hesli, and Maher (1994) report that two items related to democratic attitudes are excluded from the Index of Democratic Values because they do not covary with the other items. Thus it is obvious that some analysis of internal consistency was performed, although the results are not reported.

With respect to the Index of Pro-Democracy Orientation, Miller, Hesli, and Reisinger (1995) report on an exploratory factor analysis of the elite sample for all the items used to construct the four indices (political reform, market orientation, nationalism, and democratic orientation). Four factors tap attitudes toward reform, tendencies toward nationalism, attitudes about a market versus a controlled economy, and support for democratic principles. The applicability of the four-factor solution to the mass sample is confirmed by a factor analysis of the combined Russian and Ukrainian mass sample, using the 21 items that proved significant in the elite factor analysis. Factor loadings in the confirmatory factor analysis are not reported. We encountered no other information regarding the internal consistency of either scale.

Test–Retest

We encountered no information regarding test–retest reliability of either scale.

Validity

We encountered no information regarding validity.

Location

Reisinger, W., Miller, A., Hesli, V., & Maher, K. (1994). Political values in Russia, Ukraine and Lithuania: Sources and implications for democracy. *British Journal of Political Science, 24,* 183–223.

Miller, A., Hesli, V., & Reisinger, W. (1995). Comparing citizen and elite belief systems in post-Soviet Russia and Ukraine. *Public Opinion Quarterly, 59,* 1–40.

Miller, A. H., Reisinger, W. M., & Hesli, V. L. (1996). Understanding political change in post-Soviet societies. *American Political Science Review, 90,* 153–166.

Results and Comments

Reisinger, Miller, Hesli, and Maher (1994) report that the mean score on the Index of Democratic Values was 3.18 for Lithuania (SD = 1.2), 2.91 for Ukraine (SD = 1.46), and 2.8 for Russia (SD = 1.45). They find that prodemocratic respondents in Lithuania, Ukraine, and European Russia are less favorable to Soviet-era values and less committed to the pursuit of "order." However, those desiring stronger leadership also express more democratic than authoritarian sentiments.

Miller, Hesli, and Reisinger (1995) use surveys of Russian and Ukrainian elites and masses to explore belief systems in the two countries. The mean score on the Index of Pro-Democracy Orientation (rescaled to values between 1 and 10) was approximately 7.1 for both the Ukrainian and the Russian mass samples, 7.7 for the Russian elite sample, and 8.4 for the Ukrainian elite sample. They observed little difference in levels of attitude constraint between politically involved citizens and official elites. Even more interestingly, levels of constraint for the *least* involved citizens are higher than those found in Western democracies. Education, media exposure, and information levels were only marginally related to attitude constraint, but political involvement had a strong effect. This led the authors to attribute the relatively high level of attitude constraint among ordinary Russians and Ukrainians to the mobilization of the citizenry that preceded the collapse of the Soviet Union.

Miller, Reisinger, and Hesli (1996) report that the mean score on the index was 12.7 for Lithuania, 11.9 for Ukraine, and 12.0 for Russia.

Index of Democratic Values

Scaling: The scoring of the three items is given below. The score of the overall index is the sum of the scores of the three items and can range from 0 (least supportive) to 5 (most supportive).

1. Competition among many political parties makes the political system stronger. (response options are "agree fully," "agree," "disagree," "disagree fully," and "not able to say exactly;" the item is scored 1 for an "agree" or "fully agree" response and 0 otherwise)

2. Any individual or organization has the right to organize opposition or resistance to any governmental initiative. (response options are "agree fully," "agree," "disagree," "disagree fully," and "not able to say exactly;" the item is scored 1 for an "agree" or "fully agree" response and 0 otherwise)

3. On this card are listed some civil rights and liberties. For each of these, can you tell me if you think they should always be observed or does it depend on the situation? (response options are "should always be observed" and "depends on circumstances;" the score of the item is the sum of the responses to each of the three rights with "always be observed" = 1 and "depends on circumstances" = 0; thus, the score of the item ranges from 0 (least conscious of rights) to 3 (most conscious of rights; there is no information about whether a "don't know" option is scored as well)
   Freedom of speech
   Freedom of association, to join groups
   Religious liberty, freedom of conscience

Index of Pro-democracy Orientation
(Miller, Hesli, & Reisinger, 1995)

Scaling: The response categories for all items are "fully agree" = 1, "agree" = 2, "not able to say exactly" = 3, "disagree" = 4, "fully disagree" = 5. The score of the overall Index of Pro-Democracy Orientation is the sum of each item, with items for which disagreement represents the democratic response reverse scored. Miller, Hesli, and Reisinger (1995) rescale the index so that it ranges between 1 and 10.

I am now going to read you a number of statements. For each statement, would you please indicate whether you agree with each fully or partially or disagree partially or fully.

1. A successful political leader will often need to compromise with his political opponents (in some versions, Compromise with one's political opponents is dangerous, since it usually leads to changing one's own position).

2. Participation of the people is not necessary if decision making is left in the hands of a few trusted, competent leaders.*

3. Any individual or organization has the right to organize opposition or resistance to any governmental initiative.

4. Competition among many political parties will make the political system stronger.

5. The government has the responsibility to see that the rights of all minorities are protected.

*Disagreement represents the "democratic" response.

Attitudes towards Democracy
(S. Whitefield & G. Evans, 1996)

Variable

This is one of several batteries developed by the authors to tap the political, cultural, and economic attitudes of Russian citizens, focusing on various attitudes about democratic processes and values.

Description

Whitefield and Evans try to differentiate among support for democracy in the abstract, evaluation of the regime's democracy in practice, and support for democratic principles. The Attitudes towards Democracy items relate to the first and third concepts and consist of one item related to support for the *aim* of building democracy and six other items related to various democratic values, such as freedom of expression and political opposition. Support for the performance of democracy is assessed with an item eliciting the level of support for the *actual practice* of democracy. The item related to the normative commitment to democracy is used in a survey of Eastern Europeans reported by Evans and Whitefield (1995), and a precursor that taps support for the "ideals" of democracy is reported by Whitefield and Evans (1994). Some of the other items are used in scales reported by Heath, Evans, and Martin (1994).

Sample

The data were collected from a 1993 survey of 2030 Russians and a 1995 survey of 2003 Russians.

Reliability

Internal Consistency

We encountered no information regarding internal consistency.

Test–Retest

We encountered no information regarding test–retest reliability.

Validity

Evans and Whitefield (1995) compare responses to the normative commitment item with responses to items eliciting normative evaluations of the benefits of "democracy." These responses are correlated in similar ways in each country, and the rankings of countries according to the latter items are roughly the same as a ranking based on the normative commitment item.

Location

Whitefield, S., & Evans, G. (1996). Support for democracy and political opposition in Russia, 1993–1995. *Post-Soviet Affairs, 12,* 218–242.

Results and Comments

While agreement with Item 3 would usually be considered the democratic response, Whitefield and Evans note considerable ambiguity about the "democratic" response in the Russian context, particularly considering that supporters of antireform candidates are most supportive of this statement, while supporters of proreform candidates are least supportive.

Whitefield and Evans find a slight decrease in the normative commitment to democracy among Russian citizens between 1993 and 1995. This is combined with an even larger decrease in evaluations of the actual practice (versus the aim) of democracy in Russia.

Attitudes towards Democracy
(Whitefield & Evans, 1996)

Scaling: Whitefield and Evans assess each of the seven items separately and do not attempt to develop a composite scale. The responses for questions 2 through 7 are measured on a five-point agree-disagree scale.

1. How do you feel about the aim of building democracy in the country, in which political parties compete for government? Are you a supporter or an opponent? (response options are "supporter" and "opponent"; "Supporter" is the democratic response.)
2. People should be allowed to organize public meetings to protest against the government.
3. Political parties that wish to overthrow democracy should be allowed to stand in general elections.
4. The political opposition should not only criticize the government, but support it as well.*
5. It is not conceivable to have a viable democracy without political opposition.
6. Democracy works best if no single party is allowed to stay in power for too long a period.
7. It would be worthwhile to support a leader who could solve the main problems facing Russia today even if he overthrew democracy.*

   *Disagreement represents the "democratic" response.

Support for Democracy
(Weil, 1989, 1993, 1996)

Variable

Weil attempts to distinguish between support for democratic principles and values, on the one hand, and evaluations of democracy as a form of government, on the other.

Description

Weil (1989) uses items from surveys conducted in various countries. In Germany most of the items used as indicators of support for democracy pertain to support for a multiple party system, but some relate to evaluations of democracy versus alternative forms of governance.

In subsequent work Weil (1993, 1996) disaggregates two components of his earlier scale and differentiates between support for democratic principles, on the one hand, and evaluations of democracy as a form of government or in comparison to other forms of governance, on the other. Thus Weil (1996) reports two different scales tapping two dimensions of democratic attitudes. A scale for support for democratic principles is constructed from two items (relating to a competitive electoral system and views of Hitler and

Nazism) and a subscale composed of a number of items from Kaase's (1971) battery of items tapping key democratic principles and values.

A separate scale for the evaluation of democracy is composed of two items relating to the form of democracy in Germany and whether problems in Germany can be solved with democracy.

Sample

Weil (1989) collects data from various surveys conducted in the United States, Britain, France, West Germany, Italy, Austria, and Spain from 1945 to 1987. The resulting data set contains 15,000 data points representing responses to survey items used in various countries at various times. The data for Austria were of insufficient duration or density for inclusion in the final analysis. The data reported by Weil (1993) were collected in a 1991 survey of 1039 respondents in western Germany and 1080 respondents in eastern Germany. The data reported by Weil (1996) were collected in a 1992 survey of 1081 respondents in western Germany and 1131 respondents in eastern Germany.

Reliability

Internal Consistency

Weil (1989) observes that because most of the data used in his analysis were available only at the aggregate level, item-to-item reliability and validity checks were not possible. No estimates of internal consistency are reported.

The Democratic Ideals and the Approval of Existing Democracy scales (as well as a third scale, Socialist Values) reported by Weil (1996) are constructed using confirmatory factor analysis of the constituent items. Weil reports that attempts to extract dimensions comparable to these scales using exploratory factor analysis of the combined items from all three scales yielded dimensions close, but not identical, to the dimensions determined a priori from the research hypotheses. The factor analysis results for both scales (and the Kaase subscale) are reported for both eastern and western Germany. The factor loadings of the constituent items on the Democratic Ideals scale range from .54 to .72. The factor loadings of the constituent items on the Approval of Existing Democracy scale range from .78 to .80.

Test–Retest

We encountered no information regarding test–retest reliability.

Validity

Weil (1989) reports that standard validation procedures were employed to test the composition of the indexes, including correlating the scales, visually checking them against their component measures, and ensuring their robustness by correlating them against indexes constructed by different methods.

Weil (1996) reports the correlations of the Democratic Ideals and the Approval of Existing Democracy scales with each other, their scale components, a Socialist Values scale, and several other measures of democratic values. The Democratic Ideals and the Approval of Existing Democracy scales correlate strongly with each other. The Socialist Values scale correlates negatively with the Approval of Existing Democracy scale. There is no relationship between the Socialist Values and the Democratic Ideals scales in western Germany, but there is a moderate positive relationship in eastern Germany (a possible indication of a socialist democratic conceptualization). Nostalgia for the old East German government correlates negatively with both the Democratic Ideals and the Approval of Existing Democracy scales (and positively with the Social Values scale). In both western and eastern Germany, the Democratic Ideals and the Approval of Existing Democracy scales correlate with traditional liberal democratic values (e.g., freedom of expression and opposition, support for competitive elections), and the Democratic Ideals scale also correlates with participatory democratic values (e.g., referenda, workplace democracy) in eastern Germany.

Location

Weil, F. D. (1989). The sources and structure of legitimation in Western democracies: A consolidated model tested with time-series data in six countries since World War II. *American Sociological Review, 54,* 682–706.

Weil, F. D. (1993). The development of democratic attitudes in eastern and western Germany in a comparative perspective. In F. D. Weil (Ed.), *Research on democracy and society: Vol. 1. Democratization in eastern and western Europe* (pp. 195–225). Greenwich, CT: JAI Press.

Weil, F. D. (1996). *Western political culture and the consolidation of democracy in eastern Germany.* Paper presented at the Eighth International Conference on Socioeconomics, Geneva.

Results and Comments

Weil (1989) attempts to distinguish between political confidence and legitimation of democracy and to assess the effect of state performance and the structure of political opposition on these two indicators of political support. His results indicate that poor state performance, that is, economic crises or unfulfilled demands on the state, does lead to a decline in confidence but does not undermine support for a democratic form of government. An unresponsive structure of political opposition (e.g., polarization or fractionalization of political parties), however, not only diminishes political confidence, but also decreases the support for democracy among the citizenry. Weil suggests that these findings indicate the presence of a reservoir of legitimacy for democracy that is not responsive to negative short-term evaluations of state performance, but can only be affected by a sustained period of unresponsive opposition structure.

Weil (1993) finds eastern Germans to be much more democratically oriented than expected. In terms of support for basic democratic principles, eastern Germans are only slightly less democratic than western Germans, but have a far higher level of democratic support than those found in postwar West Germany and in Austria and Spain at similar points in their transitions to democratic rule. Eastern Germans also are more supportive of democracy than citizens of other contemporary eastern European states. Despite high levels of democratic support, eastern Germans are sharply more critical of democracy in practice than are their western compatriots, with fewer eastern Germans believing that Germany's problems can be solved with democracy.

Weil (1996) extends his analysis of western and eastern Germans by examining the bases of democratic support in transitional democracies. He finds support for "demonstration effects," in which persons who admire Western countries are more supportive of existing democracy, and "historical preferences," in which persons who prefer the new regime to the old one are more supportive of democratic values. He notes little support for the hypothesis that economic prosperity promotes democratic legitimation, finding economic evaluations to have little independent effect on support for democratic values after controlling for other factors.

Support for Democracy
(Weil, 1989)

Scaling: The response options are either given in the questions themselves or are indicated with the items presented below. Weil (1989) reports two methods of index construction. When index items are asked in the same years, the index is the mean score of the constituent items. When items are not asked in the same years, some time-points are interpolated, and the index is computed by adding the mean interannual change in the items to the previous year's index value. The initial value of the index is approximated from the beginning values of the constituent items.

1. Do you think it is better for a country to have one party, to obtain the greatest possible unity, or several parties so that the various opinions can be freely represented? (Responses: *several parties, not more than two or three parties, one party, no parties*)

2. Two men are discussing how a country should be governed. The one says: "I like it best when the people place the best politician at the top and give him complete governing power. He can then clearly and quickly decide with a few chosen experts. Not much talking is done and something really happens!" The other says: "I prefer that a number of people have to determine something in the country. They do sometimes go round and round until something is done, but it is not so easy for abuse of power to occur." Which of these two opinions is closest to your own view—the first or the second? ("Second" is the "democratic" response; exact response options are not provided.)

3. If you think about the difficulties which face us: The scarcity of raw materials, food and sources of energy, caused by the rapid growth of the population, and the growth of the economy. Do you believe that we can control these difficulties with our democratic form of state with several parties in the Parliament, or do we need a single-party system with a strong government at the top to take care of these difficulties in the future? ("Several parties" is the "democratic" response; exact response options are not provided.)

4. Which form of government do you feel is best for us as Germans? (Responses: *democracy,* * *monarchy, dictatorship/Nazism*)

5. Do you believe that the democracy which we have in the Federal Republic is the best form of state or is there another form of state which is better? ("Best form of state" is the "democratic" response; exact response options are not provided.)

6. Many say: The democratic relationships established in the Basic Law are not satisfactory in our state. In order to achieve a true democracy, we must change the whole system and write a new Basic Law. Do you also want this or are you against this? (Response options are not provided.)

7. Once again about our Constitution, the Basic Law: The Basic Law was in fact created almost 30 years ago under the supervision and control of the Western Powers. Therefore, many feel that we Germans should write a new Basic Law for ourselves and thus make it correspond better to our needs and interests. Others say, on the other hand, that the current Basic Law has lasted this long so well that we do not need a new one. Which is your opinion? (Response options are not provided.)

8. What do you think of the form of government in the Federal Republic? Is there much to object to; is there only a little bit to object to; or is everything in order?

9. Considered completely for a moment from the pragmatic view: do we actually need a Parliament with all those Representatives in Bonn or would it also work without them? ("Need a Parliament" is the "democratic" response; exact response options are not provided.)

*Indicates the "democratic" response.

Democracy Scales
(Weil, 1996)

Democratic Ideals

(Respondent scores for the scale are derived from factor analysis of the two questions and the factor score of the Democratic Principles subscale)

1. Two men are discussing how a country should be governed The one says: "I like it best when the people place the best politician at the top and give him complete governing power. He can then clearly and quickly decide with a few chosen experts. Not much talking is done and something really happens!" The other says: "I prefer that a number of people have to determine something in the country. They do sometimes go round and round until something is done, but it is not so easy for abuse of power to occur." Which of these two opinions is closest to your own view—the first or the second? ("Second" is the "democratic" response; other response options are not provided.)

2. A question about Hitler and National Socialism: Some say, if you disregard the war and the persecution of the Jews, the Third Reich was not so bad. Others say, the Third Reich was a bad thing no matter what. What is your opinion? ("Bad thing" is the "democratic" response; other response options are not provided.)

3. Democratic Principles subscale: On these cards, we have put together a series of commonly heard opinions about people's behavior. We would like to find out what people really think. Please sort out the cards on this scale according to how much you agree or disagree with each statement. ("Agree" is the "democratic" response; other response options are not provided.)
   a. A living democracy is inconceivable without a political opposition.
   b. Every democratic party should have the right in principle to enter government.
   c. Every citizen has the right to go to the streets for his convictions if necessary.
   d. Everyone should have the right to stand up for his opinion, even if the majority disagrees.

Approval of Existing Democracy

(Respondent scores for the scale are derived from factor analysis of the two questions)
1. Do you believe that the democracy which we have in the Federal Republic is the best form of state or is there another form of state which is better? ("Best form of state" is the "democratic" response; other response options are not provided.)
2. If someone says, "We can solve the problems we have in the Federal Republic with democracy," would you agree or not? ("Agree" is the "democratic" response; other response options are not provided.)

Willingness to Tolerate Nonconformists
(Stouffer, 1955)

Variable

Stouffer set out to measure the extent to which Americans respect "the civil rights of radicals and other nonconformists"—specifically admitted communists, suspected communists, socialists, and people who oppose religion.

Description

The scale contains five sets of three items, each of which Stouffer considered a "subtest." Stouffer selected items according to a Guttman scaling logic. Thus "a person who is 'tolerant' on a subtest in which *few* other people would be tolerant is also very likely to be so in a subtest on which many other people would be 'tolerant' " (Stouffer, 1955, pp. 262–263). From the five sets of items, he composed six groups of respondents, ranging from Group 0, whose members were tolerant on none of the subtests, through Group 5, whose members were tolerant on all five subtests.

Virtually without exception, the GSS has included a revised version of the Stouffer items focusing on willingness to allow three types of political activity by various groups. The original three items regarding the rights of a "person who favored government ownership of all the railroads and all big industries" were dropped after the 1974 survey. Since

1976 the GSS items have focused on the rights of five different groups: racists, communists, militarists, homosexuals, and those who oppose religion. These groups represent a more "balanced" set of target groups, politically and culturally, than the original Stouffer target groups (see Table 5–1 in the appendix).

Sample

The original survey sample (Stouffer, 1955) consisted of two parts. The mass component was a composite of two national cross-sections, one drawn by Gallup and the other by the National Opinion Research Center (NORC), with a total usable sample size of almost 5000. The elite component included 14 types of community leaders ($N = 1533$) drawn from a national sample of 123 cities with populations between 10,000 and 150,000. Both the mass and the elite interviews were conducted in 1954. Among the mass sample 19% scored 0 or 1 (least tolerant), 50% scored 2 or 3, and 31% scored 4 or 5 (most tolerant). Among the elite sample 5% scored 0 or 1, 29% scored 2 or 3, and 66% scored 4 or 5.

The Stouffer tolerance scale, or a modified version of it, has been a staple in opinion surveys conducted in the United States since 1955. Most subsequent research in the Stouffer tradition has drawn on data from one or more annual NORC General Social Surveys, which have been conducted regularly since 1972, with approximately 1500 respondents per survey. For detailed information concerning the GSS, see Davis and Smith (1996); on the GSS variant of the Stouffer items, see *GSS Data on Tolerance,* the appendix to this chapter.

Reliability

Internal Consistency

Stouffer (1955) reports a coefficient of reproducibility (a measure of the extent to which items form an acceptable Guttman scale) of .96 for the 15 tolerance items. In their follow-up study Nunn *et al.* (1978) report four different measures of Guttman scale reliability for the 1954 Stouffer data and the 1973 GSS tolerance data, respectively: the coefficient of reproducibility (.90 and .90), the minimum marginal reproducibility (.71 and .69), the percentage of improvement (.20 and .21), and the coefficient of scalability (.68 and .66). (See also Abrahamson & Carter, 1986, and Cutler & Kaufman, 1975, for Guttman scale results consistent with these.) Several studies (e.g., Bobo & Licari, 1989; Grabb, 1979; Hougland & Lacy, 1981) analyzing data from various General Social Surveys report alpha coefficients in the neighborhood of .90 for the full scale of NORC tolerance items and between .70 to .85 for three-item scales for individual target groups. However, Bobo and Licari (1989) also report an exploratory factor analysis in which two other factors emerge: One focuses on the right of extremists to teach college and another on the rights of a racist. Based on these results Bobo and Licari generate three separate tolerance scales from the GSS items rather than a single scale.

The most recent analysis of the internal consistency of the GSS items can be found in Nie, Junn, and Stehlik-Barry (1996). Nie *et al.* (1996) conduct a principal components analysis of the GSS items used from 1976 to 1994 and report the percentage of variance explained by the first principal component, the loadings of each item on the first principal component, and the coefficient *alpha* for each year. The coefficient *alpha* ranges from .91 to .94 across the thirteen years. Nie *et al.* conclude that the factor analysis and reliability estimates indicate that all of the tolerance items tap a single underlying dimension which is quite similar across time.

Test–Retest

Although we encountered no direct information regarding test–retest reliability, Gibson (1992a) reinterviewed respondents in the 1987 GSS a few months after the original interviews had been conducted and reasked nine of the tolerance questions. Unfortunately two of the original target groups were dropped, and changes in both question wording and formatting were introduced. In spite of these changes, the correlation between scores on the 15-item tolerance scale and on the 9-item reinterview variant was .72.

Validity

Although we encountered no direct tests of convergent validity, Stouffer (1955) reports that people classified as less tolerant of nonconformists according to the 15-item scale were disproportionately likely to belong to various "known" intolerant groups.

Location

Original 15-item Scale

Stouffer, S. A. (1955). *Communism, conformity and civil liberties.* Garden City, NY: Doubleday.

NORC General Social Survey Version

Davis, J. A., & Smith, T. W. (1996). *General Social Surveys, 1972–1996: Cumulative codebook.* Chicago: NORC.

Results and Comments

According to Stouffer (1955), community leaders were on average more tolerant than members of the mass public. Stouffer also observed regional and demographic differences in tolerance. Dozens of subsequent studies, following Stouffer, have attempted to pinpoint factors conducive to tolerance or to analyze tolerance toward specific target groups or among specific population groups.

Willingness to Tolerate Nonconformists Scale
(Original Stouffer Version)

Scaling: From the five sets of questions, Stouffer composed six groups of respondents, ranging from Group 0, whose members were tolerant on none of the subtests, through Group 5, whose members were tolerant on all five subtests. Respondents are assigned a score ranging from 0 (the least tolerant) to 5 (the most tolerant) depending on the highest number of the group for which they meet the criteria. The response options are indicated with the items presented below.

GROUP 5 (Give + answers to at least two out of the following three items, and to at least two items in each ensuing set):

Now, I should like to ask you some questions about a man who admits he is a Communist.

1. Suppose this admitted Communist wants to make a speech in your community. Should he be allowed to speak, or not? (+ = Yes, − = No or Don't know)

2. Suppose he wrote a book which is in your public library. Somebody in your community suggests the book should be removed from the library. Would you favor removing it, or not? (+ = Not favor, − = Favor or Don't know)

3. Suppose this admitted Communist is a radio singer. Should he be fired, or not? (+ = Not be fired, − = Should be fired or Don't know)

GROUP 4 (Do not qualify for Group 5 but give + answers to at least two of the following three questions and to at least two items in each ensuing set):

4. Should an admitted Communist be put in jail, or not? (+ = No, − = Yes or Don't know) There are always some people whose ideas are considered bad or dangerous by other people. For instance, somebody who is against all churches and religion.

5. If such a person wanted to make a speech in your city (town, community) against churches and religion, should he be allowed to speak, or not? (+ = Yes, − = No or Don't know)

6. If some people in your community suggested that a book he wrote against churches and religion should be taken out of your public library, would you favor removing this book or not? (+ = No, − = Yes or Don't know)

GROUP 3 (Do not qualify for Groups 4 or 5 but give + answers to at least two of the following three questions and to at least two items in each ensuing set):

7. Now suppose the radio program he (an admitted Communist) is on advertises a brand of soap. Somebody in your community suggests you stop buying that soap. Would you stop, or not? (+ = Would not stop, − = Would stop or Don't know)

Or consider a person who favored government ownership of all the railroads and all big industries.

8. If this person wanted to make a speech in your community favoring government ownership of all the railroads and big industries, should he be allowed to speak, or not? (+ = Yes, − = No or Don't know)

9. If some people in your community suggested that a book he wrote favoring government ownership should be taken out of your public library, would you favor removing the book, or not? (+ = No, − = Yes or Don't know)

GROUP 2 (Do not qualify for Groups 3, 4, or 5, but give + answers to at least two of the following three questions and to at least two items in the ensuing set):

Now I would like you to think of another person. A man whose loyalty has been questioned before a Congressional committee, but who swears under oath he has never been a Communist.

10. Suppose he is teaching in a college or university. Should he be fired, or not? (+ = No, − = Yes or Don't know)

11. Should he be allowed to make a speech in your community, or not? (+ = Yes, − = No or Don't know)

12. Suppose this man is a high school teacher. Should he be fired, or not? (+ = No, − = Yes or Don't know)

GROUP 1 (Do not qualify for Groups 2, 3, 4, or 5, but give + answers to two of the following three questions, which focus on the same target as in the Group 2 questions):

13. Suppose he has been working in a defense plant. Should he be fired, or not? (+ = No or Don't know, − = Yes)

14. Suppose he is a clerk in a store. Should he be fired, or not? (+ = No or Don't know, − = Yes)

15. Suppose he wrote a book which is in your public library. Somebody in your community suggests the book should be removed from the library. Would you favor removing it, or not? (+ = Not favor or Don't know, − = Favor)

GROUP 0 (Do not qualify for any of the other groups).

Willingness to Tolerate Nonconformists Scale
(NORC GSS Version)

Scaling: Each item is answered either "yes," "no," or "don't know." Numerous investigators have created tolerance scales from responses to the GSS items, though no standard means of scaling them has emerged.

There are always some people whose ideas are considered bad or dangerous by other people. For instance, somebody who is against all churches and religion . . .

1. If such a person wanted to make a speech in your (city/town/community) against churches and religion, should he be allowed to speak, or not?

2. Should such a person be allowed to teach in a college or university, or not?

3. If some people in your community suggested that a book he wrote against churches and religion should be taken out of your public library, would you favor removing this book, or not?*

Or consider a person who favored government ownership of all the railroads and all big industries.

4. If such a person wanted to make a speech in your community favoring government ownership of all the railroads and big industries, should he be allowed to speak, or not?

5. Should such a person be allowed to teach in a college or university, or not?

6. If some people in your community suggested a book he wrote favoring government ownership should be taken out of your public library, would you favor removing this book, or not?*

Or consider a person who believes that Blacks are genetically inferior.

7. If such a person wanted to make a speech in your community claiming that Blacks are inferior, should he be allowed to speak, or not?

8. Should such a person be allowed to teach in a college or university, or not?

9. If some people in your community suggested that a book he wrote which said Blacks are inferior should be taken out of your public library, would you favor removing this book or not?*

Now, I should like to ask you some questions about a man who admits he is a Communist.

10. Suppose this admitted Communist wanted to make a speech in your community. Should he be allowed to speak, or not?

11. Suppose he is teaching in a college. Should he be fired, or not?

12. Suppose he wrote a book which is in your public library. Somebody in your community suggests that the book should be removed from the library. Would you favor removing it, or not?*

Consider a person who advocates doing away with elections and letting the military run the country.

13. If such a person wanted to make a speech in your community, should he be allowed to speak, or not?

14. Should such a person be allowed to teach in a college or university, or not?

15. Suppose he wrote a book advocating doing away with elections and letting the military run the country. Somebody in your community suggests that the book be removed from the public library. Would you favor removing it, or not?*

And what about a man who admits that he is a homosexual?

16. Suppose this admitted homosexual wanted to make a speech in your community. Should he be allowed to speak, or not?

17. Should such a person be allowed to teach in a college or university, or not?

18. If some people in your community suggested that a book he wrote in favor of homosexuality should be taken out of your public library, would you favor removing this book, or not?*

*Disagreement or a negative response represents the "tolerant" response.

Repression Potential

(A. Marsh & M. Kaase, 1979)

Variable

This scale measures the tendency to grant authorities instruments of control in order to contain challenges from protesters, strikers, and other unorthodox activists.

Description

This is a four-item Guttman scale consisting of items regarding police use of force against demonstrators, severe court sentences for protestors, passage of a law forbidding protest demonstrations (see Muller, Pesonen, & Jukam, 1980, for an intensive analysis of responses to this item), and use of troops to break strikes.

Sample

Surveys based on national multistage probability samples of the national adult population were conducted in 1973 and 1974 in Austria, Britain, the Netherlands, the United States, and West Germany; the national samples ranged from approximately 1200 in the Netherlands to approximately 2300 in West Germany.

Reliability

Internal Consistency

The coefficient of reproducibility for the four-item scale ranges from .91 in Austria to .95 in Britain and the United States, though the order of the items is permitted to vary from nation to nation.

Test–Retest

We encountered no information regarding test–retest reliability.

Validity

Correlations between the Repression Potential Scale and a scale of conventional political participation (a measure of involvement in activities such as reading about politics, discussing politics, and campaigning) are minimal, ranging only from −.06 in the Netherlands to −.12 in Austria. Correlations between repression potential and protest potential (a measure of participation in and approval of various forms of protest activity) are more substantial, ranging between −.27 in Austria and −.51 in the United States.

Location

Marsh, A., & Kaase, M. (1979). Measuring political action. In S. H. Barnes & M. Kaase, (Eds.), *Political action: Mass participation in five western democracies* (pp. 57–96). Beverly Hills, CA: Sage. Reprinted by permission of Sage Publications, Inc.

Results and Comments

In every country except the United States, the most approved form of government sanction is severe court sentencing, but in the United States it is use of force by the police. Citizen approval of repression varies widely from country to country. In the Netherlands 47% scored 0 on the Repression Potential Scale, and only 5% approved of all forms of government repression. By contrast the percentages scoring 0 in Germany and Austria were only about a third that of the Netherlands, and more than five times as many achieved the maximum score of 4. The modal response was 2 for Britain and the United States (28%

of respondents for each country) and 4 for Germany and Austria (26 and 28% of respondents, respectively).

Repression Potential
(Marsh & Kaase, 1979)

Scaling: The response categories for each item are "strongly approve," "approve," "disapprove," and "strongly disapprove," with responses subsequently dichotomized into "approve" and "disapprove" categories. Nation-specific Guttman scales are created by ordering the responses to each item for each nation. Each respondent is assigned a value of 0 to 4 with 0 meaning approval of none of the repression acts and 1 to 4 corresponding to the highest ranked item on the Guttman scale of which the respondent approved (4 being most repressive). One missing data point and one scale error are allowed before a case is discarded.

Now, I'd like you to consider some kinds of action that the government and the authorities sometimes take. For each one, I would like you to tell me whether you approve strongly, approve, disapprove, or disapprove strongly.

1. The courts giving severe sentences to protesters who disregard the police.*
2. The police using force against demonstrators.*
3. The government using troops to break strikes.*
4. The government passing a law to forbid all public protest demonstrations.*

   *Disapproval represents the "tolerant" response.

Content-Controlled Measure
of Political Tolerance
(J. L. Sullivan, J. E. Piereson, & G. E. Marcus, 1982)

Variable

Tolerance is broadly understood as "a willingness to 'put up with' those things one rejects or opposes." In a political context it is defined as "a willingness to permit the expression of ideas or interests one opposes" (Sullivan, Piereson, & Marcus 1982, p. 2).

Description

The primary difference between this conceptualization and the approach associated with Stouffer is that Sullivan *et al.* pursue a "content-controlled" measurement strategy. When, in the Stouffer approach, questions are asked about the civil liberties of a particular group chosen because it is controversial, tolerance becomes confounded with the individual's feelings about the group. The content-controlled approach ensures that the group in question is not one the individual holds in high regard. That being the case, willingness to permit the exercise of civil liberties must overcome the hurdle of lack of positive affect toward the group.

Respondents are asked to select the group or groups they dislike the most from a list. In the original Sullivan *et al.* study, a list of 10 groups was provided, and respondents were also permitted to name a group not on the list. The listed groups represent a variety of points on the political spectrum. Next, subjects respond to six statements about whether members of their most disliked group should be allowed to exercise certain civil liberties.

Subsequent studies employing this approach, including studies undertaken outside the United States, have employed lists of differing composition and length. The list of potential most disliked groups varies from study to study, reflecting the need to adjust to different political systems or to changing conditions in a single system. For example, Gibson and Duch (1993a) provided Moscow respondents with the following list: believers; Jews; Stalinists; neo-Nazis; communists; members of cooperatives; nationalists; members of right-wing, pro-Slavic groups (e.g., the group Pamyat); supporters of canceling elections and introducing military dictatorship; Kalakshists; and homosexuals. In the Israeli portion of the Sullivan, Shamir, Walsh, and Roberts (1985) study, the groups were Sheli, Peace Now, Black Panthers, Mazpen, Rakah, groups in Israel supporting the Palestine Liberation Organization (PLO), Kach, Gush Emunim, and Neturei Karta. Note the considerable, but incomplete, overlap with the Israeli groups in the Caspi–Seligson (1983; Seligson & Caspi, 1983) research: Black Panthers, Peace Now, Jewish Defense League, Gush Emunim, Neturei Karta, Mazpen, communists, and PLO supporters.

Practice also varies (although within relatively narrow bounds) with regard to the recording of degrees of positive or negative affect toward the groups, the number of groups about which tolerance questions are asked, the number of tolerance questions that are asked, the number of categories on the response scale, the precise wording of the tolerance questions, and the scoring of the overall tolerance scale.

Sample

Sullivan, Piereson, and Marcus (1979, 1982) introduced the content-controlled measurement strategy in a survey of 198 residents of Minneapolis–St. Paul in 1976, in conjunction with which they also presented Stouffer's (1955) items to a random sample ($N = 200$) from the same population to facilitate comparison between the two scales. Sullivan *et al.*'s main U.S. data source was a special national survey of 1509 Americans conducted by NORC in 1978. Gibson (1989b) later posed content-controlled tolerance questions to 1210 reinterviewees from the 1987 NORC GSS.

Sullivan, Shamir, Walsh, and Roberts (1985) present comparative analyses based on the content-controlled measurement strategy for the United States, New Zealand, and Israel. The U.S. data were from the 1978 NORC survey, while the New Zealand survey ($N = 590$) was conducted in 1980 and 1981 in Christchurch, the nation's third largest city. The 1980 Israeli national sample ($N = 913$) was representative of Israeli Jews age 20 or older (see also Shamir & Sullivan, 1983).

In the Israeli survey reported by Caspi and Seligson (1983) and Seligson and Caspi (1983), 490 adult residents of the nation's four urban centers were interviewed in 1979. For the companion study in Costa Rica (Caspi & Seligson, 1983), a representative sample of 280 adult residents of San José, the capital city, was interviewed in 1980.

Barnum and Sullivan (1989) employed a content-controlled tolerance measure in a survey of a random sample of 1266 adults in England, Scotland, and Wales in 1986. Data were also collected from 77 members of Parliament in 1985.

Gibson, Duch, and Tedin (1992) also utilize a version of the content-controlled tolerance measure (asking about four political activities) as one subscale in their Multi-dimensional Scale of Democratic Values, which was used in a 1990 survey of 504

Moscow citizens. Among the other subsequent uses of this multidimensional scale, which includes the modified Sullivan *et al.* tolerance measure, are a 1990 survey of 1561 individuals in the entire European portion of the Soviet Union (Gibson & Duch, 1993a, 1993b) and a 1992 survey of 4309 persons in the former Soviet Union (Gibson, 1996). See the section on Gibson, Duch, and Tedin (1992) in this chapter for additional information about the multidimensional scale.

Reliability

Internal Consistency

Factor analyses conducted by Sullivan *et al.* (1982) strongly suggest that the six items that compose the content-controlled measure of political tolerance are unidimensional. Part–whole correlations range from .43 to .61, and alpha for the six-item scale is .78. Sullivan *et al.* (1985) report alpha coefficients of .80 for the New Zealand sample and .74 for the Israeli sample. For their four-item version of the tolerance scale, Caspi and Seligson (1983) report alpha coefficients of .96 in Israel and .78 in Costa Rica for tolerance toward the most disliked group and of .90 in Israel and .78 in Costa Rica for tolerance toward "people who say bad things about the system of government."

Test–Retest

We encountered no information regarding test–retest reliability.

Validity

While presenting no direct evidence regarding tolerance per se, Sullivan, Piereson, and Marcus (1982) and Sullivan, Shamir, *et al.* (1985) present some evidence for the validity of their content-controlled measurement strategy. First, they argue that if the measure is valid, people will select disliked target groups that are politically distant from themselves; conservatives will select left-wing groups, liberals will select right-wing groups, and so on. This pattern does hold. Second, they predict that respondents who choose one left-wing and one right-wing group as their least and second least liked groups should be close to the center of the left–right continuum. This pattern also emerges in the data. Again, both pieces of evidence pertain to the identification of the target group, not to tolerance toward the group.

Gibson (1992a) presents data bearing directly on the convergent validity of the tolerance measure based on reinterviews with 1987 GSS respondents. His primary findings concerning the convergent validity of the Sullivan *et al.* tolerance measure are as follows:

- The correlations between four- and six-item versions of the content-controlled scales of tolerance toward the most disliked and second most disliked groups are both .96.
- Correlations between pairs of tolerance scales for the four most disliked groups range from .56 to .71. Thus knowing how tolerant one is of the group one dislikes most provides some, albeit an imperfect, prediction of how tolerant one is of other groups one dislikes.
- Correlations between tolerance of disliked groups and the scale of tolerance toward communists and Klan members range from .74 to .82.

- The correlation between the most disliked tolerance scale and the 15-item Stouffer scale is .50, rising to .66 for the 9-item Stouffer scale. (The difference presumably reflects the fact that the 15-item scale was administered in the original GSS, while both the most disliked and the 9-item Stouffer scales were administered in the re-interviews.)

Location

Original U.S. Version

Piereson, J. E., Sullivan, J. L., & Marcus, G. E. (1980). Political tolerance: An overview and some new findings. In J. Pierce & J. L. Sullivan (Eds.), *The electorate reconsidered* (pp. 157–178). Beverly Hills, CA: Sage. Reprinted by permission of Sage Publications, Inc. See also Sullivan, J. L., Marcus, G. E., Feldman, S., & Piereson, J. E. (1981). The sources of political tolerance: A multivariate analysis. *American Political Science Review,* 75, 92–106; Sullivan, J. L., Piereson, J. E., & Marcus, G. E. (1979). An alternative conceptualization of political tolerance: Illusory increases 1950s–1970s. *American Political Science Review,* 73, 781–794; Sullivan, J. L., Piereson, J. E. & Marcus, G. E. (1982). *Political tolerance and American democracy.* Chicago: University of Chicago Press.

Variant Versions

Costa Rica version: Caspi, D., & Seligson, M. A. (1983). Toward an empirical theory of tolerance: Radical groups in Israel and Costa Rica. *Comparative Political Studies, 15,* 385–404.

Great Britain version: Barnum, D. G., & Sullivan, J. L. (1989). Attitudinal tolerance and political freedom in Britain. *British Journal of Political Science, 19,* 136–146.

Israel version (Caspi–Seligson): Caspi, D., & Seligson, M. A. (1983). Toward an empirical theory of tolerance: Radical groups in Israel and Costa Rica. *Comparative Political Studies, 15,* 385–404; Seligson, M. A., & Caspi, D. (1983). Arabs in Israel: Political tolerance and ethnic conflict. *Journal of Applied Behavioral Science, 19,* 55–66.

Israel version (Shamir–Sullivan): Shamir, M., & Sullivan, J. L. (1983). The political context of tolerance: The United States and Israel. *American Political Science Review, 77,* 911–928; Shamir, M., & Sullivan, J. L. (1985). Jews and Arabs in Israel: Everybody hates somebody, sometime. *Journal of Conflict Resolution* 29, 283–305; Sullivan, J. L., Shamir, M., Walsh, P., & Roberts, N. S. (1985). *Political tolerance in context: Support for unpopular minorities in Israel, New Zealand, and the United States.* Boulder, CO: Westview Press.

New Zealand version: Sullivan, J. L., Shamir, M., Walsh, P., & Roberts, N. S. (1985). *Political tolerance in context: Support for unpopular minorities in Israel, New Zealand, and the United States.* Boulder, CO: Westview Press.

U.S. version (Gibson): Gibson, J. L. (1989). The structure of attitudinal tolerance in the United States. *British Journal of Political Science, 19,* 562–570; Gibson, J. L. (1992). Must tolerance be "least-liked"? Alternative measures of political tolerance. *American Journal of Political Science, 36,* 560–577.

U.S.S.R. version: Gibson, J. L., Duch, R., & Tedin, K. (1992). Democratic values and the transformation of the Soviet Union. *Journal of Politics, 54,* 329–371; Gibson, J. L., & Duch, R. (1993). Political intolerance in the USSR: The distribution and etiology of mass opinion. *Comparative Political Studies, 26,* 286–329; Gibson, J. L. (1996). A mile wide but an inch deep (?): The structure of democratic commitments in the former USSR. *American Journal of Political Science, 40,* 396–420.

Results and Comments

The mean score of the 1978 U.S. survey (Sullivan *et al.,* 1979, 1982) was 16.1, below the scale midpoint of 18. Forty percent of the sample was categorized as "less tolerant" (scores 6–14), 45% as "in-between" (scores 15–21), and only 15% as "more tolerant" (scores 22–30). Only 38% of the respondents in the sample cited socialists, communists, or atheists (the groups used on the Stouffer measure) as their most disliked group. This finding suggests that most respondents in surveys employing the Stouffer items were asked about tolerance of groups that were not the ones they liked least. Sullivan *et al.* found the least tolerance for out-groups who were teaching and running for office (19 and 16% tolerant responses, respectively). There was more tolerance when asked about outlawing the out-group or prohibiting its public rallies (29 and 34% tolerant responses, respectively). Finally the greatest tolerance was elicited in response to items concerning whether the disliked group should be allowed to make a speech or whether the government could tap its phones (50 and 59% tolerant responses, respectively).

Gibson (1989b) found approximately the same level of overall support for each activity as Sullivan *et al.,* except for an 11-percentage-point decrease in tolerant responses to the item about preventing out-groups from running for office.

Sullivan, Shamir, Walsh, and Roberts (1985) report that the average percentages of tolerance responses on the six items were 54, 38, and 33% for the New Zealand, U.S., and Israeli samples, respectively. Caspi and Seligson (1983) report that on a 10-point scale (1 = least tolerant, 10 = most tolerant) the means for Israel and Costa Rica were 5.2 and 5.3, respectively; however, the distributions of responses were markedly different for the two countries. Sixty-three percent of the Israeli sample was located at either extreme of the scale, whereas the Costa Rica sample had a unimodal distribution, with only 9% of the sample at either extreme.

Barnum and Sullivan (1989) report that the act of which both the members of Parliament and the public were least tolerant was teaching in school (36 and 14% support, respectively). The public expressed the most tolerance with respect to whether the government could tap phones (62% disagreeing with this act), while the members of Parliament were most tolerant of public speeches (81% support).

Gibson and Duch (1993a) found intolerance to be generally widespread in the Soviet Union. Only five groups (neo-Nazis, Stalinists, homosexuals, nationalists, and supporters of military dictatorship) were identified as most disliked by more than 10% of the respondents in the Moscow and European Soviet Union samples. Neo-Nazis were the only group that was most disliked by a majority of respondents (a possible indication of focused intolerance toward this group).

Large majorities of Soviets were unwilling to allow their most disliked groups to engage in basic political activities, such as running for office, speaking in public, and holding public rallies. Approximately 60% of respondents in the 1990 Moscow and European U.S.S.R. samples were unwilling to allow their most disliked group to make a speech, while 70 to 80% held intolerant positions on the other three political acts. More than half of both the Moscow and the European Soviet Union samples were unwilling to allow their most disliked groups to engage in any of the political activities identified. These levels of intolerance were substantially higher than those found in U.S. and British studies. Gibson and Duch (1993a) found that the best predictors of intolerance were dogmatism, perceptions that a group would engage in illegal activity, support for democratic values, and age;

the latter two were significant only in the European Soviet Union sample. Education had no direct effect on tolerance (although it had an indirect effect via dogmatism, postmaterialism, and support for democratic values); neither did self-esteem, religiosity, income, wealth, and ideological self-identification.

Content-Controlled Measure of Political Intolerance (Sullivan, Piereson, & Marcus, 1982)

Scaling: Sullivan *et al.* use a five-point agree-disagree response scale with each response category receiving a value between 1 (least tolerant) and 5 (most tolerant) depending on the substantive direction of each question. The overall tolerance scale is the sum of the responses to all six items; thus, the scores on the scale can range from 6 (least tolerant) to 30 (most tolerant).

Interviewer: "I am giving you a list of groups in politics. As I read the list please follow along: socialists, fascists, communists, Ku Klux Klan, John Birch Society, Black Panthers, Symbionese Liberation Army, atheists, pro-abortionists, and anti-abortionists. Which of these groups do you like the least? If there is some group that you like even less than the groups listed here, please tell me the name of that group." The interviewer encourages respondents who have trouble deciding on a group to think which group is "the most unpleasant."
   For the least-liked group selected by a respondent:

1. Members of the [least-liked group] should be banned from being President of the United States.*
2. Members of the [least-liked group] should be allowed to teach in public schools.
3. The [least-liked group] should be outlawed.*
4. Members of the [least-liked group] should be allowed to make a speech in this city.
5. The [least-liked group] should have their phones tapped by our government.*
6. The [least-liked group] should be allowed to hold public rallies in our city.

   *Disagreement represents the "tolerant" response.

Dimensions of Political Tolerance

(J. L. Gibson & R. D. Bingham, 1982)

Variable

Political tolerance is defined as "opposition to state actions that limit opportunities for citizens, individually or in groups, to compete for political power" (p. 604).

Description

The authors define the opportunity to compete for political power in terms of the right to vote, participate in political parties, and organize politically. A person who values political tolerance therefore assigns a high priority to the opportunity for political competition, as compared to the maintenance of social and political order. Tolerance is conceptualized as composed of regard for freedom of speech, freedom of assembly, freedom of political association, and miscellaneous other civil liberties. What these freedoms have in common is that each facilitates the maintenance of political competition.

The measure consists of four subscales. (1) The Freedom of Speech subscale contains nine items regarding First Amendment protection of certain types of speech. (2) The Freedom of Assembly subscale is subdivided into sections involving the heckler's veto and majority abhorrence. The single heckler's veto item concerns the point at which a peaceful demonstration that attracts a hostile crowd should be terminated. The four-item subsection on majority abhorrence concerns whether permits for demonstrations should be granted to various groups that want to demonstrate in hostile locations. (3) The Support for Government Repression subscale measures support for official repression of communists, Nazis, and members of the Ku Klux Klan. Respondents are asked to indicate approval or disapproval of six types of government repression, ranging from banning a display of the group's symbols to outlawing membership in the group. (4) The Miscellaneous Civil Liberties subscale consists of 14 items representing a variety of civil liberties. Since Gibson and Bingham (1982) focus on the interrelatedness of the various dimensions of political tolerance, they do not develop a composite index based on the various subscales.

Sample

The data reported by Gibson and Bingham (1982) were collected in 1978 and 1979 from approximately 6000 members and leaders of the American Civil Liberties Union (ACLU) and approximately 1400 members of Common Cause.

Reliability

Internal Consistency

Guttman scaling or factor analytic results are reported for some of the subscales. Two of the nine items in the Freedom of Speech subscale (symbolic speech and obscene speech) were removed after they were determined to be undermining scalability. Without these two items the coefficients of scalability for the seven remaining items are .61 for ACLU members, .81 for ACLU leaders, and .68 for Common Cause members. Internal consistency is not at issue for the heckler's veto section of the Freedom of Assembly subscale because only a single item is used. It is reported that the four items in the majority abhorrence section of the Freedom of Assembly subscale scale in the Guttman sense.

It is also reported that a factor analysis was conducted on the Freedom of Speech and Support for Government Repression items, but the results are not provided. The results of a factor analysis of the Miscellaneous Civil Liberties items are provided. A three-factor solution is indicated. The first factor measures support for constraints for the purpose of maintaining order, the second refers to liberties of the far right, and the third represents religious freedom and separation of church and state.

The Free Speech subscale, the heckler's veto item, the majority abhorrence subsection of the Freedom of Assembly subscale, the Support for Government Repression subscale, the three factors derived from the Miscellaneous Civil Liberties subscale (liberty versus order, liberties of the far right, and separation of church and state), and a modified Stouffer tolerance subscale all tap what Gibson and Bingham (1982) describe as the eight "dimensions of political tolerance." A correlation matrix of the eight subscales and factors composing these dimensions is provided. The absolute values of the correlations range from .22 to .67. Gibson and Bingham also perform a factor analysis on these eight sub-scales and factors (factor loadings are not presented). A two-factor solution is indicated, with Gibson and Bingham interpreting the first factor as support for the rights of political opposition and the second factor as relating to freedom from government intervention in people's private lives.

Test–Retest

We encountered no information regarding test–retest reliability.

Validity

The absolute values of the correlations between a modified Stouffer (1955) measure of po-litical tolerance and the other seven "dimensions" of political tolerance (i.e., the various subscales and factors) range from .28 to .67. A regression of the Stouffer scale on the other seven dimensions produces an R^2 of .59.

Location

Gibson, J. L., & Bingham, R. D. (1982). On the conceptualization and measurement of political tolerance. *American Political Science Review, 76,* 603–620.

Results and Comments

Gibson and Bingham conclude that political tolerance is context-sensitive. As is true of the Stouffer items, when a threat of conflict is not presented in the items, tolerance appears to be relatively high. But when the likelihood of conflict is incorporated into the measure-ment scheme, tolerance declines.

Members of the groups surveyed by Gibson and Bingham would be expected to be highly tolerant. Indeed, the ACLU exists for the stated purpose of protecting civil liber-ties. Even so, there is what Gibson and Bingham describe as a "not insignificant intolerant minority" among ACLU members.

Dimensions of Political Tolerance
(Gibson & Bingham, 1982)
Support for Freedom of Speech

Scaling: Response options are a four-point Likert scale ranging from "definitely" to "definitely not." A "no opinion" option is also provided. The items in the subscale are ranked according to Guttman scale analysis with the respondent's score on the subscale being the rank of the most difficult approved item. If a "definitely should be protected" response is given to the item, .5 is added to the subscale score. The subscale score ranges from 0 (least tolerant) to 9.5 (most tolerant).

Different people have different ideas about what kinds of speech should be protected under the First Amendment to the U.S. Constitution. We are interested in getting your opinion about whether particular types of speech should be protected under the First Amendment. For each of the following types of speech, please indicate whether you believe it should definitely be protected, probably be protected, probably not be protected, or definitely not be protected by the First Amendment. That is, please mark the blank which comes closest to your opinion for each of the following types of speech.

1. Speech extremely critical of the American system of government.
2. Speech extremely critical of the First Amendment to the U.S. Constitution.
3. Symbolic speech, such as burning one's draft card in protest of the war in Vietnam.
4. Speech extremely critical of particular minority groups.
5. Speech supportive of an enemy of the U.S.
6. Obscene or profane speech.
7. Speech advocating the overthrow of the U.S. government.
8. Speech that *might* incite an audience to violence.
9. Speech *designed* to incite an audience to violence.

Support for Freedom of Assembly—Heckler's Veto

(No information on scoring Heckler's Veto subsection is provided)
1. Many public demonstrations pose a threat of violent reactions from crowds. Consider a demonstration that is itself peaceful, but which attracts a hostile crowd. Should the police be allowed to stop the demonstration in order to avoid violent crowd reactions? If so, at what point should the demonstration be stopped?
    When a crowd begins to form.
    When members of the crowd begin to taunt the group.
    When the crowd appears to be on the verge of a violent reaction.
    When a member of the crowd picks up a rock.
    When a rock is thrown in the direction of the demonstrators.
    When the demonstrators begin to fight with the crowd.
    The police should not be allowed to stop the demonstration.
    No opinion.

Support for Freedom of Assembly—Majority Abhorrence

(Responses are measured on a four-point scale ranging from "strongly support" to "strongly oppose." The score of the subsection is computed by multiplying by two the number of instances in which the respondent would allow a demonstration, adding .5 to the score for each "strongly support" response, and subtracting .5 for each "strongly oppose" response. The score of the subsection varies between −2.0 (four responses of "strongly oppose") to 10 (four responses of "strongly support")).
1. What if a black civil rights group asked to be allowed to hold a march in a white southern community—would you oppose or support granting a permit?

2. Suppose the Palestine Liberation Organization (PLO) sought to march in a Jewish community. Should a permit be granted?

3. Should the Ku Klux Klan be granted a permit to march in a black community?

4. What if the Nazis asked to be allowed to hold a march in a white Protestant community? Would you support or oppose granting a permit in such a circumstance?

Support for Government Repression

(Scores are assigned to each respondent by means of factor analysis)
What do you think the Government should do about these organizations? For instance, should the Government engage in any of the following activities?

1. I would favor the Government taking the following actions against Communists (check all of the actions you favor).
   Outlawing any organized Communist party
   Prohibiting any Communist from running for public office
   Engaging in covert surveillance of Communists (e.g., wiretapping)
   Requiring that Communists register with the government
   Ban all activities in public places by Communists
   Ban public display of Communist symbols (e.g., hammer and sickle)

2. I would favor the Government taking the following actions against Nazis (check all of the actions you favor).
   Outlawing any organized Nazi party
   Prohibiting any Nazi from running for public office
   Engaging in covert surveillance of Nazis (e.g., wiretapping)
   Requiring that Nazis register with the government
   Ban all activities in public places by Nazis
   Ban public display of Nazi symbols (e.g., swastika)

3. I would favor the Government taking the following actions against the Ku Klux Klan (check all of the actions you favor).
   Outlawing any organized Ku Klux Klan party
   Prohibiting any member of the Ku Klux Klan from running for public office
   Engaging in covert surveillance of the Ku Klux Klan (e.g., wiretapping)
   Requiring that members of the Ku Klux Klan register with the government
   Ban all activities in public places by the Ku Klux Klan
   Ban public display of Ku Klux Klan symbols (e.g., burning cross)

Miscellaneous Civil Liberties

(Respondents indicate agreement or disagreement with the allowance or repression of these liberties; no score for this subscale is calculated since it is subsequently broken up into three different dimensions based on the results of factor analysis)

1. High school students are within their rights when they express political opinions, circulate petitions and handbills, or wear political insignia in school.

2. A woman has a private right to decide whether to have a child or undergo an abortion.

3. Police should be allowed to conduct a full search of any motorist arrested for an offense such as speeding.*

4. A man should be denied unemployment compensation if fired from his job for growing a beard.*

5. Court calendars are so crowded that the right to trial by jury should be restricted to persons accused of major crimes only.*

6. Students who shout down speakers to achieve their aims subvert the principles of academic freedom.

7. The C.I.A. should be able to prevent any former employees from writing about the agency without the C.I.A.'s prior approval.*

8. Government consolidation of dossiers on individual citizens violates the right to privacy.

9. A radio station which permits the reading of an anti-Semitic poem over the air should have its F.C.C. license revoked.*

10. In their fight against crime the police should be entitled to use wiretaps and other devices for listening in on private conversations.*

11. Membership in the John Birch Society by itself is enough to bar an applicant from appointment to the police force.*

12. The use of tax funds to support parochial schools involves compulsory taxation for religious purposes and thus violates the First Amendment.

13. In light of present standards of justice and humanity, the death penalty has become "cruel and unusual punishment" in violation of the Eighth Amendment.

14. The "separation of church and state" clause of the First Amendment should be used to eliminate the tax-exempt status of religious institutions.

*Disagreement represents "tolerant" response.

Omnibus Civil Liberties Scale

(H. McClosky & A. Brill, 1983)

Variable

The Omnibus Civil Liberties Scale is designed to measure attitudes toward allowing or denying civil liberties such as free speech, free press, and freedom of assembly to people in general and to specific groups (e.g., Nazis, the PLO, student protesters, and right-to-life activists).

Description

The scale consists of 69 items, which break into nine subscales. The subscales are (1) Free Speech (5 items); (2) Free Press (10 items); (3) Symbolic Speech (3 items); (4) Freedom of Assembly (17 items); (5) Academic Freedom (6 items); (6) Freedom of Religion (4 items); (7) Due Process (13 items); (8) Privacy (5 items); and (9) Lifestyle (6 items). Items vary widely in content, focusing on a broad array of target groups and problem situations, the intent being to "cancel out" any specific cues associated with a particular group or situation through the sheer diversity of the items.

Each item presents a choice between a civil libertarian response that is generally legally sanctioned in the United States and a plausible anti–civil libertarian alternative. Respondents select one from a pair of response alternatives for each item.

Although the Due Process and Privacy subscales tap important dimensions of attitudes concerning civil liberties and are appropriate components of the Omnibus Civil Liberties Scale, they are only marginally related to the concept of political tolerance.

Sample

The civil liberties survey data were drawn from three surveys, all conducted by Gallup. Respondents in the first survey were a probability sample of 1993 adult Americans drawn from 300 communities in 1978. The second and third samples consisted of "elites" selected by Gallup, defined as individuals who by virtue of their vocation, role, or public activities could be regarded as community leaders (the "opinion leader" sample) or as members of law enforcement professions (the "legal elite" sample). The 1157 opinion leaders included public officials and officers of community service, fraternal, patriotic, union, business, environmental, political party, civil rights, political action, religious, educational, civic youth, or media organizations; the 734 legal elite members included criminal attorneys, district attorneys, public defenders, civil rights attorneys, judges, sheriffs, and police officers. Questionnaires identical to those completed by the general public sample were mailed to the two elite samples.

Reliability

Internal Consistency

Factor analysis results are reported in support of the internal consistency of the scale. Most items have positive loadings on the first factor above .40. The factor loadings of the subscales on the composite scale range from .53 to .83, generally falling between .7 and .8.

Test–Retest

We encountered no information regarding test–retest reliability.

Validity

We encountered no information regarding validity.

Location

McClosky, H., & Brill, A. (1983). *Dimensions of tolerance: What Americans believe about civil liberties.* New York: Russell Sage.

Results and Comments

The mean score on the Omnibus Civil Liberties Scale is 1.13 for the mass sample and 16.88 for the elite sample (7.67 and 16.45, respectively, after controlling for demographic differences). Eighty-three percent and 60% of the opinion leaders and legal elite samples, respectively, had a scale score greater than or equal to the top one-third of the mass sample. Opinion leaders are shown to be generally more pro–civil libertarian than are members of the general public, a finding consistent with that reached in the earlier Mc-Closky (1964) study.

Consistent with what has come to be regarded as good practice (Converse & Presser 1986, pp. 38–39), most of the items employ a forced-choice rather than an agree–disagree format to overcome a potential liability of earlier measures.

Omnibus Civil Liberties Scale
(McClosky & Brill, 1983)

Scaling: Respondents select one from a pair of response alternatives for each item. McClosky and Brill note that a respondent's score on the scale is the sum of the "relative scores he or she received on each weighted subscale." Each subscale is weighted equally, regardless of the number of items in the subscale. We could find no information on the precise method of computing the subscale scores or the weighting procedure.

Free Speech Subscale

1. Should foreigners who dislike our government and criticize it be allowed to visit or study here? a) Yes* / b) No.
2. Free speech should be granted: a) only to people who are willing to grant the same rights of free speech to everyone else / b) to everyone regardless of how intolerant they are of other people's opinions.*
3. Should groups like the Nazis and Ku Klux Klan be allowed to appear on public television to state their views? a) No, because they would offend certain racial or religious groups / b) Yes, should be allowed no matter who is offended.*
4. A group that wants to buy advertising space in a newspaper to advocate war against another country: a) should be turned down by the newspaper / b) should have as much right to buy advertising space as a group that favors world peace.*
5. If the majority votes in a referendum to ban the public expression of certain opinions, should the majority opinion be followed? a) No, because free speech is a more fundamental right than majority rule* / b) Yes, because no group has a greater right than the majority to decide which opinions can or cannot be expressed.

Free Press Subscale

1. Which of these comes closer to your own view? a) The government has no right to decide what should or should not be published* / b) To protect its moral values, a society sometimes has to forbid certain things from being published.

---

2. A newspaper should be allowed to publish its opinions: a) only if it doesn't twist the facts and tell lies / b) no matter how false and twisted its facts are.*

3. People with extreme political ideas who want to work as newspaper or TV reporters: a) should not be hired for such jobs because they can't be trusted to report the news fairly / b) should have the same chance as any other Americans to work as reporters.*

4. When a TV station reports secret information illegally taken from a government office: a) it's just doing its job of informing the public* / b) the station owners should be fined or punished in some way for reporting such information.

5. A humor magazine which ridicules or makes fun of blacks, women, or other minority groups: a) should lose its mailing privileges / b) should have the same right as any other magazine to print what it wants.*

6. Novels that describe explicit sex acts: a) have no place in a high school library and should be banned / b) should be permitted in the library if they are worthwhile literature.*

7. Books that could show terrorists how to build bombs should be: a) banned from public libraries / b) available in the library like any other book.*

8. The movie industry: a) should be free to make movies on any subject it chooses* / b) should not be permitted to make movies that offend certain minorities or religious groups.

9. Censoring obscene books: a) is necessary to protect community standards / b) is an old-fashioned idea that no longer makes sense.*

10. If the majority in a referendum votes to stop publication of newspapers that preach race hatred: a) such newspapers should be closed down / b) no one, not even the majority of voters, should have the right to close down a newspaper.*

Symbolic Speech Subscale

1. A person who publicly burns or spits on the flag: a) should be fined or punished in some way / b) may be behaving badly but should not be punished for it by law.*

2. The use of obscene gestures to express anger against a public official: a) is so rude it should be outlawed / b) should be considered a constitutionally protected form of free speech.*

3. Protesters who mock the President by wearing death masks at one of his public speeches: a) should be removed from the audience by the police / b) should have the right to appear in any kind of costume they want.*

Freedom of Assembly Subscale

1. Should a civic auditorium be used by foreign radicals who want to express their hatred of America? a) Yes* / b) No.

2. Should a civic auditorium be used by the Jewish Defense League (JDL) to advocate a war against certain Arab countries? a) Yes* / b) No.

3. Should a civic auditorium be used by revolutionaries who advocate the violent overthrow of the American government? a) Yes* / b) No.

4. Should a civic auditorium be used by right to life groups to preach against abortion? a) Yes* / b) No.

5. Should a civic auditorium be used by the American Nazi party to preach race hatred against Jews and other minorities? a) Yes* / b) No.

6. Should a civic auditorium be used by conservationists to protest the construction of a nuclear power plant? a) Yes* / b) No.

7. Should a civic auditorium be used by student protesters who call for a sit-in at city hall to shut down the city's offices? a) Yes* / b) No.

8. Should a civic auditorium be used by patriotic groups to advocate war against some foreign country? a) Yes* / b) No.

9. Should a civic auditorium be used by the Palestine Liberation Organization (PLO) to attack Jews and call for the destruction of Israel? a) Yes* / b) No.

10. When groups like the Nazis or other extreme groups require police protection at their rallies and marches, the community should: a) supply and pay for whatever police protection is needed* / b) prohibit such groups from holding rallies because of the costs and dangers involved.

11. When authorities have reason to believe that a political demonstration will become violent, they should: a) seek a court order to stop the demonstration / b) keep an eye on the demonstration but allow it to be held.*

12. If some students at a college want to form a "Campus Nazi Club": a) they should be allowed to do so* / b) college officials should ban such clubs from campus.

13. If a political group known for its violent political activities wants to picket the White House: a) it should be granted police protection like any other group* / b) it should be prevented from doing so because it might endanger the President.

14. Should a political protest group be granted a permit to hold a parade that blocks midtown traffic for two hours? a) Yes, and if necessary the city should redirect traffic to protect the group's right to parade* / b) No, because the right to assemble should not keep other people from going about their business.

15. If a group wanted to hold a protest demonstration in front of the city jail, would city officials be justified in banning it? a) Yes, because it might stir up the prisoners / b) No, because the protesters should be able to assemble wherever they believe it would be most effective.*

16. Mass student protest demonstrations: a) have no place on a college campus and the participating students should be punished / b) should be allowed by college officials as long as they are nonviolent.*

17. Should demonstrators be allowed to hold a mass protest march for some unpopular cause? a) No, not if the majority is against it / b) Yes, even if most people in the community don't want it.*

Academic Freedom Subscale

1. On issues of religion, morals, and politics, high school teachers have the right to express their opinions in class: a) even if they go against the community's most precious values and beliefs* / b) only if those opinions do not offend the community's beliefs.

2. If a professor is suspected of spreading false ideas in his class, college officials: a) should send someone into his classes to check on him / b) should not interfere since it would violate his rights.*

3. Refusing to hire a professor because he believes certain races are inferior: a) may be necessary if his views are really extreme / b) cannot be justified.*

4. Refusing to hire a professor because of his unusual political beliefs: a) is never justified* / b) may be necessary if his views are really extreme.

5. When inviting guest speakers to a college campus: a) students should be free to invite anyone they want to hear* / b) the speakers should be screened beforehand to be sure they don't advocate dangerous or extreme ideas.

6. Scientific research that might show women or minorities in a bad light: a) should be banned because the results might damage their self-respect / b) should be allowed because the goal of science is to discover the truth, whatever it may be.*

Freedom of Religion Subscale

1. Should a civic auditorium be used by atheists who want to preach against God and religion? a) Yes* / b) No.

2. The freedom of atheists to make fun of God and religion: a) should not be allowed in a public place where religious groups gather / b) should be legally protected no matter who might be offended.*

3. Freedom to worship as one pleases: a) applies to all religious groups, regardless of how extreme their beliefs are* / b) was never meant to apply to religious cults that the majority of people consider "strange," fanatical, or "weird."

4. When a young woman joins an "offbeat" cult like the Moonies or Hare Krishnas, should her parents have the legal right to force her to leave the groups and be "deprogrammed"? a) No, because that would take away her individual freedom to practice any religion she chooses* / b) Yes, because parents have the right and duty to protect their children from influences they consider harmful.

Due Process Subscale

1. All systems of justice make mistakes, but which do you think is worse? a) To convict an innocent person* / b) To let a guilty person go free.

2. Once an arrested person says he wishes to remain silent, the authorities: a) should stop all further questioning at once* / b) should keep asking questions to try to get the suspect to admit his crimes.

3. The "right to remain silent": a) is needed to protect individuals from the "third degree" and forced confessions* / b) has harmed the country by giving criminals too much protection.

4. If a person is acquitted of a crime because the judge made a mistake in legal procedure during the trial: a) it is only fair that he be set free, even if the mistake was a small one* / b) setting him free for this reason would be carrying legal technicalities too far.

5. If a person is found guilty of a crime by evidence gathered through illegal methods: a) he should be set free or granted a new trial* / b) he should still be convicted if the evidence is really convincing and strong.

6. Forcing people to testify against themselves in court: a) may be necessary when they are accused of very brutal crimes / b) is never justified, no matter how terrible the crime.*

7. In order for the government to effectively prosecute the leaders of organized crime: a) it may sometimes have to bend the rules if there is no other way to convict them / b) it should stick strictly to the rules if the government wants other people to respect the law.*

8. In dealing with muggings and other serious street crimes, which is more important? a) To protect the rights of suspects* / b) To stop such crimes and make the streets safe even if we sometimes have to violate the suspect's rights.

9. If someone is caught red-handed beating and robbing an older person on the street: a) it's just a waste of taxpayers' money to bother with the usual expensive trial / b) the suspect should still be entitled to a jury trial and all the usual legal protections.*

10. Should rapists or child molesters be given the same sort of "fair trial" as other criminals? a) Yes, because the right to fair trial should not depend on the nature of the crime* / b) No, because their crimes are so inhuman that they do not deserve the usual legal protections.

11. Keeping people in prison for long periods of time before bringing them to trial: a) should not be allowed, no matter what the crime* / b) is sometimes necessary when dealing with people who have long and dangerous criminal records.

12. Giving everyone accused of a crime a qualified lawyer even if the government has to pay for it: a) is absolutely necessary to protect individual rights* / b) is wasteful and goes beyond the requirements of justice.

13. When police catch a violent gangster, they should: a) be allowed to be a bit rough with him if he refuses to give them the information they need to solve a crime / b) treat him humanely, just as they should treat everyone they arrest.*

Privacy Subscale

1. The use of computers by the government to maintain central records on the health, employment, housing, and income of private citizens: a) is dangerous to individual liberty and privacy and should be forbidden by law* / b) would help the government fight organized crime and provide emergency assistance and other services to people who need them.

2. Should government authorities be allowed to open the mail of people suspected of being in contact with fugitives? a) Yes, as it may help the police catch criminals they have been looking for / b) No, it would violate a person's right to correspond with his friends.*

3. A student's high school and college records should be released by school officials: a) only with the consent of the student* / b) to any government agencies or potential employers who ask to see them.

4. If a police officer stops a car for a traffic violation, he should: a) be allowed to search the car if he suspects it contains narcotics or stolen goods / b) be limited to dealing with the traffic violation and nothing else.*

5. If a patient tells his psychiatrist that he is planning to commit a serious crime, the psychiatrist should: a) report it to the police / b) remain silent because his first duty is to his patient.*

Lifestyle Subscale

1. Should it be right to adopt laws which prevent "hippies" and "street people" from moving into the community? a) Yes / b) No.*

2. The custom of a woman taking her husband's last name: a) should be the woman's personal decision* / b) should be legally required because it prevents a lot of confusion.

3. Abortion during the early weeks of pregnancy should be: a) prohibited except in such extreme cases as rape, the risk of a deformed child, or danger to the mother's life / b) left entirely up to the woman.*

4. For the most part, local ordinances that guarantee equal rights to homosexuals in such matters as jobs and housing: a) damage American moral standards / b) uphold the American idea of human rights for all.*

5. Birth control devices: a) should be available to teenagers if they want them* / b) should be kept from teenagers since they are too young to handle sexual matters sensibly.

6. Suppose the majority gets a law passed making homosexuality a crime. Should homosexuals be fined or arrested? a) No, because a person's sexual preference is a private matter, beyond the majority's wishes* / b) Yes, because the voting majority has the right to decide the kind of society it wants.

*Indicates the "tolerant" response.

Political Tolerance Scale

(J. Duckitt & B. Farre, 1994)

Variable

This scale, developed to assess support for political tolerance in the new majority-rule South Africa, offers respondents a choice between tolerant and intolerant positions related to a number of democratic rights.

Description

The scale consists of six items: three dealing with expressive rights, one with suspension of "democratic rights," one with detention without trial, and one with tolerance toward political opposition. Each item asks the respondent to make a choice between a tolerant and an intolerant position. Rather than posing a choice between having or not having a specific right, Duckitt and Farre pose a choice between the right of an individual to engage in a given political activity versus the right of the state to suppress such activity.

Sample

A survey questionnaire was administered to 79 white South African university students in August 1992.

Reliability

Internal Consistency

Cronbach's alpha for the scale is .74.

Test–Retest

We encountered no information regarding the test–retest reliability of this scale.

Validity

We encountered no information regarding validity.

Location

Duckitt, J., & Farre, B. (1994). Right-wing authoritarianism and political intolerance among whites in the future majority-rule South Africa. *Journal of Social Psychology, 134,* 735–741. Reprinted with permission of the Helen Dwight Reid Educational Foundation. Published by Heldref Publications, 1319 Eighteenth St., N.W., Washington, D.C. 20036-1802. Copyright © 1994.

Results and Comments

Duckitt and Farre report that the mean of the sample was 21.5 with a standard deviation of 3.2 (although they do not report the specific values of the response options used to compute the mean).

Duckitt and Farre's study focused on the relationship between right-wing authoritarianism in South Africa and attitudes toward political tolerance. They found that authoritarian attitudes among whites were negatively associated with support for political tolerance by a newly constituted majority-rule government, despite the possibility that intolerance would be directed against conservatives opposed to the new state. The authors suggest that their findings provide support for Altemeyer's (1988) thesis that because of their fear of public disorder and anarchy, authoritarians support strong and intolerant governments even if the government is representative of social, racial, and political groups that they oppose.

Political Tolerance Scale
(Duckitt & Farre, 1994)

Scaling: Responses to each pair of opposed statements are made on a 5-point scale ranging from "strongly prefer Item A" to "strongly prefer Item B". The score of the scale is the sum of the responses to all six items, reverse-scored where appropriate. We encountered no information regarding the specific values assigned to each response option. Analyses were conducted for each item as well as for all six jointly.

Six pairs of statements are presented below indicating opposing beliefs about the kinds of rights individuals and the state should have in a new democratically constituted majority rule South Africa. When a new government truly representative of the people is established in this country, it should:

1. (a) permit complete freedom of speech* versus (b) have the right to silence those who oppose the people.
2. (a) have the right to detain enemies of the new state if necessary versus (b) never detain anyone without trial.*
3. (a) guarantee to all the right to organize peaceful protests and demonstrations against it* versus (b) have the right to suppress protests and demonstrations by reactionaries or enemies of the new state.
4. (a) be able to suspend democratic rights in the interests of the people versus (b) guarantee unconditionally all democratic rights.*
5. (a) show tolerance to all, even its opponents* versus (b) deal ruthlessly with those who oppose the new society.
6. (a) be able to prohibit the expression of beliefs and values that it feels are repugnant to the people versus (b) guarantee to all the right to express their personal beliefs and values, whatever they are.*

   *Indicates the "tolerant" response.

Appendix: GSS Data on Tolerance
(John P. Robinson)

The General Social Survey has been tracking responses to variants of the original Stouffer items since 1972. The 18 questions used in this effort over the years are shown in Table 5–1, along with the overall percentages giving each response. Except for the item on a

Table 5-1
GSS Tolerance Items

75. There are always some people whose ideas are considered bad or dangerous by other people. For instance, somebody who is against all churches and religion . . .

A. If such a person wanted to make a speech in your (city/town/community) against churches and religion, should he be allowed to speak, or not? (SPKATH)

Yes, allowed to speak	67
Not allowed	32
Don't know	1

B. Should such a person be allowed to teach in a college or university, or not? (COLATH)

Yes, allowed to teach	45
Not allowed	51
Don't know	4

C. If some people in your community suggested that a book he wrote against churches and religion should be taken out of your public library, would you favor removing this book, or not? (LIBATH)

Favor	34
Not favor	63
Don't know	3

76. Or consider a person who favored government ownership of all the railroads and all big industries.

A. If such a person wanted to make a speech in your (city/town/community) favoring government ownership of all the railroads and big industries, should he be allowed to speak, or not? (SPKSOC)

Yes, allowed to speak	77
Not allowed	20
Don't know	3

B. Should such a person be allowed to teach in a college or university, or not? (COLSOC)

Yes, allowed to teach	57
Not allowed	37
Don't know	6

C. If some people in your community suggested that a book he wrote favoring government ownership should be taken out of your public library, would you favor removing this book, or not? (LIBSOC)

Favor	26
Not favor	69
Don't know	5

77. Or consider a person who believes that Blacks are genetically inferior.

A. If such a person wanted to make a speech in your (city/town/community) claiming that Blacks are inferior, should he be allowed to speak, or not? (SPKRAC)

Yes, allowed to speak	60
Not allowed	38
Don't know	2

B. Should such a person be allowed to teach in a college or university, or not? (COLRAC)

Yes, allowed to teach	42
Not allowed	54
Don't know	4

C. If some people in your community suggested that a book he wrote in which he said Blacks are inferior should be taken out of your public library, would you favor removing this book, or not? (LIBRAC)

Favor	35
Not favor	63
Don't know	2

Table 5–1-continued
GSS Tolerance Items

78. Now, I should like to ask you some questions about a man who admits he is a Communist.

A. Suppose this admitted Communist wanted to make a speech in your community. Should he be allowed to speak, or not? (SPKCOM)

Yes, allowed to speak	59
Not allowed	38
Don't know	3

B. Suppose he is teaching in a college. Should he be fired, or not? (COLCOM)

Yes, allowed to teach	49
Not allowed	45
Don't know	6

C. Suppose he wrote a book which is in your public library. Somebody in your community suggests that the book should be removed from the library. Would you favor removing it, or not? (LIBCOM)

Favor	37
Not favor	59
Don't know	4

79. Consider a person who advocates doing away with elections and letting the military run the country.

A. If such a person wanted to make a speech in your community, should he be allowed to speak, or not? (SPKMIL)

Yes, allowed to speak	57
Not allowed	41
Don't know	2

B. Should such a person be allowed to teach in a college or university, or not? (COLMIL)

Yes, allowed to teach	40
Not allowed	56
Don't know	4

C. Suppose he wrote a book advocating doing away with elections and letting the military run the country. Somebody in your community suggests that the book be removed from the public library. Would you favor removing it, or not? (LIBMIL)

Favor	38
Not favor	59
Don't know	3

80. And what about a man who admits that he is a homosexual?

A. Suppose this admitted homosexual wanted to make a speech in your community. Should he be allowed to speak, or not? (SPKHOMO)

Yes, allowed to speak	68
Not allowed	28
Don't know	4

B. Should such a person be allowed to teach in a college or university, or not? (COLHOMO)

Yes, allowed to teach	57
Not allowed	39
Don't know	4

C. If some people in your community suggested that a book he wrote in favor of homosexuality should be taken out of your public library, would you favor removing this book, or not? (LIBHOMO)

Favor	38
Not favor	59
Don't know	3

socialist target person (not used since 1974), responses are available for more than 13,000 respondents since 1972.

Certain patterns emerge in the responses. For the same target person, more respondents would allow that person to speak or to have a book in the library than to be allowed to teach in a college or university by a margin of 10–20 percentage points.

Tolerant responses do not differ greatly across target persons, on either the left or the right, as can be seen in the "allow" percentages below:

	Speak	Teach	Library
Left Targets			
Socialist (1970s only)	77	57	69
Atheist	67	51	63
Homosexual	68	57	59
Communist	59	49	59
Right Targets			
Racist	60	42	62
Militarist	57	40	59

The responses are particularly similar for the items on the book in the library.

The inter-item correlations are also similar: all of the tolerant responses relate positively (in the .30–.50 range), suggesting a single tolerance factor that cuts across the items. This means that it makes relatively little difference whether the target person is espousing a cause on the left or right of the political spectrum (as also reflected in the low correlations of items with liberal-conservative self-identification, as noted in Table 5–2 below).

As shown in Table 5–2, the major correlates of tolerance responses are education and age.

Gender: In general, men give slightly more tolerant responses than women. These differences tend to be larger (6 to 9 points) when the target person is espousing atheist, racist, or communist causes than homosexual or socialist themes.

Age: Younger people give considerably more tolerant responses than older people. This is much less true for the racist items than for the other five sets, indicating that younger and older people are more agreed about tolerating, or not tolerating, racists.

Race: In general, African Americans tend to give less tolerant responses than whites or members of other races. This 3–16 point difference is accentuated slightly for the racist items.

Education: Education is the best predictor of responses to the tolerance questions. As with age, the lowest correlations between education and tolerance show up for the racist items.

Ideology: The ideology-tolerance correlations are modest, but in most cases reflect 15–30 point differences between extreme liberals and extreme conservatives. The smallest differences are again found for the racism items. Sharper ideological differences appear for the college teaching items than for speaking or having a controversial book in the library.

Party Identification: Again the differences are not large, but stronger Democratic Party identifiers are less tolerant than Republican identifiers, the differences being smallest on the socialist and homosexual items. For many items, however, it is both strong Republicans and strong Democrats who give the most tolerant responses.

As shown in Table 5–3 and as noted in the text above, responses to these items show progressively more widespread tolerance over time, again for target persons on both the

Table 5-2

Correlations of Background Factors with Tolerance

			Sex	Age	Race	Education	Ideology	Party ID
75	A	SPKATH	-.07	-.26	-.07	.35	-.01	.07
	B	COLATH	-.07	-.30	-.04	.32	-.08	.03
	C	LIBATH	-.05	-.23	-.08	.34	-.04	.06
76	A	SPKSOC	.01	-.23	-.03	.24	-.06	.03
	B	COLSOC	-.02	-.26	.02	.18	-.14	-.02
	C	LIBSOC	.00	-.24	-.09	.29	-.06	.04
77	A	SPKRAC	-.09	-.13	-.08	.22	-.01	.06
	B	COLRAC	-.07	-.12	-.08	.18	-.05	.04
	C	LIBRAC	-.05	-.11	-.12	.25	-.03	.06
78	A	SPKCOM	-.08	-.22	-.04	.35	-.04	.05
	B	COLCOM	-.06	-.24	.02	.29	-.09	.01
	C	LIBCOM	-.05	-.23	-.06	.36	-.04	.06
79	A	SPKMIL	-.02	-.24	-.07	.31	-.03	.06
	B	COLMIL	-.03	-.26	-.05	.27	-.08	.02
	C	LIBMIL	-.02	-.22	-.07	.33	-.04	.07
80	A	SPKHOMO	.00	-.21	-.03	.34	-.03	.03
	B	COLHOMO	.01	-.25	-.01	.34	-.07	.00
	C	LIBHOMO	-.01	-.23	-.04	.34	-.05	.04

Table 5-3

Trends in Responses to GSS Tolerance Questions

			1972	73	74	75	76	77	78	79	80	81	82	83	84	85	86	87	88	89	90	91	92	93	94	1970s–1994
75	A	SPKATH	67	66	63		65	63			67		63		69	66		69	71	73	74	73		72	74	+ 7 points
	B	COLATH	42	42	43		42	40			47		45		47	47		48	47	54	53	54		54	54	+12
	C	LIBATH	63	62	61		61	60			64		60		65	62		66	65	69	69	71		70	71	+ 8
76	A	SPKSOC	81	80	79																					NA
	B	COLSOC	60	61	61																					NA
	C	LIBSOC	72	74	73																					NA
77	A	SPKRAC					62	60			63		58		59	57		61	63	63	64	64		62	63	0
	B	COLRAC					42	42			45		42		42	44		43	43	48	47	44		45	44	+ 2
	C	LIBRAC					62	63			66		59		65	62		63	64	67	67	67		67	68	+ 6
78	A	SPKCOM	54	61	60		56	57			57		57		61	59		61	62	66	66	69		71	68	+14
	B	COLCOM	35	42	44		44	40			43		47		48	46		49	50	54	55	57		61	58	+23
	C	LIBCOM	56	60	61		58	57			59		58		62	59		62	61	64	66	69		70	68	+12
79	A	SPKMIL					55	51			58		54		58	56		57	58	60	59	64		66	65	+10
	B	COLMIL					38	35			41		39		42	41		40	37	42	45	45		50	47	+ 9
	C	LIBMIL					58	56			60		55		60	58		58	59	62	63	68		70	66	+ 8
80	A	SPKHOMO	63	63	65		64	64			68		67		71	69		69	73	78	66	78		81	81	+18
	B	COLHOMO	50	50	53		54	51			57		58		61	60		58	60	67	66	66		72	73	+23
	C	LIBHOMO	56	55	57		57	57			59		57		61	57		58	63	66	66	71		69	70	+15

left and the right. The overall gain in tolerance varies from 7 to 24 percentage points over the 20+ years of GSS studies.

References

Abrahamson, M., & Carter, V. J. (1986). Tolerance, urbanism and region. *American Sociological Review, 51,* 287–294.

Abramson, P. R. (1980). Comment on Sullivan, Piereson, and Marcus. *American Political Science Review, 74,* 780–781.

Alba, R. D. (1978). Ethnic networks and tolerant attitudes. *Public Opinion Quarterly, 42,* 1–16.

Almond, G., & Verba, S. (1963). *The civic culture.* Princeton, NJ: Princeton University Press.

Altemeyer, B. (1988). *Enemies of freedom: Understanding right-wing authoritarianism.* San Francisco: Jossey-Bass.

Altemeyer, B., & Hunsberger, B. (1992). Authoritarianism, religious fundamentalism, quest, and prejudice. *International Journal for the Psychology of Religion, 2,* 113–133.

Anderson, C., & Guillory, C. (1997). Political institutions and satisfaction with democracy: A cross-national analysis of consensus and majoritarian systems. *American Political Science Review, 91,* 66–81.

Barnum, D. G., & Sullivan, J. L. (1989). Attitudinal tolerance and political freedom in Britain. *British Journal of Political Science, 19,* 136–146.

Beatty, K. M., & Walter, O. (1984). Religious preference and practice: Reevaluating their impact on political tolerance. *Public Opinion Quarterly, 48,* 318–329.

Bobo, L., & Licari, F. C. (1989). Education and political tolerance: Testing the effects of cognitive sophistication and target group affect. *Public Opinion Quarterly, 53,* 285–308.

Caspi, D., & Seligson, M. A. (1983). Toward an empirical theory of tolerance: Radical groups in Israel and Costa Rica. *Comparative Political Studies, 15,* 385–404.

Chong, D., McClosky, H., & Zaller, J. (1983). Patterns of support for democratic and capitalist values in the United States. *British Journal of Political Science, 13,* 401–440.

Converse, J. M., & Presser, S. (1986). *Survey questions: Handcrafting the standardized questionnaire.* Beverly Hills, CA: Sage.

Corbett, M. (1980). Education and contextual tolerance: Group-relatedness and consistency reconsidered. *American Politics Quarterly, 8,* 345–359.

Corbett, M. (1982). *Political tolerance in America.* New York: Longman.

Cutler, S. J., & Kaufman, R. L. (1975). Cohort changes in political attitudes: Tolerance of ideological nonconformity. *Public Opinion Quarterly, 39,* 69–91.

Dahl, R. (1956). *A preface to democratic theory.* Chicago: University of Chicago Press.

Dahl, R. (1971). *Polyarchy.* New Haven, CT: Yale University Press.

Dalton, R. (1994). Communists and democrats: Democratic attitudes in the two Germanies. *British Journal of Political Science, 24,* 469–493.

Davis, J. A. (1975). Communism, conformity, cohorts, and categories: American tolerance in 1954 and 1972–73. *American Journal of Sociology, 81,* 491–513.

Davis, J. A., & Smith, T. W. (1989). *General Social Surveys, 1972–1989: Cumulative codebook.* Chicago, IL: National Opinion Research Center.

Davis, J. A., & Smith, T. W. (1996). *General Social Surveys, 1972–1996: Cumulative codebook.* Chicago, IL: National Opinion Research Center.

Duch, R. (1993). Tolerating economic reform: Popular support for transitions to a free market in the former Soviet Union. *American Political Science Review, 87,* 590–607.

Duch, R., & Gibson, J. L. (1992). "Putting up with" fascists in Western Europe: A comparative, cross-level analysis of political tolerance. *Western Political Quarterly, 45,* 237–273.

Duckitt, J., & Farre, B. (1994). Right-wing authoritarianism and political intolerance among whites in the future majority-rule South Africa. *Journal of Social Psychology, 134,* 735–741.

Ellison, C. G., & Musick, M. A. (1993). Southern intolerance: A fundamentalist effect. *Social Forces, 72,* 379–398.

Erskine, H. (1970). The polls: Freedom of speech. *Public Opinion Quarterly, 34,* 483–496.

Erskine, H., & Siegel, R. L. (1975). Civil liberties and the American public. *Journal of Social Issues, 31,* 13–29.

Evans, G., & Whitefield, S. (1995). The politics and economics of democratic commitment: Support for democracy in transitional societies. *British Journal of Political Science, 25,* 485–514.

Ferrar, J. W. (1976). The dimensions of tolerance. *Pacific Sociological Review, 19,* 63–81.

Finifter, A., & Mickiewicz, E. (1992). Redefining the political system of the USSR: Mass support for political change. *American Political Science Review, 86,* 857–874.

Finkel, S., Muller, E., & Seligson, M. (1989). Economic crisis, incumbent performance and regime support: A comparison of longitudinal data from West Germany and Costa Rica. *British Journal of Political Science, 19,* 329–351.

Finney, H. C. (1974). Political dimensions of college impact on civil-libertarianism and the integration of political perspective: A longitudinal analysis. *Sociology of Education, 47,* 214–250.

Fletcher, J. F. (1989). Mass and elite attitudes about wiretapping in Canada: Implications for democratic theory and politics. *Public Opinion Quarterly, 53,* 225–245.

Fuchs, D., Guidorossi, G., & Svensson, P. (1995). Support for the democratic system. In H. D. Klingemann & D. Fuchs (Eds.), *Citizens and the state* (pp. 323–353). New York: Oxford University Press.

Gay, D. A., & Ellison, C. G. (1993). Religious subcultures and political tolerance: Do denominations still matter? *Review of Religious Research, 34,* 311–332.

Gibson, J. L. (1986). Pluralistic intolerance in America: A reconsideration. *American Politics Quarterly, 14,* 267–293.

Gibson, J. L. (1988). Political intolerance and political repression during the McCarthy red scare. *American Political Science Review, 82,* 511–529.

Gibson, J. L. (1989a). The policy consequences of political intolerance: Political repression during the Vietnam War era. *Journal of Politics, 51,* 13–35.

Gibson, J. L. (1989b). The structure of attitudinal tolerance in the United States. *British Journal of Political Science, 19,* 562–570.

Gibson, J. L. (1992a). Must tolerance be "least-liked"? Alternative measures of political tolerance. *American Journal of Political Science, 36,* 560–577.

Gibson, J. L. (1992b). The political consequences of intolerance: Cultural conformity and political freedom. *American Political Science Review, 86,* 338–356.

Gibson, J. L. (1996a). A mile wide but an inch deep (?): The structure of democratic commitments in the former USSR. *American Journal of Political Science, 40,* 396–420.

Gibson, J. L. (1996b). Political and economic markets: Changes in the connections between attitudes toward political democracy and a market economy within the mass culture of Russia and Ukraine. *Journal of Politics, 58,* 954–984.

Gibson, J. L. (1997). *A sober second thought: Experiments in persuading Russians to tolerate.* Paper presented at the annual meeting of the Midwest Political Science Association, Chicago.

Gibson, J. L., & Anderson, A. J. (1985). The political implications of elite and mass tolerance. *Political Behavior, 7,* 118–146.

Gibson, J. L., & Bingham, R. D. (1982). On the conceptualization and measurement of political tolerance. *American Political Science Review, 76,* 603–620.

Gibson, J. L., & Bingham, R. (1985). *Civil liberties and Nazis: The Skokie free speech controversy.* New York: Praeger.

Gibson, J. L., & Duch, R. M. (1992). Elitist theory and political tolerance in Western Europe. *Political Behavior, 13,* 191–212.

Gibson, J. L., & Duch, R. (1993a). Political intolerance in the USSR: The distribution and etiology of mass opinion. *Comparative Political Studies, 26,* 286–329.

Gibson, J. L., & Duch, R. (1993b). Emerging democratic values in Soviet political culture. In A. Miller, W. Reisinger, & V. Hesli (Eds.), *Public opinion and regime change: The new politics of post-Soviet societies* (pp. 69–94). Boulder, CO: Westview Press.

Gibson, J. L., & Duch, R. (1993c). Support for rights in Western Europe and the Soviet Union: An analysis of the beliefs of mass public. *Research on Democracy and Society, 1,* 241–263.

Gibson, J. L., Duch, R., & Tedin, K. (1992). Democratic values and the transformation of the Soviet Union. *Journal of Politics, 54,* 329–371.

Golebiowska, E. (1996). The "pictures in our heads" and individual-targeted tolerance. *Journal of Politics, 58,* 1010–1034.

Grabb, E. G. (1979). Working-class authoritarianism and tolerance of outgroups: A reassessment. *Public Opinion Quarterly, 43,* 36–47.

Griffith, E. S., Plamenatz, J., & Pennock, J. R. (1956). Cultural prerequisites to a successfully functioning democracy: A symposium. *American Political Science Review, 50,* 101–137.

Gunther, R., Sani, G., & Shabad, G. (1986). *Spain after Franco: The making of a competitive party system.* Berkeley: University of California Press.

Hahn, J. (1991). Continuity and change in Russian political culture. *British Journal of Political Science, 21,* 393–421.

Heath, A., Evans, G., & Martin, J. (1994). The measurement of core beliefs and values: The development of balanced socialist/laissez faire and libertarian/authoritarian scales. *British Journal of Political Science, 24,* 115–132.

Herson, L. J. R., & Hofstetter, C. R. (1975). Tolerance, consensus, and the democratic creed: A contextual exploration. *Journal of Politics, 37,* 1007–1032.

Holt, N., & Tygart, C. E. (1969). Political tolerance and higher education. *Pacific Sociological Review, 12,* 27–33.

Hougland, J. G., Jr., & Lacy, W. B. (1981). Membership in voluntary organizations and support for civil liberties. *Sociological Focus, 14,* 97–110.

Hyman, H. H., & Sheatsley, P. B. (1953). Trends in public opinion on civil liberties. *Journal of Social Issues, 9,* 6–16.

Immerwahr, J. (1980). Comment on Sullivan, Piereson, and Marcus. *American Political Science Review, 74,* 781–783.

Inglehart, R. (1988). The renaissance of political culture. *American Political Science Review, 82,* 1203–1230.

Irwin, P., & Thompson, N. L. (1977). Acceptance of the rights of homosexuals: A social profile. *Journal of Homosexuality, 3,* 107–121.

Jackman, R. W. (1972). Political elites, mass publics, and support for democratic principles. *Journal of Politics, 34,* 753–773.

Jackman, R. W. (1977). Much ado about nothing. *Journal of Politics, 39,* 185–192.

Jelen, T. G., & Wilcox, C. (1990). Denominational preference and the dimensions of political tolerance. *Sociological Analysis, 51,* 69–82.

Jennings, M. K., & van Deth, J. W. (Eds.) (1990). *Continuities in political action: A longitudinal study of political orientations in three Western democracies.* New York: W. de Gruyter.

Kaase, M. (1971). Demokratische Einstellung in der Bundesrepublik Deutschland. In R. Wildenman (Ed.), *Sozialwissenschaftliches Jahrbuch für Politik* (Vol. 2, pp. 119–326). Munich: Günter Olzog Verlag.

Klingemann, H. D., & Hofferbert, R. (1994). Germany: A new "wall" in the mind? *Journal of Democracy, 5,* 30–44.

Kuklinski, J. H., Riggle, E., Ottati, V., Schwarz, N., & Wyer, R. S., Jr. (1991). The cognitive and affective bases of political tolerance judgments. *American Journal of Political Science, 35,* 1–27.

Lawrence, D. G. (1976). Procedural norms and tolerance: A reassessment. *American Political Science Review, 70,* 80–100.

Marcus, G., Sullivan, J., Theiss-Morse, E., & Wood, S. (1995). *With malice toward some: How people make civil liberties judgments.* New York: Cambridge University Press.

Marsh, A., & Kaase, M. (1979). Measuring political action. In S. H. Barnes & M. Kaase (Eds.), *Political action: Mass participation in five Western democracies* (pp. 57–96) Beverly Hills, CA: Sage.

McClosky, H. (1964). Consensus and ideology in American politics. *American Political Science Review, 58,* 361–382.

McClosky, H., & Brill, A. (1983). *Dimensions of tolerance: What Americans believe about civil liberties.* New York: Russell Sage.

McClosky, H., & Zaller, J. (1984). *The American ethos: Public attitudes toward capitalism and democracy.* Cambridge: Harvard University Press.

McCutcheon, A. L. (1985). A latent class analysis of tolerance for nonconformity in the American public. *Public Opinion Quarterly, 49,* 474–488.

McDonough, P., Barnes, S., & Pina, A. (1986). The growth of democratic legitimacy in Spain. *American Political Science Review, 80,* 735–760.

McIntosh, M., & MacIver, M. (1992). Coping with freedom and uncertainty: Public opinion in Hungary, Poland, and Czechoslovakia, 1989–1992. *International Journal of Public Opinion Research, 4,* 375–391.

Miller, A., Hesli, V., & Reisinger, W. (1994). Reassessing mass support for political and economic change in the former USSR. *American Political Science Review, 88,* 399–411.

Miller, A., Hesli, V., & Reisinger, W. (1995). Comparing citizen and elite belief systems in post-Soviet Russia and Ukraine. *Public Opinion Quarterly, 59,* 1–40.

Miller, A., Reisinger, W., & Hesli, V. (1996). Understanding political change in post-Soviet societies. *American Political Science Review, 90,* 153–166.

Mueller, J. (1988). Trends in political tolerance. *Public Opinion Quarterly, 52,* 1–25.

Muller, E., Pesonen, P., & Jukam, T. O. (1980). Support for the freedom of assembly in Western democracies. *European Journal of Political Research, 8,* 265–288.

Muller, E., & Seligson, M. (1994). Civic culture and democracy: The question of causal relationships. *American Political Science Review, 88,* 635–652.

Nie, N. H., Junn, J., & Stehlik-Barry, K. (1996). *Education and democratic citizenship in America.* Chicago: University of Chicago Press.

Nunn, C. Z., Crockett, H. J., Jr., & Williams, J. A., Jr. (1978). *Tolerance for nonconformity.* San Francisco: Jossey-Bass.

Piazza, T., Sniderman, P. M., & Tetlock, P. E. (1990). Analysis of the dynamics of political reasoning: A general-purpose computer-assisted methodology. In J. A. Stimson (Ed.), *Political analysis* (Vol. 1, pp. 99–119). Ann Arbor: University of Michigan Press.

Pierson, J. E., Sullivan, J. L., & Marcus, G. E. (1980a). Political tolerance: An overview and some new findings. In J. Pierce & J. L. Sullivan (Eds.), *The electorate reconsidered* (pp. 157–178). Beverly Hills, CA: Sage.

Pierson, J. E., Sullivan, J. L., & Marcus, G. E. (1980b). Reply [to Abramson (1980) and Immerwahr (1980)]. *American Political Science Review, 74,* 783–784.

Prothro, J. W., & Grigg, C. M. (1960). Fundamental principles of democracy: Bases of agreement and disagreement. *Journal of Politics, 22,* 276–294.

Reisinger, W., Miller, A., Hesli, V., & Maher, K. (1994). Political values in Russia, Ukraine and Lithuania: Sources and implications for democracy. *British Journal of Political Science, 24,* 183–223.

Remmer, K. (1991). The political impact of economic crisis in Latin America in the 1980s. *American Political Science Review, 85,* 777–800.

Richardson, B., & Flanagan, S. (1984). *Politics in Japan.* Boston: Little, Brown.

Rohrschneider, R. (1994). Report from the laboratory: The influence of institutions on political elites' democratic values in Germany. *American Political Science Review, 88,* 927–941.

Rose, R., & Mishler, W. (1994). Mass reaction to regime change in Eastern Europe: Polarization or leaders and laggards? *British Journal of Political Science, 24,* 159–182.

Ruggiero, J. A. (1979). Research on social class and intolerance in the context of American history and ideology. *Journal of the History of the Behavioral Sciences, 15,* 166–176.

Sani, G. (1980). The political culture of Italy. In G. Almond & S. Verba (Eds.), *The civic culture revisited* (pp. 273–324). Boston: Little, Brown.

Seligson, M., & Booth, J. (1993). Political culture and regime type: Evidence from Nicaragua and Costa Rica. *Journal of Politics, 55,* 777–792.

Seligson, M. A., & Caspi, D. (1983). Arabs in Israel: Political tolerance and ethnic conflict. *Journal of Applied Behavioral Science, 19,* 55–66.

Shamir, M. (1987). *Political intolerance among masses and elites in Israel.* Paper prepared for the annual meeting of the American Political Science Association, Chicago.

Shamir, M., & Sullivan, J. L. (1983). The political context of tolerance: The United States and Israel. *American Political Science Review, 77,* 911–928.

Shamir, M., & Sullivan, J. L. (1985). Jews and Arabs in Israel: Everybody hates somebody, sometime. *Journal of Conflict Resolution, 29,* 283–305.

Shin, D. (1995). The quality of mass support for democratization. *Social Indicators Research, 35,* 239–253.

Simon, R. J., & Barnum, D. G. (1978). Public support for civil liberties in Israel and the United States. *Research in Law and Sociology, 1,* 81–100.

Simon, R. J., & Landis, J. M. (1990). Trends in public support for civil liberties and due process in Israeli society. *Social Science Quarterly, 71,* 93–104.

Simon, R. J., & Mann, K. (1977). Public support for civil liberties in Israel. *Social Science Quarterly, 58,* 283–292.

Smith, L. W., & Petersen, K. K. (1980). Rural–urban differences in tolerance: Stouffer's "culture shock" hypothesis revisited. *Rural Sociology, 45,* 256–271.

Sniderman, P., Brody, R., & Tetlock, P. (1991). *Reasoning and choice.* New York: Cambridge University Press.

Sniderman, P. M., Fletcher, J. F., Russell, P. H., & Tetlock, P. E. (1989). Political culture and the problem of double standards: Mass and elite attitudes toward language rights and the Canadian Charter of Rights and Freedoms. *Canadian Journal of Political Science, 22,* 259–284.

Sniderman, P. M., Fletcher, J. F., Russell, P. H., & Tetlock, P. E. (1996). *The clash of rights.* New Haven, CT: Yale University Press.

Sniderman, P. M., Fletcher, J. F., Russell, P. H., Tetlock, P. E., & Boyd, R. M. (1990). *Rights of citizens and powers of the state.* Unpublished manuscript, Stanford University.

Sniderman, P. M., Fletcher, J. F., Russell, P. H., Tetlock, P. E., & Gaines, B. (1991). The fallacy of democratic elitism: Elite competition and commitment to civil liberties. *British Journal of Political Science, 21,* 349–370.

Sniderman, P. M., Tetlock, P. E., Glaser, J. M., Green, D. P., & Hout, M. (1989). Principled tolerance and the American mass public. *British Journal of Political Science, 19,* 25–45.

St. Peter, L., Williams, J. A., Jr., & Johnson. D. R. (1977). Comments on Jackman's "Political elites, mass publics, and support for democratic principles." *Journal of Politics, 39,* 176–184.

Stouffer, S. A. (1956). *Communism, conformity and civil liberties.* Garden City, NY: Doubleday.

Sullivan, J. L., & Marcus, G. E. (1988). A note on "Trends in political tolerance." *Public Opinion Quarterly, 52,* 26–32.

Sullivan, J. L., Marcus, G. E., Feldman, S., & Piereson, J. E. (1981). The sources of political tolerance: A multivariate analysis. *American Political Science Review, 75,* 92–106.

Sullivan, J. L., Piereson, J. E., & Marcus, G. E. (1979). An alternative conceptualization of political tolerance: Illusory increases, 1950s–1970s. *American Political Science Review, 73,* 781–794.

Sullivan, J. L., Piereson, J. E., & Marcus, G. E. (1982). *Political tolerance and American democracy.* Chicago: University of Chicago Press.

Sullivan, J. L., Shamir, M., Walsh, P., & Roberts, N. S. (1985). *Political tolerance in context: Support for unpopular minorities in Israel, New Zealand, and the United States.* Boulder, CO: Westview Press.

Sullivan, J. L., Walsh P., Shamir, M., Barnum, D. G., & Gibson, J. L. (1993). Why politicians are more tolerant: Selective recruitment and socialization among political elites in Britain, Israel, New Zealand and the United States. *British Journal of Political Science, 23,* 51–76.

Tedin, K. (1994). Popular support for competitive elections in the Soviet Union. *Comparative Political Studies, 27,* 241–271.

Theiss-Morse, E., Marcus, G., & Sullivan, J. L. (1993). Passion and reason in political life: The organization of affect and cognition and political tolerance. In G. Marcus & R. Hanson (Eds.), *Reconsidering the democratic public.* University Park: Penn State Press.

Thomasson, J. (1995). Support for democratic values. In H. D. Klingemann & D. Fuchs (Eds.), *Citizens and the state* (pp. 383–416). New York: Oxford University Press.

Toka, G. (1995). Political support in East-Central Europe. In H. D. Klingemann & D. Fuchs (Eds.), *Citizens and the state* (pp. 354–382). New York: Oxford University Press.

Wagner, J. (1986). Political tolerance and stages of moral development: A conceptual and empirical alternative. *Political Behavior, 8,* 45–80.

Weil, F. D. (1982). Tolerance of free speech in the United States and West Germany, 1970–79: An analysis of public opinion survey data. *Social Forces, 60,* 973–992.

Weil, F. D. (1989). The sources and structure of legitimation in Western democracies: A consolidated model tested with time-series data in six countries since World War II. *American Sociological Review, 54,* 682–706.

Weil, F. D. (1993). The development of democratic attitudes in eastern and western Germany in a comparative perspective. In F. D. Weil (Ed.), *Research on democracy and society: Vol. 1. Democratization in eastern and western Europe* (pp. 195–225). Greenwich, CT: JAI Press.

Weil, F. D. (1996). *Western political culture and the consolidation of democracy in eastern Germany.* Paper presented at the Eighth International Conference on Socio-economics, Geneva.

Westle, B. (1994). Demokratie und Sozialismus: Politische Ordnungsvorstellungen im vereinten Deutschland zwischen Ideologie, Protest und Nostalgie. *Kölner Zeitschrift für Soziologie und Sozialpsychologie, 46,* 571–596.

Weston, L. C., & Ruggiero, J. A. (1978). Change in attitudes of women toward nonconformists: A trend study. *Pacific Sociological Review, 21,* 131–140.

Whitefield, S., & Evans, G. (1994). The Russian election of December 1993. *Post-Soviet Affairs, 10,* 38–60.

Whitefield, S., & Evans, G. (1996). Support for democracy and political opposition in Russia, 1993–1995. *Post-Soviet Affairs, 12,* 218–242.

Wilcox, C., & Jelen, T. G. (1990). Evangelicals and political tolerance. *American Politics Quarterly, 18,* 25–46.

Wilson, T. C. (1985). Urbanism and tolerance: A test of some hypotheses drawn from Wirth and Stouffer. *American Sociological Review, 50,* 117–123.

Wilson, T. C. (1994). Trends in tolerance toward rightist and leftist groups, 1976–1988: Effects of attitude change and cohort succession. *Public Opinion Quarterly, 58,* 539–556.

Wilson, T. C. (1991). Urbanism, migration, and tolerance: A reassessment. *American Sociological Review, 56,* 117–123.

Zellman, G. L. (1975). Antidemocratic beliefs: A survey and some explanations. *Journal of Social Issues, 31,* 31–53.

CHAPTER 6

Racial Attitudes

Monica Biernat and Christian S. Crandall

Attitudes about race permeate American political opinion at both the mass and elite levels. A wide range of social issues, such as size of government, drug use, welfare, unemployment, affirmative action, the location of highways and landfills, crime, immigration, property taxes, Head Start, and capital punishment, appears to be linked to Americans' thinking about race (see Kinder & Sanders, 1996; Sears, 1988). Indeed, attitudes toward issues such as crime, busing, drugs, and government occasionally serve as proxies for attitudes about race. Race, in short, is one of the most complex and powerful dimensions of American political thought. American racial attitudes have their roots in the very founding of the nation: For purposes of electing U.S. representatives, Article I, Section 2 of the U.S. Constitution excludes "Indians not taxed" and counts slaves (who were almost exclusively black) by a "three-fifths of all other persons" rule.

This contrasts dramatically with another central principle of American life: that all people are fundamentally equal—in opportunity, political enfranchisement, housing, employment, and all other areas of public life. This tension between the ethic of equality and the political reality of second-class citizenship of black Americans prompted the important critique by Swedish economist Gunnar Myrdal (1944), *An American Dilemma.* Myrdal argued that the strain between the conflicting values of equality, on the one hand, and liberty to hold and express negative attitudes toward blacks, on the other, characterized the central dynamic of American politics and presented a major exception and challenge to the image of American strength and success in the late 1930s and early 1940s.

Today, there is undoubtedly *some* cause for optimism about black–white relations, as surveys reliably show that straightforward antiblack antipathy by whites has been on the decrease since Myrdal's classic work (Case & Greeley, 1990; Dovidio & Gaertner, 1991; Firebaugh & Davis, 1988; Schuman, Steeh, & Bobo, 1985; Smith & Sheatsley, 1984; Smith, 1985; Taylor, Sheatsley, & Greeley, 1978). However, white Americans continue to resist government programs that could improve the plight of blacks (Jackman, 1978; Jackman & Muha, 1984; Schuman *et al.,* 1985), and black Americans continue to be the frequent targets of whites' discriminatory behavior, sometimes in subtle forms (e.g., Crosby, Bromley, & Saxe, 1980; Gaertner & Dovidio, 1986). Whether this change in the overtness of expression represents a modification in the structure of racism or merely a modest shift in the norms of expression has been a question of much scholarly debate (e.g., see Kinder & Sanders, 1996; Kinder & Sears, 1981; McConahay, 1986; Sears, van Laar, Carrillo, & Kosterman, 1997; Sniderman & Tetlock, 1986a; Weigel & Howes, 1985). In any case, because white respondents appear to be more sensitive to and wary of racial attitude questions, a central concern in modern-day racial attitude measurement is subtlety, disguise, and misdirection in construction of attitude items.

What do we mean by "racial attitudes" and "racial prejudice"? For the most part we use these terms interchangeably; prejudice is defined as "negative attitudes toward social groups" (Stephan, 1985, p. 600). The primary emphasis in this chapter is on measures of white Americans' negative (or positive) attitudes toward black Americans. In keeping with a traditional tripartite view of the attitude construct (Greenwald, 1968; Jackman, 1977; D. Katz & Stotland, 1959; Krech & Crutchfield, 1948), these measures tap affective, cognitive, and behavioral tendencies toward blacks, although many emphasize one component more than the others. In reading the racial attitudes literature, one is struck by the variety of perspectives that have been offered regarding the dimensionality of racial attitudes. These range from Woodmansee and Cook's (1967) and Brigham, Woodmansee, and Cook's (1976) 10- or 12-dimensional perspective to Katz and Hass's (1988) 2-dimensional model of problack and antiblack attitudes and many unidimensional views. In between lies the work of Apostle, Glock, Piazza, and Suelzle (1983), who suggested that racial prejudice consists of (1) perceptions of racial differences, (2) explanations for racial differences, and (3) prescriptions regarding what should be done about these differences.

The diversity in opinion about what constitutes an attitude, and more specifically what constitutes a racial attitude, has led some to bemoan the "contamination" of racial attitude measures (Kuklinski & Parent, 1981; Sniderman & Tetlock, 1986a) and others to suggest that "there is little to be gained from searching for a single 'pure' measure of a racial attitude" (Jackman, 1981, p. 162). For example, Kuklinski and Parent (1981) argued that survey questions about racial attitudes (such as those used in the National Election Studies of the University of Michigan's Center for Political Studies) may include both "attitudes toward blacks and attitudes toward the use of the national government to impose mandatory programs" (p. 133); Sniderman and Tetlock (1986a, 1986b) further argued that racial attitude measures often do not distinguish between racial prejudice and attitudes toward race-related policy issues, such as busing and affirmative action. We agree with these authors: Although racial policy beliefs, general political ideology, and broad beliefs about the role of government may all be implicated in racial attitudes, these constructs are separable from the attitude object "black Americans."

Finally some researchers have suggested that modern-day racial attitudes cannot be successfully measured in any straightforward way. In their influential chapter on "The Aversive Form of Racism," Gaertner and Dovidio (1986) wrote that "given the high salience of race and racially symbolic issues . . . as well as aversive racists' vigilance and sensitivity to these issues, effective questionnaire measures . . . would be difficult if not impossible to develop" (p. 67). If the majority of Americans may not admit to racial prejudice on attitude scales (either to themselves or to researchers), these writers argued that social researchers must resort to unobtrusive measurement techniques, such as subliminal priming (Devine, 1989), lexical decision tasks and other reaction time indexes (Fazio, Jackson, Dunton, & Williams, 1995; Gaertner & McLaughlin, 1983; Greenwald & Banaji, 1995; Wittenbrink, Judd, & Park, 1997), or subtle contextual manipulations (Gaertner & Dovidio, 1986; Sniderman, Piazza, Tetlock, & Kendrick, 1991). Though we are sympathetic to these claims and intrigued by the novel measurement approaches, this chapter reflects our faith that the heart of modern-day racial attitudes can be successfully measured through self-report. Indeed, the measurement of racial attitudes is a flourishing area: Of the 18 instruments reviewed in this chapter, 11 have been published since 1990.

Item Content and Historical Context

In response to a changing social and normative climate, the item content of racial attitude scales has altered dramatically in the past several decades. Such development is necessary if racial attitudes are to represent the normative "fault lines" or dimensions along which respondents are arrayed. Even a cursory comparison of the racial attitude measures reviewed here with those in the 1968 edition of Robinson, Rusk, and Head's *Measures of Political Attitudes* and in Shaw and Wright's (1967) *Scales for the Measurement of Attitudes* reveals a striking difference in the face content of scale items. This difference is perhaps best described as a reduction in item offensiveness. Compare, for example, "The feeble-mindedness of the Negro limits him to a social level just a little above that of the higher animals" (Hinckley, 1932) to "Although there are exceptions, Black urban neighborhoods don't seem to have strong community organization or leadership" (Katz & Hass, 1988). Given that the expression of racial prejudice is viewed in many public contexts as inappropriate or immoral (i.e., "politically incorrect"), the introduction of less offensive item content undoubtedly reduces modern-day respondents' reactivity and leaves researchers themselves more comfortable about even *posing* racial attitude questions.

In part because of the sensitive nature of racial attitudes there has been much cross-breeding in the development of measurement scales. Valid measures of racial attitudes that still generate variability in responding (by avoiding social-desirability–based suppression) are difficult to generate, so researchers have been reluctant to bypass a well-behaved attitude question. As a result a number of items that had their introduction in one scale (e.g., Multifactorial Racial Attitudes Inventory, Modern Racism Scale) are used in other scales [e.g., Attitudes Toward Blacks (Brigham, 1993), New Racism (Jacobson, 1985), British Prejudice Scale (Lepore & Brown, 1997)]. While this is a very reasonable development strategy, it may have the unintended side effect of limiting the range and power of the "net" used to capture the complex construct of racial attitudes. One of our themes in this chapter is that diversity and plurality in measurement are good; the availability of a variety of measures and approaches to racial prejudice will serve the field well.

Another theme is that the testing of theory should be a central concern of prejudice researchers. Because many studies of racial attitudes have been based on nationally representative surveys that were not explicitly designed to test a given researcher's hypotheses, there has often not been a close connection between theory about prejudice and the content of the items used to test the theory. However, the appeal of many of the measures reviewed here is their incorporation of a theoretical perspective on the nature of prejudice, a point we will highlight as we review each measure.

A strong theoretical orientation is also notable in two scales developed by Schuman and Harding that do *not* receive review in this chapter—Sympathetic Identification with the Underdog (1963) and the Prejudice and Rationality Inventory (1964). The former index conceptualizes prejudice in largely affective terms—as the ability to sympathize with minority group members. The items tap feelings of empathy or identification in respondents' reactions to the mistreatment or distress of a minority group member. The Prejudice and Rationality Scale distinguishes between pro- and antiminority sentiments that are rational versus irrational and therefore taps not just the attitudinal direction, but also the extent to which such beliefs are "reasonable" (as defined by social scientists). We exclude these measures in the present chapter because the items are quite dated (e.g., "A group of colored teen-agers decide to picket and 'sit in' at a drug store where colored are not allowed to sit at the same part of the soda counter as Whites" from the Identification with the Underdog Scale; "It is a fairly well-established fact that Negroes have a less pleasant body odor than White people" from the Prejudice and Rationality Scale) and the scoring of responses (e.g., as sympathetic or rational) is questionable. Nonetheless, we encourage the interested researcher to review (and perhaps revamp) both of these measures, as they are good examples of prejudice conceptualizations with broad and explicit theoretical goals (see the 1968 edition of *Measures of Political Attitudes*).

Social Desirability and College Student Samples

There is little doubt that many respondents are strongly motivated to bias their attitude responses in a relatively nonprejudiced direction (Crandall, 1994; Dunton & Fazio, 1997). This is particularly true of college student populations, who tend to adopt an antiprejudice ethic during their campus stay (Altemeyer, 1988; Sears, 1986). The unfortunate fact is that many of the scales described in this chapter were developed and tested only on college student samples, limiting their known validity and reliability to the typical "college sophomore." Many of the more straightforward items and scales are highly positively skewed, suggesting that some suppressive factors (political correctness, need to maintain an egalitarian self-image) may distort the responses.

College student samples tend to be biased in predictable ways (Sears, 1986). While desiring to appear to be independent thinkers, college students generally eschew highly controversial or difficult attitudinal positions. They often have poorly developed world views and are inexperienced in a wide variety of important political and social issues. Thus they are more likely than nonstudents to appear "enlightened" in their racial attitudes, but they are also attitudinally labile. By contrast, nationally representative samples may include more attitudinally stable individuals for whom "political correctness" is a less pressing concern (Sears, 1986).

As indicated earlier, another difficulty that arises from strong social desirability pressures is that scale authors can choose to avoid the problem by using "disguised" items that ask not about one's attitudes toward blacks or whites, but rather about related issues, such as affirmative action, government activism, taxation, or perceptions of degree of antiblack discrimination. As a result the scales become confounded with beliefs and attitudes about political ideology, specific government programs, humanitarian values, or religious beliefs. Although this may be an unavoidable consequence of attempts at subtlety (or an acknowledgment of the multidimensionality of racial attitudes), the most persuasive validation evidence comes from research that separates out the effects of related variables when examining the correlates of racial attitude measures. This multiple regression approach is more typical of the researchers working with national survey samples in which a wide array of respondent characteristics is assessed.

Measures Reviewed Here

The majority of research on racial attitudes has focused on whites' attitudes toward blacks, and the content of our chapter clearly reflects that. Most of the scales reviewed here are intended for use with whites as respondents and blacks as targets, although a few incorporate other target groups (e.g., Social Distance Scale, Quick Discrimination Index, Subtle and Blatant Prejudice Scales), one measures blacks' attitudes toward whites (Attitudes Toward Whites Scale), and two can be more generally construed as prejudice-related world views (Social Dominance Orientation Scale, Universal Orientation Scale).

Because of the changing social context of racial attitudes and the parallel change in content of racial attitude items, we mainly cover scales that were either developed or published after 1975 (excepting the Multifactor Racial Attitudes Inventory, which was undergoing revision at that time, and the always relevant Social Distance Scale). In addition, we cover only those scales designed to measure "naturally occurring" attitudes rather than indexes that were developed for special, narrow purposes (e.g., scales used as dependent variables in attitude change experiments or "bogus pipeline" research). Similarly we do not touch on general methods for measuring group stereotypes (e.g., Haddock, Zanna, & Esses, 1993; Judd & Park, 1993; Judd, Park, Ryan, Brauer, & Kraus, 1995) or on scales that were specifically designed to measure attitudes toward race-related issues (e.g., affirmative action). Our primary focus is on the general social group (usually blacks) as the attitude object.

A total of 18 scales receive review in this chapter. Thirteen focus on majority perceivers' attitudes toward minority groups, and one additional scale measures blacks' attitudes toward whites. Two other scales were also developed from the perspective of white respondents, but we classified these as measures of black *stereotypes* rather than measures of prejudice per se (stereotypes are typically considered the cognitive component and prejudice the affective component of intergroup attitudes; see Dovidio, Brigham, Johnson, & Gaertner, 1996). The final two scales measure more general prejudice-related perspectives or world views. We first review the 14 out-group attitude scales, followed by the 2 stereotype measures and the 2 general scales.

Of the 14 out-group attitude measures, we classified 5 as indicators of "old-fashioned" prejudice, 8 as measures of "modern" prejudice, and 1 as a manifestly hybrid measure (Subtle and Blatant Prejudice Scales). We made these determinations on the basis of both the scale authors' conceptualizations and our own reading of item content—the old-fashioned measures include relatively blatant, obvious, or nonsubtle questions about race. Pettigrew and Meertens (1995) provided a general guide to this distinction: "Blatant prejudice is hot, close, and direct. Subtle prejudice is cool, distant, and indirect" (p. 58). Interestingly 3 of the "old-fashioned" measures were developed in the 1990s (and 1 of the "modern" scales was initially developed in the 1920s), suggesting that modern researchers do not necessarily subscribe to the view that racial prejudice is different in form today than it was decades ago.

The five "old-fashioned" scales are described in chronological order of their development, followed by the eight "modern" scales, also in chronological order, and then the hybrid scale. These are followed by the two stereotype measures and the two scales that assess prejudice-related world views. Within these groupings, the instruments are

Old-Fashioned Measures of Out-Group Attitudes
  1. Multifactor Racial Attitudes Inventory (MRAI) (Woodmansee & Cook, 1967)
  2. Multifactor Racial Attitudes Inventory—Short Scale (MRAI—SS) (Ard & Cook, 1977)
  3. Racial Attitudes Scale (RAS) (Sidanius, Pratto, Martin, & Stallworth, 1991)
  4. Attitudes toward Blacks (ATB) (Brigham, 1993)
  5. Attitudes toward Whites (ATW) (Brigham, 1993)
Modern Measures of Out-Group Attitudes
  6. Social Distance Scale (Bogardus, 1928, 1933, 1959) and variations
  7. Modern Racism Scale (MRS) (McConahay, Hardee, & Batts, 1981)
  8. New Racism Scale (NRS) (Jacobson, 1985)
  9. Pro-Black/Anti-Black Attitudes Questionnaire (PAAQ) (Katz & Hass, 1988)
  10. Social Scenarios Scale (Byrnes & Kiger, 1988)

11. Quick Discrimination Index (QDI) (Ponterotto, Burkard, Rieger, Grieger, D'Onofrio, Dubuisson, Heenehan, Millstein, Parisi, Rath, & Sax, 1995)
12. Racial Resentment Scale (RRS) (Kinder & Sanders, 1996)
13. British Prejudice Scale (Lepore & Brown, 1997)
Hybrid Measure
14. Subtle and Blatant Prejudice Scales (Pettigrew & Meertens, 1995)
Measures of Racial Stereotypes
15. Prejudice Index (Bobo & Kluegel, 1993)
16. Racial Stereotypes Measure (Peffley, Hurwitz, & Sniderman, 1997)
Prejudice-Related World Views
17. Social Dominance Orientation (SDO) Scale (Sidanius & Pratto, 1993; Pratto, Sidanius, Stallworth, & Malle, 1994)
18. Universal Orientation Scale (UOS) (Phillips & Ziller, 1997)

Overview of the Scales

The MRAI and MRAI—SS measure 10–13 dimensions or components of attitudes toward blacks, ranging from views on interracial marriage to acceptance of blacks in superior positions, to beliefs about desegregation. Scale development was based on Woodmansee and Cook's (1967) belief that racial attitudes are best assessed through a consideration of content-defined dimensions rather than the traditional tripartite (cognitive, affective, behavioral) attitude conceptualization. In the MRAI each dimension is measured with 10 items; thus the scale is likely to be too long for many researchers' objectives. The MRAI—SS includes only 1 item to measure each of 12 dimensions, making the length more reasonable, but this instrument sacrifices the possibility of considering and adequately measuring each dimension. Although the content of a number of the items is outdated, many items remain relevant even in today's social and political climate.

The Racial Attitudes Scale (Sidanius *et al.,* 1991) is a general measure of racial prejudice that has considerable diversity in its item content (attitudes toward interracial dating, policy issues, and target groups other than blacks—e.g., Mexicans, foreigners). Based on the authors' social dominance theory, the scale is designed to capture some of the "legitimizing myths" that contribute to a social dominance drive "toward group-based social inequality." The scale can be divided into three subscales: White Dominance, Racial Policy, and Caste-Maintenance Orientation.

Brigham (1993) developed two companion racial attitude scales—one for use with white respondents (Attitudes Toward Blacks) and one for black respondents (Attitudes Toward Whites). Based in the theoretical tradition of the MRAI and MRAI—SS, these 20-item scales tap a wide range of content domains that are combined to produce a single attitude score. Brigham adapted items from a number of sources, including the MRAI and the Modern Racism Scale. Despite some "modern" content, most items have an old-fashioned feel (e.g., "Generally, blacks are not as smart as whites"), which Brigham nonetheless found effective for use in college student samples. The Attitudes toward Whites Scale is, to our knowledge, the only available well-validated measure of black respondents' racial attitudes.

Since Bogardus's (1928) original conceptual development, measures of social distance have become very popular means of assessing general favorability toward or comfort with out-group members. The construct of social distance is adaptable for use with any out-group or individual target, and it is timeless—questions regarding willingness to marry, work with, live near, or share citizenship with a target are relevant across many contexts and in any era, and in this sense we consider the Social Distance Scale a "modern" measure. There is no single Social Distance Scale; Bogardus himself reported a series of versions, and many other researchers have adapted, reduced, extended, or otherwise varied the content of particular items. We focus here on the most well known seven-item version of Bogardus's scale and highlight developments and variations by Triandis (1964), Byrnes and Kiger (1988), and Crandall (1991).

Of all the instruments described here, we devote most space and attention to our review of the Modern Racism Scale (McConahay et al., 1981), as the MRS is the most widely used of the racial attitude measures (particularly by social psychologists) and the one that has most forcefully advanced the view that "modern" racism should be differentiated from "old-fashioned" racism. This scale has also been the brunt of more comment and criticism than any other instrument with regard to both its theoretical underpinnings and its specific content. Based on a general approach to symbolic/modern politics by McConahay, Sears, Kinder, and others, the scale was designed to provide a relatively nonreactive measure of whites' racial attitudes and to capture a definition of racism as "the expression in terms of abstract ideological symbols and symbolic behaviors of the feeling that blacks are violating cherished values and making illegitimate demands for changes in the racial status quo" (McConahay & Hough, 1976, p. 38). We attempt to provide a complete and balanced guide to the MRS's merits and limitations as perhaps the most popular measure of whites' attitudes toward blacks.

Like the MRS, the New Racism Scale (Jacobson, 1985) was designed to assess antiblack attitudes in a subtle form. The scale has considerable overlap with the MRS, but incorporates two items relevant to affirmative action policy. Although it has received relatively little use, the scale nonetheless provides a good example of the "modern" measurement approach.

Another scale with a strong theoretical foundation is the Pro-Black/Anti-Black Attitudes Questionnaire (Katz & Hass, 1988). The authors argued that pro- and antiblack feelings exist independently in modern-day whites (the subscales were intentionally designed to be empirically independent) and that each has its own value base: Problack attitudes derive from humanitarian–egalitarian values and antiblack attitudes from Protestant work ethic values. The combination of high pro- and high antiblack attitudes is described as racial "ambivalence," which produces instability and amplification in responses to individual black targets. The researchers have accumulated both correlational and experimental evidence supportive of their conceptualization.

The Social Scenarios Scale (Byrnes & Kiger, 1988), adapted from Kogan and Downey (1956), measures participants' "reported willingness to condone or confront discrimination in a variety of social situations" (p. 109). Respondents are presented with discriminatory scenarios and asked how they would behave; the instrument yields three subscale scores based on behavioral intentions when confronting pejorative remarks, negative judgments about interracial intimacy, and job and housing injustice. This measure conceptualizes racial prejudice in behavioral terms and may be useful as an indicator of respondents' receptivity to antidiscriminatory social norms.

The Quick Discrimination Index (Ponterotto et al., 1995) is a 30-item measure of general receptivity to diversity and multiculturalism (e.g., "I think the school system, from elementary school through college, should promote values representative of diverse cultures"). It provides three subscale scores (Multiculturalism, Racial Intimacy, and Women's Equality). This measure is unique in its conceptualization of discriminatory responses as a general (not a group-specific) tendency, but offers researchers the option of focusing separately on the race and gender components.

The Racial Resentment Scale (Kinder & Sanders, 1996) is a recent measurement offering from the modern/symbolic racism school, which the authors distinguish from measures of "biological racism" (i.e., belief in innate differences between the races). The heart of racial resentment is whites' belief "that blacks do not try hard enough to overcome the difficulties they face and that they take what they have not earned" (p. 105); thus American individualistic values are central to this construct. The six-item instrument was developed in the context of national survey data, and the validation data are noteworthy in that controls for political ideology and other constructs that may be confounded with racism were incorporated.

The British Prejudice Scale (Lepore & Brown, 1997) includes items adapted from three other instruments (Modern Racism Scale, New Racism Scale, and Subtle and Blatant Prejudice Scales), with the specific content changed to be suitable for use in a British context. We classify this as a modern measure, as many of the items reflect not direct antiblack sentiment, but rather indirect beliefs about immigration and the representation of blacks in government.

Pettigrew and Meertens (1995) developed an instrument to tap *both* old-fashioned (blatant) and modern (subtle) prejudice. Using seven representative Western European samples, the authors supported a two-factor structure of blatant prejudice (threat–rejection and opposition to intimacy) and a three-factor structure of subtle prejudice (defense of traditional values, exaggeration of cultural differences, and denial of positive emotions). An advantage of the instrument is that the scales are adaptable for use with any relevant outgroup; seven different minority groups were targeted in the validation work. Demonstrating the difference between subtle and blatant prejudice, the authors found that virtually no respondents scored low in subtle racism, but high in blatant racism; they provided further evidence that the combination of scale scores may best predict racial policy and other race-relevant attitudes.

Two of the instruments reviewed here are measures of whites' stereotypes of blacks. Both the Prejudice Index (Bobo & Kluegel, 1993) and the Racial Stereotypes Measure (Peffley *et al.*, 1997) ask respondents to indicate the extent to which they endorse various attributes as descriptive of blacks. Although the measures have some common content (e.g., laziness and violence–aggression are represented in both), they differ in one operational and one theoretical way. The operational difference is that for Bobo and Kluegel, stereotyping scores reflect the *difference* in respondents' attribution of negative traits to whites versus blacks, whereas for Peffley *et al.*, only judgments of blacks are assessed. Theoretically Bobo and Kluegel consider stereotypes as a basic component of prejudice, but for Peffley *et al.*, they are distinct from prejudice—stereotypes are "cognitive expectancies," whereas prejudice is "an affective predisposition." One might classify both of these measures as old-fashioned in nature—there is little subtlety, for example, in the item content. However, such an approach is probably necessary if one wishes to measure the extent to which traits are viewed as stereotypical of blacks as a group.

The final two scales reviewed are not direct measures of racial attitudes, but rather of broader prejudice-related orientations or world views. The Social Dominance Orientation Scale (Sidanius & Pratto, 1993; Pratto *et al.*, 1994) assesses individual differences in the tendency to prefer hierarchy and inequality among social groups. Individuals high in SDO support a variety of legitimizing myths—such as political conservatism and racial and ethnic prejudice—that align social groups on a superior–inferior dimension.

Phillips and Ziller (1997) conceptualized the Universal Orientation Scale as a measure of nonprejudice. It gauges the tendency for individuals to see similarity (rather than difference) between themselves and diverse others and is positively related to perspective-taking and egalitarian values, but negatively related to dogmatism. The authors argued that viewing others as similar to (or even interchangeable with) the self precludes tendencies toward prejudice; thus universal orientation is potentially relevant to understanding attitudes toward a wide variety of groups.

Single Items from National Surveys

Before turning to reviews of the scales, we first acknowledge that racial attitudes also have a long history of measurement with single items, as is most evident in many of the national survey series. The National Election Studies' (NES) "feeling thermometer" measure is perhaps the most notable of these items. In Appendixes A–C we provide a compendium of commonly asked racial attitude questions that have appeared in the NES (administered by the Center for Political Studies at the University of Michigan), the General Social Survey (GSS) (administered by the National Opinion Research Center of the University of Chicago), and Sniderman and Piazza's (1993) Race and Politics Survey. In some cases we indicate items that have been grouped together as scales by particular scholars. In general, however, these items have been used as individual indicators to track trends in national racial attitudes over time (e.g., see Schuman *et al.,* 1985).

Some of these trends can be noted by a brief perusal of items from the GSS.[1] The GSS has been tracking a series of racial attitude questions in its cross-sectional national samples since 1972. Nine of the most frequently asked questions over the years are shown in Table 6–1, along with the proportions of the combined 1972–1994 sample giving each response. Most of these items can be classified under the traditional racism or more blatant category, although several more of the modern racism variety have been included in more recent GSS surveys, as noted in Appendix B to this chapter.

It can be seen in Table 6–1 that over the years almost three times as many Americans disagree (71%) that there should be laws against interracial marriage as agree. Similarly almost 75% say they would not mind if a relative invited a black friend home to dinner (although less than 30% say this has happened in the recent past). That, in turn, is close to the 72% who disagree with the statement that white people have the right to keep blacks out of their neighborhood. At the same time nearly half of Americans feel that landowners can decide for themselves whether to sell to blacks, and 62% agree that blacks should not "push themselves" where they are not wanted.

Nearly 9 in 10 Americans have said that blacks and whites should go to the same schools, although they oppose interracial busing by about a 3-to-1 margin. More than 80% say they would vote for a qualified black for president, compared to only 15% who say they would not.

Correlates of Positive Attitudes

These racism items share a common set of relations with the selected GSS background questions shown in Table 6–2.

Sex: In general, women express more open (prointegration) racial attitudes than men. However, the correlations are very small (though statistically significant because of the large samples involved).

Age: Not surprisingly younger people express more open attitudes than older

[1]This section was written by John P. Robinson.

Table 6-1

GSS Race Questions (along with Variable Numbers and Names)
and Combined Response Frequencies, 1972-1994

125A. Do you think there should be laws against marriages between blacks and whites?
[RACMAR]

Yes	26%
No	71
Don't know	3

126. How strongly would you object if a member of your family wanted to bring a black
friend home to dinner? Would you object strongly, mildly, or not at all? [RACDIN]

Strongly	10%
Mildly	13
Not at all	74
Don't know	3

127. Here are some opinions other people have expressed in connection with black-white
relations. Which statement on the card comes closest to how you, yourself, feel?
   A. Blacks shouldn't push themselves where they're not wanted. [RACPUSH]

Agree strongly	33%
Agree slightly	29
Disagree slightly	18
Disagree strongly	17
No opinion	3

   B. White people have the right to keep blacks out of their neighborhoods if they
      want to, and blacks should respect that right. [RACSEG]

Agree strongly	11%
Agree slightly	14
Disagree slightly	24
Disagree strongly	48
No opinion	3

128. Suppose there is a community-wide vote on the general housing issue. There are two
possible laws to vote on. Which law would you vote for? [RACOPEN]

One law says that a homeowner can decide for himself whom to sell his house to, even if he prefers not to sell to blacks.	46%
The second law says that a homeowner cannot refuse to sell to someone because of their race or color.	50
Neither	2
Don't know	2

131. During the last few years, has anyone in your family brought a friend who was black
home for dinner? [RACHOME]

Yes	29%
No	70
Don't know	1

132. Do you think white students and black students should go to the same schools or to
separate schools? [RACSCHOL]

Same schools	88%
Separate schools	10
Don't know	2

134. In general, do you favor or oppose the busing of black and white children from one
school district to another? [BUSING]

Favor	24%
Oppose	72
Don't know	4

Table 6-1

GSS Race Questions (along with Variable Numbers and Names)
and Combined Response Frequencies, 1972–1994—cont'd

135. If your party nominated a black for president, would you vote for him if he were
qualified for the job? [RACPRES]

Yes	81%
No	15
Don't know	4

Table 6-2

Correlations between GSS Racial Attitude Questions and Background Factors, 1972–1994

| GSS questions | Demographic/background factors | | | | | |
	Sex	Age	Race	Education	Ideology	Party ID
RACMAR	−.03*	−.29***	.15**	.34***	−.04**	.02
RACDIN	.03*	−.13**	.12**	.21***	−.05**	.02
RACPUSH	.05**	−.22***	.21***	.29***	−.12**	−.04*
RACSEG	.00	−.23***	.19**	.27***	−.07**	−.02
RACOPEN	.03*	−.19***	.20**	.13**	−.10**	−.07**
RACHOME	.01	−.17**	.17**	.19**	−.07**	−.03*
RACSCHOL	−.02	−.16**	.09**	.22***	−.02	.02
BUSING	.03*	−.10**	.28***	−.01	−.14**	−.13**
RACPRES	.02	−.15**	.13**	.18**	−.02	−.04*

Notes:

All attitude questions are coded such that high values indicate more favorable (e.g., prointegra-
tion) responses.
Sex (Male = 0, Female = 1)
Race (White = 0, Black = 1)
Political Views (Liberal–Conservative)
Party ID (0 = Democrat, 1 = Republican)
*statistically significant at $p < .01$
**$p < .001$
***$p < .0001$

people, although the differences here are confounded with education. That is, most of
these correlations would be seriously reduced if adjusted for the respondent's educational
level. Nonetheless, the correlations with the interracial marriage item and other attitude
areas are almost as high as the correlations with education (and in the case of busing, the
correlation is higher for age than for education).

Race: The correlations with race are in the expectedly more open direction for
blacks, but for some items are lower than for education or age. The largest racial polarization is found for the issue of busing.

Education: The more educated are the less prejudiced. Education is most strongly
associated with favorable attitudes on the marriage, push, and segregation items and more
modestly related to the busing and integration items.

Ideology: The correlations with liberal–conservative identification are in the expected direction of liberals being more open to integration, particularly on the busing and push items. However, the relationships to ideology are notably weaker than for education, race, and age.

Party Identification: The correlations with party identification are weaker and more irregular than for ideology. Busing again turns out to be the major item separating Republicans from Democrats.

Trends Across Time

As might be predicted by the increasing presence of more educated younger people in the public, trends in these racial attitudes have become notably more open since 1972, as shown in Table 6–3. Thus the 13% who opposed interracial marriage in 1994 are only a third as large as the 39% who opposed it in 1972; much the same trend is found for the item on voting for a black president, which has declined from 26% opposition in 1972 to only 9% in 1994. The proportion agreeing strongly that whites have the right to keep blacks out of their neighborhood has dropped from 22% to 5%. Although it has shown the least change since 1972, the proportions opposed to cross-district busing have dropped 14 percentage points since 1972.

Thus these GSS items show a similar pattern of relations not only with background factors, but also across time. There is also a rather high degree of interitem correlation across these items—enough for Sears *et al.* (1997) to incorporate several of them in their traditional racism scale (see Appendix B). It appears that some of the items have reached a ceiling (or floor), such that few white respondents depart from unanimity in their responses to them. This supports the need for the more "modern" measures highlighted in this chapter.

Conclusions

Each of the racial attitude scales reviewed here has some merit in that scale reliabilities range from moderate to high and all have some demonstrated construct validity. Most have also been developed with attention to acquiescence and social desirability concerns, all are clearly written, and all focus on important racial issues. Based on our review we cannot conclude that there is any "pure" measure of racial attitudes or any one "best" racial attitude measure. Instead, we recommend that researchers carefully select an instrument based on the demands of theory and the practical considerations of their research. If a researcher is interested in racial ambivalence rather than unidimensional antiblack prejudice, the Pro-Black/Anti-Black Attitudes Questionnaire (Katz & Hass, 1988) is a good choice. If attributions about racial differences are central to one's theoretical definition of prejudice, the Racial Resentment Scale (Kinder & Sanders, 1996) may provide the best operationalization. If one needs a parallel form of whites' and blacks' racial attitudes, the Attitudes toward Blacks and Attitudes toward Whites Scales (Brigham, 1993) offer a good solution. To measure the conative component of attitudes, the Social Distance Scale (Bogardus, 1928, 1933, 1959) or the Social Scenarios Scale (Byrnes & Kiger, 1988) may be most appropriate. The Prejudice Index (Bobo & Kluegel, 1993) and the Racial Stereotypes Measure (Peffley *et al.*, 1997) assess representations of blacks as a group, and so on. Rather than relying on tradition or reputation, a specific match should be sought between

Table 6-3
Trends in Racial Attitudes, 1972–1994

Question	Year of survey																					
	72	73	74	75	76	77	78	80	81	82	83	84	85	86	87	88	89	90	91	92	93	94
RACMAR % yes	39	37	34	38	32	28	29			25		25	26	21		22	21	19	17		17	13
RACDIN % object	13	15	10		12	11	10			07		06	09									
RACPUSH % agree	44	44		46	42	44	34			25		26	26									14
RACSEG % agree	22				21	22	15			12		10	10		08	07	07	08	06		04	05
RACOPEN % decide for self		63		64	63		57	55			50	45		47	39	39	37	41	35		30	
RACHOME % no	80		77		77	77	71			68		69	71		66	68	70	71	69		63	63
RACSCHOL % same	86				83	85	87			90		90	91									
BUSING % oppose	80		79	82	84	83	79			73	75		77	70		66	71	65	64		69	66
RACPRES % no	26		17	18		22	15			10	14		15	13		18	17	12	10		11	09

Note: See Table 6–1 for question and response wording.

theory and operationalization of racial attitudes after a careful review of the appropriateness of the instrument for the population under study.

Other pitfalls to be avoided include ensuring that one's choice of attitude measures does not confound independent and dependent variables. Social researchers who investigate the role of racism in political policy issues should actively avoid racial attitude measures containing social policy items (e.g., New Racism Scale; Racial Attitudes Scale). If the link between antiblack attitudes and attributions is being investigated, then attitude scales that *include* explanations about the causes of black–white differences should be avoided. Furthermore researchers would do well to distinguish between racial attitudes and other related constructs (e.g., political ideology) as they attempt to examine the antecedents and consequences of prejudiced thought.

Despite the improvements and merits of the measures reviewed here, many are very new, and their reliability and validity information comes almost exclusively from the scale developers rather than independent researchers. Furthermore many of the instruments have been developed using only college student samples. It is important that subsequent researchers carefully document and share evidence of their successes and failures as they use these instruments in a variety of populations. To obtain a multifactorial appreciation and understanding of racial attitudes, we also recommend that whenever possible researchers should ask respondents to complete a variety of attitude measures. Different aspects, dimensions, or components of racial attitudes may have dramatically different sources, correlates, and consequences.

We also suggest that the use of multiple prejudice measures should be an end in itself. Plurality is good for the progress of science, and the availability of many measures ensures that a broad net is cast in the search for knowledge about racial attitudes (Campbell, 1974; Hull, 1988; Kitcher, 1993). Of course, the continued use of the same measures allows one to examine trends and patterns of relationship over time; this is an important goal that should not be neglected. Nonetheless, if different scientists choose to use different measures at different times, we can develop a better sense of both the limits and the generalizability of any conclusions that are drawn about the nature of racial prejudice.

Future Directions

We are sanguine about researchers' ability to adequately measure racial attitudes through self-report, but a common trend—particularly in the social psychological literature—has been to assess racial attitudes through indirect reaction time (RT) methodology. Researchers such as Greenwald and Banaji (1995), Greenwald et al. (1998), Fazio et al. (1995), Wittenbrink et al. (1997), Judd et al. (1995), Dovidio and Gaertner (1993), and others have proposed that prejudice be assessed by the speed with which respondents associate the category "blacks" (in either semantic or pictorial form) with negative versus positive attributes. By these methods prejudice scores cannot be faked (but see Blair and Banaji, 1996, for some evidence that motivational goals can disrupt the pattern of findings on semantic priming tasks). This type of measurement approach may therefore qualify as "ultramodern" in nature (see McConahay, 1986).

However, for many purposes, most notably national surveys, the RT approach is unlikely to be feasible. Furthermore not enough data have yet accumulated to indicate whether such measures are superior to self-report (and therefore worth the extra expense involved even for smaller samples). For these reasons researchers must document the extent to which RT-based prejudice scores are correlated with those based on various self-report instruments and provide evidence regarding the relative predictive power of each. Research by Fazio *et al.* (1995) and by Dovidio *et al.* (1997) on the prediction of spontaneous versus deliberative behaviors provide good examples of this approach.

Another innovation in the assessment of racial prejudice has been the use of computer-assisted telephone interviewing (CATI) technology to introduce experiments into survey research (e.g., see Sniderman *et al.*, 1991; Sniderman & Piazza, 1993; Peffley *et al.*, 1997). For example, by randomly assigning some respondents to answer a question about the extent to which they would recommend government assistance to a laid-off *white* worker and others to a comparable question regarding a laid-off *black* worker, one can determine the existence of "double standards" based on race (Sniderman *et al.*, 1991; Snidermann & Piazza, 1993). This approach precludes the calculation of an individual difference measure of racial attitudes (unless, of course, a within-subjects design is used), but provides meaningful descriptive data about the sample as a whole. Furthermore by experimentally varying other attributes of the target in this example (e.g., sex, social class, marital status, work history), one can pinpoint and distinguish the influences of many different potential sources of bias on such judgments. This approach combines the advantages of survey and experimental methods and has already proven useful in testing various accounts of how political ideology plays into racial bias (see Sniderman *et al.*, 1991). The "experiment in a survey" approach has not, to our knowledge, been used to measure group-level attitudes (e.g., asking for responses to a black versus a white version of an attitude item, such as "It is easy to understand the anger of black/white people in America"), but such an effort could prove valuable.

In addition to developments in the methods used to measure racial prejudice, another recent advance has been the recognition that to understand and predict race-relevant attitudes and behavior, the measurement of antiblack attitudes alone is not enough. Many modern theories of prejudice indicate that while there are many pressures that direct individuals *toward* the expression of prejudice (e.g., long-established prejudicial beliefs that may be automatically activated; see Devine, 1989), there are also forces that operate against this tendency. These include not only normative pressure toward political correctness, but also internalized goals, values, self-guides, and motivations toward nonprejudice. Dunton and Fazio (1997) have developed a measure of the "motivation to suppress prejudice," and Devine, Monteith, and their colleagues have developed methodologies for assessing respondents' discrepancies between their idealized goals for interracial interaction and their actual conduct (Devine, Monteith, Zuwerink, & Elliot, 1991; Monteith, 1996; Zuwerink, Devine, Monteith, & Cook, 1996). These measures, in combination with measures of antiblack attitudes, may prove effective in predicting other race-relevant attitudes as well as affective and behavioral reactions to individual blacks.

Finally the future of research on racial attitudes should, we think, involve a return to some issues of the past. The question of whether new/modern/subtle racism is substantively different from old-fashioned racism has not been definitively settled, nor have questions regarding the basic structure of racial attitudes. From the MRAI's 13 dimensions to the unidimensional affective view best reflected in a "feeling thermometer" rating of blacks, there are many conflicting views regarding the scope and structure of prejudicial attitudes. A culling of the measures reviewed here produces the following set of dimensions of whites' attitudes toward blacks: beliefs about integration, attitudes regarding intimate interracial relationships, black inferiority and other derogatory beliefs, racial policy attitudes, beliefs about government involvement in racial matters, acceptance of blacks in higher status positions, attitudes toward black militance, beliefs in white dominance, general social distance, ascription of stereotypical characteristics to blacks, affective–emotional reactions, concerns about reverse discrimination, reactions to racial injustice, sympathetic beliefs and feelings, defense of traditional values, receptivity to multiculturalism, perceived threat–rejection, exaggeration of cultural differences, and attributions for blacks' lower status relative to that of whites.

Although these can be generally grouped into affective, cognitive, and behavioral factors, the division is not neat. Rather, this list reflects the complexity of *content* that is incorporated in white Americans' opinions on race and indicates that while some things have changed, many aspects of racial attitudes have remained constant over time. Where research is needed is in *systematically* determining which dimensions are central and which are peripheral to understanding white Americans' responses to black Americans and to broader racial matters. At its core, racial prejudice is the tendency to evaluate members of a racial group unfavorably. Various contributions to this tendency have been proposed and investigated, but a coherent picture—one that accounts for the pervasiveness of race in American political life—has not yet emerged.

Multifactor Racial Attitudes Inventory (MRAI)

(J. J. Woodmansee & S. W. Cook, 1967)

Variable

This instrument measures a variety of components of attitudes toward blacks, based on 10 separate (but not independent) subscales, with 2 more dimensions reported in Brigham, Woodmansee, and Cook (1976). A scoring manual, available from the Institute of Behavioral Science at the University of Colorado, also reports a 13th subscale (apparently added by Weissbach and Cook in 1970).

Description

The original 10 subscales of the MRAI are based on cluster and factor analyses on a very large item pool, the origins of which are in the unpublished work of Collins and Haupt. Woodmansee and Cook (1967) argued that racial attitudes are best assessed through a consideration of content-defined dimensions rather than a tripartite (cognitive, affective, behavioral) conceptualization. Each of the subscales in the full inventory has 10 items; thus the full expanded MRAI consists of 13 subscales and 130 items, each answered using a dichotomous agree–disagree format. Scores on each subscale can range from 0 to 10, with high numbers indicating nonprejudiced or equalitarian attitudes. As will be seen later, no validity information is available on the 13th subscale (Black Militance), and both Woodmansee and Cook and Brigham *et al.* treat the Black Superiority subscale not as a direct measure of attitudes toward blacks, but rather as a social desirability index. We might now call this "political correctness"—an attempt to suppress, deny, or publicly gloss over "true" negative attitudes that whites have toward blacks. The researchers were very suspicious of the honesty of those respondents who scored highly on Black Superiority and so treated this subscale differently than the others. The subscale names, Cronbach alphas, sample means, and test–retest reliabilities are as follows:

Subscale	Alpha	Mean (SD)	Test–Retest r
Original MRAI			
1. Integration–Segregation Policy	.84	7.5 (2.5)	.73
2. Acceptance in Close Personal Relationships	.91	6.3 (3.9)	.95
3. Black Inferiority	.68	7.2 (2.1)	.51
4. Black Superiority	.71	2.0 (2.1)	.74
5. Ease in Interracial Contacts	.74	2.5 (1.9)	.83
6. Derogatory Beliefs	.70	4.1 (1.9)	.81
7. Local Autonomy	.86	5.3 (2.6)	.84
8. Private Rights	.89	4.0 (2.6)	.80
9. Acceptance in Status-Superior Relationships	.87	7.8 (2.5)	.82
10. Gradualism	.86	3.3 (2.6)	.87
Expanded Subscales			
11. Interracial Marriage	.84	5.6 (2.8)	—
12. Approaches to Racial Equality	.72	3.8 (2.5)	—
13. Black Militance	.82	4.6 (3.0)	—

The intersubscale correlations for the first 10 subscales reported by Woodmansee and Cook (1967) range from −.02 (between Acceptance in Status-Superior Relationships and Black Superiority) to .74 (between Local Autonomy and Private Rights), with an average of .35. Brigham *et al.* (1976) reported an average correlation of .37 between their 2 additional subscales and the original 10, with the correlations ranging from .13 to .49. These correlations suggest overlap as well as significant conceptual and empirical distinctions among the subscales.

Samples

Woodmansee and Cook (1967) used several different samples in the construction of the MRAI, including 593 white college students from different regions of the United States, a second group of 609 white college students from the Midwest and Border South, and a third group of 630 white college students from cities in the Border South or the western United States. In each of these samples, Woodmansee and Cook attempted to draw respondents with considerable diversity in their racial attitudes; thus the largest sample included 313 students who had worked for civil rights groups, had demonstrated on campus for civil rights for blacks, had belonged to right-wing political organizations, or were members of race-exclusive fraternities and sororities (the means for the first 10 subscales in the preceding table are based on this sample of 313).

Brigham *et al.* (1976) surveyed 758 white college students from Colorado, Arizona, and Tennessee. Of this larger sample 131 subjects were active in civil rights organizations, were enrolled in an elective course in minority problems, or belonged to radical right-wing political organizations or exclusionary social fraternities (the means for Interracial Marriage and Approaches to Racial Equality reported earlier are based on this subsample of 131). Data regarding the Black Militance subscale are based on a sample of 310 University of Colorado freshmen.

Reliability

Internal Consistency

As indicated previously, the scales had adequate internal consistency, with an average alpha across all 12 subscales of .80.

Test–Retest

The stability coefficients reported previously are based on a three-week test–retest study using 41 Wake Forest College students (described in the MRAI test manual available from the University of Colorado). These numbers were generally high, although the Black Inferiority index was markedly less stable than the other subscales.

Validity

Convergent

In terms of known groups Woodmansee and Cook (1967) identified four ordered criterion groups: (1) members of the NAACP, (2) students in race relations classes, (3) members of moderately right-wing political organizations, and (4) members of social fraternities with publicized exclusionary policies. These authors found that the 10 subscales were arrayed in the predicted ordering of groups in the vast majority of cases; all ANOVAs were significant at $p < .01$, and the average group effect size (eta) across all subscales was .59. These effects were larger in the Border South (eta = .66), where racial attitudes were more varied and important to everyday life, than in the West (eta = .52). Brigham *et al.* (1976) used three a priori groups (corresponding to groups 1, 2, and 4 of Woodmansee and Cook) and found an average eta of .49 across subscales, with all of the ANOVAs significant at $p < .001$—except Black Superiority, which did not differ reliably across groups.

   Woodmansee and Cook (1967) also demonstrated that several of their scales correlated moderately with Schuman and Harding's (1963) Sympathetic Identification with the Underdog Scale (e.g., $r = .23$ for Local Autonomy and $r = .21$ for Acceptance in Close Personal Relationships). Katz, Glass, and Cohen (1973) also demonstrated that college undergraduates with "ambivalent" racial attitudes (high in negative attitudes as measured by three of the MRAI subscales and high in sympathy as measured by the Schuman and Harding scale) were most likely to derogate a black victim who had received strong and undeserved electric shocks. Among other researchers who have used the MRAI as a benchmark to validate their own measures are Ard and Cook (1977), Brigham (1993), and Gaertner and McLaughlin (1983).

Discriminant

No information was provided.

Location

The validation research for the two versions of the MRAI are reported in
   Woodmansee, J. J., & Cook, S. W. (1967). Dimensions of racial attitudes: Their identification and measurement. *Journal of Personality and Social Psychology, 7,* 240–250.

Brigham, J. C., Woodmansee, J. J., & Cook, S. W. (1976). Dimensions of verbal racial attitudes: Interracial marriage and approaches to racial equality. *Journal of Social Issues, 32,* 9–21.

Results and Comments

The MRAI is a historically important scale. Several other scales have been developed out of it, the items have been adapted for use in other instruments, and the measure is based on a firm theoretical orientation in which attitude dimensions are defined by content rather than the traditional tripartite (affect, cognition, behavior) framework (see also Cook & Selltiz, 1964). Scholars interested in the structure of racial attitudes, the historical development of racial attitudes scales, or the construction of a new racial attitudes measure would be well served by a close inspection of the MRAI. However, the MRAI—SS (presented next) covers the same area in less detail and may supplant much of the need for the MRAI in its longer form. Still the modest interrelationships among some of the subscales demonstrate the value of considering the dimensions as separable facets of racial beliefs, each to be measured with its 10 items in the full MRAI. The longer version also offers researchers the opportunity to concentrate on particular aspects of racial attitudes (e.g., acceptance of blacks in superior roles) rather than measuring racial attitudes in the global manner that the MRAI—SS affords.

Of course, the length of the full MRAI (120–130 items) precludes its easy adaptation to modern use as a measurement device. Also, validation evidence was gathered solely from a version of the instrument that used the word *negroes* rather than *blacks,* and the psychometric consequences of this change are unknown. Some of the items also are outdated (we consider this an old-fashioned measure), and to the extent that the nature of prejudice has changed with time, it is also possible that the specific dimensions of whites' attitudes toward blacks have changed as well, for both whites and blacks (see also Brigham, 1977). Although some racial issues and problems are perennial, many of the racial fault lines between blacks and whites have changed course significantly since the late 1950s and early 1960s, when the MRAI scale development began.

Multifactor Racial Attitudes Inventory (MRAI) (Woodmansee & Cook, 1967)

(Low prejudiced responses are noted in parentheses; item numbers indicate recommended placement in the full questionnaire.)

Integration–Segregation Policy

2. Blacks should be accorded equal rights through integration. (A)
   1. AGREE   0. DISAGREE
19. School officials should not try placing black children and white children in the same schools because of the danger of fights and other problems. (D)
37. We should not integrate schools until blacks raise their standard of living. (D)

45. Integration will result in greater understanding between blacks and whites. (A)
61. Integration of the schools will be beneficial to both white and black children alike. (A)
71. Integration should not be attempted because of the turmoil it causes. (D)
78. Integration is more trouble than it is worth. (D)
86. I feel in sympathy with responsible blacks who are fighting for desegregation. (A)
101. Since segregation has been declared illegal, we should integrate schools. (A)
115. It is a good idea to have separate schools for blacks and whites. (D)

Acceptance in Close Personal Relationships

4. I would accept an invitation to a New Year's Eve party given by a black couple in their home. (A)
24. I would not take a black person to eat with me in a restaurant where I was well known. (D)
27. I would rather not have blacks swim in the same pool as I do. (D)
35. I am willing to have blacks as close personal friends. (A)
51. I would willingly go to a competent black dentist. (A)
63. I would rather not have blacks as dinner guests with most of my white friends. (D)
76. I have no objection to attending the movies or a play in the company of a black couple. (A)
90. If I were invited to be a guest of a mixed black and white group on a weekend pleasure trip, I would probably not go. (D)
104. I would rather not have blacks live in the same apartment building I live in. (D)
105. I would be willing to introduce black visitors to friends and neighbors in my home town. (A)

Black Inferiority

7. I think it is right that the black race should occupy a somewhat lower position socially than the white race. (D)
9. The black and the white man are inherently equal. (A)
34. I believe that the black man is entitled to the same social privileges as the white man. (A)
38. Many blacks should receive a better education than they are now getting, but the emphasis should be on training them for jobs rather than preparing them for college. (D)
50. In fields where they have been given an opportunity to advance, blacks have shown that they are good sports and gentlemen. (A)

74. The fact that blacks are human beings can be recognized without raising them to the social level of whites. (D)

77. The inability of blacks to develop outstanding leaders restricts them to a low place in society. (D)

87. Most blacks really think and feel the same way most whites do. (A)

119. I have as much respect for some blacks as I do for some white persons, but the average black person and I share little in common. (D)

127. I could trust a black person as easily as I could trust a white person if I knew him well enough. (A)

Black Superiority

6. There is nothing to the idea that the black's troubles in the past have built in him a stronger character than the white man has. (D)

23. I think that blacks have a kind of quiet courage which few white people have. (A)

33. Suffering and trouble have made blacks better able to withstand the stresses and strains of modern life than most whites. (A)

36. There is no basis in fact for the idea that blacks withstand misfortune more courageously than do most whites. (D)

62. There is no reason to believe that what blacks have suffered in the past has made them a more noble people than are whites. (D)

64. I think that blacks have a sense of dignity that you see in few white people. (A)

75. There is nothing to the idea that blacks have more sympathy for other minorities than most whites do. (D)

88. In this day of rush and hurry, the black man has met the problems of society in a much calmer manner than the white man. (A)

100. There is no basis in fact for the idea that the black person's misfortunes have made him a more understanding person than the average white. (D)

106. The black person's own experience with unfair treatment has given him a sensitivity and understanding that will make him an excellent supervisor of white people. (A)

Ease in Interracial Contacts

3. I would have no worries about going to a party with an attractive black date. (A)

20. I would probably feel somewhat self-conscious dancing with a black in a public place. (D)

32. I can easily imagine myself falling in love with and marrying a black person. (A)

44. I would feel somewhat uneasy talking about intermarriage with blacks whom I do not know well. (D)

47. I would not mind at all if my only friends were blacks. (A)

57. If I were eating lunch in a restaurant alone with a black person, I would be less self-conscious if the black were of the same sex as I rather than the opposite sex. (D)

89. Before I sponsored a black person for membership in an all-white club, I would think a lot about how this would make the other members feel toward me. (D)

91. If the blacks were of the same social class level as I am, I'd just as soon move into a black neighborhood as a white one. (A)

113. When I see a black person and a white person together as a couple, I'm inclined to be more curious about their relationship than if they were both black or both white. (D)

120. It makes no difference to me whether I'm black or white. (A)

Derogatory Beliefs

13. Blacks sometimes imagine they have been discriminated against on the basis of color even when they have been treated quite fairly. (D)

25. Some blacks are so touchy about getting their rights that it is difficult to get along with them. (D)

40. Although social equality of the races may be the democratic way, a good many blacks are not yet ready to practice the self-control that goes along with it. (D)

43. Many blacks spend money for big cars and television sets instead of spending it for better housing. (D)

59. Even if there were complete equality of opportunity tomorrow, it would still take a long time for blacks to show themselves equal to whites in some areas of life. (D)

72. Even if blacks are given the opportunity for college education it will be several generations before they are ready to take advantage of it. (D)

85. Even though blacks may have some cause for complaint, they would get what they want faster if they were a bit more patient about it. (D)

95. The problem of racial prejudice has been greatly exaggerated by a few black agitators. (D)

125. Although social mixing of the races may be right in principle, it is impractical until blacks learn to accept more "don'ts" in the relations between teenage boys and girls. (D)

129. If I were a black person, I would not want to gain entry into places where I was not really wanted. (D)

Local Autonomy

17. Society has a moral right to insist that a community desegregate even if it doesn't want to. (A)

21. The people of each state should be allowed to decide for or against integration in state matters. (D)

29. Civil rights workers should be supported in their efforts to force acceptance of desegregation. (A)

46. Since we live in a democracy, if we don't want integration it should not be forced upon us. (D)

52. It is not right to ask Americans to accept integration if they honestly don't believe in it. (D)

68. Local communities should have no right to delay the desegregation of their community facilities. (A)

79. It doesn't work to force desegregation on a community before it is ready for it. (D)

80. The federal government should take decisive steps to override the injustice which blacks suffer at the hands of local authorities. (A)

111. People who don't have to live with problems of race relations have no right to dictate to those who do. (D)

118. Race discrimination is not just a local community's problem but one which often demands action from those outside the community. (A)

Private Rights

8. A hotel owner ought to have the right to decide for himself whether he is going to rent rooms to black guests. (D)

11. There should be a strictly enforced law requiring restaurant owners to serve persons regardless of race, creed, or color. (A)

26. A person should not have the right to run a business in this country if it will not serve blacks. (A)

39. Barbers and beauticians have the right to refuse service to anyone they please, even if it means refusing blacks. (D)

49. There should be a law requiring persons who take roomers in their homes to rent to anyone regardless of race, creed, or color. (A)

66. If I were a businessman, I would resent it if I were told that I had to serve blacks. (D)

83. Real estate agents should be required to show homes to black buyers regardless of the desires of home owners. (A)

84. If I were a landlord, I would want to pick my own tenants even if this meant renting only to whites. (D)

99. Desegregation laws often violate the rights of the individual who does not want to associate with blacks. (D)

121. Regardless of his own views, an employer should be required to hire workers without regard to race. (A)

Acceptance in Status-Superior Relationships

14. If I were a teacher, I would not mind at all taking advice from a black principal. (A)

16. In a local community or campus charity drive I would rather not be represented by a black chairman even if he or she were qualified for the job. (D)

41. If I were being interviewed for a job, I would not mind at all being evaluated by a black personnel director. (A)

42. It would be a mistake ever to have blacks for foremen and leaders over whites. (D)

54. Blacks should be given every opportunity to get ahead, but they could never be capable of holding top leadership positions in this country. (D)

56. If a black person is qualified for an executive job, he should get it, even if it means that he will be supervising highly educated white persons. (A)

92. I would rather not serve on the staff of a black congressman. (D)

96. If he were qualified I would be willing to vote for a black person for Congress from my district. (A)

102. I'd be quite willing to consult a black lawyer. (A)

112. If I were working on a community or campus problem with somebody, I would rather it not be a black person. (D)

Gradualism

18. Gradual desegregation is a mistake because it just gives people a chance to cause further delay. (A)

22. It is better to work gradually toward integration than to try to bring it about all at once. (D)

30. Those who advise patience and "slow down" in desegregation are wrong. (A)

31. I favor gradual rather than sudden changes in the social relations between blacks and whites. (D)

53. I feel that moderation will do more for desegregation than the efforts of civil rights workers to force it immediately on people. (D)

70. In the long run desegregation would go more smoothly if we put it into effect immediately. (A)

81. If desegregation is pushed too fast the black people's cause will be hurt rather than helped. (D)

97. Many favor a more moderate policy, but I believe that blacks should be encouraged to picket and sit-in at places where they are not treated fairly. (A)

110. The best way to integrate schools is to do it all at once. (A)

128. School integration should begin with the first few grades rather than all grades at once. (D)

Interracial Marriage

1. The fact that an interracial married couple would be socially outcast, and rejected by both blacks and whites, indicates that such marriages should be avoided. (D)

48. Interracial marriages are quite unlikely to survive serious problems which are overlooked in the excitement of initial infatuation. (D)

58. In order to preserve the best of the culture and heritage of both the white and the black groups, the two races should *not* intermarry. (D)

65. What children of interracial marriages learn about both white and black viewpoints will help to improve relations between the races. (A)

67. The unusually strong love and trust that lead to interracial marriages will make them very rewarding. (A)

94. Neither the color of a person's skin nor the shape of his facial features are of any importance, and they should *not* even be considered in choosing a marriage partner. (A)

108. The bad feelings which are likely to arise between an interracial couple and their parents make such a marriage unwise. (D)

122. Interracial marriage should be discouraged so as to avoid the "who-am-I?" confusion which the children feel. (D)

123. The disapproval and dislike of others is of no importance if an interracial marriage is based on mutual love and respect. (A)

130. Nothing should keep you from marrying someone you love, even though he may be of a different race. (A)

Approaches to Racial Equality

12. Enforcement of laws guaranteeing the right to vote will do more for black people than will voter education programs. (A)

55. Preschool corrective programs which encourage underprivileged children to actively seek knowledge will do more for blacks than will legislation guaranteeing them access to jobs. (D)

73. Legislation to support an influx of better teachers into slum areas helps blacks more than legislation providing equal employment opportunities for people in those same areas. (D)

82. Hard work and patience will do more for the cause of black equality than will demonstrating and picketing. (D)

103. Educating blacks to hold supervisory positions will benefit them more than legislating their right to such positions. (D)

107. Black leaders who press for integration will help black people to achieve social equality sooner than those leaders who encourage blacks to develop characteristics which white men admire. (A)

109. Civil rights legislation has contributed more to the black person's progress than have programs to improve his education. (A)

114. Unless we have laws guaranteeing blacks the opportunity to hold supervisory positions in business, programs directed toward increasing the motivation of black workers will be of little value. (A)

117. Blacks will improve themselves faster by learning a trade rather than by taking jobs the government forces employers to give them. (D)

124. Unless legislation assures blacks equal employment and housing opportunities, better education will mean little. (A)

Black Militance

5. I approve of the Black Power approach to improving conditions for black people. (A)

10. When black demonstrators block city streets the crowd should be broken up and arrested. (D)

15. Violence by blacks is a justifiable reaction to prejudice and discrimination by whites. (A)

28. As long as blacks work peacefully for what they want I will support them, but I will oppose them when they make demands. (D)

60. Black people should not associate with black militants who talk tough since this will only make it harder for them to make real progress. (D)

69. Black Power leaders should be arrested and given stiff sentences for inciting blacks to riot. (D)

93. Black leaders who talk Black Power should get no help from whites. (D)

98. When I look at the way blacks have been treated, I can begin to sympathize with the riots. (A)

116. I admire blacks who march through white neighborhoods demanding desegregation. (A)

126. When blacks boycott a store that doesn't employ them, whites should join in the boycott. (A)

Multifactor Racial Attitudes Inventory—Short Scale (MRAI—SS)

(N. Ard & S. W. Cook, 1977)

Variable

This scale is a shortened version of the Multifactor Racial Attitudes Inventory (MRAI), again designed to measure whites' attitudes toward blacks.

Description

Instead of the multifaceted 12–13 subscales in the long form of the MRAI, the MRAI—SS is a 12-item short form, which provides a single summary measure of white racial attitudes. One item each from 12 of the 10-item subscales (the Black Superiority index, which Woodmansee and Cook did not consider a legitimate attitude measure, is excluded) was selected on a variety of empirical grounds. In addition to fewer items, the MRAI—SS uses a Likert-type response scale rather than a simple agree–disagree format. Scores can range from 0 to 72, with high numbers indicating less prejudicial attitudes.

Samples

Ard and Cook (1977) used six separate samples, totaling 1124 white college students from a western university. Across all respondents the mean was 43.5 (SD = 12.2).

Reliability

Internal Consistency

Ard and Cook reported an average Cronbach's alpha across all six samples of .80. In a sample of 92 residents of a small city in western Massachusetts, Weigel and Howes (1985) reported an alpha of .82 for a slightly modified version of the MRAI—SS. Brigham (1993) reported an alpha of .66 using 260 undergraduates at a mostly white southern university.

Test–Retest

No data were reported.

Validity

Convergent

Ard and Cook (1977) reported correlations between the MRAI—SS and the full form of the MRAI ranging from .86 to .93, averaging $r = .91$. Weigel and Howes (1985) reported a correlation between the Modern Racism Scale (discussed later) and the MRAI—SS of .67. They also found that supporters of Jesse Jackson (the only major black candidate in the 1984 presidential primary election) scored significantly lower on the MRAI—SS than did supporters of Ronald Reagan (the incumbent conservative Republican) (eta = .31). Brigham (1993) reported a significant relationship between the MRAI—SS and a measure of self-reported negative attitude toward blacks ($r = .57$). In the same study Brigham found the MRAI—SS correlated $r = .27$ with respondents' ranking of "Equality" among the 18 Rokeach (1982) terminal values and $r = .47$ with their ranking of "Unprejudiced" among the 19 Rokeach (1982) instrumental values. Finally Brigham (1993) reported a significant correlation ($r = -.24$) between the MRAI—SS and social contact–friendship with blacks.

Discriminant

No relevant data were reported.

Location

Ard, N., & Cook, S. W. (1977). A short scale for the measurement of change in verbal racial attitude. *Educational and Psychological Measurement, 37,* 741–744. Reprinted by permission of Sage Publications, Inc.

Results and Comments

This scale is a modestly sized version of the MRAI that focuses on the overall favorability–unfavorability of attitudes rather than attempting to "cover the waterfront" of racial attitude dimensions. What it loses in connection with the original theorizing of Woodmansee and Cook (1967) and Cook and Selltiz (1964), it gains in terms of feasibility of administration in a variety of contexts, as reflected by many scholars who switched to the MRAI—SS when the longer version proved unwieldy. There is very little subtlety in the items, and respondents are likely to have a clear idea of exactly what is being measured. Whether this affects the validity of the instrument as a measure of racial attitudes as we enter the 21st century has not been clearly established.

Multifactor Racial Attitudes Inventory—Short Scale (MRAI—SS)
(Ard & Cook, 1977)

Here are 12 questions about your opinions on controversial issues. You can state your opinion by checking one (and only one) of the seven answers listed under each question. If your exact position is not given, please choose the answer that comes closest to it. Please answer every question. Now go ahead and work fast.

1. Do you believe that integration (of schools, businesses, residences, etc.) will benefit *both* whites and blacks?

   ____ I agree *strongly* that integration will benefit both whites and blacks.

   ____ I agree *on the whole* that integration will benefit both whites and blacks.

   ____ I agree *slightly* that integration will benefit both whites and blacks.

   ____ I am *undecided* about whether integration will benefit both whites and blacks.

   ____ I disagree *slightly* that integration will benefit both whites and blacks.

   ____ I disagree *on the whole* that integration will benefit both whites and blacks.

   *____ I disagree *strongly* that integration will benefit both whites and blacks.

2. Do you think desegregation should be gradual or should it take place all at once?

   *____ I *strongly* favor gradual rather than an all-at-once desegregation.

   ____ I *moderately* favor gradual rather than an all-at-once desegregation.

   ____ I *slightly* favor gradual rather than an all-at-once desegregation.

   ____ I am *undecided* between gradual and all-at-once desegregation.

   ____ I *slightly* favor all-at-once rather than gradual desegregation.

   ____ I *moderately* favor all-at-once rather than gradual desegregation.

   ____ I *strongly* favor all-at-once rather than gradual desegregation.

3. Who do you think should decide about desegregation: the federal government, or states and local communities?

   ____ I *strongly* favor having the federal government decide about desegregation.

   ____ I *moderately* favor having the federal government decide about desegregation.

   ____ I *slightly* favor having the federal government decide about desegregation.

   ____ I am *undecided* about who should decide about desegregation.

   ____ I *slightly* favor letting states and local communities decide about desegregation.

   ____ I *moderately* favor letting states and local communities decide about desegregation.

   *____ I *strongly* favor letting states and local communities decide about desegregation.

4. Do you believe that a businessman or landlord has a right to choose whom he will deal with, even if this means refusing to deal with blacks?
    *___ I agree *strongly* that the businessman or landlord has this right.
    ___ I agree *moderately* that the businessman or landlord has this right.
    ___ I agree *slightly* that the businessman or landlord has this right.
    ___ I am *undecided* whether the businessman or landlord should have this right.
    ___ I am *slightly* opposed to giving the businessman or landlord the right to refuse to deal with blacks.
    ___ I am *moderately* opposed to giving the businessman or landlord the right to refuse to deal with blacks.
    ___ I am *strongly* opposed to giving the businessman or landlord the right to refuse to deal with blacks.

5. What is your opinion of this statement? "The fact that blacks are human beings can be recognized without raising them to the social level of whites."
    ___ I *strongly* disagree.
    ___ I *moderately* disagree.
    ___ I *slightly* disagree.
    ___ I am *uncertain*.
    ___ I *slightly* agree.
    ___ I *moderately* agree.
    *___ I *strongly* agree.

6. If a black were put in charge of you, how would you feel about taking advice and direction from him?
    *___ I would dislike it *a great deal*.
    ___ I would dislike it *on the whole*.
    ___ I would dislike it *a little*.
    ___ I am *uncertain* whether I would like it or dislike it.
    ___ I wouldn't mind it.
    ___ I would like it.
    ___ I would be very *pleased* about it.

7. If you had a chance to introduce black visitors to your friends and neighbors, how would you feel about it?
    ___ I would be very *pleased* about it.
    ___ I would like it.
    ___ I wouldn't mind it.
    ___ I am *uncertain* whether I would like it or dislike it.
    ___ I would dislike it *a little*.
    ___ I would dislike it *on the whole*.
    *___ I would dislike it *a great deal*.

8. What is your opinion of this statement? "Although social equality of the races may be the democratic way, a good many blacks are not yet ready to practice the self-control that goes with it."
    ___ I *strongly* disagree.
    ___ I disagree *on the whole*.
    ___ I disagree *a little*.
    ___ I am *uncertain* whether I agree or disagree.
    ___ I agree *a little*.
    ___ I agree *on the whole*.
    *___ I *strongly* agree.

9. How would you feel if you were eating with a black of the opposite sex in a public place?
   *____ I would feel *extremely* self-conscious.
   ____ I would feel *quite* self-conscious.
   ____ I would feel *a little* self-conscious.
   ____ I would feel at ease—but *just barely.*
   ____ I am uncertain whether I would feel at ease or self-conscious.
   ____ I would feel at ease *on the whole.*
   ____ I would feel *completely* at ease.

10. Which do you think helps blacks more: Laws preventing discrimination against blacks or programs aimed at improving blacks' ability to compete in our society?
    ____ I would give *much* more emphasis to laws preventing discrimination.
    ____ I would give *somewhat* more emphasis to laws preventing discrimination.
    ____ I would give *slightly* more emphasis to laws preventing discrimination.
    ____ I am undecided.
    ____ I would give *slightly* more emphasis to improving blacks' ability to compete.
    ____ I would give *somewhat* more emphasis to improving blacks' ability to compete.
    *____ I would give *much* more emphasis to improving blacks' ability to compete.

11. How do you feel about interracial marriage?
    *____ I am *strongly* opposed.
    ____ I am *moderately* opposed.
    ____ I am *slightly* opposed.
    ____ I am undecided whether I am in favor or opposed.
    ____ I am *slightly* in favor.
    ____ I am *moderately* in favor.
    ____ I am *strongly* in favor.

12. How do you feel about it when blacks hold mass demonstrations to demand what they want?
    ____ I am *strongly* in favor of such demonstrations.
    ____ I am *moderately* in favor of such demonstrations.
    ____ I am *slightly* in favor of such demonstrations.
    ____ I am *uncertain* whether I favor or oppose such demonstrations.
    ____ I am *slightly* opposed to such demonstrations.
    ____ I am *moderately* opposed to such demonstrations.
    *____ I am *strongly* opposed to such demonstrations.

*Indicates the most racist response (coded 0), with other responses increasing in order to 6.

Racial Attitudes Scale (RAS)

(J. Sidanius, F. Pratto, M. Martin, & L. M. Stallworth, 1991)

Variable

The authors developed their Racial Attitudes Scale in the context of their broader social dominance theory (see the later section on the Social Dominance Orientation Scale). The items appear to tap old-fashioned rather than modern or subtle prejudice, and indeed, Sidanius and his colleagues refer to a subset of the items as a measure of "classical racism" (Sidanius, Pratto, & Bobo, 1996).

Description

Designed as a general measure of racial prejudice, the RAS has considerable diversity in its item content. It incorporates attitudes toward blacks, toward policy issues (affirmative action, busing), and toward target groups other than blacks (Mexicans, foreigners). Some of the items also appear in Sidanius's (1976) Conservatism Scale. This overlap of construct operationalization makes sense, given the authors' theoretical perspective on social dominance as a "drive toward group-based social inequality" that leads to the endorsement of "legitimizing myths," including political ideology and "doctrines of racial or group superiority" (Sidanius *et al.*, 1991, p. 693; see the later section on the Social Dominance Orientation Scale). Scores are based on an average across the 14 items and can range from 1 (low prejudice) to 5 (high prejudice).

Sidanius and his colleagues reported information on the instrument in three forms—using the direct responses to the items, using the residualized responses after various factors were controlled, and using a four-item version of the scale labeled Classical Racism. The residualized form of the instrument is referred to as Consensual Racism, which the authors defined as "that portion of the spectrum of racial attitudes endorsed to the same degree by groups at differing locations in the social hierarchy; the domain in which people from different ethnic groups do not differ" (Sidanius *et al.*, 1991, p. 695). Operationally, Consensual Racism is the index based on the 14 residualized attitude items after gender, ethnicity, grade point average (GPA), and expected course grade are controlled.

Sample

The scale was administered to a random sample of 5655 University of Texas undergraduate and graduate students in 1986.

Reliability

Internal Consistency

Cronbach's alpha based on direct responses to the 14-item index was .89. Little change in reliability occurred when the items were residualized ($\alpha = .88$ for the Consensual Racism index). When these residualized items were factor-analyzed (followed by an oblique rotation), three factors emerged, accounting for 58% of the variance. These were labeled White Dominance (Items 2, 3, 4, 7, 8, 9, 10, and 12), Racial Policy (Items 1 and 11), and Caste-Maintenance Orientation (Items 5, 6, 13, and 14). The items loaded above .47 on their own factor and below .36 on the other factors. Correlations among factors were .15 (1–2), .51 (1–3), and .20 (2–3).

In later work Sidanius *et al.* (1996) reported analyses based on 3861 European Americans in the University of Texas sample, but using a four-item Classical Racism measure. As can be seen in the following instrument, these were four of the items that loaded on the White Dominance factor. Cronbach's alpha on this index was .80, and a confirmatory factor analysis supported a unidimensional solution (item factor loadings ranged from .54 to .74).

Test–Retest

No data were provided.

Validity

Convergent

In terms of known groups, male students had higher racism scores ($M = 2.3$, SD $= 0.7$) than did female students ($M = 2.2$, SD $= 0.6$) on the 14-item (nonresidualized) scale. Ethnicity groupings also revealed that European Americans and Asian Americans were significantly more racist than Hispanic Americans, who, in turn, were more racist than African Americans ($Ms = 2.3, 2.2, 2.0,$ and 1.7, respectively). Citing earlier work suggesting that academic ability is related to racial attitudes (e.g., Ekehammar, Nilsson, & Sidanius, 1987; Knoke & Isaac, 1976), the authors reported significant monotonic negative relationships between racial attitudes and GPA and between racial attitudes and expected course grades.

Consistent with social dominance theory, students preparing for careers in business and law (thus working within the "power sector") scored significantly higher on all three factors of the (residualized) Consensual Racism scale than did those in all other majors–career tracks (social work students scored the lowest). The three scales were also related to a single-item measure of political ideology (very liberal–very conservative); $rs = .31$, $.21$, and $.39$ for the White Dominance, Racial Policy, and Caste-Maintenance factors, respectively. The four-item Classical Racism index was also related to political conservatism ($r = .55$), years of education ($r = -.15$), and a single-item measure of attitudes toward affirmative action ($r = .27$). In a 1993 sample of UCLA undergraduates, a 10-item version of the instrument (with slightly different content) was significantly correlated with a measure of nationalism, rs from .28 to .56 among White, Asian, Latino, and Black student sub-samples (Sidanius, Feshbach, Levin, & Pratto, 1997).

Discriminant

No relevant data were reported.

Location

Sidanius, J., Pratto, F., Martin, M., & Stallworth, L. M. (1991). Consensual racism and career track: Some implications of social dominance theory. *Political Psychology, 12,* 691–721.

Results and Comments

Although it may be appropriate for some purposes, the 14-item Racial Attitudes Scale is problematic in that it is not on its face a "pure" measure of attitudes toward black Americans. It incorporates policy attitudes, antiforeigner sentiment, and views on black representation in university settings along with items tapping antiblack attitudes. The White Dominance index appears more appropriate as a "clean" measure of old-fashioned prejudice, and this presumably explains its use by Sidanius and his colleagues in later work. The measurement approach would also benefit from a stronger connection to the theoretical framework in which the scale was developed (Precisely how should racial attitudes be measured from a social dominance theory perspective? How are racial attitudes to be distinguished from other dominance-relevant constructs?) and from more consistency across research investigations. For example, in Sidanius *et al.* (1996) the operationalization of "classical racism" varies across three reported studies. Under the label "classical racism," Study 2 uses a measure of attributions for black–white socioeconomic differences, and Study 3 uses a hybrid and extension of the measures from the previous two studies (see also Pratto *et al.*'s 1994 measure of antiblack racism). The authors do not compare or discuss the differential measurement issue. Further validation work and refinement of the theoretical construct are clearly needed.

Racial Attitudes Scale (RAS)
(Sidanius, Pratto, Martin, & Stallworth, 1991)

Which of the following objects, statements or events do you have a positive or a negative feeling towards? Circle the number which comes closest to your feelings.

 *1. Affirmative action.
     5 = VERY POSITIVE
     4 = POSITIVE
     3 = UNCERTAIN OR NEUTRAL
     2 = NEGATIVE
     1 = VERY NEGATIVE
 *2. Racial equality. (C)
 *3. A black president of the USA.
 *4. Black neighbors in your neighborhood.
 *5. Foreigners.
  6. Interracial dating should be avoided.
  7. Each ethnic group should stay in its own place. (C)
  8. There are too many black students at the University.
 *9. Increased equality.
 10. White superiority. (C)
 *11. Busing.
 *12. A black supervisor. (C)

*13. Mexican immigrants.

*14. Interracial marriage.

*Indicates reverse scored item.
(C) Indicates items in Sidanius *et al.*'s (1996) Classical Racism Scale.

Attitudes toward Blacks (ATB)

(J. C. Brigham, 1993)

Variable

This scale is designed to measure attitudes toward blacks on a number of different dimensions; it has a companion scale for black respondents entitled Attitudes toward Whites (ATW) (see the next section).

Description

The 20-item ATB scale was designed by Brigham (1993) to represent as wide a sampling of whites' attitudes toward blacks as possible in a medium-sized inventory. The original items were adopted from a variety of sources, including the MRAI and MRAI—SS, the Modern Racism Scale, and various symbolic racism measures; new items were also developed. The items were selected on a variety of empirical and theoretical grounds, ensuring an equal number of positively and negatively coded items and covering a wide range of content in the items themselves.

Although factor analysis suggested four subscales (representing social distance, affective reactions, governmental policy, and worry about reverse discrimination), the first factor carried about three-quarters of the variance, and the interitem correlations suggested that the total scale can be used as an overall measure of the favorability of whites' attitudes toward blacks. Scores on the ATB can range from 20 to 140, with higher numbers representing a more equalitarian or favorable attitude toward blacks.

Samples

Brigham used two samples (total $N = 405$) of white undergraduates from a predominately white southern university. The mean ATB score was 89.7 (SD = 17.3).

Reliability

Internal Consistency

Cronbach's alpha across both samples was .88.

Test–Retest

No information was reported.

Validity

Convergent

The ATB correlated substantially with the MRAI—SS (Ard & Cook, 1977; $r = .86$), the Modern Racism Scale (McConahay *et al.,* 1981; $r = .70$), Kinder and Sears's (1981) index of expressive racism ($r = .45$), and a two-item scale designed by Brigham as a simple self-evaluation of having negative attitudes toward blacks ("Looking at myself as objectively and honestly as I can, I would say I feel more negatively toward blacks in general than I do toward whites in general"; $r = .64$).

The ATB also correlated $r = -.33$ with respondents' rankings of "Equality" among the 18 Rokeach terminal values, $r = -.49$ with their rankings of "Unprejudiced" among the 19 Rokeach instrumental values, and $r = .31$ with a measure of liberal political orientation. Finally, people who scored lower in prejudice on the ATB reported higher levels of interracial contact with blacks in a variety of domains, including childhood friendships, everyday contact, high school friendships, and current close friendships.

Discriminant

Although no direct data were reported on discriminant validity, Brigham (1993) did indicate that the ATB was a better predictor of overall interracial contact ($r = .22$) than were the Modern Racism Scale and Expressive Racism index ($rs = .03$ and $-.03$); the ATB did not, however, outperform the MRAI—SS (r with contact $= .24$). The ATB also correlated more strongly with the two-item self-evaluation criterion described earlier ($r = .64$) than did the MRAI—SS, the Modern Racism Scale, or the Expressive Racism scale (rs from .25 to .57). However, all of the racism scales showed comparable relationships with value rankings and various measures of sociopolitical attitudes.

Location

Brigham, J. C. (1993). College students' racial attitudes. *Journal of Applied Social Psychology, 23,* 1933–1967.

Results and Comments

The ATB represents a balanced scale of attitudes covering a wide range of race-relevant topics, and it is based on the strong theoretical tradition of the MRAI. It has acceptable psychometric properties and is of usable length for most applications (although probably not for telephone surveys). Perhaps because of its recent availability, it has not been widely used; Brigham (1993) is currently the only published article reporting its use. As a result, knowledge about the validity of the instrument rests entirely on the development studies reported in that article, which relied on a college student sample from the South. Brigham (1993) clearly acknowledges the college sample focus, as the title of his article suggests, but whether the scale is equally useful in a broader population remains to be seen. In any case the scale deserves some serious consideration, particularly in studies assessing both black and white respondents' attitudes toward their relevant out-groups; the ATW Scale (reviewed next) provides a companion instrument for black respondents.

Attitudes toward Blacks (ATB)
(Brigham, 1993)

1. If a black were put in charge of me, I would not mind taking advice and direction from him or her.

1	2	3	4	5	6	7
STRONGLY DISAGREE						STRONGLY AGREE

2. If I had a chance to introduce black visitors to my friends and neighbors, I would be pleased to do so.

*3. I would rather not have blacks live in the same apartment building I live in.

*4. I would probably feel somewhat self-conscious dancing with a black in a public place.

5. I would not mind at all if a black family with about the same income and education as me moved in next door.

*6. I think that black people look more similar to each other than white people do.

*7. Interracial marriage should be discouraged to avoid the "who-am-I?" confusion which the children feel.

8. I get very upset when I hear a white make a prejudicial remark about blacks.

9. I favor open housing laws that allow more racial integration of neighborhoods.

10. It would not bother me if my new roommate was black.

*11. It is likely that blacks will bring violence to neighborhoods when they move in.

*12. I enjoy a funny racial joke, even if some people might find it offensive.

13. The federal government should take decisive steps to override the injustices blacks suffer at the hands of local authorities.

14. Black and white people are inherently equal.

*15. Black people are demanding too much too fast in their push for equal rights.

16. Whites should support blacks in their struggle against discrimination and segregation.

*17. Generally, blacks are not as smart as whites.

*18. I worry that in the next few years I may be denied my application for a job or a promotion because of preferential treatment given to minority group members.

19. Racial integration (of schools, businesses, residences, etc.) has benefitted both whites and blacks.

*20. Some blacks are so touchy about race that it is difficult to get along with them.

*Indicates reverse scored item.

Attitudes toward Whites (ATW)

(J. C. Brigham, 1993)

Variable

This scale was designed to measure attitudes of blacks toward whites; it was created as a companion measure for the Attitudes toward Blacks Scale (ATB) just reviewed.

Description

The 20-item ATW Scale was developed as a part of Brigham's research program on the structure of racial attitudes of both blacks and whites (e.g., Brigham, 1977). Similar to the ATB Scale, Brigham designed the ATW Scale not only to represent a wide sampling of the content domains that make up blacks' attitudes toward whites, but also to produce a single overall attitude score. The items were developed at the same time as the ATB items, and most are very similar or analogous to those in the ATB Scale. The original sources for the ATB and the ATW include the MRAI and the MRAI—SS, the Modern Racism Scale, and the measure of Expressive Racism used by Kinder and Sears (1981). From an initial sample of 112 items (51 of which were identical to the ATB development pool and another 32 of which were identical except that "white" was substituted for "black" in the item text), 20 items were selected for the final scale on both empirical and theoretical grounds. Fourteen of the items are negatively worded on this index (versus 10 on the ATB measure).

When factor-analyzed, the instrument produced six subscales (social interaction between whites and blacks, integration policy, reactions to interracial couples, two social distance factors, and one unlabeled factor), with the first factor accounting for 41% of the variance. As with the ATB Scale, Brigham (1993) recommended the use of a total ATW Scale score, which can range from 20 to 140 (with higher numbers indicating more favorable, optimistic attitudes toward whites).

Sample

Brigham (1993) sampled 81 black undergraduates from a predominantly black southern university. The average ATW score was 79.1 (SD = 13.8). Comparing Brigham's two samples, blacks were less favorable toward whites than whites were toward blacks.

Reliability

Internal Consistency

Cronbach's alpha was .75; this value was significantly larger than that for a version of the MRAI that Brigham had adapted for use with black respondents ($\alpha = .46$). In general, coherence among items for blacks was less than that for whites, replicating an earlier finding (Brigham, 1977).

Test–Retest

No information was provided.

Validity

Convergent

The ATW was correlated with a variety of other racial attitude measures: $r = .53$ with a version of the MRAI adapted for blacks (Brigham, 1977), $r = .84$ with a measure of negative affect and desire for social distance, and $r = .56$ with a two-item scale measuring direct self-evaluation of attitudes toward whites (see Brigham, 1993, and the ATB Scale just reviewed). The ATW Scale was also correlated with Democratic political party preference ($r = .41$) and with a four-item measure of preference for Jesse Jackson in the 1988 presidential race ($r = .26$), but not with self-designation as a conservative or liberal ($r = .08$). Respondents who reported more positive attitudes toward whites on the ATW also reported higher levels of interracial contact with whites as childhood friends, in everyday contact situations, and as current close friends.

Discriminant

No data were reported.

Location

Brigham, J. C. (1993). College students' racial attitudes. *Journal of Applied Social Psychology, 23,* 1933–1967.

Results and Comments

Like the ATB, the ATW Scale covers a wide range of attitude topics, in roughly balanced format, using a moderate number of items with acceptable psychometric properties. Also like the ATB, the only published use of the ATW Scale is in Brigham (1993)—in a study that relied on a single small sample of black college students at a historically black institution. However, given its connection to the MRAI framework, along with the lack of other compelling and well-developed measures of blacks' attitudes toward whites, we feel the scale deserves consideration in any study that samples black respondents. Additional research is needed to address the lower internal consistency of blacks' attitudes relative to whites' and to explore the relationships between the ATW Scale and other constructs relevant to black Americans' thinking about race (e.g., racial identity, hostility toward and mistrust of whites, alienation, beliefs about discrimination; see Kinder & Sanders, 1996; Schuman & Hatchett, 1974; Schuman *et al.,* 1985).

Attitudes toward Whites (ATW)
(Brigham, 1993)

*1. Most whites feel that blacks are getting too demanding in their push for equal rights.

1	2	3	4	5	6	7
STRONGLY DISAGREE					STRONGLY AGREE	

*2. I feel that black people's troubles in the past have built in them a stronger character than white people have.

*3. Most whites can't be trusted to deal honestly with blacks.

*4. Over the past few years, blacks have gotten more economically than they deserve.

*5. Most whites can't understand what it's like to be black.

*6. Some whites are so touchy about race that it is difficult to get along with them.

*7. I would rather not have whites live in the same apartment building I live in.

8. I would accept an invitation to a New Year's Eve party given by a white couple in their home.

9. It would not bother me if my new roommate was white.

10. Racial integration (of schools, business, residences, etc.) has benefitted both whites and blacks.

*11. It's not right to ask Americans to accept integration if they honestly don't believe in it.

12. I favor open housing laws that allow more racial integration of neighborhoods.

*13. Most whites fear that blacks will bring violence to neighborhoods when they move in.

*14. By and large, I think that blacks are better athletes than whites.

*15. Local city officials often pay less attention to a request or complaint from a black person than from a white person.

*16. When I see an interracial couple I feel that they are making a mistake in dating each other.

*17. I have as much respect for whites as I do for some blacks, but the average white person and I share little in common.

*18. I think that white people look more similar to each other than black people do.

19. Whites should support blacks in their struggle against discrimination and segregation.

20. If a white were put in charge of me, I would not mind taking advice and direction from him or her.

*Indicates reverse scored item.

Social Distance Scale

(E. S. Bogardus, 1928, 1933, 1959)

Variable

The Social Distance Scale, originated by Bogardus in a series of studies (Bogardus, 1928, 1933, 1959), is designed to measure the extent to which people wish to maintain social distance and avoid increasing levels of intimate contact between themselves and members of different social, racial, ethnic, or national groups. Some have conceptualized the scale as a measure of the behavioral component of racial–ethnic attitudes (Triandis, 1964), but it incorporates a strong affective component as well.

Description

Respondents are typically given a list of social–racial–ethnic–national groups and are asked whether they would be willing, for example, to admit members of the group to their country as visitors (farthest social distance), as citizens, into employment in their occupation, into residence in their neighborhood, and into close kinship by marriage (closest social distance). The original social distance instrument was designed as a unidimensional Guttman-type scale, with each increasing level of intimacy (less social distance) entailing all of the lesser intimacies. Most uses of social distance scales follow this approach; social distance serves as a convenient metric for racial antipathy and ethnic tension.

Several different scoring methods have been used. Bogardus (1933) suggested taking the highest number of the items checked as a score. Other researchers (e.g., Brewer, 1968) added up the total number of "No" responses, and still others weighted the "No" responses according to their step values (1–7). Social distance measures have been extremely popular, and the *Social Science Citation Index* lists hundreds of citations each year to the Bogardus articles, chapters, and books that describe the measures (e.g., Bogardus, 1925, 1928, 1928/1947, 1933, 1959). Despite this popularity it is rare to find two researchers who use the same version of the instrument. Virtually all of the studies described below have incorporated some minor modifications to the scale, while retaining its essential character.

Samples

Bogardus (1925) described a sample of 110 "mature persons of experience, being of two groups, either young business men, or public school teachers" (p. 299). Bogardus (1928/1947) collected data from a sample of 1725 adults who were mostly of Northern European descent and were described as native born and younger middle class, with a high school or college education. In the latter sample Bogardus (1928) reported a median Social Distance score of 5.0 (would admit to my country) for "Negroes," "German Jews," and "Filipinos." By comparison "English," "Americans (native white)," and "Canadians" all enjoyed a median social distance of 1.0 (would admit to close kinship by marriage). Several authors have reported strong temporal trends for social distance in American samples; reported distance toward a variety of groups has significantly decreased over the decades (see Bogardus, 1959; Crull & Bruton, 1979; Payne, York, & Fagan, 1974).

Reliability

Internal Consistency

Because of the early development of the Social Distance Scale (pre-Cronbach), the first papers report little or no reliability information. Many later studies found good reliability; for example, Mielenz (1979) reported four separate Cronbach alphas greater than .90, Kleg and Yamamoto (1995) reported an alpha of .97, and Stangor, Sullivan, and Ford

(1991) reported an average alpha across four groups of .89. In Osei-Kwame and Achola (1981) alpha was .94, and the split-half reliability across 10 groups was .91; Brewer (1968) reported a split-half reliability of .99 across 30 East African tribes.

Reliability can also be reported in terms of the Guttman reproducibility index, which measures the proportion of responses that comply with the presumed ordering of items. Brewer (1968) found reproducibility coefficients across 30 tribes ranging from .91 to .99, and Osei-Kwame and Achola (1981) reported a reproducibility value of .94.

Test–Retest

We found no data on this issue.

Validity

There is no shortage of studies establishing the validity of the Social Distance Scale. We review here only a small sample of these findings, across a wide variety of content areas.

Convergent

Bogardus (1928, 1959) described a wide range of validity data, including the finding that respondents' perceived similarity to members of the target group was highly negatively correlated with Social Distance scores toward that group. Brinkerhoff and Mackie (1986) found that scores on the Social Distance Scale were lowest for people who shared similar religious beliefs with the target group and increased as religious beliefs diverged. Cox, Smith, and Insko (1996) also found that experimental manipulations of belief similarity led to lower scores on the Social Distance Scale.

To test a model of African social and political integration, Osei-Kwame and Achola (1981) measured social distance in a stratified random sample of adult members of 11 ethnic groups in Kumasi City, Ghana. They found negative correlations between preference for social distance from the other ethnic groups and willingness to join an ethnically based political party and to vote for candidates based on ethnicity.

In terms of known groups, Johnson (1977) found that highly religious Christians from churches that teach racial tolerance scored lower in social distance toward Blacks, Latin Americans, and Jews than did individuals with low religious commitment. Similarly Verma and Upadhyay (1984) found that greater commitment to religious beliefs promoting tolerance was negatively correlated with Social Distance scores toward various religious and ethnic out-groups.

Under certain conditions experience with racial and ethnic groups can lead to lower prejudice. Accordingly, greater social contact with particular groups has been associated with lower Social Distance scores for white academics working with "colored" colleagues in South Africa (Spangenberg & Nel, 1983), for white and black students in Hawaii and Durban, South Africa (Kinloch, 1974), for North American students studying for a year in Brazil (Vornberg & Grant, 1976), and for children interacting with disabled people (Hazzard, 1983). Interventions designed to create favorable conditions for intergroup contact have also lowered Social Distance scores between blacks and whites in South Africa (Taylor, Fourie, & Koorts, 1995) and have decreased "average" students' social distance ratings of severely handicapped students (Fenrick & Petersen, 1984). In one study, however, when close contact with a group led to perceived competitive threat, higher Social Distance Scale scores resulted (Rofe & Weller, 1981).

In a related vein a study on the effects of a change in church policy that permitted
black members full status in the Mormon Church demonstrated that social distance
ratings of American blacks by Mormons decreased following the policy reversal, a
change that was sustained and amplified over time (Kunz, 1979; Kunz & Oheneba-
Sakyi, 1989).

Divergent

Social Distance Scale scores have been found to correlate highly with measures of affect
(e.g., feeling thermometer ratings), but not well with measures of group stereotypes
(Stangor *et al.*, 1991). This suggests that the instrument measures general group liking and
acceptance rather than group beliefs or cognitive representations.

Location

Bogardus, E. S. (1928). *Immigration and race attitudes.* Boston: Heath. Copyright © 1928
by Houghton Mifflin Company. Title reprinted in 1971 by J. S. Ozer Publishers, New
York.
    Bogardus, E. S. (1933). A social distance scale. *Sociology and Social Research, 17,*
265–271.
    Bogardus, E. S. (1959). *Social distance.* Yellow Springs, OH: Antioch Press.

Results and Comments

The Social Distance Scale is among the most adaptable, user-friendly, and useful instruments for measuring out-group attitudes; because it has timeless appeal, we view it as a
modern measure of prejudice. The scale has been remarkably successful in generating research questions and data, and to further demonstrate this point, a few examples of interesting research applications of social distance measures are described below.
    In his classic study of prejudice and personality, Hartley (1946) used Social Distance
scores toward a variety of groups as a general individual difference measure of prejudice
or intolerance. He demonstrated that preference for a high amount of social distance from
any one out-group was strongly positively correlated with preference for distance with
virtually any other out-group.
    Several studies have used social distance measures to ascertain general changes in
prejudice over time (e.g., Crull & Bruton, 1979, 1985; Kleg & Yamamoto, 1995; Owen,
Eisner, & McFaul, 1981; Payne *et al.*, 1974). Most studies indicate that Americans have
reported less preferred social distance toward various groups as the decades have passed,
although the *relative* preference for distance among groups rated has remained remarkably
stable, ranging from about .75 to .99 and averaging about .85 across several studies. For
example, Crull and Bruton (1985) found a correlation of .92 between the social distance
ratings of groups by sociology students in 1984 and ratings of the same groups by public
school teachers and young business men in 1925. Kleg and Yamamoto (1995) found a correlation of .87 between the group social distance ratings made by the 1925 sample of businessmen and teachers (Bogardus, 1928) and comparable ratings by a 1993 sample of
Colorado middle school teachers.
    Others have used the Social Distance Scale to compare the relative acceptability
of fairly disparate groups. For example, Eisenman (1986) compared prejudice against a
person in a wheelchair with antiblack prejudice and found that rejection of blacks exceeded rejection of the physically handicapped. Pearlin and Rosenberg (1962) measured

nurse–patient social distance in a mental hospital in order to study status hierarchy and institutional structural relations.

Many other applications of the Social Distance Scale appear in the literature, and as already indicated, each of these studies seems to introduce a slightly different version of the instrument. Two goals compete when deciding whether to adapt a scale to a specific researcher's purposes: (1) the desire to compare current results with past research and (2) the desire to measure one's constructs as well and specifically as possible. In general, researchers have placed a higher value on the latter point; the *concept* of social distance has been more accepted than its specific operationalization. This precludes the possibility of direct comparison across data sets, but the need to incorporate modern and familiar language, as well as items that tap particular needs, may (appropriately) outweigh the goal of cross-study comparison (for more discussion of this issue, see Crandall, Preisler, and Aussprung, 1992).

A final issue regarding social distance is whether the construct should be considered unidimensional. Triandis and his colleagues have developed their own versions of the measure (e.g., Triandis, 1964; Triandis & Triandis, 1965), and based on findings involving a variety of item content, Triandis (1971) proposed five components of social distance: Respect (for ideas, admiration), Marital Acceptance (willingness to exogamate), Friendship Acceptance (willingness to socialize), Social Distance (social exclusion), and Superordination (appropriateness of supervision and command). Although this conceptualization maps onto other models of racial attitudes, in practice most researchers have preferred to consider social distance in its unidimensional form; very few have adapted five-dimensional scales to their research programs.

Several good reviews of the concept of social distance and the Social Distance Scale are available (e.g., Campbell, 1953; Crull & Bruton, 1979; Miller, 1977; Owen *et al.*, 1981; Triandis & Triandis, 1965). Also, of the many versions of the Social Distance Scale that have been used, two have considerable validation evidence associated with them. These variations on social distance measurement are described in detail following the original instrument (Byrnes & Kiger, 1988; Crandall, 1991).

Social Distance Scale
(Bogardus, 1928)

Remember to give your first feeling reactions in every case.

Give your reactions to each race as a group. Do not give your reactions to the best or the worst members that you have known.

Put an X below each group in as many of the rows as your feelings dictate.

Category	Blacks	Chinese	etc.
7. Would exclude from my country	——	——	
6. Would admit as visitors only to my country	——	——	
5. Would admit to citizenship in my country	——	——	
4. Would admit to employment in my occupation	——	——	
3. Would admit to my street as neighbors	——	——	
2. Would admit to my club as personal chums	——	——	
1. Would admit to close kinship by marriage	——	——	

Social Distance Scale Variation 1: Social Scale

(D. Byrnes & G. Kiger, 1988)

Variable

This is an adaptation of Bogardus's (1933) social distance measure, designed to measure willingness to interact with and accept blacks in various social roles.

Description

The Social Scale asks participants to rate how comfortable they feel in various contacts and relationships with blacks. A principal-components factor analysis of the eight items in the scale yielded a two-factor solution: Six Nonintimacy items loaded above .70 on one factor, and two Partner items loaded above .75 on a second factor; loadings on the opposite factor ranged from .09 to .45. Despite this factor solution, the authors seem to advocate use of a total scale score, which can range from 8 (low comfort) to 56 (high comfort).

Sample

The scale was developed using a sample of 286 college students (including a "large percentage" of Mormons) in the Rocky Mountain region. The sample mean was 43.6 (SD = 10.6).

Reliability

Internal Consistency

The alpha coefficient was .90 for the Nonintimacy subscale, .75 for the Partner subscale, and .90 for the total scale. The two subscales were correlated ($r = .57$).

Test–Retest

In a subsample of 30 respondents, a three-week follow-up produced a test–retest r of .94.

Validity

Convergent

The Social Scale was correlated with the Modern Racism Scale (McConahay *et al.*, 1981): $r = .48$. In terms of known groups, Neville and Furlong (1994) found that black undergraduates scored significantly higher (more comfortable) on a slightly modified version of the instrument than did Asian undergraduates, though not significantly higher than white undergraduates.

Discriminant

No relevant data were reported.

Location

Byrnes, D., & Kiger, G. (1988). Contemporary measures of attitudes toward blacks. *Educational and Psychological Measurements, 48,* 107–119. Reprinted by permission of Sage Publications, Inc.

Results and Comments

In its similarity to Bogardus's social distance instrument, the Social Scale draws on a classic and strong tradition of prejudice research. The change in language from "would admit" to "would be comfortable" seems appropriate for modern usage. However, some obvious domains of intergroup contact and relationships are surprisingly lacking from the instrument (e.g., work and school settings), and it is troubling for scale validity that the study by Neville and Furlong (1994) found no reliable difference in the scale scores of black and white undergraduates. The scale also appears to have a two-factor solution, but whether there is any reason to treat the index as two subscales has not been adequately addressed.

Social Scale
(Byrnes & Kiger, 1988)

I believe I would be happy to have a black person:

1. as governor of my state

1	2	3	4	5	6	7
VERY UNCOMFORTABLE					VERY COMFORTABLE	

2. as president of the U.S.
3. as my personal physician
4. rent my home from me
5. as my spiritual counselor
6. as my roommate
7. as someone I would date
8. as a dance partner

Items 1–6 are Nonintimacy items; Items 7 and 8 are Partner items.

Social Distance Scale Variation 2: Social Distance Questionnaire
(C. S. Crandall, 1991)

Variable

This adaptation of Bogardus's (1928/1947) Social Distance Scale is designed to measure social rejection and willingness to interact with an *individual member* of a social group (i.e., stigmatization).

Description

Like other social distance scales, this seven-item instrument was based on one of the Bogardus versions (Bogardus, 1928/1947). This scale differs from others in that the items are answered on seven-point Likert-type agree–disagree scales rather than in a yes–no or comfortable–uncomfortable format. Furthermore the scale is designed for use in measuring preferred distance from an *individual representative* of a group; this individual is typically described to the respondent in a written vignette. Most of the validation work has involved reactions to individuals with medical stigmas rather than to members of racial and ethnic groups; nonetheless, the instrument is designed for ready adaptation to any target population. Only one item in the scale is reverse scored; scores are averaged and can range from 1 (high distance) to 7 (low distance).

Sample

The scale was first developed using a sample of 393 students from the University of Florida, who responded to target individuals with varying medical problems (e.g., hepatitis, herpes, cancer, AIDS). The mean across targets (medical conditions) was 3.9 (SD = 1.2). In a separate sample of 240 Florida undergraduates, Crandall and Moriarty (1995) reported a mean of 2.5 for ratings of a "typical" male (i.e., with no discernible stigmatizing features).

Reliability

Internal Consistency

Crandall and Moriarty (1995) described a factor analysis with a single-factor solution and a reliability of .82; Crandall, Glor, and Britt (1997) reported several alphas, ranging from .84 to .98 and averaging .88. In Biernat, Vescio, and Theno's (1996) study of social distance to a black or white target individual, alpha was .89.

Test–Retest

No information was reported.

Validity

Convergent

In a validity study reported in Crandall *et al.* (1997), 10 students were asked to rate their "best friend," and 10 other students were asked to rate their "worst enemy" on the Social Distance Questionnaire. Friends averaged a rating of 1.4, and worst enemies averaged 6.5. These authors also demonstrated that reducing the contagiousness and severity of a stigmatizing illness led to decreased preferred distance from a person with that illness. Similarly, in a two-predictor analysis, Crandall and Moriarty (1995) found that the Social Distance Questionnaire correlated with perceptions of disease severity and contagiousness ($pr = .47$) and with the degree to which the target person was viewed as individually responsible for the illness ($pr = .61$).

In an experimental study focusing on race, Biernat *et al.* (1996) found that white college student participants preferred greater distance from a fictitious black male than from a comparable white male, particularly when Protestant work ethic values had been "primed" earlier in the session. Participants also viewed "hardworking" blacks and whites more favorably (with less preferred distance) than "lazy" blacks and whites.

Location

Crandall, C. S. (1991). Multiple stigma and AIDS: Medical stigma and attitudes toward homosexuals and IV-drug users in AIDS-related stigmatization. *Journal of Community and Applied Social Psychology, 1,* 165–172. Copyright John Wiley & Sons Limited. Reproduced with permission.

Results and Comments

This scale has been used to measure preferred distance from individual members of social groups; rather than responding to a group stereotype, as in Bogardus (1933), respondents are asked to read a vignette and to respond directly to the target person in that vignette. Crandall (1991) conceptualized this measure as an indicator of "stigmatization." The assumption is that preferred distance to an individual group member is a reflection of distance felt toward the group as a whole. By "fleshing out" an individual, however, respondents may feel more at ease about expressing discomfort or dislike (one can more justifiably reject a person than an entire group), and the researcher can be certain that participants are responding to precisely the *same* attitude object (rather than idiosyncratic group representations). The relationship between distance toward individual group members and that toward groups as a whole should be examined.

The main utility of this instrument is in experimental work, where information about social group members can be manipulated in a variety of ways. This measure could also be used in survey studies that implement experiments, such as those using computer-assisted telephone interviewing (CATI). The presence of only one reverse scored item is potentially problematic, although *no* items are reverse scored in the typical Guttman-type social distance scale.

Social Distance Questionnaire (Crandall, 1991)

1. This appears to be a likeable person.

1	2	3	4	5	6	7
STRONGLY DISAGREE						STRONGLY AGREE

2. I would like this person to be a close personal friend.
3. I would like this person to move into my neighborhood.
4. I would like this person to come and work at the same place I do.
5. This is a person who is similar to me.
6. I would like to have this person marry into my family.
*7. This is the kind of person that I tend to avoid.

    *Indicates reverse scored item.

Modern Racism Scale (MRS)

(J. B. McConahay, B. B. Hardee, & V. Batts, 1981)

Variable

McConahay and his colleagues sought to develop a nonreactive measure of racism that tapped their theoretical construct of symbolic or modern racism, in contrast to old-fashioned racism.

Description

McConahay initially used the term *symbolic racism* to describe this construct, but around 1978 switched to the *modern racism* label. He advocated this change to emphasize "the contemporary . . . nature of the tenets constituting the new ideology" and to reflect "that both the new racism and old-fashioned racism are symbolic in the sense that both are group-level abstractions rooted in early racial socialization and not in personal experience" (McConahay, 1986, p. 96).

In their early writing about this concept, McConahay and Hough (1976) defined modern racism as "the expression in terms of abstract ideological symbols and symbolic behaviors of the feeling that blacks are violating cherished values and making illegitimate demands for changes in the racial status quo" (p. 38). The modern racist believes that discrimination against blacks no longer exists, that blacks are "pushing too hard, too fast, and into places where they are not wanted" and that blacks' demands are unfair and therefore their societal gains undeserved (see McConahay, 1986, p. 93). Furthermore the modern racist does not see himself or herself as racist, but instead defines racism in old-fashioned terms (e.g., as endorsement of negative stereotypes of blacks, support for segregation, and advocacy and practice of obvious and open discriminatory action).

These tenets of modern racism are clearly reflected in the seven items that comprise the measurement index. In early research the item response options ranged from -2 *(Disagree Strongly)* to $+2$ *(Agree Strongly)*, and responses were summed and a value of 14 added so that scores could range from 0–28 (e.g., McConahay *et al.*, 1981). However, many researchers now use a 0–4 or 1–5 response range format. Although we present the set of items that has been used to measure modern racism since about 1981, much of the reported information regarding the reliability and the validity of the instrument is based on slightly different versions of the scale (e.g., with various questions added or dropped from this final set). In reporting this information we describe when and in what manner variations in the content of the items were implemented (for a list of the various ways in which the symbolic racism construct has been operationalized, see Bobo, 1983; Kinder, 1986; McClendon, 1985; Sears, 1988; Sears *et al.*, 1997; Sniderman & Tetlock, 1986a).

Samples

A number of samples were used in the development and refinement of the Modern Racism Scale. For example, McConahay *et al.* (1981, Study 1) reported data from 10 white Duke University undergraduates tested in front of a white experimenter [$M = 7.8$ (possible range = 0–24), SD = 4.9], McConahay (1983) sampled 81 white Duke University students [$M = 8.3$ (possible range = 0–28), SD = 5.6], and McConahay (1982) reported findings from a random sample of 879 Louisville, Kentucky, residents who were interviewed in 1976, at the height of the busing controversy [$M = 18.1$ (possible range = 6–28), SD = 5.5].

Reliability

Internal Consistency

Summarizing a series of studies using college student samples, McConahay (1986) reported reliabilities ranging from .81 to .86 [e.g., $\alpha = .86$ in McConahay's (1983) study of 81 white Duke University undergraduates].

McConahay and Hough (1976) reported a coefficient alpha of .51 in their study of 160 white Protestant seminary students in southern California, using a four-item measure of modern racism. This scale included Items 2 and 6 of the current index (with the word *Negroes* substituted for *Blacks*) and two items no longer used ("Whites should support Negroes in their struggle against discrimination and segregation" and "Negroes have it better than they ever had it before"). Scale reliability was .75 in McConahay's (1982) survey of Louisville residents. This study used a six-item measure of modern racism (Items 1, 2, 4, and 6 of the current scale plus two additional questions: "How many black people in Louisville and Jefferson County do you think miss out on good housing because white owners won't rent or sell to them?" and "How many black people in Louisville and Jefferson County do you think miss out on jobs or promotions because of racial discrimination?"). In general, McConahay (1986) reported that reliabilities for earlier versions of the scale, using various Louisville samples, ranged from .75 to .79.

Test–Retest

In McConahay *et al.'s* (1981) study of 34 white male undergraduates, the test–retest reliability (over a six-week interval) was .93 when the researcher administering the Time 2 questionnaire was white and .87 when the researcher was black (this study used an eight-item version of the scale; the item "The streets are not safe these days without a policeman around" was also included). McConahay (1986) indicated that test–retest reliabilities have ranged from .72 to .93 across a number of samples.

Validity

Convergent

Although much research (described subsequently) has been geared toward demonstrating the distinction between modern and old-fashioned varieties of racism, the MRS *is* correlated with (face valid) old-fashioned racism indexes. In McConahay's (1982) study of Louisville residents, old-fashioned and modern racism were correlated at .58, and McConahay (1986) reported that in various undergraduate samples the comparable correlation has ranged from .35 to .66 (see also Dunbar, 1995). However, in McConahay and Hough's (1973) study of white Protestant seminary students, the MRS and old-fashioned items were uncorrelated (no specific *r* reported). McConahay (1986) suggested that this lack of correlation may have been due to high levels of missing data on the old-fashioned items; when mean scores were substituted for missing values, this correlation was .23.

Convergent validity has also been demonstrated by the following:

1. Reported correlations between the MRS and other measures of racial attitudes: $r = -.30$ with Schuman and Harding's (1963) Sympathetic Identification with the Underdog Scale, $r = .38$ with an antiblack feeling thermometer measure in Louisville samples, and $r = .44$ with the feeling thermometer in college samples (see also Glover, 1994; Monteith, 1996).

2. Correlations with a variety of political, social, and value-relevant scales and questions (to support various aspects of the definition of modern–symbolic racism): $r = .41$ with a measure of conventional religious beliefs (unpublished scale), $r = .32$ with Allport and Ross's (1967) intrinsic religiosity scale, and $r = .36$ with Republican Party identification in McConahay and Hough's (1973) study of seminarians (using a four-item version of the MRS). In a 1969 study of 162 Claremont, California, voters, a two-item measure of modern racism was correlated .47 with a measure of patriotism, .40 with "preference for the old ways of teaching," .37 with preference for a high school dress code, .33 with conventional religious beliefs, and .32 with opposition to sex education.

Among white undergraduates the MRS was also correlated with perceptions that blacks (relative to whites) violate important values ($r = .18$, controlling for conservative political beliefs; Biernat et al., 1996), and with both Protestant work ethic (PWE) and egalitarian (EG) values (measured using the Katz and Hass, 1988, scales; rs from .24 to .32 for PWE values and from $-.45$ to $-.49$ for EG values in Biernat, Vescio, Theno, & Crandall, 1996; see also Glover, 1994). Pratto et al. (1994) also reported a correlation of .53 between the MRS and their Social Dominance Orientation Scale (described later); the MRS also correlated .42 with Gough's (1951) MMPI—PR (Prejudice) scale (see Dunbar, 1995) in a sample of white UCLA undergraduates.

3. Correlations with attitudes toward various racial policy issues: The MRS correlated $r = .51$ in 1976 and $r = .39$ in 1977 with opposition to busing in two samples of Louisville residents—correlations that remained significant after controlling for a variety of demographic, attitudinal, and self-interest factors (e.g., being a parent of a school-aged child, having a child in public school, having a child directly affected by busing, education, occupation, income, union membership, region of socialization, gender, authoritarianism, political efficacy, and conservatism; see McConahay, 1982). The MRS was a stronger predictor of busing opposition than was an old-fashioned racism scale ($r = .36$; McConahay, 1982; see also Bobo, 1983; McClendon, 1985; Sears & Allen, 1984). Nosworthy, Lea, and Lindsay (1995) reported that a six-item version of the MRS was significantly correlated with negative attitudes toward various forms of affirmative action programs among Canadian undergraduates (rs from $-.26$ to $-.45$) and with perceptions that affirmative action programs that earmark college scholarships for black, but not white, students are less fair and have negative consequences for self and group (rs from $-.39$ to $-.49$; see also Kluegel & Smith, 1983). In a sample of white University of Michigan undergraduates, the MRS was modestly related to indexes of racial policy attitudes and views on welfare, and these relationships increased after exposure to a 1988 news story on the "Willie Horton" case (Mendelberg, 1997).

4. Correlations with negative attitudes toward other minority and/or stigmatized groups: For example, Glick and Fiske (1995) reported correlations of .44 and .47 between the MRS and their measure of "hostile sexism" for male and female undergraduates, respectively. Fiske and Von Hendy (1992) similarly reported a correlation of .39 with the Attitudes toward Women Scale (Spence & Helmreich, 1972). Crandall (1994) found that the MRS correlated .23 with a measure of antifat attitudes, and Dunbar (1995) reported a correlation of .44 with Selznick and Sternberg's (1969) Anti-Semitism Scale (all among undergraduate samples).

5. Differences and similarities between high and low prejudiced individuals in Devine's (1989) influential work: Devine reported that high and low MRS individuals have comparable *knowledge* regarding the negative cultural stereotypes of blacks and the negative labels associated with blacks as a group and that these negative constructs are "automatically" activated by race-relevant cues for both groups. However, when asked their thoughts about blacks in a manner that prompts "controlled" processing, low MRS

individuals produce fewer pejorative *beliefs* than do high MRS individuals (high and low levels are established using a median split in various white undergraduate samples; see also Devine & Elliot, 1995). Devine *et al.* (1991) have further demonstrated that MRS scores are associated with personal standards ("should" scores) regarding how one should react in interracial situations (e.g., a black person sits next to you on the bus, a black couple moves in next door) and with actual response ("would" reactions) in these same situations. High MRS individuals report more prejudiced "should" and "would" reactions than do low MRS individuals (see also Zuwerink, Devine, Monteith, & Cook, 1996). Furthermore, low relative to high MRS individuals tend to report more discomfort and compunction when thinking about their "should–would" discrepancies (Zuwerink *et al.,* 1996).

6. Predictive studies: McConahay and Hough (1976) reported that a two-item measure of the MRS (Items 2 and 6) predicted Californians' tendencies to vote for a white Los Angeles mayoral candidate (Republican Sam Yorty) over a black candidate (Democrat Tom Bradley) in the 1969 election ($r = .39$; after controls for party identification, $pr = .32$). The authors concluded that "Yorty was victorious in 1969 because political conservatism *and* symbolic racism yielded votes in his favor; political conservatism by itself would not have been sufficient to give him the victory" (p. 26). Using a somewhat different measure of racism (labeled Expressive Racism) that incorporated several MRS items, Kinder and Sears (1981) also predicted the Yorty–Bradley voting preference in both 1969 and 1973 ($rs = .37$ and $.34$, respectively). This racism–vote relationship remained significant after controlling for party identification and for a variety of indicators of "racial threat" ($prs = .31$ and $.30$; see also Sears & Kinder, 1971).

McConahay (1983) also argued that because high modern racists are ambivalent in their racial attitudes, they should "show the greatest inconsistency of behavior between contexts fostering negative and positive behavior" (p. 552; for discussion of ambivalence, see Gaertner & Dovidio, 1986; Katz, 1981; Katz, Wackenhut, & Hass, 1986). In an experimental study involving Duke University undergraduates, participants evaluated the resume of an "average" black or white job applicant in either a positive context (the target candidate was evaluated *after* two superior white candidates, making race a highly salient issue in the black condition) or a negative context (the target candidate was evaluated first). When the applicant was white, the MRS, the context, and their interaction had no effect on evaluations, but when the applicant was black, the correlation between the MRS and the hiring decision was $-.50$ in the negative context and $.64$ in the positive context (i.e., high modern racists were affected by context, as is predicted by theories of ambivalence).

Further evidence for the criterion-related validity of the MRS has emerged from other experimental research using white college student samples.

a. Wittenbrink and Henly (1996) found that participants scoring in the upper 20th percentile of the MRS (of 1500 students) evaluated a black armed robbery defendant more guilty and assigned a longer prison sentence than did participants scoring in the lower 20th percentile of the MRS distribution.
b. Biernat and Manis (1994, Study 2) found that high MRS participants evaluated a series of white targets as significantly higher in verbal ability than a series of black targets; low MRS participants judged the two races equivalently.
c. Stangor, Lynch, Duan, and Glass (1992, Study 3) found that undergraduate participants scoring high on the MRS were more likely than low MRS participants to categorize members of a discussion group by race (as evidenced by a greater number of within-race than between-race errors in memory for "who said what" in the group).

Discriminant

Virtually all of the work on the discriminant validity of the Modern Racism Scale has been aimed at distinguishing the Modern Racism items from assorted measures of old-fashioned racism. McConahay (1986) summarized three factor analyses based on two independent samples of Louisville residents and one 1984 sample of 167 white Duke University undergraduates. Examples of the old-fashioned items used in these studies appear later; the Louisville samples included Items 1–6, and the Duke sample included Items 7–13. In each of the samples, all the modern racism items loaded together and above .30 on a single Modern factor and below .30 on a second Old-Fashioned factor; conversely the old-fashioned items loaded below .30 on the Modern factor and above .30 on the Old-Fashioned factor. (The sole exception was modern racism Item 5 in the Duke sample, which loaded .40 on the Modern factor and .41 on the Old-Fashioned factor. McConahay (1986) advocated retaining this item nonetheless, as its exclusion reduces the reliability of the Modern Racism Scale from .82 to .77 and because it has not loaded as strongly on the Old-Fashioned factor in other studies.) McConahay *et al.* (1981) also sought to establish that "whites recognize old-fashioned racial beliefs to be socially undesirable racism but do not view modern racial beliefs in the same way" (p. 565). In two studies of Duke University undergraduates, scores on an old-fashioned racism scale *were* sensitive to the experimenter's race (racism was lower when the experimenter was black than white), but scores on the MRS were not. Another sample rated the MRS items as lower than the old-fashioned items in the extent to which they "reflected a negative attitude toward blacks" (p. 574; $Ms = 5.7$ versus 7.7 on a 0–12 scale).

In the only other evidence for discriminant validity provided by McConahay and his colleagues, the Modern Racism Scale was uncorrelated with Rubin and Peplau's (1973) measure of Belief in a Just World (BJW) in two samples of Duke undergraduates (Polin, 1982, cited in McConahay, 1986). However, Nosworthy *et al.* (1995) reported a correlation of .29 with the BJW scale in a sample of Canadian undergraduates.

Location

McConahay, J. B., Hardee, B. B., & Batts, V. (1981). Has racism declined in America? It depends on who is asking and what is asked. *Journal of Conflict Resolution, 25,* 563–579. Reprinted by permission of Sage Publications, Inc.

Results and Comments

Sniderman and Tetlock (1986a, 1986b) have been the most vocal critics of the entire symbolic/modern racism approach, questioning both the theoretical and the operational definitions of the construct. They also have contested the claim that modern and old-fashioned racism are distinct constructs with "distinguishable effects" (Kinder, 1986, p. 161), as have Weigel and Howes (1985). In a study of 92 white Massachusetts residents, Weigel and Howes (1985) reported a correlation of .67 between the MRS and the short form of the (old-fashioned) MRAI (Ard & Cook, 1977). These scales had comparable response variance and internal consistency, and they were equally correlated with self-reported political ideology and with relative preference for Reagan over various potential Democratic candidates in the 1984 presidential election. Supporters of Jesse Jackson also had lower racial prejudice scores on *both* the MRS and the MRAI than did non-Jackson supporters. Swim, Aikin, Hall, and Hunter (1995) have similarly suggested that old-fashioned and modern racism items are no longer as empirically distinct as McConahay's (1986) summary suggests (see also Raden, 1994). The fact that much of the validity research on the MRS does not explicitly compare the scale to old-fashioned racism measures is clearly problematic for the claim of empirical and theoretical distinction.

Fazio *et al.* (1995) questioned another assertion—that the MRS is a "nonreactive" measure of racial prejudice. In a conceptual replication of McConahay *et al.* (1981), Fazio and his colleagues (1995) found that undergraduate students' scores on the MRS showed a significant decrease from Time 1 (a mass testing session) to Time 2 (a laboratory session in which anonymity of response was *not* ensured) when the Time 2 experimenter was black, but not when she was white (Study 3). Sears (1988) suggested that the scale reactivity issue may be particularly problematic in college student samples. Crandall (1994) has also noted that the MRS is subject to "a normative pressure (i.e., social desirability) which suppresses agreement . . . and leads to the skewing of responses at the lower end of the scale" (p. 889). Consistent with this argument, in a study by Fiske and Von Hendy (1992), the MRS was correlated $r = .31$ with the Self-Monitoring Scale (Snyder, 1974); high self-monitors tend to report less racist attitudes.

Fazio *et al.* (1995), like Weigel and Howes (1985) and Sniderman and Tetlock (1986a, 1986b), also criticized the MRS for its apparent confound with measures of political conservatism: "Given the nature of the items [in the MRS], it would appear quite difficult for a political conservative—one who does not value government intervention—to score at the low-prejudiced end of the scale" (Fazio *et al.*, 1995, p. 1021). Using a 13-item measure of issue-based conservatism (e.g., stands on abortion rights, capital punishment, defense spending, tax increases, $\alpha = .72$), Fazio *et al.* (1995) reported a correlation with the MRS of .47 in a sample of white undergraduates.

A main accomplishment of the Fazio *et al.* (1995) article is its proposal of an unobtrusive measure of racial attitudes—a reaction-time-based index of the extent to which evaluations of adjectives are facilitated by the priming of black versus white faces. Although a review of this measure is beyond the scope of this chapter, it is worth noting that the reaction-time (RT) measure, but not MRS scores, successfully predicted white students' friendliness during an interaction with a black female experimenter (Fazio *et al.*, 1995, Study 1). The MRS did, however, predict students' judgments of the justness of the 1992 Rodney King trial verdicts, the relative responsibility assigned to blacks versus whites for the postverdict violence, and the relative ratings of the attractiveness of a series of black versus white photos. MRS scores and Fazio *et al.*'s RT measure were weakly *negatively* correlated in two studies, but a further study indicated that the two measures were positively related among individuals who scored low on a measure of "motivation to control racial prejudice" (Study 4; see also Dunton & Fazio, 1997). Fazio *et al.* (1995) argued that the MRS "assesses willingness to express prejudice. . . . Truly prejudiced individuals will score high on the scale provided that they are not motivated to control prejudiced reactions. Relatively low scores on the MRS, on the other hand, can emanate either from individuals being truly unprejudiced or from their being motivated to control their prejudiced reactions" (p. 1024). Interestingly Wittenbrink *et al.* (1997) have since proposed another RT-based measure of "implicit prejudice" (based on facilitation of lexical decisions following "Black" and "White" primes). In their sample of 88 white college students, this implicit measure *was* significantly correlated with the MRS ($r = .41$).

Other criticisms of the MRS include concerns that only one of its items is worded in a problack direction and that the desegregation item (Item 5) may be outdated. Despite these problems, it must be conceded that the MRS has a considerable legacy of research evidence supportive of its value as a measure of racial prejudice. It is perhaps the most widely used instrument of its kind, having gained acceptance by both political scientists and social psychologists conducting both correlational and laboratory research. It appears to be useful as a general indicator of whites' negative attitudes toward and resentment of blacks, though claims of nonreactivity may no longer apply.

Modern Racism Scale (MRS)
(McConahay, Hardee, & Batts, 1981)

1. Over the past few years the government and news media have shown more respect to blacks than they deserve.
   4 = AGREE STRONGLY
   3 = AGREE SOMEWHAT
   2 = NEITHER AGREE NOR DISAGREE
   1 = DISAGREE SOMEWHAT
   0 = DISAGREE STRONGLY

*2. It is easy to understand the anger of black people in America.

3. Discrimination against blacks is no longer a problem in the United States.

4. Over the past few years blacks have gotten more economically than they deserve.

5. Blacks have more influence upon school desegregation plans than they ought to have.

6. Blacks are getting too demanding in their push for equal rights.

7. Blacks should not push themselves where they're not wanted.

   *Indicates reverse scored item.

Various Old-Fashioned Racism Items Used by McConahay

1. Generally speaking, do you favor full racial integration, integration in some areas of life, or full separation of the races?

2. Generally, do you feel blacks are smarter, not as smart or about as smart as whites?

3. If a black family with about the same income and education as you moved next door, would you mind it a lot, a little or not at all?*

4. How strongly would you object if a member of your family had a close relationship with a black?

5. How do you feel about the open housing law in Louisville/Jefferson County which allows more racial integration of neighborhoods?

6. In principle, do you think it is a good idea or a bad idea for children to go to schools that have about the same proportion of blacks and whites as generally exists in the Louisville–Jefferson County area?

7. I favor laws that permit black persons to rent or purchase housing even when the person offering the property for sale or rent does not wish to rent or sell it to blacks.

8. Generally speaking, I favor full racial integration.

9. I am opposed to open or fair housing laws.

10. It is a bad idea for blacks and whites to marry one another.

11. Black people are generally not as smart as whites.

12. If a black family with about the same income and education as I have moved next door, I would mind it a great deal.

13. It was wrong for the United States Supreme Court to outlaw segregation in its 1954 decision.

*Used as an indicator of "personal threat" in Kinder & Sears (1981).

Kinder and Sears's (1981) Expressive Racism Scale

1. Do you think that most Negroes/blacks who receive money from welfare programs could get along without it if they tried, or do they really need the help?

2. Negroes/blacks shouldn't push themselves where they're not wanted.

3. Because of past discrimination, it is sometimes necessary to set up quotas for admission to college of minority group students.

4. Do you think Los Angeles city officials pay more, less, or the same attention to a request or complaint from a black person as from a white person?

5. Of the groups on the card, are there any which you think have gained more than they are entitled to?*

6. It is wrong to set up quotas to admit black students to college who don't meet the usual standards.*

7. Over the past few years, blacks have got more than they deserve.

8. In Los Angeles, would you say many, some, or only a few blacks miss out on jobs or promotions because of racial discrimination?*

Items 5, 6, and 8 were deleted from analyses using the Expressive Racism Scale in Kinder & Sears (1981).

New Racism Scale (NRS)

(Jacobson, 1985)

Variable

Jacobson's instrument was developed in the tradition of the symbolic racism approach of McConahay, Sears, and Kinder; indeed, Jacobson explicitly selected items "that approximated those used previously to measure symbolic racism" (1985, p. 309).

Description

In describing his measure, Jacobson (1985) indicated that his research goal was to test the relative roles of "new racism," old-fashioned racism, and self-interest in the prediction of attitudes toward affirmative action. The instrument was designed to assess general antiblack attitudes in a more subtle manner than is possible with old-fashioned items. Scale scores can range from 7 to 25, with high scores indicating a more prejudiced attitude.

Sample

The instrument was developed in the context of a 1978 national survey conducted by Louis Harris and Associates for the National Conference of Christians and Jews. The sample described by Jacobson included 1429 white adults, whose mean racism score was 15.9 (SD = 3.9).

Reliability

Internal Consistency

Cronbach's alpha for the seven-item scale was .70, item-total correlations ranged from .31 to .48, and factor loadings ranged from .36 to .81 (Jacobson reported that several other items were dropped from the scale based on these factor analyses). Cronbach's alphas for the NRS were lower (α = .60–.62) in Carter's (1990) and Pope-Davis and Ottavi's (1992, 1994) studies of midwestern undergraduate and faculty samples.

Test–Retest

No data were reported.

Validity

Convergent

In Jacobson's (1985) sample the NRS correlated .65 with measures of "black stereotypes" and "tolerance of interpersonal intimacy" (the latter measure resembling Bogardus's social distance measure). Pope-Davis and Ottavi (1992, 1994) and Carter (1990) demonstrated that the NRS is related to the Reintegration subscale of the White Racial Identity Inventory (Helms & Carter, 1990). Reintegration reflects the "idealization of everything perceived to be White and denigration of everything thought to be Black" (Pope-Davis & Ottavi, 1992, p. 391). In separate samples of undergraduates and faculty, NRS scores were uniquely positively predicted by Reintegration scores.

Discriminant

Jacobson's (1985) study also included a two-item measure of old-fashioned racism [Item 1 from McConahay's list (see the preceding instrument) and an additional item about "why there are differences between blacks and whites"] and a three-item measure of self-interest. Jacobson reported that in a factor analysis the old-fashioned and new racism items loaded on a single factor (r = .49 between the two scales). However, the NRS was more strongly related to attitudes toward affirmative action (r = $-.38$) than was the old-fashioned scale (r = $-.28$), even after controlling for both demographic variables and measures of tolerance of interpersonal intimacy with blacks, perceived discrimination, contact with blacks, and a measure of black stereotypes (*prs* = −.25 and −.09 for the NRS and the old-fashioned scale, respectively). Similar results were obtained when attitudes toward a particular affirmative action case (the upholding of an affirmative action policy at AT&T) were examined.

Location

Jacobson, C. (1985). Resistance to affirmative action. Self interest or racism? *Journal of Conflict Resolution, 29,* 306–329. Reprinted by permission of Sage Publications, Inc.

Results and Comments

The NRS has not been widely used, and thus available reliability and validity data are limited. Using attitudes toward affirmative action as a criterion variable for the validity of the scale is potentially problematic in that two items of the NRS are themselves related to affirmative action issues. The fact that the scale is not empirically distinguishable from old-fashioned racism scales may or may not be a valid criticism, depending on one's perspective regarding the nature of modern-day racial attitudes.

New Racism Scale (NRS)
(Jacobson, 1985)

(Scoring indicated in parentheses)

1. Do you feel blacks in this country have tried to move
   (3) TOO FAST
   (2) TOO SLOW, or
   (1) AT ABOUT THE RIGHT PACE?

2. Would it upset you personally
   (4) A LOT
   (3) SOME BUT NOT A LOT
   (2) ONLY A LITTLE, or
   (1) NOT AT ALL
   if blacks moved into this neighborhood?

3. It's been said that if black children all went to school with white children, the education of white children would suffer. The reason given is that black children would hold back the white children. Do you believe that or not?
   (1) DON'T BELIEVE
   (2) NOT SURE
   (3) BELIEVE

4. Blacks are more likely to make progress in the future by being patient and not pushing so hard for change.
   (1) DISAGREE
   (2) NOT SURE
   (3) AGREE

5. If a fully qualified black whose views were acceptable to you were nominated to run for president, how likely do you think you would be to vote for that candidate?
   (1) VERY LIKELY
   (4) NOT AT ALL LIKELY

6. Whether you agree or not with the idea of affirmative action, do you think blacks are given special consideration and hired before whites for jobs
   (4) FREQUENTLY
   (3) OCCASIONALLY
   (2) HARDLY EVER, or
   (1) NEVER AT ALL?

7. How about in higher education institutions—that is, colleges and universities? Do you think blacks are given special consideration and admitted before whites in higher education institutions
   (4) FREQUENTLY
   (3) OCCASIONALLY
   (2) HARDLY EVER, or
   (1) NEVER AT ALL?

Pro-Black/Anti-Black Attitudes Questionnaire (PAAQ)

(I. Katz & R. G. Hass, 1988)

Variable

In line with their theoretical work on white Americans' *ambivalent* attitudes toward black Americans, the authors developed two empirically independent scales to capture pro- and anti-black attitude components, which are then used to create an ambivalence score.

Description

Katz and Hass (1988) argued that whites perceive blacks as both deviant and disadvantaged; therefore pro-black attitudes "reflect sympathetic beliefs and feelings about the minority group as underdog," and anti-black attitudes "include beliefs about the deviant characteristics and associated negative affect" about blacks (p. 894). To obtain independence between the Pro- and Anti-Black indexes, Katz and Hass (1988) retained items (out of an initial pool of 40) only if they were significantly correlated with the appropriate total index *and* if they had a low or zero correlation with items in the opposite index. When administering the total inventory, items from the two subscales (Pro-Black and Anti-Black) were intermixed. Scores on each index can range from 0 to 50, with high numbers indicating higher levels of the relevant attitude (pro-black or anti-black).

Samples

Initial development of the scale was conducted using various samples of white college students in New York City. Scale reliability information was based on a sample of 115 white students at Brooklyn College, whose average Pro- and Anti-Black scores were 27.4 (SD = 8.4) and 27.7 (SD = 8.6), respectively. In a separate sample of 484 white students from other northern colleges (Carnegie-Mellon University, Iowa State University, Providence College, and Manhattanville College), the mean Pro- and Anti-Black scores were 29.3 (SD = 6.7) and 23.4 (SD = 7.4), respectively.

Reliability

Internal Consistency

Item-total correlations ranged from .27 to .66 for the Anti-Black subscale items, and Cronbach's alpha coefficient for this subscale was .80. By design, the Anti-Black items were uncorrelated with the Pro-Black index (rs from −.14 to .03). For the Pro-Black subscale, item-total correlations ranged from .41 to .57, except for Items 4 and 5 (the reverse scored items), which were uncorrelated with the total scale (Katz and Hass reported, however, that in six of seven other samples, these two items did correlate significantly with the total scale). The alpha coefficient was .73, and the Pro-Black items were unrelated to the Anti-Black index (rs from −.22 to .03). The correlation between the subscales was .12 (however, the authors indicated that the subscales tend to be more highly interrelated in southern university samples).

A principal-components factor analysis (followed by either a varimax or an oblique rotation) also supported these findings. A three-factor solution accounted for 45% of the total variance; all Anti-Black items loaded above .35 on the Anti-Black factor and not on the Pro-Black factor (with the exception of Item 8, which loaded by itself on factor 3), and all the Pro-Black items loaded on the Pro-Black factor, except for Items 4 and 5, which loaded by themselves on a separate factor.

Test–Retest

No data were reported.

Validity

Convergent

In terms of known groups, white students (n = 599) scored significantly higher in anti-black attitudes and significantly lower in pro-black attitudes than did black students (n = 132) in the northern college student samples described above. Comparisons between these northern whites and 166 whites at three southern campuses (University of Delaware, University of Georgia, and Texas A & M) indicated significantly more positive Pro-Black scores for northern than southern whites, but equivalent Anti-Black scores.

In terms of relation with other measures of racial prejudice, anti-black attitudes were significantly correlated with the Derogatory Beliefs subscale of the MRAI (r = .64), as were pro-black attitudes (r = −.49), in a sample of 59 Lehman College students. The Pro-Black index was also significantly related to the Ease of Interracial Contacts subscale of the MRAI (r = .55). In Monteith's (1996) study of 203 white undergraduates, McConahay et al.'s (1981) MRS was correlated .61 with the Anti-Black index and −.60 with the Pro-Black index (see also Glover, 1994), and in a sample of 97 San Jose State University undergraduates, the Anti-Black index correlated .30 and the Pro-Black index correlated −.38 with Pratto *et al.*'s (1994) Social Dominance Orientation Scale (reviewed later). Wittenbrink *et al.*'s (1997) reaction-time-based "implicit" measure of prejudice also correlated −.33 with the Pro-Black index, but was uncorrelated with the Anti-Black subscale ($r = .17$).

Katz and Hass (1988) suggested that pro-black attitudes derive from humanitarian-egalitarian values and that anti-black attitudes derive from Protestant work ethic values. Using their own measures of these value constructs, they reported correlations of .46 between pro-black attitudes and humanitarianism–egalitarianism (HE) and .40 between anti-black attitudes and Protestant work ethic (PWE) beliefs ($Ns = 275$ to 783 white college students); the cross-value correlations were significantly lower—anti-black and HE, $r = −.28$; pro-black and PWE, $r = −.14$. In an experiment in which white college participants ($N = 122$) completed either the PWE scale or the HE scale prior to the racial attitudes measures, those "primed" with HE statements responded more favorably to the pro-black items than did those primed with PWE or control statements, and those primed with PWE statements subsequently scored higher in anti-black attitudes than did those primed with HE or control statements (the comparable reciprocal pattern also appeared when the attitude measures preceded the value measures).

Rather than view their two subscales as separate instruments, Katz and Hass and their colleagues operationalize racial ambivalence as the product of the standardized Pro- and Anti-Black scores [this ambivalence construct is uncorrelated with the MRS ($r = .01$); see Monteith, 1996]. In one study validating the utility of this ambivalence measure in complying to predictions of the "ambivalence amplification" model (Katz, Wackenhut, & Hass, 1986), Hass, Katz, Rizzo, Bailey, and Eisenstadt (1991) found that ambivalence was positively correlated with evaluations of a black partner whose performance led to a team success in a Trivia Challenge game ($r = .40$) and was negatively correlated with evaluations of a black partner who caused a team failure ($r = −.28$; $N = 60$ white Brooklyn College students).

In testing another prediction of ambivalence amplification theory, Hass, Katz, Rizzo, Bailey, and Moore (1992) also demonstrated that exposure to information regarding the controversial Howard Beach incident led to increased psychological tension and discomfort among individuals who scored high on the ambivalence index; similar results were reported by Monteith (1996). Consistent with the notion that ambivalence reflects conflict in the attitude system, Leippe and Eisenstadt (1994) reported that college participants who were high in ambivalence were more likely than those low in ambivalence to comply with an experimenter's request to write a race-relevant counterattitudinal essay (i.e., one supporting a scholarship program for black students that would take moneys away from non-black students).

Discriminant

Neither the Pro-Black index nor the Anti-Black index was significantly correlated with the Crowne–Marlowe Social Desirability Scale ($rs = .11$ and .10, respectively) in a sample of 59 white Brooklyn College students. In the Lehman College sample, the Anti-Black subscale was also unrelated to the Ease of Interracial Contacts subscale of the MRAI ($r = −.02$), presumably because the sympathy and liking necessary for interracial contact are not reflected in the Anti-Black subscale.

Location

Katz, I., & Hass, R. (1988). Racial ambivalence and American value conflict: Correlational and priming studies of dual cognitive structures. *Journal of Personality and Social Psychology, 55,* 893–905. Copyright © 1988 by the American Psychological Association. Reprinted with permission.

Results and Comments

A notable achievement of this instrument is its close link to theory; the items were developed to tap into separate and independent dimensions of pro- and anti-black feeling (each derived from relevant value systems), which together contribute to the psychological construct of ambivalence. The researchers also made unique predictions regarding ambivalence that derive from their broader model of ambivalence amplification: When activated, ambivalence prompts extremitized (and therefore unstable) responses to the corresponding attitude object (in this case, blacks). The evidence gathered thus far on this point is consistent with the theory, although more data are needed on the conditions under which ambivalence has more or less predictive power than its two subscales (see also Thompson, Zanna, & Griffin, 1995, for an alternative method of computing ambivalence scores). For researchers less interested in ambivalence than in a global indicator of prejudice, further work is also needed to determine whether the 20 items of two subscales are appropriate for use as a unidirectional prejudice measure (rather than as components of the ambivalence construct).

   Shortcomings of the PAAQ include the fact that only two items from each subscale are reverse scored and that (to our knowledge) the scale has been used only in college student samples. Its length probably limits the possibility that it will find its way into national surveys, but data from a broader range of respondents are nonetheless necessary for a fuller assessment of the scale's properties.

Pro-Black/Anti-Black Attitudes Questionnaire (PAAQ) (Katz & Hass, 1988)

Pro-Black Items

1. Black people do not have the same employment opportunities that whites do.

1	2	3	4	5
STRONGLY DISAGREE				STRONGLY AGREE

2. It's surprising that black people do as well as they do, considering all the obstacles they face.
3. Too many blacks still lose out on jobs and promotions because of their skin color.
*4. Most big corporations in America are really interested in treating their black and white employees equally.
*5. Most blacks are no longer discriminated against.

---

6. Blacks have more to offer than they have been allowed to show.
7. The typical urban ghetto public school is not as good as it should be to provide equal opportunities for blacks.
8. This country would be better off if it were more willing to assimilate the good things in black culture.
9. Sometimes black job seekers should be given special consideration in hiring.
10. Many whites show a real lack of understanding of the problems that blacks face.

Anti-Black Items

1. The root cause of most of the social and economic ills of blacks is the weakness and instability of the black family.
2. Although there are exceptions, black urban neighborhoods don't seem to have strong community organization or leadership.
3. On the whole, black people don't stress education and training.
4. Many black teenagers don't respect themselves or anyone else.
5. Blacks don't seem to use opportunities to own and operate little shops and businesses.
*6. Very few black people are just looking for a free ride.
7. Black children would do better in school if their parents had better attitudes about learning.
8. Blacks should take the jobs that are available and then work their way up to better jobs.
9. One of the biggest problems for a lot of blacks is their lack of self-respect.
*10. Most blacks have the drive and determination to get ahead.

*Indicates reverse scored item.

Social Scenarios Scale

(D. Byrnes & G. Kiger, 1988)

Variable

This adaptation of Kogan and Downey's (1956) Social Situations Scale assesses reactions to situations in which one witnesses discriminatory treatment of blacks.

Description

The Social Scenarios Scale assesses participants' "reported willingness to condone or confront discrimination in a variety of social situations" (Byrnes & Kiger, 1988, p. 109). A factor analysis of these 12 items yielded a three-factor solution: Pejorative Remarks (Items 2, 6, 9, and 12), Intimacy (Items 3, 5, and 7), and Job/Housing Injustice (Items 1, 4, 8, 10, and 11); in every case, items loaded .48 or greater on their "appropriate" factor, and loadings on other factors ranged from $-.18$ to $.39$). Scores on the total scale can range from 12 (highly discriminatory) to 38 (highly antidiscriminatory).

Sample

The authors used the same sample to develop this scale as was used in the development of the Social Scale described earlier: 286 college students (including a "large percentage" of Mormons) from the Rocky Mountain region. The sample mean was 29.9 (SD = 8.3).

Reliability

Internal Consistency

The reported alpha for the total scale was .75; reliabilities for the subscales were .65 for Pejorative Remarks, .83 for Intimacy, and .60 for Job/Housing Injustice.

Test–Retest

The authors reported a three-week test–retest reliability of .93 for the total scale in a subsample of 30 of the original respondents.

Validity

Convergent

The total Social Scenarios Scale was significantly related to McConahay *et al.*'s (1981) MRS ($r = .42$) and to the Social Scale, which Byrnes and Kiger (1988) developed using the same sample ($r = .62$) (see earlier description). In terms of known groups, Byrnes and Kiger (1992) found that women scored higher than men and that non-Mormons scored higher than Mormons (high scores indicate greater likelihood of confronting discrimination) in a separate sample of 496 Utah State University students. Neville and Furlong (1994) also found that black undergraduates scored significantly higher than both Asian and white undergraduates on a slightly modified version of the scale.

Discriminant

No data were reported.

Location

Byrnes, D., & Kiger, G. (1988). Contemporary measures of attitudes toward blacks. *Educational and Psychological Measurement, 48,* 107–119. Reprinted by permission of Sage Publications, Inc.

Results and Comments

By measuring hypothetical reactions to discriminatory situations, the Social Scenarios Scale is more distant than many other measures reviewed here from the traditional conceptualization of racial prejudice as negative attitudes toward blacks. However, it may tap a construct that is very important to understanding the expression of modern-day prejudice—respondents' behavioral intentions to confront (or ignore) discrimination. In an age of antidiscriminatory norms, measuring people's willingness to act on and enforce those norms may allow for better prediction of other race-relevant attitudes and behavior. The instrument would benefit from the collection of additional reliability and validity information, preferably from more religiously diverse samples than those noted above as well as from noncollege populations. The extent to which the items exert demand and social desirability pressures should be examined, as should the association between this measure and more general personality characteristics, such as social anxiety or perspective-taking. It is also unclear whether there is any benefit to the use of the three subscales rather than a total scale score.

Social Scenarios Scale
(Byrnes & Kiger, 1988)

1. Imagine that as you are sitting in your parents' home one day, a neighbor comes in to ask your parents to sign a letter to a neighbor discouraging her from renting or selling her house to blacks. He explains that it would not hurt blacks because there are plenty of other good places in town to live. He says keeping blacks out would keep up the value of all the houses in the neighborhood. Your folks are about to sign the letter. Under these conditions,

   ____ I would insist that they were wrong and try to persuade them not to sign the petition.*

   ____ I would probably tell my parents that I didn't think that they were doing the right thing.

   ____ I would probably keep quiet because it wouldn't make much difference one way or another.

   ____ I would understand their reasons for signing the letter, so I wouldn't say anything.

2. Imagine that you have just arrived in a large city and have a heavy suitcase to carry from the bus terminal to your hotel a few blocks away. You decide to take a cab. Waiting on the corner for a cab, you glance across the street and see a black person also waiting for a cab. After a few minutes, a cab comes by and both of you signal for it. The cab goes right by the black, turns around, and comes back to pick you up. When the driver opens the door, he remarks, "I really saw that black fellow first, but I always go by the rule that you should take care of your own first." Under these conditions,

   ____ I would figure the cabbie has good reasons for his behavior.

   ____ I would probably get into the cab without saying or doing anything.

   ____ I would let the driver know nonverbally that I didn't like what he said.

   ____ I would definitely tell the cabbie that he had done the wrong thing.*

3. Imagine that in one of your classes your instructor has broken the class into small groups to discuss race relations. One of the students in your group says it would be great if blacks and whites got along better but they shouldn't go so far as to intermarry and have children. Under these conditions,

   ____ I would voice my disagreement with the student.*

   ____ I would disagree with the student but say nothing.

   ____ I would agree with the student but not say anything.

   ____ I would voice my agreement with the student.

4. Imagine you and your friend are in a small store waiting to make a purchase. Across the aisle, a white person is asking the manager about a sales position that is open. He is given an application to complete and return. Several minutes later a black person approaches the manager about the same job opening and is told the position has already been filled. Under these conditions,

____ I would confront the manager about his discriminatory actions and tell him I was taking my business elsewhere.*

____ I would make my purchase and would probably write a letter of complaint to the manager.

____ I would stay out of it because it wouldn't make much difference to me one way or the other.

____ I would feel it is the right of the management to reject black employees if they want.

5. Imagine that you have a 19 year old brother who has been going pretty steadily with a young black woman for the past month or so. Although your parents admit that she is very nice, they have been trying to force your brother to stop taking her out because they are afraid that they might get serious about each other. Your parents don't mind him having her as a friend, but they don't want him to date her or call her "his girlfriend." One night, during an argument, when your brother is present, your parents ask you what you think. Under these conditions,

____ I would disagree with my parents and say that as long as she was a nice person, it was O.K.*

____ I would probably disagree with my parents, but I'd try to keep out of it.

____ I would probably tend to side with my parents.

____ I would definitely side with my parents.

6. Imagine that you are visiting with several good friends, chatting and sharing humorous stories. One of your friends tells a joke about blacks using the word "nigger." Under these conditions,

____ I wouldn't say anything, and would think it was a harmless joke.

____ I probably wouldn't say anything, but I would feel uncomfortable.

____ I would probably say it wasn't a very good joke.

____ I would criticize him for telling such a joke.*

7. Imagine you are standing in line at the movies waiting for the theater to empty. The person in front of you, pointing at a black man and a white woman holding hands as they walk out of the theater, turns to you and says, "Isn't that disgusting?" Under these conditions,

____ I would speak up and say, "No, it doesn't bother me."*

____ I would feel uncomfortable with his comment and I would probably give the person a disapproving look.

____ I would probably agree with him, but I wouldn't say anything back to him.

____ I would agree with the person.

8. Imagine you and some friends are talking about living arrangements for the next quarter. One of your friends says with great disgust that he was assigned a dorm room with some black guy. Under these conditions,

___ I would tell him I found his attitude offensive. *

___ I would disapprove of his attitude, but I wouldn't say anything.

___ I would figure that's just his opinion and he has a right to it.

___ I would understand why he didn't like the idea.

9. Imagine that several co-workers at your job are black. You notice that they tend to get the worst job assignments and they don't get promoted as often as the other workers. Under these conditions,

___ I would feel that the supervisor knows what's right.

___ I wouldn't want to create problems, so I would probably stay out of the situation.

___ I would express my concerns to my black co-workers.

___ I would go to the next higher supervisor and tell her or him what was going on. *

10. Imagine you are a member of a casting committee for a drama club that is in the process of casting parts for a tragic play about two young lovers. The casting committee is in complete agreement that the male lead should go to Sam Olsen. Clearly, the best actress for the part of the heroine is a beautiful young black woman. However, a number of the members of the casting committee refuse to have a black actress play opposite a white actor in a romantic play. Under these conditions,

___ I would say that if they refuse to give the part to the best qualified actress I would resign from the committee. *

___ I would say that the actress should be judged on her talent not her skin color; but I would go along with any decision the majority made.

___ I wouldn't know what to do so I'd go along with whatever the majority wanted.

___ I would side with those who felt that regardless of the talent issue it would not be a good idea to cast a biracial couple.

11. Imagine you are looking for an apartment to rent that you saw advertised in the paper. You stop a stranger who is watering his lawn to ask for directions. The person you have stopped gives you the directions but says, "You don't want to live there, that place is full of coloreds." Under these conditions,

___ I would tell him that what color of skin the people had who live there didn't make any difference to me. *

___ I would be offended by his comment, but I wouldn't say anything.

___ I wouldn't respond to his comment, but if he was right I probably wouldn't rent it.

___ I would thank him for his advice and I would no longer consider living in that apartment building.

12. Imagine you are having dinner with your parents and a well respected friend of your parents. During dinner, everyone is chatting about different sports players. At this point, your parents' friend states, "It's a good thing coloreds are good at sports because they sure aren't good at much of anything else." Under these conditions,

____ I would nod agreement.

____ I would ignore the comment not wanting to make an issue of it.

____ I would probably noticeably scowl, but I wouldn't say anything.

____ I would tell my parents' friend that I was offended by his comment.*

*Indicates the most antidiscriminatory answer (coded "4"; values for other response options decrease to 3, 2, and 1 in order from the * response).

Quick Discrimination Index (QDI)

(J. G. Ponterotto, A. Burkard, B. P. Rieger, I. Grieger, A. D'Onofrio, A. Dubuisson, M. Heenehan, B. Millstein, M. Parisi, J. F. Rath, & G. Sax, 1995)

Variable

The QDI is broader than most of the other racial attitude measures reviewed thus far. It was designed to apply across racial and ethnic groups and to provide a general measure of receptivity to multiculturalism.

Description

The QDI includes items that assess "attitudes regarding racial diversity and women's equality" (Ponterotto *et al.*, 1995, p. 1017). The instrument consists of 30 items, divided into three subscales [general (cognitive) attitudes toward racial diversity, affective attitudes toward more personal contact with racial diversity, and attitudes toward women's equality]. For the total scale, scores can range from 30 to 150, with high scores indicating more sensitivity and receptivity to racial diversity and gender equality. The subscale scores can range from 9 to 45 (Multicultural index) and from 7 to 35 (Racial Intimacy and Women's Equality indexes), again with higher numbers indicating more antidiscriminatory attitudes.

Scale development began with a 40-item version of the instrument; this was reduced to 25 items on the basis of "appropriateness and clarity" ratings of five experts. After factor and item analyses of responses to the 25 items by an initial sample of 284 New Yorkers, two items with low item-to-total correlations were rewritten, and 5 items were added.

Sample

Initial research on the 30-item version of the scale involved a sample of 220 individuals from the New York City metropolitan area who were recruited from college classrooms, high schools, businesses, and human service organizations. The sample ranged in age from 16 to 58 (*M* = 22.5 years) and was 59% female and 60% Caucasian. The average QDI total score was 103.8 (SD = 16.4), and mean scores for the Multicultural, Racial Intimacy, and Women's Equality subscales were 30.9 (SD = 6.3), 24.2 (SD = 5.7), and 24.8 (SD = 5.3), respectively.

Reliability

Internal Consistency

Cronbach's alpha on the total scale was .88. A principal-components factor analysis indicated a three-factor solution, which roughly matched the factor structure the authors found in the initial sample that responded to the 25-item version of the scale. The Multicultural factor (25% of the variance) included Items 3, 9, 13, 18, 19, 22, 23, 26, and 27; the Racial Intimacy factor (9% of the total variance) included items tapping "more personal/affective attitudes toward personal and intimate interaction with racial diversity" (Items 4, 8, 11, 15, 17, 24, and 29); and the Women's Equality factor (6% of the response variance) included Items 1, 6, 7, 14, 16, 20, and 30. With few exceptions each of the indicated items loaded at or above .40 on its factor and below .35 on the other factors. Seven items with either low or multiple high loadings (Items 2, 5, 10, 12, 21, 25, and 28) were excluded from the three-factor representation of the QDI, but remain in the total scale calculation. The Cronbach's alphas for the three subscales were .80, .83, and .76, respectively; the subscale intercorrelations ranged from .35 to .47. In a separate sample of 333 New Yorkers, a confirmatory factor analysis supported an oblique three-factor model relative to a single-factor or orthogonal three-factor solution (see Ponterotto et al., 1995, Study 3).

Test–Retest

In a separate sample of 37 suburban New York college undergraduates, the 15-week test–retest reliabilities for the three subscales were .90, .82, and .81, respectively.

Validity

Convergent

In terms of known groups, females (n = 130) scored higher (less discriminatory) than males (n = 90) on both the Multicultural and Women's Equality subscales (Ms = 32.4 versus 28.7 on the Multicultural index and 27.4 versus 21.2 on the Women's Equality index). On the Multicultural index, African-American (n = 21) and Hispanic-American (n = 51) respondents scored higher (Ms = 36.1 and 33.8) than did white respondents (n = 131, M = 29.3); on the Racial Intimacy subscale, Hispanics (28.6) scored significantly higher than both African-Americans (23.8) and whites (22.5); and on the Women's Equality index, African-Americans (26.4) and Hispanic-Americans (27.8) were more antidiscriminatory than were white Americans (23.7). The authors also reported that urban dwellers had higher scores than suburban dwellers on the Racial Intimacy and Women's Equality subscales and that Democrats scored higher than Republicans on the Multicultural and Women's Equality indexes, and higher than Independents on all three indexes.

In another validity study each of the three subscales was significantly correlated with Jacobson's (1985) New Racism Scale (rs = −.44, −.44, and −.30 for the Multicultural, Racial Intimacy, and Women's Equality subscales) in a sample of 333 New Yorkers. The three subscales were also related to the two subscales of the Multicultural Counseling Awareness Scale (Ponterotto, Rieger, Barrett, Harris, Sparks, Sanchez, & Magids, 1996), with rs from .21 to .50.

Discriminant

In the sample of 333 New Yorkers, the Social Desirability Scale (Crowne & Marlowe, 1960) was unrelated to scores on the three subscales of the QDI ($rs = -.16, -.04,$ and $-.19$). The correlations with the New Racism Scale reported earlier also provide some evidence for discriminant validity in that the two race-relevant subscales (Multicultural and Racial Intimacy) were more strongly related to the NRS than was the Women's Equality subscale.

Location

Ponterotto, J. G., Burkard, A., Rieger, B. P., Grieger, I., D'Onofrio, A., Dubuisson, A., Heenehan, M., Millstein, B., Parisi, M., Rath, J. F., & Sax, G. (1995). Development and initial validation of the Quick Discrimination Index (QDI). *Educational and Psychological Measurement, 55,* 1016–1031. Reprinted by permission of Sage Publications, Inc.

Results and Comments

Initial work indicates that the QDI is a reliable and valid indicator of sensitivity to multiculturalism and women's equality issues. Additional research is needed, however, to document whether the instrument is best used as a single scale or whether the three subscales have specific, unique, and theoretically relevant correlates (whether the seven items that did not load on any of the three subscales should be retained in the total scale is also an open question). Although the researchers have attempted to move beyond college student samples in their work, development of this instrument would nonetheless benefit (as would many of the others reviewed here) from inclusion of more diverse (and randomly selected) samples.

Quick Discrimination Index (QDI)
(Ponterotto, Burkard, Rieger, Grieger, D'Onofrio, Dubuisson, Heenehan, Millstein, Parisi, Rath, & Sax, 1995)

*1. I do think it is more appropriate for the mother of a newborn baby, rather than the father, to stay home with the baby (not work) during the first year.
  1 = STRONGLY DISAGREE
  2 = DISAGREE
  3 = NOT SURE
  4 = AGREE
  5 = STRONGLY AGREE

*2. It is as easy for women to succeed in business as it is for men.

*3. I really think affirmative action programs on college campuses constitute reverse discrimination.

4. I feel I could develop an intimate relationship with someone from a different race.

5. All Americans should learn to speak two languages.

6. It upsets (or angers) me that a woman has never been President of the United States.

*7. Generally speaking, men work harder than women.

8. My friendship network is very racially mixed.

* 9. I am against affirmative action programs in business.

*10. Generally, men seem less concerned with building relationships than women.

11. I would feel O.K. about my son or daughter dating someone from a different racial group.

12. It upsets (or angers) me that a racial minority person has never been President of the United States.

*13. In the past few years there has been too much attention directed toward multicultural or minority issues in education.

14. I think feminist perspectives should be an integral part of the higher education curriculum.

*15. Most of my close friends are from my own racial group.

*16. I feel somewhat more secure that a man rather than a woman is currently President of the United States.

17. I think that it is (or would be) important for my children to attend schools that are racially mixed.

*18. In the past few years there has been too much attention directed toward multicultural or minority issues in business.

*19. Overall, I think racial minorities in America complain too much about racial discrimination.

20. I feel (or would feel) very comfortable having a woman as my primary physician.

21. I think the President of the United States should make a concerted effort to appoint more women and racial minorities to the country's Supreme Court.

22. I think White people's racism toward racial minority groups still constitutes a major problem in America.

*23. I think the school system, from elementary school through college, should encourage minority and immigrant children to learn and fully adopt traditional American values.

24. If I were to adopt a child, I would be happy to adopt a child of any race.

*25. I think there is as much female physical violence toward men as there is male physical violence toward women.

26. I think the school system, from elementary school through college, should promote values representative of diverse cultures.

27. I believe that reading the autobiography of Malcolm X would be of value.

28. I would enjoy living in a neighborhood consisting of a racially diverse population (i.e., African American, Asian American, Hispanic, White).

*29. I think it is better if people marry within their own race.

*30. Women make too big of a deal out of sexual harassment issues in the workplace.

*Indicates reverse scored item.

Racial Resentment Scale (RRS)

(D. R. Kinder & L. M. Sanders, 1996)

Variable

This scale developed out of the symbolic/modern racism tradition, emphasizing both the value-based underpinnings of racial attitudes and the fundamentally different nature of modern as opposed to old-fashioned racial prejudice.

Description

The crux of the construct of racial resentment, evident in the measurement instrument, is the belief "that blacks do not try hard enough to overcome the difficulties they face and that they take what they have not earned. Today, we say, prejudice is expressed in the language of American individualism" (Kinder & Sanders, 1996, pp. 105–106). The authors continue:

> Like symbolic racism, racial resentment is proposed as a contemporary expression of racial discord, distinguishable from the biological racism that once dominated American institutions and white opinion. Like symbolic racism, racial resentment features indignation as a central emotional theme, one provoked by the sense that black Americans are getting and taking more than their fair share. Finally, like symbolic racism, racial resentment is thought to be the conjunction of whites' feelings toward blacks and their support for American values, especially secularized versions of the Protestant ethic. (p. 293)

The six-item scale uses a Likert-type response format; scores can range from 1 (high sympathy) to 5 (high resentment). However, Kinder and Sanders (1996) converted their scores to a 0–1 (racial sympathy–racial resentment) scaling system.

Sample

The authors relied primarily on data from the 1986 NES of the University of Michigan, which included a national probability sample of 2176 respondents. The reported analyses are based on roughly 600 white NES respondents. The sample mean (in the 0–1 format) was 0.6, with scores distributed "more or less normally" (Kinder & Sanders, 1996, p. 322).

Reliability

Internal Consistency

Cronbach's alpha was .77; item intercorrelations ranged from .16 to .56 (average $r = .36$).

Test–Retest

This information was available using the 1990–1992 NES panel data, in which only a four-item version of the RRS was available (Items 2, 4, 5, and 6). The correlation between 1990 and 1992 scores was .68 (corrected for measurement error, $r = .89$). By comparison, Kinder and Sanders (1996) noted that the RRS was more stable than the same respondents' ideological identification ($r = .49$) and slightly less stable than party identification ($r = .79$).

Validity

Convergent

In terms of known groups, 7% of white respondents chose the most racially sympathetic answers, compared to 33% of black respondents (the same pattern emerged in the 1988 and 1992 NES panels, using the four-item RRS).

In other tests of convergent validity, regressions of three items from Bobo and Kluegel's (1993) Prejudice Index on the RRS indicated significant associations: For beliefs about blacks' laziness relative to whites', unstandardized $B = .18$; for blacks' unintelligence, $B = .12$; and for blacks' violence, $B = .19$. (Kinder and Sanders argued that the weaker relationship for the intelligence item is theoretically meaningful in that this trait is highly associated with biological forms of racism, assumed to be distinct from the racism measured with the RRS.)

The RRS also reliably predicted attitudes toward six race-relevant social policies in the 1986 study (fair employment, school desegregation, federal spending for blacks, government effort to improve the conditions of blacks, preferential hiring, and college quotas; see Appendix A for question wording). Unstandardized Bs ranged from .30 to .60, controlling for self-interest, social background, views on limited government, and a six-item measure of individualism (some reduction of the effect of the RRS occurred when a six-item measure of equality was also included). Very similar patterns emerged using the four-item RRS in the 1988 and 1992 NES surveys. In Gilens (1995) a three-item version of the RRS (Items 2, 5, and 6) correlated .42 with opposition to welfare in the 1986 NES sample. Further, in the 1988 ANES, the four-item RRS was associated with negative feeling thermometer ratings of blacks, civil rights leaders, gays, people on welfare, communists, illegal aliens, Palestinians, Hispanics, and feminists (Bs from .14 to .31, median = .23).

Also in the 1988 sample, the four-item RRS was a significant predictor of reported presidential voting preference: Support for Bush was at 11% among the most racially sympathetic whites, rising monotonically to 71% among the most racially resentful whites. The RRS continued to predict voting preferences with the inclusion of various controls: party identification, assessment of national economic conditions, race of interviewer, measures of patriotism and moral conservatism, and a variety of demographic variables (e.g., gender, education, occupation, income, employment status, region, union membership). However, additional controls for attitudes about social welfare and foreign policy and evaluations of Ronald Reagan and Jesse Jackson reduced the direct effect of the RRS to near zero; Kinder and Sanders (1996) argued that racial resentment had direct effects on these variables, which, in turn, directly affected voting preference. In an interesting subsidiary analysis, Kinder and Sanders (1996) reported that the effect of the RRS on Bush preference was more than doubled for white respondents interviewed close to the election compared to those interviewed prior to the initiation of the infamous "Willie Horton" ad campaign.

Discriminant

For theoretical reasons it was important that the racism measured by the RRS be distinguished from "biological racism." The correlation between the RRS and a 1986 question about whether blacks were less well off in America because they "come from a less able race" was .12.

Kinder and Sanders (1996) also argued that the RRS should be more strongly associated with attitudes toward policies related to race than those unrelated to race. In contrast to the robust relationships between the RRS and racial policy attitudes described earlier, attitudes toward policies less associated with race (e.g., food stamps = moderate association, defense spending = no association) showed less strong relationships with the RRS in the 1992 ANES. For example, the unstandardized B for college quotas = .68, food stamps = .27, capital punishment = .33, family leave = .18, prayer in school = .07, and defense spending = .10. However, high racial resentment was unexpectedly associated with attitudes toward taking a tough posture toward the (former) Soviet Union (B = .29)

Finally Sears *et al.* (1997) also analyzed the 1986 NES data and created a symbolic racism scale using the six items of the RRS plus two additional questions ("Has there been real change in the position of black people in the past few years?" and "Are civil rights leaders trying to push too fast?"; α = .78). This measure was a stronger predictor of attitudes toward racial policy issues than was the black feeling thermometer or a two-item measure of old-fashioned racism.

Location

Kinder, D. R., & Sanders, L. M. (1996). *Divided by color.* Chicago: University of Chicago Press.

Results and Comments

This instrument's strong theoretical ties to the symbolic/modern racism perspective are appealing. Like the MRS the RRS items appear to tap appropriately into the researchers' theoretical account of the basis of modern-day racism (i.e., the resentment whites feel that blacks are getting "more than their fair share"). An obvious need is for direct comparisons of the relative predictive power of the MRS and the RRS. Some of the same criticisms that others have made of the MRS may also apply here—the RRS is heavily steeped in attributional content, which is likely to be highly correlated, for example, with conservative political ideology. However, Kinder and Sanders may have blunted some of this criticism by incorporating a number of controls (including ideology) in their validity work, adding to the appeal of this scale.

Racial Resentment Scale (RRS)
(Kinder & Sanders, 1996)

*1. Most blacks who receive money from welfare programs could get along without it if they tried.

          1 = AGREE STRONGLY
          2 = AGREE SOMEWHAT
          3 = NEITHER AGREE NOR DISAGREE
          4 = DISAGREE SOMEWHAT
          5 = DISAGREE STRONGLY

2. Over the past few years, blacks have gotten less than they deserve.

3. Government officials usually pay less attention to a request or complaint from a black person than from a white person.

*4. Irish, Italians, Jewish and many other minorities overcame prejudice and worked their way up. Blacks should do the same without any special favors.

[In past studies we have asked people why they think white people seem to get more of the good things in life in America—such as better jobs and more money—than black people do. These are some of the reasons given by both blacks and whites.]

*5. It's really a matter of some people not trying hard enough; if blacks would try harder they could be just as well off as whites.

6. Generations of slavery and discrimination have created conditions that make it difficult for blacks to work their way out of the lower class.

*Indicates reverse scored item.

British Prejudice Scale

(L. Lepore & R. Brown, 1997)

Variable

This is designed as a general measure of antiblack prejudice, suitable for use in the United Kingdom.

Description

The authors based their instrument on several existing instruments—the Modern Racism Scale, the New Racism Scale, and the Subtle and Blatant Prejudice Scales—all of which receive review in this chapter. Changes were made in the specific item content so that the measure would be suitable for use among white British respondents. Although the authors conceptualize their measure as a general indicator of antiblack prejudice, it includes a substantial component of anti-immigration–antiforeigner sentiment. These issues rarely appear in prejudice measures developed by researchers from the United States, but may well reflect an important aspect of antiblack attitudes in the United Kingdom. The authors also offer an interesting conceptualization of prejudice in cognitive terms: Prejudice is reflected in the strength of associations between the social category "Blacks" and the valence of the attributes with which the category is linked in a mental network (positive attributes for low prejudiced people, negative attributes for highly prejudiced people).

Factor analysis revealed a two-factor solution; however, these factors were highly correlated ($r = .47$), and therefore a one-dimensional solution was deemed appropriate. The scale includes 15 items, roughly balanced in pro- and antiblack directions, that are answered on 1 *(strongly disagree)* to 7 *(strongly agree)* response scales; scores are summed and can range from 15 (high prejudice) to 105 (low prejudice–greater tolerance).

Sample

Most of the validity data are based on a sample of 162 white British college students. The overall sample mean was 75.1 (SD = 13.2).

Reliability

Internal Consistency

The alpha coefficient was .85; in a second sample of 40 white students, $\alpha = .92$ (Lepore & Brown, 1997, Study 2).

Test–Retest

No relevant data were provided.

Validity

Convergent

The authors correlated their scale with a number of other measures that were also being developed for use in the United Kingdom. The British Prejudice Scale correlated $-.76$ with a measure of old-fashioned racism, $-.65$ with a measure of "aversive racism," $-.52$ with national identification, $-.61$ with "threat to national identity," and .41 with a measure of degree of contact with ethnic minorities.

   The authors also reported experimental work designed to clarify some aspects of Devine's (1989) model of automatic stereotype activation. Devine (1989) suggested that the mental priming or activation of the category "Black" elicits negative thoughts among all individuals, regardless of their levels of prejudice (see reference to Devine in the earlier section on the Modern Racism Scale). In contrast, Lepore and Brown (1997) argued that this priming activates unfavorable thoughts if one is highly prejudiced, but relatively favorable thoughts if one is low in prejudice. In their research comparing individuals who scored high versus low in prejudice on the British Prejudice Scale (based on within-sample median splits), the authors demonstrated that (1) these individuals have similar knowledge of the content of black stereotypes, though high prejudice participants have a somewhat more negative representation overall, and (2) subliminal primes designed to activate the category "Black" led high prejudice participants to judge a subsequently encountered target person more negatively and low prejudice participants to judge this target more positively than individuals in "no prime" conditions.

Discriminant

No information was reported.

Location

Lepore, L., & Brown, R. (1997). Category and stereotype activation: Is prejudice inevitable? *Journal of Personality and Social Psychology, 72,* 275–287. Copyright © 1997 by the American Psychological Association. Reprinted with permission.

Results and Comments

The scale appears to be a valid and useful measure of British students' racial attitudes, though testing on more diverse samples, and the use of better validated criterion measures, is necessary (Item 15 would require alteration for a noncollege population). To the extent that this measure represents the "modern" tradition, it may be problematic that the correlation with an old-fashioned measure of prejudice was very high (.76). Nonetheless, the instrument serves as a reminder that the content of many prejudice measures may be culture specific, even if antiblack attitudes are "as much a part of the British cultural fabric as they are in the United States and elsewhere" (p. 279). The authors' development strategy—the adaptation of items from a variety of existing U.S. scales—is a reasonable approach, although a more explicit and thorough consideration of the content domains of antiblack prejudice in the United Kingdom (as opposed to the United States) would also be useful. This approach should also be compared to the cross-cultural prejudice measurement method that is reflected in the scale reviewed next, in which item content remains the same across countries, but the targeted out-group differs (Pettigrew & Meertens's Subtle and Blatant Prejudice Scales).

British Prejudice Scale
(Lepore & Brown, 1997)

*1. It makes sense for minority groups to live in their own neighbourhoods because they share more and get along better than when mixing with Whites.

1	2	3	4	5	6	7
STRONGLY DISAGREE						STRONGLY AGREE

2. I consider our society to be unfair to Black people.

3. It should be made easier to acquire British citizenship.

4. The number of Black Members of Parliament (MPs) is too low, and political parties should take active steps to increase it.

*5. Minority groups are more likely to make progress in the future by being patient and not pushing so hard for change.

*6. Given the present high level of unemployment, foreigners should go back to their countries.

7. The rights of immigrants should be:

1	2	3	4	5	6	7
RESTRICTED			LEFT AS THEY ARE			EXTENDED

8. If many Black persons moved to my neighbourhood in a short period of time, thus changing its ethnic composition, it would not bother me.

9. If people move to another country, they should be allowed to maintain their own traditions.

*10. Once minority groups start getting jobs because of their colour, the result is bound to be fewer jobs for Whites.

*11. Those immigrants who do not have immigration documents should be sent back to their countries.

*12. Some Black people living here who receive support from the state could get along without it if they tried.

13. Suppose that a child of yours had children with a person of very different colour and physical characteristics than your own. If your grandchildren did not physically resemble the people on your side of the family, you would be:

1	2	3	4	5	6	7
VERY BOTHERED					NOT BOTHERED AT ALL	

*14. It is unfair to the people of one country if the immigrants take jobs and resources.

15. I would not be concerned if most of my peers at the university were Black.

*Indicates reverse-scored item.

Subtle and Blatant Prejudice Scales

(T. F. Pettigrew & R. W. Meertens, 1995)

Variable

This measure is designed to assess prejudice toward a variety of racial and ethnic groups, distinguishing between blatant prejudice (the "hot, close, and direct" form) and subtle prejudice (the "cool, distant, and indirect" or "modern" form of out-group antagonism) (Pettigrew & Meertens, 1995, p. 57).

Description

The authors developed their instrument in seven Western European samples, targeting seven different outgroups. For any given out-group the instrument assesses both blatant and subtle prejudice, each of which is also assumed to have component parts: for blatant prejudice, threat–rejection and opposition to intimacy; for subtle prejudice, defense of traditional values, exaggeration of cultural differences, and denial of positive emotions. Items were chosen to represent these components; as can be seen in the instrument, a number of items are similar to those that appear in the Modern Racism Scale and in other cross-sectional surveys, such as the NES and GSS. The authors reported that they chose the 10 items of each scale out of a pool of 50 items. Exploratory factor analyses supported the two-component structure of the Blatant Prejudice Scale in four of the seven samples described below; a one-factor solution emerged in the other three samples. Comparable analyses of the Subtle Prejudice Scale supported a three-factor solution in five samples and a two-factor solution (with cultural differences and positive emotions folding together) in the other two samples. The scale uses a Likert-type response format, and no scale midpoint is provided. Responses are averaged across scale items; thus scores on the Blatant Prejudice and Subtle Prejudice Scales (as well as their component subscales) can range from 1 to 5, with high numbers indicating more prejudice.

Samples

Seven independent probability samples from four countries of the European Community's Euro-Barometer Survey (No. 30) were interviewed during the fall of 1988. In the German sample "Turkish immigrants" were the targeted out-group; in France one sample considered "Asians," and another considered "North Africans"; in the Netherlands "Surinamers" and "Turks" were the out-groups in two samples; and in Great Britain the out-groups in two samples were "West Indians" and "Asians." Respectively, *N*s of the native groups were 989, 475, 455, 462, 476, 471, and 482 nonminority respondents. Sample means were not reported.

Reliability

Internal Consistency

Across the seven samples, Cronbach's alpha ranged from .87 to .90 for the Blatant Prejudice Scale and from .73 to .82 for the Subtle Prejudice Scale. Reliabilities for the Blatant Prejudice subscales ranged from .73 to .81 for Threat/Rejection and from .70 to .93 for Intimacy; for the Subtle Prejudice subscales, they ranged from .53 to .67 for Traditional Values, from .57 to .72 for Cultural Differences, and from .61 to .73 for Positive Emotions. The correlations between the Subtle Prejudice and Blatant Prejudice Indexes ranged from .48 (in the Netherlands) to .70 (in France).

The authors also reported the results of confirmatory factor analyses on the 20 items in each of seven samples. Comparisons of one-factor, uncorrelated two-factor, and correlated two-factor solutions and a second-order hierarchical model indicate that the hierarchical model provided the best fit to the data in all seven samples (blatant and subtle prejudice as first-order factors subordinate to a higher order "prejudice" factor); the correlated two-factor solution was a close second.

Test–Retest

No data were provided.

Validity

Convergent

Within each sample the authors regressed the Blatant Prejudice and Subtle Prejudice Scales on a set of nine variables (age, education, political interest, national pride, group relative deprivation, political conservatism, intergroup friendships, racist movement approval, and ethnocentrism; see Pettigrew and Meertens, 1995, for descriptions of these measures). All of these were correlated in the expected directions with both scales; the strongest correlate of both blatant and subtle prejudice was ethnocentrism (Cohen's $d = +.72$ and $+.54$, respectively). There were some distinctive patterns of correlation as well between the two scales: Controlling for other factors, group relative deprivation was a stronger predictor of blatant than of subtle prejudice, and number of intergroup friends was a stronger predictor of subtle than of blatant prejudice.

Using the same data set, Meertens and Pettigrew (1997) reported that differences between politically left and right respondents tended to be stronger on the Blatant Prejudice

Scale than on the Subtle Scale; though younger, well-educated, and left-wing respondents had relatively low scores on the Blatant scales, their mean Subtle scores were quite similar to those of older, less well-educated, and conservative respondents (see also Arcuri & Boca, 1996; Wagner & Zick, 1995). In that sense, "the Subtle Prejudice scale is most useful for detecting the covert prejudice of the political left, not the political right" (Meertens & Pettigrew, 1997, p. 65).

Supporting a Guttman-like interpretation of the Subtle Prejudice and Blatant Prejudice factors, Pettigrew and Meertens (1995) reported that less than 2% of the entire sample scored inconsistently (i.e., high on Blatant Prejudice and low on Subtle Prejudice). The high-highs (labeled "bigots") were the most likely in all samples to favor the restriction of immigrants' rights, and the low-lows ("equalitarians") were the most likely to favor the extension of immigrant rights; the high subtle–low blatants ("subtles") were the most likely to favor keeping immigrants' rights the same. Similar patterns emerged with regard to attitudes on immigration policy and preferred remedies for improving "relations with foreigners."

Also using the same data set, Pettigrew (1997) found reliable correlations between the Subtle Prejudice and Blatant Prejudice Scales and various measures of intergroup contact (e.g., with co-workers, friends, and neighbors), controlling for political conservatism, group relative deprivation, political interest, national pride, urbanism, education, and age; these correlations were strongest for the Positive Affect subscale and intergroup friendships ($r = -.25$).

Discriminant

Meertens and Pettigrew (1997) reported that Subtle Prejudice can be distinguished from Political Conservatism (a single-item 10-point "left" to "right" measure) in that it is more strongly related to low education, low political interest, few intergroup friends, and feeling high levels of group relative deprivation.

Location

Pettigrew, T. F., & Meertens, R. W. (1995). Subtle and blatant prejudice in Western Europe. *European Journal of Social Psychology, 25,* 57–75. Copyright John Wiley & Sons Limited. Reproduced with permission.

Results and Comments

The cross-national character of this work is perhaps its most impressive aspect. The use of seven representative national samples allowed for a strong demonstration of the scales' psychometric properties, and the data also indicated that the instrument can be readily adapted for use with any relevant out-group. The researchers are positing a general framework for conceptualizing and measuring out-group prejudice, and unlike other approaches to modern versus old-fashioned prejudice, they suggest that the *combination* of responses to both kinds of measures may allow for the best understanding of out-group antagonism. Their research suggests important distinctions among "bigots" (who score high on both measures), "equalitarians" (who score low on both), and the "subtles" in between. However, more direct comparison between subtle prejudice and modern racism and between blatant prejudice and various measures of old-fashioned racism, at both theoretical and operational levels, would be valuable.

Subtle and Blatant Prejudice Scales
(Pettigrew & Meertens, 1995)
(British version, West Indian out-group)

Blatant Prejudice

A. Threat/Rejection

   1. West Indians have jobs that the British should have.
      1 = STRONGLY DISAGREE
      2 = SOMEWHAT DISAGREE
      4 = SOMEWHAT AGREE
      5 = STRONGLY AGREE

   2. Most West Indians living here who receive support from welfare could get along without it if they tried.

   3. British people and West Indians can never be really comfortable with each other, even if they are close friends.

   4. Most politicians in Britain care too much about West Indians and not enough about the average British person.

   5. West Indians come from less able races and this explains why they are not as well off as most British people.

   6. How different or similar do you think West Indians living here are to other British people like yourself—in how honest they are?
      5 = VERY DIFFERENT, 4 = SOMEWHAT DIFFERENT, 2 = SOMEWHAT SIMILAR, 1 = VERY SIMILAR

B. Intimacy

   7. Suppose that a child of yours had children with a person of very different colour and physical characteristics than your own. Do you think you would be:
      5 = VERY BOTHERED, 4 = BOTHERED, 2 = BOTHERED A LITTLE, or 1 = NOT BOTHERED AT ALL
      if your grandchildren did not physically resemble the people on your side of the family?

  *8. I would be willing to have sexual relationships with a West Indian.

  *9. I would not mind if a suitably qualified West Indian person was appointed as my boss.

 *10. I would not mind if a West Indian person who had a similar economic background as mine joined my close family by marriage.

Subtle Prejudice

A. Traditional Values

   1. West Indians living here should not push themselves where they are not wanted.

   2. Many other groups have come to Britain and overcome prejudice and worked their way up. West Indians should do the same without special favour.

3. It is just a matter of some people not trying hard enough. If West Indians would only try harder they could be as well off as British people.

4. West Indians living here teach their children values and skills different from those required to be successful in Britain.

B. Cultural Differences

5. How different or similar do you think West Indians living here are to other British people like yourself . . .

. . . in the values they teach their children?
5 = VERY DIFFERENT, 4 = SOMEWHAT DIFFERENT, 2 = SOMEWHAT SIMILAR, 1 = VERY SIMILAR

6. . . . in their religious beliefs and practices?

7. . . . in their sexual values or sexual practices?

8. . . . in the language that they speak?

C. Positive Emotions

9. How often have you felt sympathy for West Indians living here?
1 = VERY OFTEN, 2 = FAIRLY OFTEN, 4 = NOT TOO OFTEN, 5 = NEVER

10. How often have you felt admiration for West Indians living here?

*Indicates reverse scored item.

Prejudice Index

(L. Bobo & J. Kluegel, 1993)

Variable

The Prejudice Index is designed to measure stereotyped perceptions of blacks relative to perceptions of whites on dimensions relevant to common black stereotypes.

Description

Respondents are asked to rate, in turn, the groups "Blacks in general" and "Whites in general" on five seven-point semantic differential items. The Prejudice Index is created by subtracting black ratings from white ratings and summing these differences, such that high numbers reflect the perception that whites possess more favorable traits than do blacks. Difference scores can range from -30 (blacks viewed more favorably than whites) to $+30$ (whites viewed more favorably than blacks). Terkildsen (1993) used a very similar scale that included one additional semantic differential item, "rich–poor," and no ratings of whites. Thus for Terkildsen the prejudice index reflects negativity in perception of blacks (ranging from 6 to 42, with high numbers indicating more favorable perceptions), not the difference in perceptions of blacks versus whites.

Samples

The instrument was developed from items that were asked in the 1990 GSS (Davis & Smith, 1990), a national survey of American adults. Complete data were available from 1150 white, English-speaking respondents. Terkildsen (1993) surveyed 348 white jury pool members from the Jefferson County, Kentucky, court system. No sample means were reported.

Reliability

Internal Consistency

Bobo and Kluegel (1993) found that the average correlation among the five items was .40 (no overall reliability coefficient was reported). The alpha coefficient for Terkildsen's (1993) six-item index of perceptions of blacks was .85.

Test–Retest

No information was reported.

Validity

Convergent

The Prejudice Index correlated .31 with respondents' tendency to attribute the black–white gap in socioeconomic status to blacks' lack of "in-born ability to learn" (Bobo & Kluegel, 1993). The authors also reported an average correlation of .27 between items on this scale and attitudes toward legal prohibition of interracial marriage and toward the right to practice residential segregation against blacks (these GSS items appear in Appendix B). Using a similar measure of prejudice in the same data set, Kinder and Mendelberg (1995) also found strong and consistent associations with attitudes toward these and other racial policy issues, particularly among respondents who had little contact with blacks. After controlling for a number of demographic and attitudinal variables, the Prejudice Index also predicted lack of support for government policies and government assistance to improve the standard of living of blacks.

In Terkildsen's (1993) research, negative stereotype ratings of blacks were associated with less favorable feeling thermometer and voter approval ratings of fictitious light- and dark-skinned black gubernatorial candidates and were unrelated to evaluations of a comparable white candidate.

Discriminant

No relevant data were reported.

Location

Bobo, L., & Kluegel, J. (1993). Opposition to race-targeting: Self-interest, stratification ideology, or racial attitudes? *American Sociological Review, 58,* 443–464.

Results and Comments

Whereas the measurement of perceived differences between blacks and whites on stereotyped attributes is intuitively appealing, little information has yet been provided on whether these difference scores are more appropriate or more predictive (e.g., of racial policy and other beliefs) than measures of perceptions of blacks alone. The use of difference scores is consistent with the theoretical work of McCauley and Stitt (1978), but more data are needed on the utility of this particular instantiation of a difference score approach. In one study that has compared the predictive power of the Prejudice Index (a three-item version) with other racial attitude measures, Sears *et al.* (1997) found this measure to be a less successful correlate of attitudes toward racial policy issues and feeling thermometer ratings of Jesse Jackson than either (1) black feeling thermometer ratings or (2) a measure of symbolic racism in the 1992 NES. This does not mean that measures of racial stereotypes have no place in understanding racial prejudice, but it highlights the importance of examining the relationships among various prejudice measures and of determining their respective domains of application.

The scale would also benefit from a more careful consideration and justification of its specific items. Bobo and Kluegel (1993) offered little discussion of precisely why or how particular attributes were selected for use in the measure. Some of the items are straightforward, but the patriotic–unpatriotic dimension seems odd, as it has little relevance to traditional stereotypes of blacks (see Devine & Elliot, 1995). The scale was clearly constructed from available data rather than from an a priori research plan, and the authors' primary research objective was *not* scale development. Nonetheless, we believe the authors should be recognized for their conceptual work. Not only did they argue that antiblack prejudice is largely based on racial stereotyping and that stereotyping is evident in perceived differences between blacks and whites, but also they suggested that prejudice of this sort is causally prior to racial policy attitudes, to attributions for poverty, and to beliefs about discrimination. We encourage additional investigation into the utility of this measure (or some variant) as a predictor of other race-relevant attitudes and behavior.

Prejudice Index
(Bobo & Kluegel, 1993)

Now I have some questions about different groups in our society. I'm going to show you a seven-point scale on which the characteristics of people in a group can be rated. . . . A score of 1 means that you think almost all of the people in that group are (X). A score of 7 means that you think almost everyone in the group are (Y). A score of 4 means you think that the group is not towards one end or another, and of course you may choose any number in between that comes closest to where you think people in the group stand.

*1. The (first) set of characteristics asks if (Blacks/Whites) tend to be hard-working or if they tend to be lazy. Where would you rate (blacks/whites) in general on this scale?

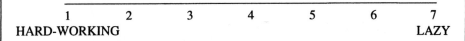

```
     1       2       3       4       5       6       7
HARD-WORKING                                      LAZY
```

2. Do (blacks/whites) tend to be violence prone or do they tend not to be prone to violence?

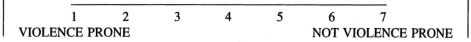

```
     1       2       3       4       5       6       7
VIOLENCE PRONE                       NOT VIOLENCE PRONE
```

3. Do (blacks/whites) tend to be unintelligent or tend to be intelligent?

1	2	3	4	5	6	7
UNINTELLIGENT						INTELLIGENT

*4. Do (blacks/whites) tend to prefer to be self-supporting or do they tend to prefer to live off welfare?

1	2	3	4	5	6	7
SELF-SUPPORTING						LIVE OFF WELFARE

*5. Do (blacks/whites) tend to be patriotic or do they tend to be unpatriotic?

1	2	3	4	5	6	7
PATRIOTIC						UNPATRIOTIC

*Indicates reverse scored item.
For each item, the "blacks in general" rating is subtracted from the "whites in general" rating.

Racial Stereotypes Measure

(M. Peffley, J. Hurwitz, & P. Sniderman, 1997)

Variable

This measure is designed to assess respondents' beliefs or stereotypes about the personal attributes of blacks.

Description

The authors conceptualized stereotypes as cognitions—"cognitive expectancies about the traits and behaviors of social groups"—rather than as prejudice—"an affective predisposition toward a group" (Peffley *et al.*, 1997, p. 56; see also Sniderman & Piazza, 1993). Respondents were asked to rate the degree to which various words or phrases accurately describe "most blacks," and two indexes were created: One included items relevant to work ethic issues; the other included the single judgment "aggressive or violent" (i.e., hostility). Five of the six items in the scale were answered using a 0 (not an accurate description) to 10 (accurate description) format, and one used a 1–4 (disagree–agree) format. The authors calculated scores by recording responses as negative (above the scale midpoint), neutral (at the scale midpoint), and positive (below the scale midpoint). We recommend that all items be answered on the 0–10 scales and that an average score be calculated, with high numbers indicating more negative stereotyping of blacks.

Sample

The items appeared in the 1991 National Race and Politics Survey, administered by the Survey Research Center at the University of California–Berkeley. Participants in the national telephone survey included 1841 whites. Although a sample mean was not reported, we used the information presented in Table 1 of Peffley et al. (1997) and calculated the mean at 2.1 (SD = .8), where 1 = positive stereotyping, 2 = neutral, and 3 = negative stereotyping.

Reliability

Internal Consistency

The alpha coefficient on the Black Work Ethic subscale was .77; the correlation between the Black Work Ethic subscale and the Black Hostility subscale was .45. No factor analytic results were reported.

Test–Retest

No data were reported.

Validity

Convergent

Overall between 13% (for the item "dependable") and 60% (for the item "lack discipline") of the sample reported negative stereotypes about "most blacks." Peffley et al. (1997) were primarily concerned with whether respondents who endorsed these stereotypes responded differently than those who did not to descriptions of individual welfare recipients and criminal suspects whose race (black or white) and fit to stereotypes (stereotype consistent or inconsistent) were manipulated in a between-subjects fashion. As predicted, respondents who endorsed negative Black Work Ethic stereotypes (the top third of the sample) were responsive to race: They made harsher judgments of a black than a white welfare mother, regardless of her fit to stereotypes (i.e., whether she was a high school dropout or not). This stood in contrast to respondents who rejected negative Black Work Ethic stereotypes (the lower third of the sample); these individuals were either equally favorable to black and white welfare mothers or more favorable toward the black high school dropout than the white dropout. Similar patterns of response emerged on items assessing support for welfare programs in general, depending on the description of likely recipients (blacks versus European immigrants); however, on this issue high stereotypers were more favorable toward blacks than European immigrants when the recipients were described as "people who have shown they want to work."

Endorsers of the negative Black Hostility stereotypes responded in a comparable manner to vignettes describing black versus white young men who were suspected of drug use and subjected to a police search. When the men fit negative stereotypes (e.g., they were using foul language), high stereotypers thought the search was more reasonable when the targets were black than white; when the men were well dressed and polite (counterstereotypical), the search was perceived as more unreasonable for blacks than whites. Those who rejected the Black Hostility stereotype were unaffected by the race or behavior of the described individuals.

Discriminant

The Black Work Ethic subscale was correlated only weakly with a two-item measure of value placed on "individualism" ($r = .12$) and with political ideology ($r = .13$).

Location

Peffley, M., Hurwitz, J., & Sniderman, P. (1997). Racial stereotypes and whites' political views of blacks in the context of welfare and crime. *American Journal of Political Science, 41,* 30–60. Reprinted by permission of the University of Wisconsin Press.

Results and Comments

This measure is new, and little validity information is available, but other national surveys have used comparable items, and these could be examined to provide additional evidence about the instrument. The single-item assessment of Black Hostility stereotypes could be improved, and the authors or other researchers should address whether the two subscales—Work Ethic and Hostility—have specific or distinct effects: For example, does the Black Work Ethic stereotype predict judgments in the "drug use" scenarios, and does the Black Hostility measure predict responses to welfare recipients? It would also be valuable to compare this scale with the other measure of stereotypes reviewed here—Bobo and Kluegel's (1993) Prejudice Index (see previous section). These sets of researchers have different theoretical conceptualizations—stereotypes are distinct from prejudice for Peffley *et al.*, but are a central component of prejudice for Bobo and Kluegel. Social psychologists seem more inclined toward the former position (e.g., see Dovidio *et al.*, 1996), but examining the relative merits of each approach would be worthwhile. Although additional research is needed, the Racial Stereotypes Measure shows some promise as an indicator of respondents' cognitive representations of black Americans and may prove an important predictor (in addition to more "affective" measures of prejudice) of policy and other judgments.

**Racial Stereotypes Measure
(Peffley, Hurwitz, & Sniderman, 1997)**

Now I'll read a few words that people sometimes use to describe blacks. Of course, no word fits absolutely everybody, but as I read each one, please tell me, using a number from 0 to 10, how well you think it describes blacks as a group. If you think it's a very good description of most blacks, give it a 10. If you feel a word is a very inaccurate description of most blacks, give it a 0.

A. Black Work Ethic

   1. Lazy

```
        1     2     3     4     5     6     7     8     9     10
     INACCURATE                                                ACCURATE
```

*2. Determined to succeed

*3. Dependable

*4. Hardworking

5. Most black parents don't teach their children the self-discipline and skills it takes to get ahead in America.
1 = DISAGREE STRONGLY, 2 = DISAGREE SOMEWHAT, 3 = AGREE SOMEWHAT, 4 = AGREE STRONGLY

B. Black Hostility

6. Aggressive/Violent

*Indicates reverse scored item.

Social Dominance Orientation (SDO) Scale

(J. Sidanius & F. Pratto, 1993; F. Pratto, J. Sidanius, L. M. Stallworth, & B. F. Malle, 1994)

Variable

The Social Dominance Orientation (SDO) Scale measures individual differences in the extent to which respondents prefer inequality among social groups.

Description

The SDO Scale is not a direct measure of racial attitudes, but a growing literature indicates that, like authoritarianism, SDO is a focal part of a social ideology that predicts a wide range of political and racial attitudes (Pratto *et al.*, 1994). We have chosen to include this scale because of its conceptual importance to politics and racial attitudes and its empirical relevance to more direct measures of racial attitudes.

Social dominance orientation is the degree of one's preference for inequality among social groups. People who score high in SDO prefer hierarchical relations among groups, as compared to equal relations among groups; they are hierarchy enhancing and support a variety of "legitimizing myths" that align social groups on a superior–inferior dimension. These myths include racial and ethnic prejudice, nationalism, patriotism, separation between "high" and "low" culture, sexism, meritocracy, political conservatism, and noblesse oblige.

Sidanius, Pratto, and their colleagues have reported at least four different, but overlapping, versions of the SDO Scale, consisting of 8, 14, 16, or 20 items. Pratto *et al.* (1994) used both the 14- and the 16-item versions, and Sidanius and Pratto (1993) used both the 8- and the 20-item versions; across these articles these various operationalizations are described as interchangeable, but Pratto (personal communication, May 1997) has noted that the 16-item version is now preferred. Responses are made on 1–7 (very positive to very negative) scales and averaged across items, with high numbers indicating a stronger social dominance orientation.

Samples

In Pratto *et al.* (1994) 13 different samples of northern California college students (total $N = 1952$) responded to a survey (these students were primarily from the University of

California at Berkeley, San Jose State University, and Stanford University). In Sidanius and Pratto (1993) several hundred undergraduates at UCLA were surveyed. The mean item mean across the 13 samples in Pratto *et al.* (1994) was 2.7 (mean item SD = .5).

Reliability

Internal Consistency

Pratto *et al.* (1994) reported an average Cronbach's alpha of .84 across all 13 samples (ranging from .80 to .89). A variety of other LISREL-based statistics suggest that SDO is best represented by a single factor.

Test–Retest

In one study 25 participants retested after a three-month interval produced a reliability coefficient of .81; in another, 46 of the highest and lowest scoring individuals from over 400 respondents were selected, and the authors reported a retest reliability "some months later" of .84. In neither of these studies did Pratto *et al.* (1994) find much evidence for regression to the mean, suggesting high stability.

Validity

Convergent

Because much of the research reported by the developers of the SDO Scale involves LISREL analysis, the statistics reported in their articles are not Pearson correlations, but estimated multivariate path coefficients (*b*s). In Sidanius and Pratto (1993) the SDO Scale was related to an unspecified measure of racism ($b = .53$) and to racial policy attitudes (opposition to affirmative action and busing, $b = .23$). Out-group denigration was more pronounced in a minimal groups experiment ($b = .18$), and more social distance was sought from out-group members ($b = .28$) by individuals high in SDO. In addition, the SDO Scale predicted conservative political ideology ($b = .57$) and racism ($b = .55$) when controlling for the shared variance in ideology and racism, suggesting that the SDO Scale can predict racism independently of its overlap with traditionally defined political ideology.

In a study of over 600 randomly selected Los Angeles County residents, Sidanius, Pratto, and Bobo (1996) reported a correlation between "classical" racism (see the Racial Attitude Scale discussed earlier) and the SDO Scale of $r = .47$ and a correlation between the SDO Scale and opposition to affirmative action of $r = .27$. Sidanius *et al.* (1996) also showed that all of the shared variance between racism and politics in a sample of 148 UCLA undergraduates could be accounted for by an individual's SDO Scale score.

In Pratto *et al.* (1994) the SDO Scale was also correlated with antifemale sentiment, including two measures of sexism (mean $rs = .49$ and .51) and rape myth acceptance (mean $r = .43$). The SDO Scale also correlated with an impressive array of political ideologies relevant to racial attitudes. In addition to antiblack racism (mean $r = .55$) and anti-Arab racism (mean $r = .25$), the SDO Scale reliably correlated with measures of nationalism (mean $r = .53$; see also Sidanius et al., 1997), patriotism (mean $r = .43$), cultural elitism (mean $r = .39$), equal opportunity (mean $r = .45$), and noblesse oblige (mean $r = -.55$).

Pratto *et al.* (1994) administered the SDO Scale during the U.S.–Iraqi War (January 1991)—a conflict with strong anti-Arab overtones—along with measures of attitudes toward war policy. The SDO Scale correlated $r = .48$ with favoring military action by the United States and $r = .45$ with favoring suspension of liberties (e.g., "Military censorship of the press is appropriate in times of war").

Furthermore, Pratto *et al.* (1994) demonstrated that the SDO Scale independently predicted negative attitudes toward gay and lesbian rights, women's rights, problack racial policy initiatives, antimiscegenation policies, and antiblack racism, over and above political party preference. This suggests that the SDO Scale is not simply a measure of conservative politics, but instead is a measure of preference for the presence of dominance hierarchies in society.

Finally, SDO theory makes several "known-group"-type predictions. Because of their relatively dominant position, males should score higher than females; Pratto *et al.* (1994) reported a mean point-biserial r of .26.

Location

Sidanius, J., & Pratto, F. (1993). The inevitability of oppression and the dynamics of social dominance. In P. M. Sniderman, P. E. Tetlock, & E. G. Carmines (Eds.), *Prejudice, politics and the American dilemma* (pp. 173–211). Stanford, CA: Stanford University Press. Reprinted with the permission of the publishers. Copyright © 1993 by the Board of Trustees of the Leland Stanford Junior University.

Pratto, F., Sidanius, J., Stallworth, L. M., & Malle, B. F. (1994). Social dominance orientation: A personality variable predicting social and political attitudes. *Journal of Personality and Social Psychology, 67,* 741–763.

Results and Comments

Social Dominance Orientation represents an ideological preference that appears to have important consequences for racial attitudes. SDO can be thought of as a predisposition to hold certain ethnic attitudes; given an appropriate opportunity, a person high in SDO will quite probably develop a negative attitude toward some group that is low in status or prestige. The route by which this attitude is justified (what Sidanius, Pratto, and their colleagues refer to as "legitimizing myths") may differ according to social, religious, or political commitment, but the ultimate result is a preference for hierarchies based on group superiority.

One problem with SDO research has been the changing nature of the scale. Almost every published paper in the SDO paradigm uses more than one version of the scale to measure the construct; together Sidanius and Pratto (1993), Pratto *et al.* (1994), and Sidanius *et al.* (1996) use a total of six different versions of the scale, with a significant amount of nonoverlap among the scale items. While all of the scales have strong face validity and each has some empirical reliability and validity associated with it, it is a confusing task to determine which scale, with what validity, has been used in which study and which scale *should* be used by other researchers. Still we find the SDO Scale to be based on a provocative and promising theory of social and political conflict that is likely to have a strong impact on social psychological and political theories of racial attitudes and policy preferences.

Social Dominance Orientation (SDO) Scale (Sidanius & Pratto, 1993; Pratto, Sidanius, Stallworth, & Malle, 1994)

Which of the following objects or statements do you have a positive or a negative feeling towards? Beside each object or statement, place a number from 1 to 7 which represents the degree of your positive or negative feeling.

From Sidanius and Pratto (1993): SDO₁

1. Some people are more worthy than others.
   - 7 = VERY POSITIVE
   - 6 = POSITIVE
   - 5 = SLIGHTLY POSITIVE
   - 4 = NEITHER POSITIVE NOR NEGATIVE
   - 3 = SLIGHTLY NEGATIVE
   - 2 = NEGATIVE
   - 1 = VERY NEGATIVE

*2. Increased economic equality.

*3. Increased social equality.

4. Winning is more important than how the game is played.

5. Getting ahead in life by any means necessary.

*6. Equality.

*7. If people were treated more equally, we would have fewer problems in the country.

8. It is not really a big problem if some people have more of a chance in life than others.

*Indicates reverse scored item.

From Sidanius and Pratto (1993): SDO₂

1. Some people are more worthy than others.

*2. Increased social equality.

3. Winning is more important than how the game is played.

4. Getting ahead in life by any means necessary.

5. This country would be better off if we cared less about how equal all people are.

*6. Equality.

*7. If people were treated more equally, we would have fewer problems in the country.

8. It is not really a big problem if some people have more of a chance in life than others.

9. Competition.

10. To get ahead in life, it is sometimes necessary to step on others.

11. This country would be better off if inferior groups stayed in their place.

*12. The world was provided with enough resources to take care of all its people.

13. Being at the top is the ONLY place to be.

14. It is important that our country continue to be the best in the world.

15. Sometimes war is necessary to put other countries in their place.

*16. In an ideal world, all nations would be equal.

17. This country must continue to lead the Free World.

18. I'd give almost anything to get rich.

19. It's about time that we put Japan in its place.

20. We should do anything necessary to increase the power of our country, even if it means war with smaller countries.

*Indicates reverse scored item.

From Pratto, Sidanius, Stallworth, & Malle (1994): SDO₃

1. Some groups of people are simply not the equals of others.

2. Some people are just more worthy than others.

3. This country would be better off if we cared less about how equal all people are.

4. Some people are just more deserving than others.

5. It is not a problem if some people have more of a chance in life than others.

6. Some people are just inferior to others.

7. To get ahead in life, it is sometimes necessary to step on others.

*8. Increased economic equality.

*9. Increased social equality.

*10. Equality.

*11. If people were treated more equally we would have fewer problems in this country.

*12. In an ideal world, all nations would be equal.

*13. We should try to treat one another as equals as much as possible. (or All humans should be treated equally.)

*14. It is important that we treat other countries as equals.

*Indicates reverse scored item.

From Pratto, Sidanius, Stallworth, & Malle (1994): SDO₄

1. Some people are just inferior to others.

2. In getting what you want, it is sometimes necessary to use force against other groups.

3. It's OK if some groups have more of a chance in life than others.

4. To get ahead in life, it is sometimes necessary to step on others.

5. If certain groups stayed in their place, we would have fewer problems.

6. It's probably a good thing that certain groups are at the top and other groups are at the bottom.

7. Inferior groups should stay in their place.

8. Sometimes other groups must be kept in their place.

*9. It would be good if groups were equal.

*10. Group equality should be our ideal.

*11. All groups should be given an equal chance in life.

*12. We should do what we can to equalize conditions for different groups.

*13. Increased social equality.

*14. We would have fewer problems if we treated people more equally.

*15. We should strive to make incomes as equal as possible.

*16. No one group should dominate in society.

*Indicates reverse scored item.

Universal Orientation Scale (UOS)
(S. T. Phillips & R. C. Ziller, 1997)

Variable

This scale measures the tendency toward *non*prejudice, which the authors define as "a universal orientation in interpersonal relations whereby the actor selectively attends to and accentuates the similarities between the self and diverse others" (Phillips & Ziller, 1997, pp. 420–421).

Description

The UOS items were designed to tap into this notion of perceived similarity between self and others (or perceived difference, for reverse scored statements). None of these items explicitly mentions race or ethnicity because the authors had "concerns about a social desirability component" to the instrument (Phillips & Ziller, 1997, p. 423). To further avoid this problem, they designed their prodifference items to be "at least as socially desirable as similarity emphasis" items, such that they would "help camouflage the purpose of the scale" (p. 423). The original scale had 26 items; 6 were later dropped because of face validity or comprehensibility problems. Scores can range from 1 (low universal orientation) to 5 (high universal orientation).

Samples

All scale development was based on various samples of University of Florida undergraduates (total $N = 1967$). In a sample of 583 introductory psychology students, the mean UOS score was 3.4 (SD = .5).

Reliability

Internal Consistency

Cronbach's alpha for the 20-item instrument was .76, and item-total correlations ranged from .11 to .40 in the sample of 583 students. Both exploratory and confirmatory factor analyses indicated that a two-factor oblique solution was somewhat more appropriate than a one-factor solution; in each case the reverse coded items (which emphasized perceived self–other differences) loaded on a separate factor from the other items. However, because the one-factor model was deemed "adequate" both empirically and theoretically (and the two subscales were correlated .23), the authors recommended using the scale in its single-factor form.

Test–Retest

In the same sample the authors found a six-week test–retest reliability of .75.

Validity

Convergent

The UOS was correlated $-.38$ with the Dogmatism Scale (Rokeach, 1960), an indicator of openness versus closedness of one's belief system, in another sample of 99 Florida undergraduates. Phillips and Ziller (1997) also reported a correlation of .37 with Katz and Hass's (1988) measure of Humanitarian/Egalitarian values ($N = 128$) and correlations of .32, .32, and .33, respectively, with the Empathic Concern, Perspective-Taking, and Fantasy subscales of Davis's (1983) Interpersonal Reactivity Index ($N = 154$).

The UOS was also meaningfully related to participants' responses to a series of nonverbal "self–social" schema measures (see Ziller, 1973). These items involve diagrams depicting self in relation to other individuals and groups, for which the respondent is asked to indicate his or her relationship to others. The resulting indexes of Openness, Marginality, Heterogeneity, Nonhierarchy, and Self–Other Unity were correlated .30, .16, .22, .23, and .16, respectively, with the UOS ($N = 158$).

From the original sample of 583 undergraduates, 66 white individuals in the top and bottom quarters of the UOS distribution participated in a laboratory study in which they rated a series of photographs (which accompanied biographical information) of minority and nonminority target individuals on perceived attractiveness, similarity to themselves, and desirability as work partners. For those scoring high on the UOS, minority and nonminority targets were judged equally acceptable–desirable; for those scoring low on the UOS, minority targets were judged significantly less desirable than nonminority targets. Low UOS participants also judged all targets as less acceptable overall than did high UOS participants.

In a second study 18 high UOS and 18 low UOS college students rated photographs of minority and nonminority fashion models on perceived attractiveness and representativeness of humankind. High UOS participants judged minority and nonminority models as equally representative of humankind; low UOS participants judged minority models as significantly less representative than nonminority models. Both high and low UOS respondents judged nonminority models more attractive than minority models, but high UOS participants judged minority models to be significantly more attractive than did low

UOS participants. Low scorers were also significantly more variable in their attractiveness judgments of minority models than were high scorers.

Discriminant

The UOS was uncorrelated with Crowne and Marlowe's (1966) Social Desirability Scale ($r = -.05$) in a sample of 251 undergraduates. In a separate sample of 712 undergraduates, the UOS was modestly correlated with, but clearly distinct from, the Modern Racism Scale ($r = -.18$) and Katz and Hass's (1988) Pro-black ($r = .11$) and Anti-black ($r = -.19$) Attitude Questionnaires. Finally the UOS was unrelated to a measure of self-complexity (Ziller, Martell, & Morrison, 1977): $r = .12$, $N = 158$.

Location

Phillips, S. T., & Ziller, R. C. (1997). Toward a theory and measure of the nature of non-prejudice. *Journal of Personality and Social Psychology, 72,* 420–434. Copyright © 1997 by the American Psychological Association. Reprinted with permission.

Results and Comments

This scale is new, and therefore there are no accumulated data outside the original lab and college student context. However, the early results are promising, and the authors' attempt to measure nonprejudice as distinct from the construct of prejudice (i.e., low scorers on the UOS are not necessarily conceptualized as high in prejudice) is welcome. The authors question the common assumption that categorization as a basic human process inevitably leads to prejudice, and this approach may indeed yield new insights into how people think about groups. Whether universal orientation is qualitatively different from prejudicial thinking remains to be established, as does the mechanism by which universal thought operates. For example, does universal thinking require the initial recognition of group differences prior to the acceptance of self–other similarity, or do universalists fail to acknowledge any such differences? The relationship between the UOS and other broad measures of sociopolitical orientation (e.g., the SDO Scale reviewed earlier) also merits further examination.

Universal Orientation Scale (UOS) (Phillips & Ziller, 1997)

1. The similarities between males and females are greater than the differences.

1	2	3	4	5
DOES NOT DESCRIBE ME WELL			DESCRIBES ME VERY WELL	

2. I tend to value similarities over differences when I meet someone.
3. At one level of thinking we are all of a kind.
4. I can understand almost anyone because I'm a little like everyone.
*5. Little differences among people mean a lot.
6. I can see myself fitting into many groups.

   7. There is a potential for good and evil in all of us.

   8. When I look into the eyes of others I see myself.

 *9. I could never get accustomed to living in another country.

*10. When I first meet someone I tend to notice differences between myself and the other person.

 11. "Between" describes my position with regard to groups better than does "in" and "out."

 12. The same spirit dwells in everyone.

*13. Older persons are very different than I am.

*14. I can tell a great deal about a person by knowing their gender.

 15. There is a certain beauty in everyone.

*16. I can tell a great deal about a person by knowing his/her age.

*17. Men and women will never totally understand each other because of their inborn differences.

 18. Everyone in the world is very much alike because in the end we all die.

*19. I have difficulty relating to persons who are much younger than I.

 20. When I meet someone I tend to notice similarities between myself and the other person.

*Indicates reverse scored item.

Appendix A: Individual Racial Attitude Items from the NES

American National Election Study (Center for Political Studies; e.g., see Rosenstone, Kinder, & Miller, 1995)

Feeling Thermometers

1. I'll read the name of a group and I'd like you to rate that group using something called the feeling thermometer. You can choose any number between 0 and 100. The higher the number, the warmer or more favorable you feel toward that group; the lower the number, the colder or less favorable. You would rate the group at the 50 degree mark if you feel neither warm nor cold toward it.

   A. Using the feeling thermometer, how would you rate BLACKS?

   B. Using the feeling thermometer, how would you rate BLACK MILITANTS?

Stereotypes

2. Which of these statements about the relative intelligence of black and white people would you agree with:

    ____ On the average, black people are born with more intelligence than white people.

    ____ On the average, white people and black people are born with equal intelligence.

    ____ On the average, white people are born with more intelligence than black people.

Views on Blacks' Efforts to Gain Civil Rights

3. Some say that the civil rights people have been trying to push too fast. Others feel they haven't pushed fast enough. How about you: Do you think that civil rights leaders are trying to push too fast, are going too slowly, or are they moving about the right speed?

4. Do you think the actions black people have taken have, on the whole, helped their cause or, on the whole, hurt their cause?

5. During the past year or so, would you say that most of the actions black people have taken to get the things they want have been violent, or have most of these actions been peaceful?

Views on Closeness Between the Races

6. Are you in favor of desegregation, strict segregation, or something in between?

7. Which of these statements would you agree with:

    ____ White people have a right to keep black people out of their neighborhoods if they want to.

    ____ Black people have a right to live wherever they can afford to, just like anybody else.

8. Some people say that it is better for America if different racial and ethnic groups maintain their distinct cultures. Others say that it is better if groups change so that they blend into the larger society as in the idea of a melting pot. Which of these positions comes closer to your own opinion: Racial and ethnic groups should maintain their distinct cultures, or groups should change so that they blend into the larger society?

Attributions

9. In past studies we have asked people why they think white people seem to get more of the good things in life in America—such as better jobs and more money—than black people do. These are some of the reasons given by both blacks and whites. Please tell me whether you agree or disagree with each reason.

    A. The differences are brought about by God; God made the races different as part of his divine plan.

    B. Blacks come from a less able race and this explains why blacks are not as well off as whites in America.

    C. A small group of powerful and wealthy white people control things and act to keep blacks down.

    D. Black Americans teach their children values and skills different from those required to be successful in American society.

Government Intervention

10. As you may know, Congress passed a bill that says that black people should have the right to go to any hotel or restaurant they can afford, just like anybody else. Some people feel that this is something the government should support. Others feel that the government should stay out of this matter. Have you been interested enough in this to favor one side over another? (If yes) Should the government support the right of black people to go to any hotel or restaurant they can afford or leave these matters to the states and local communities?

11. If you had a say in making up the federal budget this year, on which of these programs would you like to see spending increased and which decreased? Should federal spending on programs that assist blacks be increased, decreased, or kept about the same?

12. Some people feel that if black people are not getting fair treatment in jobs, the government in Washington ought to see to it that they do. Others feel that this is not the federal government's business. Have you had enough interest in this question to favor one side over the other? (If yes) Should the government in Washington see to it that black people get fair treatment in jobs or leave these matters to the states and local communities?

13. Please tell me how much you agree or disagree with the following statement. Equal opportunity for blacks and whites to succeed is important but it's not really the government's job to guarantee it. Do you agree strongly, agree somewhat, neither agree nor disagree, disagree somewhat, or disagree strongly with that?

14. Most blacks who receive money from welfare programs could get along without it if they tried. Do you agree strongly, agree somewhat, neither agree nor disagree, disagree somewhat, or disagree strongly with that?

15. Some people feel that the government in Washington should make every effort to improve the social and economic position of blacks. Others feel that the government should not make any special effort to help blacks because they should help themselves. Where would you place yourself on this scale, or haven't you thought much about this?

16. Some people say that because of past discrimination blacks should be given preference in hiring and promotion. Others say that such preference in hiring and promotion of blacks is wrong because it [gives blacks advantages they haven't earned/discriminates against whites]. What about your opinion—are you for or against preferential hiring and promotion of blacks?

17. Some people say that because of past discrimination it is sometimes necessary for colleges and universities to reserve openings for black students. Others oppose quotas because they say quotas [give blacks advantages they haven't earned/discriminate against whites]. What about your opinion—are you for or against quotas to admit black students?

18. Some people say that the government in Washington should see to it that white and black children go to the same schools. Others claim that this is not the government's business. Have you been interested enough in this question to favor one side over the other? (1 = see to it the black and white children go to same schools, 5 = government should stay out of it)

Perceptions of Opportunities for/Discrimination Against Blacks

19. In the past few years we have heard a lot about improving the position of black people in this country. How much real change do you think there has been in the position of black people in the past few years; a lot, some, or not much at all?

20. Government officials usually pay less attention to a request or complaint from a black person than from a white person.

21. Affirmative action programs for blacks have reduced whites' chances for jobs, promotions, and admission to schools and training programs.

22. What do you think the chances are these days that a white person won't get admitted to a school while an equally or less qualified black person gets admitted instead? Is this very likely, somewhat likely, or not very likely to happen these days?

23. What do you think the chances are these days that a black person will get admitted to a school while an equally qualified white person gets turned down? Is this very likely, somewhat likely, or not very likely to happen these days?

24. What do you think the chances are these days that a white person won't get a job or promotion while an equally or less qualified black person gets one instead? Is this very likely, somewhat likely, or not very likely to happen these days?

25. What do you think the chances are these days that a black person will get a job or promotion while an equally qualified white person gets turned down? Is this very likely, somewhat likely, or not very likely to happen these days?

26. What do you think the chances are these days that you or anyone in your family won't get a job or promotion while an equally or less qualified black employee receives one instead? Is this very likely, somewhat likely, or not very likely to happen these days?

27. What do you think the chances are these days that you or anyone in your family won't get admitted to a school while an equally or less qualified black person gets admitted instead? Is this very likely, somewhat likely, or not very likely to happen these days?

28. What do you think the chances are these days that you or anyone in your family will get a job or promotion while an equally qualified black employee is turned down? Is this very likely, somewhat likely, or not very likely to happen these days?

Notes:
Items 9A and 9B were used by Gilens (1995) as an index of perceived innate black inferiority, and by Sears *et al.* (1997) as a measure of old-fashioned racism, $\alpha = .54$.

Items 12, 13, and 18 were used by Gilens (1995) as a measure of attitudes toward government responsibility for ensuring equal opportunity.

Items 16 and 17 were used by Gilens (1995) to measure support for affirmative action.

Items 1A, 6, 7, 12, and 18 were used by Jackman (1977) to represent three components of racial attitudes [affect (1A), general action orientation (6 and 7), and applied action orientation (12 and 18)].

Items 11, 12, 15, 16, 17, and 18 were used by Kinder & Sanders (1996) as measures of racial policy attitudes.

Items 26 and 27 were used by Kinder & Sanders (1996) as measures of self-interest–threat.

Items 21, 22, and 24 were used by Kinder & Sanders (1996) as measures of group-interest–threat.

Appendix B: Individual Racial Attitude Items from the GSS

General Social Survey
(National Opinion Research Center; e.g., see Davis & Smith, 1990, 1994)

Views on Closeness Between the Races

1. Do you think there should be laws against marriages between blacks and whites?

2. White people have the right to keep blacks out of their neighborhoods if they want to, and blacks should respect that right.

3. How strongly would you object if a member of your family wanted to bring a Black friend home to dinner? Would you object strongly, mildly, or not at all?

4. Now I'm going to ask you about different types of contact with various groups of people. In each situation, would you please tell me whether you would be very much in favor of it happening, somewhat in favor, neither in favor nor opposed to it happening, somewhat opposed, or very much opposed to it happening.

    A. Living in a neighborhood where half of your neighbors were blacks?

    B. How about having a close relative or family member marry a black person?

5. If a black with the same income and education as you have moved into your block, would it make any difference to you?

6. How would it make you feel if a close relative of yours were planning to marry a Black? Would you be very uneasy, somewhat uneasy, or not uneasy at all?

7. If your party nominated a black for President, would you vote for him if he were qualified for the job?

8. Would you yourself have any objection to sending your children to a school where half of the children are blacks?

9. Do you think white students and black students should go to the same schools or to separate schools?

10. If you could find the housing that you would want and like, would you rather live in a neighborhood that is all black; mostly black; half black; half white; or mostly white?

11. Do Blacks attend the church that you, yourself, attend most often, or not?

12. Blacks shouldn't push themselves where they're not wanted.

13. Have you ever stopped buying certain products because of the way the company or country which makes them has treated black people?

14. Please tell me whether you agree or disagree with the following statements.

    A. You can expect special problems with marriages between Blacks and Whites.

    B. You can expect special problems with Black supervisors getting along with workers that are mostly white.

15. A school board should not hire a person to teach if that person belongs to an organization that opposes school integration.

16. If you were driving through the neighborhoods in a city, would you go out of your way to avoid going through a black section?

17. If you and your friends belonged to a social club that would not let Blacks join, would you try to change the rules so that Blacks could join?

18. If you could not get the rules changed, do you think you would resign from the club, even if your friends didn't?

19. How important is the race relations issue to you—would you say it is one of the most important, important, not very important, or not important at all?

20. How concerned are you personally about race relations? Are you very concerned, somewhat concerned, not very concerned, or not concerned at all?

Attributions

21. On the average blacks have worse jobs, income, and housing than white people. Do you think these differences are . . .

    A. Mainly due to discrimination

    B. Because most blacks have less in-born ability to learn

    C. Because most blacks don't have the chance for education that it takes to rise out of poverty

    D. Because most blacks just don't have the motivation or will power to pull themselves out of poverty

Government Intervention

22. Some people think that blacks have been discriminated against for so long that the government has a special obligation to help improve their living standards. Others believe that the government should not be giving special treatment to blacks. Where would you place yourself on this scale or haven't you made up your mind on this?

23. We are faced with many problems in this country, none of which can be solved easily or inexpensively. I'm going to name some of these problems, and for each one I'd like you to tell me whether you think we're spending too much money on it, too little money, or about the right amount: (How about) improving the conditions of blacks?

24. In general, do you favor or oppose the busing of black and white school children from one district to another?

25. Suppose there is a community-wide vote on the general housing issue. There are two possible laws to vote on. One law says that a homeowner can decide for himself whom to sell his house to, even if he prefers not to sell to blacks. The second law says that a homeowner cannot refuse to sell to someone because of their race or color. Which law would you vote for?

26. People have different opinions about the amount of influence that various groups have in American life and politics. Do you think that blacks have far too much influence, too much influence, about the right amount of influence, too little influence, or do they have far too little influence?

27. Some people think that the best way for blacks to improve their position is through civil rights groups; they would be at point 1 on this card. Other people think that the best way for blacks to improve their position is for each individual black to become better trained and more qualified. They would be located at point 7. And other people have opinions somewhere in between. Where would you place yourself on this scale?

28. Some people feel that the government in Washington should make every effort possible to improve the social and economic position of blacks and other minority groups, even if it means giving them preferential treatment. Suppose these people are at one end of the scale at point number 1. Others feel that the government should not make any special effort to help minorities because they should help themselves. Suppose these people are at the other end, at point 7. And of course, some other people have opinions somewhere in between. Where would you place yourself on this scale, or haven't you thought much about this?

29. Here are several things that the government in Washington might do to deal with the problems of poverty and unemployment among Black Americans. I would like you to tell me if you favor or oppose them. (strongly favor, favor, neither favor nor oppose, oppose, strongly oppose)

    A. Giving business and industry special tax breaks for locating in largely black areas.

    B. Spending more money on the schools in black neighborhoods, especially for preschool and early education programs.

    C. Provide special college scholarships for black children who maintain good grades.

    D. Forbidding the use of racial quotas in hiring and employment.

30. Some religious and business groups have set up programs to encourage Black people to buy houses in white suburbs. Do you favor or oppose these voluntary programs to integrate white suburbs?

31. What about the city government in white suburbs? Do you think they should encourage Black people to buy homes in the suburbs, should they discourage them, or should they leave it to private efforts?

Perceptions of Opportunity for/Discrimination Against Blacks

32. Do you feel that a black person who has the same education and qualifications can get as good a job as a white person? Would you say almost always, sometimes, or almost never?

33. If a black person has the same qualifications as a white person, do you feel that he or she can make as much money almost always, sometimes, or almost never?

34. Do you think the opportunities for blacks to get ahead have improved in the last five years, remained about the same, or gotten worse?

35. In the next 5 years, do you think that opportunities for blacks to get ahead will improve, remain about the same, or get worse?

36. How important is a person's race for getting ahead in life? (essential, very important, fairly important, not very important, not important at all)

37. Some people think that certain groups have too much influence in American life and politics, while other people feel that certain groups don't have as much influence as they deserve. For the group Blacks, just tell me the number of the statement that best says how you feel. (too much influence, right amount of influence, too little influence)

38. How much discrimination is there that hurts the chances of blacks to get good paying jobs? Would you say there is a lot, some, only a little, or none at all?

39. How much discrimination is there that makes it hard for blacks to buy or rent housing wherever they want? Would you say there is a lot, some, only a little, or none at all?

40. What do you think the chances are these days that a white person won't get a job or promotion while an equally or less qualified black person gets one instead? Is this very likely, somewhat likely, or not very likely to happen these days?

Notes:
Items 1, 2, 21, 22, and 23 were used by Bobo & Kluegel (1993) to test the validity of their Prejudice Index.
    Items 1, 2, 7, 8, 12, and 21B were scaled and used as an index of old-fashioned racism by Sears et al. (1997); in the 1994 GSS, α = .71.

Appendix C: Individual Racial Attitude
Items from the Race and Politics Survey

Race and Politics Survey
(Sniderman & Piazza, 1993)
Stereotypes

1. Now I'm going to read a few more statements about black people. No statement is true about everybody, but, speaking generally, please say whether you agree strongly, agree somewhat, disagree somewhat, or disagree strongly with each statement.

   A. How about the statement: Most blacks have a chip on their shoulder?

   B. Blacks are more violent than whites.

   C. Black neighborhoods tend to be run down because blacks simply don't take care of their property.

   D. Most blacks who are on welfare programs could get a job if they really tried.

Attributions

2. Most people—blacks and whites alike—agree that the average white person in America is more likely to have a good income, get a good education, and to have a regular job than the average black is. Here are some of the reasons that have been given as to why the average black American is not as well off as the average white American. As I read each one, please tell me whether you basically agree or disagree.

   A. First, how about the statement that rich and powerful white people who control things in America try to keep black people down—do you basically agree or basically disagree with that explanation as to why the average black American is not as well off as the average white American?

   B. How about the statement that God made the races different as part of his divine plan?

   C. If blacks would only try harder, they would be just as well off as whites.

   D. A history of slavery and being discriminated against has created conditions that make it difficult for black people to work their way up.

   E. The reason most black people are not as well off as most whites is that blacks are born with less ability.

Government Intervention

3. Some people think that the government in Washington should increase spending for programs to help blacks. Others feel that blacks should rely only on themselves. Which makes more sense to you? Should the government help improve the position of blacks, or should they rely only on themselves?

IF GOVT SHOULD HELP: Would you still feel that way even if government help means people get special treatment just because they are black or would that change your mind?

IF BLACKS SHOULD RELY ON SELVES: Would you still feel that way even if it means that blacks will continue to be poorer and more often out of work than whites or would that change your mind?

4. Suppose there were a community-wide election on a general housing law and that you had to choose between two possible laws. One law says that homeowners can decide for themselves whom to sell their houses to, even if they prefer not to sell to blacks. The second law says that homeowners are not allowed to refuse to sell to someone because of race or color. Which law would you vote for?

IF CAN DECIDE FOR SELVES: Would you feel differently if, as a result of that law, it turned out that blacks were prevented from moving into nice neighborhoods?

IF CANNOT REFUSE TO SELL: Would you feel differently if it turned out that a new government agency had to be set up to enforce that law?

5. Some people feel that (the government in Washington/state or local government) ought to see to it that blacks get fair treatment in jobs. Others feel that this is not the government's business and it should stay out of it. How do you feel?

IF GOVT SHOULD BE INVOLVED: Would you still feel the same way, even if it means that government will have more say in telling people how to run their lives, or do you think that might change your mind?

IF GOVT SHOULD STAY OUT: Would you still feel the same way even if it means that some racial discrimination will continue?

6. Sometimes you hear it said that there should be a law to ensure that a certain number of federal contracts go to minority contractors. We'd like to know what you think. Do you think that such a law is a good idea or a bad idea?

7. Some people say that because of past discrimination it is sometimes necessary for colleges and universities to reserve openings for black students who don't meet the usual standards. Others are against such quotas. What's your opinion—are you for or against quotas to admit some black students who don't meet the usual standards?

IF FAVOR QUOTAS: Would you still feel that way, even if it means fewer opportunities for qualified whites, or would you change your mind?

IF OPPOSE QUOTAS: Would you still feel that way, even if it means that hardly any blacks would be able to go to the best colleges and universities, or would you change your mind?

8. Some people think achieving racial integration of schools is so important that it justifies busing children to schools out of their own neighborhoods. Others think letting children go to their neighborhood schools is so important that they oppose busing. How about you—do you favor or oppose busing?

Appendix D: Selected Sources for Additional Measures of Race-Related Attitudes

---

Children's Racial Attitudes

Preschool Racial Attitude Measure II (PRAM II)

Williams, J. E., Best, D. L., Boswell, D. A., Mattson, L. A., & Graves, D. J. (1975). Preschool Racial Attitude Measure II. *Educational and Psychological Measurement, 35,* 3–18.

Multi-Response Racial Attitude Measure (MRA)

Doyle, A. B., Beaudet, J., & Aboud, F. E. (1988). Developmental patterns in the flexibility of children's ethnic attitudes. *Journal of Cross-cultural Psychology, 19,* 3–18.

Racial Reconciliation

Aboud, F. E. (1981). Egocentrism, conformity, and agreeing to disagree. *Developmental Psychology, 17,* 791–799.

Assorted Other Scales

Attitudes to (Australian) Aborigines Scale (AAbS)
Attitudes to Asians Scale (AAsS)

Walker, I. (1994). Attitudes to minorities: Survey evidence of western Australians' attitudes to aborigines, Asians, and women. *Australian Journal of Psychology, 46,* 137–143.

Attitudes toward Hispanics and Hispanic Integration

Green, D. P., & Citrin, J. (1994). Measurement error and the structure of attitudes—Are positive and negative judgments opposites? *American Journal of Political Science, 38,* 256–281.

Anti-Arab Racism Scale

Pratto, F., Sidanius, J., Stallworth, L. M., & Malle, B. F. (1994). Social dominance orientation: A personality variable predicting social and political attitudes. *Journal of Personality and Social Psychology, 67,* 741–763.

Attitudes toward Diversity Scale

Montei, M. S., Adams, G. A., & Eggers, L. M. (1996). Validity of scores on the Attitudes toward Diversity Scale (ATDS). *Educational and Psychological Measurement, 56,* 293–303.

Institutional Racism Scale

Barbarin, O. A., & Gilbert, R. (1981). Institutional Racism Scale: Assessing self and organizational attributes. In O. A. Barbarin, P. R. Good, O. M. Pharr, & J. A. Siskind (Eds.), *Institutional racism and community competence* (pp. 147–171). Washington, DC: U.S. Government Printing Office.

Subtle Racism

Duckitt, J. H. (1991). The development and validation of a subtle racism scale in South Africa. *South African Journal of Psychology, 21,* 233–239.

Racism Scale

Sidanius, J. (1993). The interface between racism and sexism. *Journal of Psychology, 127,* 311–322.

Manitoba Prejudice Scale

Altemeyer, B. (1988). *Enemies of freedom.* San Francisco: Jossey-Bass.

A Projective Measure of Ethnic Attitudes

Supphellen, M., Kvitastein, O. A., & Johansen, S. T. (1997). Projective questioning and ethnic discrimination: A procedure for measuring employer bias. *Public Opinion Quarterly, 61,* 208–224.

Forms of Racism

Kleinpenning, G., & Hagendoorn, L. (1993). Forms of racism and the cumulative dimension of ethnic attitudes. *Social Psychology Quarterly, 56,* 21–36.

Racial Attitudes as Explanatory Modes

Apostle, R. A., Glock, C. Y., Piazza, T., & Suelzle, M. (1983). *The anatomy of racial attitudes.* Berkeley: University of California Press.

Though not offering a validated scale, this book presents items to measure racial attitudes as three components: perceptions of racial differences, explanations for racial differences, and prescriptions regarding what should be done about these differences. Items to assess explanatory modes are provided.

Situational Attitude Scale (SAS)

Sedlacek, W. E., & Brooks, G. C., Jr. (1972). *Situational Attitude Scale (SAS) manual.* Chicago: Natural Resources.

See also Sedlacek, W. E., & Brooks, G. C., Jr. (1976). *Racism in American education: A model for change.* Chicago: Nelson-Hall.

Antiwhite Hostility

Sears, D. O., & McConahay, J. B. (1973). *The politics of violence: The new urban blacks and the Watts riot.* Boston: Houghton Mifflin.

Alienation from White Society

Schuman, H., & Hatchett, S. (1974). *Black racial attitudes: Trends and complexities.* Ann Arbor, MI: Institute for Social Research.

Racial Consciousness

Tate, K. (1994). *From protest to politics: The new black voters in American elections.* Cambridge, MA: Harvard University Press.

Racial Solidarity

Allen, R. L., Dawson, M. C., & Brown, R. E. (1989). A heuristic and systematic approach to modeling an African American belief system. *American Political Science Review, 83,* 421–441.

General Intergroup Anxiety

Stephan, W. G., & Stephan, C. W. (1985). Intergroup anxiety. *Journal of Social Issues, 41,* 157–175.

Intergroup Anxiety Scale

Britt, T. W., Boniecki, K. A., Vescio, T. K., Biernat, M., & Brown, L. M. (1996). Intergroup anxiety: A person X situation approach. *Personality and Social Psychology Bulletin, 22,* 1177–1188.

Motivation to Control Prejudiced Reactions

Dunton, B. C., & Fazio, R. H. (1997). An individual difference measure of motivation to control prejudiced reactions. *Personality and Social Psychology Bulletin, 23,* 316–326.

Blacks' Perceptions of Whites' Stereotypes of Blacks (Metastereotypes)

Sigelman, L. & Tuch, S. A. (1997). Metastereotypes: Blacks' perceptions of Whites' stereotypes of Blacks. *Public Opinion Quarterly, 61,* 87–101.

References

Allport, G. W., & Ross, J. M. (1967). Personal religious orientation and prejudice. *Journal of Personality and Social Psychology, 5,* 432–443.

Altemeyer, B. (1988). *Enemies of freedom: Understanding right wing authoritarianism.* San Francisco: Jossey-Bass.

Apostle, R. A., Glock, C. Y., Piazza, T., & Suelzle, M. (1983). *The anatomy of racial attitudes.* Berkeley: University of California Press.

Arcuri, L., & Boca, S. (1996). Pregiudizio e affiliazione politica: Destra e sinistra di fronte all'immigrazione dal terzo mondo" (Prejudice and political affiliation: Right and left confronted with immigration from the Third World). In P. Legrenzi & V. Girotto (Eds.), *Psicologia e Politica,* pp. 241–274. Milan, Italy: Raffaello Cortina.

Ard, N., & Cook, S. W. (1977). A short scale for the measurement of change in verbal racial attitude. *Educational and Psychological Measurement, 37,* 741–744.

Biernat, M., & Manis, M. (1994). Shifting standards and stereotype-based judgments. *Journal of Personality and Social Psychology, 66,* 5–20.

Biernat, M., Vescio, T. K., & Theno, S. A. (1996). Violating American values: A "value congruence" approach to understanding outgroup attitudes. *Journal of Experimental Social Psychology, 32,* 387–410.

Biernat, M., Vescio, T. K., Theno, S. A., & Crandall, C. S. (1996). Values and prejudice: Toward understanding the impact of American values on outgroup attitudes. In C. Seligman, J. M. Olson, & M. P. Zanna (Eds.), *The psychology of values: The Ontario Symposium* (Vol. 8, pp. 153–189). Hillsdale, NJ: Erlbaum.

Blair, I. V., & Banaji, M. R. (1996). Automatic and controlled processes in stereotype priming. *Journal of Personality and Social Psychology, 70,* 1142–1163.

Bobo, L. (1983). Whites' opposition to busing: Symbolic racism or realistic group conflict? *Journal of Personality and Social Psychology, 45,* 1196–1210.

Bobo, L., & Kluegel, J. (1993). Opposition to race-targeting: Self-interest, stratification ideology, or racial attitudes? *American Sociological Review, 58,* 443–464.

Bogardus, E. S. (1925). Measuring social distance. *Journal of Applied Sociology, 9,* 299–308.

Bogardus, E. S. (1928). *Immigration and race attitudes.* Boston: Heath.

Bogardus, E. S. (1928/1947). The measurement of social distance. In T. M. Newcomb & E. L. Hartley (Eds.), *Readings in social psychology* (pp. 503–507). New York: Holt.

Bogardus, E. S. (1933). A social distance scale. *Sociology and Social Research, 17,* 265–271.

Bogardus, E. S. (1959). *Social distance.* Yellow Springs, OH: Antioch Press.

Brewer, M. B. (1968). Determinants of social distance among East African tribal groups. *Journal of Personality and Social Psychology, 10,* 279–289.

Brigham, J. C. (1977). The structure of racial attitudes of blacks. *Personality and Social Psychology Bulletin, 3,* 658–661.

Brigham, J. C. (1993). College students' racial attitudes. *Journal of Applied Social Psychology, 23,* 1933–1967.

Brigham, J. C., Woodmansee, J. J., & Cook, S. W. (1976). Dimensions of verbal racial attitudes: Interracial marriage and approaches to racial equality. *Journal of Social Issues, 32,* 9–21.

Brinkerhoff, M. B., & Mackie, M. M. (1986). The applicability of social distance for religious research: An exploration. *Review of Religious Research, 28,* 151–167.

Byrnes, D., & Kiger, G. (1988). Contemporary measures of attitudes toward blacks. *Educational and Psychological Measurement, 48,* 107–119.

Byrnes, D., & Kiger, G. (1990). The effect of a prejudice-reduction simulation on attitude change. *Journal of Applied Social Psychology, 20,* 341–356.

Byrnes, D., & Kiger, G. (1992). Social factors and responses to racial discrimination. *Journal of Psychology, 126,* 631–638.

Campbell, D. T. (1953). Social distance scale. In O. K. Buros (Ed.), *Fourth mental measurements yearbook.* Highland Park, NJ: Gryphon.

Campbell, D. T. (1974). Evolutionary epistemology. In P. A. Schilpp (Ed.), *The philosophy of Karl Popper* (Vol. 1, pp. 413–463). LaSalle, IL: Open Court.

Carter, R. T. (1990). The relationship between racism and racial identity among white Americans: An exploratory investigation. *Journal of Counseling and Development, 69,* 46–50.

Case, C. E., & Greeley, A. W. (1990). Attitudes toward racial equality. *Humboldt Journal of Social Relations, 16,* 67–94.

Cook, S. W., & Selltiz, C. (1964). A multiple-indicator approach to attitude measurement. *Psychological Bulletin, 62,* 36–55.

Cox, C. L., Smith, S. L., & Insko, C. A. (1996). Categorical race versus individuating belief as determinants of discrimination: A study of southern adolescents in 1966, 1979, and 1993. *Journal of Experimental Social Psychology, 32,* 39–70.

Crandall, C. S. (1991). Multiple stigma and AIDS: Medical stigma and attitudes toward homosexuals and IV-drug users in AIDS-related stigmatization. *Journal of Community and Applied Social Psychology, 1,* 165–172.

Crandall, C. S. (1994). Prejudice against fat people: Ideology and self-interest. *Journal of Personality and Social Psychology, 66,* 882–894.

Crandall, C. S., Glor, J., & Britt, T. W. (1997). Instrumental and symbolic attitudes and AIDS-related stigma. *Journal of Applied Social Psychology, 27,* 95–123.

Crandall, C. S., & Moriarty, D. (1995). Physical illness stigma and social rejection. *British Journal of Social Psychology, 34,* 67–83.

Crandall, C. S., Preisler, J. J., & Aussprung, J. (1992). Measuring stress in the lives of college students: The Undergraduate Stress Questionnaire (USQ). *Journal of Behavioral Medicine, 15,* 627–662.

Crosby, F., Bromley, S., & Saxe, L. (1980). Recent unobtrusive studies of black and white discrimination and prejudice. *Psychological Bulletin, 87,* 546–563.

Crowne, D. P., & Marlowe, D. (1960). A new scale of social desirability independent of psychopathology. *Journal of Consulting Psychology, 24,* 349–354.

Crowne, D. P., & Marlowe, D. (1966). *The approval motive.* New York: Wiley.

Crull, S. R., & Bruton, B. T. (1979). Bogardus social distance in the 1970s. *Sociology and Social Research, 63,* 771–783.

Crull, S. R., & Bruton, B. T. (1985). Possible decline in tolerance toward minorities: Social distance on a Midwest campus. *Sociology and Social Research, 70,* 57–62.

Davis, J. A., & Smith, T. W. (1990). *The General Social Survey: Cumulative codebook and data file.* Chicago: National Opinion Research Center and University of Chicago.

Davis, J. A., & Smith, T. W. (1994). *General Social Surveys, 1972–1994: Cumulative file* [Computer file]. Chicago: National Opinion Research Center, Inter-University Consortium for Political and Social Research [Distributor].

Davis, M. H. (1983). Measuring individual differences in empathy: Evidence for a multidimensional approach. *Journal of Personality and Social Psychology, 44,* 113–126.

Devine, P. G. (1989). Stereotypes and prejudice: Their automatic and controlled components. *Journal of Personality and Social Psychology, 56,* 5–18.

Devine, P. G., & Elliot, A. J. (1995). Are racial stereotypes *really* fading? The Princeton trilogy revisited. *Personality and Social Psychology Bulletin, 21,* 1139–1150.

Devine, P. G., Monteith, M. J., Zuwerink, J. R., & Elliot, A. J. (1991). Prejudice with and without compunction. *Journal of Personality and Social Psychology, 60,* 817–830.

Dovidio, J. F., Brigham, J. C., Johnson, B. T., & Gaertner, S. L. (1996). Stereotyping, prejudice, and discrimination: Another look. In C. N. Macrae, C. Stangor, & M. Hewstone (Eds.), *Stereotypes and stereotyping* (pp. 276–319). New York: Guilford Press.

Dovidio, J. F., & Gaertner, S. L. (1991). Changes in the expression and assessment of racial prejudice. In H. J. Knopke, R. J. Norrell, & R. W. Rogers (Eds.), *Opening doors: Perspectives on race relations in contemporary America.* Tuscaloosa: University of Alabama Press.

Dovidio, J. F., & Gaertner, S. L. (1993). Stereotypes and evaluative intergroup bias. In D. M. Mackie & D. L. Hamilton (Eds.), *Affect, cognition, and stereotyping* (pp. 167–193). San Diego: Academic Press.

Dovidio, J. F., Kawakami, K., Johnson, C., Johnson, B., & Howard, H. (1997). On the nature of prejudice: Automatic and controlled processes. *Journal of Experimental Social Psychology, 33,* 510–540.

Dunbar, E. (1995). The prejudiced personality, racism, and anti-Semitism: The PR scale forty years later. *Journal of Personality Assessment, 65,* 270–277.

Dunton, B. C., & Fazio, R. H. (1997). An individual difference measure of motivation to control prejudiced reactions. *Personality and Social Psychology Bulletin, 23,* 316–326.

Eisenman, R. (1986). Social distance ratings toward Blacks and the physically disabled. *College Student Journal, 20,* 189–190.

Ekehammar, B., Nilsson, I., & Sidanius, J. (1987). Education and ideology: Basic aspects of education related to adolescents' sociopolitical attitudes. *Political Psychology, 8,* 395–410.

Fazio, R. H., Jackson, J. R., Dunton, B. C., & Williams, C. J. (1995). Variability in automatic activation as an unobtrusive measure of racial attitudes: A bona fide pipeline? *Journal of Personality and Social Psychology, 69,* 1013–1027.

Fenrick, N. J., & Petersen, T. K. (1984). Developing positive changes in attitudes toward moderately/severely handicapped students through a peer tutoring program. *Education and Training of the Mentally Retarded, 19,* 83–90.

Firebaugh, G., & Davis, K. E. (1988). Trends in anti-black prejudice: Region and cohort effects. *American Journal of Sociology, 94,* 251–272.

Fiske, S. T., & Von Hendy, H. M. (1992). Personality feedback and situational norms can control stereotyping processes. *Journal of Personality and Social Psychology, 62,* 577–596.

Gaertner, S. L., & Dovidio, J. (1986). The aversive form of racism. In J. Dovidio & S. L. Gaertner (Eds.), *Prejudice, discrimination, and racism* (pp. 61–89). New York: Academic Press.

Gaertner, S. L., & McLaughlin, J. P. (1983). Racial stereotypes: Associations and ascriptions of positive and negative characteristics. *Social Psychology Quarterly, 46,* 23–30.

Gilens, M. (1995). Racial attitudes and opposition to welfare. *Journal of Politics, 57,* 994–1014.

Glick, P., & Fiske, S. T. (1995). The ambivalent sexism inventory: Differentiating hostile and benevolent sexism. *Journal of Personality and Social Psychology, 70,* 491–512.

Glover, R. (1994). Using moral and epistemological reasoning as predictors of prejudice. *Journal of Social Psychology, 134,* 633–640.

Gough, H. G. (1951). Studies of social intolerance: I. Psychological and sociological correlates of anti-Semitism. *Journal of Social Psychology, 33,* 237–246.

Greenwald, A. G. (1968). On defining attitude and attitude theory. In A. G. Greenwald, T. C. Brock, & T. M. Ostrom (Eds.), *Psychological foundations of attitudes* (pp. 1021–1061). New York: Academic Press.

Greenwald, A. G., & Banaji, M. R. (1995). Implicit social cognition: Attitudes, self-esteem, and stereotypes. *Psychological Review, 102,* 4–27.

Greenwald, A. G., McGhee, D. E., & Schwartz, J. L. K. (1998). Measuring individual differences in implicit cognition: The implicit association test. *Journal of Personality and Social Psychology, 74,* 1464–1480.

Haddock, G., Zanna, M. P., & Esses, V. M. (1993). Assessing the structure of prejudicial attitudes: The case of attitudes toward homosexuals. *Journal of Personality and Social Psychology, 65,* 1105–1118.

Hartley, E. L. (1946). *Problems in prejudice.* New York: Octagon.

Hass, R. G., Katz, I., Rizzo, N., Bailey, J., & Eisenstadt, D. (1991). Cross-racial appraisal as related to attitude ambivalence and cognitive complexity. *Personality and Social Psychology Bulletin, 17,* 83–92.

Hass, R. G., Katz, I., Rizzo, N., Bailey, J., & Moore, L. (1992). When racial ambivalence evokes negative affect, using a disguised measure of mood. *Personality and Social Psychology Bulletin, 18,* 786–797.

Hazzard, A. (1983). Children's experience with, knowledge of, and attitude toward disabled persons. *Journal of Special Education, 17,* 131–139.

Helms, J. E., & Carter, R. T. (1990). Development of the White Racial Identity Inventory. In J. E. Helms (Ed.), *Black and white racial identity: Theory, research, and practice* (pp. 67–80). Westport, CT: Greenwood.

Hinckley, E. D. (1932). The influence of individual opinion on construction of an attitude scale. *Journal of Social Psychology, 3,* 283–296.

Hull, D. L. (1988). *Science as a process.* Chicago: University of Chicago Press.

Jackman, M. R. (1977). Prejudice, tolerance, and attitudes toward ethnic groups. *Social Science Research, 6,* 145–169.

Jackman, M. R. (1978). General and applied tolerance: Does education increase commitment to racial integration? *American Journal of Political Science, 22,* 302–324.

Jackman, M. R. (1981). Issues in measurement of commitment to racial integration. *Political Methodology, 7,* 160–172.

Jackman, M., & Muha, M. (1984). Education and intergroup attitudes: Moral enlightenment, superficial democratic commitment, or ideological refinement? *American Sociological Review, 49,* 751–769.

Jacobson, C. (1985). Resistance to affirmative action. Self interest or racism? *Journal of Conflict Resolution, 29,* 306–329.

Johnson, D. (1992). Racial preference and biculturality in biracial preschoolers. *Merrill-Palmer Quarterly, 38,* 233–244.

Johnson, D. P. (1977). Religious commitment, social distance, and authoritarianism. *Review of Religious Research, 18,* 99–113.

Judd, C. M., & Park, B. (1993). Definition and assessment of accuracy in social stereotypes. *Psychological Review, 100,* 109–128.

Judd, C. M., Park, B., Ryan, C. S., Brauer, M., & Kraus, S. (1995). Stereotypes and ethnocentrism: Diverging interethnic perceptions of African American and white youth. *Journal of Personality and Social Psychology, 69,* 460–481.

Katz, D., & Stotland, E. (1959). A preliminary statement to a theory of attitude structure and change. In S. Koch (Ed.), *Psychology: A study of a science* (Vol. 3, pp. 423–475). New York: McGraw-Hill.

Katz, I. (1981). *Stigma: A social psychological analysis.* Hillsdale, NJ: Erlbaum.

Katz, I., Glass, D. C., & Cohen, S. (1973). Ambivalence, guilt, and the scapegoating of minority group victims. *Journal of Experimental Social Psychology, 9,* 423–436.

Katz, I., & Hass, R. (1988). Racial ambivalence and American value conflict: Correlational and priming studies of dual cognitive structures. *Journal of Personality and Social Psychology, 55,* 893–905.

Katz, I., Wackenhut, J., & Hass, R. G. (1986). Racial ambivalence, value duality, and behavior. In J. Dovidio & S. L. Gaertner (Eds.), *Prejudice, discrimination, and racism* (pp. 35–59). New York: Academic Press.

Kinder, D. R. (1986). The continuing American dilemma: White resistance to racial change 40 years after Myrdal. *Journal of Social Issues, 42,* 151–171.

Kinder, D. R., & Mendelberg, T. (1995). Cracks in American apartheid: The political impact of prejudice among desegregated whites. *Journal of Politics, 57,* 402–424.

Kinder, D. R., & Sanders, L. M. (1996). *Divided by color.* Chicago: University of Chicago Press.

Kinder, D. R., & Sears, D. O. (1981). Prejudice and politics: Symbolic racism versus racial threats to the good life. *Journal of Personality and Social Psychology, 40,* 414–431.

Kinloch, G. (1974). Racial prejudice in highly and less racist societies: Social distance preferences among white college students in South Africa and Hawaii. *Sociology and Social Research, 59,* 1–13.

Kitcher, P. (1993). *The advancement of science.* New York: Oxford University Press.

Kleg, M., & Yamamoto, K. (1995). Ethnic and racial social distance: Seven decades apart. *Psychological Reports, 76,* 65–66.

Kluegel, J. (1987). Macro-economic problems, beliefs about the poor and attitudes toward welfare spending. *Social Problems, 34,* 82–99.

Kluegel, J. (1990). Trends in whites' explanations of the black–white gap in socioeconomic status, 1977–1989. *American Sociological Review, 55,* 512–525.

Kluegel, J., & Smith, E. (1983). Affirmative action attitudes: Effects of self-interest, racial affect, and stratification beliefs on whites' views. *Social Forces, 61,* 797–824.

Knoke, D., & Isaac, L. (1976). Quality of higher education and sociopolitical attitudes. *Social Forces, 54,* 524–529.

Kogan, N., & Downey, J. F. (1956). Scaling norm conflicts in prejudice and discrimination. *Journal of Abnormal Social Psychology, 53,* 292–295.

Krech, D., & Crutchfield, R. S. (1948). *Theory and problems of social psychology.* New York: McGraw-Hill.

Kuklinski, J. H., & Parent, W. (1981). Race and big government: Contamination in measuring racial attitudes. *Political Methodology, 7,* 131–159.

Kunz, P. R. (1979). Blacks and Mormonism: A social distance change. *Psychological Reports, 45,* 81–82.

Kunz, P. R., & Oheneba-Sakyi, Y. (1989). Social distance: A study of changing views of young Mormons toward black individuals. *Psychological Reports, 65,* 195–200.

Leippe, M. R., & Eisenstadt, D. (1994). Generalization of dissonance reduction: Decreasing prejudice through induced compliance. *Journal of Personality and Social Psychology, 67,* 395–413.

Lepore, L., & Brown, R. (1997). Category and stereotype activation: Is prejudice inevitable? *Journal of Personality and Social Psychology, 72,* 275–287.

McCauley, C., & Stitt, C. L. (1978). An individual and quantitative measure of stereotypes. *Journal of Personality and Social Psychology, 36,* 929–940.

McClendon, M. (1985). Racism, rational choice, and white opposition to racial change: A case study of busing. *Public Opinion Quarterly, 49,* 214–233.

McConahay, J. B. (1982). Self-interest versus racial attitudes as correlates of anti-busing attitudes in Louisville: Is it the buses or the blacks? *Journal of Politics, 44,* 692–720.

McConahay, J. B. (1983). Modern racism and modern discrimination: The effects of race, racial attitudes, and context on simulated hiring decisions. *Personality and Social Psychology Bulletin, 9,* 551–558.

McConahay, J. B. (1986). Modern racism, ambivalence, and the Modern Racism Scale. In J. Dovidio & S. L. Gaertner (Eds.), *Prejudice, discrimination, and racism* (pp. 91–125). New York: Academic Press.

McConahay, J. B., Hardee, B. B., & Batts, V. (1981). Has racism declined in America? It depends on who is asking and what is asked. *Journal of Conflict Resolution, 25,* 563–579.

McConahay, J. B., & Hough, J. C., Jr. (1973). Love and guilt oriented dimensions of Christian belief. *Journal for the Scientific Study of Religion, 12,* 53–64.

McConahay, J. B., & Hough, J. C., Jr. (1976). Symbolic racism. *Journal of Social Issues, 32,* 23–45.

Meertens, R. W., & Pettigrew, T. F. (1997). Is subtle prejudice really prejudice? *Public Opinion Quarterly, 61,* 54–71.

Mendelberg, T. (1997). Executing Hortons: Racial crime in the 1988 presidential campaign. *Public Opinion Quarterly, 61,* 134–157.

Mielenz, C. C. (1979). Non-prejudiced Caucasian parents and attitudes of their children toward Negroes. *Journal of Negro Education, 48,* 84–91.

Miller, D. C. (1971). *Handbook of research design and social measurement* (3rd ed.). New York: David McKay.

Monteith, M. J. (1996). Contemporary forms of prejudice-related conflict: In search of a nutshell. *Personality and Social Psychology Bulletin, 22,* 461–473.

Myrdal, G. (1944). *An American dilemma.* New York: Harper and Row.

Neville, H., & Furlong, M. (1994). The impact of participation in a cultural awareness program on the racial attitudes and social behaviors of first-year college students. *Journal of College Student Development, 35,* 371–377.

Nosworthy, G., Lea, J., & Lindsay, R. (1995). Opposition to affirmative action: Racial affect and traditional value predictors across four programs. *Journal of Applied Social Psychology, 25,* 314–337.

Osei-Kwame, P., & Achola, P. P. W. (1981). A new conceptual model for the study of political integration in Africa. *Journal of Developing Areas, 15,* 585–604.

Owen, C. A., Eisner, H. C., & McFaul, T. R. (1981). A half-century of social distance research: National replication of the Bogardus studies. *Sociology and Social Research, 66,* 80–98.

Payne, M. C., Jr., York, C. M., & Fagan, J. (1974). Changes in measured social distance over time. *Sociometry, 37,* 131–136.

Pearlin, L. I., & Rosenberg, M. (1962). Nurse–patient social distance and the structural context of a mental hospital. *American Sociological Review, 27,* 517–531.

Peffley, M., Hurwitz, J., & Sniderman, P. (1997). Racial stereotypes and whites' political views of blacks in the context of welfare and crime. *American Journal of Political Science, 41,* 30–60.

Pettigrew, T. F. (1985). New black–white patterns: How best to conceptualize them? *Annual Reviews of Sociology, 11,* 329–346.

Pettigrew, T. F. (1997). Generalized intergroup contact effects on prejudice. *Personality and Social Psychology Bulletin, 23,* 173–185.

Pettigrew, T. F., & Meertens, R. W. (1995). Subtle and blatant prejudice in Western Europe. *European Journal of Social Psychology, 25,* 57–75.

Phillips, S. T., & Ziller, R. C. (1997). Toward a theory and measure of the nature of nonprejudice. *Journal of Personality and Social Psychology, 72,* 420–434.

Ponterotto, J. G., Burkard, A., Rieger, B. P., Grieger, I., D'Onofrio, A., Dubuisson, A., Heenehan, M., Millstein, B., Parisi, M., Rath, J. F., & Sax, G. (1995). Development and initial validation of the Quick Discrimination Index (QDI). *Educational and Psychological Measurement, 55,* 1016–1031.

Ponterotto, J. G., Rieger, B. P., Barrett, A., Harris, G., Sparks, R., Sanchez, C. M., & Magids, D. (in press). Development and initial validation of the multicultural counseling awareness scale. In G. R. Sodowsky & J. C. Impara (Eds.), *Multicultural assessment in counseling and clinical psychology.* Lincoln, NE: Buros Institute of Mental Measurements.

Pope-Davis, D. B., & Ottavi, T. M. (1992). The influence of white racial identity attitudes on racism among faculty members: A preliminary examination. *Journal of College Student Development, 33,* 389–394.

Pope-Davis, D. B., & Ottavi, T. M. (1994). The relationship between racism and racial identity among white Americans: A replication and extension. *Journal of Counseling and Development, 72,* 293–297.

Pratto, F., Sidanius, J., Stallworth, L. M., & Malle, B. F. (1994). Social dominance orientation: A personality variable predicting social and political attitudes. *Journal of Personality and Social Psychology, 67,* 741–763.

Raden, D. (1989). Interrelationships between prejudice and other social attitudes in the General Social Survey. *Sociological Focus, 22,* 53–67.

Raden, D. (1994). Are symbolic racism and traditional prejudice part of a contemporary authoritarian attitude syndrome? *Political Behavior, 16,* 365–385.

Robinson, J. P., Rusk, J. G., & Head, K. B. (1968). *Measures of political attitudes.* Ann Arbor, MI: Institute for Social Research.

Rofe, Y., & Weller, L. (1981). Attitudes toward the enemy as a function of level of threat. *British Journal of Social Psychology, 20,* 217–218.

Rokeach, M. (1960). *The open and closed mind.* New York: Basic Books.

Rokeach, M. (1982). *Value survey.* Palo Alto: CA: Consulting Psychologists Press.

Rosenstone, S. J., Kinder, D. R., & Miller, W. E. (1995). *American National Election Study, 1994: Post-election survey* [Computer file]. Ann Arbor: University of Michigan, Center for Political Studies/Inter-University Consortium for Political and Social Research [Distributor].

Rubin, Z., & Peplau, A. (1973). Belief in a just world and reactions to another's lot: A study of participation in the national draft lottery. *Journal of Social Issues, 29,* 73–93.

Schuman, H., & Harding, J. (1963). Sympathetic identification with the underdog. *Public Opinion Quarterly, 27,* 230–241.

Schuman, H., & Harding, J. (1964). Prejudice and the norm of rationality. *Sociometry, 27,* 353–371.

Schuman, H., & Hatchett, S. (1974). *Black racial attitudes: Trends and complexities.* Ann Arbor, MI: Institute for Social Research.

Schuman, H., Steeh, C., & Bobo, L. (1985). *Racial attitudes in America: Trends and interpretations.* Cambridge, MA: Harvard University Press.

Sears, D. O. (1986). College sophomores in the laboratory: Influences of a narrow data base on psychology's view of human nature. *Journal of Personality and Social Psychology, 51,* 515–530.

Sears, D. O. (1988). Symbolic racism. In P. Katz & D. Taylor (Eds.), *Eliminating racism: Profiles in controversy* (pp. 53–84). New York: Plenum.

Sears, D. O., & Allen, H. M., Jr. (1984). The trajectory of local desegregation controversies and whites' opposition to busing. In N. Miller & M. B. Brewer (Eds.), *Groups in contact: The psychology of desegregation* (pp. 123–151). New York: Academic Press.

Sears, D. O., & Kinder, D. R. (1971). Racial tensions and voting in Los Angeles. In W. Z. Hirsch (Ed.), *Los Angeles: Viability and prospects for metropolitan leadership* (pp. 51–88). New York: Praeger.

Sears, D. O., van Laar, C., Carrillo, M., & Kosterman, R. (1997). Is it really racism? The origins of white Americans' opposition to race-targeted policies. *Public Opinion Quarterly, 61,* 16–53.

Selznick, G. J., & Sternberg, S. (1969). *The tenacity of prejudice.* New York: Harper and Row.

Shaw, M. E., & Wright, J. M. (1967). *Scales for the measurement of attitudes.* New York: McGraw-Hill.

Sidanius, J. (1976). *Further tests of a Swedish scale of conservatism* (Report No. 467). Stockholm: Department of Psychology, University of Stockholm.

Sidanius, J., Feshbach, S., Levin, S., & Pratto, F. (1997). The interface between ethnic and national attachment: Ethnic pluralism or ethnic dominance? *Public Opinion Quarterly, 61,* 102–133.

Sidanius, J., & Pratto, F. (1993). The inevitability of oppression and the dynamics of social dominance. In P. M. Sniderman, P. E. Tetlock, & E. G. Carmines (Eds.), *Prejudice, politics and the American dilemma* (pp. 173–211). Stanford, CA: Stanford University Press.

Sidanius, J., Pratto, F., & Bobo, L. (1996). Racism, conservatism, affirmative action, and intellectual sophistication: A matter of principled conservatism or group dominance? *Journal of Personality and Social Psychology, 70,* 476–490.

Sidanius, J., Pratto, F., Martin, M., & Stallworth, L. M. (1991). Consensual racism and career track: Some implications of social dominance theory. *Political Psychology, 12,* 691–721.

Smith, A. W. (1985). Cohorts, education, and the evolution of tolerance. *Social Science Research, 14,* 205–225.

Smith, T. W., & Sheatsley, P. B. (1984). American attitudes toward race relations. *Public Opinion, 14–15,* 50–53.

Sniderman, P. M., & Piazza, T. (1993). *The scar of race.* Cambridge, MA: Belknap Press of Harvard University Press.

Sniderman, P. M., Piazza, T., Tetlock, P. E., & Kendrick, A. (1991). The new racism. *American Journal of Political Science, 35,* 423–447.

Sniderman, P., & Tetlock, P. (1986a). Symbolic racism: Problems of motive attribution in political analysis. *Journal of Social Issues, 42,* 129–150.

Sniderman, P., & Tetlock, P. (1986b). Reflections on American racism. *Journal of Social Issues, 42,* 173–187.

Snyder, M. (1974). Self-monitoring and expressive behavior. *Journal of Personality and Social Psychology, 30,* 526–537.

Spangenberg, J., & Nel, E. M. (1983). The effect of equal status contact on ethnic attitudes. *Journal of Social Psychology, 121,* 173–180.

Spence, J. T., & Helmreich, R. (1972). The Attitudes toward Women Scale: An objective instrument to measure attitudes toward the rights and roles of women in contemporary society. *JSAS: Catalog of Selected Documents in Psychology, 2,* 66.

Stangor, C., Lynch, L., Duan, C., & Glass, B. (1992). Categorization of individuals on the basis of multiple social features. *Journal of Personality and Social Psychology, 62,* 207–218.

Stangor, C., Sullivan, L. A., & Ford, T. E. (1991). Affective and cognitive determinants of prejudice. *Social Cognition, 9,* 359–380.

Stephan, W. G. (1985). Intergroup relations. In G. Lindzey & E. Aronson (Eds.), *Handbook of social psychology* (3rd ed., Vol. 2, pp. 599–658). Hillsdale, NJ: Erlbaum.

Swim, J. K., Aikin, K. J., Hall, W. S., & Hunter, B. A. (1995). Sexism and racism: Old-fashioned and modern prejudices. *Journal of Personality and Social Psychology, 68,* 199–214.

411

Taylor, C. A., Fourie, R. J., & Koorts, A. S. (1995). The design of an instrument to measure change in attitudes in white and black children. *South African Journal of Psychology, 25,* 116–121.

Taylor, D. G., Sheatsley, P. B., & Greeley, A. M. (1978). Attitudes toward racial integration. *Scientific American, 238,* 42–49.

Terkildsen, N. (1993). When white voters evaluate black candidates: The processing implications of candidate skin color, prejudice, and self-monitoring. *American Journal of Political Science, 37,* 1032–1053.

Thompson, M. M., Zanna, M. P., & Griffin, D. W. (1995). Let's not be indifferent about (attitudinal) ambivalence. In R. E. Petty & J. A. Krosnick (Eds.), *Attitude strength: Antecedents and consequences* (pp. 361–386). Mahwah, NJ: Lawrence Erlbaum Associates.

Triandis, H. C. (1964). Exploratory factor analyses of the behavioral component of social attitudes. *Journal of Abnormal and Social Psychology, 68,* 420–430.

Triandis, H. C. (1971). *Attitude and attitude change.* New York: Wiley.

Triandis, H. C., & Triandis, L. M. (1965). Some studies of social distance. In I. D. Steiner & M. Fishbein (Eds.), *Current studies in social psychology* (pp. 207–217). New York: Holt, Rinehart & Winston.

Verma, O. P., & Upadhyay, S. N. (1984). Religiosity and social distance. *Indian Psychological Review, 26,* 29–34.

Vornberg, J. A., & Grant, R. T. (1976). Adolescent cultural acquaintance experiences and ethnic group attitudes. *Adolescence, 11,* 601–608.

Wagner, U., & Zick, A. (1995). The relation of formal education to ethnic prejudice: Its reliability, validity, and explanation. *European Journal of Social Psychology, 25,* 41–56.

Weigel, R., & Howes, P. (1985). Conceptions of racial prejudice: Symbolic racism reconsidered. *Journal of Social Issues, 41,* 117–138.

Wittenbrink, B., & Henly, J. R. (1996). Creating social reality: Informational social influence and the content of stereotypic beliefs. *Personality and Social Psychology Bulletin, 22,* 598–610.

Wittenbrink, B., Judd, C. M., & Park, B. (1997). Evidence for racial prejudice at the implicit level and its relationship with questionnaire measures. *Journal of Personality and Social Psychology, 72,* 262–274.

Woodmansee, J. J., & Cook, S. W. (1967). Dimensions of racial attitudes: Their identification and measurement. *Journal of Personality and Social Psychology, 7,* 240–250.

Ziller, R. C. (1973). *The social self.* New York: Pergamon Press.

Ziller, R. C., Martell, R. T., & Morrison, R. H. (1977). Social insulation, self-complexity, and social interactions: A theory chain. *Journal of Research in Personality, 11,* 398–415.

Zuwerink, J. R., Devine, P. G., Monteith, M. J., & Cook, D. A. (1996). Prejudice toward blacks: With and without compunction? *Basic and Applied Social Psychology, 18,* 131–150.

CHAPTER 7

Political Alienation and Efficacy

Mary Jo Reef and David Knoke

Political alienation refers to a social condition in which citizens have or feel minimal connection with the exercise of political power. The roots of political alienation extend back to the formation of a mass citizenry in the constitutional democracies of Western Europe and the United States in the late 1700s and early 1800s. Through their struggles to secure membership rights in the polity—to create and join political parties, to participate in elections by voting and running for office—ordinary men (and eventually women) for the first time confronted the nature of their attachments to the political system and its incumbent officials.

Initial scholarly efforts to create a vocabulary and a conceptual framework with which to analyze political alienation thus concentrated on the structural *relationships* between citizens and their governments. The young Karl Marx examined alienation as an *objective* social phenomenon, adapting Hegel's philosophical concept of alienation *(Entfremdung)* as a condition under which a person's own powers were reified as an external force controlling the individual's actions. Religion, private property, and the capitalist state were inhumane institutions that separated man from Nature, labor, and the political community. They were "the projection of the social forces of man onto an external power which is an incarnation of arbitrariness and injustice" (Bottomore, 1956, p. 27)—much as in Durkheim's (1933) concept of *anomie* as a societal condition of general normlessness and Simmel's (1950) analysis of uprooted individualism of the modern metropolis. Both these concepts greatly shaped the classical sociological understanding of alienation as an *objective* condition of social estrangement—a property of the *social system* virtually independent of citizens.

In contrast, almost all the empirical work on political alienation in the late 20th century has approached it as a social psychological or subjective attitudinal orientation of the individual. The heavy reliance on batteries of survey items designed to reveal a respondent's beliefs about officials holding political power has inevitably meant that these earlier classical structural concepts are ignored. For contemporary researchers political alienation has focused exclusively on psychological attachments to, identifications with, or estrangements from the various actors and institutions of the political system. Virtually all definitions and measures of political alienation (or its antonym, political efficacy) produced over the past 40 years have abandoned the original structural meaning in favor of the citizens' subjective feelings about their abilities to affect the political system's performance at the individual level (see Almond & Verba, 1965; Campbell, Gurin, & Miller,

1954; Citrin, McClosky, Shanks, & Sniderman, 1975; Craig, Niemi, & Silver, 1990; Dennis, 1987; Easton, 1965; Finifter, 1970; Gamson, 1968; Hamilton & Wright, 1986, pp. 361–373; Herring, 1987a, 1987b; House & Mason, 1975; Mason, House, & Martin, 1985; Miller, Miller, & Schneider, 1980; Muller, 1979; Olsen, 1969; Schwartz, 1973; Seeman, 1959, 1975; Southwell, 1986, 1995; Weatherford, 1991; Wright, 1976).

Despite this convergence on a narrowed scope, considerable disagreement still surrounds the theoretical concepts of political alienation and political efficacy. Lane (1962, pp. 161–162) asserted that "[p]olitical alienation refers to a person's sense of estrangement from the politics and government of his society." Schwartz (1973, p. 7) defined political alienation as a sense of estrangement of the self from the polity; the individual simply does not identify with the political system. Other definitions are less sweeping than those of Lane and Schwartz, while still recognizing that political alienation remains fundamentally a multidimensional construct. Individuals may become estranged in many ways from many different political referents. In practice the more narrow definitions of political alienation tend to examine in depth only one among several dimensions of this multifaceted concept.

One primary theoretical perspective behind most recent efforts to specify the distinct dimensions of political alienation derives from Seeman's (1959, 1989) refinement of general alienation into six underlying factors. Based on Seeman's typology, Finifter (1970) defined four analogous dimensions within political alienation: political powerlessness, political meaninglessness, political normlessness, and political isolation (not included were analogues to Seeman's categories of self-estranged activity and cultural estrangement). *Political powerlessness* refers to political inefficacy, or a person's perceived inability to influence governmental policy. Finifter's *political meaninglessness* is the perception that political decisions are unpredictable. *Political normlessness* concerns the government's responsiveness and equity, beliefs that the norms and rules governing political relations have broken down. Finally *political isolation* is a rejection of the political norms held by most other members of the society. The common focal point in all four dimensions is the individual citizen as a political actor, ignoring the political system itself as an object worthy of loyalty and support.

A second theoretical approach to political alienation stems from speculations about the necessary conditions for effective functioning of a democratic political system, as emphasized by such macro-political analysts as Almond and Verba (1965), Easton (1965), and Gamson (1968). These authors were concerned about how various components are articulated as a coherent political system, including formal governing institutions, administrative incumbents, the philosophy or rules of the game (regime), and the larger polity or political community. These authors distinguish political efficacy as a system *input* or demand measure from political trust as a system *output* or support indicator of system performance (Gamson, 1968, p. 42). *Political efficacy* refers to an individual's sense of personal competence in influencing the political system. In its focus on subjective potency, efficacy resembles the inverse of Seeman's powerlessness dimension. *Political trust* stresses perceptions that the political system and authorities are responsive to the public's interests and demands. The objects of evaluation are the institutional complex and its incumbent officials rather than the citizen. These two dimensions are conceptually orthogonal: Individuals may have a high sense of their own political potency vis-à-vis the system, yet be very distrustful of the officials running the government. Hence high efficacy combined with low trust may lead to political protest, whereas low efficacy reinforced by distrust produces political apathy and withdrawal from political participation (Gamson, 1968, p. 48). Although these system theorists did not propose empirical measures to test their theoretical ideas, other researchers have developed operational indicators supporting the conceptual distinction between efficacy and trust (Aberbach, 1969; Abramson, 1972; Balch, 1974; Craig *et al.,* 1990; House & Mason, 1975; Jennings & Niemi, 1981; Mason *et al.,* 1985; Wright, 1976; Yin & Lucas, 1973).

While many investigations of political alienation have been clearly influenced by these two analytic frameworks, other approaches cannot be neatly pigeonholed under either rubric. For instance, some definitions of political alienation have attempted to make it wholly synonymous with just one of its many dimensions, such as normlessness, powerlessness, or distrust (Agnello, 1973; Clarke & Levine, 1971). Other scholars have distinguished among separate elements of political alienation, but conflated them with elements from Seeman's social psychological perspective and the system-level efficacy–trust approach. For example, Olsen (1969) defined political alienation as estrangement from the political system, which he argued could be broken down into two broad categories: political incapability (an aspect of powerlessness) and political discontent or cynicism (a systemic-trust component). Similarly Watts (1973) viewed political alienation as an immensely diverse concept under whose umbrella are found three distinct dimensions: efficacy–powerlessness, process commitment, and political trust. Political efficacy and powerlessness anchor opposite ends of one continuum. That is, efficacy is an individual's belief that he or she can readily influence the political system, while powerlessness is the perception that an individual can do nothing to affect government action. Process commitment measures beliefs in the appropriateness of working within the established political system—an individual's commitment to the norms of a democratic government—and feelings of loss of diffuse support for the government. Finally political trust is conceived as a disaffection for and distrust of politicians and authorities.

Current theoretical practice usually asserts a sharp conceptual separation between political trust (covered in Chapter 8) and political efficacy. The trust domain targets current incumbents of political offices, while efficacy concentrates more broadly on the political system rather than on specific officeholders or public policy decisions. Despite varying terminology, a general consensus about these two fundamental concepts seemed to have emerged by the end of the 1970s. Easton (1975, p. 445) coined the term *diffuse support* to connote support for the governing regime and the general political community. He conceptualized diffuse support as citizens' sense of the system's legitimacy, perceptions that it conforms to their values about what is right politically (see Dennis, 1987, and Weatherford, 1991, for more recent discussions of the alienation–legitimacy relationship). Almond and Verba (1965, p. 63) referred to "system affect" to signify a general positive feeling toward the political system. Muller and his colleagues (1977, 1979, 1982; also Seligson, 1983) also treated political support–alienation in terms of affect toward a regime's institutions, norms, and values rather than the incumbent administration's officials.

On the other hand, Citrin *et al.* (1975, p. 4) proposed that "the term alienation is reserved for negative responses that go beyond the activities of incumbent leaders to the essential principles and institutions of the system itself." In contrast to citizens who give their allegiance to the political system, the politically alienated experience "a relatively enduring sense of estrangement from existing political institutions, values and leaders." Thus "at the far end of the continuum, the politically alienated feel themselves outsiders, gripped in an alien political order; they would welcome fundamental changes in the ongoing regime" (p. 3).

We follow these conventional distinctions in the present chapter, restricting ourselves to an examination of political alienation and political efficacy scales that refer primarily to powerlessness and estrangement from the political system. The next chapter in this volume examines those measures that deal exclusively with citizen trust in government officials.

Measures of Political Alienation and Efficacy

The scales and subscales offered here for detailed discussion are presented in chronological order from 1954 to the present. In this section we provide a comparative summary and interpretation of scales grouped according to their substantive contents.

1. Political Efficacy Scale (Campbell *et al.*, 1954)
2. Political Efficacy Scale (Verba, Schlozman, & Brady, 1995)

   Probably the most commonly used measure of political alienation is Campbell *et al.*'s (1954) four-item Political Efficacy Scale (see the later sections for the specific items comprising each scale). Although the efficacy items were created prior to most theoretical discussions of political alienation, this scale has been widely replicated in the Survey Research Center's ongoing series of American National Election Studies (SRC/ANES) and in other surveys (e.g., Agnello, 1973; House & Mason, 1975; Kahn & Mason, 1987; Wright, 1976; Yin & Lucas, 1973).

   Researchers' general tendencies have been to treat the political efficacy scale as though it measures Seeman's powerlessness concept, or what Easton (1965) and Gamson (1968) called "input" alienation or inefficacy. However, evidence soon accumulated that the link between these theoretical concepts and the empirical estimates of the constructs was less than perfect. Converse (1972, pp. 334–335) demonstrated that the four SRC/ANES political efficacy items did not covary over time and, therefore, could not be considered a simple unidimensional measure. Two of the items (Don't Care and No Say) appeared to measure Gamson's trust dimension, one (Complex) measured efficacy, and the fourth (Voting) seemed to be related to both. Both Balch (1974) and Jennings and Niemi (1981), while describing the indicators as efficacy items, supplied corroborative evidence that the scale was not unidimensional. These authors also suggested that the Don't Care and No Say items may measure trust, while the Voting and Complex items may be better indicators of efficacy. Both House and Mason's (1975) cross-sectional analysis and McPherson, Welch, and Clark's (1977) panel analysis reached similar conclusions. In their factor analysis of 27 SRC/ANES items, Mason *et al.* (1985) further confirmed that No Say and Don't Care are both indicators of the same underlying alienation construct. Like House and Mason (1975), they concluded that Voting and Complex do not reflect the same latent factor as No Say and Don't Care. Most recently Craig *et al.* (1990) suggested that No Say and Don't Care actually combine to measure both regime and incumbent effects of governmental responsiveness to citizen demand, with Complex measuring internal efficacy and Voting being an indicator of regime-based trust.

   Mason *et al.* (1985, p. 112) identified a major problem in political alienation research as the disjuncture between the development of theoretical constructs and their empirical indicators. Thus theorists who proposed clarifying conceptual distinctions about political alienation never specified their operational measures clearly enough that researchers could use them to test their propositions. Consequently survey researchers' political alienation and political efficacy measures were simply unconnected to the proposed theories. Instead, the four-item SRC/ANES efficacy scale has continued to gain wide attention and acceptance among empirical analysts as it is replicated from one survey to the next. Indeed, Wright (1976, pp. 91, 95) argued that the scale had achieved consensual validity simply because it was "well established, widely recognized, and commonly employed."

Thus the obvious dimensional problems in the Campbell *et al.* efficacy measure need to be acknowledged by any researchers who propose to use it. Moreover, further methodological investigation is still needed about how each of the four SRC/ANES items relates to the other efficacy and alienation measures reviewed in this chapter so that substitute and/or additional indicators might be developed to produce a conceptually sounder political efficacy scale. Unfortunately the SRC/ANES surveys, now spanning five decades, offer secondary analysts the only existing series of national political alienation benchmarks. Therefore researchers should analyze the four political efficacy items separately rather than simply combining them into a single multi-item scale.

The dimensionality of the Verba *et al.* (1995) Political Efficacy Scale has fewer problems. It exhibits a rather higher level of internal consistency for a four-item scale. It also is relatively new and based on a large representative sample whose respondents were asked a variety of interesting political behavior questions.

As with the majority of the research on political alienation that has conceptualized it as a multidimensional construct combining two components—(in)efficacy or powerlessness and lack of trust—the next five scales include items tapping both components.

3. Political Alienation Scale (Thompson & Horton, 1960)
4. Political Alienation Scale (McDill & Ridley, 1962)
5. Political Alienation Scale (Malik, 1982)
6. Political Alienation Scale (General Social Survey) (Davis & Smith, 1996)
7. Local Government Alienation Scales (Zimmer, 1983)

While the national government is the referent for most political alienation scales, three of these five scales involve alienation from the local political scene.

One of Thompson and Horton's (1960) items asks respondents whether they feel they are involved in community decision making. The other items focus on the responsiveness of the political authorities to their constituents, as in this item: "It doesn't matter which party wins the elections, the interests of the little man don't count." Several questions refer to politicians, thereby emphasizing officials of the incumbent administration rather than the political system in general terms. Thompson and Horton's scale includes items related to the respondent's view of himself/herself as influential in the community, the unresponsiveness of government, and trust in political officials and in the government as a whole.

McDill and Ridley (1962) also mixed items measuring efficacy and trust, but more clearly focused on the *local community's* politics rather than on attitudes toward the national government. Their items tap feelings of unresponsiveness of the local government to its constituents. All items mention the city of Nashville, Tennessee, such as "The average person can't get any satisfaction out of talking to the officials of a big city government like Nashville." Presumably their scale could be translated to a national frame of reference by appropriately substituting "the government in Washington."

Reversing this process, Zimmer (1983) borrowed items from the SRC/ANES's Internal Efficacy scale, External Efficacy scale, and Trust in Government scale. He simply substituted "local government" into these existing indicators; for instance, "People like me have no say in what *local government* does" (emphasis added). This measure also taps system responsiveness and issues of trust. Although Zimmer failed to define political alienation, his scale combined items measuring both efficacy and trust.

The political alienation items appearing in the 1978 General Social Survey (GSS) were derived from items originally asked in the Harris Poll. The main values of this scale lie in its relatively high internal consistency, the large number of correlates available in the annual GSS, and the quality of the national sample. Its disadvantages include openness to agreement response set and meager evidence about its validity.

Malik (1982) also borrowed the Complex and Voting items from the original Campbell *et al.* (1954) efficacy scale and added three more items, including one referring explicitly to distrust of civil servants and politicians.

In contrast, Schwartz's (1973) theoretical perspective incorporated social–psychological measures contributing to the development of political alienation.

8. Political Estrangement Scales (Schwartz, 1973)

Schwartz attempted to bypass those theories that assumed political alienation to be a product of social alienation or of low socioeconomic status and other disadvantaged social states. His research differs from other studies in that only weak and indirect links are found between social background indicators, and in that no relationship occurs between social alienation and political alienation. Schwartz's Estrangement from Municipal Government scale tends to focus on the individual's generalized sense of estrangement; for example, "When I think about Philadelphia government and politics, I generally feel like an outsider." Attempting to capture this general feeling of estrangement from the political realm sets Schwartz's local political alienation scale apart from the others.

In contrast to the preceding scales, which combine elements of both political efficacy and political trust, the following three scales are premised on further differentiation within the efficacy dimension and on the separation of political efficacy from political trust (covered in Chapter 8).

9. Political Incapability and Political Discontent Scales (Olsen, 1969)
10. Efficacy/Powerlessness and Process Commitment Scales (Watts, 1973)
11. Political Estrangement and Political Powerlessness Scales (Ross, 1975)

Olsen (1969) defined political alienation as estrangement from the political system. He identified political incapability and political discontent (or cynicism) as components of this broader concept. However, his Incapability scale is simply a new label for Campbell *et al.*'s (1954) four SRC/ANES efficacy items discussed earlier. What is new is Olsen's focus on the opposite end of the continuum, namely, respondent feelings of inefficacy. His index of cynicism includes statements about the inability of the government to do a good job of governing. He attempts to measure feelings of "dissatisfaction, dissimilarity, and disillusionment" at a system level (1969, p. 292).

Watts's (1973) two scales measure political efficacy and commitment to the political process, each targeted on the national government. She argued that respondents who score low on political efficacy and trust (measured by a third scale) are the least committed to the democratic process.

Ross (1975) developed two scales: (1) A two-item Political Powerlessness index assesses feelings of efficacy, as indicated by the question "Do you think there are things that a person like yourself can do to get the government to change its policies?" This Political Powerlessness index captures respondents' perceptions that they can influence governmental policies and their political environments. (2) A Political Estrangement scale taps mainly issues of governmental responsiveness, reflecting a negative attitude toward public officials in terms of their reluctance to listen to the problems of their constituents, their lack of regard for the general welfare, the amount of payment received for their services, and the government's lack of understanding of and action toward resolving problems. Ross applied these measures in one of the few political alienation studies conducted outside the United States, namely, in Nairobi, Kenya. He found that perceptions of political powerlessness and estrangement were related to Kenyan tribal ethnicity. While some re-searchers have examined American racial differences in political alienation, examining ethnic differences with this construct is rare.

The next two scales are based on Seeman's (1959) dimensions.

12. Political Powerlessness and Political Normlessness Scales (Finifter, 1970)
13. Political Normlessness Scale (Schoultz, 1978)

As noted previously, Finifter (1970) used Seeman's typology of general alienation as the theoretical basis for her work, perhaps the only analyst who has tried to link theoreti-cal dimensions to indicators of political alienation in order to justify them empirically. Finifter assumed that each of the four types of political alienation—political powerless-ness, political meaninglessness, perceived political normlessness, and political isolation—might differently affect political behavior. However, in her effort to identify these four components from 21 candidate items included in Almond and Verba's (1965) five-nation study, she uncovered only two dimensions from the U.S. data. The referents of both di-mensions included the national government, local government, the police, and political parties. Her first dimension, Political Powerlessness, referred to an individual's ability to understand and affect the political process, as in this item: "If you made an effort to change this law, how likely is it that you would succeed?"

Finifter's second dimension of Political Normlessness reflected the extent to which political powerholders observe the norms of the political culture. Some of these items concerned the role of political parties in the country's welfare and the trustworthiness of political officials. Other items attempted to assess the treatment respondents would expect from various political agents, as in this item: "Suppose there were some question that you had to take to a government office—for example, a tax question or housing regulation. Do you think you would be given equal treatment?" Finifter concluded that people who feel that they would receive unfair treatment are questioning "the norm of equal and consid-erate treatment of citizens by government officials" (1970, p. 395). In such instances re-spondents do not have feelings of anomie, but perceive occurrences of normative devia-tion in the political process.

Schoultz's (1978) Political Normlessness Scale is derivative of Finifter's work, using only 4 of the 10 items from her scale. His factor analysis of Kirkpatrick's 1965 survey of 2014 adults in Argentina revealed that these 4 items loaded highly on a single dimension. In the Argentine context the pattern of covariations between Schoultz's Political Norm-lessness Scale and social status or political attitudes differed notably from the relationships among the same 4 items in the U.S. survey analyzed by Finifter.

The impetus for the final scale was the theoretical concern that without an underlying and generalized feeling of citizen support for the political system, the system would suc-cumb to a state of political jeopardy or crisis.

14. Political Support–Alienation Scale (Muller, Jukam, & Seligson, 1982)

Thus, Easton (1965) argued that diffuse public support for the political system is im-portant if the system is to survive. According to Miller (1974), when diffuse support de-creases, a discontent will result that gives rise to opportunities for revolutionary changes of the political system.

For these authors, and for Muller and his colleagues (1977, 1979, 1982; also Selig-son, 1983), whose primary interest is to measure diffuse support, positive system affect contributes to political stability. They are concerned with the relationship between affect for the system and aggressive political behavior. They hypothesize that "if system affect is positive among either powerful or sizable segments of the polity, the threat to the stability of the prevailing regime will be small." Conversely, if system affect is negative among either a powerful or a sizable portion of the polity, the threat to the present administration will be more substantial (1977, p. 1563).

Muller and his colleagues further tried to clarify empirically the meaning of political alienation. They sought to validate Easton's (1965, 1975) theoretical work on political support. The support–alienation concept forms a continuum ranging from support at the positive end to alienation at the negative end. Specifically the authors wanted to test whether respondents make distinctions between officials of an incumbent administration and the general political system.

Like several other scholars (Citrin, 1974; Citrin *et al.,* 1975; Miller, Erbring, & Goldenberg, 1979), Muller concluded that the SRC/ANES political trust scale merely measures support for the incumbent administration and, therefore, is an inadequate indicator of system affect. He expressed two goals for his scale. The first was to measure affect for the political system, that is, to distinguish support for political institutions from positive affect toward an incumbent administration. "The intent of the scale is to measure what Easton calls the 'legitimacy' dimension of the diffuse support concept; that is, to evaluate how well the political system and political institutions conform to a person's general sense of what is right and proper and how well the system and institutions uphold basic political values of importance to citizens" (Muller *et al.,* 1982, p. 246). His second goal was to elicit responses along a continuum from very strong positive affect (support) to very strong negative affect (alienation). Muller *et al.*'s Political Support–Alienation Scale attempts to measure legitimacy of the political system, in general and over time. It is not concerned so much with the attitudes toward a specific incumbent administration. Alienation from a specific regime need not connote a lack of support for the governmental system itself, as in this item that attempts to elicit regime affect: "To what extent do you have respect for the political institutions in [country]?" A timely negative response to current leaders does not necessarily diminish one's positive affect for the system.

Trends and Correlates of Political
Alienation from the General Social Survey

The GSS has been asking alienation items since 1973, and this series provides a valuable way to track trends in such feelings across time. However, only one of the GSS cross-time items taps political alienation ("Most public officials are not really interested in the problems of the average man"). As can be seen in Figure 7–1, this item has become more popular since 1973, with 37% agreeing then, as compared to 44% in 1994. However, the other two general alienation items ("In spite of what some people say, the lot of the average man is getting worse, not better"; "It's hardly fair to bring a child into the world with the way things look for the future") also rose. The lot of the average man question increased from 55 to 69%, and the child-future question rose from 59 to 75%. Thus, these two nonpolitical alienation items have increased in popularity much more than the political item.

Much the same impression of convergence between political and nonpolitical alienation emerges from examining the items' demographic correlates in Table 7–1. Correlations of both items with sex and age are minimal (women and the young being slightly more alienated), and both are significantly more likely to be agreed to by blacks than by

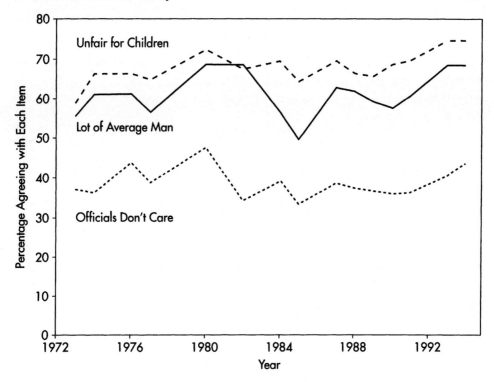

Fig. 7.1   GSS Trends in Alienation 1973–1994

whites. Part of this covariation is due to the correlation of race with the most powerful predictor of all alienation responses, namely, the respondents' levels of education. Moreover, in terms of all nine items in the Srole scale (of which these three are part), the overall education–general alienation correlation is substantial (−.40), while race shows a more moderate correlation (.20). Further, political and nonpolitical alienation responses have been significantly more popular among Democrats than Republicans. During the same period political ideology was unrelated (partly because extreme liberals and extreme conservatives are more likely to feel alienated than are centrist respondents).

Thus, both Figure 7–1 and Table 7–1 indicate that, while conceptually distinct, there seems to be a good deal of empirical correspondence between the two types of alienation. Further evidence in Table 7–1 to support that conclusion comes from the correlates of the Harris–GSS political alienation scale reviewed later in this chapter. Here again we find

Table 7-1

Correlations of GSS Alienation Items with Social Background Factors

	Sex	Age	Race	Educ	Party	Lib–Cons
1978 Harris items	.01	−.02	.05	−.27	.03	.02
1972–1996 Public officials	.01	.04	.07	−.18	.06	.00
1972–1996 Lot/child worse	.05	.03	.13	−.23	.11	.03
1972–1978 All Srole items	.03	.07	.20	−.40	.10	.02

minimal correlation of alienation with sex, age, and ideology, but significantly higher alienation scores among the less educated, black, and Democratic respondents. Here also we find no relation of alienation with income, but significantly higher alienation among those respondents dissatisfied with their income or unhappy with life in general. Nonetheless, this area deserves a good deal more research. [It should be noted that the general alienation measures were reviewed in the first volume of this series by Seeman (1991).]

Recommendations

The best research on measuring the social psychology of political alienation is more than two decades old. Because the four original SRC/ANES items remain the most salient measures of political efficacy, all researchers undertaking investigations of this concept must familiarize themselves with the Campbell *et al.* (1954) appendix. Finifter's (1970) reanalysis of the Almond and Verba (1965) items also provides the most detailed discussion of theoretical issues related to political powerlessness and political normlessness. While lacking a theoretical basis, the recent Verba *et al.* (1995) Political Efficacy Scale offers a short scale with good measurement properties. Using non-national samples Schwartz (1973) conducted original research that yielded several political estrangement scales. Researchers interested in conducting secondary data analysis with good national samples are limited to the biennial ANES and the single item in the annual GSS.

Future Research

Several suggestions for future research have emerged from our review of the existing literature on political alienation and efficacy, as research in this area seems to have become largely inactive during the last decade. They fall into four basic categories: (1) the causes of political alienation, (2) the consequences of political alienation, (3) the development of more efficient and parsimonious measures, and (4) issues of methodology and data collection.

Some speculation, but relatively little research, has been undertaken on the causes and preconditions of political alienation. Schwartz (1973) stressed the need to understand the impact of macro-sociopolitical trends and events on the creation of political alienation. Individuals' attributes might also foster alienation. For example, several researchers have reported race to be an important predictor of political alienation in the United States, with blacks in general being more alienated than whites (Abramson, 1972; Finifter, 1970; Herring, 1987a; Long, 1975, 1978; Schwartz, 1973). Hence further explorations of the origins of racial differences in efficacy and alienation would appear warranted. Contemporary political controversies may exacerbate racial tensions and foster majority–minority antagonism—for example, the backlash against affirmative action policies manifested in events such as the passage of California Proposition 209. Conceivably racial discord may translate into rising levels of political alienation or more specifically into distrust by racial minorities of the political officials and institutions perceived as working against their collective interests.

Very little research on the relationship of ethnicity to political alienation has been undertaken apart from that of Ross (1975). Specific cultural values within particular ethnic groups may heighten or diminish the potential for developing political disaffection. More-over, the fundamental personality traits contributing to political alienation or efficacy have yet to be investigated. Are introverted pessimists more likely to be alienated than optimis-tic extroverts? In addition, the exclusive reliance on cross-sectional research designs means that little understanding exists about how alienation develops and how its levels of expression interact with other social forces over time.

In terms of our second concern, while several studies have examined the consequences of political alienation, they are incomplete. Their findings indicate that the expected inverse relationship exists between political alienation and various forms of po-litical participation, such as voting, interest in political issues, political discussion, making political contributions to parties or candidates, working for candidates, party affiliation, political organization involvement, and support for term limits (Campbell, Converse, Stokes, & Miller, 1960; Mason et al., 1985; McDill & Ridley, 1962; Olsen, 1969; Ross, 1975; Schwartz, 1973; Southwell, 1986, 1995; Thompson & Horton, 1960; Watts, 1973). However, little of this research specifies the range of conditions across which the inverse relationship holds.

Our third concern is over the proliferation in the research literature of political alien-ation indicators having questionable value. For example, Mason et al. (1985) identified 7 indexes and 6 items from an initial list of 27 indicators from the SRC/ANES series. Simi-larly Craig et al. (1990) examined 35 efficacy and trust items from the ANES and found only four of the five hypothesized dimensions. Such reassessments of the factor structure of political alienation could winnow the candidate lists down to a more parsimonious and workable set of indicators. In addition, a shortened list of items could be more intensively analyzed to determine their dimensionality. Because so much of the early research on po-litical alienation was based on SRC/ANES data, comparisons should be made between the findings using those data and results from new data collection efforts.

Our final source of concern is the limited research focus on political alienation from government at the national level. A further refinement would be to examine alienation from specific national institutions, such as the presidency, the Congress, or the Supreme Court, to parallel the well-known Gallup and GSS series on confidence in these institu-tions' performance. Additional distinctions might be drawn with respect to more local lev-els of government, such as state, county, and municipal governments. Within these levels analysts should assess contextual variables, such as the characteristics of local political structures.

Mason et al. (1985) have pointed to further potential problems that may arise from the use of SRC/ANES items. The items in a scale are generally presented to respondents in a series even though the context and order of items may influence responses. Abramson, Silver, and Anderson (1987) demonstrated how question order influenced a decline in scores for the separate SRC/ANES scale of citizen duty. Hence future survey analysts could determine whether the clustering of items may be responsible for inducing high in-tercorrelations.

Finally more investigation of political alienation across cultural settings is desirable. Although several notable cross-cultural studies have been undertaken (Almond & Verba, 1965; Muller et al., 1982; Ross, 1975; Schoultz, 1978; Seligson, 1983), few have appeared recently, with the bulk of research concentrated on the United States. The upheavals in Eastern Europe and the former Soviet Union, coupled with an increased openness to so-cial science research in those nations, present political scientists and sociologists with a golden opportunity to track the shifting tides of alienation and efficacy within the citizenry of political systems undergoing major transformations.

Political Efficacy Scale

(A. Campbell, G. Gurin, & W. E. Miller, 1954)

Variable

Political efficacy was defined as "the feeling that political and social change is possible, and that the individual citizen can play a part in bringing about this change" (Campbell *et al.*, 1954, p. 188).

Description

With political efficacy at one end of the continuum of political potency, political alienation seems to anchor the opposite pole of the construct. Initially five items were proposed for the Political Efficacy Scale. An agree–disagree response format was used. Disagreement with Items 1, 3, 4, and 5 and agreement with Item 2 indicated efficaciousness. Thus, political alienation was suggested by the opposite pattern of responses. Guttman scale analysis (discussed later) disclosed a relatively large error for the second item ("The way people vote is the main thing that decides how things are run in this country"). Campbell *et al.* (1954, p. 189) decided that "[s]ince this was a somewhat ambiguous question with a relatively large per cent error, it was dropped from the scale."

Scores thus range from 0 (low efficacy) to 4 (high efficacy). The mean score for the 1594 respondents in the 1952 sample was 1.80 (SD = 1.39), with the following distribution:

0	20.7%
1	12.7
2	39.5
3	20.5
4	6.6
	100.0%

Sample

All analyses of political efficacy discussed here are based on data from the 1952–1996 American National Election Studies conducted during national election years initially by the Survey Research Center and later by the Center for Political Studies, both located at the University of Michigan. The survey sample sizes ranged from 1139 to 2705 respondents. These data were obtained by personal interviews with representative samples of voting-age citizens living in private households in the contiguous United States. Miller *et al.* (1980) give a complete description of the sampling methods for the surveys conducted until 1978.

Reliability

Internal Consistency

The Political Efficacy Scale's coefficient of reproducibility based on a Guttman scale procedure was .92 for all five items and .94 with Item 2 excluded. The range of error was 6 to 8% for Items 1, 3, 4, and 5 and 11% for the second item. Further evidence of the scale's internal consistency is discussed under Results and Comments.

Test–Retest

No information was reported.

Validity

Convergent

Campbell *et al.* (1954) reported that political efficacy was positively correlated with measures of political participation: The higher one's sense of efficacy, the higher one's level of participation in elections. The authors also found that, as expected, political efficacy covaried positively with such socioeconomic variables as income, occupation, and education. (Significant differences in efficacy also were found for respondents' sex, race, and geographic location. Men scored higher than women, whites scored higher than blacks, and southerners scored lower than residents of other regions. Further, as population density increased, so did the sense of political efficacy.)

Discriminant

No information was reported.

Location

Original Citations

Campbell, A., Gurin, G., & Miller, W. E. (1954). *The voter decides.* Evanston, IL: Row, Peterson.

   Campbell, A., Converse, P. E., Stokes, D. E., & Miller, W. E. (1960). *The American voter.* New York: Wiley.

Later Sources

Agnello, T. (1973). Aging and the sense of political powerlessness. *Public Opinion Quarterly, 37,* 251–259.

   House, J. S., & Mason, W. M. (1975). Political alienation in America, 1952–1968. *American Sociological Review, 40,* 123–147.

   Wright, J. D. (1976). *The dissent of the governed: Alienation and democracy in America.* New York: Academic Press.

   Yin, R. K., & Lucas, W. (1973). Decentralization and alienation. *Policy Sciences, 4,* 327–336.

Results and Comments

Campbell *et al.* originally developed these items as an indicator of political efficacy, which they defined as "the feeling that individual political action does have, or can have, an impact on the political process" (Campbell *et al.*, 1954, p. 187). Since its original development, the ANES Political Efficacy scale has frequently been used as a measure of political alienation.

   Many authors describe this measure of political alienation as comprised of two separate dimensions: political efficacy (sometimes referred to as political powerlessness) and political trust. Agnello (1973), for example, described powerlessness as one of several possible dimensions of political alienation. He combined SRC Items 1, 4, and 5 from the 1952, 1960, and 1968 ANES surveys as an index of powerlessness. He reported that feelings of powerlessness decrease among the young, but tend to increase for the old. While interest in voting may be low among the young, other forms of political participation and interest may be substituted. Yin and Lucas (1973) defined political alienation as having two independent dimensions, political powerlessness and distrust of government. They hypothesized that four forms of decentralization would reduce political alienation. Item 2 from the 1970 ANES was used as one indicator of powerlessness, while distrust was measured by a Trust in Government scale in the survey. Similar findings were reported by other authors (e.g., Finifter, 1970; Verba & Nie, 1972), who found that although political efficacy was related to political participation, trust in the political system was not. Other elements of decentralization (citizen awareness of decentralized facilities, service improvements) were also associated with a sense of efficacy, but not with feelings of trust.

House and Mason (1975) also conceptualized political alienation as having two dimensions, efficacy and trust. Their findings were based on ANES presidential year surveys from 1952 through 1968. They took four items from Campbell *et al.*'s (1954) original Political Efficacy Scale to measure the two alienation dimensions (Items 1, 3, 4, and 5). Based on canonical analysis, Items 1, 4, and 5 (Don't Care, No Say, and Complex) were combined into a single alienation index. However, analysis of the 1968 ANES data led them to conclude that only Items 1 and 4 (Don't Care and No Say) comprised a valid system trust measure. Items 3 and 5 (Complex and Voting) were not examined for their validity. House and Mason's initial focus was to demonstrate that little change in both dimensions of political alienation occurred during the 1950s and 1960s among specific demographic groups. Their subsequent focus was on the distinction between political efficacy and system trust. They found support for the hypothesis that, over time, system trust decreased among persons with initial attitudes favorable to existing public policies. Political trust decreased as respondent attitudes became more opposed to such policy developments.

Wright (1976) defined political alienation to include both an efficacy (or input) dimension and a trust (or output) dimension. One component was a sense of confidence in one's ability to influence the system, and the other was a sense of competence by the governmental system. The data came from four ANES presidential election studies (1960 to 1972). The political efficacy measure consisted of four items (1, 3, 4, and 5). The political trust scale was measured by means of the ANES Political Trust index. The low level of association (gamma = .29) between the trust and efficacy scales supported Wright's conclusion that they are essentially distinct components of political alienation. The average interitem correlation for the political efficacy items was .64 in the 1968 survey. The four efficacy scale items correlated moderately with eight alternative efficacy items in the 1966 survey (gamma = .49). In an exploratory discriminant validity analysis, a varimax rotated factor analysis produced four distinct factors: political efficacy, political trust, individual efficacy, and trust in people. Wright failed to find any relationship between alienation and political negativism and found only minor differences between alienated and nonalienated voters in terms of their political motivations or the influence of social background (sex, race, age, and socioeconomic indicators) and political interests (party identification, political ideology) on their voting behavior.

Political Efficacy Scale (ANES Mnemonics) (Campbell, Gurin, & Miller, 1954)

1. I don't think public officials care much what people like me think. (Don't Care)
   0. AGREE   *1. DISAGREE

2. The way people vote is the main thing that decides how things are run in this country. (Vote)
   *0. AGREE   1. DISAGREE

3. Voting is the only way that people like me can have any say about how the government runs things. (Voting)
   0. AGREE   *1. DISAGREE

4. People like me don't have any say about what the government does. (No Say)
   0. AGREE   *1. DISAGREE

5. Sometimes politics and the government seem so complicated that a person like me can't really understand what's going on. (Complex)
   0. AGREE   *1. DISAGREE

*Indicates efficacious response.

Political Efficacy Scale

(S. Verba, K. Schlozman, & H. Brady, 1995)

Variable

The authors define efficacy in terms of how much attention a local and a national government official would pay if the respondent had a complaint and how much influence the respondent has over local or national government decisions.

Description

This is a four-item scale with four alternatives each; the scores thus vary between 4 (low efficacy) to 16 (high efficacy). The average score was 9.2 (SD = 2.4).

Sample

This scale was administered in 1990 during in-person interviews with a national probability sample of 2517 respondents 18 years or older. This sample was the second stage selected from a 15,053-person sample initially interviewed by telephone in 1989.

Reliability

Internal Consistency

The scale had an alpha coefficient of .79.

Test–Retest

No information was reported.

Validity

Convergent

Mean scores on the Political Efficacy Scale increased with level of education and income. Anglo-white respondents had higher mean scores than African Americans and Latinos, but the gender difference was very small. In a multiple regression equation with overall political participation as the dependent variable, political efficacy had a significant positive coefficient.

Discriminant

The authors consider political efficacy as one of four overlapping measures of political engagement, including political interest, political information, and partisanship. Political efficacy had significant correlations with political interest (.21) and political information (.21), but not with partisanship (.01).

Location

Verba, S., Schlozman, K., & Brady, H. (1995). *Voice and equality: Civic voluntarism in American politics.* Cambridge, MA: Harvard University Press. Reprinted by permission of the publisher. Copyright © 1995 by the President and Fellows of Harvard College.

Results and Comments

The authors were more interested in explaining overall political participation than in understanding the origins of political efficacy. The impact of efficacy on participation is lower than that of education and political information, and equal to that of political information.

Political Efficacy Scale
(Verba, Schlozman, & Brady, 1995)

1. If you had some complaint about a *local government* activity and took that complaint to a member of the local government council, do you think that he or she would pay:
   1. NO ATTENTION AT ALL 2. VERY LITTLE ATTENTION 3. SOME ATTENTION *4. A LOT OF ATTENTION

2. If you had some complaint about a *national government* activity and took that complaint to a member of the national government, do you think that he or she would pay:
   1. NO ATTENTION AT ALL 2. VERY LITTLE ATTENTION 3. SOME ATTENTION *4. A LOT OF ATTENTION

> 3. How much influence do you think someone like you can have over *local* government decisions?
> 1. NONE AT ALL 2. VERY LITTLE 3. SOME *4. A LOT
> 4. How much influence do you think someone like you can have over *national* government decisions?
> 1. NONE AT ALL 2. VERY LITTLE 3. SOME *4. A LOT
>
> *Indicates most efficacious response.

Political Alienation Scale
(W. E. Thompson & J. E. Horton, 1960)

Variable

Political alienation involves both (1) an awareness of and a displeasure in being powerless and (2) an element of distrust of those in power.

Description

Thompson and Horton saw political alienation as a reaction to political inefficacy, a perception of being unable to influence or control public policy.

The index of political alienation combined five items. The first response to the first question about one's participation in community affairs was categorized as active; the last two responses denoted more passive individuals. The four remaining items were constructed using the Guttman scaling technique. Persons who were passive in community affairs and gave negative responses to the remaining four items were considered to be highly alienated. Scores range from 0 (low alienation) to 5 (high alienation).

Sample

The data came from an upstate New York community that had voted on a school bond proposal in March 1957. Of the 227 face-to-face interviews completed, 207 were used in the analyses. At least 5 interviews were obtained from each of several tracts of the community that were roughly based on different socioeconomic levels. This was the only systematic attempt to produce a representative sample.

Reliability

Internal Consistency

The coefficient of reproducibility for the measure was .94. The error ratio was .57.

Test–Retest

No information was reported.

Validity

Convergent

The authors hypothesized that alienated persons would be more apt to use their vote as a demonstration of resentment or opposition and that alienation would be correlated with lower socioeconomic status. Both of these hypotheses were substantiated empirically.

Discriminant

No information was reported.

Location

Thompson, W. E., & Horton, J. E. (1960). Political alienation as a force in political action. *Social Forces, 38,* 190–195.

Results and Comments

The authors reported that younger and older voters were apt to be more alienated than middle-aged respondents. Rural residents were more alienated that those living in town. In support of previous researchers (Campbell *et al.,* 1954; Lane, 1959, p. 190), alienated individuals were slightly less likely to turn out to vote. Further, politically alienated respondents were more likely to demonstrate less faith in people. When overall feelings of alienation were used as a control variable, the positive relationship between political alienation and protest voting remained unchanged.

Political Alienation Scale
(Thompson & Horton, 1960)

1. People have different ideas of just how they fit into community affairs. Would you say that you are:
   - 0. A PERSON WHO CONTRIBUTES TO COMMUNITY DECISIONS
   - *1. A PERSON WHO IS ACTIVE, BUT NOT ONE OF THE DECISION-MAKERS, JUST AN ORDINARY PERSON IN THE COMMUNITY
   - *1. NOT REALLY PART OF THE COMMUNITY AT ALL

2. Some people say you can usually trust local officials because they are your neighbors and friends, others say that elected officials become tools of special interests no matter who they are. What do you think?
   - 0. TRUST   *1. BECOME TOOLS

3. It doesn't matter which party wins the elections, the interests of the little man don't count.
   - *1. AGREE   0. DISAGREE

4. Local officials soon lose touch with the people who elected them.
   *1. AGREE   0. DISAGREE
5. If people knew what was really going on in high places, it would blow the lid off things.
   *1. AGREE   0. DISAGREE

*Indicates alienated response.

Political Alienation Scale
(E. L. McDill & J. C. Ridley, 1962)

Variable

McDill and Ridley (1962) drew on Thompson and Horton (1960) to define political alienation as containing (1) elements of apathy in response to political powerlessness or inefficacy and (2) elements of distrust of political leaders.

Description

The Political Alienation Scale has five items that refer to city government. Scores range from 0 (low alienation) to 5 (high alienation).

Sample

Data were obtained from an area probability sample of 283 white, nonfarm households of Davidson County, Tennessee, excluding the city of Nashville. The findings are based on responses to structured interviews with 268 suburban heads-of-household, or the closest relative of the head who was eligible to vote in a June 1958 referendum to consolidate the county government with the Nashville city government.

Reliability

Internal Consistency

A Kuder–Richardson coefficient of .69 showed the internal consistency of the political alienation scale.

Test–Retest

No information was reported.

Validity

Convergent

The authors hypothesized that low socioeconomic status leads to anomia and political alienation, which, in turn, affect voting behavior. Specifically, alienated individuals are more likely to vote against the agendas of political leaders (in their study, against the referendum for a consolidated city–county government). The findings supported the hypothesis.

Discriminant

No information was reported.

Location

McDill, E. L., & Ridley, J. C. (1962). Status, anomia, political alienation, and political participation. *American Journal of Sociology, 68,* 205–213.

Results and Comments

Politically alienated respondents were less likely to vote in the referendum, but if they voted, they were more apt to vote against the proposal for a consolidated metropolitan city–county government. Also as hypothesized, politically alienated respondents had less clearly defined attitudes on the referendum.

Political Alienation Scale
(McDill & Ridley, 1962)

1. The government of a big city like Nashville doesn't take much interest in a person's neighborhood.
   *1. AGREE   0. DISAGREE
2. The government of a big city like Nashville is too costly to the average taxpayer.
3. The average person can't get any satisfaction out of talking to the officials of a big city government like Nashville.
4. The government of a big city like Nashville is controlled too much by machine politics.
5. The average person doesn't have much to say about the running of a big city like Nashville.

   *Indicates alienated response.

Political Alienation Scale

(Y. K. Malik, 1982)

Variable

Alienation is viewed as powerlessness, self-estrangement, political ineffectiveness, and disorientation toward the political system.

Description

A five-item scale was used to measure the respondents' sense of political efficacy and attitudes toward the political system, with all items in an agree–disagree format. Scores range from 0 (low alienation) to 5 (high alienation).

Sample

The survey was conducted in 1979 in Jullundur City in India. The sample was drawn from the university and 12 colleges within the community. The author reported that 2500 usable questionnaires were returned from students in their first year and third (last) year of classes.

Reliability

Internal Consistency

No information was reported.

Test–Retest

No information was reported.

Validity

Convergent

No information was reported.

Discriminant

No information was reported.

Location

Malik, Y. K. (1982). Attitudinal and political implications of diffusion of technology: The case of north Indian youth. *Journal of Asian and African Studies, 17,* 45–73.

Results and Comments

A large majority of respondents were highly alienated, with only a minority expressing favorable views of the political system. Malik's hypothesis that a positive relationship would exist between exposure to technology and alienation was not supported. Alienated youth were more predisposed to political violence and to the acceptance of revolutionary solutions to social problems.

Alienation Scale
(Malik, 1982)

1. Sometimes governmental and political affairs look so complex that I am unable to understand them.
   *1. AGREE   0. DISAGREE

2. I think that other than voting there is no way whereby we can influence the governmental decision-making.
   *1. AGREE   0. DISAGREE

3. If the government officials mistreat us we are unable to do anything against them.
   *1. AGREE   0. DISAGREE

4. The government does not care for men like me; it is influenced only by the leaders of the groups or the capitalist class.
   *1. AGREE   0. DISAGREE

5. Even though the civil servants and the politicians of our country are incompetent and they do not deserve our trust, I am still proud of the political achievements of my country.**
   0. AGREE   *1. DISAGREE

   *Indicates alienated response.
   **Item reverse coded for scale consistency.

Political Alienation Scale (General Social Survey)

(J. A. Davis & T. W. Smith, 1996)

Variable

This six-item scale taps various sentiments related to feeling a lack of power in social and political relations.

Description

The items were adapted from items developed in Harris (1976), and further and more recent updates can be found in Harris Poll studies available through the University of North Carolina Survey Archives.

The items are in simple yes–no format, with a *yes* response indicating a more alienated response. Scores thus range between 0 (lowest alienation, namely, disagreement with all six items) and 6 (agreement with all six items). The distribution for those respondents answering all six items in this 1978 survey was as follows:

0	9%
1	12
2	14
3	16
4	16
5	17
6	16
	100%

The average score was 3.3 (SD = 1.9).

Sample

The questions were asked in the 1978 GSS, with a national cross-section of 1432 respondents and a response rate of nearly 80%.

Reliability

Internal Consistency

The alpha coefficient was .74 for all six items, and they all loaded on a single common factor in a factor analysis. The average interitem correlation was about .35.

Test–Retest

No information was reported.

Validity

Convergent

The scale correlated .17 with voting in the 1976 election, which is significant at the .001 level although not very high. Higher relations were found with measures of life satisfaction (.21), satisfaction with one's financial condition (.24), and judging one's income as above average (.23). (The latter correlations held up after multivariate control for income and education; income per se was not related to alienation.)

Discriminant

No information was reported.

Location

Davis, J. A., & Smith, T. W. (1996). *General Social Surveys 1972–96: Cumulative codebook.* Chicago: National Opinion Research Center.

　　Harris, L. (1976). *Report 2521.* New York: Louis Harris.

Results and Comments

This scale, like others in this chapter, is flawed by its reliance on items all phrased in the same direction, which may account for a large part of its high internal consistency. Its main value lies in the availability of norms from a national probability sample with a wealth of other opinion questions with which it can be related. Not all of the items deal specifically with political alienation, but those that do seem to relate to the other items as highly as those that do not. That is, they seem to be tapping a common sentiment.

A related set of alienation items has been asked by the GSS since 1973 and has similar measurement properties and problems (see text).

Political Alienation Scale
(Davis & Smith, 1996)

Do you tend to feel or not . . .

1. The people running the country don't really care what happens to you.
   *1. YES (Feel) (54%**)   0. NO (Don't feel)
2. The rich get rich and the poor get poorer. (76%)
3. What you feel doesn't count very much anymore. (58%)
4. You're left out of things going on around you. (30%)
5. Most people with power try to take advantage of people like yourself. (57%)
6. The people in Washington, D.C., are out of touch with the rest of the country. (58%)

   *Indicates alienated response.
   **Agreement among those with an opinion.

Local Government Alienation Scales
(T. A. Zimmer, 1983)

Variable

Zimmer (1983) devised two separate measures of political alienation: (1) general local government alienation and (2) specific local government alienation.

Description

General local government alienation was measured using a summed scale of five dichotomous agree–disagree items. Higher scores denoted feelings of alienation. Specific local government alienation was measured by a two-item index. The first item used a nine-point rating scale, and the second used a seven-point scale. Scores can thus range from 0 (low alienation) to 14 (high alienation).

Sample

The data for the study derived from the 1976 ANES survey of 2248 adult U.S. citizens. The average score on the scale was 2.2 (SD = 1.8).

Reliability

Internal Consistency

The internal consistency of the general Local Government Alienation Scale was reflected in a Spearman–Brown r of .82 and a Cronbach's alpha of .79. A factor analysis of the local government alienation items revealed a one-factor solution with all factor loadings ranging from .50 to .74.

Test–Retest

No information was reported.

Validity

Convergent

No direct measures of convergent validity were reported.

Discriminant

The correlation between the two specific alienation items was low (r = .17). The relationships of these two items differed with respect to the general alienation scale. Whether the government was seen as doing a good job was more closely related to the general local alienation (r = .45) than was the amount of power a local government *should* have (r = .13).

Location

Zimmer, T. A. (1983). Local news exposure and local government alienation. *Social Science Quarterly, 64*, 634–640. Reprinted by permission of the author and the University of Texas Press. All rights retained by the University of Texas Press.

Results and Comments

Zimmer tested three hypotheses. He found support for the hypothesis that local news exposure (not television) was negatively associated with general alienation. A hypothesis regarding community context found the above relationships to be significantly stronger for suburban compared to urban or rural communities. A third hypothesis suggesting that an increase in news exposure for those more generally alienated would be associated with regarding local government as not doing a good job or as not deserving more power was not supported.

Local Government Alienation Scale
(Zimmer, 1983)

1. Local government is run by a few big interests looking out for themselves.
   *1. AGREE   0. DISAGREE
2. Those elected to local government quickly lose touch with the people.
3. I trust local government to do what is right only some of the time.
4. People like me have no say in what local government does.
5. Local government seems so complicated for a person like me to understand.

   *Indicates alienated response.

Specific Local Government Alienation Scale
(Zimmer, 1983)

1. How good a job do you think the local government is doing?

   *0   1   2   3   4   5   6   7   8
   VERY POOR   VERY GOOD

2. Rate how much influence and power local government should have.

   *0   1   2   3   4   5   6
   ALMOST NONE   A GREAT DEAL

   *Indicates alienated response.

Political Estrangement Scales
(D. C. Schwartz, 1973)

Variable

Political estrangement is defined as a sense of separation from the polity, "a perception that one does not identify oneself with the political system" (Schwartz, 1973, p. 7).

Description

The scales focus on a person's lack of connection to the political system rather than on the level of trust in the officials who are in charge of the political system.

Seven distinct estrangement scales were developed by the author: (1) Estrangement from Municipal Government, (2) Political Srole Scale, (3) Estrangement from National Polity I, (4) Estrangement from Nationality Polity II, (5) Estrangement from National Polity III, (6) Estrangement from State Polity, and (7) Estrangement from Local Polity. All scale items used a dichotomous agree–disagree format.

Sample

Empirical tests of the scales were conducted between 1968 and 1970. Various aspects of the author's theory were tested in 16 separate studies using a variety of methods, including 3 laboratory experiments and 13 field studies. Of the latter, 2 were personal interviews, 7 involved direct contact followed by self-administered questionnaires, and 4 employed a mailed questionnaire. The studies were conducted in the northeastern region of the United States, predominately in Pennsylvania.

An attempt was made to sample diverse elements of the population. A citywide sample was used in Newark, New Jersey. Philadelphia's black ghetto communities and white lower-middle- and middle-class suburbs were surveyed. A prestigious private liberal arts college was sampled, as were a large urban state-related university, a community college, and a medium-sized urban engineering and technical college. The sizes of the survey samples range from 49 to 854. Overall there were 2687 respondents who responded to personal interviews or questionnaires.

Reliability

Internal Consistency

The range of average interitem correlations across all the scales was .24–.64.

Test–Retest

No information was reported.

Validity

Convergent

As hypothesized, general feelings of alienation and political alienation were not significantly associated with one another. In general there was not a strong relationship between sociocultural and political alienation. Schwartz also hypothesized no correlation between social background variables and political alienation, and he found none. Further he hypothesized strong relationships among the perceived threat from value conflict, political inefficacy, perceived systemic inefficacy, and political alienation at local, state, and national levels. The correlations between pairs of these psychopolitical variables were modest to moderate (.11 to .56).

Discriminant

No information was reported.

Location

Schwartz, D. C. (1973). *Political alienation and political behavior.* Chicago: Aldine.

Results and Comments

In addition to the process variables that influence the development of political estrangement, the author also investigated the behavioral consequences of political alienation, such
as nonconformist political orientations. Estrangement was strongly associated with nonconformity and significantly correlated with revolutionism and ritualism. Politically alienated persons read as much political information as the nonalienated.

Estrangement from Municipal Government Scale
(Schwartz, 1973)

**1. I generally think of myself as a part of Philadelphia government and poli-
   tics.
   0. AGREE   *1. DISAGREE

2. When I think about Philadelphia government and politics, I generally feel
   like an outsider.

3. Many people feel they used to be a part of Philadelphia government and
   politics, but no longer. I feel the same way.

*Indicates alienated response.
**Indicates reverse scored item.

Political Srole Scale
(Schwartz, 1973)

1. When I think of the direction things are going in the government, I feel
   frightened for the kids growing up.
   *0. AGREE   1. DISAGREE

2. I'm just not sure I can rely on representatives in government.

3. One never knows what the government is going to do next.

**4. Most public officials are concerned with the interests of the average man.

5. Public officials come and go but government seems to keep getting worse.

*Indicates alienated response.
**Indicates reverse scored item.

Estrangement from National Polity Scale I
(Schwartz, 1973)

1. When I think about politics and government in America, I consider myself an outsider.
   *0. AGREE   1. DISAGREE

2. In American politics and government, power is maintained by secrecy and collusion which excludes people like me.

3. The way things are in government now, people like me are no longer interested.

**4. I tend to identify myself (feel closely associated) with American politics and government.

**5. When I hear or read about the politics and governmental system in the United States, I feel that I am a part of that system.

   *Indicates alienated response.
   **Indicates reverse scored item.

Estrangement from National Polity Scale II
(Schwartz, 1973)

**1. I generally share the basic values exhibited in the policies and processes of American politics.
   0. AGREE   *1. DISAGREE

**2. I usually identify myself (feel closely associated) with American politics and government.

3. In American politics, power is maintained by secrecy and collusion which excludes even the interested citizen.
   *0. AGREE   1. DISAGREE

4. The way things are going in our society, my friends and I aren't really represented anymore.

   *Indicates alienated response.
   **Indicates reverse scored item.

Estrangement from National Polity Scale III
(Schwartz, 1973)

1. The government no longer seems to represent people like me.
   *0. AGREE   1. DISAGREE

2. In American politics, power is maintained in secret, shutting out even interested citizens.

3. The government seems to be unwilling to do the things I think need to be done.

*Indicates alienated response.

Estrangement from State Polity Scale
(Schwartz, 1973)

1. When I think about the politics in Harrisburg [the state capital], I feel like an outsider.
   *0. AGREE   1. DISAGREE
2. When I think about the government in Harrisburg, I don't feel as if it's my government.
3. People like me aren't represented in Harrisburg.

*Indicates alienated response.

Estrangement from Local Polity Scale
(Schwartz, 1973)

1. When I think about the politics in my town, I feel like an outsider.
   *0. AGREE   1. DISAGREE
2. When I think about the government in my town, I don't feel as if it's my government.
3. People like me aren't represented in my town.

*Indicates alienated response.

Political Incapability and Political Discontent Scales
(M. E. Olsen, 1969)

Variable

Olsen (1969) suggested that the broader concept of estrangement from the political system was divided into two dimensions: (1) political incapability–futility and (2) discontent–cynicism.

Description

The Political Incapability scale involves feelings of powerlessness, meaninglessness, and guidelessness (individual normlessness) that are forced on people by their environment. Olsen (1969) measured incapability using four of the five items in Campbell *et al.*'s (1954) Political Efficacy Scale with only minor wording changes.

The Political Discontent scale encompasses attitudes of dissimilarity, dissatisfaction, and disillusionment that are chosen by the person. The two dimensions are derived from Seeman's (1989) five types of alienation: powerlessness, meaninglessness, normlessness, isolation, and self-estrangement. Olsen's two scales also incorporated Dean's concept of social isolation, or "feelings of loneliness and impersonality" (Olsen, 1969, p. 290).

The two scales attempt to answer these questions: Are there forms of "middle class" political alienation, or is it limited to the "working class"? Does alienation predict political participation? How do the different types of alienation relate to party membership and voting? Each scale consists of four statements with which respondents agree or disagree. Scores range from 0 (low incapability) to 4 (high incapability) and similarly from 0 to 4 for discontent.

Sample

Both scales were included in a survey conducted in Ann Arbor, Michigan, in 1965. A sample was drawn from two census tracts, one lower middle class and one upper middle class. Interviews were administered to 154 of the 200 residents selected, a 77% completion rate.

Reliability

Internal Consistency

The coefficient of reproducibility (alpha) was .89 for the Political Incapability scale and .92 for the Political Discontent scale.

Test–Retest

No information was reported.

Validity

Convergent

No information was reported.

Discriminant

To assess whether these two scales were measuring the same concept, Olsen performed a multiple classification analysis. The scales were only moderately correlated (eta = .46). Hence, though related, the two scales represent distinct aspects of the broader concept of political alienation.

Neither form of alienation is highly correlated with political participation in four realms—mass media, informal discussions, voting, and personal involvement. However, persons with high incapability and low discontent voted overwhelmingly Democratic, while those with high discontent and low incapability voted Republican.

Location

Olsen, M. E. (1969). Two categories of political alienation. *Social Forces, 47,* 288–299.

Results and Comments

Both forms of alienation were present within the middle-class sample. According to Olsen's findings, the two scales are better predictors of voting patterns than of political participation.

Political incapability is negatively related to demographic variables, such as occupation, education, and income. It is more highly associated with persons over 60 and with women. These zero-order correlations hold even when the other demographic variables are held constant. Political incapability occurs more frequently among persons who have lower educational levels, lower incomes, and lower status occupations and who are older and nonwhite.

The findings are similar, but not as strong, for attitudes of political discontent. This dimension is inversely correlated to education and income. The relationship between occupation and discontent is nonmonotonic. This attitude is somewhat more prevalent among the elderly and women. When controlling for education, the relationship between sex and discontent disappears, and the relationship between discontentment and income is greatly reduced. Further, when education is used as a control, the business and professional occupational category has the highest level of discontent. (At the zero-order, this category had the lowest level of discontent.) This form of alienation is more prevalent among the elderly, the less educated, and small businesspersons.

Political Incapability Scale
(Olsen, 1969)

1. I believe public officials don't care much what people like me think.
   *1. AGREE   0. DISAGREE
2. There is no way other than voting that people like me can influence actions of the government.
3. Sometimes politics and government seem so complicated that I can't really understand what's going on.
4. People like me don't have any say about what the government does.

   *Indicates alienated response.

Discontent Scale
(Olsen, 1969)

1. These days the government is trying to do too many things, including some activities that I don't think it has the right to do.
   *1. AGREE   0. DISAGREE
2. For the most part, the government serves the interests of a few organized groups, such as business or labor, and isn't very concerned about the needs of people like myself.
3. It seems to me that the government often fails to take necessary actions on important matters, even when most people favor such actions.

4. As the government is now organized and operated, I think it is hopelessly incapable of dealing with all the crucial problems facing the country today.

*Indicates alienated response.

Efficacy/Powerlessness and Process Commitment Scales

(M. W. Watts, 1973)

Variable

Watts's Efficacy/Powerlessness and Process Commitment scales are components of a three-part Alienation Scale that measures political efficacy, process commitment, and trust.

Description

Political efficacy is the individual's belief that he or she can influence the political process; the inverse of efficacy is powerlessness, the individual's belief that he or she cannot affect government action. Process commitment measures an individual's belief in the appropriateness of working within the established political system. The political trust component concerns disaffection and distrust of politicians and politics in general.

Scale items were selected from commonly used measures of political attitudes (see Robinson, Rusk & Head, 1968). The Efficacy/Powerlessness scale consists of four items, while the Process Commitment scale has five items. Watts reported constructing both scales "using Likert-style scoring and item analysis" (Watts, 1973, p. 625). If dichotomous agree–disagree responses are used instead, scores would range from 0 to 4 for the Efficacy/Powerlessness scale and from 0 to 5 for the Process Commitment scale.

Sample

Two studies were conducted, the first of which gathered data on 471 predominately white social science students at three midwestern universities. Data for the second study came from almost 400 students at an urban midwestern university, nearly one-half of whom were selected for their involvement in nonpartisan, but predominantly liberal–left, political action groups.

Reliability

Internal Consistency

Item–scale correlations were computed as measures of internal consistency (Watts, 1974). These correlations ranged from .60 to .72 for the items in the Efficacy/Powerlessness scale and from .61 to .73 for those in the Process Commitment scale.

Test–Retest

No information was reported.

Validity

Convergent

Previous researchers had found that political efficacy was not strongly related to voters' party affiliations (Aberbach, 1969). Watts found only a slight difference between Republicans and Democrats. Republicans were less alienated on all three measures. Independents and Democrats with weaker party affiliations exhibited a higher level of political alienation. A related hypothesis by Dennis (1966) was that strength of party affiliation was related to political alienation. Watts's study indicated a significant positive relationship between the intensity of party affiliation and the three alienation measures. Watts hypothesized that all three concepts would be inversely related to election attitudes. He found that respondents who felt less efficacious had a lower opinion about elections, as did those who lacked commitment to the political process. None of these alienation measures was highly correlated with the norm of voter duty: No matter how alienated, people felt that voting was a civic obligation.

Discriminant

A factor analysis conducted on all items revealed three distinct dimensions, leading to the Efficacy/Powerlessness, Process Commitment, and Political Trust scales (Watts, 1974). All three alienation measures covaried positively with strength of party identification—Political Trust (.42), Powerlessness/Efficacy (.30), and Process Commitment (.19)—suggesting that each scale contributed differentially to political orientations.

Location

Watts, M. W. (1973). Efficacy, trust and commitment to the political process. *Social Science Quarterly, 54,* 623–631. Reprinted by permission of the author and the University of Texas Press. All rights retained by the University of Texas Press.

   Watts, M. W. (1974). Alienation and support for the political system among college students. In A. R. Wilcox (Ed.), *Public opinion and political attitudes* (pp. 105–127). New York: Wiley.

Results and Comments

The basic purpose of Watts's research was to determine whether the concept of political alienation might be a more effective predictor of political activity if it were separated into several components. His findings about each scale's relation to several types of political support were as expected. Both of Watts's studies were designed to test Gamson's (1968) hypothesis that political participation would be highest among persons whose political trust is low, while their political efficacy is high. However, the findings indicate that a combination of high efficacy and high trust were related to high process commitment, thus failing to support Gamson's hypothesis.

Efficacy/Powerlessness Scale
(Watts, 1973)

1. It is only wishful thinking to believe that one can really influence what happens in society at large.
   *1. AGREE   0. DISAGREE
**2. The way people vote is the main thing that decides how things are run in this country.
3. It seems that whoever people vote for, things go on pretty much the same.
4. Government officials don't care much about what people like me think.

*Indicates alienated response.
**This item was reverse coded for consistency in scale scoring.

Process Commitment Scale
(Watts, 1973)

**1. The individual is obligated to obey the law for the good of society as a whole, even if he finds it personally unjustifiable.
   1. AGREE   *0. DISAGREE
**2. Working within the established party system is the best way to bring about change in the long run.
3. It is sometimes necessary to resort to force to advance a cause one strongly believes in.
**4. Working within the system is the only way to accomplish meaningful change in America.
5. There are times when it almost seems better for the people to take the law into their own hands than to wait for the machinery to act.

*Indicates alienated response.
**These items were reverse coded for consistency in scale scoring.

Political Estrangement and Political Powerlessness Scales

(M. H. Ross, 1975)

Variable

Political alienation is viewed as combining feelings of political estrangement and political powerlessness.

Description

Estrangement refers to an individual's belief that the governmental system, which includes both the institutions and the political authorities, is not responsive to the needs and interests of the populace. Political powerlessness is the perception that one has little input into the political decision-making process.

Political estrangement is measured by a five-item scale. Scores range from 5 to 15. Political powerlessness is measured by a two-item dichotomous response index. Scores range from 2 to 6.

Sample

The data were collected in 1967 through interviews with randomly selected adults from two neighborhoods of Nairobi, Kenya. Shauri Moyo was a working-class neighborhood of about 900 single-room apartments, while residents of Kariokor were predominately white-collar and civil service employees living in 240 five-room apartments. According to the author, the demographic characteristics of these communities were similar to those of the entire city (Ross, 1975a, p. 294).

Reliability

Internal Consistency

The five items of political estrangement were subjected to a factor analysis, and one factor was extracted, indicating unidimensionality.

Test–Retest

No information was reported.

Validity

Convergent

Ross (1975a) found that both political estrangement and political powerlessness were affected by ethnicity and related to differences in social support and participation opportunities. The Kikuyu tribe, which was in power at the time of the study, felt less estranged from the Kenyan government and, in general, felt more powerful or efficacious than the Luo, a tribe whose organizations had been banned and whose leaders had been murdered or jailed.

Ross (1975a) hypothesized that political estrangement would be negatively associated with income and education. To the contrary there was no relationship for the Luo, and the association was in the opposite direction for the Kikuyu tribe. Membership in voluntary associations was related to feelings of estrangement for the Luo, but not for the Kikuyus, again contrary to expectations. Political powerlessness was expected to be correlated with measures of deprivation or exposure to new ideas (land ownership, income, education, and cinema attendance). Findings varied along ethnic lines. Among the Luo, those who had less education or who did not attend the cinema felt politically powerless. The lack of land was related to a feeling of powerlessness among the Kikuyu. Ross found support for the proposition that those who felt powerless would be less likely to participate politically.

Among the Luo, however, highly estranged individuals were more likely to participate in political activity.

Discriminant

The two indices of political estrangement and political powerlessness were found to co-vary independently.

Location

Ross, M. H. (1975a). Political alienation, participation, and ethnicity: An African case. *American Journal of Political Science, 19,* 291–311.

   Ross, M. H. (1975). *Grass roots in an African city: Political behavior in Nairobi.* Cambridge, MA: MIT Press.

Results and Comments

Ross's research is one of a handful of studies of political alienation in non-Western populations. His findings that feelings of political estrangement and powerlessness varied in unexpected ways with socioeconomic status, and were very strongly related to tribal ethnicity, underscore the importance of encompassing the historical etiology and contemporary social structures of the communities and societies under study.

Political Estrangement Scale
(Ross, 1975)

1. Some people say that there are many MPs who do not listen to the problems of people in their constituency. How satisfied are you that the MP from this constituency listens to the problems of the people here?
   1. SATISFIED
   2. SOMETIMES SATISFIED AND SOMETIMES DISSATISFIED
   *3. DISSATISFIED
2. Some people say that certain individuals or groups have so much influence over the way the government is run that the interests of the majority are ignored. Do you agree or disagree that there are such people or groups in Kenya today?
   *1. AGREE   2. DON'T KNOW   3. DISAGREE
3. Do you think that the government really understands the problems of the people?
   1. YES   2. DON'T KNOW   *3. NO
4. To improve the lives of the people since independence, has the government done:
   (1) MORE THAN YOU HAD EXPECTED IT WOULD DO
   (2) ABOUT WHAT YOU HAD EXPECTED IT WOULD DO
   *(3) LESS THAN YOU HAD EXPECTED IT WOULD DO

---

5. Do you think that politicians get too much money for the work that they do?
   *1. YES   2. DON'T KNOW   3. NO

   *Indicates alienated response.

Political Powerlessness Scale
(Ross, 1975a)

1. Do you think there are things that a person like yourself can do to get the government to change its policies?
   1. YES   2. DON'T KNOW   *3. NO

2. Nowadays we hear a great deal about self-reliance. Do you think there is a great deal that individuals can do to improve their lives in the city?
   1. YES   2. DON'T KNOW   *3. NO

   *Indicates alienated response.

Political Powerlessness and Political Normlessness Scales

(A. W. Finifter, 1970)

Variable

These two scales, Political Powerlessness and Political Normlessness, are viewed as separate dimensions of the underlying concept of political alienation.

Description

Powerlessness connotes a feeling of being unable to affect the government or political system and is the inverse of political efficacy. Normlessness concerns being critical of the operations of the political system, measuring respondents' beliefs that public officials violate legal procedures and community norms.

All items were taken from Almond and Verba's (1965) Civic Culture Questionnaire. Eleven items comprise the Political Powerlessness scale, with scores ranging from 0 to 11. Ten items were used to measure perceived political normlessness, with scores ranging from 0 to 10. Finifter did not report descriptive statistics about the scales.

Sample

Data were obtained from 970 interviews from a multistage stratified national probability sample early in 1960. Persons 18 and older residing within a family in the United States had equal probability of selection. See Almond and Verba (1965, pp. 519–523) for more complete sampling information.

Reliability

Internal Consistency

The reliability coefficients were .77 for the Political Powerlessness scale and .62 for the Political Normlessness measure. The correlation coefficients were factor-analyzed by the principal components method, and three of the four components were then varimax rotated. The results identified 5 items that were only weakly related to the underlying factors, and these were eliminated. A second principal-components analysis of the remaining 21 items was conducted, and all of the items were related to two components, identified as powerlessness and perceived political normlessness.

Test–Retest

No information was reported.

Validity

Convergent

Because previous ANES surveys had demonstrated a positive relationship between efficacy (the inverse of powerlessness) and socioeconomic status (education, occupation, and income), the opposite relationship was anticipated for Finifter's Political Powerlessness scale. Indeed, the Political Powerlessness measure was inversely correlated with education ($-.44$), occupation ($-.32$), and income ($-.31$), and positively correlated with male gender (.12). Powerlessness was most strongly related to political participation ($-.64$). The scale also covaried with organizational membership ($-.38$) and faith in people ($-.37$). A faith-in-people measure of interpersonal trust was strongly correlated with the Political Normlessness scale ($-.37$), while race (.22) and education ($-.16$) were the next highest predictors.

Discriminant

The two scales were only weakly related ($r = .26$) and had different patterns of correlation with demographic factors and attitude questions (see Results and Comments).

Location

Finifter, A. W. (1970). Dimensions of political alienation. *American Political Science Review, 64,* 389–410.

Results and Comments

The author hypothesized that the two alienation dimensions would be differentially related to other variables, and this was the case. Blacks had higher perceived normlessness scores than did whites, while race was only weakly related to powerlessness. Differences also occurred for sex and country of origin. Men felt less powerless than did women, but women tended to perceive fewer norm violations. Persons born in the United States felt less powerless than did foreign-born persons, but foreign-born persons felt less normlessness. Political participation was strongly correlated to powerlessness ($-.64$), but only slightly related to feelings of normlessness ($-.10$).

A stepwise regression revealed two subsets of variables that best predicted the two types of alienation. Persons who scored high on powerlessness were less likely to participate in either secular or church-related community activities. They were more apt to be older, be less educated, and possess less faith in people. Being Jewish and living in a small community reduced this type of alienation. Those who scored high on the Political Normlessness scale were characterized by having low faith in people, being black and male, having lower incomes, living in large cities, and attending church infrequently.

Political Powerlessness Scale
(Finifter, 1970)

1. If you wanted to discuss political and governmental affairs, are there some people you definitely wouldn't turn to—that is, people with whom you feel it is better not to discuss such topics?
   *1. YES   0. NO
   About how many people would you say there are with whom you would avoid discussing politics?
   0. NO ONE   *1. ONE OR MORE

2. Some people say that politics and government are so complicated that the average man cannot really understand what is going on.
   *1. AGREE   0. DISAGREE

3. How do you feel about this: Thinking of the important national and international issues facing the country, how well do you think you can understand these issues?
   *1. NOT AT ALL   0. SOME UNDERSTANDING

4. How about local issues in this town or part of the country? How well do you understand them?
   *1. NOT AT ALL   0. SOME UNDERSTANDING

5. If you made an effort to change this regulation (a hypothetical local regulation considered to be "very unjust or harmful"), how likely is it that you would succeed?
   *1. NOT AT ALL LIKELY   0. SOME CHANCE OF SUCCESS

6. If such a case (a local regulation) arose, how likely is it that you would actually try to do something about it?
   *1. NOT AT ALL LIKELY   0. SOME LIKELIHOOD

7. If you made an effort to change this law (a hypothetical national law considered to be "very unjust or harmful"), how likely is it that you would succeed?
   *1. NOT AT ALL LIKELY   0. SOME CHANCE OF SUCCESS

8. If such a case (a national law) arose, how likely is it you would actually try to do something about it?
   *1. NOT AT ALL LIKELY   0. SOME LIKELIHOOD

9. Thinking now about the national government in Washington, about how much effect do you think its activities, the laws passed and so on, have on your day-to-day life?
   0. A GREAT EFFECT   0. SOME EFFECT   *1. NONE

10. Now take the local government: about how much effect do you think its activities have on your day-to-day life?
    0. A GREAT EFFECT   0. SOME EFFECT   *1. NONE

11. People like me don't have any say about what the government does.
    *1. AGREE   0. DISAGREE

   *Indicates alienated response.

Political Normlessness Scale
(Finifter, 1970)

1. One sometimes hears that some people or groups have so much influence over the way the government is run that the interests of the majority are ignored.
   *1. AGREE   0. DISAGREE

2. On the whole, do the activities of the national government tend to improve conditions in this country, or would we be better off without them?
   0. IMPROVE   *1. BETTER OFF WITHOUT

3. On the whole, do the activities of the local government tend to improve conditions in this area, or would we be better off without them?
   0. IMPROVE   *1. BETTER OFF WITHOUT

4. Suppose there were some question that you had to take to a government office—for example, a tax question or housing regulation. Do you think you would be given equal treatment? I mean, would you be treated as well as anyone else?
   0. YES, EQUAL   *1. NO

5. If you explained your point of view to the officials, what effect do you think it would have? Would they give your point of view serious consideration, would they pay only a little attention, or would they ignore what you had to say?
   0. SERIOUS   0. LITTLE   *1. IGNORE

6. If you had some trouble with police—a traffic violation, maybe, or being accused of a minor offense—do you think you would be given equal treatment? That is, would you be treated as well as anyone else?
   0. YES, EQUAL   *1. NO

7. If you explained your point of view to the police, what effect do you think it would have? Would they give your point of view serious consideration, would they pay only a little attention, or would they ignore what you had to say?
   0. SERIOUS   0. LITTLE   *1. IGNORE

8. The Republican party now controls the administration in Washington. Do you think that its policies and activities would ever seriously endanger the country's welfare? Do you think that this probably would happen, that it might happen, or that it probably wouldn't happen?
   0. MIGHT   0. PROBABLY WON'T   *1. PROBABLY WOULD

9. If the Democratic party were to take control of the government, how likely is it that it would seriously endanger the country's welfare? Do you think that this would probably happen, that it might happen, or that it probably wouldn't happen?
   0. MIGHT   0. PROBABLY WON'T   *1. PROBABLY WOULD

10. All candidates sound good in their speeches, but you can never tell what they will do after they are elected.
    *1. AGREE   0. DISAGREE

*Indicates alienated response.

Political Normlessness Scale

(L. Schoultz, 1978)

Variable

Schoultz relied on theoretical writings by Seeman and Finifter to define political normlessness as a perception that the rules and norms that should be used in the political arena are not being followed.

Description

While Schoultz suggested that lawful violations of procedures are the most obvious indicators of political normlessness, this behavior is not limited to deviant officials, but is necessary in successful political activity.

   This scale is based on four items from Kirkpatrick's (1971) survey of Argentineans, drawn originally from Almond and Verba (1965). Scores range from 0 (low normlessness) to 4 (high normlessness).

Sample

The data come from personal interviews with 2014 Argentineans conducted in 1965 by Kirkpatrick, whose *Leader and Vanguard in Mass Society* (1971) contains details about the sampling and the data collection procedures.

Reliability

Internal Consistency

A factor analysis of the four normlessness items revealed a one-factor solution.

Test–Retest

No information was reported.

Validity

Convergent

Schoultz hypothesized that persons in a culture exhibiting high levels of political normlessness (such as Peronist Argentineans) would exhibit different social characteristics and political attitudes from persons in a society with high levels of political compliance (such as the United States). He found that social status and social cohesion were only weakly related to political normlessness in Argentina, while the correlations were much higher in analyses of the same scale in the U.S. survey conducted by Almond and Verba. Geocultural measures were also not highly associated with political normlessness in either nation.

An expected inverse relation between normlessness and feelings of personal political competence was not borne out, while a hypothesized positive relationship between political normlessness and political powerlessness was identified. In the United States these two components were separate, but positively related. Schoultz's factor analysis of the Argentine data failed to produce separate dimensions. As expected, he found that persons who perceived higher levels of political normlessness were the least supportive of the Argentine status quo. However, a positive relationship between normlessness and stronger government control was not found. Further, because in 1965 the centrist government was foundering, political normlessness was positively related to pro-Peronist sentiments and negatively related to support for the governmental party.

Discriminant

No information was reported.

Location

Schoultz, L. (1978). Political normlessness in comparative perspective. *Journal of Politics, 40,* 82–111.

Kirkpatrick, J. (1971). *Leader and vanguard in mass society.* Cambridge, MA: MIT Press.

Results and Comments

Schoultz showed that the cultural context of political normlessness conditions its relations with other political attitudes and behaviors.

Political Normlessness Scale
(Schoultz, 1978)

1. Suppose there were some question that you had to take to a government office, for example, a tax question or housing regulation. Do you think you would be given fair treatment or not?
   0. FAIR   *1. NOT

2. If you had some trouble with the law and authorities, do you think it would be probable, or not very probable, that you would receive fair treatment from the police and the courts?
   0. PROBABLE   *1. NOT VERY PROBABLE

3. All candidates sound good in their speeches, but you can never tell what they will do when they are elected.
   *1. AGREE   0. DISAGREE

4. One sometimes hears that some people have so much influence over the way government is run that the interests of the people are ignored and only the needs of the influential people receive attention. Do you think this is true?
   *1. YES   0. NO

*Indicates alienated response.

Political Support–Alienation Scale

(E. N. Muller, T. O. Jukam, & M. A. Seligson, 1982)

Variable

This scale is a revised form of the political support–alienation measure first used in West Germany.

Description

The two stated purposes of this scale are (1) to record sentiments toward the political system or political institutions versus affect for an incumbent administration and (2) to elicit responses along a continuum from very strong positive affect (support) to very strong negative affect (alienation).

"The intent of the scale is to measure what Easton calls the 'legitimacy' dimension of the diffuse support concept; that is, to evaluate how well the political system and political institutions conform to a person's general sense of what is right and proper and how well the system and institutions uphold basic political values of importance to citizens" (Muller *et al.*, 1982, p. 246). The Political Support–Alienation Scale consists of eight items. Respondents were asked to give magnitude ratings using a card with the following response continuum printed on it:

NONE AT ALL   A GREAT DEAL

1	2	3	4	5	6	7

The scale was originally administered in face-to-face interviews, but later versions also used self-administration techniques.

Using the response continuum, scores range from 7 (low support) to 56 (high support).

Sample

Two samples were initially tested: (1) Personal interviews were conducted in a 1978 probability sample of 778 adults from the five boroughs of New York City in which three forms of the interview schedule were made available in English and Spanish, and (2) a self-administered version of the instrument was completed in 1978 by 240 undergraduates, graduate students, and faculty from the liberal arts colleges at Columbia University and New York University.

Reliability

Internal Consistency

The eight-item scale had $\alpha = .87$ for the New York City general public sample and $\alpha = .90$ for the university sample. The average interitem correlations for the two samples were .45 and .53, respectively. A similar version of this scale was administered to a sample of over 2500 West Germans in 1974, with an overall reliability score of $\alpha = .82$.

Test–Retest

No information was reported.

Validity

Convergent

This scale has been administered to several different samples: two in New York, one in West Germany, two in Mexico, and one in Costa Rica. The findings were similar for the measure of political support–alienation for all of these samples. Though the scale correlated positively with trust-in-government measures, it was more strongly related to measures of aggressive political behavior than were the trust scales.

Discriminant

A partial correlation analysis for three samples (New York public and university, and Costa Rica) revealed that though the support–alienation and trust variables were correlated ($rs = .44, .52,$ and $.44$, respectively), support–alienation demonstrates a much stronger bivariate correlation with aggressive political behavior than does trust. Further the relationship between aggressive behavior and trust is essentially eliminated when support–alienation is used as a control variable, although when trust is used as a control, the correlations between aggressive behavior and alienation remain.

Further supporting evidence emerged when the Political Support–Alienation Scale and the Political Trust–Distrust measure (which is analogous to the ANES Trust in Government index) were entered into a regression equation predicting participation in aggressive political behavior. While the Political Support–Alienation Scale was a strong predictor of such behavior, political trust–distrust was estimated to have no direct effect.

Seligson (1983) performed a factor analysis on items from both the Political Support–Alienation Scale and the Trust in Government scale. A two-factor solution emerged, in which each scale formed a distinct factor. The factor analysis revealed that the Political Support–Alienation Scale and the Trust in Government scale were independent of one another.

Location

Muller, E. N., Jukam, T. O., and Seligson, M. A. (1982). Diffuse political support and antisystem political behavior: A comparative analysis. *American Journal of Political Science, 26,* 240–264. Reprinted by permission of the University of Wisconsin Press.

Seligson, M. A. (1983). On the measurement of diffuse support: Some evidence from Mexico. *Social Indicators Research, 12,* 1–24.

Results and Comments

The Political Support–Alienation Scale presented here contains eight items. The German version omitted the item about "leading" politicians and another item about the police, since the police in West Germany are part of the federal legal system. The original agree–disagree response format has been replaced by one that allows respondents to indicate the intensity of their affect better.

Seligson (1983), in an effort to replicate the scale in a cross-national perspective, included the scale in his study of blue-collar factory workers from six Mexican cities. The version he used included only six of the eight items (Items 2 through 7). Seligson planned further studies that were conducted by others. For instance, seven of the eight original items (Items 1 through 7) were included in 201 personal interviews of urban residents of Costa Rica. In addition, a 10-point response format was used for a five-item form (Items 3 through 7) that was administered to 169 middle-class residents of Guadalajara. These alternative versions achieved internal consistency reliabilities ranging from .83 to .87.

Political Support–Alienation Scale
(Muller, Jukam, & Seligson)

1. To what extent do you have respect for the political institutions in [COUNTRY]?

*NONE AT ALL   A GREAT DEAL

| 1 | 2 | 3 | 4 | 5 | 6 | 7 |

2. To what extent do you think that the courts in [COUNTRY] guarantee a fair trial?

3. To what extent do you feel that the basic rights of citizens are well protected by our political system?

4. To what extent are you proud to live under our political system?

5. To what extent do you feel our system of government is the best possible system?

6. To what extent do you feel you should support our system of government?

7. To what extent do you feel you and your friends are well-represented in our political system?

8. To what extent do you feel that your own political values differ from those of our political system?

*Indicates alienated response.

Political Support Scale

(E. N. Muller & T. O. Jukam, 1977)

Variable

This scale contains items intended to measure "affect for authorities in general, for the values, norms, and institutions of a regime, and for the political community" (Muller & Jukam, 1977, p. 1566).

Description

The authors attempted to provide a measure of affect for the governmental system in general rather than toward a specific incumbent administration. Their Political Support Scale was influenced by Easton's conceptualization of diffuse support or legitimacy of the political system and is composed of eight items that are related to the legitimacy of the political system. In face-to-face interviews respondents were handed a deck of cards, each one printed with one of the legitimacy items. They were asked to report how strongly they agreed or disagreed with each statement. The agree–disagree response format used the seven-point Likert-response categories, ranging from $+3$ *(agree completely)* to -3 *(disagree completely)*. Scores can thus range from $+24$ (high support) to -24 (low support).

Sample

The sample consisted of 2663 residents from 12 communities in the Federal Republic of Germany (4 rural, 2 urban, and 6 university communities). These sites were selected because behavior connoting opposition to the administration had occurred in these communities at higher than average levels within five years of the personal interviews in 1974. From the rural communities 569 persons were interviewed, 479 of whom were randomly drawn from lists of eligible voters. Ninety persons were drawn from lists of community elites obtained from the mayors and other community influentials. Of the 990 urban residents interviewed, 928 came from lists of eligible voters, and 62 came from lists of local influentials. And of the 1104 university students and faculty interviewed, 956 were drawn from quota sampling, and 148 came from lists of persons influential in campus organizations.

Reliability

Internal Consistency

The interitem correlations were moderate, ranging from −.21 to .58 (75% of the correlations were .30 or higher). The overall scale reliability was indicated by a Kuder–Richardson reliability coefficient (KR–20) of .82. The authors also reported that this reliability coefficient yielded an estimated correlation of test scores with true scores of .91.

Test–Retest

No information was reported.

Validity

Convergent

No information was reported.

Discriminant

In this study four types of political affect were measured. As hypothesized, these scales of political affect covary. Positive correlations occurred between political support measures and measures of political trust, incumbent evaluation, and policy output evaluation (tau-b of .48, .34, and .35, respectively). Further, as predicted, the Political Support Scale was highly related to aggressive political behavior (gamma = .66); the other affect measures were also related to the Aggressive Behavior Index: political trust (gamma = .38), incumbent performance evaluation (gamma = .30), and policy output evaluation (gamma = .42). These zero-order correlations appeared to be spurious when political support was used as a control variable. The relationship between political support and aggressive behavior remained significant after controlling for the other affect variables.

Location

Muller, E. N. (1979). *Aggressive political participation.* Princeton, NJ: Princeton University Press.

Muller, E. N., & Jukam, T. O. (1977). On the meaning of political support. *American Political Science Review, 71,* 1561–1595.

Results and Comments

The conceptual distinction between incumbent support and system support suggests that affect for the political system is a more powerful explanatory variable of aggressive political behavior. According to this study, the Political Trust, Incumbent Evaluation, and Policy Output Evaluation scales were more sensitive to support for an incumbent administration, while the measure of political support was more sensitive to affect toward the system of government. The authors also used other control variables to examine the additional relationships between the measures of system affect and aggressive political behavior.

Ideological commitment (a self-rating of one's political location on a continuum, left or right) was used as a specification variable, as was community. The findings suggest that the relationship between political support and aggressive behavior is sustained, even among those with different ideological orientations or within communities more or less conducive to aggressive behavior. These relationships are considerably stronger than those involving the other affect measures.

The authors attempted to measure legitimacy of the political system in general and across time. They were not much concerned with the attitudes toward a specific incumbent administration because alienation from a specific regime does not necessarily connote lack of support for the governmental system itself. In other words, a timely negative response to current leaders does not diminish one's positive affect for the system. The authors were concerned with the relationship between affect for the system and aggressive political behavior, hypothesizing that "if system affect is positive among either powerful or sizable segments of the polity, the threat to the stability of the prevailing regime will be small"; conversely, widespread negative system affect could substantially increase threats to an incumbent administration (Muller & Jukam, 1997, p. 1563).

Political Support Scale
(Muller & Jukam, 1977)

**1. It makes me concerned when I think about the difference between what people like me value in life and what actually happens in our political system.

+3	+2	+1	0	−1	−2	−3

*AGREE COMPLETELY   DISAGREE COMPLETELY

2. I have great respect and affection for the political institutions in the Federal Republic.

3. My friends and I feel that we are quite well represented in our political system.

**4. I find it very alarming that the basic rights of citizens are so little respected in our political system.

**5. At present, I feel very critical of our political system.

6. The courts in the Federal Republic guarantee everyone a fair trial regardless of whether they are rich or poor, educated or uneducated.

7. Looking back, the leading politicians in the Federal Republic have always had good intentions.

8. Considering everything, the police in the Federal Republic deserve great respect.

*Indicates alienated response.
**Phrased in the negative direction; indicates reverse scoring.

462   Mary Jo Reef and David Knoke

References

Aberbach, J. D. (1969). Alienation and political behavior. *American Political Science Review, 62,* 86–99.

Abramson, P. R. (1972). Political efficacy and political trust among black schoolchildren: Two explanations. *Journal of Politics, 34,* 1243–1275.

Abramson, P. R., Silver, B. D., & Anderson, B. A. (1987). The effects of question order in attitude surveys: The case of the SRC/CPS citizen duty items. *American Journal of Political Science, 31,* 900–908.

Agnello, T. (1973). Aging and the sense of political powerlessness. *Public Opinion Quarterly, 37,* 251–259.

Almond, G., & Verba, S. (1965). *The civic culture.* Boston: Little, Brown.

Balch, G. I. (1974). Multiple indicators in survey research: The concept "sense of political efficacy." *Political Methodology, 1,* 1–43.

Bottomore, T. B. (1956). Marx's sociology and social philosophy. In T. B. Bottomore (Ed.), *Karl Marx: Selected writings in sociology and social philosophy* (pp. 1–28). New York: McGraw-Hill.

Campbell, A., Converse, P. E., Stokes, D. E., & Miller, W. E. (1960). *The American voter.* New York: Wiley.

Campbell, A., Gurin, G., & Miller, W. E. (1954). *The voter decides.* Evanston, IL: Row, Peterson.

Citrin, J. (1974). Comment: The political relevance of trust in government. *American Political Science Review, 68,* 973–988.

Citrin, J., McClosky, H., Shanks, J. M., & Sniderman, P. M. (1975). Personal and political sources of political alienation. *British Journal of Political Science, 5,* 1–31.

Clarke, J. W., & Levine, E. L. (1971). Marijuana use, social discontent and political alienation: A study of high school youth. *American Political Science Review, 65,* 120–130.

Converse, P. E. (1972). Change in the American electorate. In A. Campbell & P. E. Converse (Eds.), *The human meaning of social change* (pp. 263–337). New York: Russell Sage Foundation.

Craig, S. C., Niemi, R. G., & Silver, G. E. (1990). Political efficacy and trust: A report on the NES Pilot Study items. *Political Behavior, 12,* 289–314.

Davis, J. A., & Smith, T. W. (1996). *General Social Surveys 1972–96: Cumulative codebook.* Chicago: National Opinion Research Center.

Dennis, J. (1966). Support for the American party system by the mass public. *American Political Science Review, 60,* 600–615.

Dennis, J. (1987). Groups and political behavior: Legitimation, deprivation, and competing values. *Political Behavior, 9,* 232–272.

Durkheim, E. (1933). *The division of labor in society.* New York: Free Press.

Easton, D. (1965). *A systems analysis of political life.* New York: Wiley.

Easton, D. (1975). A re-assessment of the concept of political support. *British Journal of Political Science, 5,* 435–457.

Finifter, A. W. (1970). Dimensions of political alienation. *American Political Science Review, 64,* 389–410.

Gamson, W. A. (1968). *Power and discontent.* Homewood, IL: Dorsey Press.

Hamilton, R. F., & Wright, J. D. (1986). *The state of the masses.* New York: Aldine.

Harris, L. (1976). *Report 2521.* New York: Louis Harris.

Herring, C. (1987a). Changes in political alienation, 1964–1980. *National Journal of Sociology, 1,* 73–100.

Herring, C. (1987b). Alienated politics and state legitimacy: An assessment of three neo-Marxian theories. *Journal of Political and Military Sociology, 15,* 17–31.

House, J. S., & Mason, W. M. (1975). Political alienation in America, 1952–1968. *American Sociological Review, 40,* 123–147.

Jennings, M. K., & Niemi, R. G. (1981). *Generations and politics: A panel study of young adults and their parents.* Princeton, NJ: Princeton University Press.

Kahn, J. R., & Mason, W. M. (1987). Political alienation, cohort size, and the Easterlin hypothesis. *American Sociological Review, 52,* 155–169.

Kirkpatrick, J. (1971). *Leader and vanguard in mass society.* Cambridge, MA: MIT Press.

Lane, R. E. (1962). *Political ideology.* New York: Free Press.

Long, S. (1975). Malevolent estrangement: Political alienation and political justification among black and white adolescents. *Youth and Society, 7,* 99–129.

Long, S. (1978). Personality and political alienation among white and black youth: A test of the social deprivation model. *Journal of Politics, 40,* 433–457.

McDill, E. L., & Ridley, J. C. (1962). Status, anomia, political alienation, and political participation. *American Journal of Sociology, 68,* 205–213.

McPherson, J. M., Welch, S., & Clark, C. (1977). The stability and reliability of political efficacy: Using path analysis to test alternative models. *American Journal of Political Science, 71,* 509–521.

Malik, Y. K. (1982). Attitudinal and political implications of diffusion of technology: The case of north Indian youth. *Journal of Asian and African Studies, 17,* 45–73.

Mason, W. M., House, J. S., & Martin, S. S. (1985). On the dimensions of political alienation in America. *Sociological Methodology, 5,* 111–151.

Miller, A. H. (1974). Political issues and trust in government. *American Political Science Review, 68,* 951–972.

Miller, A., Erbring, L., & Goldenberg, E. (1979). Type-set politics: Impact of newspapers on public confidence. *American Political Science Review, 73,* 67–84.

Miller, W. E., Miller, A. H. & Schneider, E. J. (1980). *American national election studies data sourcebook, 1952–1978.* Cambridge, MA: Harvard University Press.

Muller, E. N. (1979). *Aggressive political participation.* Princeton, NJ: Princeton University Press.

Muller, E. N., & Jukam, T. O. (1977). On the meaning of political support. *American Political Science Review, 71,* 1561–1595.

Muller, E. N., Jukam, T. O., & Seligson, M. A. (1982). Diffuse political support and antisystem political behavior: A comparative analysis. *American Journal of Political Science, 26,* 240–264.

Olsen, M. E. (1969). Two categories of political alienation. *Social Forces, 47,* 288–299.

Robinson, J. P., Rusk, J. G., & Head, K. B. (1968). *Measures of political attitudes.* Ann Arbor, MI: Institute for Social Research.

Ross, M. H. (1975a). Political alienation, participation, and ethnicity: An African case. *American Journal of Political Science, 19,* 291–311.

Ross, M. H. (1975b). *Grass roots in an African city: Political behavior in Nairobi.* Cambridge, MA: MIT Press.

Schoultz, L. (1978). Political normlessness in comparative perspective. *Journal of Politics, 40,* 82–111.

Schwartz, D. C. (1973). *Political alienation and political behavior.* Chicago: Aldine.

Seeman, M. (1959). On the meaning of alienation. *American Sociological Review, 24,* 783–791.

Seeman, M. (1975). Alienation studies. *Annual Review of Sociology, 1,* 91–123.

Seeman, M. (1991). Alienation and anomie. In J. P. Robinson, P. R. Shaver, & L. S. Wrightsman (Eds.), *Measures of personality and social psychological attitudes* (Vol. 1, pp. 291–371). New York: Academic Press.

Seligson, M. A. (1983). On the measurement of diffuse support: Some evidence from Mexico. *Social Indicators Research, 12,* 1–24.

Simmel, G. (1950). *The sociology of Georg Simmel* (K. H. Wolff, Ed. and Trans.). New York: Free Press.

Southwell, P. L. (1986). Alienation and nonvoting in the United States: Crucial interactive effects among independent variables. *Journal of Political and Military Sociology, 14,* 249–261.

Southwell, P. L. (1995). "Throwing the rascals out" versus "Throwing in the towel": Alienation, support for term limits, and congressional voting behavior. *Social Science Quarterly, 76,* 741–748.

Thompson, W. E., & Horton, J. E. (1960). Political alienation as a force in political action. *Social Forces, 38,* 190–195.

Verba, S. & Nie, N. (1972). *Participation in America.* New York: Harper & Row.

Verba, S., Schlozman, K., & Brady, H. (1995). *Voice and equality: Civic voluntarism in American politics.* Cambridge, MA: Harvard University Press.

Watts, M. W. (1973). Efficacy, trust and commitment to the political process. *Social Science Quarterly, 54,* 623–631.

Watts, M. W. (1974). Alienation and support for the political system among college students. In A. R. Wilcox (Ed.), *Public opinion and political attitudes* (pp. 105–127). New York: Wiley.

Weatherford, M. S. (1991). Mapping the ties that bind: Legitimacy, representation, and alienation. *Western Political Quarterly, 44,* 251–276.

Wright, J. D. (1976). *The dissent of the governed: Alienation and democracy in America.* New York: Academic Press.

Yin, R. K., & Lucas, W. (1973). Decentralization and alienation. *Policy Sciences, 4,* 327–336.

Zimmer, T. A. (1983). Local news exposure and local government alienation. *Social Science Quarterly, 64,* 634–640.

CHAPTER 8

Trust in Government

Jack Citrin and Christopher Muste

Political trust refers to the faith people have in their government. This concept belongs to a large family of terms regarding the subjective level of support citizens give their political system. Prominent relatives in this family tree include political allegiance, commitment, and legitimacy—as well as their opposites, mainly covered in Chapter 7, namely, political alienation, disaffection, and estrangement.

These concepts share the common goal of capturing the citizenry's attitudinal underpinnings for the effectiveness of government policies. It is widely believed that the level of political trust can affect the stability of the institutions that make or enforce these policies. Partly for this reason the initial family resemblance of trust and support can blind one to what, if anything, makes them distinct.

Concepts related to political support go beyond whether citizens simply approve or disapprove of their government to ask whether they feel a part of it. Do people feel that they truly belong to the political community in which they live? Do they believe that the government operates fairly and is deserving of respect and obedience?

Underlying the scholarly belief in the importance of properly measuring political trust and related concepts, therefore, is the presumption that governments enjoying greater public support are able to function more smoothly and effectively than those with less public trust. It is assumed that belief in the fairness of the prevailing political processes enhances one's willingness to comply voluntarily with official policies and commands that entail personal costs or sacrifice.

To trust a person or thing is to assume their reliability, to believe that they will act "as they should" (Barber, 1983). Political trust thus indicates confidence that authorities will observe the rules of the game and serve the general interest. Political trust is an important construct because diffuse expectations of appropriate conduct are widely believed to have significant consequences for the *effectiveness, continuity,* and *morality* of social systems. Indeed, a certain level of mutual trust probably is essential for all stable social relationships (Blau, 1964).

For the individual, trust reduces the complexity of choice. Faith in the reliability of others makes it possible to take much for granted; one can accept the veracity of their claims and go about one's daily business without worrying about every possible contingent future. Trust in government thus allows citizens and private institutions to plan and not to worry.

But trust is also a resource for government, providing authorities with the freedom to act and expect to be obeyed. Widespread public trust thus endows the political system with a basic source of power. The maintenance of trust ultimately depends on the use of such power in competent and responsible ways. When trust is lacking, citizens limit discretionary authority and create auditing and monitoring arrangements to protect their interests. Bereft of public confidence, government is forced to turn to bribery or coercion to obtain compliance with its commands.

Moreover, in a democratic political system in which policies should be based on consent, the level of political trust or support has normative implications that go beyond its impact on effectiveness. In this context a high level of trust, if it is earned, signifies a healthier political quality of life in the sense that there is a greater sense of harmony, tranquillity, and commitment. More generally a high level of political trust implies that as much as disagreements and conflicts may arise over public policies, a basic respect for the system remains. By the same token, as political trust decreases or disintegrates, the public is assumed to be more receptive to political change—even radical change achieved by drastic means.

Although not reviewed in this chapter, trust at the basic interpersonal level ("trust in people") also is related to overall political trust. The argument that increasing cynicism about politics is worrisome because political trust undergirds democratic legitimacy thus finds a parallel in the concern about declining "personal trust" or "social capital" expressed in Putnam's provocative *Making Democracy Work* (1993) and "Bowling Alone: America's Declining Social Capital" (1995). Putnam and others (e.g., Fukuyama, 1995) argue that a society in which people believe that others can be trusted to follow the rules and keep their word will have higher levels of civic engagement, economic innovation, and political responsiveness. They worry about the recent decline of general trust in people, as measured by survey items such as "Generally speaking, would you say that most people can be trusted or that you can't be too careful in dealing with people?"

At the same time, however, Putnam correctly points out that the relationship between personal and political trust is a separate matter. Indeed, it is clear (Brehm & Rahn, 1996; Putnam, 1993) that despite the concomitant erosion of both personal and political trust in America, the determinants of these attitudes are quite distinct. Thus the present chapter deals solely with *political* trust and support, with the "object" of trust being government in its varied manifestations. It excludes as well trust in other societal institutions, such as the press or financial institutions (although these attitudes are briefly tracked below for comparative purposes).

Conceptual and Measurement Issues

Despite numerous attempts to disentangle the meanings of various putatively "basic" orientations toward government (Citrin, 1977; Easton, 1975; Keniston, 1965; Muller & Jukam, 1977; Rogowski, 1983; Schact, 1970; Seeman, 1968), there is no settled consensus on important conceptual issues. For example, when trust in government is defined as the perceived correspondence between the ideals and the realities of the political process, it becomes a virtual synonym of support. Yet debate continues over whether mistrust of government should be regarded as a variant, an indicator, or a cause of political alienation or support, and over whether support for a political regime may usefully be distinguished from its legitimacy.

Another theoretical problem is that knowing that someone supports or rejects the political regime rarely tells us why this is so. For example, what is the relative importance of instrumental and normative concerns in determining a citizen's level of political support? (Tyler, Rasinski, & Griffin, 1986). Some theories stress the effectiveness of a regime, as indicated by satisfaction with the *outcomes* of government actions, as a source of support (Citrin & Green, 1986; Wright, 1981). Others emphasize the connection between support and the fairness of a regime, focusing on satisfaction with the governmental *process* and how one is treated (Gurr, 1970; Tyler, 1990). Over time, however, satisfaction with the prevailing pattern of outcomes and belief in the fairness of political processes should be mutually reinforcing. It is unlikely that anyone will regard an institution's rules and practices as just if he or she always ends up on the losing end.

In inventorying measures of political trust and system support, it is necessary to skirt many of the controversies regarding their family ties. We simply note at the outset that murky concepts yield measures of dubious discriminant validity (Campbell & Fiske, 1959) and that Chapter 7 in this volume reviews attitude scales with different labels (referring to supposedly distinct concepts) that are composed of rather similar items— although with a separate conceptual genealogy and focus.

Developing an operational definition of *trust* or *support* involves not only different types of psychological attitudes, but also different political referents and levels of abstraction. Like other attitudes, political trust and support have specific *objects*. One does not simply support or trust; one supports or trusts some politician, political group, process, or institution. In characterizing the individual's orientations toward government, therefore, one needs to specify what aspect of government is being evaluated. As shown in Figure 8–1, the *basis* for that assessment also can vary. Some measures focus on the object's trustworthiness, others on its effectiveness or on its responsiveness. To examine either the level of consistency across distinct political objects or the extent of differentiation in beliefs about a political object involves empirical issues that can be settled only with the availability of multiple measures.

Figure 8–1 presents one useful way of mapping the individual's attitudes of political support and estrangement. The columns in this two-dimensional matrix refer to many of the objects of support in extant scales—politicians as a class, the legislature, the political regime, and so forth. The rows refer to the attributes by which each object is being judged—fairness, responsiveness, competence, and trustworthiness, among others. A typical item in the survey-based measures we review here thus can be represented as a cell in

Object of Support

Bases of Support	Community	Regime	Officials	National Government	Local Government	President	Legislature	Judiciary
Trustworthiness								
Fairness								
Worthy of Pride								
Effectiveness								
Efficiency								
Responsiveness								
Compassion								
Integrity								

Fig. 8–1   A Matrix for Measuring Citizens' Support for the Political System

this matrix—a particular kind of assessment of a specified object. A typical scale is composed of a number of these cells, moving either vertically to sum different assessments of a single object or horizontally to combine evaluations of several objects on the same criterion. Few researchers have chosen to create a comprehensive measure in which one combines responses across multiple objects and multiple dimensions of judgment.

In practice, one persistent problem in interpreting citizens' responses to survey questions is the use of phrases such as the "government in Washington," the "political system," and the "people running" an institution to indicate the object of the attitude being measured (Citrin, 1974; Miller, 1974). The meanings of these ambiguous terms are likely to vary widely across respondents, no matter how clear they may seem to the investigator.

Support for some political actor or institution similarly can vary from action taken on its behalf by an individual to just a favorable orientation toward it. In principle virtually any positive sentiment could generate this approving attitude. Accordingly a wide range of meanings—pride, loyalty, and simple liking—have been regarded as roughly equivalent to support. Perceptions of the competence, integrity, fairness, or strength of an object frequently are employed as indicators of support for it. Researchers assume that these traits are consensually valued by the public and that support derives from confidence that political authorities and institutions behave according to the prevailing normative standards (Finifter, 1972). The particular items used to measure support, therefore, may vary as a reflection of the differences in expectations concerning morally appropriate conduct across political systems or across institutions within a given system.

Among the many possible objects of political support are such broad referents as a society's constitutional order, its present national administration, and local government agencies. The research literature includes examples of support measures for each of these as well as for specific institutions, such as the legislature, military, police, and judiciary. Nevertheless, the main preoccupation of scholarship has been distinguishing support for the three levels of the political system identified by Easton (1965):

1. the political community, which refers to the territorial and social boundaries of the system;
2. the regime, which refers to its institutional order and fundamental values; and
3. the current political leaders and their policies.

This concern is based on the entrenched belief that attitudes toward these objects have significantly different political consequences. The conventional prediction is that a loss of support for the *regime* threatens its stability and diminishes the voluntary compliance of citizens with government policy, whereas the impact of support for *authorities* is confined to the domain of conventional electoral activity (Easton, 1965; Muller & Jukam, 1977).

It is easier, of course, to make the conceptual distinction between support for the "system" and support for incumbent authorities than to invent the operational procedures that will adequately realize it. As noted previously, one problem is that the idea of "the regime level of the system," in Easton's sense of this term, may have little meaning to many ordinary citizens, for whom politics is a remote world of little interest. The face validity of items asking for evaluations of "the way our government operates regardless of which party is in power" thus is questionable.

Moreover, the same verbal response may have several meanings of varied significance. For example, expressions of doubt that government will "do what is right most the time" are an amalgam of enduring disaffection from the regime's basic institutional arrangements and underlying values, partisan reactions to those in power, short-run assessments of the current state of the nation, and ritualistic complaints about "politics" and "politicians," a familiar and clichéd sentiment that is neither deeply felt nor behaviorally potent (Citrin, 1974; Citrin & Green, 1986). These distinctions should be kept in mind in assessing the implications of trends in the aggregate level of trust.

Thus it has been found that attitude scales that putatively measure support for the political regime usually are positively correlated with conventional indicators of support for authorities, such as party affiliation, approval of the incumbent national leader, and agreement with his or her policies (Citrin, McClosky, Shanks, & Sniderman, 1975.) But since theory would lead one to expect *rejection* of the ongoing political order to color evaluations of current rulers, these statistical associations need not reflect negatively on the validity of such scales. Without longitudinal or cross-cultural data, it can be difficult to settle the question of how respondents define a measure's object. Ultimately the strongest evidence for discriminant validity in measuring support for the regime is the results showing that scores on it have the "correct" relationships to theoretically predicted behaviors.

Measures Reviewed Here

The first set of measures discussed in this chapter deals with general trends in government, usually at the short-term, incumbent level.

1. Trust in Government Scale (Miller, 1974)
2. Political Trust and System Evaluation Scales (Mason, House, & Martin, 1985)
3. Trust in Government Scale (Muller & Jukam, 1977)

More specific aspects or objects of trust are examined in the next set of measures.

4. Trust in the Incumbent Congress and the Presidency Items (Abramson & Finifter, 1981)
5. Trust in Member of Congress Scale (Parker & Parker, 1989)
6. Trust in Local Government Scale (Baldassare, 1985)
7. Incumbent-Based Trust Scale (Craig, Niemi, & Silver, 1990)
8. Governmental Attentiveness Scale (Bennett, 1984)
9. Confidence in Government and Other Institutions Scale (Smith, 1981)

The next four scales deal with the opposite of trust in the form of political cynicism and assess this outlook toward "politicians" or "politics in general."

10. Political Cynicism Scale (Agger, Goldstein, & Pearl, 1961)
11. Political Cynicism Scale (Citrin & Elkins, 1975)
12. Political Cynicism (Baloyra, 1979)
13. Political Cynicism (Sniderman, 1981)

The final set of scales deals with longer-term regime-level support.

14. Regime-Based Trust Scale (Craig, Niemi, & Silver, 1990)
15. Political Allegiance Index (Citrin, McClosky, Shanks, & Sniderman, 1975)
16. Political Support Typology (Sniderman, 1981)
17. Political Support Scale (Muller & Jukam, 1977)
18. Judicial Legitimacy Scale (Tyler, 1990)
19. Democratic Legitimacy (McDonough, Barnes, & Lopez-Pina, 1986)
20. Political Support Index (Miller, 1991)
21. Political Criticism Scale (Baloyra, 1979)
22. Support for Democratic Institutions Scale (Schmitt, 1983)

23. Support for the Political Community Scale (Sniderman, 1981)
24. Affective Support Scale (Kornberg & Clarke, 1992)
25. Government Power Scale (Bennett & Bennett, 1990)

The scales are discussed in roughly chronological order within each category. Several variants of these indices and a number of single-item measures are also summarized in the Recommendations and Future Directions section of this chapter.

The Michigan Trust in Government Scale and Its Offshoots

The most widely used measure of political trust is based on five questions that were first included in the 1964 American National Election Studies (ANES) conducted by the Survey Research Center and Center for Political Studies at the University of Michigan. These items have achieved wide currency through the accessibility of the resulting data through the Inter-University Consortium for Political and Social Research and their suitability for trend analysis—rather than for their explicit reference to the theoretical ideas of Easton (1965) or Seeman (1959).

The Michigan (ANES) questions differ in both their format and their object (or target) from those making up the political cynicism measures described later. Rather than using agree–disagree response options or a forced-choice format, the items are posed as questions with concrete alternatives like "almost always," "most of the time," or "not very many."

More important, they ask about the "government in Washington" and "officials" rather than "politicians" and "politics." Two of the Michigan questions refer to "the government in Washington," asking how often it can be trusted to "do what is right" and whether it is run just on behalf of "a few big interests." The remaining three items ask about the "people in government" or "people running the government," focusing on how "wasteful," "crooked," and "smart" they are. Exploratory factor analysis of these and other questions pertaining to the individual's perceptions of government indicated that the five Trust in Government items do define one underlying dimension. Miller (1974) used Guttman scaling techniques to score respondents on this measure, whereas Citrin (1974) and Sniderman and Brody (1977) used slightly different scoring techniques to construct additive indices. Hill (1982) analyzed the 1972 ANES data, which included the Trust in Government items in both the preelection and the postelection waves of its panel, and found only a .57 test–retest reliability for the scale, lower than expected of a "basic" orientation toward the political system.

As indicated earlier, both Citrin (1974) and Muller and Jukam (1977) have questioned the validity of the ANES Trust in Government index as a measure of support for the political regime. Citrin argued that the verbal representation of the attitude object and the lack of extremity of the negative response options suggest that scores largely reflect respondents' evaluations of incumbent officeholders and their performance. Citrin and Green (1986) buttressed this conclusion by demonstrating that the Trust in Government index, unlike the Political Cynicism scales discussed here, fluctuated with approval of the incumbent president's performance and a positive image of his persona.

Moreover, the findings of Muller and Jukam (1977), Seligson (1983), and Finkel, Muller, and Seligson (1989) were consistent across American, German, Mexican, and Costa Rican data: Political trust as operationalized by the ANES items was associated with support for the incumbent national administration, but was unrelated to "aggressive" or antiregime political activity. Armed with such results, these and other researchers have proposed alternative scales to measure support for "the system," occasionally incorporating one or more of the Trust in Government items.

The second scale presented in this chapter was devised by Mason *et al.* (1985), who revisited the structure of the pool of "political alienation" items contained in the ANES studies. They employed confirmatory factor analysis and canonical techniques and concluded that two of the five Trust in Government items (Trust Government to Do Right and Big Interests) are indicators of a single latent construct of confidence in the ability of the federal government to act in ways that people regard as right and fair. They recommended treating the remaining items (relating to the wastefulness, competence, and honesty of people in government) as evaluations of public officials in general. Other internal item analyses, however, have suggested a four-item Trust in Government scale (Parker, 1986), excluding just the question about whether government officials are "smart people who usually know what they are doing." The basis for retaining four items in a single scale was their cohesion in confirmatory factor analysis. Beginning in 1983 only these four items have been retained in the biennial ANES surveys.

Without necessarily taking a stand on whether the ANES items measure affect toward the regime rather than toward incumbents, scholars have employed them to assess citizens' attitudes in a variety of settings (in scales not included here because of their redundant quality). For example, Barnes, Kaase, *et al.* (1979) combined the Trust Government and Big Interests items in their cross-national study of political dissatisfaction and protest in Western Europe. McDonough *et al.* (1986) added the Waste Tax Money item to build a political trust measure for Spanish respondents. Tanaka (1984) employed the same three items to measure political trust in Japan. This can also be said about the third scale on the present list, devised by Muller and Jukam (1977) in a West German survey.

Clearly questions about the trustworthiness, responsiveness, or efficiency of government can be aimed at a wide range of targets, as indicated earlier in Figure 8–1. Such questions also can be posed in different formats. Based on the 1987 ANES Pilot Study, Craig *et al.* (1990) proposed a new version of the original Trust in Government measure, which they labeled the Incumbent-Based Trust Scale. This scale used Likert-style items, such as "Those we elected to public office usually try to keep the promises they have made during the election." Craig *et al.* contrasted this scale with a measure of Regime-Based Trust, which we discuss later.

Other researchers have reformulated the questions to focus on feelings about specific institutions, as in the next group of scales we briefly mention. Thus, Abramson and Finifter (1981) compared trust in Congress and in the presidency. Parker and Parker (1989) asked about the Florida legislature, the respondent's congressman, the Supreme Court, the presidency, Congress, and "the government in general." Baldassare (1985), by contrast, developed a Trust in Local Government Scale from three questions, including the ANES item about waste.

The impact of differences in question wording and question order on the internal structure and correlates of these measures deserves further exploration. For example, Mason *et al.* (1985) noted that the items defining the Trust, Responsiveness, and Efficacy factors, respectively, happen to be grouped together in the interview schedule. In another context, Green (1988) has shown that nonrandom measurement error due to the proximity of items and their common format is another influence on the observed dimensionality of attitudes. Such response bias problems underscore the need for a sustained analysis of the construct validity of these proposed measures.

Confidence in Institutions

Another simple measure of political trust involves asking respondents how much *confidence* they have in specific institutions. Gallup has developed a time-series of this kind, using a question that simply names the institution as its object—Congress, the military, television, religion, big business, and so on. The National Opinion Research Center (NORC) version of this question asks about "the *people running* some institutions in this country," whereas at various times Harris has asked about the people running them, the people in charge of running them, and the people in charge of managing them. As indicated previously, some institutions on the list are political; others are social or economic in nature.

After an extensive comparison of the NORC and Harris data, Smith (1981) identified minor, though noticeable, "house," context, and order effects in these measures. He also suggested that responses to the confidence items are often uncrystallized opinions, although this appears to be less of a problem for the institutions of government in that on these items a majority of respondents (57%) *are* able to give a reasonable definition of confidence. Almost 35% chose *trust* as the meaning of confidence, and the closely related terms *having faith* or *believing in an institution's leaders* were mentioned by another 22% (Smith, 1981, p. 169).

Researchers generally have analyzed responses to these questions about particular institutions separately rather than creating composite political or social confidence scales. Viewed as social indicators, the NORC–Harris–Gallup confidence items and the ANES political trust questions provide consistent evidence of historical trends. Both measures show that favorable orientations toward government institutions declined fairly steadily between 1964 and 1980, rebounded between 1980 and 1986, but have turned downward since then.

Lipset and Schneider (1987) identify two cross-cutting components of this attitude change. First, *dissatisfaction with the nation's performance* in significant domains of economic and social life engendered an across-the-board loss of confidence in most institutions. Second, however, *partisan* and *ideological* concerns partially shaped opinions about specific institutions: Republicans and conservatives were more likely than Democrats and liberals to shift toward a favorable evaluation of the executive branch during the Reagan presidency. Similarly, when events made the adversary relationship between institutions such as the presidency and the press or the presidency and Congress highly salient, feelings about them, which are colored by partisan and ideological orientations, tended to move in opposite directions.

GSS Trends in Political Confidence

The General Social Survey (GSS) provides probably the most complete and richest set of benchmark data to track public confidence and trust in a variety of American institutions, including the three main branches of national government. The GSS data indicate the patterns and trends since 1973 shown in Figure 8–2.

Across time, as noted previously and shown in Figure 8–2, there has been a general tendency of long-term decline in confidence in all types of organizations. Some of the largest declines have occurred in confidence in the executive (from 30% having a great deal of confidence in 1973 to just 11% in 1996) and legislative (from 24 to 8%) branches. Similar 10- to 15-point declines in confidence are found for banks, medicine, education, religion, the press, and television. At the same time, confidence in the judicial branch of government (along with science) has not declined, and confidence in the

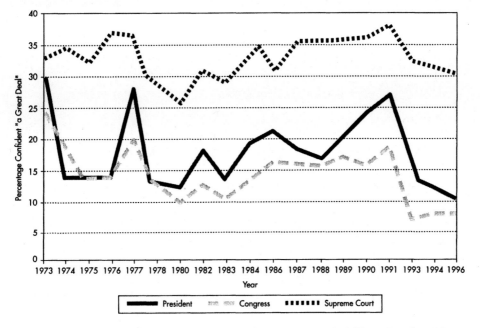

Fig. 8–2 Percentage of Respondents with "a Great Deal" of Confidence in the Different Branches of Government (GSS data, 1973–1996)

military, doubtless at a low ebb when the time-series was begun during the Vietnam War, has actually increased, with a particular boost given by the Gulf War.

In general, then, it appears that trust in both the presidency and Congress has declined—particularly during the early Clinton administration years. However, that decline in trust in governmental institutions has not been shared by the Supreme Court, whereas most other nongovernment institutions have also suffered a loss in public confidence.

Table 8–1 reports the differences in confidence in institutions across social and political groups:

1. *Gender* differences are small, although women tend to have more confidence in education and organized labor, while men have more confidence in the scientific community.

2. When it comes to *race,* blacks also tend to have more confidence in education and organized labor (and television), while whites have more confidence in the scientific community and business.

3. *Age* differences also emerge, with younger people having more confidence in organized labor, the scientific community, medicine, and the press, while older people have more trust in banks and financial institutions, major companies, organized religion, and the military.

4. *Education* has a stronger connection to feelings of confidence than other demographic factors. The less educated have more trust in the military, television, banks and financial institutions, organized religion, and education, while college graduates have more confidence in the scientific community, the U.S. Supreme Court, and business.

5. *Party* differences are quite predictable. Republicans have expressed more confidence in business, the scientific community, the military, and the executive branch, while Democrats have had more trust in organized labor, the press, television, and Congress.

Table 8-1
Correlates of Confidence Items

Confidence in	Sex	Age	Education	Race	Party identification	Ideology
Executive branch of federal government	−.03**	.03**	.01	−.02**	.09**	.06**
Congress	−.00	.01	−.06**	.02**	−.03**	−.01
U.S. Supreme Court	−.06**	−.03**	.10**	−.03**	.03**	−.03**
Education	.00	.03**	−.08**	.07**	−.05**	−.01
Press	−.03**	−.04**	−.06**	.02	−.07**	−.08**
Banks and financial institutions	.01	.09**	−.08**	−.01	.01	.05**
Major companies	−.06**	.07**	.08**	−.08**	.13**	.10**
Organized religion	.02*	.08**	−.08**	.00	.01	.05**
Organized labor	−.03**	−.02*	−.12**	.05**	−.10**	−.05**
Medicine	−.03**	−.08**	−.00	−.01	.03**	.01
Television	−.03**	−.01	−.13**	.05**	−.05**	−.03**
Scientific community	−.09**	−.06**	.17**	−.09**	.06**	−.02
Military	−.05**	.05**	−.13**	−.01	.04**	.09**

Entries are Pearson's r.
Sample: Pooled GSS respondents (1972–1994).
Number of cases: 17,035.
One-tailed significance: *—.01, **—.001.

6. *Ideological* differences roughly parallel those related to partisanship. Conservatives have had more trust in the military, business, and organized religion, while liberals trust organized labor and the press more.

In terms of the structure of confidence reactions, two separate patterns emerge: (1) a general, overall confidence factor and (2) a few separate subdomains (organized religion and education; the scientific community, medicine, and the U.S. Supreme Court; the press and television). Included in a separate subdomain are the three branches of government, with Congress and the executive branch linked more tightly to each other ($r = .44$) than either is linked with the Court ($r = .39$ and $.35$, respectively).

Governmental Attentiveness and Responsiveness

The next scale approaches the topic from a somewhat different perspective, asking about the public's views regarding the government's willingness to listen to its citizens, rather than the competence or truthfulness of leaders. That government should be sensitive to popular opinion is a fundamental tenet of democracy. This suggests that public perceptions of how sensitive political elites are to the desires and needs of ordinary citizens comprise another indicator of the prevailing level of satisfaction with existing institutions. With this in mind, the ANES surveys have posed a series of questions that ask, "Over the years, how much attention does the government (the political parties, elections, most Congressmen) pay to what the people think?" When included with the familiar ANES political trust and political efficacy items in factor analyses, these four similarly worded governmental attentiveness (or institutional responsiveness) items appear to define a distinct attitudinal dimension. Bennett (1984) combined them into a single additive index, reporting that this measure has a standardized alpha reliability ranging from .65 in the 1980 ANES survey to .75 in the 1964 and 1968 data. The test–retest correlation for this measure in the 1972 and 1974 waves of the 1972–1974–1976 panel study was .38.

At the same time perceptions of the government as highly attentive to "what people think" were positively associated with trust in the national government, with feelings of pride in "the American form of government," and with approval of the performance of the presidency, Congress, the Supreme Court, and the federal government in general. Despite these findings and its availability for secondary analysis, the Governmental Attentiveness Scale has been passed over by researchers in favor of the Trust in Government measure described previously. Only the Government Attentive and Elections Attentive items were included in ANES surveys after 1980.

Political Cynicism

A number of the earliest scales in this area focused on the other end of the governmental trust continuum and were labeled political cynicism measures. These were constructed from agree–disagree items that tapped a generalized disdain for politicians and politics. These scales resemble the measures of political normlessness described in Chapter 7.

For example, Agger *et al.* (1961) analyzed the responses of diverse samples in Oregon and three southern cities to items such as "Politicians spend most of their time getting re-elected or reappointed" and "People are frequently manipulated by politicians" to construct a six-item Guttman scale with a coefficient of reproducibility of .94. Representative items from the Political Cynicism Scale, built by Citrin and Elkins (1975) from a study of British and American students, include "Most politicians are in politics for what they can get out of it personally" and "Most politicians are practically the agents of some pressure group or other." Another version based on Venezuelan data is Baloyra's (1979) five-item Guttman scale composed of statements such as "Parties only care about winning elections" and "Government would be better off without the interference of politicians." Sniderman (1981) employed a forced choice between pairs of items, such as "Most of our political leaders can be trusted to tell the truth" versus "Our political leaders are prepared to lie to us whenever it suits their purposes."

Measured in these ways political cynicism is strongly related to socioeconomic status. Lower-class, less well educated respondents consistently have higher political cynicism scores. Political cynicism is also significantly related to low scores on measures of interpersonal trust, but has weaker and inconsistent associations with dissatisfaction with the government's policies and performance. These findings led Baloyra (1979) to characterize the standard operational definition of political cynicism as measuring a social-psychological as much as a political attitude. The standard measures of political cynicism appear to tap a more generalized suspiciousness and pessimism rooted in the social circumstances of disadvantaged strata rather than a critical evaluation of current politics. This broad psychological orientation may, of course, have significant political implications.

Regime Support and Political Legitimacy

In the wake of the doubts raised concerning the theoretical status of the ANES political trust questions, a number of alternative approaches to measuring support for the political regime have emerged. Characteristic of these efforts is the greater care taken to define the attitude object in "systemic" terms and a focus on the fairness and representative quality of political processes as the basis for evaluating them.

Citrin (1974) suggested that questions about respondents' pride in the American "form of government" and their beliefs about whether it needed substantial change could be employed as measures of support for the regime. The results of Mason et al.'s (1985) factor analysis of the 1972 ANES data confirmed that these items identified an attitudinal dimension that should be distinguished from political trust, political efficacy, and perceptions of the government's attentiveness to the public. The Pride and Change items, along with two others expressing diffuse affect toward "our system of government," comprise the Regime-Based Trust Scale built by Craig et al. (1990) from the 1987 ANES Pilot Study survey, which is the first of the *regime*-oriented measures presented here.

Weatherford (1992) analyzed the extended set of items from the 1987 ANES Pilot Study and constructed a model of relationships among different dimensions of legitimacy orientations. The two main dimensions in this model were *judgments of system performance* (further divided into representational procedures and governmental performance) and *personal–citizenship traits* (consisting of political involvement and interpersonal assurance measures). Structural equation estimation of this alternative conceptualization and the standard one focusing exclusively on the one dimension of performance produced several goodness-of-fit statistics supporting the alternative model.

The Political Allegiance Index developed from the 1972 Bay Area Survey is the second regime measure reviewed here. It used the phrases "our system of government" and "our system of national government, regardless of which party is in power" as the foci of its constituent items (Citrin et al., 1975). This index consisted of eight items asked in three different formats. It combined responses tapping diffuse affect with questions about the trustworthiness and representative quality of national institutions and leaders.

In order to explore whether people hold a differentiated image of the political process, the Bay Area Survey asked respondents to rate the American national government "as it operates regardless of which party is in power" on 46 scales, each one consisting of defined paired antonyms, similar to the semantic differential. A factor analysis of the intercorrelations among these rating scales identified a powerful first factor that accounted for almost half the variance (Citrin, 1977). This underlying dimension is best characterized as a diffuse evaluative orientation on which "good" attributes have high positive loadings and "bad" qualities high negative ones.

Citrin (1977) found that the adjective pairs whose face content closely approximates that of the ANES trust, efficacy, and attentiveness measures had similar high loadings on this underlying evaluative dimension. This suggests that the oft-cited "dimensionality" of these items in the ANES samples may be a reflection of differences in their referents, order, and format rather than an indication that people differentiate in their use of the above criteria for assessing a given political object.

Sniderman (1981) employed the same *semantic differential* ratings from the Bay Area Survey in a different manner. He assumed that the willingness to hold balanced and restrained beliefs about the polity is an important feature of democratic commitment and created a typology of supportive and alienated attitudes based on the ratio of the positive and negative attributions made by respondents.

Muller and Jukam (1977) measured support for the regime with a set of items that are intended to capture affect for the political system stemming from a belief in the good intentions of political authorities, a sense of being well represented, and confidence in the fairness of the courts and police. Muller developed his initial measure in a study of West German attitudes conducted in 1974. The inclusion of items about the judicial system is especially appropriate in this cultural context, since Germany is a legalistic society that stresses conformity to prescribed norms concerning what is right and proper. The Political Support Scale composed of these items satisfies the standard Kuder–Richardson criteria for reliability (Muller & Jukam, 1977, p. 1567). Its discriminant validity as a measure of *system* affect rather than *incumbent* support rests primarily on the finding that the Political Support Scale rather than a version of the ANES Trust in Government measure predicts aggressive political behavior.

The Tyler (1990) scale presented next conceptualizes legitimacy as a combination of diffuse positive affect and the perceived obligation to obey the law. Since his interest was in explaining compliance with the law, Tyler's items refer specifically to the police and the courts. In capturing feelings of trust, pride, and respect rather than assessing satisfaction with outcomes, however, this measure resembles the regime support measures summarized earlier.

Situations in which alternative regimes compete for support provide the strongest test of the significance of favorable "basic orientations toward the system" for political stability. In a fundamental sense support for a particular regime means that one prefers one set of underlying values and institutional arrangements to other possibilities. Recognizing this, some scholars have built scales from items that refer to contested institutions and values rather than to "our system" in the abstract. Thus, McDonough *et al.*'s (1986) study of democratic legitimacy in Spain measured support for the regime with items asking whether there was a need for a legislature, whether elections are the best system for selecting authorities, and whether Spain should be a republic or a monarchy. Miller's (1991) study of political legitimacy in the Soviet Union during its death throes developed a Political Support Index that combined questions about the trustworthiness of national leaders, feelings about the Communist Party and the Supreme Soviet, and opinions about the worth of a competitive party system.

Baloyra's (1979) study of Venezuela generated a measure of political criticism that focused on assessments of the long-term performance of recent democratic governments in a country that had experienced changes in regime. The questions asked whether the *democratic* regimes generally had served the public interest and spent money wisely.

A final regime measure from the ANES is analyzed by Bennett and Bennett (1990). They used multiple discriminant analyses to show that the item asking about whether or not the federal government is "too powerful" related significantly to decreased trust in government and presidential approval as well as to a number of demographic and political orientation variables.

Love of Country

One common observation about American political culture is the absence of any prominent image of a rival to the established constitutional order. Despite the rise of political mistrust after 1964 and the intensity of criticism of established authorities and institutions, patriotic sentiment and belief in the superiority of the American system (albeit in its idealized form) have remained largely unchanged. Moreover, the foundation of American national identity, unlike those of most other countries, rests on a shared ideological creed rather than on a common ethnic heritage (Huntington, 1981). In this context support for the political community, a sense of we-feeling, and allegiance to the political regime are closely related.

Several political support scales include an item asking whether the respondent perceives his or her political system as "the best possible." Sniderman (1981) constructed a measure of support for the community from questions in the 1972 Bay Area Survey that asked respondents to compare the United States with other modern countries in areas such as protecting freedom of speech and safeguarding the rights of minority groups. Related questions assessed feelings of belonging to the country and reactions to the idea of emigration.

The Pride in Britain Scale constructed by Citrin and Elkins (1975) to measure support for the national *community* also has a political component. It included items such as "Despite some faults, our form of government is better than any practiced elsewhere" and "I want to participate actively in my country's national life." Kornberg and Clarke (1992) used the so-called feeling thermometer to ask respondents how warmly they felt about their country (Canada) as well as about particular levels and branches of government. One difficulty with these measures is the presence of response bias, so it is important that such affective measures be embedded in a larger study exploring the specific cognitive bases of "warm" or "cold" attitudes.

Recommendations and Future Directions

This chapter has reviewed a multiplicity of attitude scales constructed to measure political trust and support. There are a variety of other indices and single-item measures circulating in the research literature, such as the EuroBarometer question, asking respondents about how satisfied they are with "democracy in this country" (Schmitt, 1983). But since much of the interest in political support centers on its presumed relationship to the effectiveness and stability of regimes, we have concentrated here on the efforts to operationalize Easton's notion of affect toward different aspects of the political system.

The measures reviewed above indicate that political support and disaffection are multifaceted phenomena with a range of specific targets. The unifying thread among these
measures is the intention to capture the feeling of closeness to or estrangement from some
aspect of one's government. We have identified three main categories of indicators: measures that capture trust in the incumbent national leadership (measures 1–9), measures that
tap a generalized cynicism about the motives and conduct of professional politicians (measures 10–13), and measures of diffuse affect for the political regime based on perceptions
of the fairness and responsiveness of major institutions (measures 14–25). Although empirical relationships among these alternative conceptualizations of support tend to be positive, they frequently have distinctive relationships to demographic variables (such as race,
age, income, and education) as well as to political orientation variables (such as party
identification and political ideology) and to political behavior variables (such as voting
turnout and unconventional protest activities).

Specifically social background variables are more strongly and consistently related to
cynicism about politicians and diffuse feelings of disengagement from the political process than to the other measures of support. Approval of incumbent national leaders and
their policies has the strongest impact on the scales developed from the ANES Trust in
Government items. Finally only measures of disaffection from the political regime have
significant effects in the statistical models explaining participation in political protests.
Thus it seems clear that multiple indicators of support are needed to measure adequately
the psychic bonds between citizens and their government.

In making recommendations concerning which measures to use, we begin by returning to the core meaning of trust: the truster's confidence that the trusted (political actor or
institution) will act in the interests of the trusting. The "object" of trust (or potential trust)
must be specified. In the political realm measurement thus is system-specific, reflecting
the particular institutional structures or regime norms of the population being surveyed.
This said, the following basic dimensions of trust should be assessed with different measures:

1. trust in incumbent authorities versus trust in regime structures and norms,
2. confidence in the competence of the trusted versus confidence in their fiduciary
   qualities (or integrity), and
3. trust in the flow of satisfactory outcomes versus trust in the fairness of political and
   legal processes.

One difficulty in discriminating among these attitudes empirically is that ordinary
citizens may not hold such differentiated cognitions about such vague objects as the "government" or "political system." In addition, political discourse often takes on a ritualistic
quality, and many mistrusting or cynical responses may constitute the repetition of familiar clichés or low-level grousing rather than the expression of genuine discontent.

With these caveats in mind, we recommend the following measures from those in the
present inventory. The Trust in Government Scale (Miller, 1974) and the NORC Confidence in Government and Other Institutions items (Smith, 1981) should be used in tandem
as indicators of satisfaction with the performance of existing authorities. One obvious advantage of these items is the existence of a time-series; another is the fact that the political
trust items have been used in cross-national research. The ANES items can safely be limited to two, the Trust Government to Do What Is Right and the Big Interests items, as indicated in the Political Trust and System Evaluation scales (Mason et al., 1985). Because
responses to these questions about "the government in Washington" apparently subsume
feelings about both the presidency and Congress, the NORC items, with their more specific referents, are a useful complement. To measure support for the political regime and

belief in the fairness and integrity of political processes, the Political Allegiance Index (Citrin *et al.*, 1975), the Political Support Typology (Sniderman, 1981), and the Political Support Scale (Miller & Jukam, 1977) are sources of good items in terms of both face validity and construct validity.

The literature on political trust is substantial, with certain sources being particularly helpful. Gambetta (1988) and Hardin (1993) provide excellent conceptual accounts of trust and emphasize both early socialization and ongoing experience as the foundations of trusting (or mistrusting) attitudes. Easton (1975) explains the relationship between trust and support for the political system, clarifying his earlier theory (1965) in the light of empirical evidence. Miller (1974), Citrin (1974), Muller and Jukam (1977), Citrin and Green (1986), and Craig (1993) debate the meaning of the most commonly used measure of political trust, the ANES Trust in Government index, while Smith (1981) and Lipset and Schneider (1987) cover the same substantive ground using the NORC Confidence in Institutions items.

With respect to methodological guidelines for assessing existing scales or constructing new measures of trust, we emphasize the following:

1. Specify the attitude object as unambiguously as possible (e.g., specific institution or political leaders);
2. Ask for the object to be evaluated according to normative standards appropriate to the political context being studied (e.g., responsiveness to public opinion in a democracy, fairness of judicial hearing);
3. Include items that make comparisons with rival systems of governance when measuring support for a given political regime;
4. Collect test–retest evidence concerning the stability of respondents' answers in order to confirm that these reflect enduring attitudes rather than fleeting emotional reactions;
5. Use a multiformat approach to item construction in order to minimize the possible influence of response sets inherent in agree–disagree and yes–no formats; and
6. Strengthen evidence of validity by testing predictions across a broader range of political theories, including evidence of attitude–behavior relations looking at such actions as tax compliance, willingness to serve in the military, obedience to the law, varieties of participation, and social cooperation.

The recent collapse of communism and subsequent political convulsions in Europe dramatically illustrate the importance of people's underlying allegiances and identifications. After 70 years the Soviet regime still lacked enough popular legitimacy to withstand the loosening of social control. What level of trust or support among citizens matters, whose support matters, and what conditions the loss of trust and the transfer of loyalty are vital questions of enduring practical as well as theoretical interest. One cannot investigate these issues empirically without acquiring the proper measurement instruments. This inventory of attitude scales has examined the strengths and weaknesses of the available tools in order to provide a starting point for the continuing search.

We conclude, however, by briefly indicating some ways to broaden the traditional horizons of research about political trust and support. One useful departure would be to move beyond the measurement of affect to learn what both ordinary citizens and institutional elites expect from government, both instrumentally and normatively. What types of outcomes are judged as effective? What kinds of processes are considered to be fair, and how are standards of fairness changing over time in response to social and cultural transformations? And how do variations in political structures and contexts influence popular perceptions of the trustworthiness and fairness of government?

Another new direction for research involves extending our concern beyond the distinction between support for *incumbents* and support for the *regime* and the related fixation with the wholesale transformation of political systems. We need to examine as well the attitudinal underpinnings of less comprehensive, yet consequential, changes in the functioning of institutions, such as new electoral rules or enhanced legal protection for the individual and for groups.

A final suggestion is for clarification of the relationship between the politically focused variables considered here and broader social attitudes, such as a generalized disposition toward authority or what psychologist Erik Erikson (1963) labeled "basic trust." How these orientations interact in explaining political engagement and civic cooperation is an issue of general relevance.

Political theorists are concerned with what might be called system trust because they suppose, implicitly at least, that trust in human relations can lead to successful and mutually beneficial interactions and, therefore, that a political culture of trust serves the collective welfare. Yet trusting political leaders involves an act of faith because we cannot plausibly know a great deal about them, as we do about our family, friends, or coworkers (Hardin, 1993). To the extent that this is true, the problem of political trust becomes more acute as society becomes larger, more complex, and more economically and culturally differentiated.

In this context where does trust come from, and how can it be sustained? If trust is *learned,* then citizens come to political maturity with varying levels of trust that reflect their socialization, both personal and political. And there are likely to be significant aggregate differences in political trust, reflecting different patterns of experience and political education, both formal and informal. Yet one important lesson of the research summarized briefly in this chapter is that trust is *earned.* The loss of confidence in government in the United States in recent decades resulted largely from a succession of political failures. The difficulty is that, once lost, trust is not easily regained, since citizens rationally base their attitudes toward new leaders on the basis of recent past experience. Moreover, since how satisfied we are depends on our expectations, governments will always find it difficult to build a solid reservoir of popular trust and goodwill if expectations are constantly rising. The development of a political environment in which there is widespread, well-founded confidence in government is a collective problem requiring improved communication between elites and ordinary citizens.

Trust in Government Scale
(A. H. Miller, 1974)

Variable

This scale taps the public's general trust in the national government in Washington, D.C.

Description

This scale consists of five items in multiple-choice format initially developed to measure public cynicism concerning the political process. The content deals with assessments of the national government's general trustworthiness, competence, honesty, wastefulness, and concern for the public interest.

The items are scored straightforwardly, with one point for each trusting alternative (underlined in the scale), so that the lowest trusting score is 0 and the highest trusting score is 5.

Sample

The national samples in the ANES are drawn using a multistage area probability sample design. The questions have been in the biennial surveys from 1964 to 1996. In recent years some of the items have been omitted from the interview schedule.

Reliability

Internal Consistency

The items have been extensively factor-analyzed, mainly by Miller (1974, p. 954), who found that the five items formed a single factor in the context of other political attitude items. Across the 1964–1970 period, all five items had factor loadings above .70, with a .90 coefficient of reproducibility using Guttman scale criteria. Hill (1982) found McKennell's alpha to be .68 for both the pre- and post-1972 election studies. Abramson and Finifter (1981) used the same five items in the 1978 ANES survey, with each item scored as a trichotomy to create an index, resulting in a Cronbach's alpha of .57.

More recently Parker (1986) performed a LISREL confirmatory factor analysis on the items across 1964–1980 and found wide discrepancies in their individual reliabilities— from .41 on the Trust Government and Big Interests items to .32 on the Crooked item to .22 on the Waste Money item to only .14 on the Smart People item. As a result, the scale was modified in the ANES in subsequent years to include just four items, omitting the Smart People item (Item 4).

Test–Retest

Using the 1972 pre- and postelection data on the ANES, Hill (1982) found individual items with test–retest coefficients of .39 to .47 across time. Overall scale reliability was .57 (Pearson's r).

Validity

Convergent

Citrin (1977) found political trust correlated .31 with internal political efficacy in the 1968–1974 ANES studies and .43 with a measure of institutional responsiveness.

Discriminant

Citrin (1974, p. 980) found no consistent relation between trust and "unconventional political participation" in the form of protest marches, sit-ins, refusal to obey, and the like.

In a West German study, Muller and Jukam (1977) found that a four-item adapted version of the trust scale correlated .38 (gamma) with aggressive political participation, although that relationship dropped to −.06 (partial gamma) after controlling for political support.

Location

Miller, A. H. (1974). Political issues and trust in government: 1964–1970. *American Political Science Review, 68*, 951–972.

Results and Comments

Citrin and Green (1986) showed that the Trust in Government index is consistently related to evaluations of the incumbent president and his performance. These findings led them and other scholars to conclude that this measure focuses more heavily on the incumbent authorities than on the regime level of the political system.

Trust in Government Scale
(ANES 1964)

People have different ideas about the government in Washington. These ideas don't refer to Democrats or Republicans in particular, but just to the *GOVERNMENT IN GENERAL.* We want to see how you feel about these ideas. For example:

1. How much of the time do you think you can trust the government in Washington to do what is right:
   1. JUST ABOUT ALWAYS*
   2. MOST OF THE TIME
   3. OR ONLY SOME OF THE TIME

2. Would you say the government is:
   1. PRETTY MUCH RUN BY A FEW BIG INTERESTS LOOKING OUT FOR THEMSELVES
   2. OR THAT IT IS RUN FOR THE BENEFIT OF ALL THE PEOPLE

3. Do you think that people in government:
   1. WASTE A LOT OF THE MONEY WE PAY IN TAXES
   2. WASTE SOME OF IT
   3. OR DON'T WASTE VERY MUCH OF IT

4. Do you feel that:
   1. ALMOST ALL OF THE PEOPLE RUNNING THE GOVERNMENT ARE SMART PEOPLE WHO USUALLY KNOW WHAT THEY ARE DOING
   2. OR DO YOU THINK THAT QUITE A FEW OF THEM DON'T SEEM TO KNOW WHAT THEY'RE DOING

5. Do you think that:
   1. QUITE A FEW OF THE PEOPLE RUNNING THE GOVERNMENT ARE A LITTLE CROOKED
   2. NOT VERY MANY ARE
   3. OR DO YOU THINK HARDLY ANY OF THEM ARE CROOKED AT ALL

*Trusting responses are underlined.

Political Trust and System Evaluation Scales

(W. M. Mason, J. S. House, & S. S. Martin, 1985)

Variable

These two scales tap public confidence in the federal government to act in ways perceived as right and fair. They represent a modification of the ANES Trust in Government measure.

Description

These variables emerged from a reanalysis of the ANES Trust in Government items discussed in the preceding review, along with 23 other measures (Mason *et al.*, 1985). The Political Trust scale consists of two of the five multiple-choice ANES Trust in Government items (Trust Government and Big Interests) detailed in #1 above. The other three questions (Waste Money, Crooked, Smart People) were treated as separate measures of beliefs about public officials, similar in some ways to the political cynicism items in measures described later in this chapter. These conclusions derived from an extended interitem analysis, using factor analytic and canonical techniques, of 27 ANES questions measuring diverse aspects of political disaffection and personal efficacy.

The Political Trust scale items are scored in the same manner as described for the Trust in Government scale. Dichotomies of the two items are formed from the underlined response options and then added to form a scale ranging from 0 (low trust) to 2 (high trust). The distributions in six ANES surveys were

	1964	1980	1984	1988	1992	1996
Low trust—0	15%	65%	42%	48%	62%	56
1	22	23	29	31	26	27
High trust—2	63%	12%	29%	21%	12	16
	100%	100%	100%	100%	100%	100%
	(mean = 1.47)	(mean = .48)	(mean = .86)	(mean = .73)	(mean = .50)	(mean = .60)

The breakdown of the 1996 Two-item Political Trust index by demographic groups is as follows:

	Age					Income				
	18–29	30–39	40–49	50–59	60 or Older	Low	Lower middle	Middle	Upper middle	High
Low trust—0	55%	61%	54%	54%	55%	49%	55%	64%	59%	57%
1	31	24	28	26	30	32	28	25	24	28
High trust—2	14	15	18	20	15	20	17	12	17	15

	Race		Gender		Education			
	White	Black	Male	Female	Some high school	High school grad	Some college	College grad
Low trust—0	58%	53%	54%	58%	48%	57%	61%	55%
1	26	27	31	25	34	28	23	27
High trust—2	16	20	15	18	18	15	16	18

Sample

The data come from national probability samples in the ANES from 1964 to 1978.

Reliability

Internal Consistency

Exploratory factor analysis on 21 items in the ANES surveys from 1964 to 1976 confirmed the dimensionality of the six factors commonly cited and used in research, including the five-item Trust in Government measure (Mason *et al.*, 1985, p. 122). However, a constrained factor analysis (LISREL IV) indicated that the Waste Money and Crooked items cross-load with factors other than the Political Trust factor and that the Smart People item has very low factor loadings for all the dimensions.

Test–Retest

No data were reported.

Validity

No data were reported.

Location

Mason, W. M., House, J. S., & Martin, S. S. (1985). On the dimensions of political alienation in America. *Sociological Methodology, 15,* 111–151.

Results and Comments

The same two-item measure of political trust was used to analyze trends in the ANES data by Citrin and Green (1986). Barnes *et al.* (1979) used the two-item measure in a five-nation comparative study of political protest. Gabriel (1995) used the two-item measure of trust drawn from EuroBarometer surveys in analyzing trust in Western Europe.

Mason *et al.* (1985) used the results of their LISREL analysis to propose another index, the System Evaluation scale, referring to the feelings of pride in and the perceived need for change in the "form of government." The scoring is a simple additive index of the two dichotomized items. This measure might be more properly thought of as an index of support for the political regime, as are measures 14–25 reviewed here.

Political Trust Scale
(ANES, 1964)

People have different ideas about the government in Washington. These ideas don't refer to Democrats or Republicans in particular, but just to the *GOVERNMENT IN GENERAL*. We want to see how you feel about these ideas. For example:

1. How much of the time do you think you can trust the government in Washington to do what is right:
   1. <u>JUST ABOUT ALWAYS</u>*
   2. <u>MOST OF THE TIME</u>
   3. ONLY SOME OF THE TIME

2. Would you say the government is:
   1. PRETTY MUCH RUN BY A FEW BIG INTERESTS LOOKING OUT FOR THEMSELVES
   2. OR THAT IT IS RUN FOR THE <u>BENEFIT OF ALL THE PEOPLE</u>

   *Trusting responses are underlined.

System Evaluation Scale
(Mason, House, & Martin, 1985)

1. (Proud) Would you say
   1. I AM <u>PROUD OF MANY THINGS</u> ABOUT OUR FORM OF GOVERNMENT*
   2. OR I CAN'T FIND MUCH IN OUR GOVERNMENT TO BE PROUD OF

2. (Need Change) Some people believe a change in our whole form of government is needed to solve the problems facing our country, while others feel no real change is necessary. Do you:
   1. THINK A BIG CHANGE IS NEEDED IN OUR FORM OF GOVERNMENT
   2. OR SHOULD IT BE <u>KEPT PRETTY MUCH AS IT IS</u>

   Note: Volunteered "some change" responses to Item 2 were coded 2, with "change needed" coded 3 and "kept as is" coded 1.
   *Trusting responses are underlined.

Trust in Government Scale
(E. N. Muller & T. O. Jukam, 1977)

Variable

This scale taps different aspects of attitudes toward the federal government and government officials.

Description

The items in the scale were initially developed to tap attitudes of political trust in cross-national surveys. This scale consists of four items, one in a seven-point agree–disagree format and the other three in a five-option multiple-response format. The item content refers to the trustworthiness of the national government as well as to the integrity and concern for the public interest of elected representatives.

The seven-point scale item was reduced to five response categories by collapsing the three middle responses. With all four items thus coded 0 to 4, they were then summed to form a scale from 0 (positive) to 16 (negative). This scale was then divided into five levels of affect (Muller & Jukam, 1977, p. 1569), with the distribution in the 1974 West German sample as follows:

Very negative	(13–16)	8%
Negative	(10–12)	20
Intermediate	(7–9)	43
Positive	(4–6)	25
Very positive	(0–3)	4
		100%

Sample

Data came from a survey of 2663 West German adults, interviewed during the fall of 1974. Twelve sites were selected in which opposition to the regime had been stronger than in other parts of the country. The sites were rural, urban, and university in character. Sampling at each site was done separately, using combinations of eligible voter rolls, lists of community influentials, and quota samples of students and faculties in the universities.

Reliability

Internal Consistency

The authors report that the Kuder–Richardson 20 reliability coefficient was .77, with an estimated correlation of test with true scores of .88 (Muller & Jukam, 1977, p. 1569).

Test–Retest

No data were reported.

Validity

Convergent

Political trust had strong bivariate relationships with measures of political support (tau-b = .48), incumbent evaluation (tau-b = .44), and policy output evaluation (tau-b = .36).

Discriminant

The Political Trust scale (scored with low values in the trusting direction) correlated .38 (gamma) with a measure of aggressive political participation. However, after controlling for a measure of regime support, gamma dropped to −.06.

Location

Muller, E. N., & Jukam, T. O. (1977). On the meaning of political support. *American Political Science Review, 71,* 1561–1595.

Results and Comments

This scale was used as part of a larger effort to distinguish support for the political regime from support for authorities.

Trust in Government Scale
(Muller & Jukam, 1977)

1. In general, one can rely on the federal government to do the right thing.

1	2	3	4	5	6	7
STRONGLY AGREE						STRONGLY DISAGREE

2. How much do you trust the government in Bonn to act as it really should?
   1. ABOUT ALWAYS 2. MOSTLY 3. SOMETIMES
   4. ONLY VERY SELDOM 5. NEVER
3. When members of Parliament or cabinet ministers speak on television or in Parliament with journalists, how often in your opinion do they tell the truth?
4. How much do you trust members of the government to put the interests of the people over the interests of their own parties?

Trust in the Incumbent Congress and the Presidency Items
(P. R. Abramson & A. W. Finifter, 1981)

Variable

These items focus specifically on trust in the incumbent president and Congress.

Description

The analysis utilizes four items, two referring to the president and two referring to the Congress, in multiple-response formats. The item content refers to beliefs about the trustworthiness of the person or the institution (Abramson & Finifter, 1981).

The purpose of these measures was to distinguish trust in the incumbent president and Congress from the more general attitude of trust in government that the ANES items seek to capture (see the review of Trust in Government Scale, Miller, 1974). The new items asked the Trust Government and Big Interests questions about President Jimmy Carter and Congress.

The distribution of the items was not reported, although scores run from 1 (low trust) to 4 (high trust).

Sample

Data come from the 1978 ANES postelection survey, an in-person interview with 2304 adults. The sample was drawn using a stratified cluster sampling design based on congressional districts, resulting in a national probability sample. (In the authors' analysis, respondents with two or more "don't know" or "not ascertained" responses were excluded from the five-item Michigan Trust in Government scale, for a resulting effective sample of 2245.)

Reliability

Internal Consistency

Exploratory factor analysis of the five Trust in Government scale items (see the previous scale review) and the four new items produced a one-factor solution (Abramson & Finifter, 1981). The factor loadings of the four new items ranged from .69 for the Congress Big Interests item to .50 for the Trust Carter item. Single-factor solutions resulted when two other factor analyses were run, omitting first the Trust Government item and then the Government Run by Big Interests item.

Test–Retest

No information was reported.

Validity

Convergent

The four Carter and Congress items were related to the full five-item Trust in Government scale, with Pearson's r ranging from .32 for Trust Carter to .53 for Congress Big Interests. When the Trust Government item is dropped from the five-item Trust in Government scale, the correlations drop by about .05 for the Trust Carter and Trust Congress items, but the drop is negligible for the Carter Big Interests and Congress Big Interests items. Similarly, when the Big Interests item is dropped from the five-item Trust in Government scale, the corresponding Carter Big Interests and Congress Big Interests correlations drop .10 and .08, respectively, compared to .02 and .05 for the Trust Carter and Trust Congress items, respectively (Abramson & Finifter, 1981, pp. 301–303).

Discriminant

No information was reported.

Location

Abramson, P. R., & Finifter, A. W. (1981). On the meaning of political trust: New evidence from items introduced in 1978. *American Journal of Political Science, 25,* 297–307. Reprinted by permission of the University of Wisconsin Press.

Results and Comments

The authors conclude from these results that the new items have the virtue of greater specificity in their objects and, therefore, are good measures of support for the incumbent authorities. They argue further that the referents of the Trust in Government index items are too ambiguous to enable one to conclude that they measure support for the regime.

Trust in the Incumbent Congress and the Presidency Items (Abramson & Finifter, 1981)

1. How much of the time do you think you can trust President Carter to do what is right
   1. <u>JUST ABOUT ALWAYS</u>*
   2. <u>MOST OF THE TIME</u>
   3. OR ONLY SOME OF THE TIME
2. Would you say that the Carter administration is
   1. PRETTY MUCH RUN BY A FEW BIG INTERESTS LOOKING OUT FOR THEMSELVES OR
   2. THAT IT IS RUN FOR THE <u>BENEFIT OF ALL THE PEOPLE</u>
3. How much of the time do you think you can trust the U.S. Congress to do what is right
   1. <u>JUST ABOUT ALWAYS</u>
   2. <u>MOST OF THE TIME</u>
   3. OR ONLY SOME OF THE TIME
4. Would you say that the U.S. Congress is
   1. PRETTY MUCH RUN BY A FEW BIG INTERESTS LOOKING OUT FOR THEMSELVES OR
   2. THAT IT IS RUN FOR THE <u>BENEFIT OF ALL THE PEOPLE</u>

   *Trusting responses are underlined.

Trust in Member of Congress Scale

(G. R. Parker & S. L. Parker, 1989)

Variable

This scale specifically assesses respondents' trust in their congressional representative.

Description

This scale consists of five items in multiple-option format. The item content refers to the representative's promise-keeping, personal benefits, honesty, trustworthiness, and responsiveness to constituents' policy preferences. The items in the scale were initially developed by Parker and Parker (1989) to tap the factors shaping respondents' likes and dislikes about their congressman.

The item scoring technique was not reported, nor was the distribution of the scale scores.

Sample

In January and February of 1988, 989 adult Florida residents were interviewed in a telephone survey. The five Trust-in-Representative questions were posed only to the 49% of the sample who chose a response other than "don't know who the representative is" on a screening question asking for an evaluation of the job performance of the U.S. House member.

Reliability

Internal Consistency

Guttman analysis of the Trust-in-Representative questions resulted in a coefficient of reproducibility of .91 and a coefficient of scalability of .65. Exploratory factor analysis of the five Trust-in-Representative questions and five system trust items revealed two distinct dimensions, with little overlap between the two factors; however, statistics from this procedure were not reported.

Confirmatory factor analysis, using LISREL, generated reliability estimates, expressed as the square of lambda for each item, or its relationship to the unmeasured latent concept. The lambda-squared values for these five items ranged from .12 for the Constituents' Opinion item (indicating that 12% of the variance in this item is explained by the latent concept of Trust in Representative) and .18 for the Benefits Himself Personally item to .58 for the Trust House Member item. The mean value for all five items is .34 (Parker & Parker, 1989, pp. 13–14). The Trust House Member item also loads slightly on the System Trust concept, with a lambda-squared of .03.

Test–Retest

No information was reported.

Validity

Convergent

Using regression analysis, Trust in Representative has a significant effect on voter turnout, even with controls for Strength of Party Identification, Age, and Level of Education. However, Parker and Parker utilize LISREL to test hypothesized relationships between Trust in Representative and Waste Taxes, Economic Outlook, Impersonal Contact with Representative, Personal Contact with Representative, Socioeconomic Status, and System Trust. The LISREL findings indicate a poor initial fit to the model, with System Trust not supported as an exogenous variable and Waste Taxes, Economic Outlook, and Socioeconomic Status only weakly related to Trust in Representative.

Discriminant

No information was reported.

Location

Parker, G. R., & Parker, S. L. (1989, August–September). *Why do we trust our congress-man and does it matter?* Paper presented at the annual meeting of the American Political Science Association, Atlanta.

Results and Comments

Trust in Member of Congress Scale
(Parker & Parker, 1989)

1. How often do you feel that your member in the U.S. House of Representatives keeps the promises he makes:
   1. JUST ABOUT ALWAYS*
   2. MOST OF THE TIME
   3. ONLY SOME OF THE TIME
   4. OR NEVER

2. How often do you feel your U.S. House member uses his position to benefit himself personally:
   1. MOST OF THE TIME
   2. ONLY SOME OF THE TIME
   3. RARELY OR
   4. NEVER

3. How would you rate the honesty of your U.S. House member:
   1. VERY HONEST
   2. FAIRLY HONEST
   3. SOMEWHAT DISHONEST OR
   4. VERY DISHONEST

4. How often do you feel you can trust your U.S. House member to do what is right:
   1. ALMOST ALWAYS
   2. MOST OF THE TIME
   3. ONLY SOME OF THE TIME
   4. OR NEVER

5. How closely do you feel your U.S. House member follows the opinions of his constituents when voting in Washington:
   1. VERY CLOSELY
   2. FAIRLY CLOSELY
   3. NOT CLOSELY AT ALL

*Trusting responses are underlined.

Trust in Local Government Scale
(M. Baldassare, 1985)

Variable

This scale taps feelings of trust in *local* (rather than national) government.

Description

The scale was adapted from measures of Trust in Government and External Political Efficacy in the ANES (Baldassare, 1985) and consists of three items in multiple-option format. The item content refers to governmental performance and to officials' efficiency in using tax money and attentiveness to the public's policy preferences.

The items are scored 1 to 3 and then summed to form a scale with a range of 3 to 9, with high scores indicating low trust. The distribution of the scale was

High trusting	3–4	9%
Moderate trusting	5–6	37
Moderate mistrusting	7	24
High mistrusting	8–9	30
		100%

Sample

Telephone interviews were conducted in July 1983 with 1003 adults in Orange County, California. The sample was stratified into north and south Orange County, and then random digit dialing of working telephone blocks was employed to select households.

Reliability

Internal Consistency

The alpha coefficient of the composite scale was .65.

Test–Retest

No data were reported.

Validity

No data were reported.

Location

Baldassare, M. (1985). Trust in local government. *Social Science Quarterly, 66,* 704–712. Reprinted by permission of the author and the University of Texas Press. All rights retained by the University of Texas Press.

Results and Comments

In this study Trust in Local Government is significantly related to characteristics of the respondent's community such as density, population size, social heterogeneity, and rate of social change. In a regression analysis with controls for age, education, home ownership, length of residence, and family income, only social heterogeneity remained significantly related to Trust in Local Government.

Trust in Local Government Scale
(Baldassare, 1985)

1. How would you rate the performance of your local government in solving problems in your community:
   1. EXCELLENT*   2. GOOD   **3. FAIR   **4. POOR

2. In general, do you think that the people who run your local government:
   3. WASTE A LOT OF THE MONEY WE PAY IN TAXES
   2. WASTE SOME OF THE MONEY WE PAY IN TAXES
   1. WASTE VERY LITTLE OF THE MONEY WE PAY IN TAXES

3. When your local government leaders decide what policies to adopt, how much attention do you think they pay to what the people think:
   1. A LOT   2. SOME   3. VERY LITTLE ATTENTION

   *Trusting responses are underlined.
   **The last two responses were combined in scale construction.

Incumbent-Based Trust Scale

(S. C. Craig, R. G. Niemi, & G. E. Silver, 1990)

Variable

This scale specifically taps trust in incumbent officeholders, as distinguished from support for the political regime.

Description

This scale consists of four items in agree–disagree format. The items' content refers to public officials' trustworthiness and honesty. In order to reduce response set bias, the authors recommend rewording the items, with two in multiple-option format and two in paired-choice format (Craig et al., 1990).

The items in the scale were initially developed by contributors to the 1987 ANES Pilot Study in order to develop clear distinctions between incumbent and regime-based trust and between internal and external efficacy. A total of 37 items were included in the original analysis.

The item responses are summed into a scale with a range of 0 (low trust) to 4 (high trust), although the distribution of scale scores was not reported.

Sample

The 1987 ANES Pilot Study survey was administered by telephone from May to July 1987 to a subset of the 1986 ANES postelection cross-section sample. Due to the split-sample design in the pilot study, 360 respondents were asked these trust and efficacy items on Form 2.

Reliability

Internal Consistency

The authors hypothesized that the 37 items would form five distinct factors: Incumbent-Based Efficacy, Incumbent-Based Trust, Internal Efficacy, Regime-Based Efficacy, and Regime-Based Trust/Diffuse Support. Initial exploratory factor analysis of all 37 items with five factors specified showed that the 4 items from the standard Trust in Government scale clustered together, along with 6 of the 9 hypothesized incumbent-based trust items and 1 incumbent-based efficacy item (Craig *et al.*, 1990, p. 293). The four Trust in Government items had the lowest factor loadings of this cluster and also loaded between .28 and .35 on the factor labeled Incumbency Efficacy/Trust. The Big Interests and Trust Government items also loaded .31 and .21, respectively, on a third factor, labeled Regime Efficacy.

The reliability of the resulting four-item Trust in Government scale ($\alpha = .64$) is somewhat lower than that for the authors' proposed four-item Incumbent-Based Trust Scale ($\alpha = .70$). The authors attribute this difference to response set bias associated with the agree–disagree format of the latter scale (Craig *et al.*, 1990, pp. 301–302).

Confirmatory factor analysis (using LISREL) of only those items proposed for the final scale indicates a high adjusted goodness-of-fit index of .95. Incumbent-Based trust was significantly correlated (phi) with External Efficacy (phi = .25, $p < .01$), but not with Internal Efficacy (Craig *et al.*, 1990, p. 304).

Validity

Convergent

Comparing the construct validity of the four-item Trust in Government and Incumbent-Based Trust measures, the authors indicate that these scales have similar relationships to presidential and congressional job approval, government performance on the country's most important problem, and the strength of the U.S. position in the world (Craig *et al.*, 1990, p. 302).

Discriminant

No data were reported.

Location

Craig, S. C., Niemi, R. G., & Silver, G. E. (1990). Political efficacy and trust: A report on the NES Pilot Study items." *Political Behavior, 12,* 289–314.

Results and Comments

The four agree–disagree items constituted the Incumbent-Based Trust Scale. The authors proposed replacing the Trust in Government scale with items similar to these four, but with the questions reworded to avoid the agree–disagree format.

Incumbent-Based Trust Scale
(Craig, Niemi, & Silver, 1990)

1. You can generally trust the people who run our government to do what is right.
   1. AGREE*   2. DISAGREE
2. When government leaders make statements to the American people on television or in the newspapers, they are usually telling the truth.
3. Those we elected to public office usually try to keep the promises they have made during the election.
4. Most public officials can be trusted to do what is right without our having to constantly check on them.

   *Trusting response is underlined.

Governmental Attentiveness Scale
(S. E. Bennett, 1984)

Variable

This scale taps respondent perceptions regarding the attentiveness of national government officials and institutions to the public.

Description

This scale consists of four items first included in the 1964 ANES in multiple-response format. The item content deals with the attention paid by the government and congressional representative to "the people" and with the role played by elections and political parties in assuring the government's attention to what "the people" want (Bennett, 1984).

The item scoring consists of a simple linear summation of the three response options on each item, forming a scale with scores ranging from 4 (low attentiveness) to 12 (high attentiveness). This scale was then collapsed into five categories, although category scores are not reported. Respondents with missing data on any of the items were excluded from the scale.

The distribution of the five-category scale employing all four items in 1964 and 1980 was:

	1964	1980
Very attentive	34%	6%
Slightly attentive	32	34
Pro–con	16	21
Slightly inattentive	13	28
Very inattentive	5	11
	100%	100%

In recent years only the two items referring to government and elections have been included in the ANES biennial surveys. The distribution of a simple summed two-item scale has been

		1964	1980	1984	1988	1992	1996	1964–1996
Attentive	4	31	7	13	11	10	14	−17
	3	29	31	24	23	30	26	−3
	2	25	33	33	39	40	37	+12
	1	10	19	15	14	12	13	+3
Inattentive	0	5%	10%	14%	13%	8%	10	+5
		101%	101%	100%	100%	100%	101%	0

Sample

Data come from national samples in the ANES, drawn using a multistage area probability sample design. The four questions were included in the biennial surveys from 1964 to 1992. After that the items referring to congressional representatives and political parties were omitted from the interview schedule.

Reliability

Internal Consistency

In a principal-components factor analysis of 13 items covering Trust in Government (see review earlier in this chapter), Political Efficacy, and Governmental Attentiveness, all four governmental Attentiveness items have had factor loadings above .40 on a single factor in every year from 1964 to 1980.

The internal consistency of the four-item Governmental Attentiveness Scale was measured using Cronbach's alpha. During the 1964–1980 period, the standardized alpha ranged from .65 (1980) to .75 (1964, 1968), with a mean of .71.

Test–Retest

Test–retest reliability of the four-item index using the ANES 1972–1974–1976 panel data was .37 (Pearson's r) over the four-year 1972–1976 period, .38 for 1972–1974, and .48 for 1974–1976.

Validity

Convergent

The four-item scale is correlated between .20 and .35 with Pride in the American Form of Government (1972, 1976), Perceived Need for Change in Form of Government (1972, 1976), Perceived Representation by the Political System (1976), and feeling thermometers of the Supreme Court, Congress, "people working for the federal government," and the federal government itself (1980). The author reports that these correlations are similar to those for the Trust in Government and External Efficacy scales and that these three measures "form a general syndrome of basic evaluative orientations toward government" (Bennett, 1984, p. 342).

Correlations (Pearson's *r*) with feeling thermometers of the incumbent president and major party presidential nominees are below .20 in every year available, as is the correlation between presidential Job Approval and Governmental Attentiveness.

Discriminant

No data were reported.

Location

Bennett, S. E. (1984). Change in the public's perceptions of governmental attentiveness, 1964–1980. *Micropolitics, 3*, 309–348.

Governmental Attentiveness Scale
(Bennett, 1984)

1. Over the years, how much attention do you feel the government pays to what the people think when it decides what to do:
   1. A GOOD DEAL*   2. SOME   3. NOT MUCH

2. How much do you feel the political parties help to make the government pay attention to what the people think:

3. And how much do you feel having elections makes the government pay attention to what the people think:

4. How much attention do you think most Congressmen pay to the people who elected them when they decide what to do in Congress:

   *Attentive response is underlined.

Confidence in Governmental and Other Institutions Scale

(T. W. Smith, 1981)

Variable

These items tap confidence in the leaders of a variety of social and political institutions, of which three are national government agencies and two are related to government (military and education).

Description

The items in the scale were initially developed by Harris in 1966 and subsequently have been slightly modified in both question wording and response options by Gallup, the GSS (NORC), the Opinion Research Corporation (ORC), and others (see Smith, 1981, and Lipset & Schneider, 1987, for extensive analyses of item content and meaning). Batteries of these items are presented to the respondent in a multiple-choice format that varies, depending on the survey organization conducting the study.

The items are scored differently by each survey organization, with three response options (GSS/NORC and Harris), four options (Gallup), or a seven-point scale (ORC).

The distribution of the GSS/NORC items for those with an opinion was

	1973–1994			1973–1975	1994
	Great deal	Only some	Hardly any	Great deal	Great deal
1. Executive branch	18%	54%	28%	30%	12%
2. Congress	15	60	25	24	8
3. Supreme Court	33	52	15	33	31
4. Military	36	51	14	33	38
5. Education	33	55	12	38	25
6. Medicine	50	43	7	54	42
7. Press	19	57	24	23	10
8. Television	15	55	28	19	10
9. Major companies	26	60	14	31	26
10. Banks	27	57	16	33	18
11. Organized Religion	31	49	20	36	25
12. Organized Labor	12	54	34	16	10
13. Science	43	50	7	41	41

Sample

These questions are typically posed in national surveys by the above-mentioned survey organizations, using random sampling designs or stratified cluster designs in personal or telephone interviews. The questions have been included annually or biennially in surveys since 1966 (Harris), 1972 (GSS/NORC), and 1973 (Gallup).

Reliability

Internal Consistency

Intercorrelations among the individual items of Confidence in Institutions in the GSS for 1973–1977 were all positive and ranged from .08 (between science and organized labor) to .40 (between Congress and Supreme Court) over the five-year period (Lipset & Schneider, 1987, pp. 96–99). (See the comments in text for more recent analyses.)

Exploratory factor analysis indicated that all of the 12 items tested loaded on a single factor (Lipset & Schneider, 1987). Using principal components, a one-factor solution was derived, with factor loadings between .65 for Congress and .43 for organized labor. In addition, the authors reported that a second factor was extracted (presumably in a later analysis), but that only confidence in the press and in television loaded significantly on this additional factor.

Test–Retest

Smith (1981) discusses the results from efforts to measure the stability of responses to the Confidence in Institutions questions using a subsample of the 738 respondents who were reinterviewed one month following the initial interview. An average of 63% of respondents gave the same response as previously. A dichotomization of the data shows a test–retest average of 81% agreement, slightly lower than the agreement levels of 85%, 86%, and 83% reported from the 1972, 1973, and 1974 GSSs, respectively.

Validity

To explore the content validity of these items, Smith (1981) debriefed a randomly selected subsample of the 1978 GSS respondents using two questions intended to explore what content respondents had in mind in answering the Confidence in Institutions items. Respondents were first asked what the word *confidence* meant to them and then whether another word would be clearer to them. Most respondents gave answers that could be considered reasonable definitions of confidence, with the largest single response being "trust" (35%). About 7% could not offer a reasonable definition of the term (Smith, 1981, p. 169).

When asked to name a concrete referent for the institutions being evaluated, respondents gave answers that varied from individual leaders, to groups, to more impersonal definitions. In addition, between 12 and 39% could not give a specific referent to the specific institutions (Smith, 1981, pp. 169–176).

Location

Smith, T. W. (1981). Can we have confidence in confidence? Revisited. In D. F. Johnston (Ed.), *Measurement of subjective phenomena* (pp. 119–189). Washington, DC: U.S. Bureau of the Census.

Lipset, S. M., & Schneider, W. (1987). *The confidence gap: Business, labor and government in the public mind* (Rev. ed.). New York: Free Press.

Results and Comments

The GSS data indicate that levels of Confidence in the presidency and Congress, while experiencing some fluctuations, have declined in the 1973–1994 period. Similar declines have occurred in Confidence in other types of organizations and institutions. At the same time, Confidence in the Supreme Court and in the Scientific Community has remained basically stable, and Confidence in the Military has increased somewhat.

Confidence in Government and Other Institutions Scale
(Smith, 1981)
GSS/NORC and Harris

As far as the people running [institution] are concerned, would you say you have
1. A GREAT DEAL OF CONFIDENCE*
2. ONLY SOME CONFIDENCE
3. OR HARDLY ANY CONFIDENCE AT ALL IN THEM

The institutions are Medicine, Education, Military, Organized Religion, Major Companies, *Supreme Court*, Press, *Executive Branch, Congress,* and Organized Labor.

Gallup

I am going to read you a list of institutions in American society. Would you tell me how much confidence you, yourself, have in each one:
1. A GREAT DEAL   2. QUITE A LOT   3. SOME   4. OR VERY LITTLE

The institutions are the Church or Organized Religion, the Public Schools, the *Supreme Court, Congress,* Organized Labor, Big Business, the Military, Medicine, Newspapers, Television, Free Enterprise, and Banks and Banking.

*Confident responses are underlined.

Political Cynicism Scale
(R. E. Agger, M. N. Goldstein, & S. Pearl, 1961)

Variable

This scale was an early attempt to tap beliefs about politicians and the political process.

Description

This scale consists of six questions initially developed by Agger *et al.* (1961) that were posed to respondents in a six-point agree–disagree scale format. The items deal with political candidacy, the role of money in policy making, and the perceptions of politicians as hacks, manipulators, and representatives of general versus special interests.

The item responses were dichotomized and then summed into an additive scale, with scores ranging from 0 to 6. These scores were then trichotomized, combining those scoring 0 or 1 (cynical), 2 or 3 (neutral), and 4, 5, and 6 (trusting) (Agger *et al.*, 1961, p. 481). The distribution was as follows:

Cynical (0, 1)	18%
Neutral (2, 3)	31%
Trusting (4, 5, 6)	51%

Sample

The data came from a random sample of 1230 adult residents of Eugene and Springfield, Oregon, conducted during the summer of 1959. The Political Cynicism items were included on a mailback, 62-item self-administered attitudinal inventory, completed and returned by 779 (63%) of the original 1230 interviewees.

Reliability

Internal Consistency

Guttman scaling techniques were used to build a composite Political Cynicism score, and the resultant scale had a reproducibility coefficient of .94. The Kuder–Richardson coefficient of reliability was .62 (Agger *et al.*, 1961, p. 480).

Test–Retest

No data were reported.

Validity

Convergent

Cross-tabulations showed that the Political Cynicism Scale was related to three scales measuring Personal Cynicism, Political Potency (Efficacy), and Political Discussion. The relationship to Personal Cynicism remained strong even after separate controls were applied for level of education and age. Political Potency is also strongly related to Political Cynicism, and this relationship remained after controls were applied for educational level.

Discriminant

Political Discussion was related to Political Cynicism, but this relationship was weaker and less consistent under controls for education than were the other two scales (Agger *et al.*, 1961, pp. 489–499).

Location

Agger, R. E., Goldstein, M. N., & Pearl, S. (1961). Political cynicism: Measurement and meaning. *Journal of Politics, 23,* 477–506. Reprinted by permission of the authors and the University of Texas Press. All rights retained by the University of Texas Press.

Political Cynicism Scale
(Agger, Goldstein, & Pearl, 1961)

1. In order to get nominated, most candidates for political office have to make basic compromises and undesirable commitments.
   1. STRONGLY AGREE*
   2. SOMEWHAT AGREE
   3. SLIGHTLY AGREE
   4. SLIGHTLY DISAGREE
   5. SOMEWHAT DISAGREE
   6. STRONGLY DISAGREE

2. Politicians spend most of their time getting re-elected or reappointed.

3. Money is the most important factor influencing public policies.

4. A large number of city and county politicians are political hacks.

5. People are very frequently manipulated by politicians.

**6. Politicians represent the general interest more frequently than they represent special interests.

   *Cynical response is underlined.
   **Indicates reverse scored item.

Political Cynicism Scale

(J. Citrin & D. J. Elkins, 1975)

Variable

This scale taps cynical versus trusting attitudes toward British politicians and government officials.

Description

The items in the scale were initially developed by Citrin and Elkins (1975) to measure cynicism about political figures in Great Britain using 13 items in agree–disagree format. Item content refers to politicians' and officials' concern for the public interest, ideals, honesty, campaign promises, responsiveness to pressure groups, idealism, problem solving, personal gain from politics, role as public servants, quality, dedication, and willingness to stand up for their beliefs. Questions were worded so that agreement was the cynical response on 8 of the 13 items.

The scoring technique was a simple linear addition of dichotomized items, running from 0 (least cynical) to 13 (most cynical). The distribution of scale scores was not reported.

Sample

Samples of university students from five British universities were selected using every *n*th name on university registration lists. Those selected were mailed extensive questionnaires in the spring of 1968. One hundred questionnaires were mailed at the universities of Sussex, Edinburgh, and Manchester, with 75 mailed at King's College (University of London) and Surrey. The total number of responses was 234, for an average response rate of 52%, with a low of 43% at King's College and a high of 61% at Surrey.

Reliability

Internal Consistency

The 13 items comprising the Political Cynicism Scale emerged as a single dimension under factor analysis of 108 agree–disagree items. Reliability was measured using a Kuder–Richardson procedure, yielding a coefficient value of .86. The coefficient of reproducibility using Guttman scale criteria was .87.

Test–Retest

No data were reported.

Validity

Convergent

The Political Cynicism Scale correlated .43 (Pearson's *r*) with the number of negative responses on an adjective checklist of politicians' qualities and correlated .51 with an open-ended question about what politicians in Britain are like. Political Cynicism was also correlated (Pearson's *r*) with Political Moralism (.32) and Political Disinterest (.21).

Political Cynicism was negatively correlated (Pearson's *r*) with Perceived System Responsiveness (−.52) and Political Efficacy (−.30).

Discriminant

The Political Cynicism Scale was not significantly related to a Britain First Scale, Pride in Britain, Civic Duty, or a Political Contacts–Participation Index.

Location

Citrin, J., & Elkins, D. J. (1975). *Political disaffection among university students: Concepts, measurement and causes.* Berkeley: Institute of International Studies, University of California.

Political Cynicism Scale
(Citrin & Elkins, 1975)

1. Most government officials try to serve the public interest even if it goes against their own personal interests.
   1. AGREE   2. DISAGREE*

**2. If a politician sticks to his ideals and principles, he is unlikely to reach the top of his profession.

**3. No man can hope to stay honest once he enters politics.

4. Despite what some people say, most politicians try to keep their campaign promises.

**5. Most politicians are practically the agents of some pressure group or other.

**6. Almost all politicians will sell out their ideals or break their promises if it will increase their power.

**7. Most politicians do a lot of talking but they do little to solve the really important issues facing the country.

**8. Most politicians are in politics for what they can get out of it personally.

9. Most politicians are really willing to be truthful with the voters.

**10. Politicians are supposed to be servants of the people, but too many of them try to be our masters.

**11. All politicians are bad—some are just worse than others.

12. Most politicians are dedicated men and we should be grateful to them for the work they do.

13. Most politicians are willing to stand up for what they believe is right even when the going gets rough.

*Cynical response is underlined.
**Indicates reverse scored item.

Political Cynicism Scale
(E. A. Baloyra, 1979)

Variable

This scale taps attitudes of extreme cynicism regarding the motives and competence of government officials and political parties.

Description

This scale consists of five items worded to invite agreement with extreme statements concerning whether politicians hurt government, whether parties care only about winning elections, and government officials' ability to make appropriate decisions, their competence, and their attentiveness to ordinary citizens.

The items in the scale were initially developed by Baloyra and Martz (1979) in an effort to distinguish levels of deep cynicism from less behaviorally potent forms of political criticism (see the review of Political Criticism Scale, Baloyra, 1979) in a political culture notable for its "generalized sense of distrust and suspicion" (Baloyra, 1979, p. 989).

The items were first standardized and then summed into a linear combination scale. The author reported that none of these items could be scaled using Guttman criteria.

The distribution of scale scores was not reported, although the scale runs from 0 (lowest cynicism) to 5 (highest cynicism).

Sample

The data came from a national sample of 1521 adult Venezuelans, interviewed in the fall of 1973.

Reliability

Internal Consistency

The mean interitem correlation (Pearson's r) for the five scale items was .21. The mean correlation between the scale and each item was .58. Other reliability data were not reported.

Test–Retest

No data were reported.

Validity

Convergent

The Political Cynicism Scale correlated .51 (Pearson's r) with a composite measure of Political Criticism and .22 with Interpersonal Distrust. In a path analysis with Political Cynicism as the dependent variable, these relationships were only somewhat diminished, with a second-order partial beta of .48 for Political Criticism and .11 for Interpersonal Distrust. Interpersonal Distrust also has an indirect effect on Political Cynicism through Political Criticism (Pearson's $r = .17$).

Political Cynicism was negatively correlated with Political Efficacy (Pearson's $r = -.26$) and Ideological Tendency (Pearson's $r = -.15$).

Discriminant

Political Cynicism had a zero-order correlation of .22 with a preference for not voting, but this relationship disappeared in path analysis due to the presence of Political Criticism, which was related to not voting (partial beta = .21).

Location

Baloyra, E. A. (1979). Criticism, cynicism and political evaluation: A Venezuelan example. *American Political Science Review, 72*, 987–1002.

Political Cynicism Scale
(Baloyra, 1979)

Exact wording is not reported; however, the items cover the following topics, with the presumed cynical responses in parentheses:

1. How frequently government officials fail to do what is right. (ALWAYS)
2. The capacity of government officials. (BUREAUCRATIC INCOMPETENCE)
3. How much attention government officials pay to ordinary citizens. (BUREAU-CRATIC INDOLENCE)
4. Government would be better off without the interference of politicians. (AGREE)
5. Parties only care about winning elections. (AGREE)

Political Cynicism
(P. M. Sniderman, 1981)

Variable

These items tap feelings of trust in political authorities in general.

Description

The items were initially developed by Sniderman (1981) to present respondents with a choice of two contrasting, but not highly polarized, response options on the same evaluative dimension of government. The Bay Area Survey included six paired-choice items, referring to the integrity of government officials. These are similar to the items in the first three measures reviewed. They were not combined into an index, but each was strongly related to the Political Support Index (Sniderman, 1981), reviewed later.

The items were not formed into a scale.

Sample

Personal interviews were conducted in 1972 by the Survey Research Center of the University of California, Berkeley, with 963 adults in a full probability cluster sample in the five-county San Francisco–Oakland Standard Metropolitan Statistical Area (SMSA). Responses to these six items were from a subsample of 143 completed mailback questionnaires.

Reliability

No reliability information was reported.

Validity

Convergent

The construct validity of these items is indicated by their strong relationship to a measure of Political Support (Sniderman, 1981), #16 reviewed later. Cross-tabulations of the six paired-choice cynicism measures with this Political Support Typology showed that all the relationships were strong (Sniderman, 1981, pp. 56–57).

Discriminant

No data were reported.

Location

Sniderman, P. M. (1981). *A question of loyalty.* Berkeley: University of California Press. Copyright © 1981 The Regents of the University of California.

Political Cynicism
(Sniderman, 1981)

Choose one of the two statements, whichever comes closer to how you feel:

1. 1. Our government officials usually tell us the truth, vs
   2. Most of what our government leaders say can't be believed.
2. 1. Most of our political leaders can be trusted to tell the truth, vs
   2. Our political leaders are prepared to lie to us whenever it suits their purposes.
3. 1. When presidents keep facts from the public it's usually because they want to protect the national security, vs
   2. The main reason presidents keep information secret is so they can hide things the public would object to.
4. 1. I'm more likely to trust what a government spokesman says than what the newspapers or television tell us, vs
   2. Newspapers and television are more likely to tell us the truth about public affairs than the people who speak for the government.
5. 1. Corruption is a serious problem in our government—Too many of our officials are simply not honest, vs
   2. Given the pressures they face, most of our political leaders are surprisingly honest.

> 6. 1. These days almost every citizen has to be careful about what he says, be-
>   cause the government may be listening in, vs
>   2. All the talk these days about the government spying on people is not really
>   true.

Regime-Based Trust Scale

(S. C. Craig, R. G. Niemi, & G. E. Silver, 1990)

Variable

This scale taps support for the American political regime—as distinguished from trust in incumbent officeholders.

Description

The items in the scale were initially developed by contributors to the 1987 ANES Pilot Study in order to establish clear distinctions between regime- and incumbent-based trust and between internal and external efficacy (Craig *et al.*, 1990). A total of 37 items were included in the analysis.

This scale consists of four items in agree–disagree format. The item content refers to evaluations of and willingness to change the form of government. The item scoring method and distribution of the scale were not reported.

Sample

The ANES 1987 Pilot Study was administered by telephone in May and July 1987 to a subset of the 1986 ANES postelection cross-section sample. Due to the split-sample design in the Pilot Study, 360 respondents were asked these trust and efficacy items on Form 2.

Reliability

Internal Consistency

The authors expected the four items to compose a single dimension of Regime-Based Trust/Diffuse Support. Exploratory factor analysis showed that only three of the four items loaded highly on their own dimension, while the fourth item had a higher loading on a dimension named Incumbent-Based Efficacy/Trust. Further, one of the three items also loaded relatively highly on Incumbent-Based Efficacy/Trust.

The four-item index had an alpha reliability of .47 and a mean interitem correlation of only .21. Two of the items (Best Government and Rather Live Here), however, correlated .44. On the basis of the factor analysis, reliabilities, and interitem correlations, the authors recommend provisional use of this two-item version of the index.

Test–Retest

No data were reported.

Validity

Convergent

The authors find evidence of the construct validity of the two-item measure of Regime-Based Trust in its moderate correlation (Pearson's *r*) with measures of Patriotism (.33), External Efficacy (.23), and Incumbent-Based Trust (.16).

Discriminant

No data were reported.

Location

Craig, S. C., Niemi, R. G., & Silver, G. E. (1990). Political efficacy and trust: A report on the NES Pilot Study items. *Political Behavior, 12*, 289–314.

Regime-Based Trust Scale
(Craig, Niemi, & Silver, 1990)

1. Whatever its faults may be, the American form of government is still the best for us.
   1. <u>AGREE*</u>   0. DISAGREE
2. There is not much about our form of government to be proud of.
   0. AGREE   1. <u>DISAGREE</u>
3. It may be necessary to make some major changes in our form of government in order to solve the problems facing our country.
   0. AGREE   1. <u>DISAGREE</u>
4. I would rather live under our system of government than any other that I can think of.
   1. <u>AGREE</u>   0. DISAGREE

   *Trusting responses are underlined.

Political Allegiance Index
(J. Citrin, H. McClosky, J. M. Shanks, & P. M. Sniderman, 1975)

Variable

This scale taps general feelings of separation, distance, or rejection from the political process at the national level.

Description

The items in the scale were initially developed by Citrin *et al.* (1975) to provide a multiple-indicator measure of subjective allegience to political institutions, values, and leaders. Item selection was based on intercorrelations of approximately 30 items and evaluations of their face validity by the authors and six other raters.

The final scale consists of eight items: three in paired-choice format, two in multiple-response format, and three from an adjective checklist. The item content refers to openness of the political system; pride in that system; the honesty, integrity, and corruption of government officials; and perceptions of whether the adjectives *fair, corrupt,* and *disgusting* describe respondents' feelings about the national government (Citrin *et al.,* 1975).

The items were dichotomized and then summed to produce simple linear index scores, with low scores indicating more allegiant responses. These scores were then divided into quintiles for subsequent analysis, although the distribution of scale scores was not reported.

Sample

Personal interviews were conducted in 1972 by the Survey Research Center of the University of California, Berkeley, with 963 adults in a full probability cluster sample in the five-county San Francisco–Oakland SMSA.

Reliability

Internal Consistency

The mean interitem correlation of the eight items was .36; the split-half reliability was .82 (Spearman–Brown, with correction for attenuation). Factor analysis showed that the items all loaded on a single factor.

Test–Retest

No test–retest data were reported.

Validity

Convergent

The Political Allegiance Index was strongly related to responses to 15 items on the adjective checklist. The most allegiant quintile was much less likely to attribute negative qualities to the national government (and more likely to attribute positive qualities) than was the alienated quintile, regardless of the adjective content.

In a test of construct validity, the Political Allegiance Index correlated .36 (Pearson's *r*) with a summary measure of participation in unconventional political protest. The Political Allegiance Index was also associated with lack of support for the political authorities, regime, and community.

Discriminant

No data were reported.

Location

Citrin, J., McClosky, H., Shanks, J. M., & Sniderman, P. M. (1975). Personal and political sources of political alienation. *British Journal of Political Science, 5,* 1–31.

Political Allegiance Index
(Citrin, McClosky, Shanks, & Sniderman, 1975)

1. "The way our system of government operates, almost every group has a say in running things,"* or "This country is really run by a small number of men at the top who only speak for a few special groups."
2. "I am proud of many things about our system of government," or "I can't find much in our system of government to be proud of."
3. "Our government officials usually tell us the truth," or "Most of the things that government leaders say can't be believed."
4, 5, 6. Adjective checklist—"Which describes your feelings about the national government? Corrupt; Disgusting; and Fair."
7. "How much of the time do you think you can trust the government to do what is right? Just about always, most of the time, only some of the time, or none of the time?"
8. "Would you say that most of the political leaders in this country stand for the things you really believe in, that only some of them do, that only a few do, or that none of them do?"

*Allegiant responses are underlined.

Political Support Typology
(P. M. Sniderman, 1981)

Variable

This typology covers different kinds of allegiance to, and disaffection from, the American national government.

Description

The items in the scale were initially developed by the authors of the Bay Area Survey to examine the structure of beliefs and affect toward political institutions and processes. This typology consists of 18 items in an adjective checklist format. The item content refers to descriptive terms, such as "fair" or "wasteful."

Sniderman (1981) divided the adjectives into favorable (10) and unfavorable (8) groups. The ratio of positive to negative assessments was used as the basis of classification. See Sniderman (1981, pp. 17–20, 47–48) for a more detailed description.

The distribution of the 1972 Bay Area Survey on this typology was

Committed	23%
Supportive	26
Middle	15
Disenchanted	19
Disaffected	17
	100%

Sample

Personal interviews were conducted with 963 adults in a full probability cluster sample in 1972 by the Survey Research Center of the University of California, Berkeley, in the five-county San Francisco–Oakland SMSA.

Reliability

Internal Consistency

Since these items were employed to construct a typology, as distinct from a scale or an index, reliability information was not reported.

Test–Retest

No data were reported.

Validity

Convergent

The Political Support Typology was strongly negatively related to six paired-choice questions tapping cynical feelings about government officials (Sniderman, 1981, pp. 56–57) and was also strongly related to evaluations of American government on a variety of dimensions.

Discriminant

No data were reported.

Location

Sniderman, P. M. (1981). *A question of loyalty.* Berkeley: University of California Press. Copyright © 1981 The Regents of the University of California.

Results and Comments

Sniderman (1981) presents evidence concerning the protest participation of respondents in each group in order to argue that they represent qualitatively different types rather than points along a single dimension. No information concerning statistical tests of this hypothesis is reported.

Political Support Typology
(Sniderman, 1981)

Place an "X" beside each adjective you consider to be a good description of what the national government is like (Sniderman, 1981, p. 17). The adjectives were:

*Honest	___	*Trustworthy	___
Unfair	___	*Unselfish	___
*Helpful	___	Wasteful	___
Corrupt	___	Stubborn	___
*Kind	___	*Honorable	___
Unfriendly	___	Confusing	___
*Fair	___	*Democratic	___
*Dependable	___	Disgusting	___
Stupid	___	*Efficient	___

*Indicates favorable response.

Political Support Scale
(E. N. Muller & T. O. Jukam, 1977)

Variable

This index taps affect toward the regime level of the political system, as distinct from both the incumbent authorities and the political community.

Description

The items in the scale were initially developed by Muller and Jukam (1977) to provide a multifaceted measure of political system affect "which stems from belief that the authorities in general do or do not conform to a person's sense of what is right and proper behavior" (p. 1567). Four of the items were based on measures developed by Schwartz (1973).

This scale consists of eight items in seven-point agree–disagree format. The item content refers to respondents' perceived congruence between their own attitudes and those of governmental authorities, respect for political institutions, a feeling of being well represented, the political system's respect for rights, politicians' good intentions, and respect for the police.

The items are scored from 0 to 6 and then summed to form an index, with scores ranging from 0 (support for the system) to 48 (alienation from the system). The distribution of scale scores was not reported.

Sample

The data come from a survey of 2663 West German adults interviewed during the fall of 1974. Twelve sites were selected in which opposition to the regime had been stronger than in other parts of the country. The sites were rural, urban, and university in character. Sampling at each site was done separately, using combinations of eligible voter rolls, lists of community influentials, and quota samples of students and faculties in the universities.

Reliability

Internal Consistency

Mean interitem correlation among the eight items was .37. The Kuder–Richardson 20 reliability coefficient was .82, with an estimated correlation of test with true scores of .91.

Test–Retest

No data were reported.

Validity

Convergent

The Political Support Scale had strong bivariate relationships with a measure of Trust in Government (tau-b = .48; see the review of Trust in Government Scale, Muller & Jukam, 1977) as well as to Incumbent Evaluation (tau-b = .34) and Policy Output Evaluation (tau-b = .35).

Unlike many measures intended to tap behaviorally potent beliefs, the Political Support Scale was also strongly related to a measure of aggressive political participation (gamma = .66). This relationship remained strong under controls for Political Trust (partial gamma = .61), Incumbent Evaluation (partial gamma = .62), and Evaluations of Policy Outputs (partial gamma = .58).

Discriminant

No data were reported.

Location

Muller, E. N., & Jukam, T. O. (1977). On the meaning of political support. *American Political Science Review, 71,* 1561–1595.

Remarks and Comments

This scale has been slightly modified by Seligson (1983) in a study of regime support in Mexico and by Finkel *et al.* (1989) in a study of regime support in Costa Rica.

Political Support Scale
(Muller & Jukam, 1977)

*1. It makes me concerned when I think about the difference between what people like me value in life and what actually happens in our political system.
   1. STRONGLY AGREE
   2. SOMEWHAT AGREE
   3. SLIGHTLY AGREE
   4. NEITHER AGREE NOR DISAGREE
   5. SLIGHTLY DISAGREE
   6. SOMEWHAT DISAGREE
   7. STRONGLY DISAGREE**

2. I have great respect and affection for the political institutions in the Federal Republic.

3. My friends and I feel that we are quite well represented in our political system.

*4. I find it very alarming that the basic rights of citizens are so little respected in our political system.

*5. At present, I feel very critical of our political system.

6. The courts in the Federal Republic guarantee everyone a fair trial regardless of whether they are rich or poor, educated or uneducated.

7. Looking back, the leading politicians in the Federal Republic have always had good intentions.

8. Considering everything, the police in the Federal Republic deserve great respect.

   *Indicates reverse scored item.
   **Supportive response is underlined.

Judicial Legitimacy Scale
(T. R. Tyler, 1990)

Variable

This scale taps general positive affect toward the court system and toward police.

Description

The items in the scale were initially developed by Tyler (1990) to distinguish between a concept of *legitimacy* that emphasizes general positive evaluations of governmental leaders and institutions and one that refers to people's willingness to comply with rules with which they disagree.

This scale consists of eight items in Likert-style agree–disagree format. Four items refer to perceptions of fairness, honesty, and protection of rights by the courts and four items to similar beliefs about the Chicago police.

The scale construction method is not reported. However, Tyler (1990) constructed separate court support and police support scales and then combined them into a scale that he describes as a measure of judicial legitimacy. The distributions of Court Support and Police Support scales were not reported. However, the combined Judicial Legitimacy (Courts and Police) Scale distribution was

Low 1.00–1.5	4%
1.51–2.0	15
2.01–2.5	33
2.51–3.0	35
3.01–3.5	11
High 3.51–4.0	2
	100%

Sample

A random sample of 1575 Chicago citizens was interviewed by telephone in the spring of 1984. One year later 804 of these respondents were randomly selected and reinterviewed.

Reliability

Internal Consistency

For the four Court Support measures, the mean interitem correlation (Pearson's r) was .48, and the alpha was .79. For the Police Support measures, the mean interitem correlation was .51, with an alpha of .81 (first wave). Reliability data for the Judicial Legitimacy Scale were not reported.

Test–Retest

No data were reported.

Validity

Convergent

The Court Support and Police Support subscales were highly intercorrelated, with a Pearson's r = .51. The correlation between the Judicial Legitimacy Scale and the Obligation to Obey the Law Scale was .26 (Pearson's r) in the first wave and .25 in the second wave.

Another indication of the convergent validity of the measure was the strength of its relationship to measures of concepts that should be theoretically linked. As hypothesized, Judicial Legitimacy was correlated with a measure of Compliance with the Law (Pearson's r = .11), significant at the .001 level.

Discriminant

No data were reported.

Location

Tyler, T. R. (1990). *Why people obey the law.* New Haven, CT: Yale University Press.

Results and Comments

Tyler's primary interest lay in explaining compliance with the law. In this context he developed a second indicator, a measure of perceived obligation to obey the law, and treated this as another aspect of the underlying construct of legitimacy. This measure was composed of six Likert-style items, such as "Disobeying the law is seldom justified." The correlation between this index and the Court Support subscale was only moderately strong (Pearson's $r = .26$).

Judicial Legitimacy Scale
(Tyler, 1990)

A. Court Support:

1. The courts in Chicago generally guarantee everyone a fair trial.
   1. STRONGLY AGREE*
   2. SOMEWHAT AGREE
   3. SOMEWHAT DISAGREE
   4. STRONGLY DISAGREE
2. The basic rights of citizens are well protected in the Chicago courts.
3. On the whole Chicago judges are honest.
4. Court decisions in Chicago are almost always fair.

B. Police Support:

1. I have a great deal of respect for the Chicago police.
2. On the whole Chicago police officers are honest.
3. I feel proud of the Chicago police.
4. I feel that I should support the Chicago police.

*Supportive response is underlined.

Democratic Legitimacy
(P. McDonough, S. H. Barnes, & A. Lopez-Pina, 1986)

Variable

These items tap support for democratic institutions.

Description

The six items were initially developed by McDonough *et al.* (1986) to measure political affect and support for democratic institutions in a country changing from an authoritarian to a democratic political system. Three are similar to items from the Trust in Government Index (see review referring to Trust Government, Big Interests, and Waste Money). The other three items assess support for representative institutions.

The items were not combined into a single composite measure.

Sample

Data were collected in national samples at three different times: in June 1978, December to January 1979–1980, and November 1984. The first two samples were drawn using probability-proportional-to-size criteria applied to provinces, then counties, and then polling areas. At this stage a quota sample for age and sex was employed. In the third survey an area probability sample was used, followed by random selection of households and then of individuals within households. The total numbers of adults (age 16 and over) in the surveys were 3004 in 1978, 3014 in 1979–1980, and 2994 in 1984 (McDonough *et al.*, 1986, p. 756).

Reliability

Internal Consistency

The items were not combined into a scale, so no reliability information was reported.

Test–Retest

No data were reported.

Validity

Convergent

The six legitimacy items have varying relationships with ratings of how the government had performed in several domains under the democratic and authoritarian regimes, respectively.

In the 1984 sample the Trust in Government items had relatively higher correlations (.32 to .40) with a measure of Satisfaction with Democracy. Satisfaction with Democracy was less strongly related to Elections (.20), Congress (.23), and Monarchy/Republic (.16 in 1980, not asked in 1984).

Discriminant

No data were reported.

Location

McDonough, P., Barnes, S. H., & Lopez-Pina, A. (1986). The growth of democratic legitimacy in Spain. *American Political Science Review, 80,* 735–760.

Democratic Legitimacy
(McDonough, Barnes, & Lopez-Pina, 1986)

Three of the items were direct translations of items from the Trust in Government scale (see the first review in this chapter):

1. How much of the time do you think you can trust the government in Washington to do what is right:
   1. <u>JUST ABOUT ALWAYS</u>*
   2. <u>MOST OF THE TIME</u>
   3. OR ONLY SOME OF THE TIME

2. Would you say the government is:
   1. PRETTY MUCH RUN BY A FEW BIG INTERESTS LOOKING OUT FOR THEMSELVES
   2. OR THAT IT IS RUN FOR THE <u>BENEFIT OF ALL THE PEOPLE</u>

3. Do you think that people in government:
   1. WASTE A LOT OF THE MONEY WE PAY IN TAXES
   2. <u>WASTE SOME OF IT</u>
   3. <u>OR DON'T WASTE VERY MUCH OF IT</u>

The other three items were:

4. Do you believe that elections are the best system for choosing the government and the authorities of the country, or do you believe that they are not the best system?
   1. <u>ARE</u>   2. ARE NOT

5. Do you believe that we need a congress of deputies and a senate or could we get along without them?
   1. <u>NEED CONGRESS AND SENATE</u>   2. GET ALONG WITHOUT

6. Do you think that Spain should be a monarchy, or that Spain should be a republic?
   1. MONARCHY   2. <u>REPUBLIC</u>

*Supportive responses are underlined.

Political Support Index
(A. H. Miller, 1991)

Variable

This scale taps attitudes toward political authorities and rules in a political system under-going regime instability.

Description

The items in the scale were initially developed by Miller (1991) to measure attitudes to-ward the incumbent authorities, politically powerful institutions, and basic democratic forms of government in the Russian Federation. The scale consists of seven items: three agree–disagree questions, three five-point feeling thermometers, and one multiple-option item. The item content refers to beliefs about the national political leaders, the Communist Party Supreme Soviet, the Military and the value of competitive political institutions.

The items were dichotomized and the alienated responses summed in an additive in-dex, with scores ranging from 0 (supportive) to 7 (alienated).

The distribution of scale scores was

Supportive	0	8%
	1	15
	2	17
	3	17
	4	18
	5	14
	6	8
Alienated	7	3
		100%

Sample

Data are from the New Soviet Citizen Survey, 1800 in-person interviews conducted in the Russian Federation (west of the Ural Mountains), the Ukraine, and Lithuania during May and June of 1990. A multistage, stratified random sample design was employed.

Reliability

Internal Consistency

All seven items were positively intercorrelated, with a mean interitem correlation of .39. Each item correlated a minimum of .8 with the scale, and the overall standardized item al-pha was .83.

In a factor analysis of 16 attitudinal items, all 7 Political Support items formed a separate factor, although the factor loadings were not reported.

Test–Retest

No data were reported.

Validity

Convergent

Miller (1991) cites as evidence of convergent validity the relationships between this scale and items "measuring assessments of political authorities, institutions and broader political principles."

Discriminant

No data were reported.

Location

Miller, A. H. (1991). *In search of regime legitimacy.* Paper presented at the annual meeting of the International Political Science Association, Buenes Aires.

Political Support Index
(Miller, 1991)

1. Would you say that you trust the All-Union political leadership to do what is right
   1. ALMOST ALWAYS
   2. MOST OF THE TIME
   3. ONLY SOME OF THE TIME*
   4. ALMOST NEVER
2. The All-Union political leadership doesn't care much about what people like me think.
   1. AGREE   2. DISAGREE

Now we would like to get your feelings toward certain groups using a five-point scale, where 5 indicates a very positive view and 1 a very negative view. You may use any number between 1 and 5 to tell me how favorable or unfavorable your feelings are for each group. If you don't recognize a particular group, just tell me and we will go on to the next one.

3. How would you rate the Communist Party of the Soviet Union?

1	2	3	4	5
VERY NEGATIVE**				VERY POSITIVE

4. How would you rate the Supreme Soviet of the USSR?
5. How would you rate the Military?
6. Competition among many political parties makes the political system stronger.
   1. AGREE   2. DISAGREE

7. It is better to live in an orderly society than to allow people so much freedom that they can become disruptive.
   1. AGREE   2. <u>DISAGREE</u>

   *Alienated responses are underlined.
   **Scores of 1 or 2 were considered alienated.

Political Criticism Scale

(E. A. Baloyra, 1979)

Variable

This scale taps assessments of the long-term performance of recent democratic governments.

Description

The items in the scale were initially developed by Baloyra and Martz (1979) and were employed by Baloyra (1979) to distinguish between more behaviorally potent political cynicism (see the review of Political Cynicism Scale, Baloyra, 1979) and less corrosive political criticism. Baloyra has developed three other Political Criticism measures in addition to the scale discussed here, which Baloyra characterizes as focusing on the policies of the democratic regime: Cynicism toward the Incumbent Administration, the Role of Politicians, and the Institution of Elections.

This scale consists of four items, the format of which was not reported. The content of three of the items is similar to that of the Trust in Government scale items—whether public funds have been spent wisely, whether the public interest has been served, and whether public officials are honest. The fourth refers to whether recent governments have generally been beneficial to the country.

The items are scaled using Guttman criteria. No other information about item scoring was provided, although the distribution of the scale in the 1973 Venezuelan study was

Very low criticism	18%
Low	30
Moderate	39
Very high criticism	13
	100%

Sample

Data come from a national sample of 1521 adult Venezuelans interviewed in the fall of 1973.

Reliability

Internal Consistency

The Political Criticism Scale has a coefficient of reproducibility of .90 and a coefficient of scalability of .67.

Test–Retest

No data were reported.

Validity

Convergent

Correlations between the Political Criticism Scale and the three other Political Criticism scales indicated that these different "modes" of criticism were related. Pearson's *r*s range from .29 to .35, with an average of .32 (Baloyra, 1979, p. 993). These four composite measures of the "modes" of Political Criticism were combined into a summary measure of criticism by simple linear combination of their standardized scores. All four of the composite scales correlate between .58 and .70 with the resultant scale.

Discriminant

Path analysis was employed to evaluate potential determinants of Political Criticism. The impacts of Party Sympathy (.18) and Ideological Tendency (−.16) are small, but significant, while Sense of Political Efficacy is not significant.

Location

Baloyra, E. A. (1979). Criticism, cynicism and political evaluation: A Venezuelan example. *American Political Science Review, 72,* 987–1002.

Results and Comments

In path analysis of the determinants of Political Cynicism, Political Criticism had a strong impact, with a second-order partial beta of .48. Political Criticism also acted as a path through which Interpersonal Distrust and Stratification had indirect effects in addition to their direct effects on Political Cynicism. In addition, Political Criticism acted as a conduit for the effects of Ideological Tendency, Party Sympathy, Class Image, and Political Self-Image, ranging from .11 to .22 (Baloyra, 1979, pp. 994–996).

Given the similarity of these items to the ANES Trust in Government items and the absence of information about these items' relationships to feelings about alternative regimes or to political protest, the construct validity of this measure as an indicator of support for a type of political system is uncertain.

Political Criticism Scale
(Baloyra, 1979)

Question Wording: Exact question wording was not reported in this article. However, the items cover the following topics:

1. Have the democratic governments of the last fifteen years (1958–1973) been beneficial to Venezuela?
   1. NO*   2. YES

2. Have the democratic governments of the last fifteen years spent public monies judiciously, or have they <u>wasted them</u>?

3. Have the democratic governments of the last fifteen years served the public interest or the <u>interests of very powerful groups</u>?

4. Have the democratic governments of the last fifteen years been staffed with honest people, or <u>with crooks</u>?

*More critical responses are underlined.

Support for Democratic Institutions
(H. Schmitt, 1983)

Variable

The 1979 EuroBarometer, the cross-national European Election Study, included two items developed to tap specific and diffuse support for democratic forms of government.

Description

The items were initially developed by Schmitt (1983) to measure Satisfaction with Democracy and Support for Party Government. These items are both in multiple-response format and could be summed to form a scale running from 2 (high support) to 10 (low support).

Sample

A sample of 10 nations in Western Europe in the EuroBarometer 11 survey, conducted by the European Elections Study, was used.

Reliability

No data were reported.

Validity

Support for Party Government was correlated with respondents' Party Identification between .20 and .40 for the 10 nations, with a mean correlation of .30.

Location

Schmitt, H. (1983). Party government in public opinion: A European cross-national comparison. *European Journal of Political Research, 11,* 353–376.

Results and Comments

In most of the nations in the survey, these two items were only weakly related to each other. Only in West Germany (.28) was Pearson's r above .20.

Support for Democratic Institutions Scale
(Schmitt, 1983)

1. People hold different opinions on whether political parties should play a very important role in politics. What is your opinion? Please tell me . . . how far are you in favor or against political parties playing a very important role in the national government of (country):
   1. STRONGLY IN FAVOR*
   2. MODERATELY IN FAVOR
   3. NEITHER IN FAVOR NOR AGAINST
   4. MODERATELY AGAINST
   5. STRONGLY AGAINST

2. On the whole, are you
   1. VERY SATISFIED
   2. FAIRLY SATISFIED
   3. NOT VERY SATISFIED
   4. NOT AT ALL SATISFIED
   with the way democracy works in (country)?

   *Supportive responses are underlined.

Support for the Political Community
(P. M. Sniderman, 1981)

Variable

This battery taps supportive feelings toward the national political community.

Description

These 10 items are in multiple-response format, and tap comparative evaluations of the United States with other countries.

Sample

The 1972 San Francisco–Oakland Bay Area Survey included 10 items as indicators of support for the political community in the United States (Sniderman, 1981).

Reliability

No data were reported.

Validity

No data were reported.

Location

Sniderman, P. M. (1981). *A question of loyalty.* Berkeley: University of California Press. Copyright © 1981 The Regents of the University of California.

Results and Comments

Sniderman found little criticism of the "fundamental aspects of the political order." Even respondents categorized as alienated from the political system (Sniderman's 1981 Political-cal Support Typology, #16) perceived the United States as better than, or at least neither better nor worse than other countries in terms of freedom to live as one pleases, minority rights, and the quality of government (p. 119).

Support for the Political Community Scale (Sniderman, 1981)

How do you think the United States compares with most modern countries in these areas of life? Is it:
1. MUCH BETTER
2. SOMEWHAT BETTER
3. NEITHER BETTER NOR WORSE
4. SOMEWHAT WORSE
5. MUCH WORSE

The areas of life were

  Freedom of Speech
  Opportunity to Get Ahead
  Personal Safety from Crime
  Protection of the Environment
  Quality of Education
  Rights of Minority Groups
  Health Care for Everyone
  Treatment of the Poor
  Quality of Government
  Freedom to Live as You Choose

Affective Support Scales
(A. Kornberg & H. D. Clarke, 1992)

Variable

These items employ the Feeling Thermometer to tap feelings toward a variety of political agencies and actors at the national level.

Description

Affective support was ascertained at the levels of the national political community, the political regime, and political authorities using a 100-point feeling thermometer (see Chapters 3 and 12).

Sample

Canadian national cross-section surveys were done in 1974, 1979, 1980, 1983, 1984, 1987, and 1988; panel data are available for 1974–1979, 1979–1980, 1980–1983, 1983–1984, and 1984–1988.

Reliability

Internal Consistency

No data were reported.

Test–Retest

For support for the national political community, panel gammas ranged from .60 (1983–1984) to .76 (1980–1983); for support for the political regime, gammas ranged from .06 (1979–1980) to .40 (1980–1983); for support for political authorities, gammas ranged from .30 (1983–1984) to .59 (1979–1980).

Validity

Convergent and Discriminant

Factor analysis on the 1983 and 1988 data, using the feeling thermometers of support for the community, parliament, civil service, judiciary, incumbent party, and incumbent party leader, indicated that a four-factor model best fit the data, with four clear factors emerging: one for the Community, one for the Incumbent Authorities, and two separate factors for the regime: a Parliament–Civil Service factor and a Judiciary factor.

Location

Kornberg, A., & Clarke, H. D. (1992). *Citizens and community: Political support in a representative democracy.* New York: Cambridge University Press.

Results and Comments

The interfactor correlations, using weighted least squares estimates, indicated that, as expected, the relationships among all four factors, but in particular the relationship between Incumbent Authorities and Parliament–Civil Service was stronger in 1983 than in 1988, after the postwar one-party dominance of the Liberal Party had been broken. The interfactor correlations ranged from .11 (Community—Incumbent Authorities, in 1988) to .69 (Parliament–Civil Service—Incumbent Authorities, in 1983).

Affective Support Scales
(Kornberg & Clarke, 1992)

A. *Support for the national political community:*

1. How do you feel in general about Canada on the (thermometer) scale?

B. *Regime support:*

2. How do you feel about the government of Canada?
3. How do you feel about the national parliament of Canada?
4. How do you feel about the civil service of Canada?
5. How do you feel about the judiciary of Canada?

C. *Support for political authorities:*

6. How do you feel about the national Liberal party and its leaders?
7. How do you feel about the national Progressive party and its leaders?
8. How do you feel about the national Conservative party and its leaders?
9. How do you feel about the national New Democratic party and its leaders?

Government Power Scale
(L. L. M. Bennett & S. E. Bennett, 1990)

Variable

This measure taps perceptions of the power of the federal government.

Description

The measure consists of a single item asking respondents to evaluate whether or not the federal government has too much power.

	1964	1980	1984	1988	1992
Too powerful	46%	76%	59%	63%	70%
Not too strong	54	24	41	37	30
	100%	100%	100%	100%	100%

Sample

The national samples in the ANES are drawn using a multistage area probability sample design. This question has been included in the biennial surveys from 1964 to 1996, with the exception of 1986.

Reliability

No reliability information was reported.

Validity

Convergent

Bennett and Bennett (1990) employed multiple discriminant analyses to determine which of a set of hypothesized factors contributed to opinions about the role of the federal government. Trust in Government, Race, Ideology, and, to a lesser extent, Partisanship, Socioeconomic Status, and Presidential Approval were related to beliefs about the power of the federal government from 1964 to 1988.

Discriminant

No data were reported.

Location

Bennett, L. L. M., & Bennett, S. E. (1990). *Living with Leviathan: Americans coming to terms with big government.* Lawrence: University Press of Kansas.

Government Power Scale
(Bennett & Bennett, 1990)

"Some people are afraid the government in Washington is getting too powerful for the good of the country and the individual person. Others feel that the government has not gotten too strong for the good of the country. Have you been interested enough in this to favor one side over the other? [If yes] What is your feeling, do you think?"

1. THE GOVERNMENT IS GETTING TOO POWERFUL
2. THE GOVERNMENT HAS NOT GOTTEN TOO STRONG

References

Abramson, P. R., & Finifter, A. W. (1981). On the meaning of political trust: New evidence from items introduced in 1978. *American Journal of Political Science, 25,* 297–307.

Agger, R. E., Goldstein, M. N., & Pearl, S. (1961). Political cynicism: Measurement and meaning. *Journal of Politics, 23,* 477–506.

Baldassare, M. (1985). Trust in local government. *Social Science Quarterly, 66,* 704–712.

Baloyra, E. A. (1979). Criticism, cynicism and political evaluation: A Venezuelan example. *American Political Science Review, 72,* 987–1002.

Baloyra, E. A., & J. D. Martz. (1979). *Political attitudes in Venezuela.* Austin & London: University of Texas Press.

Barber, B. (1983). *The logic and limits of trust*. New Brunswick, NJ: Rutgers University Press.

Barnes, S. H., Kaase, M., et al. (1979). *Political action: Mass participation in five western democracies*. Beverly Hills, CA: Sage.

Bennett, L. L. M., & Bennett, S. E. (1990). *Living with Leviathan: Americans coming to terms with big government*. Lawrence: University Press of Kansas.

Bennett, S. E. (1984). Change in the public's perceptions of governmental attentiveness, 1964–1980. *Micropolitics, 3*, 309–348.

Blau, P. M. (1964). *Exchange and power in social life*. New York: Wiley.

Brehm, J., & Rahn, W. (1996, July). *Individual-level evidence for the causes and consequences of social capital*. Paper presented at the annual meeting of the International Society for Political Psychology, Vancouver, Canada.

Campbell, D. T., & Fiske, D. W. (1959). Convergent and discriminant validation by the multitrait multimethod matrix. *Psychological Bulletin, 56*, 81–105.

Citrin, J. (1974). Comment: The political relevance of trust in government. *American Political Science Review, 68*, 973–988.

Citrin, J. (1977). Political alienation as a social indicator. *Social Indicators Research, 4*, 381–419.

Citrin, J., & Elkins, D. J. (1975). *Political disaffection among university students: Concepts, measurement and causes*. Berkeley: Institute of International Studies, University of California.

Citrin, J., & Green, D. P. (1986). Presidential leadership and the resurgence of trust in government. *British Journal of Political Science, 16*, 431–435.

Citrin, J., McClosky, H., Shanks, J. M., & Sniderman, P. M. (1975). Personal and political sources of political alienation. *British Journal of Political Science, 5*, 1–31.

Craig, S. C. (1993). *The malevolent leaders: Popular discontent in America*. Boulder: Westview Press.

Craig, S. C., Niemi, R. G., & Silver, G. E. (1990). Political efficacy and trust: A report on the NES Pilot Study items. *Political Behavior, 12*, 289–314.

Easton, D. A. (1965). *A systems analysis of political life*. New York: Wiley.

Easton, D. (1975). A re-assessment of the concept of political support. *British Journal of Political Science, 5*, 435–457.

Erikson, E. H. (1963). *Childhood and society*. New York: Norton.

Finifter, A. W. (1972). Dimensions of political alienation. In A. W. Finifter (Ed.), *Alienation and the social system* (pp. 189–212). New York: Wiley.

Finkel, S. E., Muller, E. N., & Seligson, M. A. (1989). Economic crisis, incumbent performance, and regime support: A comparison of longitudinal data from West Germany and Costa Rica. *British Journal of Political Science, 19*, 329–351.

Fukuyama, F. (1995). *Trust: The social virtues and the creation of prosperity*. New York: Free Press.

Gabriel, O. W. (1995). Political efficacy and trust. In J. W. Van Deth & E. Scarbrough (Eds.), *Beliefs in government: Vol. 4. The impact of values* (pp. 357–389) New York: Oxford University Press.

Gambetta, D. (Ed.). (1988). *Trust: Making and breaking cooperative relations*. New York: Blackwell.

Green, D. P. (1988). On the dimensionality of public sentiment toward partisan and ideological groups. *American Journal of Political Science, 52*, 758–780.

Gurr, T. (1970). *Why men rebel*. Princeton, NJ: Princeton University Press.

Hardin, R. (1993). The street-level epistemology of trust. *Politics and Society, 21*, 505–529.

Hill, K. Q. (1982). Retest reliability for trust in government and governmental responsiveness measures: A research note. *Political Methodology, 8*, 33–46.

Huntington S. P. (1981). *American politics: The promise of disharmony*. Cambridge, MA: Harvard University Press.

Keniston, K. (1965). *The uncommitted: Alienated youth in American society*. New York: Harcourt, Brace and World.

Kornberg, A., & Clarke, H. D. (1992). *Citizens and community: Political support in a representative democracy*. New York: Cambridge University Press.

Lipset, S. M., & Schneider, W. (1987). *The confidence gap: Business, labor and government in the public mind* (Rev. ed.). New York: Free Press.

Mason, W. M., House, J. S., & Martin, S. S. (1985). On the dimensions of political alienation in America. *Sociological Methodology, 15,* 111–151.

McDonough, P., Barnes, S. H., & Lopez-Pina, A. (1986). The growth of democratic legitimacy in Spain. *American Political Science Review, 80,* 735–760.

Miller, A. H. (1974). Political issues and trust in government: 1964–1970. *American Political Science Review, 68,* 951–972.

Miller, A. H. (1991). *In search of regime legitimacy.* Paper presented at the annual meeting of the International Political Science Association, Buenos Aires.

Muller, E. N., & Jukam, T. O. (1977). On the meaning of political support. *American Political Science Review, 71,* 1561–1595.

Parker, G. R., & Parker, S. L. (1989, August–September). *Why do we trust our congressman and does it matter?* Paper presented at the annual meeting of the American Political Science Association, Atlanta.

Parker, S. L. (1986). *The dynamics of changing system support in the United States, 1964–1980.* Unpublished doctoral dissertation, Florida State University.

Putnam, R. D. (with Leonardi, R., & Nanetti, R. Y.). (1993). *Making democracy work: Civic traditions in modern Italy.* Princeton, NJ: Princeton University Press.

Putnam, R. D. (1995). Bowling alone: America's declining social capital. *Journal of Democracy, 6,* 65–78.

Rogowski, R. (1983). Political support for regimes: A theoretical inventory and critique. In A. Kornberg & H. D. Clarke (Eds.), *Political support in Canada: The crisis years* (pp. 27–48). Durham, NC: Duke University Press.

Schacht, R. (1970). *Alienation.* Garden City, NY: Doubleday.

Schmitt, H. (1983). Party government in public opinion: A European cross-national comparison. *European Journal of Political Research, 11,* 353–376.

Schwartz, D. C. (1973). *Political alienation and political behavior.* Chicago: Aldine.

Seeman, M. (1959). On the meaning of alienation. *American Sociological Review, 24,* 783–791.

Seeman, M. (1972). Alienation and engagement. In A. Campbell & P. E. Converse (Eds.), *The human meaning of social change* (pp. 467–527). New York: Russell Sage.

Seligson, M. A. (1983). On the measurement of diffuse support: Some evidence from Mexico. *Social Indicators Research, 12,* 1–24.

Smith, T. W. (1981). Can we have confidence in confidence? Revisited. In D. F. Johnston (Ed.), *Measurement of subjective phenomena* (pp. 119–189). Washington, DC: U.S. Bureau of the Census.

Sniderman, P. M. (1981). *A question of loyalty.* Berkeley: University of California Press.

Sniderman, P. M., & Brody, R. A. (1977). Coping: The ethics of self-reliance. *American Journal of Political Science, 21,* 501–521.

Tanaka, A. (1984, August–September). *System support in Japan: Political culture explanations vs. system performance explanations.* Paper presented at the annual meeting of the American Political Science Association, Washington, DC.

Tyler, T. R. (1990). *Why people obey the law.* New Haven, CT: Yale University Press.

Tyler, T. R., Rasinski, K. A., & Griffin, E. (1986). Alternative images of the citizen: Implications for public policy. *American Psychologist, 41,* 970–978.

Weatherford, M. S. (1992). Measuring political legitimacy. *American Political Science Review, 86,* 149–166.

Wright, J. D. (1981). Political disaffection. In S. Long (Ed.), *Research in micropolitics* (Vol. 1, pp. 1–79). New York: Greenwood Press.

CHAPTER 9

International Attitudes

Jon Hurwitz and Mark Peffley

Public opinion on foreign policy issues has received relatively little research attention until recent years, at least partly because of the pervasive scholarly assumption that the American electorate is more concerned with domestic than with international concerns. Specifically scholars had concluded that the American electorate is poorly informed about, and disinterested in, foreign affairs (e.g., Erskine, 1963; Free & Cantril, 1968; Simon, 1974) and that few citizens hold foreign policy attitudes that are stable or coherently organized within a belief system (e.g., Converse, 1964). Converse, in fact, maintained that foreign policy attitudes, even more than most domestic policy attitudes, are more appropriately labeled "nonattitudes," given their alleged incoherence and transience. Moreover, international attitudes were found to be only minimally related to important political decisions, such as the vote choice (Stokes, 1966). Given the likely irrelevance of international beliefs to many Americans, then, students of public opinion turned to a study of domestic policy attitudes in an effort to understand the landscape of electoral attitudes.

But a series of studies published over the past several decades has served to resurrect interest in the domain of international attitudes, largely because of findings that Americans actually do indeed seem to possess foreign policy attitudes that are reasonably well structured (e.g., see Holsti, 1992, 1996, for comprehensive reviews; Hurwitz & Peffley, 1987a; Maggiotto & Wittkopf, 1981; Modigliani, 1972; Wittkopf, 1990; Zaller, 1991), reasonably stable (e.g., Achen, 1975; Page & Shapiro, 1992; Peffley & Hurwitz, 1992, 1993), and, more important, demonstrably linked to political choices, such as presidential support (Hurwitz & Peffley, 1987b; Krosnick & Brannon, 1993) and voting (Aldrich, Sullivan, & Borgida, 1989). Thus, while the volume of scholarship in this domain clearly is not on a par with the massive attention devoted to economic and racial politics, the study of international attitudes has become an important area of study for students of political behavior.

Unfortunately, however, scholars who are investigating the international attitudes and beliefs of citizens and who are searching for well-researched off-the-shelf measures of their constructs may be disappointed. Put simply, until recently the international (foreign policy) domain of public opinion was both data-poor and measurement-poor, and while improvements have been made, there is much that remains to be done. Thus, while other chapters of this volume—particularly those that deal with ideology, race and ethnicity, system support, participation, and party identification—can offer readers a large set of frequently employed scales, the measurement properties of which are well understood, this chapter will be somewhat more limited in terms of both the quantity and the quality of the measures that it includes. A major part of the problem, of course, has arisen because of the shifting international landscape, particularly as the pressures of the Cold War have receded.

To what do we attribute these measurement problems in the study of international beliefs? One explanation relates to the nature of the policy domain—a domain in which both the actors and the policies are fluid. Students of racial attitudes, for example, are able to study responses toward a historical referent (i.e., blacks) that is relatively fixed over time. And for the most part the policies have also remained constant, at least over a period of several decades. While the Fair Employment Practices Commission may not be a salient policy stimulus today, as it was during the 1950s, the last several decades have witnessed a constellation of policies (including busing, affirmative action, and welfare, among others) that have been consistent in their salience.

In international politics, on the other hand, the agenda experiences a great deal more variation from year to year, given the fluidity of world events. In the first place the actors change frequently. If nothing else, the pivotal events of the past few years have reminded us that nations that once seemed menacing may today seem unthreatening and countries that once seemed irrelevant may quite suddenly become prominent. The preeminence of the Soviet Union for much of the postwar era, therefore, has given way to an era in which Iraq, China, and Japan appear to pose greater threats.

Adding to the changing cast of characters is our nation's changing international agenda, in which the relevance or salience of particular policies fluctuates to a great extent. During the Cold War era, for instance, discussion centered on Pentagon spending, support for various weapon systems (the particulars of which also changed rapidly as new technologies introduced new weapons), human rights problems, and other policies regarding various types of relations with the former Soviet Union. In the new era, however, these concerns have been joined by a new set of issues that are more closely related to the nations that have now become prominent on the international stage. The focus on the Middle East, for instance, has generated an interest in antiterrorist policies, while the increasing prominence of Japan and China has focused attention on international trade policies.

A quite different cause of the limitations of data and measurement in the international domain is the fact that major omnibus political surveys—most notably the questionnaires designed by the Center for Political Studies at the University of Michigan—have devoted very little space or attention to the measurement of foreign policy attitudes. Mostly, we contend, this neglect of the policy domain can be attributed to the previously noted conventional wisdom among many electoral behavior scholars that foreign policy simply does not "matter" to most Americans. While this scholarly view of an internationally ignorant and indifferent public has now been widely criticized (e.g., Hurwitz & Peffley, 1987a, 1990; Page & Shapiro, 1992), an important result of this conventional wisdom has been to limit severely the attention devoted by survey researchers to the foreign policy domain. Why "waste" valuable questionnaire space and time on matters assumed to be unimportant to the majority of respondents?

One important consequence of these dual conditions—that is, the fluidity of international politics and the failure of omnibus surveys to address this issue area in any depth—is that investigators of this domain of public opinion do not enjoy access to measures that have been frequently used in a variety of different studies. This limitation is especially noticeable in the fact that we have very few measures with extended time-series, thus hampering our understanding of the test–retest properties of the measures.

In sum, while we do not mean to exaggerate the differences between measurement of international politics and measurement in other political domains, we do believe it important to begin this chapter with the caveat that survey instrumentation in this domain of public opinion is both less plentiful and less well understood scientifically than that in most other political attitude domains.

Chapter Organization

The coverage of this chapter is both eclectic and wide-ranging, united by an underlying focus on perceptions, beliefs, and affective orientations toward world powers (i.e., nations) as well as policy preferences regarding the role of the United States in international affairs. The first portion is devoted to nationalism, that is, perceptions and attitudes toward world actors, beginning with the individual's own nation (mainly the United States) as the attitude object. While it may appear odd to begin a chapter on foreign policy attitude measurement with a series of scales designed to measure orientations toward one's own homeland, the choice makes sense in light of the frequent findings (discussed later) that foreign policy attitudes are driven in part by the attitudes of the citizen toward his or her own nation. Thus we start with a discussion of measures of patriotism and nationalism—two beliefs that are central to an understanding of opinions regarding world politics.

We then turn to measures that have been used to study perceptions and attitudes of citizens toward other nations—that is, the "objects" of foreign policy. To a considerable degree international policy preferences are motivated by the images that citizens hold of various world actors. A wide assortment of specific foreign policy attitudes—including defense spending, support for nuclear weapon systems, and the sending of U.S. troops to Central America—has been closely linked to Americans' perceptions and judgments of the former Soviet Union during the Cold War era. At least until recently citizens who viewed the former USSR as aggressive and deceitful had been found to favor more "hawkish" defense-related policies (Hurwitz & Peffley, 1990). And while the topic has not yet been explored, it is likely that Americans' perceptions of the Middle Eastern nations underlie preferences regarding antiterrorism policy, while views of Japan may motivate international economic attitudes. Thus, given this relationship between assessments of important world actors (both nations and leaders) and foreign policy preferences, we review one scale that measures such perceptions and another that uses the same approach to measure differences between two specific countries.

The third section of this chapter deals with a diverse assortment of policy-relevant attitudes. There are, of course, dozens of different specific foreign policies that have been examined, including attitudes toward defense spending, various weapon systems, employment of U.S. troops abroad, free trade, and foreign aid, among others. Our coverage, however, will not include such specific policy scales and will instead focus on more general or abstract policy-relevant beliefs. Such generic beliefs, which have been found to be related to more specific foreign policy positions (Hurwitz & Peffley, 1987a), transcend specific policies and, consequently, are necessarily less likely to become obsolete when new policies rise or fall in salience.

A more detailed litany of what is covered in this chapter includes 10 scales, organized under the three basic topics previously described:

A. Orientations toward Individuals' Own Nation
   1. Patriotism Scale (American National Election Study [ANES], 1987)
   2. Patriotism–Nationalism Questionnaire (Kosterman & Feshbach, 1989)
   3. Patriotism Scale (Sullivan, Fried, Theiss-Morse, & Dietz, 1992)
   4. National Involvement Scales (DeLamater, Katz, & Kelman, 1969)

    B. Perceptions and Attitudes Regarding Other Nations
        5. National Image Scale (Hurwitz, Peffley, & Seligson, 1993)
        6. Differential National Image Scale (Kurbanov & Robinson, 1997)
    C. Policy-Related Attitudes
        7. Militant and Cooperative Internationalism Scale (Wittkopf, 1990)
        8. Militant and Cooperative Internationalism Scales (Holsti & Rosenau, 1990)
        9. Militarism Scale (Peffley & Hurwitz, 1987)
      10. Attitude toward War Scale (Stagner, 1942)

Orientations toward Individuals' Own Nation

The empirical study of patriotism and nationalism dates back to the prewar era, while theoretical and conceptual (English language) treatments of these orientations can be traced back to the sixteenth century in English usage (see Sullivan *et al.,* 1992, for an overview of the historical changes in the treatment of patriotism). Clearly the measurement of patriotism–nationalism has been hampered by a lack of conceptual clarity and by a lack of consensus as to the meanings of these terms.

    While a complete clarification of these terms is beyond the scope of this chapter, it is essential at a minimum to provide the conventional distinction between the more emotional term *patriotism* on the one hand and the more cognitive term *nationalism* on the other. A standard dictionary definition of patriotism typically invokes a phrase such as "love of country," defining a patriot as "one who loves his country." The concept of patriotism, in other words, is a heavily affect-laden one that is closely related to the intensity of positive regard that a citizen holds toward his or her homeland.

    Nationalism on the other hand focuses on the implicit relative evaluation of one's country vis-à-vis foreign countries or international groups. *Webster's Dictionary,* for instance, defines the term as "a sense of national consciousness exalting one nation above all others and placing primary emphasis on promotion of its culture and interests as opposed to those of other nations or supranational groups." While affect is certainly an important component of nationalism (it seems unlikely that a highly nationalistic individual would not love his or her country), it is important to bear in mind the distinction Kosterman and Feshbach (1989) made between the patriot and the nationalist: The patriot does not *necessarily* consider his or her country to be superior to others. Moreover, the nationalist, unlike the patriot, generally advocates an international policy designed to promote the national interest of his or her country. In short, patriotism has conventionally been described in affective terms, while nationalism has typically been viewed as a cognitive set of beliefs in national superiority, together with a conative predisposition to advocate supporting policies.

    While this distinction is useful for the purpose of conceptual clarification, measurement scales do not always fall neatly within one of these two categories. One of the seminal measures of patriotism was formulated as one of three subscales of the Ethnocentrism Scale, developed by Adorno, Frenkel-Brunswick, Levinson, and Sanford (1950). The researchers' own definition of their concept—"blind attachment to certain national cultural values, uncritical conformity with the prevailing group ways, and rejection of other nations as outgroups" (Adorno *et al.,* 1950, p. 107)—clearly characterizes the scale as an amalgam of beliefs rather than as a simple affective orientation toward one's country (see also Levinson, 1957).

    On the other hand the Ferguson (1942) Nationalism Scale, as the name implies, represents an attempt to discern the respondents' belief that the United States is a country that is preferable to those in the communist world, though some of the questions tap affect-laden ties to the United States. This scale (included in the first edition of this volume [Robinson, Rusk, & Head, 1968]) is of historical interest in that it has been widely employed and cited.

The ANES Patriotism Scale on the other hand is perhaps the best current example of a purely affective measure of support for the United States. None of the scale items requires the respondent to pass judgment on another nation; rather, each item assesses a particular emotion (e.g., pride, anger, love) as applied to the United States and its various symbols.

The other three scales in this genre are explicitly multidimensional in nature, though quite different in execution and purpose. Kosterman and Feshbach (1989) factor-analyzed 120 relevant survey items to derive a six-factor solution, which they label Patriotism, Nationalism, Internationalism, Civil Liberties, World Government, and Smugness. While the first two factors (and perhaps the sixth) are obviously germane to the concepts, it is unclear whether the authors consider the Internationalism, Civil Liberties, and World Government factors as representing various dimensions of nationalism–patriotism or instead believe them to be policy preferences that happen to be empirically related to orientations toward the United States. In any event Kosterman and Feshbach (1989) contend that it is crucial for students of public opinion to be sensitive to the dimensionality problem of studying international orientations.

The Sullivan *et al.* (1992) treatment of patriotism is also multidimensional in approach, yet it differs fundamentally from the other scales in its self-conscious attempt to derive measures of patriotism that are based on the wide range of public definitions of the concept. Beginning with the assumption that patriotism has been frequently mislabeled to apply only to a chauvinistic, my-country-right-or-wrong mentality, the authors combed the conceptual literature and uncovered numerous and quite different meanings of the term—meanings that include not only an affective attachment, but also concepts such as commitment to the preservation of the land, loyalty for the regime, support for democratic principles and procedures, and love of free enterprise, among others. They then devised attitude scales to reflect each of these definitions, asking respondents to indicate the degree to which the scales' statements corresponded to patriotism, *as they would define it.* Sullivan *et al.* (1992) found that different individuals define patriotism in quite different ways, indicating that there are numerous different kinds of patriots in the public.

These three treatments of patriotism–nationalism are intended to give the reader a more contemporary sampling of the different approaches. As noted, readers interested in an early attempt to assess national orientations should consult the Ferguson (1942) scale. While dated, this influential index is important for the contrasts that it asks the respondent to draw between the U.S. and communist systems.

The final measure of interest here is the DeLamater, Katz, and Kelman (1969) National Involvement Scales, which attempt to distinguish between three mechanisms by which citizens can be attached to their country. Specifically the authors partition their items into a Symbolic Commitment scale (characterized by "strong emotional investment in the nation and its values and a positive affective orientation to its symbols"), a Normative Commitment scale ("an orientation toward the sanctions attached to the national role expectations as the individual perceives them"), and a Functional Commitment scale ("based on an instrumental relationship to the ongoing system—on the rewards he perceives as the outcome of participation in the system"). These scales represent a laudable attempt to unpack systematically the various conceptual sources and varieties of nationalism. While the scales appear face valid, they do suffer from low levels of reliability in terms of interitem correlations. It is their strong and valid conceptual development that warrants their inclusion here.

For measures of nationalism in a multiethnic context, Forbes (1985) has developed a set of scales designed to tap attitudes toward Canadian provincial orientations, especially views of provincial (Quebec) separatism, national unity, and Canadian versus Quebecois national identity. The abbreviated Ethnocentrism Scale of Hurwitz and Peffley (1987a) also requires explicit comparison between one's own and other systems, thus placing it under the label of nationalism as defined above. Researchers interested in a brief (four-item) inventory may find this scale useful. Although this short index has relatively low reliability, it was found to have desirable degrees of convergent and discriminant validity.

Perceptions–Attitudes Regarding Other Nations

Attitudes and beliefs about foreign countries have been linked to foreign policy preferences among both citizens (Hurwitz & Peffley, 1990; Peffley & Hurwitz, 1992) and elites (e.g., Herrmann, 1986). Although the explanations behind these linkages are varied, Hurwitz and Peffley contend that images (particularly of enemy nations) serve as a heuristic (cognitive shortcut) by which individuals derive their policy attitudes. Thus, just as many persons may formulate their racial policy positions based on their views of blacks (Sniderman & Tetlock, 1986), it has been argued that citizens operating in an environment of uncertainty and a shortage of information may base their foreign policy preferences on their judgments of the nations to which these policies are intended to apply.

A large number of formats have been used to assess reactions toward other nations. While many of these measures are purely affective in nature (such as the thermometer ratings of foreign countries and leaders included in the Chicago Council on Foreign Relations [CCFR] time-series), others are more cognitive in nature (i.e., stereotypic), in the sense that they gauge various beliefs and perceptions about foreign nations. Lambert and Klineberg (1967) used open-ended questions to investigate children's stereotyped images of 11 areas of the world; earlier Buchanan and Cantril (1953) examined adult Americans' stereotypes of the United States and the Soviet Union using 12 varied adjectives (see Bronfenbrenner, 1961, and Oskamp, 1965, for other influential studies of U.S. and Soviet images). More recent discussions of national stereotypes of and affective responses to other nations are contained in the *Journal of Social Issues* (1989, Vol. 45, No. 2), which is devoted entirely to articles on enemy images; the Yatani and Bramel (1989) review of Americans' attitudes toward the former Soviet Union is especially recommended. Also recommended is Part One of Kelman's (1965) *International Behavior: A Social Psychological Analysis.*

While assessments of national images are plentiful, it is difficult to evaluate the measurement properties of measures not utilized in ways that lend themselves to reliability analysis. While most of the measures of nationalism–patriotism rely on a multiple-indicator approach in which the internal consistency of the scale components can be estimated, the national image measures are ordinarily based on a single indicator. Thus, rather than relying on multiple indicators regarding a common attitude object, these measures typically employ a number of single items, each related to a different attitude object (i.e., country or leader). These measures, in other words, are designed to provide comparative judgments and evaluations across nations (or leaders) rather than to examine intensively the responses regarding a common object.

An important example of the comparative image measure can be found in Merritt's (1968) analysis of United States Information Agency (USIA) data collected in five western nations (France, West Germany, Italy, Great Britain, and the United States) and the Soviet Union. Merritt, who is concerned primarily with the degree to which one nation perceives another in terms of hostility, plots images in three-dimensional space: The first dimension is based on the hostility–friendliness perception, the second based on the

degree of "salience" or importance of a particular nation (based on the percentage of respondents with a "firm" opinion of that country), and the third corresponding to changes
in the friendliness and salience perceptions over time. The Merritt and Puchala (1968)
volume also describes the entire USIA survey with accompanying marginal results.

The most widely used and referenced comparative image measures have appeared on
the Chicago Council instrument, which is administered every fourth year. As noted, the
CCFR routinely asks respondents to rate a number of foreign countries on a feeling thermometer according to the degree of warmth felt for that nation. Ranging from 100 degrees
(maximum positive affect) to 0 degrees (maximum negative affect), respondent scores are
presumed to reflect a somewhat visceral emotional attachment toward foreign nations as
well as to provide useful evaluative comparisons between nations. Moreover, the CCFR
time-series permits useful over-time comparisons. Interested readers should consult the
series of reports by Rielly (1975, 1979, 1983, 1987) for details on these measures.

Given the importance of the former Soviet Union and the communist bloc during the
post–World War II era, it is not surprising that most of the multiple-indicator measures designed to gauge international images have been created to study foreign policy attitudes
toward the former Soviet Union and toward communism more generally (e.g., Hurwitz &
Peffley, 1990; Peffley & Hurwitz, 1992). The Soviet Image Scale designed by Hurwitz and
Peffley (1990; Peffley & Hurwitz, 1992) focuses on two attribute dimensions general to
"enemy" nations—belligerence and trust, both of which were found to be important determinants of attitudes toward national security issues; thus individuals who viewed the
Soviets as expansionist and dishonest were much more likely to adopt "hawkish" policy
stands than were those whose images were less enemy-oriented (Hurwitz & Peffley,
1990). Moreover, after Soviet President Gorbachev's peace initiatives of the 1980s, more
benevolent perceptions of this traditional U.S. "enemy" clearly anticipated a movement
toward more "dovish" public attitudes on a variety of national security issues (Peffley &
Hurwitz, 1992).

To the extent that national security concerns drive foreign policy agendas, "enemies"
are likely to be the focus of public attention. But the chief lesson of the collapse of the
Eastern bloc in terms of mass foreign policy attitudes is that a dynamic and multipolar
world requires a more general measurement strategy for tapping images of a variety of
different types of nations. Included in this chapter, consequently, is the Hurwitz, Peffley,
and Seligson (1993) National Image Scale, a context-free scale that is applicable to any
nation, regardless of its geographic location, form of government, historical conditions, or
leadership characteristics. The Kurbanov and Robinson (1997) scale uses the same basic
measurement approach to tap differences between images of one's own country and images of another.

Policy-Related Attitudes

Despite the attention paid to citizen evaluations and perceptions of nations, most research
on foreign affairs opinions has focused on attitudes and beliefs related to foreign policy.
Much of this work has examined attitudes on a variety of specific policy issues, such as
defense spending, support for particular weapon systems, willingness to employ U.S.
troops in various parts of the world, human rights, free trade, or foreign aid. As noted, we
focus instead on instrumentation designed to gauge opinions regarding more general or
abstract foreign policy views—views that transcend specific policies and are sufficiently
general to encompass a number of such specific policies.

Specific foreign policy attitudes are often found to be disorganized and unstable over
time (see, e.g., Converse, 1964; Converse & Markus, 1979; but see also Achen, 1975;
Feldman, 1989). More general foreign policy preferences, on the other hand, have been

found to exhibit greater stability (Peffley & Hurwitz, 1993) and, importantly, to constrain or predict attitudes on specific issues. Thus general orientations appear to play a more meaningful role in the cognitive structures of most citizens.

While specific foreign policy issues wax and wane in salience over time, general orientations do not. Thus attitudes toward the Strategic Defense Initiative or U.S. military involvement in Iraq—cases in which, in all likelihood, both the weapons and the site of conflict will change—are limited to specific circumstances.

For these reasons we focus on the most fundamental foreign policy decision that political elites must make, namely, whether to entangle a government in the affairs of another nation. Whether the nature of the entanglement is military or economic (or hostile or supportive), the decision to intervene is the most basic governmental choice in the domain of international relations. For citizens, consequently, the isolationism–internationalism dimension emerges as important in attempting to follow or influence governmental behavior.

An early attempt to measure internationalism–isolationism can be found in McClosky's (1967) Isolationism Scale (included in the first edition of this volume [Robinson *et al.*, 1968]), which he defines as a "sense of disengagement from other nations." The items in his index require the respondent to indicate support for various types of U.S. involvement with other nations, including military, economic, and diplomatic involvements. Implicit in both the scale and its scoring is the assumption that internationalism and isolationism lie on opposite ends of a single continuum. One who objects to an isolationist position, in other words, is dubiously assumed to be supportive of almost *any* type of intervention (i.e., economic, diplomatic, and militaristic) in world affairs.

More recent treatments of the concepts of isolationism and internationalism, however, have avoided such assumptions of unidimensionality and have instead adopted a multipolar perspective. While the various conceptualizations have differed in their particulars (see the *International Studies Quarterly* symposium issue [1986, Volume 30] for a review of this debate), they share a common contention that few individuals advocate internationalism as a generic principle; rather, citizens tend to support international engagements *of particular types,* while rejecting entanglements of other forms.

While the most heated debates in this recent literature have centered around the nature and number of dimensions necessary to describe international opinion adequately (e.g., Chittick & Billingsley, 1989; Mandelbaum & Schneider, 1979), there now appears to be some scholarly agreement on the utility of the framework developed by Wittkopf and his associates (e.g., Wittkopf, 1981, 1986, 1987, 1990, 1993; Maggiotto & Wittkopf, 1981; Wittkopf & Maggiotto, 1983). Maggiotto and Wittkopf (1981, p. 601) first describe the unidimensional internationalist–isolationist continuum as a "casualty of Vietnam," in the sense that after Vietnam, many former internationalists became more skeptical about U.S. involvement in other nations, while many former isolationists now saw particular advantages to involvement. More specifically, using Chicago Council data, the authors empirically presented a fourfold typology derived from the intersections of two orthogonal attitude dimensions: cooperative internationalism (CI) and militant internationalism (MI). The resultant types include (1) Internationalists (who support both militant and cooperative internationalism), (2) Isolationists (who support neither type of intervention), (3) Accommodationists (who favor cooperative, but not militant, intervention), and (4) Hardliners (who support militant, but oppose cooperative, intervention). In Wittkopf's analysis of the Chicago Council data series, in which masses and elites were interviewed every four years from 1975 to 1987, he finds considerable support for this fourfold typology and the dimensions on which it is based for both masses and elites across the 1975–1987 time period (see especially Wittkopf, 1986). While the 1990 version of Wittkopf's scale is included in this chapter, other permutations of Wittkopf's

CI–MI construct have been usefully employed by Hinckley (1988), Zeigler (1987), and others.

One characteristic of Wittkopf's particular operationalization of this typology is that the dimensions are measured by factor scores based on a principal-components analysis of Chicago Council items (included in this chapter). Although the 1990 Holsti and Rosenau survey measures of these dimensions use a different methodology and different data sources (the Foreign Policy Leadership Project [FPLP] surveys of foreign policy elites, who have been interviewed at four-year intervals since 1976), the authors find considerable support for the typology suggested by Wittkopf and his colleagues, both in the stable percentage of elites who fit the four types over time (a finding that concurs with Wittkopf's analysis of CCFR data) and in the distinctive international orientations of elites so characterized by the fourfold typology. The items measuring the two dimensions are reported here; for an insightful analysis of elite opinion spanning two decades of important change in the international environment, readers are referred to earlier works by Holsti and Rosenau (1984, 1986, 1988).

Implicit in these multidimensional conceptualizations of internationalism–isolationism, of course, is the assumption that levels of support for government action abroad depend on both a willingness to become entangled with other nations (in any form) and a relative preference for either military or nonmilitary orientations to the nation's foreign policy. Support for militant policy orientations thus became an important and fundamental component of a citizen's foreign policy belief system.

Measures designed for the express purpose of gauging preferences for, or aversions to, militaristic foreign policies have been used successfully over many decades. Readers interested in an early (prewar) instrument should consult the first edition of this volume (Robinson et al., 1968) for two early Attitude toward War scales by Day and Quackenbush (1942) and Putney (1962). In this chapter we conclude with another early Attitude toward War Scale (Stagner, 1942) as well as a more contemporary index developed by Peffley and Hurwitz (1987).

International Attitudes in the General Social Survey

The General Social Survey (GSS) has asked a number of individual questions on international attitudes since 1973, and these provide a comprehensive picture of the public's general international attitudes for over 8000 respondents (if only on specific individual items rather than scales). These GSS items can be grouped into three categories:

1. Expectations of war, mainly for a world war (since 1976)
2. Isolationism, in general and in terms of UN membership and rejection of communism as a system of government
3. Ratings of the public's liking of eight specific countries on 10-point rating scales (from +5 to −5)

The distribution of responses to and correlates of these questions since 1973 are shown in Figure 9–1 and Tables 9–1 and 9–2.

Across Time: Expectation of a world war was at 46% in 1986 and dropped to around 30% in 1989–1990, but it has risen back to about 46% since then. Expectations about smaller wars dropped to 57% in 1985 after reaching 74% in 1982; the question has not been asked since 1985. The proportion wanting to be internationally involved rose to 75%

Table 9–1

International Attitude Questions on the GSS

Q97. Do you expect the United States to fight in another war within the next ten years?

1. YES (62%)   2. NO (33%)   8. DON'T KNOW (5%)

(n = 9491)

Q98. Do you expect the United States to fight in another world war within the next ten years?

1. YES (41%)   2. NO (54%)   8. DON'T KNOW (5%)

(n = 9878)

Q99. Do you think it will be best for the future of this country if we take an active part in world affairs, or if we stay
out of world affairs?

1. ACTIVE PARTICIPATION (65%)   2. STAY OUT (31%)   8. DON'T KNOW (4%)

(n = 18,601)

Q100. Do you think our government should continue to belong to the United Nations, or should we pull out of it now?

1. CONTINUE TO BELONG (79%)   2. PULL OUT NOW (15%)   8. DON'T KNOW (6%)

(n = 17,963)

Q101. Thinking about all the different kinds of governments in the world today, which of these statements comes closest
to how you feel about Communism as a form of government? CODE ONE.

1. IT'S THE WORST ONE OF ALL   52

2. IT'S BAD, BUT NO WORSE THAN SOME OTHERS   28

3. IT'S ALL RIGHT FOR SOME COUNTRIES   15

4. IT'S A GOOD FORM OF GOVERNMENT   2

8. DON'T KNOW   3
                                                                  ─────
                                                                   100%

(n = 19,584)

Q103. You will notice that the boxes on this card go from the highest position of "plus 5" for a country which you *like* very much, to the lowest position of "minus 5" for a country you *dislike* very much. How far up the scale or how far down the scale would you rate the following countries? READ EACH ITEM.

	A. Russia (15,531)	B. Japan (15,564)	C. England (8196)	D. Canada (15,742)	E. Brazil (7497)	F. China (15,309)	G. Israel (15,202)	H. Egypt (14,899)
+5	3	8	20	40	6	5	12	6
+4	3	9	19	22	8	5	9	6
+3	10	20	24	18	15	11	14	12
+2	9	15	14	9	16	12	12	13
+1	18	19	13	8	28	22	19	26
−1	11	9	4	1	12	14	12	14
−2	6	5	2	1	5	8	6	7
−3	9	5	2	1	4	7	6	6
−4	5	4	1	*	2	5	3	3
−5	26	7	2	1	3	10	7	6
	100%*	100	100	100	100	100	100	100
% Positive	43	71	90	97	73	55	66	63
Average (1974–1994)	−1.5	1.3	2.8	3.6	1.4	−.2	1.2	0.8
Average (since 1990)	1.0	1.1	NA	3.5	NA	0	1.6	1.2

*Figures have been rounded and, therefore, do not add to 100%.

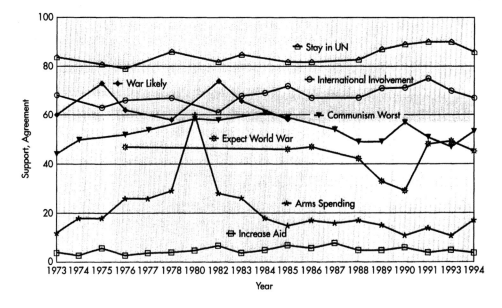

Fig. 9–1 GSS Trends in International Attitudes, 1973–1994

in 1991 (following the Gulf War and the fall of the Berlin Wall) after having dropped to only 61% in 1982. The percentage wanting to stay in the UN was also low in 1982 and also reached its peak of 91% in 1991, declining since then. The greatest opposition to communism was evident in the early 1980s, but has slipped to about 50% in the 1990s—although still above the 44% total opposition in 1973.

Much the same picture emerges for ratings of Russia, which were at their lowest point in the early 1980s (the time of the Flight 007 disaster); ratings for Russia have become about as positive as those for Japan in the 1990s. Japan has slipped some from its generally positive rating in the 1970s and 1980s. Even Canada is viewed less positively, and China is now viewed least positively—although still more positively than Russia was during the "Soviet detente period" of the 1970s.

By Gender: In general, male–female differences are not large, although women are slightly more likely to expect war, reject communism, be isolationist, and feel less positive toward Russia and Japan. However, they are more supportive of the United Nations.

Table 9–2
Demographic Correlates of International Attitudes (GSS 1973–1994)

	NAT ARMS	NAT AID	US UN	US INTL	US WAR	Communism
Sex	−.05**	.01	.02	−.09**	.02	.10**
Age	.07**	−.07**	−.09**	−.03	−.11	.14**
Race	−.05**	.10**	−.05**	−.13**	.12**	−.08**
Education	−.08**	−.04*	.13**	.24**	−.08**	−.15**
Party ID	.04*	−.01	−.01	.08**	−.07**	.02
Ideology	.09**	−.04*	.08**	.02	−.03	.14**

*p < .05
**p < .001

By Age: Young adults are more likely to express a range of responses than are older adults. Thus they are more likely to expect a war and to support foreign aid, but are much less opposed to communism and more opposed to the UN.

By Race: In general blacks express more isolationist attitudes and less UN support. They are much more likely to expect war, but less likely to oppose communism.

By Education: College-educated people are much more "open" in terms of their international attitudes, being twice as likely to take an activist stance than are those with no high school education and 20 points less fearful about war, the UN, and communism. They are far more positive toward Russia and Japan, but less positive toward China. These differences have remained about the same across the 20 years of GSS studies.

By Ideology: As might be expected, conservatives are 7–20 points more opposed to the UN and communism than are liberals and are less positive to Russia and Japan as well. However, on expectations of war and general isolationism, one finds surprising agreement between extreme liberals and conservatives.

By Party: In general, party differences are smaller than ideological differences, strong Republicans being more isolationist and opposed to communism than are Democrats or Independents; however, Democrats are more fearful of wars. Strong Republicans and strong Democrats emerge as more negative toward Russia and China.

Directions for Future Research

Despite the caveats issued at the start of this chapter about the dearth of foreign policy measures, substantial progress has been made over the past decade. Scholars are clearly convinced of the need to take a multidimensional approach to concepts such as patriotism and internationalism and, consequently, have developed measures capable of tapping more refined dimensions of these constructs. Methodological advances, such as those proposed in the Sullivan *et al.* (1992) patriotism measure, have made users more aware of the desired scientific properties of their measures.

However, more work is needed to improve the measurement in this domain. Most urgently needed since the dramatic realignment in the international arena that accompanied the collapse of the Soviet empire are instruments that reflect the current world situation. These need to be developed, and developed in such a way that they will not become as obsolete over time as those associated with a Cold War mentality became outmoded with the dismantling of the Soviet bloc. We have not seen many new instruments that reflect more current concerns, such as Middle Eastern hegemony, multinational corporations, international trade, European integration, or human rights and peacekeeping interventions in other countries.

An appropriate strategy would, therefore, be to develop measures of broad, abstract foreign policy dimensions that transcend specific nations or policies. The Wittkopf work on internationalism and the Hurwitz and Peffley work on militarism exemplify this approach, but other postures are surely important for structuring belief systems in the post–Cold War era, such as human rights and nationalism.

Further, standardized measures of national images are needed to tap the various attributes of salient world actors. As noted, most national image measures (e.g., the Chicago Council ratings of various countries) do not use a multiple-indicator approach, which would permit analysis of the multifaceted properties of these measures. And very few multiple-indicator measures exist beyond those developed to study perceptions of the former Soviet Union.

We need to develop, in other words, multi-item batteries that gauge perceptions and evaluations of nations that will still be relevant in the long run. Toward this end interested readers might consult the conceptual framework developed by Cottam (1977) and Herrmann (1985) for studying elite images of allies and enemies, or colonies and imperialist nations. Such images of these nations then need to be linked to the foreign policies associated with each country.

Finally there needs to be a greater focus on issues that are likely to have greater currency in the post–Cold War era, such as human rights, environmental degradation, and issues surrounding an international globalized economy.

Patriotism Scale
(ANES, 1987)

Variable

The Patriotism scale was designed to measure a "deeply felt affective attachment to the nation which constitutes the symbolic side of citizenship" (Conover & Feldman, 1987), a concept held to be distinct from "nationalism."

Description

Nationalism is seen as involving feelings of the superiority of one's own country relative to others. Hence a person may feel patriotic toward his or her country without feeling nationalistic. Patriotism was measured by eight items dealing with emotional reactions to the country and its symbols, such as the flag and the national anthem. All eight items were used in the 1987 ANES Pilot Study, and four have been included in subsequent ANES surveys (indicated on the scale with an asterisk).

Sample

The eight-item scale was administered to a random national survey of 360 respondents in the 1987 ANES Pilot Study. The abbreviated four-item scale was subsequently administered to the 1500 respondents included in the 1988 ANES survey. Both surveys are national probability studies.

Reliability

Internal Consistency

Cronbach's alpha for the eight-item scale is .86.

Test–Retest

No test–retest information was encountered.

Validity

Convergent

Responses to the Patriotism scale are correlated with a wide range of foreign policy attitudes, with more patriotic individuals being more anticommunist ($r = .43$) and militaristic ($r = .34$) and being more supportive of increasing defense spending ($r = .28$), building more nuclear arms ($r = .33$), and increasing U.S. military involvement in Central America ($r = .26$). An emotional attachment to national symbols is thus strongly associated with more conservative or "hard-line" foreign policy views.

Discriminant

As noted, the Patriotism scale is most highly correlated with anticommunism, which may be viewed as evidence either for the tendency for in-group loyalty to translate into out-group hostility or for the fact that those who feel the strongest attachment to national symbols perceive the greatest threat to national security from an alien and hostile system. The relationship between patriotism and opinions on specific national security issues would seem to be indirect, mediated by militarism and anticommunism, since the zero-order correlation between patriotism and most national security issues all but disappears when the effects of these two general orientations are partialled out.

Location

The items were first reported in a memo written by Conover and Feldman (1987), "Measuring Patriotism and Nationalism," to the National Election Studies Board of Overseers (obtainable from ANES). Also see the analysis of this scale compared to alternative measures of patriotism in Sullivan *et al.*'s Twin Cities survey, reported in Sullivan *et al.* (1992), "Patriotism, Politics, and the Presidential Election of 1988," *American Journal of Political Science, 36,* 200–234 (reviewed in this chapter).

Results and Comments

With only a few exceptions, responses in the 1987 survey were skewed toward the most patriotic response, with large majorities of Americans reporting feeling either "extremely" or "very" with respect to the following: "proud to be an American" (92%), "good to see the American flag flying" (87%), "proud when you hear the national anthem" (85%), and "strong respect for the United States" (71%). Conover and Feldman (1987) noted that it seems unlikely that a change in question format would produce more evenly distributed responses, since the concept of patriotism is so laden with social desirability bias.

As the review of Sullivan *et al.*'s (1992) work demonstrates, "love of country" may be defined quite differently by survey respondents as well as scholars. It is perhaps not surprising that when patriotism is defined as an emotional and unthinking attachment to national symbols, "patriots" are found to be more conservative generally and to take a more militant hard line on foreign policy. Defined differently (e.g., as a love of country based on its commitment to individual freedoms), the resulting measure of patriotism would doubtless produce a very different set of "patriots" with different views in foreign affairs.

One may adopt the strategy of Sullivan *et al.* (1992) and survey respondents' subjective meanings of patriotism. Alternatively one may simply relabel the ANES measure as emotional or symbolic patriotism, with the knowledge that it taps a severely restricted definition of patriotism that does not apply to all individuals. Adopting the latter course raises questions about the conceptual overlap between concepts like patriotism, which are defined as a form of "diffuse" support for one's nation, and specific support for incumbent presidents and their policies, since pride in one's country is likely to be dependent on what kind of policies the government is pursuing and how well it solves national and international problems (e.g., Easton, 1965). For example, in the 1987 ANES survey, patriotism was associated with positive thermometer ratings of President Ronald Reagan ($r = .31$). While this relationship might be expected, given President Reagan's repeated emphasis of patriotic themes, it also raises questions about the degree to which measures designed to tap diffuse, unconditional support for the country also reflect more specific support for the incumbent president and his policies.

Patriotism Scale
(ANES, 1987)

1. How strong is the respect you have for the United States these days . . . EXTREMELY STRONG, VERY STRONG, SOMEWHAT STRONG, OR NOT VERY STRONG?

2. How angry does it make you feel when you hear someone criticizing the United States . . . EXTREMELY ANGRY, VERY ANGRY, SOMEWHAT ANGRY, OR NOT VERY ANGRY?

*3. How proud are you to be an American . . . EXTREMELY PROUD, VERY PROUD, SOMEWHAT PROUD, OR NOT VERY PROUD?

4. How angry does it make you feel when people burn the American flag in protest . . . EXTREMELY ANGRY, VERY ANGRY, SOMEWHAT ANGRY, OR NOT VERY ANGRY?

*5. How good does it make you feel when you see the American flag flying . . . EXTREMELY GOOD, VERY GOOD, SOMEWHAT GOOD, OR NOT VERY GOOD?

*6. How strong is your love for your country . . . EXTREMELY STRONG, VERY STRONG, SOMEWHAT STRONG, OR NOT VERY STRONG?

7. How mad do people who sell government secrets make you feel . . . EXTREMELY MAD, VERY MAD, SOMEWHAT MAD, OR NOT VERY MAD?

*8. How proud do you feel when you hear the national anthem . . . EXTREMELY PROUD, VERY PROUD, SOMEWHAT PROUD, OR NOT VERY PROUD?

*Indicates item was included in the abbreviated Patriotism scale in the 1988 ANES.

Patriotism–Nationalism Questionnaire

(R. Kosterman & S. Feshbach, 1989)

Variable

This measure is explicitly designed to capture the multidimensionality of the constructs of patriotism ("feelings of attachment to America"), nationalism ("the view that America is superior and should be dominant"), and internationalism ("attitudes toward other nations"), among other beliefs.

Description

The authors assembled 120 five-point Likert-format opinion statements (response options: *Strongly Agree, Moderately Agree, Neutral, Moderately Disagree,* and *Strongly Disagree*) that were deliberately designed to "assess various dimensions believed to contribute differentially to patriotism and nationalism" (Kosterman & Feshbach, 1989, p. 262). While approximately half of the items were devised by the authors, the rest were taken—either conceptually or verbatim—from extant measures, including 30 from the National Involvement Scales of DeLamater *et al.* (1969), 9 from Ferguson's (1942) Nationalism Scale, 6 from Campbell's (1973) Foreign Policy Scale, 6 from the Human Loyalty Expressionnaire (Lentz, 1976), 5 from Loh's (1975) Nationalism Scales, 5 from the Worldmindedness Scale (Sampson & Smith, 1957), 4 from Comrey and Newmeyer's (1965) Radical–Conservatism Scale, 2 from Levinson's (1957) Internationalism–Nationalism Scale, and 1 from Stagner's (1940) Survey of Opinions on Methods of Preventing War. Several items were modified or reversed in direction in order to balance the scales and avoid response acquiescence. Respondents completed the written questionnaire in approximately 30 to 40 minutes and were informed that the survey concerned "the United States in general and its role in international affairs."

All items were subjected to an iterated principal-component factor analysis (varimax rotation). A six-factor solution emerged, and factors were defined by selecting items loading above a specified criterion value ($\pm.50$ for factors 1, 2, 3, and 5; $\pm.45$ for factor 4; and $\pm.40$ for factor 6). In several instances items loading below these threshold values were added to improve scale balance in the event that highly loading items loaded in a consistent direction.

The emergent factors are labeled

1. *Patriotism:* affect for America or "my country";
2. *Nationalism:* an "America-first" or "American superiority" view relative to other countries;
3. *Internationalism:* concern for global welfare versus concern for taking care of America's problems first;
4. *Civil Liberties:* the right to hold beliefs critical of one's country;
5. *World Government:* support for international (or transnational) authority and government; and
6. *Smugness:* the belief that "America, its symbols, and its people are simply 'the best.' "

Sample

The 120-item questionnaire was administered to a total (nonprobability) sample of 239 subjects from three different populations: 194 were students at the University of California at Los Angeles (106 females and 88 males), 24 were high school students from a "small town in Washington state" (12 females and 12 males), and 21 were from an association of building contractors from Washington state (14 males and 7 females). While those from the last group ranged in age from 21 to over 50 years old, 89% of the students were under 21 years old. While the small sizes of two of the subsamples precluded comparisons of the factor structures among the three groups, the authors report that a "separate factor analysis . . . carried out only for the college student sample . . . yielded very similar findings to the analysis based on the entire sample" (Kosterman & Feshbach, 1989, p. 263).

Reliability

Internal Consistency

The authors report alpha coefficients for the six subscales as Patriotism = .88, Nationalism = .78, Internationalism = .87, Civil Liberties = .74, World Government = .81, and Smugness = .77.

Test–Retest

No test–retest information was encountered.

Validity

Convergent

Given the authors' purpose of establishing the multidimensionality of patriotism–nationalism, most of their effort with regard to validation is an attempt to demonstrate differential performance of the various subsamples. The authors neither argue nor attempt to establish as fact that the separate subscales form a coherent measure of a single construct. Using analysis of variance, however, the authors do establish theoretically consistent relationships between partisanship and scale responses, with Democrats scoring significantly higher on the Internationalism, Civil Liberties, and World Government subscales and significantly lower on the Patriotism, Nationalism, and Smugness subscales.

Discriminant

As noted, most of the attention is devoted to establishing that the six subscales tap different dimensions of the construct and, consequently, are associated with different criteria. Toward this end the authors present interfactor correlations that, they claim, demonstrate a high degree of orthogonality.

Factors	2	3	4	5	6
1	.28	−.17	−.24	−.28	.15
2	—	−.18	−.23	−.18	.33
3	—	—	.28	.29	−.08
4	—	—	—	.25	−.02
5	—	—	—	—	−.04

The authors also demonstrate discriminant validity using a modification of White and Feshbach's (1987) Nuclear Policy Questionnaire, which measures three "factors": attitudes toward the Soviet Union, negative attitudes toward people supporting a nuclear freeze, and attitudes regarding the survivability of a nuclear war. Among the other findings, the authors stress that Nationalism, but not Patriotism, is very closely associated with the Nuclear Policy Questionnaire, which they take as evidence that the two are "functionally different psychological dimensions" (Kosterman & Feshbach, 1989, p. 272). Further, even though Nationalism and Internationalism are not conceptualized as opposite poles on the same dimension, the authors conclude that "each of the positive correlations of the Nationalism factor with the Nuclear Policy scale and subscales is counterbalanced by negative correlations of similar magnitude of the Internationalism factor with these subscales" (p. 272).

Location

Kosterman, R., & Feshbach, S. (1989). Toward a measure of patriotic and nationalistic attitudes. *Political Psychology, 10,* 257–274.

Results and Comments

While the authors have made a conscious attempt to develop a multidimensional measure of patriotism–nationalism, they do not address the issue of whether the various component dimensions share sufficient commonality that they address a common construct. Whether the six subscales tap six different constructs or instead measure six different components of the same construct is an unanswered question. Further, if the authors advocate the latter interpretation, they do not identify the nature of the construct that allegedly integrates the individual factors.

Patriotism–Nationalism Questionnaire (Kosterman & Feshbach, 1989)

Factor I: Patriotism

*10. I love my country. (.73)

25. I am proud to be an American. (.69)

76. In a sense, I am emotionally attached to my country and emotionally affected by its actions. (.67)

39. Although at times I may not agree with the government, my commitment to the U.S. always remains strong. (.63)

113. I feel a great pride in that land that is our America. (.63)

29. It is not that important for me to serve my country. (−.61)

23. When I see the American flag flying I feel great. (.61)

9. The fact that I am an American is an important part of my identity. (.57)

48. It is not constructive for one to develop an emotional attachment to his/her country. (−.52)

7. In general, I have very little respect for the American people. (−.50)

20. It bothers me to see children made to pledge allegiance to the flag or sing the national anthem or otherwise induced to adopt such strong patriotic attitudes. (−.49)

50. The U.S. is really just an institution, big and powerful yes, but just an institution. (−.46)

Factor II: Nationalism

28. In view of America's moral and material superiority, it is only right that we should have the biggest say in deciding United Nations policy. (.59)

88. The first duty of every young American is to honor the national American history and heritage. (.55)

2. The important thing for the U.S. foreign aid program is to see to it that the U.S. gains a political advantage. (.54)

85. Other countries should try to make their government as much like ours as possible. (.54)

92. Generally, the more influence America has on other nations, the better off they are. (.52)

40. Foreign nations have done some very fine things but it takes America to do things in a big way. (.52)

34. It is important that the U.S. win in international sporting competition like the Olympics. (.50)

67. It is really not important that the U.S. be number one in whatever it does. (−.37)

Factor III: Internationalism

44. If necessary, we ought to be willing to lower our standard of living to co-operate with other countries in getting an equal standard for every person in the world. (.68)

74. The alleviation of poverty in other countries is their problem, not ours. (−.66)

103. America should be more willing to share its wealth with other suffering nations, even if it doesn't necessarily coincide with our political interests. (.64)

93. We should teach our children to uphold the welfare of all people everywhere even though it may be against the best interests of our own country. (.59)

32. I would not be willing to decrease my living standard by ten percent to increase that of persons in poorer countries of the world. (−.57)

110. Children should be educated to be international minded—to support any movement which contributes to the welfare of the world as a whole, regardless of special national interests. (.56)

84. The agricultural surpluses of all countries should be shared with the have-nots of the world. (.54)

78. The position a U.S. citizen takes on an international issue should depend on how much good it does for how many people in the world, regardless of their nation. (.51)

116. Countries needing our agricultural surpluses should pay for them instead of getting something for nothing. (−.40)

Factor IV: Civil Liberties

57. A person who preferred jail to serving in the U.S. Army could still be a good American. (.50)

17. A person who does not believe in God could still be a good American. (.49)

4. A person who believes in socialism could still be a good American. (.49)

12. A person who doesn't stand when the Star Spangled Banner is being played could still be a good American. (.47)

102. It is O.K. to criticize the government. (.46)

109. We should have complete freedom of speech even for those who criticize the country. (.46)

49. People who do not want to fight for America should live somewhere else. (−.37)

Factor V: World Government

60. All national governments ought to be abolished and replaced by one central world government. (.65)

56. I am not willing to surrender my allegiance to my country in order to give it to a world authority represented by all nations. (−.56)

58. We should immediately take steps toward establishing a world government. (.55)

100. We should give the United Nations more power. (.53)

55. The U.S. should never give up its military power to a strong world government. (−.52)

18. I could never be as loyal to a world government as I am to my national government. (−.52)

Factor VI: Smugness

114. I would never settle in another country. (.46)

21. The American flag is the best in the world. (.43)

15. I think the American people are the finest in the world. (.42)

26. America is the best country in the world. (.42)

*Numbers prior to items indicate the placement of the statement on the 120-item questionnaire. Parenthetical entries reflect the items' factor analytic loadings (varimax rotation) on the relevant factors. Readers should consult Kosterman and Feshbach (1989, pp. 264–268) for each item's loadings on the other five factors.

Patriotism Scale
(J. L. Sullivan, A. Fried, E. Theiss-Morse, & M. Dietz, 1992)

Variable

The Sullivan *et al.* (1992) measure of patriotism differs from traditional treatments in its multidimensional rejection of the ANES assumption that patriots differ from nonpatriots only in their levels of affective attachment toward their nation.

Description

Rather than imposing a set definition of the concept on respondents, the authors' approach explicitly permits respondents to conceptualize patriotism in different ways. The various understandings of the construct, consequently, are determined, at least in part, by respondents, not totally by the researcher.

Beginning with the assumption that patriotism has been frequently mislabeled to apply only to a chauvinistic, "my-country-right-or-wrong mentality," the authors combed the conceptual literature and uncovered numerous and quite different meanings of the term—meanings that include not only an affective attachment ("Instinctive Patriotism"), but also concepts such as a commitment to the preservation of the land ("Environmental Patriotism"), a belief that one's country has a special character ("American Exceptionalism"), a loyalty for the regime ("Institutional Patriotism"), a support for democratic principles and procedures ("Democratic Patriotism"), a love of free enterprise ("Liberal, Capitalist Patriotism"), and "a commitment to the whole of humankind and a loyalty to world order and peace" ("Supra-Nationalist Patriotism").

They then devised 49 statements to reflect each of these conceptions and asked respondents to indicate the degree to which these statements correspond to patriotism, *as they tend to see it.* Subjects of their Q-methodology (see Brown, 1980) study were asked to judge the degree to which each statement reflects their own understanding of patriotism, sorting the items into 1 of 11 piles labeled "most patriotic" to "least patriotic."

A Q-factor analysis program (QUANAL) was used to group respondents with shared perspectives regarding patriotism, deriving a factor solution that becomes increasingly differentiated to the degree that different types of individuals hold different perspectives on the construct. The authors' analysis yielded a five-factor solution (so labeled when the eigenvalue for the factor exceeded 1.0):

Type 1. *Iconoclastic Patriotism:* Distinguished by a strong reaction against purely symbolic and emotional appeals, this conception "does not associate patriotism with wearing the military uniform, flying the flag or celebrating the Fourth of July." Rather, these individuals contend that "patriots who love their country must work toward economic and political change. . . ."

Type 2. *Symbolic Patriotism:* These patriots have a strong, affective bond with their country, combined with a positive orientation toward traditional patriotic symbols (e.g., the flag) and a high level of chauvinism.

Type 3. *Instinctive Environmental Patriotism:* Distinguished "by a tendency to see people who despoil the environment for profits as traitors" and emphasizing love and preservation of land in addition to love of country, these people also share with symbolic patriots a positive attachment to patriotic symbols.

Type 4. *Capitalistic Patriotism:* Defined "as much by economic as by political heroes," this perspective blends economic growth with love of country; the "conquest of nature and development of natural resources seem to be viewed as viable expressions of patriotic devotion."

Type 5. *Nationalistic Symbolic Patriotism:* This perception is distinguished from Symbolic Patriotism by an assumption that one's nation is clearly "at the top of God's current order." (These persons refuse to reject, for example, the view that "[w]henever there are strong differences of opinion between the United States and the Soviet Union, we are always right and they are always wrong. We almost seem destined to be favored by God to be on the right side.")

In the table of items, 11 statements are designated as distinguishing statements (selected by QUANAL "if the ranking of the statement by one type was at least one standard deviation away from the average of all other types"). Such items most clearly differentiate one type of patriot from all others.

Sample

A group of 43 diverse subjects participated in the initial item sorting for the purpose of identifying differing perspectives, including students at the University of Minnesota (students from a left-wing campus organization, R.O.T.C., the Minnesota Public Interest Research Group, and Students for Freedom and Democracy [a right-wing organization] and nonactivist students) and community members (from the Veterans of Foreign Wars, the Unitarian–Universalist Church, and a local labor union). In their effort to validate their interpretations of the resultant factors from their Q-study, the authors then administered the 11 unique items (which distinguish each view of patriotism) to a probability sample of approximately 400 individuals in the Minneapolis–St. Paul, Minnesota, area. Respondents were assigned to a particular patriotism perspective "based on the match between their response profile and each of the five perspectives." Respondents were assigned to a perspective on patriotism as follows: They were assigned to the iconoclastic perspective if they agreed with four of the five unique responses for Iconoclastic Patriotism (statements 1, 2, 11, 36, and 39); if they agreed with statements 16 and 39, they were classified as symbolic patriots; with statements 10, 29, and 39, they were classified as instinctive environmental patriots; with three of the four statements (10, 17, 21, and 39), they were classified as capitalistic patriots; and with statements 32 and 39, they were classified as nationalistic symbolic patriots. In the sample, 16, 38, 31, and 16% were classified as iconoclastic, symbolic, instinctive environmental, and capitalistic patriots, respectively. Only one respondent (who was eliminated from subsequent analyses) was classified as a nationalistic symbolic patriot.

Reliability

Internal Consistency

The traditional meaning of internal consistency is not germane to these measures because the construct is assumed to be interpreted differently by different individuals. Thus the various items are not expected to converge to measure a common construct.

Test–Retest

No test–retest data were encountered.

Validity

Convergent

Support for the validity of the types was derived from a number of survey-based findings. Iconoclastic patriots, for example, are significantly more participatory—including both conventional and unconventional (e.g., protest activities) behaviors—than are others.

Instinctive environmental patriots are (not significantly) more participatory than either symbolic or capitalistic patriots. Thus the two types most emphatic about the importance of activism do in fact exhibit higher levels of political participation.

Second, as expected, iconoclasts are far less likely to report flying the flag or attending patriotic parades, relative to others. And third, the authors report voting patterns in the 1988 election consistent with their expectations: Given candidate George Bush's emphasis on "flag waving patriotism" during the campaign, it is not surprising that symbolic patriots reported stronger support for Bush than did other types, with iconoclasts predictably being least supportive. (The associations were found in fully specified models that controlled for a variety of potentially spurious associations.) Importantly, the traditional ANES patriotism measure (which comes close to measuring symbolic patriotism) does not predict the vote choice.

Location

Sullivan, J. L., Fried, A., Theiss-Morse, E., & Dietz, M. (1992). Patriotism, politics, and the presidential election of 1988. *American Journal of Political Science, 36,* 200–234. Reprinted by permission of the University of Wisconsin Press.

Results and Comments

It is inappropriate to apply traditional standards of classical test theory to these measures of patriotism. Q-methodology compares individuals' overall response profiles rather than variables in identifying alternative understandings of patriotism. Because of the multiplicity of meanings, a given measure of patriotism does not discriminate between those who are "high" and those who are "low" on the construct. While researchers may want to use some of the items below to begin the process of constructing scales that assess various components of patriotism, these items are not currently suited for this purpose.

Patriotism Scale
(Sullivan, Fried, Theiss-Morse, & Dietz, 1992)

	Patriotism Type[1]				
	1	2	3	4	5
1. No one can convince me that Ollie North and the rest of the Contragate crew are true patriots. They may think that what they did was good for the country, but they just trampled all over the law and the Constitution.	+3*	−3	−1	−1	−2
2. Wearing the uniform of the United States is a great privilege. To serve in the armed forces is the ultimate expression of loyalty to our country.	−3*	+2	+2	+3	+4

3. America is special because of its willingness to accept immigrants fleeing persecution, seeking freedom, and struggling to establish new lives. No other country in the world is as open to the people of other lands as we are. People everywhere want to become U.S. citizens.   −1   +1   +5   +4   +4

4. Powerful corporations and the military have asserted too much power in recent years. We have a responsibility to rebuild our democratic processes and institutions in ways that limit their power and reassert the authority of the citizens.   +2   0   0   −2   −2

5. The major advantage of being an American is that we can afford to have so many nice things and to live a comfortable life. The rest of the world could too, if they would only follow our example and let freedom and capitalism have a chance in their countries. It is therefore our responsibility to let the rest of the world know about our successes and to learn from them.   −4   −2   −1   −1   −1

6. For heavens sake, what is so glorious about the geography of a country or where its boundaries happen to be drawn? A nation's territory is a matter of luck and circumstance. Its true glory (or shame) rests in the political values and ideals it cherishes and preserves, and in the political life it offers its citizens.   0   +1   +3   +1   0

7. A patriotic attitude is something that must be developed with a lot of thought and hard work. It cannot be merely a gut reaction based on simple emotions learned at an early age.   +4   +1   −3   −1   +1

8. It is the fashion to speak of the United States as "the greatest nation on earth" and as the "leader of the free world." But such words encourage us to idolize rather than scrutinize our political practices and principles.   +1   −2   0   −5   −3

9. I love my country because of the way I was brought up. I was taught to respect and care for it, just like the way I learned that it's not right to steal.   −2   +2   +1   +2   +5

10. Those who exploit our natural resources for profit do not act in the true spirit of this country. They are destroying our most precious heritage and it is not too extreme to call them traitors.   +1   −1   +4*   −3*   0

11. America has failed to fulfill its promise to its citizens. The poor and the underprivileged are not treated equally with the rest of us. Good citizens must therefore work to change the economic and political systems in order to provide the benefits of our wealth to more of our citizens.   +2* 0 −5 −5 −5

12. This country is my home. I can't imagine feeling as comfortable anywhere else. I also can't imagine living anywhere else.   −1 +2 +1 +3 +1

13. In America, our hard work has created a nation second to none. We are more powerful than any nation on earth, and if more countries begin to imitate us, they can reap the same rewards.   −4 +1 −4 −4 +1

14. The Constitution, as originally written, does not present an especially strong vision of democracy. It is not the original document which should be celebrated, but the amendments and the people who fought to extend freedom and rights to women and minorities. +2   0 +2   0 −2

15. We must insist that our children and grandchildren shall inherit a land which they can truly call America the beautiful. Prosperity should not be purchased by poisoning the air, the rivers, and the natural resources that are the greatest gift of this country.   +2 +3 +4 +3 +1

16. The way I feel about my country has little or nothing to do with complicated ideas. It's very close, deeply emotional, and nearly instinctive—like how a parent feels about an infant or how that child feels about that parent.   −1 +3* +2   0 −2

17. In my mind the giants of American industry, such as John D. Rockefeller, Henry Ford, and Andrew Carnegie were patriots as great as Washington, Jefferson, and Lincoln.   −3 −4 −4 +2* −3

18. Simple patriots are not equal to such tasks as nuclear disarmament and world peace. They are too narrow in their loyalties. We need internationalists, people with broader views.   0 −4 −4 −2 −5

19. We must stand by our country, but that does not mean we must always support, condone, participate in or refuse to criticize wrongful actions and policies of our country. Where such wrongful actions and policies harm the country, to support and participate in them would be to act against, not for, the good of the country.   +4 +2 +1 +4 +2

20. In this Bicentennial year of the Constitution, we must remember our great founders, who gave us a special document that created political institutions that are stable, yet able to deal with changing circumstances. Our political system is so special because of its system of checks and balances, where no one segment—whether the President and the executive branch, the Congress, or the Courts—takes all the power.   +2 +3 +3 +2 +4

21. It is just fine to talk about protecting our environment, but as good Americans we must take a broader view. In order to have enough economic development and jobs for our people, we must be willing to accept some damage to our environment.   −2 −3 −1 +3* −3

22. Patriotism is not an expression or a feeling, but rather a way of being and acting, as a citizen. Patriotism is active participation in political affairs, engagement with others in the public realm.   +4 +4 −1 +4 +2

23. I think the American people are pretty much like people anywhere. But our land is exceptional. It is the most beautiful and special land in the world and anyone who inherited it could have made it work and would have become a great people.   −1   0 −4 −2 −3

24. A patriot's basic focus should be his or her local community. The nation is too large and too complex for people to make much of a difference, and is too remote to feel close to.   −2 −4 −2   0 −4

25. We can enter the next century having achieved a level unsurpassed in history if we guarantee that government does everything possible to promote America's ability to compete.   −2   0 +1   0   0

26. Many Americans think they are a free and happy people. What they fail to realize is that their fate is dependent on the fate of all people on earth and they cannot be truly free and happy in the long run until they begin to help the other people on earth.   +3   0   0 +1 −2

27. I just can't help it. I don't like or trust the Russians and I think every good American should feel that way.   −5 −5 −3 −3 +1

28. Elegance is the word for the American Midwest—enormous plains of beautifully inlaid rectangles, the grain running different ways, walnut, satinwood, or oatcake, the whole of it tortoiseshelled with thickets and shadows of clouds.   0   −2 +2   0   0

29. Our political leaders have not worked hard enough to achieve peace and human rights in the world. All Americans must put pressure on them to work harder toward peace and human rights, and people who do nothing about it are not good citizens.   +1 −1 +3* −2 −2

30. The great gift of the Constitution of the United States is the economic freedom it promises and protects—free trade, free commerce, free enterprise. These are among the most valuable legacies of our Founding Fathers.   0   +3 −2 +1 +3

31. Handling scandals like Watergate and the Iran–Contra affair honestly and openly, without letting our Presidents off the hook, is one of the things that makes this country great. It proves we are a nation committed to the rule of law and to democracy.   +3 +1 +4   0 +3

32. Whenever there are strong differences of opinion between the United States and the Soviet Union, we are always right and they are always wrong. We almost seem destined to be favored by God to be on the right side.   −5 −5 −5 −5   0*

33. Symbols such as flags, national songs, nationalistic statuary, and so on can be very dangerous. They can be used to arouse people emotionally and to get them to do irrational things in order to demonstrate their love of country.   0   −5 −3 −1 −4

34. Nationality is just a state of mind and should not be all that important to people. Americans should think of themselves as citizens of the world first and citizens of the U.S. only secondarily.   0   −1 −3 +1 −5

35. Loss of our national past is a supreme human tragedy, and we Americans have forgotten our past. With the failure to remember comes our failure to understand what belonging to our country truly means. An intimate knowledge of American history and democratic political traditions is essential for all true patriots so that freedom might flourish.   +1 +4   0 +2 +5

36. When I see Old Glory flying on the Fourth of July, or watch our veterans march in the Memorial Day parades, or sing the Star Spangled Banner with thousands of other Americans, I know the true meaning of patriotism.   −3* +4 +4 +2 +2

37. Many Americans make it easy for our government to interfere in their lives. They do so out of a mistaken belief that their government is all good and all-knowing. In fact, the government often gets things wrong and creates more problems than it solves.   0 −1 +1 −2 −1

38. It's things like freedom of religion and freedom of speech that makes this country great. An individual doesn't have to go to church or agree with government officials to be considered a good American.   +5 +4 −5 +5 +2

39. It is important not to accept all government decisions as valid. Some are unjust and should be protested or met with civil disobedience. If unjust decisions become the rule, then the government and its officials should be toppled.   +3* −2* +3* −4* −4*

40. Oliver North is a true patriot because he realizes that, in this dangerous world, we have to do everything possible to combat our nation's enemies. People who do not agree with him and fail to support the contras are not patriotic Americans.   −5 −3 0 −3 −1

41. The United Nations is a dangerous force in the world today. It is attempting to promote the idea of "one world" and trying to destroy Americans' love for their own country.   −4 −4 +1 −4 0

42. A good American today is someone who buys American made products, rather than foreign goods made with cheap labor.   −2 −1 −2 −4 0

**43. The greatness of our country depends on a sense of community and a spirit of cooperation and toleration, which can be developed by active participation by all citizens.   +5 +5 +5 +4 +5

44. During times of conflict between the President and Congress on foreign policy, we the people should rally around the President because he is elected by all the people and has the interests of our great nation at heart. Congress, on the other hand, is merely concerned with special interests and getting reelected.   −4 −3   0 −3 −1

**45. The true patriot is the person who tries to make the government do what is right and live up to its ideals, by contacting government officials, working in political campaigns, or voting.   +4 +5 +5 +5 +4

46. To understand the glory of America, just remember that we were the first nation on earth to land a man on the moon. Whenever we do something first or best, I feel a surge of pride that reminds me that the U.S.A. is number one.   −3 +2 −2 −1 +2

**47. In America, disagreement with the policies of the government is not evidence of lack of patriotism. Indeed, it's the very fact that Americans can openly criticize their government, openly and without fear or reprisal, that is the essence of our freedom and that will keep us free.   +5 +5 +2 +5 +3

48. The U.S. has made its share of mistakes, just as other nations have. Because of our great power, our mistakes have had more disastrous consequences.   +1 −2   0   0 −4

49. When Americans go overseas, they feel homesick for our beautiful country—for its cosmopolitan cities, its lush farmlands, its lofty mountains and shining seas. There is no place on earth as beautiful, as spectacular, as diverse, as the United States.   −1   0 −2 +1 +3

[1]Type 1 = Iconoclastic Patriotism; type 2 = Symbolic Patriotism; type 3 = Instinctive Environmental Patriotism; type 4 = Capitalistic Patriotism; type 5 = Nationalistic Symbolic Patriotism.

*Unique (or distinguishing) statements significantly distinguish the type in question from the other perspectives; the ranking of the statement by one type is one standard deviation or more from the average ranking of all other types.

**Consensual items are accepted by all types; Z-scores of the rankings for all types are within one standard deviation.

National Involvement Scales

(J. DeLamater, D. Katz, & H. C. Kelman, 1969)

Variable

These scales represent an attempt to separate three different mechanisms by which an individual can be nationalistic: symbolic (by national symbols), normative (by rewards and sanctions), and functional (by material benefits).

Description

The three mechanisms follow from Katz and Kahn's (1966) distinctions among the major means by which a role system is integrated: through values, norms, and roles. Below are some of the different orientations that are hypothesized to be associated with each role:

Attitude toward	Symbolic	Normative	Functional
1. Flag, leaders, etc.	Strong and positive	Mild positive	Low
2. Role of an "American"	Most important to learn and low tolerance	As important as other roles	In terms of political and social responsibilities
3. Criticism of American way of life	Defensive and hostile		Tolerated if in the national interest
4. Extending American way of life	Approve	Disapprove because want to preserve	Only if in other countries' national interest
5. Policies that might weaken U.S. power	Oppose	Accept if agreed on by national leaders	Support if in national interest
6. Involvement in political life		Passive (as reflected in their political apathy)	Active (as reflected in their greater participation)

Initially, 15–20 items tapping each orientation were included in the interview schedule, but only those were finally included that either (1) correlated at the .05 level with one other item or (2) seemed on an a priori basis to tap the aspect in question. Eight items remained in the symbolic and normative scales and six in the functional scale. Items on each scale employ a variety of question formats. The score categories and the percentage of the sample falling into each score category are as follows:

Score Category	Symbolic	Normative	Functional
High	5–8 (28%)	4–5 (19%)	3–5 (26%)
High-medium	3–4 (28%)	3 (23%)	2 (23%)
Low-medium	1–2 (22%)	1–2 (38%)	1 (35%)
Low	−4–0 (22%)	−4–0 (20%)	0 (16%)
	100%	100%	100%

Sample

A probability sample of 129 residents of Ann Arbor, Michigan, was used. People affiliated with the University of Michigan were excluded from the sample.

Reliability

The following average interitem correlation coefficients (phi) were obtained (with values of .17 being significant at the .05 level for this size sample):

> Symbolic   .16
> Normative   .11
> Functional .08

The correlations among the three scales were .19 between symbolic and normative, −.11 between normative and functional, and −.11 between functional and symbolic.

Validity

As might be expected, there was a strong relation between education and type of role involvement. While 84% of the Functional group had been to college, only 40% of the Normative group and 0% of the Symbolic group had. The same relation held in terms of fathers' education—47% of the Functional group had fathers who had been to college, as compared to 30% of the Normative group and 14% of the Symbolic group. Other indirect evidence of validity is provided by the verbal behavior of the various types of respondents when asked open-ended questions about political issues and events. For example, the Symbolic group was especially likely to report strong affect (e.g., anger, sorrow) as their reaction to the assassination of President John Kennedy. These respondents also placed the highest value on children's learning to be "good Americans" and were least tolerant of deviation from role prescriptions (e.g., by not believing in God or being an ex-Communist). On the other hand the Normative group members (mainly working-class people) were most likely to feel that violators of norms are not "good" Americans, mentioning interpersonal morality as something "a person ought to do to be a good American." They are most likely also to accept government policies that are generally agreed on.

Finally, those in the Functional group were better informed politically, more likely to stress helping one's fellow man as a value in child-rearing, more favorable toward the United Nations, more favorable toward disarmament and international negotiation, and least likely to do nothing if a dictatorship came to power in the country.

Location

DeLamater, J., Katz, D., & Kelman, H. C. (1969). On the nature of national involvement: A preliminary study. *Journal of Conflict Resolution,* 13:320–357.

Results and Comments

As the authors note, this is a pilot study conducted with a relatively small sample. Undoubtedly, controls for education (possible with a larger sample) would result in considerably attenuated relations from those found here. For now, these scales constitute a most interesting way of conceptualizing educational differences in the manner in which people identify themselves with their country.

Symbolic Commitment Scale
(DeLamater, Katz, & Kelman, 1969)

1. "Suppose a person criticizes the government in time of national crisis. In your opinion, could he be a good American?"
    Could be; yes (0)
    Depends: on kind of criticism, nature of crisis (0)
    No, unqualified (1)

2. "Suppose a person doesn't stand when the Star Spangled Banner is being played. Do you think he could be a good American?"
    Yes, unqualified (−1)
    Yes, if he had a reason—physical, religious (0)
    No, qualified (1)
    No, unqualified (2)

3. "Do you happen to own a flag?"
    Yes (1)
    No (0)
    Other: once did, NA (0)

    (For those who own a flag) "Do you ever display it on national Holidays?"

    Always; yes (1)
    Usually; sometimes (1)
    Never; no (0)
    Other: inappropriate (0)

4. "Some observers have complained that the American public nowadays does not pay proper respect to the American flag. Would you agree or disagree with this complaint?"
    Agree (1)
    Disagree (0)
    Other (0)

5. "What would you think of an American who says that he takes no particular pride in our armed forces?"
    Approve; he has a right to say that (−1)
    Indifferent; nothing; don't know (0)
    Disapprove, general (1)
    Disapprove: not a good American (0)
    Other (0)

6. "Imagine the American Peace Corps comes up in a conversation between yourself and a foreigner and he laughs at it. How do you think you would react when this occurs—would you regard this as:
    An insult (1)
    A sign of poor taste (0)
    An opinion to which he is entitled (0)

7a. "How would you feel if a foreigner criticized racial segregation in the U.S.?"

An insult; poor taste; would be mad (1)*
He is wrong; would argue with him (0)
Depends: where he's from, what he says (0)
An opinion to which he's entitled (0)
Would like to talk to him (0)
He is right; would agree with him (0)
Other (0)

7b. "How would you feel if a foreigner attacked the free enterprise system?"

8. "Whereas some people feel that they are citizens of the world, that they be-
long to mankind and not to any one nation, I, for my part, feel that I am first,
last, and always an American." Do you:
Strongly agree (1)
Slightly agree (0)
Slightly disagree (−1)
Strongly disagree (−2)

*One point only if coded in this category on both items.

Normative Commitment Scale
(DeLamater, Katz, & Kelman, 1969)

1. "What do you think a person ought to do in order to be a good American?"
Mentioned formal requirements: vote, pay taxes, serve in Army, support
constitution (1)
Did not mention the above (0)

2. "What do you think a person ought to do in order to be a good American?"
Mentioned conformity to norms: obey laws, be honest, stay out of
trouble, do the right things, be loyal, live properly, live a clean life, etc.
(1)
Did not mention the above (0)

3. "Some people say that a person should go along with whatever his country
does even if he disagrees with it. How do you feel about that?"
Agree, unqualified; he should (1)
He should go along with majority (1)
Has no choice, has to go along (1)
Depends: on the issue, the person (0)
Disagree: he has a right to criticize (0)
Disagree: government could be wrong (−1)

4. "Suppose a law was passed raising income taxes by fifty percent. Would
you:
Pay the tax without question (1)
Refuse if others did (0)
Refuse regardless of what others did (−1)

5. "Suppose a law was passed requiring all citizens to be fingerprinted and to
carry identity cards. Would you:
Obey without question (1)
Refuse if others did (0)
Refuse regardless (−1)

6. "Serve in the armed forces."
   Government should require people to (0)
   Government should encourage people to (−1)
   Government should leave to the individual (−2)

7. "Pay taxes."
   Government should require people to (0)
   Government should encourage people to (−1)
   Government should leave to the individual (−2)

8. "Send their children to school."
   Government should require people to (0)
   Government should encourage people to (−1)
   Government should leave to the individual (−2)

Functional Commitment Scale
(DeLamater, Katz, & Kelman, 1969)

1. "What are some of the things that particularly remind you that you are an American?"
   Mentioned opportunity: affluence, standard of living, free enterprise; accomplishment, progress (1)
   Did not mention the above (0)

2. "What do you think a person ought to do in order to be a good American?"
   Mentioned participation: be informed, participate in public affairs, use citizenship rights, take part in community, vote intelligently, etc. (1)
   Did not mention the above (0)

3. "Are there any people you know or have heard about who you think are *not* good Americans?"
   Mentioned apathetic persons: people who don't appreciate what they have, our opportunities; people who don't accept their responsibilities as citizens (1)
   Did not mention the above (0)

4. "What do you think people mean when they talk about the American way of life?"
   Mentioned affluence: high standard of living, free enterprise, freedom (defined in terms of consumption), security, happiness (1)
   Did not mention the above (0)

5. "What do you think are the most important things that make America different from other countries?"
   Mentioned opportunity: advancement, chance to get ahead (1)
   Did not mention the above (0)

6. "What do you think are the most important things that make America different from other countries?"
   Mentioned affluence: high standard of living, ease of living, convenience; modern civilization; industrialization; free enterprise (1)
   Did not mention the above (0)

National Image Scale

(J. Hurwitz, M. Peffley, & M. A. Seligson, 1993)

Variable

The National Image Scale was designed to measure public perceptions of the properties of other nations in a way that permits both intensive analyses of images of one nation and comparisons of images across nations.

Description

The authors used nine semantic differential scales to tap citizen perceptions of a certain nation. The purposes of the scale are threefold: (1) to tap national images in a manner that is sufficiently generic so that it can be applied to *any* nation, regardless of geographic location, form of government, historical condition, or leadership characteristics; (2) to investigate intensively the various image dimensions of a given nation; and (3) to compare images *across* nations along particular image dimensions.

Respondents to the paper-and-pencil questionnaire were asked to respond to nine bipolar adjective pairs, with each pair separated on a five-point scale. (Pretesting revealed the five-point dimensions to be more reliable than analogous seven-point scales.) In order to make the comparative judgments across nations more explicit, respondents were asked to rate all nations (in this case, the United States, Cuba, and Nicaragua) on each adjective pair question before moving on to the next adjective pair question.

Two different versions of the National Image Scale have been employed. (1) The full scale consists of nine adjective pairs that tap both internal and external characteristics of the nation. (2) The more restricted seven-adjective version eliminates two adjective pairs that assess the internal images (i.e., "repressive–free" and "authoritarian–democratic") and retains only the characteristics relevant to the external traits of the nation—traits that both theoretically and empirically are more closely related to the judgments of the nation held by a citizen of a different country. Scale scores range from 9 (low image) to 45 (high image).

Sample

Hurwitz *et al.* (1993) report findings from a probability sample in the greater metropolitan region of San Jose, Costa Rica, conducted by the Department of Statistics at the University of Costa Rica. In-home personal interviews were conducted with 597 adults in October and November of 1990.

Reliability

Internal Consistency

Cronbach's alpha for the nine-item comprehensive scale ranges from .90 (Nicaragua) to .89 (Cuba) to .83 (United States). Reliability for the seven-item external trait scale ranges from .88 (Nicaragua) to .87 (Cuba) to .81 (United States). While such reliability estimates are obviously inflated by response set on the part of respondents, such bias should be minimal given the strategy of forcing respondents to apply an adjective pair to each country before proceeding to the next adjective pair.

Test–Retest

No test–retest data were encountered.

Validity

Convergent

The authors' intention in the study was to explore the linkage between a Costa Rican citizen's image of a foreign country and policies related to that country. Consequently only the external trait scales were employed in the analysis. In LISREL models, images of the United States were found to be highly related to attitudes toward foreign policies pertaining to the United States, in that Costa Ricans with more positive perceptions of the United States were significantly more likely to support Costa Rica's asking the United States to deploy soldiers to help combat drug trafficking and to support the U.S. invasion of Panama to capture General Manuel Noriega (b = .41)—even after controlling for a number of other political orientations and values. Similarly perceptions of Cuba were found to be strongly related (b = .48) to support for initiating trade relations between Costa Rica and Cuba.

Discriminant

In support of the discriminant validity of these measures, the authors report that images of Nicaragua are not significantly predictive (at the .01 level) of policies related to either the United States or Cuba and that U.S. images are unrelated to Cuban trade policy, while Cuban images are not linked to U.S.-related policies.

Location

Hurwitz, J., Peffley, M., & Seligson, M. A. (1993). Foreign policy belief systems in comparative perspective: The United States and Costa Rica. *International Studies Quarterly,* *37,* 245–270.

Results and Comments

With the end of the Cold War, images of the primary U.S. postwar antagonist (i.e., the Soviet Union) no longer have the dominant importance in foreign policy belief systems that they once had. Consequently it is important to develop generic measures of international images that permit investigators to explore perceptions of any nation. Toward this end the authors investigated the international perceptions of Costa Ricans and found them to play an important role in guiding foreign policy attitudes of the citizens. Although the scales have not been evaluated outside of Costa Rica, more widespread analysis of national images can be easily obtained using the method. Interested readers should consult the conceptual framework developed by Cottam (1977) and Herrmann (1985, 1988) for studying *elite* images of various countries using this basic approach.

National Image Scale
(Hurwitz, Peffley, & Seligson, 1993)

*1. Trustworthy   ___ ___ ___ ___ ___   Not Trustworthy

  2. Dishonest   ___ ___ ___ ___ ___   Honest

  3. Repressive   ___ ___ ___ ___ ___   Free

*4. Friend   ___ ___ ___ ___ ___   Enemy

*5. Responsible   ___ ___ ___ ___ ___ Irresponsible

  6. Aggressive   ___ ___ ___ ___ ___   Peaceful

*7. Good   ___ ___ ___ ___ ___   Bad

  8. Authoritarian ___ ___ ___ ___ ___ Democratic

  9. Threatening   ___ ___ ___ ___ ___   Not Threatening

*Item reversed before scaling.

Differential National Image Scale

(E. Kurbanov & J. Robinson, 1997)

Variable

This scale was designed to measure general images and perceptions of one's country relative to other countries, using a series of semantic differential scales.

Description

Based on a factor analysis of pilot scale image dimensions, the authors chose 10 items to reflect two main dimensions of the semantic differential, namely, evaluative (good–bad) and potency (strong–weak). Six items tap the evaluative dimension and four the potency dimension, using five-point rating scales.

The overall scale score is based on the differences between the rating of one's own country and that of a comparative country. With six items and five points per scale, evaluation scores can range from 30 (completely positive) to 6 (completely negative) for any country. The differential image is thus the difference between the score for one's own country and that for some other country; to the extent that one's own country is seen more positively, higher positive scores will be obtained—negative scores are possible if the other country is rated more positively than one's own. Scores can thus range from +30 to −30.

Sample

Data have been collected from national probability surveys of 1000–2000 high school students in 12 of the 15 former republics of the Soviet Union using these scales between 1993 and 1997. Earlier comparable data are available from urban samples in most of these countries.

For illustrative purposes data are presented from the 1996 Ukrainian national sample of 2046 students aged 13–17. The overall score was 2.1, but it varied as follows, depending on the respondent's ethnic identification:

	Means	n	sd
Very strong Ukrainian	9.3	(569)	1.4
Strong Ukrainian	5.8	(651)	1.8
Not strong Ukrainian	6.8	(411)	1.5
Not strong Russian	−2.1	(111)	2.6
Strong Russian	−2.4	(102)	1.8
Very strong Russian	−6.1	(54)	2.4

Reliability

Internal Consistency

The average interitem correlation for the six evaluative items is .36 and for the four potency items .17. Both factors emerged for ratings of Russians and for ratings of Ukrainians.

Test–Retest

No test–retest data are available.

Validity

Convergent

The demonstrated monotonic relation with one's ethnic identification provides a basic indicator of the ethnic identity of one's parents and of the language mainly spoken (Russian or Ukrainian). The scale also correlated with a separate set of scales asking how much each nationality group was liked.

Discriminant

The differential potency ratings correlate only .11 with the evaluation ratings, indicating that the latter ratings are not a function of differences in how rich or free respondents see these peoples as being.

Location

Kurbanov, E., & Robinson, J. (1997). *Differential ethnic images within the former Soviet Union.* Paper presented at the annual meeting of the American Sociological Association, Toronto, Canada.

Results and Comments

The items have been asked about one's own and the major minority group (as well as about Americans) in each former Soviet republic. In general, ratings of Russians in each republic were higher than Russians gave to each of these respective nationalities; that is, native Russians rate Uzbeks lower than native Uzbeks rate Russians.

Differential National Image Scale
(Kurbanov & Robinson, 1997)

Please check one position on each of the following scales to reflect how you feel about that national/ethnic group:

Russians

1. Friendly	:__:__:__:__:__:	Unfriendly
2. Hardworking	:__:__:__:__:__:	Lazy
3. Peaceful	:__:__:__:__:__:	Aggressive
4. Willing to help others	:__:__:__:__:__:	Indifferent to others
5. Open	:__:__:__:__:__:	Not open
6. Trustworthy	:__:__:__:__:__:	Untrustworthy

Ukrainians

1. Friendly	:__:__:__:__:__:	Unfriendly
2. Hardworking	:__:__:__:__:__:	Lazy
3. Peaceful	:__:__:__:__:__:	Aggressive
4. Willing to help others	:__:__:__:__:__:	Indifferent to others
5. Open	:__:__:__:__:__:	Not open
6. Trusworthy	:__:__:__:__:__:	Untrustworthy

Cooperative and Militant Internationalism Scale
(E. R. Wittkopf, 1990)

Variable

Designed to tap the "two faces" of internationalism, this measure posits two orthogonal dimensions: Cooperative Internationalism (CI) and Militant Internationalism (MI). The intersection of the CI and MI continua yields a fourfold typology: Internationalists (proponents of both types of internationalism), Isolationists (opponents of both types), Hardliners (supporters only of MI), and Accommodationists (supporters only of CI).

Description

Proponents and opponents of these two faces of internationalism are assumed to differ in their attitudes toward communism, the use of military force, and relations with the Soviet Union, with the Hardliners being most adamant, the Internationalists least adamant, and the others in between. The author analyzed more than 300 items on the quadrennial (1974,

1978, 1982, and 1986) Chicago Council on Foreign Relations surveys. (Because of space constraints, we present only the most recent [i.e., 1986] indices; interested readers can consult Wittkopf, 1990, for prior scales.) Wittkopf first constructed subscales consisting of items closely related in a substantive sense. Where possible, the author attempted to attain reliability coefficients for each subscale of .7 or above (although this criterion was not adhered to in every instance) and deleted questions that depressed alpha levels.

For the 1986 study, six subscales were formed, of which 1, 3, and much of 4 are too dated for current use.

1. *Active Cooperation–Apartheid:* The United States should pursue an active role in world affairs, but with an emphasis on cooperative ties with other nations. (For the 1986 scale only one item—an apartheid question—was used because CCFR included only a small number of more general active cooperation items, and these did not contribute to a reliable scale.)
2. *Communist:* The larger the number of nations that become communist, the more threatened would be American interests.
3. *Detente:* Closer ties between the United States and the Soviet Union are desirable.
4. *Troops:* Some circumstances might justify the use of U.S. troops abroad.
5. *U.S. Goals:* The goals of American foreign policy should embrace a wide range of security and nonsecurity issue areas.
6. *Vital Interests:* The United States has vital interests in many countries.

In prior years the Chicago Council study also included questions pertaining to both military and economic aid, and Wittkopf, consequently, was able to construct scales germane to these issue areas. Aid items were not, however, included on the 1986 survey. Wittkopf (1990) describes the measurement properties of these military and economic aid items.

Wittkopf performed a principal-component factor analysis of the scale scores (rather than of the individual items) and, for 1986, extracted a two-factor solution (though solutions differed slightly for data from previous years). The Communist, Troops, U.S. Goals, and Vital Interests subscales loaded at .76, .68, .71, and .56, respectively, on factor I; the Detente and Active Cooperation–Apartheid items, on the other hand, loaded at only −.03 and .07 on this factor. The Detente and Active Cooperation–Apartheid subscales loaded at .78 and .73, respectively, on factor II, with the other subscales loading as follows: Communist (−.05), Troops (−.10), U.S. Goals (.07), and Vital Interests (.26). To determine a respondent's MI and CI scale scores, Wittkopf multiplied the respondent's score on each of the six subscales by the loading weight of each scale. (Thus these loadings are only applicable to the 1986 survey; loadings for previous years are presented in Table 2.3 (Wittkopf, 1990, p. 24).

Sample

The data are from the Chicago Council on Foreign Relations national probability surveys of the mass public conducted in 1974, 1978, 1982, and 1986. The sample size and weighted *N,* from which Wittkopf worked, for the 1986 sample are 1585 and 2872, respectively.

Reliability

Internal Consistency

The author reports alpha coefficients for all subscales employing multiple indicators.

	No. of Items	Alpha
Active Cooperation–Apartheid	1	—
Communist	6	.84
Detente	6	.55
Troops	11	.82
U.S. Goals	14	.80
Vital Interests	22	.76

Test–Retest

No explicit test–retest information was encountered. The CCFR conducts repeated cross-sectional (rather than panel) surveys. Even though Wittkopf reports a high degree of response stability across surveys, this finding is not intended as a report on item reliability for three reasons: (1) Different respondents were interviewed for each survey, (2) items often changed—in either format or substance—between surveys, and (3) environmental changes between surveys were often sufficiently profound to encourage intersurvey response patterns, irrespective of question reliability.

Validity

Convergent

Convergent validity of the MI and CI measures is demonstrated to the extent that the subscales differentiate respondents in their attitudes toward communism, the use of military force, and relations with the Soviet Union. Toward this end Wittkopf demonstrates proponents of MI (i.e., Internationalists and Hardliners) to be substantially more supportive of using U.S. troops abroad in a variety of situations relative to opponents of MI (Accommodationists and Isolationists) (1990, Table 2.4) and also to feel a higher level of threat "if communists came to power" in a number of countries (1990, Table 2.6). Advocates of CI (Internationalists and Accommodationists) were found, compared to opponents of CI (Hardliners and Isolationists), to be more likely to support nonmilitary relations with the Soviet Union, such as arms control agreements, cultural and educational exchanges, grain sales, and trade promotion (1990, Table 2.7).

Discriminant

Wittkopf demonstrates (1990, Table 3.4) that both the CI and the MI dimensions are strongly and positively associated with the belief that it is best if the United States takes an active part in world affairs, indicating that while CI and MI supporters differ in their preferred methods of international relationships, they concur that an active U.S. role is essential.

Location

Wittkopf, E. R. (1990). *Faces of internationalism: Public opinion and American foreign policy.* Tables A.1.2, A.1.3, A.1.4, A.1.7, A.1.8, A.1.10 (pp. 240–243, 247, 248, 250, 251, 253, 254). Durham, NC: Duke University Press. Copyright 1990, Duke University Press. Reprinted with permission. This work presents and extensively discusses the measures. Previous analyses using the same CI–MI perspective with earlier CCFR data sets can be found in Wittkopf (1987) and Wittkopf and Maggiotto (1983), as well as in several other articles attributed to Wittkopf in the References section. For a replication of the CI–MI typology in the post–Cold War era, see Wittkopf (1993).

Results and Comments

The CI–MI perspective on foreign policy beliefs has influenced a number of different researchers. See especially Hinckley (1988) and Zeigler (1987) for applications.

Cooperative and Militant Internationalism Scale (Wittkopf, 1990)

Apartheid

Which of the statements on this card comes closest to your view of how the United States should respond to the situation in South Africa?

	Percent
We should support the South African government.	8
We should take no position.	23
Don't know	12
We should impose limited economic sanctions if the South African government does not dismantle its apartheid system.	28
We should ban all trade with or investment in South Africa if the South African government does not dismantle its apartheid system.	28

Note: The item was reversed before being used as a scale.

Communist

I am going to read a list of countries. For each, tell me how much of a threat it should be to the U.S. if the communists came to power. First, what if the Communist party came to power in. . . . Do you think this would be a great threat to the United States, somewhat of a threat to the United States, not very much of a threat to the United States, or no threat at all to the United States?

	Great Threat	Somewhat of a Threat	Don't Know	Not Very Much of a Threat	No Threat at All
El Salvador	27	43	9	17	4
France	30	38	6	18	8

Saudi Arabia	39	35	9	12	5
Mexico	62	18	5	10	5
Philippines	37	35	7	15	6
South Africa	21	40	9	22	8

Detente

Relations between the Soviet Union and the United States have been the subject of disagreement for some time. Please tell me if you would favor or oppose the following types of relationships with the Soviet Union.

	Favor	Not Sure/ Don't Know	Oppose
*Restricting U.S.–Soviet trade	37	11	52
Sharing technical information with the Soviet Union about defending against missile attacks	23	10	67
*Prohibiting the exchange of scientists between the U.S. and the Soviet Union	36	11	53
Negotiating arms control agreements between the U.S. and the Soviet Union	81	7	13
Resuming cultural and educational exchanges between the U.S. and Soviets	78	7	15
Increasing grain sales to the Soviet Union	57	12	31

*Items were reversed in creating the scale.

Troops

There has been some discussion about the circumstances that might justify using U.S. troops in other parts of the world. I'd like to ask your opinion about several situations. [W]ould you favor or oppose the use of U.S. troops if . . .

	Favor	Not Sure/ Don't Know	Oppose
Japan were invaded by the Soviet Union	53	10	36
The Nicaraguan government allowed the Soviet Union to set up a missile base in Nicaragua	45	13	42
The Arabs cut off all oil shipments to the U.S.	36	12	51
North Korea invaded South Korea	24	12	64
The government of El Salvador were about to be defeated by leftist rebels	25	19	56
Iran invaded Saudi Arabia	26	15	59
Arab forces invaded Israel	33	14	54

The People's Republic of China invaded Taiwan	19	17	64
Soviet troops invaded Western Europe	68	8	24
The Soviet Union invaded the People's Republic of China	27	12	61
Nicaragua invaded Honduras in order to destroy Contra rebels' bases there	24	16	60

U.S. Goals

I am going to read a list of possible foreign policy goals that the United States might have. For each one please say whether you think that should be a very important foreign policy goal of the United States, a somewhat important foreign policy goal, or not an important goal at all.

	Very Important	Somewhat Important	Not Sure/ Don't Know	Not Important
Containing communism	57	30	4	9
Helping to improve the standard of living of less developed countries	37	50	4	9
Worldwide arms control	69	22	4	6
Defending our allies' security	56	36	4	5
Securing adequate supplies of energy	69	25	3	3
Helping to bring a democratic form of government to other nations	30	48	5	17
Protecting the interests of American business abroad	43	42	4	12
Protecting the jobs of American workers	78	18	2	3
Matching Soviet military power	53	34	4	9
Combating world hunger	63	31	3	4
Strengthening the United Nations	46	33	5	16
Reducing our trade deficit with foreign countries	62	26	7	5
Promoting and defending human rights in other countries	42	45	4	10

Protecting weaker nations against foreign aggression	32	54	6	8

Vital Interests

Many people believe that the United States has a vital interest in certain areas of the world and not in others. That is, certain countries of the world are important to the U.S. for political, economic or security reasons. I am going to read a list of countries. For each, tell me whether you feel the U.S. does or does not have a vital interest in that country.

	Does	Don't Know	Does Not
Italy	41	21	38
Egypt	61	19	20
West Germany	77	13	10
Iran	50	15	34
Japan	78	12	11
Mexico	74	12	14
Israel	76	13	11
Syria	48	20	33
India	36	22	42
Canada	78	11	11
Brazil	44	25	31
Great Britain	83	6	11
Saudi Arabia	77	9	14
China (PRC)	60	13	27
France	56	13	31
Taiwan (Formosa)	53	19	28
South Korea	58	16	26
Poland	35	22	43
South Africa	59	12	30
Nigeria	31	27	42
Philippines	73	10	16
Nicaragua	60	15	25

Militant and Cooperative Internationalism Scales

(O. R. Holsti & J. N. Rosenau, 1990)

Variable

The authors rely on Wittkopf's (1990) definitions of Militant Internationalism (MI) and Cooperative Internationalism (CI) to create four types: *hard-liners, internationalists, isolationists,* and *accommodationists.*

Description

Holsti and Rosenau (1990) used batteries of items from their quadrennial surveys of American leaders on foreign policy (the 1976, 1980, and 1984 Foreign Policy Leadership Project surveys) to measure both types of internationalism. Militant Internationalism and Cooperative Internationalism are assumed to correspond closely to two basic views or theories of international affairs: *Realism* (corresponding to MI) views conflict (and warfare) among nations as natural, fixed, and zero-sum, while *idealism* (corresponding to CI) views international conflict as manageable if nations emphasize cooperation through mechanisms such as institution building, improved international education and communication, and trade.

Like Wittkopf, the authors assume the two constructs are superordinate dimensions that organize and constrain more specific foreign policy attitudes. Unlike Wittkopf, however, who factor-analyzed indices of batteries of items to *induce* the superordinate dimensions, Holsti and Rosenau (1990) measured the dimensions *directly,* using correlational methods to verify the existence and validity of the two dimensions. By relying on different data and different measurement procedures, Holsti and Rosenau thus provide a stringent "test" of the applicability of Wittkopf's scheme as well as providing survey items that might be adapted for use in mass surveys.

The seven items used to measure MI and the seven items used to measure CI rely on two different formats—a standard Likert format, where respondents are presented with statements and asked how much they agree or disagree on a four-point scale, and a format where respondents indicate whether they think various goals are very important, somewhat important, or not important. Responses are summed over the items in the scale.

Sample

The FPLP surveys of 1976 ($N = 2282$), 1980 ($N = 2502$), and 1984 ($N = 2515$) were long questionnaires covering a broad range of foreign policy issues mailed to an elite range of American leaders whose names were listed in *Who's Who* and other directories. Return rates averaged between 53 and 63% (for further details on the sampling design, questionnaires, and respondents, see Holsti, 1985).

Reliability

Internal Consistency

The average correlations among the MI scale items in the three surveys range from .41 to .43, with Cronbach's alpha ranging between .83 and .84 across the surveys. The mean correlation for the CI scale is .35 in each of the surveys, with an alpha coefficient of .79 for all three surveys.

Test–Retest

Because the surveys are cross-sectional, this information was not available (though see Holsti and Rosenau, 1984, for an examination of continuity and change in these items over the 1976 and 1980 cross-sections).

Validity

Convergent

Validity assessments were conducted by first classifying respondents into the four groups mentioned earlier, with (1) *hard-liners* supporting MI and opposing CI, (2) *internationalists* supporting both MI and CI, (3) *isolationists* opposing both MI and CI, and (4) *accommodationists* opposing MI, but supporting CI. In keeping with the associations outlined earlier between MI and the "realist" perspective and between CI and the "idealist" perspective, the four types were found to differ significantly in their general beliefs about the causes of war and ways to prevent it. For example, hard-liners and internationalists—that is, those with a favorable attitude toward militant internationalism—ranked national aggression and nationalism as more important causes of war than did other groups. Even more striking were differences in the evaluations of different approaches to peace, with U.S. military superiority being the only approach given strong support by hard-liners (who also rejected approaches supported by accommodationists, such as implementing arms control, narrowing the gap between rich and poor nations, and strengthening the UN). Moreover, the four groups differed significantly in their attitudes on specific foreign policy issues assessed in the three surveys.

The political and demographic characteristics of the four groups also differed in expected ways, with hard-liners much more likely to be Republicans, conservatives, military officers, and business executives and accommodationists more likely to be Democrats, liberals, educators, clergy, and media leaders. In contrast, internationalists and isolationists were marked by an absence of distinguishing background characteristics.

Discriminant

An assessment of the performance of the two scales vis-à-vis other dissimilar constructs was not encountered.

Location

Holsti, O. R., & Rosenau, J. N. (1990). The structure of foreign policy attitudes among American leaders. *Journal of Politics, 52,* 94–125. Reprinted by permission of the authors and the University of Texas Press. All rights retained by the University of Texas Press.

Results and Comments

The Holsti–Rosenau (1990) measures of militant and cooperative forms of internationalism (and the scheme by Wittkopf on which their measures are based) represent a vast improvement over traditional measures of isolationism–internationalism, which assumed that isolationism and internationalism were two poles on opposite ends of a single continuum.

Moreover, the authors realize that these two separate dimensions of internationalism do not subsume all important international attitudes and that the content and meaning of the dimensions may change over time. This would certainly be true in the post–Cold War period for their obsolete Militant Internationalism scale, given that their scale is defined largely by beliefs about containing communism and the Soviet Union.

Obviously some adjustments would be necessary to adapt the items for use in a mass survey. Nevertheless, as the Holsti–Rosenau and Wittkopf studies demonstrate, some of the better theoretical studies in this area have examined elite foreign policy belief systems, and the interested reader is encouraged to examine this important literature (such as in Kegley's 1986 review article).

Militant and Cooperative Internationalism Scales (Holsti & Rosenau, 1990)

Militant Internationalism Scale

1. There is considerable validity in the "domino theory" that when one nation falls to communism, others nearby will soon follow a similar path.[a]
2. Any communist victory is a defeat for America's national interest.[a]
3. The Soviet Union is generally expansionist rather than defensive in its foreign policy goals.[a]
4. There is nothing wrong with using the C.I.A. to try to undermine hostile governments.[a]
5. The United States should take all steps including the use of force to prevent the spread of communism.[a]
6. Containing communism (as a policy goal).[b]
7. It is not in our interest to have better relations with the Soviet Union because we are getting less than we are giving to them.[a]

Cooperative Internationalism Scale

1. It is vital to enlist the cooperation of the U.N. in settling international disputes.[a]
2. The United States should give economic aid to poorer countries even if it means higher prices at home.[a]
3. Helping to improve the standard of living in less developed countries (as a foreign policy goal).[b]
4. Worldwide arms control (as a foreign policy goal).[b]
5. Combatting world hunger (as a foreign policy goal).[b]
6. Strengthening the United Nations (as a foreign policy goal).[b]
7. Fostering international cooperation to solve common problems, such as food, inflation, and energy (as a foreign policy goal).[b]

[a]Scale: 1. AGREE STRONGLY to 4. DISAGREE STRONGLY.
[b]Scale: 1. VERY IMPORTANT to 3. NOT IMPORTANT AT ALL.

Militarism Scale

(M. Peffley & J. Hurwitz, 1987)

Variable

This scale taps a general desire for the government to assume an assertive posture in foreign affairs emphasizing military strength versus a more flexible, accommodating stance through negotiations.

Description

Of the five items used to tap this dimension, the first two are five-point branching scales posing a trade-off between "toughness" and "flexibility" in dealing with other countries and between an emphasis on military strength versus an emphasis on negotiation as the preferred method of keeping peace. The next two items are five-point Likert scales that measure the extent to which respondents agree that we should go to the brink of war to preserve our country's military dominance and that the only way to resolve disputes with other countries is through negotiation. The final item is a four-point scale that asks how important it is that the United States is militarily strong enough to get its way with its adversaries.

Peffley and Hurwitz (1987) note that while it is possible for respondents to find both alternatives presented in the first two branching items—being tough *and* flexible, emphasizing strength *and* negotiations—desirable, the *relative emphasis* that people attach to each of the poles of these two scales is highly predictive of attitudes on specific foreign policy issues.

Sample

The first three items in the Militarism Scale were developed through extensive pretesting in a local telephone survey of the general population of Lexington, Kentucky, conducted in 1986 ($N = 501$). For the most part the item analysis reported here draws from telephone survey data collected in the second wave of the 1987 ANES Pilot Study, in which a representative sample of 360 voting-age residents of the United States was interviewed. These findings are supplemented with analysis from the Lexington survey, where appropriate.

Reliability

Internal Consistency

Cronbach's alpha for the five-item scale is .63. The items are listed roughly in descending order of the magnitude of the item–total correlations.

Test–Retest

The over-time correlation for a three-item Militarism Scale (the first three items presented here) is .97 across interviews conducted in Lexington, Kentucky, in February 1986 and March 1987 ($N = 301$) (Peffley & Hurwitz, 1993). The stability coefficient was estimated by full-information maximum likelihood methods using LISREL VI and so is "corrected" for attenuation due to random measurement error.

Validity

Convergent

The Militarism Scale is highly predictive of Americans' attitudes on a wide range of specific foreign policy issues. Most generally militarism plays a predominant role in shaping preferences on national security issues. In regression analysis of various policy attitudes involving several other independent variables (e.g., party identification, liberalism–conservatism, anticommunism, isolationism, and patriotism), individuals favoring a tough, assertive stance are especially likely to favor increased defense spending (beta = .46), more nuclear weapons (beta = .33), and military responses to deal with terrorism (beta = .28). In addition, militarism plays an important role (second only to anticommunism) in predicting support for U.S. military involvement in Central America.

Discriminant

The low correlations between militarism and various domestic orientations, such as partisan identification ($r = .14$) and liberalism–conservatism (.20), provide some evidence that superordinate dimensions in the public mind involve separate attitudinal domains.

Moreover, the militarism dimension was found to be largely orthogonal to a general measure of isolationism ($r = -.15$), suggesting that the question of whether the United States should become involved in *any* fashion with other countries is independent of the question of what the *nature* of that involvement should be.

While militarism *was* found to be strongly related to a two-item measure of anticommunism ($r = .35$), this relationship is to be expected, since, until recently, the USSR was America's principal adversary and containing Soviet influence was the principal rationale for using military force. More to the point, while both dimensions were important predictors of national security attitudes, militarism was an especially important predictor of attitudes on primarily military issues (e.g., defense spending and nuclear arms policy), whereas anticommunism was of predominant importance on issues invoking anti-Soviet sentiment, such as limiting Soviet trade or keeping the communists from power in Central America.

Location

Peffley, M., & Hurwitz, J. (1987). *Report on foreign policy items, 1987 Pilot Study.* Prepared for the American National Election Study Pilot Committee. See also Hurwitz and Peffley (1987a).

Results and Comments

Given the lack of public information about the details of specific foreign policy issues, it seems likely that broad foreign policy orientations, like militarism, play a large role in guiding mass thinking and policy responses in the international arena.

The centrality of the militarism dimension for American public opinion in foreign affairs is undeniable. Certainly one's orientation toward military force—its procurement as well as its use—is a fundamental one that involves controversial issues of life and death, morality and economics. Issues connected with militarism and the proper use of military force have polarized the American public at least since the Vietnam War. Regardless of which particular country is designated as the enemy of the United States—whether it be the Soviet Union or Iraq—the question of whether the United States should use military force to achieve its objectives overseas should continue to be a central one in the foreseeable future.

Militarism Scale
(Peffley & Hurwitz, 1987)

	Mean	SD	Skew	Item–Total Correlation
*1. Some people feel that in dealing with other nations our government should be strong and tough. Others feel that our government should be understanding and flexible. Which comes closer to the way you feel— that our government should be strong and tough or understanding and flexible?	2.86	1.67	.122	.405
*2. Which do you think is the better way for us to keep the peace—by having a very strong military so other countries won't attack us, or by working out our disagreements at the bargaining table?	1.27	1.67	.553	.456
**3. The U.S. should maintain its position as the world's most powerful nation, even if it means going to the brink of war.	3.04	1.49	.029	.358
**4. The only way to settle disputes with other countries is to negotiate with them, not by using military force.	2.10	1.19	.895	.315
5. How important is it for the U.S. to have a strong military force in order to get our way with our adversaries? Is it extremely important, very important, somewhat important, or not at all important? (four-point scale)	1.94	.866	.405	.425

Note: Item 4 has been recoded so that lower values indicate more militarist positions.

*Indicates a five-point branching scale where respondents were asked to choose the position that was closer to their own and then asked whether they felt strongly or not so strongly about that position, with "uncertain" and "both/neither" coded to the midpoint of the scale.

**Indicates a five-point Likert scale: 1. AGREE STRONGLY, 2. AGREE SOMEWHAT, 3. UNCERTAIN (volunteered), 4. DISAGREE SOMEWHAT, or 5. DISAGREE STRONGLY with the statement.

Attitude toward War Scale

(R. Stagner, 1942)

Variable

This scale was designed to measure general attitudes toward war as an institution.

Description

In a variation of the Thurstone scale construction technique, items were rated by judges who were instructed to apply "absolute judgments" on a five-point scale in which 5 represented a rating of most favorable to war and 1 a rating of least favorable to war.

Subjects indicate agreement with an item by marking it with a check. The respondent's score is the mean of scale values of checked items. Possible scores range from 1.2 to 4.8, with higher scores indicating the more favorable attitude toward war.

Sample

The judges were described as five graduate and undergraduate classes with a total of 125 students. The evaluation sample consisted of four groups—265 adult men, 191 adult women, 229 college men, and 181 college women—who were administered the scale in 1938.

Reliability

Internal Consistency

A corrected split-half reliability coefficient of .58 was reported for the short form of the scale as tested on a group of 100 college men.

Test–Retest

The author administered the short form of the Attitude toward War Scale again in the fall of 1940, with five responses per item instead of two and with differential item weights eliminated. The sample was 157 students at Dartmouth College, and the test–retest reliability (corrected) was .83 on 93 students, with an intertest interval of one month. Eighteen months later, after the United States had entered World War II, a retest on 50 of the subjects produced a much reduced test–retest coefficient of .40.

Validity

In one test of validity by known groups, it was found that military training groups and veterans groups scored significantly higher than did men with no military training. In another known-groups validity test, differences in the responses of the Dartmouth students and those of 27 members of the Young People's Socialist League were highly significant.

Location

Stagner, R. (1942). Some factors related to attitude toward war, 1938. *Journal of Social Psychology, 16,* 131–142. Reprinted with permission of the Helen Dwight Reid Educational Foundation. Published by Heldref Publications, 1319 Eighteenth St., N.W., Washington, D.C. 20036-1802. Copyright © 1942.

    Stagner, R. (1946). Studies of aggressive social attitudes: I. Measurement and interrelation of selected attitudes; II. Changes from peace to war. *Journal of Social Psychology, 24,* 187–215.

Results and Comments

While the wording of some of the items may need to be updated, several have been adapted for use in recent studies to tap general beliefs about the morality of warfare (e.g., Conover & Feldman, 1984; Hurwitz & Peffley, 1987a; Peffley & Hurwitz, 1987). A short form of the scale consists of 14 of the 27 items included in the original long form (i.e., the 14 items not preceded by an asterisk).

Attitude toward War Scale
(Stagner, 1942)

Item	Median Rat- ing**	Range of scoring Means	Value
*1. War brings out the best qualities in men. 1. AGREE 0. DISAGREE	4.76	0.51	—
2. War is often the only means of preserving the national honor.	4.24	0.33	7
3. The desirable results of war have not received the attention they deserve.	4.24	0.32	7
4. There can be no progress without war.	4.67	0.38	7
5. War is the only way to right tremendous wrongs.	4.72	0.30	8
6. Patriotism demands that the citizens of a nation participate in any war.	4.26	0.20	7
*7. The United States has never fought an unjust war.	4.10	0.34	6
8. The United States should always be armed to the limit of its treaty rights.	4.10	0.26	6
*9. War is necessary to avoid overpopulation of nations.	4.62	0.30	7
*10. The Biblical command against killing not does apply to warfare.	4.19	0.37	6
*11. Nations should pay high honor to their military leaders.	4.05	0.38	6

*12. College students should be trained in times of peace to assume military duties.	3.90	0.33	6
*13. Modern warfare provides a glorious adventure for men not afraid of danger.	4.52	0.40	7
14. Under some conditions, war is necessary to maintain justice.	3.76	0.36	6
15. Although war is terrible, it has some value.	3.81	0.31	6
16. Defensive war is justified but other wars are not.	3.48	0.49	5
*17. We should abolish military armaments for offensive purposes.	1.97	0.53	—
*18. The average citizen can do nothing to oppose war.	3.29	0.82	—
19. Those who profit by war profit by the preparations for war.	2.33	0.47	3
*20. We expect war to endanger life and property rather than protect it.	1.72	0.52	—
21. The benefits of war rarely pay for its losses even for the victor.	1.72	0.42	2
22. There is no conceivable justification for war.	1.24	0.34	1
23. War is a futile struggle resulting in self-destruction.	1.45	0.29	1
24. The evils of war are greater than any possible benefits.	1.32	0.47	1
*25. International disputes should be settled without war.	1.48	0.47	1
*26. War breeds disrespect for human life.	1.36	0.59	—
*27. It is good judgment to sacrifice certain rights in order to prevent war.	1.43	0.63	—

*These items were omitted in the short form.

**Original Judges' Rating Scale:* Consider each of the statements below. Regardless of your own opinion, mark it as to whether you consider it to be favorable to war or to peace. Let 5 be the statements most favorable to war, and 1 those most favorable to peace. If a statement is somewhat favorable to war, mark it 4. If somewhat favorable to peace, mark it 2. If a statement is not favorable to either, mark it 3. Be sure not to consider your own agreement or disagreement, but just the question, Does this statement indicate an attitude favoring war or peace?

References

Achen, C. H. (1975). Mass political attitudes and the survey response. *American Political Science Review, 69,* 1218–1231.

Adorno, T. W., Frenkel-Brunswick, E., Levinson, D. J., & Sanford, R. N. (1950). *The authoritarian personality.* New York: Harper and Row.

Aldrich, J. H., Sullivan, J. L., & Borgida, E. (1989). Waltzing before a blind audience: The anomaly of foreign affairs and issue voting. *American Political Science Review, 83,* 123–142.

Bronfenbrenner, U. (1961). The mirror image in Soviet–American relations: A social psychologist's report. *Journal of Social Issues, 17,* 45–56.

Brown, S. R. (1980). *Political subjectivity.* New Haven: Yale University Press.

Buchanan, W., & Cantril, H. (1953). *How nations see each other: A study in public opinion.* Urbana: University of Illinois Press.

Campbell, D. T. (1973). Various social attitudes scales. In J. Robinson & P. Shaver (Eds.), *Measures of social psychological attitudes.* Ann Arbor, MI: Institute for Social Research.

Chittick, W. O., & Billingsley, K. R. (1989). The structure of elite foreign policy beliefs. *Western Political Quarterly, 42,* 201–224.

Comrey, A. L., & Newmeyer, J. (1965). Measurement of radicalism–conservatism. *Journal of Social Psychology, 67,* 357–369.

Conover, P. J., & Feldman, S. (1984). How people organize the political world: A schematic model. *American Journal of Political Science, 28,* 95–126.

Conover, P. J., & Feldman, S. (1987). Measuring patriotism and nationalism. Report to the National Election Studies Board of Overseers.

Converse, P. E. (1964). The nature of belief systems in mass publics. In E. Apter (Ed.), *Ideology and discontent.* New York: Free Press.

Converse, P. E., & Markus, G. (1979). Plus ça change . . . The new CPS election study panel. *American Political Science Review, 73,* 32–49.

Cottam, R. W. (1977). *Foreign policy motivation: A general theory and a case study.* Pittsburgh: University of Pittsburgh Press.

Day, D., & Quackenbush, O. F. (1942). Attitudes toward defensive, cooperative, and aggressive war. *Journal of Social Psychology, 16,* 11–20.

DeLamater, J., Katz, D., & Kelman, H. C. (1969). On the nature of national involvement: A preliminary study. *Journal of Conflict Resolution, 13,* 320–357.

Easton, D. (1965). *A systems analysis of political life.* New York: Wiley.

Erskine, H. G. (1963). The polls: Exposure to international information. *Public Opinion Quarterly, 27,* 658–662.

Feldman, S. (1989). Measuring issue preferences: The problem of response instability. *Political Analysis, 1,* 25–60.

Ferguson, L. W. (1942). The isolation and measurement of nationalism. *Journal of Social Psychology, 16,* 215–228.

Forbes, H. D. (1985). *Nationalism, ethnocentrism, and personality.* Chicago: University of Chicago Press.

Free, L. A., & Cantril, H. (1968). *The political beliefs of Americans.* New York: Simon and Schuster.

Herrmann, R. (1985). *Perceptions and behavior in Soviet foreign policy.* Pittsburgh: University of Pittsburgh Press.

Herrmann, R. (1986). The power of perceptions in foreign policy decision making: Do views of the Soviet Union determine the policy choices of American leaders? *American Journal of Political Science, 30,* 831–875.

Herrmann, R. (1988). The empirical challenge of the cognitive revolution: A strategy for drawing inferences from perceptions. *International Studies Quarterly, 32,* 175–203.

Hinckley, R. H. (1988). Public attitudes toward key foreign policy events. *Journal of Conflict Resolution, 32,* 295–318.

Holsti, O. R. (1985). *The lessons of Vietnam and the breakdown of consensus on foreign and domestic policy: A study of American leadership.* Final report on NSF Grant No. SES 83-09036.

Holsti, O. R. (1992). Public opinion and foreign policy: Challenges to the Almond–Lippmann consensus. *International Studies Quarterly, 36,* 439–466.

Holsti, O. R. (1996). *Public opinion and American foreign policy.* Ann Arbor: University of Michigan Press.

Holsti, O. R., & Rosenau, J. N. (1984). *American leadership in world affairs: Vietnam and the breakdown of consensus.* London: Allen & Unwin.

Holsti, O. R., & Rosenau, J. N. (1986). Consensus lost. Consensus regained? Foreign policy beliefs of American leaders, 1976–1980. *International Studies Quarterly, 30,* 375–409.

Holsti, O. R., & Rosenau, J. N. (1988). The domestic and foreign policy beliefs of American leaders. *Journal of Conflict Resolution, 32,* 248–294.

Holsti, O. R., & Rosenau, J. N. (1990). The structure of foreign policy attitudes among American leaders. *Journal of Politics, 52,* 94–125.

Hurwitz, J., & Peffley, M. (1987a). How are foreign policy attitudes structured? A hierarchical model. *American Political Science Review, 81,* 1099–1120.

Hurwitz, J., & Peffley, M. (1987b). The means and ends of foreign policy as determinants of presidential support. *American Journal of Political Science, 31,* 236–258.

Hurwitz, J., & Peffley, M. (1990). Public images of the Soviet Union: The impact on foreign policy attitudes. *Journal of Politics, 52,* 3–28.

Hurwitz, J., Peffley, M., & Seligson, M. A. (1993). Foreign policy belief systems in comparative perspective: The United States and Costa Rica. *International Studies Quarterly, 37,* 245–270.

Katz, D., & Kahn, R. (1966). *The social psychology of organizations.* New York: Wiley.

Kelman, H. C. (Ed.). (1965). *International behavior: A social psychological analysis.* New York: Holt, Rinehart and Winston.

Kosterman, R., & Feshbach, S. (1989). Toward a measure of patriotic and nationalistic attitudes. *Political Psychology, 10,* 257–274.

Krosnick, J., & Brannon, L. A. (1993). The impact of the Gulf War on the ingredients of presidential evaluations: Multidimensional effects of political involvement. *American Political Science Review, 87,* 963–978.

Kurbanov, E., & Robinson, J. (1997). *Differential ethnic images within the former Soviet Union.* Paper presented at annual meeting of the American Sociological Association, Toronto, Canada.

Lambert, W. E., & Klineberg, O. (1967). *Children's views of foreign peoples.* New York: Appleton-Century-Crofts.

Lentz, T. F. (1976). *Humatriotism.* St. Louis: Futures Press.

Levinson, D. J. (1957). Authoritarian personality and foreign policy. *Journal of Conflict Resolution, 1,* 37–47.

Loh, W. D. (1975). Nationalist attitudes in Quebec and Belgium. *Journal of Conflict Resolution, 19,* 217–249.

Maggiotto, M. A., & Wittkopf, E. R. (1981). American public attitudes toward foreign policy. *International Studies Quarterly, 25,* 601–631.

Mandelbaum, M., & Schneider, W. (1979). The new internationalisms. In K. Oye, D. Rothchild, & R. J. Lieber (Eds.), *Eagle entangled: U.S. foreign policy in a complex world.* New York: Longman.

McClosky, H. (1967). Personality and attitude correlates of foreign policy orientation. In J. Rosenau (Ed.), *Domestic sources of foreign policy.* New York: Free Press.

Merritt, R. L. (1968). Visual representation of mutual friendliness. In R. L. Merritt & D. J. Puchala (Eds.), *Western European perspectives on international affairs: Public opinion studies and evaluations.* New York: Praeger.

Merritt, R. L., & D. J. Puchala (Eds.) (1968). *Western European perspectives on international affairs: Public opinion studies and evaluations.* New York: Praeger.

Modigliani, A. (1972). Hawks and doves, isolation and political distrust: An analysis of public opinion on military policy. *American Political Science Review, 66,* 960–978.

Oskamp, S. (1965). Attitudes toward U.S. and Russian actions: A double standard. *Psychological Reports, 16,* 43–46.

Page, B. I., & Shapiro, R. Y. (1992). *The rational public: Fifty years of trends in Americans' policy preferences.* Chicago: University of Chicago Press.

Peffley, M., & Hurwitz, J. (1987). *Report on foreign policy items, 1987 Pilot Study.* Prepared for the American National Election Study Pilot Committee.

Peffley, M., & Hurwitz, J. (1992). International events and foreign policy beliefs: Public response to changing Soviet–U.S. relations. *American Journal of Political Science, 36,* 431–461.

Peffley, M., & Hurwitz, J. (1993). Models of attitude constraint in foreign affairs. *Political Behavior, 15,* 61–90.

Putney, S. (1962). Some factors associated with student acceptance or rejection of war. *American Sociological Review, 27,* 655–667.

Rielly, J. E. (Ed.). (1975). *American public opinion and U.S. foreign policy, 1975.* Chicago: Chicago Council on Foreign Relations.

Rielly, J. E. (Ed.). (1979). *American public opinion and U.S. foreign policy, 1979.* Chicago: Chicago Council on Foreign Relations.

Rielly, J. E. (Ed.). (1983). *American public opinion and U.S. foreign policy, 1983.* Chicago: Chicago Council on Foreign Relations.

Rielly, J. E. (Ed.). (1987). *American public opinion and U.S. foreign policy, 1987.* Chicago: Chicago Council on Foreign Relations.

Robinson, J., Rusk, J. G., & Head, K. B. (1968). *Measures of political attitudes.* Ann Arbor, MI: Institute for Social Research.

Robinson, J., & Shaver, P. (Eds.). (1973). *Measures of social psychological attitudes.* Ann Arbor, MI: Institute for Social Research.

Sampson, D. L., & Smith, H. P. (1957). A scale to measure world-minded attitudes. *Journal of Social Psychology, 45,* 99–106.

Simon, R. (1974). *Public opinion in America, 1936–1970.* Chicago: Rand-McNally.

Sniderman, P. M., & Tetlock, P. E. (1986). Interrelationship of political ideology and public opinion. In M. E. Hermann (Ed.), *Political psychology.* San Francisco: Jossey-Bass.

Stagner, R. (1940). A correlational analysis of nationalistic opinions. *Journal of Social Psychology, 12,* 197–212.

Stagner, R. (1942). Some factors related to attitude toward war, 1938. *Journal of Social Psychology, 16,* 131–142.

Stagner, R. (1946). Studies of aggressive social attitudes: I. Measurement and interrelation of selected attitudes; II. Changes from peace to war. *Journal of Social Psychology, 24,* 187–215.

Stokes, D. E. (1966). Some dynamic elements of contests for the presidency. *American Political Science Review, 60,* 19–28.

Sullivan, J. L., Fried, A., Theiss-Morse, E., & Dietz, M. (1992). Patriotism, politics, and the presidential election of 1988. *American Journal of Political Science, 36,* 200–234.

White, M. J., & Feshbach, S. (1987). Who in Middletown supports a nuclear freeze? *Political Psychology, 8,* 201–209.

Wittkopf, E. R. (1981). The structure of foreign policy attitudes: An alternative view. *Social Science Quarterly, 62,* 108–123.

Wittkopf, E. R. (1986). On the foreign policy beliefs of the American public: A critique and some evidence. *International Studies Quarterly, 30,* 425–446.

Wittkopf, E. R. (1987). Elites and masses: Another look at attitudes toward America's world role. *International Studies Quarterly, 31,* 131–159.

Wittkopf, E. R. (1990). *Faces of internationalism: Public opinion and American foreign policy.* Durham, NC: Duke University Press.

Wittkopf, E. R. (1993). *Faces of internationalism in a transitional environment.* Paper presented at the annual meeting of the International Studies Association, Acapulco, Mexico.

Wittkopf, E. R., & Maggiotto, M. A. (1983). Elites and masses: A comparative analysis of attitudes toward America's world role. *Journal of Politics, 45,* 303–334.

Yatani, C., & Bramel, D. (1989). Trends and patterns in Americans' attitudes toward the Soviet Union. *Journal of Social Issues, 45,* 13–32.

Zaller, J. (1991). Information, values, and opinion. *American Political Science Review, 85,* 1215–1237.

Zeigler, A. (1987). The structure of Western European attitudes toward Atlantic cooperation. *British Journal of Political Science, 17,* 457–477.

CHAPTER 10

Political Information

Vincent Price

Underlying the assumptions of an ideal democracy is a well-informed citizenry. Unless checked by an informed and active public, political leaders are too easily tempted by lazy, arrogant, or tyrannical impulses. Without the lively exchanges of information that took place in town meetings of the late 1700s, our country's Constitution might not have developed into the rather enduring and supple instrument that lives to this day.

The concept of political information thus plays a crucial role in political science, public opinion research, political psychology, and survey research. Concerns about the ability of the citizenry to marshal adequate information date from writings of Plato and Aristotle and were prominent during the 18th century's Age of Enlightenment, when so much of the modern lexicon of public opinion and democracy was articulated (Berelson, 1950; Lazarsfeld, 1957; Minar, 1960; Price, 1992). Worries about the public's fitness for democratic life have persisted ever since. Contemporary scholars are fond of citing Lippmann's (1922, 1925) withering attacks on the virtually complete lack of knowledge of ordinary citizens as they confront the complex and confusing world of modern political affairs. With the growth of empirical social science in the 1940s and 1950s, questions about how well informed the public was on matters of political concern naturally rose to the fore, since these questions go directly to the heart of public competence for forming and expressing sound opinions, selecting leaders, and deciding on government policies (e.g., Berelson, 1950).

In spite of this long theoretical pedigree and a half-century of involvement in empirical research, political information has only recently come under sustained attention from scholars focusing explicitly on its conceptual and empirical properties. In the first edition of this volume, Robinson (1968) identified only four developed scale measures of political information, noting at the time a lack of evidence concerning their validity. Evidence of scale reliability was available in only a single case, and there correlations among scale items were rather low.

Fortunately the past decade and a half have witnessed a mushrooming interest in political information and produced a number of careful empirical studies dedicated to the conceptualization and measurement of the concept (e.g., Delli Carpini & Keeter, 1992, 1996; Iyengar, 1986; Luskin, 1987; Smith, 1989; Zaller, 1985, 1986, 1990). Many of these have been carried out as part of the American National Election Studies (ANES), of the University of Michigan, with its generalizable samples and rich set of political correlates. Scale measures of political information are increasingly informing research, particularly on political behavior. For example, political information scales play a central role in Zaller's (1992) research on the means by which elite arguments diffuse throughout society and shape mass opinion. Capping the trend toward more sustained and focused empirical work on the concept was the publication of Delli Carpini and Keeter's (1996) *What Americans Know about Politics and Why It Matters,* dedicated entirely to political knowledge. The authors examine carefully what Americans know about politics, stability and change in political knowledge from the late 1940s to the late 1980s, social and demographic patterns in its distribution, and its causes and consequences. With these efforts, we are in a much better position to understand and measure political information than at the time of this volume's initial publication 30 years ago.

This chapter is intended to offer a distillation of key issues surrounding the conceptualization and measurement of political information. After a brief look at the origins and development of contemporary scholarly interest in the concept, we will turn to a closer investigation of its conceptual and empirical properties.

Origins and Development of Scholarly Interest

We can trace the prominent role of political information in contemporary political research to at least three basic concerns: (1) interests in levels of citizen knowledge, rooted in democratic political theory; (2) debates over the political sophistication and "ideological" thinking among the mass electorate; and (3) interests in psychological processes underlying information diffusion, information processing, and opinion change. These concerns correspond to three broad developmental phases of social–scientific research that unfolded in rough chronological order, beginning in the 1940s.

Citizen Knowledge

As noted earlier, much of the scientific interest in political information stems from debates over the capacity of ordinary people to participate in democratic life. Without systematic empirical observation, early writers on democracy and public opinion worried that citizens were uninterested and largely uninformed about current affairs (e.g., Bryce, 1888, p. 8). Most prominent and persuasive were Lippmann's (1922, 1925) arguments that people invest little or no energy in learning about political affairs, basing opinions on vague and incomplete information from casual exposure to superficial press accounts. Not surprisingly, then, some of the earliest measures of political information were simple descriptive soundings of public knowledge. In a series of articles published in the early 1960s, Erskine (1962, 1963a, 1963b, 1963c) reviewed results from surveys gauging public understanding of domestic affairs, international affairs, and "textbook knowledge." Similar descriptions of public knowledge followed in Lane and Sears (1964), Robinson (1967), Verba and Nie (1972), Glenn, (1972), Neuman (1986), and Delli Carpini and Keeter (1991, 1996).

These authors have greeted the findings with a range of interpretations and prognoses for democratic government. But the accumulated findings clearly suggest that Bryce, Lippmann, and others were correct in supposing that most Americans know relatively little about matters of politics (Bennett, 1988, 1989; Lane & Sears, 1964; Neuman, 1986). The evidence is clear that the American public is poorly informed "by anything approaching

elite standards" (Luskin, 1987, p. 889). Delli Carpini and Keeter (1996) have most recently documented that political knowledge continues to be quite limited and "does not
run very deep" (p. 91).

On the other hand, Delli Carpini and Keeter conclude that Americans are not peculiar
in this regard. They appear to lag only slightly behind citizens of many Western nations
in their political knowledge (though perhaps the lag is greater for knowledge of foreign
affairs; see Dimock & Popkin, 1997). And despite possessing limited information, a *majority* of the American public was nonetheless able in 1992 to (1) identify presidential candidates; (2) place them relative to one another on controversial issues like abortion, job
programs, and defense spending; (3) identify which political party controlled the U.S.
Senate and House of Representatives; and (4) place the major parties in relative positions
on several key issues (Delli Carpini & Keeter, 1996).

Ideological Thinking and Political Sophistication

Growing out of studies of public knowledge is a long line of research focused on the extent of ideological thinking among the mass electorate (Achen, 1975; Campbell, Converse,
Miller, & Stokes, 1960; Converse, 1964, 1970; Hamill & Lodge, 1986; Judd & Milburn,
1980; Lane, 1962, 1973; Luskin, 1987, 1990; Luttbeg, 1968; Nie, Verba, & Petrocik, 1976;
Stimson, 1975). Here the concern is that poor information carries over to the central ideological distinction—between liberal and conservative—that generally structures political
debate in the United States. One implication of this ignorance is that people's opinions are
not much constrained by ideology. Campbell *et al.* (1960), and later Converse (1964,
1970), found that responses to the same opinion questions in 1956, 1958, and 1960 were
so unstable as to be nearly random. Moreover, people would inconsistently hold a liberal
position on one issue and a conservative position on the next. Converse concluded that,
beyond being uninterested and uninformed, most voters also failed to possess a system of
attitudes or opinions organized in any coherent fashion. They were, in short, unsophisti-
cated, at least in the ideological terms commonly employed by political analysts. Only half
even recognized the basic terms *liberal* and *conservative*.

Converse's conclusion that citizens' opinions were not constrained by ideological
thinking was challenged in a variety of ways. Some argued that each person could
maintain his or her own idiosyncratic ideology that simply did not conform to the liberal–
conservative worldviews expected by political scientists (Bennett, 1975; Brown, 1970;
Lane, 1962). Others raised methodological issues, arguing that the over-time response instability Converse saw as evidence of citizen "non-attitudes" could as easily stem from
vague survey questions or other sources of unreliable measurement (Achen, 1975). Another challenge came from scholars who argued that mass political sophistication and
ideological thinking, even if limited in the late 1950s, increased significantly in the 1960s
due to increased political protest and confrontation (Nie *et al.*, 1976; Pomper, 1972). Debates over each of these points have occupied political science for many years (Luskin,
1987; Smith, 1989), although recent reviews suggest that Converse's general conclusions
about the public's lack of sophistication were on the mark (Kinder & Sears, 1985; Luskin,
1987; Smith, 1989).

Most research on political sophistication did not actually make much use of direct
measures of information or knowledge. It relied instead on other kinds of operational
measures. Some scholars employed survey respondents' identifications of themselves as
liberal or conservative (e.g., Bennett, Oldendick, Tuchfarber, & Bishop, 1979). Many relied on responses to open-ended questions probing likes and dislikes of parties and candidates. These responses were coded into ordinal "levels of conceptualization" based on

the extent to which they reflected the use of ideological abstractions (Campbell *et al.*, 1960; Converse, 1964; Hagner & Pierce, 1983; Pierce, 1970). The most common approach was to assess the consistency of respondents' policy opinions, using mean interitem correlations (Bennett, 1973; Campbell *et al.*, 1960; Converse, 1964; Nie *et al.*, 1976).

Recently, however, several researchers have concluded that knowledge and information measures may actually offer superior indicators of general political sophistication (Luskin, 1987; Smith, 1989; Zaller, 1990). Willingness to identify oneself as liberal or conservative does not seem to require much sophistication. Correlations between opinion items are only aggregate measures. They impose sampling bias because of large numbers of "don't know" responses to opinion questions, and the covariance they tap may stem from many factors other than ideological constraint (Luskin, 1987). The levels of conceptualization index, according to Smith (1989), suffers from a variety of faults and depends too heavily on short-term election influences.

Although political sophistication and political knowledge are not quite the same thing, they are closely enough related to make separation difficult. As Luskin (1987, p. 860) notes, a person is politically sophisticated to the extent that his or her system of political beliefs is large (containing many elements), wide ranging (covering many aspects of politics), and highly organized (or "constrained," in the sense that ideas are associated with others in the system). Much sophistication research has tended to focus on the third of these aspects, while political information scales tend to tap the first two. However, all three aspects of belief systems tend to go hand in hand. One cannot maintain a large and differentiated store of knowledge without some effective inventory system. So citizens who are knowledgeable about politics will also tend to be sophisticated or organized political thinkers, and vice versa.

Information Diffusion, Information Processing, and Opinion Change

A third stream of research, more general and more recent than the other two, focuses on the role of existing knowledge in information diffusion and opinion change. This line of research actually groups together several different streams of scholarship. What they share is an attempt to move beyond the distributional questions—How informed is the public? How sophisticated is the electorate?—to address the process of knowledge acquisition and its consequences.

Information diffusion research has focused mainly on learning from the mass media, examining audience comprehension of information presented in the media. These studies have employed a variety of designs, including cross-sectional and longitudinal survey designs, field experiments, and laboratory experiments (e.g., Gunter, 1987; Jacoby & Hoyer, 1987; Jacoby, Hoyer, & Sheluga, 1980; Neuman, 1976; Robinson, 1972; Robinson & Levy, 1986). Although the research on comprehending media messages deals with a range of information topics, a reasonably large number of studies have focused on the learning of political information (e.g., Patterson, 1980; Patterson & McClure, 1976; Price & Czilli, 1996; Price & Zaller, 1990, 1993; Robinson, 1967, 1976). These studies have typically demonstrated strong relationships between audience learning and education, and even stronger relationships between existing knowledge and the reception of new information. Thus considerable "knowledge gaps" exist between better- and less-well-educated segments of the population, in terms of both existing information levels and the acquisition of new knowledge (Tichenor, Donohue, & Olien, 1970, 1980). Such gaps appear in part because better educated and better informed members of the audience can marshal greater cognitive resources than others and in part because they tend to pay closer attention to public affairs programming and use more informative media (often print sources or "high brow" broadcast media).

Complementing these basic studies of information diffusion are studies focusing on the role of prior knowledge in message processing. The rise to prominence of the "cognitive perspective" in the 1970s and 1980s (Markus & Zajonc, 1985) has greatly affected political science, communication studies, and related fields. This perspective generally emphasizes the role of cognition in mediating political behavior and, more specifically, the processes related to encoding, decoding, storing, and retrieving information. In examinations of these processes, political "expertise" has become a central variable (Krosnick, 1990). Political experts think about politics differently than do novices (Fiske & Kinder, 1981; Fiske, Kinder, & Larter, 1983; Judd & Downing, 1990; McGraw, Lodge, & Stroh, 1990; McGraw & Pinney, 1990). They tend to identify large, meaningful patterns in sets of information; encode information in broader, more abstract ways; and process information in a deeper, more analytic fashion (Krosnick, 1990). In many ways, then, research on political information processing has extended longstanding concerns with sophistication by coupling them with more detailed analyses of the "black box" processes that underlie opinion formation and voting decisions (Lau & Erber, 1985; Lodge, Stroh, & Wahlke, 1990).

Recognition that political knowledge may be a powerful mediator of information processing has consequently influenced research on opinion change, especially media-induced opinion change. Political scientists had for years generally downplayed the role of the media in shaping policy opinions or considered it largely inconsequential. However, recent research has increasingly focused on modeling opinion change dynamically in tandem with the flow of news and information (Bartels, 1988; MacKuen, 1984; Zaller, 1987, 1990, 1992). Importantly, emerging models of opinion change take account of interactions among knowledge, exposure to information, and political predispositions. Zaller's (1992) account, drawn from the work of Converse (1962) and McGuire (1968), proposes nonmonotonic relationships between political knowledge and opinion change in response to persuasive communications. Politically aware citizens are much more likely than their poorly informed counterparts to attend to and comprehend such communications; at the same time they are less likely, by virtue of their preexisting knowledge, to be swayed by these messages. Thus moderately well informed people may often show the greatest levels of media-induced change. Moreover, politically knowledgeable citizens will respond differently to political information, depending on the congruence of that information with their predispositions. The ability of politically aware people to reject messages they find disagreeable and accept those that are more congenial can produce complex patterns of opinion polarization. These would not be detectable were the analyst to overlook the central role of political knowledge.

Conceptual Definition

For each of these reasons, political information has become increasingly central to the study of public opinion, media effects, and political behavior more generally. According to Zaller (1990, p. 125), "[p]olitical awareness deserves to rank alongside party identification and ideology as one of the central constructs of the public opinion field." Nevertheless, one encounters a certain degree of confusion in the literature about the conceptualization and measurement of political information. Much of this confusion stems not from political information itself, but from its employment for so many different research purposes. On the one hand political information is a relatively narrow and straightforward construct relating to factual knowledge in the political domain (which will be our primary focus here). On the other hand it is often used—for both theoretical and practical reasons—as an operational surrogate for other related constructs, including political "sophistication," "expertise," "involvement," and even "media exposure" (Price & Zaller, 1993). In this respect it resembles education, a variable that is very often used as a surrogate for the same class of concepts (although, as we will discuss later, information tends to serve better in this role). As Delli Carpini and Keeter (1996, p. 10) note, there are some good reasons for the "conceptual blurring" of knowledge, information, sophistication, involvement, interest, and other kindred terms. Theory leads us to expect that how much one knows about politics is closely connected to becoming educated, participating in political affairs, following the news, learning from it, carefully considering policy issues, and forming and holding consistent and stable opinions.

As an empirical matter we do in fact find these variables to be strongly intercorrelated (Smith, 1989; Zaller, 1990). Yet, at least conceptually speaking, they are not all the same. The two terms that come closest to conceptual interchangeability are *information* and *knowledge*. Political information is at its root knowledge. This knowledge, as with all, resides in one's mind. It is also shared between minds through communication. Consequently one finds the term *information* used to refer to the content of communications as well as to the content of a person's knowledge store. Here we focus only on the latter usage.

The concept of political information is restricted in several other important ways: It refers to knowledge that is in the political domain, and it refers to factual knowledge. Delli Carpini and Keeter define political knowledge as "the range of factual information about politics that is stored in long-term memory" (1996, p. 10). They thus distinguish it from other cognitive concepts, such as attitudes, values, opinions, and beliefs; from cognitive processes, such as logic, reasoning, problem solving, and decision making; and from behavioral experiences, such as participation, education, and media use. Conceptualized this way, political information is also distinguished from expertise, which refers to "especially good performance in some domain" (Krosnick, 1990, p. 3), unless the performance domain is restricted to the retrieval of factual political information from long-term memory.

As Delli Carpini and Keeter (1996) admit, other analysts might quibble with aspects of this definition. Establishing information as *fact* can be problematic. The aim, however, is to identify cognitions that are objectively verifiable—what person holds the office of vice-president, whether or not a military conflict is occurring in some region of the world, which party is more liberal than another on a policy issue—as opposed to beliefs that cannot be so verified—whether the vice-president is doing a good job, whether a military conflict is likely to worsen, or whether a liberal response to a certain policy issue is wise. Restricting knowledge to information stored in *long-term memory* aims at identifying ideas that are not only processed in the mind as some point, but also retained over time and available for future use. By the *range* of information, Delli Carpini and Keeter (1996) refer to the different kinds of cognitions people possess that are relevant to politics. These include knowledge about how the political system is structured, how it works, who the main political actors are, and what they are doing.

Many of the debates over the measurement of political information relate in one way or another to these basic conceptual distinctions. How unambiguously can we determine whether the knowledge someone possesses is correct (Belli & Schuman, 1996; Graber, 1994)? How relevant to politics does an item of information need be in order to be included within the conceptual range of the construct (Graber, 1994)? Is political knowledge a single dimension or a differentiated concept with multiple subdimensions? That is, do people tend to specialize in particular political matters? If so, they could be quite knowledgeable in one domain (say, women's issues), while being quite poorly informed in others, forcing researchers to take separate account of each subdomain (Iyengar, 1986; McGraw & Pinney, 1990). If not, on the other hand, then global information measures may be generally quite adequate (Delli Capini & Keeter, 1996; Price & Zaller, 1993; Zaller, 1992). How long does information need to be retained in long-term memory, if at all, for it to have impact? What if, as Lodge's "on-line" model of opinion change proposes, people use new information to update their attitudes and opinions during message processing, but then promptly discard that information (Lodge, McGraw, & Stroh, 1989; Lodge, Steenbergen, & Brau, 1995)?

Ultimately such conceptual and theoretical questions will be answered only through careful empirical study. Fortunately research has begun to settle at least some of these debates—for instance, questions about the dimensionality of political knowledge (Delli Carpini & Keeter, 1996). Answers to other questions—for example, whether or not memory of political information plays a critical mediating role in opinion change, and the conditions under which it does or does not—will require much more research.

Alternative Measurement Strategies

The critical first step is to come to some common understanding of political information and preferred ways of measuring it (Delli Carpini & Keeter, 1993; Zaller, 1985). Political information can be measured in a variety of ways. Direct knowledge tests—essentially quizzes designed to test whether respondents know basic facts—are the simplest and most straightforward means of assessing political knowledge. Unfortunately, such questions have rarely been included in general population surveys of political behavior and attitudes. Smith (1989) notes that they dwindled after the late 1940s. Erskine (1963a), for example, found that the number of textbook political knowledge questions in national surveys declined markedly in the 15 years from 1947 to 1962. Many of the extant data holdings bearing on mass attitudes and behavior do not contain direct tests of political knowledge. The General Social Surveys have only rarely included political knowledge questions. The 1987 GSS carried three political knowledge questions (identification of the respondent's congressional representative, state governor, and local school superintendent).[1] Otherwise, the only knowledge scale available on the GSS is a ten-item vocabulary test designed to assess verbal intelligence (Thorndike & Gallup, 1944). For this measure, respondents are presented with ten test words. For each, they are asked to select which of five other words comes closest to the meaning of the test word. Alwin (1991) reports that, for the period from 1974 to 1990, GSS respondents averaged around 6.5 out of 10 correct, and that a simple summative scale had an internal consistency reliability of .71. However, the GSS verbal intelligence scale is clearly not a measure of political knowledge. For such data, analysts generally must turn to the National Election Studies, which began to include more knowledge items in the late 1980s.

One reason for the dearth of knowledge questions was apparently a fear that respondents would find quizzes annoying or embarrassing (Smith, 1989). Including them risked jeopardizing interviewer rapport and respondent cooperation. Or so it was thought. As it turns out, recent experience from the ANES and other surveys suggests that such concerns

[1]The GSS has occasionally carried other knowledge questions, although not directly related to politics. For instance, the 1993–94 GSS contained a battery of knowledge items focusing on science and technology.

are greatly overblown and that posing direct knowledge questions to respondents does not create any undue resistance (Delli Carpini & Keeter, 1996).[2]

Indirect Means of Assessing Information

At any rate the absence of knowledge items led many researchers to rely on surrogate measures—most commonly education or media use. Another indirect approach to measuring political information has been to rely on measures of opinionation. For example, Campbell *et al.* (1960) computed an "index of issue familiarity," which ranked people on their willingness to express an opinion on 16 issues and on their willingness to judge government performance on those issues. Along similar lines researchers have sometimes assessed the willingness of respondents to rate political figures on feeling thermometers— 100-point scales ranging from "very cold" to "very warm" (Bartels, 1988; Mann & Wolfinger, 1980; Zaller, 1992). These latter variables are indeed correlated with political information (as discussed later in connection with construct validity), but they are clearly distinct concepts and are comparatively weak indicators of information per se.

On the other hand a much stronger empirical case can be made for two other indirect measures of political information. Both come from items regularly carried on surveys by the ANES.

1) Sum of Likes and Dislikes
Since 1952 the ANES has asked respondents whether "there was anything in particular" that they "liked [or disliked] about" the political parties and candidates. Respondents are probed for answers, and up to five separate likes and dislikes are coded for each candidate or party. As an indirect measure of political information, Kessel (1980) and Smith (1989) employed a simple index of the total number of likes and dislikes given. They acknowledge that the measure suffers from several fundamental problems: It gauges interest and loquacity rather than knowledge and takes no account of whether or not respondents' comments are factually correct. Nevertheless, the simple count of like–dislike responses, when included with a large set of direct knowledge items in a scale analysis, produced a corrected item–total correlation of .57 (Delli Carpini & Keeter, 1996). In analyses of ANES data from 1956 to 1976, the count indices also produced high factor loadings, ranging from .60 to .75, on a general information factor (Smith, 1989).

2) Interviewer Ratings
The second indirect measure draws on a global assessment of the respondents' "general level of information about politics and public affairs" made by the survey interviewers at the conclusion of the ANES interviews (Zaller, 1986, 1992). Interviewers rate the respondents' information level on a five-point scale ranging from "very high" to "very low." This measure is, of course, problematic in its inherent subjectivity. If interviewers do not ask direct questions about knowledge, then they must base their estimates on other clues, for example, their face-to-face interactions with respondents. Ratings may thus be susceptible to a bias in favor of higher-status respondents or those with better interviewer rapport. Despite these clear limitations, Zaller (1986) reports that the interviewer ratings have great discriminating power. Specifically he recoded the ratings into four hierarchical

[2]Knowledge questions can, like all survey questions, produce consequential context effects. Bishop, Oldendick, and Tuchfarber (1984) found, for example, that respondents who were not able to answer a political knowledge question subsequently reported significantly less interest in public affairs. Recently Schwarz and Schuman (1997) reported that this effect could be substantially reduced by a buffer item that provides respondents with an external explanation for their lack of knowledge (e.g., a question asking how well politicians or the media keep them informed).

dichotomies (distinguishing the bottom level from the top four, the bottom two levels from the top three, and so on) and evaluated these items in a scale analysis with direct knowledge tests. Each of the dichotomous variables from the interviewer ratings performed as well as the very best of the direct knowledge items. Zaller (1992, p. 338) also reports that further analysis uncovered no evidence of bias favoring higher-status respondents.

More-Direct Means of Assessment

Turning to more direct measures of knowledge, we find that three general types of questions have been used: opinion placements of parties and candidates; questions soliciting identifications of prominent political figures; and questions soliciting information about other political events, governmental structures, or processes.

Opinion Placements

The ANES surveys have often asked respondents, after giving their opinions on policy issues using seven-point response scales, to then place political parties, groups, or candidates on those same scales. In cases where the party positions or candidate stands are clear and public—an important caveat, since in some cases their positions can be ambiguous—researchers can use these measures to determine whether respondents correctly understand this information (Delli Carpini & Keeter, 1996; Luskin, 1987; Smith, 1989; Zaller, 1986, 1992). Even if the exact location of a party or candidate is hard to determine, there is often an unambiguously correct comparative placement—for example, Democrats to the left of Republicans on federal spending for social welfare programs.

Methods of coding these data, and the names given to the resulting scales, have varied. Hamill, Lodge, and Blake (1985) proposed a measure they termed "partisan schema usage," which required not only correct relative placements of the parties, but also placements on the correct side of the scale midpoint. Luskin's (1987) measure of "information holding" required only that the order of placements be correct. Zaller (1992) also required only a correct ordering of the comparative placements, but in some cases (e.g., placements of Democrats and Republicans on defense and social services in 1986–1987) he credited respondents with correct placements only if they were several scale points apart. As is clear from these examples, researchers must make important judgments in transforming respondents' opinion placements into information items. Yet the measures can yield quite useful results. For example, Delli Carpini and Keeter (1996) report an analysis using ANES surveys from 1990–1991 in which six comparative placements were used in a 20-item information scale. Item–total correlations ranged from .49 (for the relative location of the parties on aid to blacks) to .54 (for the relative location of the parties on a general ideology scale).

Such comparative placements (what Zaller calls "location tests") are very similar in spirit to the index of "issue awareness" used by Patterson and McClure (1976), although the latter measure used single questions with a different format. Patterson and McClure's respondents were asked about the certainty with which they believed a particular candidate held a position on key election issues (e.g., "George McGovern favors spending less money on the military"). Answers were given on a seven-point scale from "extremely likely" to "extremely unlikely." It is unclear how much the multiple-question sequence used in the ANES—respondents first placing themselves; next, one party; finally, the second party—contributes to the reliability of the comparative placement tests. Before 1970, surveys by the ANES occasionally asked respondents which of the two parties was more likely to favor a particular policy (e.g., government medical care). Although these questions would appear to be a close substitute for placements, Zaller (1992, p. 338, n. 5) reports that they registered poor item reliability in information scales. On the other hand a single question asking which party is more conservative has generally worked well (Delli Carpini & Keeter, 1996; Price & Zaller, 1993).

Identifications

Some of the simplest, most common, and most direct information tests are those requiring respondents to identify prominent political figures. Delli Carpini and Keeter (1996) searched survey holdings of the Roper Center and the ANES for all factual knowledge questions asked in surveys from 1940 to 1994. They found that of all the questions dealing clearly with political matters, a full 37% asked respondents about contemporary public figures, political parties, and other groups (compared with 27% about international affairs, 20% about political and economic institutions, and 16% about domestic affairs).

A variety of question formats is possible, but two are most common. One approach involves providing the respondent with a political office or public role and requesting the name of the person filling that position (e.g., "Do you happen to know the name of the U.S. secretary of state?"). This format is similar to that used in the ANES questions measuring knowledge of congressional candidates. A second format, also used in the ANES, provides the respondent with a name and then requests the position or office they hold (e.g., "Do you happen to know what job or office is now held by Madeleine K. Albright?"). Commonly such items are administered in a list format with a common question stem, which reduces interviewing time. Both kinds of questions appear to function extremely well in scale measures of political information, provided that—if over-time comparisons are important—they are not too reactive to very short-term influences (Delli Carpini & Keeter, 1996; Zaller, 1986, 1992). Thus for a short-form scale Delli Carpini and Keeter (1996) recommend identification of the current vice-president, while Zaller (1985) suggests identifications of the Supreme Court justices.

Other Direct Information Questions

Myriad other questions can solicit direct items of information concerning politics and public affairs. Teachers who have written student examinations probably understand well the trade-offs involved in different test-question formats. Many surveys have used questions eliciting a "true–false" or "yes–no" response (e.g., "So far as you know, is France now able to make a nuclear bomb?"). Somewhat less frequently used are multiple-choice formats (e.g., "Whose responsibility is it to determine if a law is constitutional—the president, Congress, or the Supreme Court?"). Geography questions have typically involved asking respondents to identify states or countries on a map. The most common approach involves asking respondents to provide open-ended answers (e.g., "How long is a senator's term?" or "Just your best guess—What is the population of China?"), with the hope that responses to these open-ended questions will be concise and easily codable as correct or incorrect.

Issues in Measuring Political Information

There are, then, a number of question types suitable for measuring political information. As with many tests it is often advantageous to employ a number of formats, with the hope that each will present unique advantages and suffer from different sources of error. Several of the omnibus scales used in the literature (e.g., Delli Carpini & Keeter, 1996; Zaller, 1992) take advantage of four or more distinct question types. Prior to combining items into a scale measure, analysts render the data in a common form, usually coded dichotomously (1 = correct, 0 = incorrect). Issues of question type aside, however, there are a number of other important issues that arise in constructing political information scales.

1) Range of Knowledge Assessed

First, decisions must be made about the scope of the test. How much ground will the scale attempt to cover? Even if the scale seeks to assess a fairly specific form of knowledge—say, issue awareness—domains could include political issues (e.g., campaign reform), economic matters (e.g., jobs programs or tax policies), and social issues (e.g., abortion, gender equity, or affirmative action). Is information sought related to domestic affairs, international affairs, or both? In the case of domestic matters, a fourth question concerns the levels of government involved—state, local, or national. Even more generally will the measure cover only expressly political matters (e.g., political candidates, public officials, and governmental processes) or quasi-political matters as well (e.g., knowledge of news and popular culture that has only indirect bearings on politics)?

A key concern here is the potential multidimensionality of political knowledge. Results to date, discussed later, indicate that political information does resemble a general trait, such that knowledge in one domain is highly correlated with knowledge in others. Sampling from a variety of subdomains can improve the content validity of a scale, but as a practical matter, which areas of knowledge are represented is often not of great concern (Delli Carpini & Keeter, 1990, 1996; Zaller, 1986). On the other hand a researcher with strong theoretical interests in a specific domain or domains would be well advised to consider domain-specific information measures, since these can sometimes have distinct effects (Delli Carpini & Keeter, 1996; Iyengar, 1986).

2) Item Difficulty

Another key issue concerns the difficulty of knowledge tests. Adequate discrimination in the highest and lowest ranges of the knowledge continuum requires inclusion of some easy and some difficult items. As Delli Carpini and Keeter (1996) note, items with maximal variance (i.e., those with marginals close to 50% correct) will be favored in the calculation of the item correlations and the squared multiple correlation coefficients that inform standard scale analysis. This is appropriate when the principal task is to discriminate among respondents toward the center of the scale distribution.

The problem, however, is that information tests need to discriminate among respondents at the tails of the distribution as well. Items that do this—namely, those with more extreme marginals (i.e., those with very high or very low percentages of correct responses)—will produce attenuated correlations and squared multiple correlation coefficients. Theoretically the item-response curve relating each dichotomous knowledge item to the general underlying trait would not be a straight line, but instead a logistic curve. Consequently both Zaller (1985) and Delli Carpini and Keeter (1996) use logistic regression to examine item characteristics. When each item is regressed on all others in the full scale, the resulting logistic regression coefficients can be interpreted as reflecting the discriminatory power of each item. Results of such analysis can reveal the utility of retaining some scale items with extreme marginals (Delli Carpini & Keeter, 1996, Table A2.2). For example, only 5% of respondents correctly identified William Rehnquist as chief justice of the Supreme Court in 1990–1991. The question's corrected item–total correlation was only .33 (compared with .47 for all other items in the 20-item scale). Nevertheless, its logistic regression coefficient indicated superior discriminatory power—in fact, better than all but 1 other item (2.59 for the Rehnquist question, compared with an average for all items of 1.64).

3) Changes over Time

The difficulty of any particular information item will change as the general news and information context changes. The more salient an item in the news is, the easier it is to know. People also forget, unless reminded. Recall of congressional candidates is easier in presidential election years, when the flows of electoral information are stronger. Knowing which party controls the House of Representatives or the Senate can be easier or harder, depending on whether or not control of Congress and the White House is unified or divided and on whether control has recently shifted from one party to another (Smith, 1989). In the 1950s sizable majorities of Americans knew about Orval Faubus, who figured prominently in battles over civil rights; no doubt far fewer would know of him today. Events, celebrities, and issues come and go.

Although people's standing relative to their peers on political information appears highly stable over time (Smith, 1989), the specific elements of knowledge they possess will certainly change. For many research purposes comparability of items over time is of no great concern. In other instances—for example, in the study of learning and forgetting the news—it is precisely the change in "difficulty" that is of theoretical interest. Alternatively a researcher may wish to determine whether the aggregate public is becoming any better informed. In this case the analyst must try to identify changes in item difficulty and attempt to adjust over-time comparisons accordingly. "That is," notes Smith (1989), "one must try to get past superficial changes in the method of measuring information so changes in general information over time can be measured" (p. 162).

4) Affective Responses to Information Questions

Another problem is that some people may treat information questions as opinion items (Zaller, 1985). In other words respondents might reject items of information they find disagreeable and more easily assent to items of information that are more palatable. The danger is that if an information scale is not ideologically neutral, correlations between information and various opinions and values may be biased. For example, Zaller (1985) examined a set of information questions about legally supported civil liberties. Many of the facts addressed in the knowledge scale were (entirely consistent with legal trends at the time) probably more amenable to liberals. His results suggested that the strong positive correlation observed between the information measure and support for mainstream civil liberties norms might have been slightly inflated as a consequence. The lesson is that care must be taken to ensure that information items are, as much as possible, politically neutral.

5) Scoring Answers

A final issue surrounds scoring answers to information questions. Even when designed to elicit clear responses that are unambiguously correct or incorrect, questions will inevitably yield responses that are sometimes difficult to score. For this reason answers are often coded as "partially" correct. Depending on the proportion of such answers, the difficulty of an item can be increased if only completely correct answers are allowed or decreased if responses that are only partly right are counted as correct. Various rules can be developed that assign variable credit for different responses, depending on whether the answer is judged completely or only partly correct (e.g., Zaller, 1986).

So long as the eventual scoring rule is consistent across respondents, for scaling purposes this problem is not severe. Yet sometimes unforeseen biases can affect the scoring of answers. For example, Belli and Schuman (1996) conducted a careful qualitative examination of incorrect responses given to a series of questions about historical public figures and events. They discovered that answers coded as "wrong" were in fact sometimes correct, and were sometimes systematic forms of misremembering—as when respondents identified Joe McCarthy as a U.S. senator accused of being a Communist rather than as one who gained notoriety *hunting* alleged Communists.

Empirical Performance

Both practical and theoretical uncertainties, then, surround the measurement of political information. Yet evidence to date warrants the following generalizations: (1) Acceptably reliable scales measuring political information can be readily constructed using one or more of the approaches described previously; (2) political information is a reasonably general trait, in spite of some discernible subdimensions; (3) scales of political information exhibit strong construct validity; and (4) political information has demonstrated high stability at both the individual and the aggregate levels.

Scale Reliability

Internal consistency for scale measures of political information is generally high. As Zaller (1992) indicates, reliable scales can be constructed from most surveys of the ANES. They draw on different combinations of question formats, along the lines described earlier, and vary in their specific components from survey to survey, depending on the supply of items. Nevertheless, with few exceptions, the scales have alpha reliabilities ranging from .80 to .90, with most hovering around .85 (Zaller, 1992, p. 340; Zaller provides specific scale items for a variety of ANES surveys on pages 340–344).

Acceptable reliability may be obtained for long-form and short-form scales alike. Delli Carpini and Keeter (1996) report an alpha coefficient of .87 for a 20-item information scale combining eight identification questions, four comparative party placements, two questions about which party controls the U.S. House of Representatives and the Senate, and six questions soliciting a variety of "textbook" facts. A short form of the scale containing just 5 items (described later in the scale review) also scaled reasonably well (α = .71). Price and Zaller (1993) report an alpha coefficient of .82 for a 10-item scale along the same lines and an alpha coefficient of .75 for a shorter scale containing just four questions—identifications of Yasser Arafat and Margaret Thatcher and questions about which party controls the U.S. House of Representatives and the Senate.

Scale Dimensionality

Questions about the dimensionality of political information—specifically about the extent to which information and its effects might be domain-specific—have been addressed in a number of studies (Delli Carpini & Keeter, 1990, 1996; Iyengar, 1986; Price & Zaller, 1993; Smith, 1989; Zaller, 1986). Some have made a case for domain specificity. Notably, Iyengar (1986) analyzed data from the 1985 ANES Pilot Study, which included questions about four distinct subject domains: race, the economy, foreign affairs, and group politics. He constructed separate scales comprising the four or five items best capturing each domain. Evidence was mixed with respect to the construct validity of the separate scales. On the other hand Iyengar determined that, when compared with a general information measure, the domain-specific information scales interacted more strongly with domain-specific opinion measures in predicting evaluations of President Ronald Reagan. He concluded that in some information domains—especially race—domain-specific questions boost the observed impact of information.

Analyzing the same data Zaller (1986) concurred that the effects of political information on public opinion are, to some extent, domain-specific. Nevertheless, the increased predictive value of domain-specific information measures was modest and uneven. In a variety of different empirical tests, general information scales produced results that were almost as strong as those generated using more specific information scales. His conclusion is that information is a relatively general trait that is adequately assessed with a general-purpose scale (see also Price & Zaller, 1993).

Delli Carpini and Keeter (1990) reviewed a series of studies in which information items had been factor analyzed, finding conflicting evidence on the matter. In their own analysis of political information questions using structural equation modeling, they drew from several ANES surveys and from an extensive 1989 Survey of Political Knowledge containing 51 questions tapping knowledge of a wide array of topics (Delli Carpini & Keeter, 1996). They found that in knowledge of national politics, a unidimensional model provided an acceptable simplification of the data. Increasing the number of dimensions slightly improved the statistical performance of their structural models (e.g., in the 1989 data a one-factor model had an adjusted goodness of fit $= .97$ [$\chi^2/d.f. = 2.1$], while a three-factor model produced a goodness of fit of .98 [$\chi^2/d.f. = 1.7$]). However, the sub-dimensions were all highly correlated, with interfactor correlations across their five data sets averaging close to .80. Even domains that were conceptually distant were nonetheless highly correlated, as in the case of knowledge about racial issues and foreign policy information (interfactor $r = .85$).

Patterns of relationships between various domain-specific knowledge scales and many other variables—education, interest in politics, media use, income, age, gender, race, trust in government—tended to be quite similar. Such findings parallel those of Smith (1989), who found in factor analyses of ANES information items from 1956 to 1976 that a single factor generally explained between one-half and two-thirds of the collective variance. Delli Carpini and Keeter (1996) find that the strongest case for the distinctiveness of political knowledge can be made for levels of government, with the greatest differences observed in comparisons of national and local political information.

At least with respect to national politics, then, general political knowledge scales tap the likelihood that respondents will know about public affairs in many domains. Delli Carpini and Keeter (1990, 1996) conclude that the concept may be reasonably construed as a unidimensional phenomenon or, more accurately, as the combination of highly correlated subdomains. "To the general question of whether the U.S. public is composed of information specialists," they write, "the answer is no" (p. 142). The fact that people instead tend to be information generalists means that, as a practical matter, analysts can construct reliable and valid omnibus scales with a limited number of knowledge items, more or less regardless of their specific content.

Scale Validity

As Kaplan (1964) notes, measurement research validates not a scale itself, but the *use* to which a measure is put. The question, in other words, is not how valid the scale, but how valid the scale for a given purpose. Studies to date, including the structural analyses discussed previously, suggest that political information scales (even those based on a limited sample of knowledge domains) are indeed valid measures of the knowledge people possess about politics. Moreover, owing to their empirical properties, information scales can even serve as reasonably valid indicators of other conceptually distinct concepts, such as political sophistication and the likelihood of news reception.

In general, construct validity concerns "the extent to which a particular measure relates to other measures consistent with theoretically derived hypotheses concerning the concepts (or constructs) being measured" (Carmines & Zeller, 1979, p. 23). Theoretically we would expect the principal correlates of political information to include education, political interest, participation, and news media exposure. Studies to date have demonstrated consistent and substantial positive relationships between each of these variables and political information. Correlations between education and general political knowledge typically hover between .40 and .60, as do correlations between interest in politics and political knowledge. Correlations with print media exposure (e.g., reading of daily newspapers) are generally around .30, although exposure to television news is often weakly related to political information (Robinson & Levy, 1986). Political information is also correlated with voter turnout. Delli Carpini and Keeter (1996) estimate that the probability of voting in the 1988 presidential election was only .50 for ANES respondents who scored one standard deviation below the mean in political information, rising to .69 for respondents scoring one standard deviation above the mean. Studies also find that information scales are consistently related to gender (with males scoring higher than females), race (with whites scoring higher than blacks), and income (with upper-income groups scoring highest).

More detailed analyses suggest that education can be treated as a cause of political information (Delli Carpini & Keeter, 1996). Smith (1989) argues that the effect could be more apparent than real, in no small part because of selection bias: Those who attain a higher level of education are already better informed politically. Delli Carpini and Keeter (1996), on the other hand, find that even though the selectivity of access to education has declined over the past 40 years, the estimated impact of education on political knowledge has remained constant. Luskin (1990) presents results suggesting that much of the effect of education could in fact be attributable to intelligence rather than educational experience per se, although his measure of intelligence may have been biased toward inflated relationships with political knowledge (Delli Carpini & Keeter, 1996).

In addition to education, multivariate analyses find that political involvement and interest have large effects—usually comparable in size to those of education (Delli Carpini & Keeter, 1996; Luskin, 1990; Smith, 1989). Smaller effects are sometimes obtained for attention to the mass media, though usually only for print media use. The weak performance of media use measures appears to stem in part from measurement problems (Price & Zaller, 1993) and, in the case of television exposure, from audience selection biases (Neuman, Just, & Crigler, 1992).

The overall patterning of correlates of political information is, then, largely as one would expect. Even more impressive, political information scales quite successfully predict a number of consequential theoretical outcomes. People who score higher on information demonstrate higher levels of opinionation (Krosnick & Milburn, 1990). Information scales predict—more strongly than education, political interest, participation, or media exposure—the test–retest stability and measurement reliability of opinion measures (Delli Carpini & Keeter, 1996; Zaller, 1990). Higher information scores also predict greater consistency of political attitudes, in line with traditional liberal–conservative ideology (Delli Carpini & Keeter, 1996; Stimson, 1975). They also predict greater correspondence between basic predispositions and political evaluations (Delli Carpini & Keeter, 1996; Zaller, 1992), and more detailed processing of new political information (Fiske, Lau, & Smith, 1990). Perhaps for these reasons Luskin (1987) found that an information measure (built of 11 comparative opinion placements from the ANES) performed just as well as an indicator of political sophistication as did a scale combining several of the more traditional sophistication measures assessing levels of conceptualization and understanding of liberal and conservative terms.

Research by Price and Zaller (1993) suggests that a political information scale is also a useful empirical indicator of individual differences in news reception. Examining audience awareness of 16 news stories that broke during the summer of 1989, Price and Zaller found that a measure of political information actually proved more successful at predicting basic news awareness than did education or scales measuring exposure and attention to the news. This was so even in the case of nonpolitical stories, such as a major airline disaster and the trial of actress Zsa Zsa Gabor for slapping a police officer—and in spite of the fact that the information measure was gathered close to a year beforehand and included only standard political knowledge questions. The accuracy of political information as a predictor of news reception can make it an attractive surrogate for media exposure in studies of opinion change, where it has been found to better specify media-induced opinion changes than do measures of media exposure (Price & Zaller, 1990, 1996; Zaller, 1992).

Stability over Time

Analyses to date indicate that individual differences in political information are extremely stable over time. Delli Carpini and Keeter (1990) report test–retest correlations greater than .50 for single knowledge items over a one-year interval. Data gathered in a panel study of parents and their children by Jennings and Niemi (1981) show that test–retest correlations for a five-item knowledge index, even over eight- or nine-year intervals, ranged from .66 to .73 (from Jennings, 1996, Table 1). Comparisons with test–retest correlations for the standard seven-point party identification measure, which ranged from .49 to .83 for the same period, suggest that political information is about as stable as the most enduring political attitudes. Jennings's (1996) analysis suggests that, like other political characteristics, a person's political knowledge crystallizes and stabilizes in young adulthood.

The stability of political information in the aggregate is also remarkable. Numerous scholars now agree that, despite large gains in educational attainment over the past 30 to 40 years, the public's knowledge of politics has not increased (Bennett, 1988, 1989; Delli Carpini & Keeter, 1996; Neuman, 1986; Smith, 1989). For example, Delli Carpini and Keeter (1996) compared marginals on 15 knowledge questions asked from 1945 to 1957 and again in 1989. On 9 questions they found increases ranging from 1 to 15%. The other 6 questions, on the other hand, showed declines of between 1 and 10%. They also identified 749 cases in which political knowledge questions were repeated in general population surveys. Sixty percent of the cases showed an average yearly change of one percentage point or less, and only 9% averaged yearly changes of 10 percent or more. Instances of greatest change were mainly explained by the shifting information context (e.g., large increases in knowledge about Washington, D.C.'s Mayor Marion Barry resulting from charges that he had used illegal drugs). Delli Carpini and Keeter also found that differences in knowledge by gender, income, and race have not declined over the past 30 to 40 years.

The fact that information levels have not grown much over the past four decades, despite large increases in aggregate educational levels, has been a source of some puzzlement to analysts (Delli Carpini & Keeter, 1996; Smith, 1989). Smith (1989) concludes that, once other factors influencing information and the selectivity of higher education are taken into account, the modest effects of education are not strong enough "to cause more than minor change over decades" (p. 219). From the Jennings and Niemi (1981) Youth Socialization Panel Study, Smith estimates that the gain in political knowledge associated with going from a high school diploma to a doctorate would be less than one additional question correct on a six-question quiz. For their part Delli Carpini and Keeter (1996) speculate that a number of factors—declining levels of interest in political campaigns, weakened psychological attachment to parties, and dropping confidence that government is responsive to citizens—may well have offset the positive effects of education.

Scales Selected for Review

Following are eight sample scale measures of political information culled from the available literature. Most emphasize knowledge of national public affairs, and the majority employ data from surveys conducted by the ANES. Information on hundreds of individual knowledge questions can be obtained from Delli Carpini and Keeter (1996), especially Chapter 2 and Appendix 3.

1. Political Knowledge Scale (Delli Carpini & Keeter, 1996)
2. Political Awareness Scale (Zaller, 1986, 1992)
3. News Recall (Robinson & Levy, 1986; Price & Zaller, 1993; Price, 1993)
4. Political Information Scale (Iyengar, 1986; Zaller, 1986)
5. Candidate Like/Dislike Responses (Kessel, 1980; Smith, 1989)
6. Information Holding (Luskin, 1987)
7. Issue Awareness Index (Patterson & McClure, 1976)
8. Information about Foreign Countries (Robinson, 1967)

Several of these are omnibus political knowledge scales that combine a variety of question formats. The Political Knowledge Scale of Delli Carpini and Keeter (1996) makes use of comparative opinion placements, identifications, and several other direct information questions. Zaller's (1992) Political Awareness Scale uses comparative placements and identifications as well, but also adds the survey interviewer ratings of respondents' apparent levels of political information. Both scales can be viewed as excellent "general duty" information measures. They focus on national public affairs, and both demonstrate good internal consistency and construct validity. Both also draw from questions included in the National Election Studies, and rely upon items that tap relatively long-term information. Although the particular scales described below drew from ANES surveys that included a fairly rich selection of information questions, they offer secondary analysts good examples of the kinds of scales that can be built from standard ANES items, even when the supply of questions is more limited.

The largely unidimensional nature of political knowledge (as discussed above) means that such general measures may be useful in a wide variety of empirical applications. Nevertheless, analysts interested in specific political domains (e.g., economic issues or environmental issues) might wish to develop items tapping knowledge in those domains more directly, as illustrated by items included in the Iyengar (1986) and Zaller (1986) Political Information Scale. That scale includes a range of topical questions intended to form subscales in the areas of economics, racial issues, and foreign affairs. The question formats used—identifications, definitions, questions about the political leanings of a variety of groups and people—are more direct than many included in the general awareness scales built by Zaller (1992) from more regularly appearing ANES survey questions. Aside from the identifications, however, the topical knowledge questions included in the Political Information Scale have not been adopted for regular use by the ANES.

Whereas most of the information scales reviewed here emphasize general and enduring forms of political knowledge, the News Recall measures used by Robinson and Levy (1986) and Price and Zaller (1993) are intended to capture shorter-term knowledge. One potential advantage of these items is their directness and specificity: They capture basic awareness of recent and discrete news events. In principle, they offer a mechanism for linking specific information gains (e.g., about a new charge of wrongdoing against a party or public official) to some outcome of interest, such as opinion change, in a relatively unambiguous fashion. Because the questions tap entirely *new* pieces of information, there are few temporal ambiguities surrounding knowledge acquisition—as there inevitably are when longer-term information is measured. Although the utility of such news recall measures in the study of political persuasion remains untested, they have proven useful in studies of the diffusion of news and information. One important practical difficulty is that, because the questions aim at awareness of breaking stories in the news, researchers must operate with a survey design flexible enough to accommodate items developed either just before or during the field period. Another major difficulty is that researchers are seldom in a position to know, in advance, what particular news items will prove most effectual, politically speaking.

As discussed above, the Sum of Candidate Likes and Dislikes (Kessel, 1980; Smith, 1989) is a much less direct measure of political knowledge. It is a simple count of the number of things respondents report liking—or disliking—about candidates for office. The measure confounds political information-holding with loquacity. Moreover, because the content of responses is completely disregarded, the measure does not directly tap knowledge per se. Delli Carpini and Keeter (1996) also point out that like and dislike responses are often used as dependent variables in analyses; and in this case, uses of the same items as independent variables would clearly not be appropriate. Nonetheless, data from Smith (1989) and Delli Carpini and Keeter (1996) illustrate that the total number of like/dislike responses, despite its limitations, can serve as a potentially useful index of political knowledge. Perhaps the principal advantage is that it has become a staple of the ANES surveys, and in some cases may be one of the few alternatives available to secondary analysts.

Luskin's (1987) Information Holding Scale and the Issue Awareness Index of Patterson and McClure (1976) both focus on the ability of survey respondents to identify the issue positions of key political actors—parties in the former case and presidential candidates in the latter. In this respect, the two scales are somewhat more specialized than others reviewed here. As a practical matter, this form of knowledge is highly correlated with others (for instance, identification of political figures and knowledge of how government works). That is why the same ANES questions used by Luskin to build the Information Holding Scale (comparative placements of the parties on 7-point opinion scales) are incorporated by Zaller, Delli Carpini, and others into their omnibus scales. The Patterson and McClure items, although conceptually similar to those included in the ANES, use a very different format that was designed to track *increases* in citizens' issue knowledge over the course of a campaign. The authors did not compute comparative placements of the candidates, but the questions could certainly be employed for that purpose. Empirical evidence of scale reliability and validity has been presented for the ANES comparative placements, but not for the Patterson and McClure questions. One potential difficulty with the latter is that the agree/disagree response scale may invite respondents to report their own opinions, thus confounding these with the opinions believed to be held by candidates.

The earliest of the scale measures reviewed is Robinson's (1967) Information about Foreign Countries Scale. These items assess basic knowledge about the form of government and geographical location of a set of the world's nations, along with awareness of which countries have (or have not yet) developed and tested atomic weapons. Although the questions are dated and would need to be adapted to a contemporary application, they offer researchers an example of simple and quick question formats that can be used to measure foreign affairs knowledge.

Recommendations and Future Lines of Development

Information scales are fast becoming a standard part of the analysis of political behavior. The recent growth of theoretical interest in political information has quite naturally spawned concerns about its proper measurement. As noted at the beginning of this chapter, the result has been an expanded base of findings, many accumulated over the past decade, bearing on the assessment of political knowledge in survey research.

The findings to date are mainly good news for political scientists. Reliable scales measuring political information can be readily constructed using one or more of the approaches described here. Indeed, the reliability and over-time stability of information scales rival other central constructs of the field. Because people tend to be information generalists rather than specialists, a reliable omnibus measure built from a reasonably varied collection of test questions is likely to perform quite well in many research applications, regardless of the specific domains of content covered in the scale. The tendency of political information to behave as a general trait—or as a constellation of highly correlated subdimensions—means that short-form scales with a half-dozen or fewer items also achieve acceptable (though naturally somewhat lower) reliability. Findings from measurement studies, as well as those from substantive research studies making use of political information scales, give ample indications of construct validity.

Although much has been learned about the measurement of political information in the past several decades, there certainly remain open questions. Although evidence to date does suggest we can reasonably construe political information as a single dimension, there is little doubt that topical subdimensions do exist. At times domain-specific knowledge may be fundamentally implicated in important political persuasion processes, with effects that are distinguishable from those of general knowledge (e.g., Iyengar, 1986; McGraw & Pinney, 1990; Price & Zaller, 1993). Unfortunately, it is difficult to know when domain-specific knowledge will have such effects, or when a general measure will fail to identify them adequately. It would seem from findings to date that knowledge of local public affairs is the most unique subdimension of political information (Delli Carpini & Keeter, 1996), unique enough that analysts interested in local politics would do well not to rely exclusively on the general scales presented here. More research in the coming years should give us a more elaborate understanding of topical specificity in political information and its effects.

A second, even more basic question concerns the extent to which the persuasive effects of political communications are—or are not—generally mediated by stored knowledge of those communications. Much contemporary research in the field is based, implicitly if not explicitly, on a learning model of opinion change. Analysts often adopt the view that communications produce cognitive changes (i.e., changes in the salience or structure of knowledge), which subsequently influence evaluations and opinions. But the long-term duration of cognitive effects and their relation to evaluations has been questioned by theorists adopting the "on-line" model of political information processing (e.g., Lodge, McGraw, & Stroh, 1989). According to this model, people adjust their evaluations directly in response to communications, without storing in memory much of the information itself. Survey-based research by Zaller (1992) and others, in that it finds substantive changes in mass opinion that are clearly and understandably linked to political knowledge, certainly suggests that political learning figures prominently in opinion change. At the same time, recent experimental studies (e.g., Lodge, Steenbergen, & Brau, 1995) offer evidence of on-line communication effects and suggest a much weaker role for memory of messages.

Future research could help to reconcile these findings, perhaps by better clarifying the conditions under which on-line processing is most likely to occur and the prevalence of such conditions in everyday political experience.

A third question concerns the surprising stability of political information at the aggregate level, given increases in schooling over the past decades. As noted above, recent research investigating this phenomenon has not come to any firm conclusions or explanations. It is interesting to note that measures of non-political knowledge have shown similar stability—even declines—over the same period. There have been continuing debates, for example, about declines in standardized test scores and college entrance examinations, and reasons for these trends. Alwin's (1995) analysis of verbal ability measures carried on the General Social Surveys from 1974 to 1990 did indeed find a declining trend for successive birth cohorts dating from 1950 (i.e., for people graduating from high school in the late 1960s and afterward). His analysis aimed primarily at examining whether changes in the family, such as larger family sizes due to the post-war baby boom, dramatic increases in maternal employment, or growth in the number of single-parent families, might have accounted for the trends. These aspects of family life—which might conceivably have affected trends in political knowledge as well—do not, however, explain the trends in verbal ability (Alwin, 1995, p. 635). There are, of course, other possibilities for declines in various measures of academic performance or cognitive ability, which could also provide clues to explanations for the trends in political information over time. These include weakening academic values in families and schools, declines in academic rigor and/or practice associated with schooling (e.g., fewer hours spent on homework), increases in time spent with television, or changes in the content or structure of schooling (e.g., larger class sizes). It is possible that social trends such as these could affect the general preparedness of citizens to deal with the complexities of public affairs, and thus underlie overtime patterns in political knowledge.

Political Knowledge Scale

(M. X. Delli Carpini & S. Keeter, 1996)

Variable

This scale measures knowledge of basic civics, political parties, and people prominent in public affairs.

Description

Items are in general very similar to those used by Zaller in his political awareness scales (see the following review). Items were selected to cover political figures, political parties, and basic processes of government. The focus of the scale, however, was on national politics, with no items designed to tap knowledge of local government. Several scale measures were constructed, including a long-form (20-item) scale and a short-form (5-item) scale. Respondents scored one point for each item answered correctly and no points for items not answered or answered incorrectly. Consequently the long-form scale scores ranged from 0 to 20 and the short-form scale scores from 0–5. Across all items the mean proportion of respondents answering correctly was 43%. Scale distributions were normal.

Delli Carpini and Keeter employ the scale in describing three general "knowledge classes" (1996, p. 154). In the upper class are the top 30% of respondents, who, on average, answer about 70% of the questions correctly. The middle class is made up of the middle 40% of respondents, who, on average, answer about half the questions correctly. The remaining 30% of respondents make up the lower class, who, on average, answer only about a quarter of the questions correctly.

Sample

The study was conducted by the Center for Political Studies at the University of Michigan, by telephone, in the summer of 1991. The items were administered to a subsample ($N = 449$) of respondents to the 1990 ANES survey, a representative sample of the adult U.S. population.

Reliability

Reported scale reliability (alpha) for the short-form (5-item) scale was .71 and for the long-form (20-item) scale, .87. Corrected item–total correlations for individual items ranged from .28 to .52, averaging .47.

Validity

After presenting the most comprehensive analysis of political information scale items published to date, the authors conclude that a strong case can be made for unidimensionality. Latent variable structural equation modeling did reveal a discernible number of meaningful dimensions, but estimated interfactor correlations were very high, and a unidimensional model also fit the data well. Tests of construct validity indicated that each subdimension tended to correlate similarly with a variety of other variables (education, political interest, age, and other demographic variables).

Correlations with other variables (gender, race, income, education, interest in politics) were as hypothesized (see the previous text), indicating construct validity. Women, blacks, and lower-income groups tended to score consistently lower on the knowledge scales.

Location

Delli Carpini, M. X., & Keeter, S. (1996). *What Americans know about politics and why it matters.* New Haven, CT: Yale University Press. Data are available from the Inter-University Consortium for Political and Social Research (ICPSR Study No. 9548 and No. 9673).

Results and Comments

The authors also developed a longer, 39-item scale in a separate study drawing from a sample of 610 U.S. adults contacted from March to May of 1989. That scale used similar items, but included a more extensive set of questions bearing on political issues (e.g., defining the Superfund, knowing whether one's state can prohibit abortion, defining the term *recession*). Reliability and validity analyses produced results similar to those noted here.

Political Knowledge Scale
(Delli Carpini & Keeter, 1996)

Following is a description of the scale items used in the 1991 ANES Pilot Study.

Do you happen to remember the names of the candidates for Congress—
that is, for the House of Representatives in Washington—who ran in this
district this November? Who were they? [Probe: Any others?]

1. What was [candidate's name]'s party? (23% correct) (V111)

Now we have a set of questions concerning various public figures. We
want to see how much information about them gets out to the public from
television, newspapers, and the like.

2. The first name is Dan Quayle. What job or political office does he
   now hold? (Answer: Vice President; 84% correct) (V395)

3. (Do you happen to know what job or political office) George
   Mitchell (holds now)? (Answer: Senate Majority Leader; 3% correct) (V396)

4. William Rehnquist? (Answer: Chief Justice of Supreme Court; 5%
   correct) (V397)

5. Mikhail Gorbachev? (Answer: Head of Soviet Union, Russia, or
   Communist Party; 71% correct) (V398)

6. Margaret Thatcher? (Answer: Prime Minister (former) of U.K.; 53%
   correct) (V399)

7. Nelson Mandela? (Answer: Black leader in South Africa, or of
   A.N.C.; 17% correct) (V400)

8. Tom Foley? (Answer: Speaker of the House; 12% correct) (V401)

We hear a lot of talk these days about liberals and conservatives. Here is
a seven-point scale on which the political views that people might hold are
arranged from extremely liberal to extremely conservative.

Where would you place yourself on this scale, or haven't you thought
much about this? [If DK or HAVEN'T THOUGHT MUCH] If you had to
choose, would you consider yourself a liberal or conservative?

9a. (Where would you place) the Democratic Party? (V413)

9b. (Where would you place) the Republican Party? (V414) (Correct
   only if Democrats are rated more liberal than Republicans)

I am going to read you several statements. After each one, I would like you
to tell me whether you AGREE STRONGLY with the statement, AGREE
SOMEWHAT, NEITHER AGREE NOR DISAGREE, DISAGREE SOME-
WHAT, or DISAGREE STRONGLY. You can just give me the number of your
choice from the booklet. (VERIFY BY READING CHOICE BACK TO
RESPONDENT.) The first statement is:

Some people believe that we should spend much less money for defense. (Suppose these people are at one end of the scale, at point number 1.) Others feel that defense spending should be greatly increased. (Suppose these people are at the other end, at point 7. And, of course, some people have opinions somewhere in between, at points 2, 3, 4, 5 or 6.)

> Where would you place yourself on this scale, or haven't you thought much about this?
>
> 10a. (Where would you place) the Democratic Party? (V443)
>
> 10b. (Where would you place) the Republican Party? (V444) (Correct only if Republicans are rated as more supportive of cuts)

Some people feel that the government in Washington should make every effort to improve the social and economic position of blacks. Others feel that the government should not make any special effort to help blacks because they should help themselves.

> Where would you place yourself on this scale, or haven't you thought much about this?
>
> 11a. (Where would you place) the Democratic Party? (V449)
>
> 11b. (Where would you place) the Republican Party? (V450) (Correct only if Democrats are rated as more favorable toward making every effort)

Some people feel that the government should provide fewer services, even in such areas as health and education in order to reduce spending. Other people feel it is important for the government to provide many more services even if it means an increase in spending.

> Where would you place yourself on this scale, or haven't you thought much about this?
>
> 12a. (Where would you place) the Democratic Party? (V456)
>
> 12b. (Where would you place) the Republican Party? (V457) (Correct only if Democrats are rated as more favorable toward providing many services)

13. Do you happen to know which party had the most members in the House of Representatives in Washington BEFORE the election (this/last) month? Answer: Democrats; 55% correct) (V402)

14. Do you happen to know which party had the most members in the Senate in Washington BEFORE the election (this/last) month? Answer: Democrats; 47% correct) (V403)

Last, here are a few questions about the government in Washington. Many people don't know the answers to these questions, so if there are some you don't know just tell me and we'll go on.

> 15. What are the first ten amendments to the U.S. Constitution called? (Answer: The Bill of Rights; 43% correct) (V2848)

16. Whose responsibility is it to determine if a law is constitutional or not . . . is it the President, the Congress, or the Supreme Court? (Answer: Supreme Court; 68% correct) (V2849)

17. And whose responsibility is it to nominate judges to the Federal Courts . . . is it the President, the Congress, or the Supreme Court? (Answer: The President; 51% correct) (V2850)

18. How much of a majority is required for the U.S. Senate and House to override a presidential veto? (Answer: Two thirds of both houses; 37% correct) (V2851)

19. Do you happen to know how many times an individual can be elected President? (Answer: Two times; 73% correct) (V2852)

20. How long is the term of a United States Senator? (Answer: Six years; 25% correct) (V2853)

Scale Items for Short Form

(Following are the recommended wordings for a five-item scale.)

Last, here are a few questions about the government in Washington. Many people don't know the answers to these questions, so if there are some you don't know just tell me and we'll go on.

1. Do you happen to know what job or political office is now held by [insert current vice-president]?

2. Whose responsibility is it to determine if a law is constitutional or not . . . is it the president, the Congress, or the Supreme Court? (Answer: the Supreme Court)

3. How much of a majority is required for the U.S. Senate and House to override a presidential veto? (Answer: Two-thirds of both houses)

4. Do you happen to know which party had the most members in the House of Representatives in Washington before the election (this/last) month?

5. Would you say that one of the parties is more conservative than the other at the national level? Which party is more conservative? (Answer: Republican Party)

Political Awareness
(J. Zaller, 1986, 1992)

Variable

This scale is designed to measure respondents' ability to recall "political ideas that have been encountered, comprehended, and remain available for use" (Zaller, 1990, p. 131).

Description

Scales have been constructed for many different ANES survey collections. The composition of each scale varies, depending on the particular supply of items available on a given survey. In general, however, they are built from comparative placements of parties and candidates on opinion scales; a sampling of direct knowledge questions, usually identifications of political figures; and ANES interviewer ratings of the respondents' general level of information. The focus of the scale is generally national politics, with some items measuring foreign affairs information. Respondents typically score one point for each item answered correctly and no points for items not answered or answered incorrectly. In the 1984 ANES study, the measure was a 24-point scale, with a mean of 9.8.

Sample

The sample scale below was drawn from the 1984 ANES, conducted by the Center for Political Studies at the University of Michigan. The study was based on a national, multistage area probability sample representative of citizens of voting age ($N = 2257$).

Reliability

The 1984 scale reproduced here has an alpha reliability of .87 (Zaller, 1986). Zaller (1992) reports that for all ANES surveys except those in 1951, 1978 (House elections), and 1990 (Senate elections), alpha reliability coefficients ranged from .80 to .90, with most typically about .85.

Validity

Although some of the composite items are only indirect tests of information, evidence suggests that they do tap the intended construct. Zaller (1986) reports a series of tests in which the 1984 political awareness scale and a 27-item scale built entirely of direct knowledge tests (see the review of the Political Information Scale) were correlated with a series of criterion variables. He found that the two scales showed close to identical patterns of correlations with issue salience, opinion stability, and opinion consistency. Zaller (1990) also reports that a Political Awareness Scale from the 1972–1974–1976 ANES Panel Study successfully predicted opinion crystallization (as measured by the test–retest stability and measurement reliability of opinion measures). In that case it proved to be a consistently better predictor than education, political interest, participation, or media exposure.

Location

Zaller, J. (1992). *The nature and origins of mass opinion.* Oxford: Oxford University Press. Data from the 1984 ANES are available from the Inter-University Consortium for Political and Social Research (ICPSR Study No. 8298).

Results and Comments

Zaller uses measures of political awareness to model patterns of mass opinion change in response to both one-sided and two-sided flows of political information. In cases of elite consensus, mass opinion follows a "mainstream" pattern such that better-informed citizens, regardless of their predispositions, are most likely to change their views in line with the flow of political news. In cases of elite conflict, on the other hand, mass opinion follows a "polarization" pattern. Better-informed citizens are likely to change only when the flow of information supports their predispositions, leading to increased opinion gaps between better-informed liberals and conservatives (the model is fully described in Zaller, 1992).

Political Awareness Scale
(Zaller, 1992)

(Following is a description of the scale items used in the 1984 ANES. All variables were scored one if correct and zero otherwise, unless indicated differently here.)

We hear a lot of talk these days about liberals and conservatives. Here is a seven-point scale on which the political views that people might hold are arranged from extremely liberal to extremely conservative.

Where would you place yourself on this scale, or haven't you thought much about this? [If DK or HAVEN'T THOUGHT MUCH] If you had to choose, would you consider yourself a liberal or conservative?

1a, 2a. (Where would you place) Ronald Reagan? (Preelection wave, V371; Postelection wave, V1017)

1b, 2b. (Where would you place) Walter Mondale? (Preelection wave, V372; Postelection wave, V1018) (Scored correct only if Reagan is rated 2 points to right of Walter Mondale on preelection measures 1a and 1b, and 3 points to the right on the post-election measures 2a and 2b)

I am going to read you several statements. After each one, I would like you to tell me whether you AGREE STRONGLY with the statement, AGREE SOMEWHAT, NEITHER AGREE NOR DISAGREE, DISAGREE SOMEWHAT, or DISAGREE STRONGLY. You can just give me the number of your choice from the booklet. (VERIFY BY READING CHOICE BACK TO RESPONDENT.) The first statement is:

Some people feel that the government should provide fewer services, even in such areas as health and education in order to reduce spending. (Suppose these people are at one end of the scale, at point number 1.) Other people feel it is important for the government to provide many more services even if it means an increase in spending. (Suppose these people are at the other end, at point 7. And, of course, some people have opinions somewhere in between, at points 2, 3, 4, 5 or 6.)

Where would you place yourself on this scale, or haven't you thought much about this?

3a. (Where would you place) Ronald Reagan? (Pre-election wave, V376)

3b. (Where would you place) Walter Mondale? (Preelection wave, V377) (Scored correct only if Reagan is at least 2 points to right of Mondale)

4a. (Where would you place) most liberals? (Postelection wave, V1034)

4b. (Where would you place) most conservatives? (Postelection wave, V1035) (Scored correct only if liberals are rated at least 3 points to left of conservatives)

Some people feel that the government in Washington should make every effort to improve the social and economic position of blacks and other minorities. Others feel that the government should not make any special effort to help minorities because they should help themselves.

Where would you place yourself on this scale, or haven't you thought much about this?

5a. (Where would you place) Ronald Reagan? (Preelection wave, V383)

5b. (Where would you place) Walter Mondale? (Preelection wave, V384) (Scored correct only if Reagan is to right of Mondale)

Some people think that the United States should become much more involved in the internal affairs of Central American countries. Others believe that the U.S. should become much less involved in this area.

Where would you place yourself on this scale, or haven't you thought much about this?

6a. (Where would you place) Ronald Reagan? (Preelection wave, V389)

6b. (Where would you place) Walter Mondale? (Preelection wave, V390) (Scored correct only if Reagan is at least 2 points to right of Mondale)

7a. (Where would you place) most liberals? (Postelection wave, V1045)

7b. (Where would you place) most conservatives? (Postelection wave, V1046) (Scored correct only if at least 3 points to left of conservatives)

Some people believe that we should spend much less money for defense. Others feel that defense spending should be greatly increased.

Where would you place yourself on this scale, or haven't you thought much about this?

8a. (Where would you place) Ronald Reagan? (Preelection wave, V396)

8b. (Where would you place) Walter Mondale? (Preelection wave, V397) (Scored correct only if Reagan is to right of Mondale)

Some people feel it is important for us to try to cooperate more with Russia, while others believe we should be much tougher in our dealings with Russia.

Where would you place yourself on this scale, or haven't you thought much about this?

        9a. (Where would you place) Ronald Reagan? (Preelection wave, V409)

        9b. (Where would you place) Walter Mondale? (Preelection wave, V410) (Scored correct only if Reagan is to right of Mondale)

Some people feel that the government in Washington should see to it that every person has a job and a good standard of living. Others think the government should just let each person get ahead on his own.

        Where would you place yourself on this scale, or haven't you thought much about this?

        10a. (Where would you place) Ronald Reagan? (Preelection wave, V415)

        10b. (Where would you place) Walter Mondale? (Preelection wave, V416) (Scored correct only if Reagan is to right of Mondale)

        11a. (Where would you place) most liberals? (Postelection wave, V1054) (Scored correct only if at least 3 points to left of conservatives)

        11b. (Where would you place) most conservatives? (Postelection wave, V1055) (Scored correct only if liberals are to right of liberals)

    12a. Do you happen to remember the names of the candidates for Congress—that is, for the House of Representatives in Washington—who ran in this district this November? Who were they? [Probe: Any others?]

    12b. What was [candidate's name]'s party? (Two candidates, Postelection wave, V741 & V745; each coded 2 points if name and party correct, 1 if name correct, 0 otherwise)

13. Would you say that one party is more conservative than the other at the national level? (If yes) Which party is more conservative? (Postelection wave, V875)

14. Do you happen to know which party had the most members in the House of Representatives in Washington BEFORE the election? (Postelection wave, V1006)

15. As a result of the election this month, which party *will now have* the most members in the House of Representatives? (Postelection wave, V1007)

16. Do you happen to know which party had the most members in the U.S. Senate *before* the election? (Postelection wave, V1008)

17. As a result of the election this month, which party *will now have* the most members in the U.S. Senate? (Postelection wave, V1009)

I'd like to get your feelings toward some of our political leaders and other people who are in the news these days. I will use something we call the feeling thermometer and here is how it works: I'll read the name of a person and I'd like you to rate that person using the feeling thermometer. Ratings between 50 degrees and 100 degrees mean that you feel favorable and warm toward the person. Ratings between 0 degrees and 50 degrees mean that you don't feel favorable toward the person and that you don't care too much for that person. If we come to a person whose name you don't recognize, you don't need to rate that person. Just tell me and we'll move on to the next one. If you do recognize the name, but you don't feel particularly warm or cold toward the person, you would rate the person at the 50 degree mark.

Our first person is Ronald Reagan. How would you rate him using the thermometer? [Probe for "I don't know" response: When you say "don't know" do you mean that you don't know who the person is, or do you have something else in mind?]

18. George Bush? (Preelection wave, V292) (Correct if other than "don't know")

19. Geraldine Ferraro? (Preelection wave, V304) (Correct if other than "don't know")

20, 21. [Interviewer Rating at conclusion of interview] Respondent's general level of information about politics seemed: very high, fairly high, average, fairly low, very low. (Pre-election wave, V713; Post-election wave, V1112; each coded from 4 = very high to 0 = very low)

News Recall Scale

(J. P. Robinson & M. R. Levy, 1986; V. Price & J. Zaller, 1993; V. Price, 1993)

Variable

These items measure basic awareness of recent stories prominent in the news.

Description

Items developed by Robinson and Levy (1986) were part of an effort to assess audience comprehension of a week's news. Those developed by Price and Zaller (1993) were quite similar in form, but were intended to serve as a validating criterion for various survey measures of news media exposure and attention. In both cases, for each news story respondents were asked in general terms whether they had seen or heard anything about the news item. If they answered yes, an open-ended question was asked to confirm whether they knew rudimentary elements of the story. Respondents were given one point for any minimally correct response to the open-ended follow-up question and zero otherwise. Robinson and Levy combined 14 single items into a cumulative scale, with scores ranging from 0 to 14. Owing to the fact that most questions in the Price and Zaller study were rotated on the survey, overlapping cases were insufficient to create a large, multi-item scale. Price (1993) did, however, compute a scale by combining five questions that were administered to all wave one respondents (noted with an asterisk in the list below; scale scores ranged from 0 to 5).

Wordings of the questions used by Robinson and Levy can be found in Appendix C of their book (Robinson & Levy, 1986, pp. 252–255). The Price and Zaller questions, which refer to more recent news events, are presented below. These questions covered awareness of a wide range of news items, including low-profile international and domestic political affairs (e.g., an arms proposal by Soviet leader Mikhail Gorbachev, debates in Congress over repeal of catastrophic health insurance), and higher-profile political news (e.g., a Supreme Court decision on abortion) as well as some nonpolitical news (e.g., an airline disaster and the trial of a movie actress).

Sample

The two-wave panel study was conducted by the Center for Political Studies at the University of Michigan, by telephone, in the summer of 1989. The items were administered to a subsample of respondents to the 1988 ANES, a representative sample of the adult U.S. population (wave one: $N = 614$; wave two: $N = 494$). Cases varied considerably for different news items because questions were rotated on and off the telephone interview schedule.

Reliability

As noted above, the fact that most questions were rotated on the survey left too few cases for computing reliable inter-item correlations for many stories. However, a scale formed by combining five questions that were administered to all wave one respondents (noted with an asterisk in the list below) produced an internal consistency reliability (alpha) of .75 (Price, 1993).

Validity

Strong bivariate relationships were observed between the news recall items and education, general political knowledge (assessed with items similar to those in the Zaller and Delli Carpini and Keeter scales reviewed earlier), media exposure and attention (especially to print media), and political discussion. Multivariate analyses reported by Price and Zaller (1993) showed that the strongest and most consistent indicator of news reception was general political knowledge, measured along the lines of Zaller's (1992) political awareness scale (described earlier).

Location

Price, V., & Zaller, J. (1993). Who gets the news? Alternative measures of news reception and implications for research. *Public Opinion Quarterly, 57,* 133–164. Data are available from the Inter-University Consortium for Political and Social Research (ICPSR Study No. 9295).

Results and Comments

These questions were designed to assess only the short-term current information retained rather than more enduring knowledge inventories. Results showed that the two kinds of knowledge are strongly related. By itself a scale measure of political information could correctly classify an average of nearly 80% of cases as having recalled the news stories or not (a 46% reduction in classification errors; Price & Zaller, 1993). Furthermore, Zaller and Price (1990) found that levels of general knowledge predicted the rate at which respondents forgot about these news stories. The better informed tended to retain the information over a 90-day period, while it quickly decayed among the poorly informed.

Price and Zaller (1993) also found several cases of domain-specific news reception, whereby certain members of the audience were more likely than others to receive news stories that were especially relevant to them (e.g., older people in the case of news about catastrophic health insurance). These effects, however, tended to supplement rather than override the consistently strong association between general political information and news reception.

The authors conclude that, "as a practical matter, the measurable effects of self-reported media use on learning are more or less completely swamped by the stronger, overall tendency of the better informed to stay that way" (1993, p. 158). When the analyst wishes to estimate the likelihood that a person actually received a particular item of news, they argue, the preferred indicator would be general political knowledge rather than self-reports of media use.

News Recall Scale
(Price & Zaller, 1993)

(Following is a description of the scale items from the 1989 ANES Pilot Study used by Price and Zaller [1993]. Items noted with an asterisk were combined by Price [1993] into a five-item scale.)

Now we have a set of questions concerning recent stories in the news. We want to see how much information gets out to the public from television, newspapers, and the like.

1. Have you read or heard any news articles about the resignation of Congressman Jim Wright? (If yes) Do you happen to recall why he resigned? (44% recalled) (V7450)*

2. Do you recall any stories about a U.S. Supreme Court decision this summer on the death penalty? (If yes) Do you remember what the court decided? (17% recalled) (V7454)*

3. Have you heard or read any stories about the Department of Housing and Urban Development, also known as HUD? (If yes) Do you happen to remember why this agency was in the news? (50% recalled) (V7456)*

4. Do you remember any recent stories about Marine Colonel Oliver North receiving a sentence for his conviction in the Iran-Contra affair? (If yes) Do you recall anything about what sentence he received? (67% recalled) (V7458)*

5. Do you recall any stories about a U.S. Supreme Court decision this summer on abortion? (If yes) Do you remember what the court decided? (52% recalled) (V7460)*

6. Do you remember any stories about former President Reagan undergoing surgery? (If yes) Do you recall why he underwent surgery? (78% recalled) (V7462)

7. Have you heard or read any stories about Soviet leader Gorbachev making an arms control proposal during his recent visit to France? (If yes) Do you remember anything about what he proposed? (27% recalled) (V7466)

8. Have you heard or read any stories about President Bush leaving Washington to go on an official trip? (If yes) Do you happen to recall where he went? (65% recalled) (V7468)

9. Have you seen or heard any stories about the B2 Stealth Bomber? (If yes) Do you happen to recall why the Stealth Bomber was in the news? (54% recalled) (V7472)

10. Have you seen any stories about a major airline disaster? (If yes) What exactly happened? (85% recalled) (V7476)

11. Have you seen or heard any stories about a major televised speech to the nation by President George Bush? (If yes) Do you remember what the main points of his speech were? (61% recalled) (V8602)

12. Do you remember any stories about the Solidarity labor movement gaining a new position in the Polish government? (If yes) Do you recall what position that was? (40% recalled) (V8606)

13. Have you seen or heard any stories about the trial of TV evangelist Jim Bakker? (If yes) Do you recall what's going on with the trial right now? (78% recalled) (V8612)

14. Have you seen or heard any news stories about the actress Zsa Zsa Gabor? (If yes) Do you recall why she was in the news? (72% recalled) (V8622)

15. Have you heard or seen any stories about Ed Koch's defeat in his effort to be re-elected as mayor of New York? (If yes) Do you recall anything about the candidate who beat him? (30% recalled) (V8624)

16. Do you remember any stories about proposals in Congress to change the Government's catastrophic health insurance program? (If yes) Do you recall what these proposals are mainly about? (14% recalled) (V8626)

Political Information Scale

(S. Iyengar, 1986; J. Zaller, 1986)

Variable

This instrument is based on a variety of factual questions intended to measure a person's general political knowledge.

Description

The 27 items test current public affairs information rather than "textbook" knowledge. Questions tap knowledge in several domains, including international political affairs, domestic politics, race, and economics. With each item scored 1 if correct and 0 otherwise, scale scores range from 0 to 27.

The items were designed to explore a variety of issues in the measurement of political information, including the degree to which knowledge measures should be domain-specific (Iyengar, 1986; Zaller, 1986) and the extent to which standard items carried on the ANES served as good indicators of political knowledge.

Sample

The two-wave panel study was conducted by the Center for Political Studies at the University of Michigan, by telephone, in the summer of 1985. The items were administered to a subsample of respondents to the 1984 ANES, a representative sample of the adult U.S. population. The knowledge items were asked only in the final wave ($N = 345$). Zaller (1986) reports that, owing to panel attrition, the sample was upwardly biased in the distribution of political information.

Reliability

Zaller (1986) combined all items into a single scale, for which he reports a reliability coefficient (alpha) of .89. Iyengar (1986) analyzed the pattern of correlations within and across substantive information domains to produce a set of four, maximally independent domain-specific scales. A four-item race information scale (selected items are each noted "R" below) had a reliability (alpha) of .58. A three-item economic information scale (items noted "E" below) had a reliability of .59. A four-item foreign-affairs information scale (items noted "F" below) had a reliability of .78, and a four-item scale of information about group politics (items noted "G" below) had a reliability of .71.

Validity

Zaller demonstrated that the general knowledge scale (using all 27 items) effectively predicted issue salience, opinion stability, and opinion consistency, across a range of issues (U.S. involvement in Central America, government spending, and aid to minorities). Iyengar found that blacks were lower than whites, after controls, in foreign affairs information and economic knowledge, but higher than whites in race information. Using scales similar (though not identical) to the domain-specific scales developed by Iyengar, Zaller found that topical knowledge did correlate slightly better with salience, stability, and consistency within the relevant domain (e.g., race information with opinions on affirmative action) than did general knowledge. Overall, however, such differences were small.

Location

Iyengar, S. (1986). *Whither political information.* Report to the National Election Studies Board of Overseers, Center for Political Studies, University of Michigan. Also Zaller, J. (1986). *Analysis of information items on the 1985 NES Pilot Study.* Report to the National Election Studies Board of Overseers, Center for Political Studies, University of Michigan. Data are available from the Inter-University Consortium for Political and Social Research (ICPSR Study Number 8476).

Results and Comments

The authors reach somewhat different conclusions and offer distinct recommendations based upon their review of the data. Iyengar concluded that domain-specific scales—in the area of race information—are superior to general information measures for detecting knowledge effects on opinion formation (specifically, evaluations of President Reagan). He recommended inclusion of race-specific knowledge items on ANES surveys for this reason. Zaller agreed that there are some advantages to measures of domain-specific knowledge. However, because in most instances these advantages are small to modest, a general measure of information suffices. Moreover, he concluded that a general political awareness measure constructed entirely of standard ANES election survey questions (see above) performs just as well as the 27-item knowledge scale.

Political Information Scale
(Iyengar, 1986; Zaller, 1986)

(Following is a description of the knowledge items from the 1985 ANES Pilot Study used by Iyengar [1986] and Zaller [1986]. Percentages correct and "partially correct" given here are as reported by Iyengar [1986]. Items noted *R* were included in Iyengar's race information scale, while those labeled *E, F,* and *G* were used to measure knowledge of economics, foreign affairs, and group politics, respectively.)

Now we have a set of questions concerning public affairs information. These questions do not represent a "test" of any sort; rather, we want to assess what kind of information gets through to the public and whether different people find out about different issues.

I'm going to read a list of individuals, groups and terms. Please try to identify each. [Do not probe "don't know" responses]

1. Martin Luther King (Answer: Black civil rights leader; 41% correct, 41% partially correct) (V8501)

2. Caspar Weinberger (Answer: Secretary of Defense; 19% correct, 16% partially correct) (V8502)

3. Thurgood Marshall (Answer: Supreme Court Justice; 18% correct, 5% partially correct) (V8503)—R

4. George Bush (Answer: Vice-President) (V8504)

5. N.A.A.C.P. (Answer: National Association for the Advancement of Colored People; 45% correct, 15% partially correct) (V8505)—R

6. Daniel Ortega (Answer: President of Nicaragua; 7% correct, 5% partially correct) (V8506)

7. Richard Nixon (Answer: Former President) (V8507)

8. Dow Jones Index (Answer: Stock market index; 22% correct, 47% partially correct) (V8508)

9. NATO (Answer: North Atlantic Treaty Organization; 21% correct, 18% partially correct) (V8509)—F

10. Affirmative Action (Answer: Program for employment advancement of minorities; 13% correct, 17% partially correct) (V8510)—R

11. Paul Volker (Answer: Head of Federal Reserve Board; 10% correct, 7% partially correct) (V8511)

12. What do you think is the current unemployment rate? (Answer: 6–8.5%; 42% correct) (V8512)—E

13. What do you think is the current rate of inflation—that is, by what percent have prices increased this year over last? (Answer: 2–5%; 42% correct) (V8513)—*E*

14. Is the federal budget deficit larger or smaller than it was when Ronald Reagan took office? (Answer: Larger; 83% correct) (V8514)—*E*

Now I'm going to read a list of groups and individuals. For each, please indicate what you consider their political party preference to be, if they have one—generally Democrat, generally Republican, or no clear preference. The first group is . . .

15. Corporate executives. (Answer: Republican; 60% correct) (V8515)—*G*

16. Blacks (Answer: Democrat; 69% correct) (V8516)—*G*

17. Jack Kemp (Answer: Republican; 27% correct) (V8517)

18. Mario Cuomo (Answer: Democrat; 40% correct) (V8518)

19. People on welfare (Answer: Democrat; 59% correct) (V8519)—*G*

20. Feminists (Answer: Democrat; 46% correct) (V8520)

21. Stock brokers (Answer: Republican; 62% correct) (V8521)—*G*

Now I would like to ask you about the international situation.

22. Is the government of Poland an ally of the United States, an ally of Russia, an ally of neither, or aren't you sure about this? (Answer: Russia; 47% correct) (V8522)—*F*

23. How about Turkey? Is the government of Turkey an ally of the United States, an ally of Russia, an ally of neither, or aren't you sure about this? (Answer: United States; 20% correct) (8523)

24. This is a question about mainland China. Have you paid attention to the kind of government China has—is it a democracy, a communist system, or something else? (Answer: Communist; 70% correct) (8524)

25. How about India? Is the government of India a democracy, a communist system, or something else? (Answer: Democracy; 30% correct) (8525)—*F*

26. Is the United States a member of the United Nations? (Answer: Yes; 96% correct) (8526)

27. Do you happen to know in what country the headquarters and General Assembly of the United Nations are located? (Answer: U.S. or New York; 58% correct) (V8527)—*F*

Candidate Like/Dislike Responses

(J. H. Kessel, 1980; E. R. A. N. Smith, 1989)

Variable

This scale is based on the number of responses given to open-ended questions asking what the respondent likes and dislikes about the two major parties and their candidates.

Description

Respondents are asked to think about the good and bad points about parties and candidates and to tell the interviewer separately their likes and dislikes. Interviewers probe for up to five separate likes and five dislikes for each of four questions (two parties, and two candidates). Thus the total number of responses ranges from 0 to 40. In this particular measure the content of the responses is disregarded; only a sum is calculated.

Sample

Multiple surveys conducted by the ANES included these questions. The studies were based on multistage area probability samples representative of citizens of voting age, with sample sizes generally ranging from 1000 to 2000.

Reliability

Delli Carpini and Keeter (1996, p. 304) analyzed this measure in conjunction with a scale of 20 other information items (see the earlier review) and reported a corrected item–total correlation of .57. Smith (1989) reports split-half reliability coefficients for surveys from 1956 to 1976 ranging from .50 to .56.

Validity

In ANES surveys from 1956 to 1976, the correlation between total count of likes/dislikes and education was approximately .35 (Smith, 1989). Average correlations with other criterion variables were as follows: political activity, .29; number of media used in following the election, .34; and knowledge of which party controls the U.S. House of Representatives, .38. In factor analyses along with other information items, loadings for the sum of party responses and the sum of candidate responses (treated as separate items) were generally above .65 (Smith, 1989). Kessel (1980) reports a correlation (*Tau*-c) of .44 with survey interviewers' ratings of respondents' general levels of political information.

Location

Kessel, J. H. (1980). *Presidential campaign politics: Coalition strategies and citizen response.* Washington, DC: CQ Press.

Smith, E. R. A. N. (1989). *The unchanging American voter.* Berkeley: University of California Press. Data are available from the Inter-University Consortium for Political and Social Research (ICPSR).

Results and Comments

As Kessel (1980) points out, the measure confounds political information holding with loquacity. Smith (1989) also notes that results may vary as a function of interviewer behavior, with interviewers who probe more carefully and consistently eliciting more responses. Because the content of responses is disregarded, the measure does not directly tap knowledge per se. Another limitation, noted by Delli Carpini and Keeter (1996), is that like and dislike responses are often used as dependent variables in substantive analyses (for an example, see Zaller, 1992, chap. 10); use of the same items as independent variables in these cases would be inappropriate.

Nonetheless, Smith (1989) argues that the total number of responses is a useful indicator of political knowledge and, more generally, sophistication. The number of responses is, for instance, more reliable and more stable than the traditional "levels of conceptualization" indices based on the content of responses. The sum of party responses appears somewhat more reliable than the sum of candidate responses.

Smith reports that the number of responses given to the ANES likes–dislikes questions has remained stable over time (1989, p. 164). From 1956 to 1976 the average total number of responses hovered close to 7.5 (just over 3 party responses and between 4 and 4.5 candidate responses).

Likes/Dislikes Response Index
(Kessel, 1980; Smith, 1989)

Following is a description of the scale items currently included in the National Election Studies. One point is given for each response, no matter what the content.

1. I'd like to ask you what you think are the good and bad points about the two national parties. Is there anything in particular you like about the Democratic Party? [If necessary] What is that?

   Record responses 1–5 [Probe: Anything else you like about the Democratic Party? until respondent says "No"]

2. Is there anything in particular you don't like about the Democratic Party? [If necessary] What is that?

   Record responses 1–5 [Probe: Anything else you don't like about the Democratic Party? until respondent says "No"]

3. Is there anything in particular you like about the Republican Party? [If necessary] What is that?

   Responses 1–5 [Probe: Anything else you like about the Republican Party? until respondent says "No"]

4. Is there anything in particular you don't like about the Republican Party? [If necessary] What is that?

   Responses 1–5 [Probe: Anything else you don't like about the Republican Party? until respondent says "No"]

5. Next I would like to ask you what you think about the candidate(s) who ran for [name office]. Was there anything in particular you liked about [name candidate], the Democratic candidate for [name office]. [If necessary] What was that?

   Record responses 1–5 [Probe: Anything else you liked about this candidate? until respondent says "No"]

6. Is there anything in particular you didn't like about [name candidate]? [If necessary] What was that?

   Record responses 1–5 [Probe: Anything else you didn't like about this candidate? until respondent says "No"]

7. Is there anything in particular you liked about [name candidate], the Republican candidate for [name office]? [If necessary] What was that?

Record responses 1–5 [Probe: Anything else you liked about this candidate? until respondent says "No"]

8. Is there anything in particular you didn't like about [name candidate]? [If necessary] What was that?

Record responses 1–5 [Probe: Anything else you didn't like about this candidate? until respondent says "No"]

Information Holding

(R. C. Luskin, 1987)

Variable

This scale is based on knowledge of the relative position of the major parties on a range of issues.

Description

After giving their opinions on 11 policy issues using seven-point response scales, respondents are asked to place the two major political parties on those same scales. Respondents are given one point for each issue if they (1) place themselves on the opinion scale, (2) place both parties on the same scale, and (3) correctly order the two parties' programs. The measure is similar to an index of "partisan schema usage" developed by Hamill *et al.* (1985), except that the latter did not require the respondent to offer an opinion and did require placement on the correct side of the scale midpoint. Most ANES composite measures of general political knowledge (see the scales from Zaller and from Delli Carpini & Keeter reviewed previously) make use of comparative placements as component items. Scores on Luskin's scale range from 0 to 11.

Sample

Multiple surveys conducted by the ANES included opinion-placement questions, with the specific issues varying from election to election. The studies are based on multistage area probability samples representative of citizens of voting age, with sample sizes generally ranging from 1000 to 2000. Luskin (1987) based his analysis on the 1976 ANES.

Reliability

Luskin (1987) does not report reliability statistics. However, Delli Carpini and Keeter (1996) reported an analysis using ANES surveys from 1990–1991 in which six very similar comparative placements were used in a 20-item information scale. Item–total correlations ranged from .49 (for the relative location of the parties on aid to blacks) to .54 (for the relative location of the parties on a general ideology scale).

Validity

The information holding measure correlated positively with several criterion variables, including self-location on a liberal–conservative scale (.48); correct identification of the party controlling the U.S. House of Representatives, both before and after the election (.60); and the interviewer's rating of the respondent's level of political information (.58).

Location

Luskin, R. C. (1987). Measuring political sophistication. *American Journal of Political Science, 31,* 856–899. Reprinted by permission of the University of Wisconsin Press. Data are available from the Inter-University Consortium for Political and Social Research (ICPSR Study No. 7381).

Results and Comments

Researchers must exercise judgment in transforming respondents' opinion placements into information items. Luskin notes that, in 1976, the parties' positions on two issues—penalties for marijuana smoking and an equal role for women in business, industry, and government—were not sufficiently clear to consider any ordering necessarily incorrect (thus, apparently, all respondents expressing an opinion and placing both parties on those two issues, regardless of the ordering, received credit for these items).

Information Holding Scale
(Luskin, 1987)

(Following is a description of the scale items from the 1976 ANES used by Luskin [1987].)

Some people feel that the government in Washington should see to it that every person has a job and a good standard of living. Suppose that these people are at one end of this scale—at point number 1. Others think the government should just let each person get ahead on his own. Suppose that these people are at the other end—at point number 7. And, of course, some other people have opinions in between.

    1a. Where would you place yourself on this scale, or haven't you thought much about this? (V3241)

    1b. (Where would you place) the Democratic Party ⟨on this scale⟩? (V3244)

    1c. (Where would you place) the Republican Party ⟨on this scale⟩? (V3245) (Scored correct if respondent places self in part [a], and then places Republicans higher than Democrats in parts [b] and [c])

Some people are primarily concerned with doing everything possible to protect the legal rights of those accused of committing crimes. Others feel that it is more important to stop criminal activity even at the risk of reducing the rights of the accused.

    2a. Where would you place yourself on this scale, or haven't you thought much about this? (V3248)

2b. (Where would you place) the Democratic Party ⟨on this scale⟩? (V3251)

2c. (Where would you place) the Republican Party ⟨on this scale⟩? (V3252) (Scored correct if respondent places self in part [a], and then places Republicans higher than Democrats in parts [b] and [c])

There is much discussion about the best way to deal with racial problems. Some people think achieving racial integration of schools is so important that it justifies busing children to schools out of their own neighborhoods. Others think letting children go to their neighborhood schools is so important that they oppose busing.

3a. Where would you place yourself on this scale, or haven't you thought much about this? (V3257)

3b. (Where would you place) the Democratic Party ⟨on this scale⟩? (V3261)

3c. (Where would you place) the Republican Party ⟨on this scale⟩? (V3262) (Scored correct if respondent places self in part [a], and then places Republicans higher than Democrats in parts [b] and [c])

Some people feel that the government in Washington should make every possible effort to improve the social and economic position of blacks and other minority groups. Others feel that the government should not make any special effort to help minorities because they should help themselves.

4a. Where would you place yourself on this scale, or haven't you thought much about this? (V3264)

4b. (Where would you place) the Democratic Party ⟨on this scale⟩? (V3267)

4c. (Where would you place) the Republican Party ⟨on this scale⟩? (V3268) (Scored correct if respondent places self in part [a], and then places Republicans higher than Democrats in parts [b] and [c])

There is much concern about the rapid rise in medical and hospital costs. Some feel there should be a government insurance plan which would cover all medical and hospital expenses. Others feel that medical expenses should be paid by individuals, and through private insurance like Blue Cross.

5a. Where would you place yourself on this scale, or haven't you thought much about this? (V3273)

5b. (Where would you place) the Democratic Party ⟨on this scale⟩? (V3276)

5c. (Where would you place) the Republican Party ⟨on this scale⟩? (V3277) (Scored correct if respondent places self in part [a], and then places Republicans higher than Democrats in parts [b] and [c])

Over the past few years there has been much discussion about the best way to deal with the problem of urban unrest and rioting. Some say it is more important to use all available force to maintain law and order—no matter what results. Others say it is more important to correct the problems of poverty and unemployment that give rise to the disturbances.

6a. Where would you place yourself on this scale, or haven't you thought much about this? (V3767)

6b. (Where would you place) the Democratic Party ⟨on this scale⟩? (V3770)

6c. (Where would you place) the Republican Party ⟨on this scale⟩? (V3771) (Scored correct if respondent places self in part [a], and then places Republicans lower than Democrats in parts [b] and [c])

Some people think that the use of marijuana should be made legal. Others think that the penalties for using marijuana should be set higher than they are now.

7a. Where would you place yourself on this scale, or haven't you thought much about this? (V3772)

7b. (Where would you place) the Democratic Party ⟨on this scale⟩? (V3775)

7c. (Where would you place) the Republican Party ⟨on this scale⟩? (V3776) (Scored correct if respondent places self in part [a], and then places Republicans and Democrats in parts [b] and [c])

As you know, in our tax system people who earn a lot of money already have to pay higher rates of income tax than those who earn less. Some people think that those with high incomes should pay even more of their income into taxes than they do now. Others think that the rates shouldn't be different at all—that everyone should pay the same portion of their income, no matter how much they make.

8a. Where would you place yourself on this scale, or haven't you thought much about this? (V3779)

8b. (Where would you place) the Democratic Party ⟨on this scale⟩? (V3782)

8c. (Where would you place) the Republican Party ⟨on this scale⟩? (V3783) (Scored correct if respondent places self in part [a], and then places Republicans lower than Democrats in parts [b] and [c])

Recently there has been a lot of talk about women's rights. Some people feel that women should have an equal role with men in running business, industry, and government. Others feel that women's place is in the home.

9a. Where would you place yourself on this scale, or haven't you thought much about this? (V3787)

9b. (Where would you place) the Democratic Party ⟨on this scale⟩? (V3790)

9c. (Where would you place) the Republican Party ⟨on this scale⟩? (V3791) (Scored correct if respondent places self in part [a], and then places Republicans and Democrats in parts [b] and [c])

Some people are afraid the government in Washington is getting too powerful for the good of the country and the individual person. Others feel that
the government in Washington is not getting too strong. Do you have an
opinion on this? (V3224)

10a. [If yes] What is your feeling, do you think the government is getting too powerful or do you think the government is not getting
too strong? (V3225)

10b. Which party do you think is more likely to favor stronger government in Washington—the Democrats, the Republicans, or
wouldn't there be much difference between them on this?
(V3226) (Scored correct if respondent places self in part [a], and
then indicates Democrats in part [b])

Some people believe that our armed forces are powerful enough and ⟨that⟩
we should spend less money for defense. Others feel that military spending
should at least continue at the present level.

11a. How do you feel—should military spending be cut, or should it
continue at least at the present level? (v3357)

11b. Which political party do you think is more in favor of cutting military spending—the Democrats or the Republicans, or wouldn't
there be much difference between them? (V3359) (Scored correct if respondent places self in part [a], and then indicates
Democrats in part [b])

Issue Awareness Index
(T. E. Patterson & R. D. McClure, 1976)

Variable

This scale is based on knowledge of presidential candidates' stands on a series of campaign issues.

Description

Respondents were asked to indicate the certainty with which they believed that 1972
presidential candidates, Richard Nixon and George McGovern, held a position on important election issues. People were given a series of statements about each candidate (e.g.,
"Richard Nixon favors spending less money on the military") and responded on seven-
point scales ranging from "extremely likely" to "extremely unlikely." Respondents completed these items in September, in October, and again in November, after the presidential
election.

The items were used by Patterson and McClure (1976) to assess learning over the
course of the 1972 campaign. If a candidate publicly favored a particular issue position,
then any change from September to November toward the "likely" end of the scale was
considered an increase in issue awareness, while any change toward "unlikely" was considered a decrease in issue awareness. A percentage increase (or decrease) was calculated
as $100 \times (n$ increasing $- n$ decreasing)/(total n changing in any direction). Thus, positive
scores result when more people gain than lose awareness and negative scores result when

more people lose than gain awareness. The scale theoretically ranges from +100 (everybody gaining) to −100 (everybody decreasing).

Sample

The three-wave panel study drew a random sample of adults over 18 from the metropolitan Syracuse area. The sample was stratified in order to increase variation in partisan loyalty. The first wave of interviews was held in September 1972 ($N = 731$). Respondents were reinterviewed in October ($N = 650$) and in November ($N = 650$).

Reliability

No assessments of reliability are reported.

Validity

No explicit tests of validity are reported. As one would expect, the measures indicated that issue awareness increased from September to November by an average of over 25%. Gains were correlated positively with education and income.

Location

Patterson, T. E., & McClure, R. D. (1976). *The unseeing eye: The myth of television power in national politics.* New York: G. P. Putnam's Sons. Data are available from the Inter-University Consortium for Political and Social Research (ICPSR Study No. 7989).

Results and Comments

Regular viewers of television network news were no more likely than non-regular viewers to increase in their issue awareness, but newspaper reading did identify information gains. Frequent readers had a 35% increase in issue awareness, compared with 18% among infrequent readers. Exposure to political advertising also appeared to contribute to issue awareness: Those respondents exposed to many spots registered an average 36% increase across issues, compared with 25% among those reporting little exposure to ads.

Issue Awareness Index
(Patterson & McClure, 1976)

(Following is a description of the basic issue items used in the study. For all items the response scale was extremely likely; quite likely; slightly likely; not sure; slightly unlikely; quite unlikely; extremely unlikely. Items were asked separately for each candidate.)

1, 2. George McGovern [Richard Nixon] favors a guaranteed annual income for everyone.

3, 4. George McGovern [Richard Nixon] favors spending less money on the military.

5, 6. George McGovern [Richard Nixon] favors granting amnesty to Vietnam draft evaders.

7, 8. George McGovern [Richard Nixon] favors requiring persons with incomes over $20,000 to pay more taxes.

9, 10. George McGovern [Richard Nixon] favors holding down government spending.

11, 12. George McGovern [Richard Nixon] favors a tougher stand on law and order.

13, 14. George McGovern [Richard Nixon] favors government support for parochial schools.

15, 16. George McGovern [Richard Nixon] favors an immediate pullout of all U.S. troops from Vietnam.

17, 18. George McGovern [Richard Nixon] favors honoring our commitments to other nations.

19, 20. George McGovern [Richard Nixon] favors putting a stop to busing.

21, 22. George McGovern [Richard Nixon] favors a government-guaranteed job for everyone who wants to work.

23, 24. George McGovern [Richard Nixon] favors wiping out all political corruption and favoritism.

Information about Foreign Countries

(J. P. Robinson, 1967)

Variable

This series of questions assesses a person's knowledge of certain characteristics of foreign countries.

Description

The scale consists of 16 items, 5 dealing with whether certain countries have Communist governments, 5 dealing with countries that are in Africa, and 6 dealing with which countries have developed their own atomic weapons. One point is given for each correct answer, one is subtracted for each incorrect answer, and no points are given for "don't know" responses. Scores can thus range from −16 (all items incorrect) to +16 (all items correct).

Sample

The sample consisted of a representative cross-section of Detroit, Michigan, area adults interviewed in early 1964.

Reliability

The average item–total correlation was .37 (.41 if the item on whether England had tested atomic weapons is deleted). The average interitem correlation was .13 (.15 if the England item is deleted).

Validity

No direct evidence of validity is reported, but the scale did correlate highly with educational background. Most of the items were relatively easy (with more than 60% answering correctly), so the scale may not discriminate well at the upper end of the knowledge continuum.

Location

Robinson, J. P. (1967). *Public information about world affairs.* Ann Arbor, MI: Survey Research Center.

Results and Comments

The average score was 7.0. Degree of education was the major correlate, while persons who were heavier in media use tended to have higher scores. The test is dated, so items (e.g., Poland's form of government) should be screened for updating.

Information about Foreign Countries (Robinson, 1967)

(Following is a description of the scale items used.)

Now we have three short questions about some things you might not hear about from the newspapers or TV.

First of all, which of these countries have communist governments and which do not?

1. Egypt (Answer: Noncommunist; 61% correct)
2. Poland (Answer: Communist; 70% correct)
3. Spain (Answer: Noncommunist; 65% correct)
4. Mainland China (Answer: Communist; 70% correct)
5. India (Answer: Noncommunist; 64% correct)

Very good, now which of these countries are located in Africa? Again name ALL the African countries on the list.

6. Ecuador (Answer: Not African; 64% correct)
7. Ghana (Answer: African; 63% correct)
8. Afghanistan (Answer: Not African; 34% correct)
9. Mongolia (Answer: Not African; 51% correct)
10. Morocco (Answer: African; 45% correct)

Finally which of these countries have developed and tested their own atomic weapons?

11. West Germany (Answer: Has not; 62% correct)
12. Algeria (Answer: Has not; 76% correct)
13. France (Answer: Has; 60% correct)

14. Japan (Answer: Has not; 66% correct)
15. England (Answer: Has; 52% correct)
16. Russia (Answer: Has; 95% correct)

References

Achen, C. (1975). Mass political attitudes and the survey response. *American Political Science Review, 69*, 1218–1231.

Alwin, D. F. (1991). Family of origin and cohort differences in verbal ability. *American Sociological Review, 56*, 625–638.

Bartels, L. M. (1988). *Presidential primaries and the dynamics of public choice.* Princeton, NJ: Princeton University Press.

Belli, R. F., & Schuman, H. (1996). The complexity of ignorance. *Qualitative Sociology, 19*, 423–430.

Bennett, L. W. (1975). *The political mind and the political environment* (pp. 3–25). Lexington, MA: D.C. Heath and Co.

Bennett, S. E. (1973). Consistency among the public's social welfare policy attitudes in the 1960s. *American Journal of Political Science, 17*, 544–570.

Bennett, S. E. (1988). Know-nothings revisited: The meaning of political ignorance today. *Social Science Quarterly, 69*, 476–490.

Bennett, S. E. (1989). Trends in Americans' political information, 1967–1987. *American Politics Quarterly, 17*, 422–435.

Bennett, S. E., Oldendick, R. W., Tuchfarber, A. J., & Bishop, G. F. (1979). Education and mass belief systems: An extension and some new questions. *Political Behavior, 1*, 53–71.

Berelson, B. (1950). Democratic theory and public opinion. *Public Opinion Quarterly, 16*, 313–330.

Brown, S. (1970). Consistency and the persistence of ideology. *Public Opinion Quarterly, 34*, 60–68.

Bryce, J. (1888). *The American commonwealth* (Vol. 3). London: Macmillan.

Campbell, A., Converse, P. E., Miller, W. E., & Stokes, D. E. (1960). *The American voter.* New York: John Wiley & Sons.

Carmines, E. G., & Zeller, R. A. (1979). *Reliability and validity assessment.* Sage University paper series on quantitative applications in the social sciences, no. 17. Beverly Hills, CA: Sage.

Converse, P. E. (1962). Information flow and the stability of partisan attitudes. *Public Opinion Quarterly, 26*, 578–599.

Converse, P. E. (1964). The nature of belief systems in mass publics. In D. E. Apter (Ed.), *Ideology and discontent* (pp. 206–261). New York: Free Press.

Converse, P. E. (1970). Attitudes and non-attitudes: Continuation of a dialogue. In E. R. Tufte (Ed.), *The quantitative analysis of social problems.* Reading, MA: Addison-Wesley.

Delli Carpini, M. X., & Keeter, S. (1990). *The structure of political knowledge.* Paper presented at the annual meeting of the American Political Science Association, San Francisco.

Delli Carpini, M. X., & Keeter, S. (1991). Stability and change in the U.S. public's knowledge of politics. *Public Opinion Quarterly, 55*, 583–612.

Delli Carpini, M. X., & Keeter, S. (1992). *An analysis of information items on the 1990 and 1991 NES surveys.* Report to the National Election Studies Board of Overseers, Center for Political Studies, University of Michigan.

Delli Carpini, M. X., & Keeter, S. (1993). Measuring political knowledge: Putting first things first. *American Journal of Political Science, 37*, 1179–1206.

Delli Carpini, M. X., & Keeter, S. (1996). *What Americans know about politics and why it matters.* New Haven, CT: Yale University Press.

Dimock, M. A., & Popkin, S. L. (1997). Political knowledge in comparative perspective. In S. Iyengar & R. Reeves (Eds.), *Do the media govern? Politicians, voters, and reporters in America.* Thousand Oaks, CA: Sage.

Erskine, H. G. (1962). The polls: The informed public. *Public Opinion Quarterly, 26*, 668–677.

Erskine, H. G. (1963a). The polls: Textbook knowledge. *Public Opinion Quarterly, 27,* 133–141.

Erskine, H. G. (1963b). The polls: Exposure to domestic information. *Public Opinion Quarterly, 27,* 491–500.

Erskine, H. G. (1963c). The polls: Exposure to international information. *Public Opinion Quarterly, 27,* 658–662.

Fiske, S. T., & Kinder, D. (1981). Involvement, expertise, and schema usage: Evidence from political cognition. In N. Cantor & J. Kihlstrom (Eds.), *Personality, cognition, and social interaction.* Hillsdale, NJ: Erlbaum.

Fiske, S. T., Kinder, D. R., & Larter, W. M. (1983). The novice and the expert: Knowledge-based strategies in political cognition. *Journal of Experimental Social Psychology, 19,* 381–400.

Fiske, S. T., Lau, R. R., & Smith, R. A. (1990). On the varieties and utilities of political expertise. *Social Cognition, 8,* 31–48.

Glenn, N. (1972). The distribution of political knowledge in the United States. In D. Nimmo & C. Bonjean (Eds.), *Political attitudes and public opinion.* New York: McKay.

Graber, D. (1994). Why voters fail information tests: Can the hurdles be overcome? *Political Communication, 11,* 331–346.

Gunter, B. (1987). *Poor reception: Misunderstanding and forgetting broadcast news.* Hillsdale, NJ: Erlbaum.

Hagner, P. R., & Pierce, J. C. (1983). Levels of conceptualization and political belief consistency. *Micropolitics, 2,* 311–348.

Hamill, R., & Lodge, M. (1986). Cognitive consequences of political sophistication. In R. R. Lau & D. O. Sears (Eds.), *Political cognition.* Hillsdale, NJ: Erlbaum.

Hamill, R., Lodge, M., & Blake, F. (1985). The breadth, depth, and utility of class, partisan, and ideological schemata. *American Journal of Political Science, 29,* 850–870.

Iyengar, S. (1986). *Wither political information.* Report to the National Election Studies Board of Overseers, Center for Political Studies, University of Michigan.

Jacoby, J., & Hoyer, W. D. (1987). *Comprehension and miscomprehension of print communications.* New York: Advertising Educational Foundation, Inc.

Jacoby, J., Hoyer, W. D., & Sheluga, D. A. (1980). *Miscomprehension of televised communications.* New York: Advertising Educational Foundation of the American Association of Advertising Agencies.

Jennings, M. K. (1996). Political knowledge over time and across generations. *Public Opinion Quarterly, 60,* 228–252.

Jennings, M. K., & Niemi, R. G. (1981). *Generations and politics: A panel study of young adults and their parents.* Princeton, NJ: Princeton University Press.

Judd, C. M., & Downing, J. W. (1990). Political expertise and development of attitude consistency. *Social Cognition, 8,* 104–124.

Judd, C. M., & Milburn, M. A. (1980). The structure of attitude systems in the general public: Comparison of a structural equation model. *American Sociological Review, 45,* 627–643.

Kaplan, A. (1964). *The conduct of inquiry.* Scranton, PA: Chandler.

Kessel, J. H. (1980). *Presidential campaign politics: Coalition strategies and citizen response.* Washington, DC: CQ Press.

Kinder, D. R., & Sears, D. O. (1985). Public opinion and political action. In G. Lindzey & E. Aronson (Eds.), *The handbook of social psychology* (3rd ed., Vol. 2, pp. 659–741). New York: Random House.

Krosnick, J. A. (1990). Expertise and political psychology. *Social Cognition, 8,* 1–8.

Krosnick, J. A., & Milburn, M. A. (1990). Psychological determinants of political opinionation. *Social Cognition, 8,* 49–72.

Lane, R. E. (1962). *Political ideology.* New York: Free Press.

Lane, R. E. (1973). Patterns of political belief. In J. N. Knutson (Ed.), *Handbook of political psychology* (pp. 83–116). San Francisco: Jossey-Bass.

Lane, R. E., & Sears, D. O. (1964). *Public opinion.* Englewood Cliffs, NJ: Prentice-Hall.

Lau, R. R., & Erber, R. (1985). Political sophistication: An information processing perspective. In S. Kraus & R. Perloff (Eds.), *Mass media and political thought.* Newbury Park, CA: Sage.

Lazarsfeld, P. F. (1957). Public opinion and the classical tradition. *Public Opinion Quarterly, 21,* 39–53.

Lippmann, W. (1922). *Public opinion.* New York: Harcourt Brace Jovanovich.

Lippmann, W. (1925). *The phantom public.* New York: Harcourt Brace Jovanovich.

Lodge, M., McGraw, K. M., & Stroh, P. (1989). An impression-driven model of candidate formation. *American Political Science Review, 83,* 399–420.

Lodge, M. A., Steenbergen, M. R., & Brau, S. (1995). The responsive voter: Campaign information and the dynamics of candidate evaluation. *American Political Science Review, 89,* 309–326.

Lodge, M., Stroh, P., & Wahlke, J. (1990). Black-box models of candidate evaluation. *Political Behavior, 12,* 5–18.

Luskin, R. C. (1987). Measuring political sophistication. *American Journal of Political Science, 31,* 856–899.

Luskin, R. C. (1990). Explaining political sophistication. *Political Behavior, 12,* 331–362.

Luttbeg, N. (1968). The structure of beliefs among leaders and the public. *Public Opinion Quarterly, 32,* 388–409.

MacKuen, M. (1984). Exposure to information, belief integration, and individual responsiveness to agenda change. *American Political Science Review, 78,* 372–391.

Mann, T., & Wolfinger, R. (1980). Candidates and parties in congressional elections. *American Political Science Review, 74,* 617–632.

Markus, H., & Zajonc, R. B. (1985). The cognitive perspective in social psychology. In G. Lindzey & E. Aronson (Eds.), *The handbook of social psychology* (3rd ed., Vol. 1, pp. 137–230). New York: Random House.

McGuire, W. J. (1968). Personality and susceptibility to social influence. In E. F. Borgatta & W. W. Lambert (Eds.), *Handbook of personality theory and research* (pp. 1130–1187). Chicago: Rand-McNally.

McGraw, K. M., Lodge, M., & Stroh, P. (1990). On-line processing in candidate evaluation: The effects of issue order, issue importance, and sophistication. *Political Behavior, 12,* 41–58.

McGraw, K. M., & Pinney, N. (1990). The effects of general and domain-specific expertise on political memory and judgment. *Social Cognition, 8,* 9–30.

Minar, D. W. (1960). Public opinion in the perspective of political theory. *Western Political Quarterly, 23,* 31–44.

Neuman, W. R. (1976). Patterns of recall among television viewers. *Public Opinion Quarterly, 40,* 115–123.

Neuman, W. R. (1986). *The paradox of mass politics: Knowledge and opinion in the American electorate.* Cambridge, MA: Harvard University Press.

Neuman, W. R., Just, M. R., & Crigler, A. N. (1992). *Common knowledge: News and the construction of political meaning.* Chicago: University of Chicago Press.

Nie, N. H., Verba, S., & Petrocik, J. R. (1976). *The changing American voter.* Cambridge, MA: Harvard University Press.

Patterson, T. E. (1980). *The mass media election: How Americans choose their president.* New York: Praeger.

Patterson, T. E., & McClure, R. D. (1976). *The unseeing eye: The myth of television power in national politics.* New York: G. P. Putnam's Sons.

Pierce, J. C. (1970). Party identification and the changing role of ideology in American politics. *Midwest Journal of Political Science, 14,* 25–42.

Pomper, G. M. (1972). From confusion to clarity: Issues and American voters, 1956–1968. *American Political Science Review, 66,* 415–428.

Price, V. (1992). *Public opinion.* Newbury Park, CA: Sage.

Price, V. (1993). The impact of varying reference periods in survey questions about media use. *Journalism Quarterly, 70,* 615–627.

Price, V., & Czilli, E. J. (1996). Modeling patterns of news recognition and recall. *Journal of Communication, 46,* 55–78.

Price, V., & Zaller, J. (1990). *In one ear and out the other: Learning and forgetting the news.* Paper presented at the annual meeting of the Midwest Political Science Association, Chicago.

Price, V., & Zaller, J. (1993). Who gets the news? An examination of news reception and its implications for research. *Public Opinion Quarterly, 57,* 133–164.

Price, V., & Zaller, J. (1996). *Measuring media exposure and gauging its effects in general population surveys.* Paper presented to the annual conference of the American Political Science Association, San Francisco, CA.

Robinson, J. P. (1967). World affairs information and mass media exposure. *Journalism Quarterly,
44,* 23–30.

Robinson, J. P. (1968). Political information. In J. P. Robinson, G. Rusk, & K. Head (Eds.), *Measures of political attitudes.* Ann Arbor, MI: Institute for Social Research.

Robinson, J. P. (1972). Mass communication and information diffusion. In F. G. Kline & P. J.
Tichenor (Eds.), *Current perspectives in mass communication research.* Newbury Park, CA:
Sage.

Robinson, J. P. (1976). Interpersonal influences in election campaigns: Two-step flow hypotheses.
Public Opinion Quarterly, 40, 304–319.

Robinson, J. P., & Levy, M. R. (1986). *The main source: Learning from television news.* Newbury
Park, CA: Sage.

Smith, E. R. A. N. (1989). *The unchanging American voter.* Berkeley: University of California Press.

Stimson, J. A. (1975). Belief systems: Constraint, complexity and the 1972 election. *American Journal of Political Science, 19,* 393–417.

Tichenor, P. J., Donohue, G. A., & Olien, C. (1970). Mass media flow and differential growth in
knowledge. *Public Opinion Quarterly, 34,* 159–170.

Tichenor, P. J., Donohue, G. A., & Olien, C. (1980). *Community conflict and the press.* Newbury
Park, CA: Sage.

Verba, S., & Nie, N. H. (1972). *Participation in America: Political democracy and social equality.*
New York: Harper & Row.

Zaller, J. (1985). *Improved measures of political information.* Proposal to the National Election
Studies Board of Overseers, Center for Political Studies, University of Michigan.

Zaller, J. (1986). *Analysis of information items on the 1985 NES Pilot Study.* Report to the National
Election Studies Board of Overseers, Center for Political Studies, University of Michigan.

Zaller, J. (1987). The diffusion of political attitudes. *Journal of Personality and Social Psychology,
53,* 821–833.

Zaller, J. (1990). Political awareness, elite opinion leadership, and the mass survey response. *Social
Cognition, 8,* 125–153.

Zaller, J. (1992). *The nature and origins of mass opinion.* New York: Cambridge University Press.

Zaller, J., & Price, V. (1990). *In one ear and out the other: Learning and forgetting the news.* Paper
presented at the meeting of the Midwest Political Science Association, Chicago.

CHAPTER 11

Political Agendas

J. Merrill Shanks
with the assistance of Douglas A. Strand

Previous chapters have focused on public *opinions* about particular issues, such as race or foreign affairs. This chapter reviews procedures for assessing the public *importance* or salience of specific issues—for example, do people *care more* about race than foreign affairs? In psychological terms the measurement here is the *potency* of an issue, not its evaluation.

Since the beginning of public opinion research, both consumers and producers of survey-based evidence have wanted to compare issues in terms of their apparent political importance. For most of the topics that compete for attention in the national political agenda, they want to know: "How important is that issue to ordinary citizens, in comparison to all the other concerns they have?" Getting issues on the national agenda has become a prime political objective for lobby groups, politicians, and the mass media.

A primary motivation for continuing popular and academic interest in the "importance" issue is that it may be important in a particular *election*. Presidential election campaigns are often remembered in terms of issue-related slogans long after other aspects of the contests are no longer salient. Some of those campaign themes may reflect dominant conflicts that had a major impact on voters' choices for President, while others may conceal as much as they reveal.

Perhaps the clearest historical example of an "issue" that played a dominant role is the disagreement about slavery that preceded the 1860 election—a conflict that led to the Civil War and that continues in the concerns over civil rights and racial equality in contemporary American politics. Other issue-related campaign themes include the conflict over "free silver" in 1896, the importance of "keeping us out of the war" in 1916, the emphasis on continued national prosperity (with "a chicken in every pot") in 1928, Franklin Roosevelt's "New Deal" in 1932, Republican charges concerning "Korea, Corruption, and Communism" in 1952, and Richard Nixon's emphasis on the "silent majority" concerning large scale domestic protests before the 1968 election.

Such summary statements about electoral issue "importance" are difficult to separate from statements about the degree to which the candidates emphasized that topic during the campaign. Despite such difficulties, however, journalists and academic researchers have found it impossible to discuss specific elections without discussing the importance of specific issues. As a consequence, a great deal has been written about the role of issues in American presidential elections, using a wide variety of quantitative and qualitative evidence. (See for example Asher, 1988; Campbell *et al.,* 1960; Kessel, 1987, Miller &

Shanks, 1996; Pomper, 1989, 1993, 1997; Polsby & Wildavsky, 1988; Popkin, 1990; and White, 1982).

From the outset, it must be emphasized that different researchers can easily arrive at different conclusions about the salience of various issues, either because they examine different kinds of empirical evidence or because they are motivated by different substantive questions. For example, contrasting interpretations of the 1964 presidential election focused on the relative importance of voters' attitudes toward Barry Goldwater's conservative positions on issues versus Lyndon Johnson's position as the incumbent Democrat after President John Kennedy's assassination. Conflicting views of the 1968 and 1972 elections focused on the relative importance of various issues concerning the war in Vietnam and race-related conflicts, and rival interpretations of the 1980 election focused on the importance of Ronald Reagan's conservative agenda versus President Jimmy Carter's performance in handling the national economy and the Iran hostage crisis (Markus, 1982; Miller & Shanks, 1982). More recently, alternative accounts of the 1992 election disagreed about the relative importance of the state of the economy versus social issues like abortion (Abramowitz, 1997; Miller & Shanks, 1996). As discussed later, most of these apparent conflicts in electoral interpretation can be traced to the authors' use of different criteria for relative importance or different aspects of public opinion about those topics as well as different approaches to survey analysis. Given the variety of ways in which the term "important" is used in everyday conversation, any review concerning political importance must consider a variety of alternative criteria for such comparisons.

Public opinion data have been used in many different ways to suggest that one topic is more politically important than another, but all of those procedures can be grouped into two general categories or approaches. The first and simplest involves *direct measurement* of individual survey respondents' opinions about the "importance" of various topics or issues, in which an issue is characterized as more important if a larger *proportion of respondents* describe some aspect of that topic as having greater salience, relevance, urgency, or priority.

The second and more complex kind of assessment of the importance of different topics is based on the *apparent impact* of voters' opinions (about each topic) on some political or electoral *decision*, based on *statistical relationships* between those opinions and the vote. For both types of procedures or criteria, a given topic may be much more important for some individuals than for others, and the overall or average importance of that topic may fluctuate a great deal over time.

Within these two general approaches, public opinion researchers have used a substantial variety of different concepts, measures, and statistical procedures to assess the importance of specific topics or issues. This conceptual and methodological diversity is suggested by the following list of alternative substantive questions.

Type A: Direct Evaluations by Survey Respondents

- On average, which aspects of national life do individual citizens regard as the "most important *problem*" or the "most serious *issue*" *facing the country?*
- On average, how do individual citizens evaluate the *"seriousness"* of a variety of potential *problems?*
- Which consensual goals do more citizens feel the country is *very far from achieving?*
- Which potential objectives seem to be the most (or least) important to the electorate, based on the number of citizens who give a high (or low) *ranking* to those *values* or *goals?*

- Which specific *issues* appear to be the most important in the sense that more respondents describe governmental policy in those areas as very *"important to them"?*
- Which potential *objectives* or purposes *for the national government* appear to have the greatest popular *support* or the least opposition?
- Which current governmental objectives or programs appear to have the highest *priority,* based on the number of citizens who prefer *increased* (instead of decreased) governmental *effort* or *spending* in those areas?
- Which issues do voters most frequently identify as having the *greatest influence* on their own *candidate preferences?*

Type B: Electoral Relevance Based on Statistical
Relationships

- How important do voters' opinions about a variety of issues (such as abortion or the state of the economy) appear to be, based on simple bivariate relationships (or correlations) between those opinions and vote *choice?*
- How important do voters' opinions on specific issues appear to be in influencing vote choice *after other political attitudes* (such as party identification or other issues) *are taken into account?*
- Which substantive topics or issues were the most important in a given election in the sense that voters' opinions concerning those topics made the *greatest contribution to the aggregate results of the election* or to the winner's margin of victory?
- How much *change* is there *from one election to the next* in the issues that appeared to have shaped individual or aggregate decisions in those contests?

This chapter reviews survey-based measures and procedures that have been used to answer each of these different types of questions concerning the importance of specific issues. Specific survey procedures are presented in the second section of this chapter if the descriptive question involves direct measurement of respondents' own evaluations (as in the eight Type A questions) and in the third section if it involves indirect assessment based on statistical relationships with vote choice (as in the four Type B questions).

Within both of these general approaches, discussion of specific procedures begins by clarifying the conceptual criteria involved, or the *rationale* that has led some researchers to use that approach to the apparent importance of different kinds of opinions. For several of these procedures, the underlying rationale is based on a general distinction between more general substantive "topics" and specific political "issues." The following section clarifies that general distinction and places different types of political issues within a broader analytic framework.

Putting Specific Issues in a Broader Political Context

Any discussion of the relative importance of different political issues is difficult to separate from the central motivating question for most electoral surveys: What was that election really *about,* in addition to the competition for power between major party candidates and their allies? Most such inquiries try to identify specific "issues" that played a more important role in the sense that major candidates appeared to have been more successful in activating voters' opinions about those issues (instead of others) in shaping their eventual votes. A similar question arises between elections when no behavioral choice is available as the "dependent variable" to be explained: Which of several different kinds of political attitudes seems to have been most important in shaping citizens' approval (or disapproval) of the incumbent president or the majority party's leadership in Congress?

In most political contests voters have opinions about a large number of different topics, problems, or other kinds of issues that *may* play some role in shaping their impressions of national leaders—and their eventual choices between candidates. A central problem for all electoral surveys is to *classify* this large collection of potentially relevant subjects into a smaller number of categories or general *measurement objectives* in order to develop survey questions that will permit analysts to examine all of the topics or issues that may play some role in shaping the vote. Given the substantial number of topics involved and the possibility of multiple issues within each general topic, electoral researchers have used a variety of measurement strategies to "cover" all of the potential issues in the current election—so that they can assess the relative importance of specific issues after the election is over.

Substantive Topics versus Electoral Issues: The Role of Political Disagreement

In general, discussions of political importance involve the specification of alternative general topics (such as taxes, poverty, crime, discrimination, foreign affairs, or morality) and more specific disagreements within the society concerning one or more *aspects* of each topic. In conventional terminology we often ask: "What is (or was) the real *issue* in that election concerning (a given topic)?" As emphasized later, the content of specific potential issues concerning a more general political topic may take several different forms. Were one or more issues about that topic defined in terms of disagreement concerning particular conditions in the country? Or conflicting assessments of the seriousness of specific (suggested) problems? Or disagreement about the appropriateness of specific governmental objectives or responsibilities? Or conflict about relative priorities for existing governmental objectives? Or some other aspect of that topic? For any general topic (such as taxes, foreign affairs, or poverty), several different "issues" may acquire some political importance based on different aspects of that topic whenever disagreements within the electorate (concerning those specific issues) are activated by conflicting appeals from rival parties or candidates.

Any attempt to assess the importance of specific political issues, however, must acknowledge that several other kinds of individual characteristics are often discussed in terms of their political importance—in addition to several different types of "issues." For that reason the following paragraphs review the different types of individual characteristics that are often used to explain political preferences and the role that different types of political issues may play within that broader explanatory context.

Other Types of Explanatory Variables

Nonpolitical versus Political Characteristics

One of the earliest—and most persistent—distinctions between alternative types of explanatory variables rests on the assumption that individual characteristics that are not defined in political terms can play a substantial—although indirect—role in influencing political preferences. In particular, social or economic characteristics are often included in explanations of political preference (even though they are largely acquired outside the world of politics) because they are assumed to influence a variety of election-related opinions, which (in turn) determine political preferences or vote choice. Such characteristics include voters' race or ethnicity, age, gender, religion, education, marital status, income, union membership, and social class and the geographic area (or region) in which they live. Most such variables represent individual characteristics that are highly stable in the sense that they were acquired long before the current political period—even though their electoral effects may not arise until the current (or most recent) campaign. Electoral analysts often refer to the "importance" of these nonpolitical characteristics, as in the continuing emphasis on the "gender gap" and other differences in electoral preferences between groups defined by race and religion. The importance of these characteristics, however, will not be discussed in the rest of this chapter because they are not defined in terms of political attitudes.

Parties versus Issues versus Candidates

Within the diverse set of explicitly political attitudes that have been used to explain electoral preferences, the most frequently used distinction between different types of explanatory variables concerns the *object* of the attitude involved—that is, whether a specific type of opinion is "about" the parties, about a specific issue that has arisen during the campaign, or about the personal characteristics of the candidates.[1] No matter what other distinctions are used, these traditional categories are reflected in most (if not all) comprehensive explanations of electoral preferences, and major controversies continue concerning the role or importance of voters' partisan identifications and their assessments of candidates' personal qualities. As stated earlier, however, this chapter will concentrate on the relative importance of different political *issues*—instead of attitudes about specific parties or candidates.

Long-Term Predispositions versus Short-Term Forces

The distinction between attitudes toward parties (or candidates) is hard to separate from the suggestion that some of those attitudes represent more general "long-term" characteristics that were established before the current election and have remained fairly stable for quite some time—while other opinions were created (or have changed) recently in response to specific "short-term forces" in the current campaign. In principle any political attitude can be assigned to a position on a continuum from extremely stable (or long-term) predispositions to highly volatile opinions (based on short-term issues). In over four decades of publications based on the American National Election Studies (ANES), many analysts have concluded that the initial question in those surveys concerning partisan identification represents the most stable political attitude, that measures based on perceptions of national conditions and evaluations of specific candidates represent the most volatile potential causes of the vote, and that policy-related preferences occupy an intermediate (and uncertain) position on that continuum.

Chapter 12 of this book (by Herbert Weisberg) discusses alternative measures concerning partisan identification or partisanship, and Chapter 4 (by Stanley Feldman) reviews a series of measures concerning general policy-related predispositions. Each of the measures reviewed by Feldman is designed to capture general—and fairly stable—beliefs

---

[1]See Kinder, Peters, Abelson, and Fiske (1980) and Funk (1997) for additional discussion of measurement objectives and analytic procedures concerning different kinds of candidate evaluations.

about continuing policy-related conflicts within one general area: economic equality, individual responsibility, or the role of government. Because of those two chapters, measurement procedures concerning partisan and policy-related predispositions will not be reviewed in this chapter. Some of the resulting variables, however, will be mentioned in the final sections of this chapter concerning the importance of alternative issue-related variables in shaping electoral decisions.

Two Types of "Issues"

In the early years of survey-based electoral research, researchers at both Columbia and Michigan universities suggested that any assessment of the role or importance of different aspects of a given campaign should distinguish between two fundamentally different types of issues.[2] As discussed later, this separation of political issues into two contrasting categories has been described in various terms, based on whether the electorally relevant aspect of a given issue involves differences between candidates in their policy-related *positions* versus differences in their *style* or *valence*, *conflict* versus *consensus* among voters concerning the appropriateness of specific governmental objectives, or preferences concerning *policy direction* versus evaluations of candidate (or incumbent) *performance*. Others have suggested a distinction between campaign issues in which candidate evaluations are based on voters' beliefs that a particular policy or objective is *right or wrong* versus issues in which reactions to candidates are based on whether they have been a *success* or a *failure* in achieving some consensual objective. Electoral analysts do not agree on the necessity or feasibility of this kind of distinction, but it persists as a major component in many explanations of vote choice—and it will play a pivotal role in this chapter's review of alternative procedures for assessing relative importance.

Other Competing Distinctions

The previous paragraphs provide a somewhat arbitrary subset of distinctions that have been used to classify attitudes that may influence the vote. Other analysts have focused on such distinctions as voters' individual versus group-related economic interests, their evaluations of their own (personal) versus national (or societal) conditions, the degree of specificity (concerning particular controversies) versus generality (concerning broader substantive domains) in their issue-related attitudes, the degree to which specific issues are complex or difficult for voters to understand, and the degree to which candidate evaluations represent retrospective judgments (based on previous activities) versus prospective expectations (concerning future performance).

Measurement Strategies Based on Governmental Objectives

Survey evidence concerning the importance of alternative political issues will often be discussed in terms of potential governmental objectives—based on a wide variety of alternative ideas about what the national government should (or should not) be trying to accomplish. As emphasized later, election-related issues may be defined in many different ways, but most questions in political surveys involve some kind of (explicit or implicit) statement concerning a current or potential goal for the federal government.

For some potential issues in a given election, the relevant goals or objectives for the national government may be both implicit and highly consensual, as in the universal desirability of a "strong economy" and general agreement that the federal government has a substantial responsibility for national economic conditions. Other potential issues may

---

[2]See "Spatial Models of Party Competition" (Stokes, 1966) and Chapters 8, 10, and 13 in *The New American Voter* (Miller & Shanks, 1996) for more extensive discussions of these alternative formulations.

involve an implicit conflict over governmental objectives based on disagreement concerning the seriousness (or existence) of alternative "problems" that different leaders have suggested the government should address, such as "the size of the budget deficit" or "the number of Americans living in poverty." A third type of political issue involves more explicit (if not fundamental) conflict about alternative goals or objectives that the government should—or should not—be trying to achieve, while a fourth type of issue is based on disagreement about the relative priority of existing objectives where most citizens would agree on some kind of governmental responsibility.

To be sure, any comprehensive explanation of electoral decisions must include direct evaluations of the candidates in terms of their personal or nongovernmental characteristics (such as their "honesty" or "morality") as well as evaluations of their past and future effectiveness in handling consensual governmental objectives. Discussions about the relative importance of different political topics often refer to such candidate-related attitudes, but they will not be discussed in this chapter, which concentrates on the potential *sources* of candidate evaluations that are defined in terms of voters' opinions about alternative governmental objectives.

In attempting to describe voters' opinions about issues that may affect the vote, some researchers (including the present authors) believe that electoral surveys must also consider this general question: In what aspects of national life *do* almost all citizens share a basic *consensus* concerning the federal government's general responsibilities, specific objectives, and policy-related priorities? And what (other) aspects of national life involve substantial *conflicts* concerning the government's responsibilities, objectives, or priorities?

This kind of distinction is hardly new, since previous electoral research has often divided all potential "issues" into two different categories, depending on the degree of consensus concerning the implicit purposes or objectives involved. In addition to previous studies using that distinction, an experimental project called the Survey of Governmental Objectives (SGO) has developed a questionnaire designed to "cover" the full range of potential issues that may become important in national electoral politics (Shanks & Strand, 1997). The SGO project pays close attention to the conceptual distinction between aspects of national life where broad agreement exists concerning the federal government's objectives and priorities and those where there are substantial policy-related conflicts.

Direct Individual-Level Measures

Public opinion researchers have developed several kinds of questions to identify issues having greater priority or importance to individual survey respondents. In general, direct measures of this sort have been used to capture respondents' opinions about a specific aspect of potentially important topics. As shown in Table 11–1, these alternative questions assess individual respondents' views concerning the perceived "seriousness" of alternative problems; the degree to which the country has achieved specific goals; the centrality of general values, goals, or issues; preferences for (or against) alternative governmental objectives; preferences for more (or less) governmental emphasis on existing governmental objectives; and the degree to which different topics represent "reasons" for preferring one electoral candidate over another.

With the exception of the last two questions in Table 11–1, each of these approaches asks respondents for their own opinions about the importance or priority of one or more problems, values, goals, objectives, or issues and does not make any reference to alternative candidates or parties. The following paragraphs review the rationale and analytic procedures for each of these kinds of direct measurement.

Table 11–1

Alternative Questions for Direct Measurement of Importance

Aspect of topic	Type of question	Surveys used in	Approximate text of specific survey question
Problem	Open-ended	ANES and others	What do you think are the most important problems facing this country?
Problem	Rating	SGO	Is (specific condition) not really a problem, a minor problem, a serious problem, or an extremely serious problem?
Condition	Rating	SGO	How close is the country to (specific desirable condition)?
Value	Ranking	ANES	Which of these (values) is most important to you (in your life)? Which is next, and so on?
Goal	Ranking	ANES	Which one of these (national goals) seems most desirable to you? Which is second?
Campaign issue	Ranking	ANES	Which of these (issues) is most important to you? Which is next most important, and so on?
Policy issue	Rating	ANES	How important is it (to you) for the government to take your position concerning (a specific issue)?
Policy issue	Rating	SGO	To what extent are you concerned about what the federal government does—or does not do—concerning (a specific topic)?
Government responsibility	Rating	SGO	Do you think the federal government should—or should not—try to (a specific objective)?
Spending priority	Rating	ANES General Social Survey SGO	Is the government spending too much, too little, or about the right amount on a (specific national objective or program)?
Effort priority	Rating	SGO	Do you think the federal government is putting too much, about the right amount, or too little effort in trying to reach that objective?
Reasons for choice	Ranking	Media polls	Which of these (issues) was the most important reason for your vote choice?
Reasons for choice	Open-ended	ANES	Is there anything that you (like or dislike) about the (Democratic or Republican) (candidate or party) that would make you want to vote for or against that (person or party)?

Open-Ended Questions Concerning the "Most Important Problem"

In this approach voters are simply asked to describe the "most important problems facing the nation" from their own point of view.

Exhibit A documents several versions of this question that have been used in recent years by selected public opinion polls and survey organizations. Many other survey organizations and specific questions could be included in this list but were omitted for

Exhibit A
Questions about "Most Important Problems" Used by Different Organizations

Organization/year	Question text
Gallup Poll 1986	Most important problem facing the US today (open-ended question)
Harris Poll 1996	What do you think are the two most important issues for the government to address?
Los Angeles Times Poll 1996	(a) What's the most important problem facing this country today? Is there another problem you think is almost as important? (b) What do you believe is the country's major problem today? Is there another equally important?
NBC/Wall Street Journal 1995	(a) What would you say are the two or three most important issues or problems facing the nation today that you personally would like to see the federal government in Washington do something about? (b) Which one of the following six issues do you think needs the greatest attention from the federal government at the present time? Improving education, strengthening the economy, combating street crime and violence, reforming the welfare system, reducing the budget deficit, reforming the health care system.
NYT/CBS Poll 1996	What do you think is the most important problem facing the country today?
Pew Research Center 1996	What do you think is the most important problem facing the country today?
Princeton Survey Research Associates 1995	(a) In your opinion, what is the most important problem facing the country today? (b) What do you think is the most important problem facing this country today?
Roper Starch 1993	Here is a list of things people have told us they are concerned about today. Would you read over that list and then tell me which two or three you personally are most concerned about today? The free trade agreement between the U.S., Canada, and Mexico. Our relations with foreign countries. Wrongdoing by elected government officials. Crime and lawlessness. Inflation and high prices. Pollution of air and water.
Time/CNN Poll 1996	What do you think is the main problem facing the country today?
Times Mirror 1995	(a) What things are you most dissatisfied with—the health care system, the economy, crime, the political system, or taxes being too high? (b) What is the most important problem facing the country today?
Washington Post/ABC 1995	What do you think is the most important problem facing this country today?

Source: *American Public Opinion Index* for 1986, 1993, 1995, and 1996.

simplicity. Readers should note that some of these items ask respondents to compare or rank specific problem areas, while others rely on open-ended questions that do not mention any particular topics. As discussed below, the consequence of this methodological difference is not well understood. (For an exception to this rule, see Schuman & Presser, 1981, pp. 79–89.)

This type of question was introduced by The Gallup Poll in 1935 (Gallup, 1969) and remains a fixture in periodic reports by several polling organizations; Smith (1995) contains a long-range review of responses to this question over the years. Since 1960, a version of this question (often referred to as "MIP") has also been included in the ANES. The ANES question is asked in an open-ended fashion, without any precoded categories, and interviewers are instructed to prompt for "any other" problems as well as an initial response. The resulting text is then converted to one or more numeric values with a three-digit code that identifies broad topics or themes, like social welfare or foreign affairs, as well as more specific concerns. By convention the first response to this open-ended question is designated as the "most important problem" for that person. As shown in Table 11–2, these coded responses can be aggregated to generate indicators of the salience of specific topics based on the percentages of all respondents who described some aspect of those topics as most important.

Since 1960 the relative frequency with which ANES respondents mention various general topics in identifying the "most important" national problem has fluctuated fairly dramatically. As shown in Table 11–2, substantial changes have occurred in the relative frequency with which U.S. citizens describe the nation's "most important problem" in terms of economic conditions, foreign affairs, public order, racial issues, or social welfare. For example, the percentage who described the "most important problem" in economic terms has varied from a low of 8% in 1960 (and 1964) to a high of 46% in 1980 (with continuing percentages at approximately that level in each of the following elections), while the percentage who designated some aspect of foreign affairs declined from a high of 62% in 1960 to a low of only 3% in 1992.

Most of the fluctuations in Table 11–2 "make sense" in the context of national political history and specific presidential campaigns. Based on several decades of research, however, many scholars have concluded that the percentages of respondents who mention a specific topic in a given year are primarily a reflection of the simple *visibility* of that

Table 11-2

ANES Trends in the Most Important Problem* (% of respondents who described the "most important problem" in that category)

Election year	Economy	Foreign affairs	Public order	Race	Social welfare	Other
1960	9	62	0	6	15	8
1964	8	37	4	20	24	7
1968	6	51	19	9	12	3
1972	22	34	20	6	11	7
1976	45	5	8	1	35	6
1980	46	32	2	0	15	5
1984	34	34	4	0	23	5
1988	39	10	21	1	22	7
1992	42	3	12	1	37	5

*Full text of the MIP question for most of these ANES surveys: "What do you think are the most important problems facing the country?"

topic in media coverage and other political discussions. To be sure, individual respondents are different from one another in the degree to which specific topics are personally relevant or "central" based on their own values, current circumstances, and personal problems. That kind of interpersonal variation concerning the psychological importance of a given topic, however, may not be captured by dichotomous indicators based on whether each individual does (or does not) mention that topic in response to the ANES MIP question. Instead, the "problems" mentioned by most respondents may represent little more than those topics that have been emphasized most frequently in recent media coverage.

In general, electoral researchers have been unsuccessful in using the ANES MIP questions to identify respondents whose opinions about specific topics appear to have had a larger influence on their vote choice. In such analyses persons who mention a given problem as "most important" should be more likely to mention that topic as a reason for their choice, or their opinion about issues in that area should exhibit a stronger (statistical) relationship with vote choice. Electoral analysts do not agree whether this failure of the ANES MIP question (to identify voters whose choices are more clearly linked to specific topics) should be attributed to (1) the influence of media coverage on responses to that question (instead of true differences in its personal centrality), (2) the absence of any electoral references in the wording of that question, (3) respondents' inability to identify those topics that are *really* important in shaping their vote choice, or (4) more general problems associated with open-ended questions. As a consequence, many analysts regard the coded answers to the ANES MIP question as an uninterpretable combination of the strength or intensity of real concerns, simple awareness of the topics that are most frequently emphasized in the national media, and measurement error.

Precoded Questions for Specific Potential Problems

One alternative to this open-ended question is a more structured approach that asks respondents to rate the perceived severity of alternative suggestions about current national "problems" on a standardized rating scale. The 1996 SGO included a battery of questions about a series of specific circumstances that some national leaders described as "problems." In particular, respondents were asked whether they personally thought that each of the circumstances listed in Table 11–3 was "not really a problem," a "small problem," a "serious problem," or an "extremely serious problem."

Most of these suggested problems were seen as either "serious" or "extremely serious" by a clear majority of respondents. Thus, 88% of SGO96 respondents said that "the number of people who commit crimes and then aren't punished severely enough" was a serious or extremely serious problem, the same percentage as for "illegal drug use"; that was followed by 87% for "the number of people who can't afford health insurance," 75% for "the size of the federal budget deficit," 73% for "the amount of poverty," and 71% for "the amount of crime that you think will be faced by the average person 20 years or so from now." Several of these suggested problems, however, were *not* viewed so unanimously, and substantial numbers of respondents classified some suggestions as only a "small problem" or "not really a problem." In particular, 56% of the SGO sample regarded "the number of black people who face discrimination in hiring or promotion" as a small or nonexistent problem, followed by 35% for "the number of people who have to pay the federal government too much in taxes" and 33% for "the condition of our environment and natural resources." In the United States the two major parties have usually emphasized different sets of problems or "agendas" for the country as a whole, and SGO96 respondents were no different in that respect.

Table 11-3

Distribution of Responses Concerning the Seriousness of Alternative Problems* (% of 657 SGO respondents who selected that response)

What about _____? Do you think it is:	Not really a problem	Small problem	Serious problem	Extremely serious problem	Don't know, not ascertained
The size of the federal budget deficit	4%	12%	48%	27%	8%**
The number of black people who face discrimination in hiring or promotion	19	37	29	7	8
The condition of our environment and natural resources	7	26	42	17	8
The amount of poverty in the United States	4	18	50	23	6
The number of people who have to pay the federal government too much in taxes	14	21	38	19	8
The number of people who can't afford health insurance	3	8	50	37	2
The number of people who commit crimes and then aren't punished severely enough by the justice system	2	7	43	45	4
The amount of illegal drug use	2	7	45	43	3
The number of middle-income people who are likely to face economic difficulty over the next 10 years or so	5	24	46	19	5
The amount of crime that you think will be faced by the average person 20 years or so from now	2	15	44	27	12

*Text of question, including introduction:

**Figures have been rounded and, therefore, may not add to 100%.

The next few questions involve aspects of the United States today that some people believe are serious problems. Other people, however, disagree and say that these things are not really problems at all. For each topic, we want to know what YOU PERSONALLY think. If you aren't sure about a topic, just say so and we will move on to the next one.

What about the size of the federal budget deficit? Do you personally think that is NOT REALLY A PROBLEM, is it a PROBLEM, BUT NOT SERIOUS, is it a SERIOUS PROBLEM, or an EXTREMELY SERIOUS PROBLEM—or aren't you sure?

Perceptions of Current Conditions: The Potential Relevance
of Consensual Objectives

In some aspects of national life, almost all American citizens presumably agree that the federal government is at least partially responsible for some general goals or objectives. Thus almost every U.S. citizen agrees that the federal government is responsible for maintaining a strong economy and military defense. For such aspects of national life, where a pervasive consensus exists concerning both a general national objective and the federal government's responsibilities, electoral "issues" may refer to the possibility that the incumbent administration gains popular support when current conditions are perceived in positive terms—or loses support when such perceptions are clearly negative.

This chapter and the SGO project are based on a general belief that this kind of consensus about the federal government's goals or objectives is *not* as pervasive as has sometimes been suggested. Like many other researchers the present authors suspect that American citizens (and their leaders) do not in fact agree on both the appropriateness and the priority of most of the objectives that are often attributed to the federal government, and that these disagreements play a crucial role in shaping electoral decisions. In many aspects of national life, both leaders and voters maintain sharply conflicting ideas about the objectives that the federal government should—or should not—be pursuing in some (or any) way. In other aspects of national life, an overwhelming majority may endorse a very general governmental objective or responsibility, but may not agree that current conditions are particularly problematic or that efforts to achieve that objective should be given a high priority in the competition for scarce governmental resources.

Despite that general caveat about the potential for conflict (instead of consensus) concerning many governmental objectives, any assessment of the potential relative importance of alternative political issues should include the electorate's perceptions of current conditions in those aspects of national life where there *is* a national consensus concerning a specific objective and the federal government's responsibility in that area. For such objectives the incumbent administration *may* be rewarded (or punished) because of sharply positive (or negative) perceptions of current conditions. For electoral researchers, however, it is not clear which governmental objectives should be covered by direct survey questions about current conditions because of uncertainty about the existence (or extent) of national agreement about the appropriateness or priority of those (implicit) objectives.

To address these questions, each SGO96 interview began with a series of questions that asked "how close" the respondent thought current conditions in the United States were to goals or objectives that are presumably shared by the overwhelming majority of citizens: "very close to," "somewhat close to," "not too close to," or "a long way from" the stated goal. The percentage distributions for all six goals across those fixed response categories are shown in Table 11–4.

The percentages who chose these fixed categories in 1996 are not strictly comparable across the six conditions because of inevitable differences among topics in the thresholds used to define positive or desirable conditions. Despite that caveat, political analysts may be interested in comparing different aspects of national life in terms of the percentages who described the United States as "very close" or "somewhat close" to the stated circumstances. Thus, 56% of SGO96 respondents saw the United States as currently very or somewhat close to having a "strong economy," 57% saw the United States as very or somewhat close to "where citizens who work hard over time have a decent chance of achieving financial success," 64% saw the United States as very or somewhat close to "where anyone who wants to work can find a job," and 72% saw the United States as very or somewhat close to having an "effective defense" against any military attack. In contrast

J. Merrill Shanks

Table 11-4

Distribution of Responses Concerning Current Conditions* (% of 657 SGO respondents who selected that response)

As of today, how close do you think the U.S. is to:	Very close	Somewhat close	Not too close	A long way from	Don't know, not ascertained
Having a strong economy?	13	43	25	11	8
Where most people can walk in their own neighborhoods without much danger of theft or violence?	4	28	39	25	4
Where anyone who wants to work can find a job?	23	41	22	10	4
Having an effective defense against any military attack on this country or its allies?	44	28	12	3	13
Where citizens who work hard over time have a decent chance of achieving financial success?	17	40	28	11	4
In twenty years or so, how close do you think most of today's teenagers will be to having a good economic standard of living when they are adults?	5	34	33	15	13

*Text of question, including introduction:

First, we would like to know how you see the current situation in the United States. For a variety of topics, we will ask you which of several descriptions is most accurate for our country today. If you aren't sure about an area, just say so and we will move to the next question.

Let's start with a familiar subject: How close do you think the United States is to where anyone who wants to work can find a job? Are we VERY CLOSE, SOMEWHAT CLOSE, NOT TOO CLOSE, or A LONG WAY FROM a country in which anyone can find a job——or aren't you sure about that?

only 32% saw the current United States as very or somewhat close to "where most people can walk in their own neighborhoods without much danger of theft or violence," and only 39% said that the country was very or somewhat close to where most of today's teenagers will have a "good economic standard of living when they are adults."

Relatively few aspects of national life can be described in terms of implicit goals or objectives that are almost universally shared or accepted. In the course of testing and revising the SGO96 interview schedule, questions about current "conditions" in several areas (such as universal access to health care) were rewritten in terms of the perceived seriousness of a suggested national problem (discussed earlier) because test respondents did *not* agree about the appropriateness of that implicit objective for the federal government.

Preferences Concerning the Appropriateness of Specific Governmental Objectives

In many discussions of public opinion, statements about the political importance of different topics may refer to citizens' preferences concerning the particular goals that should be included in the government's current policy-related "agenda." This criterion for the importance of different topics is based on that individual's *prescriptions* concerning the appropriateness of specific *governmental objectives* or their *policy-related* preferences concerning governmental *priorities* and should not be confused with the apparent psychological importance (to the respondent) of specific problems, values, goals, or issues—or with the impact of such opinions on electoral preferences.

The most powerful policy-related conflicts presumably arise when enough citizens believe that the federal government *should* be trying to reach some (stated) goal or objective, while many others believe that the government *should not* be pursuing that objective at all. Disagreements over basic purposes or objectives may have more powerful electoral consequences because the policy-related conflicts involved are (by definition) more fundamental than differences of opinion concerning the relative priority of different consensual objectives.

Despite the potentially greater electoral influence of this more fundamental kind of policy-related disagreement, social scientists know relatively little about the degree to which a clear majority of Americans endorse a wide variety of alternative potential objectives that are often discussed in electoral campaigns. Furthermore, it is difficult to compare the extent of support for different objectives because of the diversity in question formats that have been used. As electoral analysts we need to know what proportion of the electorate believes that the federal government should try to reach a wide variety of potential objectives.

For that reason the SGO project has developed a battery of questions that rely on the same format and response alternatives in order to answer this kind of descriptive question about the different objectives. For each of these suggested objectives, it was expected that many respondents would quickly indicate their view that the federal government *should* try to achieve that objective, while another group would have no difficulty saying that the government *should not*. This battery of questions was primarily designed to document those aspects of national life where a substantial amount of conflict was expected concerning the federal government's basic purposes or objectives. For many potential objectives, however, participating researchers were unsure how much conflict (or disagreement) would emerge.

The SGO96 list of suggested objectives is fairly long and covers most of those aspects of national life where observers have suggested some kind of underlying disagreement concerning the objectives of the federal government. Table 11–5 presents the precise

Table 11-5

Distribution of Responses Concerning the Appropriateness of Alternative Objectives (% of 657 SGO respondents who selected that response)

Do you think the federal government should or should not:	Yes, government should	Depends	No, government should not	Don't know, not ascertained
Make sure that every American who wants to work can find a job?	64	3	27	6*
Maintain military forces that are stronger than those of any other country?	83	2	8	7
Use American military forces to try to stop internal fighting or civil wars in other countries?	19	15	54	12
Try to reduce the size of income differences between rich and poor Americans?	37	3	48	11
Make it illegal to sell or distribute pornography to anyone?	55	3	35	6
Give racial minorities some preferential treatment in hiring for government jobs?	19	4	70	7
Make sure that all public school students have the opportunity to pray as a part of some official school activity?	57	4	33	6
Make persons with higher incomes pay a larger percentage of their income in taxes than persons with lower incomes?	56	3	33	8
Tax an individual's income from capital gains at a much lower rate than all other types of income, including salaries and wages?	36	2	39	22
Allow homosexuals to serve in the U.S. armed forces?	59	4	28	8
Give tax credits or vouchers to people who send their children to private schools?	35	2	52	10
Put any restrictions on abortion?	37	3	54	5
Make sure that all Americans have health insurance?	74	3	17	5
Cut income taxes in some way?	67	5	20	9
Eliminate the Department of Education in Washington?	17	0	68	14
Do you think the U.S. Constitution should or should not be changed to add an amendment that requires the federal budget to be balanced every year?	58	1	32	10

*Figures have been rounded and, therefore, may not add to 100%.

wording and the distribution of responses for each of those suggestions, based on the simple choice between "Yes, the government should" and "No, the government should not" try to pursue that objective—with separate categories for those who said their answer would "depend" on some clarification and those who did not know or did not provide any response.

Several of these suggested objectives were endorsed by substantial majorities. Thus 83% said that the federal government *should* "maintain military forces that are stronger than those of any other country," followed by 74% for making sure that "all Americans have health insurance," 67% for cutting income taxes "in some way," and 64% for making sure that "every American who wants to work can find a job." Smaller majorities indicated that the federal government should "allow homosexuals to serve in the U.S. armed forces" (59%), change the U.S. Constitution to add an amendment that "requires the federal budget to be balanced every year" (58%), make sure that "all public school students have the opportunity to pray as a part of some official school activity" (57%), make "persons with higher incomes pay a larger percentage of their income in taxes than persons with lower incomes" (56%), and make it "illegal to sell or distribute pornography to anyone" (55%).

Other suggested objectives, however, were opposed by majorities of SGO respondents, led by the 70% who thought that the federal government should *not* "give racial minorities some preferential treatment in hiring for government jobs," the 68% who thought that the federal government should *not* "eliminate the Department of Education in Washington," the 54% who thought that the federal government should *not* "use American military forces to try to stop internal fighting or civil wars in other countries," the 54% who thought that the federal government should not "put any restrictions on abortion," and the 52% who opposed giving "tax credits or vouchers to people who send their children to private schools." Of the 16 questions about suggested objectives that were included in this SGO96 battery, 9 are more often advocated by conservative politicians, and 7 are more frequently advocated by liberals. Because of the visibility of these ongoing conflicts, it was expected (and confirmed) that SGO respondents' views concerning the appropriateness of these potential objectives would be strongly related to their electoral preferences in 1996.

Conflicts Over Policy-Related Priorities

Finally, disagreements may also arise among voters concerning governmental objectives that are seen as legitimate or "appropriate" by a clear majority of citizens. That is, voters who agree that the federal government has some responsibility for a given objective may have divergent preferences about the attention or money that should be devoted to that objective. These kinds of policy-related priorities have been captured by questions about national "spending" in both the GSS and the ANES. As discussed below, the SGO96 pilot survey has extended that kind of question to include governmental activities in which policy-related priorities are expressed in terms of "effort" rather than financial or budgetary support. The basic policy-related question is the same, however—whether the federal government should be putting more, the same, or less emphasis on a particular (stated) objective than it is currently doing.

Voters' policy-related priorities for the federal government can have a substantial impact on their vote. For example, voters' choices in most recent U.S. presidential elections have been strongly related to their preferences for more or less emphasis by the federal government on assistance to persons with very low incomes (i.e., welfare-related programs). Voters' preferences for increased or reduced emphasis on a given governmental objective, however, are *not the same thing* as the impact of those preferences (concerning governmental priorities) on their electoral decisions. Thus a given voter may believe that a specific objective (such as assistance to the poor) is currently "very important" in the sense of its urgency in the competition for governmental priorities, but that same individual may make voting decisions that are unaffected by his or her preference concerning that objective's priority—because rival candidates have taken similar positions concerning that objective or because neither candidate has emphasized that topic or because the voter really does not care much about that issue. Also voters for whom a specific topic is *not* important *may* still make electoral decisions that are powerfully influenced by their own negative attitudes toward that objective—if the major candidates present very different positions concerning the appropriateness or priority of that objective.

Questions about the most appropriate priorities for the federal government represent a familiar kind of assessment in several contexts. Public opinion surveys have often concentrated on this kind of policy-related statement, as have major policy essays that recommend changes in "national goals" (President's Commission on National Goals, 1960). In practice, however, this distinction between preferences concerning policy-related priorities and other types of evaluations concerning relative importance can be problematic or elusive. Everyday conversations about politics often fluctuate between statements about most voters' preferences concerning those objectives that should be given the highest priority by the government and statements about the psychological importance of those topics to most people—or the electoral impact of voters' policy-related preferences in those areas. For that reason it may be impossible to determine if informal comments about the importance of any topic or issue (e.g., abortion) refer to impressions about most voters' preferences concerning the priority of specific objectives in that area (e.g., reducing the number of abortions), the psychological importance of that topic, or the impact of policy preferences concerning that topic in shaping electoral decisions. At this point we can only emphasize the conceptual distinction between voters' own preferences about the government's priorities in an area and all other psychological or explanatory criteria.

Trends in Spending-Related Priorities

Since the 1970s direct measures of voters' policy-related preferences concerning governmental priorities have been included in both the GSS and the ANES. To date both of these surveys have based their battery of questions about the priority of different objectives on the amount of *money* that is currently being spent on those kinds of programs. In particular the GSS questions in this series ask respondents whether the country is "spending too much money, too little money, or about the right amount" in over 10 different programmatic areas. Parallel questions in the ANES series ask respondents whether the federal government's spending in a given area should be "increased, decreased, or kept about the same."

National results from both of these surveys suggest that different governmental objectives are given quite different priorities by the electorate as a whole and that fluctuations over time in these apparent priorities do seem to reflect shifting national debates concerning those topics. Table 11–6 presents pooled two-year GSS estimates for the percentages of citizens who said that the country is currently spending "too little" on nine types of governmental programs or objectives. For each type of program, these estimates indicate the percentages of citizens (in that period) who believed that spending should be increased.[3]

---

[3]The parallel questions concerning "spending" in the biennial ANES surveys permit comparisons over time for a smaller set of programmatic areas and a shorter period of time (beginning in 1984). For that reason most of this discussion is limited to the GSS time series. GSS questions also cover other types of programs (aid to cities, social security, drugs, national parks, roads, and mass transportation) that have been omitted from Table 11–6 because they were not asked for the entire 22-year period. Parallel results for ANES questions about spending are presented after this initial table.

Table 11-6

Change over Time in Spending-Related Priorities (% of GSS respondents who said that "too little" money is currently being spent in that area)

Year	Defense	Crime	Health	Education	Environment	Blacks	Welfare	Space	Foreign Aid
1972	12	69	63	51	65	35	21	8	4
1974	18	70	66	52	60	31	24	8	4
1976	26	70	61	51	54	28	13	10	3
1978	29	67	58	54	55	26	14	12	4
1980	60	72	57	55	51	26	14	20	5
1982	27	73	61	62	57	38	25	13	7
1984	16	67	60	63	60	35	21	12	6
1986	17	69	66	64	66	41	25	13	7
1988	16	73	69	68	72	37	24	17	5
1990	13	70	72	71	72	39	23	12	5
1992	11	74	74	69	59	39	17	9	5
1994	16	77	67	72	61	34	13	10	4
1996	18	69	68	70	61	35	16	12	4

As indicated in Table 11–6, popular support for increased spending concerning one governmental objective (defense) has fluctuated substantially since 1972: The percentage who said that current spending is "too little" began at only 12% during the Vietnam War, rose to a high of 60% in 1980, fell quickly to only 27% after Ronald Reagan's sharp increase in military expenditures, and has fluctuated between 11 and 17% since 1986. In contrast, public support for increased spending concerning crime, health, education, and the environment remained fairly high throughout this 22-year period. Thus the level of support for additional spending to stop crime has not gone below 67 percent or above 77 percent. The corresponding (low and high) percentages concerning health are 57 and 74% and are identical for education and the environment (51 and 72%).

In contrast, popular support for increased spending in other areas has stayed at a fairly low level throughout this period. In particular, preferences for increased levels of spending for welfare or assistance to the poor range from only 13 to 25%, and parallel percentages (for increased spending) on space exploration and foreign aid range from 8 to 20% and 3 to 7%, respectively. During the same period public support for increased spending on assistance to blacks has fluctuated from a low of 26% in 1978 and 1980 to a high of 41% in 1986.

For some areas not included in Table 11–6, popular support for increased spending was also fairly high and did not fluctuate a great deal. In particular, support for additional spending on "problems of the big cities" fluctuated between 45 and 62% between 1973 and 1994, support for additional spending on "social security" ranged between 46 and 57%, and support for "dealing with drug addiction" varied between 58 and 74%. From 1984 through 1994, support for additional spending was somewhat lower for "parks and recreation" (between 31 and 35%), for "highways and bridges" (from 36 to 48%), and for "mass transportation" (from 32 to 38%).

Beginning in 1980, similar kinds of results can be obtained from ANES surveys, based on a somewhat different question about the federal government's spending in a smaller number of areas. Table 11–7 presents the percentages of ANES respondents who said that federal spending should be increased for "food stamps," "the environment,"

Table 11-7

ANES-Based Preferences for Increased Federal Spending* (% of ANES
respondents who preferred an increase in that area)

	Food stamps	Environment	Science	Social security	Assistance to blacks
1984	21	36	38	52	26
1988	22	63	30	59	24
1992	18	61	42	49	25
1996	12	43	—	51	—

*Text of question:

If you had a say in making up the federal budget this year, for which programs would you like
to see spending increased and for which would you like to see spending decreased:

Should federal spending on [item] be increased, decreased, or kept about the same?

"science," "social security," and "assistance to blacks." As in the GSS series, popular support for additional spending on the poor (food stamps) and racial minorities (blacks) was visibly lower than that for other kinds of programs.

Priority-Related Preferences Based on Spending versus Effort

To extend this kind of description concerning different governmental programs, the SGO96 questionnaire included two batteries of questions with similar kinds of response categories concerning relative priority. The first of these batteries asked respondents whether the federal government should be placing more, less, or the same *"effort"* in each area. The objectives covered by this battery involved programs where the government's priorities are difficult to discuss in terms of "spending," such as punishment of criminals and job discrimination against blacks. Table 11-8 presents the precise wording for each of these current objectives along with the distribution of responses, including a combined category for "don't know" and "not ascertained."

For five of these nine objectives, a majority of SGO96 respondents expressed a preference for "more effort," with 83% saying they wanted the government to put more effort into "making sure that people convicted of violent crimes are punished severely" and into "punishing people caught with any illegal drugs." Somewhat smaller majorities favored more effort on "protecting the environment and natural resources" (62%), "restricting the kinds of guns that people can buy" (62%), and "restricting the number of legal immigrants" (57%). In contrast only a minority of respondents preferred more effort in each of the other four areas, from 49% for "trying to stop job discrimination against women," to 36% for "trying to stop job discrimination against blacks," to 33% for "trying to stop job discrimination against homosexuals," to only 28% for "eliminating many of the regulations that businesses have to follow"; that last area also had the highest percentage who preferred less or no effort by the federal government (25%). Researchers anticipated that disagreement about the priority of these nonbudgetary objectives would be clearly related to voters' voting preferences in 1996, and most of those expectations (except those for business regulation and limits on legal immigration) were strongly confirmed.

The final battery of questions about alternative governmental objectives in the SGO96 questionnaire asked respondents if they thought the federal government should spend more, the same, less, or no money on areas like food stamps and the military. Table 11-9

Table 11-8

Distribution of Responses Concerning Governmental Priorities in Effort*

(% of 657 SGO respondents who selected that response)

Should the federal government put more, same, or less into:	More effort	Same amount of effort	Less effort	No effort at all	Don't know, not ascertained
Protecting the environment and natural resources?	62	28	5	1	3**
Making sure that people convicted of violent crimes are punished severely?	83	10	2	0	4
Trying to stop job discrimination against blacks?	36	40	14	5	6
Eliminating many of the regulations that businesses have to follow?	28	33	20	5	14
Trying to stop job discrimination against gay men and lesbians, in other words, homosexuals?	33	34	14	10	9
Restricting the number of legal immigrants into the U.S. from other countries?	57	25	9	4	5
Punishing people caught with any illegal drugs?	83	10	2	0	4
Trying to stop job discrimination against women?	49	35	8	4	4
Restricting the kinds of guns that people can buy?	62	15	12	7	4

*Text of question, including introduction:

**Figures have been rounded and, therefore, may not add to 100%.

Now we're going to ask what you think of the federal government's CURRENT ACTIVITIES in several different areas. In each case, I will ask whether you think the federal government should put LESS, the SAME amount of effort, or MORE EFFORT into that area, compared to its current activities. If you aren't sure about an area, just say so and we will move on to the next question.

First, do you think the federal government should put LESS effort, the SAME amount of effort, or MORE EFFORT into "reducing the federal deficit"?

presents the precise wording for each of these questions concerning federal spending and the distribution of responses across the same alternatives as for the "effort" battery.

Only two of these objectives or programs received majority support for increased spending, led by "health care for elderly people" (56%) and "financial assistance to public elementary and secondary schools" (53%). However, none of these programs received less than 20% support for more spending (as was true for "providing food stamps to poor people" in Table 11–9). The largest percentages in favor of *less* or no spending were for "providing food stamps to poor people" (30%), followed by "developing a system that would defend the U.S. against a nuclear missile attack" (21%), "providing assistance to poor mothers with young children" (17%), and "maintaining a strong military defense" (15%). Because of the visibility of ongoing budgetary conflicts between the Clinton administration and Republican leaders, it was expected and confirmed that all of these disagreements concerning federal spending would be sharply related to the vote.

Comparisons between "Importance" Based on MIP and Priorities

To some observers, statements about the relative importance based on some "problematic" aspect of those topics may reflect a very different orientation than statements about the relative priority of governmental objectives in that area. Uncertainty about the relevance of this distinction, however, should be reduced by comparing the apparent importance of some of the topics covered in both Tables 11–2 and 11–6 concerning MIPs and spending-related preferences. For example, 34% of ANES respondents in 1972 named some aspect of "foreign affairs" as the most important problem (Table 11–2), a percentage that was considerably higher than for any other general topic. At the same time, however, only 12% of the GSS respondents in that year thought "defense spending" was important in the sense that federal spending should be increased in that area (Table 11–6), a substantially lower percentage than the corresponding percentages for crime (69%), health (63%), education (50%), the environment (65%), blacks (35%), and welfare (21%). The opposite kind of discrepancy arose in 1976, when only 8% of ANES respondents mentioned some aspect of public order (including crime) as the nation's most important problem, compared to 45% for the economy and 35% for social welfare; but 70% of the same respondents indicated that federal spending concerning crime should be increased, the largest percentage favoring an increase in any programmatic area. Clearly, survey-based reports concerning the public's views about the nation's most important problems may be based on very different aspects of alternative topics than preferences for additional spending in those areas.

Direct Assessments of "Importance" for Values, Goals, and Issues

Only the 1976 ANES survey included questions that ask respondents to evaluate the personal importance of alternative personal values or national goals. In particular the 1976 ANES survey asked respondents to rank five general aspects of life in terms of their personal importance "as a guiding principle," based on the degree to which they are seen as "ambitious or hard working"; a "pleasant person or well-liked"; "self-reliant or independent"; "helpful to others"; and "responsible or dependable." In 1976 and subsequent ANES surveys, a second set of questions asked respondents to rank four general goals for

Table 11-9

Distribution of Responses Concerning Governmental Priorities in Spending (% of 657 SGO respondents who selected that response)

Should the federal government put more, same, or less into:	More spending	Same amount	Reduce rate of growth	Less spending	No spending at all	Don't know or refused
Providing food stamps to poor people?	20	42	1	27	3	7
Maintaining a strong military defense?	27	52	1	15	0	4
Providing health care for poor people?	46	40	1	9	1	4
Developing a system that would defend the U.S. against a nuclear missile attack?	34	38	0	16	5	6
Providing health care for elderly people?	56	38	0	3	0	3
Social security benefits?	48	40	1	6	0	5
Providing assistance to poor mothers with young children?	34	42	0	15	2	5
Providing financial assistance to students attending universities or junior colleges?	49	38	0	6	2	4
Providing financial assistance to public elementary and secondary schools?	53	32	0	5	3	7

the country that were defined in terms of "maintaining order," "giving the people more say," "fighting rising prices," and "protecting freedom of speech." In 1976 similar kinds of rankings were also obtained for the relative importance (to the respondent) of alternative political "issues" that were defined in terms of "honesty in government," "high taxes," "inflation," "energy shortages," unemployment," "relations with other countries," "racial issues," "combating crime and drugs," "consumer protection," and "pollution."

Researchers hoped to use respondent ratings to identify voters for whom certain kinds of issues would appear to have the greatest influence on vote choice. Unfortunately analyses of these rankings have yet to yield any consistent ability to identify voters for whom specific topics or issues appear to have played a more important role in shaping their electoral preferences.

The possibility of substantial differences (between voters) in the electoral importance of specific policy issues was examined in a somewhat different way in the 1980 and 1984 ANES surveys. As in previous ANES surveys, 1980 and 1984 respondents were asked to place themselves on several seven-point scales concerning a single policy-related controversy and then to "place" the major candidates, parties, and "current federal policy" on the same scale. After placing current federal policy on the same seven-point scale, respondents in 1980 and 1984 were also asked: "How important is it to you that the federal government change its policy so that it is close to your own position on that issue?"

As before, the rationale for introducing these direct questions about "issue importance" was based on rational choice theory from economics, according to which the apparent importance of each issue could be used as a "weight" to reflect the degree to which that individual's own position on that issue influences his or her vote. As with the previous approaches, however, analyses have failed to exhibit consistent differences between those who rated specific policy issues as more versus less important, with the exception of the limited success reported in Krosnick (1988).

In general, then, survey questions concerning the relative importance of specific topics or issues have not played a prominent role in survey-based explanations of political or electoral choices. The limited success of such direct measures in electoral explanation may be due to a variety of factors:

- The electoral relevance of some topics may not be revealed by the specific survey question because that question did not mention an explicit electoral criterion and because other topics may be "important" to the respondent in some nonelectoral context.
- Differences in the real causal importance of a given topic are likely to be strongly correlated with the apparent extremity of policy-related preferences in that area, so that only voters who feel strongly about a given issue make choices correlated with their policy-related preferences—without using any direct measure of psychological importance.
- Voters may not know or be able to describe how important a topic has been in shaping their vote, so that direct assessment of that kind of individual-level relevance for electoral choices has no causal-analytic value.

Direct Measurement of Factors That Influence Candidate Evaluations

Finally, the pervasive interest in identifying issues that are more important in shaping electoral decisions has led many researchers to rely entirely on survey respondents to answer such questions. Exit polls and other media-based surveys routinely present respondents with a list of alternative issues or topics that were discussed during the current campaign and ask, "Which of these topics were the most important in your decision to support (candidate)?" Social scientists and media analysts have both expressed reservations about the validity of these explanations. Such questions will no doubt continue to be used, however, because of their simplicity in presentation and the short period of time within each interview that is required.

A more intensive form of this approach has been used by the ANES since 1952. In this more detailed approach, respondents are asked open-ended questions concerning those aspects of the two major party candidates and two major parties that they "like" and parallel questions about those aspects that they "dislike." Up to five positive responses are recorded for each major candidate and each party, and similar procedures are used to code negative responses. In this approach the political importance of any given subject can be assessed by calculating the proportion of respondents who mentioned that subject as a "reason" for either liking or disliking any of the candidates or parties. As discussed in the following section, these respondent-described reasons for candidate evaluations can produce results similar to those of other methods. The same procedures, however, can also produce quite different impressions for selected topics and issues.

Importance Based on Statistical Relationships

As emphasized previously, one of the traditional criteria for issue importance is the extent to which voters' opinions about that issue appear to have influenced their electoral preferences. Issues that are described as electorally "important" in a campaign are those that seem relevant to many voters and that are emphasized by at least one of the opposing candidates.

Electoral analysts, however, have not agreed on the most effective way to use survey data to identify the most important sources of differences between voters. As discussed in the preceding section, some analysts are worried about the validity of respondents' own explanations. But if we do not rely on respondents' own "reasons" for choice, how *can* we decide which issues should be given the most credit for affecting the vote? This section reviews statistical procedures that have been used to assess the relative importance of issues in producing the observed differences in vote, analyses that have been used to compare the most important factors in different election years and to compare elections conducted in different states or countries.

For example, two countries may be compared in terms of the relative electoral importance of religious conflicts or the degree to which such conflicts are correlated with or cut across other social or economic cleavages. In such comparisons religious differences are seen as less "important" in a given country insofar as that country is relatively homogeneous in terms of religious beliefs *or* such beliefs are unrelated to electoral issues. In contrast, religious cleavages reach their maximum electoral importance when voters are highly divided in their religious affiliations *and* campaign issues are clearly linked to those affiliations.

While a comprehensive review of the different procedures that have been used is beyond the scope of this volume, several of the issues involved arise in reviewing one of the most frequently used procedures for multivariate analyses and then comparing the results of that approach with parallel analyses based on open-ended questions. Without some understanding of the potential differences between the two contrasting procedures, electoral analysts may find it difficult to make decisive recommendations concerning the most appropriate survey questions to ask—or to resolve continuing controversies involving alternative explanations of the same election.

Frequently Used Analytic Procedures

The most familiar statistical technique for assessing the electoral importance of a given explanatory variable is to calculate a "standardized" measure of association between that variable and vote choice. Such an analysis often begins with calculating the simple correlation coefficient to summarize the strength of the bivariate statistical connection between each variable and vote choice and then compares that correlation with standardized regression coefficients for the same variable produced by analyses in which other predictors are included in the analysis or "controlled."

Table 11–10 presents a series of alternative coefficients of that sort for several issue variables that appeared to have some influence on voters' choices for George Bush or Michael Dukakis in the 1988 presidential election (Shanks & Miller, 1991). In particular,

Table 11–10

Apparent Impact of Political Attitudes in Shaping Individual Vote Choice in 1988 (Standardized regression coefficients or * if <1.0 standard error)

	Bivariate correl. (r)	Socioeconomic characteristics held constant	Party ID also held constant	Policy-related predisp's also held constant	Current issues also held constant
Partisan identification					
Party ID	.634	.565		.429	.346
Policy-related predispositions					
Ideology (lib/con)	.508	.439	.258	.168	.088
Union vs. business	.317	.259	.133	.088	.057
Egalitarianism	.375	.286	.196	.100	.045
Anti-Communism	.210	.204	.142	.041	*
Feminists vs. pro-life	.258	.234	.146	.076	.040
Patriotism	.203	.145	.106	.054	*
Blacks vs. whites	.290	.191	.149	.070	.050
Current policy preferences					
Military	.475	.431	.270	.172	.142
Aid to the disadvantaged	.471	.380	.242	.136	.101
Abortion	.123	.137	.125	.049	.069
Death penalty	.304	.215	.148	.080	.079
Perceptions of current conditions					
Country as a whole	.362	.299	.185	.141	.097
Unemployment	.408	.327	.180	.134	.077
U.S. position in the world	.280	.219	.110	.089	.038
Worry about jobs in the household	.121	.079	.058	.048	.047

Table 11–10 presents standardized coefficients for voters' liberal versus conservative self-designations, their general predispositions toward equality and Communism and their attitudes toward unions versus corporations, feminists versus pro-life activists, blacks versus whites, and patriotism—as well as their current policy preferences concerning the military, assistance to the disadvantaged, abortion, and the death penalty and their evaluations of current conditions in the country. The first column of Table 11–10 presents simple correlations, or standardized coefficients from bivariate analyses in which no other variables have been held constant. Based on those bivariate results, it is clear that voters' opinions on all of these issues were clearly related to vote choice in 1988.

The second column presents comparable (standardized) coefficients from analyses in which standard social and economic characteristics are controlled in order to eliminate any confounding effects of those (clearly prior) variables. The general similarity between the first and second columns of Table 11–10 suggests that statistical controls for potentially confounding social and economic factors had only a modest impact on the apparent relevance of various issue-related variables in the 1988 election.

The third column of Table 11–10 presents comparable coefficients for each of our issue-related variables that are produced by controlling for voters' partisan identifications as well as their social and economic characteristics. From that column it is clear that the impact of each issue-related variable is substantially reduced when we review the potentially confounding influence of long-term partisan identification—a predisposition that is presumably stronger, having been acquired before other issue-related opinions. For example, the electoral influence of general liberal versus conservative orientations is reduced from .44 to .26 when we "hold constant" voters' general partisan identifications, and the corresponding reduction for general beliefs about equality is from .29 to .20. The same kind of reduction can be seen for current policy issues (such as aid to the disadvantaged, which declines from .38 to .24) and for perceptions of current conditions (such as unemployment, with a decline from .33 to .18).

Finally, columns 4 and 5 of Table 11–10 document the consequences when we also control for other issue-related variables. The coefficients in column 4 were produced by including all of our general predispositions, and the coefficients in column 5 were produced by including all of the other variables in this table, in addition to social and economic characteristics. These two columns represent different approaches to assessing the electoral effects of specific variables that should be attributed to those specific issues rather than to voters' opinions about other potentially confounding topics. Analysts prefer somewhat different estimates for the apparent importance of specific variables, and these two columns are intended to suggest the range of choices involved. In any event, all but the issues of Communism and patriotism maintain a significant relationship with the vote after we control for all of the other issue-related variables.

Alternative Approaches to Explaining the Vote[4]

Any attempt to explain a respondent's vote as a deliberate "choice" or decision may encounter the following sequence of arguments:

- Most voters do not consciously "choose" between candidates by weighing or combining all of the considerations that may be involved in evaluating those candidates. Instead, their preferences evolve over time in response to the *accumulation*

---

[4]For an earlier version of the argument in that short section, see Shanks and Strand (1994).

of positive and negative *impressions* about the candidates; many of these impressions were created by specific experiences or events that are no longer remembered by the voter.

- Thus all that remains from many of those experiences concerning a specific candidate is a residual positive or negative impression, whether the voter was ever conscious of which aspect of the experience was responsible for that residual impression. At the time of "decision" (or the survey interview), voters simply "select" the candidate about whom their cumulative impression is the most positive, or least negative.

- *If* voters did "decide" at a specific point in time by consciously reviewing and weighing their impression of the candidates with respect to a list of different criteria, they would almost certainly not remember *all* the factors or considerations that produced the positive or negative impressions that led to their decision.

- *If* voters did make a conscious decision *and* remembered all the experiences that produced their impressions of the candidate, they would *differ* significantly from each other in the causal *weights* that were attached to specific factors or considerations. Moreover, they would not remember which ones had a major influence and which ones were less important.

- Finally, even *if* voters remembered all of the factors involved *and* their associated weights, they might be unlikely to accurately *report* those factors and weights when asked by an interviewer, either because of the tendency for respondents to reconstruct such causes in ways that make them appear in a favorable light or because of other deficiencies in respondents or measurement procedures. Measurement-related problems are particularly serious in assessing the importance of causal weight for both major traditions in vote explanation—that is, regardless of whether we use "reasons" based on open-ended questions (and use the number of responses in a given area as an indication of its importance to that respondent) or we carry out multivariate analyses based on structured questions that include direct measurement of the "importance" of each area for each respondent.

Given these arguments or possibilities, why do so many analysts of ANES materials and exit polls rely on respondents' explanations of their own electoral "choice"? Are such analyses necessarily misleading—or can they make an important contribution to any comprehensive account that would not otherwise be possible?[5] If such analyses *are* inevitably misleading, do any viable alternatives exist—besides abandoning questions on the direct causes of choice in favor of less proximate explanatory variables?

Direct Measurement of Reasons versus Multivariate
Analyses of Variables

We have emphasized the simple dichotomy between the use of "reasons" versus "variables" as contrasting strategies for using survey data to explain individual vote choice. Although easy to state and remember, the dichotomy should be seen as the ends of a continuum that represents the variety of strategies that analysts have adopted to explain voters' decision-making processes. Such a continuum thus ranges from complete reliance on respondents' own self-reports concerning their vote rationale to complete

[5]Voters' own "reasons" for preferring one candidate over another were featured in *The American Voter* (Campbell, Converse, Miller, & Stokes, 1960) and numerous subsequent publications (including Kelley, 1983). For an impressions-based approach that challenges the validity of self-reported causes, see Lodge and Hammill (1986).

disregard of them. This continuum may also be clarified by identifying a sequence of specific analytic strategies for using information from respondents' own decisions:

- Relying on respondents' explanations, using open-ended questions concerning their reasons for choice—without any multivariate analysis to estimate differential "weights" for specific areas.
- Using summary measures for different types of reasons, with some multivariate analysis to assess the overall importance of several issue areas.
- Using structured questions to ask respondents for comparative evaluations of the candidates with respect to specific criteria or areas—as well as their own ratings of the importance (or weight) of each such area (as in the candidate placement and importance ratings introduced in the 1980 ANES survey). Using such variables, multivariate analyses can be carried out for equations in which comparative evaluations (or proximity scores) are multiplied by salience weights based on respondents' own reports.
- Using respondents' perceptions or evaluations of candidates with respect to specific criteria independent of respondent salience weights. In such analyses coefficients for specific areas thus presumably represent some kind of average across respondents for whom the "true" effect is somewhat different.
- Disregarding the placements, ratings, or comparative candidate evaluations in order to estimate the overall impact of respondents' own positions on each issue. Such analyses rest on the assumption that any apparent impact that remains after other appropriate variables are held constant must be attributable to mechanisms by which respondents' impressions of the candidates were at least partially shaped by their own positions on those issues.

Assessments Based on Contrasting Procedures in the 1988
ANES Survey

Alternative interpretations of the same election can be attributed to different assumptions among analysts about concepts, measurement, and causality. It would require an extraordinarily comprehensive survey instrument to encompass these alternative approaches. Interview schedules for such a survey would at least need to include the traditional ANES battery of open-ended questions about the candidates and a large number of structured questions about different issues using several different formats.

Unfortunately the perennial conflict over the content of ANES questionnaires attests to how difficult it is to satisfy all of the above measurement objectives within a single survey—even with the two-hour-plus interviews and the traditional ANES pre- and post-election design. Inevitable limitations in respondent patience and project funds require that interview schedules for election surveys exclude significant numbers of potentially relevant questions—about respondents' social and economic circumstances; their own predispositions, preferences, or perceptions in some "issue" areas; and their evaluations of the candidates in the same or other issue areas. Since no survey can include all of the questions required by the alternative competing approaches to vote explanation encompassing all potentially relevant issues, other strategies must be found to test or compare those approaches.

One such strategy is to compare the results based on the most divergent approaches: *only* structured questions about the respondents' circumstances, preferences, and perceptions versus *only* open-ended questions about the "reasons" why respondents like or dislike each of the major candidates. This section presents the results of one such effort to compare these two approaches as used to examine several potential causes of the 1988 vote, deferring consideration of intermediate approaches based on issue "proximities" or respondents' own reports concerning the salience of specific issues.

It would be convenient if one approach or method led to consistently different conclusions, but method-related differences may be difficult to predict or summarize, given the number of simultaneous issues involved. For example, even the harshest critic of the ANES "likes and dislikes" approach might expect *some* correspondence between results based on structured questions and those based on responses to open-ended questions in the same substantive areas.[6] Such similarities do emerge in some areas, but emphasis has been placed on areas where these two types of methods suggest different conclusions concerning the role played by different sources of candidate evaluations or vote choice.

Critics of respondent-based accounts of the vote anticipated finding several potential "issues" where the results of these contrasting approaches would suggest very different conclusions about the 1988 election. In particular they expected to find some policy issues (or general policy areas, like the strength or use of U.S. military forces) for which the apparent effects of respondents' own preferences (based on structured questions without any candidate perceptions or evaluations) would be quite substantial; but the corresponding coefficients for measures based on the open-ended "likes and dislikes" questions would be small, if not invisible—because of the indirect effect of such preferences through mechanisms other than conscious deliberation and because of general measurement-related problems associated with open-ended questions. Other researchers would not have been surprised if issues not "covered" by 1988 structured questions emerged from the ANES 1988 open-ended questions. Other researchers anticipated results defined in terms of candidate evaluations (and, therefore, presumably "closer" to the vote, such as presidential performance or candidate traits) that would seem more "important" than noncandidate factors (i.e., less the respondents' own policy- or ideology-related preferences)—when both types of variables were measured with the ANES open-ended questions.

Still other researchers suggested that the apparent importance of *every* explanatory theme in explaining vote choice would be greater for measures based on structured as opposed to open-ended questions—because of widely shared beliefs about the extent of measurement error inherent in simple "counts" from open-ended questions. As shown here, however, these expectations have not been supported by the results of analyses of the 1988 ANES data.

To identify areas where the two approaches produce similar results, a series of regression analyses was carried out with two sets of approximately matched measures concerning the same general explanatory theme (e.g., preferences concerning policy direction). For each comparison one set of measures was constructed from responses to structured questions and a parallel set (dealing with the same specific topics) from responses to the open-ended ("likes and dislikes") questions about George Bush and Michael Dukakis. At the outset it should be noted that these "likes and dislikes" measures are explicitly evaluative in nature and represent a subset of all positive or negative reasons that each respondent mentioned as "reasons" for voting for or against the candidates. For issue-related areas the counterpart measures based on structured questions are defined in terms of either the respondents' own preferences independent of evaluations of the candidates in that area *or* their self-reports concerning the relevance or importance of that area for the respondent's vote. Because of these built-in differences, the results of these comparisons should be interpreted with caution.

---

[6]For an influential summary of the reasons why individuals may be unreliable informants concerning the causes of their own choices, see Nisbett and Wilson (1977).

General Predispositions Concerning Policy Direction
or Values

Since 1984, ANES presidential surveys have included questions concerning general if not ideological predispositions, beliefs, or "values" that represent the background for attitudes toward more specific issues that might arise in a campaign. The 1988 ANES interviews included five sets of questions that can be used to generate summary measures of respondents' apparent predispositions concerning the issues of equality, Communism, blacks and discrimination, traditional morality, and patriotism.

To compare the apparent effects of these two alternative approaches to vote explanation (structured versus open-ended questions), parallel regression analyses were carried out that included summary measures for all five policy-related topics as well as six social or economic characteristics and party identification. Table 11-11 presents the standardized regression coefficients for three equations, depending on whether the policy-related measures were all based on structured questions, were all based on open-ended questions, or included both sets of measures in the same "head-to-head" equation. Standardized coefficients have been selected for these comparisons because there is no basis for meaningful comparison between the artificial units of measurement for the two sets of explanatory variables and because such coefficients provide an appropriate descriptive statistic for the kind of "importance" we have in mind—that is, for the degree to which a given variable is apparently responsible for producing the observed differences between respondents in their vote choice.

Based on the results in Table 11-11, it seems tempting to conclude that analysts who estimate the apparent impact of these 1988 general predispositions with structured questions will conclude that those predispositions were "more predictive" than are variables for the same substantive areas that are constructed from the ANES "likes and dislikes." In other words the statistical "connection" between issue opinions and vote choice is stronger for measures based on structured questions than for open-end measures—despite the potential advantage of reasons-based measures in terms of causal

Table 11-11

Apparent Importance of Predispositions in 1988: Explaining Vote Choice Based on Structured versus Open-Ended Questions (Standardized regression coefficients or * if <1.0 standard error)

Name and format of explanatory variables	Based on structured questions	Based on open-ended questions	Includes both types of variables
Egalitarianism (structured)	.157		.157
Egalitarianism (open-ended)		.045	.044
Anti-Communism (structured)	.082		.079
Anti-Communism (open-ended)		*	*
Blacks and discrimination (structured)	.051		*
Blacks and discrimination (open-ended)		.038	*
Traditional morality (structured)	.073		.066
Traditional morality (open-ended)		.056	.040
Patriotism (structured)	.051		.048
Patriotism (open-ended)		.072	.052
Party identification	.506	.575	.499
Multiple R	.704	.667	.709

proximity and electoral relevance. In the two areas of egalitarianism and anti-Communism, the strength of those relationships is *much* greater for measures based on structured questions, and the same result emerges for an analysis that includes both types of questions in direct, "head-to-head" competition for vote prediction. The same result does not apply to the issue of patriotism, where slightly larger coefficients are found for the open-ended questions.

Supporters of the two contrasting methods would likely reach quite different conclusions about the relative importance of specific predispositions. Analyses based only on structured questions suggest a much larger role for general views concerning equality and (to a lesser extent) Communism, while the counterpart coefficients based on open-ended questions are smaller than the coefficients for patriotism and morality.

Table 11–11 suggests that only a portion of the apparent effects of respondents' own predispositions is mediated by a process in which their candidate evaluations are consciously based on their preferences or predispositions. For all but anti-Communism, the apparent effect of respondents' structured responses remains after adding the parallel reasons-based measure into the equation. At this point, we are unsure whether these remaining coefficients represent "true" effects not mediated by conscious candidate evaluations or reflect greater measurement error in open-ended questions.

It should be noted that the small coefficients for the open-ended questions undoubtedly reflect the infrequent nature of such responses. The percentages of voters who mentioned any response in those five areas range from 0.8 (for anti-Communist) to 3.7 (for morality).

Preference Concerning Current Policy Issues

In assessing the strength of these statistical relationships for measures based on the ANES open-ended questions, the most encouraging comparisons concern reasons for "liking or disliking" one of the candidates. Shanks and Miller's (1991) analysis of the 1988 election used parallel measures based on structured questions and policy-related responses to open-ended questions that concerned military strength or defense, assistance to economically disadvantaged citizens, the death penalty, and abortion. When these four policy-related measures and ideological self-designation are added to the three (separate) regression analyses described previously, Table 11–12 presents the same general picture concerning the impact of policy preferences on the 1988 vote—regardless of which method is employed. With the exception of the smaller coefficients for abortion and the death penalty, the same general conclusions emerge concerning specific policy issue areas. Furthermore, both methods fail to identify any other issues for which the corresponding coefficients are as large as for these four. Also the standardized coefficients for policy issues suggest approximately the same ranking of these issues as for the simple open-ended percentages who mentioned each issue (20% for both the military and the disadvantaged, 16% for abortion, and 6% for the death penalty).

These policy-related preferences are also consistent with the general hypothesis concerning the greater predictive importance of variables defined in terms of structured questions. In three of these four policy areas, standardized coefficients are larger for measures based on structured questions, and the only exception (abortion) shows only a small reversal for open-ended questions. Finally the apparent effect of policy preferences remains after we add the presumably intervening reasons concerning these substantive areas. As before, it is unclear whether these (remaining) coefficients are true effects mediated through other intervening mechanisms or an inevitable by-product of greater measurement error.

Table 11-12

Apparent Importance of Policy Preferences in 1988: Explaining Vote Choice Based on Structured versus Open-Ended Questions (Standardized regression coefficients or * if <1.0 standard error)

Name and format of explanatory variables	Based on structured questions	Based on open-ended questions	Includes both types of variables
Egalitarianism (structured)	.093		.076
Egalitarianism (open-ended)		.042	*
Anti-Communism (structured)	*		*
Anti-Communism (open-ended)		*	*
Blacks and discrimination (structured)	*		*
Blacks and discrimination (open-ended)		.037	*
Traditional morality (structured)	*		*
Traditional morality (open-ended)		.039	*
Patriotism (structured)	*		*
Patriotism (open-ended)		.046	*
Party Identification	.408	.451	.384
Ideology (lib–cons)	.057	.157	.060
Military/defense (structured)	.179		.145
Military/defense (open-ended)		.127	.081
Assistance to disadvantaged (structured)	.133		.116
Assistance to disadvantaged (open-ended)		.134	.089
Death penalty (structured)	.083		.080
Death penalty (open-ended)		*	.007
Abortion (structured)	.066		.050
Abortion (open-ended)		.072	.046
Multiple R	.741	.718	.754

Perceptions of Economic Conditions

The 1988 ANES interview schedule also included structured questions concerning several personal or national conditions, including respondents' comparisons of their current economic circumstances to past and future years and parallel comparisons for the national economy and for the U.S. "position" in the world as well as for the overall condition of the country. While some of these areas were not mentioned as "reasons" for liking or disliking either of the candidates, enough responses about the state of the economy were made to construct a summary measure for all "reasons" in that area—including references to inflation, employment, and simply the "economy." When that measure and its structured counterpart (combining perceptions of how the U.S. economy had performed in the past year and how it would perform in the next year) were added to the previously described policy-related analysis, the two methods produced rather similar conclusions about the impact of general economic conditions on the vote in 1988. Specifically when those variables are added to those in Table 11–12, the standardized coefficients for the two alternative measures in separate analyses were .074 (structured) and .060 (open-ended), and those coefficients were reduced to .055 and .045, respectively, when both variables are included in the same "head-to-head" equation.

Evaluations of Other Candidate Characteristics

In sharp contrast to the preceding results concerning policy direction and economic *conditions,* the structured and open-ended approaches yield *strikingly* different results concerning the importance of candidate evaluations with respect to personal characteristics or "traits." The 1988 ANES survey includes several candidate attributes that might lead citizens to prefer one of them over the other, and many of these same criteria are mentioned by ANES respondents in response to the standard open-ended questions. For this analysis parallel measures were constructed from both structured and open-ended questions to provide comparative evaluations concerning the candidates' (1) integrity (or honesty), (2) competence (including intelligence), (3) empathy (with ordinary citizens), (4) leadership-related qualities, and (5) anticipated (or prospective) effectiveness in "controlling crime" and "protecting the environment."

Table 11–13 presents the results of those analyses in the same format as in Table 11–12. In this context, however, the apparent importance of specific characteristics is *not* the same for both methods. The candidates' "empathy" seemed to play a significant role with both types of measures, but the apparent role of the other candidate characteristics is nearly the opposite for the two approaches.

As before, standardized coefficients are generally higher for explanatory variables based on structured (instead of open-ended) questions about candidate "traits" when both sets of variables are included in the same equation (as shown in the last column of Table 11–13). Given the explicitly evaluative nature of both measures, it is tempting to interpret this consistent difference in terms of the general superiority of structured questions in reducing measurement error. The differences between these two methods in their coefficients for integrity, competence, leadership, crime, and the environment, however, do raise questions about the proper interpretation of coefficients based on either method.

This cautionary note is reinforced when both sets of coefficients are compared with the simple percentages of voters in the 1988 ANES sample who reported "reasons" for voting for (or against) Bush or Dukakis that could be classified into one of these categories. These percentages were 20% for leadership, 19% for both integrity and empathy, 13% for crime, 10% for competence, and 6% for the environment—and 34% for the candidates' governmental "experience" (a characteristic not covered in the 1988 structured "traits" question). These percentages do not correspond to the rank order of these alternative criteria suggested by either multivariate procedure.

The Search for Other Method-Related Differences

The preceding results are drawn from a continuing effort to identify circumstances in which markedly different impressions emerge concerning the importance of specific topics based on structured versus open-ended questions. The preceding analyses are restricted to the 1988 election, but somewhat different comparisons have also been done for the 1992 election (Miller & Shanks, 1996). (It seems appropriate to note that the preceding results include the most significant differences between the two contrasting approaches found for 1988.) Parallel measures have been constructed for several other "issue" areas, including taxes and aid to education, but none of those measures has generated results that suggest a significant difference between the two approaches in the sense that a specific kind of content appeared to play a significant role based on one "method," but not on the other. It should be noted, however, that the specific measures and statistical procedures used in the above analysis can be replaced by several alternative formulations. For that reason more analyses of this sort are needed before drawing any definitive conclusions about these two methods.

In the meantime, however, the above analyses suggest the following tentative conclusions:

1. *Similar Coefficients within Some Explanatory Themes.* Assessments of the relative importance of different issues for vote choice appear to be fairly similar—regardless of whether the explanatory variables are based on (a) the respondent's own preferences in a

Table 11-13

Apparent Importance of Candidate Traits in 1988: Explaining Vote Choice Based on Structured versus Open-Ended Questions (Standardized regression coefficients or * if <1.0 standard error)

Name and format of explanatory variables	Based on structured questions	Based on open-ended questions	Includes both types of variables
Egalitarianism (structured)	.053		.047
Egalitarianism (open-ended)		.042	*
Patriotism (structured)	*		.040
Patriotism (open-ended)		.044	*
Party Identification	.240	.417	.239
Ideology (lib–cons)	.040	.133	.040
Military/defense (structured)	.065		.049
Military/defense (open-ended)		.120	.065
Assistance to disadvantaged (structured)	.059		.055
Assistance to disadvantaged (open-ended)		.120	.036
Death penalty (structured)	.065		.067
Death penalty (open-ended)		*	*
Abortion (structured)	.043		.027
Abortion (open-ended)		.080	.037
Integrity (structured)	*		*
Integrity (open-ended)		.115	*
Competence (structured)	*		*
Competence (open-ended)		.063	*
Empathy (structured)	.148		.137
Empathy (open-ended)		.083	*
Leadership (structured)	.186		.174
Leadership (open-ended)		.046	*
Crime (structured)	.107		.106
Crime (open-ended)		*	*
Environment (structured)	.103		.101
Environment (open-ended)		*	−.034
Multiple R	.813	.737	.819

Note: Variables for which all entries were insignificant (*) in Table 11–12 have been deleted from this table.

given policy area or (b) the respondent's references to the same area as "reasons" for liking (or disliking) the candidates. That is, when analyses are carried out that use similarly defined measures as explanatory variables that are either all based on the respondents' own policy preferences or all based on their "reasons" that deal with the same topic, the relative importance of each policy area seems to be about the same. This pattern of approximate similarity in the relative importance of specific factors also appears to hold (although less clearly) for perceptions of national economic conditions, but *not* for policy-related predispositions or traitlike characteristics of the candidates. These results could be very helpful in future instrument design if they hold for other elections.

2. *Measurement-Related Advantages of Structured Questions.* Despite this general similarity in overall importance within some explanatory themes, measures based on structured questions seem to provide better indicators of the overall impact of voters' "positions" on those issues. When both types of measures are included as "head-to-head" competitors in the same explanatory equation, the coefficients for structured questions are at least as large, and generally larger, than the corresponding coefficients for measures

based on responses to parallel open-ended questions for 1988 ANES measures concerning policy preferences, perceptions of economic conditions, and candidate traits.

3. *Noncomparability Concerning Indirect Effects.* Measures based on structured questions offer another potential advantage concerning multistage causation (or indirect effects) that seems difficult to achieve with measures based on "reasons" or "likes and dislikes." Specifically, by using measures of issue-related questions, policy preferences, and perceptions of current economic conditions independent of candidates, the analyst can examine the apparent impact of these preferences or perceptions on performance-related variables and evaluations of candidate "traits" in addition to their apparent impact on all measures based on open-ended questions. That is, analytic strategies that rely entirely on open-ended questions do not permit analysts to examine the *indirect* effects of noncandidate-related preferences (or perceptions) on vote choice—effects that are presumably mediated by more proximate variables that *are* defined in terms of candidate evaluations.

Importance in Explaining Aggregate Electoral Results

Up to this point our discussion of the importance of specific issues has concentrated on their role in individual voter decisions. It should be noted, however, that academic, journalistic, and political *use* of such results is often linked to a conceptually different analytic question in terms of the *aggregate* result of the election; namely, "Why did the victorious candidate win?" or "Why was the margin of victory as big (or small) as it was?" In quantitative terms such analyses are attempts to decompose the aggregate division of the two-party vote into a set of positive and negative contributions of specific factors that (in combination) produced the winner's plurality.

This distinction between the explanation of differences between voters in their electoral choices and the decomposition of aggregate results has a long history that emphasizes the following points:

- Issues that play a major role in determining individual choice may *not* make a significant contribution to the winning candidate's victory *if* the numbers of voters with opinions on the two sides of that issue are evenly balanced with respect to a neutral position, so that neither candidate had an advantage in that area.
- Issues that play only a modest role in explaining individual differences in voting behavior may still make a major contribution to the aggregate result—*if* the distribution of opinions in that area is heavily skewed to favor one of the candidates. (Such factors, however, must explain at least some of the variation in choice between voters if we are to estimate their contribution to the winner's plurality.)
- All techniques for interpreting the aggregate decision are necessarily based on some kind of "explanation" at the individual level, and they will be suspect insofar as that individual-level account is incorrect.

Because of the dependence of any aggregate decomposition on an underlying individual-level explanation, interpretations of the aggregate "results" of any election are subject to the same kinds of controversies discussed previously concerning the validity of respondents' self-reported reasons for their vote. If we trust voters' own reports concerning those reasons, we can adopt an interpretation of the aggregate result that is based on those (self-reported) reasons. If not, we must rely on less direct approaches.

Alternative Interpretations of "Contributions
to the Aggregate Result"

Any questions about the overall contribution of a given issue to the aggregate vote must
be defined in terms of the differences between specific survey-based results and alternative results that would have appeared *if* that topic had *no* net impact on the result of the
election. All answers to such questions, therefore, must be based on the hypothetical comparison between the actual division of the votes between the two major candidates and a
result that would have occurred in a version of that election in which "everything else"
was the same except for this one factor. For some readers, however, it may be difficult to
imagine in what sense the national electorate might have behaved in an election that was
identical to the context being examined except that the aggregate contribution of one factor (or group of factors) was nonexistent.

The easiest way to define such a hypothetical "other things equal" election is to imagine that a distribution of voter attitudes on that issue is evenly balanced at 0.0, or no further from 0.0 than we would expect, given their scores on all rival issues that have been
assigned to causal stages that precede the factor in question. In that alternative election all
of the apparent effects are the same, and all of the other variables have the same distribution as in the actual election—so that the *only* difference is in the distribution of scores for
the variable being discussed. In this sense the apparent "contribution" of a given variable
to the national aggregate results is the degree to which those results would have been different if the distribution of scores on that factor had been evenly balanced.

In the opposite hypothetical formulation, voters retain the same distributions on all
the variables in the analysis, and all but one of the explanatory variables have the same
influence on vote choice, but the total effect of this one variable is set to 0.0. This kind of
alternative election might take place, for example, if the distribution of voters' preferences
and perceptions on all the major issues remained the same, but the major candidates took
identical positions on this one (given) issue.

Importance of Specific Variables for Individual versus
Aggregate Decisions in 1988

To illustrate the difference between these two criteria for electoral importance, Table
11–14 presents side-by-side results for the apparent role of voters' attitudes concerning
specific topics in influencing individual choices and for the contributions of those attitudes
toward George Bush's plurality in 1988. Entries in the first column of Table 11–14 must
be positive and less than 1.0, thus representing standardized regression coefficients. Entries in the second column represent apparent contributions to the winner's plurality as the
products of the unstandardized regression coefficient for each variable adjusted for its average score among respondents who voted for Bush.[7]

Even a cursory inspection of these two columns suggests that these two criteria lead
to *very* different conclusions about issue importance. For example, while equality had a visible influence on individual choices, these issue attitudes actually made a negative contribution to Bush's victory, as did issue preferences on aid to the disadvantaged. Perceptions
of current conditions clearly played some role in shaping individual decisions, but their apparent combined contribution to Bush's victory was quite small. Similar kinds of contrasts
can be found in most of the recent national election surveys conducted by the ANES.

[7]For a discussion of these statistical procedures, see Chapter 17 of *The New American Voter* (Miller &
Shanks, 1996).

Table 11–14

Alternative Criteria for Relative Importance in the 1988 Election: Sources of Individual
Differences in Vote Choice versus Contributions to the Aggregate Result

Name of explanatory theme and specific variable	Sources of individual differences	Contributions to George Bush's victory
Partisan identification		
Party ID	.43	−.01
Policy-related predispositions		
Lib–cons. self-designation	.17	.05
Equality	.10	−.05
Anti-Communism	.04	.03
Union versus business	.09	.02
Blacks versus whites	.07	.04
Feminists versus pro-life supporters	.07	.00
Patriotism	.05	.01
Current policy preferences		
Military	.14	−.06
Aid to the disadvantaged	.10	−.04
Abortion	.07	−.02
Death penalty	.08	.05
Perceptions of current conditions		
Country as a whole	.09	.03
Unemployment	.08	.02
U.S. position in the world	.04	−.01
Worry about jobs in household	.05	−.02
Retrospective evaluations of President Reagan		
General	.15	.04
Economy	.06	.00
Economic policies since 1980	.08	.02
Foreign affairs	.05	.01
Personal economic help	.04	.00
Honesty since 1980	.04	−.02
Personal qualities of the candidates		
Empathy (cares, compassionate)	.16	−.03
Integrity (honest and moral)	.04	.00
Leadership (inspiring)	.09	−.01

Conclusion

Any statement about the importance of specific issues to average citizens should be treated
with considerable caution. Since such statements often reflect the advocate's own issue
preferences rather than quantitative evidence, disagreements about issue importance may
be expressed without empirical evidence. Readers or audience members must ask: "Important in what sense?"

This chapter has repeatedly distinguished between conclusions based on respondents'
own opinions about importance and those based on statistical analyses of apparent influence. When political analysts fail to make clear which of these two kinds of statements
about political importance they are trying to make, their audiences should simply refuse
to consider such conclusions seriously. Additional clarification is essential.

Alternative Criteria for Importance Based on Direct
Respondent Evaluations

As discussed previously, respondent-based ratings of issue importance may be influenced
by several considerations, in addition to the format and construct of specific survey questions:

1. Issue visibility in media coverage
2. Alternative definitions of national problems
3. The degree of issue consensus
4. The psychological centrality of related values, goals, or issues
5. The legitimacy or priority of different issues
6. Respondents' personal "reasons" for their vote choice

These aspects of an issue may influence its apparent importance, even if the survey
question involved does not ask for respondents' opinions about that aspect. As we have
seen, the apparent importance of a given topic can vary dramatically, depending on
whether the survey question is defined in terms of problems, conditions, values, general
goals (or objectives), specific policy issues, or the relevance of those considerations for
one's vote. Because of these conflicting possibilities, readers should be cautious about the
validity of direct respondent ratings of importance—especially when the survey questionnaire does not clarify the intended criteria for such assessments.

Alternative Criteria for Importance Based
on Electoral Explanations

Statistical relationships with vote are often used to assess the relative importance of
voters' attitudes toward political issues. A simple and traditional approach to assessing
the strength of such relationships is the standardized regression coefficient, or the
multivariate extension of the simple correlation between each issue and the vote. Such
coefficients represent the product of the apparent impact of a one-unit shift in attitudes
toward that topic on vote choice and the variability of those attitudes among voters.
Issues for which the apparent (per unit) impact on the vote is very small will be
designated as "unimportant" in generating the observed differences between voters in
their vote choice—as will issues on which voters largely agree, so that variability is
small.

Such conclusions based on standardized coefficients may be determined by respondents' own attitudes toward specific issues or by the "reasons" they provide to explain
their own candidate evaluations. Conclusions about the relative importance of different issues may be approximately the same, regardless of whether the analyst uses respondent-
based "reasons" behind the vote or respondents' own opinions about the different issues
involved.

Finally, statements about relative issue importance may also refer to each variable's
contribution to the aggregate result of the election—instead of its role in explaining
individual-level differences in vote. Factors that appear to play important roles in shaping
individual decisions may make no net contribution to the aggregate result of an election,
and they can make a *negative* contribution to the winner's plurality. Conclusions about the
political importance of an issue, then, *must* be accompanied by a clear statement describing the empirical criteria involved.

References

Abramowitz, A. (1995). It's abortion, stupid—Policy voting in the 1992 presidential election. *Journal of Politics, 57,* 176–186.

Achen, C. H. (1982). *Interpreting and using regression.* Beverly Hills, CA: Sage.

Asher, H. B. (1988). *Presidential elections and American politics: Voters, candidates, and campaigns since 1952* (4th ed.). Chicago, IL: Dorsey Press.

Barber, J. D. (1980). *The pulse of presidential politics: The rhythm of presidential elections in the twentieth century.* New York: Norton.

Campbell, A., Converse, P. E., Miller, W. E., & Stokes, D. E. (1960). *The American voter.* New York: John Wiley and Sons.

Chase, S. (1942). *Goals for America.* New York: Twentieth Century Fund.

Funk, C. L. (1997). *Candidate-based voting behavior: Understanding images of U.S. presidents.* Paper presented at the annual meeting of the American Political Science Association, Washington, DC.

Gallup Poll reprints. (1969). Princeton, NJ: American Institute of Public Opinion.

Kelley, S. (1983). *Interpreting elections.* Princeton, NJ: Princeton University Press.

Kinder, D. R., Peters, M. D., Abelson, R. P., & Fiske, S. T. (1980). Presidential prototypes. *Political Behavior, 2,* 315–338.

Krosnick, J. A. (1988). The role of attitude importance in social evaluation: A study of policy preferences, presidential candidate evaluations, and voting behavior. *Journal of Personality and Social Psychology, 55,* 196–210.

Lodge, M., & Hammill, R. (1986). A partisan schema for political information processing. *American Political Science Review, 80,* 505–519.

Markus, G. B. (1982). Political attitudes during an election year: A report on the 1980 NES Panel Study. *American Political Science Review, 76,* 538–560.

Miller, W. E., & Shanks, J. M. (1982). Policy directions and presidential leadership: Alternative interpretations of presidential elections. *British Journal of Political Science, 12,* 299–356.

Miller, W. E., & Shanks, J. M. (1996). *The new American voter.* Cambridge, MA: Harvard University Press.

Nisbett, R. E., & Wilson, T. D. (1977). Telling more than we can know: Verbal reports of mental processes. *Psychological Review, 84,* 231–259.

Polsby, N., & Wildavsky, A. (1988). *Presidential elections* (7th ed.). New York: Free Press.

Popkin, S. L. (1990). *The reasoning voter: Communication and persuasion in the presidential campaigns.* Chicago, IL: University of Chicago Press.

President's Commission on National Goals. (1960). *Goals for Americans.* Englewood Cliffs, NJ: Prentice-Hall.

Schuman, H., & Presser, S. (1981). *Questions and answers in attitude surveys: Experiments on question form, wording, and context.* New York: Academic Press.

Shanks, J. M., & Miller, W. E. (1991). Partisanship, policy, and performance: The Reagan legacy in the 1988 election. *British Journal of Political Science, 21,* 129–197.

Shanks, J. M., & Strand, D. A. (1994). Unresolved issues in electoral decisions: Alternative perspectives on the explanation of individual choice. In *Elections at home and abroad: Essays in honor of Warren E. Miller.* Ann Arbor, MI: The University of Michigan Press.

Shanks, J. M., & Strand, D. A. (1997). *Conflict and consensus in presidential elections: Initial results from the 1996 Survey of Governmental Objectives.* Paper presented at the annual meeting of the Midwest Political Science Association. Chicago.

Smith, T. (1985) The polls: America's most important problems, part I: National and international. *Public Opinion Quarterly,* 264–274.

Stokes, D. E. (1966). Spatial models of party competition. In A. Campbell (Ed.), *Elections and the political order.* New York: John Wiley & Sons.

White, T. H. (1982). *America in search of itself: The making of the president 1956–1980.* New York: Harper and Row.

Political Partisanship

Herbert F. Weisberg

Partisanship is the central concept in the field of voting behavior because political conflict in modern democracies is usually organized around political parties. While these parties have elite and organizational bases, they also have a basis in their support among the mass electorate. Political partisanship questions are designed to measure that mass basis of party support.

Starting in the 1952 election, the University of Michigan's Survey Research Center (SRC) developed a party identification question series that has been at the core of their influential model of the vote decision at the individual level (Campbell, Gurin, & Miller, 1954; Campbell, Converse, Miller, & Stokes, 1960). This scale and its variants have received wide attention both in academic publications and in the popular press, particularly when political developments suggest that party fortunes might be shifting. While several alternative measures have been proposed and used, the traditional "Michigan questions" remain the most important—regardless of potentially serious measurement issues that have been raised. The theoretical importance of political partisanship has been restated in *The New American Voter,* which vigorously argues that it "is the most enduring of political attitudes, responsible for shaping a wide variety of values and perceptions, and, therefore, an appropriate starting point for any analysis of a partisan political preference, such as a choice between presidential candidates" (W. Miller & Shanks, 1996, p. 117).

Academic study of voting behavior began in earnest in the 1950s, as Republican Dwight Eisenhower was elected president after 20 years of Democratic presidential victories—despite Democratic control of Congress after 1954. Researchers were confronted with the need to explain simultaneously the Democratic dominance of the legislative branch and the Republican capture of the presidency.

That was the context in which the Michigan researchers developed their more sophisticated model of the individual vote decision, one based on the distinction between long-term attitudes toward the political parties and short-term election-year attitudes toward the candidates and issues. Thus long-term partisan factors were found to favor the Democratic Party in the 1950s, leading to Democratic control of Congress through most of this period, while short-term factors (mainly Eisenhower's popularity) led to the election of a Republican president at the same time.

Individual partisanship became the linchpin of this theory of voting, in which voters were considered to develop long-term identifications with the political parties. Partisanship could directly affect the individual's vote decision, but it could also affect the voter's issue attitudes and candidate orientations, which, in turn, affect the vote. Additionally partisanship was seen to serve as a screening device, affecting how people process political information, as when Democratic citizens pay less attention to Republican campaign ads or when Republican loyalists tend to disbelieve claims by Democratic candidates. Partisanship was viewed as a decisional short-cut, one particularly useful for those least interested in following individual campaigns (Shively, 1977). While this identification could certainly change, the long-term conception of partisanship led to the notion that it was highly stable. People were thought to identify with a party as a child, usually maintaining that identification through their adult life and generally passing that identification on to their children. Partisanship was the stable long-term element in the theory, the base from which short-term election-specific elements could operate.

The logic of this argument requires that partisanship be highly stable at the individual level and presumably at the aggregate level as well. Instability of partisanship during periods of normal politics would undermine the special status accorded to it in this theory. Additionally its special status could be undermined if partisanship were the composite of several separate dimensions rather than a single dimension and if its theoretical basis in the reference group theory of the late 1940s and early 1950s were challenged. As a result, these three aspects of party identification—its stability, its dimensionality, and its theoretical underpinnings—have been subsequently scrutinized in the research literature.

Treating partisanship as long-term at the individual level has important system-level implications. For one thing the stability of partisanship helps explain the stability of party systems in most democracies. Second, this individual stability underlies the important system-level concept of *party realignment*—when the party balance of the electorate shifts in an enduring way, due either to large-scale switching from one party to another *(conversion)* or to large-scale voting for one party by people who previously were nonvoters *(mobilization)*.

In the first article to discuss party identification as a concept, Belknap and Campbell (1952) used the simple question "If a presidential election were being held today, do you think you would vote for the Democratic, Republican, or for some other party?" as their measure of party identification. Respondents were grouped into four categories on the basis of their responses: Democratic, Republican, Independent (depends on the candidates), and Don't know. However, it was obvious from the beginning that this question wording was too short-term in its focus on current vote intentions rather than examining long-term orientations. By their 1952 election study, the Michigan researchers developed the longer-term question wording that remains the dominant measure today. Given this focus on partisanship as a long-term concept, it is important to check how long-term other proposed partisanship measures are.

Types of Partisanship Measures Reviewed in This Chapter

Three main aspects of partisanship will be reviewed in this chapter. The most important is the direction of partisanship—the political party with which people identify. The second is the strength of that identification. The third is political independence—whether people see themselves as independents rather than as partisans. Party system support—the extent to which people support the current party system—will be considered along with independence.

While these aspects of partisanship may be conceptually separate, the partisanship scale developed by the University of Michigan researchers in the early 1950s is traditionally used to measure all three: partisan direction, strength, and independence. As a result, in practice it has been difficult to differentiate the separate aspects of partisanship. This has led to a controversy regarding the dimensionality of partisanship, a controversy that will be reviewed after the different partisanship scales are described.

Most of the discussion in this chapter will focus on measures developed for the U.S. system of two major parties, with political independence as a separate tradition. There have been numerous attempts to "export" the concept of party identification to other countries, but scholars in many nations doubt its usefulness for describing electoral behavior in their polities. Some of the problems encountered in measuring partisanship in other countries will also be described, along with alternative approaches developed in those nations.

Partisanship can be measured in either behavioral or attitudinal ways. Many of the early measures were behavioral, using people's voting registration or voting history to reveal their partisanship. These behavioral measures were soon supplanted by attitudinal measures, partly because problems arose with these behavioral measures and partly because attitudinal measures fit better with the voting theory that was developed in the 1950s. There have been occasional rediscoveries of behavioral measures, but attitudinal measures continue to be used more often.

It is important to recognize that the validation of partisanship measures has been complicated by the nature of the theorized relationship between partisanship and the vote. While partisanship should have a high correlation with the vote, too high a correlation suggests that the measure is overly sensitive to short-term election-specific factors instead of measuring the long-term element of partisanship. The inability to validate partisanship directly through a high correlation with the vote decision has led to a focus instead on the "transitivity" of its relationship to other variables. That is, at a minimum a proper measure of partisanship should have a monotonic relationship with criterion variables that are related to partisan direction, and strength of partisanship should have a monotonic relationship with criterion variables that are related to partisanship strength. Thus the demonstration of "intransitivities" in the relationship of the standard partisanship scale to several criterion variables points to important validation problems (Petrocik, 1974).

Direction of Partisanship

The first set of measures discussed in this chapter is composed of those that focus on the *direction* of partisanship—whether the person is a Republican or a Democrat. The main measure described is the Michigan Party Identification scale, along with slight variants of that scale used by the Gallup Poll and other commercial polling firms and the variants of the response alternatives that have been used in methodological experimentation. Three additional attitudinal measures of direction are presented in this section, including thermometer-based measures, a scale of party closeness, and a party image scale based on open-ended questions, along with several related variants.

Behavioral measures of partisan direction, such as official voting registration, have also been advocated. The utility of the respondent's official party registration as a measure of partisanship is limited by the fact that many states (22 in 1982 according to Finkel &

Scarrow, 1984) do not employ registration by party and by the strategic choices that may be involved (such as registering to participate in the primary of the party with the more exciting contests). Evidence of the low validity of survey questions about party registration is that 76% of the respondents from states that did not have enrollment by party still answered the question in the 1980 American National Election Studies (ANES) survey.

Party voting history is another possible behavioral measure, as in Ladd and Hadley's (1973) definition of "behavioral Republicans" as those who voted for Republican candidates in the two most recent presidential elections, with "behavioral Democrats" being similarly defined. Because that measure is based on past vote recall questions, the validity of such recall questions is debatable. Party voting regularity can also be judged from a question in the ANES surveys: "Have you always voted for the same party or have you voted for different parties for President?" (Keith *et al.*, 1986, pp. 176–180). Again, the accuracy of these self-reports of past behavior can be challenged, given social psychological research on the accuracy of recall of past behavior. As a result of these validity issues, the attitudinal measures of partisan direction described in this section are employed more frequently than behavioral measures.

The ANES Party Identification Scale

The ANES Party Identification scale in Table 12–1 is the main measure of partisanship used in academic studies in the United States, and it is likely to remain the main measure of partisanship, regardless of the extensive critiques of its measurement properties in the research literature.

The full distribution of the ANES scale from 1952 through 1996 is given in Table 12–2. The Democrats had an average 19% advantage in partisanship over the Republicans

Table 12–1
The ANES Party Identification Questions and Scale

---

1. Generally speaking, do you usually think of yourself as a Republican, a Democrat, an Independent, or what?

    1a. (IF REPUBLICAN OR DEMOCRAT) Would you call yourself a strong (Republican/ Democrat) or a not very strong (Republican/Democrat)?

    1b. (IF INDEPENDENT) Do you think of yourself as closer to the Republican or Democratic Party?

    The standard seven-point scale coding is as follows:
    0. Strong Democrat (SD: D on Q1 and strong D on Q1a)
    1. Weak Democrat (WD: D on Q1 and not very strong D on Q1a)
    2. Independent Democrat (ID: Independent on Q1 and D on Q1b)
    3. Pure Independent (PI: Independent on Q1 and no on Q1b; or no preference on Q1, no on Q1b, and expression of some interest in politics during the interview)
    4. Independent Republican (IR: Independent on Q1 and R on Q1b)
    5. Weak Republican (WR: R on Q1 and not very strong R on Q1a)
    6. Strong Republican (SR: R on Q1 and strong R on Q1a)

    Two additional categories for this scale are
    7. Other (other political party names on Q1 and no on Q1b)
    8. Apolitical (no preference on Q1, no on Q1b, and no expression of interest in politics throughout the interview)

Table 12-2

ANES Party Identification Scale Distribution, 1952–1996

	1952	1954	1956	1958	1960	1962	1964	1966	1968	1970	1972	1974	1976	1978	1980	1982	1984	1986	1988	1990	1992	1994	1996
Strong Dem	22	22	21	27	20	23	27	18	20	20	15	17	15	15	18	20	17	18	17	20	18	15	18
Weak Dem	25	25	23	22	25	23	25	28	25	24	26	21	25	24	23	24	20	22	18	19	18	19	19
Indep Dem	10	9	6	7	6	7	9	9	10	10	11	13	12	14	11	11	11	10	12	12	14	13	13
Pure Indep	6	7	9	7	10	8	8	12	11	13	13	15	15	14	13	8	12	11	11	10	12	10	8
Indep Rep	7	6	8	5	7	6	6	7	9	8	10	9	10	10	10	8	12	11	13	12	12	12	11
Weak Rep	14	14	14	16	14	16	14	15	15	15	13	14	14	13	14	14	15	15	14	15	14	15	16
Strong Rep	14	13	15	11	16	12	11	10	10	9	10	8	9	8	9	10	12	10	14	10	11	16	13
Apolitical	3	4	4	4	2	4	1	1	1	1	1	3	1	3	2	2	2	2	2	2	1	1	1

Source: American National Election Studies, based on tables at the ANES Web Site.

from 1952 through 1980, but that advantage fell to an average of 9% in the 1984–1996 period, as shown in the table below:

	Party Strength (in percent)											
	1952	1956	1960	1964	1968	1972	1976	1980	1984	1988	1992	1996
Dem	47%	44%	45%	52%	45%	40%	40%	41%	37%	35%	35%	38%
Ind	23	23	23	23	29	35	36	34	34	36	38	33
Rep	27	29	29	24	24	23	23	22	27	28	26	29
Dem–Rep diff	+20	+15	+16	+28	+21	+17	+17	+19	+10	+7	+9	+9

Source: Based on Weisberg and Kimball (1995), Table 3.1, using ANES data, supplemented with data from the 1996 ANES survey.

Stability Issues

Early studies (Campbell *et al.,* 1960) claimed a high degree of stability of party identification. This was especially true when aggregate marginals from separate cross-section surveys were compared over time. The first indication of instability in partisanship was Dreyer's (1973) report of only a .73 correlation (tau-b) between pre- and postelection readings of party identification (using a five-point classification with leaners combined with pure independents) in the 1960 ANES survey, a figure that was similar to the comparable statistics over two-year time periods for the 1956–1958–1960 ANES Panel Study. Some degree of change was found for 40% of the respondents during the 1960 presidential campaign, with the most change for independents and weak partisans.

One change in the party identification distribution occurred in the late 1960s and early 1970s, when the proportion of independents began to climb. About the same time, the correlation of the Party Identification scale with the vote declined, a decline that in retrospect may have had more to do with the weakness of the Goldwater candidacy in 1964 and the McGovern candidacy in 1972 than with a permanent diminution of the effect of party identification on vote. Still, by the mid-1970s these changes led to some disenchantment with the usefulness of the Party Identification scale (see, for example, Nie, Verba, & Petrocik, 1979), which resulted in more extensive examinations of its measurement properties.

Partisanship was originally regarded as exogenous to the contemporaneous vote decision (i.e., changes in partisanship were thought to affect vote, but not vice versa), giving it a status that has become known as the "unmoved mover." That status was challenged in causal models of the vote decision (Jackson, 1975; Page & Jones, 1979; cf. Markus & Converse, 1979), which found that vote could actually affect partisanship, as when long-time Democratic identifiers voted Republican over a series of elections and then began to think of themselves as Republicans. Fiorina (1981) provided a theoretical basis for this endogenous view of party identification (i.e., for the view that partisanship was affected by political variables, such as vote) with an analysis that supported that interpretation. Franklin and Jackson (1983) and Franklin (1984, 1992) demonstrated the effects of policy preferences on changing partisanship, particularly for younger people (cf. Schickler & Green, 1996). Marks (1993) confirmed similar endogeneity of party identification in Australia, with short-term issue and candidate leadership effects on partisanship having to be removed in order to estimate the true impact of party identification on the vote. Similarly, changes in party identification at the individual level across waves of the Jennings–Niemi socialization study can partially be accounted for by attitudes toward presidential candidates (Rapoport, 1997).

The stability of partisanship was further challenged by a series of studies in the 1980s and 1990s. Changes in party identification at the individual level across waves of the 1980 ANES Panel Study could be accounted for by issues (Brody & Rothenberg, 1988). Considerable partisan instability was found over a year of repeated interviewing of two dozen Twin Cities residents (Flanigan, Rahn, & Zingale, 1989), but these results must be viewed as only suggestive, given the small sample size. Substantial systematic aggregate shifts in party identification have now been found in nightly tracking polls during a presidential campaign (Allsop & Weisberg, 1988), monthly readings of party identification during the 1981–1986 (Weisberg & Smith, 1991) and 1989–1992 (Weisberg & Kimball, 1995) periods, and Gallup data from the 1940s through the 1980s (MacKuen, Erikson, & Stimson, 1989). Converse (1976) suggested that instability of partisanship would be confined to the least involved, but Weisberg and Allsop (1990) found that the systematic instability during the 1984 presidential campaign was actually greater among respondents who were registered to vote than those who were not.

Not only does partisanship vary over time, but also it varies systematically with other variables. Aggregate partisanship (or "macropartisanship," as MacKuen, Erikson, and Stimson term it) is responsive to changes in presidential approval and in the economy. The macropartisanship distribution has been accounted for statistically by regression analysis, using as predictors the Gallup presidential approval series plus either subjective evaluations (MacKuen *et al.*, 1989; cf. Green, Palmquist, & Schickler, 1996) of the economy (measured by the University of Michigan Index of Consumer Sentiment) or objective indicators (Weisberg & Kimball, 1995; Weisberg & Smith, 1991) of the economy (measured by unemployment and inflation rates).

The stability of partisanship remains at issue. Abramson and Ostrom (1991) have partially challenged the MacKuen, Erikson, and Stimson work, showing that the Gallup party identification question has greater variability than the ANES question wording and that the ANES version is less responsive to changes in the economy or presidential approval. However, in a response, MacKuen, Erikson, and Stimson (1992) show that the difference in variability between the Gallup and ANES results is not due to question wording effects: they found that the party identification question in the CBS News/*New York Times* surveys since 1976 (which use the ANES question wording) varied in nearly the same way as the Gallup Poll version (although Abramson and Ostrom, 1992, respond that the CBS News/*New York Times* telephone surveys are not necessarily comparable to Gallup's personal interviews). Bishop, Tuchfarber, and Smith (1994) report that the Gallup wording was not more responsive to short-term factors than the ANES wording in their Ohio experimental surveys, but Abramson and Ostrom (1994b) still argue that the Gallup wording would show greater instability during a more volatile political period, and they (Abramson & Ostrom, 1994a) find such an effect in their Michigan statewide surveys.

Whiteley (1988) did not find partisanship to vary as a result of changing views of issues, candidates, or vote intentions over the short-term period covered by the ANES continuous monitoring study through the 1984 campaign year. Green and Palmquist (1990) argue that the endogeneity is largely artifactual; after correcting for reliability, they find minimal effects of candidate evaluations, issue proximity, presidential approval, or presidential vote on party identification in the ANES surveys during the 1980 presidential election year. Green (1991) shows that nonrandom error actually decreases the estimate of the effect of party identification on presidential approval. W. Miller (1991) finds that responses to the first party identification question were stable in the aggregate from 1952 to after 1980 for northern white voters; he describes realignment in the white male South during this period along with significant changes for blacks, but he argues that the stability for northern white voters calls into question the research explaining national changes in party identification by national economic trends. W. Miller and Shanks (1996) similarly argue that partisanship is the most stable of political attitudes. Analyzing a continuous monitoring study, Johnston (1992a) shows that party identification in the 1988 Canadian general election campaign was not moved by campaign forces that had large effects on vote intention. Thus the evidence about instability of partisanship remains debatable.

The controversy over the stability of partisanship suggests that the party identification scale itself probably has long-term and short-term aspects. Smith, Harding, and Crone (1990) attempt to estimate the relative magnitude of these components. Their analysis accounts for nearly all of the variance in party identification, with the reliability being .94. The long-term aspect loading is .92, versus .10 for the short-term. The exact proportions are probably sensitive to the researchers' modeling criteria, but the fundamental notion of a mixture of long-term and short-term elements underlying the measure, with long-term predominating, has intuitive appeal. Yet even if the measure is mainly long-term, the short-term element may be substantial enough to permit some degree of instability.

The party identification series can be analyzed to determine its dynamic properties. Box-Steffensmeier and Smith (1996) discover fractional integration in the Gallup time series, with a "persistence parameter" of .84 for macropartisanship. This means that shocks in the party system would have effects that last for years, but not decades.

Several explanations have been offered for how party identification can be more unstable at the macrolevel than at the individual level. Green and Palmquist (1994) argue that it could be a matter of people maintaining their relative locations on a partisanship continuum as the whole continuum shifts in unison to benefit one party or the other. Box-Steffensmeier and Smith (1996) instead contend that this dynamic is due to heterogeneity of the electorate and/or persistence of the exogenous factors that affect individual partisanship. Erikson, MacKuen, and Stimson (1996) suggest that small changes in individual partisanship are large enough to produce important changes in macropartisanship. Weisberg (1994) offers an explanation in terms of the time-intervals involved, with greater change found when more frequent measures are obtained (as is the case in studies of macropartisanship measured on a monthly or quarterly basis) than when measures are less frequent (as in most studies of change in individual party identification through multiyear panel studies).

Theoretical Issues

The Party Identification scale has been understood from several different theoretical perspectives over the years. The original presentations by Campbell and his colleagues (1954, 1960) were based on the reference group theory of the 1950s. Just as people identify with religious groups, such as Catholics or Protestants, so people would identify with political groups, such as Republicans or Democrats. Additionally it has often been interpreted as a low-information rational shortcut for obtaining more complete information about an election (Popkin, 1991). Fiorina (1977, 1981) developed a definition of party identification as "the difference between an individual's past political experiences with the two parties, perturbed by a factor . . . that represents effects not included directly in an individual's political experiences (e.g., parents' party ID)" (Fiorina, 1981, p. 89). This "running-tally" reinterpretation of party identification has been highly influential, in large part because it fits in with the new view of partisanship as endogenous (Jackson, 1975; Page & Jones, 1979) and because it has a rational choice basis. Achen (1989, 1992) has

formalized this view of party identification as Bayesian updating of long-term party identification into current party identification (see also the information theory perspective of
Smith, 1993). The voting behavior literature of the 1980s and 1990s was influenced by the
cognitive revolution in psychology, but there has not yet been an accepted reinterpretation
of party identification from that theoretical perspective.

Considerable attention has been given to the meaning of the specific scale categories,
particularly the independent leaners. Campbell *et al.* (1960) suggest that some leaners may
be "closet partisans"—real partisans who feel (perhaps because of their socialization) that
the independent response is more socially acceptable. Shively (1980; cf. Keith *et al.,* 1992,
pp. 92–95) instead argues that leaners are actually "vote announcers"—independents
whose choice of party indicates how they plan to vote at the election.

While the original research on mass partisanship was from the United States, similar
research has now been conducted in many other nations. Partisanship questions have been
adapted to other countries with varied degrees of success. While many political questions
can be adapted to other political systems with ease, partisanship questions must be re-
worked to be sensitive to the nature of the party system. In particular, the usual wording
of the American question cannot be easily applied to countries with more than two major
parties and without the concept of political independence. Moreover, translating the concept of *identification* to other languages can be tricky. For example, West German studies
obtained very different results, depending on whether they asked about adhering to a party,
liking a party, or leaning long-term toward a political party (Norpoth, 1978).

When partisanship was measured in other countries, it was found that partisanship
was actually as variable as the vote decision in some countries. Panel studies in the
United States showed that many respondents change their vote between elections, but
not their partisanship, while the opposite is unusual. However, panel studies of such
other countries as the Netherlands (Thomassen, 1976; see also LeDuc, 1981, and
Holmberg, 1994), for example, showed that in some political systems more people
changed their partisanship between elections, while maintaining their vote stable, than
vice versa. This high level of volatility severely challenges the utility of the long-term
partisanship concept in those countries. Indeed, many researchers would argue that
left–right political orientation is the important long-term political attitude in those
countries, rather than partisanship.

Finally, the Bayesian and information-processing interpretations of partisanship have
important implications for analysis of the party identification scale. As Achen (1992) and
Smith (1993) show, these perspectives are not compatible with the usual ordinary least-
squares approach. That is, linear regression models cannot be used to study the determinants of partisanship. Smith (1993) gives examples of interactive relationships that are
more appropriate to employ.

Alternative Question Wordings

Several variations of the party identification question have been used in major national surveys, as shown in part A of Table 12–3. Some of these wordings tap mainly the
long-term aspect of partisanship, while others also measure its short-term component. In
particular, the "as of today" phrase in the Gallup Poll wording is more short-term in orientation (Converse, 1976, p. 36), whereas such phrases as "generally," "usually," and "regardless of how you vote," used in the CBS News/*New York Times* Poll, convey a longer
"time horizon" (Bishop *et al.,* 1994). Eulau (1994) follows Gallup in calling the short-term
version "party affiliation" to emphasize that its time perspective is different from that in
the ANES wording.

Table 12–3
Variants of the ANES Party Identification Question

A. Alternative Party Identification Question Wordings

1. Gallup: "In politics, as of today, do you consider yourself a Republican, a Democrat, or an Independent?"

2. Harris: "Regardless of how you (voted in the last election/may vote), what do you usually consider yourself—a Republican, a Democrat, an Independent, or what?"

3. Media General/Associated Press: "Do you consider yourself a Democrat, Republican, or Independent?"

4. *Time*/Yankelovich, Skelley, and White: "Are you a Democrat, Republican, or what?"

5. NBC News: "In politics today, do you usually think of yourself as a Republican, a Democrat, an Independent, or something else?"

6. CBS News/*New York Times*: "Generally speaking, do you usually consider yourself a Republican, Democrat, or Independent?"

7. ABC News/*Washington Post*: "Generally speaking, do you think of yourself as a Republican, Democrat, or Independent?"

8. Roper: "Regardless of how you may have voted in the past, what do you usually consider yourself—a Democrat, a Republican, some other party, or what?"

Source: Question wordings are taken from *Public Opinion* (1985, October–November), 8(5), 22–23.

B. Alternative Party Identification Response Categories

1. Filtered: "Generally speaking, do you usually think of yourself as a Republican, a Democrat, an Independent, or *don't you usually think of yourself that way?*"

2. Forced choice: "Generally speaking, do you usually think of yourself as a Republican or a Democrat?" (There are two additional coding categories for volunteered responses to the forced-choice version: Independent and Neither.)

Borrelli, Lockerbie, and Niemi (1987) find that during a presidential campaign the "as of today" wording leads to a 5% greater difference in Democratic versus Republican support, advantaging the party that is leading in the presidential polls. Additionally Abramson and Ostrom (1991) show that the variance in partisanship as measured with the Gallup question is much larger than for the Michigan wording, presumably because of its shorter-term focus. Nie *et al.* (1979, p. 421) report that administration of the standard ANES wording and the Gallup "as of today" wording to the same National Opinion Research Center sample in 1973 obtained similar results, though about 10% of the sample gave different responses about whether they considered themselves Republicans, Democrats, or Independents.

Different Response Categories

Some experiments have asked the party identification question with different response categories in order to test wording effects on partisanship. For example, not providing the "independent" option resulted in 10% fewer people giving that response in comparing two separate statewide polls a year apart (Kenney & Rice, 1988).

The 1987 ANES Pilot Study obtained responses from 349 respondents to the traditional wording and the two experimental wordings shown in part B of Table 12–3. Niemi, Reed, and Weisberg (1991) used the results of this study to analyze the commitment of respondents to their partisanship category on the standard Party Identification scale. Comparing responses to these three wordings, they classified about two-thirds of the respondents as committed, either giving the same partisan response each time or responding independent when that option was offered and a partisan category otherwise. They coded other response patterns as uncommitted partisans (gave partisan answers to the forced-choice and one other version, but an independent response to the third version), nonpartisans (responded "neither" on the forced-choice version, but independent on the other two), apartisans (did not think of themselves as partisans or independents), or inconsistent (responded Republican on one version, but Democratic on another). A quarter of the respondents gave apartisan or inconsistent answers, which suggests that their response to the traditional party identification question may not be meaningful.

Multiple Partisanship

The standard party identification question series makes no reference to levels of government. That has resulted in concern about which level of government respondents in federal systems have in mind when answering the question. Some studies have measured partisanship separately at different levels in order to assess the extent of "dual partisanship" or "segmented partisanship." For example, Jennings and Niemi (1966) used separate questions for the national, state, and local levels: "Generally speaking, at the local level of politics, do you generally think of yourself as a Republican, a Democrat, an Independent, or what? How about at the state level of politics? Finally, at the national level of politics?" They report that most respondents have consistent identifications across the different levels, but some, particularly in the American South, have different identifications at multiple levels. Hadley (1985) further documented the prevalence of such multiple identifications in the South. Perkins and Guynes (1976) showed the effect of question wording on the level of multiple partisanship that is found. Niemi, Wright, and Powell (1987) provided a summary of work on this topic.

This topic has been of concern in other federal systems, particularly the Canadian system, which is even more complicated in that the same parties do not always compete at both the federal and the provincial levels (Clarke, Jenson, LeDuc, & Pammett, 1979). The Canadian data have been analyzed from several different perspectives (Blake, 1982). Uslaner (1990) and Martinez (1990) analyzed the determinants of this "split-level identification."

Additionally people may identify with more than one party—even at the same level of government. Weisberg's (1980) dimensional theory of partisanship allows for this possibility. Multiple identification was found to be prevalent in the Netherlands (Van der Eijk & Niemöller, 1983), with about half of party adherents identifying with multiple parties.

Apartisans and Partisan Misfits

The original reports of the success of the Party Identification scale (Campbell *et al.*, 1954; Campbell *et al.*, 1960) derived much of their power from the result that over 95% of respondents could be located on the scale. However, several studies found a far greater level of "partisan misfits" (a term coined by Niemi *et al.*, 1991): 10% of respondents have no partisan preference (A. Miller & Wattenberg, 1983), 28% are unattached to partisanship (Dennis, 1988a), 28–30% are neither partisan supporters nor independents when asked separate questions on both (Weisberg, 1980, table 2; Kessel, 1984, table 16–3A), and 24% either do not think of themselves in partisan terms or answer three partisanship questions in inconsistent ways (Niemi *et al.*, 1991). The exact definitions used in these different studies vary considerably, but they agree in suggesting that the fit of the Party Identification scale is much less complete than it first seemed and that, as is the case for many other survey questions, a substantial part of the citizenry may lack a meaningful position on the scale.

Correlates

The sociological correlates of partisan direction inevitably change over time as the party system undergoes major or minor realignments. As shown in Table 12–4, the standard results for the United States in the second half of the 20th century are that blacks, Jews, people in union households, and those with lower incomes are more Democratic in their partisanship, while the college educated and people with higher incomes are more Republican. Catholics are more Democratic than Protestants, though this relationship is weaker than it was in the 1950s. While the South used to be predominately Democratic, the link between region and party identification has declined. A new relationship is that between gender and partisanship, with women remaining more Democratic, while men are becoming less Democratic.

The Thermometer Approach

The thermometer question was originally intended to be an easily administered measure of affect toward a number of different social and political groups. Once the basic thermometer introduction is read to the respondent, affect toward many different groups can be measured quickly. Respondents are told to rate groups to which they feel very warm 100°, groups to which they feel very cool 0°, and groups to which they are neutral 50°, so their numerical response shows how warm or cold they feel toward the groups. (A thermometer card is often shown to the respondents in personal interviews, but the question can be easily used in phone surveys without a card.)

The thermometer question was first included in the ANES surveys in 1964. That survey included "Republicans" and "Democrats" in the list of political and social groups on the thermometer. Some subsequent ANES surveys have instead used the more specific stimuli "Republican party" and "Democratic party," while others have gone back to the original usage of "Republicans" and "Democrats." While the intention of the *party* wording is clearly to obtain a more specific reading on the political party rather than to follow Americans who happen to consider themselves Republicans or Democrats, there is no published methodological treatment of the differences produced by these different sets of stimuli. Since 1980 the surveys have sometimes also measured thermometer ratings of "people who call themselves political independents" and "political parties in general," as discussed later in this chapter.

Table 12-4

Correlates of Partisanship, 1952, 1972, and 1992 (in percent)

	1952		1972		1992	
	Dem	Rep	Dem	Rep	Dem	Rep
Gender						
Male	58%	33%	49%	35%	45%	42%
Female	56	35	54	32	54	34
Race						
White	56	36	49	36	46	42
Black	63	16	76	10	77	7
Education						
Not grad high school	61	28	56	27	58	26
High school diploma	53	40	51	34	53	33
Some college	48	48	50	37	46	41
College degree	44	53	43	48	44	48
Income						
0–16 percentile	57	28	57	30	55	27
17–33 percentile	58	32	53	30	57	30
34–67 percentile	61	32	53	30	53	35
68–95 percentile	58	37	49	40	44	47
96–100 percentile	28	59	35	52	30	60
Occupation						
Professional	51	42	45	44	47	43
White collar	55	37	53	34	50	38
Blue collar	66	27	56	27	55	30
Unskilled	59	21	58	24	46	36
Farmers	57	37	49	38	35	53
Housewives	54	38	50	35	50	39
Union membership						
Union household	66	28	58	25	61	29
Nonunion household	54	36	49	37	48	39
Region						
South	75	14	58	26	51	33
Non-South	51	41	49	37	49	40
Age cohort:						
Born 1975 or later					31	38
Born 1959–1974					45	38
Born 1943–1958			51	29	50	38
Born 1927–1942	61	29	50	34	51	37
Born 1911–1926	61	31	54	36	56	36
Born 1895–1910	56	35	53	36	54	36
Born before 1895	49	41	41	52		

Source: American National Election Studies, based on tables at the ANES Web Site. Leaners are combined with partisans.

Thermometer ratings of both parties have fallen since 1964, as shown below:

Party	Average Thermometer Ratings of Political Parties								
	1964	1968	1972	1976	1980	1984	1988	1992	1996
Democrats	72	65	66	63	61	62	62	58	58
Republicans	59	62	63	57	57	58	59	52	53
Dem–Rep diff	+13	+3	+3	+6	+4	+4	+3	+6	+5

Source: Based on Weisberg and Kimball (1995), Table 3.2, using ANES data, supplemented with data from the 1996 ANES survey.

European studies often employ a similar rating task, sometimes using a 0–10 scale instead of the 0–100 scale. The 1996 ANES postelection survey included such a 0–10 scale as part of the multination Comparative Study of Electoral Systems project. The question used was

> I'd like to know what you think about each of our political parties. After I read the name of a political party, please rate it on a scale from 0 to 10, where 0 means you strongly dislike that party and 10 means that you strongly like that party. If I come to a party you haven't heard of or you feel you do not know enough about, just say so. The first party is the Democratic party. [Next the interviewer asks:] The Republican party.

The mean response to the Democratic Party was 5.78 and to the Republican Party, 5.19—values in line with the preelection thermometer averages for those parties shown above.

Thermometer-based measures are probably the second most common measures of partisan direction, second only to the party identification scale described previously. Yet they are controversial in the study of voting behavior. Some analysts like them because of their ambitious attempt at interval-level measurement; others (e.g., Fiorina, 1981) dislike them because they are undifferentiated summary measures. The work of McDonald and Howell (1982) and Converse and Pierce (1985) demonstrated that they are more short-term than the party identification scale is. Yet they have the advantage of being more transitive in relationships with other variables than is the party identification scale. Overall the ease of collecting thermometers makes it likely that they will remain an important measure of partisanship, even if they are somewhat more short-term in their time perspective.

Party Image Scales

A more open-ended approach to party identification is provided by the party image scales used first by Matthews and Prothro (1966). They simply totaled up the number of positive and negative statements made by respondents in reacting to the parties.

The party image questions and scales based on them would usually be considered short-term measures of partisanship. That is, they are affected by recent events that are favorable or unfavorable to a party as well as by long-term allegiance to a party. The higher relationship with vote for the Party Image scale as opposed to the Party Identification scale presumably reflects this short-term orientation of the party image questions. Yet even if it is an excellent predictor of the vote for people who make comments about the parties, its predictive power is limited by the growing number of Americans who make no comments about the parties on any of the four open-ended questions.

The party image questions have also been used to develop a typology of people's views of the parties. Wattenberg (1981, 1994) divides the separate measures for each party into three categories:

1. Positive (more positive reactions than negative)
2. Neutral (an equal number of positive and negative reactions)
3. Negative (more negative reactions than positive)

Combining attitudes toward the two U.S. parties, Wattenberg developed six categories of respondents: positive–positive (like both parties), positive–neutral (like one party, neutral on the other), neutral–negative (neutral on one party, negative on the other), positive–negative (positive on one party, negative on the other), negative–negative (negative on both parties), and neutral–neutral (neutral on both parties). Wattenberg traced the distribution of this variable since 1952, showing a growth in the proportion of the public who are neutrals. However, Stanga and Sheffield (1987) pointed out that the neutral–neutral category is mainly composed of what they term "artificial neutrals," people who give no answers to any of the four original questions, and that this is the category that has increased over the years.

This approach is also useful in comparative research. Wattenberg (1982) showed how four Anglo-American democracies differ from one another in terms of these evaluations of the parties. Whereas neutrality had increased over time in the United States, the views of parties in Canada were nonpolarized (low negativity), Australia was marked by negativity that permitted the emergence of flash parties, and Britain was marked by growing polarization of party images. Thus the party image analysis permits a richer examination of party direction than does a single party identification scale.

Party Closeness Scale

Another approach is provided by Barnes, Jennings, Inglehart, and Farah (1988), who advocate simply asking people which party they feel closest to. The Party Closeness Scale is likely to be a good measure of long-term partisanship, though not as long term as the traditional ANES scale.

Whereas the Party Identification scale works only for two-party systems, the Party Closeness Scale is easily used, regardless of the number of parties in a political system. The Party Closeness Scale identifies more than four out of five U.S. respondents who consider themselves closer to one of the parties, with the remaining people not having a preference. Comparable figures are similar for the Netherlands, Finland, and Britain, versus only 73% of Italian respondents expressing a party preference and 59% of Swiss respondents (Barnes et al., 1988). Thus the party closeness questions and scale are very useful for comparative research, even though they are not usually used in U.S. studies. This scale is being used in many nations in the Comparative Study of Electoral Systems project, with a revised version included in the 1996 ANES.

Other Measures

In addition to the major scales of partisan direction described so far, a few other measures have been proposed, but have not been widely used. Some are idiosyncratic scales developed as part of methodological experiments, while others are frequently included in surveys, but are rarely used as the basic measure of partisanship.

Party Support Scales

As part of a major methodological exploration of the measurement of party identification, several new questions were tested in a 1979 ANES Pilot Study, and some were used in the 1980–1982 ANES surveys. They are designed to provide unidimensional measures of partisanship that are fully transitive in their relationships to other variables. Several party support and closeness scales have been based on these measures. The question series is as follows:

> 1) In your own mind, do you think of yourself as a supporter of one of the political parties, or not? 2) (If yes,) Which political party do you support? 3) On this scale from 1 to 7 where 1 means "not very strongly" and 7 means "very strongly," please choose the number that describes how strongly you support the (Republican/Democratic) Party. 4) (If no,) Do you ever think of yourself as closer to one of the major political parties, or not? 5) (If yes,) Here is a scale from 1 to 7 where 1 means feeling very close to the Republican Party and 7 means feeling very close to the Democratic Party. Where would you place yourself on this scale? 6) Do you ever think of yourself as a political independent or not?

Weisberg (1980) used the responses to the first three support questions to develop a scale of party support, ranging from -7 for strong Republican support to -1 for weak Republican support, 0 for not supporting either party, and 1 for weak Democrat support to 7 for strong Democrat support. Weisberg (1983) used the responses to the first, second, fourth, and fifth questions to develop a Party Support–Closeness Scale consisting of five categories:

- Republican supporter (yes on the first question, Republican on the second)
- Closer to Republican Party (no on the first question, yes on the fourth, and at the Republican end of the scale on the fifth)
- Not closer to a party (no on the first and fourth questions)
- Closer to Democratic Party (no on the first question, yes on the fourth, and at the Democrat end of the scale on the fifth)
- Democratic supporter (yes on the first question, Democrat on the second)

The reliability of this Party Support–Closeness Scale, as tested by the correlation between January–February and September–October 1980 measures, is .78. Applying Blalock's (1970) method for multiple-wave, multiple-indicator data, the relationship with the underlying concept is .90. Barnes *et al.* (1988) criticize this scale because one-third of the sample is in the middle category, presumably understating the level of partisanship.

Dennis (1981) used these same questions to develop a "partisan supporter typology." The 6-category version of this typology consists of

- Ordinary Democrats (yes on the first question, Democratic on the second, and no on the last question)
- Independent Democrats (yes on the first question, Democratic on the second, but yes on the last question)
- Unattached (no on the first and last questions)
- Ordinary independents (no on the first question, but yes on the last)
- Independent Republicans (yes on the first question, Republican on the second, but yes on the last)
- Ordinary Republicans (yes on the first question, Republican on the second, and no on the last)

The closeness question was asked of all respondents in the 1979 ANES survey. Dennis used that additional information to construct a 14-category version of this typology:

- "close to party, ordinary Democrats" (yes on the first question, Democratic on the second, yes on the fourth, and no on the last)
- "close to party, independent Democrats" (same pattern, except yes on the last question)
- "close to Democratic party, unattached" (no on the first question, yes on the fourth, on the Democratic side on the fifth, and no on the last)
- "not close to party, ordinary Democrats" (yes on the first question, Democratic on the second, and no on the fourth and last)
- "close to Democratic party, ordinary independents" (no on the first question, yes on the fourth, on the Democratic side on the fifth, and yes on the last)
- "not close to party, independent Democrats" (yes on the first question, Democratic on the second, no on the fourth, and yes on the last)
- "not close to either party, unattached" (no on the first, fourth, and last questions)
- "not close to either party, ordinary independents" (no on the first and fourth questions, but yes on the last)

Six additional patterns correspond to Republican rather than Democratic identification. Dennis (1981) shows that the test–retest correlation between the first and third waves of the 1980 ANES Panel Study was .64 for the 6-category version of the partisan supporter typology and .74 for the 14-category version.

Direct Rating Scale

Much of the difficulty with intransitivities for the Party Identification scale results from its use of a "branching" format. As an alternative, Krosnick and Berent (1993) have reported on experiments using a seven-point scale format. Respondents are asked:

> Some people consider themselves to be strong Republicans. Suppose these people are at one end of a seven-point scale, at point number 1. Other people consider themselves to be strong Democrats. Suppose these people are at the other end of the scale, at point number 7. Of course other people think of themselves as somewhere in between, at points 2, 3, 4, 5, and 6. Where would you place yourself on this scale (remembering that 1 is a strong Republican and 7 is a strong Democrat), or haven't you thought much about this?

They find the reliability of this measure to be less than that of the conventional Party Identification scale. However, Green and Schickler (1993) conclude that a similar seven-point self-placement scale in a 1973 NORC survey has desirable technical properties, including a slightly higher reliability (.92 v. .89) and a larger correlation with vote (.72 v. .67) than the conventional Party Identification scale.

Party Competence Evaluations

The *party competence evaluations* variable is designed to see which party has an advantage on short-term political issues. Respondents are asked which political party is best able to handle the national problem that they personally consider most important. They are first asked about important problems they see facing this country, and they are then asked: "Which political party do you think would be most likely to get the government to do a better job in dealing with this problem—the Republicans, the Democrats, or wouldn't there be much difference between them?" Answers are used to show if the person thinks the Republicans are better able to handle the problem, if the respondent sees no difference, or if Democrats are better able to handle the problem. The question has been included in the ANES surveys since 1960. There are no published studies of the reliability of this measure. This variable is analyzed in Abramowitz, Cover, and Norpoth (1986), who find it an important predictor of voting for Congress in midterm elections. This variable is a short-term measure of partisanship; as such, it may be an excellent predictor of the vote for offices in which voting is more partisan than candidate-based.

Party Identification Scale

(A. Campbell, G. Gurin, & W. E. Miller, 1954; A. Campbell, P. E. Converse, W. E. Miller, & D. E. Stokes, 1960)

Variable

The Party Identification (Party ID, PID, or Michigan Party ID) scale was designed to measure long-term identification with a political party.

Description

The standard Party Identification scale is based on a set of three questions. First, respondents are asked whether they generally consider themselves Republicans, Democrats, or Independents. Those answering that they are partisans are then asked a strength of identification question, while those answering that they are independents (or that they identify with another party) are instead asked if they consider themselves closer to the Republican Party or the Democratic Party. As detailed later, slightly different question wordings are used in some political polls, and variants of response alternatives have been used for methodological exploration.

The standard scale uses this set of questions to put respondents in one of seven ordered categories:

- Strong Democrat (SD: Democrat on the first question, "strong" on the second)
- Weak Democrat (WD: Democrat on the first question, but "not very strong" on the second)
- Independent leaning to the Democrats (ID: Independent on the first question, but closer to the Democrats on the last)
- Pure Independent (PI: Independent on the first question, and not closer to either party on the last)
- Independent leaning to the Republicans (IR: Independent on the first question, but closer to the Republicans on the last)
- Weak Republican (WR: Republican on the first question, but "not very strong" on the second)
- Strong Republican (SR: Republican on the first question, "strong" on the second)

There are two additional categories that do not fit the ordinal scale and are generally treated as missing data: other (for people who identify with a third party) and apolitical (for people who do not understand the question series enough to respond). People who answer that they have no preference to the first question are also asked if they are closer to one party or the other; those who indicate they are not closer to either party are treated as pure Independents if they have some political interest on other questions in the survey, but are treated as apoliticals if they do not have any interest in politics.

Several scorings of the main seven-point scale have been used. The most common is integer scoring: 0 SD, 1 WD, 2 ID, 3 PI, 4 IR, 5 WR, 6 SR. However, weak partisans and independent leaners have similar behavior (Keith *et al.,* 1977, 1992; A. Miller & W. Miller, 1977). A magnitude scaling study of the proper scoring of the partisan categories also found small differences on average between weak partisans and independent leaners (Lodge & Tursky, 1979). As a result, it is common to combine those categories and instead use the following scoring: 0 SD, 1 WD and ID, 2 PI, 3 IR and WR, 4 SR. The Abelson and Tukey (1970) procedure to find an optimal scoring for an ordinal variable (maximizing the correlation with vote as the criterion variable) would be more consistent with this scoring: 0 SD, 1 WD and ID, 3 PI, 5 IR and WR, 6 SR (J. Campbell, 1984).

Fiorina (1981) challenged the stable equal-interval scoring on the basis of his probit analysis for several ANES surveys. He found that the weak Republican and weak Democratic categories were of similar length, but that they were 2.5–4 times longer than any of the three independent categories for 1958 and 1960 and less than twice that length for 1974 and 1976. On the basis of this analysis, Fiorina advocated simply treating party identification as a series of ordinal categories; that obviates the need to assign interval-level scores to the separate categories. This same approach has been used by Franklin and Jackson (1983) and Franklin (1984, 1992).

Moreover, one of the authors of the Michigan Party Identification scale (W. Miller, 1991) has proposed that a measure of partisanship more in line with the original theoretical treatment of party identification would be the first party identification question (which asks people whether they consider themselves Republicans, Democrats, or Independents) by itself. Instead of using the seven-point scale, he argues that analysts should use only a classification of Republicans versus Democrats as proportions of the total sample. This position is reiterated in W. Miller and Shanks (1996). Indeed, this is the version used through most of one of the two major voting behavior textbooks (Flanigan & Zingale, 1994), though the other uses mainly the seven-point scale version (Abramson, Aldrich, & Rohde, 1995).

Sample

Campbell, Gurin, and Miller (1954) reported data from a 1952 national probability survey of 2021 personal interviews taken for the preelection wave, including a double sample of the West. All but 4% of the respondents were able to relate themselves to the classification; these "apoliticals" were mainly southern blacks who at that time were blocked from registering and voting by a variety of legal and extralegal devices. This scale has subsequently been administered in all the University of Michigan–based election surveys since 1952 as well as in the General Social Survey (GSS) since 1972.

Reliability

Internal Consistency

The ANES Party Identification scale correlates highly with other measures of partisan direction described in this chapter. However, the average party thermometer difference is not always monotonic with the Party Identification scale (Weisberg, 1980). For example, in 1968 the average difference in thermometer ratings of the Republicans and Democrats was 40.6 for strong Republicans, 19.6 for weak Republicans, and 20.9 for Republican leaners. This difference in 1972 was -30.5 for strong Democrats, -10.9 for weak Democrats, and

−12.6 for leaning Democrats. This anomaly is usually interpreted as further evidence of Petrocik's (1974) demonstration of "intransitivities" in the Party Identification scale, as discussed later.

Test–Retest

The over-time consistency of party identification has been measured in several panel studies. Correlations over two-year periods are in the low .80s, while corrected reliability values are in the high .80s.

Converse and Markus (1979) reported that the average two-year continuity coefficient for the 1956–1958–1960 panel was .84, .84 for a 1964–1966 "mini-panel," and .81 for the 1972–1974–1976 panel. The over-time stabilities averaged .95 for the 1950s panel using the Heise (1971) method, which assumes a constant reliability, versus an average of .96 for the Wiley and Wiley (1970) method, which permits varying reliabilities; the stabilities were .97 for the 1970s panel, using both the Heise and the Wiley and Wiley methods. The estimated reliabilities averaged .88 in the 1956–1958–1960 panel and .84 in the 1972–1974–1976 panel (see also Asher, 1974; Achen, 1975; Sullivan & Feldman, 1979; Markus, 1979; McDonald & Howell, 1982; Green & Palmquist, 1994). The average test–retest correlation between adjacent waves of the 1980 ANES Panel Study (Markus, 1982) was .86. Using the Heise (1971) procedure, which assumes constant reliability for the items, the average stability across the four waves of the 1980 ANES Panel Study was .98, with a reliability of .89 (Weisberg, 1983, fn. 5; see also Green & Palmquist, 1990). Using tests that followed age cohorts across time, Krosnick (1991) found standardized stability coefficients averaging in the .92–.95 range for the 1956–1958–1960, 1972–1976, and 1980 Panel Studies.

McDonald and Howell (1982) used the Wiley and Wiley (1970) procedure to estimate the reliability of categories of the Party Identification scale for the 1956–1958–1960 ANES Panel Study. Lower reliabilities were found for independent leaners, ranging from .70 to .75, with stability coefficients of .71 to .85.

Validity

Convergent

The Party ID scale has been consistently and significantly related to vote. The tau-c correlation between party identification and presidential vote has generally been in the .70s (Kessel, 1984, p. 523). This correlation has fallen in years in which sharp short-term forces caused large-scale vote deviations from partisanship, down to .62 in 1964 and .54 in 1972. It is still routinely found to be one of the best single predictors of vote, though Krosnick (1991) argues that this is simply due to its being measured more reliably than other vote predictors.

A potential problem with this validity test is whether the results are biased by asking a vote question before asking the party identification question. Heath and Pierce (1992) suggest this hypothesis in their analysis of the 1983–1986–1987 British Election Studies panel survey. Bishop, Tuchfarber, and Smith (1994) also find more independents when the vote question is asked before the party identification item. However, McAllister and Wattenberg (1995) find very little question-order effect in a split-sample experiment in the 1992 British Election Survey and no effect in the 1992–1993 ANES.

Perhaps the most influential challenge to the Party Identification scale was due to Petrocik's (1974) demonstration of "intransitivities" in the relationship of the scale to criterion variables. In particular, independent leaners were sometimes found to be more partisan in their behavior on some questions than were weak partisans. The measurement of party identification had not been seriously challenged before that article. Later research challenged the measurement in many ways, from questioning the dimensionality of the concept to testing the meaning of the various categories. Most of these later works have returned to Petrocik's original demonstration of intransitivity to suggest that their perspective accounts for the divergence from transitivity.

Discriminant

Several studies contrast the ability to predict the vote from the Party Identification scale with the predictability level using other measures of partisanship. While these results will be summarized in discussing those other measures later in this chapter, in general the evidence is that measures such as the party thermometer difference and the index of party image have a higher correlation with the vote. This is usually interpreted as evidence that those measures are too short-term in their orientation and that the Party Identification scale is a preferable measure of long-term partisanship even if it has a lower correlation with vote.

Location

Campbell, A., Gurin, G., & Miller, W. E. (1954). *The voter decides.* Evanston, IL: Row, Peterson.

Campbell, A., Converse, P. E., Miller, W. E., & Stokes, D. E. (1960). *The American voter.* New York: Wiley.

Party Thermometer Scales

Variables

The party thermometers are designed to measure general affect toward each political party separately, with a "party thermometer difference" calculated to measure differential affect toward the two major parties.

Description

Generally the (signed) difference in thermometer ratings given to the two parties is used as the thermometer-based measure of partisan direction. However, the two party thermometers are sometimes used separately. Weisberg (1980) used them separately to suggest that Republican and Democratic partisanship are not polar opposites of one another, with the correlation between these thermometers often near zero; however, later work argued that the lack of correlation is at least partially due to measurement artifacts (Green, 1988; Krosnick & Weisberg, 1988).

Additionally the thermometer rating of the person's least preferred party is sometimes analyzed separately from the thermometer rating of the person's favorite party. Maggiotto and Pierson (1977) tested the "hostility hypothesis" that partisan defection depends mainly on the voter's evaluation of his or her least preferred party, with greater defection the more the voter likes that party. Crewe (1976) distinguished four types of partisans in Britain: (1) the "polarized," who strongly favor their party and strongly dislike the other party; (2) the "loyal," who strongly favor their party, but do not strongly dislike the other party; (3) the "negative," who strongly dislike the other party, though they do not strongly favor their own party; and (4) the "apathetic," who have strong feelings toward neither party. The Crewe categorization is actually based on a different set of questions, but it could very easily be operationalized in terms of the separate thermometers for the different parties. Indeed, Richardson (1991) showed how the thermometer rating of parties in Europe can be used to gauge hostility toward those parties, finding high levels of such hostility between traditional cleavage parties.

Sample

The party thermometers were first included in the ANES surveys in 1964. In that survey the average rating for Republicans was 59 and for Democrats 72.

Reliability

Internal Consistency

The Pearson r correlations between the party thermometer difference and the ANES Party Identification scale in the 1964–1976 ANES surveys ranged from .55 to .76 (Weisberg, 1980).

Test–Retest

The party thermometer difference is less stable over time than is the Party Identification scale. Converse and Pierce (1985) showed that the average continuity coefficient for 1972–1974 and 1974–1976 for the thermometer difference was .60. McDonald and Howell (1982) used the Wiley and Wiley (1970) procedure for the 1972–1974–1976 ANES Panel Study, obtaining reliabilities for the thermometer difference of .67 to .70, with stabilities of .82 to .92. The test–retest correlations over the 1980 ANES Panel Study for the separate party thermometers were .54 (Republican) and .65 (Democrat), with a .66 correlation for the party thermometer difference (Dennis, 1981). Using the Heise (1971) procedure, the average stability across waves of the 1980 ANES Panel Study was .93, with a reliability of .83 (Weisberg, 1983, fn. 5).

Validity

Convergent

Studies show that current vote is very well predicted by the thermometer difference both in the United States (Weisberg, 1980) and in Britain (Feldman & Zuckerman, 1982). For example, in Britain in 1970 only 2–3% of the respondents who rated one major party higher than the other major party voted for the other major party, with comparable figures for the United States in 1976 being 6–10%. However, this relationship may be considered too high, suggesting that the thermometer difference is overly sensitive to short-term factors associated with the election rather than long-term partisanship. The relationship between the thermometer difference and vote is fairly monotonic, especially when the thermometer difference (which can take on 201 distinct values) is collapsed into a reasonable number of smaller categories (Weisberg, 1980).

As noted above, the two separate party thermometers can also be used as predictors. Weisberg (1982) shows that thermometer ratings of a party's politicians are predicted almost exclusively by the thermometer rating of that party, with the rating of the other party exerting little independent effect even after controlling for the Party Identification scale. Additionally Converse and Pierce (1992) demonstrated a large effect of distance from parties on party thermometers in four European multiparty systems. Thus responses on party thermometers vary systematically with relevant aspects of the party system.

Discriminant

The correlation between party thermometer difference and presidential vote is higher than that between the Party Identification scale and the vote (Weisberg, 1980). Converse and Pierce (1985) also show that the current vote in 1972 could be predicted better with the current thermometer difference (a correlation of .58 between 1972 vote and 1972 thermometer difference, versus .51 using the Party Identification scale as the predictor), while subsequent 1976 vote could be better predicted from earlier party identification (a correlation of .52 between 1976 vote and 1972 party identification, versus .41 using the thermometer difference as the predictor). They obtain similar results for their French survey. In a more elaborate two-stage least-squares analysis, McDonald and Howell (1982) show that the 1976 Party Identification scale had a greater effect on the 1976 presidential vote than did the 1976 thermometer difference, when the 1976 partisanship measures are predicted from the 1972 vote and partisanship (taking into account the lower reliability and stability of the thermometer-based measure). Additionally Dennis (1982) found that the error variance for the thermometer difference in a LISREL model of the vote was higher than for the Party Identification scale when both are considered measured indicators of the same latent variable of partisan direction.

Location

There is no report on the first use of the party thermometers in 1964, nor is there a research article focusing exclusively on the thermometer difference, even though it has been a heavily used measure. The following two studies give considerable attention to the thermometer measures.

Weisberg, H. F. (1980). A multidimensional conceptualization of party identification. *Political Behavior, 2,* 33–60.

Feldman, S., & Zuckerman, A. S. (1982). Partisan attitudes and the vote. *Comparative Political Studies, 15,* 197–222.

Party Thermometer Questions and Thermometer Difference Scale

A. There are many groups in America that try to get the government of the American people to see things more their way. We would like to get your feelings towards some of these groups.

   I have here a card on which there is something that looks like a thermometer. We call it a "feeling thermometer" because it measures your feelings towards groups.

   Here's how it works. If you don't know too much about a group, or don't feel particularly warm or cold toward them, then you should place them in the middle, at the 50 degree mark.

   If you have a warm feeling toward a group, or feel favorably toward it, you would give it a score somewhere between 50° and 100° depending on how warm your feeling is toward the group.

   On the other hand, it you don't feel very favorably toward some of these groups—if there are some you don't care for too much—then you would place them somewhere between 0° and 50°.

1a. Republicans. Where would you put them on the thermometer? ____

1b. Democrats ____

(Generally reactions to one to two dozen groups are obtained at the same time, the others being social or ideological groups rather than political parties.)

B. Thermometer difference = Democrat thermometer minus Republican thermometer

---

Party Image Scales

(D. R. Matthews & J. W. Prothro, 1966)

Variables

The party image scales were developed to measure separate reactions to each political party based on the respondent's open-ended comments.

Description

Respondents are asked to list what they like and dislike about both political parties. The positive and negative comments about each party are counted. Net reactions to each party separately are computed. Composite scales of net reactions to each party are computed along with a summary (the index of party image), showing how much more positive the respondent is to one party than to the other.

   An overall net reaction to the parties can also be obtained from these open-ended questions as a measure of the respondents' partisan directions. The net party image index is the view of the Democratic Party minus the view of the Republican Party (number of likes about Democrats + number of dislikes about Republicans − number of likes about

Republicans − number of dislikes about Democrats). Positive values reflect a surplus of positive comments about the Democrats and negative comments about the Republicans as opposed to negative comments about the Democrats and positive comments about the Republicans. The Index of Party Image used by Matthews and Prothro (1966) and by Trilling (1976) divides this sum into five categories:

0. Strongly pro-Democratic (3 and up)
1. Mildly pro-Democratic (2 to 1)
2. Neutral (0)
3. Mildly pro-Republican (−1 to −2)
4. Strongly pro-Republican (−3 and down)

Trilling (1976) traced the distribution on this variable from 1952 to 1972. Baumer and Gold (1995) reviewed the content of party images and the determinants of the dominant images of each party from 1976 through 1992.

Sample

The party image questions were first included in the ANES surveys in 1952. The sample was the same as described previously for the Party Identification scale. The first extensive use of the party image material was in the Matthews and Prothro (1966) study, based on a cross-section sample of citizens of voting age in the 11 southern states of the former Confederacy. Blacks were triple-sampled, leading to 694 interviews with whites and 618 with blacks. Personal interviews were conducted in March and June 1961; black interviewers were used for black respondents.

Reliability

Internal Consistency

The correlation between the index of party image and the ANES party identification question, as measured by Goodman and Kruskal's gamma, was in the .78–.83 range from 1952 through 1964, falling to .72–.73 for 1968 and 1972 (Trilling, 1976).

Test–Retest

No published studies of the test–retest reliability of this measure were found.

Validity

Convergent

Matthews and Prothro (1966) reported a strong relationship between party image and presidential vote for southern whites and blacks in 1960 and for southern whites in 1964. (All blacks in their 1964 sample voted Democratic.)

Discriminant

The relationship between the index of party image and the presidential vote for the South in 1960 and 1964 was higher than the relationship between party identification and presidential vote (Matthews & Prothro, 1966). A strong relationship between party image and presidential vote remains when holding party identification constant.

Location

Matthews, D. R., & Prothro, J. W. (1966). *Negroes and the new southern politics.* New York: Harcourt, Brace and World.

Party Image Scale
(Matthews & Prothro, 1966)

I'd like to ask you what you think are the good and bad points about the two national parties.

1. Is there anything in particular that you like about the Democratic Party? (If yes,) What is that? Anything else?
2. Is there anything in particular that you don't like about the Democratic Party? (If yes,) What is that? Anything else?
3. Is there anything in particular that you like about the Republican Party? (If yes,) What is that? Anything else?
4. Is there anything in particular that you don't like about the Republican Party? (If yes,) What is that? Anything else?

> *Note:* Up to five answers are usually coded per question.
> Three additional variables are generated from the responses:

View of Republican Party = Number of answers given to Q1 minus number given to Q2.
View of Democratic Party = Number of answers given to Q3 minus number given to Q4.

The index of party Image is the difference between these variables: view of Democratic Party minus view of Republican Party.

Party Closeness Scale
(S. Barnes, M. K. Jennings, R. Inglehart, & B. Farah, 1988)

Variable

The party closeness question was designed as a general partisanship direction measure that could be used in multiple-party systems as well as in two-party systems.

Description

Respondents are asked to which party they feel closest as well as their degree of closeness to that party. This is also the question used in the Converse and Pierce (1986) surveys of partisanship in France in 1968. The alternate version was used in the 1996 ANES as part of the Comparative Study of Electoral Systems project.

Sample

The party closeness questions were first measured in the United States by Barnes and his colleagues in a 1974 national survey of 1719 people age 16 and above. Results are reported for the 1651 people who are age 18 and above.

Reliability

Internal Consistency

The Pearson r correlation between the Party Closeness scale and the ANES party identification question was .85 in 1974 and .88 in 1981 (Barnes et al., 1988).

Test–Retest

Over a 1974–1981 U.S. panel, the Pearson r correlation was .71 versus .72 for the standard Party Identification scale (Barnes et al., 1988).

Validity

Convergent

The Party Closeness scale is a very good predictor of the presidential vote. Barnes et al. (1988) report the predictive success of 1974 measures of party identification and party closeness on the 1980 presidential vote, finding virtually identical predictive success.

Discriminant

In contrast to the Party Identification scale, explanation of presidential vote and other variables from contemporaneous party closeness is not marked by intransitivities (Barnes et al., 1988, Table 7 & fn. 12).

Location

Barnes, S., Jennings, M. K., Inglehart, R., & Farah, B. 1988. Party identification and party closeness in comparative perspective. *Political Behavior, 10,* 215–231.

Party Closeness Scale
(Barnes, Jennings, Inglehart, & Farah, 1988)

1. Which political party do you usually feel closest to?
2. (Those who name a party are then asked,) Would you say you feel very close, fairly close, or not very close to that party?

This leads to a seven-category scale:
> very close Dem (D on Q1, very close on Q2)
> fairly close Dem (D on Q1, fairly close on Q2)
> not close Dem (D on Q1, not very close on Q2)
> no preference (neither on Q1)
> not close Rep (R on Q1, not very close on Q2)
> fairly close Rep (R on Q1, fairly close on Q2)
> very close Rep (R on Q1, very close on Q2)

Alternative (1996) Version

1. Do you usually think of yourself as close to any particular party?

1a. (If yes,) Which party is that?

1b. (If more than one party is mentioned in answering Q1a), Do you feel yourself a little closer to one of the political parties than the others? (If yes,) Which party is that?

2. (Those who name a party are then asked,) Do you feel very close to this party, somewhat close, or not very close?

This leads to a seven-category scale
> very close Dem (D on Q1a or Q1b, very close on Q2)
> somewhat close Dem (D on Q1a or Q1b, somewhat close on Q2)
> not close Dem (D on Q1a or Q1b, not very close on Q2)
> no preference (no on Q1 and no on Q1b)
> not close Rep (R on Q1a or Q1b, not very close on Q2)
> somewhat close Rep (R on Q1a or Q1b, somewhat close on Q2)
> very close Rep (R on Q1a or Q1b, very close on Q2)

Strength of Partisanship

From the first election studies, it has been seen as important to measure the intensity of partisanship along with its direction. Once again, attitudinal measures of strength of partisanship are more common than behavioral measures. The most common measure of strength of partisanship is obtained by "folding" the standard Party Identification scale presented above. This measure will be discussed, after which some other measures will be mentioned.

Standard Folded Party Strength Scale

The folded strength scale is a heavily used measure of partisan intensity, with respondents classified as strong partisans, weak partisans, independent leaners, or pure independents. Whereas the direction of partisanship was originally seen as very stable, some variability in its strength has been acknowledged since the beginning. In particular, party identification was found to strengthen with age (Campbell *et al.*, 1960; Converse, 1969). This was challenged by Abramson (1975, 1979), who applied cohort analysis to the election studies and found that the change in strength of identification for white Americans was mainly generational change rather than an aging effect, though Converse (1976, 1979) still dissents and indicates that there was a definite (though slight) strengthening of partisanship with age during the 1952–1964 period. A second type of individual change that is widely accepted is a weakening of partisanship with geographic mobility (Brown, 1981).

The status of this measure is controversial because its four points are based on two separate questions for two different groups of respondents. As part of the reconsideration of partisanship in the late 1970s and early 1980s, it was realized that the scale actually combines two separate processes. In particular, Valentine and Van Wingen (1980) show that the requirement that strong partisans be more partisan than weak ones and that independent leaners be more partisan than pure independents does not imply that weak partisans are more partisan than independent leaners. Also Claggett (1981) shows how the acquisition of partisanship (moving from independence to partisanship) is different from the intensification of partisanship (moving from weak to strong partisanship). The analysis of independent leaners by Keith et al. (1986, 1992) further bolsters the view that the distinction between leaners and weak partisans is invalid, though Dennis (1992) uses 1980 data to show that the leaners are like strong partisans in terms of political involvement and partisan commitment, but more like independents in terms of attitudes toward independence and views of party differences.

The meaning of the strength of partisan categories is of particular interest, so the 1980 ANES survey asked people to explain their responses. After respondents were classified into party identification categories on the basis of the usual questions, they were shown a series of statements and asked: "Do any of these statements come close to what you mean when you say you think of yourself as a (strong/weak Democrat, closer to the Democratic party, etc.)." According to Kessel (1984, p. 528), strong partisans tended to agree with three statements: that they "almost always support the Democratic (Republican) candidates" (65%), that "ever since I can remember, I've always been a Democratic (Republican)" (63%), and that they are "enthusiastic about what the Democratic (Republican) party stands for" (60%). The only statement agreed to by a majority of weak partisans was that they would "vote for the person, not the party" (66%). None of the statements was agreed to by a majority of the independent partisans. A majority of independents agreed to two statements: "I decide on the person, not the party" (70%) and "I decide on the issues, not the party label" (56%). This evidence as to the meaning of these terms is problematic, however, because many individual respondents in each category agreed with each of the 6–11 statements offered and because no statement was agreed to by as many as three-quarters of the respondents in a category. Additionally these responses should not be taken overly literally, given the known difficulties with self-explanations of people's behaviors. Finally, people in different partisanship categories were shown different statements, precluding comparisons across categories.

Also, the four-point folded scale is problematic in that combining the responses to the two separate questions does not lead to a unitary scale. On the other hand, there is less problem in using it as a three-point scale—strong identifier, weak identifier, and independent, with leaners generally included with weak identifiers (Keith et al., 1992).

Other Measures

Several other measures of party direction can also be folded to obtain measures of partisan strength. For example, how much more people like their favored party on the thermometers than the other party is a possible measure, and another is how much people like their favored party using the thermometer approach. The seven-point scale used to measure party support can be used, as can the seven-point scale used to measure party closeness. The Weisberg (1983) Party Support–Closeness scale gives a three-category ordered distinction: party supporter, closer to a party, and neither. The Barnes (1988) Party Closeness scale leads to a four-category measure: very close, fairly close, not close, and no preference. Weisberg's (1980) factor analysis of several of these measures that were included in the 1980 ANES survey found a single strength factor on which the unsigned party thermometer difference, the Folded Party Closeness scale, the Folded Party Support scale, the Standard Strength of Partisanship scale, and the Maximum Party Thermometer scale all loaded highly.

Furthermore, other questions can be used to measure this component of partisanship. For example, Butler and Stokes's (1969) study of party affiliation in Britain included an intensity question: "How strongly (Conservative/Labour/Liberal) do you generally feel— very strongly, fairly strongly, or not very strongly." Some later British studies (Särlvik & Crewe, 1983) also inquired about the strength of negative partisanship by asking "I should also like to ask what you think about the parties that you don't support. Would you say you were very strongly against the (Conservative/Labour/Liberal) party?" Another possibility is to ask an importance follow-up question. In a local survey, for example, Kessel (personal communication) has followed the standard party identification question with a simple probe asking the respondent "How important is that to you?" Also, measures of the centrality of partisanship to the respondent could be devised.

Finally, Wattenberg (1994) has developed a Partisanship scale that sums up four separate measures of partisanship: (1) whether the person identifies with a party (which Wattenberg calls the "affiliative" dimension of partisanship), (2) whether the person makes positive comments about one party and negative ones about the other or whether the person is neutral about both parties ("cognitive"), (3) whether the person is positive about one party and negative about the other on the feeling thermometer or whether the person is neutral about both ("affective"), and (4) whether the person sees a difference between the parties in handling the nation's most important problem ("performance"). Wattenberg shows that this scale is related to voting for Perot for president in 1992, with Perot obtaining only 11% of the vote of those who were partisan on all four measures as compared to more than 60% of the vote of those who were nonpartisan on three or four of the measures.

Standard Folded Party Strength Scale

*(A. Campbell, G. Gurin, & W. E. Miller, 1954; A. Campbell, P.
E. Converse, W. E. Miller, & D. E. Stokes, 1960)*

Variable

The Folded Party Strength scale is designed to measure strength of identification with a political party.

Description

The standard ANES party identification question series presented earlier includes questions to differentiate strong partisans from weak partisans and independent leaners from pure independents. The resultant strength scale is thus a "folded" version of the Party Identification scale described early in this chapter. The four categories are

1. Strong identifier (R or D on Q1 and strong on Q1a)
2. Weak identifier (R or D on Q1 and not very strong on Q1a)
3. Independent leaner (I on Q1 and R or D on Q1b)
4. Pure independent (I on Q1 and no on Q1b)

Several scorings have been used. The most common (e.g., Converse, 1976) is integer scoring: 3 for strong identifiers, 2 for weak identifiers, 1 for independent leaners, and 0 for pure independents. Keith *et al.* (1977, 1992) and A. Miller and W. Miller (1977) find little difference between weak identifiers and independent leaners, which suggests that it might be better to use the scoring of 2 for strong identifiers, 1 for weak identifiers and independent leaners, and 0 for pure independents. W. Miller (1990, Table 5.2) essentially used a variant of this scoring ($+1$ for strong identifiers, 0 for weak identifiers and independent leaners, and -1 for pure independents) in his analysis of change in strength of partisanship across age cohorts. Markus (1983) scored strength of identification 10 for strong partisans, 5 for weak partisans, 4 for leaners, and 0 for pure independents, reporting that this scoring is consistent with Weisberg's (1980) analysis of the party thermometer difference by strength of identification. An equivalent scoring maximizes correlations with criterion variables for the 1952–1982 ANES data, according to the Abelson and Tukey (1970) procedure for finding a scoring of ordinal variables when voting turnout is used as the criterion variable (J. Campbell, 1984).

Sample

The sample is the same 1952 ANES sample described under the Party Identification scale itself earlier in this chapter.

Reliability

Internal Consistency

The Folded Party Strength scale is not always fully monotonic with the average party thermometer difference (Weisberg, 1980). For example, in 1968 the average difference in thermometer ratings of the Republicans and Democrats, averaged for the two parties, was 35.6 for strong partisans, 15.2 for weak partisans, and 16.8 for independent leaners. This is further evidence that the distinction between weak partisans and independent leaners is not entirely reliable.

Test–Retest

Markus (1983) used the Wiley and Wiley (1970) procedure on the ANES 1956–1958–1960 and 1972–1974–1976 Panel Studies to estimate the reliability of the Folded Party Strength scale (using a 10–5–4–0 scoring). The average reliability for strength of partisanship was .58, with an autoregressive coefficient of .95. Brody's (1991) analysis showed that strength of identification changed more in two panel studies (1956–1958 and 1972–1974) than did direction of identification.

Validity

Convergent

In their original report on the Party Identification scale, Campbell, Gurin, and Miller (1954) validated it by comparing it to two party loyalty questions. Strong partisans were found more likely to vote for a candidate of their party whom they do not like because of party loyalty than were weak partisans. Strength of partisanship was also related to whether the person felt that voters should vote for the same party for Congress and president. In each case the proportion of strong partisans who might be disloyal to their party was greater than might have been anticipated. Campbell, Gurin, and Miller (1954, p. 97) conclude that strong identifiers do have greater partisan attachments than do weak identifiers, but that the strong category includes some people whose intensity of partisanship is not as great as the term *strong* implies. Campbell *et al.* (1960, pp. 125–126) also report that strength of partisanship is strongly related to regularity of voting for the same party for president, especially for people old enough to have participated in several presidential elections. It is also one of the best predictors of straight-ticket voting (Brody, Brady, & Heitshusen, 1994).

However, Petrocik's (1974) demonstration of "intransitivities" in the Party Identification scale focused directly on the strength component, showing that it is not monotonic with most measures of political involvement. Pooling 1952–1972 election studies, he found that weak identifiers are not higher than independent leaners with regard to political interest, interest in the campaign, concern about the election outcome, voting turnout regularity, turnout in the current election, political efficacy, political participation, or media use to follow the campaign. Indeed, weak identifiers are not higher than pure independents with regard to interest in politics or in the present campaign.

Discriminant

No studies of the discriminant validity of this measure were found.

Location

Campbell, A., Gurin, G., & Miller, W. E. (1954). *The voter decides.* Evanston, IL: Row, Peterson.

Campbell, A., Converse, P. E., Miller, W. E., & Stokes, D. E. (1960). *The American voter.* New York: Wiley.

Political Independence and Party System Support

Political independence has a long tradition in the United States, dating back at least as far as the Mugwumps of 1884, namely, those Republicans who defected to vote for Democrat Grover Cleveland over the Republican nominee, James Blaine. Rather than being viewed as a separate party per se, independence is more an indication that the person prefers not to identify with one of the existing political parties. Early discussions of the concept are provided by Eldersveld (1952) and Agger (1959). Incidentally, note that the independence concept is employed mainly in the United States; there is not a similar concept for most other countries.

A related concern is the respondent's support for the party system. Indeed, this may be the obverse of independence, with independents being less supportive of the party system. Measures of party system support are mentioned briefly in this section along with measures of independence.

The most common measure of political independence is again based on the standard Michigan Party Identification scale. This measure will be reviewed in this section along with Dennis's scales of independence and party system support.

The ANES Independence Classification

The ANES party identification classification basically treats as independents those citizens who self-identify as independents rather than Republicans or Democrats (along with people who are interested in politics but do not self-identify as independents or partisans). While based on self-identifications, the Michigan researchers' treatment of independence was less theoretical than their use of reference group theory to understand identification with the Republican and Democratic Parties. Independence was virtually seen as a residual category, combining those who lack positive attraction to any party, those who are repelled by parties, and those who value independence as an ideal (Campbell *et al.*, 1960, p. 123).

Whereas the usual interpretation (Campbell *et al.*, 1960) is that empirical studies have disproved the traditional view that independents would pay close attention to politics, an alternative possibility is that this measurement of independence is not valid. For one thing, if independent leaners are more like weak partisans, then descriptions of independents should be based solely on pure independents (Asher, 1988). For another, the no-partisan-preference group dilutes the competence level of those pure independents (A. Miller & Wattenberg, 1983). However, defining independence as only pure independents makes the group so small that any concern over their competence becomes fairly academic.

The proportion of independents has increased since the 1950s, as shown here:

	Party Independents (in percent)											
	1952	1956	1960	1964	1968	1972	1976	1980	1984	1988	1992	1996
All Indep	23%	23%	23%	23%	29%	35%	36%	34%	34%	36%	38%	33%
Pure Indep	6	9	10	8	11	13	15	13	11	11	12	8

Source: Based on Weisberg and Kimball (1995), Table 3.1, using ANES data, supplemented with data from the 1996 ANES survey.

A substantial increase in the proportion of independents would be one indicator of a "dealignment" of the party system, in which citizens are moving away from the political parties (Beck, 1979). Many would interpret the increase in independents since the 1950s as indicating that such dealignment has occurred, though the major study of independents by Keith *et al.* (1992, p. 203) concludes that "the surface-level increase in Independents does not portend a decline in political stability, the decay of the party system, nor any of the other unwelcome developments heralded by some scholars."

The dynamics of independence have been studied by Clarke and Suzuki (1993) in the quarterly Gallup series from 1953 to mid-1988. Using a switching regression model, they find that the proportion of independents increased during the period starting in the third quarter of 1967 as both the inflation and unemployment rates increased, but that independence did not vary with economic variables prior to mid-1967. The proportion of independents increased with the number of fatalities in the Vietnam war during both periods, fell during the first period in response to "rally-around-the-flag" events, and increased during the second period in response to scandals (such as Watergate). Thus, economic and political events both affect rates of independents after 1967.

The proportion of independents in the electorate has increased when there is a strong minor party candidacy for the presidency, such as Wallace in 1968, Anderson in 1980, and Perot in 1992 and 1996. The theoretical question of importance is which is the causal variable: Is there strong support for a minor presidential candidate when more people are independents, or is it simply that people who vote for a minor presidential candidate feel that they cannot claim to be Republicans or Democrats and so respond that they are independents? The use of the term *independent* in the name of some third parties (such as George Wallace's American Independent Party) further confuses this issue.

Weisberg and Mockabee (1997) have called attention to the decline in independents in the 1996 ANES survey. The proportion of independents in 1996 was the lowest in any presidential election since 1968, while the proportion of pure independents fell to single digits for the first time in a presidential election year since 1964. Part of the decline may have to do with not having as strong a minor presidential candidate as in 1992, but Weisberg and Mockabee use CBS News/*New York Times* poll data to show that the decline occurred as politics became more polarized during the Republican 104th Congress.

One issue involves the extent to which independence is a clear stimulus to the public. Bastedo and Lodge (1980) show that it is more ambiguously defined for citizens than are the stimuli "Republicans" and "Democrats." While academics do not view political independence as a separate party, that may be less clear for the public. The increase in independence during the years in which there is a third-party candidacy for the president suggests that independence reflects contemporary political trends. Finally, studies that do not include the "independence" option find that relatively fewer people volunteer that response (Barnes *et al.*, 1988; Kenney & Rice, 1988; Niemi *et al.*, 1991).

Little is known about the sociological correlates of political independence because independence has rarely been measured separately from strength of partisanship. People with less education are more likely to identify as independents. Young people are more independent than older people who have been attached to the party system for a longer period of time. Some general correlations are shown in Table 12–5.

Dennis Independence Scales

An alternative approach has been proposed by Dennis (1988b). He suggests that there are four separate aspects of independence: (1) political autonomy (a positive view of independence in terms of such values as individualism), (2) antipartyism (independence due to a negative view of parties), (3) partisan neutrality (independence due to neutrality between the parties), and (4) partisan variability (a view of oneself as switching between the parties). He helped develop questions tapping each of these dimensions that were used in the 1980 ANES survey. Factor analysis shows that these are four separate factors.

Over the years Dennis (1966, 1975, 1986) has developed several other measures of attitudes toward political independence and toward the party system. The samples have often been from Wisconsin surveys, rather than full national samples. These scales have often used some of the same questions employed here, though combined in different ways, as when Dennis (1986) used the five questions reproduced later in the scale review as a measure of "diffuse party support." Presumably some of the dimensions that Dennis (1988b) obtains are a more differentiated version of this measure. However, this usefully points out that Dennis's independence measures are also measures of attitudes toward the party system.

To this point, the Dennis questions and scales have received little further use. Nevertheless, they remain significant as a commentary on the importance of measuring the full diversity of independence and studying its meaning.

Table 12-5

Correlates of Independence, 1952, 1972, and 1992 (in percent)

	1952	1972	1992	Increase
Gender				
Male	9	16	13	+4
Female	9	14	12	+3
Race				
White	8	15	12	+4
Black	21	14	16	−5
Education				
Not grad high school	11	17	16	+5
High school diploma	7	15	14	+7
Some college	4	13	13	+9
College degree	3	9	8	+5
Income				
0–16 percentile	15	13	18	+3
17–33 percentile	10	17	13	+3
34–67 percentile	7	17	12	+5
68–95 percentile	5	11	9	+4
96–100 percentile	13	13	10	−3
Occupation				
Professional	7	11	10	+3
White collar	8	13	12	+4
Blue collar	7	17	15	+8
Unskilled	20	18	18	−2
Farmers	6	13	12	+6
Housewives	8	15	11	+3
Union Membership				
Union household	6	17	10	+4
Nonunion household	10	14	13	+3
Region				
South	11	16	16	+5
Non-South	8	14	11	+3
Age Cohort				
Born 1975 or later			31	
Born 1959–1974			17	
Born 1943–1958		20	12	
Born 1927–1942	10	16	12	+2
Born 1911–1926	8	10	8	0
Born 1895–1910	9	11	10	+1
Born before 1895	10	7		

Source: American National Election Studies, based on tables at the ANES Web Site. Independent leaners are not included, but apoliticals are included.

Other Measures

Some other measures of independence and party system support have been employed. There have not been reports of the reliability of these measures, and there have been few studies of their validity.

Attitudinal Measures

One attitudinal measure is a *thermometer* variable, which measures the respondent's affect toward political independence. The standard thermometer introduction is used (given in full earlier in this chapter), followed by this item: "People who consider themselves political independents." This item has been used in the ANES surveys, starting in 1980. This is a controversial measure in that some analysts regard the referent as unclear. Fiorina (1981, p. 105), in particular, objects to including in party identification "such strange notions as affect toward 'independence.' " A related measure is the thermometer rating of "political parties in general." It is intended as a measure of support for the party system and would be expected to have a negative relationship to attitudes toward political independence. There have not been studies of the reliability or validity of these items.

A separate series of political independence questions is intended to measure political independence separately from strength of party identification. Respondents are asked: "Do you ever think of yourself as a political independent, or not?" If they answer yes, they are then asked: "On this scale from 1 to 7 (where 1 means "not very strongly," and 7 means "very strongly"), please choose the number that describes how strongly independent in politics you feel." The political independence questions were first used in the 1980 ANES survey (after experimentation in a 1979 ANES Pilot Study). Weisberg (1983) uses the first question by itself. Also, Weisberg (1980) and Kamieniecki (1985, 1988) constructed an eight-category Strength of Independence scale from the two questions together: 0 for those who do not think of themselves as independents on the opening question and, for those who think of themselves as independents, the number they choose on the scale. Using this scale, strong independents are actually better educated than weak independents and nonindependents (Weisberg, 1980), and they are also more interested in the campaign, are more knowledgeable about politics, and pay more attention to political matters in the media (Kamieniecki, 1988). These correlates are very different than usual results. If this measurement is valid, it seriously challenges the validity of the traditional independence measurement. Dennis (1988a, 1988b) also uses this first political independence question in developing his partisan support typology, discussed earlier in this chapter.

Another attitudinal measure of independence is the "divided government question," which determines the respondent's attitude toward having the control of the U.S. government split between different political parties. For example, the wording used by the CBS News/*New York Times* poll in September 1989 was "Do you think it is better for the country to have a President who comes from the same political party that controls Congress, or do you think it is better to have a President from one political party and Congress controlled by another?" The flurry of attention in the political science literature of the 1990s to divided government (Cox & Kernell, 1991; Fiorina, 1991) suggests there will be further use of divided government questions. Press polls are also likely to continue to measure this attitude, especially in years like 1996, when one presidential candidate is considerably ahead in the polls and the other party's campaign emphasizes the need to give its party a majority in Congress as a check on the president.

Finally, although political independence is rarely measured directly outside of the United States, it is sometimes treated as the residual category of people not supporting any political party. This form of independence can be important in a party system undergoing change. For example, Tanaka and Weisberg (1996) report a large increase in independence in Japan during the early 1990s, during which time their party system changed considerably, with half of the Japanese electorate being independent in 1995.

Behavioral Measures

Behavioral measures of independence are also possible. The *split-ticket* measure is intended to determine the extent to which the respondent has voted for a single party. Respondents are asked about their votes for several different political offices at the same election (such as president, senator, U.S. representative, state governor, and other state and local offices). Respondents are then coded according to whether they voted a "straight ticket" (supporting the same party for every office) or a "split ticket" (supporting different parties for different offices). DeVries and Tarrance (1972) used this as a measure of independence. Eldersveld (1952, p. 735) defined independent voting even more broadly as an "absence of party loyalty or . . . periodic transference of party allegiances" and operationalized this as a combination of split-ticket voting, voting for one party while identifying with the other party, voting for minor parties (excluding long-time supporters of those parties), regularly shifting from one major party to another, and deciding late on their voting decision; this broad definition leads to a large number of behavioral independents (37% in the 1948 University of Michigan Survey Research Center [SRC] study), though many self-classified independents are not found to be behavioral independents.

Finally, *official registration* can be used as a measure of independence. This measure determines if the respondent has chosen not to register officially as a partisan. In some states a citizen can register as an independent; in other states not registering as a partisan can be considered the equivalent of independent registration. A major difficulty with this measure is that registration by party does not exist in many states, so this measure is applicable in only a subset of the states.

Measuring Independence

All in all the measurement of independence remains more controversial than the measurement of direction or strength of partisanship. Treating independence as simply the obverse of strength of partisanship confounds two concepts that could be separate. Yet independence may be too diffuse a stimulus for the public to have a clear referent. The Dennis scales begin to hint at the complexity involved in understanding independence. The political media give much attention to the growth in political independence, sometimes portraying poll results as showing that independents are the second largest (or at times the very largest) political party in the United States. These measurement considerations argue that much caution is necessary in interpreting such results. Indeed, Eldersveld's (1952) words remain appropriate today:

> Independents may be many or few; they may be increasing or not; areal patterns may or may not exist; independents may be of many undetermined types; they may be intelligent or fickle; and the effects of independent voting on the political system may be beneficent or dangerous. The state of our knowledge about independent voting is obviously not precise, well documented, or unanimous. (p. 735)

NES Independence Classification

(A. Campbell, G. Gurin, & W. E. Miller, 1954; A. Campbell, P. E. Converse, W. E. Miller, & D. E. Stokes, 1960)

Variable

The Michigan independence classification is designed to measure independence in terms of psychological self-identification.

Description

The standard treatment of independence is to code as an independent anyone who chooses that category in response to the party identification questions given at the beginning of this chapter. Strength of independence is not measured per se, except as the complement of strength of partisanship—pure independents are treated as the most independent, leaners the next most independent, weak partisans next, and strong partisans least.

The precise coding of independents is actually more complicated than this (A. Miller & Wattenberg, 1983). Some respondents answer the first party identification question ("Generally speaking, do you usually think of yourself as a Republican, a Democrat, an Independent, or what?") in a manner to indicate that none of those terms applies to them and do not lean to a party on the follow-up question. These "no preference" respondents are coded as independents if they have an interest in politics; they are instead coded as apoliticals if they show little interest in politics. A. Miller and Wattenberg (1983) showed that much of the increase in independents from 1968 through 1980 was actually due to this no-preference category. Further, they show that these respondents were different from self-proclaimed independents in their level of political involvement and attitudes toward political independence. Craig (1985), however, sharply disagrees, finding that they differ more on symbols of independence than on views of the parties.

Sample

The Michigan independence classification was first used in the 1952 ANES, which was described early in this chapter. Originally about a quarter of the American electorate was found to be independent. That proportion grew in the 1960s and 1970s to a peak of nearly 40% from 1978 to 1994, but fell in 1996. The growth in independence is documented and explained in many works, including Nie, Verba, and Petrocik (1979) and Asher (1988). However, the percentage of respondents who are self-professed independents that do not lean toward either party is much lower.

Reliability

Internal Consistency

The thermometer ratings of the Democratic and Republican Parties by pure independents are generally fairly equal. For example, in 1996 the average rating given by pure independents to the Democratic Party was 53.67 versus 52.87 to the Republican Party, a difference that is not statistically significant. Thus pure independents are neutral between the parties, whereas leaners and partisans give significantly higher ratings to their preferred parties.

Test–Retest

No published studies of the reliability of this measure were found beyond studies of the reliability of the Michigan Party Identification scale and its Folded Party Strength scale, discussed previously.

Validity

Convergent

The traditional ideal of political independence was that citizens would pay close attention to politics and rationally choose the best candidate in a given election, instead of following party ties. This view implies that independents would be attentive to politics, interested in campaigns, and informed about government. However, from the first empirical studies in 1952, it was clear that this informed image of independents did not hold. Campbell *et al.* (1960, pp. 142–145) showed that independents actually are less interested in politics, care less about the election outcome, and thus are less competent in political matters than partisans. This result was treated as showing that the traditional understanding of independence was incorrect rather than as disconfirming the validity of the measurement of independence.

Discriminant

No studies of the discriminant validity of this measure were found.

Location

Campbell, A., Gurin, G., & Miller, W. E. (1954). *The voter decides.* Evanston, IL.: Row, Peterson.

Campbell, A., Converse, P. E., Miller, W. E., & Stokes, D. E. (1960). *The American voter.* New York: Wiley.

Dennis Independence Scales

(J. Dennis, 1988b)

Variable

The Dennis Independence scales are intended to measure several separate dimensions of attitudes toward independence.

Description

The Positive Autonomy factor includes four questions, covering the feeling thermometer on "political independents," whether the person is registered as an independent, an index of acceptability of voting for nonparty candidates, and feelings toward being a firm party supporter. The Negative Antipartyism factor includes four questions, covering whether political parties are still needed, attitudes on whether party labels should be put on the ballot, views about whether the parties confuse the issues, and a feeling thermometer on "political parties." The Partisan Neutrality factor includes three questions, covering a folded index of prospective party leadership, whether the person cares which party wins the election, and an index of the number of important issues on which the person perceives party differences. Finally, Partisan Variability includes four questions, covering self-perceived party regularity, whether it is better to vote for the candidate than the party, whether one should be a firm party supporter, and the feeling thermometer on "political parties." Note that the latter two items each have high loadings on two of the factors; Dennis assigned each to the factor on which it had the highest loading—being a firm party supporter to the Partisan Variability factor and the political parties thermometer to the Negative Antipartyism factor. The factors were scored by simple addition, with equal weights for each item. There are moderate correlations (.14 to .33) among indices based on these four factors.

Sample

The Dennis independence questions were first used on a full national sample in the 1980 ANES. That was a panel study, but the Dennis report is based on only the September–October preelection wave. This study used personal interviews and was based on a national probability sample.

Reliability

Internal Consistency

Dennis shows that a greater proportion of pure independents than any partisan category score high on Negative Antipartyism, Partisan Neutrality, and Partisan Variability, though independent leaners are higher on Positive Autonomy.

Test–Retest

No reports on the test–retest reliability of these measures were found.

Validity

Convergent

Dennis finds that independents tend to have higher values on all of these factors. The four-point Michigan Independence scale has positive correlations with each index, but the correlation with Negative Antipartyism is only .08.

Discriminant

The better educated are higher on Positive Autonomy and Partisan Variability, but lower on Negative Antipartyism and Partisan Neutrality. Variability is positively related to turnout, while antipartyism and neutrality are negatively related to it. Looking at several variables, Dennis concludes that neutrality and, to a lesser extent, antipartyism are associated with lower involvement and political awareness, whereas variability is related to higher involvement and awareness.

Location

Dennis, J. (1988b). Political independence in America, Part II: Towards a theory. *British Journal of Political Science, 18,* 197–219.

Dennis Independence Scales (Dennis, 1988b)

Next I will read some general statements about political parties. Please use the scale on this page to tell me how strongly you agree or disagree with each statement. The scale runs from "disagree very strongly" at point 1 to "agree very strongly" at point 7. After I read each statement, you can just give me the number from the scale that applies.

1. The best rule in voting is to pick a candidate regardless of party label.
2. It is better to be a firm party supporter than to be a political independent. (Reverse)
3. The parties do more to confuse the issues than to provide a clear choice on issues.
4. It would be better if, in all elections, we put no party label on the ballot.
5. The truth is we probably don't need political parties in America anymore.

    Questions 3–5 had their highest loading on Negative Antipartyism, as did the feeling thermometer on "political parties" (reversed); questions 1 and 2 had their highest loading on Partisan Variability. The variables with their highest loadings on Positive Autonomy were the feeling thermometer on "political independents," political party registration (presumably scored with party registrants low), and an index of acceptability of voting for nonparty candidates, which is not explained in the article. The variables with their highest loadings on Partisan Neutrality were a folded index of prospective party leadership, which is not explained in the article; caring which party wins the election (presumably not caring which party wins is scored high), and the number of important issues on which the person perceives differences between the parties (reversed).

Dimensionality of Partisanship

Having discussed measures of three different aspects of partisanship, it is appropriate to question directly the unidimensionality of partisanship. The original view of partisanship was unidimensional. In particular, the standard Party Identification scale was considered a unidimensional scale, running from strong Democrats to strong Republicans, with Independents in the middle. However, this unidimensionality was presumed rather than tested directly. The presumed unidimensionality allowed direction of partisanship, strength of partisanship, and independence all to be measured from the same question series.

The dimensionality of partisanship has become a controversial topic. Weisberg (1980) provided a broad theoretical statement of dimensional perspectives on partisanship. He showed how the most general view of partisanship permits separate dimensions for partisanship and independence, as well as having attitudes toward the Republican and Democratic Parties be separate dimensions, though most work on the topic has focused only on the former. Several researchers (Alvarez, 1990; Dennis, 1986; Howell, 1980; Jacoby, 1982; Kamieniecki, 1985, 1988; Katz, 1979; Valentine & Van Wingen, 1980; Weisberg, 1980) have found evidence of multidimensionality, while others (Green, 1988; McDonald & Howell, 1982) have provided evidence to the contrary. A typical conclusion is that of Kessel (1984), who also provided evidence of multidimensionality, but argued that the unidimensional fit suffices. The preponderant position at this time appears to be an acceptance that the traditional Party Identification scale works well in the contemporary United States, even if some multidimensionality or intransitivities may exist.

Evidence in Support of Multidimensionality

Several studies published around 1980 simultaneously suggested that partisanship and independence should be seen as separate dimensions: Katz (1979) found that patterns of partisan change across panel studies could best be accounted for by a two-dimensional view of partisanship, with a direction dimension (Democrats versus Republicans) and an intensity direction (partisans versus independents). Howell (1980) also found patterns of change in partisanship that she considered compatible with separate partisanship and independence dimensions. Valentine and Van Wingen (1980) provided a major demonstration that partisan strength for identifiers was incomparable to whether independents leaned toward a party, so that weak partisans are not necessarily more partisan than independent leaners, leading to the conclusion that partisanship and independence are separate dimensions. Jacoby (1982) used Coombs's (1964) unfolding analysis on responses by a sample of 101 college undergraduates who were asked to "list the order in which you yourself would like to be known by the labels" "strong Democrat," "weak Democrat," and so on. Only 65 percent gave preference orders that were consistent with the usual unidimensional ordering from strong Democrat to strong Republican. Multidimensional scaling produced a two-dimensional fit, with the party labels falling in a horseshoe-pattern; Jacoby labeled the dimensions Democratic to Republican and partisan to independent.

   Partly as a result of this early work, the 1980 ANES surveys included several new questions on partisanship. Weisberg (1980) showed that only 52% of respondents in the January–February 1980 ANES survey gave responses to the party and independent thermometers that were compatible with the usual Democratic–Independent–Republican dimension. Also, he reported that the correlations between the Democratic and Republican Party thermometers ranged from mildly negative to zero, rather than the strongly negative thermometers that a single dimension would imply. Furthermore, 16% of the sample of 954 respondents thought of themselves as both party supporters and independents, and 28% thought of themselves as neither. (Similarly, in the fall 1980 ANES survey, Kessel (1984, p. 527) showed that 15% of the sample viewed themselves as both party supporters and independents and 30% as neither.) Factor analysis of several scales from that 1980 study provided multiple factors. Weisberg reported separate Partisan Direction, Partisanship Strength, Independence, and Party System factors, though Kamieniecki (1985, 1988) found only the Partisan Direction, Partisanship Strength, and Independence factors.

   In his analysis of the same new ANES questions, Dennis (1986) found three separate dimensions underlying his partisan supporter typology: a partisan dimension; a party system support dimension, with ordinary partisan supporters at one end and ordinary independents at the opposite end; and a political involvement function, with independent partisan supporters at the high end and the unattached at the low end. He reported a similar factor analysis, except that Republican and Democratic Party variables were on two separate factors. Additionally Dennis (1988b) found four separate dimensions of political independence, as described previously.

Kamieniecki (1985, 1988) correlated the traditional Strength of Partisanship scale and his Strength of Independence scale with many variables in the 1980 and 1984 ANES surveys. If the traditional Strength of Partisanship scale measured the same continuum as the Strength of Independence scale, the two should have opposite-sign correlations with other variables. However, the two had same-sign correlations with many variables, including interest in the election. From this evidence, Kamieniecki (1988, p. 364) concluded that "partisan strength and independence are separate components of party identification."

Alvarez (1990) used ANES data to test the dimensionality of party identification. He found that in 1980, 1982, and 1984, at most 37% of party identifiers had transitive preferences, giving the highest thermometer score to their party, the second highest to independents, and the lowest to the other party. Second, the correlation of party thermometers was only weakly negative from 1964 through 1986. Third, the expectation for party identifiers that strength of identification would correlate positively with their own party's thermometer and negatively with the opposite party's thermometer was met with weaker correlations than expected. Further, in predicting candidate preference and vote for 1980 and 1984, the thermometers provided stronger predictive power than did the Party Identification scale by 2–4%. He interpreted these results as supporting a multidimensional view of partisanship.

Evidence against Multidimensionality

The finding of multidimensionality has been challenged by studies that correct for the lack of full reliability of partisanship measures. McDonald and Howell (1982) used the Wiley and Wiley (1970) procedure to estimate the reliability of the Party Identification scale and the party thermometer difference for the 1950s and 1970s ANES Panel Studies. The thermometer difference had lower reliability and stability. Taking into account that lower reliability and lower stability, they found that, controlling on the 1972 presidential vote, the party thermometer difference in 1972 has less effect on 1976 partisanship than does the Party Identification scale. They concluded that the thermometer measure is contaminated by short-term political forces and that there is little need to accept a multidimensional perspective on partisanship.

There also have been arguments against viewing attitudes toward the Republican and Democratic Parties as orthogonal. Green (1988) used confirmatory factor analysis of the 1972 and 1976 ANES surveys, with a control for response biases due to how charitable respondents are across the thermometer items. He reported a corrected correlation of −.81 between the latent party factors, but there is a correlation of .35 (1972) to .43 (1976) between the measurement errors for the feeling thermometers. For 1976 the random measurement errors reduced the correlation of the party thermometers to −.30, and nonrandom error further reduced it to −.03. Measurement error makes the thermometers look independent when in fact they are unidimensional. Krosnick and Weisberg (1988) obtained similar results in their confirmatory factor analysis, using a Methods factor on which all of the thermometers load equally, after which the Republican and Democratic factors are strongly negatively correlated. Yet these models are based only on a series of assumptions about the structure of the measurement error, and the quality of fit of the final models is not excellent. This suggests that viewing the Republican and Democratic thermometers as polar opposites may be a case of overcorrection, in the same way that viewing them as independent is a case of undercorrection.

In his important text Kessel (1984, p. 529) offers the following reasonable conclusion about the dimensionality of partisanship: "It appears that some citizens have multiple (partisan and independent) reference groups, some citizens have only one such reference group, and some citizens have no such reference group. No one-dimensional taxonomy is going to capture all of this, but the traditional classification is a good first approximation." Fiorina (1981, p. 105) takes the stronger position that the concept of party identification is one-dimensional, arguing that multidimensional views of partisanship would "let methodology run away with the substance."

Yet the discussion in this chapter demonstrates the utility in separating different dimensions of partisanship. The standard Party Identification scale is usually used as the only measure of partisanship, but it may do better at measuring some ideas than others. Partisan direction is easy to measure. The standard scale measures it well, though some would prefer the affect measures of the thermometers, the richer measurement of party images, or the greater cross-national generalizability of the Party Closeness scale. Partisan strength is more awkward to measure, and the usual scale may confound strength of partisanship and independence. Independence has been measured separately so infrequently that it is difficult to gauge which measures are valid and which are not; in itself, independence is a complex multidimensional phenomenon that requires more extensive measurement than it is usually accorded.

Partisanship Outside of the United States

Attempts to "export" the concept of partisanship to other countries began very soon after the importance of partisanship in the United States was first proclaimed. However, it has turned out to be a classic instance of a concept that does not "travel" well. The questions must be adapted to the political system being studied. For example, in some countries citizens are actually members of political parties, so it is more appropriate to ask about party membership, which presumably requires more commitment than does the American concept of identification with a party. Further, scholars in other countries have generally found the concept of limited usefulness, partly because partisanship seems to shift with changes in voting more than in the United States.

Question Formats

There is no single partisanship question format that is used universally outside of the United States. Instead, most of the question forms reviewed in this chapter have been used in some nations. The main exception has to do with measuring independence. That seems to be mainly an American concept, so questions about independence are rarely used elsewhere.

In asking a party identification direction question in other countries, two important decisions involve (1) whether to list the parties and (2) what type of affiliation to ask about. The usual question in the United States lists the parties: "a Republican, a Democrat, ..." That format can be used when the number of parties is small, but it is more awkward to use when the number of parties is large. It would be truly impossible to use that format when there are 12 parties contesting an election. Instead, an open-ended format is typically used in this situation, asking people "which party . . ." without supplying a list of possible answers. That wording tends to obtain lower levels of identification than when the actual parties are listed, since respondents are not being reminded of the party names. Still it is the only practical format in countries with large numbers of political parties.

The other important decision is what type of affiliation to ask about. The U.S. question asks about "identification" when it asks people if they "think of themselves" as Republican, Democrat, and so on. Questions in other countries vary considerably in this respect. Some ask about party membership. Others ask about affiliation, party support, or leaning toward a party. In a real sense there is a cumulative relationship underlying possible wordings, where giving financial support to a party might be the most difficult form, followed by becoming a member of a party, adhering to a party, affiliating with a party, identifying with a party, liking a party, and leaning toward a party, in roughly that order. As would be expected, different results are obtained from different question wordings. Norpoth (1978) reported that less than 30% of the West German public were found to be partisans when asked if they adhere to a party without being given a list of parties versus 80% when they were instead asked if they lean toward a particular party.

A few examples are useful in showing the range of variation in question wording. The Butler and Stokes (1969) study of Britain basically used the American question wording— "Generally speaking, do you usually think of yourself as Conservative, Labour, or Liberal?"—with these follow-ups: (for those with a party affiliation) "How strongly (Conservative/Labour/Liberal) do you generally feel—very strongly, fairly strongly, or not very strongly?" and (for those without a party affiliation) "Do you generally feel a little closer to one of the parties than the others? (If yes,) Which party is that?" Ninety percent of their respondents in a summer 1963 survey had a party affiliation, with half of the remaining respondents feeling closer to one party than the others.

The Van der Eijk and Niemöller (1983) Dutch study asked, "Many people think of themselves as adherents of a certain party, but there are also people who do not. Do you usually think of yourself as an adherent of a certain party? (If yes,) "Of which party? Would you consider yourself a convinced adherent of that party or do you consider yourself not to be a convinced adherent?" (If no,) "Is there any party you feel more attracted to than other parties, or not? Which party is that?" In their January–February 1981 study, they found 21% of the public were convinced adherents, another 16% were nonconvinced adherents, 34% were leaners, and 29% had no identification.

The 1983 Japanese Election Study (JES) (Watanuki, Miyake, Inoguchi, & Kabashima, 1986) asked, "Which of Japan's contemporary political parties do you usually support, apart from this election? And, how strongly do you support that party: enthusiastically or not so enthusiastically?" Those who do not support a party were asked, "Is there some political party that you ordinarily like? If so, which is that?" About 70 percent of their respondents indicated party support, though it was enthusiastic for under a quarter of those party supporters. About 30% of those who do not support a party said that they did ordinarily like a particular party.

The wording used in a 1972 study in West Germany asked, "Many people in the Federal Republic lean toward a particular party for a long time, although they may occasionally vote for a different party. How about you: do you in general lean toward a particular party? If so, which one? (If yes,) How strongly or weakly do you lean toward this party: very strongly, fairly strongly, moderately, fairly weakly, or very weakly?" Roughly 80% of the sample were found to be party identifiers according to this question (Norpoth, 1978).

The other partisanship direction questions have also been used in other countries. The party thermometer question has been used extensively outside of the United States. It is particularly well suited for countries with a large number of parties, as it takes only a few extra seconds to ask about reactions to another party. The one variation to mention here involves the response categories. Some surveys in other countries do use the 100-degree scale, though the thermometer analogy may work differently for countries measuring temperature in Celsius than for those using the Fahrenheit scale. An alternative is to ask people to rate the parties on a 0–10 scale, sometimes termed a *skalometer.* Richardson (1991) used thermometer scores to develop an "index of party difference," which is the difference between the rating of the person's most preferred party and the person's average rating of the remaining parties.

Party image questions are frequently used in other countries, asking people what they like and dislike about each party so that net party evaluations can be computed. Wattenberg (1982) reported on a comparison of such party images for four English-speaking democracies.

The party closeness question was originally developed for use outside of the United States. It is an explicit attempt to adapt the party identification idea to countries where identification might not be the appropriate concept. The usual format is to list the parties when asking to which party the respondent is closest, but the question can be used in a more open-ended format when the number of parties is very large. For example, the 1967–1968–1969 French study of Converse and Pierce (1986) asked, "To which party do you usually feel closest? Would you say that you feel very close to this party, rather close, or not very close?"

Strength of identification is usually determined in the same way as in the United States, with only occasional variations in response categories. As stated above, political independence is rarely measured outside of the United States. Party system support would be a fascinating concept to explore in other countries, but it has received remarkably little attention cross-nationally.

Cross-National Validity

The early research on party identification in other countries (Campbell & Valen, 1961; Converse & Dupeux, 1962) found that the American concept was equally applicable to those settings. Indeed, the Converse and Dupeux (1962) study comparing France and the United States suggested that partisanship operated in similar ways in the different countries. They found that in both countries about 80% of the adults who knew their parents' partisanship themselves identified with a party, whereas only 50% of the adults who did not know their parents' partisanship themselves identified with a party.

Early studies also focused on cross-national differences in partisanship. The Almond and Verba (1963) cross-national study developed a typology of partisanship based on two sets of questions. One set measured intensity of partisanship by asking about attitudes toward interparty marriage ("How would you feel if your son or daughter married a supporter of the _____ party? Would you be pleased, would you be displeased, or would it make no difference?"), while the other measured feelings toward electoral contests ("Do you ever get angry at some of the things that go on in election campaigns? Do you ever find election campaigns pleasant and enjoyable? Do you ever find election campaigns silly or ridiculous?" Response categories were "often," "sometimes," and "never."). Open partisans were defined as those who are indifferent toward interparty marriage, but who are emotionally involved in election campaigns. Apathetic partisans were those who voted for a major party, but who were indifferent about interparty marriage and who did not feel anger, pleasure, or contempt toward campaigns. Intense partisans were both concerned about interparty marriages and emotionally involved in elections. Finally, parochial partisans were concerned about interparty marriage, but were not emotionally involved in elections.

The Almond and Verba five-nation study found the greatest proportion of open partisans in the United States (82% versus 14–61% in the other countries). Italy had the highest proportion of apathetic partisans (30%). Intense partisanship was most common in Germany and Mexico (25% each). Parochial partisanship was mainly an Italian phenomenon (36% of that sample versus at most 13% in any other country), due mainly to religious women. The questions used to develop this typology are unusual, but they certainly demonstrated differences in the role of partisanship across countries.

The search for empirical generalizations with cross-national validity came to an end as researchers began to challenge more strongly the role of partisanship in other countries (see especially Budge, Crewe, & Farlie, 1976). As described earlier, partisanship was discovered to be as variable as the vote decision in panel studies in some countries. Butler and Stokes (1969) first showed that party moved with the vote more in Britain than in the United States, though Cain and Ferejohn (1981) have found great similarity between the two countries when Liberals in Britain and Independents in the United States are excluded. Thomassen's (1976) work on the Netherlands was the most emphatic statement of the instability of partisanship, with half of Dutch identifiers changing parties at least once in a five-month period. The U.S. pattern is for more people to change in their vote direction from one election to the next, while maintaining their partisanship direction, than to change their partisanship direction, while voting for the same party. Thomassen finds the opposite true in the Netherlands, which considerably undermines any claim for long-term status for partisanship in that nation. The usual argument is that left–right ideology is a more important long-term political force in such countries than is partisanship.

More recent work on partisanship in other countries has gone past arguments about the degree of similarity with the United States and has instead taken advantage of the unique aspects of the party systems in other countries. The result has been that some of the most innovative research on partisanship has been conducted outside of the United States. As one example take the idea of multiple partisanship. Most treatments in the United States have assumed that people are Republicans *or* Democrats *or* Independents, but not more than one of the above (cf. Weisberg, 1980). By contrast, in their exploration of the dozen-party Dutch system, Van der Eijk and Niemöller (1983) permitted people to indicate identification with more than one party. After being asked if they think of themselves as adherents to a party, respondents in a 1981 survey were asked, "Are there any other parties to which you feel attracted? Which party (or parties)?" to determine if multiple identifications occur. Indeed, multiple identification was found, with half of the respondents having multiple identifications. Some of the distinctions between the political parties in the Netherlands are relatively minor, so such multiple identification should not be surprising. Thus many identifiers with one Calvinist party also identify with another Calvinist party. There is enough variation in party systems around the world to expect many variations like this in particular countries.

The idea of negative partisanship has also been analyzed more in other countries than in the United States (cf. Maggiotto & Piereson, 1977). Crewe (1976), in particular, has examined responses to a question asking Britons if there is a political party that they do not like. Crewe used the answers to distinguish "polarized partisans," who are very strongly for their party and against the other party, from other types of partisans.

The possibility of different party identifications at different levels of government has also been examined extensively in some countries. The Canadian system is especially interesting in this regard, since the parties at the federal level are not the same parties that are important in some provinces and vice versa. For example, the New Democratic Party and the Social Credits are much more important than the Liberals and Conservatives in British Columbia. The Parti Québécois is similarly more important in Quebec than are the

Conservatives. Different party loyalties at the different levels of Canadian government have been termed "split identification" and "dual loyalty" (Blake, 1982), "inconsistent partisanship" (Clarke et al., 1979), and "split-level identification" (Uslaner, 1990). The 1974 Canadian federal election study found 18% of party identifiers having split loyalties, with a high of 35% in British Columbia. Stewart and Clarke (1998) also find that provincial party identification has an effect on federal party identification in Canada, showing that party performance evaluations occur at both national and provincial levels.

The greater variety of political parties outside of the United States leads to the possibility of different forms of identification with different types of parties. Richardson (1991) has explored this possibility, contrasting traditional cleavage-based parties that evoke interparty hostilities based on a century of conflict with newer noncleavage parties. He found greater vote stability in panel studies of the Netherlands, Germany, and Britain for followers of the cleavage-based parties. His index of party distance was greater for supporters of cleavage parties in Britain and moderately so for the Netherlands, but polarization was weak for Germany.

Finally, the concept of multidimensional partisanship may be particularly useful for studying multiple-party systems. Thus, Miyake (1991) finds that a multidimensional perspective is useful in understanding partisanship in Japan. Using Hayashi quantification scaling of several partisanship variables, two dimensions are found. A cognitive dimension distinguishes between people with feelings toward the parties and people without partisan feelings, while an affective dimension contrasts strong identifiers and independents. Miyake used these dimensions to describe four types of partisanship: (1) loyal partisans (high on both dimensions, with awareness of parties and positive affect toward their own parties), (2) negative partisans (high cognitive awareness of parties, but lacking positive affective ties with their own parties), (3) nonpartisans (low on both dimensions), and (4) uninformed partisans (positive affect toward their own parties, but having little knowledge about politics). This is somewhat similar to Granberg and Holmberg's (1988, pp. 185–189) distinction among partisans as identifiers who are interested in politics; independents who are highly interested in politics, but who do not identify with a party; apathetics who lack partisanship and interest; and habituals who identify with a party, while lacking political interest. Tanaka and Weisberg (1996) used factor analysis of thermometers to show that independence is a separate dimension from partisan dimensions in Japan.

All in all the concept of partisanship is likely to remain controversial outside of the United States. The early cross-national work was too closely tied to American research, not sufficiently taking into account the pertinent details of the party systems being studied. The result was often a demonstration that the American approach did not work in other countries and so should be totally dismissed. Gradually more sophisticated moderate positions are being developed, as researchers find that some variant of the American concept has utility for studying other political systems, though party identification may never have the primary importance in those countries that it does in the United States.

Future Directions

The vigor of the debate over the theoretical underpinnings, stability, and measurement of partisanship is likely to continue undiminished. The explosion of research on this topic in the early 1990s shows little sign of abatement. The concept is so central to our modern understanding of voting behavior that the topic will continue to receive considerable attention. At the same time the terrain of the debate is likely to shift.

For one thing the original theoretical justification of the Party Identification scale was the social psychology of the 1940s and 1950s. The social psychology field has developed considerably since then, and that is bound to lead to new understandings of partisanship based on the newest political psychology perspectives. In particular, a reinterpretation of partisanship that is more in line with modern cognitive perspectives is likely, using such perspectives as information theory and social identity theory.

The impact of social psychology should be particularly great in measuring the strength of partisanship. Current measures of strength are fairly naïve. New questions are necessary that better measure the strength, salience, and centrality of partisanship. New measures of independence may not be necessary, but independence should routinely be measured separately from strength of partisanship rather than confounding the two concepts, as in the traditional party identification question series.

Furthermore, a more complete understanding of the dynamics of partisanship is likely. One of the most dramatic developments in the literature in the past 20 years has involved challenging the traditional view of partisanship as stable and tracing the determinants of the changes. There have been important arguments to the contrary, which will spur further debate. At the same time the availability of more extensive data sets and data over longer time frames should permit more extensive mapping of changes in partisanship.

Barring the unanticipated emergence of a new major party, there is no reason to expect that the traditional Party Identification scale will lose its preeminent status in research in the United States, though there is equally little reason to expect that this scale will achieve that status in other nations. However, the use of multiple partisanship questions is likely to become more common in order to measure different aspects of partisanship as well as to continue methodological explorations.

To summarize, the traditional party identification question series may suffice as a measure of long-term partisan direction. However, more work is required on measuring the strength of partisanship. Also, political independence should be gauged separately from the Party Identification scale. Our theoretical understanding of partisanship should be modernized, and this probably requires adding further partisanship questions to surveys. Also, longitudinal study designs should be employed that allow better testing of the stability of party ties. All in all, partisanship will probably remain the central concept of the voting behavior field, but our understanding of that concept should become richer.

References

Abelson, R. P., & Tukey, J. W. (1970). Efficient conversion of non-metric information into metric information. In E. R. Tufte (Ed.), *The quantitative analysis of social problems* (pp. 407–417). Reading, MA: Addison-Wesley.

Abramowitz, A. I., Cover, A. D., & Norpoth, H. (1986). The president's party in midterm elections. *American Journal of Political Science, 30,* 562–576.

Abramson, P. R. (1975). *Generational change in American politics.* Lexington, MA: Lexington Books, D. C. Heath.

Abramson, P. R. (1976). Generational change and the decline of party identification. *American Political Science Review, 70,* 469–478.

Abramson, P. R. (1979). Developing party identification. *American Journal of Political Science, 23,* 78–96.

Abramson, P. R., Aldrich, J. H., & Rohde, D. W. (1995). *Change and continuity in the 1992 elections* (rev. ed). Washington, DC: Congressional Quarterly Press.

Abramson, P. R., & Ostrom, C. W. (1991). Macropartisanship: An empirical reassessment. *American Political Science Review, 85,* 181–192.

Abramson, P. R., & Ostrom, C. W. (1992). Response. *American Political Science Review, 86,* 481–486.

Abramson, P. R., & Ostrom, C. W. (1994a). Question wording and partisanship. *Public Opinion Quarterly, 58,* 21–48.

Abramson, P. R., & Ostrom, C. W. (1994b). Response. *American Political Science Review, 88,* 955–958.

Achen, C. H. (1975). Mass political attitudes and the survey response. *American Political Science Review, 69,* 1218–1231.

Achen, C. H. (1979). The bias in normal vote estimates. *Political Methodology, 6,* 343–356.

Achen, C. H. (1989). *Prospective voting and the theory of party identification.* Paper presented at the annual meeting of the American Political Science Association, Atlanta.

Achen, C. H. (1992). Social psychology, demographic variables, and linear regression: Breaking the iron triangle in voting research. *Political Behavior, 14,* 195–211.

Agger, R. E. (1959). Independents and party identifiers: Characteristics and behavior in 1952. In E. Burdick & A. J. Brodbeck (Eds.), *American voting behavior.* New York: Free Press.

Allsop, D. (1988). *The dynamic nature of party identification during an election campaign.* Unpublished doctoral dissertation, Ohio State University.

Allsop, D., & Weisberg, H. F. (1988). Measuring change in party identification in an election campaign. *American Journal of Political Science, 32,* 996–1017.

Almond, G. A., & Verba, S. (1963). *The civic culture.* Princeton, NJ: Princeton University Press.

Alvarez, M. (1990). The puzzle of party identification. *American Politics Quarterly, 18,* 476–491.

Asher, H. B. (1974). Some consequences of measurement error in survey data. *American Journal of Political Science, 18,* 469–485.

Asher, H. B. (1988). *Presidential elections and American politics* (4th ed.). Chicago: Dorsey.

Barnes, S., Jennings, M. K., Inglehart, R., & Farah, B. (1988). Party identification and party closeness in comparative perspective. *Political Behavior, 10,* 215–231.

Bassilli, J. N. (1995). On the psychological reality of party identification. *Political Behavior, 17,* 339–358.

Bastedo, R., & Lodge, M. (1980). The meaning of party labels. *Political Behavior, 2,* 287–308.

Baumer, D. C., & Gold, H. J. (1995). Party images and the American electorate. *American Politics Quarterly, 23,* 33–61.

Beck, P. A. (1979). The electoral cycle and patterns of American politics. *British Journal of Political Science, 9,* 129–156.

Beck, P. A. (1986). Choice, context, and consequence: Beaten and unbeaten paths toward a science of electoral behavior. In H. F. Weisberg (Ed.), *Political science: The science of politics* (pp. 241–283). New York: Agathon Press.

Belknap, G., & Campbell, A. (1952). Political party identification and attitudes toward foreign policy. *Public Opinion Quarterly, 15,* 601–623.

Bishop, G. F., Tuchfarber, A. J., & Smith, A. E. (1994). Question form and context effects in the measurement of partisanship: Experimental tests of the artifact hypothesis. *American Political Science Review, 88,* 945–954.

Blake, D. E. (1982). The consistency of inconsistency: Party identification in federal and provincial politics. *Canadian Journal of Political Science, 15,* 691–710.

Blalock, H. M. (1970). Estimating measurement error using multiple indicators and several points in time. *American Sociological Review, 35,* 101–111.

Borrelli, S., Lockerbie, B., & Niemi, R. G. (1987). Why the Democrat–Republican partisanship gap varies from poll to poll. *Public Opinion Quarterly, 51,* 115–119.

Box-Steffensmeier, J. M., & Smith, R. M. (1996). The dynamics of aggregate partisanship. *American Political Science Review, 90,* 567–580.

Brody, R. A. (1991). Stability and change in party identification: Presidential to off-years. In P. M. Sniderman, R. A. Brody, & P. E. Tetlock (Eds.), *Reasoning and choice: Explorations in political psychology* (pp. 179–205). Cambridge: Cambridge University Press.

Brody, R. A., Brady, D. W., & Heitshusen, V. (1994). Accounting for divided government. In M. K. Jennings & T. E. Mann (Eds.), *Elections at home and abroad* (pp. 157–177). Ann Arbor: University of Michigan Press.

Brody, R. A., & Rothenberg, L. (1988). The instability of partisanship: An analysis of the 1980 presidential election. *British Journal of Political Science, 18,* 445–465.

Brown, T. A. (1981). On contextual change and partisan attributes. *British Journal of Political Science, 18,* 445–465.

Budge, I., Crewe, I., & Farlie, D. (Eds.). (1976). *Party identification and beyond.* London: Wiley.

Butler, D., & Stokes, D. E. (1969). *Political change in Britain.* New York: St. Martin's.

Cain, B. E., & Ferejohn, J. (1981). A comparison of party identification in the United States and Great Britain. *Comparative Political Studies, 14,* 31–47.

Campbell, A., Converse, P. E., Miller, W. E., & Stokes, D. E. (1960). *The American voter.* New York: Wiley.

Campbell, A., Converse, P. E., Miller, W. E., & Stokes, D. E. (1966). *Elections and the political order.* New York: Wiley.

Campbell, A., Gurin, G., & Miller, W. E. (1954). *The voter decides.* Evanston, IL: Row, Peterson.

Campbell, A., & Valen, H. (1961). Party identification in Norway and the United States. *Public Opinion Quarterly, 25,* 505–525.

Campbell, J. (1984). *The intervals of party identification: Rescaling the partisan categories.* Paper presented at the annual meeting of the American Political Science Association, Washington, DC.

Carmines, E. G., & Stanley, H. W. (1992). The transformation of the New Deal party system: Social groups, political ideology, and changing partisanship among northern whites, 1972–1988. *Political Behavior, 14,* 213–237.

Claggett, W. (1981). Partisan acquisition versus partisan intensity: Life-cycle, generation, and period effects, 1952–1976. *American Journal of Political Science, 25,* 193–214.

Clarke, H. D., Jenson, J., LeDuc, L., & Pammett, J. H. (1979). *Political choice in Canada.* Toronto: McGraw-Hill Ryerson.

Clarke, H. D., & Suzuki, M. (1993). Partisan dealignment and the dynamics of independence in the American electorate, 1953–88. *British Journal of Political Science, 24,* 57–77.

Converse, P. E. (1964). The nature of belief systems in mass publics. In D. E. Apter (Ed.), *Ideology and discontent* (pp. 206–261). New York: Free Press.

Converse, P. E. (1966). The concept of the normal vote. In A. Campbell, P. E. Converse, W. E. Miller, and D. E. Stokes, *Elections and the political order* (pp. 9–39). New York: Wiley.

Converse, P. E. (1969). Of time and partisan stability. *Comparative Political Studies, 2,* 139–171.

Converse, P. E. (1970). Attitudes and non-attitudes: Continuation of a dialogue. In E. R. Tufte (Ed.), *The quantitative analysis of social problems* (pp. 168–189). Reading, MA: Addison-Wesley.

Converse, P. E. (1976). *The dynamics of party support.* Beverly Hills, CA: Sage.

Converse, P. E. (1979). Reply to Abramson. *American Journal of Political Science, 23,* 97–100.

Converse, P. E., & Dupeux, G. (1962). Politicization of the electorate in France and the United States. *Public Opinion Quarterly, 26,* 1–23.

Converse, P. E., & Markus, G. B. (1979). Plus ça change . . . : The new CPS Election Study Panel. *American Political Science Review, 73,* 2–49.

Converse, P. E., Miller, W. E., Rusk, J. G., & Wolfe, A. C. (1969). Continuity and change in American politics: Parties and issues in the 1968 election. *American Political Science Review, 63,* 1083–1105.

Converse, P. E., & Pierce, R. (1985). Measuring partisanship. *Political Methodology, 11,* 143–166.

Converse, P. E., & Pierce, R. (1986). *Political representation in France.* Cambridge, MA: Belknap/ Harvard University Press.

Converse, P. E., & Pierce, R. (1992). Partisanship and the party system. *Political Behavior, 14,* 239–259.

Coombs, C. H. (1964). *A theory of data.* New York: Wiley.

Cox, G., & Kernell, S. (Eds.). (1991). *The causes and consequences of divided government in America.* Boulder, CO: Westview.

Craig, S. C. (1985). Partisanship, independence, and no preference: Another look at the measurement of party identification. *American Journal of Political Science, 29,* 274–290.

Crewe, I. (1976). Party identification theory and political change in Britain. In I. Budge, I. Crewe, & D. Farlie (Eds.), *Party identification and beyond* (pp. 33–61). London: Wiley.

Dean, G., & Moran, T. (1977). Measuring mass political attitudes: Change and unreliability. *Political Methodology, 4*, 383–413.

Dennis, J. (1966). Support for the party system by the mass public. *American Political Science Review, 60*, 600–615.

Dennis, J. (1975). Trends in public support for the American party system. *British Journal of Political Science, 5*, 187–230.

Dennis, J. (1981). *Some properties of measures of partisanship.* Paper presented at the annual meeting of the American Political Science Association, New York.

Dennis, J. (1982). *New measures of partisanship in models of voting.* Paper presented at the annual meeting of the Midwest Political Science Association, Milwaukee.

Dennis, J. (1986). *Public support for the party system, 1964–1984.* Paper presented at the annual meeting of the American Political Science Association, Washington, DC.

Dennis, J. (1988a). Political independence in America, Part I: On being an independent partisan supporter. *British Journal of Political Science, 18*, 77–109.

Dennis, J. (1988b). Political independence in America, Part II: Towards a theory. *British Journal of Political Science, 18*, 197–219.

Dennis, J. (1992). Political independence in America, Part III: In search of closet partisans. *Political Behavior, 14*, 261–296.

DeVries, W., & Tarrance, V. L. (1972). *The ticket-splitter.* Grand Rapids, MI: Eerdmans.

Dobson, D., & Meeter, D. (1974). Alternative Markov models for describing change in party identification. *American Journal of Political Science, 18*, 487–500.

Downs, A. (1957). *An economic theory of democracy.* New York: Harper and Row.

Dreyer, E. C. (1973). Change and stability in party identification. *Journal of Politics, 35*, 712–722.

Eldersveld, S. (1952). The independent vote: Measurement, characteristics, and implications for party strategy. *American Political Science Review, 46*, 732–753.

Erikson, R. S., MacKuen, M. B., & Stimson, J. A. (1996). *Party identification and macropartisanship: Resolving the paradox of micro-level stability and macro-level dynamics.* Paper presented at the annual meeting of the American Political Science Association, San Francisco.

Eulau, H. (1994). Electoral survey data and the temporal dimension. In M. K. Jennings & T. E. Mann (Eds.), *Elections at home and abroad* (pp. 39–70). Ann Arbor: University of Michigan Press.

Feldman, S., & Zuckerman, A. S. (1982). Partisan attitudes and the vote. *Comparative Political Studies, 15*, 197–222.

Finkel, S. E., & Scarrow, H. A. (1984). *Party identification and party enrollment: The difference and the consequence.* Paper presented at the annual meeting of the American Political Science Association, Washington, DC.

Fiorina, M. P. (1977). An outline for a model of party choice. *American Journal of Political Science, 21*, 601–626.

Fiorina, M. P. (1981). *Retrospective voting in American national elections.* New Haven, CT: Yale University Press.

Fiorina, M. P. (1991). An era of divided government. In B. Cain & G. Peele (Eds.), *Developments in American politics.* London: Macmillan.

Flanigan, W. H., Rahn, W. M., & Zingale, N. H. (1989). *Political parties as objects of identification and orientation.* Paper presented at the annual meeting of the Western Political Science Association, Salt Lake City, Utah.

Flanigan, W. H., & Zingale, N. H. (1994). *Political behavior of the American electorate* (8th ed.). Washington, DC: Congressional Quarterly Press.

Franklin, C. H. (1984). Issue preferences, socialization, and the evolution of party identification. *American Journal of Political Science, 28*, 459–478.

Franklin, C. H. (1992). Measurement and the dynamics of party identification. *Political Behavior, 14*, 297–309.

Franklin, C. H., & Jackson, J. E. (1983). The dynamics of party identification. *American Political Science Review, 77*, 957–973.

Granberg, D., & Holmberg, S. (1988). *The political system matters.* Cambridge: Cambridge University Press.

Green, D. P. (1988). On the dimensionality of public sentiment toward partisan and ideological groups. *American Journal of Political Science, 32,* 758–780.

Green, D. P. (1991). The effects of measurement error on two-stage least-squares estimates. *Political Analysis, 1990, 2,* 57–74.

Green, D. P., & Palmquist, B. (1990). Of artifacts and partisan instability. *American Journal of Political Science, 34,* 872–902.

Green, D. P., & Palmquist, B. (1994). How stable is party identification? *Political Behavior, 16,* 437–466.

Green, D. P., Palmquist, B., & Schickler, E. (1996). *Macropartisanship: A replication and a critique.* Paper presented at the annual meeting of the American Political Science Association, San Francisco.

Green, D. P., & Schickler, E. (1993). Multiple-measure assessment of party identification. *Public Opinion Quarterly, 57,* 503–535.

Hadley, C. D. (1985). Dual partisan identification in the South. *Journal of Politics, 47,* 254–268.

Heath, A., & Pierce, R. E. (1992). It was party identification all along: Question order effects on reports of party identification in Britain. *Electoral Studies, 11,* 93–105.

Heise, D. R. (1971). Separating reliability and stability in test–retest correlation. In H. M. Blalock (Ed.), *Causal models in the social sciences* (pp. 348–363). Chicago: Aldine.

Holmberg, S. (1994). Party identification compared across the Atlantic. In M. K. Jennings & T. E. Mann (Eds.), *Elections at home and abroad* (pp. 93–121). Ann Arbor: University of Michigan Press.

Howell, S. E. (1980). The behavioral component of changing partisanship. *American Politics Quarterly, 8,* 279–302.

Howell, S. E. (1981). Short term forces and changing partisanship. *Political Behavior, 3,* 163–180.

Jackson, J. E. (1975). Issues, party choice, and presidential votes. *American Journal of Political Science, 19,* 161–185.

Jacoby, W. G. (1982). Unfolding the party identification scale. *Political Methodology, 9,* 33–59.

Jennings, M. K., & Markus, G. B. (1984). Partisan orientations over the long haul: Results from the three-wave Political Socialization Panel Study. *American Political Science Review, 78,* 1000–1018.

Jennings, M. K., & Niemi, R. G. (1966). Party identification at multiple levels of government. *American Journal of Sociology, 72,* 86–101.

Johnston, R. (1992a). Party identification and campaign dynamics. *Political Behavior, 14,* 311–331.

Johnston, R. (1992b). Party identification measures in the Anglo-American democracies: A national survey experiment. *American Journal of Political Science, 36,* 542–559.

Kamieniecki, S. (1985). *Party identification, political behavior, and the American electorate.* Westport, CT: Greenwood Press.

Kamieniecki, S. (1988). The dimensionality of partisan strength and political independence. *Political Behavior, 10,* 364–376.

Katz, R. S. (1979). The dimensionality of party identification: Cross-national perspectives. *Comparative Politics, 11,* 147–163.

Keith, B. E., Magleby, D. B., Nelson, C. J., Orr, E., Westlye, M. C., & Wolfinger, R. E. (1977). *The myth of the independent voter.* Paper presented at the annual meeting of the American Political Science Association, Washington, DC.

Keith, B. E., Magleby, D. B., Nelson, C. J., Orr, E., Westlye, M. C., & Wolfinger, R. E. (1986). The partisan affinities of independent "Leaners." *British Journal of Political Science, 16,* 155–185.

Keith, B. E., Magleby, D. B., Nelson, C. J., Orr, E., Westlye, M. C., & Wolfinger, R. E. (1992). *The myth of the independent voter.* Berkeley: University of California Press.

Kenney, P., & Rice, T. (1988). The evaporating independents. *Public Opinion Quarterly, 52,* 231–239.

Kessel, J. H. (1984). *Presidential parties.* Homewood, IL: Dorsey.

Key, V. O., Jr. (1960). *Public opinion and American democracy.* New York: Alfred Knopf.

Key, V. O., Jr. (1966). *The responsible electorate.* New York: Vintage Books.

Krosnick, J. A. (1991). The stability of political preferences: Comparisons of symbolic and nonsymbolic attitudes. *American Journal of Political Science, 35,* 547–576.

Krosnick, J. A., & Berent, M. K. (1993). Comparisons of party identification and policy preferences: The impact of survey question format. *American Journal of Political Science, 37,* 941–964.

Krosnick, J. A., & Weisberg, H. F. (1988). *Ideological structuring of public attitudes toward social groups and politicians.* Paper presented at the annual meeting of the American Political Science Association, Washington, DC.

Ladd, E. C., Jr., & Hadley, C. D. (1973). Party definition and party differentiation. *Public Opinion Quarterly, 37,* 21–34.

LeDuc, L. (1981). The dynamic properties of party identification. *European Journal of Political Research, 9,* 257–268.

Lodge, M., & Tursky, B. (1979). Comparisons between category and magnitude scaling of political opinion employing SRC/CPS items. *American Political Science Review, 73,* 50–66.

MacKuen, M. B., Erikson, R. S., & Stimson, J. A. (1989). Macropartisanship. *American Political Science Review, 83,* 1125–1142.

MacKuen, M. B., Erikson, R. S., & Stimson, J. A. (1992). Question wording and macropartisanship. *American Political Science Review, 85,* 475–481.

Maggiotto, M. A., & Piereson, J. E. (1977). Partisan identification and electoral choice: The hostility hypothesis. *American Journal of Political Science, 21,* 745–767.

Maggiotto, M. A., & Wekkin, G. D. (1992). *Federalism and party identification.* Paper presented at the annual meeting of the Southern Political Science Association, Atlanta.

Marchant-Shapiro, T., & Patterson, K. D. (1995). Partisan change in the mountain west. *Political Behavior, 17,* 359–378.

Marks, G. N. (1993). Partisanship and the vote in Australia. *Political Behavior, 15,* 137–166.

Markus, G. B. (1979). *Analyzing panel data.* Beverly Hills, CA: Sage.

Markus, G. B. (1982). Political attitudes during an election year: A report on the 1980 NES Panel Study. *American Political Science Review, 76,* 538–560.

Markus, G. B. (1983). Dynamic modeling of cohort change: The case of political partisanship. *American Journal of Political Science, 27,* 717–739.

Markus, G. B., & Converse, P. E. (1979). A dynamic simultaneous equation model of electoral choice. *American Political Science Review, 73,* 1055–1070.

Martinez, M. D. (1990). Partisan reinforcement in context and cognition: Canadian federal partisanships, 1974–79. *American Journal of Political Science, 34,* 822–845.

Martinez, M. D., & Gant, M. M. (1990). Partisan issue preferences and partisan change. *Political Behavior, 12,* 243–264.

Matthews, D. R., & Prothro, J. W. (1966). *Negroes and the new southern politics.* New York: Harcourt, Brace and World.

McAllister, I., & Wattenberg, M. P. (1995). Measuring levels of party identification: Does question order matter? *Public Opinion Quarterly, 59,* 259–268.

McDonald, M., & Howell, S. E. (1982). Reconsidering the reconceptualizations of party identification. *Political Methodology, 9,* 73–92.

Miller, A. H., & Miller, W. E. (1977). *Partisanship and performance: "Rational" choice in the 1976 presidential election.* Paper presented at the annual meeting of the American Political Science Association, Washington, DC.

Miller, A. H., & Wattenberg, M. P. (1983). Measuring party identification: Independence or no preference? *American Journal of Political Science, 27,* 106–121.

Miller, W. E. (1976). The cross-national use of party identification as a stimulus to political inquiry. In I. Budge, I. Crewe, & D. Farlie (Eds.), *Party identification and beyond* (pp. 21–31). New York: Wiley.

Miller, W. E. (1987). A new context for presidential politics: The Reagan legacy. *Political Behavior, 9,* 91–113.

Miller, W. E. (1990). The electorate's view of the parties. In S. Maisel (Ed.), *The parties respond* (pp. 97–115). Boulder, CO: Westview.

Miller, W. E. (1991). Party identification, realignment, and party voting: Back to basics. *American Political Science Review, 85,* 557–568.

Miller, W. E. (1992). Generational changes and party identification. *Political Behavior, 14,* 333–352.

Miller, W. E., & Shanks, J. M. (1982). Policy directions and presidential leadership: Alternative interpretations of the 1980 presidential election. *British Journal of Political Science, 12,* 299–356.

Miller, W. E., & Shanks, J. M. (1989). *Alternative interpretations of the 1988 election.* Paper presented at the annual meeting of the American Political Science Association, Atlanta.

Miller, W. E., & Shanks, J. M. (1996). *The new American voter.* Cambridge: Harvard University Press.

Miyake, I. (1991). Types of partisanship, political attitudes, and voting choices. In S. Flanagan, S. Kohei, I. Miyake, B. M. Richardson, & J. Watanuki, *The Japanese voter* (pp. 226–264). New Haven, CT: Yale University Press.

Nie, N. H., Verba, S., & Petrocik, J. R. (1979). *The changing American voter* (enlarged edition). Cambridge: Harvard University Press.

Niemi, R. G., & Jennings, M. K. (1991). Issues and inheritance in the formation of party identification. *American Journal of Political Science, 35,* 970–988.

Niemi, R. G., Reed, D., & Weisberg, H. F. (1991). Partisan commitment. *Political Behavior, 13,* 213–220.

Niemi, R. G., & Weisberg, H. F. (1992). *Controversies in voting behavior* (3rd ed.). Washington, DC: Congressional Quarterly Press.

Niemi, R. G., Wright, S., & Powell, L. (1987). Multiple party identifiers and the measurement of party identification. *Journal of Politics, 49,* 1093–1103.

Norpoth, H. (1978). Party identification in West Germany: Tracing an elusive concept. *Comparative Political Studies, 11,* 36–59.

Norrander, B. (1989). Explaining cross-state variation in independent identification. *American Journal of Political Science, 33,* 516–536.

Page, B. I., & Jones, C. C. (1979). Reciprocal effects of policy preferences, party loyalties and the vote. *American Political Science Review, 73,* 1071–1089.

Perkins, J., & Guynes, R. (1976). Partisanship in national and state politics. *Public Opinion Quarterly, 40,* 376–378.

Petrocik, J. R. (1974). An analysis of the intransitivities in the index of party identification. *Political Methodology, 1,* 31–47.

Petrocik, J. R. (1989). An expected party vote. *American Journal of Political Science, 33,* 44–66.

Popkin, S. L. (1991). *The reasoning voter.* Chicago: University of Chicago Press.

Rapoport, R. B. (1997). Partisanship change in a candidate-centered era. *Journal of Politics, 59,* 185–199.

Richardson, B. M. (1991). European party loyalties revisited. *American Political Science Review, 85,* 751–775.

Särlvik, B., & Crewe, I. (1983). *Decade of dealignment.* Cambridge: Cambridge University Press.

Schickler, E., & Green, D. (1996). Issues and the dynamics of party identification. *Political Analysis, 5,* 151–181.

Shanks, J. M., & Miller, W. E. (1990). Policy direction and performance evaluation: Complementary explanations of the Reagan elections. *British Journal of Political Science, 20,* 143–235.

Shanks, J. M., & Miller, W. E. (1991). Partisanship, policy and performance: The Reagan legacy in the 1988 election. *British Journal of Political Science, 21,* 129–197.

Shively, W. P. (1977). *Information costs and the partisan life cycle.* Paper presented at the annual meeting of the American Political Science Association, Washington, DC.

Shively, W. P. (1979). The development of party identification among adults: Explanation of a functional model. *American Political Science Review, 73,* 1039–1054.

Shively, W. P. (1980). The nature of party identification: A review of recent developments. In J. C. Pierce & J. L. Sullivan (Eds.), *The electorate reconsidered* (pp. 219–236). Beverly Hills, CA: Sage.

Smith, C. E. (1993). *An information-processing theory of party identification.* Unpublished doctoral dissertation, Ohio State University.

Smith, C. E., Harding, D. R., Jr., & Crone, M. (1990). *Estimating the separate effects of party iden-*
tification and short-term partisan forces on the vote. Paper presented at the annual meeting of
the Southern Political Science Association, Tampa, FL.

Stanga, J. E., & Sheffield, J. F. (1987). The myth of zero partisanship: Attitudes toward American
political parties, 1964–1984. *American Journal of Political Science, 31,* 829–855.

Stewart M. C., & Clarke, M. D. (1998). The dynamics of party identification in federal systems: The
Canadian case. *American Journal of Political Science, 42,* 97–116.

Sullivan, J. L., & Feldman, S. (1979). *Multiple indicators.* Beverly Hills, CA: Sage.

Tanaka, A., & Weisberg, H. F. (1996). *Political independence in Japan in the 1990s: Multidimen-*
sional party identification during a dealignment. Paper presented at the annual meeting of the
American Political Science Association, San Francisco.

Thomassen, J. (1976). Party identification as a cross-national concept: Its meaning in the Netherlands. In I. Budge, I. Crewe, & D. Farlie (Eds.), *Party identification and beyond* (pp. 63–80).
New York: Wiley.

Trilling, R. J. (1976). *Party image and electoral behavior.* New York: Wiley.

Uslaner, E. M. (1990). Splitting image: Partisan affiliations in Canada's "two political worlds."
American Journal of Political Science, 34, 961–981.

Valentine, D. C., & Van Wingen, J. R. (1980). Partisanship, independence, and the partisan identification question. *American Politics Quarterly, 8,* 168–186.

Van der Eijk, C., & Niemöller, B. (1983). *Electoral change in the Netherlands.* Amsterdam: CT
Press.

Watanuki, J., Miyake, I., Inoguchi, T., & Kabashima, I. (1986). *Electoral behavior in the 1983 Japa-*
nese elections. Tokyo: Institute of International Relations, Sophia University.

Wattenberg, M. P. (1981). The decline of political partisanship in the United States: Negativity or
neutrality? *American Political Science Review, 75,* 941–950.

Wattenberg, M. P. (1982). Party identification and party image. *Comparative Politics, 14,* 23–40.

Wattenberg, M. P. (1994). *The decline of American political parties.* Cambridge: Harvard University
Press.

Weisberg, H. F. (1980). A multidimensional conceptualization of party identification. *Political Be-*
havior, 2, 33–60.

Weisberg, H. F. (1982). *Party evaluations: A theory of separate effects.* Paper presented at the annual meeting of the Midwest Political Science Association, Milwaukee.

Weisberg, H. F. (1983). A new scale of partisanship. *Political Behavior, 5,* 363–376.

Weisberg, H. F. (1994). *Of political time and electoral change: Plus ça change, plus ça change.* Paper presented at the annual meeting of the American Political Science Association, New York.

Weisberg, H. F., & Allsop, D. (1990). *Sources of short-term change in party identification.* Paper
presented at the annual meeting of the Midwest Political Science Association, Chicago.

Weisberg, H. F., & Kimball, D. C. (1995). Attitudinal correlates of the 1992 presidential vote: Party
identification and beyond. In H. F. Weisberg (Ed.), *Democracy's feast* (pp. 72–111). Chatham,
NJ: Chatham House.

Weisberg, H. F., & Mockabee, S. T. (1997). *Attitudinal correlates of the 1996 presidential vote: The*
people reelect a president. Paper presented at the annual meeting of the American Political Science Association, Washington, DC.

Weisberg, H. F., & Smith, C. E. (1991). The influence of the economy on party identification in the
Reagan years. *Journal of Politics, 53,* 1077–1092.

Wekkin, G. D. (1991). Why crossover voters are not "mischievous voters." *American Politics Quar-*
terly, 19, 229–247.

Whiteley, P. (1988). The causal relationships between issues, candidate evaluations, party identification, and vote choice—The view from "Rolling Thunder." *Journal of Politics, 50,* 961–984.

Wiley, D. E., & Wiley, J. A. (1970). The estimation of measurement error in panel data. *American*
Sociological Review, 35, 112–117.

Wright, G., Erikson, R., & McIver, J. (1985). Measuring state partisanship and ideology with survey
data. *Journal of Politics, 47,* 469–489.

CHAPTER 13

Political Participation

Henry E. Brady

Political participation is surely one of the central concepts in the study of mass politics. Through political participation people can voice their needs, concerns, and problems to their government. Free and autonomous participation establishes the democratic character of a regime, while staged mobilization of citizens marks authoritarian societies. Through the ebbs and flows of voting turnout, political protest, or revolutionary action, the fates of governments are determined. Seeking to define political participation, then, provides crucial indicators of the health and functioning of political systems.

Almost all definitions of political participation include four basic concepts: *activities or actions, ordinary citizens, politics,* and *influence.* Nagel's (1987, p. 1) definition is typical: "Participation refers to actions through which ordinary members of a political system influence or attempt to influence outcomes." Kaase and Marsh (1979, p. 42) offer a similar formulation, in which political participation includes "all voluntary activities by individual citizens intended to influence either directly or indirectly political choices at various levels of the political system." Parry, Moyser, and Day (1992, p. 16) join the chorus by proposing that political participation includes "action by citizens which is aimed at influencing decisions which are, in most cases, ultimately taken by public representatives and officials." These more recent definitions are virtually the same as Verba and Nie's (1972, p. 2) classic formulation, in which "[p]olitical participation refers to those activities by private citizens that are more or less directly aimed at influencing the selection of governmental personnel and/or the actions they take."

Political participation, then, requires *action* by *ordinary citizens* directed toward *influencing* some *political outcomes.* All four elements—actions, citizens, influence, and political outcomes—are necessary for political participation.

The first element, an *action,* is something that a person does. It is not just thoughts or tendencies. Measures of political engagement, such as political interest, political efficacy, political information, strength of partisanship, and intense concern about a political issue, only gauge the motivations or dispositions inclining people to become involved in politics; they do not tell us whether someone undertakes political activity. Similarly, approving of a political activity or being willing to do it is not the same as actually doing it. Political engagement and willingness to do an activity may be highly correlated with political activity, but they are not measures of political activity.

The second aspect is an emphasis on actions by *ordinary citizens.* Actions by political elites, such as a senator voting in Congress, a bureaucrat writing a memorandum, a political candidate giving a speech, or a paid lobbyist making a contact, are not mass political participation. Political participation refers to actions by non-elites.

Another element of the definition, *politics,* is, according to a classic definition, the authoritative allocation of values by the government. *Political* participation, therefore, does not include the many daily actions citizens undertake at home, at work, at church, or in other organizations that are not attempts to affect governmental actions—even though these actions may indirectly shape politics because of the public policy problems they create or solve. Joining a church, being laid off from a job, recycling garbage, divorcing a spouse, engaging in a work strike, and joining the homeowners' association are all nonpolitical actions. They may be important determinants of political activity, but they do not become political activity itself until they directly attempt to affect governmental action. Political participation, then, must be directed at some government policy or activity.

These examples demonstrate that actions must have some political content before they can qualify as political participation. Yet even more than this is required. Political participation involves a final element—an attempt to *influence* outcomes. This excludes actions such as getting information about politics by reading a newspaper or watching a television program; being contacted by a person, party, or organization soliciting involvement in some political activity; and going to a governmental office to pick up a welfare check. These activities border political activity, but they are not in and of themselves attempts to influence politics.[1] The person watching political discussions on television may be engaging in an action with political content, but watching, listening, or reading does not constitute an attempt to influence politics. Similarly a person asked to participate in politics is engaging in an activity with political content, but this does not constitute an attempt by this person to influence politics.[2] And the person going to a governmental office to receive a welfare check is certainly interacting with government, but this (usually) does not constitute an attempt to influence public officials.

Table 13–1 summarizes this discussion of indicators that are sometimes treated as measures of political participation, but that are not. We shall not discuss passive indicators of engagement with politics (I.A) or ways that people get information about politics (II.A). Readers interested in these topics can consult Chapter 10 of this book and other sources. We shall, however, consider attitudes toward infrequent forms of participation (I.B), such as political protest, because some authors have tried to overcome the limitations of small numbers of protestors in mass surveys by substituting attitudes toward protest for actual reports of protesting. We shall also consider recruitment to politics (II.B) even though being contacted by a party or an organization does not constitute political participation by our definition. We include recruitment because these attempts sometimes provide a direct route for a person to become involved in politics, and these attempts certainly involve po-

---

[1]These kinds of actions are close enough to the borderline that they are often treated as if they were political participation. For example, in the questionnaire for the eight-nation political action study undertaken during the 1970s, a series of questions is introduced with "Some people do quite a lot in politics while others find they haven't the time or perhaps the interest to participate in political activities. I'll read you briefly some of the things that people do and I would like you to tell me how often you do each of them. The first is: How often do you read about politics in the newspapers?" (Barnes & Kaase, 1979, pp. 161–162). Similarly Verba and Nie (1972) treat inquiries about a welfare check as "personalized" or "particularized" contacting (pp. 64–73). They note that "[t]he unique position of particularized contacting suggests that we have found a mode of political activity that is not 'political' in the ordinary sense of the word" (p. 71).

[2]Presumably the person doing the recruiting may be trying to influence political action, and the commentators on a television show may be trying to do the same.

Table 13-1

Indicators That Are Not Measures of True Political Activity, But That Are Sometimes Treated
as Such Because They Involve Ordinary Citizens and Politics

I. *Passive Indicators of Concern with Politics or Participation*—These involve ordinary citizens and politics, but not influence or activity.
  A. Engagement with politics
      1. General political engagements
          a. Interest in politics
          b. Political efficacy
          c. Political information
          d. Partisanship
      2. Specific issue engagements—concern with specific policy issues
  B. Attitudes toward participation
      1. Approval of political acts
      2. Willingness to perform acts
II. *Actions Through Which People Learn about Politics or Participation*—These involve ordinary citizens and politics, but not attempts to exert influence.
  A. Information about politics
      1. Follow media
      2. Other people or sources
  B. Recruitment to politics
      1. Contacted by party or organization
      2. Contacted by individuals

---

litical participation on the part of those asking people to become involved. Although questions about recruitment do not directly measure political activity, they do measure events that are very proximate to activity.[3]

Chapter Outline

This chapter differs from previous chapters because it focuses on political behavior instead of attitudes and because it is primarily an exercise in classifying and describing the many ways people participate in politics.[4] Naming, distinguishing, and counting things are often thought of as pedestrian scientific tasks—suitable for museum curators, genteel amateurs, librarians, and government statisticians, but not for first-rate scientists. This perspective has changed as philosophers of science, linguists, cognitive psychologists, and practicing scientists have shown how our conceptualizations, taxonomies, and classifications underlie our world views.[5] How we name and classify things has a lot to do with how we understand them. For social scientists this insight is doubly important because we must be

---

[3]We have also included attitudes toward participation and questions about recruitment to politics because these are not covered elsewhere in this book or other standard references.

[4]Those interested in a review of theories of political participation should consult Aldrich (1993), Leighley (1995), and Whiteley (1995).

[5]See, for example, Collier and Levitsky (1997), Collier and Mahon (1993), Hempel (1965), Lakoff (1987), Suppe (1989), Taylor (1989), and Thagard (1992).

concerned with natural categories—with how ordinary people name and classify things and with how they understand the world—as well as with how our scientific enterprise names and classifies things.

The need to be sensitive to natural categories poses substantial problems for those studying political participation across nations because it requires a great deal of contextual understanding (Verba, 1971). Party membership, for example, means quite different things in different countries, and the legality, acceptability, and efficacy of political protest differ from one country to the next. An analytical framework that neglects this context will probably miss something important. This chapter cannot hope to provide in-depth contextual knowledge about each area of the world, but it can provide a foundation for thinking about how political participation might differ over time, across places, and among people.

This chapter lays this foundation by paying careful attention to how we define, classify, and measure political participation. The preceding subsection explored the complexities of defining political participation, and the next subsection describes our analytical stance toward studying political participation. Then we distinguish three major approaches to studying political participation—through the direct enumeration of political actions, through the study of institutions where actions might occur, and through the identification of political problems leading to participation. Before going on to devote separate sections to each approach, we review six major sets of studies that have collected important data on political participation, that involve more than one survey, that are publicly available, and that have generated important scholarly literature. This section provides a short history of the development of items on political participation and a great deal of basic data on participation scales, including frequency distributions of items, correlations among them, and the relationships of the scales to demographic, attitudinal, and other characteristics of respondents. It also includes information on how political participation, as measured by basic items and scales, has changed over time in the United States.

This overview of the field is followed by separate sections devoted to the major approaches for studying political participation. The first section on *political activities* is the largest because most studies take this direct approach, which asks about participation in the activity, and because the other two approaches ultimately rely on questions about specific activities. The *institutions* approach starts by identifying places, such as work, church, or organizations, where people might participate and then moves to questions about participation. The *problems and needs* approach asks about people's concerns and then follows up with questions about activities.

The penultimate section assesses the meaningfulness of survey responses about participation by reviewing a small number of validation studies that have been undertaken. This leads to a discussion of how social desirability bias, often thought to be the major defect of self-reports of participatory behavior, might affect survey research on political participation. Although it might be a problem, the evidence and theory are not clear-cut. The concluding section of the chapter contains some suggestions for scales to measure political participation and some suggestions for future research.

The reader can use this chapter to get an overview of political participation studies, to learn about the problems of measuring political participation, or as a resource for particular items and scales. The section on "Six Major Participation Studies" provides a brief overview of the major political participation studies. The "Introduction" and the section on "Validity of Measures and Social Desirability Bias" provide a general discussion of the problems of measuring political participation. The sections on approaches discuss in detail particular approaches, items, and scales—some of which are also mentioned in the section on major participation studies. The "Conclusions" section provides a convenient summary of the chapter.

The Stance of This Chapter

The study of political participation using survey data began with the efforts of Lane (1959, pp. 93–94), Milbrath (1965, pp. 18–19), and others to develop unidimensional scales of political participation that exhibited a "hierarchy of political involvement" with "a kind of internal logic, a natural progression of becoming involved in politics" (Milbrath, 1965, pp.18–19),[6] but recent research (including the second edition of Milbrath [Milbrath & Goel, 1977, chap. 1]) suggests that political participation is so varied and complex that simple multi-item scales cannot summarize a person's political activities.[7] Different forms of participation vary so much in the concerns that motivate them, in their duration and intensity, in their target, and in their outcomes that a complete analysis must go beyond unidimensional scales. Consequently, unlike other chapters in this volume on specific attitudes, it is impossible to present a single valid and reliable scale for political participation. Instead, one can provide a multidimensional conceptual framework for thinking about political participation, a broad and diverse set of items for measuring all the important characteristics and types of political activity, some discussion of what can be done with unidimensional "scales" for overall participation, and some suggestions for scales for particular subdomains of political activity where items can more closely approximate a true scale.

As well as requiring a different conceptual framework than the study of particular political attitudes, the study of political participation requires a somewhat different analytical stance. Political attitudes are dispositions or beliefs measurable at any point in time, but political participation is episodic and irregular, so that respondent memories of it become corrupted with time. As the discussion of nonattitudes (Converse, 1964) has made clear, there are certainly reasons to worry about the meaningfulness of attitudes recorded during a survey interview, but this is not because a reported attitude may differ from a concrete, real attitude that is befogged by memory lapses. The problem, rather, may be that there is no attitude there to begin with.[8] In contrast, there should be a real behavioral event behind every report of political participation, although the details surrounding this event may become clouded with time. Retrieving these details is the problem of "episodic memory" (Tulving, 1983).

Researchers try to guard against meaningless attitudes by establishing their reliability with test–retest correlations and other techniques for testing internal consistency, by ascertaining their stability by evaluating change over several time periods, and by determining their validity by correlating attitudes with other attitudes or socioeconomic characteristics. Roughly speaking, a meaningful attitude is one that is reasonably reliable, stable at least

---

[6]The same basic approach is taken in Robinsion, Rusk, and Head (1968, chap. 11).

[7]The classic critique of the unidimensional perspective is Verba and Nie (1972, chaps. 3–4). They find that "it is meaningful to talk of a common dimension that can be described as a propensity for political activity or a prime 'activeness' component" (p. 61), but this dimension "by no means describes all of the patterned structure among the political activists" (p. 63). In Verba and Nie's initial four-dimensional principal components representation for 13 political acts (p. 62), the three additional components explain as much variance as the first component, and the authors conclude their chapter with the observation that "the analysis in this chapter substantiates our multidimensional view of participation" (p. 81). Kaase and Marsh (1979, p. 44) prefer to retain the assumption of unidimensionality for "conventional activities oriented exclusively toward the electoral process," but they propose that unconventional political participation (such as protest) is a separate dimension.

[8]Converse (1964) started the debate about nonattitudes that has led to an enormous literature. More recent literature on the nature of the survey response includes Tourangeau and Rasinski (1988) and Zaller and Feldman (1992).

over short periods of time, and correlated with (theoretically) similar attitudes and uncorrelated with dissimilar ones. We can, of course, compute reliabilities, stabilities, and discriminant and convergent validity through multitrait–multimethod matrices (Campbell & Fiske, 1959) for survey measures of political participation, but the ideal tool for assessing the worth of survey reports of political participation is the existence of some independent observation or written record of the activity, such as a voter log. Without an independent confirmation of a political activity, we must fall back on measures of reliability, stability, or validity from surveys, but we must always remember that they are second-best approaches.

Approaches to Studying Political Participation

Once we have defined what we mean by political activity, we must find a way to get ordinary individuals to provide valid reports of their political activities. Three different approaches are listed in Table 13–2. The most straightforward and most often used approach is simply to describe political acts and ask respondents whether they have engaged in them. This *political actions approach* is certainly the most direct and obvious way to find out about political participation—just ask respondents whether they have voted or sent a political letter.

Despite its simplicity, asking respondents about political activities makes some strong demands on them. They must identify the act in the same way as the researcher, and their memories must be sufficiently jogged by the question so that they will recall all instances of that particular kind of act (Clark & Schober, 1992). Complete recall of events and a common understanding between the researcher and the respondent are most likely for visible electoral activities, such as voting or working in a campaign, where there is common agreement that these acts are political and where the regular scheduling of the events makes it easier to remember them. Adequate recall and common understanding are somewhat less likely for political protest and political contacting because of the difficulty of defining these acts comprehensively and the lack of a regular schedule for their performance, which probably makes it harder for respondents to remember them. These problems are probably most severe for activities such as attending a meeting of a hobby organization that culminated in someone writing a letter to the local park authority or attending

Table 13-2
Three Approaches to Eliciting Information about Participation

I. *Political Actions Approach*—Describing political acts
   A. Actions meant to influence politics indirectly
   B. Electoral activity
   C. Nonelectoral activity
II. *Institutions Approach*—Describing institutional venues where acts can occur
   A. Workplace activity and union membership
   B. Organizational memberships
   C. Religious institutions
   D. Family
III. *Problems Approach*—Describing problems, issues, or needs that can motivate acts
   A. General elicitation of areas
   B. Enumeration of specific problem areas

a religious meeting where a resolution on abortion was passed and reported in the local news media. Respondents may not remember (or even realize) that these activities connected with their institutional attachments are meant to influence politics. For these reasons just asking about political activities may not produce a complete listing of a citizen's actual activities.

In addition, asking about political activities, perforce, neglects those instances where respondents had some need or concern, but did not participate, or those cases where they were asked by someone to take some political action, but they did not participate. Moreover, the approach fails to consider those situations where respondents may have taken some action to solve a problem, but their action did not involve influencing politics. Neglecting these situations may make it hard to identify the factors that distinguish the cases where people decide to participate in politics and those situations where they decide not to do so.

To overcome these problems, researchers have turned to the next two methods for eliciting information about political participation listed in Table 13–2. The *institutions approach* recognizes that political activity intended to influence politics must be rooted in the respondents' daily activities—in the basic relationships or organizations of a culture, such as family, work, religion, and voluntary groups. Asking respondents about their institutional ties and activities provides an inventory of possible locations for political action.[9] Respondents first describe their work, their organizational memberships, their religious preferences and involvements, and their family life; then questions are asked about whether they ever contacted a governmental official as part of their work, whether they engaged in a protest organized by their church, or whether they became engaged in electoral activities because of their membership in some voluntary organization. Properly employed, this approach ensures that respondents are asked about each possible site for participation, but it can be very time consuming. It can also overlook such obvious forms of participation as voting or protesting that have no obvious connection with the family, workplace, church, or organizational life.

The *problems approach* recognizes that political actions to influence politics are almost always rooted in citizens' problems, needs, and concerns. Consequently, asking about problems, needs, and concerns can provide an inventory of the respondents' motivations for political action. This can be done either through open-ended solicitations of concerns and problems or through closed-ended enumerations of specific concerns and problems that people might have. After they are asked about each concern, respondents are then asked whether they engaged in some political activity to express their needs or desires. This approach provides a solid link between motivations and actions, but it may miss those activities that are undertaken solely in response to requests from others.

In principle, we could identify all instances of political participation by relying on any one of the three methods in Table 13–2, but the complexity of human endeavors and the fallibility of respondent memory mean that each approach can sometimes usefully supplement the others. In fact, most researchers have employed a combination of these methods to study political participation, although the political activities approach remains the most popular method because it is so simple and direct. Even when the other two methods are used, respondents are usually asked direct questions about political participation in the context of their institutional affiliations or their enumerations of problems and needs. For these reasons the place to begin is with a discussion of political activities. Before doing

[9]Another way to get an inventory of respondents' daily activities is to use daily time diaries to see how people spend their time (Robinson, 1977).

this, however, it will prove valuable to review six major studies of political participation that have largely shaped this field of research.

Six Major Political Participation Studies

Most of the items now used to measure political activity have been drawn from a small number of landmark studies of political participation. Six are considered in this section, each of which contributed some major innovations in the measurement of political participation.[10]

American National Election Studies

The oldest continuing effort at measuring political participation are the American National Election Studies (ANES), which have undertaken a national survey in the United States every two years since 1952. As well as being the major source of data on campaigns and elections in the United States, these studies have provided the template for election studies around the world. Consequently the questions used on the ANES have had a great impact on the study of political participation in many countries.[11]

Although the ANES questionnaire has changed over time, several political activity items have been repeated in the ANES studies almost every two years since 1952, except for 1954.[12] Table 13–3 presents the wording of this core set of items for which the responses have been either "yes" or "no," and Table 13–4 presents frequencies and correlations for these items for both 1990 and 1992. Note that one item, Give Money, is constructed from the two questions about giving money to candidates and giving money to parties because the responses to these two questions are highly correlated in both years (.51 in 1990 and .43 in 1992). Not surprisingly this constructed variable has a high correlation with each of its components in both years (at least .72 in every case).

If one considers the composite question on giving money to be the only measure of monetary donations, then there are six distinct activities in this table (Vote, Try to Persuade, Display Preferences, Go to Meetings, Give Money, and Political Work). Milbrath (1965, pp. 155–156) used these six items along with a seventh—"Do you belong to any

---

[10]These six sets of studies were chosen because each of them includes a study of the United States, because many of the questions from them have been used as the basis for studies of countries other than the United States, because each has served as the basis for one or more major scholarly studies on political participation, and because each has been archived at the Inter-University Consortium for Political and Social Research (ICPSR) or Roper Center data archives.

[11]The ANES data have been used in many studies of participation, including Milbrath (1965), Milbrath and Goel (1977), Conway (1991), Teixeira (1992), and Rosenstone and Hansen (1993). The ANES participation questions have been used in many election studies around the world.

[12]None of these questions was asked in the small 1954 study. The vote question and the question about trying to persuade others have been asked every biennium since 1952, except for 1954. The question about displaying preferences was not asked in 1952, 1954, 1958, and 1966. The go to meetings and work questions were asked in 1952, but not in 1954, 1958, and 1966. For 1952, 1956, 1960, 1962–1968, 1972–1978, and 1986, only a single question about money was asked. For 1980–1992 (except for 1986), one question about giving money to candidates and another about giving money to parties were asked. Starting in 1984, a third question was asked about giving money to other groups. See Miller and the National Election Studies (1994).

Table 13–3

Core Set of Participation Items in the American National Election Studies

1. *Vote:* "In talking to people about the election we often find that a lot of people weren't able to vote because they weren't registered or they were sick or they just didn't have the time. How about you, did you vote in the elections this November?"

2. *Try to Persuade:* "During the campaign, did you talk to any people and try to show them why they should vote for or against one of the parties or candidates?"

3. *Display Preferences:* [During the campaign] "Did you wear a campaign button, put a campaign sticker on your car, or place a sign in your window or in front of your house?"

4. *Go to Meetings:* [During the campaign] "Did you go to any political meetings, rallies, speeches, dinners or things like that in support of a particular candidate?"

5. *Give Money:* Constructed by taking a "yes" to either the question about money given to candidates (7) or the question about money given to parties (8).

6. *Political Work:* [During the campaign] "Did you do any work for one of the parties or candidates?"

7. *Money to Candidate:* [During the campaign] "Did you give money to an individual candidate running for public office?"

8. *Money to Party:* [During the campaign] "Did you give money to a political party during this election year?"

9. *Other Group Money:* [During the campaign] "Did you give any money to any other group that supported or opposed candidates?"

Source: American National Election Studies.

political club or organization?"[13]—to form a "campaign activity index," which he described as follows:

> Nonvoters were given a score of zero and are generally spoken of in this book as apathetics. Voters who had not participated in any other way received a score of 1. Voters who had talked to someone else or had worn a button or put a sticker on their car were given a score of 2. Persons with scores of 1 or 2 are classified as spectators in this book. Persons who had voted and performed any one of the other four acts (give money, attend a meeting, do work, join a club) were given a score of 3. If they had done two or more of the four acts, they were given a score of 4. Persons scoring 3 or 4 are called gladiators in this book. (p. 156)

This index was used throughout the first edition of Milbrath's book, and it was the basis for treating participation as unidimensional. A quick glance at the correlations in Table 13–4, however, suggests that voting does not fit easily into this scale because it has an average correlation of only about .15 with the other items.[14]

The ANES have traditionally created a zero- to five-point *campaign participation count* by counting the number of these activities, excluding voting and membership in clubs, that respondents have engaged in. These five items (Try to Persuade, Display Preferences, Go to Meetings, Give Money, and Political Work) listed after Vote in Table 13–4

---

[13]The question about membership in political clubs actually appeared in the 1952 ANES survey and was repeated at least in 1956, 1960–1964, 1968, and 1970, but it has been dropped from more recent ANES surveys.

[14]This is confirmed by a factor analysis of the six items in which voting has the lowest loading (.23 for the 1992 data) and by an item analysis in which Cronbach's alpha is higher for the five items without voting (.64) than for the six items (.63).

Table 13-4

Frequency of Activity and Correlations among Acts for the 1990 and 1992 ANES Data on Political Participation

1990 ANES Data Correlation Matrix

	Vote	Pers.	Disp.	Mtg.	$	Work	$Can.	$Party	$Other	% Doing it
1. Vote	1.00	.26	.16	.17	.18	.12	.19	.12	.13	46.2%
2. Try to persuade	.26	1.00	.20	.25	.25	.21	.24	.16	.18	17.2
3. Display preferences	.16	.20	1.00	.37	.25	.43	.26	.15	.08	6.6
4. Go to meetings	.17	.25	.37	1.00	.41	.41	.43	.29	.14	6.0
5. Give money	.18	.25	.25	.41	1.00	.28	.89	.73	.22	6.6
6. Political work	.12	.21	.43	.41	.28	1.00	.27	.28	.12	2.6
7. Money to candidate	.19	.24	.26	.43	.89	.27	1.00	.51	.18	5.4
8. Money to party	.12	.16	.15	.29	.73	.28	.51	1.00	.14	3.7
9. Other group money	.13	.18	.08	.14	.22	.12	.18	.14	1.00	5.0

1992 ANES Data Correlation Matrix

	Vote	Pers.	Disp.	Mtg.	$	Work	$Can.	$Party	$Other	% Doing it
10. Vote	1.00	.21	.13	.14	.13	.08	.12	.10	.12	75.4%
11. Try to persuade	.21	1.00	.22	.19	.17	.17	.17	.11	.15	37.6
12. Display preferences	.13	.22	1.00	.35	.22	.27	.24	.15	.11	11.2
13. Go to meetings	.14	.19	.35	1.00	.37	.39	.34	.25	.14	8.1
14. Give money	.13	.17	.22	.37	1.00	.30	.86	.72	.17	7.3
15. Political work	.08	.17	.27	.39	.30	1.00	.33	.17	.09	3.4
16. Money to candidate	.12	.17	.24	.34	.86	.33	1.00	.43	.16	5.5
17. Money to party	.10	.11	.15	.25	.72	.17	.43	1.00	.15	4.0
18. Other group money	.12	.15	.11	.14	.17	.09	.16	.15	1.00	5.2

Source: Miller, Warren E. and the National Election Studies. *American National Election Studies Cumulative Data File, 1952–1994.* ICPSR Study #8475. Ann Arbor, Michigan, Inter-University Consortium for Political and Social Research.

form a reasonable scale, with a Cronbach's alpha of .69 for the 1990 data and .64 for the 1992 data. Moreover, the maximum likelihood estimates of factor loadings for both the 1990 and the 1992 data are all above .32, and they are above .49 if the Try to Persuade item is excluded. This low factor loading may not be reason enough to exclude the persuasion item from the campaign participation count, but its average correlation with the other four items is clearly lower than their average correlations with one another. As will be seen, trying to persuade someone to vote in one way or another is somewhat different from the other items in this scale.

The high correlation in each year between Money to Candidate and Money to Party suggests that it makes sense to use the composite measure of giving money instead of each of these two separate questions, but the low correlation of Other Group Money with all of the other activities (even the composite measure of giving money to candidates or parties) suggests that this form of giving is another kind of activity.[15] This question was added in 1984 to capture the increasing role of political action committees, and it does seem to represent a distinct form of giving.

The last column in Table 13–4 indicates the percentages of the sample reporting having performed the activity. Not surprisingly in every case the level of activity is higher in 1992, a presidential election year, than in 1990, when only congressional elections were held at the national level. The differences between the two elections in reported voting, in trying to persuade people how to vote, and in displaying political preferences are especially large. In both years the reported turnout is much higher than the actual turnout. More will be said about this toward the end of this chapter.

Voting plus the five activities in the political participation count are arrayed in both parts of Table 13–4 in terms of their frequency of occurrence during the 1992 election. This ordering works for the 1990 data as well, except for the statistically insignificant difference between the fractions of people going to meetings and giving money. An examination of the items in the table suggests that this ordering by frequency is roughly the same as an ordering from the easiest to the hardest activity, and this provides a further rationale for the campaign participation count. Figure 13–1 shows how this count has changed over time by fitting separate ordinary least-squares regression lines for congressional (dashed line) and presidential (solid line) election years from 1956 to 1992. Although these (practically) biennial measures have standard errors of about .025 and there are just 10 points for presidential elections and only 6 for congressional elections, there is at least some evidence for a decrease in the campaign participation count of about one-tenth of an act in the nearly 40-year period from 1956 to 1992. This is about a 13% decline in participation. In addition, there seems to be a difference of about one-fifth of an act in participation between congressional and presidential election years.

Political Participation and Equality in Seven Nations and Participation in America

Because they are election studies, the ANES and their many cousins around the world have typically focused on the electoral activities in Table 13–3.[16] Starting with their 1967 Participation in America (PIA) survey, Verba, Nie, and their collaborators undertook studies (collectively known as the Political Participation and Equality Surveys) in seven

---

[15]Whereas the five items in the campaign participation count are typically intercorrelated at .20 and even .30, other group giving is typically correlated only about .15 with these items.

[16]The ANES have asked about some other activities, but they have not asked about that many, and they have not asked very often.

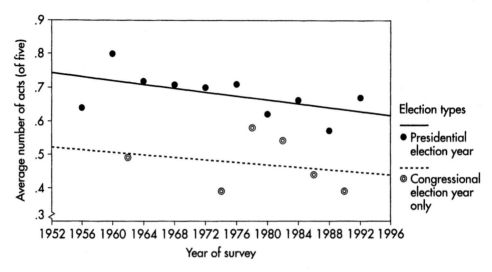

Fig. 13-1   ANES Campaign Participation Count for Congressional and Presidential Elections over Time

countries that were explicitly designed to study political participation.[17] These studies went beyond electoral activities by asking about citizen contacts with governmental officials, cooperative activities at the local level, and involvements with political and nonpolitical groups. One of the major contributions of this work was its demonstration that political participation was diverse and multidimensional.

Table 13–5 lists 11 of the basic participation items in the Verba–Nie (1972) PIA study, and Table 13–6 presents correlations and frequencies for these items from the 1967 survey. Table 13–6 also includes data from a replication of these questions in the 1987 General Social Survey (GSS). In both cases questions were dichotomized to simplify the presentation and to allow for comparable presentations across data sets.

These questions are different from those in the ANES in two ways. First of all, there are questions about a broader array of activities, including contacting and local problem-solving and group formation. Second, whereas the ANES questions typically ask about the recent election campaign, these questions ask about activity during elections in general, during the last few years, or even over the course of the person's lifetime ("Have you ever . . ."). And for those questions about elections in general, the answers are graded from "always" through "sometimes" to "rarely or never." This difference in wording undoubtedly explains the differences in percentages between the ANES data in Table 13–4 and the GSS data in Table 13–6 for comparable activities (voting, trying to persuade, going to meetings, giving money, or engaging in political work). The most striking differences are between the percentages for giving money, working, or going to meetings in the ANES data in 1990 or 1992 and in the GSS data from 1987. For each of these three activities, the GSS replication of the PIA survey questions yields substantially higher fractions of people doing the activity than in the ANES, but in each case the GSS questions cast their net much wider than do the ANES questions, either by referring to the last three or four years instead of the last campaign or by asking about elections in general. As we shall see later, there may be some dangers in such broadly constructed questions.

[17]Results from these surveys were reported in Verba and Nie (1972); Verba, Nie, and Kim (1971); and Verba, Nie, and Kim (1978). The seven countries were Austria, India, Japan, the Netherlands, Nigeria, the United States, and Yugoslavia.

Table 13-5

Participation Items on the Verba and Nie Study of Political Participation in America

---

1. *National Voting:* Constructed from questions about voting in 1960 and 1964. Score 1 if reported voting in both 1960 and 1964 and 0 otherwise.

2. *Local Voting:* "What about local elections—do you always vote in those [1], do you sometimes miss one [1], or do you rarely vote [0], or do you never vote [0]?"

3. *Try to Persuade:* "During elections, do you ever try to show people why they should vote for one of the parties or candidates? Do you do that often [1], sometimes [1], rarely [0], or never [0]?"

4. *Political Work:* "Have you done (other) work for one of the parties or candidates in most elections [1], some elections [1], only a few [0], or have you never done such work [0]?"

5. *Go to Meetings:* "In the past three or four years, have you attended any political meetings or rallies?" [1 if yes; 0 otherwise]

6. *Give Money:* "In the past three or four years, have you contributed money to a political party or candidate or to any other political cause?" [1 if yes; 0 otherwise]

7. *Political Group Membership:* "Now we would like to know something about the groups or organizations to which individuals belong. Here is a list of various organizations. Could you tell me whether or not you are a member of each type? . . . D. Political groups?" [1 if yes; 0 otherwise]

8. *Local Contacting:* "Have you ever personally gone to see, or spoken to, or written to some member of local government or some other person of influence in the community about some needs or problems?" [1 if yes; 0 otherwise]

9. *National Contacting:* "What about some representatives or governmental officials outside of the local community—on the county, state, or national level? Have you ever contacted or written to such a person on some need or problem?" [1 if yes; 0 otherwise]

10. *Local Problem Solving:* "Have you ever worked with others in this community to try to solve some community problems?" [1 if yes; 0 otherwise]

11. *Local Group Formation:* "Have you ever taken part in forming a new group or a new organization to try to solve some community problems?" [1 if yes; 0 otherwise]

Source: Verba & Nie (1972).

Verba and Nie's factor analysis of these questions led them to propose that participation was multidimensional. In their initial analysis of the data (Verba & Nie, 1972, pp. 56–63), they proposed four dimensions: voting, campaign activity, contacting, and cooperative activity. We have organized the data by these four dimensions. Voting at the national level and voting at the local level are highly correlated with one another (.54 in both tables), and they do not correlate at more than .28 with any other activity. These obviously constitute the *voting* dimension.

Four questions (trying to persuade, doing political work, going to meetings, and giving money) are very similar to 4 of the 5 ANES items in the campaign participation count, and they (along with an item about membership in a political group) constitute the *campaign activity* dimension. Nine of the 10 pairwise correlations for these 5 items are over .30 in both studies. Only the correlation for campaign giving and persuading how to vote is below this (about .25 in both studies). The Cronbach's alpha for these five items is .70 for the 1967 PIA study and .67 for the 1987 GSS replication. Factor analyses of these items[18] yield loadings of .48 for all of them on both studies, with the lowest loading found for the persuasion item, as in the ANES data.

---

[18]Maximum likelihood factor analysis with oblimin rotation.

Henry E. Brady

Table 13-6

Frequency of Activity and Correlations Among Acts for the 1967 Participation in America Survey and the 1987 General Social Survey Replication

Participation in America, 1967

	National voting	Local voting	Try to persuade	Political work	Go to meetings	Give money	Political group member	Local contact	National contact	Local problem solving	Local group formation	%Doing
1. National Voting	1.00	.54	.17	.22	.22	.19	.16	.15	.15	.21	.12	66.8%
2. Local Voting	.54	1.00	.19	.26	.25	.21	.21	.16	.17	.21	.15	46.8
3. Try to Persuade	.17	.19	1.00	.37	.30	.24	.25	.20	.20	.22	.19	27.9
4. Political Work	.22	.26	.37	1.00	.38	.33	.34	.22	.20	.31	.22	25.1
5. Go to Meetings	.22	.25	.30	.38	1.00	.34	.39	.24	.22	.24	.23	19.2
6. Give Money	.19	.21	.24	.33	.34	1.00	.35	.19	.22	.21	.13	13.1
7. Political Group Member	.16	.21	.25	.34	.39	.35	1.00	.17	.17	.22	.22	8.2
8. Local Contact	.15	.16	.20	.22	.24	.19	.17	1.00	.24	.28	.21	19.3
9. National Contact	.15	.17	.20	.20	.22	.22	.17	.24	1.00	.21	.18	16.2
10. Local Problem Solving	.21	.21	.22	.31	.24	.21	.22	.28	.21	1.00	.39	30.2
11. Local Group Formation	.12	.15	.19	.22	.23	.13	.22	.21	.18	.39	1.00	14.0

General Social Survey, 1987

	National voting	Local voting	Try to persuade	Political work	Go to meetings	Give money	Political group member	Local contact	National contact	Local problem solving	Local group formation	%Doing
1. National Voting	1.00	.54	.20	.26	.21	.28	.13	.26	.27	.22	.15	58.1%
2. Local Voting	.54	1.00	.18	.27	.21	.20	.14	.27	.24	.24	.18	34.8
3. Try to Persuade	.20	.18	1.00	.33	.31	.25	.19	.24	.26	.16	.13	31.9
4. Political Work	.26	.27	.33	1.00	.38	.32	.28	.32	.31	.29	.25	26.6
5. Go to Meetings	.21	.21	.31	.38	1.00	.37	.34	.35	.27	.26	.21	18.8
6. Give Money	.28	.20	.25	.32	.37	1.00	.38	.28	.29	.24	.19	22.7
7. Political Group Member	.13	.14	.19	.28	.34	.30	1.00	.17	.17	.15	.16	4.2
8. Local Contact	.26	.27	.24	.32	.35	.28	.17	1.00	.48	.41	.33	34.3
9. National Contact	.27	.24	.26	.31	.27	.29	.17	.48	1.00	.30	.30	29.8
10. Local Problem Solving	.22	.24	.16	.29	.26	.24	.15	.41	.30	1.00	.40	33.6
11. Local Group Formation	.15	.18	.13	.25	.21	.19	.16	.33	.30	.40	1.00	17.3

Notes: Definitions of items are the same as in Table 13–5 except that item 7 of the GSS questions asks about political clubs instead of about political groups.
Sources: Participation in America (1967) and General Social Survey (1987). Analysis by the author.

Contacting public officials constitutes a third dimension. The two questions on contacting local and national officials are highly correlated with one another at .48 in the GSS data, but less highly correlated at only .24 in the original Verba–Nie data. This is probably partly an artifact of the somewhat different wordings of the contacting questions in these studies.

Finally, the *cooperative* activities are correlated at .39 to .40 in both studies, suggesting a fourth dimension. The data, especially the 1987 data, also suggest that cooperative activity and contacting are closely related to one another, but there is still a clear indication of multidimensionality even in the 1987 data.[19]

It is interesting to compare the changes over time in these data because there is an ongoing debate about trends in civic participation (Ladd, 1996; Putnam, 1995a, 1995b). The decline in voting is well documented, and the drop from 67% in 1967 to 58% in 1987 is no surprise. Furthermore, these figures are consistent with the turnout data presented in Figure 13–4 later in this chapter. What is surprising is that every other activity (except for membership in political clubs) has stayed about the same or gone up. The decline in political club membership may be the result of the decline of political machines in the cities, but it also may be the result of a change in the wording of this question from "political groups" in the 1967 study to "political clubs" in the 1987 study. The increasing importance of money in politics and the development of sophisticated mobilization techniques through political and nonpolitical organizations probably account for the dramatic rise in campaign giving and in political contacting.

Political Action Studies

The Eight Nation Political Action Studies (PAS),[20] conducted (mostly) in 1974, utilized several innovations in the study of political participation. Almost all survey research prior to 1970 had focused on such conventional political participation as electoral activity and had ignored such unconventional participation as protest. With the wave of political protest that swept the advanced industrial democracies in the late 1960s, protest behavior could no longer be ignored, but studying protest behavior presented some serious problems. Protesting had been neglected partly because of the difficulty of measuring "behaviors that occur irregularly, infrequently, and in specific, often local, contexts of mobilization" (Barnes, Kaase, *et al.*, 1979, p. 42).

The designers of the PAS proposed overcoming the problems of measurement by concentrating on protest potential—a combination of whether respondents approved or disapproved of various forms of protest and whether or not they had ever engaged, would engage, might engage, or would never engage in various forms of protest. This innovation overcame the main problem of using surveys to study infrequent protest behaviors, but it did so at the cost of substituting intentions and dispositions for

---

[19]In fact, Verba and Nie went on to refine their analysis by distinguishing between particularized and social contacting. The latter was closely related to other forms of cooperative activity, while the former formed a separate dimension.

[20]Two major volumes from this work are Barnes, Kaase, *et al.* (1979) and Jennings, van Deth, *et al.* (1989). The first volume deals with the Netherlands, Britain, the United States, West Germany, and Austria. The data set is described in Barnes and Kaase (1979). The data set also includes data on Italy, Switzerland, and Finland. The second volume combines the original data with a second wave of interviews in 1979–1981 in the Netherlands, West Germany, and the United States. The 1979–1981 data included a new cross-section as well as reinterviews with original respondents from the 1974 studies.

Table 13–7

Frequency of Conventional Political Participation for Three Countries

	Often	Sometimes	Rarely	Never	Missing data	
Netherlands						
Read about politics in papers	35%	29%	20%	16%	(0)%	(=100%)
Discuss politics with friends	17	35	27	21	(0)	
Convince friends to vote as self	3	7	12	77	(1)	
Work to solve community problems	5	13	16	66	(1)	
Attend political meetings	1	5	8	85	(1)	
Contact officials or politicians	5	8	13	73	(1)	
Campaign for candidate	1	2	6	90	(1)	
Britain						
Read about politics in papers	36	30	19	15	(1)	
Discuss politics with friends	16	30	23	30	(1)	
Convince friends to vote as self	3	6	8	82	(1)	
Work to solve community problems	4	13	13	69	(2)	
Attend political meetings	2	7	12	78	(2)	
Contact officials or politicians	2	9	13	74	(2)	
Campaign for candidate	1	3	3	91	(2)	
United States						
Read about politics in papers	47	27	17	8	(1)	
Discuss politics with friends	27	37	24	11	(1)	
Convince friends to vote as self	6	13	21	59	(1)	
Work to solve community problems	8	28	25	38	(1)	
Attend political meetings	3	15	25	57	(1)	
Contact officials or politicians	4	23	24	48	(1)	
Campaign for candidate	2	12	15	70	(0)	

Source: Barnes, Kaase, *et al. Political Action: An Eight Nation Study, 1973–1976.* ICPSR Study #7777. Ann Arbor, Michigan, Inter-University Consortium for Political and Social Research. Reprinted by permission of Sage Publications, Inc.

behaviors.[21] We shall discuss the costs and benefits of this strategy in more detail later.

Although the PAS were especially innovative in measuring unconventional political behavior, they also considered conventional participation by constructing a Guttman scale using the seven items listed in Table 13–7. These items are similar to those on the ANES

---

[21]We discuss the PAS measures because they have had the greatest impact, but Muller (1972) appears to have been the first to develop a full list of unconventional activities and the first to systematically use behavioral intention. He also used questions about approving or disapproving of each activity, but these "approve–disapprove items were adapted from the Survey Research Center 1968 Election Study schedule" (p. 956), which had three items on approving or disapproving of lawful meetings or marches, refusing to obey a law that one thinks is unjust, and stopping the government from going about its activities with sit-ins, mass meetings, and demonstrations. These items were repeated every two years through 1974 and formed a basis for an Approve of Protest scale. The research tradition begun by Muller has produced at least one book and many articles. See, for example, Muller (1979); Muller and Opp (1986); and Muller, Dietz, and Finkel (1991).

and the PIA, except that the PAS asked about them as a battery of questions with the following introduction: "Some people do quite a lot in politics while others find they haven't the time or perhaps the interest to participate in political activities. I'll read you briefly some of the things people do and I would like you to tell me how often you do each of them." [Each activity was then described.] The answer options were "often," "sometimes," "seldom," and "never." Table 13–7 also presents the frequencies of these items for three countries in the PAS. Note that even in this scale of conventional participation, the PAS included at least one item—the frequency of reading about politics in the newspaper—that is not, by our earlier definition, a form of political participation.

The Guttman scale was constructed by dichotomizing the answers (see Barnes, Kaase, *et al.*, 1979, "Technical Appendix," p. 543) to the seven items. The order of these items for the Guttman scale for the United States[22] was similar, but not identical, to the ordering for the other countries. Guttman scaling yields a coefficient of reproducibility (CR) that measures the accuracy of the scale, but this measure is sometimes misleadingly close to its theoretical maximum of 1.0 (Robinson, 1973). The CR of .91 for the U.S. scale appears to be an acceptable figure, and the CRs of .94 to .95 for the European countries seem even better. But despite the rule of thumb that CRs above .90 are acceptable, the American figure is still relatively low. Indeed, Barnes and Kaase (1979, p. 86) concluded that "[i]f one dug vigorously enough into the factor structure of the American data, one would probably find traces of the Verba and Nie multifactor model; but, clearly, in Europe the unidimensional model is a fully appropriate way to proceed."

For the sake of comparison, we constructed a Guttman scale for the conventional activities reported in the American Citizen Participation Study described in the next subsection. Using the same rules as the PAS and employing eight of the nine items (all but protesting) listed in Table 13–11, we also obtained a CR of .91 even though these items appear to be even more diverse than those in the PAS and they definitely have some multifactor structure.[23] This does not mean that it is wrong to treat the PAS index of conventional participation as a unidimensional index; it only suggests that researchers seeking the simplicity of unidimensionality should be aware that it can mask significant differences among forms of participation.

Barnes, Kaase, *et al.* put a great deal of effort into measuring unconventional protest activity by carefully specifying a range of unconventional political behaviors, listed in Table 13–8, and by developing a method for reliably gauging protest potential, which is the "readiness of individuals to pursue political goals by direct means" (Barnes, Kaase, *et al.*, 1979, p. 65). Their rationale for considering protest potential is the following:

> In our view, actual involvement in protest behavior may be contingent upon strong and hence infrequent stimuli, such as the location of a new airport or an atomic power station, the passing of laws related to powerful moral dilemmas such as abortion, the opposition to war, and so on. But the *potential to participate,* the individual readiness to be mobilized, is an abiding property of a wide sector of the whole political community, whether currently active or not. (Barnes, Kaase, *et al.*, 1979, p. 58)

[22]Namely, from easiest to hardest: read about politics in the papers, discuss politics with friends, work to solve community problems, campaign for candidates, contact officials or politicians, convince friends to vote as self, and attend political meetings.

[23]The PAS did not include voting in their scale on the grounds that "voting is a unique form of political behavior" (Barnes, Kaase, *et al.*, 1979, p. 86) and would not scale well, but the scale based on the Citizen Participation Study (CPS) data includes voting. This would tend to produce a lower CR. At the same time the PAS scale excluded fewer cases because of "errors" (situations where the Guttman scaling assumption was violated) than did the CPS scale. The PAS rule was to exclude a case if it had more than three errors, but fewer than 1% of the total cases had to be excluded on these grounds. Applying the same rule to the CPS data excluded about 4.5% of the total cases. If these cases are included, then the CR goes down to .893.

Table 13-8

Protest Activity and Behavioral Intentions toward Unconventional Political Behaviors

	Have done	Would do	Might do	Would never do	Missing data	
Netherlands						
Petitions	21%	54%	13%	9%	(3)%	(=100%)*
Lawful demonstrations	7	39	22	29	(2)	
Boycotts	5	27	22	41	(6)	
Rent strikes	3	23	25	46	(3)	
Unofficial strikes	2	14	17	64	(4)	
Occupying buildings	2	23	19	54	(3)	
Blocking traffic	1	13	15	68	(3)	
Painting slogans	2	5	8	82	(3)	
Damaging property	1	1	3	93	(2)	
Personal violence	0	2	4	91	(3)	
Britain						
Petitions	22	31	22	21	(4)	
Lawful demonstrations	6	25	24	42	(4)	
Boycotts	5	17	23	47	(7)	
Rent strikes	2	10	20	65	(4)	
Unofficial strikes	5	7	15	69	(3)	
Occupying buildings	1	6	13	77	(3)	
Blocking traffic	1	7	15	74	(2)	
Painting slogans	0	1	2	95	(2)	
Damaging property	1	1	2	95	(2)	
Personal violence	0	1	4	93	(2)	
United States						
Petitions	58	20	13	6	(3)	
Lawful demonstrations	11	28	29	28	(4)	
Boycotts	15	20	27	31	(8)	
Rent strikes	2	8	22	65	(3)	
Unofficial strikes	2	5	21	59	(14)	
Occupying buildings	2	5	17	71	(6)	
Blocking traffic	1	2	15	79	(2)	
Painting slogans	1	1	7	88	(3)	
Damaging property	1	0	3	94	(2)	
Personal violence	1	0	5	92	(2)	

*Figures have been rounded and, therefore, may not add to 100%.

Source: Barnes, Kaase, *et al. Political Action: An Eight Nation Study, 1973–1976.* ICPSR Study #7777. Ann Arbor, Michigan, Inter-University Consortium for Political and Social Research. Reprinted by permission of Sage Publications, Inc.

Whereas electoral participation is constantly stimulated by regularly scheduled elections, protest behavior is only infrequently called forth even though the potential for it may always be there. This suggests that it makes sense to create a scale of protest potential from questions about protest activity and about approval or disapproval of protest even though this is not a true measure of political participation.

The development of the protest potential scale is complicated, and it begins with the construction of two other scales for protest activity and protest approval. Questions about protest activity and protest approval were asked for the 10 different activities listed in Tables 13–8 and 13–9, but three items (painting slogans, damaging property, and personal violence) were omitted from the protest activity and approval scales because the first one

Table 13–9

Approval of Unconventional Political Behaviors

	Approve very much	Approve	Disapprove	Disapprove very much	Missing data	
Netherlands						
Petitions	44%	48%	3%	1%	(3)%	(=100%)*
Lawful demonstrations	30	50	12	5	(3)	
Boycotts	9	33	38	13	(7)	
Rent strikes	5	26	45	19	(5)	
Unofficial strikes	3	17	50	24	(6)	
Occupying buildings	7	35	36	18	(5)	
Blocking traffic	4	18	45	30	(3)	
Painting slogans	2	9	47	39	(3)	
Damaging property	0	1	24	72	(2)	
Personal violence	1	1	25	73	(2)	
Britain						
Petitions	24	58	10	3	(5)	
Lawful demonstrations	13	52	22	7	(5)	
Boycotts	5	30	39	15	(11)	
Rent strikes	4	19	48	23	(7)	
Unofficial strikes	2	11	45	38	(4)	
Occupying buildings	2	12	41	39	(6)	
Blocking traffic	1	13	44	38	(4)	
Painting slogans	1	1	31	65	(2)	
Damaging property	1	0	21	76	(2)	
Personal violence	1	1	18	79	(2)	
United States						
Petitions	47%	42%	5%	2%	(4)%	
Lawful demonstrations	26	47	16	8	(4)	
Boycotts	13	39	27	13	(9)	
Rent strikes	4	16	40	37	(4)	
Unofficial strikes	1	12	40	31	(15)	
Occupying buildings	2	13	39	40	(6)	
Blocking traffic	1	6	40	50	(2)	
Painting slogans	1	3	34	59	(3)	
Damaging property	0	1	17	81	(2)	
Personal violence	1	1	17	80	(1)	

*Figures have been rounded and, therefore, may not add to 100%.

Source: Barnes, Kaase, *et al. Political Action: An Eight Nation Study, 1973–1976.* ICPSR Study #7777. Ann Arbor, Michigan, Inter-University Consortium for Political and Social Research. Reprinted by permission of Sage Publications, Inc.

did not fit the scales and there was virtually no variance in the second two. For the seven remaining activities, respondents were first asked whether or not they ever engaged in the behavior or were likely to do so. The responses are displayed in Table 13–8. A Guttman scale for *protest activity,* with a CR of .96 for the United States, was created by dichotomizing and scaling these responses. Respondents were also asked whether they approved or disapproved of these activities, and these responses are displayed in Table 13–9. A Guttman scale for *protest approval,* with a CR of .96 for the United States, was created by dichotomizing and scaling these responses. The scales of protest activity and protest approval correlated at .60 to .67, depending on the cutpoints used, suggesting that they measured essentially the same thing.

Responses about protest activity and protest approval were then used to produce a *protest potential* measure by taking each activity separately and constructing an intermediate variable of potential protest participation.[24] A person scored as a potential participant in an activity if he or she both approved (or strongly approved) of the activity *and* indicated that he or she had done, would do, or might do it. Otherwise the person scored as not being a potential participant in that activity. This formulation of potential protest served as a cross-check on people too easily saying that they might do an activity even though they disapproved of it or people saying that they approved of an activity even though they would never undertake it themselves. Respondents had to both approve of the activity and say they might do it. The seven activities were then Guttman scaled to create a scale of protest potential, with a CR of .96. Not surprisingly the three scales—protest activity, approval, and potential—are highly intercorrelated.

Protest potential is an ingenious measure producing interesting results, but it has been criticized because of doubts about the cumulativeness and unidimensionality of the scale (Uehlinger, 1988) and because it does not measure actual political participation (Budge, 1981). The technical scaling issues are discussed in an appendix (Kaase, 1989b) to the 1989 book by Jennings *et al.,* which used the PAS. These technical objections are worthy of consideration, but are not a sufficient basis for rejecting the scales. Criticisms of protest potential based on the obvious fact that it does not measure actual political participation seem more fundamental, but not because these criticisms are obviously right. If protest potential were only a gimmick to overcome the low base rates of political protest in mass surveys, then these criticisms would be very telling, but protest potential is more theoretically interesting than that.

The theory behind protest potential is that many people may be ready to protest, but simply lack the opportunity or need to do so. This is a powerful notion. It is similar to the argument that some people are more prone to disease than others because they have weak immune systems, genetic predispositions, or nutritional shortfalls. What is lacking in Barnes and Kaase's *Political Action* (1979) is a clear demonstration that when these susceptible people are given the need or opportunity, they are more likely to engage in unconventional forms of participation than others.

In a chapter entitled "Mass Participation," Kaase (1989a) provides some validation of the PAS measures by using a second wave of data collected from 1979 to 1981. He shows that the protest potential scales for the two time periods are highly correlated for the three countries reported in the study (Netherlands, .52; West Germany, .29; United States, .48). He also shows that in cross-tabulations of protest activity (would not do, would or might do, and have done) for the two time periods for each of three protest activities (petitions, boycotts, and demonstrations), 53% or more of the entries lie along the diagonals for the Netherlands, Germany, and the United States, which indicates that people gave the same responses in both waves of the survey.

Probably most importantly, across the six countries and two acts (demonstrations and boycotts), a positive response in 1980 was most likely if you said in 1974 that you had done the act, somewhat less likely if you said that you would or might do it in 1974, and very unlikely if you said you would not do it in 1974. An average of 35% of those who said they did a particular act in 1974 also did it again by 1980, 7% of those who said they would or might do an act in 1974 then actually did it by 1980, and only 1% of those who said they would not do it in 1974 then went on to do it by 1980. Because in 1974 an

---

[24]For discussions of this step, see Barnes, Kaase, *et al.* (1979, pp. 74–78, 554–555).

average of 33% said they would not do the act, 58% said they might do it, and 9% said they did it, these data suggest that those doing each act by 1980 came about equally from those who did it before and those who had said they might (or would) do it. Only a very small number (less than 4%) came from those who said they would not do it.[25] Finally, mean changes in orientation toward unconventional acts[26] are highly correlated with age, sex, education, and level of ideological conceptualization in a way that suggests that "[P]eople who move into or are closer to action resemble those who have already been close to the action mode. People who move out of or away from action resemble those who have already been distant from it" (Kaase, 1989a, p. 50). These results suggest the utility of the PAS measures, especially the protest activity measure, but they do not directly validate the theory on which the protest potential measure is based.

Whatever the strengths or limitations of protest potential, it has not been repeated in many other studies. This may be because it requires two sets of questions, one about activity and another about approval. It may also be because it is complicated to construct, or it may be because it is a hybrid measure combining attitudes and behaviors.

Although protest potential has not been used much, the protest activity measure, based on a battery of questions about a number of protest activities (scored with "have done," "would do," "might do," and "would never do"), has been used as a convenient measure of unconventional participation in a number of studies.[27] This measure is still a bit of a hybrid because it combines actual behavior with predictions about behavior, but it seems closer to standard participation measures. It is also easy to administer.

Citizen Participation Studies

The 1989–1990 American Citizen Participation Study (CPS) undertaken by Verba, Schlozman, Brady, and Nie sought to go beyond previous studies by obtaining oversamples of activists through a two-stage sampling procedure; developing more elaborate measures of the amounts and kinds of political participation; and constructing more detailed questions about the motivations, resources, and social networks that lead to political participation.[28] These same steps were followed by Kaplan and Brady in the Estonian CPS and in the Russian CPS.[29] For the purposes of this chapter, the most important of these innovations is the development of more elaborate measures of the nature and circumstances of people's political participation.

Table 13–10 presents the basic questions for nine of the more important kinds of political participation in the 1990 U.S. CPS. All of the questions yield dichotomous responses, and all are designed to be very specific about the time period involved. Table 13–11 presents a correlation matrix for these activities. The questions about voting, campaign work, campaign money, contacting, and informal community activity are similar to ones on the ANES or on the PIA survey. The item measuring involvement in political organizations has its roots in an organizational inventory first used in the PIA study. The innovation here is the use of a more detailed inventory (described in a later section) and more detailed questions about the political activities of the organization. The question

---

[25]The figures in this sentence and in the preceding three sentences in the text were calculated by the author from Kaase (1989a, Table 8, p. 48).

[26]The results are presented in Kaase's Table 9 (1989a, p. 51), and the orientation toward unconventional acts is scored as described in his Table 7 (p. 47). This scale relies only on the protest activity measures.

[27]It was used, for example, in the first stages of the Estonian and Russian Citizen Participation Studies.

[28]Reports on these data are in Verba, Schlozman, and Brady (1995) and in Nie, Junn, and Stehlik-Berry (1996).

[29]Articles using these data include Kaplan and Brady (1995, 1997) and Brady and Kaplan (1994).

Table 13–10

Participation Questions in the American Citizen Participation Study

1. *National Vote:* "Thinking back to the national election in November 1988, when the presidential candidates were Michael Dukakis, the Democrat, and George Bush, the Republican, did you happen to vote in that election?" (Respondents were first asked how often they voted in national elections. If they responded with "All," "Never," "Not old enough," or "Never eligible," then they were not asked this follow-up question.)

2. *Campaign Work:* "Since January 1988, the start of the last national election year, have you worked as a volunteer—that is, for no pay at all or for only a token amount—for a candidate running for national, state, or local office?"

3. *Campaign Money:* "Since January 1988, did you contribute money—to an individual candidate, a party group, a political action committee, or any other organization that supported candidates?"

4. *Mail Donations:* "How often do you receive requests through the mail asking you to donate to political organizations, political causes, or candidates? [If ever] In the past twelve months, have you sent any money in response to such mail requests?"

5. *Political Groups:* A respondent is involved with a political group if for any one of twenty categories of groups the respondent (a) says "yes" to "Are you a member of . . ." *or* the respondent says "yes" to "Not counting any membership dues, have you contributed money in the past twelve months to any organization of this type?" and (b) if for at least one of these groups the respondent says "yes" to "Does this organization sometimes take stands on any public issues—either locally or nationally?"

6. *Contacting:* Score a 1 if a "yes" response to any of the following four questions: (1) "In the past twelve months, have you initiated any contacts with a federal elected official or someone on the staff of such an official?" (2) "What about a non-elected official in a federal government agency?" (3) "What about an elected official on the state or local level?" (4) "And what about a non-elected official in a state or local government agency or board?"

7. *Informal Community:* "Aside from membership on a board or council or attendance at meetings, I'd like to ask also about informal activity in your community or neighborhood. In the past twelve months, have you gotten together informally with or worked with others in your community or neighborhood to try to deal with some community issue or problem?"

8. *Boards or Meetings:* Constructed from responses to the following questions: "In the past two years, since [current month, 1988], have you served in a voluntary capacity—that is, for no pay at all or for only a token amount—on any official local governmental board or council that deals with community problems and issues such as a town council, a school board, a zoning board, a planning board, or the like?" "Have you attended a meeting of such an official local government board or council in the past twelve months? [If yes] Do you attend these meetings regularly or have you attended only once in a while?" Serving on a board or attending meetings regularly produced a score of 1.

9. *Protest:* "In the past two years, since [current month, 1988], have you taken part in a protest, march, or demonstration on some national or local issue (other than a strike against your employer)?"

Source: American Citizen Participation Study Questionnaire.

Table 13-11

Frequency of Activity and Correlations among Acts for the 1990 American Citizen Participation Survey

	Vote	Campaign work	Campaign money	Mail donations	Political groups	Contacting	Informal community	Boards or meetings	Protest	% Doing it
Vote	1.00	.15	.28	.13	.26	.22	.13	.10	.04	69.7%
Campaign work	.15	1.00	.27	.14	.18	.21	.13	.16	.13	8.4
Campaign money	.28	.27	1.00	.38	.37	.26	.15	.13	.15	23.6
Mail donations	.13	.14	.38	1.00	.20	.16	.11	.07	.15	6.6
Political groups	.26	.18	.37	.20	1.00	.31	.19	.12	.16	48.1
Contacting	.22	.21	.26	.16	.31	1.00	.23	.16	.15	34.0
Informal community	.13	.13	.15	.11	.19	.23	1.00	.15	.10	17.0
Boards or meetings	.10	.16	.13	.07	.12	.16	.15	1.00	.08	4.3
Protest	.04	.13	.15	.15	.16	.15	.10	.08	1.00	5.7

Source: American Citizen Participation Survey.

about protest is a general one covering several kinds of activity. The questions about mail donations and involvement with community boards or meetings are new.

The Estonian and Russian studies added some other new kinds of questions. In both studies a detailed inventory of political parties was developed, and respondents were asked for each party whether they recognized it, supported it, or were members of it. This battery is described in more detail later. Both the Estonian and Russian studies followed the lead of the PAS by asking about multiple forms of protest behavior, but in keeping with the approach of the CPS, they also asked detailed questions about the way that people became involved in each activity, their reasons for doing so, and their issue concerns.

In all of these studies, the participation questions were designed to capture very different kinds of participatory behavior. Consequently it is not surprising that there are only a few large correlations in Table 13–11, such as those between voting in local and presidential elections (.77) and between giving money to campaigns and giving money in response to mail solicitations (.38). Otherwise, all of the other correlations are below .30, and many of them are below .20. This confirms the multidimensionality of political participation.

Despite this multidimensionality, it is often convenient to have a summary measure of participation, and Verba, Schlozman, and Brady (1995) used a simple one that added up the number of eight of the nine activities (excluding mail donations) performed by each respondent. This "scale" has a coefficient of reproducibility of .92,[30] but in a principal components analysis of these items, the first dimension explains only about 29% of the variance, and the Cronbach's alpha is just .59.[31] Because of these limitations of this scale, Verba, Schlozman, and Brady also broke down their analyses by specific kinds and groups of acts.

Correlates of Participation

Table 13–12 shows how the eight-item scale of political participation is related to four types of explanatory variables used in Verba, Schlozman, and Brady (1995) to construct the Civic Voluntarism Model of political participation. The variables range from demographic characteristics that are highly visible, fixed, and remote from participation to attitudes that are much less visible, more changeable, and possibly more proximate to participation. Activities, information, and skills are in between on these dimensions. The first column in Table 13–12 presents the bivariate correlation between each variable and the political participation scale, the second column presents the beta weights[32] for a regression of the scale on just the variables within the block (e.g., the beta weights for the demographic variables are for a regression of the scale on just these six demographic variables), and the third column includes all variables in one regression.

It is not surprising to find that among the *demographic* variables, education is by far the most important (as measured by its large bivariate correlation and its large beta weight in the second column), and it remains important in the overall regression as well. Family income is also important. Being Hispanic, female, or black is negatively correlated with participation, but only the first two relationships persist once other demographics are

----

[30]This is based on excluding the 125 cases (about 5% of the total) that had more than three errors. If the number of errors is allowed to be up to five, then the CR goes down to .90, and only 13, or 0.5%, of the cases are excluded.

[31]Moreover, as we might expect, the protest item has the lowest factor loading.

[32]The beta weight equals the regression coefficient of an independent variable times the standard deviation of the independent variable divided by the standard deviation of the dependent variable. It provides a rough-and-ready way to compare the impact of variables with different units. The beta weight for a bivariate regression is just the bivariate correlation. Hence beta weights can be thought of as a generalization of correlations to multivariate relationships.

Table 13-12

Impacts of Demographic Characteristics, Activities, Information and Skills,
and Attitudes on the Eight-Item Scale of Political Participation from the American
Citizen Participation Study

Block of variables	Bivariate correlations	Beta weights for regressions for each block	Beta weights for overall regression
Demographics			
Education	.442***	.382***	.136***
Family income	.308***	.176***	.098***
Hispanic	−.140***	−.059***	−.012
Age	.124***	.186***	.113***
Female	−.096***	−.053**	−.016
Black	−.042*	.010	.015
Activities			
Member nonpolitical organization	.319***	.260***	.010
Occupational level	.291***	.233***	.024
Religious attendance	.121***	.092***	.025
Working	.085***	.015	−.026
Information and skills			
Political information	.441***	.276***	.120***
Civic skills	.424***	.292***	.162***
Vocabulary skill	.363***	.151***	.041*
Attitudes			
Political interest	.488***	.394***	.244***
Political efficacy	.374***	.220***	.125***
Strength of party identication	.148***	.054**	.046**
Strength of lib–con opinion	.141***	.063***	.040*
Party identification	.069***	.032	−.020
Lib–con opinion	.001	−.040*	−.035*

Note: One asterisk indicates significance at the .05 level or better, two asterisks indicate significance at the .01 level or better, and three asterisks indicate significance at the .001 level or better.

Source: American Citizen Participation Study. The sample size is close to the total of 2517 (weighted) for all correlations. Detailed descriptions of the variables are in Appendix B of Verba, Schlozman, and Brady (1995) and in Brady, Verba, and Schlozman (1995).

controlled, and all three seem to disappear in the full equation.[33] Increasing age appears to increase participation, but the complete story is somewhat more complicated. Participation increases steeply from an average of about 1 act on the eight-point scale at age 20 to 2.3 acts at age 40; then it hits a plateau until about age 60, when it declines somewhat to about 1.8 acts by age 70.

Activities such as being a member of a nonpolitical organization, working at a job, working at a higher status job (as measured by occupational level), and attending church have a strong bivariate relationship with political participation, but none of these relationships persists in the final regression equation, and their impact appears to be mediated by information, skills, and attitudes.

Information and skills are measured by three different scales. Political information is based on eight items tapping civic and political knowledge. Civic skills are a measure of

---

[33]For a much more detailed and nuanced picture of women's participation, see Schlozman, Burns, and Verba (1994).

whether the person has written a letter, gone to a meeting, planned or chaired a meeting, or given a presentation or speech on the job, in a nonpolitical organization, or at church. Vocabulary skill is measured by how many words a person could define in a short multiple-choice test that is also used on the GSS. All three scales have a strong bivariate relationship to political participation, and the first two remain highly significant in the full regression equation.

The strength of *attitudes* matters much more than the direction of attitudes for political participation. Those with high levels of political interest and a strong sense of efficacy are more likely to participate even after controlling for many other characteristics. There is some evidence to suggest that Republicans participate more than Democrats (see Party Identification in Table 13–12), but this difference goes away once other factors are controlled. Similarly there are no clear-cut results about liberals versus conservatives, but those who identify more strongly with political parties or who have strong liberal or conservative sentiments are more likely to participate. A much more detailed elaboration of these results is provided in Verba, Schlozman, and Brady (1995).

Innovations in the Citizen Participation Studies

Perhaps the most important questionnaire innovations on the CPS in America, Estonia, and Russia are an elicitation of the amount of time or money involved in each act and a detailed characterization of the issues and reasons that led to the act. By asking about time or money, the study obtained a much more detailed picture of the levels of political participation. Asking about time and money requires careful question formulation and careful editing of the data to avoid errant responses, but it provides an important extra dimension in our understanding of political participation. It matters, for example, that some people give $1000 to campaigns and others give only $25. This information was used extensively in *Voice and Equality* (Verba, Schlozman, & Brady, 1995) to demonstrate that there were often significant differences between those who gave some money or time and those who gave a great deal of money or time.

The CPS also asked respondents an open-ended question for each kind of activity: "What were the issues or problems ranging from public policy issues to community, family or personal concerns that led you to take part in this [activity]?" This was followed up with a list of about 10 reasons why respondents might have taken part in the activity, and for each reason they were asked whether it was very important, somewhat important, or not very important. These reasons were designed to cover such major domains of motivation as selective material benefits (e.g., get a job, get help from an official, run for office someday), selective social gratifications (e.g., feel excitement, meet important and influential people), selective civic gratifications (e.g., doing one's share or one's duty), and collective outcomes (influence government policy).

Rational choice theorists argue that substantial selective material benefits are theoretically necessary for participation, but that they are seldom available in sufficient quantities to explain why people participate. Participation, therefore, is a paradox. In "Participation's Not a Paradox," Schlozman, Verba, and Brady (1995) show that political activists find reasons beyond material self-interest that seem sufficient to motivate their actions.

Roper Studies

In their analysis of political participation over time in the United States, Rosenstone and Hansen (1993) used a set of seven items from 173 Roper polls from September 1973 to December 1990. The polls themselves asked about 12 different activities listed in Table 13–13, and they extend until 1994, when there were some changes in question wording.

Table 13-13

Roper Political Participation Questions

Political activity	Percentage taking part, 1974–1994
Signed a petition	33.6%
Attended a public meeting on town or school affairs	17.2
Wrote your congressman or senator	14.2
Served as an officer of some club or organization	9.1
Attended a political rally or speech	8.6
Served on a committee for some local organization	8.3
Wrote a letter to the paper	4.9
Made a speech	4.4
Worked for a political party	4.3
Belonged to some group like the League of Women Voters or some other group that is interested in better government	3.5
Wrote an article for a magazine or newspaper	2.3
Held or ran for political office	.9

Note: The stem question is "Now here is a list of things some people do about government and politics. Have you happened to have done any of those things in the past year? [If yes] Which ones?" The results are based on 210 Roper polls from 1974–1994 involving 417,902 respondents.
Source: Roper files, 1974–1994.

There are 10 polls nearly every year, with almost 20,000 total respondents. Rosenstone and Hansen analyzed how 3 of the 12 items (signing a petition, attending a meeting, and writing a representative or senator) changed over time. They justify this choice on both substantive and methodological grounds: "First, taken together, these three activities represent participation both in national and in local government, in high-cost activities and in low-cost activities. Second, each has a range of observed values that well exceeds sampling error" (p. 42). All 12 items have the virtue of being available at frequent intervals over a long period of time, but the question format suffers from a lack of specificity about both the activities and the time frame and from the possibility that respondents would too easily lapse into responding positively to the questions.

Figure 13–2 shows how five of these activities have changed over time. All of them decline over time, lending some support to Putnam's (1995a, 1995b) thesis about the decline of civic participation. Two of these activities (attended a political rally or speech and worked for a political party) are closely linked to electoral campaigns, and the other three (signed a petition, attended a public meeting on town or school affairs, and wrote a congressman or senator) are not. The two campaign measures show a discernible up-tick in the year after presidential campaigns, which appears to capture the activity that occurs at the end of each campaign. Because the questions ask about activity during the last year, almost all of the surveys in the year after an election year will capture election year activity, whereas most of those fielded during the election year take place before the intensive activity at the end of the campaign. The large sample sizes and these up-ticks suggest that the Roper data could be a very valuable source of yearly and even monthly changes in political participation.

General Social Survey

In addition to the 1987 replication of the PIA study, the American General Social Survey (GSS) has also asked the organizational membership questions from that study on 15

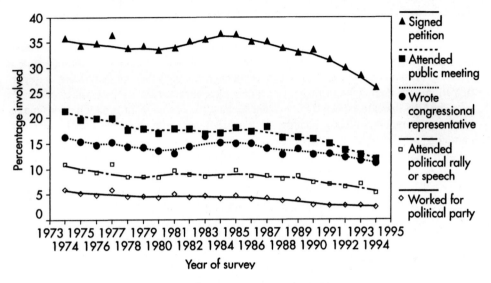

Fig. 13-2 Percent in Various Political Activities, 1974–1994 (LOWESS fit)

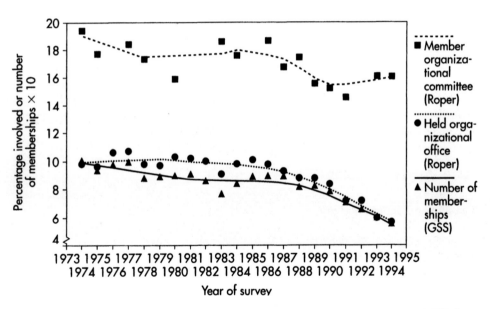

Fig. 13-3 Memberships and Percent Involved in Organizations over Time Using Roper and GSS Data (LOWESS fit)

surveys between 1974 and 1994.[34] These questions have yielded important data in the debate over the putative decline in civic participation (Ladd, 1996; Putnam, 1995a, 1995b). The top of Figure 13–3 plots the average number of such memberships (the scale is times 10, so that the overall average is about 1.8 memberships) from 1974 to 1994 and shows a general downward trend—once again providing some evidence that civic involvement

---

[34]The questions are identical to those in the PIA, except for a slight difference in the question about membership in political groups.

has decreased. This figure also presents the fraction of Roper respondents holding organizational offices or belonging to organizational committees. These time series also decline, although the curves look somewhat different from that for the GSS data. Although these data support the notion that participation has declined, Table 13–6, based on data from the PIA and the GSS replication 20 years later, suggests that only some forms of participation have declined and that many others have increased.

The GSS data are especially important because they provide information over time on trust in government, efficacy, confidence in institutions, and many other factors related to participation. Unfortunately the only continuous-participation time series are the organizational memberships battery and the vote in last election. The International Social Survey Program, which grew out of the GSS and which now covers 29 countries, does not have organizational memberships as part of the basic core questions, although there have been some cross-country modules, such as one on the environment in 1993 that asked about petitioning, joining a group, and other forms of participation.

Summary of the Major Studies

Four of these studies (ANES, PPE/PIA, PAS, and CPS) have produced major innovations in the way we study political participation, including the campaign participation count (ANES); questions about nonelectoral forms of conventional participation, such as contacting, organizational membership, and local problem-solving and group formation (PPE/PIA); measures of unconventional participation (PAS); and quantitative measures of participation, such as the amount of money or time devoted to an activity (CPS). At least three of the studies (PPE/PIA, PAS, and CPS) have ranged beyond the United States.[35] Methodologically, three (ANES, PAS, and CPS) have included at least two-wave panels, and three (ANES, Roper, and GSS) provide very important time series of civic and political participation. These studies provide a rich source of questions and data on political participation. The next three sections explore in further detail the specific questions that these and other studies have used to measure political participation.

The Political Activities Approach

Classifying Political Activity

To obtain a sense of the range of approaches for studying political participation, a review was conducted of the major studies of participation that could be identified from the ICPSR catalog and other sources, and other studies including interesting questions were consulted.[36]

Table 13–14 provides a convenient and common, if somewhat arbitrary, way of classifying political activities considered in these studies. There are numerous ways to classify forms of political participation, and this table uses several of them at once. One distinction is whether activity is meant to influence politics directly or indirectly. This is the basis for distinguishing between the first set of activities and all the rest. Discussing politics and trying to recruit people to political activity do not directly send a message to

---

[35]In addition, there are now international versions of the GSS, and the ANES has been widely copied in other election studies.

[36]These studies are listed in the list of "Datasets Referenced and Used." Not all available studies were consulted, and the author apologizes for any important work that was missed.

Table 13-14

Political Activities Approach: A Classification of Acts

I. Actions Meant to Influence Politics Indirectly

    A. Discuss politics

    B. Recruitment—try to persuade or convince someone to do something

II. Electoral Activity—scheduled by the political system

    A. Voting

        1. Vote intention

        2. Registration

        3. Report of vote

        4. Parent's vote

    B. Campaign activity

        1. Meetings

        2. Work

        3. Money

        4. Display preferences through signs, buttons, or stickers

        5. List of activities

    C. Party membership or member of a political club

III. Nonelectoral—with others or alone

    A. Nonelectoral—conventional

        1. Informal community

        2. Contacting

        3. Organizational memberships

        4. Attending meetings or serving on boards

    B. Nonelectoral—unconventional

        1. Petitioning

        2. Lawful demonstration

        3. Boycotts

        4. Joining in wildcat strikes

        5. Refusing to pay rent or taxes

        6. Occupying buildings

        7. Blocking traffic

        8. Destroying property

        9. Terrorism and assassination

---

political leaders or institutions, but they can and do indirectly influence the political system.

Another distinction is whether or not the activity revolves around elections. Voting, campaigning, and belonging to a party typically focus on elections, and this is the basis for the second category versus the third. Electoral activities are more regularized and standardized[37] than nonelectoral activities, and they are the essential features of a democratic

---

[37]This is true even in parliamentary systems, where the exact timing of elections is unknown, but where there are usually requirements for calling elections within four or five years of the last election.

system of government. In addition, there are many national election studies that ask questions about electoral activities, so there is a much better survey record of these kinds of participation. Within the nonelectoral activities we make use of another distinction taken from the PAS—whether an activity is conventional or unconventional. This distinction is useful only if one knows where to draw the line. In the 1970s the designers of the PAS treated petitioning as an unconventional activity. Today lawful demonstrations and even boycotts would probably be considered more conventional than unconventional. More will be said about this distinction later in this chapter.

Basic Characteristics of Political Activity

What should be asked about the activities in Table 13–14? For each activity one could ask about its core characteristics—the nature of the activity, the target of the attempt to influence politics, and the nature of the issue involved. These questions are summarized at the top of Table 13–15. The core characteristics are roughly keyed to the basic definition of political participation. An *activity* must be performed by some *ordinary citizen;* it must involve attempts to *influence* some governmental actor or agency at some political level; and it must involve one or more *political* issues, needs, or concerns. Asking questions about all these aspects allows the researcher to make sure that the respondent really did engage in political participation.

One can also go beyond the core characteristics of the activity and ask about its proximate causes and effects, as indicated at the bottom of Table 13–15. These proximate causes and effects can be thought of as extensions of the definition because they get at people's reasons, expectations, and evaluations of an activity. Asking about the reasons behind participation might be especially useful for determining the intent of an action. We might, for example, interpret political protest activity in one way for someone who told us he became involved "to go along with friends" and in another way for someone who told us she "cared deeply about some issue." Moreover, this kind of interpretation might be fundamental for understanding voting and nonvoting in an authoritarian regime where voting is required and nonvoting is punished. In this case those not voting in order to protest are the true political activists, and voters who voted only to avoid punishment could hardly be said to be exercising political influence.

Most of the questions in Table 13–15 are straightforward, but the definition of the nature of an act has varied substantially from one study to another because there are so many ways to describe political acts and to measure how much people have become involved in them. Moreover, many activities occur so rarely that some studies have tried to enlarge their chances of capturing events by asking about the activity of other people or the potential activity of the respondent. Much of the rest of this chapter will elaborate on the different ways political activity has been described and measured.

Once an act is defined, the most basic question about it is the amount of activity, and this depends on the time period considered. Are respondents asked about their activity in the past week? Month? Year? Over their lifetime? Once the time period is defined, the survey can ask follow-up questions about the amount of the activity by asking how many times the act was performed, how much time was devoted to it, or how much money was expended? Frequency, time, and money cannot be asked about for all acts, but most lend themselves to at least two of these questions.

Asking a respondent about how much family members, neighbors, or others engage in some act can increase the number of reported instances of the activity, although the results are prone to substantial biases in reporting and may be very hard to interpret. Another approach to increasing the variance in responses for rare and unusual events beyond

Table 13-15
Basic Characteristics of Political Acts

I. **Core Characteristics**—nature of activity, influencing whom, and political issue or concern at stake

  A. **Nature of the act?**

    1. What is the act?

    2. How much?

      a. Has person done it

        i. Ever?

        ii. Over some time period?

      b. Amount it has been done

        i. Frequency over some time period

        ii. Time expended over some time period

        iii. Money expended

    3. Who does it?

      a. Respondent

      b. Anyone respondent knows—spouse or family member, family, parents, neighbors, friends, co-workers, coreligionists

      c. Would respondent do it?

  B. **What political level and what actor or agency are the targets?**

    1. Target level?

      a. International

      b. National

      c. State or provincial

      d. Local

    2. Target actor or agency?

      a. Media

      b. Politician

      c. Government official

      d. Other people, such as friends, family, or neighbors

  C. **Characteristics of the issue involved?**

    1. Was there a particular issue?

    2. Whom did it affect?

    3. What was it?

II. **Proximate Causes and Effects**

  A. **Reasons for doing it?**

    1. How did you get idea to take action?

    2. Specific reasons?

      a. Material benefits

      b. Social benefits

      c. Civic gratifications

      d. Policy gratifications

  B. **Did it have an impact?**

  C. **Satisfaction with result?**

---

merely recording whether or not the respondent has actually performed the action is to ask if the respondent would do an activity. As noted above, Marsh and Kaase (1979, p. 58) have done this for political protest by measuring the potential to participate, which they define as "the individual readiness to be mobilized," which is an "attitude wedded to individual behavioral intentions." This approach is prone to standard criticisms about the gap between attitudes and behavior, and Marsh and Kaase discuss this difficulty at great length (pp. 61–65).

At one time or another, surveys have asked a great many of the questions in Table 13–15 about each of the activities in Table 13–14. The following pages describe the kinds of questions that make the most sense and some of the more interesting approaches in the literature.

Being Contacted about or Recruited to Politics

The line between contacting people and recruiting them is very fine—presumably most political contacts try to get people to do something, but we can think of contacting as a milder and less insistent form of recruitment. Although neither activity is, strictly speaking, an indicator of political participation, they are both closely related to political acts in two ways. First, the person being recruited or contacted often undertakes some political action, even if it is merely engaging in a political discussion with the contactor, as a result of the contact. Second, the person doing the recruiting is clearly performing a political act. For these reasons recruitment and contacting of citizens are considered in this chapter.

The classic question, repeated again and again in election studies, asks respondents whether they have been contacted through letters or pamphlets or in person during an electoral campaign. The question varies slightly from one study to another, but the ANES query is typical: "Did anyone from one of the political parties call you up or come around and talk to you about the campaign? [If yes] Which party was that?" This question figures prominently in Rosenstone and Hansen (1993) as an explanation for political activity. The 1974 Canadian study asked about personal contact, but followed up with this question: "Were you contacted in any other ways by the parties during the campaign, for example, by telephone or by having a pamphlet left in your mailbox? [If yes] Which parties?"

In 1968, the ANES also asked, "Did any of the people listed on this card [wife/husband, a relative, a friend, someone you work with, anyone else] talk to you about why you should vote for one of the parties or candidates?" and followed up by asking, "Does this person pay more attention or less attention to politics than you?" The answers to this question and to a question described later about whether the respondent tried to persuade people to vote one way or another were used by Robinson (1976) in a test of the "two-step flow" hypothesis of Lazarsfeld, Berelson, and Gaudet (1948). Robinson describes the close relationship between being contacted and contacting others about politics (what he calls "opinion taking" and "opinion giving") and thereby provides part of the justification for us including being contacted as part of a discussion of political participation.

Most contacting questions are quite limited because they ask only about recruitment efforts during campaigns. They focus on voting and vote choice, and they do not ask for any details about who contacted the respondent except the recruiter's party affiliation. The CPS in the United States, Estonia, and Russia include a much more extensive battery about recruitment for campaign activity, protesting, contacting of government officials, community involvement, and other activities. This set of questions ascertains the number of recruitment attempts in the past 12 months, whether the person making the request was known personally, and many other details about the recruiter—such as his or her sex, race, and party identification and whether the recruiter was a neighbor, fellow worker, or member of the same religion or the same organization as the respondent. The final question in the battery asks whether the respondent reacted positively to the request and took the action requested.

Not surprisingly there is always a substantial correlation between being asked to do some political activity and actually doing it. But there are great dangers in using questions about recruitment to explain political activity because those who are recruited to politics are undoubtedly asked partly because they are likely to say yes (Brady, Schlozman, & Verba, 1996). One of the tasks facing students of political participation is to develop better ways to use these questions because there are ample reasons to believe that being asked to participate has an independent impact on political participation.

Discussing Politics or Persuading Someone to Perform a Political Act

The most offhand and frequent political activity is discussing politics with someone,[38] and many studies of political attitudes and behavior have asked respondents, "How often do you talk about [or discuss] politics with other people?" This question is asked in various ways, but most of its core characteristics remain the same from one version to another. The question is invariably asked about just the respondent, often about politics in general (although some versions ask about a specific political level), and usually with respect to discussion with other people. There are never any queries about the issue involved. The biggest variation is in the way respondents are asked about the frequency of discussing politics. A common approach is to provide response categories, such as "often," "sometimes," "seldom," and "never," but this approach provides no way for the respondent to calibrate the responses, and a better method, used in some studies, is to provide concrete frequencies: "every day," "nearly every day," "once or twice a week," "less than once a week," "never."

Although most queries about political discussion ask about discussions with "other people" or with "friends," a few studies have asked about "working mates," "fathers" or "mothers," or even a list of possible partners in political conversation. When lists are used, one typically finds that political discussions are mostly with relatives (especially spouses), with friends, and with fellow workers (see, for example, Verba & Nie, 1976, p. 156). This information is useful, but a further understanding of networks of political discussion will be better served by the institutional approach described later, in which respondents are first asked about their social networks and then asked about the content of their interactions. This in fact was done on the 1987 GSS, where up to three people were identified who are "the people with whom you discussed matters important to you," and for each person a follow-up question was asked: "How often do you talk to [the person] about political matters?"

Nothing could seem simpler than this "discuss politics" question, but it ignores some important nuances, such as whether someone joins in a discussion passively by just listening, becomes actively involved by giving an opinion, or actually tries to convince

---

[38]Not everyone believes that discussing politics is a form of political participation. "Relatedly, activities such as talking about politics, reading about politics, keeping current with political issues and public affairs, pledging allegiance to a flag or other political symbol, or feeling supportive of the government are largely symbolic in nature. They are usually not intended to influence the selection of government officials or decisions and therefore are not political activities" (Mishler, 1979, p. 18). Indeed, if being the object of a political contact is not a form of political participation—even though it must involve some discussion of politics—then it is hard to see why discussing politics should always be considered a form of political participation.

someone of his or her views. Very few attempts have been made to determine the intensity of participation in political discussion, but this question from the Dutch Election Study of 1970–1973 is a welcome exception:

> What do you usually do when you are with people who start talking about politics? Which of the descriptions on this card do you think is most appropriate in your case?
> (1) I hardly ever listen when people start talking about politics (21%);
> (2) I usually listen, but I never participate in the discussion (21%);
> (3) It sometimes happens, but not often that I give my opinion (26%);
> (4) Usually I participate in the discussion and give my opinion (32%).

The percentages of responses in each category (indicated in parentheses) are fairly evenly spread out, suggesting that something valuable is being captured by this question, but this approach has not been used in many other studies.[39]

Although very few studies have tried to distinguish the intensity of political discussion, many studies have asked respondents whether they were involved in a strong form of discussion, namely, whether they tried to persuade or convince someone of their views. The canonical question, from the ANES, is "During the campaign, did you talk to any people and try to show them why they should vote for one of the parties or candidates?" Except for one case (the 1976 German Election Study, where respondents were asked whether they tried to convince others of their opinions), this question has always been asked about voting.

Somewhat surprisingly, no examples could be found in which people have been asked whether they tried to get people to work in a political campaign, become engaged in local political activity, or join a protest. Consequently, very little is known about who asks whom to participate.[40] In the 1968 ANES, follow-ups to the basic question asked, "Which of the people listed on this card [wife or husband, relative, friend, someone you work with, anyone else] did you talk to?" and "Does this person pay more attention or less attention to politics than you?" These questions are analogous to those described earlier about contacting, and they allowed Robinson (1976) to form a typology of opinion givers and takers in his test of the two-step flow hypothesis.

It was noted earlier that the ANES campaign participation count included the persuasion question, but also noted that this question had a relatively low correlation with the other items. This led to the suspicion that the persuasion question might not really belong with the other items on this scale, and in this section the persuasion question has been treated as a strong form of discussion. In fact, using the 1967 PIA data, one finds that the persuasion question is correlated .35 with discussion and .34 with interest in politics. This is lower than the correlation of .52 between interest in politics and discussion, but it is higher than the average correlation (.30) of persuasion with the other items on the campaign participation count. A (maximum likelihood oblique) factor analysis of interest, discussion, persuasion, campaign work, campaign meetings, campaign giving, and membership in a political club produces two dimensions explaining 40% of the variance in the items. Interest and discussion load heavily on the first dimension, with loadings of about .72; membership in a political club and campaign work, meetings, and giving load over

[39]The American, Estonian, and Russian CPS ask people "how free they feel to speak about controversial political issues" with friends, at church, or at work. These questions imply certain behaviors, but they really ask about attitudes toward behaviors. The Dutch question asks about actual behavior. A similar question appears on the 1948 panel study of Elmira, New York (see Berelson, Lazarsfeld, & McPhee, 1954, p. 357).

[40]One can, however, infer something about who does the asking from the extensive battery of questions in the CPS about the person making the request.

.55 on the second dimension. Persuasion has a loading of .33 on the first dimension and .30 on the second dimension. These results suggest that political discussion is a weak form of participation, possibly more akin to interest in politics than to other forms of activity, and they suggest that trying to persuade someone how to vote is midway between interest and other forms of electoral activity.

Voting

Voting is easily the most studied political activity. Because of its fundamental importance for democracy, surveys regularly ask people about their voting behavior in primary elections; general elections; referendums; and national, provincial or state, and local elections. Where applicable, questions are also asked about voting for all kinds of political offices, such as the presidential, congressional, and gubernatorial races in the United States. Because voting is scheduled for a set time, people can be asked about their voting intention before the election and their voting behavior after the election. Intentions and behaviors can be of two sorts: the decision to turn out and the choice among the candidates or parties. Participation studies focus on the turnout decision, and election studies consider the choice.

Election polls regularly ask citizens if they are registered to vote in upcoming elections and if they intend to vote. Many election studies interview people before the election to determine their voting intention, and some studies even follow the dynamics of preelection vote intention, as with the 1988 and 1993 Canadian Election Studies. All election studies of which the author is aware go back after the election and ask people whether they voted and how they voted. The Current Population Survey[41] asks people at what time of day they voted.

Most surveys focus on the upcoming or most recent election, but there are often questions about previous elections. The ANES, for example, usually asks respondents if they voted in the elections two years earlier. A few studies concerned with political participation, including the 1974 Canadian Election Study, the 1967 PIA study, and the 1990 American CPS, have asked respondents about how often they have voted since reaching voting age. It is very rare for studies to ask about the voting behavior of anyone other than the respondent, but the Current Population Survey does rely on an informant for the entire household. Very few studies ask about the issues that led people to vote (as opposed to the issues that affected their decision to vote for one candidate instead of another), but the 1990 American CPS did ask this question. Only about 50% of those who reported voting in the 1988 presidential election could offer a specific issue that motivated them to vote.[42]

A few studies have asked respondents why they did not vote, and a smaller number have asked why they voted. The 1983 British Participation Study, the 1965 Norwegian Election Study, and the 1974 Canadian Election Study, for example, listed reasons why people might not vote and asked whether they applied to the respondents.[43] The American, Estonian, and Russian CPS asked respondents about the importance of various reasons for voting. The 10 questions in the American battery are analyzed extensively in

---

[41]The Current Population Survey is often referenced by the acronym CPS, but here these letters have already been used for the Citizen Participation Studies.

[42]For the purposes of comparison, it is worth noting that two-thirds of those who worked in a campaign named an issue, and 90% of those who engaged in informal community activity identified a particular issue.

[43]These reasons included, "I could not vote because I was ill; because I was away; because I was too busy; elections are not important enough to make me bother to vote; my name was not on the Electoral register where I live; I couldn't get enough information to make a decision about voting."

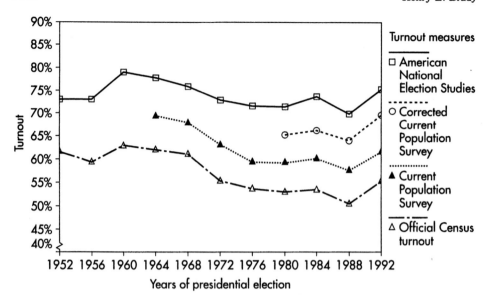

Fig. 13-4   Measures of U.S. Turnout over Time

Schlozman, Verba, and Brady (1995), which also reviews the extensive psychological literature that identifies the dangers of interpreting people's reasons or retrospective con-
structions of motivations too literally.

Perhaps the biggest problem with voting surveys is finding ways to reduce overreporting resulting from people saying they voted when they did not.[44] The standard approach to this problem has been to provide people with excuses for not voting, such as the
following Current Population Survey question: "In any election some people are not able
to vote because they are sick or busy or have some other reason, and others do not want
to vote. Did you vote. . . ?" This and other approaches will be discussed in detail in the
section on the reliability of measures and social desirability bias.

Figure 13–4 provides an indication of how much overreporting there might be.[45] This
figure depicts the change in American presidential election turnout over time, as reported
by several different methods. The top line is based on the ANES surveys, and the bottom
line is based on the official turnout statistics compiled by the U.S. Census Bureau from actual election results and estimates of the voting-age population. The lines roughly track
one another, but they also differ by about 11 percentage points at the beginning of the period and 20 percentage points by the end of the period. Part of this difference is undoubtedly due to overreporting on the ANES survey, but this is not the only difference between
the way turnout is calculated in each case. Turnout calculations are the ratio of numerator
data on the number of people who voted and denominator data on the number of potential
voters. Discrepancies in turnout can arise from differences in the way the numerator or the
denominator or both are defined.

The numerator for the bottom line on Figure 13–4 is based on the official statistics
from the registrars of voters for the number of people turning out, and this probably
provides the best estimate of who votes. But the overall turnout figure is probably an

[44]Voter validation studies (e.g., Wolfinger, 1993b) have shown that up to a quarter of those who did not vote
report having voted on surveys. It is very rare for someone to report not having voted when he or she did vote.

[45]I am indebted to Benjamin Highton and Raymond Wolfinger for these data. This discussion owes a great
deal to Wolfinger (1993a, 1993b).

underestimate because it is based on an inflated denominator defined as the resident population of voting age. This denominator includes noncitizens who are not eligible to vote. The top line, from the ANES, is based on interviews with the right group of people—citizens of voting age—but it uses survey self-reports of voting, which tend to produce inflated reports of the number of people voting. In addition, the sample selection effects of nonresponse to the interview probably produce a respondent population that is more likely to vote than all citizens of voting age (Brehm, 1993), and this leads to an even greater overestimate of turnout. The top and bottom lines are the upper and lower bounds for the true turnout figures.

The intermediate lines are from the Current Population Survey. The lower turnout figure (the dotted line) is based on those who reported voting on the survey divided by the voting-age population—noncitizens and those reported as "do not know" and "not reported" are classified as nonvoters and included in the denominator. Because both the numerator and the denominator are probably too big in this estimate, they tend to cancel one another out to produce an intermediate turnout figure. The dashed line excludes from the denominator noncitizens (based on a question about citizenship that was added to the Current Population Survey in 1980) and those reported as "do not know" and "not reported." This produces a turnout figure whose denominator is more likely to be correct (and more like that used in the ANES), but that may still suffer from biases in the numerator from self-reports. In addition, although the Current Population Survey has a higher response rate than the ANES, it also suffers from sample selection effects that bias the results toward higher turnout. All in all the corrected Current Population Survey (the dashed line) is probably a better upper bound than the line for the ANES data, but this still leaves a 12- to 14-percentage-point gap between the corrected Current Population Survey figures and the official turnout rate.

Some of this 12- to 14-percentage-point gap is due to survey overreports on the Current Population Survey, which inflates the turnout from that source, but part of it is due to the inclusion of noncitizens in the official figures, which deflates them. Wolfinger and Highton (personal communication) estimate that the inclusion of noncitizens in the denominator of the official figures deflates them by about 3 percentage points, so that the net inflation attributable to overreporting is 9 to 11%. This is very close to the results obtained from ANES voter validation studies (Wolfinger, 1993b, p. 17), which conclude that the turnout from ANES studies is inflated by about 7 to 13 percentage points by overreporting.

The clear differences among the four lines suggest the difficulty of estimating turnout, and they also suggest that reported declines in turnout since 1952 must be treated cautiously. All four lines have a downward trend (although 1992 produced a significant upturn), but very different rates of decline. The official turnout statistics decrease (in a linear regression) by about one percentage point every quadrennium, whereas the ANES figures decrease by only about one-third of a percentage point every four years—for a total of only about three percentage points over the entire period. Because immigration increased enormously over some of this period, it is tempting to think that the ANES figure, which excludes noncitizens in its denominator, might be more accurate than that derived from the official statistics. This makes the much ballyhooed decline in turnout seem less serious than do the official statistics.

Campaign–Electoral Activities

Beyond voting, the most studied forms of political participation are those associated with political campaigns and elections. As noted previously, five items listed in Table 13–3 (Try to Persuade, Display Preferences, Go to Meetings, Give Money, and Political Work) dating back to the 1952 and 1956 ANES have been used almost continuously in the United States and widely replicated elsewhere.[46] The Try to Persuade item has already been discussed in detail. The remaining items usually refer to the campaign period, and the biggest variation from one study to the next is in the way the act is described.

Almost all of the Display Preferences items mention putting a sticker on one's car, displaying a sign, or wearing a campaign button. The Go to Meetings items ask, not surprisingly, about going to political meetings, rallies, speeches, debates, or entertainment. Some studies employ follow-up questions about either the types of meetings (Japanese Election Study, 1967) or which party or parties organized the meetings (Norwegian Election Study, 1965). The Political Work items ask whether respondents have worked for a party or a candidate. The British studies usually mention "canvassing" as a form of work, and the Japanese Election Study of 1967 asks about the sorts of things that were done. The most basic form of the Give Money item asks if the respondent gave money to a candidate or a party.[47] These items have become more complicated as campaign financing has become more complex. The ANES, for example, started asking in 1980, "Did you use the one-dollar check-off option on your federal income tax return to make a political contribution this year?" and in 1984 "Did you give money to any other group [e.g., a political action committee] that supported or opposed candidates?" The Japanese Election Study of 1967 asked whether contributions were given through school or work and whether they were given to a candidate, to a party, through a union, through groups, through friends, or by other methods. The 1990 American CPS asked respondents whether they have sent any money in the past 12 months in response to "requests through the mail asking you to donate to political organizations, political causes, or candidates?" Finally, the 1988 Canadian Election Study asked an omnibus question that included going to a meeting, working for a candidate, or putting a sticker on a car.

For most studies, respondents are asked only whether or how often they undertake these activities, but in the American, Estonian, and Russian CPS, respondents were asked detailed questions about how much money in dollars or time in hours was given to candidates, parties, or groups. Questions were also asked about the office a candidate was running for; the party he or she represented; and the candidate's sex, race, and political views. Respondents were also asked about the issue or problem and the reasons that motivated the donation of time or money. In the American study a battery of about 15 reasons was administered, covering material, social, civic, and policy motivations. Finally, respondents were asked how much difference their efforts made.

Party Membership

Neither political party nor party membership is a straightforward concept. In some countries, such as the emerging democracies in Eastern Europe and the former Soviet Union, political parties are often no more than associations of people with some political interests. And party memberships may not exist in any formal sense even in well-developed

---

[46]All five of these items appear on the ANES from 1952 to 1992 and on the Canadian National Election Survey, 1974. All but Display Preferences appear on the 1967 Japanese Election Study. Three of them (Try to Persuade, Display Preferences, and Political Work) appear on the Political Action Studies, 1973 to 1976; Political Participation in America, 1967; Norwegian National Election Survey, 1965; German Election Panel Study, 1976; and Dutch Election Study, 1970–1973. The question about giving money is not relevant in some political systems, and the question about displaying preferences may be deemed too easy an item by some researchers. The Roper polls, used extensively by Rosenstone and Hansen (1993), regularly ask only whether citizens have "worked for a political party."

[47]It is often not clear whether or not party membership dues are considered monetary contributions.

democracies, such as the United States—not to mention the emerging democracies.[48] Consequently many studies rely on attitudinal measures of party identification or support for parties instead of behavioral measures of membership, such as paying dues and taking out a membership card. This has been the standard practice in the United States, but questions about party membership do appear in the Political Participation and Equality (PPE) Seven Nation study (but not for Japan or the United States), in the EuroBarometer studies, and in studies of countries such as Australia, Canada, France, Great Britain, Norway, and the Netherlands.

Party membership is often defined in terms of paying dues, but general queries such as "Are you a member of a political party?" have been used on the EuroBarometers and in studies in Britain and Canada. The British Participation Study even asks whether a respondent's father was a member of a political party when the respondent was in his or her teens. A few studies (e.g., Norwegian National Election Survey, 1965) follow up membership questions with whether or not respondents take an active part in the work of the party, such as meetings, study groups, or electoral work. The 1958 French Election Study asks how long the person has been a member by mentioning important dates (1957, 1953, 1945, "the days of the Resistance [1940–44]," and "since before the War"). Party involvements are also sometimes a part of larger organizational inventories, such as those described in the section on the institutions approach. The most detailed exploration of party involvements occurs in surveys of party members, such as Seyd and Whiteley's (1992) survey of British Labour Party members.

The Estonian and Russian CPS employed a grid in which about 30 political parties or associations were mentioned, and respondents were asked whether they were *familiar* with the party, whether they *supported* it, and in the Russian study, whether they were *members* of the party, or in the Estonian study, whether "within the last two years you had occasion to *donate money or to otherwise materially help [the party] or to participate in events, affairs, meetings or demonstrations, [or] marches of [the party]?*" This more complicated approach was taken with the Estonian study because dues-paying memberships are rare and involvement in these other ways with a party would be a strong indicator of attachment to the party. The Estonian and Russian studies also asked respondents whether they or their parents had ever been members of the Communist Party.

Although there has been scholarly reflection on the meaning of party identification across different political systems (Budge, Crewe, & Farlie, 1976; Cain & Ferejohn, 1981; Johnston, 1992), there has not been a similar degree of thought about the meaning of party membership. Paying dues is one simple definition of party membership, but this approach neglects the possibility that membership could consist of working for a party without providing money. A comparative study of this topic would be useful.

Political Contacting

More than any other form of participation, political contacting allows citizens to communicate a specific message to targeted political or governmental officials or even to their fellow citizens through the media. Contacting can occur through at least three *modes*—in

---

[48]Nie, Powell, and Prewitt (1969) constructed a five-item political participation index from the five-country Almond–Verba *Civic Culture* data set (Almond & Verba, 1963). This index included talking about public affairs, trying to influence a local decision, influencing an act of the national legislature, being a member of some group concerned with governmental affairs, and being involved in a party. In all countries but the United States, they asked whether the respondent was currently or ever a member of a political party or organization. In the United States they asked whether the respondent had ever been active in a political campaign "due to the absence of the phenomena of memberships in political parties in this country" (p. 377).

person, through a telephone call, or through writing—and it can be targeted toward at least three different *levels* (national, state, and local) and three types of *actors* (elected official or his or her staff, nonelected governmental official, and the media).[49] In addition, as with all forms of activity, the *time period* can vary from the past year to ever, or respondents can be asked how often they engage in contacting without a specific time period as a reference. The many choices for modes, target levels, target actors, and time periods make it possible to ask about contacting in many different ways.

The Roper question, "Have you written [in the past year] your congressman or senator?" is explicit about the mode, the target level, the target actors, and the time period, but it ignores a great many other ways that people can engage in political contacting. The American CPS mentions all three modes of contacting and asks four separate questions about the target level and actor. The questions are about two kinds of actors (elected officials or their staff and nonelected officials) and two levels (federal and state or local). The 1967 PIA question asks separately about local contacting and about state and federal contacting, and it allows open-ended responses on who was contacted and on the subject of the contact. The 1983 British Participation Study asks about these four kinds of situations and about radio or television programs and newspapers as well. The standard ANES question, which has been asked since 1952 (except for 1954, 1956, and 1970), mentions only writing letters and refers vaguely to "any public officials,"[50] and the PAS question is vague in the time period, the target actor and level, and the mode: "How often do you contact public officials or politicians?" These kinds of questions seem awfully vague, but they have the virtue of being quick and easy to ask.

As the modes of contacting expanded, new questions had to be devised. The 1990 American CPS asked whether those who listen to "talk shows" on the radio have "called up such a show" to express their opinions in the last 12 months. Future studies of contacting will no doubt have to mention e-mail, the Internet, and interactive television.

One of the core distinctions in Verba and Nie's (1972) work is between particularized contacting and contacts with broad social referents. They defined particularized contacts as those "in which the issue refers only to the respondent or his immediate family, and in which a government decision responsive to that contact would presumably have little or no direct impact on others in the society" (p. 66). Contacts about solving a Social Security problem, fixing a pothole in front of the respondent's house, getting a patronage job, and getting a relative into West Point are all particularized. Contacts with broad social referents "refer to issues or problems that are more public in nature and in which government actions would affect a significant segment of the population, if not the entire community or society" (p. 66). These include contacts about prices received by farmers, housing for African Americans, and environmental issues. Verba and Nie (1972) found that contacts with broad social referents had a strong relationship to other forms of "communal activity," such as holding membership in community problem-solving organizations and forming a group to work on local problems, whereas particularized contacts formed a separate dimension unrelated to other forms of political activity. Indeed, particularized contacts are just barely political in many instances.

---

[49]If one also allows other citizens to be targeted directly, then discussing politics and trying to persuade others could be considered forms of political contacting. If contacting political interest groups were added, then one would have a continuum ranging from contacting personal friends to interest groups to the media to governmental officials. This seems like too broad a definition, and one should be wary about including contacting the media because it is a much more indirect way to influence politics than contacting governmental officials directly.

[50]The 1968 ANES also asked, "Have you ever written a letter to the editor of a newspaper or magazine giving any political opinions?"

Making this distinction requires either asking and coding open-ended questions about the content of the contact, as was done by Verba and Nie (1972), or asking the respondent to think about the issue involved and to describe who was affected by the problem, as was done the CPS. This second method seems to work well, and it is much easier than coding open-ended responses. Nevertheless, it still requires follow-up questions, so that only a few studies have explored this distinction in detail.

In addition to asking about the issues involved and who were affected by them, the British Participation Study and the American, Estonian, and Russian CPS have also asked whether the contact had any results and whether the respondent was satisfied with the outcome. The CPS also asked a battery of questions about the reasons for contacting and a set of questions about the characteristics (race, party affiliation, sex) of the person contacted.

Local Community Activity

For many people the most salient and important type of political participation is involvement with others in nonelectoral political activities in their local community. Despite their importance, however, these forms of participation are not easy to characterize, and this has led to a number of useful—but perhaps incompletely worked-out—notions of how to ask about local political activity.

One common distinction is between informal and formal activities. The goal here is to make sure that survey research does not miss those cases where people get together on their own to solve community problems. The 1990 American CPS asked, "I'd like to ask also about *informal* activity in your community or neighborhood. In the past twelve months, have you gotten together *informally* with or worked with others in your community or neighborhood to try to deal with some community issue or problem?" This can be contrasted with the British Participation Study of 1983, which asked, "Have you supported or worked in, an *organized* group to raise an issue?" (Emphasis has been added to both questions.) Although the distinction seems clear, informal groups almost always quickly gain some organized structure, so that the line between formal and informal becomes blurred.

Perhaps it is better to distinguish between old and new groups and to ask, as the 1967 PIA did, "Have you ever taken part in forming a new group or a new organization to try to solve some community problem?" Old and new groups are probably easier to distinguish than organized and informal groups, but this is undoubtedly quite a different kind of distinction. It may be useful to know whether someone has started a group, but certainly it would be wrong to assume that someone must start a group to have engaged in informal participation.[51]

One approach to this problem is to simply jettison the distinction, as did the 1974 PAS, 1974 Canadian Election Study, 1967 PIA, and 1976 ANES, all of which used the simple variant of "Worked with others or joined an organization in your community to do something about some community problem?" Another approach was taken in the 1990 American CPS, where respondents were first asked about activities that were clearly

---

[51]One way out is to use a question like the following from the 1967 PIA, which allows those who did not really start the group still to climb on board: "Have you ever taken part in forming a new group or a new organization to try to solve some community problem?" That 14% of the American public said "yes" to this suggests that it is a very elastic question, but it is not clear that much is gained from this. The 1990 American CPS takes another approach by following up its question about engaging in informal activity with this question: "Did you take the lead in starting this informal effort?" Whereas 17% of the public said they engaged in informal activity in the past year, only 3% said they took the lead in it.

formal and organized. Once these questions had been asked, it was easier to use the question about informal activity to "mop up" all other local community activity.

Attending meetings and serving on local boards are the two kinds of formal activity that are most often considered. Of the two, people are more likely to attend meetings on local affairs. Three studies—Roper, the 1976 ANES, and the 1990 American CPS—ask about attending meetings on local affairs, and they all ask roughly the same question: "Have you attended in the last year [or two or three] a public meeting on town, school, or community affairs of the city council, school board, zoning board, planning board, or the like?" All three sources produce roughly the same base participation rate of about 15%.

There is a much lower rate for serving on a board or council. The 1990 American CPS, for example, asked about serving in the last two years on a local governmental board or council that deals with community problems. Only about 3% of the respondents replied affirmatively, and this is one reason why this question is so seldom asked. Nevertheless, this is a very interesting group of highly committed participators.

Unconventional Political Participation

Unconventional political acts present substantial problems for those studying political participation. In most cases they are infrequently performed. They are sometimes illegal, so that respondents will be unwilling to report having done them. And their meaning depends a great deal on the legal and cultural environment of a society. Not voting, for example, can be an act of protest in a totalitarian society that makes nonvoting a crime. Nevertheless, through the work of Muller (1972), Marsh (1977), and Barnes and Kaase (1979), there has been real progress in measuring this kind of participation.

Table 13–16 lists along the left-hand side a number of unconventional acts culled from the studies canvassed for this chapter. Based on the work by Marsh and Kaase (1979), they are listed in a "continuum from the relatively innocuous behaviors such as petitioning through increasingly severe forms of protest such as demonstrations, boycotts, strikes, occupations, blockades, damaging property, and violence" (p. 68). Activities in section A are usually lawful in democratic countries, while those in section B involve only the passive withdrawal of labor or patronage, although they are still sometimes legally restricted in various ways. The activities in section C are nonviolent and nonobstructive, but they do involve an individual disobeying a law, which can lead to criminal prosecution. The usually illegal activities in section D have a wider impact because they block access or occupy areas through picketing, staging sit-ins, or blocking traffic, but they do not actively do violence to property or people, as do the more serious acts in section E and especially in section F.

Table 13–16 also lists five important studies across the top that have employed five or more items on unconventional behavior, and the entries in the table indicate the percentage performing each act. As we would expect, the percentages near the top of the table are higher than those near the bottom. An asterisk next to a percentage indicates that the item was used to form a scale. The PAS scale of unconventional behavior was already discussed in this chapter.

Beginning in the early 1970s, Muller and his collaborators began their independent line of research on aggressive political behavior,[52] and the first column in Table 13–16

---

[52]Muller defines aggressive political behavior as (1) antiregime or illegal, (2) with political significance, and (3) involving group activity on the part of nonelites. It may or may not involve violence; "if it does not involve violence, it will be called *civil disobedience,* as distinguished from *political violence"* (Muller, 1979, p. 6). Muller sometimes refers to this as unconventional behavior, but this can cause confusion with the somewhat different concept defined in the PAS.

Table 13-16

Types of Unconventional Activities and Surveys with Five or More Items

	Percentage performing the act in five major studies				
Unconventional activities	FRG APP 1974	USA PAS 1974	BPS 1983	ANES PILOT 1985	EST CPS 1992
A. Usually Lawful—petition and assembly					
1. Signing a petition	48	58*	63	67	14
2. Organizing a petition			8		
3. Public meeting to protest			15		
4. Protest, march, or demonstration	34	11*	5	15	9
B. Passive Withdrawal of Labor or Patronage					
1. Boycotts		15*	4	20	1
2. Wildcat strikes or political strikes	6*	2*	7		6
C. Nonviolent and Nonobstructive Refusal to Obey Laws					
1. Refusing to pay rent, taxes, etc.	6*	2*		4	
2. Refusing military service	6				
D. Blocking Access to or Occupying Areas					
1. Picketing				13	3
2. Sit-ins or occupying buildings	4*	2*		3	
3. Blocking traffic		1*	1		
E. Violence against Property					
1. Painting slogans on walls		1			
2. Breaking windows, destroying signs		1			
F. Violence against People					
1. Participating in fights	3*	1	<1		
2. In group endorsing violent means	1*				

Note: Wording differs somewhat from one study to another. All studies except the FRG APP are random samples of the country's citizens. The FRG APP used a mixed random and purposive sampling scheme.

Sources and Key:

FRG APP—Federal Republic of Germany Aggressive Political Participation Study
USA PAS—Political Action Study for the USA
BPS—British Participation Study
ANES PILOT—American National Election Study Pilot
EST CPS—Estonian Citizen Participation Study

*Item used in a scale

presents data from Muller's study of Aggressive Political Participation (APP) done in the Federal Republic of Germany. As in the PAS, Muller (1979, p. 37) asked respondents "(1) whether or not they approved of each behavior; (2) in their view, how large a percentage of the Federal Republic would approve of each behavior; (3) whether or not they personally would engage in each behavior; and (4) whether or not they had done each behavior." Each of the five acts (sections A, B, C, D, and F) was then scored (see Muller, 1979, pp. 42–45) based on actual participation in the behavior (question 4), behavioral intention (question 3), and mean perceived social disapproval rating (question 2). This scoring differs from the PAS scale of protest potential because the individual's *own* approval or disapproval of the act (question 1) is not used to form the scale. After performing a factor analysis to establish the strong unidimensionality of these five acts, Muller combined them into a scale of aggressive political participation, which he used throughout his work.

There is some overlap between the PAS scale of protest potential and Muller's APP scale, but they differ in important ways. Because it does not use the respondent's approval or disapproval of the activity, Muller's scale seems closer to the PAS protest activity scale than to the protest potential scale. In addition, all of the PAS scales omit violent acts (even though they were on the PAS surveys) and include acts from all other categories (sections A–D) on Table 13–16, including the usually lawful acts of petition and assembly, whereas the APP scale omits lawful acts (even though they were included on the survey) and includes items from all other areas except violence against property. Muller's approach makes sense, given his theoretical interest in aggressive behavior that requires breaking the law. The authors of the PAS had no principled reason for omitting violent acts, but they justified their omission on the grounds that "[t]he level of positive support for damage and violence is so low that very little variance remains for survey analysis" (Marsh & Kaase, 1979, pp. 71–72).

Despite their differences, the PAS and APP scales do converge in their claim that unconventional political participation is unidimensional. Although lawyers might argue that there are significant differences among lawful forms of petition and assembly (the acts in section A of Table 13–16), civil disobedience (roughly sections B, C, and D), and political violence (sections E and F), Muller (1979, pp. 46–51) and Marsh and Kaase (1979, pp. 65–81) have argued forcefully for a unidimensional conception. There is certainly substantial evidence on this side of the argument, but there is no denying that certain lines are crossed when people pass first from legal to illegal and then to violent actions. Furthermore, the PAS found that the order of activities in Guttman scaling varied somewhat from country to country, suggesting that they at least had different meanings (or at least different "difficulty levels") across societies.

Two of the three other studies listed on Table 13–16 are notable because they asked follow-up questions that elaborated on the features of political protest, but the major innovation of the 1985 ANES Pilot Study items is three questions that ask about protesting specific issues. Each question began by asking, "Have you ever participated in some kind of public protest concerning," and respondents were then asked about "either supporting or opposing prayer in the schools," "either the right to an abortion or the 'right to life,' " and "restricting the distribution or requiring labelling the contents of magazines, books, TV programs, movies or records." These questions provide a very useful way to link problems and concerns with protesting. The two other studies ask extensive follow-up questions about protesting. Both the 1983 British Participation Study and the 1992 Estonian CPS asked about the issue involved, the impact of the act, and the respondent's satisfaction with the result. All of the CPS also asked about the reasons for protesting.

Strengths and Limitations of the Political Actions Approach

The political actions approach forms the core of all political participation studies, and it can produce an excellent inventory of political participation. At the same time it might miss some activities, such as organizational involvements or workplace mobilization, by failing to mention particular settings where people might participate or specific problems that might motivate them. To overcome these problems, we turn to the institutions approach and the problems and needs approach.

Institutions Approach

Rationale for the Institutions Approach

Of all the forms of political participation, electoral behavior is the easiest to measure because it takes place within the framework of regularly scheduled elections. No other form of participation is as regularized and as widely practiced, but many other forms are rooted in institutional behaviors that can serve as reference points for those recording and studying them. Trade unions and other workplace organizations, for example, have traditionally been a locus of political activity. Religious organizations have been a fountainhead of such American political movements as abolition, temperance, and civil rights. Organizational memberships are often a source of political motivations and actions. Families and schools provide the resources, skills, knowledge, and contacts for political activity. These are the institutions we consider in this section. Not every act of participation has a clear-cut link to a particular institution, so that the institutions approach has to be supplemented by other methods, but some forms of participation, such as voting on the issue position of an organization that takes political stands, are hard to identity in any other way.

To use the institutions approach, three steps must be taken. First, a list of institutional locations for political participation must be developed that covers the relevant possibilities. Second, the extent of the respondent's involvement in each institution must be determined. Third, some method must be devised to determine whether the respondent undertook some form of political participation through his or her involvement. Each of these steps leads to a host of difficulties that can be illustrated by inventories of voluntary organizations.

Inventories of Group Memberships

The institutions approach to measuring political participation is most often used in conjunction with inventories of group and organizational memberships. Baumgartner and Walker (1988) trace these inventories back to the famous 1924 Middletown study of Muncie, Indiana (Lynd & Lynd, 1929, p. 527), which placed groups in 10 categories: trade union, business or professional, athletic, benevolent, literary or musical, military or patriotic, social, civic, juvenile clubs, and civic (see Table 13–17). A very similar list was used in the coding of an open-ended question about organizational memberships in the 1948 Elmira campaign study (Berelson, Lazarsfeld, & McPhee, 1954, p. 51). Verba and Nie (1972) adapted this list, mostly by expanding it to 15 categories, for their 1967 survey. They also broadened the question to include national groups, and they presented respondents with the list to jog their memory. Most importantly, they were the first to ask whether the groups did "anything to try to solve individual or community problems" and whether there was "any discussion of public affairs or of politics at the meetings." This provided a way to determine whether the organizations were the sites for political participation. Baumgartner and Walker (1988) call the Verba–Nie version the "Standard Question" because a variant of it has been used repeatedly in the GSS,[53] in the PAS, and in other studies.

Unfortunately the Standard Question developed three serious flaws as time passed:

> First, the probes were not changed in response to changes in the nature of American voluntary association, so they failed to record the growing number of affiliations with new

---

[53]Smith (1990) discusses the GSS and other questions in detail.

Table 13-17

Comparison of Organizational Categories across Major Studies

Middletown—1924	Elmira—1948	PIA—1967	PAS—1974	ANES Pilot—1985	CPS—1990
Athletic	Sports, hobby, recreational	Sports/hobby, garden	Athletic clubs or teams/ special interest or hobbies	Sports, recreation, community, neighborhood, school, youth	Sports, hobbies
Benevolent	Lodge, fraternal	Fraternal	Fraternal	Fraternities, lodges, nationality, ethnic	Fraternal
Business, professional	Economic, occup., professional	Professional, academic	Business assn./professional assn.	Business or profession	Business, professional, farm
Church affiliated	Church affiliated	Church affiliated	Church or religious	(Church affiliated)	Religiously affiliated
Literary, musical, study	Cultural	Literary, art, discussion, study		Cultural, literary, art organizations	Cultural/literary, art, discussion, study
Military, patriotic	Military, patriotic, veterans	Veterans	Veterans	Veterans	Veterans
Social	Neighborhood, card clubs, discussion		Neighborhood assn./social or cardplaying	[See Sports, recreation, community, etc.]	Neighborhood, block

Civic	Civic	Youth club	Civic	[See Sports, recreation, community, etc.]	Nonpartisan, civic
Juvenile club			Youth		Youth
Trade union	(Trade union)	Labor union	(Labor union)	Labor union	Labor union
	Political, political party	Political groups	Political party		Electoral, party
	Service	Service	Charity or social welfare	Charities	Charitable, service
					[See Business, professional, farm]
		Farm organization	Farm organization		
		Nationality groups	Racial or ethnic	[See Fraternities, lodges, nationality, ethnic]	Nationality, ethnic, racial
		School fraternities, sororities/School service			Educational
			Other political clubs or orgs.	Social issue	Senior citizens
			Cooperative		Women's rights
					Liberal, conservative/political issue

Key: Parentheses indicate that the category is not included in the battery, but that there are separate questions about it in the study. Slashes indicate separate questions in the battery.

types of groups. Second, the data collection techniques suited to the computer technology of the mid-1960s allowed for only one affiliation within each category, overlooking the explosive growth of the number of groups within certain types. And third, the concept of affiliation did not include sending money without being a formal member of the organization, though direct-mail solicitation and other developments have made this form of affiliation more and more common among Americans. (Baumgartner & Walker, 1988, p. 914)

The 1985 ANES Pilot Study (Baumgartner & Walker, 1988) and the 1990 CPS (Schlozman, 1994) tried to correct these flaws by including additional organizational types, by allowing respondents to mention more than one affiliation within each category, and by asking about both holding membership in and giving money to the organization. For example, the 1990 CPS lists 19 different categories, and for each category it asks respondents the questions in Table 13–18 (see Schlozman, 1994). These questions allow the researcher to experiment with different definitions of organizational involvement and of political involvement in the organization.

Baumgartner and Walker (1988) show that their modifications of the Standard Question create a much different picture of the interest group system, with 78% of their sample reporting holding membership in one or more groups and 90% reporting holding membership or giving money. Even more importantly, many respondents report multiple memberships in specific categories. Baumgartner and Walker (1988, p. 920) conclude that "[b]y recording all memberships and financial contributions, we uncovered 187 percent more group affiliations than we would have with the Standard Question." Similarly the CPS indicates that 71% of the American public are members of one or more organizations and 79% are members of or give money to one or more groups.[54]

The last step toward identifying political participation resulting from organizational involvements is asking whether the respondent engaged in some political activity. There are several ways this can be done using the questions in Table 13–18. A person could be counted as politically active in an organization if people sometimes chatted informally about politics at meetings, but this is too low a standard because it requires neither the respondent's involvement in the informal chats nor the organization's involvement in politics. A somewhat harder test would be to require that there be discussions of politics or public affairs on the agenda of these meetings. A still harder test would be to require that the organization take stands on public issues.

Baumgartner and Walker (1988, p. 918) required only an affirmative response to "Does [the group] take stands on or discuss public issues or try to influence governmental actions?" The CPS used the tougher standard of requiring that the organization take stands on public issues (Schlozman, 1994). An even harder standard would be to require that the respondent protested, contacted, voted, or campaigned as a result of organizational involvement, but this would establish too a high a standard by requiring an action above and beyond the respondent's holding membership or giving money to the organization.

Whatever the standard for political participation, there is some question about whether respondents, especially those with limited attachments to organizations, know very much about the political involvement of their organizations. It is certainly true that those organizations that respondents claim take stands are ones that we would expect to do so, but it is also true that respondents who are members are more likely to claim that their organizations take political stands than those who just give money. Unfortunately it

---

[54]The differences in these figures between the two studies could be the result of differences in the sample or the year of the survey.

Table 13-18

Questions about Organizational Membership from the American Citizen Participation Study

1. Are you a member of. . . ?
2. Not counting any membership dues, have you contributed money in the past twelve months to any organization of this type?
3. How many such organizations are you involved with?
4. What is the name of the organization?
5. Have you attended a meeting of the organization in the past twelve months?
   a. Are there sometimes political discussions on the agendas of these meetings?
   b. Do people at these meetings sometimes chat informally about politics or government?
   c. Do you consider yourself an active member of the organization—that is, *in the past twelve months* have you served on a committee, given time for special projects, or helped organize meetings?
6. In the past five years, have you served on the board or been an officer of the organization?
7. Does this organization sometimes take stands on any public issues—either locally or nationally?
8. Does this organization fund or provide charitable or social services to benefit people who are not members of the organization?

Source: American Citizen Participation Study Questionnaire.

is an almost impossible task to check out the political activities of every organization mentioned by every respondent, so researchers must rely on these self-reports.

Questions about Participation through Work, Church, or Family

Some studies have focused on only one or two institutional locations for political participation. Questions about union membership have been a staple of political surveys since they began, and perhaps because unions are assumed to be politically active, these studies do not ask about political discussion at meetings or political stands by the unions. A few studies (e.g., 1988 Canadian Election Study), however, have asked whether the union contacted the respondent or a family member about supporting a candidate or party. The 1990 American CPS asked respondents whether the organization where they worked or their superiors suggested voting one way or another, making a political contribution, or taking some other political action.

The 1990 American CPS also asked respondents whether the clergy in their church discussed local or national political issues from the pulpit, whether the respondents attended a meeting about some local or national political issue at their church or synagogue, and whether anyone in an official position at their church made suggestions about voting for or against candidates or taking some political action. The answers to these questions suggest that a good deal of mobilizing might be taking place in these institutions, so that we might learn a great deal about the genesis of political action by repeating and elaborating these kinds of questions.[55]

[55]The several waves of the Youth–Parent Socialization Panel Study also asked respondents about political activity in their households when they were in high school and about political activity in their high schools and colleges. The American CPS used retrospective versions of these questions (e.g., "When you were sixteen. . . ?").

Problems and Needs Approach

The Approach

The 1967 PIA study alternates between questions about the respondents' concerns and questions about their political participation. After a series of questions about "the most [and next most] important problem of this community," the questionnaire asks the respondent:

> How often do you usually discuss local community problems with others in this community?
>
> Have you ever worked with others in this community to try to solve some community problem?
>
> Have you ever taken part in forming a new group or a new organization to try to solve some community problem?

This approach is repeated at the national level with questions about "the most [and next most] important problem facing the United States these days," followed by a series of questions about holding organizational memberships, discussing politics, persuading others, performing campaign work, attending political meetings, voting, and contacting governmental officials. Similarly the 1979–1981 PAS started with a series of questions about life problems and how to cope with them before launching into queries about political participation. These questions are used in at least two chapters of Jennings *et al.* (1989) to explore the boundary between personal and governmental responsibilities along the lines of Sniderman and Brody's (1977) discussion of "coping."

British Participation Study

This approach is very appealing because it starts at the very beginning with people's needs and concerns. Yet a careful examination of both the PIA and the PAS suggests that the questions about problems and needs are not linked directly to political activity. Instead, they serve as a convenient way to introduce questions about political participation by getting people talking about things they care about. Parry, Moyser, and Day (1992) go one step further and try to make a direct link between problems and participation because "people take action in response to issues, needs and problems" (Parry, Moyser, & Day, 1992, p. 241). Table 13–19 extracts some of the basic questions from the British Participation Study of Parry, Moyser, and Day, but the full schedule is worth perusing for anyone interested in this approach.

The British Participation Study begins by asking about "issues, needs, and problems that people might consider taking action on." By including the last phrase, they narrow the range from all possible issues, needs, and problems in order to eliminate those that have no public dimension, such as losing a girlfriend, leaking roofs, or car trouble. They allowed the respondent to list as many as four issues, needs, or problems in an open-ended format, which they later coded. They found that 65% mentioned an issue and 42% reported taking an action (Parry *et al.*, 1992, p. 247). They followed up these actions with a battery of questions, including what was done, how the respondent had gotten the idea of doing it, and whether or not it was a "political" action. There was also a series of questions about how much effort was expended, what results were obtained, and how satisfied the respondent was with the results.

Table 13-19

Problems and Needs Approach as Used in the British Participation Study, 1984–1985

---

4. Next I'd like to ask about the issues, needs and problems that people might consider taking action on: actions such as contacting a Local Councillor or official, signing a petition, joining in a national protest or working in a small group.

   a) *Whether or not* you have taken any action on them, what particular issues, needs or problems have been important to you over the past five years or so? . . .

   b) [For each issue/need/problem] Would you say that [it] is the sort of thing that people might take action about, for example, actions such as contacting an MP or Local Councillor?"

   c) What issues, needs or problems are there at a local level, or that affect you or your family, or that affect the country as a whole that people might take action about?

   d) About how much action have you, yourself taken on [it]—a lot, some, a little, or none at all?

8. [Follow-up if respondent took action]

   a) First, could you describe the main action that you took? (I mean the action that took most effort.)

   b) How did you first get the idea of taking this action?

12. Generally speaking would you describe this action as political in any way?

Source: British Political Participation Study. (Parry, Moyser, & Day, 1992, pages 443, 445, 446)

These questions are one way to determine people's political agendas and to link their political participation to their problems and needs. But it seems likely that starting with problems and needs has some of the same problems as asking people about their most important problem (Iyengar & Kinder, 1987). Too often people rely on recent media reports or top-of-the-head responses. Asking people to link their problems to political participation probably improves the quality of the responses, but it still seems likely that much is missed through this procedure. It probably makes more sense to start by using either the political activities or the institutions approach to identify acts of political participation and to then ask about the issue, need, or problem that motivated the act. In fact, Parry *et al.* used this approach as well.

Validity of Measures and Social Desirability Bias

No matter which of the three methods survey researchers use to assess political participation, they must ultimately rely on responses to questions about (usually) socially desirable political participation and group affiliations. It is well known that responses to questions can vary dramatically, depending on the way the questions are worded,[56] and this may affect the results obtained. Answers to questions about political participation can depend on the specificity of the stimulus, the time period mentioned, and the context of the question. In addition, a number of authors[57] have noted that respondents typically overreport

---

[56]See, for example, Bradburn, Rips, and Shevell (1987) and Tanur (1984, pt. III).

[57]See, for example, Anderson and Silver (1986); Quaile-Hill and Hurley (1984); Katosh and Traugott (1981); Silver, Abramson, and Anderson (1986); Silver, Anderson, and Abramson (1986); Volgy and Schwarz (1984); and Weiss (1968).

forms of participation like these because of a social desirability bias "in which cognitive dissonance can lead to a rather consistent distortion of memory in order to reinforce continued perception of oneself as a good citizen" (Cahalan, 1968).

These results could lead to three ways that data on political participation might either differ from source to source or, more seriously, be biased. First, studies differ in the degree of specificity when they ask about political participation. This makes comparisons difficult, and it might mean that some data are better than others. Second, reports of activity might be inflated by social desirability bias or other factors. Third, if these same biases inflate reports of church attendance, civic skills, involvement in high school governance, organizational affiliations, and other activities, then there may be spurious correlations with political participation. This could mean that many models of political participation that explain participation in terms of these factors are confounded by spurious correlations.

Different Question Wordings

Much of the available data on political participation comes from questions asked on public opinion polls or the ANES. None of these surveys has as its primary purpose the study of political participation, so that each must depend on short batteries of items and abbreviated questions to inquire about participation. Most political participation studies have the luxury of focusing on political participation. As a consequence they utilize detailed batteries of questions with extensive descriptions of exactly what is meant by giving a contribution or contacting an official. This approach increases the number of people claiming to engage in an activity, but this method might provide a closer approximation to the truth than do short and often vague questions about political activity.

It is known, for example, from comparing the screener data on the 1989 CPS with the more detailed follow-up questionnaire administered in 1990 that administering more extensive questions to the same people increases the amount of reported participation. Whereas 49% of screener respondents said they belonged to an organization when asked a simple question about organizational membership on the screener, almost 80% of the respondents on the follow-up said they were associated with an organization when presented with a list of over 20 organizations.

Turning to contacting, when a question on the screener was used to ask whether people had contacted at any level in the past year, 26% said "yes." On the follow-up questionnaire 34% of the same respondents reported contacting at the federal or local level in the last year. The two questions cover the same time period (one year), but on the follow-up, people were asked whether they had contacted a "federal elected official or someone on the staff of such an official," "a non-elected official in a federal government agency," "an elected official on the state or local level," or "a non-elected official in a state or local government agency or board." By specifying four different targets for their contacting, the number of people who said they had made such contacts increased quite substantially.

Turning to comparisons with other studies, the Roper studies described in Rosenstone and Hansen (1993) report that 14% of the population contacted their senator or congressman within the last year. This is substantially smaller than the results of either the CPS screener or the follow-up percentage for contacting, and it seems likely that the Roper question underestimates the amount of contacting. The Roper question is embedded within a battery of items, and it states, "Please look at this list of activities and tell me if you have done any of them in the last year: Spoken to or written your congressman or some other national leader." The screener question on the 1989 CPS covers the same time period (12 months), but it asks about a broader range of activities within the confines of one question. And as noted previously, the follow-up question employs four questions. One of these asks whether the respondent has contacted a "federal elected official or someone on the staff of such an official." This seems closest to the Roper item, and 13% of the CPS sample reported having contacted a federal elected official or someone on the staff of such an official in the last year. This seems about right, given the Roper figure of 14%.[58]

Similar disparities arise when one turns to other questions. In the 1990 CPS follow-up study, for example, 24% of the American population had contributed to an individual candidate, a party group, a political action committee, or any other organization that supported candidates between January 1988 and the interview in the spring of 1990. This is a substantially larger figure than the 9–10% of the respondents on ANES who answered "yes" to either one or both of two questions about contributing to a party or a candidate,[59] but the question asked on the 1990 CPS covers a longer time period than the ANES questions, and it asks about a broader range of activities. Similarly, 9% of the CPS sample said that between January 1988 and spring 1990 they had "worked as a volunteer . . . for a candidate running for national, state, or local office." This is almost double the 4–5% who said "yes" to the ANES question, "Did you do any (other) work for one of the parties or candidates during the campaign?" but the CPS question covers a longer period of time, and it explicitly mentions all levels of government.[60]

For activities in the local community, about 17% of the population surveyed by Roper report attending "meetings of city council or school board" in the last year. The CPS reports a much smaller figure of 5% with a series of questions about serving on a local board or attending meetings within the last 12 months.

These data suggest that responses about political participation vary a great deal, depending on the question wording, and that there is no way to be sure which results give the closest approximation to the truth without some independent information on performance of these activities. One can, however, turn to recent research on the cognitive bases of surveys (Tanur, 1992) to obtain a framework for thinking about good and bad questions. This research is still in its infancy, but there is a growing body of literature on how people understand questions (Tanur, 1992, pt. II) and how they access memory (Tanur, 1992, pt. III) to answer them.

Probably the most frequently used method for aiding recall is to convert the task into one of recognition by presenting respondents with extensive lists of possible actions they might have taken. As noted earlier, this increases the percentage of people saying they engaged in an action. The work by Loftus, Smith, Klinger, and Fiedler (1992) on "Memory and Mismemory for Health Events" suggests that the recall task may lead to underreporting, while the recognition task may lead to overreporting, but one cannot say much more than that.

---

[58]On the CPS screener, respondents were asked in one question whether they had contacted at any level in the past year. Twenty-six per-cent said "yes." When the time period was expanded to five years, 36% of the sample said "yes."

[59]The two questions are "Did you give money to a political party during this election year?" and "Did you give any money to an individual candidate running for public office?" The 9–10% figure represents the number of people saying "yes" to either question.

[60]The CPS question, however, only mentions working for a "candidate" and not a "party or candidate," but almost all campaign work seems to be for some candidate. For the CPS screener question, which covers the time between the beginning of the 1988 campaign and the screener interview, which was in the summer and fall of 1989, only 4.8% of the sample said they participated in a campaign. The question and time period are much closer to the ANES query, and the results are closer as well.

Pearson, Ross, and Dawes (1992, p. 87) summarize some techniques that might be used to improve questions:

(1) emphasizing to respondents through instruction and reinforcement the importance and need for accurate and precise answers;

(2) reinstating the context of the event or attribute being recalled;

(3) using "aided recall" methods in which respondents are provided with lists related to the event being recalled and then asked to recognize events or objects, as compared to the more difficult task of recalling them;

(4) keeping the reference period short (e.g., less than six months);

(5) using landmark events as memory anchors (e.g., an earthquake, the Shuttle disaster, Christmas);

(6) in panel studies "bounding" the recall period by explicit reference to periods and information provided in previous interviews; and

(7) asking respondents to date events—if such dating is required—only after other questions about the events have provided contextual information to assist recall.

Very few participation studies have used even one or two of these methods, and none has really tried to put an extensive amount of effort into aiding respondents' recall of events or verifying the results. In fact, only in the area of voting do we have extensive efforts to verify the vote and to improve reporting.

Bias in Reports of Activity

Voting is the only form of participation for which there are readily available aggregate baseline data for comparing what survey respondents say and their actual behavior. As shown in Figure 13–4, the ANES routinely reports turnout levels that are 15 to 20% higher than the actual vote totals suggest.[61] These substantial differences have led the ANES to engage in a long-term program of voter validation, in which survey interviewers check local voting registration records of respondents. This research has found a very low level of underreporting by those who actually vote, but a substantial level of overreporting by those who did not vote. "In the four vote validation studies conducted by the University of Michigan Survey Research Center (SRC) and Center for Political Studies, a large proportion of respondents who did not vote, according to checks of local registration and voting records, claimed that they voted: 27.4% in 1964, 31.4% in 1976, 22.6% in 1978, and 27.4% in 1980" (Silver, Anderson, & Abramson, 1986, p. 613).

The most common explanation for this is "that people like to see themselves as good citizens or, more generally, to present themselves in a socially desirable light" (Presser, 1990, p. 587). In contrast, Abelson, Loftus, and Greenwald (1994, p. 152) have proposed a low salience explanation in which "people who failed to vote in the target election may have only a vague general impression of having gone to the polls at some past time, but be unable to retrieve the specifics that would permit them to identify a vote as having been an old one rather than the recent one."[62] Whatever the explanation, researchers (Abelson, Loftus, & Greenwald, 1994; Presser, 1990) have found it very hard to eliminate overreporting by increasing the context; by trying to make nonvoting

---

[61]This problem is discussed in detail in Appendix A of Wolfinger and Rosenstone (1980, pp. 115–118) and in Wolfinger (1993b).

[62]Brady, Verba, and Schlozman (1995, p. 616) make the same point.

more socially desirable; or by providing an outlet for social desirability, while stressing the importance of precision by asking about voting during a longer and a shorter time frame.

Spurious Correlations

Every survey of voting has found some upward biases in the reporting of the one form of activity for which there is a good social accounting system. This raises concerns about results from surveys of political participation. Could social desirability bias invalidate the causal inferences researchers try to make from their data?

For spurious results to occur, social desirability bias has to enter in a very specific way, so that some subgroups are more prone to it than others (Brady, 1985). Silver, Anderson, and Abramson (1986, p. 620) apparently believe that it does enter in the required fashion. They show that "the tendency to overreport voting is related to respondent characteristics," so that "measures of the relation between respondent characteristics and self-reported voting will overestimate the strength of the relation between the dependent and independent variables." They reject earlier findings by Sigelman (1982) and Katosh and Traugott (1981) that showed that validated and self-report measures of voting yield the same results.

Verba, Schlozman, and Brady (1995, Appendix E) present a model that accounts for exaggerated reports of activity and many of the empirical findings in the vote validation literature without leading to spurious correlations. In this model when an interviewer asks a question about political participation (often substantially after the act might have been performed), every respondent forms a sense of the likelihood of having performed the act based on the relevant clues or considerations (Bradburn *et al.*, 1987; Zaller & Feldman, 1992), and every respondent exaggerates this likelihood by adding some quantity drawn from a distribution with a positive mean that is independent of their characteristics. If the resulting likelihood is above some threshold, then the respondent says that he or she performed the activity. Those who actually are more likely to have done it (and in fact often do the activity, but perhaps not in the period asked about by the interviewer) are more likely to go over the threshold and to report they did it because of the exaggeration factor. Those who are less likely to have done it are less likely to go over the threshold, even though they add in the same exaggeration factor. Hence we tend to find that overreporters look a lot like truthful reporters—although maybe somewhat less educated, less interested in politics, and so forth because it is these people who are closest to the threshold.

This is exactly what has been found in the literature cited earlier. Volgy and Schwarz (1984), for example, find that "these findings suggest that those who claim to participate and those who actually do participate have a good deal in common, . . . both undocumented and documented participants may come from a similar 'pool' of potential activists" (p. 760), and Silver, Anderson, and Abramson (1986) find that "Americans who are more concerned about the outcome of the election are also more likely to overreport voting" (p. 614). Furthermore, several studies that have either devised experimental manipulations to increase social desirability (Presser, 1990) or looked for factors in the interview situation that would have increased social desirability (Silver, Abramson, & Anderson, 1986) have failed to find any effects, although the race of the interviewer may be an exception (Anderson, Silver, & Abramson, 1988).

The most compelling evidence for spurious correlations comes from Presser and Traugott (1992), who consider the hypothesis that "misreporters regularly voted in earlier elections" (p. 77). They found the following: "A comparison of regressions predicting turnout using the validated reports versus the self-reports shows that the respondent errors can distort conclusions about the correlates of voting. For example, controlling for three other variables, education was related to self-reported voting but not to validated voting" (p. 77). Presser and Traugott also found that the impact of income was larger for the validated vote equation than for the self-report equation. This suggests that both upward and downward biases are possible.

There are still reasons to believe that social desirability may not be a serious problem for research on political participation. For example, if there are different forms of social desirability—some people think that church attendance is desirable, but others do not—then social desirability may lead to an underestimation of the importance of some factors because of what amounts to a classic errors-in-variables situation. These observations are encouraging, but until we have better validation studies of political participation, we will have to worry that biases in reports can lead us astray.

Conclusions

Because political participation is multidimensional and multifaceted, this chapter cannot end with a simple or single recommendation for a specific set of items to measure political participation. Instead, one can make some recommendations about the strengths and weaknesses of the three approaches to measuring political participation, about several scales that might be useful, about the best formats for questions, and about areas for further research.

Strengths and Weaknesses of the Three Approaches

The mainstay of all political participation studies has been the political activities approach, and this will undoubtedly remain the best way to measure political participation. Table 13–14 provides a useful checklist of political activities, and Table 13–15 lists all of the characteristics that might be considered. The political activities approach works best when it is easy to name and describe acts, but it tends to miss participation that takes place incidentally or through organizational affiliations, so it must be supplemented with the institutions approach. A thorough study of political participation certainly requires the use of an inventory of political organizations along with questions about the respondent's political involvement in each organization. A complete study probably also requires very detailed questions about involvement and participation within especially important institutions, such as the workplace and churches. An exploration of individual activity within these institutions in fact may be the best way to get a better understanding of how social networks foster political activity. Finally, although we should always ask about the problems, issues, or needs that motivated political actions, more may be lost than gained by asking about these problems and needs before asking about participation. Most people are not very good at articulating their problems and needs, and even after identifying them, most people may not find them very helpful in recounting instances of political participation. It is probably best to ask about problems, issues, or needs after identifying political actions.

Most studies have used a combination of the political activities and institutions approaches, and that is the proper mixture. In most cases there is not much need to turn to the problems and needs approach. Ultimately, however, each study must combine the available methods to maximize recall, data quality, the coverage of activities, and the collection of ancillary information that can be useful in explaining political participation.

Some Useful Scales

No one item or scale can adequately measure political participation, but at least two scales of participation are used fairly widely, and a third seems very promising.

The *ANES campaign participation count* (see items 2 through 6 in Table 13–3) has been used since 1952 in the United States and in many studies in other countries. Earlier it was argued that the "trying to persuade someone to vote" item is somewhat different from the other items on the scale, but this scale is still an excellent starting place for anyone studying political participation during election campaigns.

The 1974 *PAS scale for protest activity* (see the items in Table 13–8 for the scale, and consult Table 13–16 to compare them with other items) is widely used to measure unconventional forms of political participation, and it has the virtue of asking about potential participation as well as actual participation.

The eight-item *CPS participation count* (see items 1 through 8 in Table 13–10) is harder to administer than the ANES campaign participation count, but it is a promising new measure that goes beyond campaign participation. Researchers might choose some of the more easily administered items from this scale (e.g., those on voting, campaign work, campaign contributions, contacting, informal community participation, and protesting) to get a broad array of activities and to maintain comparability with other data sets. One of the advantages of the CPS questions is that there are follow-up items on the intensity of involvement as measured by time expended, money donated, or frequency of performance. These quantitative measures provide a much more detailed view of political participation.

In addition to using these scales, some variant of the organizational inventory first developed by Verba and Nie's PIA (see Table 13–17) must be used in any serious study of participation, but users will find themselves torn between wanting to replicate the version used by the GSS and solving some of the problems identified by Baumgartner and Walker (1988) by using the new inventory in the 1990 American CPS (see Table 13–18) or the inventory in the 1996 ANES. The best solution may be a version that allows replication of the PIA inventory, while adding additional groups and questions about giving money and belonging to multiple groups.[63]

These three scales and one of the organizational inventories provide very good coverage of all possible forms of participation. They might all be profitably included in a study of political participation. If a study is restricted to a very small number of items, however, subsets from these scales and inventories could be chosen, depending on the theoretical purposes of the study.

Best Formats for Questions

The growing literature on survey responses and the substantial experience now obtained with questions about political participation suggest the following rules for improving survey items:

- Aim for concreteness through detailed description of the act.
- Ask about a short and definite time interval (e.g., one year).
- Ask for details of the activity to help the respondent remember it.
- Ask for amounts of time or money, if possible.
- Design questions to discourage overreporting and social desirability bias.

[63]Schlozman (1994), however, makes a strong case for the particular order and wording used in the American CPS.

These rules make sense based on our experience, but they have not been rigorously tested with adequate validity studies for any form of participation except possibly voting.

Areas for Further Research

Perhaps the greatest need for future research is the validation of political participation measures. Figure 13–4 dramatically indicates the complexities in the measurement of even such a simple concept as voting turnout. Future research should consider different question wordings on surveys, and it should compare the results with actual behaviors. This research should explore how response biases affect not only the correct reporting of events, but also the multivariate analyses of political participation. In addition to these methodological studies, students of political participation should work to develop measures of the context within which people decide to participate. Most models of participation emphasize factors affecting the supply of participation (e.g., political interest, money, time, skills, education). Little attention is given to those factors, typically the political and social context of an individual, that create a demand for political participation. These factors include the issues that motivate participation, the social networks and local context that support or impede it, and the recruitment mechanisms that draw people into participation.

Issues present the greatest challenge. Most people get involved in politics because they care about some issue or cause, but most models of participation give short shrift to issues. The problems and needs approach to asking about political participation was designed to overcome this limitation, but it has not been very successful. Verba, Schlozman, and Brady (1995, ch. 14) had some success with issue information from open-ended questions asked after respondents said they engaged in an activity.

Although there is only a small literature on social networks (e.g., Knoke, 1990), local context (e.g., Oliver, 1997), and recruitment (e.g., Brady, Schlozman, & Verba, 1996), the problems here seem less daunting. The work that has been done to measure social networks, local context, and recruitment seems very promising, and the major impediment to further progress is the lack of questions about these factors on the existing surveys of political participation.

Acknowledgments

Andrea Campbell, John Mark Hansen, Benjamin Highton, M. Kent Jennings, Jane Junn, Cynthia Kaplan, John Robinson, Kay L. Schlozman, and Sidney Verba provided very useful comments. Andrea Campbell compiled the Roper data, and Benjamin Highton prepared several of the tables and figures.

References

Abelson, R. P., Loftus, E. F., & Greenwald, A. G. (1992). Attempts to improve the accuracy of self-reports of voting. In J. M. Tanur (Ed.), *Questions about questions: Inquiries into the cognitive bases of surveys* (pp. 138–153). New York: Russell Sage Foundation.

Aldrich, J. H. (1993). Rational choice and turnout. *American Journal of Political Science, 37,* 246–278.

Almond, G., & Verba, S. (1963). *The civic culture.* Princeton, NJ: Princeton University Press.

Anderson, B. A., & Silver, B. D. (1986). Measurement and mismeasurement of the validity of the self-reported vote. *American Journal of Political Science, 30,* 771–785.

Anderson, B. A., Silver, B. D., & Abramson, P. F. (1986). Who overreports voting? *American Political Science Review, 80,* 613–624.

Anderson, B. A., Silver, B. D., & Abramson, P. R. (1988). Effects of race of the interviewer on measures of electoral participation by blacks in SRC National Election Studies. *Public Opinion Quarterly, 52,* 53–83.

Barnes, S. H., & Kaase, M. (1979). *Political action: An eight nation study.* Ann Arbor, MI: Inter-University Consortium for Political and Social Research, 1979.

Barnes, S. H., Kaase, M., Allerbeck, K., Farah, B. G., Heunks, F., Inglehart, R., Jennings, M. K., Klingemann, H. D., Marsh, A., & Rosenmayr, L. (1979). *Political action: Mass participation in five Western democracies.* Beverly Hills: Sage Publications.

Baumgartner, F. R., & Walker, J. L. (1988). Survey research and membership in voluntary associations. *American Journal of Political Science, 32,* 908–928.

Berelson, B. R., Lazarsfeld, P. F., & McPhee, W. N. (1954). *Voting.* Chicago: University of Chicago Press.

Bradburn, N., Rips, L. J., & Shevell, S. K. (1987). Answering autobiographical questions: The impact of memory and inference in surveys. *Science, 236,* 157–161.

Brady, H. E. (1985). The perils of survey research: Interpersonally incomparable responses. *Political Methodology, 11,* 269–291.

Brady, H. E., & Kaplan, C. A. (1994). Referendums in Eastern Europe and the former Soviet Union. In D. Butler & A. Ranney (Eds.), *Referendums around the world: The growing use of direct democracy.* Washington, DC: American Enterprise Institute.

Brady, H. E., Schlozman, K. L., & Verba, S. (1996). *Prospecting for participants: Rational expectations and the recruitment of political activists.* Paper presented at the annual meeting of the American Political Science Association, Chicago.

Brady, H. E., Verba, S., & Schlozman, K. L. (1995). Beyond SES: A resource model of political participation. *American Political Science Review, 89,* 271–294.

Brehm, J. (1993). *The phantom respondents: Opinion surveys and political representation.* Ann Arbor: University of Michigan Press.

Budge, I. (1981). Review of the book *Political Action. American Political Science Review, 75,* 221–222.

Budge, I., Crewe, I., & Farlie, D. (Eds.). (1976). *Party identification and beyond: Representations of voting and party competition.* New York: Wiley.

Cahalan, D. (1968). Correlates of respondent accuracy in the Denver Validity Survey. *Public Opinion Quarterly, 32,* 607–621.

Cain, B. E., & Ferejohn, J. A. (1981). A comparison of party identification in the United States and Great Britain. *Comparative Political Studies, 14,* 31–47.

Campbell, D. A., & Fiske, D. W. (1959). Convergent and discriminant validity by the multitrait–multimethod matrix. *Psychological Bulletin, 56,* 81–105.

Clark, H. H., & Schober, M. F. (1992). Asking questions and influencing answers. In J. M. Tanur (Ed.), *Questions about questions: Inquiries into the cognitive bases of surveys* (pp. 15–48). New York: Russell Sage Foundation.

Collier, D., & Levitsky, S. (1997). Democracy with adjectives: Conceptual innovation in comparative research. *World Politics 49,* 430–451.

Collier, D., & Mahon, J. E. (1993). Conceptual "stretching" revisited: Adapting categories in comparative analysis. *American Political Science Review, 87,* 845–855.

Converse, P. E. (1964). The nature of belief systems in mass publics. In D. A. Apter (Ed.), *Ideology and discontent* (pp. 206–261). New York: Free Press.

Conway, M. M. (1991). *Political participation in the United States* (2nd ed.). Washington, DC: CQ Press.

Hempel, C. (1965). "Fundamentals of taxonomy" and "Typological methods in the natural and the social sciences." In *Aspects of scientific methodology* (pp. 137–171). New York: Free Press.

Iyengar, S., & Kinder, D. R. (1987). *News that matters: Television and American opinion.* Chicago: University of Chicago Press.

Jennings, M. K., van Deth, J. W., Barnes, S. H., Fuchs, D., Heunks, F. J., Inglehart, R., Kaase, M., Klingemann, H. D., & Thomassen, J. A. (1990). *Continuities in political action: A longitudinal study of political orientations in three Western democracies.* Berlin: Walter de Gruyter.

Johnston, R. (1992). Party identification measures in the Anglo-American democracies: A national survey experiment. *American Journal of Political Science, 36,* 542–559.

Kaase, M. (1989a). Mass participation. In M. K. Jennings, J. W. van Deth, et al., *Continuities in political action* (pp. 23–64). Berlin: Walter de Gruyter.

Kaase, M. (1989b). Appendix C: The cumulativeness and dimensionality of the participation scales. In M. K. Jennings, J. W. van Deth, et al., *Continuities in political action* (pp. 393–395). Berlin: Walter de Gruyter.

Kaase, M., & Marsh, A. (1979). Political action: A theoretical perspective. In S. H. Barnes, M. Kaase, et al., *Political action: Mass participation in five Western democracies* (pp. 27–56). Beverly Hills, CA: Sage.

Kaplan, C. S. & Brady, H. E. (1995) Igaunija: divu kopienu raksturojums, Estonia: A profile of two communities. In E. Veber & R. Karklins (Eds.), *Politika Baltijas Valstia* (pp. 7–36). Riga: Zinatne.

Kaplan, C. A., & Brady, H. E. (1997). The Communist Party on the eve of collapse. In J. S. Zacek & I. J. Kim (Eds.), *Legacy of the Soviet Bloc* (pp. 52–72). Gainesville: University Press of Florida.

Katosh, J. P., & Traugott. M. W. (1981). The consequences of validated and self-reported voting measures. *Public Opinion Quarterly, 45,* 519–535.

Knoke, D. (1990). *Political networks: The structural perspective.* Cambridge: Cambridge University Press.

Ladd, E. C. (1996). The data just don't show erosion of America's social capital. *Public Perspective, 7,* 1–6.

Lakoff, G. (1987). *Women, fire, and dangerous things: What categories reveal about the mind.* Chicago: University of Chicago Press.

Lane, R. E. (1959). *Political life: Why people get involved in politics,* Glencoe, IL: Free Press.

Lazarsfeld, P., Berelson, B., & Gaudet, H. (1948). *The people's choice* (2nd ed.). New York: Columbia University Press.

Leighley, J. E. (1995). Attitudes, opportunities and incentives: A field essay on political participation. *Political Research Quarterly, 48,* 181–209.

Loftus, E. F., Smith, K. D., Klinger, M. R., & Fiedler, J. (1992). Memory and mismemory for health events. In J. M. Tanur (Ed.), *Questions about questions: Inquiries into the cognitive bases of surveys* (pp. 102–137). New York: Russell Sage Foundation.

Lynd, R. S., & Lynd, H. M. (1929). *Middletown: A study in American culture.* New York: Harcourt Brace.

Marsh, A. (1977). *Protest and political consciousness.* Beverly Hills, CA: Sage.

Marsh, A., & Kaase, M. (1979). Measuring political action. In S. H. Barnes, M. Kaase, et al., *Political action: Mass participation in five Western democracies* (pp. 57–96). Beverly Hills, CA: Sage.

Milbrath, L. W. (1965). *Political participation.* Chicago: Rand McNally.

Milbrath, L. W., & Joel, M. L. (1977). *Political participation* (rev. ed.). Chicago: Rand McNally.

Miller, W. E., & National Election Studies. (1994). *American National Election Studies Cumulative Data File, 1952–1992.* Ann Arbor, MI: Inter-University Consortium for Political and Social Research.

Mishler, W. (1979). *Political participation in Canada: Prospects for democratic citizenship.* Toronto: Macmillan of Canada.

Muller, E. (1972). A test of a partial theory of potential for political violence. *American Political Science Review, 66,* 928–959.

Muller, E. N. (1979). *Aggressive political participation.* Princeton, NJ: Princeton University Press.

Muller, E. N., Dietz, H. A., & Finkel, S. (1991). Discontent and the expected utility of a rebellion: The case of Peru. *American Political Science Review, 85,* 1261–1282.

Muller, E. N., & Opp, K.-D. (1986). Rational choice and rebellious collective action. *American Political Science Review, 80,* 471–489.

Nagel, J. H. (1987). *Participation.* Englewood Cliffs, NJ: Prentice-Hall.

Nie, N., Junn, J., & Stehlik-Berry, K. (1996). *Education and citizenship in America.* Chicago: University of Chicago Press.

Nie, N., Powell, G. B., Jr., & Prewitt, K. (1969). Social structure and political participation: Developmental relationships, Part I. *American Political Science Review, 63,* 361–378.

Oliver, E. (1997). *Civil society in suburbia: The effects of metropolitan social context on participation in voluntary organizations.* Unpublished doctoral dissertation, University of California, Berkeley.

Parry, G., Moyser, G., & Day, N. (1992). *Political participation and democracy in Britain.* Cambridge: Cambridge University Press.

Pearson, R. W., Ross, M., & Dawes, R. M. (1994). Personal recall and the limits of retrospective questions in surveys. In J. M. Tanur (Ed.), *Questions about questions: Inquiries into the cognitive bases of surveys* (pp. 65–94). New York: Russell Sage Foundation.

Presser, S. (1990). Can context changes reduce vote overreporting? *Public Opinion Quarterly, 54,* 586–593.

Presser, S. & Traugott, M. (1992). Little white lies and social science models: Correlated response errors in a panel study of voting. *Public Opinion Quarterly, 56,* 77–86.

Putnam, R. D. (1995a). Bowling alone: America's declining social capital. *Journal of Democracy, 6,* 65–78.

Putnam, R. D. (1995b). Tuning in, tuning out: The strange disappearance of social capital in America. *PS: Political Science and Politics, 28,* 664–683.

Quaile-Hill, K., & Hurley, P. A. (1984). Nonvoters in voters' clothing: The impact of voting behavior misreporting on voting behavior research. *Social Science Quarterly, 65,* 199–206.

Robinson, J. P. (1973). Toward a more appropriate use of Guttman scaling. *Public Opinion Quarterly, 37,* 260–267.

Robinson, J. P. (1976). Interpersonal influence in election campaigns: Two Step-Flow Hypotheses. *Public Opinion Quarterly, 40,* 304–319.

Robinson, J. P. (1977). *How Americans use time: A social psychological analysis of everyday behavior.* Boulder, CO: Praeger.

Robinson, J. P., Rusk, J. G., & Head, K. B. (1968). *Measures of political attitudes.* Ann Arbor: Center for Political Studies, University of Michigan.

Rosenstone, S. J., & Hansen, J. M. (1993). *Mobilization, participation, and democracy in America.* New York: Macmillan.

Schlozman, K. L. (1994). Voluntary organizations in politics: Who gets involved? In W. Crotty, M. Schwartz, & J. C. Green (Eds.), *Representing interests and interest group representation* (pp. 67–83). Lanham, MD: University Press of America.

Schlozman, K. L., Burns, N., & Verba, S. (1994). Gender and the pathways to participation: The role of resources. *Journal of Politics, 56,* 963–990.

Schlozman, K. L., Verba, S., & Brady, H. E. (1995). Participation's not a paradox: The view from American activists. *British Journal of Political Science, 25,* 1–36.

Seyd, P., & Whiteley, P. (1992). *Labour's grass roots: The politics of party membership.* Oxford, England: Clarendon Press.

Sigelman, L. (1982). The nonvoting voter in voting research. *American Journal of Political Science, 26,* 47–56.

Silver, B. D., Abramson, P. R., & Anderson, B. A. (1986). The presence of others and overreporting of voting in American national elections. *Public Opinion Quarterly, 50,* 228–239.

Silver, B. D., Anderson, B. A., & Abramson, P. R. (1986). Who over-reports voting. *American Political Science Review, 80,* 613–624.

Smith, T. (1990). Trends in voluntary group membership: Comments on Baumgartner and Walker. *American Journal of Political Science, 34,* 646–661.

Sniderman, P. M., & Brody, R. A. (1977). Coping: The ethic of self-reliance. *American Journal of Political Science, 21,* 501–521.

Suppe, F. (1989). Some philosophical problems in biological speciation and taxonomy. In *The semantic conception of theories and scientific realism* (pp. 201–265). Urbana: University of Illinois Press.

Tanur, J. M. (Ed.). (1994). *Questions about questions: Inquiries into the cognitive bases of surveys.* New York: Russell Sage Foundation.

Taylor, J. R. (1989). *Linguistic categorization: Prototypes in linguistic theory.* Oxford, England: Clarendon Press.

Teixeira, R. A. (1992). *The disappearing American voter.* Washington, DC: Brookings Institution.

Thagard, P. (1992). *Conceptual revolutions.* Princeton, NJ: Princeton University Press.

Tourangeau, R., & Rasinski, K. A. (1988). Cognitive processes underlying context effects in attitude measurement. *Psychological Bulletin, 103,* 299–314.

Tulving, E. (1983). *Elements of episodic memory.* New York: Oxford University Press.

Uehlinger, H.-M. (1988). *Politische partizipation in der Bundesrepublik.* Opladen, Germany: Westdeutscher Verlag.

Verba, S. (1971). Cross-national survey research: The problem of credibility. In I. Vallier (Ed.), *Comparative methods in sociology: Essays on trends and applications* (pp. 309–356). Berkeley: University of California Press.

Verba, S., & Nie, N. H. (1972). *Participation in America.* New York: Harper & Row.

Verba, S., & Nie, N. H. (1976). *Political participation in America.* Ann Arbor, MI: Inter-University Consortium for Political and Social Research.

Verba, S., Nie, N. H., & Kim, J. (1971). *The modes of democratic participation: A cross national analysis* (Sage Professional Papers in Comparative Politics 2, No. 01-103). Beverly Hills, CA: Sage.

Verba, S., Nie, N. H., & Kim, J. (1978). *Participation and political equality: A seven-nation comparison.* Cambridge: Cambridge University Press.

Verba, S., Schlozman, K., & Brady, H. E. (1995). *Voice and equality: Civic voluntarism in American politics.* Cambridge: Harvard University Press.

Volgy, T. J., & Schwarz, J. E., (1984). Misreporting and vicarious political participation at the local level. *Public Opinion Quarterly, 48,* 757–765.

Weiss, C. H. (1968). Validity of welfare mothers' interview responses. *Public Opinion Quarterly, 32,* 622–633.

Whiteley, P. F. (1995). Rational choice and political participation—Evaluating the debate. *Political Research Quarterly, 48,* 211–233.

Wolfinger, R. E. (1993a). *Building a coalition to ease voter registration.* Paper prepared for presentation at the annual meeting of the American Political Science Association, Washington, DC.

Wolfinger, R. E. (1993b). *Improving voter participation.* Paper prepared for the National Conference on Improving the Electoral Process, Northeastern University, Boston.

Wolfinger, R. E., & Rosenstone, S. (1980). *Who votes?* New Haven, CT: Yale University Press.

Zaller, J., & Feldman, S. (1992). A simple theory of the survey response: Answering questions versus revealing preferences. *American Journal of Political Science, 36,* 579–616.

Data Sets Referenced and Used

Aitkin, D., Kahan, M., & Stokes, D. E. *Australian national political attitudes, 1967.* ICPSR Study #7282. Ann Arbor, MI: Inter-University Consortium for Political and Social Research.

Apollonio, D., Elms, L., & Brady, H. E. *Trends in American political participation from Roper surveys, 1973–1994.* Berkeley, CA: UC DATA, University of California, Berkeley.

Barnes, S. H., Kaase, M., et al. *Political action: An eight nation study, 1973–1976.* ICPSR Study #7777. Ann Arbor, MI: Inter-University Consortium for Political and Social Research.

Clarke, H., Jenson, J., LeDuc, L., & Pammett, J. *Canadian national election study, 1974.* ICPSR Study #7379. Ann Arbor, MI: Inter-University Consortium for Political and Social Research.

Converse, P. E., McDonough, P. J., DeSouza, A. G., & Cohen, Y. *Representation and development in Brazil, 1972–1973*. ICPSR Study #7712. Ann Arbor, MI: Inter-University Consortium for Political and Social Research.

Davis, J. A., & Smith, T. W. *General social surveys, 1972–1996 [cumulative file]*. ICPSR Study #6870. Ann Arbor, MI: Inter-University Consortium for Political and Social Research.

Dupeux, G. *French election study, 1958*. ICPSR Study #7278. Ann Arbor, MI: Inter-University Consortium for Political and Social Research.

Forschungsgruppe Wahlen E. V. Mannheim. *German election panel study, 1976*. ICPSR Study #7513. Ann Arbor, MI: Inter-University Consortium for Political and Social Research.

Heath, A. F., Jowell, R. M., Curtice, J. K., Brand, J. A., & Mitchell, J. C. *British election study, [June] 1983*. ICPSR Study #8409. Ann Arbor, MI: Inter-University Consortium for Political and Social Research.

Heunks, F., Jennings, M. K., Miller, W. E., Stouthard, P. C., & Thomassen, J. *Dutch election study, 1970–1973*. ICPSR Study #7261. Ann Arbor, MI: Inter-University Consortium for Political and Social Research.

Jennings, M. K., Markus, G. B., & Niemi, R. G. *Youth-parent socialization study, 1965–1982: Three waves combined*. ICPSR Study #9553. Ann Arbor, MI: Inter-University Consortium for Political and Social Research.

Johnston, R., Blais, A., Brady, H., & Crete, J. *Canadian national election study, 1988*. ICPSR Study #9386. Ann Arbor, MI: Inter-University Consortium for Political and Social Research.

Kaplan, C., Brady, H. E., & Saar, A. (1991–1992). *The Estonian citizen participation study*. Final dataset in preparation.

Kaplan, C., Brady, H. E., Andreenkov, V., & Smirnov, W. (1991–1992). *The Russian citizen participation study*. Final dataset in preparation.

Lazarsfeld, P. F., Berelson, B. R., & McPhee, W. N. *Elmira community study, 1948*. ICPSR Study #7203. Ann Arbor, MI: Inter-University Consortium for Political and Social Research.

Miller, W. E., & the National Election Studies. *American national election studies cumulative data file, 1952–1994*. ICPSR Study #8475. Ann Arbor, MI: Inter-University Consortium for Political and Social Research.

Miller, W. E., & the National Election Studies. *American national election studies pilot study, 1985*. ICPSR Study #8476. Ann Arbor, MI: Inter-University Consortium for Political and Social Research.

Parry, G., Moyser, G., & Day, N. *British political participation study, 1984–1985*.

United States Department of Commerce, Bureau of the Census. *Current population survey: Voter supplement files, 1972–1994*. ICPSR Study numbers #60, #7558, #7699, #7876, #7875, #8193, #8457, #8707, #9318, #9715, #6365, #6548. Ann Arbor, MI: Inter-University Consortium for Political and Social Research.

Valen, H. *Norwegian election study, 1965*. ICPSR Study #7256. Ann Arbor, MI: Inter-University Consortium for Political and Social Research.

Verba, S., & Nie, N. *Political participation in America, 1967*. ICPSR Study #7015. Ann Arbor, MI: Inter-University Consortium for Political and Social Research.

Verba, S., Schlozman, K. L., Brady, H. E., & Nie, N. *American citizen participation study, 1990*. ICPSR Study #6635. Ann Arbor, MI: Inter-University Consortium for Political and Social Research.

Ward, R. E., & Kubota, A. *Japanese national election study, 1967*. ICPSR Study #7294. Ann Arbor, MI: Inter-University Consortium for Political and Social Research.